TED SENNETT'S
ON-SCREEN/OFF-SCREEN
MOVIE GUIDE

Ted Sennett

Associate: Curtis F. Brown

A FIRESIDE BOOK
Published by Simon & Schuster
New York   London   Toronto   Sydney   Tokyo   Singapore

Fireside
Simon & Schuster Building
Rockefeller Center
1230 Avenue of the Americas
New York, New York 10020

Designed by Irving Perkins Associates
Manufactured in the United States of America

10 9 8 7 6 5 4 3 2 1

Library of Congress Cataloging-in-Publication Data is available.

ISBN 0-671-76818-2

INTRODUCTION

My earliest memories are memories of movies. Of my brother, pulling me on a sled to our local Bijou to see a horror film with Bela Lugosi that scared me half out of my wits. Of my father carrying me out of the theater as I cried inconsolably about some misfortune that had befallen Jackie Cooper. Of my parents returning from seeing *Footlight Parade* and singing "By a Waterfall" ("I'm calling you-ou-ou-ou"). Ever since I can remember, the flickering images on a movie screen have been an integral part of my life, a source of wonder and pleasure, a bottomless repository of dreams. Lucky me to have made the movies the source of my livelihood as well.

This book represents the sum total of my moviegoing experience, the happy (and sometimes frightening, thought-provoking, or exasperating) memories of a lifetime. I have written other books, but this one is the amalgam, the crucible of everything I have loved, or thought, about films across the decades.

I have used several criteria in choosing the movies. First, the films are all from the sound era and all American—to include silent and foreign films would have made the book unwieldy. Then, inevitably, I selected the films that have stood the test of time: those that can entertain us, or surprise us, or make us think, no matter how many times they are viewed. I added films that are worth seeing for extraordinary performances or memorable sequences, or perhaps they represent the early work of a major star or director. These are the movies that offer the delicious possibility of a new discovery. Then, as seasoning, I sprinkled the book with movies that simply gave me enormous pleasure, movies I would like to share with the reader. The result is in your hands.

The On-Screen section for each movie will tell the reader what is good, bad, or indifferent about the movie, and why it may be worth watching, even if it fails to live up to expectations. The Off-Screen section will, I hope, be of special interest not only to movie buffs but also to everyone who is fascinated by the behind-the-scenes activity that goes into the making of every film—that unpredictable mixture of luck, opportunity, talent, and ambition that fuses into a movie that people will pay money to see. Who was considered for the role? How were the special effects achieved? What was the original title? The answers are here, the cumulation of intensive research.

A few words about what the book does *not* have. You will not find star ratings, which I consider a gratuitous device that tells you little or nothing about the movie. Nor will you find notations indicating whether the movie has been colorized. It is sufficient to say that I regard the colorizing process as an abomination and a serious setback to film history. I choose not to acknowledge it in these pages. One small disclaimer: It is virtually impossible to state the exact running time for many movies. Like many other film historians, I have listed the running time that is a consensus in most references.

It has been a rewarding journey, growing, alongside these and other films, from that small boy in the local Bijou into the author of this book. I hope you will enjoy taking that journey with me, once again.

ACKNOWLEDGMENTS

I should like to thank a number of people who provided their help and support in carrying out this enormous project.

First and foremost, I am deeply and everlastingly grateful to Curtis Brown, my associate, whose contribution to this book has been invaluable. He not only wrote a number of the entries but gave me the benefit of his support, his generosity, and a wit that kept me smiling when there was little to smile about. Thanks also to Burt Lehrenbaum and to Judy Kass for their contributions.

Writing this book required my seeing scores of movies, both new and old, and I am grateful to Jerry Vermilye and John Springer for making their vast collections of tapes available to me. I also want to thank Jerome S. Ozer for allowing me to pore over his indispensable multivolume *Film Review Annual*. Thanks, as well, are due the ever-helpful staff at the Billy Rose Collection of the New York Public Library at Lincoln Center. In addition, I would like to acknowledge the unswerving support of my editor, David Dunton.

As always, my deepest love and gratitude go to my wife and children. I provide the words, but they provide the strength and the devotion that keep me going.

In loving memory of my father,
who took me to see my first movie . . .

NOTE: Entries contributed by writers
other than Ted Sennett are cited as follows:

CFB—Curtis F. Brown
BL—Burton Lehrenbaum
JMK—Judith M. Kass

KEY TO NOTATIONS:

Dir—Director
Sp—Screenplay written by
b/o—based on
MS—Music score written by
C—filmed in color

The Accidental Tourist

Warners, 1988. (C-121m.) Dir: Lawrence Kasdan. Sp: Frank Galati and Lawrence Kasdan, b/o book by Anne Tyler. Cast: William Hurt, Kathleen Turner, Geena Davis, Amy Wright, David Ogden Stiers, Ed Begley, Jr., Bill Pullman.

On-Screen: *A grieving man is awakened to life*. Derived from Anne Tyler's novel, *The Accidental Tourist* is a movie that is every bit as becalmed and enervated as its protagonist. Macon Leary (Hurt) is a travel writer whose life has been brutally shattered by the shooting death of his young son. His marriage to Sarah (Turner) ended, Macon has deliberately cut himself off from all feelings. That is, until he meets Muriel (Davis), an oddball dog trainer whose outgoing attitude baffles and irritates him until he surrenders to her warmth and spirit. Complications develop when Sarah wants to return to Macon. From the first, the film is caught in a fatal trap: Hurt must play a disengaged man in a disengaged style, but his uninflected voice and zombielike manner pall in a short time. Turner seems miscast, and Davis plays the sort of "kooky," adorable character that was all the rage in films and the theater a few decades ago. The only real fun in this drab movie is contributed by Macon's eccentric family, played by Amy Wright, Ed Begley, Jr., and David Ogden Stiers.

Off-Screen: *The Accidental Tourist* obviously had its share of admirers, among them the New York Film Critics Circle, which voted it the Best Film of 1988. Geena Davis received a Best Supporting Actress Oscar for her performance. The author of the screenplay is actually Lawrence Kasdan; although Frank Galati wrote a first draft, his version was not used. His name was still cited in the credits for contractual reasons.

The Accused

Paramount, 1988. (C-110m.) Dir: Jonathan Kaplan. Sp: Tom Topor. Cast: Jodie Foster, Kelly McGillis, Bernie Coulson, Leo Rossi, Ann Hearn, Carmen Argenziano, Steve Antin.

On-Screen: *A rape victim has her day in court*. A riveting and sometimes harrowing melodrama, *The Accused* is based on an actual notorious incident in which a woman was repeatedly raped in a bar as others watched and cheered the rapists on. In a fierce, Oscar-winning performance, Jodie Foster plays the victim, a tough, provocative young woman named Sarah Tobias who demands justice for the brutal assault. The public prosecutor (McGillis), at first sympathetic but remote, becomes emotionally committed to Sarah's cause and insists on bringing the bystanders to trial. Some viewers may think that the shockingly graphic reenactment of the crime, late in the film, was included for merely prurient reasons; others may believe that it was essential to show that rape is an act of violence. But scarcely anyone will dispute the stunning power of Jodie Foster's acting.

Off-Screen: Jodie Foster had this comment on *The Accused:* "The film doesn't show bullets, just basic human cruelty—what happens when people are in a room together. It's not inhuman, which is why it's so scary." And screenwriter Tom Topor said, "We wanted to lull the audience and then turn things around. We were saying, 'As a spectator, you're part of the problem. What would *you* have done?'"

Ace in the Hole aka The Big Carnival

Paramount, 1951. (112m.) Dir: Billy Wilder. Sp: Billy Wilder, Lesser Samuels, and Walter Newman. Cast: Kirk Douglas, Jan Sterling, Bob Arthur, Porter Hall, Richard Benedict, Frank Cady, Ray Teal.

On-Screen: *An opportunistic reporter manipulates a news story.* Writer-director Billy Wilder's jaundiced view of humanity has seldom been more vividly demonstrated than in this caustic film. Unrelenting in its cynicism, *Ace in the Hole* (later retitled *The Big Carnival*) stars Kirk Douglas at his most intense as Chuck Tatum, a down-on-his-luck reporter looking for his "big" story. He finds it in Albuquerque, New Mexico, when a man is trapped in an underground cave. Cold-bloodedly, Tatum turns the poor man's plight into a three-ring circus, manipulating events until there is too little time to save the victim. The screenplay's sharp-edged, vitriolic dialogue ranges across the least attractive aspects of man's behavior, from idle curiosity and indifference in the face of tragedy to outright greed and corruption. Jan Sterling is memorably sleazy as the trapped victim's sluttish wife (she won't pray for him—"kneeling bags my nylons"), and Douglas sinks his teeth into the sort of role he does best.

Off-Screen: Call it *Ace in the Hole* or *The Big Carnival,* this film is strong medicine, apparently too strong for most viewers since it failed at the box office. The movie was loosely based on the Floyd Collins cave-in incident in Kentucky, which caused a stir in the twenties. (The script was updated and the locale changed to Albuquerque.) To Wilder, Douglas expressed his concern about his character's total lack of human feeling, but the director refused to soften him. "Give it both knees. Right from the beginning," Wilder told Douglas. And he did.

Across the Pacific

Warners, 1942. (97m.) Dir: John Huston. Sp: Richard Macaulay, b/o story by Robert Carson. Cast: Humphrey Bogart, Mary Astor, Sydney Greenstreet, Victor Sen Yung, Keye Luke, Richard Loo, Charles Halton.

On-Screen: *Bogart tangles again with those "Falcon" people.* After their success as the devious protagonists of Huston's *The Maltese Falcon,* the studio decided to reteam Bogart, Astor, and Greenstreet in another movie, again under Huston's direction. This time, however, the result was not half as good. A routine melodrama set just before the start of World War II, *Across the Pacific* sends Bogart on a secret government mission to ferret out and then thwart a Japanese plan to destroy the Panama Canal. Along the way he encounters a beautiful woman (Astor) with a mysterious past and equally mysterious motives, and a portly, Japanese-worshiping professor (Greenstreet) in charge of the insidious plan against the canal. There are some echoes of *The Maltese Falcon* and several evocative scenes, notably an encounter between Bogart and an informant in a Chinese theater, but on the whole the film has a perfunctory air and little distinction.

Off-Screen: The movie was started shortly before Pearl Harbor and resumed shooting in March of 1942. But John Huston was required to leave for the Army Signal Corps before the last scenes could be filmed. As a parting gesture, Huston wrote a cliff-hanger ending in which Bogart was trapped in a room with Japanese soldiers. Director Vincent Sherman was called in to the project to extricate Bogart from his dilemma in a hectic, slapdash climax.

Adam's Rib

MGM, 1949. (100m.) Dir: George Cukor. Sp: Ruth Gordon and Garson Kanin. Cast: Katharine Hepburn, Spencer Tracy, Judy Holliday, Tom Ewell, David Wayne, Jean Hagen, Hope Emerson, Polly Moran, Marvin Kaplan.

On-Screen: *Two married lawyers battle over the same case.* When a woman (Holliday) tries to kill her straying husband (Ewell) and his mistress (Hagen), two happily married lawyers (Hepburn and Tracy) become opponents in the case. She sees it as a cause for the woman's right to defend herself and her family; he, an assistant district attorney, sees it as attempted murder. Soon their marriage is not so happy. Around this premise Ruth Gordon and Garson Kanin spin a witty and adroit screenplay with provocative overtones about feminism and the law. Hepburn and Tracy are in peak form, she all fired-up by her cause, and he amused when she turns "cause-y." They get splendid support from Tom Ewell as the befuddled husband in the case, David Wayne as an effete neighbor, and especially Judy Holliday as the neglected wife with a gun. Holliday, in fact, walks off with the movie in a funny, touching performance—her thoughts and even her speech patterns move to her own private rhythm. *Adam's Rib* is sophisticated film comedy at its best.

Off-Screen: When Columbia mogul Harry Cohn proved extremely reluctant to cast Judy Holliday in her stage role of Billie Dawn in *Born Yesterday,* Katharine Hepburn, George Cukor, and the Kanins were determined to get her the part. Hepburn used *Adam's Rib* as a kind of screen test, favoring the highly nervous Holliday in key scenes, and encouraging her to do her best. The result: Holliday won the role in *Born Yesterday*—and a Best Actress Oscar. "Farewell, Amanda," the song rendered by David Wayne, was written for the film by Cole Porter. The story became the basis for a short-lived television series in 1973, with Blythe Danner and Ken Howard.

The Addams Family

Paramount, 1991. (C-102m.) Dir: Barry Sonnenfeld. Sp: Caroline Thompson and Larry Wilson, b/o characters created by Charles Addams. Cast: Anjelica Huston, Raul Julia, Christopher Lloyd, Dan Hedaya, Elizabeth Wilson, Judith Malina, Carel Struycken, Christopher Hart, Christina Ricci, Jimmy Workman.

On-Screen: *Not the usual folks next door.* Reaching their peak of popularity during the forties and fifties, Addams's one-liner cartoons, created for *The New Yorker,* chronicled the ghoulish goings-on in what came to be known as the Addams family. Overblown and wearisomely long, the movie benefits most from its own one-liners: "Don't torture yourself, Gomez," Morticia (Huston) cautions her husband (Julia). "That's *my* job." Okay, that and many other gags raise laughs. The endearingly nasty banter, however, is weighted down by a who-cares plot involving an imposter (Lloyd) posing as Gomez's long-lost brother, Fester. A seemingly endless ballroom sequence isn't much fun, either. Huston brings her customary elegance and aplomb to her role as mother of two diabolical tots (Ricci and Workman), but Julia and Lloyd are leaden in their not-very-funny roles. Stick with the classic, single-jab cartoons.

Off-Screen: That the macabre ménage could exist beyond the confines of the printed page, its campy wickedness intact, was proven by the popular half-hour television series of the mid-sixties, "The Addams Family," with Carolyn Jones as Morticia and John Astin as Gomez. It was Addams himself, in fact, who provided the sitcom characters with their memorable names, which were carried over into the movie. Thing, the heroic, disembodied member of the horrific household, is the agile right hand of Hart. The 1993 sequel was entitled *Addams Family Values.* (CFB)

The Adventures of Robin Hood

Warners, 1938. (C-102m.) Dir: Michael Curtiz and William Keighley. Sp: Norman Reilly Raine and Seton I. Miller. Cast: Errol Flynn, Olivia de Havilland, Basil Rathbone, Claude Rains, Patric Knowles, Eugene Pallette, Alan Hale, Ian Hunter, Melville Cooper.

On-Screen: *Errol Flynn aids the Saxons' struggle against Norman oppression and wins the hand of Olivia de Havilland.* A handsome, youthful Flynn makes the ideal Robin Hood, legend's dashing outlaw with a social conscience. Leading his band of lovable rogues—Little John (Hale) and Friar Tuck (Pallette) among them—Robin pits his superior prowess in archery and fencing against the scheming of nasty Sir Guy (Rathbone) and wicked Prince John (Rains), who plot to usurp the English throne from kindly King Richard the Lion-Hearted (Hunter). Over five decades after its release, the movie remains unequaled in the Swashbuckler Sweepstakes. It's a perfect blend of inspired Anglo-American casting, heart-stopping thrills, and tender romance. Erich Wolfgang Korngold's music is stirring; the sets and costumes are sumptuous. And it's all in gorgeous Technicolor.

Off-Screen: Warners first planned a film about Robin Hood in 1935, with James Cagney in the title role and Guy Kibbee as Friar Tuck. Shelved for three years, it became the studio's most expensive production up to that time ($2 million). Soon after filming began, it was clear that William Keighley's direction was uninspired. Michael Curtiz, who replaced him, brought out all the wit and rousing adventure in Raine and Miller's superior screenplay. The imaginative staging of the lengthy duel between Flynn and Rathbone—the winding stone staircase, ominous shadows, overturned candelabra crashing to the floor—makes for a thrilling fencing sequence that remains unsurpassed. The film won three Academy awards, for music score (Korngold's second Oscar), art direction, and editing.(CFB)

Advise and Consent

Columbia, 1962. (139m.) Dir: Otto Preminger. Sp: Wendell Mayes, b/o novel by Allen Drury. Cast: Henry Fonda, Charles Laughton, Don Murray, Walter Pidgeon, Franchot Tone, Lew Ayres, Peter Lawford, Gene Tierney, George Grizzard, Inga Swenson, Burgess Meredith, Paul Ford, Eddie Hodges.

On-Screen: *Political skulduggery on the Washington merry-go-round, via Allen Drury's novel.* A slickly produced and entertaining movie, *Advise and Consent* revolves about the political storm that ensues in the nation's capital after the president (Tone) nominates Robert Leffingwell (Fonda) as secretary of state. When Leffingwell lies under oath about his past, the storm intensifies. Caught up in the fracas is every shade of political belief, from Laughton's conservative Southern senator (his last performance) to Grizzard's fire-breathing, unscrupulous liberal. Don Murray plays the idealistic senator whose involvement has tragic consequences. The movie's star-filled cast includes Lew Ayres as the benign vice president and Walter Pidgeon (giving the film's best performance) as the Senate majority whip. Amusingly, the movie aroused the anger of *New York Times* critic Bosley Crowther, who objected to its concentration on Washington rascals. In our post-Watergate era, *Advise and Consent* begins to seem like fiction verging on fact.

Off-Screen: Charles Laughton worked strenuously to acquire a convincing Southern accent. To lick the problem, he used a voice coach and studied a record of Southern Senator John C. Stennis's keynote address to the Democratic Convention in 1952. Knowing of Gene Tierney's long history of mental illness, Laughton took special pains to protect her from director Preminger's badgering. Preminger wanted Martin Luther King, Jr., to play a senator from Georgia. King was interested, but declined at the last moment.

The African Queen

United Artists, 1951. (105m.) Dir: John Huston. Sp: James Agee, b/o novel by C. S. Forester. Cast: Katharine Hepburn, Humphrey Bogart, Robert Morley, Peter Bull, Theodore Bikel.

On-Screen: *Hepburn and Bogart join forces to battle the Germans in Africa.* One of the most entertaining movies ever made, *The African Queen* combines rousing adventure and quirky romance with high-voltage star power. Set in Africa at the start of World

War I, it stars Humphrey Bogart as Charlie Allnut, the disreputable owner of the ramshackle *African Queen,* who joins prim spinster Rose Sayer (Hepburn) in a wildly adventurous trip downriver. Battling the elements and the odds as they attempt to elude the Germans, the mismatched duo find themselves falling in love. The movie never for a minute takes itself seriously as Rose and Charlie survive an attack by leeches, a perilous ride over a waterfall, and a dual hanging. Their sniping exchanges, before they become lovers, are funny indeed. Bogart is quite wonderful as Charlie, whose stomach growls at teatime, and his Best Actor Oscar was well-deserved. Hepburn received her fifth Oscar nomination for her spirited performance.

Off-Screen: The making of *The African Queen* has become almost as legendary as the film itself. Anecdotes abound about the shooting on location in Africa, concerning Hepburn's amazing resilience in the face of terrible conditions, and how she retained her cool demeanor while Bogart and John Huston shared liquor and dirty jokes. Amazingly, they all ended up genuinely fond of each other. Hepburn credits Huston with giving her the key to her characterization by telling her to play Rose like Eleanor Roosevelt. She wrote of her experiences in *The Making of "The African Queen"* (Knopf, 1987). Before Hepburn and Bogart were signed, there was talk of casting David Niven or John Mills as Charlie and Deborah Kerr or Bette Davis as Rose. Occasionally, good fortune does indeed smile on us all.

After Hours

Warners, 1985. (C-97m.) Dir: Martin Scorsese. Sp: Joseph Minion. Cast: Griffin Dunne, Rosanna Arquette, Teri Garr, John Heard, Verna Bloom, Thomas Chong, Cheech Marin, Catherine O'Hara, Bronson Pinchot, Dick Miller.

On-Screen: *One man's journey into urban hell.* A nightmare comedy from Martin Scorsese, *After Hours* foregoes all the usual movie trappings of plot and characterization and instead offers an exercise in writing and directorial style. You'll find the result either fascinating or bewildering, or possibly both. Griffin Dunne plays Paul, a young word-processor operator who goes down to New York's SoHo for a date and becomes immersed in a frightening, inexplicable series of events. On his night in hell, he meets a number of people, mainly women, who appear to be seriously disturbed. Eventually, he is fleeing in terror from a crowd who believes he is a neighborhood thief. The movie is played for black humor, but you may not find yourself laughing at Paul's plight. There are attempts to make it all seem more complex and portentous than it really is, and even a touch of Kafka emerges when the beleaguered Paul shouts to the world at large, "What do you want from me? What have I done?" But *After Hours* is only a minor entry from Scorsese.

Off-Screen: The script was written by Joseph Minion as an assignment when he was a graduate student at the Columbia University Film School. Bronson Pinchot (Balki in television's "Perfect Strangers") can be seen briefly as a colleague of Paul's. The two harried thieves are played by the comedy team of Cheech and Chong.

Air Force

Warners, 1943. (124m.) Dir: Howard Hawks. Sp: Dudley Nichols. Cast: John

Garfield, Arthur Kennedy, Gig Young, John Ridgely, Harry Carey, George Tobias, Faye Emerson, Charles Drake.

On-Screen: *The crew of a B-17 faces action at the start of World War II.* If you wanted to watch one movie that typified the wartime military drama, Howard Hawks's *Air Force* would be a dependable choice. The story of the crew of the bomber *Mary Ann,* just before and immediately after the onset of World War II, it contains all the elements that usually went into these combat movies: a plane crew made up of familiar ethnic and regional types, yards of come-out-fighting dialogue ("We're going to play the 'Star-Spangled Banner' with two-ton bombs!"), and well-photographed scenes of aerial battles. In keeping with the pent-up feelings of the times, there are now wince-inducing remarks by crew members. (As gunner George Tobias shoots down a plane, he exclaims, "Fried Jap going down!") Hawks directs with his usual skill, and the climactic battle scene is rousing.

Off-Screen: An amusing censorship note: Although the Breen Office allowed virtually every jingoistic piece of dialogue to remain in the screenplay, it objected to such inoffensive lines as "Let's go after those sons of heaven," "This place is a hell hole," and "He's a pain in the pants." Since the government did not want the war to be criticized in any way, particularly at a time when U.S. forces were faring badly in the Pacific, the censors also insisted on deleting the line, "This is a lousy war." The movie received Oscar nominations for writing and photography.

Airplane!

Paramount, 1980. (C-86m.) Dir and Sp: Jim Abrahams, Jerry Zucker, and David Zucker. Cast: Robert Hays, Julie Hagerty, Robert Stack, Lloyd Bridges, Leslie Nielsen, Peter Graves, Kareem Abdul-Jabbar, Lorna Patterson, Stephen Stucker.

On-Screen: *Off-the-wall spoof of airplane disaster movies.* If you're relaxed and in the mood for outrageous humor, you will probably find *Airplane!* wildly hilarious. Its nonstop parade of puns, sight gags, parodies, and wordplays contains as many duds as gems, but you're not likely to count them while you're laughing. The movie takes off from a serious 1957 movie called *Zero Hour,* in which the crew of a plane is felled with ptomaine poisoning. Here the poisoning includes many of the passengers. The wittiest idea is to have actors spoofing the very roles they played in earlier years with straight faces, including Robert Stack as a hotshot pilot, Leslie Nielsen as a dense doctor, and Lloyd Bridges as a madly addicted airport-traffic controller. Robert Hays plays the traumatized—and thick-skulled—ex-pilot who is forced to take over for the poisoned crew (and who literally bores some of his fellow passengers to death). Watch for Lieutenant Hurwitz and his peculiar problem, and stay around for the final credits.

Off-Screen: The agile writer-directors can be seen in walk-on roles: Abrahams as a religious zealot, the Zucker brothers as ground controllers. Among the parodied films are *From Here to Eternity* (1953), *Jaws* (1975), and *Saturday Night Fever* (1977). A sequel, bluntly titled *Airplane II: The Sequel,* appeared in 1982.

Airport

Universal, 1970. (C-137m.) Dir: George Seaton. Sp: George Seaton, b/o novel by Arthur Hailey. Cast: Burt Lancaster, Dean Martin, Jean Seberg, Jacqueline Bisset, George Kennedy, Helen Hayes, Van Heflin, Maureen Stapleton, Barry Nelson, Dana Wynter, Lloyd Nolan, Barbara Hale.

On-Screen: *A jetliner in big trouble.* One of the first and most popular of the all-star disaster movies that surfaced in the seventies (*The Poseidon Adventure, The Towering Inferno, Earthquake,* etc.), *Airport* sets the formula: Take a group of new and slightly faded stars and place them in terrible peril. Then let the audience guess which of them will survive by the final credits. This time Disaster Central is a giant jetliner flying through a midwestern blizzard with a mad bomber (Heflin) aboard. Naturally the passengers, the crew, and the officials waiting at the airport have personal problems that compound the imminent disaster. Among them are the airport manager (Lancaster), the married pilot (Martin), the stewardess (Bisset) carrying his baby, and a sweet little old stowaway (Hayes). Maureen Stapleton is at least touching as the bomber's frightened wife, and George Kennedy has a gruff, take-charge attitude as the chief of the maintenance men. Adapted from Arthur Hailey's best-selling novel, *Airport* is terribly silly, but then the makers don't pretend that it's anything more than a neatly turned-out exercise in cinematic terror.

Off-Screen: Helen Hayes, billed imperiously as "Miss" Helen Hayes, won the year's Oscar as Best Supporting Actress. There were eight other nominations, including one for Best Picture. *Airport* spawned three sequels: *Airport 1975* (1974), *Airport '77* (1977), and *The Concorde—Airport '79* (1979). In 1980, *Airplane!* came along with a wicked and often hilarious spoof of these movies.

Alexander's Ragtime Band

Fox, 1938. (105m.) Dir: Henry King. Sp: Kathryn Scola and Lamar Trotti. MS: Irving Berlin. Cast: Alice Faye, Tyrone Power, Don Ameche, Ethel Merman, Jack Haley, Jean Hersholt, Helen Westley.

On-Screen: *"C'mon and hear" Irving Berlin's music in its full glory.* One of Fox's most popular musicals of the thirties, *Alexander's Ragtime Band* offers a heady tribute to the foot-tapping, tuneful, proudly American music of Irving Berlin. The story, an over-the-years chronicle focusing on the lives of Faye, Power, and Ameche (they never age), has little interest, but with a wonderful Berlin score, who cares? Usually undervalued as a singer, Alice Faye gives creamy, unaffected renditions of "Everybody's Doin' It," "Now It Can Be Told," and the rousing title song, while Ethel Merman uses her inimitable trumpet voice to belt out such tunes as "Blue Skies," "Heat Wave," and "My Walking Stick." She does not get to join the others in "The International Rag" but made up for this lapse fifteen years later by singing it in *Call Me Madam* (1953).

Off-Screen: At first Darryl Zanuck asked Irving Berlin to work on the screenplay for the film, but when the result was severely disappointing, he assigned it to the studio's in-house writers. Some of Ethel Merman's footage in the film was cut in order to expand Alice Faye's screen time. The score contains twenty-six old Berlin songs and two new songs ("Now It Can Be Told" and "My Walking Stick"). Alfred Newman's background score won an Oscar. Henry King called the movie the one he most enjoyed directing.

Alice

Orion, 1990. (C-106m.) Dir: Woody Allen. Sp: Woody Allen. Cast: Mia Farrow, William Hurt, Joe Mantegna, Cybill Shepherd, Alec Baldwin, Blythe Danner, Gwen Verdon, Bernadette Peters, Judy Davis, Julie Kavner, Keye Luke.

On-Screen: *A woman reviews her life, Woody Allen style.* Blessed with a good life, Alice Tate (Farrow) has a rich husband (Hurt), two darling children, and more than enough creature comforts. Vaguely discontent, however, she drifts into a guilt-ridden affair with a divorced musician (Mantegna). She also visits a mysterious Oriental herbalist (Luke) whose concoctions have her exploring her "needs, limits, gifts, and innermost feelings." Rendered invisible, she eavesdrops on other people's lives or remembers a past lover (Baldwin) with whom she flies over the nighttime city in the movie's most memorable sequence. She also comes to grips with past and present relationships with family members. A richly textured mixture of fantasy and satire, *Alice* is yet another in the series of early-nineties movies (*The Doctor, Regarding Henry*) that ask us to discard the greed and selfishness of the eighties for the altruism and "reaching out" of a new decade. At least this spin on the overworked theme is informed by Woody Allen's wit and perceptiveness. Funniest scene: All the men at a Christmas party, having had an aphrodisiac drug stirred into their eggnog by mistake, come lusting after Alice.

Off-Screen: Woody Allen won an Oscar nomination for his original screenplay. Dr. Yang, the dispenser of the potent herbs, was played by veteran actor Keye Luke, who years earlier had appeared as detective Charlie Chan's Number One Son in a dozen movies and as the servant Kato in the "Green Hornet" serials. He died soon after making *Alice* at age eighty-six.

Alice Adams

RKO, 1935. (99m.) Dir: George Stevens. Sp: Dorothy Yost and Mortimer Offner, b/o novel by Booth Tarkington. Cast: Katharine Hepburn, Fred MacMurray, Fred Stone, Evelyn Venable, Frank Albertson, Ann Shoemaker, Hattie McDaniel.

On-Screen: *Katharine Hepburn longs for love and acceptance in small-town America.* One of Hepburn's better vehicles of the thirties, *Alice Adams* allowed the actress to make good use of her special combination of charm and eccentricity. She plays Booth Tarkington's wistful heroine yearning to become a member of a small town's social circle. Burdened with a vulgar family and too proud to modify her offbeat attitudes, she suffers quietly until she wins MacMurray, the town "catch" and the man of her dreams. With her affected ways, Alice comes close to being an irritating character, but Hepburn makes her credible and even appealing under George Stevens's sympathetic direction. The movie's outstanding scene is the disastrous dinner Alice gives for MacMurray. With Hattie McDaniel leading the way as a slovenly maid, one thing after another goes terribly, hilariously wrong. Hepburn made only a few good films during her RKO years in the thirties, and this is one of them.

Off-Screen: For the film's director, studio executives had to choose between William Wyler, then approaching the peak of his career, and a thirty-year-old beginner, George Stevens. They chose Stevens. Long afterward, Stevens recalled a dispute with Hepburn over the scene in which she cries at the window of her bedroom. Hepburn was reluctant to expose her emotions so fully in this fashion, but Stevens persisted, and the result was a memorable moment. The actress received an Oscar nomination, as did the picture. Tarkington's story was filmed before, in 1923.

Alice Doesn't Live Here Anymore

Warners, 1975. (C-113m.) Dir: Martin Scorsese. Sp: Robert Getchell. Cast: Ellen Burstyn, Kris Kristofferson, Alfred Lutter, Diane Ladd, Vic Tayback, Harvey Keitel, Jodie Foster, Valerie Curtin, Billy Green Bush.

On-Screen: *Ellen Burstyn's Oscar as a struggling woman.* When we first meet her, Alice Hyatt (Burstyn) is the embodiment of a prefeminist woman. Suddenly widowed after the death of her abusive husband (Green Bush) and left with a young, wisecracking son (Lutter), she is helpless and ineffectual. ("My idea of a man was strong and dominating.") That is, until she becomes a waitress at Mel and Ruby's Cafe. With the help of a salty friend (Ladd), also a waitress at Mel's, and the love of a caring rancher (Kristofferson), Alice finds some happiness on her terms. Ellen Burstyn's vibrant performance deserved the Best Actress Acad-

emy Award, and under Martin Scorsese's direction—this was his most conventionally commercial movie of the period—*Alice* is undeniably entertaining. The climax, however, is one of those hopelessly false sequences Hollywood regards as "surefire": In the crowded diner, Alice and the rancher have a lovers' quarrel, making up to vociferous cheers from the customers. Uh-huh.

Off-Screen: Diane Ladd won an Oscar nomination for her performance as waitress Flo, and Robert Getchell's original screenplay was also nominated. Look for a preteen Jodie Foster as Audrey, free-spirited friend of Alice's son, Tommy. *Alice Doesn't Live Here Anymore,* shortened to simply "Alice," became a long-running television show in 1976, with Linda Lavin as Alice. Only Vic Tayback as Mel was retained from the movie cast.

Alice's Restaurant

United Artists, 1969. (C-111m.) Dir: Arthur Penn. Sp: Venable Herndon and Arthur Penn, b/o song by Arlo Guthrie. Cast: Arlo Guthrie, Pat Quinn, James Broderick, Michael McClanathan, Geoff Outlaw, Pete Seeger, Joseph Boley.

On-Screen: *Farewell to the youth counterculture of the sixties, as optimism is confronted by reality.* The story is an expansion of "The Alice's Restaurant Massacree," Guthrie's autobiographical "talking blues" record hit. The movie's elegiac tone is set when Guthrie visits his father, legendary folksinger Woody (Boley), who lies dying in a Brooklyn hospital. Amid the Berkshire hills of Stockbridge, Massachusetts, young Guthrie mingles with restaurateur Alice Brock (Quinn) and her husband, Ray (Broderick), who manage a hippie commune. The film has genuinely funny moments, as when Guthrie, a Candide-like innocent, is arrested by an implacable Stockbridge cop for littering. The wintertime funeral of a young, self-destructive sculptor (McClanathan), dead of a drug overdose, stresses the overall melancholic, end-of-an-era mood. Undervalued, this is one of director Penn's best.

Off-Screen: The real-life Alice Brock, reluctant to play herself because she "had already done it," can be seen playing a small part in the sequences filmed in Stockbridge. Though her marriage to Ray is depicted as a generally happy one, they were actually in the throes of divorce during the filming. William Obenhein, the policeman who arrested Guthrie, plays himself. He proved so adept at taking direction, that he was nicknamed "One-Shot Obie." Penn's direction won him an Oscar nomination. (CFB)

Alien

Fox, 1979. (C-117m.) Dir: Ridley Scott. Sp: Dan O'Bannion, b/o story by Dan O'Bannion and Ronald Slusett. Cast: Sigourney Weaver, Tom Skerritt, John Hurt, Ian Holm, Harry Dean Stanton, Yaphet Kotto, Veronica Cartwright.

On-Screen: *An alien monster decimates a spaceship crew.* The first, and probably the most conventional, of the three Alien movies, *Alien* offers a few jolting scenes and some vivid special effects. Otherwise, the basic premise is old hat: A spaceship returning to earth from a long mission becomes the feasting ground for a hideous alien creature inadvertently brought aboard by one of its crew members. One by one the creature destroys its victims until the only one remaining is the feisty, resourceful Ripley (Weaver), who becomes the heroine of the subsequent Alien movies. The dialogue comes out of previous films of the "monster-from-outer-space" subgenre ("I've never seen anything like it!" "Whatever it was, it was *big!*," etc.), but even the sequels found it hard to match the horrifying sequence in which the alien creature explodes out of John Hurt's chest. Inevitably, the climax is a fierce battle to the death between Ripley and the creature.

Off-Screen: Carlo Rambaldi won his second Oscar (the first was for the 1976 *King Kong*) for his visual effects. He later contributed importantly to *E.T.: The Extra-Terrestrial* (1982), this time creating a *lovable* outer-space creature. *Alien³*, the third, and presumably last, film in the Alien series, was released in 1992.

Aliens

Fox, 1986. (C-137m.) Dir: James Cameron. Sp: James Cameron, b/o story by David Giler, Walter Hill, and James Cameron. Cast: Sigourney Weaver, Michael Biehn, Carrie Henn, Paul Reiser, Lance Henriksen, Bill Paxton, Jenette Goldstein.

On-Screen: *Sigourney Weaver returns to battle alien monsters.* On the surface *Aliens* resembles other science-fiction-plus-horror films: Intrepid souls venture to a strange planet where they must confront ghoulish alien creatures. Many perish; a few survive. But *Aliens*, a sequel to Ridley Scott's 1979 *Alien*, has several elements that raise it a few notches above the usual fare. For one, the Oscar-winning special effects are stunning, not only impressive in scope but in execution. For another, the central character, fiercely played by Sigourney Weaver, is a heroine for the nineties. The very same Lieutenant Ripley who battled the demons in *Alien,* she is asked to return to the planet from which she barely escaped to investigate missing settlers. Ripley is not only shown to be superior in resilience and intelligence to all the men aboard her spaceship, she is also depicted as a nurturing mother to the child (Henn) who survived the alien destruction. In essence, Ripley is both aggressor and defender, and terrifically capable at both. All in all, *Aliens* is good, scary fun.

Off-Screen: Little Carrie Henn won a talent search conducted among American girls living in England, where the film was shot at Pinewood Studios. Sigourney Weaver was said to have refused to shoot scenes involving "gore" and would not allow a cast of her body to be taken for some planned effects for dream sequences—nightmares of the original expedition that still troubled her character. The queen alien designed for the film was some thirteen feet high and twenty feet long. Another sequel, *Alien³,* turned up in 1992.

All About Eve

Fox, 1950. (138m.) Dir: Joseph L. Mankiewicz. Sp: Joseph L. Mankiewicz, b/o story by Mary Orr. Cast: Bette Davis, Anne Baxter, George Sanders, Celeste Holm, Gary Merrill, Hugh Marlowe, Thelma Ritter, Gregory Ratoff, Marilyn Monroe.

On-Screen: *Stage star Bette Davis clashes with understudy Anne Baxter, fang and talon, in the Broadway jungle.* Everything about this movie is just right: Mankiewicz's dialogue crackles; cast members seem born for their roles, and the Great White Way was never more glamorous, nor more threatening. In her relentless march toward Having It All, Eve Harrington (Baxter, all sugar and strychnine) convinces nearly everyone that she's just a naive kid trying to make it in the tough world of the Broadway theater. Aging Margo Channing (Davis, giving a bravura performance), her maid Birdie (Ritter, as her usual lovable sourpuss), and influential critic Addison De Witt (Sanders, at his most poisonous) know better. Taken in by dewy-eyed Eve are Margo's fiancé and director (Merrill), her best friend (Holm), and Holm's playwright husband (Marlowe). Most quoted line: "Fasten your seat belts," Margo advises her party guests. "It's going to be a bumpy night!" Funny and dramatic at the same time, *All About Eve* is probably the definitive show-biz movie.

Off-Screen: In its casting, the movie is so perfect that it seems impossible that others were even considered for the principal roles. According to Mankiewicz, studio head Darryl F. Zanuck wanted Marlene Dietrich as Margo, Jeanne Crain as Eve, and Jose Ferrer as De Witt. Mankiewicz's own preference for Claudette Colbert over Dietrich, among other cast changes, prevailed, but a severe back injury eliminated her. After British star Gertrude Lawrence turned down the role, Davis was approached and, wisely, she grabbed it. Davis's off-camera romance with Merrill resulted in their marriage. The movie won six Oscars: Best Picture, Supporting Actor (Sanders), Director, Screenplay, Costume Design (black-and-white), and Sound Recording. In 1970, *All About Eve* was turned into a Broadway musical called *Applause.* (CFB)

All Quiet on the Western Front

Universal, 1930. (130m.) Dir: Lewis Milestone. Sp: Dell Andrews, Maxwell Anderson, and George Abbott, b/o novel by Erich Maria Remarque. Cast: Lew Ayres, Louis Wolheim, Slim Summerville, John Wray, Russell Gleason, Ben Alexander, Beryl Mercer.

On-Screen: *Intensely realistic drama of World War I.* The first major antiwar movie of the sound era, *All Quiet on the Western Front* strips war of all glamour. Based on the sensational best-selling novel, this powerful film depicts the horror and futility of war from the point of view of seven German youths who enlist idealistically to fight for the Fatherland. Instead, they find destruction, despair, and death on the battlefield. Ayres is sympathetic as the central character who returns home on leave only to find his townsfolk still trumpeting the "glories" of war. Disillusioned, he returns to the front. Among the film's many unforgettable moments is the final one, in which, just before the armistice, Ayres reaches out to grasp a butterfly and is mortally wounded.

Off-Screen: The film was awarded two Oscars, for Best Picture and for Milestone's direction; it was nominated for its screenplay and Arthur Edeson's photography. In order to convincingly depict the battlefields of France, a military site was built covering nearly a thousand acres on the Irvine Ranch in southern California. The realistic German village later provided the studio with exterior sets for *Frankenstein* and its sequels. ZaSu Pitts, who had played a serious role in von Stroheim's silent classic, *Greed,* was cast as Ayres's mother; her comically whiny voice, however, evoked laughter, and her scenes were reshot with British character actress Mercer. George Cukor, soon to become a director himself, assisted Milestone (whose hand, incidentally, is seen clutching the butterfly) as dialogue coach. Another budding director, Fred Zinnemann, played a small role. (CFB)

All That Jazz

Fox, 1979. (C–123m.) Dir: Bob Fosse. Sp: Robert Alan Aurthur and Bob Fosse. MS: Various writers. Cast: Roy Scheider, Ann Reinking, Leland Palmer, Jessica Lange, Cliff Gorman, Erzebet Foldi, Ben Vereen, John Lithgow, Anthony Holland, Max Wright.

On-Screen: *Bob Fosse's semiautobiographical musical drama.* You may be exasperated and baffled, or you may be fascinated and enthralled, but chances are you won't be bored by Bob Fosse's film about a dance director's life and death. From its stunning opening musical sequence, "On Broadway," *All That Jazz* follows Joe Gideon (Scheider) through a day of auditions, rehearsals, and impulsive womanizing. When he suffers a heart attack, his hospital becomes a setting for a series of hallucinatory musical numbers. These are climaxed by a rousing "Bye, Bye, Life" (originally "Bye, Bye, Love"), in which Gideon bids farewell to the world. True, much of the film is self-indulgent, and some of the dramatic portions are overstated or heavy-handed, but the musical numbers are brilliantly conceived and staged. (Best is "Take Off with Us.") Despite its flaws, *All That Jazz* is a scintillating portrait of that combination of dedication, talent, fear, and egomania called the theater.

Off-Screen: Bob Fosse's style was clearly influenced by Italian director Federico Fellini. In fact, his photographer, Giuseppe Totunno, worked with Fellini. Fosse first cast Richard Dreyfuss as Joe Gideon, but he left the project after "artistic differences." Jack Nicholson and Keith Carradine were also considered. The role of Gideon's ex-wife, Audrey, modeled on Gwen Verdon and played by Leland Palmer, was written for Shirley MacLaine, who finally declined. Director Sidney Lumet was supposed to play Lucas Sargent but bowed out. The movie won three Oscars: for original song score, film editing, and costume design. It was nominated for five others, including Best Picture, Best Actor (Scheider), and Best Director.

All That Money Can Buy aka The Devil and Daniel Webster

RKO, 1941. (84m., 106m. in restored version) Dir: William Dieterle. Sp: Dan Totheroh and Stephen Vincent Benet, b/o story by Benet. Cast: Edward Arnold, Walter Huston, James Craig, Anne Shirley, Simone Simon, Jane Darwell, Gene Lockhart, John Qualen, H. B. Warner.

On-Screen: *A New Hampshire farmer must give the Devil his due.* After Jabez Stone (Craig) sells his soul to a certain Mr. Scratch (Huston) in exchange for seven years of prosperity, he enlists the aid of famed lawyer and statesman Daniel Webster (Arnold) to save him from eternal damnation. Based on Benet's "The Devil and Daniel Webster," a homespun version of the Faust legend, the movie excels when Arnold and Huston are on-screen. Arnold is ideal as go-getter Web-

ster, and Huston's cigar-chomping Prince of Darkness is such a genial Yankee that one pulls for him, rather than worry about Jabez Stone. The young leads (Craig and Shirley) are earnest but colorless, but French import Simon, a home-wrecking temptress, and Qualen, one of Scratch's doomed clients, are effective in lesser roles. A spectral ball waltzed to Bernard Herrmann's eerie music and the climactic trial scene provide drama otherwise missing from this film.

Off-Screen: Thomas Mitchell was originally cast in the role of Mr. Scratch but an injury soon after filming began prevented him from continuing. Huston, an inspired choice to replace him, won an Oscar nomination as Best Actor. Herrmann's evocative score won an Oscar for this film, though he was also nominated for *Citizen Kane.* The movie has a checkered history: It previewed as *Here Is a Man* in July 1941 but was released several months later as *All That Money Can Buy.* It was later distributed as *The Devil and Daniel Webster,* then cut down to the bare-bones, 84-minute version that was shown for many years. The original, 106-minute version is now available on laser disc. (CFB)

All the King's Men

Columbia, 1949. (109m.) Dir: Robert Rossen. Sp: Robert Rossen, b/o novel by Robert Penn Warren. Cast: Broderick Crawford, John Ireland, Mercedes McCambridge, Joanne Dru, John Derek, Shepperd Strudwick.

On-Screen: *A Southern demagogue rises to power.* Rossen's skill as both director and adaptor turns Warren's Pulitzer Prize–winning novel, a thinly disguised account of the meteoric career of Louisiana governor Huey Long, into an explosive film. Crawford's bulldozer performance makes Willie Stark, a hayseed lawyer whose growing lust for political power very nearly turns him into a fascist dictator, frighteningly plausible. (Just watch him at a barbecue where his bare-knuckled speech rouses the crowd to fever pitch.) McCambridge, in her film debut, also stands out as Stark's hard-boiled hatchet woman who becomes embittered when he throws her over for society belle Dru. Other cast members are fine, including Ireland as a reporter covering Stark's career and Strudwick as the ruthless politico's disillusioned nemesis. But it's Crawford's movie all the way.

Off-Screen: Studio chief Harry Cohn had little confidence in this offbeat movie. He had wanted Spencer Tracy to play the lead as box-office insurance but Rossen insisted on a lesser-known actor. He had favored Crawford after seeing him in *Of Mice and Men,* and won out after much opposition. Rossen shot most of the film in Stockton, California, using hundreds of citizens as extras and bit players At Oscar time, awards went to the film and to both Crawford and McCambridge. Rossen (direction and screenplay), Ireland (supporting actor), and the film's editors were nominated.

All the President's Men

Warners, 1976. (C-138m.) Dir: Alan J. Pakula. Sp: William Goldman, b/o book by Carl Bernstein and Bob Woodward. Cast: Robert Redford, Dustin Hoffman, Jason Robards, Jack Warden, Martin Balsam, Jane Alexander, Ned Beatty, Hal Holbrook.

On-Screen: *Bold, enthralling exposé of the Watergate scandal.* Based on the best-selling book by a Washington *Post* investigative team, the movie traces, step by step, the disclosure of the White House conspiracy to cover up the break-in at the Watergate office complex that led, uncoincidentally, to the resignation of President Nixon two years later. Redford and Hoffman are terrific as the journalists whose dogged persistence revealed what lay behind the infamous scandal that had such shattering results. Robards also excels as the fearless *Post* editor Ben Bradlee, and Alexander is splendid as the jumpy secretary with the shady Committee to Re-elect the President ("CREEP"). Holbrook is the mysterious informant "Deep Throat." Newspaper adventure, political drama, detective-story thriller—this movie has it all.

Off-Screen: Although some of the movie was shot in Washington, D.C., scenes occurring in the busy, sprawling newsroom were filmed in a 33,000-square-foot studio replica. Astute viewers will spot Frank Wills in his real-life role as the Watergate security guard who blew the whistle on the break-in. The movie, Pakula, and Alexander were nominated for Oscars, but awards went to Goldman (Best Screenplay Based on Material from Another Medium) and Robards (Best Supporting Actor). (CFB)

All This and Heaven, Too

Warners, 1940. (143m.) Dir: Anatole Litvak. Sp: Casey Robinson, b/o novel by Rachel Field. Cast: Bette Davis, Charles Boyer, Jeffrey Lynn, Barbara O'Neil, Virginia Weidler, Helen Westley, Walter Hampden, Henry Daniell, Harry Davenport.

On-Screen: *A romantic scandal rocks mid-nineteenth-century France.* A long, elaborate, and rather musty drama, *All This and Heaven, Too* adapts Rachel Field's best-selling novel (based on a celebrated true case) concerning a French governess (Davis) and her shocking purported romance with her employer (Boyer). Despite the fact that murder, passion, and other ungenteel activities are involved, their love affair, as depicted in the film, is remarkably chaste and platonic. Still, Davis gives an affecting performance as the long-suffering governess, reaching the heights in the courtroom scene in which she denies her complicity in a murder, and Boyer is especially fine as the duke who finally, on his deathbed, confesses to loving Davis "with every drop of blood" in him. Barbara O'Neil won an Oscar nomination for her performance as his insanely jealous wife. The movie is heavy going, but there are some compensations along the way.

Off-Screen: Although they had been lovers, Davis and director "Tola" Litvak clashed openly during the making of this film. Davis resented his abrasive manner of directing, and his refusal to permit spontaneity or flexibility in his actors. Later Davis also recalled that he ruined Barbara O'Neil's performance by not allowing her to play the frowsy, unkempt, and utterly unattractive woman described in Rachel Field's book. Davis said, "It was heartbreaking to Barbara, as it robbed her of a far greater performance."

Always

Universal–United Artists, 1989. (C-121m.) Dir: Steven Spielberg. Sp: Jerry Belson, b/o screenplay by Dalton Trumbo; adaptation: Frederick Hazlitt Brennan, b/o story by Chandler Sprague and David Boehm. Cast: Richard Dreyfuss, Holly Hunter, John Goodman, Brad Johnson, Audrey Hepburn, Roberts Blossom, Keith David.

On-Screen: *A romantic fantasy from Steven Spielberg.* Steven Spielberg has spent much of his career trying to recreate the sort of exuberant feeling once generated by the very act of "going to the movies." When he succeeds, the result is triumphant, such as in *E.T.: The Extra-Terrestrial.* But when he fails, as in *Always,* it's simply an embarrassment. *Always* advances Hollywood's perennial idea of death as an extended vacation at a blissful, puffy-clouded resort. Richard Dreyfuss is a daredevil, fire-fighting pilot in love with Holly Hunter. When he dies in a crash, Head Angel Audrey Hepburn sends him back to earth to imbue a young pilot (Johnson) with divine inspiration. Trouble is young Johnson also loves Hunter, and Dreyfuss must release his lost love so that she can go on with her life. It's all very gauzy and tear-streaked and silly, and despite all the tender gazes, the Dreyfuss-Hunter romance is never believable. *Always* is not even "now."

Off-Screen: The movie is a remake of the 1943 film *A Guy Named Joe,* in which Spencer Tracy and Irene Dunne played the romantic leads. Even then, despite the Tracy-Dunne star power, the story was rather hard to take. Curious casting note: In the 1943 movie, Audrey Hepburn's role of the welcoming Head Angel (called "the General") was played by Lionel Barrymore.

Amadeus

Orion, 1984. (C-158m.) Dir: Milos Forman. Sp: Peter Shaffer, b/o his play. Cast:

F. Murray Abraham, Tom Hulce, Elizabeth Berridge, Simon Callow, Roy Dotrice, Christine Ebersole, Jeffrey Jones.

On-Screen: *Music, madness—and murder?* This lavishly produced, superbly acted movie is as far from those lifeless and-then-he-wrote musical biopics of yesteryear as Vienna is from Tin Pan Alley. Imaginatively mixing fact with fiction, the Forman-Shaffer team focuses on the conflict between composer Antonio Salieri (Abraham), a favorite at the court of Emperor Joseph II (Jones), and his young rival, Wolfang Amadeus Mozart (Hulce). Salieri, a grave, virtuous man and a musician of conventional talent, is outraged at the rambunctious, vulgar upstart whose creative gifts seem preternaturally inspired. Abraham is heartbreaking as an artist driven mad by an incomprehensible truth; Hulce is endearing as "Wolfie," the giggling, seeming nincompoop whom the gods have blessed. Purists may balk at liberties taken with fact. Others will enjoy this drama for what it sets out to be: a gripping and exhilarating paean to genius.

Off-Screen: In transferring the London-Broadway stage hit to the screen, Shaffer and Forman were able to film many of the movie's scenes in actual sites in Czechoslovakia (standing in for Austrian locations as well). One sequence, for example, shows Mozart conducting his opera *Don Giovanni* in Prague's Tyl Theater, the very place where such an event actually occurred. The inspired casting of Hulce, who had played a college fraternity zany in *National Lampoon's Animal House,* derives from Shaffer's concept of Mozart as a modern-day cutup. The movie won eight Oscars, including Best Picture, Direction, Screenplay, and Abraham as Best Actor, in which category Hulce was also nominated. (CFB)

American Graffiti

Universal, 1973. (C-112m.) Dir: George Lucas. Sp: George Lucas, Gloria Katz, and Willard Huyck. Cast: Richard Dreyfuss, Ronny Howard, Paul Le Mat, Charlie Martin Smith, Cindy Williams, Candy Clark, Mackenzie Phillips, Bo Hopkins, Harrison Ford, Suzanne Somers.

On-Screen: *Lucas's pre-*Star Wars *surprise hit.* "Where were you in '62?" queried the ads for this funny, nostalgic evocation of teenage life in a small California town. More a summation of the complacent fifties than a comment on the turbulent sixties, the movie covers twelve hours in the lives of four friends: Curt (Dreyfuss), about to head for college; Steve (Howard), also college-bound but emotionally tied to the town and his girlfriend, Lauri (Williams); Terry (Smith), bumbling but amiable; and John (Le Mat), a strutting hot-rodder. At the center are their mishaps, mostly comic, and their crucial decisions, all to the sounds of rock 'n' roll and "cruising" cars. An epilogue reveals what eventually happens to the four young men. Nominated for five Oscars, including Best Picture and Director.

Off-Screen: Because the movie lacked "big names" (at the time), the studio doubted its box-office appeal, so Lucas had to limit his shooting schedule to less than a month on a budget of well under a million dollars. To help insure its success, he got his friend Francis Ford Coppola, fresh from his triumph as director of *The Godfather,* to lend his name as coproducer. An instant hit, Lucas's movie grossed over $55 million. In a small role is Johnny Weissmuller, Jr., son of the famous movie Tarzan. *More American Graffiti* (1979), with another director and several members of the original cast, disappointed. (CFB)

An American in Paris

MGM, 1951. (C-115m.) Dir: Vincente Minnelli. Sp: Alan Jay Lerner. MS: George and Ira Gershwin. Cast: Gene Kelly, Leslie Caron, Georges Guetary, Oscar Levant, Nina Foch.

On-Screen: *Gershwin, Kelly, and Paris—who could ask for anything more?* One of the glorious peaks in movie musicals during the fabled Arthur Freed period at MGM, *An American in Paris* enchants the viewer with its glittering color, superb dancing (Gene Kelly at his energetic best), and brace of marvelous Gershwin songs. Among the bountiful musical treasures: Kelly's song-and-dance to "I Got Rhythm" with a streetful of Paris urchins, and his romantic dance on the banks of the Seine with the delectable Leslie Caron (her film debut) to "Our Love Is Here to Stay." The famous seventeen-minute ballet that closes the film is everything its admirers and detractors claim: imaginative, audacious, and too ambitious for its own good. Yes, there are flaws: The story line is serviceable, no more; the film's Paris is clearly studio-bound, despite the lavish decor; and there is perhaps a bit too much of Oscar Levant as Kelly's caustic friend. In all, the spirit is festive, the Gershwin music is hard to resist, and Kelly wraps it all up with his infectious grin.

Off-Screen: Vincente Minnelli wanted Maurice Chevalier to play the French entertainer affianced to Leslie Caron, then chose Georges Guetary when Chevalier was unavailable. He also thought of Celeste Holm for the Nina Foch role but changed his mind after Foch read. The expensive ($450,000) ballet sequence had many detractors, but Minnelli and Lerner, with Louis B. Mayer's support, persevered. Amazingly, the film won seven Academy Awards, and Gene Kelly received a Special Oscar. For a full account of the making of this film, see *The Magic Factory* by Donald Knox (Praeger, 1973).

The Americanization of Emily

MGM, 1964. (117m.) Dir: Arthur Hiller. Sp: Paddy Chayefsky, b/o novel by William Bradford Huie. Cast: James Garner, Julie Andrews, Melvyn Douglas, James Coburn, Joyce Grenfell, Keenan Wynn, Judy Carne, Liz Fraser, Edward Binns, William Windom.

On-Screen: *Paddy Chayefsky's sardonic reflection on wartime bravery and romance.* In May 1944, shortly before D Day, Charlie Madison (Garner) is a "dog-robber": a naval officer who tends to all the needs of his admiral (Douglas). A champion wheeler-dealer, Charlie is also a self-confessed coward who believes that we "perpetuate war by exalting its sacrifices." Charlie meets and falls for a young British war widow (Andrews) whose ideas are diametrically opposed to his. When his loony admiral insists that the first dead man on Omaha Beach must be a sailor, a surprised and reluctant Charlie finds himself at the spearhead of the invasion. Paddy Chayefsky's sharp-edged screenplay is guaranteed to offend some viewers with its skewered view of wartime behavior but like much of Chayefsky's latter-day work (*The Hospital, Network*), it is clearly intended to stir up arguments. Andrews's widow sums up the movie's attitude when, believing that Charlie is gone, she chooses not to mourn his death but to celebrate his "cowardly, greedy, selfish appreciation of life." Food for thought in a caustic comedy.

Off-Screen: It was no surprise when the Pentagon refused to help the film in any way. It would not cooperate at all when the filmmakers wanted to borrow landing craft for the invasion scenes, and an old craft had to be found. MGM originally wanted William Wyler to direct the film, with William Holden in the leading role, but both were unavailable because of contractual difficulties.

Anastasia

Fox, 1956. (C–105m.) Dir: Anatole Litvak. Sp: Arthur Laurents, b/o play by Marcelle Maurette as translated by Guy Bolton. Cast: Ingrid Bergman, Yul Brynner, Helen Hayes, Akim Tamiroff, Martita Hunt, Felix Aylmer.

On-Screen: *A woman claims to be the surviving daughter of the last Russian czar.* For many decades an aura of mystery has surrounded some aspects of the assassination of Russia's Czar Nicholas and his family in 1918. Did Nicholas's daughter Anastasia survive? Marcelle Maurette's 1954 play, translated by Guy Bolton, dramatized this possibility, and was brought to the screen two years later in this lavish, compelling film. After a six-year absence, Ingrid Bergman returned to American films as the poor, half-mad woman who is chosen by an exiled general (Brynner) and his confederates to impersonate Anastasia so that they can claim her large inheritance. Strange coincidences suggest that she may *indeed* be Anastasia, and in the best-remembered sequence, the Dowager Empress (Hayes) finally accepts her as her true granddaughter. A twist of the plot leaves the mystery tantalizingly unsolved. Bergman gives a stunning, Oscar-winning performance as the street-girl-turned-regal-beauty. The role of the Dowager Empress needs a more imposing actress than Helen Hayes but she is moving as her emotions overwhelm her reason in that private interview with Anastasia.

Off-Screen: During the filming, Bergman received many vituperative letters about her relationship with director Roberto Rossellini. Although the two had been married since 1950, many apparently were unwilling to forgive her early "scandalous" relationship with him. According to Yul Brynner, the letters affected her acting: "She'd forget her lines, bump into chairs, and face the wrong camera. I tried to calm her down." Nevertheless, the actress was warmly welcomed back to America in January 1957. Two months later she received an Academy Award. *Anya,* a musical version of *Anastasia,* had a brief Broadway run in 1965.

Anatomy of a Murder

Columbia, 1959. (160m.) Dir: Otto Preminger. Sp: Wendell Mayes, b/o novel by Robert Traver. Cast: James Stewart, Lee Remick, Ben Gazzara, George C. Scott, Eve Arden, Arthur O'Connell, Kathryn Grant, Orson Bean, Murray Hamilton.

On-Screen: *A murder trial rocks a quiet Michigan town.* Lieutenant Frederick Manion (Gazzara) has been accused of murdering local resident Barney Quill, allegedly after Quill raped his wife, Laura (Remick). What really happened—and why? And how can lawyer Paul Biegler (Stewart) successfully defend his arrogant client? From these questions *Anatomy of a Murder* fashions a long but gripping courtroom melodrama laced with enough ironies and ambiguities to raise it several notches above the conventional film of this sort. Derived from Robert Traver's best-selling novel, the screenplay leaves a number of questions unanswered, but this never diminishes the force of the narrative. Stewart, George C. Scott (as a prosecuting attorney), and Arthur O'Connell (as Stewart's alcoholic colleague) give exceptionally good performances, and real-life Judge Joseph N. Welch, famous for the Army-McCarthy hearings, is delightful as the presiding judge. The film's only flaw is Duke Ellington's inappropriate jazz score.

Off-Screen: The first choice for the female lead was Lana Turner, but after a flap about her wardrobe for the film she was released, and Lee Remick replaced her. Joseph Welch was signed to play the judge after Spencer Tracy and Burl Ives turned down the role. The movie was filmed in Ishpeming and Marquette, two small communities in Michigan's northern peninsula. Robert Traver was the pen name for Judge John D. Voelker.

Anchors Aweigh

MGM, 1945. (C-140m.) Dir: George Sidney. Sp: Isobel Lennart, b/o story by Natalie Marcin. MS: Jule Styne and Sammy Cahn. Cast: Gene Kelly, Frank Sinatra, Kathryn Grayson, José Iturbi, Pamela Britton, Dean Stockwell, Rags Ragland.

On-Screen: *Kelly and Sinatra on the town in Hollywood.* Four years before their triumph in *On the Town,* MGM's film version of the Broadway musical, Gene Kelly and Frank Sinatra starred in this amiable and splashy forerunner, also as two gobs on leave. Here they are loose in Hollywood, trying to help singer Kathryn Grayson arrange an audition with pianist-conductor José Iturbi. The movie is too long, and the plot, replete with romantic misunderstandings, is tiresome. Still, there is pleasure to be had in the musical numbers, especially Kelly and Sinatra's exuberant song-and-dance to "I Begged Her," Sinatra's smooth rendition of "I Fall in Love Too Easily," and Kelly's charming Mexican dance with little Sharon McManus. Best of all, and worth waiting for, is Kelly's classic dance with the cartoon character Jerry the Mouse. The tale of a sad mouse king and the sailor who teaches him how to dance is an ingenious delight.

Off-Screen: Stanley Donen, Gene Kelly's assistant on the film, was required to teach Sharon McManus her dance routine. It required three hours in the morning and four in the afternoon for Sharon to learn a single step that involved skipping rope. By the time she had mastered the step, she and Donen despised each other. The number was shot on a reconstruction of Olvera Street in the Mexican settlement of Los Angeles. Surprisingly, the movie received several Oscar nominations, including Best Picture and Best Actor (Kelly). It won for Best Scoring of a Musical Picture (George Stoll).

... And Justice for All

Columbia, 1979. (C-117m.) Dir: Norman Jewison. Sp: Valerie Curtin and Barry Levinson. Cast: Al Pacino, Jack Warden, John Forsythe, Christine Lahti, Lee Strasberg, Jeffrey Tambor, Sam Levene, Craig T. Nelson, Robert Christian, Thomas Waites.

On-Screen: *A dedicated lawyer battles the judicial system.* Can a movie suffer a nervous breakdown before your very eyes? The ironically titled *. . . And Justice for All* proves that it's possible. Part black comedy, part blistering satire, and part stark drama, the film never seems certain about where it wants to take us. The result is well-intentioned but incoherent. Al Pacino is Arthur Kirkland, a fiercely committed, caring lawyer who must deal with a judicial system that is corrupt and life-destroying at worst, expedient at best. His clients include a desperate young man (Waites) who cannot get out of jail for a minor offense, a terrified transvestite (Christian), and, worst of all, a truly evil judge (Forsythe) whom he is forced to defend. Al Pacino gives a sturdy, passionate performance that fully conveys Arthur Kirkland's despair and rage, but the muddled, overwrought screenplay defeats him. That excellent actress Christine Lahti makes her film debut as Kirkland's lover and a lawyer whose legal opinions are the opposite of his.

Off-Screen: The movie was shot largely in co-author Barry Levinson's home town of Baltimore, the city he later celebrated when he turned to directing such films as *Diner* (1982) and *Avalon* (1990). Al Pacino was nominated for an Academy Award, as were Levinson and Valerie Curtin for their original screenplay. Christine Lahti was signed after Norman Jewison spotted her in *The Last Tenant,* a television play that starred famed acting coach-turned-actor Lee Strasberg. Strasberg plays Pacino's senile grandfather in the film.

Angels with Dirty Faces

Warners, 1938. (97m.) Dir: Michael Curtiz. Sp: John Wexley and Warren Duff, b/o story by Rowland Brown. Cast: James Cagney, Pat O'Brien, Ann Sheridan, Humphrey Bogart, George Bancroft, Billy Halop, Leo Gorcey, Huntz Hall, Bobby Jordan, Gabriel Dell.

On-Screen: *Two slum friends share different fates.* A ripe target for parody over many years, *Angels with Dirty Faces* is vintage Warners fare: melodramatic, hard-hitting, and noisily scored. It's the one about the two slum boys who move in opposite directions—one (Cagney) becomes an arrogant thug, the other (O'Brien) a kindly priest. The movie advances the idea that a corrupt, poverty-stricken society breeds crime, but most of the time is taken with the action. Ann Sheridan is on hand as Cagney's loyal girlfriend, as is Humphrey Bogart as Cagney's treacherous colleague. Also present are the rowdy Dead End Kids, who must learn not to admire Cagney as a role model. In one of his most memorable moments on film, Cagney teaches them by pretending to turn "yellow" as he is dragged off to his execution. (Or does he? See below.)

Off-Screen: Cagney's own comment on the ending: "I think in looking at the film it is virtually impossible to say which course Rocky took—which is just the way I wanted it. I played it with deliberate ambiguity so that the spectator can take his choice." Sam Goldwyn objected to the studio's using the words "The Dead End Kids," claiming that the actors were associated exclusively with the Sidney Kingsley play *Dead End* he had adapted for the screen. Warners's lawyers made it clear that the use of the "Dead End" name was in no way "misleading" or "unfair" (it was not in the film's title), and the name remained for additional films.

Animal Crackers

Paramount, 1930. (98m.) Dir: Victor Heerman. Sp: Morrie Ryskind, b/o musical play by George S. Kaufman and Morrie Ryskind. MS: Bert Kalmar and Harry Ruby. Cast: Groucho, Harpo, Chico, and Zeppo Marx, Margaret Dumont, Lillian Roth, Louis Sorin, Hal Thompson, Margaret Irving, Robert Greig.

On-Screen: *"Hooray for Captain Spaulding!"* An antique piece of Marxian mayhem, *Animal Crackers,* their second feature film, is every bit as stagebound and creaky as their first, *The Cocoanuts.* Marx fans won't mind, however, since it contains some gloriously funny moments. This time the boys are set loose on a palatial Long Island estate where they become involved with a stolen painting. And with Margaret Dumont as Mrs. Rittenhouse, the mistress of the manor, there's ample mirth and mischief. As the not exactly reputable explorer, Captain Spaulding, Groucho gets to perform his famous number, "Hooray for Captain Spaulding!" and to deliver his hilarious monologue about his African exploits. Of course he also mixes it up with Chico, playing a musician named Ravelli, and with Harpo as a demented soul called the Professor (of what, nobody knows). A choice sequence: Chico and Harpo play bridge with Mrs. Rittenhouse and her friend (Irving). Harpo wins the game by playing thirteen aces.

Off-Screen: Like *The Cocoanuts, Animal Crackers* was filmed at Paramount's Astoria studio. The director, Victor Heerman, had worked for Mack Sennett, and so was used to the sort of slapstick mayhem perpetrated by the Marxes, both in front of and behind the cameras. The film's ingenue is Lillian Roth, later known as the actress-singer who wrote about her life as an alcoholic in *I'll Cry Tomorrow.*

Anna and the King of Siam

Fox, 1946. (128m.) Dir: John Cromwell. Sp: Talbot Jennings and Sally Benson, b/o biography by Margaret Landon. Cast: Irene Dunne, Rex Harrison, Linda Darnell, Lee J. Cobb, Gale Sondergaard, Mikhail Rasumny, Dennis Hoey, Richard Lyon.

On-Screen: *An English governess clashes with the Siamese king.* Before *The King and I,* there was *Anna and the King of Siam,* a non-musical account of the determined governess (Dunne) who comes to Siam in 1862 to tutor the many children of the country's imperious king (Harrison). The movie follows the now-familiar story: Anna Leonowens (here called Owens) finds herself confronting the ancient, implacable ways of a proud, inquisitive ruler (Harrison) and comes to admire and even love him in the end. Even without the lilting Rodgers and Hammerstein score, *Anna and the King of Siam* is a touching, enjoyable film, lavishly produced and impeccably acted by Dunne and Harrison. In his first American film, Harrison gives a bravura, Oscar-winning performance of a complex man who is puzzled by change. There is perhaps too much Hollywood in Linda Darnell's portrayal of a harem favorite who has a clandestine, tragic love affair. But this *Anna* is well worth the viewing.

Off-Screen: In his autobiography Rex Harrison claimed to have had "no real contact" with director Cromwell: "I had to take my own course. This only widened the gap between us, because Cromwell saw that I wasn't waiting for him. I'd play each scene as I'd prepared it, to the best of my ability, always suspecting that I could never really get inside the mind of the King of Siam, and John Cromwell, from the beginning, just left it, never trying to make suggestions or improvements." Oscars were also awarded for cinematography (Arthur Miller) and for art direction/set decoration.

Anna Christie

MGM, 1930. (74m.) Dir: Clarence Brown. Sp: Frances Marion, b/o play by Eugene O'Neill. Cast: Greta Garbo, Charles Bickford, Marie Dressler, George F. Marion.

On-Screen: *The supreme goddess of the silents strides into the sound era.* Unlike the well-heeled woman of affairs that she often portrayed in her silent movies, Garbo became a down-at-the-heels streetwalker for her talkie debut, an adaptation of Eugene O'Neill's Pulitzer Prize–winning drama. She plays Anna, a disillusioned girl recently released from prison who comes to a waterfront saloon in search of her estranged father (Marion,), a barge captain. (Her first lines: "Gimme a whiskey, ginger ale on the side. And don't be stingy, baby.") Later, during a raging storm, Anna and her father rescue Matt (Bickford), a burly Irish sailor. Anna and Matt fall in love, although his feeling for her is sorely tested when he learns of her crimson past. Garbo, as always, is never less than riveting; at age twenty-four, she was blessed with a throaty voice that perfectly matched her smoldering aura. As good as she is, it is Marie Dressler, as Marthy, a boozy old barfly and friend to Anna's father, who comes close to stealing the film.

Off-Screen: Garbo regarded O'Neill's play as belittling to Swedes, but she agreed to appear in the film when the studio threatened to suspend her if she refused. The picture proved a career booster for Dressler, who was considered washed up before the arrival of sound. *Anna Christie* had been filmed once before, in 1923, with Blanche Sweet in the title role. In 1957 it was made into a Broadway musical, *New Girl in Town,* with Gwen Verdon as Anna and Thelma Ritter as Marthy. (CFB)

Anna Karenina

MGM, 1935. (95m.) Dir: Clarence Brown. Sp: Clemence Dane, Salka Viertel, and S. N. Behrman, b/o novel by Leo Tolstoy. Cast: Greta Garbo, Fredric March, Basil Rathbone, Reginald Owen, Freddie Bartholomew, Maureen O'Sullivan, May Robson.

On-Screen: *Garbo leaves her husband and son for the man she loves.* More a Garbo fan's collection of moments to treasure than Tolstoy's biting novel of social criticism, the movie nonetheless allows the legendary actress to glow as the tragic Russian adulteress who learns too late that she lives in a man's world. Her anguished voice ("I feel pain. I feel tears. Only because I am so happy."), her look first of hope, then of steely resolve at the end—the subtle eloquence of Garbo's art is to be savored, as always. The production aspires to czarist splendor, but much of the opulence is visually numbing. Basil Rathbone gives an outstanding performance as cold, dispassionate Karenin, to whom social position is all. The serious flaw is March as Anna's lover, Vronsky. Ill at ease, he's no match for Garbo's smoldering eroticism.

Off-Screen: When Garbo told producer David O. Selznick that she wanted to appear again as Anna Karenina (in 1927 she played the part in an updated version, *Love,* opposite John Gilbert), he tried in vain to interest her in *Dark Victory,* a modern drama and a recent Broadway hit. In 1939 the role became one of Bette Davis's biggest successes. Selznick's first choice for Vronsky was Clark Gable, but he was unavailable. March, who wanted a respite from costume films, replaced him at the insistence of his home studio, Fox. In the novel, Anna bears an illegitimate child, but the censors eliminated that and other unappetizing plot elements. Vivien Leigh starred in a British version released in 1948, and many years later, in 1992, a stage-musical adaptation was a short-lived failure on Broadway. (CFB)

Annie Get Your Gun

MGM, 1950. (C-107m.) Dir: George Sidney. Sp: Sidney Sheldon, b/o the 1946 musical play. MS: Irving Berlin. Cast: Betty Hutton, Howard Keel, Louis Calhern, J. Carrol Naish, Edward Arnold, Keenan Wynn, Benay Venuta.

On-Screen: *Annie Oakley gets her man to a Berlin score.* On stage, *Annie Get Your Gun* was a memorable triumph for Ethel Merman, her voice trumpeting the wonderful Berlin songs to the theater's last row. As the unlettered backwoods sharpshooter who totes a gun and pines for Frank Butler (Keel), brash Betty Hutton was no Merman, but her tireless energy and spirit carried her

through and helped to make this film version lively, splashy entertainment. There are some colorful production numbers, topped by the massive finale, a rodeo staged to Berlin's anthem "There's No Business Like Show Business." Hutton brings her frenetic style to such songs as "Doin' What Comes Naturally" and "You Can't Get a Man with a Gun," and joins Keel (in his film debut) in the challenge duet "Anything You Can Do." In robust voice, Keel gets to perform "The Girl That I Marry" and "My Defenses Are Down." In all, not a great musical film but a distinctly enjoyable one.

Off-Screen: Few musical films were ever plagued with so many problems. Judy Garland, the original movie Annie, had to be replaced when her mental state became unmanageable from the use of too many drugs and too much liquor. The production also had to be delayed when Howard Keel broke his ankle, and when Frank Morgan, cast as Buffalo Bill, died suddenly and had to be replaced by Louis Calhern. Annie (real name Phoebe Annie Oakley Mozee) was also played by Barbara Stanwyck in *Annie Oakley* (1935).

Annie Hall

United Artists, 1977. (C-94m.) Dir: Woody Allen. Sp: Woody Allen and Marshall Brickman. Cast: Woody Allen, Diane Keaton, Tony Roberts, Paul Simon, Shelley Duvall, Carol Kane, Colleen Dewhurst, Christopher Walken, Janet Margolin.

On-Screen: *Woody Allen's Oscar-winning comedy about urban neurotics.* Still the most popular and most lauded of Woody Allen's films, *Annie Hall* warrants its honored status by dint of its wit and originality. Allen's first fully rounded view of the bright, intense, angst-ridden New Yorkers who would populate many of his later films, *Annie Hall* centers on writer and world-class neurotic Alvy Singer (Allen). Alvy's thoughts range across his life: he remembers his childhood, his ex-wives, his ex-girlfriends, and mostly his on-and-off relationship with quirky, enchanting Annie Hall (Keaton). The requisite Allen quips are present (and hilarious), but the "triple-threat" director, star, and coauthor also uses a freewheeling style that goes from reality to fantasy and back again without missing a beat. Diane Keaton gives the film's key performance; her dithering Annie is a unique creation that the actress imbues with considerable charm. *Annie Hall* is studded with familiar Allen themes (his pessimism; his obsession with anti-Semitism; his dislike of California; etc.), but they are so smoothly integrated into the Alvy-Annie romance that they never seem like intrusions. You'll love meeting *Annie Hall* every time.

Off-Screen: For a while, the film was called *Anhedonia,* a disease in which the victim (i.e., Alvy) is incapable of experiencing pleasure. *Annie Hall* won Oscars for Best Picture, Best Actress (Keaton), Best Direction, and Best Original Screenplay. Diane Keaton, whose true surname is Hall, really does have a Grammy Hall. Sharp-eyed Future Stargazers may be able to spot Jeff Goldblum, Shelley Hack, Beverly D'Angelo, and Sigourney Weaver.

The Apartment

United Artists, 1960. (125m.) Dir: Billy Wilder. Sp: Billy Wilder and I.A.L. Diamond. Cast: Jack Lemmon, Shirley MacLaine, Fred MacMurray, Ray Walston, Jack Kruschen, Edie Adams, David Lewis, Joan Shawlee.

On-Screen: *Billy Wilder's bittersweet comedy of morals and manners in the business world.* Sharp-witted and bold for its day, and more than a little sardonic, *The Apartment* returned Billy Wilder to his satirical style after his more romantic comedies of the fifties. Jack Lemmon stars as C. C. ("Bud") Baxter, an ambitious office worker who, on the promise of advancement, agrees to lend his apartment to higher-ranking colleagues for sexual assignations. Secretly, Bud loves Fran Kubelik (MacLaine), an elevator operator who turns out to be the discarded mistress of a womanizing married executive (MacMurray) in the company. In the end, Bud regains his integrity and pride and also wins Fran's admiration and love. The Wilder-Diamond screenplay is polished and observant, but the movie leaves an unpleasant residue. The central character is not particularly attractive, and his groveling before his cheating superiors makes him less than palatable. There are many pleasurable moments, however, mostly the scenes between Lemmon and MacLaine—a lonely man and a wounded girl grasping at a relationship. And who can forget Jack Lemmon straining spaghetti through a tennis racket?

Off-Screen: According to a Lemmon biographer, Shirley MacLaine drove Billy Wilder to distraction with her habit of ad-libbing her own dialogue, plus a marked reluctance to rehearse. Paul Douglas was originally assigned to the Fred MacMurray role but died two weeks before filming began. A huge hit in 1960, *The Apartment* garnered five Oscars: Best Picture, Director, Screenplay, Editing, and Art Direction/Set Decoration. Jack Lemmon and Shirley MacLaine were both nominated but lost, respectively, to Burt Lancaster for *Elmer Gantry* and Elizabeth Taylor for *Butterfield 8*. In 1968, *The Apartment* was turned into a Broadway musical entitled *Promises, Promises*.

Apocalypse Now

United Artists, 1979. (C-150m.) Dir: Francis Coppola. Sp: John Milius and Francis Coppola. Cast: Marlon Brando, Martin Sheen, Robert Duvall, Frederick Forrest, Albert Hall, Sam Bottoms, Dennis Hopper.

On-Screen: *Unsparing drama of the Vietnam War's horror*. A flawed but powerful and haunting war film, *Apocalypse Now* uses the Vietnam experience as a metaphor for a vision of war as a demonic voyage into the deepest pit of hell. In 1968 Captain Willard (Sheen) is sent into the Cambodian jungle to locate and to "terminate with extreme prejudice" a renegade colonel named Kurtz (Brando) who has gone mad, deserted, and set himself up as a brutal dictator-god of a Cambodian island. In his search for Kurtz, Willard is plunged into the nightmarish and disorienting heart of battle. A memorable character is Lieutenant Colonel Kilgore (Duvall), who has also become unglued by the war's absurdity. Kilgore leads helicopter attackers to Wagner's whooping "Ride of the Valkyries" blasting over loudspeakers. Willard's ultimate confrontation with Kurtz is chilling although somewhat anticlimactic after all the "horror" that preceded it. Not a pretty picture, but a brilliant one.

Off-Screen: The screenplay is derived from Joseph Conrad's short novel *Heart of Darkness,* in which a man named Kurtz succumbs to

madness through his blind conquest of a region in Africa. More than five years in the planning and making, the movie was filmed primarily in the Philippines. After a typhoon destroyed sets and equipment, Sheen suffered a heart attack, necessitating the use of doubles. A winner of the Grand Prize at the Cannes Film Festival, the movie received eight Oscar nominations, including director and supporting actor (Duvall), but it was awarded only two statuettes, for Vittorio Storaro's superb photography and for sound. A 1991 documentary by Coppola's wife, called *Hearts of Darkness: A Filmmaker's Apocalypse,* reveals a great deal about the making of the film.(CFB)

Applause

Paramount, 1929. (78m.) Dir: Rouben Mamoulian. Sp: Garrett Fort, b/o novel by Beth Brown. MS: E. Y. Harburg, Jay Gorney, Dolly Morse, and Joe Burke. Cast: Helen Morgan, Joan Peers, Fuller Mellish, Jr., Joe King, Henry Wadsworth.

On-Screen: *Singer Helen Morgan stars in Rouben Mamoulian's landmark musical drama*. A singer whose high, sweet, poignant voice barely concealed the pain and despair of a short life, Helen Morgan made few film appearances. Rouben Mamoulian's pioneer drama with music marks her first—she plays an aging, blowsy burlesque queen whose virginal daughter (Peers) emerges from a convent. Trouble—and eventually tragedy—ensue, provoked by Morgan's no-good boyfriend (Mellish). Morgan gets to sing a few tunes in her inimitable style, but the story told is harsh and uncompromising. *Applause* creaks by now, but mostly it is famous for director Mamoulian's striking innovations in the use of camera and sound. Mamoulian works to give his first film the virtue of motion, not only in the camera movement, but also in the swift way he segues from period to period.

Off-Screen: A distinguished stage director (*Porgy and Bess, Oklahoma!*, etc.), Rouben Mamoulian was lured to Hollywood by an offer from Jesse Lasky and Walter Wanger of Paramount Pictures. After watching and absorbing the mechanics of filmmaking at the Astoria studio in Queens, New York, he plunged into his first movie. For the film, he created a now-common sound technique whereby two related but separate scenes can be recorded simultaneously.

Around the World in 80 Days

United Artists, 1956. (C-167m.) Dir: Michael Anderson. Sp: S. J. Perelman. Cast: David Niven, Cantinflas, Shirley MacLaine, Robert Newton, Robert Morley, Trevor Howard, and many guest stars, including Marlene Dietrich, Ronald Colman, Charles Boyer, Noel Coward, Beatrice Lillie, Red Skelton, Peter Lorre, Buster Keaton.

On-Screen: *Michael Todd's extravagant, star-studded travelogue via Jules Verne.* Stargazers will enjoy identifying the celebrities who keep turning up in cameo roles in this elaborate, entertaining spectacle produced by master showman Michael Todd. Brilliant humorist S. J. Perelman (with uncredited help from James Poe and John Farrow) adapted Jules Verne's 1872 novel about Phileas Fogg (Niven), a very proper Englishman, who makes a wager with his men's club that he can travel around the world in eighty days. With his valet Passepartout (Cantinflas), he makes his way to the world's capitals by train, boat, balloon, and even an ostrich, picking up an imperiled princess (MacLaine) along the way. The scenic views of Bombay, Hong Kong, Yokohama, and other cities are beautiful indeed, and the screenplay, a mixture of travelogue, slapstick, and satire, is generally amusing, especially in its spoof of British rectitude and formality. The movie gives too much footage to Mexican comedian Cantinflas, who is seldom as funny as intended. Still, the trip is worth taking—and how many stars can *you* spot?

Off-Screen: Filmed in the wide-screen Todd-AO process, *Around the World in 80 Days* won the Academy Award as the year's Best Picture. Victor Young's score also won, as did the screenplay adaptation (S. J. Perelman), the cinematography (Lionel Lindon), and the editing (Gene Ruggiero, Paul Weatherwax). Perelman's award was disputed by the Writers Guild, which claimed that James Poe had worked on the script. Poe's contribution, along with director John Farrow's, was later acknowledged. Michael Todd used almost 70,000 people in thirteen countries for the film. There were also 140 actual locations, plus interiors on soundstages in London, Hong Kong, Tokyo, and Hollywood. John Farrow was replaced as director by Michael Anderson after the first day's shooting.

Arthur

Orion, 1981. (C-97m.) Dir: Steve Gordon. Sp: Steve Gordon. Cast: Dudley Moore, Liza Minnelli, John Gielgud, Geraldine Fitzgerald, Jill Eikenberry, Stephen Elliott, Barney Martin, Ted Ross.

On-Screen: *An eccentric millionaire falls for a waitress. Arthur* attempts to revive the well-remembered "screwball" comedies of the thirties, and succeeds within reason. British comedian Dudley Moore plays the title role, an infantile, alcoholic millionaire who is being pushed into marriage with a rich girl (Eikenberry) he doesn't love. Instead he falls for waitress Liza Minnelli, with comically devastating results. Moore's incessant cackling may irritate you, and sodden drunks are no longer amusing, but there's a prize for those who forbear: John Gielgud. The actor delights in his Oscar-winning performance as Arthur's acerbic, imperious, and very funny valet Hobson. An indisputable highlight of the movie is his hospital scene with Arthur. Geraldine Fitzgerald tries to infuse some life into the role of Arthur's salty, plain-speaking grandmother, but this stock character was already wearing thin in the thirties. *Arthur* has a contrived and hectic climactic sequence in a wedding chapel, but until then the movie has some scintillating dialogue and a good number of laughs.

Off-Screen: The movie's theme song, "Best That You Can Do," won an Oscar. Steve Gordon's screenplay was also nominated for an Academy Award. Sadly, shortly after the success of *Arthur,* Gordon died at age forty-two. A stage-musical version of the story, appropriately called *Arthur: The Musical,* turned up at several theaters around the country in 1992.

The Asphalt Jungle

MGM, 1950. (112m.) Dir: John Huston. Sp: Ben Maddow and John Huston, b/o novel by W. R. Burnett. Cast: Sterling Hayden, Louis Calhern, Jean Hagen, Sam Jaffe, James Whitmore, John McIntyre, Marc Lawrence, Marilyn Monroe.

On-Screen: *A classic heist movie, taut and gripping.* Unlike Cagney or Robinson's snarling paranoids of the thirties, the crooks who come together for a bank heist in *The Asphalt Jungle* are simple people with modest dreams of personal fulfillment. They include Dix Handley (Hayden), a quick-trigger killer who wants to reclaim his Kentucky farm and settle down, and lecherous Doc Riedenschneider (Jaffe), who masterminds the robbery and longs to retire to a life of ease and easy women in Mexico. Louis Calhern excels as Emmerich, the suave, philandering lawyer who bankrolls the caper while indulging his blonde "niece" Angela (Marilyn Monroe in one of her early roles). The sequence of the jewel heist is justly famous, generating suspense without resorting to tricky editing. *The Asphalt Jungle* has strong *noir* elements, but the subtle interplay of characters gives it a special strength and power.

Off-Screen: The movie received Oscar nominations for Best Direction, Best Supporting Actor (Jaffe), Best Screenplay, and Best Cinematography (black-and-white). Originally, Huston wanted Lola Albright as Angela, but Monroe's ingenuous, childlike reading for the part impressed the director, and she won the role. The violent, and poignant, conclusion in which Hayden returns to the farm and his beloved horses, was filmed in Lexington, Kentucky. The studio remade the movie three times—as *The Badlanders* in 1958, *Cairo* in 1963, and *Cool Breeze* in 1972—but lightning struck only once.(CFB)

Auntie Mame

Warners, 1958. (C-143m.) Dir: Morton Da-Costa. Sp: Betty Comden and Adolph Green, b/o novel by Patrick Dennis and play by Jerome Lawrence and Robert E. Lee. Cast: Rosalind Russell, Forrest Tucker, Coral Browne, Peggy Cass, Fred Clark, Roger Smith, Jan Handzlik.

On-Screen: *Rosalind Russell embodies Patrick Dennis's irrepressible aunt.* The long and colorful career of Mame Dennis had its origins in Patrick Dennis's best-selling novel, which purported to be the account of life with his rowdy, outrageous, and loving aunt. The story was adapted successfully to the stage and then brought to the screen in this sprawling, unsubtle, but often funny comedy. (Later it became a stage and screen musical.) Rosalind Russell repeats her Broadway role as Mame, whose fortunes rise and fall over the years as she teaches her nephew (Handzlik as a boy, Smith as an adult) all about tolerance, bigotry, individuality, and life itself. The movie is too long and lacks finesse, but many laughs are generated by Russell's warmly expansive Mame and by Peggy Cass, who is hilarious as Mame's dowdy, myopic secretary, Agnes Gooch.

Off-Screen: Rosalind Russell claimed to have a sister who resembled Mame Dennis in many ways. (She called her "the Duchess.") She had taken copious notes about her sister and later asserted, good-humoredly, that Patrick Dennis had "beaten" her to writing the book. Travis Banton had designed the costumes for Broadway and was signed to repeat for the screen. When he died, he was replaced by Orry-Kelly. Russell and Cass received Oscar nominations, as did the picture, the cinematography, the art direction, and the editing.

Avalon

TriStar, 1990. (C-126m.) Dir: Barry Levinson. Sp: Barry Levinson. Cast: Armin Mueller-Stahl, Aidan Quinn, Elizabeth Perkins, Joan Plowright, Lou Jacobi, Kevin Pollak, Elijah Wood.

On-Screen: *An over-the-years chronicle of a Jewish family.* Although it tends to ramble, Barry Levinson's affectionate, bittersweet film entertains with its portrait of Jewish family life in Baltimore over several decades. The central figure, Sam Krichinsky (Mueller-Stahl), arrives in America as an awed immigrant on July 4, 1914, experiences the joys and tragedies of his family, and ends his days in a nursing home, a sad, confused old man lost in memory. Much of the film concerns the strivings of his son Jules (Quinn). The central theme is really the decline of family life—the Krichinsky Thanksgiving dinner begins as a festive occasion for the family circle and ends, many years later, with only a few people watching television as they consume their turkey. Although *Avalon* is well-acted and the period details are beautifully handled, it is never quite as impressive as it would like to be. A few of the incidents fail to ring true or have become frayed by overuse. On balance, however, *Avalon* takes a worthwhile journey to the past.

Off-Screen: For the 1914 Fourth of July celebration, hundreds of flags had to be sewn by hand. Most of the early television sets came from a collection in New Jersey. Almost everything else came from Baltimore-based collectors. Barry Levinson relied on memories of his own childhood and on family experiences. His parents acted as uniquely qualified technical advisers. Several members of the true-life Krichinsky family worked as extras or had small parts.

Awakenings

Columbia, 1990. (C-121m.) Dir: Penny Marshall. Sp: Steven Zaillian, b/o book by Oliver Sacks. Cast: Robert De Niro, Robin Williams, Julie Kavner, John Heard, Ruth Nelson, Max von Sydow, Anne Meara.

On-Screen: *A doctor tries to recall his "sleeping" patients to life.* Based on a true story, *Awakenings* concerns a neurologist named Oliver Sacks, here called Malcolm Sayer and played by Robin Williams, who, in 1966, experimented with patients stricken many years before with encephalitis, or sleeping sickness. Now in a trancelike state, these people exist in a closed world of their own. Given permission to test L-DOPA, Sayer manages to "awaken" Leonard Lowe (De Niro), who has not functioned since contracting sleeping sickness thirty years earlier. For a while, Leonard is ecstatically recalled to life as a feeling and thinking human being. Sadly, however, the cure is only temporary. Despite a downbeat ending and a depressing milieu, *Awakenings* somehow manages to impart a feeling of exhilaration in Leonard's deep if fleeting pleasure as he rediscovers the simple things. Robert De Niro's Oscar-nominated performance makes him a touching and believable figure, and Robin Williams forgoes his usual quicksilver comic style to play a shy and compassionate doctor with a mission.

Off-Screen: Oliver Sacks worked on the set with the actors, helping them to understand the disease they were simulating. A 1973 documentary, made for British television, showed the real Leonard, "frozen" since the twenties, who was able to tap out book reviews one letter at a time for the hospital magazine. Oscar nominations also went to the film itself and to Steven Zaillian's screenplay.

The Awful Truth

Columbia, 1937. (92m.) Dir: Leo McCarey. Sp: Viña Delmar, b/o play by Arthur Richman. Cast: Irene Dunne, Cary Grant, Ralph Bellamy, Cecil Cunningham, Alexander D'Arcy, Molly Lamont, Esther Dale, Joyce Compton.

On-Screen: *Irene Dunne and Cary Grant head for Splitsville.* One of the breeziest screwball comedies of the thirties, *The Awful Truth* has stayed fresh and funny for decades. The premise is actually as simple as can be: Lucy and Jerry Warriner (Dunne and Grant), who are clearly meant for each other, nevertheless split up when Jerry is caught in a lie. They each find separate prospective new mates, but they are really still in love. By film's end they are reunited. That's about it, but what a pleasure it is to watch Dunne, airy and deliciously tongue-in-cheek, exchange banter with quizzical, ironic Grant. They make the dialogue sound wittier than it is, and with McCarey's improvisational style carrying them along—he won an Oscar as Best Director—they are ideally matched. Two scenes are peerless, one in which Jerry disrupts Lucy's song recital and another in which Lucy, pretending to be Jerry's flamboyant Southern sister, arrives at the home of Jerry's new fiancée and promptly stirs up some mischief. Dunne and Grant are at their sparkling best, but note Cecil Cunningham's wry performance as Lucy's plain-speaking aunt.

Off-Screen: Although its plot seems thoroughly modern, the film is based on a 1922 stage hit, which was followed by two silent-movie versions. There's no evidence of it on-screen, but Grant was uncomfortable with McCarey's encouraging him and Dunne to improvise some of their dialogue. Exasperated, at one point he even offered to exchange roles with Bellamy, who played Dunne's fiancé. "Mr. Smith," the pet that Grant and Dunne squabble over for custody rights, is "Asta," Nick and Nora Charles's wirehaired fox terrier in the Thin Man series. In addition to the Academy Award for direction, the movie was nominated as Best Picture, and Dunne as Best Actress. *Let's Do It Again* (bad idea) was Columbia's 1953 musical remake.

Babes in Arms

MGM, 1939. (97m.) Dir: Busby Berkeley. Sp: Jack McGowan and Kay Van Riper, b/o musical play by Richard Rodgers and Lorenz Hart. MS: Richard Rodgers, Lorenz Hart, Arthur Freed, Nacio Herb Brown, and others. Cast: Mickey Rooney, Judy Garland, Charles Winninger, Guy Kibbee, June Preisser, Betty Jaynes, Douglas McPhail.

On-Screen: *Mickey Rooney and Judy Garland "put on a show" in the first of their musicals together.* There is a moment early in this dated but entertaining musical in which Rooney and Garland sing "Good Morning" and explode with energy and talent. This exuberant duet signals the start of an ongoing professional relationship that resulted in a series of movies affectionately known as the "Mickey-Judy" musicals. *Babes in Arms* sets the standard, with a sentimental plot, a fairly modest production, and, best of all, a batch of musical numbers that range from pure "camp" (the distressing "God's Country" finale) to pleasing (Garland's solo rendition of "I Cried for You"). In his first assignment away from Warner Bros., director Busby Berkeley keeps it all lively. His handling of the title number—Mickey and the kids asserting their independence in song—is the film's highlight.

Off-Screen: *Babes in Arms* stems only vaguely from the 1937 Broadway musical—just two Rodgers and Hart songs were retained. Many writers worked on the screenplay but only two were finally credited. Exhausted from making *The Wizard of Oz,* Judy Garland may have already been taking the diet and pep pills that made her hyperactive one minute and lethargic the next during the shooting. She often quarreled with Busby Berkeley, who relied on her good friend Rooney to keep her under control.

Babes on Broadway

MGM, 1941. (118m.) Dir: Busby Berkeley. Sp: Fred Finklehoffe and Elaine Ryan, b/o story by Fred Finklehoffe. MS: Burton Lane, Yip Harburg, and Ralph Freed. Cast: Mickey Rooney, Judy Garland, Fay Bainter, Virginia Weidler, Ray MacDonald, Richard Quine, James Gleason, Donna Adams (Donna Reed), Donald Meek.

On-Screen: *Mickey and Judy, still climbing that ladder to success.* The third entry in the series of Mickey Rooney–Judy Garland musicals, and the third directed by Busby Berkeley, *Babes on Broadway* is probably the weakest of the trio. Once again, the story had them striving to make it big on Broadway, battling odds that might have stymied the Theatre Guild. There are some good musical moments: Garland singing Harold Rome's "Franklin D. Roosevelt Jones," originally performed in the 1938 stage musical *Sing Out the News,* and the pleasing Rooney-Garland duet of "How About You." There are also some low points: a long number called "Ghost Theatre," in which the stars impersonate such past celebrities as Sarah Bernhardt and Harry Lauder, and especially a wince-inducing scene in which British refugee children relay a radio message to their beleaguered parents in London, after which Garland renders the song "Chin Up! Cheerio! Carry On!"

Off-Screen: Shirley Temple was offered a role in the film but declined. The movie's climax was an elaborate minstrel show, with the stars in blackface. At the first previews, it was poorly received; Roger Edens, who arranged the number, realized that the audience was unable to recognize Mickey and Judy in blackface. He did a retake showing the pair getting into blackface, and the number was a hit. Look for little Margaret O'Brien, making her film debut at age four.

Baby Doll

Warners, 1956. (114m.) Dir: Elia Kazan. Sp: Tennessee Williams, b/o play by Tennessee Williams. Cast: Carroll Baker, Karl Malden, Eli Wallach, Mildred Dunnock, Rip Torn.

On-Screen: *Comedy-drama of young bride's sexual awakening.* Archie Lee Meighan (Malden), a loutish, middle-aged businessman in rural Mississippi, has just married a young, and fairly dim, local beauty (Baker). But their union can't be consummated until Baby Doll turns twenty. When the nubile bride coyly rebuffs her husband's feverish advances on the eve of her twentieth birthday, Archie, in a frustrated rage, torches the cotton mill of business rival Silva Vacarro (Wallach). No fair guessing how the wily Sicilian gets his revenge. Kazan extracts all the raunchiness in Williams's psychosexual hothouse of a screenplay, and the small cast plays it out with every drop of perspiration they can muster. Intended as a droll, steamy romp, the film seems more than ever a shallow showcase for the hyperrealistic style of Method acting.

Off-Screen: In the glaring light of latter-day film fare, this once-controversial movie now pales. At the time of its release, however, the Catholic Legion of Decency denounced it as "morally repellent." Kazan replied that he "wasn't trying to be moral or immoral, only truthful," and Williams called his screenplay merely "a funny story." The knock turned into a boost, for the movie exceeded studio expectations. Filming mainly in Benoit, Mississippi, Kazan used many of the townspeople as actors, and a local abandoned mansion served as Archie's ramshackle home. Though nominated for four Oscars, the film won none. (CFB)

Bachelor Mother

RKO, 1939. (81m.) Dir: Garson Kanin. Sp: Norman Krasna, b/o story by Felix Jackson. Cast: Ginger Rogers, David Niven, Charles Coburn, Frank Albertson, Ernest Truex, Ferike Boros, Jane Wilkins.

On-Screen: *Ginger Rogers has her very own baby boom.* In one of her best nondancing roles at the time she was separating from longtime partner Fred Astaire, Ginger Rogers plays a department store salesgirl who is mistaken by everyone for an unwed mother when she finds an abandoned baby. Rather racy for its time, *Bachelor Mother* involves the girl with the playboy son (Niven) of the owner of the department store. By the time everything is straightened out, the two are in love. Still a pert and unaffected actress rather than the lacquered icon she would become, Rogers gives a charming, believable performance as the beleaguered heroine, and she gets expert support from Niven (always an excellent light comedian), and from Charles Coburn as Niven's crusty father. Watch for Rogers's hilarious encounter with Niven's jealous girlfriend (Wilkins).

Off-Screen: The movie was originally called *Nobody's Wife* and then *Little Mother* before the studio finally settled on *Bachelor Mother*. At first Ginger Rogers disliked the project, calling the story thin and the characters cardboard, but producer Pandro Berman changed her mind. Felix Jackson's original story won an Oscar nomination. The film was poorly remade as a musical, *Bundle of Joy* (1956), with Debbie Reynolds and Eddie Fisher.

Back to the Future

Universal, 1985. (C–116m.) Dir: Robert Zemeckis. Sp: Robert Zemeckis and Bob Gale. Cast: Michael J. Fox, Christopher Lloyd, Lea Thompson, Crispin Glover, Thomas F. Wilson, Wendie Jo Sperber, Marc McClure, Claudia Wells, James Tolkan.

On-Screen: *A teenager travels back thirty years.* The year is 1985. Teenage Marty McFly (Fox) has a crackpot inventor friend, Doc Brown (Lloyd), who has concocted a time machine from an old DeLorean car. Circumstances place Marty in the machine, where he is projected back to 1955. Now he has three problems: to get back to the future, to make certain his parents fall in love and marry (otherwise he doesn't exist), and to keep Doc Brown from dying in 1985 at the hands of Libyan terrorists. (Don't ask.) This hugely popular comedy-fantasy begins badly—the pace is slow and the middle-age makeup for Marty's parents is atrocious—but once Marty goes back to 1955, the jokes are clever and the pace accelerates. There's a great chase sequence in which Marty, in flight from some bullies, rides an improvised skateboard, and a funny scene in which he stuns a 1955 audience of high-school kids with a wild rock solo on his guitar. Director Zemeckis keeps the film moving so swiftly that there's no time to notice the gaping holes in the narrative. (Why, for example, are there no other residents and no police in Marty's town when it's time to noisily launch the time machine?) The ending is pure wish fulfillment for most every teenager, but it's not in keeping with the rest of the movie.

Off-Screen: The success of *Back to the Future* sparked two sequels, *Back to the Future Part II* (1989) and *Back to the Future Part III* (1990). Both starred Michael J. Fox and Christopher Lloyd. Lloyd is remembered for his role as the very weird Reverend Jim in the long-running television comedy "Taxi."

The Bad and the Beautiful

MGM, 1952. (118m.) Dir: Vincente Minnelli. Sp: Charles Schnee, b/o story by George Bradshaw. Cast: Kirk Douglas, Lana Turner, Dick Powell, Barry Sullivan, Gloria Grahame, Walter Pidgeon, Gilbert Roland, Leo G. Carroll, Ivan Triesault.

On-Screen: *A tyrannical movie tycoon's fate hangs in the balance.* Hollywood on the subject of Hollywood rarely makes for great box office, although *A Star Is Born* proved otherwise in its several incarnations. *The Bad and the Beautiful,* another notable exception to the rule, traces with style and candor producer Douglas's ruthless rise to and fall from power. Now, three people whose careers he made and nearly destroyed are in a position to help him make a comeback: Turner, an alcoholic actress once in love with Douglas who was nearly ruined when he proved unfaithful; Powell, a novelist and screenwriter who suffered personal tragedy through his treachery; and Sullivan, a director who helped boost the producer's career, then was betrayed. Douglas's powerhouse of a mogul-on-the-make is both fascinating and properly unsympathetic, and Turner is totally believable as the gorgeous young hopeful who, through determination and innate star quality, rises to the top. Grahame won a Supporting Oscar for her performance as Powell's neglected, pathetic Southern-belle wife.

Off-Screen: Clark Gable was offered the Douglas role but refused it. David O. Selznick, hearing Tinseltown gossip, considered suing the studio over the Douglas character, but others thought that the part more closely fitted Val Lewton, producer of "classy" horror films (*Cat People, The Body Snatcher,* e.g.) in the forties. Turner's role was possibly inspired by the career of Diana Barrymore. The voice of her actor father, heard on the phonograph reciting Shakespeare, is that of Louis Calhern. Because of the highly dramatic nature of Turner's solo scene in which her car runs out of control, the actress became temporarily hysterical after completing it.(CFB)

Bad Day at Black Rock

MGM, 1955. (C-81m.) Dir: John Sturges. Sp: Millard Kaufman, b/o story by Howard Breslin. Cast: Spencer Tracy, Robert Ryan, Anne Francis, Walter Brennan, Dean Jagger, Ernest Borgnine, Lee Marvin, John Ericson, Russell Collins.

On-Screen: *A stranger uncovers a town's darkest secret.* Taut, trim, and absorbing, *Bad Day at Black Rock* relates its bleak story with few wasted words or motions. A one-armed man (Tracy) arrives in a dusty Western town to deliver a posthumous medal to the father of a fallen Japanese-American hero. Instead he finds hostility and worse—a long-buried secret about the father's grim fate. Eventually he faces a deadly confrontation with the town's nasty tyrant (Ryan) and his bullying hoods. Tracy gives a solid performance with exemplary support from the others, including Dean Jagger as a cowed sheriff, Walter Brennan as the only apparent townsman with a conscience, and Lee Marvin as a sadistic thug. Filmed in the CinemaScope process, the movie conveys the sense of a pitiless Western wasteland, but it's the high-voltage action, and Tracy's heroic if a mite improbable battle against all odds, that will keep you riveted to your seat.

Off-Screen: Spencer Tracy was reluctant to do the film but was persuaded by MGM's production head Dore Schary, especially after the leading character became a man who had been crippled in the war. Schary also decided to make the film without a musical score to emphasize the bleakness of the setting, but he changed his mind after the first preview. Much of the film was shot on location in the sweltering heat of the Mojave Desert during the summer of 1954. The film won Oscar nominations for Best Actor (Tracy), Screenplay, and Direction.

Badlands

Warners, 1973. (C-95m.) Dir: Terrence Malick. Sp: Terrence Malick. Cast: Martin Sheen, Sissy Spacek, Warren Oates, Ramon Bieri, Alan Vint.

On-Screen: *A young couple goes on a killing spree*. Terrence Malick's artful debut film is based on a true story. Martin Sheen plays Kit, an aimless young man who meets fifteen-year-old Holly (Spacek), a girl whose life and dreams are formed by soap opera and movie fan magazines. After he kills her father on impulse, the two begin a wave of killings that ends only with their capture. The horror derives from the couple's blank indifference to their crimes—as if the arid bleakness of the midwestern landscape and the mindlessness of popular culture have left them unable to feel either fear or remorse. The movie fascinates even while it repels, but it's also somewhat overcalculated in its effects. Sheen and Spacek are fine—there's a

wonderful moment in which, isolated from the world in the middle of the desert, they dance at night to "A Blossom Fell." The ending is hugely ironic: Pleased to be told that he looks like James Dean, captured Kit basks in the glow of being a new culture hero. "Boy, we rang the bell, didn't we?" he remarks as he is led away by the police. A postscript tells us that he was executed for the crimes.

Off-Screen: The take-off point for the story was an actual case in which nineteen-year-old Charlie Starkweather went on a murder spree in Nebraska and Wyoming in January 1958. Among his victims were the mother, stepfather, and half-sister of fourteen-year-old Caril Fugate, who accompanied him on his spree. Both were convicted of murder; Starkweather was executed, and Fugate was sentenced to life imprisonment. The movie was plagued by money problems and equipment failures, and it was a year in the editing, partly because Terrence Malick had to take writing jobs to raise the money for postproduction work. Several years after it failed at the box office, *Badlands* was reissued to many enthusiastic reviews.

Ball of Fire

Goldwyn-RKO, 1941. (111m.) Dir: Howard Hawks. Sp: Charles Brackett and Billy Wilder, b/o story by Billy Wilder and Thomas Monroe. Cast: Gary Cooper, Barbara Stanwyck, Dana Andrews, Dan Duryea, Oscar Homolka, S. Z. Sakall, Henry Travers, Richard Haydn, Aubrey Mather, Allen Jenkins, Tully Marshall.

On-Screen: *A burlesque queen invades the world of academia.* A sly variation on *Snow White and the Seven Dwarfs,* this comedy casts Barbara

Stanwyck (in an Oscar-nominated performance) as a not-exactly-snow-white burlesque dancer named Sugarpuss O'Shea. Fleeing from a subpoena that would incriminate her boyfriend (Andrews), she hides out in a home where seven staid old professors have been working on an encyclopedia. Ostensibly she is in residence to teach them all about "slang," but when she meets an eighth professor (Cooper), younger and not quite as stuffy as the others, she soon has other things on her mind. And so, to his bewilderment, does he. The Brackett-Wilder screenplay offers some amusing variations on the worldly woman–naive man theme, and if Hawks's direction grows slack too often, it's certainly better than his feeble 1948 remake *A Song Is Born,* with Danny Kaye and Virginia Mayo.

Off-Screen: The screenplay was based on "The Professor and the Burlesque Queen," a story Billy Wilder had written before coming to America. Sam Goldwyn paid $7,500 for the story, with the understanding that Wilder would get a $2,500 bonus if the film was a hit. Goldwyn first asked Ginger Rogers to play the lead, but she declined, claiming that she only wanted to play ladylike roles. Goldwyn was furious: "You tell Ginger Rogers for me that ladies stink up the place!"

Bambi

Disney-RKO, 1942. (C-69m., animated) Supervising Dir: David Hand. Story Direction: Perce Pearce. Story Adaptation: Larry Morey, b/o story by Felix Salten. MS: Frank Churchill and Edward Plumb.

On-Screen: *Disney's animated classic on the life and coming-of-age of a deer.* One of Walt Disney's most exquisitely animated feature films, *Bambi* combines haunting images of beauty and terror in its tale of the young deer Bambi. The first part of the movie is idyllic as the seasons change and newborn Bambi learns to walk and talk, makes friends with the rabbit Thumper and the skunk Flower, and comes to fear the enemy, Man. After the death of his mother (a sequence that must have upset generations of youngsters), Bambi grows to adulthood, finds love with the graceful Faline, and rescues her from a consuming forest fire. The characters (especially Thumper) are delightful, and the songs are syrupy but pleasant. *Bambi* could be called an anti-hunting film in a way (would *you* shoot any of these charming creatures?), or even a religious parable (the Great Prince of the Forest as Christ, Bambi as his disciple), but in any case, it's a classic entry in the Disney catalog.

Off-Screen: To make the forest scenery as realistic as possible, Disney sent a cameraman to Maine to photograph thousands of feet of forests, snowfall, rainstorms, spiderwebs, and changes of seasons. Two live fawns were provided by the state to be sketched and photographed as they grew. Rabbits, skunks, owls, and other species were added until the Disney studio resembled a zoo.

Bananas

United Artists, 1971. (C-82m.) Dir: Woody Allen. Sp: Woody Allen and Mickey Rose. Cast: Woody Allen, Louise Lasser, Carlos Montalban, Howard Cosell, Rene Enriquez, Charlotte Rae, Conrad Bain.

On-Screen: *Woody Allen's second film, and a laugh riot.* Here's rampant hilarity from Woody Allen in his early mode. Fans of Allen's still enjoy trading gags from this uproarious movie. He plays Fielding Mellish, a products tester who travels to the Latin American country of San Marcos, where a revolution is raging. He not only joins the rebels but ends up being president of the country. (Don't ask how.) It's all here: the purely Allenesque gags ("I was a bed wetter. I used to sleep with an electric blanket and I was constantly electrocuting myself."); the ludicrously funny twists (he brings a box of cookies to dinner with San Marco's president, and with the rebels, he orders a thousand grilled-cheese sandwiches at a lunch counter); the borrowings from his idols, especially Chaplin (note the *Modern Times* food-testing machine at the beginning). Allen also gets in a few digs at television's penchant for showing *any* event—the movie begins with an official assassination of San Marcos's current president and ends with the televising of Fielding's wedding night. Favorite scene: Fielding on trial, at which he cross-examines himself and interrogates a sweetly dim Miss America. A treat for Allen fans.

Off-Screen: Look quickly for Sylvester Stallone as a subway hoodlum. The movie's heroine, Louise Lasser, was Mrs. Woody Allen at the time. Playing Vargas, San Marcos's dictator, is Carlos Montalban, Ricardo's brother, and the well-remembered "Juan Valdez" of Columbian coffee commercials. The movie's jaunty musical score is by Marvin Hamlisch.

The Band Wagon

MGM, 1952. (C-112m.) Dir: Vincente Minelli. Sp: Betty Comden and Adolph Green. MS: Arthur Schwartz and Howard Dietz. Cast: Fred Astaire, Cyd Charisse, Jack Buchanan, Nanette Fabray, Oscar Levant.

On-Screen: *Fred Astaire stars in the ultimate backstage musical.* One of the durable joys among film musicals, *The Band Wagon* offers an abundance of riches: a witty book about the perilous journey of a Broadway-bound musical; a bouquet of lovely Dietz-and-Schwartz songs; a stylish production helmed by Vincente Minnelli at his most assured; and the unchanging artistry of Fred Astaire. *The Band Wagon* even adds a poignant touch, casting Astaire as a dancing film star on the skids who is trying for a comeback in a Broadway musical. (His opening number, "All by Myself," is the very essence of Astaire magic, and he doesn't even dance.) As a haughty ballerina, Cyd Charisse makes a beautiful dancing partner, and British star Jack Buchanan is marvelous as an eccentric director. Add Nanette Fabray and Oscar Levant as a married writing team, and you have an ideal cast. The musical highlights are too numerous to mention, but viewers are not likely to forget Astaire's dazzling song-and-dance to "Shine on My Shoes" in a penny arcade, or the imaginative "Girl Hunt" ballet that closes this delectable musical.

Off-Screen: Clifton Webb was sought to play the flamboyant director, and after he declined Edward G. Robinson and Vincent Price were considered. This was not a happy production. Jack Buchanan was in a foul humor because of dental surgery. Oscar Levant had had a heart attack some weeks earlier, and he was more waspish than ever. According to Fabray, Astaire was "aloof, cold, remote." At one point, uncharacteristically, he bolted from the set when he could no longer take Minnelli's confusing direction. A short while later, he returned and apologized.

The Bank Dick

Universal, 1940. (74m.) Dir: Edward Cline. Sp: Mahatma Kane Jeeves (W. C. Fields). Cast: W. C. Fields, Cora Witherspoon, Una Merkel, Evelyn Del Rio, Grady Sutton, Jessie Ralph, Franklin Pangborn, Shemp Howard, Richard Purcell, Russell Hicks.

On-Screen: *The comic master at his very best.* Ramshackle but deliriously funny, *The Bank Dick* represents the apex of W. C. Fields's film career. Once again firing his barbs at middle-class values, Fields plays Egbert Sousé, the town drunkard and foremost customer of the Black Pussy Cat Café in the town of Lompoc. Saddled with the usual dreadful family, Sousé finally gets his big chance when he foils not one but two bank robberies (both by accident, of course) and is named the bank detective. He also gets to direct a movie being made in town—but don't ask how. Imagine the larceny-minded Sousé in charge of protecting the bank, and you have some idea of the ample fun in store. His main job turns out to be keeping a bank auditor named J. Pinkerton Snoopington (Pangborn) from examining the books—Sousé and his shiftless son-in-law (Sutton) just happen to have "borrowed" bank money to pay for some beefsteak bonds. In the end, fortune smiles on Sousé, proving that larceny and alcoholism have their rewards.

Off-Screen: The working title for the film was *The Great Man.* Fields wrote the screenplay under the pseudonym of "Mahatma Kane Jeeves." He enjoyed drawing-room dramas and liked when the leading man would say to his butler, "My hat, my cane, Jeeves." Hence, the pseudonym. The citizens of the real-life community of Lompoc, a small town near the Vandenberg Air Force base, were furious at being depicted as stupid and backward.

The Barefoot Contessa

United Artists, 1954. (C-128m.) Dir: Joseph L. Mankiewicz. Sp: Joseph L. Mankiewicz. Cast: Humphrey Bogart, Ava Gardner, Edmond O'Brien, Marius Goring, Rossano Brazzi, Valentina Cortesa, Warren Stevens.

On-Screen: *A sexy flamenco dancer rises to Hollywood fame.* "You name it. Whether you're born with it, or catch it from a public drinking cup, Maria had it." So says toadying press agent Edmond O'Brien about Maria Vargas. Ava Gardner plays Maria as a voluptuous waif, seeking guidance from sardonic, has-been director Humphrey Bogart, and love in the arms of numerous men. Told at Maria's funeral from the perspective of the men who knew her best, *The Barefoot Contessa* is a mixture of fevered soap opera, gilded trash, and half-baked philosophy. Maria was one of Gardner's best roles, and although stuck with some awkward dialogue, she gives the part her all. Bogart plays Mankiewicz's spokesman, the man who sets the tone for the entire film, as a rueful cynic. Brazzi, as Maria's fatally jealous, impotent husband, furrows his brow to show emotion. O'Brien is a joy to watch, sweating anxiously as he tries to please everyone. He won the year's Oscar as Best Supporting Actor.

Off-Screen: A Cinderella story with a twist, *The Barefoot Contessa* is a movie à clef in which the characters are based on real people: Gardner on Rita Hayworth and Ava herself; Bogart on writer-director Joseph L. Mankiewicz (and as Bogart said, " . . . after most of my friends who are ex-drunks"); Marius Goring on playboy Porfirio Rubirosa; ruthless millionaire Warren Stevens on Howard Hughes; and O'Brien on Johnny Meyer, a Hughes associate. The European locations were gloriously photographed by Jack Cardiff. (JMK)

Barefoot in the Park

Warners, 1967. (C-105m.) Dir: Gene Saks. Sp: Neil Simon, b/o his play. Cast: Jane Fonda, Robert Redford, Charles Boyer, Mildred Natwick, Herb Edelman.

On-Screen: *Newlyweds squabble and make up, via Neil Simon's Broadway play.* When *Barefoot in the Park* opened on Broadway in the fall of 1963, the *New York Times* reviewer called it "a bubbling, rib-tickling comedy." Transcribed to the screen, its essential thinness shows through, and there are fewer bubbles and fewer occasions for tickled ribs. Jane Fonda (strenuous and a bit trying) and Robert Redford (in his stage role as an aspiring lawyer) play very cutesy newlyweds whose passion for each other collapses in a noisy argument and brief separation. Do they kiss and make up? Of course. Mildred Natwick (repeating her Broadway role) is marvelous as Fonda's sensible mother who unwinds under the influence of rakish neighbor Boyer. Some of Simon's relentless jokes are genuinely funny, but far too much is made of the cast members' exhausting five-flight climb to the newlyweds' apartment. All in

all, with viewers in a frivolous frame of mind, *Barefoot in the Park* may suffice.

Off-Screen: Elizabeth Ashley, who originated the role of Corie Bratter on Broadway, was anxious to play it on-screen, but it went to Jane Fonda. Producer Hal Wallis cast Fonda because she was becoming a major star and he needed her to bolster the casting of the relatively unknown Redford. The movie was filmed primarily on the Paramount soundstage in Los Angeles, with two weeks on location in New York City. A 1970 television series based on the play had an all-black cast.

Barfly

Cannon, 1987. (C-97m.) Dir: Barbet Schroeder. Sp: Charles Bukowski. Cast: Mickey Rourke, Faye Dunaway, Alice Krige, J. C. Quinn, Frank Stallone, Jack Nance, Gloria Leroy.

On-Screen: *Two Los Angeles alcoholics sustain each other.* "It takes a special talent to be a drunk. It takes endurance. Endurance is more important than truth." These words are spoken by Henry Chinaski (Rourke), and he should know. A boozy, battered barfly, Henry spends his time either drinking and provoking fights with a bartender (Stallone) or writing in his room. His companion and soulmate is Wanda (Dunaway), another alcoholic with a dark streak of despair. ("We're all in some kind of hell.") Nothing much happens, except that Tully (Krige), the elegant publisher of a highbrow magazine, recognizes Henry's latent talent and buys one of his stories. She also tries in vain to strike up a relationship with her "protégé." The movie is quirkily amusing, even funny at times, and Rourke, with his shuffling gait and W. C. Fields–like voice, performs a comic spin on the sort of low-life characters he usually plays. Dunaway is also good and even touching in some scenes. In the forties, Henry's relationship with Tully would have made a Joan Crawford–John Garfield movie, and it's no less foolish in the late eighties.

Off-Screen: Charles Bukowski, a longtime and highly regarded writer of poems, stories, and novels, based his screenplay on incidents in his own life. It took French director Schroeder eight years to bring it to the screen. Every Hollywood studio rejected it as "too depressing." Much of the movie was shot at a Los Angeles bar called Big Ed's, and many of the customers seen are authentic barflies. Veteran actor Fritz Feld has a bit as an old man who gives Dunaway a light.

The Barkleys of Broadway

MGM, 1949. (C-109m.) Dir: Charles Walters. Sp: Betty Comden and Adolph Green. MS: Harry Warren and Ira Gershwin. Cast: Fred Astaire, Ginger Rogers, Oscar Levant, Billie Burke, Gale Robbins, Jacques François, Clinton Sundberg, Hans Conreid.

On-Screen: *The peerless dance team of Astaire and Rogers, reunited.* Brought back together again after a ten-year separation, the celebrated team of Fred Astaire and Ginger Rogers made their legion of fans happy with this Technicolor musical. In truth, the film's story line, concerning a popular married stage couple who are eternally bickering, was surprisingly flat considering that it was written by Betty Comden and Adolph Green (*On the Town, Singin' in the Rain,*

etc.). But the musical numbers compensate in large part, especially their smooth romantic pairing for George and Ira Gershwin's lovely "They Can't Take That Away from Me," which had originally appeared in *Shall We Dance* (1937). Other musical highlights: Astaire's tricky solo dance to "Shoes with Wings On," and the duo's charming duet to "My One and Only Highland Fling." Best neglected song: "You'd Be So Hard to Replace." Most excruciating moment: Rogers, turning dramatic to play Sarah Bernhardt, recites "La Marseillaise."

Off-Screen: The movie was originally meant to reteam Astaire with Judy Garland after *Easter Parade*. However, Garland's behavior became increasingly erratic, and when she collapsed, Rogers took over. The screenplay was rewritten to accommodate her. Astaire commented on his "Shoes with Wings On" number: "I love those mechanical things, using the medium as much as you can. You couldn't do those things on the stage if you tried."

Barton Fink

Fox, 1991. (C-117m.) Dir: Joel Coen. Sp: Ethan Coen and Joel Coen. Cast: John Turturro, John Goodman, Judy Davis, Michael Lerner, John Mahoney, Tony Shalhoub, Jon Polito.

On-Screen: *Offbeat hilarity and horror, via the Coen team.* Millions of stories wait to be written, but goggle-eyed dramatist Barton Fink (Turturro), champion of the Common Man, can't dream up even one. His Clifford Odets knockoff rocked Broadway, but now Hollywood studio pasha Jack Lipnick (Lerner) wants Fink to dash off a B-movie script. Holed up in his spooky Los Angeles hotel room, he struggles to earn his princely salary (by 1941 standards). A seemingly affable next-door neighbor, Charlie Meadows (Goodman), offers to help Fink overcome his writer's block. Even the mistress (Davis) of a boozy writer (Mahoney) agrees to share her scriptwriting talents, and more. Abruptly, what appears to be satirical takes a sudden turn into bizarre violence, leaving Barton Fink as bewildered and unsettled as the audience. What is really happening to Fink—and why? The blazing, apocalyptic climax provides more questions than answers—for example, how did Fink sleep through the murder committed in his bed?—but the flawless acting and the decaying Art Deco sets are spellbinding.

Off-Screen: The young Coen brothers made their mark with 1984's *Blood Simple,* a gruesome but slyly witty homage to *film noir.* Three years later came *Raising Arizona,* and in 1990 *Miller's Crossing,* a stylish mobster bash set in the twenties. It was during the writing of the latter that they themselves experienced Fink's syndrome. To freshen the creative juices, they wrote *Barton Fink,* then set it aside to film after *Miller's Crossing.* The scene in which Fink confesses the failure of his muse to tycoon Lipnick was shot on the grounds of the old Gloria Swanson mansion in Beverly Hills. Lerner received an Oscar nomination for his performance as Lipnick.(CFB)

Bataan

MGM, 1943. (114m.) Dir: Tay Garnett. Sp: Robert D. Andrews. Cast: Robert Taylor, Robert Walker, George Murphy, Lloyd Nolan, Thomas Mitchell, Lee Bowman, Desi Arnaz, Kenneth Spencer, Philip Terry, Barry Nelson.

On-Screen: *A patrol's last-ditch defense of Bataan.* One of the darkest hours of World War II occurred early on when Japanese forces overran and conquered the armies stationed on the peninsula of Bataan. MGM's film recreates that grim event in this pounding war film, focusing on a single American patrol as it makes one last desperate stand. The men are made up of the familiar mix, ranging from hardened (Sergeant Robert Taylor) to naive (sailor Robert Walker, attached to the patrol), with some racial and ethnic flavoring added for good measure. One by one the soldiers are picked off, until only Taylor survives to go down fighting. The battle scenes are well staged, but there is also the expected melodramatic excess, epithets hurled at the enemy ("no-tailed baboons!"), and some lofty speechifying ("We figure that the men who died here may have done more than we'll ever know to save the whole world").

Off-Screen: To create the illusion of ground fog customary in jungle country, the special effects man dumped dry ice into tubs of water. Immediately, a heavy white vapor formed on the surface of the water. By using an electric fan at low speed, the technicians were able to blow this vapor into the desired areas of the set. Being heavier than air, the "fog" settled into prearranged hollows.

Batman

Warners, 1989. (C-126m.) Dir: Tim Burton. Sp: Sam Hamm and Warren Skaaren, b/o characters created by Bob Kane. Cast:

Michael Keaton, Jack Nicholson, Kim Basinger, Robert Wuhl, Michael Gough, Pat Hingle, Billy Dee Williams, Jack Palance.

On-Screen: *Not what the kiddies expected. Witty, imaginative, and surprisingly dark-edged.* Set aside fond memories of the comic strip and the 1966 movie version of the campy television series. This is a *Batman* for a more knowing generation. Nicholson is outlandishly cartoonish as the grinning Joker, an archcriminal plotting to subvert the populace with toxic toiletries. Basinger is romantically vulnerable as photojournalist Vicky Vale, set on revealing debonair Bruce Wayne (Keaton) as crime-fighter Batman. The movie dazzles with its depiction of the tawdry underbelly of Gotham City (think New York), but it positively stuns with its kinky characterization of Wayne, whose Batman alter ego finds expression in vengeful, even sadistic, overkill. Keaton wisely underplays his complex role, leaving the welcome histrionics to Nicholson. A bit overlong, but brilliant.

Off-Screen: Filmed entirely in a London studio, the movie is worth seeing for Anton Furst's Oscar-winning production design, which recalls the futuristic structures in Fritz Lang's German film, *Metropolis* (1926). Movie buffs will also note that the Joker, who schemes to take over the world, is reminiscent of the evil masterminds in other Lang movies, *Dr. Mabuse, the Gambler* (1922) and *The Last Will of Dr. Mabuse* (1932). Danny Elfman's score, supplemented by rock performer Prince's songs, is outstanding. Bob Kane, creator of the Caped Crusader, appears in a cameo role. A disappointing 1992 sequel, *Batman Returns,* lacked the dark thrust of the original and was merely raucous and violent. (CFB)

Battleground

MGM, 1949. (118m.) Dir: William Wellman. Sp: Robert Pirosh. Cast: Van Johnson, George Murphy, John Hodiak, Ricardo Montalban, James Whitmore, Marshall Thompson, Denise Darcel, Richard Jaeckel, James Arness, Scotty Beckett, Douglas Fowley, Leon Ames.

On-Screen: *The Battle of the Bulge revisited.* A solid, gritty war film, *Battleground* recreates the crucial Battle of the Bulge of World War II with all its despair, terror, and heroism. Robert Pirosh's Oscar-winning screenplay follows a single army platoon through the battle, starting with the usual soldier horseplay and taking the men into the heat of combat as their situation becomes increasingly desperate. The characters are all cut from familiar cloth: there's the good-natured rowdy (Johnson), the intellectual (Hodiak), the older man (Murphy) who's about to be discharged, the hard-bitten sergeant (Whitmore), the naive youngster (Thompson), etc. A number of scenes are strikingly handled (Paul C. Vogel won an Oscar for his cinematography), and many of the images of the weary soldiers marching through a snow-covered wasteland are haunting. At one point the narrative pauses while a chaplain (Ames) explains what the men are fighting for: "Don't let anyone tell you you were a sucker to fight in the war against fascism!"

Off-Screen: Louis B. Mayer was unenthusiastic about producing a war film at MGM, but Dore Schary, the new vice president in charge of production, argued that it depended on the treatment of the subject. (He had bought the screen rights from RKO when he moved to MGM.) The studio felt that the movie would be a disaster, but it was an enormous hit, even winning a Best Picture Oscar nomination.

Beaches

Touchstone, 1988. (C-123m.) Dir: Garry Marshall. Sp: Mary Agnes Donoghue, b/o novel by Iris Rainer Dart. Cast: Bette Midler, Barbara Hershey, John Heard, Spalding Gray, Lainie Kazan, James Read, Mayim Bialik, Marcie Leeds.

On-Screen: *Two women share a lifelong friendship.* Friends since childhood, C. C. Bloom (Midler) and Hillary Whitney (Hershey) couldn't be less alike. An earthy, brazen New Yorker, C. C. dreams only of becoming a singing star, while wealthy and beautiful Hillary has aspirations to be a lawyer. Meeting and corresponding over the years, both women marry, happily for a while, then quarrel bitterly and separate, only to be reunited when tragedy strikes. Immersed in soapsuds, *Beaches* scarcely has a scene that isn't telegraphed. Still, Bette Midler is a strong and vibrant presence, and she gets to deliver several songs, one of which, "The Wind Beneath My Wings," won that year's Oscar. Barbara Hershey, a talented actress, plays Hillary with appropriate highborn restraint, and her final scenes should have you sniffling. *Beaches* is well-seasoned corn, but corn nonetheless.

Off-Screen: *Beaches* was the first movie to emerge from Bette Midler's company, All-Girl Productions. The song "The Wind Beneath My Wings" not only won an Oscar but also became the first number-one hit of Midler's career. Young Mayim Bialik, who plays Midler as a child, comes close to steal-ing the movie. She needed brown contact lenses and a flaming red wig for the role.

Beat the Devil

United Artists, 1954. (89m.) Dir: John Huston. Sp: John Huston and Truman Capote, b/o novel by James Helvick. Cast: Humphrey Bogart, Jennifer Jones, Gina Lollobrigida, Robert Morley, Peter Lorre, Edward Underdown.

On-Screen: *Bogart and conspirators in an offbeat caper comedy.* A top director and a great cast are clearly having a ball with this bizarre tale, so you may as well have a good time, too. Don't expect to make much sense of the story involving an odd assortment of crooks situated in an Italian seaport and their schemes to acquire uranium-rich land in East Africa. Instead, relish Bogart's wry delivery of lines like "Without money I become dull, listless, and have trouble with my complexion," and enjoy Jones as a compulsive liar who prefaces each whopper with "In point of fact. . . ." Adding to the fun are Lollobrigida as Bogart's sexy wife, Lorre as an unlikely Chilean named Julius O'Hara, and Morley as a jaunty and ineffectual racketeer. Relax, and enjoy.

Off-Screen: The movie's playful allusions to other Huston movies, especially *The Maltese Falcon,* have kept it a camp-cult favorite for many years. As the glib drifter, Bogart plays off his Sam Spade role, and as the habitual prevaricator, Jones recalls Mary Astor's Brigid O'Shaughnessy. Bug-eyed Lorre's craven whining pays homage to Elisha Cook, Jr.'s pop-eyed gunsel, and Morley is a seedier version of Greenstreet's Gutman. The first screenplay, by Huston and others, was a close adaptation of Helvick's thriller. Bogart, however, disliked the script, and though filming had already begun, Capote was engaged to furnish a new version, which he improvised on location in Ravello, Italy, barely staying ahead of the shooting schedule.(CFB)

Beau Geste

Paramount, 1939. (114m.) Dir: William Wellman. Sp: Robert Carson, b/o novel by Percival Christopher Wren. Cast: Gary Cooper, Ray Milland, Robert Preston, Susan Hayward, Brian Donlevy, J. Carroll Naish, Donald O'Connor, Albert Dekker, Broderick Crawford.

On-Screen: *First sound version of the famous adventure tale*. Older viewers will certainly recall the memorable opening scene in which soldiers come upon a desert fort "guarded" by dead legionnaires. Except for Brian Donlevy's sadistic villainy as Sergeant Markoff, not much else is worth remembering in this decent but rather uninspired scene-by-scene remake of the 1926 silent film. Once again the devoted Geste brothers (Cooper, Milland, and Preston) join the Foreign Legion after the theft of the fabulous Blue Water sapphire. The true identity of the thief is only one of several mysteries that occupy the brothers once they are legionnaires in the desert under the thumb of nasty Sergeant Markoff. Cooper and Preston are not very believable as stiff-upper-lip Englishmen, and much of their dialogue is faintly absurd, but the action scenes are handled with dispatch by Wellman.

Off-Screen: The movie was filmed in Buttercup Valley, in the desert near Yuma, Arizona (the same location as the silent film).

An entire tent city, accommodating a thousand men, was built on the site, with electricity, running water, and even a movie theater. Actor Brian Donlevy, detested on-screen, was apparently detested off-screen as well, for lording it over the cast and crew. Still, he won an Oscar nomination for his performance. The story of *Beau Geste* was remade in 1966, and in 1977 Marty Feldman wrote, directed, and starred in a fitfully amusing parody, *The Last Remake of Beau Geste*.

Beauty and the Beast

Disney, 1991. (C-85m., animated) Dir: Gary Trousdale and Kirk Wise. Sp: Linda Woolverton. MS: Alan Menken and Howard Ashman.

On-Screen: *Disney version of the classic tale*. Enchanting is the word for this animated feature from the Disney studio. It's a contemporary spin on the fable of Beauty and the Beast, boasting first-class animation, a story with surprising emotional resonance, and a Broadway-caliber musical score. This time around, Beauty (called Belle) is a bright and bookish girl from a provincial French town who becomes the prisoner of the Beast in his enchanted castle. The Beast, of course, is actually a prince under an enchantress's hideous spell that can be broken only when he falls in love, and that love is reciprocated. The castle is chock-full of delightfully humanized household fixtures (a candle holder called Lumiere, a mantel clock named Cogswold, and the teapot Mrs. Potts), also under the spell. And yes, there is a villain—a scheming, insufferably vain scoundrel named Gaston. Several of the production numbers are among the most imaginative and diverting Disney has ever produced, most notably "Be My Guest" and the title song, beautifully sung by Angela Lansbury as the voice of Mrs. Potts. As usual, there are several scenes that may frighten very young children. (One has Belle pursued by wolves in the forest.) Still, *Beauty and the Beast* is prime Disney, and a treat for everyone except grumps.

Off-Screen: *Beauty and the Beast* made film history by becoming the first feature-length animated movie to be nominated for a Best Picture Oscar. The Ashman-Menken score won an Academy Award, as did the title song. Among the voices used are Paige O'Hara as Belle, Robby Benson as the Beast, Jerry Orbach as Lumiere, David Ogden Stiers as Cogswold, and Rex Everhart as Belle's father. *Beauty and the Beast* was first visualized as a straightforward, nonmusical version of the fairy tale, but the direction changed after the successful release of *The Little Mermaid*. For a complete account of the making of the movie, see Bob Thomas's *Disney's Art of Animation: From Mickey Mouse to Beauty and the Beast* (Hyperion, 1991).

Becket

Paramount, 1964. (C-148m.) Dir: Peter Glenville. Sp: Edward Anhalt, b/o play by Jean Anouilh. Cast: Richard Burton, Peter O'Toole, Donald Wolfit, John Gielgud, Martita Hunt, Pamela Brown, Sian Phillips, Paola Stoppa, Felix Aylmer, Gino Cervi.

On-Screen: *An archbishop and his king battle for supremacy.* The historic twelfth-century contention between Thomas Becket, Archbishop of Canterbury, and King Henry II formed the basis for Jean Anouilh's play *Becket,* which enjoyed a successful Broad-

way run in 1960 with Laurence Olivier (Becket) and Anthony Quinn (King). Opened up for the screen by Peter Glenville (who also directed the stage production), the story takes full advantage of the opportunity for pageantry on a grand scale. Still, Edward Anhalt's Oscar-winning screenplay seldom loses sight of the central conflict between an inflexible churchman who assumes "the honor of God" and a hot-tempered, tormented king who feels betrayed by his former friend. Much of the dispute between the two men takes the form of wearisome talk, but the pace quickens toward the end when they meet for the last time on a windswept beach. The sequence in which Becket is brutally murdered has a horrific power. Richard Burton's Becket and Peter O'Toole's King Henry are apparently quite different from their stage counterparts, but they convey the force of their conflict.

Off-Screen: Producer Hal Wallis had to work hard to convince Paramount to make this film. Studio executives felt that historical spectacles were passé, but Wallis insisted that the story involved deep and important human emotions. He finally won the day. Richard Burton was reluctant to play Becket until he was told that Peter O'Toole would costar as the king. The film, Glenville, Burton, and O'Toole were all Oscar-nominated.

Becky Sharp

RKO, 1935. (C-83m.) Dir: Rouben Mamoulian. Sp: Francis Edwards Faragoh, b/o play by Langdon Mitchell from the novel by William Makepeace Thackeray. Cast: Miriam Hopkins, Frances Dee, Sir Cedric Hardwicke, Nigel Bruce, Alan Mowbray, Billie Burke, Alison Skipworth.

On-Screen: *The first feature film photographed in full Technicolor*. Considering its relative brevity, this version of *Vanity Fair* is a satisfying "highlights" account of Thackeray's sprawling social satire set in England's Regency period. While Hopkins's brittle acting style would seem ideally suited for the scheming heroine, she seems less a youthful adventuress than a hyperactive society matron. Many of the novel's colorful personages are well portrayed—Hardwicke's foxy Lord Steyne; Dee's sentimental Amelia Bradley; Bruce's blundering Joe Sedley; Mowbray's weak Rawdon Crawley. Mamoulian's use of the enhanced color process is sometimes gaudy but reaches its potential at a grand ball on the eve of Waterloo. The blues, greens, yellows, and oranges of the gowns yield to the blazing crimson of the British officers' uniforms—a color-drenched sequence of unforgettable moviemaking.

Off-Screen: Former actor Lowell Sherman was the original director, but he died after a few weeks of filming. Mamoulian began the movie again, and his creative use of the new, three-strip Technicolor process made the film both an aesthetic and a technical milestone. In 1984, a print was made that restored the movie to its original colors. Viewers may spot an extra named Thelma Ryan, later known as Pat Nixon, in the ballroom scene. Hopkins was nominated for a Best Actress Oscar. The novel was also filmed in 1923 and in 1932. (CFB)

Being There

United Artists, 1979. (C-130m.) Dir: Hal Ashby. Sp: Jerzy Kosinski, b/o his story. Cast: Peter Sellers, Shirley MacLaine, Melvyn Douglas, Jack Warden, Richard Dysart, Richard Basehart, James Noble, David Clennon.

On-Screen: *Simple-minded Peter Sellers is treated as a sage*. Chance (Sellers), a childlike gardener, lives in his private world where the only things he knows are his job and whatever he sees on television. When his employer dies, Chance is cast into the world of Washington, D.C, where he ends up living in the home of dying financier Douglas and his wife MacLaine. Soon, all of Chance's meaningless remarks are interpreted as profoundly wise, and he becomes a media celebrity and a sounding board for policymakers. *Being There* takes a savage swipe at America's obsession with the media and its tendency to take any pronouncement in print or on television as the gospel truth. But once the point has been made that America's media madness can turn a fool into a prophet, the movie has little place to go, and its single joke eventually wears thin. Sellers is amusing in his penultimate role, and Douglas, in his last role, won a Supporting Oscar.

Off-Screen: Peter Sellers's heart condition worsened during the production, making the filming difficult, but he gamely sought the right look and sound for Chance. After trying out various voices, he finally found the voice he wanted in Stan Laurel. His performance won him an Oscar nomination, but he lost to Dustin Hoffman's divorced father in *Kramer vs. Kramer*.

Belle of the Nineties

Paramount, 1934. (73m.) Dir: Leo McCarey. Sp: Mae West, b/o her story. Cast: Mae West, Roger Pryor, John Mack Brown, John Miljan, Katherine DeMille,

Libby Taylor, James Donlan, Duke Ellington and His Orchestra.

On-Screen: *Mae West conquers New Orleans and its men.* Riding the crest of her popularity, Mae West stars as Ruby Carter, a music-hall entertainer and courtesan who is "the most talked about woman in America." The plot is the usual melodramatic mix involving West with jealous and ardent lovers, but as always, we mostly recall the lady's no-nonsense quips. "The wildest men make the best pets," she announces, and when she arrives in New Orleans, she is asked, "Are you in the city for good?" Without missing a beat, she replies, "I expect to be here, but not for good." She even offers a bit of philosophy: "Don't let a man put anything over on ya except an umbrella." Once again, she gets to render a few music-hall songs, this time accompanied by no less than Duke Ellington and His Orchestra. *Belle of the Nineties* is surely one of the best of the Wests.

Off-Screen: George Raft was announced for the male lead but balked at playing second fiddle to West; he was replaced by Roger Pryor. One musical number, "American Beauty," has Mae appearing in a variety of outlandish costumes: as a rose, a butterfly, a bat, a spider, and the Statue of Liberty. Critic George Jean Nathan commented that the latter might have been better described as "the Statue of Libido."

Bells Are Ringing

MGM, 1960. (C-127m.) Dir: Vincente Minnelli. Sp: Betty Comden and Adolph Green, b/o their musical play. MS: Jule Styne, Betty Comden, and Adolph Green. Cast: Judy Holliday, Dean Martin, Fred Clark, Eddie Foy, Jr., Jean Stapleton, Frank Gorshin, Gerry Mulligan.

On-Screen: *Judy Holliday repeats her Broadway musical role.* With her inimitable voice and dumb-as-a-fox demeanor, Judy Holliday was a unique movie presence in the fifties. From her first major film, *Adam's Rib* (1949), to this, her last, she endeared herself to audiences in a series of winning comedies. *Bells Are Ringing* records her stage triumph in her first musical attempt. As such, it's a valuable document, but as a musical film it leaves much to be desired. As a lovelorn answering-service operator, Holliday displays all the warmth, charm, and comic skill that had made her a popular actress. Whether singing and dancing to "Just in Time" with boyfriend Dean Martin (barely awake in his role as a playwright) or mourning the demise of a love affair in "The Party's Over," she is completely endearing. The screenplay is weak, however, and the score is no better than average. Even the gifted Vincente Minnelli seems to direct listlessly. But there's always Judy Holliday, and that may be enough.

Off-Screen: Sadly, the making of Judy Holliday's last movie was far from smooth. Moody and intensely critical of her performance even though she had played the role many times on stage, Holliday asked to be released after only a week of shooting, even offering to give up her entire salary, but the studio refused to replace her. Neither Vincente Minnelli nor Arthur Freed could gain her confidence. Her frequent crying jags and recurring illnesses constantly disrupted the filming. Dean Martin believed that his role was a waste of his time and talent. One of his numbers, a song called "My Guiding Star," was cut from the final print.

The Bells of St. Mary's

RKO, 1945. (126m.) Dir: Leo McCarey. Sp: Dudley Nichols, b/o story by Leo McCarey. Cast: Bing Crosby, Ingrid Bergman, Henry Travers, Ruth Donnelly, William Gargan, Joan Carroll, Martha Sleeper.

On-Screen: *Priest and nun contrive to save a parochial school.* In this tissue-thin sequel to *Going My Way,* Father Chuck O'Malley (Crosby, reprising his role in that film) meets Sister Benedict (Bergman). The priest, still breezy but accommodating ("If you're ever in trouble, dial O for O'Malley"), and the nun, who's made of sterner stuff, persuade a Scrooge-like industrialist (Travers) to part with a building that will better house the nun's school. By the movie's hankie-soaker end, she's rewarded for her labors by the love of her pupils and the admiration of the priest. Along the way, Crosby gets to sing "Aren't You Glad You're You?," "Ave Maria," and "The Bells of St. Mary's." Bergman solos in a Swedish song. A charming highlight has a group of tots actually ad-libbing a reenactment of the Nativity story.

Off-Screen: During the filming of the movie, Oscars were awarded to Crosby and McCarey for *Going My Way* and to Bergman for *Gaslight.* Despite generally lukewarm critical reception, the movie proved a box-office bonanza, drawing even larger audiences than its predecessor. Only after McCarey agreed to David O. Selznick's stiff terms for lending his star contract-player was he able to cast Bergman. The movie received nominations for eight Oscars, including encore nominations for Crosby, Bergman, and McCarey, but it garnered only one, for sound recording.(CFB)

Ben-Hur

MGM, 1959. (C–212m.) Dir: William Wyler. Sp: Karl Tunberg, b/o novel by Lew Wallace. Cast: Charlton Heston, Jack Hawkins, Stephen Boyd, Haya Harareet, Hugh Griffith, Martha Scott, Cathy O'Donnell, Sam Jaffe, Finlay Currie.

On-Screen: *William Wyler's epic Biblical drama.* Among the many sin-and-sandal films that proliferated in the fifties and sixties, *Ben-Hur* can probably be rated the most successful, not only because of its many awards but because of its intelligent screenplay and opulent production. A remake of the 1926 silent version of Lew Wallace's novel, *Ben-Hur* begins with a prologue on the birth of Christ, then proceeds to tell the story of Judah Ben-Hur (Heston), stalwart prince of Judea. When he and his family are betrayed by former friend Messala (Boyd), now tribune of Rome, Judah moves from vengeful galley slave to adopted son of Roman admiral Quintus Arrius (Hawkins) and ultimately to devout believer in the crucified Jesus. Throughout its long running time, the film offers sequences of sweeping grandeur, climaxed, of course, by the celebrated chariot race between Judah and Messala. The last section, in which Judah searches for his mother (Scott) and sister (O'Donnell) in the Valley of the Lepers, than has them restored to him by a miracle after the crucifixion, is genuinely moving. Charlton Heston and Stephen Boyd vie to see who can clench his teeth more often, and the huge cast works largely to good effect.

Off-Screen: *Ben-Hur* won an unprecedented eleven Oscars, including Best Picture and Best Direction. Awards also went to Heston, Hugh Griffith (as a bulging-eyed

Arab chieftain), Robert Surtees (cinematography), and Miklos Rozsa (scoring). Kirk Douglas wanted to play Ben-Hur, and when Wyler offered him the role of Messala instead, he turned it down. Thirty years earlier, Wyler had worked as an assistant on the silent version. Many uncredited writers, including Gore Vidal and Christopher Fry, worked on the screenplay. The chariot race was staged by Andrew Marton and Yakima Canutt on eighteen acres of Rome's Cinecittà Studios. The entire massive production was supervised by producer Sam Zimbalist, who died shortly before the film's completion.

The Best Man

United Artists, 1964. (102m.) Dir: Franklin Schaffner. Sp: Gore Vidal, b/o his play. Cast: Henry Fonda, Cliff Robertson, Lee Tracy, Edie Adams, Margaret Leighton, Ann Sothern, Gene Raymond, Kevin McCarthy, Shelley Berman, John Henry Faulk, Richard Arlen.

On-Screen: *Two men vie bitterly for the presidential nomination.* The fierce, turbulent, and back-stabbing world of presidential politics is the arena for this intelligent comedy-drama. Adapted by Gore Vidal from his 1960 Broadway play, *The Best Man* centers on two men of vastly different temperaments and beliefs who come to their party's presidential convention, each seeking—and fighting for—the nomination. Henry Fonda is Secretary of State William Russell, witty, cerebral, and liberal, and Senator Joe Cantwell (Cliff Robertson) is his arch-rival, a ruthless, conservative, self-appointed "man of the people." As the hoopla of the convention swirls around them, each man tries to repudiate the other with "dirty" secrets about the past. Razor-sharp dialogue combines with sturdy performances to make an entertaining movie. Top acting honors go to veteran actor (and Oscar-nominated) Lee Tracy in his last role. As former President Art Hockstader, Tracy shows vestiges of the vigor and forcefulness that made him a popular performer in the thirties.

Off-Screen: One need not be too astute to sense that author Gore Vidal had certain real-life figures in mind when he wrote *The Best Man*. William Russell suggests Adlai Stevenson in many particulars, while Joe Cantwell is not too far from Richard Nixon as he is perceived by many people. Also, ex-President Art Hockstader is strongly reminiscent of Harry S. Truman. Frank Capra was scheduled to direct the movie and collaborated with Myles Connolly on a screenplay, but ultimately Franklin Schaffner replaced Capra and Vidal wrote his own script.

The Best Years of Our Lives

Goldwyn-RKO, 1946. (170m.) Dir: William Wyler. Sp: Robert E. Sherwood, b/o novel by MacKinlay Kantor. Cast: Myrna Loy, Fredric March, Dana Andrews, Teresa Wright, Virginia Mayo, Cathy O'Donnell, Harold Russell, Hoagy Carmichael, Gladys George.

On-Screen: *Three World War II veterans face readjustment.* This emotional drama presents a cross section of veterans who served bravely and came home to face trials of a different nature: an infantry sergeant (March) unsure of his reception by his wife (Loy) and the bank where he worked; an Air Force captain (Andrews) with no real job prospects and a bored, sluttish wife (Mayo); and a sailor (Russell) who lost his hands and is afraid to face his family and girlfriend (O'Donnell). Superlatively written, directed, and played, the movie is best remembered for its tensely dramatic scenes: Loy's "Who's at the door?" as she senses her husband has come home; Andrews, in the nose of an abandoned bomber, reliving wartime memories; and Russell, exploding with anger and frustration, asking his girl, "You wanna see how the hooks work?" A deeply felt movie, marvelously expressive of its time and place.

Off-Screen: Based on Kantor's *Glory for Me,* a novel in blank verse, the movie proved an instant success. It was honored with seven Academy Award "Bests": Picture, Director, Actor (March), Supporting Actor (Russell), Screenplay, Scoring (Hugo Friedhofer), and Editing. Double-amputee Russell received a special statuette "for bringing hope and courage to his fellow veterans" through his appearance in the movie. (A business executive today, Russell made only one other film, *Inside Moves,* in 1980.) A made-for-television adaptation, *Returning Home,* was shown in 1975.(CFB)

Beverly Hills Cop

Paramount, 1984. (C-105m.) Dir: Martin Brest. Sp: Daniel Petrie, Jr., b/o story by Danilo Bach and Daniel Petrie, Jr. Cast: Eddie Murphy, Lisa Eilbacher, Steven Berkoff, Judge Reinhold, Ronny Cox, Stephen Elliott, Paul Reiser, James Russo.

On-Screen: *Detroit cop Eddie Murphy descends on Beverly Hills.* After scoring a hit in his film debut as a streetwise convict in *48HRS.* (1982), then playing a wily hustler in *Trad-*

ing Places (1983), Eddie Murphy turned to the right side of the law with this fast, violent action comedy. The story is ordinary: Detroit cop Axel Foley (Murphy) comes to Beverly Hills to track down the killer of his friend and stays to destroy a major drug-smuggling ring headed by a suave art dealer (Berkoff). What makes the movie work is the single overriding joke: loose-cannon Foley as a cop who is smarter, more resourceful, and more effective than all the by-the-numbers police in posh Los Angeles. Scene after scene—in a fancy hotel, in a suspicious warehouse, in an exclusive club—has him either blustering his way to success, or risking his life to catch the killers. After so many foolhardy gestures or narrow escapes, he becomes a fantasy figure, but a likable one. It's Murphy's movie all the way, but watch for Bronson Pinchot's funny bit as a gay art-gallery worker with an indeterminate accent.

Off-Screen: The screenplay went through six versions over a number of years. Both Mickey Rourke and Sylvester Stallone were scheduled to play the lead, but Rourke left to star in *The Pope of Greenwich Village* and Stallone pulled out only a fortnight before shooting began. Eddie Murphy took the role with sensational results. Murphy was encouraged to ad-lib during the filming, and he improvised the scene in which he bluffs his way into an exclusive club to confront the villain. A sequel, *Beverly Hills Cop II,* turned up in 1987.

Big

Fox, 1988. (C-102m.) Dir: Penny Marshall. Sp: Gary Ross and Anne Spielberg. Cast: Tom Hanks, Elizabeth Perkins, John Heard, Robert Loggia, Jared Rushton, Mercedes Ruehl, Jon Lovitz, David Moscow.

On-Screen: *A young boy gets his wish to be "big."* Thirteen-year-old Josh Baskin (Moscow) would like to be grown-up without a kid's dependency and hang-ups. He expresses his wish to a mysterious figure at an amusement park and lo! he wakes up in the body of a thirty-year-old man (Hanks). On this premise, director Marshall and writers Ross and Spielberg spin a surprisingly funny and endearing fantasy. Behaving like a child in a man's body, Josh finds himself rising in the ranks of a toy company and even enjoys his first sexual experience with a coworker (Perkins) who finds his innocence irresistible. Tom Hanks is simply wonderful as the boy-man, whether cavorting in F.A.O. Schwarz with his boss (Loggia), enjoying a luxury car for the first time, or reacting to Perkins's question, "How do you feel about me?" He gets firm support from Perkins, delightful as the ambitious but bewildered Susan, and from Loggia, Mercedes Ruehl as his mother, and Jared Rushton as his best friend. But mostly *Big* is Hanks's show, and he comes through with abundant charm and superb timing. A favorite moment: Josh confronts the special taste of caviar.

Off-Screen: Tom Hanks received a Best Actor Oscar nomination, an honor rarely bestowed on a comedy performance. The carnival scenes were shot at Ross Dock Park along the Hudson River in Fort Lee, New Jersey. Other scenes were shot on and off Anderson Avenue in Cliffside Park, New Jersey.

The Big Chill

Columbia, 1983. (C-103m.) Dir: Lawrence Kasdan. Sp: Lawrence Kasdan and Barbara Benedek. Cast: Glenn Close, Kevin Kline, William Hurt, JoBeth Williams, Jeff Goldblum, Tom Berenger, Mary Kay Place, Meg Tilly, Don Galloway.

On-Screen: *Friends from the sixties assemble twenty years later.* First-rate acting and a witty, probing screenplay make this serious comedy worth viewing. A group of friends from the sixties, former students at the University of Michigan, come together for the funeral of a mutual friend, a suicide. Two decades past their bright years of hope and rebellion, they include Close and husband Kline; television star Berenger; bitter, rootless Hurt; acerbic journalist Goldblum; unhappily married Williams; and lawyer Place. Over a weekend, they reflect on the past and the present, while rekindling old relationships. The screenplay looks at the characters without blinkers, examining their delusions and anxieties with a mixture of candor and affection. Under Kasdan's adroit direction, no single actor is permitted to dominate a scene, and the cast comes through with a well-meshed ensemble performance.

Off-Screen: Originally, a ten-minute flashback was included showing Alex, the friend who committed suicide. He was played by future star Kevin Costner. The screenplay was turned down by many studios as "not funny enough, too narrow, or not commercial." Finally, it became the first film produced by Johnny Carson's production company. The movie was shot on location in Beaufort, South Carolina, and in Atlanta.

The Big Country

United Artists, 1958. (C-166m.) Dir: William Wyler. Sp: James R. Webb, Sy Bartlett, and Robert Wilder; adaptation: Jessamyn West and Robert Wilder, b/o novel by Donald Hamilton. Cast: Gregory Peck, Charlton Heston, Jean Simmons, Carroll Baker, Burl Ives, Charles Bickford, Alfonso Bedoya, Chuck Connors.

On-Screen: *Two Western families battle to the death.* William Wyler's long, elaborate Western focuses on the murderous feud for control of vital water rights between rancher Henry Terrill (Bickford) and scruffy Rufus Hannassey (Ives). Involved in the feud are Terrill's daughter (Baker), a schoolteacher (Simmons) who owns the ranch on which the contested water runs, and especially the Eastern dude (Peck) who expects to marry Baker. Villainy is supplied by Heston, the lecherous foreman of Terrill's ranch. The churning action and the spectacular photography (by Franz Planer) help to carry the familiar story line, but the only real excitement comes in the climactic sequence in which arch-enemies Terrill and Hannassey confront each other against the austere landscape. *The Big Country* is a visually stunning but dramatically diffuse Western.

Off-Screen: Many writers worked on the screenplay before the final shooting script was deemed acceptable. Coproducers Peck and Wyler disagreed on a number of points throughout the filming. Things came to a head when Peck wanted to reshoot a scene with Carroll Baker in a horse-drawn wagon and Wyler refused adamantly. Peck walked off the film for a while, and the rift between the two lasted for several years. Charlton Heston had to learn how to deal with Wyler's insistence on countless retakes of virtually every shot.

The Big Heat

Columbia, 1953. (90m.) Dir: Fritz Lang. Sp: Sydney Boehm, b/o novel by William McGivern. Cast: Glenn Ford, Gloria Grahame, Jocelyn Brando, Lee Marvin, Alexander Scourby, Jeanette Nolan, Adam Williams, Carolyn Jones.

On-Screen: *A revenge-minded cop tangles with a nest of vipers.* Blistering and uncompromising from its first scene—a police officer commits suicide—to its violent climax, Fritz Lang's *film noir* still packs quite a wallop. Glenn Ford stars as a cop determined to get the goods on a big-time gang lord (Scourby). When his young wife (Brando) is murdered by the mob, he sets out on a fierce, implacable crusade to nail the killers. Soon he finds himself embroiled with the gang lord, his sadistic aide (Marvin), and the aide's good-time girlfriend (Grahame). As he gets dangerously close to committing his own acts of violence, the sense of corruption becomes almost palpable. The most jolting moment, one that is hard to forget, occurs when Marvin, in a rage at his girl's betrayal, flings a pot of scalding coffee in her face. Ford is quietly forceful as another of Fritz Lang's driven heroes, and Grahame, playing in her usual pouting, insinuating style, is most effective and finally even touching.

Off-Screen: Director Fritz Lang was widely feared and hated for his bullying ways with actors. According to all reports. Gloria Grahame bore the brunt of his ill will during the filming of *The Big Heat.* He was relentless in his criticisms, but she bore his badgering with a reasonable amount of humor, as did the other cast members. On her first day of shooting, Lang had Jocelyn Brando cutting a piece of steak and serving it to Glenn Ford twenty-five times. By the end of the day, she was in tears and wanted to quit. Ford persuaded her to stay.

The Big Sleep

Warners, 1946. (114m.) Dir: Howard Hawks. Sp: William Faulkner, Leigh Brackett, and Jules Furthman, b/o novel by Raymond Chandler. Cast: Humphrey Bogart, Lauren Bacall, Martha Vickers, John Ridgely, Louis Jean Heydt, Elisha Cook, Jr., Dorothy Malone.

On-Screen: *Private eye Philip Marlowe tangles with some shady characters.* A remarkably faithful adaptation of Chandler's novel, this classic whodunit (who indeed? many viewers still wonder) is one of the best *films noir*— a murky brew that's mordantly witty in all the right moments, a Rubik's Cube of a puzzler that gives its charismatic stars two of their most potent roles. Sid Hickox's shadowy camera work and Max Steiner's richly thematic score enhance Hawks's taut direction of a first-rate script, notable for its deft blend of dark decadence and tangy dialogue. The tangled plot has private eye Philip Marlowe (Bogart) uncovering such unsavory matters as extortion, blackmail, pornography, and murder as he becomes involved in the lives of the rich Sternwood sisters, alluring Vivian (Bacall) and nymphomaniacal Carmen (Vickers). Enjoy the movie for the high-voltage rapport between the stars and for its splendid acting in supporting roles, especially Cook's seedy grifter, who dies a gallant death.

Off-Screen: The studio capitalized on Bogart and Bacall's marriage during the filming by adding scenes that exploited their off-camera relationship. As for the vexing question, "Who killed Taylor?" (even Chandler couldn't recall offhand when Hawks asked him), it's giving nothing away to clarify a minor point: Joe Brody (Heydt) is the culprit. In *Harper*, two decades later, Bacall does an amusing spin-off of her *Big Sleep* role. An even closer version of the novel (this time set in England) appeared in 1978, with Robert Mitchum. A big snooze.(CFB)

Billy Bathgate

Touchstone, 1991. (C-108m.) Dir: Robert Benton. Sp: Tom Stoppard, b/o novel by E. L. Doctorow. Cast: Dustin Hoffman, Nicole Kidman, Loren Dean, Bruce Willis, Steven Hill.

On-Screen: *A Bronx boy enters the underworld.* The credentials are impeccable: an adaptation of a novel by a popular author; a proven director of quality films (*Kramer vs. Kramer, Places in the Heart,* etc.); a top-ranking star in the leading role. Then how did they manage to create such a flat and lifeless movie? In the Bronx in 1935, Billy (Dean) is an ambitious teenager who admires kingpin mobster Dutch Schultz (Hoffman). When Billy becomes Schultz's protégé (Schultz calls him his "prodigy"), he learns the hard way that his mentor is a vicious, cold-blooded killer. Young Billy's involvement with Schultz's rich, married mistress (Kidman) puts him in a dangerous spot. The production values are fine, but the characters are one-dimensional, the pace slack, and the acting no better than competent. Using a kind of raspy growl, Dustin Hoffman seems to be giving a performance rather than occupying the role. Nicole Kidman is decorative as the woman who turns to

Schultz after her lover, Bo Weinberg (Willis), is murdered. (Guess who kills him. Right.) Loren Dean's Billy is merely a cypher who witnesses the most brutal deeds with the blankest stare.

Off-Screen: Amid much gossip about a troublesome star and temper tantrums by Disney executives, a new ending was shot for the film. The company returned to a New York City location on Riverside Drive to reshoot the scene. Some time afterward, a heated Hoffman asked, "What was it? Was it a love story, a gangster story, a coming-of-age story?" Good question.

Biloxi Blues

Rastar, 1988. (C-106m.) Dir: Mike Nichols. Sp: Neil Simon, b/o his play. Cast: Matthew Broderick, Christopher Walken, Matt Mulhern, Corey Parker, Markus Flanagan, Penelope Ann Miller, Casey Siemaszko, Park Overall, Michael Dolan.

On-Screen: *Neil Simon's Eugene Jerome is drafted into the World War II army*. The second entry in Neil Simon's autobiographical trilogy on young Brooklynite Eugene Jerome, *Biloxi Blues* transposes the Broadway hit into an amusing service comedy with distinctly serious overtones. Here, Eugene finds himself in basic training in Biloxi, Mississippi, near the end of World War II. His experiences not only involve his army buddies and their tough sergeant (Walken), but also his inauguration into sex (with prostitute Overall) and his first fleeting romance with a local girl (Miller). A far distance from the old service comedies with Bob Hope or Abbott and Costello, *Biloxi Blues* also touches on such nonfrivolous matters as anti-Semitism

and homosexuality. The film's highlight is Eugene's tense final confrontation with his sergeant, who is not only drunk but also armed and dangerous. Matthew Broderick performs well as the compulsively wisecracking Eugene, but Corey Parker hits only one note as his intellectual fellow soldier Epstein—an expression of pained disapproval never seems to leave his face.

Off-Screen: Matthew Broderick repeated his Broadway role as Eugene, and Penelope Ann Miller and Matt Mulhern (as Private Wykowski) were also taken from the stage cast. Barry Miller appeared onstage as Epstein. In 1992, *Broadway Bound* (officially known as *Neil Simon's "Broadway Bound"*), the third and final entry in the trilogy, was adapted for television.

Bird

Warners, 1988. (C-160m.) Dir: Clint Eastwood. Sp: Joel Oliansky. Cast: Forest Whitaker, Diane Venora, Michael Zelniker, Samuel E. Wright, Keith David, Michael McGuire, James Handy.

On-Screen: *A jazz legend's painful descent to oblivion*. Forest Whitaker's electrifying performance as Charlie ("Yardbird") Parker (1920–1955), the famed jazz musician, along with Bird's brilliant music, are the centerpieces of this overlong but gripping drama. Clint Eastwood does an expert job of directing the sad story of Bird's short, tragic life, including his relationship with his steadfast wife, Chan (Venora), and his torment from addiction to drugs. The death of his young daughter is seen as a turning point that sends him reeling into self-destructive excesses of every kind. Also figuring importantly in his story are fellow musicians Red Rodney (Zelniker) and Dizzy Gillepsie (Wright). The boldness and the beauty of Bird's jazz improvisations fill the soundtrack, making the movie a genuine treat for jazz fans. Personal favorite: the breathtaking rendition of "Laura."

Off-Screen: Charlie Parker's famous original recordings were used, including cuts never released before. The backgrounds were eliminated electronically and the music was rerecorded, using modern-day musicians who were attuned to Bird's brilliant improvisations. At one point in 1980, Joel Oliansky was set to write and direct *The Charlie Parker Story,* with Richard Pryor producing and playing the title role, but the project never got off the ground. *Bird* won an Oscar for sound recording.

Birdman of Alcatraz

United Artists, 1962. (143m.) Dir: John Frankenheimer. Sp: Guy Trosper, b/o book by Thomas E. Gaddis. Cast: Burt Lancaster, Karl Malden, Thelma Ritter, Betty Field, Edmond O'Brien, Telly Savalas, Neville Brand, Whit Bissell, Hugh Marlowe.

On-Screen: *True story of a convict turned bird expert.* Narrated by author Tom Gaddis (O'Brien), who wrote the book about Robert Stroud (Lancaster), the prison "lifer" who became an expert on ornithology, *Birdman of Alcatraz* is an absorbing if diffuse film. Lancaster plays Stroud as a sullen, bitter man, imprisoned on a murder charge and placed in solitary confinement, who develops a pervading interest in birds. He creates a makeshift haven and laboratory for feathered creatures in his cell and eventually

writes a book on bird diseases. Since Stroud is an essentially unchanging figure, the screenplay injects some dramatic life into other characters: his possessive mother (Ritter), the woman (Field) who helps him and whom he later marries, and the warden (Malden) who alternates between sympathy for Stroud and deep resentment of Stroud's unbreakable nature and his criticism of the prison system. There's also a vivid prison breakout late in the film. Oscar-nominated Lancaster gives a fierce, firm performance.

Off-Screen: With a longtime interest in the subject, producer–star Burt Lancaster first hired British director Charles Crichton for the film. They argued about the concept of the film, and after several weeks the production was shut down. John Frankenheimer was signed as the new director. Frankenheimer had wanted to do the story years before on television, but he had been warned by the networks that there would be pressure from the Bureau of Prisons.

The Birds

Universal, 1963. (C-120m.) Dir: Alfred Hitchcock. Sp: Evan Hunter, b/o story by Daphne du Maurier. Cast: Rod Taylor, Tippi Hedren, Jessica Tandy, Suzanne Pleshette, Ethel Griffies, Veronica Cartwright.

On-Screen: *California town is besieged by feathered guided missiles.* If the contrived plot doesn't get to you, the thought of birds bent on wiping out humanity probably will. You'll find yourself not much caring whether lawyer Mitch Brenner (Taylor) yields to the charms of Melanie Daniels (Hedren). But when all sorts of birds wreak havoc on the village's homes, attack schoolchildren, and kill their teacher (Pleshette), you'll fall willingly under the spell of the Master of Suspense. Since the story begins in a fancy San Francisco pet shop, perhaps we're meant to face the possibility of an upset in the natural order, birds and beasts finally turning the tables on their captors. While the special effects—swarms of birds take ominous counsel, then swoop down on their human prey—can be distractingly ingenious, there's no denying their power to shock.

Off-Screen: Alfred Hitchcock wanted to omit the customary, and comforting, THE END as Taylor and Hedren confront a multitude of threatening birds, but the studio vetoed his idea. Some of the birds are replicas, but the real ones were trained by Ray Berwick to nip, peck, and dive at their "victims." The special visual effects, supervised by Ub Iwerks, won an Oscar nomination. Blooper Spotters will notice that in a scene in which the children flee their attacker, the tots cast shadows but the birds do not. Hitchcock makes his trademark appearance leading his own pair of Sealyham terriers out of the pet shop. (CFB)

Blackboard Jungle

MGM, 1955. (101m.) Dir: Richard Brooks. Sp: Richard Brooks b/o novel by Evan Hunter. Cast: Glenn Ford, Anne Francis, Sidney Poitier, Louis Calhern, Vic Morrow, Richard Kiley, Margaret Hayes, Warner Anderson, Emile Meyer, John Hoyt, Rafael Campos.

On-Screen: *Teenagers terrorize an inner-city school.* Controversial in its day for showing violent student behavior, Richard Brooks's melodrama is noteworthy now as a foreshadowing of the social upheaval of the sixties. Glenn Ford plays a new teacher at a vocational high school located in a New York City slum. Soon, instead of teaching, his days are spent dealing with such non-academic matters as attempted rape, grand-scale vandalism, and open contempt or indifference from his students. Anonymous letters are even sent to his pregnant wife (Francis), suggesting her husband is two-timing her. Only after born-leader Gregory Miller (Poitier) stops a classmate (Morrow) from committing murder do the boys stop beating up on the faculty and hit the books instead. Despite Brooks's lively direction and his vigorous screenplay (from Evan Hunter's best-selling novel), the movie seems simplistic today. But Poitier and Brando-wannabe Morrow stand out in the cast.

Off-Screen: The movie's innovative scoring— Bill Haley and His Comets accompany the credits with "Rock Around the Clock," and additional music is by jazz artists Stan Kenton and Bix Beiderbecke—created something of a sensation. A dozen years later, Poitier found himself on the opposite side of the schoolroom desk as another harassed teacher in *To Sir with Love*. Actor Jameel Farah, playing Santini, would become better known as Jamie Farr, the cross-dresser in television's "M*A*S*H" series. (CFB)

Blade Runner

The Ladd Company, 1982. (C-118m.) Dir: Ridley Scott. Sp: Hampton Fancher and David Peoples, b/o novel by Philip K. Dick. Cast: Harrison Ford, Rutger Hauer, Sean Young, Daryl Hannah, Edward James

Olmos, William Sanderson, Joe Turkel, Joanna Cassidy, Brion James.

On-Screen: *Ridley Scott's futuristic melodrama*. In the year 2019, Los Angeles is a waking nightmare: a decaying, dreary, cluttered metropolis in which advanced high-tech machinery overwhelms the populace. Deckard (Ford) is a "blade runner," a professional assassin charged with finding and killing four dangerous replicants—strong, agile, intelligent near-humans. In time, he fulfills his mission but runs off with one replicant (Young), with whom he has fallen in love. On this simple plot, *Blade Runner* hangs a remarkable physical production built around an apocalyptic view of twenty-first-century Los Angeles, a terrifying city strewn with debris and ravaged by fires, where people seem like either ghosts or demons. Without characters a viewer can care about, this unrelentingly bleak view of a civilization ruined by "progress" becomes oppressive and off-putting. Yet many regard the film as an extraordinarily imaginative masterwork. Others, however, may find it a pretentious *film noir*. Note: The videocassette version contains several extremely gory sequences, so beware.

Off-Screen: In the fall of 1992, the so-called "director's cut" of *Blade Runner* was released to theaters. In point of fact, except for a brief shot of Deckard daydreaming about a unicorn, there was no new footage in this version. Some material was deleted rather than added, including the gory sequences mentioned above. Also excised, to the movie's benefit, was the nearly parodistic, Philip Marlowe-like narration spoken by Harrison Ford. The sound in this version was much improved, but on the whole the changes were not major. Coauthor Peoples later wrote *Unforgiven* and *Hero* (both 1992).

Blazing Saddles

Warners, 1974. (C-93m.) Dir: Mel Brooks. Sp: Mel Brooks, Richard Pryor, Andrew Bergman, and Norman Steinberg. Cast: Cleavon Little, Gene Wilder, Madeline Kahn, Harvey Korman, Slim Pickens, David Huddleston, Alex Karras, Burton Gilliam, Liam Dunn, Mel Brooks, John Hillerman.

On-Screen: *Mel Brooks takes on the Wild West*. One of Mel Brooks's funniest, most popular movies, *Blazing Saddles* is a freewheeling burlesque of the Western. The plot is only a peg on which to hang the gags: A black drifter named Bart (Little), who becomes sheriff of the town of Rock Ridge, not only wipes out the corruption but also bests the state's idiot governor (Brooks) and scheming attorney general (Korman). The film is a compendium of Brooksian humor: the scatological jokes, the shameless anachronisms, the startling reversal of stereotypes (the homespun townfolk use four-letter words), and the cheerful disregard of time and place. Also taking part in the rampant confusion are the Waco Kid (Wilder), a once-famous gunslinger, and Lili Von Shtupp (Kahn), an uproarious spoof of Marlene Dietrich's "Frenchy" in *Destry Rides Again*. The jokes come as thick and fast as bullets, and many of them hit the target; others land with a heavy thud. Personal favorite: Asked to sing "a good ole nigger work song," a black chain gang breaks into a chorus of "I Get a Kick Out of You."

Off-Screen: Warners rejected Richard Pryor in the leading role, claiming that he lacked box-office stature. Dan Dailey was originally signed to play the Waco Kid but he bowed out at the last minute. After a disastrous preview for studio executives, the movie was shown at a public screening to an enthusiastic reception. It became one of the year's major successes.

Blood and Sand

Fox, 1941. (C-123m.) Dir: Rouben Mamoulian. Sp: Jo Swerling, b/o novel by Vicente Blasco-Ibañez. Cast: Tyrone Power, Linda Darnell, Rita Hayworth, Nazimova, Anthony Quinn, J. Carrol Naish, John Carradine, Lynn Bari, Laird Cregar.

On-Screen: *Bullfighting and redemption, by way of Rouben Mamoulian.* Stunningly beautiful, Oscar-winning Technicolor photography by Ernest Palmer and Ray Rennahan is the principal, and probably sole, virtue of Rouben Mamoulian's remake of the 1922 film. Tyrone Power replaces Rudolph Valentino as the ardent young Spanish matador who allows fame to go to his head, with tragic consequences. Abandoning his young wife (Darnell) and ignoring his devoted mother (Nazimova), he falls prey to the alluring Hayworth. Redemption comes too late in the bullring. Although the hard-breathing theatrics are foolish, *Blood and Sand* occasionally captures the pagentry and excitement of the bullfight in a flaring scarlet cape and charging bull or in the tense faces of the waiting matadors as the frenzied audience cheers another "moment of truth."

Off-Screen: Working closely with the art directors, Rouben Mamoulian styled some sequences in the film after certain painters (Goya for the bullring, Velazquez for Hayworth's mansion, El Greco for the matador's chapel, etc.) He also sent Tyrone Power to Mexico City to see several bullfights and to observe the elaborate ritual surrounding the matador on the eve of the fight. A Spanish version of the novel was released in 1989.

Blood Simple

Circle Films, 1985. (C-97m.) Dir: Joel Coen. Sp: Joel Coen and Ethan Coen. Cast: John Getz, Frances McDormand, Dan Hedaya, M. Emmet Walsh, Samm-Art Williams.

On-Screen: *Low-budget but high-tension thriller of jealousy and murder.* You'll have lots of grisly fun as you follow the abrupt twists and turns in this decidedly offbeat shocker. The surprises mount after Marty (Hedaya), a Texas saloon owner, hires a sleazy private eye (Walsh) to kill his faithless wife (McDormand) and her lover (Getz). Murphy's Law takes over, however, and absolutely everything goes wrong with Marty's plan. One of the conspirators is shot instead, and the lovers come to suspect each other of betrayal, theft, and foul play. Much of the enjoyment of this wildly improbable yet compelling movie derives from your being a step ahead of the characters (most of the film, anyway) as they blunder their way toward the gruesome climax. The actors may be unfamiliar, but they seem all the more real for that reason, with Walsh a standout as the slimy detective. Recurring shots of a string of putrifying fish nicely sum up the grubby goings-on.

Off-Screen: This is the first of the redoubtable Coen brothers' bizarre movies—*Raising Arizona* (1987), *Miller's Crossing* (1990), and *Barton Fink* (1991) were to follow. Praised as a superior black comedy when shown at the Cannes Film Festival in May of 1984, it reached theaters early the following year, when its freewheeling spin on the *film noir* genre quickly captured an enthusiastic cult following. The movie's cinematographer, Barry Sonnenfeld, later directed *The Addams Family* (1991). (CFB)

Blow Out

Orion, 1981. (C-107m.) Dir: Brian De Palma. Sp: Brian De Palma. Cast: John Travolta, Nancy Allen, John Lithgow, Dennis Franz, John Aquino, Peter Boyden.

On-Screen: *A sound-effects man is entangled in a political murder.* Suspend your disbelief for 107 minutes, and you may find yourself caught up in the mayhem and mystery of Brian De Palma's film. John Travolta plays Jack Terry, a sound-effects wizard who, on one dark night in Philadelphia, records what seems to be an accident in which a car plunges into a river. His painstaking investigation of the recording proves that it was no accident but the political murder of a presidential aspirant. Of course nobody believes him. Also deeply involved is Sally (Allen), a bimbo who was in the car with the victim, and a cold-blooded serial killer (Lithgow) who is after both Jack and Sally. *Blow Out* clearly takes its cue not only from Antonioni's *Blowup* (1966), but also from a number of Alfred Hitchcock movies. The movie suffers, however, from a downbeat ending that violates the implicit pact between the viewer and the filmmaker in thrillers of this kind. Hitchcock, for one, understood that a twisty melodrama that places a hero in severe jeopardy demands that he triumph in the end. Here, the audience leaves puzzled, glum, and unsettled.

Off-Screen: The climax takes place against the background of a massive parade. When several thousand feet of footage of the parade was stolen from a van parked in midtown Manhattan, De Palma had to recall thousands of extras dressed in parade costumes, as well as cameramen and technicians, to Philadelphia to reshoot the sequence that ran only two minutes in the finished movie. De Palma rummaged through trash cans in the Times Square area before deciding to reshoot.

The Blue Dahlia

Paramount, 1946. (99m.) Dir: George Marshall. Sp: Raymond Chandler. Cast: Alan Ladd, Veronica Lake, William Bendix, Howard Da Silva, Doris Dowling, Frank Faylen, Hugh Beaumont, Will Wright.

On-Screen: *Veteran becomes suspect in wife's murder.* Returning from the war, veteran Johnny Morrison (Ladd) discovers that his wife (Dowling) has become an easy-living, hard-drinking tramp. When she's murdered, he becomes the prime suspect. Swirling around him are other *film noir* types, including a mysteriously helpful blonde (Lake), a shell-shocked war buddy (Bendix), and a sleazy nightclub owner (Da Silva). Written by novelist Raymond Chandler, *The Blue Dahlia* is a competent but essentially routine melodrama with the requisite amount of *noir* dialogue ("I told you she was poison. They're *all* poison, sooner or later.") More interesting than either Ladd or Lake, who seem to be working under the influence of Novocain, are the colorful supporting characters, especially Will Wright as a blackmailing house detective.

Off-Screen: Paramount bought *The Blue Dahlia* as an unfinished novel by Raymond Chandler, which Chandler used as the basis for his screenplay. The author was apparently less than enthusiastic about his leading man, remarking that "Ladd is hard, bitter, and occasionally charming, but he is, after all, a small boy's idea of a tough guy." The movie was the first produced by John Houseman under a newly signed contract.

Blue Skies

Paramount, 1946. (C-104m.) Dir: Stuart Heisler. Sp: Arthur Sheekman, adapted by Allan Scott and b/o idea by Irving Berlin. MS: Irving Berlin. Cast: Bing Crosby, Fred Astaire, Joan Caulfield, Billy De Wolfe, Olga San Juan, Mikhail Rasumny.

On-Screen: *A parade of Irving Berlin music, sung by Crosby and danced by Astaire.* Berlin's songs, gloriously melodic and expressing basic emotions with deceptive simplicity and truth, are the mainstay of this movie. The old favorites—"Always," "You'd Be Surprised," "Heat Wave," etc.—are still a joy, but so are the new entries, such as the lovely "You Keep Coming Back Like a Song." Astaire does a virtuosic song-and-dance to "Puttin' on the Ritz" and joins Crosby for a delightful rendition of "A Couple of Song-and-Dance Men." There are problems, however: Some of the production numbers are marred by the truly ugly costumes and decor of forties musicals, and the story, concerning the changing relationship of Crosby and Astaire over the years, as well as their mutual love for Caulfield, is dull and uninvolving. Still, Berlin's music sweeps away objections, even as it lifts the heart and the spirit.

Off-Screen: Dancer Paul Draper was originally cast in the Astaire role, but apparently he couldn't get along with the other cast members and was replaced by Astaire. After the film was completed, Astaire announced his retirement from films. (He returned two years later.) Director Mark Sandrich died before production began and was replaced by Stuart Heisler.

Blue Velvet

De Laurentiis, 1986. (C-120m.) Dir: David Lynch. Sp: David Lynch. Cast: Kyle MacLachlan, Isabella Rossellini, Dennis Hopper, Laura Dern, Dean Stockwell, Hope Lange, Jack Nance, Brad Dourif.

On-Screen: *David Lynch's shocker about covert evil.* Which movie will you see? Will it be the one critic Rex Reed called "one of the sickest movies ever made"? Or the movie that was named Best Film of 1986 by the National Society of Film Critics? You judge, but beware. A bizarre, disorienting, and often repellent film, *Blue Velvet* is an exercise in style and a kinky thriller, but no "work of art" (*New York* magazine). A young man named Jeffrey Beaumont (MacLachlan) discovers a severed ear in the grass, which leads him into a nightmare world of hallucinatory drugs and strange sexual rituals. Inhabiting this world are a masochistic nightclub singer (Rossellini), an obscenity-spouting, drug-inhaling, sadistic drug dealer (Hopper), and other depraved types. Only one person, the angelic Sandy (Dern), has the reactions of a normal human being. The film impressed some critics and scholars, but curiously, some were careful to praise and condemn it simultaneously —"A bizarre thriller, deliriously erotic, perversely funny, appallingly cruel" (*Newsday*). "It's a strange world, isn't it?" says the young hero at several points. Strange indeed, and not for every taste.

Off-Screen: Isabella Rossellini is the daughter of Ingrid Bergman, who might have been appalled by Isabella's role in *Blue Velvet*. A grotesque drag queen is played by former child star Dean Stockwell (*Anchors Aweigh, The Green Years*), whose father, Harry Stockwell, provided the voice for the Prince in Disney's *Snow White and the Seven Dwarfs*. Little did Harry know that many years later, his son would be playing the wicked queen.

Bob & Carol & Ted & Alice

Columbia, 1969. (C-104m.) Dir: Paul Mazursky. Sp: Paul Mazursky and Larry Tucker. Cast: Natalie Wood, Robert Culp, Dyan Cannon, Elliott Gould, Horst Ebersberg, Donald F. Muhich.

On-Screen: *Two married couples unleash their inhibitions—with devastating results.* Once considered a bold new approach to depicting marital relationships on-screen, *Bob & Carol & Ted & Alice* now seems heavily dated. Yet it's still quite entertaining in its account of two married couples (Wood and Culp, Cannon and Gould) who pretend to seek sexual freedom and honesty in their marriages and then find themselves in situations for which they had never bargained. When Bob and Carol release their deepest feelings at an encounter group, they convince their inhibited friends Ted and Alice to join them in the experience. The result is catastrophic—and comic. Elliott Gould's Ted, caught up in his sexual fantasies, is exceptionally funny, but it is Dyan Cannon as Alice, a

mass of neuroses and repressions, who walks away with the movie. *Bob & Carol* opts for a conventional ending, but along the way there are some well-earned laughs.

Off-Screen: Performing since the age of five, Natalie Wood blossomed into a beautiful and capable leading actress; tragically, she died in a drowning accident in 1981. Dyan Cannon's funniest scene in the film is with her unflappable psychiatrist, played by a true analyst named Donald F. Muhich. A short-lived television series based on the movie appeared in 1973.

Bob Roberts

Paramount, 1992. (C-102m.) Dir: Tim Robbins. Sp: Tim Robbins. Cast: Tim Robbins, Giancarlo Esposito, Ray Wise, Rebecca Jenkins, Allan Rickman, Gore Vidal, Brian Murray.

On-Screen: *Chilling comedy-satire of millionaire folksinger's bid for political office.* "I don't have any idea who he is," says Senator Brickley Paiste (Vidal), the pouchy, patrician incumbent whose upstart opponent is dimpled, guitar-strumming Bob Roberts (Robbins). If Paiste were to view this mock documentary tracing the scary rise and rise of "rebel conservative" Roberts, however, he'd get a very good idea. The opening sequences are funny, as an on-camera interviewer (Murray) follows Roberts on his rounds at rallies ("It's show time!") and in television appearances. The wicked fun in discovering that behind his charm and steady gaze Bob is really a dangerous hatemonger is offset by a plot hole wide enough to drive the "Vote Bob" campaign bus through, and some heavy lecturing by Esposito's character at the end underlines the obvious. Still, this boldly original movie places Robbins among that rare breed of triple-threat filmmakers.

Off-Screen: "Times Are Changin' Back," "This Land Was Made for Me," "Retake America"—these are among the thirteen mean-spirited, thoroughly in-character songs that Robbins not only performs in the movie but also cowrote with his brother David. (Their father, Gil, was a member of the sixties' popular folk group The Highwaymen.) In cameo roles are John Cusack, as a harried live-television host, and Susan Sarandon, James Spader, Pamela Reed, Fred Ward, and Peter Gallagher as television-news anchors. Robbins introduced his fictional character in a "Saturday Night Live" skit in 1985. Vidal, of course, is the well-known novelist and biographer. (CFB)

Body and Soul

United Artists, 1947. (104m.) Dir: Robert Rossen. Sp: Abraham Polonsky. Cast: John Garfield, Lilli Palmer, Hazel Brooks, Anne Revere, Canada Lee, William Conrad, Joseph Pevney.

On-Screen: *Powerful rags-to-riches boxing tale.* "Fight for something, but not for money," Revere begs her son. Upwardly mobile Garfield does both. Struggling to escape from a Manhattan slum, he first tastes success as an amateur boxer. Later, as a pro, he heads for the big time and the big bucks. And big trouble. He neglects his widowed mother, ditches good woman Palmer for bad woman Brooks, then accepts a bribe from crooked sports promoters to take a dive. The movie climaxes with a rousing fight sequence (James Wong Howe's photography here seems amazingly authentic) but leaves the inevitable consequences of its conclusion unexplored. Garfield's strong performance is one of his best; Lee is superb as his doomed, punch-drunk trainer.

Off-Screen: Surprisingly, the newsreel-like boxing scenes, in which Howe followed the blow-by-blow action with a hand-held camera as he whirled about on roller skates, failed to earn him an Oscar nomination for cinematography. However, Garfield's vigorous portrait garnered him a Best Actor nomination, and Polonsky's rather pretentious original screenplay was similarly recognized. One Oscar went to editors Francis Lyon and Robert Parrish. Garfield suffered a heart attack, one of a series that would later prove fatal, during the filming of a rope-skipping scene. Conrad became the bulky star of the "Cannon" and "Jake and the Fatman" television series. The movie was remade, forgettably, in 1981. (CFB)

Body Heat

The Ladd Company–Warners, 1981. (C-113m.) Dir and Sp: Lawrence Kasdan. Cast: William Hurt, Kathleen Turner, Richard Crenna, Ted Danson, J. A. Preston, Mickey Rourke.

On-Screen: *Smitten lawyer is trapped into murder.* "When it gets hot, people start to kill each other." That's the comment of a dogged cop (Preston) in this steamy *film noir,* and he's certainly right. A melodrama in the classic *noir* style, *Body Heat* has a familiar story line: In a heat-stricken Florida community, a none-too-bright, easily corruptible lawyer (Hurt) is seduced by a ravishing socialite (Turner) into killing her loathed husband (Crenna). Fans of *Double Indemnity* will know that their plan will start to unravel, and that the lady has depths of wickedness her lover cannot fathom until it is too late. William Hurt gives a sterling performance, and Kathleen Turner is alluring in her film debut. At several points, Mickey Rourke appears as a seedy arsonist and immediately rivets the attention. Lawrence Kasdan's dialogue encapsulates the *noir* style. Cop (to Hurt): "She's trouble, Ned. Real big-time major-league trouble." Turner: "I'd kill myself if I thought this thing would destroy us." *Body Heat* marks writer Kasdan's directorial debut.

Off-Screen: It was William Hurt's idea to dye his pale blonde hair a darker shade and to grow a mustache for the role of Ned Racine. Lawrence Kasdan offered this comment on his dialogue: "*Body Heat* is talk heavy and it was meant to be. That is one of the things I wanted to do with it. I wanted to make a movie that you have to listen to, because I don't think there have been many in America lately and I miss them."

Bombshell

MGM, 1933. (95m.) Dir: Victor Fleming. Sp: Jules Furthman and John Lee Mahin, b/o play by Caroline Francke and Mack Crane. Cast: Jean Harlow, Lee Tracy, Frank Morgan, Franchot Tone, Pat O'Brien, Una Merkel, C. Aubrey Smith, Ted Healy, Ivan Lebedeff.

On-Screen: *Jean Harlow shines as a flamboyant thirties movie star.* One of the best comedies about Hollywood in the thirties, *Bombshell* stars Jean Harlow as Lola Burns, a volatile film star who is forever caught up in head-lined scandals engineered by her aggressive press agent, Space Hanlon (Tracy). Space thwarts Lola's plans to adopt a baby and involves her in a bogus romance with an actor (Tone) impersonating a Boston scion. Zeroing in on the movie colony's madcap, self-promoting ways, *Bombshell* (later retitled *Blonde Bombshell* to avoid the impression that it was a war film) crackles with funny dialogue and satirical moments. As the brassy, temperamental Lola, Jean Harlow is clearly in her element—most hilarious when she tries to behave like a lady—and Lee Tracy, a first-rate comic actor, stays right in step with her as the unscrupulous Space. Frank Morgan harrumphs his way through the role of Lola's disreputable father. *Bombshell* is vintage fun.

Off-Screen: *Bombshell* is virtually a *film à clef*. Lola Burns was modeled after actress Clara Bow, not Harlow herself, as some have suggested. Frank Morgan's role in the film was obviously inspired by Harlow's real-life stepfather, Marino Bello. Also, Lola's titled fiancé (Lebedeff) suggests the real-life Henri de la Coudraye, who was married first to Gloria Swanson and later to Constance Bennett. Franchot Tone replaced Nils Asther in the role of Lola's bogus suitor.

The Bonfire of the Vanities

Warners, 1990. (C-125m.) Dir: Brian De Palma. Sp: Michael Cristofer, b/o novel by Tom Wolfe. Cast: Tom Hanks, Melanie Griffith, Bruce Willis, Morgan Freeman, Kim Cattrall, Saul Rubinek, Alan King, John Hancock.

On-Screen: *A hotshot Wall Street broker's world collapses.* Yes, *The Bonfire of the Vanities* died an ignominious death at the box office. And yes, the movie bears scant relation to the popular novel. But wait. There are two schools of thought possible about this movie. Those who read the book may be justified in scorning it as an unrecognizable blunder. But those who come to it knowing nothing about the travails of Tom Wolfe's Sherman McCoy, Wall Street's "Master of the Universe," might view the movie in a different light: as a nasty black comedy, an urban nightmare made disturbingly real. When the movie's McCoy (Hanks) becomes involved in a hit-and-run accident with his mistress (Griffith), he opens a Pandora's box out of which emerge darkly satiric versions of all-too-familiar types of the nineties. Each has his own agenda, especially an alcoholic reporter (Willis) who looks at the incident as a step toward fame and fortune. At first Tom Hanks seems blatantly miscast as Sherman McCoy, but viewed as the hapless victim of an out-of-control society, the actor's comic persona seems almost justified. No doubt *The Bonfire of the Vanities* is a serious miscalculation by De Palma, but it hardly deserves to be trashed.

Off-Screen: Those who want to follow the film's inexorable, step-by-step path to disaster should read Julie Salamon's book *The Devil's Candy: "The Bonfire of the Vanities" Goes to Hollywood* (Houghton Mifflin, 1991).

Bonnie and Clyde

Warners, 1967. (C-111m.) Dir: Arthur Penn. Sp: David Newman and Robert Benton. Cast: Warren Beatty, Faye Dunaway, Gene Hackman, Michael J. Pollard, Estelle Parsons, Gene Wilder, Denver Pyle, Dub Taylor.

On-Screen: *Stunning, influential comedy-drama about Kansas outlaws.* A landmark film of the sixties, *Bonnie and Clyde* provoked both outraged and admiring criticism with its startlingly original approach to the crime film. Juxtaposing boisterous comedy and explicit violence, the movie glamorized Clyde Barrow (Beatty) and Bonnie Parker (Dunaway), two small-time thieves and murderers of the Depression era, into folk heroes not unlike the antiestablishment rebels of the sixties. Despite their murderous ways, we come to sympathize with these losers as they try to survive the Depression, however violently and self-destructively. The other Barrow gang members—Clyde's "good ol' country boy" brother Buck (Hackman); Buck's frumpy, hysterical wife (Parsons); and nitwit C. W. Moss (Pollard)—are equally ordinary people who turn to robbing and killing almost as an impulse or an afterthought. Shown in slow motion, as well as real time, the now-classic final ambush sequence is still imitated in action films.

Off-Screen: Producer Beatty wanted New Wave filmmakers Jean-Luc Godard and François Truffaut to direct; when they declined, Penn, another top director, got the job. Jane Fonda and Tuesday Weld were asked to play Bonnie, but they declined. Exterior "Kansas" scenes were filmed in and around Dallas. The movie received ten Oscar nominations, but only Parsons and cinematographer Burnett Guffey won statuettes. *You Only Live Once* (1937), *They Live by Night, Gun Crazy* (1949), *The Bonnie Parker Story* (1958), and *Thieves Like Us* (1974) are similar in content, but *Bonnie and Clyde* is a true original.

Boom Town

MGM, 1940. (116m.) Dir: Jack Conway. Sp: John Lee Mahin, b/o story by James

Edward Grant. Cast: Clark Gable, Claudette Colbert, Spencer Tracy, Hedy Lamarr, Frank Morgan, Chill Wills.

On-Screen: *Gable and Tracy fight over oil and women.* A lively but familiar tale that reprises the old "two battling buddies" plot of countless B movies, *Boom Town* stars Clark Gable and Spencer Tracy as wildcatters hunting for oil and finding plenty of trouble. Claudette Colbert costars as Gable's loyal wife, and Hedy Lamarr is the beautiful distraction who leads him temporarily astray. The early sequences are best as the persevering men are rewarded with a gusher of oil and battle a blazing well by "shooting" it with nitroglycerin. Interest lags, however, when domestic problems take over and Gable must play the neglectful husband chastised by Tracy. Colbert's role gives her little to do, and Lamarr, as always, is inexpressive. In the oil fields *Boom Town* has some vigor and excitement; elsewhere it loses momentum.

Off-Screen: Feeling that he was being exploited by MGM, Spencer Tracy requested that there be no more films in which he played "second fiddle" to Clark Gable or Joan Crawford. Following *Men of Boys Town* (1941), a sequel to his popular *Boys Town,* he received full-star status with *Dr. Jekyll and Mr. Hyde* (1941)—not a wise choice—then found his most compatible costar in Katharine Hepburn with *Woman of the Year* (1942).

Boomerang!

Fox, 1947. (88m.) Dir: Elia Kazan. Sp: Richard Murphy, b/o article by Anthony Abbot. Cast: Dana Andrews, Jane Wyatt, Lee J. Cobb, Arthur Kennedy, Ed Begley, Karl Malden, Sam Levene, Taylor Holmes, Robert Keith, Cara Williams.

On-Screen: *The murder of a priest rocks a small Connecticut town.* Having revolutionized film journalism with his celebrated March of Time series (1935–51), producer Louis de Rochement applied his realistic techniques to feature films. Drawing on actual events, he created semidocumentary dramas such as *The House on 92nd Street* and this absorbing movie. Under Elia Kazan's skilled direction, it centers on the events in a small Connecticut town after a popular priest is shot dead in the street. Public and political pressure insist on a quick arrest of the murderer, and soon a drifter (Kennedy) is charged with the crime. The state's attorney (Andrews), assigned to prosecute the case, has growing doubts about the man's guilt, and his investigation leads to an explosive conclusion. There are clichéd characters, such as Wyatt as Andrews's loyal, loving wife, but the story is trimly told, with no wasted footage and an air of realism.

Off-Screen: The film cites Homer S. Cummings, the lawyer who became attorney general in Franklin Roosevelt's administration, as the source for the character played by Dana Andrews. Some of the facts, however, are not accurate. Cummings did preside as the state's attorney at the 1924 trial of the accused murderer, but at this time he was already a prestigious national figure, not the obscure attorney played by Andrews. A small role as a witness to the crime was filled by Kazan's colorful Uncle Joseph, and one of the men in the police lineup is famed playwright Arthur Miller, then a friend of Elia Kazan's.

Born on the Fourth of July

Universal, 1989. (C-144m.) Dir: Oliver Stone. Sp: Oliver Stone and Ron Kovic b/o book by Ron Kovic. Cast: Tom Cruise, Kyra Sedgwick, Raymond J. Barry, Caroline Kava, Bryan Larkin, Jerry Levine, Frank Whaley, Willem Dafoe, Tom Berenger.

On-Screen: *One man's Vietnam ordeal.* Based on Ron Kovic's true story, this powerful film beings with Kovic as a devout, patriotic young man who sets tough, unforgiving standards for himself. Then, in 1963, he is plunged into combat as a U.S. Marine in Vietnam. War is hell, but the war in Vietnam was a special hell of physical danger and moral chaos, and Kovic emerges damaged in body and spirit. Paralyzed from mid-chest down, he embarks on a long journey of self-discovery and self-repair that takes him, among other places, to a Vietnam veterans' enclave in Mexico. Here the insanity of the Vietnam experience comes clear: Kovic and another veteran (Dafoe) wrestle each other in wheelchairs over claims of killing children. Director Oliver Stone lets the story speak for itself, with near-total realism and no sentimentality. Led by Cruise, the cast performs flawlessly. At the end, when Kovic has reached his resolution, we have reached our own resolution, and his triumph leaves us triumphant as well. *Born on the Fourth of July* will leave you shaken but proud.

Off-Screen: Ron Kovic can be seen in the opening parade sequence, and Oliver Stone plays a television reporter. Stone's direction and the editing won Academy Awards. His comment on the film: "My story and that of other vets is subsumed in Ron's. We experienced one war over there, then came home and slammed our heads into another war of indifference. I felt like I was in the 'Twilight Zone.' " (BL)

Born to Dance

MGM, 1936. (105m.) Dir: Roy Del Ruth. Sp: Sid Silvers and Jack McGowan. MS: Cole Porter. Cast: Eleanor Powell, James Stewart, Virginia Bruce, Una Merkel, Buddy Ebsen, Francis Langford, Sid Silvers, Raymond Walburn.

On-Screen: *Eleanor Powell taps her heart out to a Cole Porter score.* A typical MGM musical of the period, lavish, entertaining, and a trifle cumbersome, *Born to Dance* has much to recommend, but this does not include the plot, a frail business about an ambitious dancer (Eleanor Powell) who finds fame on Broadway (replacing a *singer,* no less). James Stewart plays the sailor who loves her and gets to sing Cole Porter's "Easy to Love" in his own plaintive, untrained voice. The movie's pleasures are all musical: a jaunty rendition of "Hey, Babe, Hey" by the cast principals, a dubbed Virginia Bruce (as the star Powell replaces) singing "I've Got You Under My Skin" to an embarrassed Stewart, and an elaborate nautical finale, "Swingin' the Jinx Away," in which Powell, teeth flashing, taps up a storm. As usual in MGM's thirties musicals, some irrelevant but amusing specialty acts are tossed in for no good reason, most notably Reginald Gardiner's hilarious miming of a symphony conductor.

Off-Screen: The song "Easy to Love" was originally written for William Gaxton in the stage version of *Anything Goes.* Gaxton complained that the song was not suitable for his voice and "All Through the Night" was substituted. The finale, "Swingin' the Jinx Away," was staged by Roger Edens, who had recently joined MGM as a composer and arranger, and would become an important member of the prestigious Arthur Freed unit at the studio. Seven years later the same number was cut into another, and lesser, MGM musical, *I Dood It* (1943).

Born Yesterday

Columbia, 1950. (103m.) Dir: George Cukor. Sp: Albert Mannheimer, b/o play by Garson Kanin. Cast: Judy Holliday, William Holden, Broderick Crawford, Howard St. John.

On-Screen: *Holliday repeats her stage triumph, and wins an Oscar.* Although it's a little dated now, this spin on the Pygmalion-Galatea theme is worth seeing for Holliday's uproariously funny performance as Billie Dawn, a brawling, not-so-dumb blonde, and mistress of blustering Harry Brock (Crawford). A crooked junk tycoon, he's brought her with him to Washington, where he plans to wheel and deal his way into forming an illegal cartel. Harry makes a big mistake by hiring urbane reporter Paul Verrall (Holden) to give Billie polish and social mobility. Verrall also enlightens her on constitutional law. Their budding romance is no surprise; what remain fresh are Billie's brickbats hurled at Harry: "You're just not couth!" and "Would you do me a favor? . . . Drop dead!" Holden is good as Billie's Pygmalion, but Crawford overplays, making Brock less a likable oaf than a raging bull.

Off-Screen: After buying the screen rights to Kanin's 1946 comedy, studio head Harry Cohn intended to cast glamorous contract star Rita Hayworth as Billie Dawn. Holliday's hilarious appearance in *Adam's Rib* (1949), however, had so impressed Cukor, Katharine Hepburn, Spencer Tracy, and Kanin, all involved in the making of that film, that Cohn was persuaded to go with Holliday. He wasn't taking much of a chance: The actress had introduced the role on Broadway (replacing an indisposed Jean Arthur), playing Billie for more than 1,600 performances. Holliday's success was complete; she crowded out favorites Bette Davis (*All About Eve*) and Gloria Swanson (*Sunset Boulevard*) for the Best Actress Academy Award. A 1993 remake starred Melanie Griffith and John Goodman. (CFB)

Bound for Glory

United Artists, 1976. (C-147m.) Dir: Hal Ashby. Sp: Robert Getchell. Cast: David Carradine, Melinda Dillon, Ronny Cox, Gail Strickland, John Lehne, Randy Quaid, Ji-Tu Cumbuka.

On-Screen: *The life and music of folksinger-composer Woody Guthrie.* Haskell Wexler's stunning, Oscar-winning photography is the principal virtue of this long, rambling film about Woody Guthrie (Carradine), the folksinger-composer whose vibrant songs of hope and protest were a hallmark of the Depression years. Wexler's images are unforgettable: the worn faces in a migrant workers' camp, the hoboes riding the rails, Guthrie singing to children in a field school, and many others. The story shows Guthrie as a restless, uncompromising man who insisted on "touching" the people with his music and refused to sing bland, inoffensive songs for the benefit of his radio sponsors. His attitude and his wanderlust cost him his family, but he remained close to his roots.

For all of his committed social sense and wonderful music, Guthrie does not come off as a completely sympathetic figure. And Randy Quaid carries too heavy a symbolic burden as a militant migrant worker. But *Bound for Glory* is a visual treasure.

Off-Screen: Leonard Rosenman's score adaptation also won an Oscar, and the film itself and Robert Getchell's screenplay were nominated. Production designer Michael Haller was required to transform the little town of Isleton, near Stockton, California, into the run-down town of Pampa, Texas, in the thirties. He also built a huge California migrant workers' camp outside Isleton and constructed a complete Los Angeles radio station of the period on a soundstage.

The Boys from Brazil

Fox, 1978. (C-123m.) Dir: Franklin J. Schaffner. Sp: Heywood Gould, b/o novel by Ira Levin. Cast: Gregory Peck, Laurence Olivier, James Mason, Lilli Palmer, Uta Hagen, Rosemary Harris, Steven Guttenberg, Denholm Elliott, John Dehner, Anne Meara, John Rubinstein, Jeremy Black.

On-Screen: *A Nazi hunter versus a Nazi chieftain*. If you believe this story, we can sell you Adolf Hitler's authentic memoirs. It appears that notorious Nazi bigwig Dr. Josef Mengele (Peck), alive and well in Paraguay, has been plotting for years to clone duplicates of Hitler, creating a race of future dictators from a group of specially selected boys. Aging Nazi hunter Ezra Lieberman (Olivier) gets on Mengele's trail, finally realizing the enormity of his insidious scheme. The two men finally do violent battle in a Pennsylvania farmhouse. Considering the stature of the cast and the credits of the director (*Planet of the Apes, Patton,* etc.), one might justifiably expect a better movie than this preposterous melodrama. Scarcely any of it is credible, and the climax in the farmhouse, also involving one of the cloned boys, is laughably bad. As Lieberman, Laurence Olivier does try, trotting out the accent he would use again two years later in *The Jazz Singer*. But it's all in vain.

Off-Screen: Portugal—mainly Lisbon and a town named Rosario De Molta—stood in for Brazil in the movie. Other filming took place in Vienna, London, and Lancaster, Pennsylvania. Gregory Peck's comment on playing an evil character: "Being obsessed and sadistic is not so hard to do. I am thoroughly enjoying myself."

Boys Town

MGM, 1938. (96m.) Dir: Norman Taurog. Sp: John Meehan and Dore Schary, b/o story by Eleanore Griffin and Dore Schary. Cast: Spencer Tracy, Mickey Rooney, Henry Hull, Gene Reynolds, Leslie Fenton, Edward Norris, Frankie Thomas, Bobs Watson, Addison Richards.

On-Screen: *Father Flanagan builds a school for problem boys*. "There's no such thing in the world as a bad boy," says Father Edward J. Flanagan, founder of Nebraska's Boys Town for boys in trouble. Unfortunately, there *is* such a thing in the world as a bad movie, and for all its good intentions and huge popularity, *Boys Town* cannot be considered a winner. So stickily sentimental it may make your teeth ache, it relates how Father Flanagan created his refuge despite overwhelming odds. Mostly it deals with the reformation of the town's toughest, most arrogant resident, Whitey Marsh

(Rooney). Brother of a convicted hoodlum (Norris), Whitey must learn the hard way about caring, decency, and all those values cherished by Louis B. Mayer. Young Rooney plays Whitey with scenery-chewing relish and gets heavily involved in the movie's melodramatic climax. Spencer Tracy won the Best Actor Oscar for his earnest performance as Father Flanagan, and Griffin and Schary's original story also received a trophy. A sequel, *Men of Boys Town,* turned up in 1941.

Off-Screen: Spencer Tracy modeled his performance on the real Father Flanagan, whom he admired greatly. Much of the movie was filmed at the actual Boys Town in Nebraska, and some of the residents appear in the background. Tracy gave Father Flanagan his Oscar with the inscription, "To Father Edward J. Flanagan, whose great human qualities, timely simplicity, and inspiring courage were strong enough to shine through my humble effort."

Boyz N the Hood

Columbia, 1991. (C-107m.) Dir: John Singleton. Sp: John Singleton. Cast: Cuba Gooding, Jr., Larry Fishburne, Ice Cube, Morris Chestnut, Angela Bassett, Mia Long, Tyra Ferrell, Whitman Mayo.

On-Screen: *Struggling to survive in black Los Angeles.* Centering on a group of male black high school students, *Boyz N the Hood* is writer-director Singleton's plea for an end to violence in the black community. The story is told through Tre (Gooding), living with his father (Fishburne) in an all-black section of Los Angeles. Tre hangs out after school with some basically decent kids who face normal high school growing pains, plus too-early sex and children, random crime, and the presence of drugs. Still they manage to cope until they are caught up, almost by chance, in a sudden whirlpool of murder and revenge. There are too many places where Singleton steps in to deliver a message, and sometimes the dialogue (straight from the streets) is hard to make out. But there's also so much truth in it, and it's played with such conviction, that in the end we forget the flaws and remember its honesty and its final glimmer of hope.

Off-Screen: Twenty-three-year-old John Singleton began filming *Boyz N the Hood* only months after completing a film-writing course at the University of Southern California. He became the first black director to be nominated for an Academy Award. The film was shot entirely on location in South Central Los Angeles in the midst of patrolling police helicopters, street gangs, and a supportive neighborhood. Despite the movie's antiviolence message, gunfire and pandemonium broke out at theaters across the country at its opening. (BL)

Breakfast at Tiffany's

Paramount, 1961. (C-115m.) Dir: Blake Edwards. Sp: George Axelrod, b/o novella by Truman Capote. Cast: Audrey Hepburn, George Peppard, Mickey Rooney, Patricia Neal, Martin Balsam, Buddy Ebsen, John McGiver.

On-Screen: *Call girl leads the hedonistic life in Manhattan.* "I don't know who I am!" wails Holly Golightly (Hepburn) as she prepares to ditch boyfriend Peppard to decamp for the rich-husband hunting grounds of Brazil.

Identity and commitment are only two of the problems faced by lovers star-crossed in ways Hollywood had seldom dealt with before the sixties. Although it tones down Capote's more serious, explicit novella, the movie deals candidly with the romance that develops between a kept man (Peppard by Neal) and a café-society call girl (Hepburn) with a surprising past and unsuspected ties to the Mafia. The best performances are by Oscar-nominated Hepburn, whose sophistication covers her fears, and Neal, stylishly accepting her fate as an older woman doomed to paying for sex. Manhattan locations, expertly employed by director Edwards, lend the film authenticity. Henry Mancini's score and his theme song, "Moon River," won Academy Awards.

Off-Screen: The film's first day of shooting took place outside Tiffany's on Fifth Avenue in New York City. A crowd gathered to watch the crew working in the early hours of the morning. Seeing the mob, many thought there had been a robbery. What they saw was a rather frightened and ill-at-ease Audrey Hepburn, who hated to be watched when she was working. She was merely required to gaze in Tiffany's window as she munched on a danish, but she flubbed take after take. Eventually, she got it right. A Broadway musical adaptation starring Mary Tyler Moore closed during previews in 1966. (JMK)

Breaking Away

Fox, 1979. (C-100m.) Dir: Peter Yates. Sp: Steve Tesich. Cast: Dennis Christopher, Dennis Quaid, Daniel Stern, Jackie Earle Haley, Paul Dooley, Barbara Barrie, Robyn Douglass, Amy Wright.

On-Screen: *A young man's tribulations—and ultimate triumph.* A genial and perceptive comedy, *Breaking Away* stars Dennis Christopher as Dave, one of the working-class fellows known as "cutters" in Bloomington, Indiana. (Their fathers were once stonecutters.) Enamored of all things Italian (he calls his cat "Fellini"), nineteen-year-old Dave is a trial to his bewildered parents (Dooley and Barrie). He and his "cutter" friends (Quaid, Stern, Haley) dream of winning the annual bicycle race over the snobbish college kids. And win they do after a few setbacks and humiliations. It's all predictable, but Steve Tesich's screenplay has a feeling for the dreams and frustrations of the working-class boys. He also manages to make an amusing character out of Dave's insensitive father, played convincingly by Paul Dooley. A key scene with his son as they walk around the campus he helped to build provides a revealing glimpse into the man behind the boorish behavior of this used-car salesman. A nice surprise, and a sleeper in its year.

Off-Screen: Steve Tesich's script won an Oscar, and nominations went to the movie and Peter Yates. The film was shot entirely in Bloomington. Dennis Quaid, who plays Dave's friend Mike, went on to star in such films as *The Right Stuff, Suspect,* and *The Big Easy.* Daniel Stern, appearing as Dave's friend Cyril, later played leads in *Diner* and *City Slickers,* and was the voice of the narrator on the television series "The Wonder Years." A television series based on *Breaking Away* turned up in 1980.

The Bride of Frankenstein

Universal, 1935. (75m.) Dir: James Whale. Sp: John L. Balderston and William Hurlbut. Cast: Boris Karloff, Colin Clive, Valerie Hobson, Elsa Lanchester, Ernest Thesiger, Dwight Frye, O. P. Heggie, Una O'Connor.

On-Screen: *A marriage is attempted in the laboratory*. It seems the monster (Karloff) didn't burn to a crisp at the end of *Frankenstein* after all. In a stagy prologue, poets Shelley and Byron persuade novelist Mary Shelley (Lanchester) to continue her gruesome story. More sophisticated than its predecessor, the movie strikes a giddy balance between stark horror (the monster still has it in for the villagers, and who can blame it?) and campy comedy. The latter element is introduced when a mincingly dainty, thoroughly dotty old scientist, Dr. Praetorius (Thesiger), suggests to Dr. Frankenstein (Clive) that the monster should have a mate. Suspenseful complications ensue involving Frankenstein's new bride (Hobson). When the mate (Lanchester again) is finally "born" amid a pyrotechnic display of crackling lab equipment, each monster's response to the other (Lanchester is no prize herself) results in a classic sequence that combines hilarity with horror. Still, a genuinely touching scene occurs when a blind old hermit (Heggie), unaware of the monster's grotesque appearance, teaches it to utter a few words and to enjoy the pleasure of tobacco.

Off-Screen: Lanchester modeled the jerky, robotic movements of the monster's intended bride on those of German actress Brigitte Helm in Fritz Lang's silent classic, *Metropolis*. Both Helm and Louise Brooks were considered for the part, and Claude Rains for the role of the zany Praetorius. For this sequel, British actress Hobson replaced Mae Clarke as Dr. Frankenstein's new bride. Franz Waxman's score was his first Hollywood effort; the resemblance of Lanchester's monster theme to a song from a forties Broadway musical by a preeminent collaborating team is, one may be certain, purely coincidental. (CFB)

The Bridge on the River Kwai

Columbia, 1957. (C-161m.) Dir: David Lean. Sp: Carl Foreman and Michael Wilson, credited to Pierre Boule, b/o novel by Pierre Boule. Cast: William Holden, Alec Guinness, Sessue Hayakawa, Jack Hawkins, Geoffrey Horne, James Donald.

On-Screen: *David Lean's complex, towering war drama*. By far the most prestigious war film of the fifties, *The Bridge on the River Kwai* poses thought-provoking questions about the nature of war and the men who fight it, while, at the same time, offering its share of large-scale action scenes. Set in a Japanese prison camp in the Burmese jungle during 1943, the film focuses on the fierce battle of wills between British Colonel Nicholson (Guinness), brave, imperious, and dangerously obtuse, and Colonel Saito (Hayakawa), the camp's harsh, intelligent commander. At issue is the bridge that Nicholson and his men are commanded to build. Before the explosive climax, the two men expose the layers of the military mind in scenes of cumulative power. As a resilient American prisoner named Shears, William Holden is the nominal star, but acting honors go to Guinness, who etches an unforgettable portrait of misguided pride and military rectitude. A former silent-screen star, Oscar-nominated Sessue Hayakawa is superb as the secretly tormented colonel.

Off-Screen: Producer Sam Spiegel's first choice for Colonel Nicholson was Humphrey Bogart. Laurence Olivier was asked to play the role but declined. Howard Hawks, John Ford, and other Hollywood directors were considered before David Lean was signed. Blacklisted authors Carl Foreman and Michael Wilson had written the screenplay with Pierre Boule, but only Boule (who could speak no English) was credited. The jungle sequences were filmed deep inside the Ceylon interior at Kitulgala. The weather was oppressive and the housing dreadful. The film received seven Academy Awards, including Best Picture, Best Direction, and Best Actor (Guinness).

Brighton Beach Memoirs

Rastar, 1986. (C-110m.) Dir: Gene Saks. Sp: Neil Simon, b/o his play. Cast: Blythe Danner, Jonathan Silverman, Bob Dishy, Judith Ivey, Brian Drillinger, Lisa Waltz, Stacey Glick.

On-Screen: *Neil Simon's nostalgic comedy of a boy's coming of age in thirties Brooklyn.* There is too little space here to discuss why Neil Simon's hugely successful stage comedies so often seem flat on the screen. *Brighton Beach Memoirs,* alas, is no exception. Its story of young Eugene Jerome (Silverman) and his family in Brighton Beach in 1937 was amusing on the stage, and here it draws a number of laughs and some heartwarming chuckles. But it never seems real, and Eugene's nonstop wisecracks as he copes with raging puberty become wearisome after a while. Another problem is the central character of Eugene's mother Kate (Danner). She is intended to be a tenacious but loving woman forced to deal with traumatic family events, but comes across as a bigoted, mean-spirited drudge. (Danner, a fine actress, is also miscast.) Kate has a strong scene with her timid sister Blanche (Ivey), in which the women reveal the resentment they have built up over the years. The film's best performance is given by Bob Dishy as Eugene's worn-down but essentially kindly father.

Off-Screen: After scouting locations in and around New York City, the filmmakers finally returned to Brighton Beach itself, where they were surprised to learn how little the neighborhood had changed. The Jerome house was built at the Kaufman Astoria Studios, using the dimensions of an actual Brighton Beach house. Simon completed his trilogy on Eugene Jerome with *Biloxi Blues* (filmed in 1988) and *Broadway Bound* (on television in 1992).

Bringing Up Baby

RKO, 1938. (102m.) Dir: Howard Hawks. Sp: Dudley Nichols and Hagar Wilde, b/o story by Hagar Wilde. Cast: Cary Grant, Katharine Hepburn, May Robson, Charles Ruggles, Barry Fitzgerald, Walter Catlett, Fritz Feld, Ward Bond.

On-Screen: *Hepburn and Grant scramble about with a leopard named "Baby."* Not a hit when it was first released, *Bringing Up Baby* is now regarded as one of the definitive screwball comedies. Cary Grant is the serious-minded archeologist whose life is turned into a shambles by dizzy heiress Katharine Hepburn and her pet leopard Baby. Surrounding them are some rightfully bewildered characters, including Hepburn's crusty aunt (Robson), a baffled explorer (Ruggles), and an indignant psychiatrist (Feld). There are any number of highlights, but most viewers recall Hepburn and Grant chasing Baby through the woods while singing the leopard's favorite song, "I Can't Give You Anything But Love." As the madcap Susan, Hepburn comes perilously close to being a nuisance to the audience as well as to Grant, but she comes through with an expert comic performance (actually her first in films). Already accomplished at holding on to his dignity under trying circumstances, Grant makes a delightful foil for Hepburn's harebrained antics. *Bringing Up Baby* is classic fun.

Off-Screen: A Grant biographer asserts that his role was first offered to Robert Montgomery, Ronald Colman, and Ray Milland. Hepburn recalled that Grant didn't like cats and was afraid of Baby. "I was the only one who could work with the leopard," she said. "I was too dumb to be afraid." Hepburn constantly astonished Howard Hawks with her gift for improvisation. In one scene, while on camera, she broke the heel of a shoe, and as she limped, she improvised the line, "I was born on the side of a hill." Hawks also praised her "amazing sense of timing": "I've never seen a girl that had that odd rhythm and control."

Broadcast News

Fox, 1987. (C-131m.) Dir: James L. Brooks. Sp: James L. Brooks. Cast: William Hurt, Holly Hunter, Albert Brooks, Robert Prosky, Lois Chiles, Joan Cusack, Peter Hackes, Jack Nicholson (unbilled).

On-Screen: *Romance and ratings at a television news station*. In many romantic comedies of the eighties, career considerations were of-

ten as crucial as sex (and, in some cases, even more important). James L. Brooks's crackling, intelligent comedy focuses on three people who interact in more ways than one at the news organization of a Washington, D.C., television station: take-charge producer Holly Hunter; handsome but superficial anchorman William Hurt; and erudite but uncharismatic news writer Albert Brooks, who gets most of the screenplay's best lines. All three Oscar-nominated players give fine performances as they try to contend with each other's disparate personalities, while, at the same time, they take part in the station's fierce, high-pressure battle for ratings. Joan Cusack is hilarious as a manic worker at the station, and Jack Nicholson makes a brief, unbilled appearance as the station's star anchorman. You'll be amused by the opening prologue, which depicts the early lives of the three principals.

Off-Screen: The film also received Oscar nominations for Best Picture, Best Original Screenplay (James L. Brooks), Best Cinematography (Michael Ballhaus), and Best Film Editing (Richard Marks).

Broadway Danny Rose

Orion, 1984. (86m.) Dir: Woody Allen. Sp: Woody Allen. Cast: Woody Allen, Mia Farrow, Nick Apollo Forte, Sandy Baron, Corbett Monica, Morty Gunty, Will Jordan, Milton Berle, Edwin Bordo.

On-Screen: *Woody Allen's small-time agent in big trouble*. Poor Danny Rose (Allen). A two-bit theatrical agent whose clients include a blind xylophonist and a stammering ventriloquist, Danny finds himself in hot water involving his one promising client, an Italian singer named Lou Canova (Forte). Lou's mistress Tina (Farrow) has ties to a jealous mobster (Bordo), and when Danny is mistakenly identified as her boyfriend, there's plenty of trouble. *Broadway Danny Rose* has little substance, but it's genial, funny, and even a bit poignant. Danny is another of Allen's jittery but resilient losers who must accept his wretched fate. ("It's important to have some laughs, but you have to suffer a little, too.") Mia Farrow is hilarious—and barely recognizable—as the brassy blonde who triggers all the complications, and Nick Apollo Forte, an actual lounge singer, wins laughs with his rendition of "Agita." Minor but enjoyable Allen.

Off-Screen: The movie won two Oscar nominations for Allen: as director and as author of the screenplay. The actors relating Danny's story were all working comedians who must have known many Danny Roses. Other real-life figures making brief appearances in the film are Joe Franklin, Howard Cosell, and Allen's manager, Jack Rollins.

The Broadway Melody

MGM, 1929. (104m.) Dir: Harry Beaumont. Sp: Sarah Y. Mason, Norman Houston, and James Gleason, b/o story by Edmund Goulding. MS: Nacio Herb Brown and Arthur Freed. Cast: Charles King, Bessie Love, Anita Page, Jed Prouty, Edward Dillon.

On-Screen: *The granddaddy of all film musicals*. A pioneer film musical, and the first sound film to win a Best Picture Oscar, *The Broadway Melody* is more historic than entertaining, but for all its primitive style, it has some diverting moments and even a few virtues.

The plot creaks—two sisters, seeking fame in show business, fall for the same man. Yet Bessie Love gives a surprisingly credible performance as the more sensible sister, and the musical numbers, now pure camp, were widely admired in their time. There's an elaborate color sequence (now apparently lost) built around "The Wedding of the Painted Doll," and a hit song, "You Were Meant for Me," rendered by Charles King to Anita Page in a hotel room. Occasional boredom can be overcome by counting the number of times King sings the title tune.

Off-Screen: Since the sound techniques were new, problems constantly turned up on the set of *The Broadway Melody*. It was discovered that the swish of beads embroidered on silver costumes reverberated loudly through the recording machine. (The costumes became more pliable when the beads were strung on rubber bands.) Also, dresses with metallic fringes had to be discarded since their rustle recorded noisily. At one point a persistent echo was removed by hanging heavy curtains on the set. The movie survived all problems to win acclaim from critics and audiences. The story was remade in 1940 as *Two Girls on Broadway*.

Broken Arrow

Fox, 1950. (C-93m.) Dir: Delmer Daves. Sp: Albert Maltz, originally credited to Michael Blankfort, b/o novel by Elliott Arnold. Cast: James Stewart, Jeff Chandler, Debra Paget, Will Geer, Arthur Hunnicut, Jay Silverheels, Basil Ruysdael.

On-Screen: *Sympathetic treatment of Native Americans in the world of treacherous white men*. A major breakthrough in the screen's perception of Indians, *Broken Arrow* portrays the Apaches as proud people who retaliated only after their land was pillaged. The film centers on the romance between Civil War veteran James Stewart and Apache maiden Debra Paget, awkwardly played out against a backdrop of treaty negotiations between the U.S. and the Apaches. Led by an overly articulate Cochise (Chandler), the Apaches are too noble. The age discrepancy between Stewart and Paget makes casting her as his ill-fated young wife somewhat incongruous. Perhaps sensing this, Stewart uses his celebrated awkwardness to cover flaws better dealt with by more felicitous writing. The film's plea for justice and equality does come across, however, and the movie rightly sparked Chandler's career as a leading man, albeit in B movies.

Off-Screen: In 1991, after more than four decades, it was finally acknowledged that blacklisted author Albert Maltz was actually the author of the screenplay. Michael Blankfort had served only as his front. As progressive as the film's approach was at the time, Canadian Jay Silverheels was the only true Indian in the cast. (JMK)

Brute Force

Universal, 1947. (98m.) Dir: Jules Dassin. Sp: Richard Brooks, b/o story by Robert Patterson. Cast: Burt Lancaster, Hume Cronyn, Charles Bickford, Yvonne De Carlo, Ann Blyth, Ella Raines, Anita Colby, Sam Levene, Howard Duff, John Hoyt, Jeff Corey, Whit Bissell.

On-Screen: *Convicts rebel in a prison from hell.* Talk about the screen's most sadistic prison warden—Hume Cronyn's Wagner-loving Captain Munsey wins that dubious distinction hands down in this blistering melodrama. Written by Richard Brooks several years before he turned to directing as well, *Brute Force* centers on five prison inmates who organize a break that leads to a pitched battle. Their leader is Joe Collins (Lancaster), a crook obsessed with getting to his ill young wife (Blyth). The movie has some brutal sequences, especially one in which an informer is forced to his death in a huge printing press by vindictive convicts. The jailbreak, ending with Captain Munsey hurled to his death from a high guide-tower, is staged vividly. The women, including Yvonne De Carlo and Ella Raines, are only peripheral memories in this savage film.

Off-Screen: Director Dassin later recalled: "The character of the warden . . . was based on a real warden that I knew. . . . He was a man of enormous charm and considerable cruelty; a very cultivated, educated man. I tried to re-create him on the screen, but it was cut to hell." Many years afterward, Hume Cronyn remembered his climactic fight with Lancaster, which he called "one of the most murderously filthy fights ever photographed. . . . It was considered altogether too violent for the public and portions of it were eliminated. Today, it would probably seem commonplace."

Buck Privates

Universal, 1941. (84m.) Dir: Arthur Lubin. Sp: Arthur T. Horman. Cast: Bud Abbott, Lou Costello, the Andrews Sisters, Lee Bowman, Alan Curtis, Jane Frazee, Nat Pendleton, Samuel S. Hinds.

On-Screen: *The first starring film for Abbott and Costello.* After years in vaudeville and burlesque, and a stint on radio's "Kate Smith

Hour," the comedy team of Bud Abbott and Lou Costello moved to Hollywood and fame. Costello's rotund, childlike clown and Abbott's fast-talking straight man created a sensation in this, their first starring film. The movie is little more than a collection of the material they had fashioned in vaudeville, especially their "Who's on First?" baseball routine, all sprinkled with some songs by the Andrews Sisters. But audiences, especially younger viewers, loved them and roared with laughter when Costello, forced into difficult situations by Abbott or their tough sergeant (Pendleton), fumbled his way through a drill routine or found himself in a prizefight with Pendleton as referee.

Off-Screen: Surprisingly, *Buck Privates* was one of the year's top grossers and even won some admiring reviews. (The *New York Times* called it "an hour and a half of uproarious monkeyshines.") The movie catapulted the team into the front rank in the national popularity polls, right behind Mickey Rooney and Clark Gable. "I'll Be with You in Apple Blossom Time," sung by the Andrews Sisters, was one of the singing trio's most durable hits. A sequel, *Buck Privates Come Home,* turned up in 1947.

The Buddy Holly Story

Columbia, 1978. (C-113m.) Dir: Steve Rash. Sp: Robert Gittler, b/o story by Alan Swyer and source material by John Coldrosen. Cast: Gary Busey, Charles Martin Smith, Don Stroud, Maria Richwine, Amy Johnston, Conrad Janis, Dick O'Neill.

On-Screen: *The short life of an influential rock-'n'-roll singer.* In the fifties, singer Buddy Holly enjoyed great popularity as a singer whose new style combined elements of country music with rhythm and blues. In 1959, Holly was killed with others (including Richie Valens) in a plane crash. *The Buddy Holly Story* tells how Holly (Busey) came out of Lubbock, Texas, with his small band (Smith, Stroud) and offered a new "sound" that either baffled or enthused listeners. The events of his short life, at least as related here, fit the conventional mold for movie biographies of modern-day musicians: heavy resistance to his "sound," sudden fame and fortune, romance with a Puerto Rican girl (Richwine), dissension in the band, and, in this case, premature death. There is one notable variance from the cut-and-dried material: Gary Busey's galvanizing performance as Buddy Holly. He not only plays the role with conviction but also sings, in his own voice, many of Holly's songs ("That'll Be the Day," "Peggy Sue," "It's So Easy," and others) with driving force.

Off-Screen: Gary Busey won an Oscar nomination for his performance, and the movie received an Academy Award for score adaptation. The voice of Ed Sullivan, heard during Holly's appearance on "The Ed Sullivan Show," belongs to impressionist Will Jordan. *Buddy,* a stage musical based on Holly's life, had a modest run on Broadway in 1990. For a movie view of singer Richie Valens, see *La Bamba* (1987).

Buffalo Bill and the Indians or Sitting Bull's History Lesson

United Artists, 1976. (C-120m.) Dir: Robert Altman. Sp: Robert Altman and Alan Rudolph, b/o play by Arthur Kopit. Cast: Paul Newman, Joel Grey, Kevin McCarthy, Burt Lancaster, Harvey Keitel, Geraldine Chaplin, Frank Kaquitts, Will Sampson.

On-Screen: *"Buffalo Bill" Cody—but not the legend.* History tells us that William Frederick ("Buffalo Bill") Cody was an army scout and buffalo hunter. That is, until a dime-novel writer named Ned Buntline turned him into a mythical Western Hero. Robert Altman's Western, one of the many "revisionist" Westerns of the seventies, does no such thing. In this movie, loosely based on Arthur Kopit's play *Indians,* Buffalo Bill (Newman) is an aging, flamboyant showman who is partly a fraud and partly a victim of his own legend, forced to indulge in Wild West fakery to hold his audience. Despite Altman's lavish, affectionate recreation of a Wild West show, the film is a harsh and jaundiced view of "Buffalo Bill" and his cohorts, including Annie Oakley (Chaplin). The only true note comes from a brooding Sitting Bull (Frank Kaquitts), who is determined not to debase history through the fraudulent melodrama of the Wild West shows. Burt Lancaster appears as writer Ned Buntline.

Off-Screen: The movie's screenplay shifted the emphasis of the stage play away from the plight of the Indians and toward the enigma of "Buffalo Bill." Paul Newman's comment at the time about his role: "A combination of Custer, Gable, Redford, and me. . . . Symbolically the first star . . . someone who cannot live up to his legend."

Bugsy

TriStar, 1991. (C-135m.) Dir: Barry Levinson. Sp: James Toback. Cast: Warren Beatty, Annette Bening, Harvey Keitel, Ben Kingsley, Elliott Gould, Joe Mantegna, Bebe Neuwirth.

On-Screen: *The rise and fall of mobster "Bugsy" Siegel.* Warren Beatty gives his best performance since *Bonnie and Clyde,* and delineates his most fascinating and complex character, in Barry Levinson's film about the true-life big-time gangster, Benjamin ("Bugsy") Siegel. Set largely in California in the forties, artfully reconstructed in a stylized production, the movie traces Siegel's ignominious career as a criminal in league with Meyer Lansky (Kingsley), Mickey Cohen (Keitel), and other notorious figures; his tempestuous romance with Virginia Hill (Bening); and his vision of turning the Las Vegas desert into a golden mecca for tourists and gamblers. In Toback's expertly handled screenplay, Bugsy emerges as a devoted father, a cold-blooded killer given to blind rages, an egoist who fancies himself as a movie actor, and a dreamer who sees his Flamingo Hotel as "a palace, an oasis, a city." One dazzling sequence reveals all facets at once: In his home, while trying to celebrate his daughter's birthday, he meets with his gangster cronies about his Las Vegas business, all the time frantically telephoning to learn Virginia Hill's whereabouts. In the end, he expires in a hail of bullets while watching his own screen test. If *Bugsy* is ultimately less than the sum of its parts, it is still a gripping portrait of the many faces of evil.

Off-Screen: The film, Levinson, Beatty, Keitel, and Toback were all nominated for Oscars, along with five others. Two were awarded, for art direction-set direction and for costume design. Other Bugsy Siegels include Richard Grieco in *Mobsters* (1991), Armand

Assante in *The Marrying Man* (1991), Joe Penny in the TV miniseries "The Gangster Chronicles," Harvey Keitel in *The Virginia Hill Story* (1974), and Alex Rocco as a thinly disguised Bugsy named Moe Green in *The Godfather* (1972).

Bull Durham

Orion, 1988. (C-108m.) Dir: Ron Shelton. Sp: Ron Shelton. Cast: Kevin Costner, Susan Sarandon, Tim Robbins, Trey Wilson, Robert Wuhl, Jenny Robertson, Max Patkin, William O'Leary, David Neidorf.

On-Screen: *The games of baseball and sex, as played by a minor-league team.* Movies about baseball often strike out at the box office, but here's a happy, ribald exception. Kevin Costner stars as Crash Davis, a veteran player hired by the Carolina League's Durham Bulls, ostensibly as a catcher, but actually to look after Ebby ("Nuke") La-Loosh (Robbins), a promising but wildly undisciplined young pitcher. Susan Sarandon is Annie Savoy, a baseball devotee whose mission is to choose one player each year and teach him to "mature" in her own womanly way. When she chooses "Nuke," a conflict erupts inevitably between Crash and Annie. And just as inevitably, Crash and Annie come to appreciate each other. The character of Annie may trouble feminists—she's intelligent and attractive, yet defines her purpose in life by the baseball players she beds every year. Still, *Bull Durham* is rowdy, pungent, and original.

Off-Screen: Ron Shelton's first screenplay was an earlier version of *Bull Durham,* which he called *A Player to Be Named Later.* After writing *Under Fire* and *The Best of Times,* he dusted off the script, reconceived it, and added some dimension to the character of Annie. He still found it hard to sell, despite a commitment from Kevin Costner. It finally went to Orion and became a big success. Shelton had spent five years as a second baseman in the Baltimore Orioles' farm system.

Bullitt

Warners, 1968. (C-113m.) Dir: Peter Yates. Sp: Alan R. Trustman and Barry Kleiner, b/o novel by Robert Pike. Cast: Steve McQueen, Robert Vaughn, Jacqueline Bisset, Don Gordon, Robert Duvall, Simon Oakland, Norman Fell.

On-Screen: *A San Francisco cop—and a classic chase.* Fast-moving, scenic, and exciting, *Bullitt* stars Steve McQueen as Frank Bullitt, a renegade San Francisco detective who is assigned to guard a key witness against the top crime organization. When the witness is critically wounded, Bullitt starts his own investigation, leading him into deep trouble. The plot twists are not always credible, but the film's pace is furious, with the busy photography and tricky editing characteristic of the late sixties. Particularly suspenseful scenes are set at a hospital, where a second attempt is made against the witness, and at San Francisco's airport, where Bullitt and the police pursue a villain. Most memorable is the car chase, complete with hairpin turns and screeching tires, over the hills of the city. McQueen again demonstrates his skill at playing tough but sympathetic heroes, and Robert Vaughn is properly obnoxious as a self-aggrandizing politician.

Off-Screen: To prepare for his role as Frank Bullitt, Steve McQueen spent weeks driving around in a squad car with actual police detectives. The car-chase scene ran for eleven minutes and required weeks of preparation, with the cars specially rigged for the punishment they would take. McQueen insisted on doing his own stunt driving. Frank Keller won an Oscar for his editing.

Bus Stop

Fox, 1956. (C-96m.) Dir: Joshua Logan. Sp: George Axelrod, b/o play by William Inge. Cast: Marilyn Monroe, Don Murray, Arthur O'Connell, Betty Field, Eileen Heckart, Hope Lange, Robert Bray, Hans Conried, Casey Adams.

On-Screen: *Monroe in peak form, in adaptation of Broadway hit.* After appearing in two dozen films, the voluptuous "dumb blonde" at last does more than slink across the screen, wide-eyed and compliant. Logan's directorial alchemy gets a real performance from his star. Cherie (Monroe), a "chantoose" with her roots in the Ozarks and her eyes on Hollywood, meets along the way lusty, blustering Bo (Murray), a young Montana rancher. After he gets a sobering comeuppance at the hands of a burly bus driver (Bray), and a waitress pal (Heckart) helps Cherie wise up to the world and its ways, the pair learn the meaning of shared respect and love. Murray was nominated for the Best Supporting Actor Oscar in his movie debut, and the other cast members couldn't be better. Monroe's Cherie, caught between conflicting goals—possible fame and probable security—is both a funny and a deeply moving portrait.

Off-Screen: Although her request that Rock Hudson play Bo didn't work out, Monroe insisted that her costumes be consistent with Cherie's unsophisticated nature, that her makeup match Bo's description of her as his "angel, so pale and white," and that Lange's hair be darkened to contrast with her own. Because of Monroe's poor memory, Logan had to retake her lines over and over and skillfully patch together the best readings. Whatever the director's off-screen means, they produced an on-screen performance. A television series loosely based on the play and movie had a run in the 1961–62 season. (CFB)

Butch Cassidy and the Sundance Kid

Fox, 1969. (C-112m.) Dir: George Roy Hill. Sp: William Goldman. Cast: Paul Newman, Robert Redford, Katharine Ross, Strother Martin, Henry Jones, Jeff Corey, George Furth, Cloris Leachman, Ted Cassidy, Kenneth Mars.

On-Screen: *Newman and Redford, thinly disguised as Butch and Sundance.* In the annals of the West, Robert LeRoy Parker was a cowhand who drifted into outlawry and called himself Butch Cassidy. Harry Longabaugh was a fellow outlaw who gave himself the name of the Sundance Kid. Now forget history and enjoy the legend: an enormously popular, entertaining mixture of impudent comedy, antiestablishment sentiment, and conventional Western action. *Butch Cassidy and the Sundance Kid* stars Paul Newman and Robert Redford as the mischievous outlaws who hurtle from adventure to adventure, accompanied part of the way by teacher Etta Place (Katharine Ross). Many of the movie's diverting sequences are send-ups of

Western conventions—the bank robbery, for example, becomes a slapstick caper in which the robbers are almost as bewildered as the victims. Some critics abhorred the movie's facetious attitude, but moviegoers found it all hugely enjoyable.

Off-Screen: Darryl Zanuck wanted Steve McQueen to play Cassidy opposite Marlon Brando or Warren Beatty, but director Hill and others held out for Newman and Redford. Oscars went to the movie's screenplay, cinematography (Conrad Hall), music score (Burt Bacharach), and hit song, "Raindrops Keep Fallin' on My Head," written by Bacharach and Hal David. A decade later, Richard Lester directed *Butch and Sundance: The Early Days* (1979), a "prequel" that concerned events before the 1969 movie. This time audiences were much less responsive.

Butterfield 8

MGM, 1960. (C-109m.) Dir: Daniel Mann. Sp: Charles Schnee and John Michael Hayes, b/o novel by John O'Hara. Cast: Elizabeth Taylor, Laurence Harvey, Eddie Fisher, Dina Merrill, Mildred Dunnock, Susan Oliver, Betty Field, Kay Medford, Jeffrey Lynn.

On-Screen: *Elizabeth Taylor's first Oscar.* As Gloria Wandrous, John O'Hara's "bad" girl striving for respectability, Elizabeth Taylor pulls out all emotional stops to give a performance that won her a Best Actress Academy Award. From her long, almost wordless opening scene, she works hard and well, but shorn of the novel's bite, *Butterfield 8* is overblown romantic nonsense, brimming with self-consciously "wicked" dia-

logue. As her wealthy, married lover, Laurence Harvey is required to play a character so surly and disagreeable that it is difficult to fathom Gloria's passion for him. Eddie Fisher is merely adequate as her disapproving but loyal friend, and Mildred Dunnock is good as her worried mother. Taylor has two strong confessional scenes, one with her mother—"Mama, I was the slut of all time!"—the other with Fisher, in which she reveals the sordid secret of her childhood. It all glistens in bright color, but *Butterfield 8* is junk jewelry.

Off-Screen: At first Taylor turned down the role, calling Gloria "a sick nymphomaniac" and declaring the story "unpalatable," but she finally consented. During the filming, she was very ill and was treated by at least six different doctors. She disliked making the movie, telling her costar Laurence Harvey, "This is going to be a rough one, but don't take it personally." Producer Pandro Berman wanted David Janssen to play her platonic, piano-playing friend, but Taylor insisted on Eddie Fisher for the role.

Bye Bye Birdie

Columbia, 1963. (C-112m.) Dir: George Sidney. Sp: Irving Brecher, b/o musical play by Michael Stewart. MS: Charles Strouse and Lee Adams. Cast: Janet Leigh, Dick Van Dyke, Ann-Margret, Maureen Stapleton, Paul Lynde, Jesse Pearson, Bobby Rydell.

On-Screen: *A wildly popular crooner invades an Ohio town.* Adapted from the long-running stage musical, *Bye Bye Birdie* should keep you awake and reasonably entertained. Brash and energetic, if not much else, it concerns one Conrad Birdie, an Elvis Presley–like singer (Pearson) who overwhelms a small Ohio town before his induction into the army. Dick Van Dyke repeats his stage role as the put-upon composer who wants to get Birdie and his own song on "The Ed Sullivan Show," and Janet Leigh is decorative as his long-suffering secretary and girlfriend. As Birdie's most worshipful fan, Ann-Margret seems more like a bump-and-grind stripper than a demure Ohio teenager, but she sings and dances vivaciously. Paul Lynde is amusing as her harried father. The score ("Put On a Happy Face," "Kids," etc.) is pleasant but unexceptional. Much of the material now dates badly, but *Bye Bye Birdie* has enough merit to warrant a look.

Off-Screen: Paul Lynde, like Dick Van Dyke, was repeating his stage role. A sequel, called *Bring Back Birdie,* had a brief Broadway run in March 1981, with Donald O'Connor in the Van Dyke role and Chita Rivera returning to her stage role of Rosie.

Cabaret

Allied Artists, 1972. (C-128m.) Dir: Bob Fosse. Sp: Jay Allen, b/o musical play by Joe Masteroff, adapted from a play by John Van Druten and story by Christopher Isherwood. MS: John Kander and Fred Ebb. Cast: Liza Minnelli, Michael York, Joel Grey, Helmut Griem, Marisa Berenson, Fritz Wepper.

On-Screen: *Life is a cabaret, old chum.* The most unusual—and arguably the greatest—musical of the seventies, *Cabaret* (originally *I Am a Camera*) went through a number of permutations (story to stage play to movie to musical play) before reaching the screen a second time. The place is prewar Berlin, where writer Brian Roberts (York) arrives to confront a hedonistic, increasingly dangerous society. Front and center he finds Sally Bowles (Minnelli), the deliberately shocking, cheerfully promiscuous waif who sings in a cabaret. Overseen by the androgynous master of ceremonies (Grey), the cabaret reflects the amoral lives of the film's characters and the rotting world outside its walls. In music and performance, *Cabaret* is a stunning achievement. Most of the songs ("Willkommen," "The Money Song," "If You Could See Her (With My Eyes)," etc.) are not the usual set pieces but a commentary on—and a reflection of—the sinister events enveloping Germany. As Sally, Minnelli gives an electrifying performance that makes good use of her quicksilver style and nervous mannerisms, and Joel Grey, repeating his stage role, is brilliant, his chalk-white makeup and crimson lips barely concealing the mockery and malice.

Off-Screen: Jay Allen's screenplay was rewritten by an uncredited Hugh Wheeler. In the hiring period before filming began, there was considerable ill will and vituperation between Bob Fosse and the film's producer, Cy Feuer. From dissension, however, came a triumph: The film swept the Oscars in its year, winning awards for Best Actress (Minnelli) and Best Supporting Actor (Grey), as well as for direction, cinematography, sound, editing, art direction, and scoring.

Cabin in the Sky

MGM, 1943. (100m.) Dir: Vincente Minnelli. Sp: Joseph Schrank, b/o musical play by Lynn Root. MS: Vernon Duke and John Latouche. Additional songs by Harold Arlen and E. Y. Harburg. Cast: Ethel Waters, Eddie "Rochester" Anderson, Lena Horne, John W. ("Bubbles") Sublett, Kenneth Spencer, Rex Ingram, Butterfly McQueen, Louis Armstrong, Duke Ellington and His Orchestra.

On-Screen: *Ethel Waters glows in Vincente Minnelli's first musical.* For many years Ethel Waters enchanted audiences with her full-bodied singing and earthy, infectious manner. *Cabin in the Sky* records her performance as Petunia Jackson in the stage-musical fantasy and affords the opportunity to hear her sing "Takin' a Chance on Love" and other wonderful songs. The movie has its shortcomings: Its attitude toward blacks as shiftless, irresponsible, and highly sexed is unmistakably racist, and some of the heaven-and-hell fantasy weighs a ton. But then there's Lena Horne's seductive rendition of "Honey in the Honeycomb," John W. ("Bubbles") Sublett's insinuating "Shine," and, throughout, Ethel Waters's soulful voice and expressive face. *Cabin in the Sky* also contains elements of future Minnelli musicals, including a penchant for fantasy, touches of stylization, and, above all, a creative imagination.

Off-Screen: When the original composers weren't available, MGM turned to Harold Arlen and "Yip" Harburg, who wrote "Happiness Is Just a Thing Called Joe" and "Life's Full of Consequence." Vincente Minnelli wanted Dooley Wilson to repeat his stage role as Little Joe, but the studio felt that Eddie ("Rochester") Anderson was a bigger name. The tornado that wrecks the nightclub in the film was the same as the one used in *The Wizard of Oz*. It was rear-projected so that it could be seen through the nightclub window.

The Caine Mutiny

Columbia, 1954. (C-125m.) Dir: Edward Dmytryk. Sp: Stanley Roberts, b/o novel by Herman Wouk. Cast: Humphrey Bogart, Jose Ferrer, Fred MacMurray, Van Johnson, Robert Francis, May Wynn, E. G. Marshall, Lee Marvin, Tom Tully.

On-Screen: *Herman Wouk's novel of rebellion at sea.* What actually happened aboard the minesweeper *Caine,* at the height of World War II? It seems that the ship's executive officer, Steve Maryk (Johnson), seized command of the *Caine* when its captain (Bogart) appeared to lose control during a typhoon. Under the prodding of Lieutenant Keefer (MacMurray), Maryk had come to believe that Captain Queeg was dangerously unbalanced. At Maryk's court-martial, Queeg is goaded into incoherence by Maryk's cynical defense lawyer, Barney Greenwald (Ferrer). Herman Wouk's Pulitzer Prize–winning book becomes an absorbing, if uneven and not very profound, reflection on the stresses of military command in wartime. At the center of the conflict is Captain Queeg, expertly played by Humphrey Bogart in an Oscar-nominated performance. The crux of the film, of course, is the court-martial sequence, at which Queeg crumbles under questioning. There is an ironic but debatable coda in which Greenwald, arriving drunk at a celebration party, denounces the intellectual but devious Keefer as the true "villain" in the case and praises the Queegs of the Navy.

Off-Screen: According to director Dmytryk, Herman Wouk wrote an unsatisfactory adaptation of his novel, so Stanley Roberts was assigned to replace him. When Columbia insisted on adding a romantic interest, Roberts quit and was replaced by uncredited Michael Blankfort. The film won seven Oscar nominations in all, including one for Best Picture. *The Caine Mutiny Court Martial,* a stage dramatization of the court-martial, opened on Broadway seven months before the movie. It starred Lloyd Nolan as Queeg. Robert Altman directed a television version in 1988, with Brad Davis playing Queeg.

Camelot

Warners, 1967. (C-178m.) Dir: Joshua Logan. Sp: Alan Jay Lerner, b/o his musical play. MS: Alan Jay Lerner and Frederick Loewe. Cast: Richard Harris, Vanessa Redgrave, Franco Nero, David Hemmings, Lionel Jeffries.

On-Screen: *Film version of musical about King Arthur and his court.* Opening on Broadway to high expectations in 1960, the new Alan Jay Lerner–Frederick Loewe musical, *Camelot,* proved disappointing, in spite of the star presences of Richard Burton and Julie Andrews. Transferred to the screen seven years later, it again failed to make its mark. The production is sumptuous, the score richly melodic, and there are some moving moments in the tale of King Arthur (Harris) and his Queen Guinevere (Redgrave), but the gargantuan sets, the heavy-handed direction, and the oppressively nonstop close-ups conspire to smother the theme of a chivalrous and gallant world brought to ruin by an illicit love affair. Vanessa Redgrave makes a charming Guinevere, but Richard Harris plays Arthur almost entirely in a hoarse whisper and with a disconcerting touch of effeminacy. Hang on for some of the music, especially "How to Handle a Woman" and "If Ever I Would Leave You." The rest is heavy going indeed.

Off-Screen: Jack Warner suggested to Joshua Logan that he get Richard Burton and Julie Andrews to repeat their Broadway roles in the film, but Logan rejected the idea. Vanessa Redgrave wanted to wear the same costume throughout the film until it was pointed out that the story spanned twenty-four years. She also wanted to sing a key song translated into French, but neither Warner nor Alan Jay Lerner would approve. The movie won Oscars for its scoring, its set direction/set decoration, and its costumes.

Camille

MGM, 1936. (109m.) Dir: George Cukor. Sp: Zoe Akins, Frances Marion, and James Hilton, b/o play and novel by Alexandre Dumas, *fils.* Cast: Greta Garbo, Robert Taylor, Lionel Barrymore, Henry Daniell, Laura Hope Crews, Jessie Ralph, Lenore Ulric, Rex O'Malley.

On-Screen: *Garbo glows in her most famous role.* Justly counted among the screen's greatest achievements, Garbo's bravura performance as the ill-fated courtesan is exquisitely nuanced and altogether captivating. Responding to Cukor's sensitive direction, the legendary actress convinces, whether frivolously gay, darkly brooding, or passionately romantic. Taylor perfectly embodies the callow, handsome youth swept away by love for an older woman despite knowledge of her past; Daniell is all ice as the baron who wants merely to add Garbo to his possessions; and Barrymore is properly grumpy as Taylor's protective father. One of the movie's most memorable scenes occurs when Daniell appears unexpectedly as Garbo awaits Taylor for a supper for two. A knowing Daniell thunders on the piano as Garbo simultaneously laughs with pretended casualness and brokenheartedly sobs for a love she has lost forever. Expertly directed and lavishly produced, *Camille* is Hollywood at its most proficient. Garbo's performance is art.

Off-Screen: Director Cukor said about Garbo, "She always knew what she was doing, what the camera was doing, she understood, she worked hard, she was all there on the screen. What else can one say?" To honor the memory of MGM producer Irving Thalberg, who had died prematurely at age thirty-seven, Garbo made one of her rare public appearances at the premiere in California. She was nominated for a Best Actress Oscar, but she lost it to Luise Rainer, the studio's newest import, for her performance in *The Good Earth*. An indisposed John Barrymore was replaced by brother Lionel. (CFB)

Cape Fear

Universal, 1962. (105m.) Dir: J. Lee Thompson. Sp: James R. Webb, b/o novel by John D. MacDonald. Cast: Gregory Peck, Robert Mitchum, Polly Bergen, Lori Martin, Martin Balsam.

On-Screen: *A revenge-minded man stalks a family.* Don't let sleepy-eyed, soft-spoken Max Cady (Mitchum) fool you. A ticking time-bomb, he's just done time as a convicted rapist. Now he's out to destroy Sam Bowden (Peck), a small-town Georgia lawyer whose incriminating testimony sent him away. With cold calculation, Cady also targets Bowden's attractive wife (Bergen) and

young daughter (Martin) for revenge. Cady's terrorizing cat-and-mouse game goes according to plan until the violent climax, when Bowden confronts him. Chances are the ending will surprise you. Peck is strong as a decent man struggling to have a psychopath brought once again to justice. Mitchum's creature of reptilian evil, though, makes it his movie.

Off-Screen: Location filming in Georgia placed Mitchum in a perilous position. As a teenager in the early thirties, he was convicted of vagrancy, and served six days on a Georgia chain gang before escaping and becoming a fugitive. Technically, he could have been made to serve out his sentence. The passage of thirty years, however, as well as his celebrity, combined to wipe the slate clean. To show there were no hard feelings, a local paper playfully displayed his youthful mug shot on the front page. Martin Scorsese directed a 1991 remake. (CFB)

Cape Fear

Universal, 1991. (C-123m.) Dir: Martin Scorsese. Sp: Wesley Strick, b/o novel by John D. MacDonald. Cast: Robert De Niro, Nick Nolte, Jessica Lange, Juliette Lewis, Joe Don Baker, Illeana Douglas, Robert Mitchum, Gregory Peck, Martin Balsam.

On-Screen: *Updated, high-octane remake.* This version of the 1962 thriller gives lawyer Sam Bowden (Nolte) plenty to worry about. His reputation will be wrecked when ex-con Max Cady (De Niro) reveals Sam's unethical conduct at Cady's rape trial. What's more, Sam and his wife (Lange), whose marriage is faltering, have a teenage daughter (Lewis) ripe for sexual awakening, if the wrong man comes along. He does. In the original movie, Cady's lazy charm deceptively masks his sadism. This Cady, all muscles and Bible-quoting tattoos, is still a world-class psychopath, and with the anything-can-be-shown attitude of the nineties, his encounters with Bowden's family and associates become gruesomely explicit. Yet the movie is more exhausting than terrifying; Scorsese's relentless approach, with his endlessly swooping and zooming camera, pushes every scene into the viewer's face. (It's as if the ghost of Hitchcock had turned inexplicably demented and seized control of the director.) The violent climax strains credulity; *Cape Fear* is a thriller that leaves you worn-out and depressed rather than exhilarated.

Off-Screen: At first Scorsese had doubts about directing a remake of the highly regarded original; but as he and screenwriter Strick began elaborating on De Niro's character and fleshing out the Bowden family, it was clear that the story could be given a fresh approach. Reunited from the previous version, Mitchum, Peck, and Balsam appear in cameo roles, and film composer Elmer Bernstein recycled Bernard Herrmann's original score. (CFB)

Captain Blood

Warners, 1935. (99m.) Dir: Michael Curtiz. Sp: Casey Robinson, b/o novel by Rafael Sabatini. Cast: Errol Flynn, Olivia de Havilland, Basil Rathbone, Lionel Atwill, Ross Alexander, Guy Kibbee, Henry Stephenson, Robert Barrat, Donald Meek.

On-Screen: *Errol Flynn's star-making role in a vintage swashbuckler.* After playing tiny roles in several minor Warners movies, Errol Flynn leaped to stardom as the doctor-turned-

pirate in this rousing version of the Rafael Sabatini novel. (A silent version was made in 1923.) A full-rigged adventure film, *Captain Blood* overcomes its grade-school primer dialogue with many sequences of vigorous action, as Peter Blood leads his "Brotherhood of Buccaneers" against villainous James II. The best scenes include the commandeering of a Spanish pirate ship by desperate slaves and the climactic battle in which French ships clash with Blood's pirates. Olivia de Havilland makes a pretty picture of a heroine, one worth defending. Until dissipation wrecked his career, Errol Flynn was the King of Swashbucklers (and the definitive Robin Hood) in the thirties and early forties.

Off-Screen: Many actors were considered for the title role before Errol Flynn was signed. Robert Donat had been signed but had to bow out for a number of reasons, including his health. Brian Aherne was tested, but Leslie Howard refused to consider the role. A September 1935 memorandum from Hal Wallis to Michael Curtiz indicated that he was indignant over Curtiz's dressing Flynn like "a molly-coddle" rather than a pirate, with velvet coat, lace cuffs, and lace collar.

Captains Courageous

MGM, 1937. (116m.) Dir: Victor Fleming. Sp: John Lee Mahin, Marc Connelly, and Dale Van Every, b/o novel by Rudyard Kipling. Cast: Spencer Tracy, Freddie Bartholomew, Melvyn Douglas, Lionel Barrymore, Mickey Rooney, John Carradine, Charley Grapewin.

On-Screen: *Film version of Rudyard Kipling's seafaring story.* Spencer Tracy won his first Academy Award for his performance as

Portuguese fisherman Manuel in this respectable, immensely popular adaptation of Kipling's novel. Although his accent wavers, he's likable and occasionally touching as he teaches Harvey (Bartholomew), the spoiled-rotten rich boy, all about life, honesty, and fishing. Harvey, son of tycoon Douglas, has fallen off an ocean liner and been rescued by Manuel, who adopts him as his "leetle feesh" aboard the schooner *We're Here*. There are some good, burly fishing scenes, and a climactic scene involving Manuel that will doubtlessly move you to tears. In all, the movie is an unexceptional but fairly sturdy boys' adventure. Bartholomew is a capable young actor, although his piping British voice can induce a case of teeth-gnashing. Cap'n Barrymore and young Rooney (as his son Dan) offer competent support.

Off-Screen: Tracy was extremely reluctant to play Manuel, feeling that he could never manage the Portuguese accent. Encouraged by his wife and director Fleming, he took the part. He allowed his hair to be curled and learned several sea chanteys written especially for him. Later he said, "I used to pray that something would happen to halt production. I was positive I was doing the worst job of my life." When Tracy was given the Oscar statuette, it was found to be inscribed To DICK TRACY rather than Spencer. A stage musical adaptation of the story turned up at Ford's Theater in Washington in the fall of 1992.

Carefree

RKO, 1938. (80m.) Dir: Mark Sandrich. Sp: Allan Scott and Ernest Pagano, b/o story by Dudley Nichols and Hagar Wilde.

MS: Irving Berlin. Cast: Ginger Rogers, Fred Astaire, Ralph Bellamy, Luella Gear, Jack Carson, Clarence Kolb.

On-Screen: *Rogers and Astaire team up again with Irving Berlin*. The glorious dance team's next-to-last film before *The Barkleys of Broadway* in 1949, *Carefree* is not one of their best, but it will do. For once, Astaire didn't play a debonair dancer but an unlikely psychiatrist whose rather light-headed patient is Ginger Rogers. Without music, this would be a fairly intolerable screwball comedy but fortunately, the two fall in and out of love to the strains of some grand Irving Berlin tunes. The best song, "Change Partners," has one of Berlin's loveliest, most haunting melodies, but so does the lesser-known "I Used to Be Color Blind," performed by the team in a dreamlike setting (literally, since this is Rogers's dream). In keeping with the fashion of the times, they also whirl about to a new "dance craze" called "The Yam." Note the presence of Broadway actress Luella Gear, who plays the Helen Broderick role of Rogers's confidante with wry good humor but less acerbity.

Off-Screen: Several songs rendered by Fred Astaire were deleted from the release print. One was a ballad, "The Night Is Filled with Music," the other a song intended for Astaire's golf dance, which was used only as background music. For "I Used to Be Color Blind," Astaire devised the novelty of a dance in slow motion. He wanted Rogers to seem to be floating in space, so he included a series of lifts, a strenuous feat for any male dancer. To maintain the dreamlike quality of the dance, Astaire and Rogers shared their first on-screen kiss.

Carnal Knowledge

Avco Embassy, 1971. (C-96m.) Dir: Mike Nichols. Sp: Jules Feiffer. Cast: Jack Nicholson, Candice Bergen, Arthur Garfunkel, Ann-Margret, Rita Moreno, Cynthia O'Neal, Carol Kane.

On-Screen: *Blistering comedy-drama of two perennially adolescent men*. Under the credits, you hear college roommates Jonathan (Nicholson) and Sandy (Garfunkel) discuss their favorite topic. "If you had a choice," Jonathan asks, "would you rather love a girl or have her love you?" As this corrosive story traces their intertwined lives over the years, you get to understand each man's problem. For Jonathan, love is mere sexual conquest, neither the giving nor the receiving of affection. His grudging marriage to a model (Ann-Margret), who loves him despite his cruelty to her, ends disastrously. Sandy, though romantically inclined, is overly shy and sensitive, and marriage to his college sweetheart (Bergen) eventually falls apart. Certain scenes are presented as blackout skits; others, like Jonathan's revelation of his impotence, alleviated by visits to a prostitute (Moreno), are filmed as monologues. This is a stunningly directed, flawlessly acted, and brutally candid portrait of two mixed-up, modern Peter Pans.

Off-Screen: Until they appeared in the movie, both Ann-Margret and Garfunkel were regarded primarily as musical talents. The latter, fastidiously billed as Arthur in the credits, is better known as Art, half of the famous (Paul) Simon and Garfunkel pop-music team. The actress gained a reputation primarily as a song-and-dance star in both films and cabaret. Her performance as the embittered Bobbie brought her a Best Supporting Actress Oscar nomination. Bergen, best known today as "Murphy Brown" in the hit television series, referred to the movie as the one she was "proudest to be in." Feiffer's script was originally written as a play, and in 1990 it was produced off-Broadway. The film was banned in Georgia as pornographic. (CFB)

Carousel

Fox, 1956. (C-128m.) Dir: Henry King. Sp: Phoebe and Henry Ephron, b/o musical play by Richard Rodgers and Oscar Hammerstein II and play by Ferenc Molnar. MS: Richard Rodgers and Oscar Hammerstein II. Cast: Gordon MacRae, Shirley Jones, Cameron Mitchell, Barbara Ruick, Claramae Turner, Robert Rounseville, Gene Lockhart.

On-Screen: *Rodgers and Hammerstein's poignant musical drama on the screen*. Graced with one of the best—if not the best—of Rodgers and Hammerstein's musical scores, *Carousel* brims over with words and music that are lovely, infectious, and inspirational. Such songs as "If I Loved You," "June Is Bustin' Out All Over," and "You'll Never Walk Alone" are permanent treasures in our collective memory. This film version of the long-running stage musical does reasonable justice to the material despite one serious miscalculation. The story of ill-fated lovers (MacRae and Jones) in a New England fishing village in the 1870s has some genuinely touching moments. The production numbers, especially a "real nice" clambake, are expansive and attractive, and the cast works enthusiastically. The movie errs, however, in trying to blend stylized and surrealistic sequences (such as the hero's encounter with the Starkeeper in heaven) with sequences filmed on location. Generally, however, *Carousel* works as a respectable film transcription of a memorable musical play.

Off-Screen: Ferenc Molnar's play *Liliom,* the source for *Carousel,* was previously adapted to the screen in 1930, with Charles Farrell and Rose Hobart, and again in 1934, with Charles Boyer. *Carousel* was filmed in Fox's wide-screen CinemaScope 55 process. The movie was overshadowed that year by Fox's version of another Rodgers and Hammerstein musical, *The King and I,* which won a number of Oscars.

Carrie

United Artists, 1976. (C-97m.) Dir: Brian De Palma. Sp: Lawrence D. Cohen, b/o novel by Stephen King. Cast: Sissy Spacek, Piper Laurie, Amy Irving, John Travolta, William Katt, Nancy Allen, Betty Buckley, P. J. Soles, Sydney Lassick.

On-Screen: *Brian De Palma's shocker about a girl with telekinetic powers.* Lurid and preposterous, and clearly aimed at a teenage audience, *Carrie* has its share of Hitchcockian jolts but very little of the Hitchcockian finesse. It was also director De Palma's first big hit. Sissy Spacek is Carrie White, an unhappy, repressed high-school girl whose mother (Laurie) is an off-the-wall religious fanatic who despises men and makes Carrie pray in a closet. Carrie's cruel classmates pretend to make her the prom queen so that they can prepare an elaborate joke to humiliate her. What they don't know is that poor Carrie has telekinetic powers that can cause objects to move at will. When she realizes the truth about her "popular" status at school, those powers go berserk, destroy-

ing the school and many of the students and faculty members. Carrie also ends her own and her mother's miserable existence. The ending is cagily designed to shock. De Palma uses all sorts of stylistic tricks to grip the viewer, and sometimes they work. Other times they merely call attention to the threadbare material. Sissy Spacek is very good as Carrie, and John Travolta makes his film debut as one of her tormenters.

Off-Screen: Sissy Spacek and Piper Laurie were both Oscar-nominated for their performances, Spacek as Best Actress and Laurie as Best Supporting Actress. A stage-musical version was presented by the Royal Shakespeare Company at Stratford-on-Avon, England, in February 1988. The musical was received hostilely when it opened on Broadway in May of 1988. Several years later, Ken Mandelbaum used this show in the title of his book, *Not Since Carrie* (St. Martin's Press, 1992), which dealt with musical failures over the years.

Casablanca

Warners, 1942. (102m.) Dir: Michael Curtiz. Sp: Julius J. and Philip G. Epstein and Howard Koch, b/o play by Murray Burnett and Joan Alison. Cast: Humphrey Bogart, Ingrid Bergman, Paul Henreid, Claude Rains, Conrad Veidt, Sydney Greenstreet, Peter Lorre, Dooley Wilson, S. Z. Sakall.

On-Screen: *You must remember this.* A compelling script, flawless direction, and above all, the miraculous pairing of costars make this one of the most cherished movies of all time. Bogart is Rick Blaine, a cynical expatriate American who runs a café where refugees go for anything that will lead to escape from pursuing Nazis. Also in Casablanca are Victor Laszlo (Henreid), a Czech Resistance leader, and his wife Ilsa (Bergman), Rick's former lover. Still in love with Ilsa, Rick is drawn reluctantly into helping her and Laszlo flee to America. The fascinating gallery of intriguers includes Captain Renault (Rains), "a poor corrupt official"; Ugarte (Lorre), a jittery informer; and Señor Ferrari (Greenstreet), a black marketeer. Among the movie's classic moments are Wilson's playing of "As Time Goes By," rekindling bittersweet memories of Rick and Ilsa's Paris days, and that final, legendary scene on the rainwashed airstrip.

Off-Screen: Ronald Reagan and Ann Sheridan were first announced to play Rick and Ilsa, with Dennis Morgan as Laszlo. The script was often improvised on the set; the tangled plot was resolved only just before the final scene was shot. Among the many fondly remembered lines, Bergman's plea to Wilson is usually misquoted. For the record: "Play it once, Sam, for old times' sake. Play it, Sam. Play 'As Time Goes By.' " Although Dooley Wilson strokes the keys convincingly, it's studio musician Elliott Carpenter whose playing you hear on the soundtrack. Unsurprisingly, the movie won Oscars for Best Picture, Best Director, and Best Screenplay. Recent books on the movie include Howard Koch's *Casablanca: Script and Legend* (Overlook, 1992), Aljean Harmetz's *Round Up the Usual Suspects* (Hyperion, 1992), and Harlan Lebo's *Casablanca: Behind the Scenes* (Simon & Schuster, 1992). (CFB)

Casualties of War

Columbia, 1989. (C-113m.) Dir: Brian De Palma. Sp: David Rabe, b/o book by Daniel Lang. Cast: Michael J. Fox, Sean Penn, Don Harvey, John C. Reilly, Thuy Thu Le, John Leguizamo, Erik King, Jack Gwaltney.

On-Screen: *A searing war drama based on a true incident.* The Vietnam War dramas that surfaced in the late eighties usually attempted to encompass a fairly broad spectrum of events. In *Casualties of War,* Brian De Palma focuses instead on a single true incident and brings about a highly disturbing film. In Vietnam, a patrol of terrified, disoriented soldiers sets out on a mission, and at the instigation of their rage-filled, revenge-minded sergeant (Penn), they kidnap, rape, and ultimately murder a young Vietnamese girl (Thuy Thu Le). Only one member of the patrol (Fox) expresses horror at the deed, and conscience-stricken at being unable to save the girl, he reveals all to his less-than-supportive superiors. The soldiers are tried and sentenced, and Fox remains haunted by the memory of what happened. The film is undeniably stark, yet its story should have considerable impact on those who are challenged enough to confront a painful truth. Michael J. Fox is good in a difficult role that requires him to sound a single note of righteous concern, and Penn, a fine young actor, gives a sterling performance as the sergeant whom the war has turned into a conscienceless killer. And Brian De Palma forgoes his usual stylistic flourishes to offer a straightforward account of the incident.

Off-Screen: The true story began as a long article by Daniel Lang in a 1969 issue of *The New Yorker.* It offered a true account of the October 1966 incident in which five soldiers on patrol in Vietnam's central highlands kidnapped, raped, and then murdered a teenage Vietnamese girl. Four of the men were court-martialed and convicted in

March 1967. The young man played by Michael J. Fox still lives somewhere under an assumed name in the Southwest. The film was shot in seventy-five days near the resort island of Phuket in Thailand.

The Cat and the Canary

Paramount, 1939. (72m.) Dir: Elliott Nugent. Sp: Walter DeLeon and Lynn Starling, b/o play by John Willard. Cast: Bob Hope, Paulette Goddard, John Beal, Douglass Montgomery, Gale Sondergaard, Nydia Westman, George Zucco, Elizabeth Patterson.

On-Screen: *The old haunted-house chiller gets the Bob Hope treatment.* With his jutting nose and chin, his shark's smile, and his rapid-fire wisecracks, Bob Hope had made a number of comedies before affirming his stardom with *The Cat and the Canary*. The movie has Hope as a jittery, quipping fellow who joins heiress Paulette Goddard and others at a haunted mansion where skulduggery is afoot. While doors slide open mysteriously and hands clutch at terrified victims, Hope cracks jokes, and many of them are amusing in his brash style ("I'm so scared even my goose pimples have goose pimples!"). Surprisingly, the mystery elements evoke genuine suspense in some sequences, making the movie as frightening as it is funny.

Off-Screen: John Willard's play first appeared on Broadway in February 1922. A 1927 silent-film version, directed by Paul Leni, starred Laura La Plante and Creighton Hale, and a 1930 sound version, called *The Cat Creeps,* featured Helen Twelvetrees and Raymond Hackett. A 1978 British version of the story was mediocre.

Cat on a Hot Tin Roof

MGM, 1958. (C-108m.) Dir: Richard Brooks. Sp: Richard Brooks and James Poe, b/o play by Tennessee Williams. Cast: Elizabeth Taylor, Paul Newman, Burl Ives, Judith Anderson, Jack Carson, Madeleine Sherwood.

On-Screen: *Pulitzer Prize–winning Broadway drama of greed and sexual frustration.* "You started drinking with your friend Skipper's death," Big Daddy (Ives) tells his son Brick (Newman). Big Mamma (Anderson) puts it another way. "When a marriage goes on the rocks," she says to daughter-in-law Maggie (Taylor), thwacking a bed for emphasis, "the rocks are right there." Those clues help explain why guilt-ridden Brick and his passionate wife are emotionally unfulfilled and childless. By today's standards, the play is skittish about Brick's homosexual attachment to a college football buddy, and the movie is even more oblique on the matter. Ives and Anderson are powerful as the ailing patriarch and his wife; Carson and Sherwood are amusing as parents of obnoxious "no-neck monsters," who stand to inherit Big Daddy's fortune. But it's Taylor's desperate Maggie the Cat and Newman's tormented Brick that give the movie its drive and momentum.

Off-Screen: Although Barbara Bel Geddes had enjoyed great success on Broadway as Maggie, an established star was needed to help offset the movie's controversial theme. Grace Kelly was the studio's first choice; however, her marriage to Monaco's Prince Rainier intervened, and Taylor was cast instead. The actress experienced personal tragedy during filming when her husband, showman Mike Todd, was killed in a plane crash. The film was nominated for six Academy Awards: Best Picture, Newman and Taylor as Best Actor and Actress, and for Best Direction, Screen Adaptation, and William Daniels's Color Cinematography. (CFB)

Cat People

RKO, 1942. (73m.) Dir: Jacques Tourneur. Sp: DeWitt Bodeen. Cast: Simone Simon, Kent Smith, Jane Randolph, Tom Conway, Jack Holt.

On-Screen: *An ancient curse haunts a modern-day young woman.* On a dark night in Central Park, a terrified woman, fleeing from something unseen, rushes to board a bus, and the hiss of the bus as it stops sounds like that of a giant cat. Alone in an indoor swimming pool, the same woman becomes aware that she is being stalked by an angry, screeching animal. These two frightening moments are well-remembered by fans of *Cat People,* one of the best of producer Val Lewton's series of low-budget but effective thrillers of the early forties. Simone Simon plays a young Serbian girl haunted by an ancient curse that turns her into a murderous cat when her passions are aroused. This makes life difficult for her new husband (Smith) and his coworker (Randolph), who has loved him for years. (She's the lady in peril). The story is patently nonsense and the production is skimpy, but unlike the 1982 remake, the movie relies on suggestion rather than explicit gore. *Cat People* overrides its limitations to become a chilling fable.

Off-Screen: The film was the first of producer Val Lewton's nine superior, though low-budget, thrillers for RKO. French actress Simone Simon had worked for Fox from 1936 to 1938, cast mainly as a pert innocent, but she returned to France dissatisfied with her career. A striking performance in Jean Renoir's *The Human Beast* (1938) brought her an invitation to return to Hollywood for roles in this film and several others. She returned to France at the end of World War II and remained there.

Catch-22

Paramount, 1970. (C-121m.) Dir: Mike Nichols. Sp: Buck Henry, b/o novel by Joseph Heller. Cast: Alan Arkin, Martin Balsam, Richard Benjamin, Art Garfunkel, Jack Gilford, Bob Newhart, Anthony Perkins, Paula Prentiss, Martin Sheen, Jon Voight, Orson Welles.

On-Screen: *World War II satire.* This heavy-handed adaptation of Heller's devastating look at the madness of war misses the novel's spark of divine lunacy. As members of a bomber squadron stationed on an island off the Italian coast, most of the cast is merely stereotypically funny in the fashion of television sitcoms. Outstanding, however, are Newhart as timid Major Major, Welles as the hopelessly befuddled General Dreedle, and Balsam as Colonel Cathcart, whose fondest wish is to be written up in *The Saturday Evening Post.* Arkin is brilliant as Captain Yossarian, the panic-stricken and all-too-sane bombardier who learns from Gilford's Dr. Daneeka what Catch-22 is all about: "Anyone who wants to get out of combat isn't really crazy, so I can't ground him." The war-is-hell message is too often handled ponderously.

Orson Welles himself had wanted to film the novel, but when he failed to acquire the rights, he accepted the role of Dreedle instead. Nichols replaced Stacy Keach with Balsam, and offered George C. Scott a part, but Scott thought the script "just awful." Screenwriter Henry appears as Colonel Korn. An air base was built in Guaymas, Mexico, to represent the tiny Mediterranean island of Pianosa. Other scenes were filmed in Rome and Hollywood. (CFB)

Champion

United Artists, 1949. (99m.) Dir: Mark Robson. Sp: Carl Foreman, b/o story by Ring Lardner. Cast: Kirk Douglas, Marilyn Maxwell, Arthur Kennedy, Paul Stewart, Ruth Roman, Lola Albright.

On-Screen: *Ruthlessly ambitious prizefighter slugs his way to the top.* Midge Kelly (Douglas) is more than a champion boxer. He's also a world-class heel. True, he sends money to his mother and helps his crippled brother, Connie (Kennedy), who idolizes him. After Midge callously tosses aside the manager (Stewart) who made him into a pro, leaves his wife (Roman) for a nightclub warbler (Maxwell), and then takes up with his new manager's seductive spouse (Albright), Connie risks some plain speaking ("You stink from corruption!") and is rewarded with one of Midge's famous right hooks. The fight sequences are convincing, the dialogue is pungent, and Douglas's subtly shaded portrayal of a pathetically flawed human being is both powerful and credible. His almost unbearably moving scene in the locker room at the film's conclusion will stay with you for a long time.

Off-Screen: Lardner's short story gives Midge Kelly no redeeming qualities whatsoever. In making him less villainous and more dramatically interesting, Robson, Foreman, and Douglas softened details of the character. The result brought the actor his first Oscar nomination. Douglas had no boxing experience before this movie, though he had been on St. Lawrence University's wrestling team. After training for little more than a month, he was able to enter the studio ring with actual former prizefighters. The movie's editor, Harry Gerstad, won an Oscar. (CFB)

Chaplin

TriStar, 1992. (C-142m.) Dir: Richard Attenborough. Sp: William Boyd, Bryan Forbes, and William Goldman, b/o story by Diana Hawkins and books by Charlie Chaplin and David Robinson. Cast: Robert Downey, Jr., Geraldine Chaplin, Anthony Hopkins, Dan Aykroyd, Kevin Kline, Marisa Tomei, Penelope Ann Miller, Nancy Travis, James Woods, John Thaw.

On-Screen: *All about the master comedian.* Making a film biography on the life and career of Charlie Chaplin was, at best, a daunting task, and if director Richard Attenborough fails to carry it off, neither is the movie the abysmal failure some reviewers would have you believe. Handsomely produced, *Chaplin* skims lightly and unrevealingly across the events: his impoverished childhood, his music-hall days, his rise to superstardom in silent movies, the attacks on his morality and loyalty that led to his banishment and exile, and finally, his triumphant return to America. We are given only a fleeting sense of his unique film artistry (that famous last shot in *City Lights* is oddly missing) so that younger viewers (if there are any) might wonder what the fuss was all about. The movie's best feature by far is Robert Downey, Jr.'s exemplary, Oscar-nominated performance as Chaplin—in voice, demeanor, and style, he embodies one of the seminal figures of this century. The cast is studded with well-known names, but Chaplin's daughter Geraldine stands out in the role of her mentally ill grandmother Hannah.

On-Screen: Getting *Chaplin* onto the screen proved to be a long and arduous task. Richard Attenborough spent two years developing the project at Universal, only to have the studio eventually back out. The screenplay went through many versions, including contributions by playwright Tom Stoppard. Ultimately, William Boyd's original script was reworked by William Goldman. Dustin Hoffman, Billy Crystal, and Robin Williams all wanted to play Chaplin, but Downey was chosen, according to Attenborough, for "the combination of his youth, his mimicry, his ability to play age, his balletic skills, his ear, his height, and his similarity to Chaplin." It took seven hours to transform young Downey into the eighty-three-year-old Chaplin. In addition to his nomination for best actor, the film's art direction was also nominated for an Oscar.

Charade

Universal-International, 1963. (C-114m.) Dir: Stanley Donen. Sp: Peter Stone, b/o story by Peter Stone and Marc Behm. Cast: Cary Grant, Audrey Hepburn, Walter Matthau, George Kennedy, James Coburn, Ned Glass, Jacques Marin.

On-Screen: *Grant and Hepburn (Audrey) in a twisty comedy-thriller*. Highly scenic, diverting, and suspenseful, *Charade* is one of the few Hitchcockian melodramas that comes reasonably close to the master. Chic and lovely Audrey Hepburn stars as a bewildered young wife in Paris whose husband is brutally murdered. Soon she is entangled with the killers, who want the money they claim her husband stole from them. With her life in jeopardy, she is helped (or is she?) by a suave but mysterious man (Grant) who takes on various identities. Walter Matthau is also on hand as an ambiguous government official. It all makes little sense, and much of the action is surprisingly violent, but the leading players and the scenery are so attractive, and the pace is so swift, that you are bound to be entertained. There's also a lilting Henry Mancini score that helps to make *Charade* an enjoyable dip into the Hitchcock pool.

Off-Screen: Worried about the discrepancy between his age and that of his leading lady, Cary Grant was reassured when first-time writer Peter Stone added a number of lines that made light of his apparent maturity. At first Grant vehemently refused to do the scene in which he must take a shower fully clothed, but the director and writer held firm, and he carried it off with aplomb. Audrey Hepburn remarked, "Working with him was a joy. There was something special, which is quite undefinable, about Cary."

The Charge of the Light Brigade

Warners, 1936. (116m.) Dir: Michael Curtiz. Sp: Michel Jacoby and Rowland Leigh, b/o story by Michel Jacoby. Cast: Errol Flynn, Olivia de Havilland, Patric Knowles, Henry Stephenson, Donald Crisp, Nigel Bruce, David Niven, C. Henry Gordon, Spring Byington.

On-Screen: *A dashing British soldier finds romance and a tragic fate.* Viewers of a certain age will surely remember the rousing charge of the Light Brigade that ends this epic adventure film. One of the great action sequences of the thirties, it begins with the camera sweeping across the line of mounted soldiers as they prepare for the charge and ends with their heroic demise. The rest of the film is lavish and stirring in Warners' Anglophile tradition, with Errol Flynn in top form as the brave lieutenant who, while defending British sovereignty on the Crimean frontier, romances young Olivia de Havilland. Unfortunately for him, she loves his younger brother (Knowles). The love story, however, is merely secondary to the large-scale action sequences. Jack Sullivan received an Oscar as Best Assistant Director, a category dropped from the awards in 1938. A 1968 British version offered a quite different view of the celebrated charge.

Off-Screen: It was during the making of this film that Hungarian-born director Michael Curtiz was reputed to have yelled "Bring on the empty horses!" During the filming of the action sequences, trip wires were used to create realistic falls by the horses; many horses broke their legs and had to be shot. A campaign by the furious Society for the Prevention of Cruelty to Animals resulted in new film-production rules that guaranteed animal safety. Flynn, who called this "the toughest picture I ever made," despised the autocratic Curtiz. The famous charge was filmed near Chatsworth in the San Fernando Valley.

Charly

Cinerama, 1968. (C-103m.) Dir: Ralph Nelson. Sp: Stirling Silliphant, b/o his television play and on short story and novel by Daniel Keyes. Cast: Cliff Robertson, Claire Bloom, Leon Janney, Lilia Skala, Dick Van Patten, Ruth White, Barney Martin, William Dwyer.

On-Screen: *Robertson's Oscar as a retarded-man-turned-genius.* The story of *Charly* has undergone many permutations over the years, but this version is the best known, primarily because it won Cliff Robertson a Best Actor Academy Award. He plays Charly Gordon, a mentally retarded man who becomes the subject of an experimental brain operation that turns him into a mental giant. He falls in love with his beautiful psychiatric counselor (Bloom), and eventually she reciprocates the feeling. Sadly, however, he reverts to his retarded state by the film's end. Though certainly well-intentioned, the movie now seems almost laughably simplistic, with many unanswered questions. Just for starters: Why do Charly's coworkers treat him so nastily when he's retarded? What is the nature of the vaguely defined operation? How could a sophisticated woman fall in love with a man like Charly? And why didn't the filmmakers consider these questions and others? Ralph Nelson's direction, with its self-conscious camera trickery, is no help. Cliff Robertson works hard and gives a good performance, but all in vain.

Off-Screen: Before *Charly* reached the screen, it had been a short story and novel by Daniel Keyes called *Flowers for Algernon* and then a 1961 television play by Stirling Silliphant, entitled *The Two Worlds of Charly Gordon,* also with Robertson in the leading role. Many years after the movie, the story was turned into an unsuccessful stage musical, variously called *Flowers for Algernon* and *Charlie and Algernon. Charly* was filmed at various locations in and around Boston.

Cheyenne Autumn

Warners, 1964. (C-145m.) Dir: John Ford. Sp: James R. Webb, b/o novel by Mari Sandoz. Cast: Richard Widmark, Carroll Baker, Karl Malden, Dolores Del Rio, Sal Mineo, Edward G. Robinson, James Stewart, Ricardo Montalban, Gilbert Roland, John Carradine, John Qualen.

On-Screen: *John Ford's elegy to the plight of the Indian.* For years, director Ford had painted the Indians as little more than a hostile or threatening presence in his Western films. In *Cheyenne Autumn,* Ford tries to set the record straight with a blistering indictment of America's abuse of Indians. The story is based on fact: the devastating trek of nearly three hundred Cheyenne Indians to their ancestral lands in the Dakota mountains. Facing cold, starvation, and attacks by American troops, the Cheyennes were virtually annihilated over their fifteen-hundred-mile journey. Under Ford's assured direction, an impressive cast tells this mournful story. The movie is occasionally eloquent but also too long and diffuse—too many side issues are left unresolved. One curious note: A disconcerting sequence in the middle of the film seems to come out of nowhere. It involves James Stewart as Wyatt Earp in an encounter with three cowboys who are exposed as the killers of a starving Cheyenne. Originally, this was part of a larger sequence in which the poker

players and townspeople ride out to jeer the passing Indians. This segment was cut from the film after initial showings.

Off-Screen: Talking about the film with Peter Bogdanovich, John Ford noted, "Let's face it, we've treated them [the Indians] very badly—it's a blot on our shield; we've cheated and robbed, killed, murdered, massacred, and everything else, but they kill one white man and God, out come the troops."

Children of a Lesser God

Paramount, 1986. (C-110m.) Dir: Randa Haines. Sp: Hesper Anderson and Mark Medoff, b/o play by Mark Medoff. Cast: William Hurt, Marlee Matlin, Piper Laurie, Philip Bosco, Alison Gompf, William Byrd, Frank Carter, Jr.

On-Screen: *A teacher of the deaf falls for a deaf girl.* Adapted from the long-running and award-winning Broadway play, *Children of a Lesser God* stars William Hurt as a teacher of the deaf who meets a defiant, uncommunicative deaf girl (deaf actress Marlee Matlin) who works as the school's janitor. Eventually, their scratchy, contentious relationship ripens into a love affair, but they find themselves at cross purposes, unable to deal with the differences between them and their separate needs. By the film's end, they have learned from each other and are reconciled. Essentially a two-person drama, the film benefits from the capable acting of the leads, especially Matlin's heartfelt, Oscar-winning performance. The scene in which she responds to the vibrations of unheard music is exceptionally fine. The work of the deaf students at Hurt's school (played by hearing-impaired youngsters) forms an interesting background for this poignant story.

Off-Screen: Set in Maine, the film was actually shot on the New Brunswick, Canada, shore. Matlin, who built on her own experiences for the role, had a complex relationship with her costar. She has said, "We had fights a lot, heavy things we used in our scenes. It was difficult working with him, but I stood on my own two feet."

The China Syndrome

Columbia, 1979. (C-123m.) Dir: James Bridges. Sp: Mike Gray, T. S. Cook, and James Bridges. Cast: Jane Fonda, Jack Lemmon, Michael Douglas, Wilford Brimley, Scott Brady, James Hampton, Peter Donat.

On-Screen: *The threat of a nuclear disaster galvanizes many people.* Movie trailers used to emphasize a film's timeliness by shouting, "Ripped from today's headlines!" Few recent films could make the point so dramatically as this exciting—and disturbing—drama. (See below.) At a California nuclear plant, an accident is quickly covered up, but it leads one plant executive (Lemmon) to the horrifying conclusion that the plant is *not* safe and that the possibility exists of a nuclear holocaust that would devastate a wide area and kill indeterminate numbers. A spunky television reporter (Fonda) and an activist photographer (Douglas) rally to Lemmon's cause, leading to a final and deadly encounter in the plant. The characters are lightly sketched, but the tension is nonstop and the climax is truly riveting. By now Jack Lemmon had played a number of men at the end of their tether, and he gives another charged performance as the desper-

ate whistle-blower. Both he and Jane Fonda won Oscar nominations, as did the screenplay.

Off-Screen: On March 28, 1979, an accident deemed the worst in the history of the United States occurred at Three Mile Island, south of Harrisburg, Pennsylvania. Through a combination of human error and stuck valves, the plant's cooling system failed, causing the core of the reactor to begin to melt and release radioactive gases. Although the damage was contained, the accident raised serious doubt about the safety of nuclear energy and, incidentally, gave *The China Syndrome* abundant free publicity. The role of the television reporter was originally supposed to be played by Richard Dreyfuss, but the character was changed to a woman.

Chinatown

Paramount, 1974. (131m.) Dir: Roman Polanski. Sp: Robert Towne. Cast: Jack Nicholson, Faye Dunaway, John Huston, Perry Lopez, Joe Mantell, John Hillerman, Darrell Zwerling, Diane Ladd, Burt Young.

On-Screen: *Powerful mystery thriller set in L.A. of the thirties.* Towne's Oscar-winning screenplay has enough action, intrigue, and tart dialogue to satisfy the most demanding Hammett-Chandler fans. In taking on what seems at first to be just another seedy divorce case, detective J. J. Gittes (Nicholson) stumbles on more than what his fee covers when he becomes involved in a cesspool of public and private corruption. Obstacles mount before he can learn the true connection between the murdered water commissioner's widow (Dunaway) and a ruthless millionaire (Huston). Nicholson is both funny and moving as the private eye whose probings scar him in more ways than one; Dunaway is properly enigmatic as the glamorous woman in question. Huston's hearty tycoon turns chilling in his dark hint to Nicholson that "most people never have to face the fact—the right time, the right place—they're capable of anything." A stunner.

Off-Screen: In addition to its Academy Award for Best Screenplay, *Chinatown* was nominated for Best Picture, Nicholson and Dunaway for Best Actor and Actress, and Polanski for Best Director. (There were a number of other nominations as well.) Ali McGraw was eliminated from the Dunaway role because of her divorce from the film's producer Robert Evans; Jane Fonda turned it down. Polanski, briefly seen as a knife-wielding hood, departed from the script by giving the movie a more violent ending. *The Two Jakes,* a 1990 sequel directed by Nicholson, seemed a parody of its predecessor. (CFB)

A Chorus Line

Embassy, 1985. (C-113m.) Dir: Richard Attenborough. Sp: Arnold Schulman, b/o musical play by James Kirkwood and Nicholas Dante. MS: Marvin Hamlisch and Edward Kleban. Cast: Michael Douglas, Alyson Reed, Terrence Mann, Cameron English, Vicki Frederick, Audrey Landers, Gregg Burge, Nicole Fosse.

On-Screen: *Film version of the landmark stage musical.* The longest-running show in Broadway history, Michael Bennett's *A Chorus Line* opened in 1975 after an off-Broadway

run and closed in 1990 after 6,137 official performances. It was inevitable that some day this musical psychodrama about the theater's dogged, eternally hopeful "gypsies" would reach the screen, and when it did, it received a mostly scathing reception. Critics had little good to say about the movie in which dancers, trying out for a show, reveal in song and dance their poignant, bitter, hopeful feelings. In fact, the movie is nowhere as bad as its reputation, and it is probably as good a version of the stage show as possible, considering that the material resists filming. Some of the performers lack charisma, and some of the dances are photographed awkwardly, but in general the singing and dancing are far from mediocre and, in some cases, excellent. Highlights include Gregg Burge's exuberant "Surprise!" the lovely, touching "At the Ballet," and Alyson Reed's striking "The Girl in the Mirror." There are others as well. Try it, even if you've seen the show.

Off-Screen: *A Chorus Line* began filming at the Mark Hellinger Theater in Manhattan nearly ten years after the movie rights were sold. A number of prominent producers, directors, and writers, including Joseph Papp, Michael Bennett, Mike Nichols, Sidney Lumet, and Joel Schumacher, became involved in the project at one time or another. The full story of the movie's long and difficult journey to the screen can be found in the Arts and Leisure section of *The New York Times* of November 11, 1984. The film's editing and the song "Surprise!" were Oscar-nominated.

The Chosen

Fox, 1981. (C-108m.) Dir: Jeremy Paul Kagan. Sp: Edwin Gordon, b/o novel by

Chaim Potok. Cast: Rod Steiger, Maximilian Schell, Robby Benson, Barry Miller, Hildy Brooks, Ron Rifkin, Val Avery.

On-Screen: *Two boys from different worlds become friends*. Adapted from Chaim Potok's best-selling novel, *The Chosen* is an intriguing but curiously undramatic film. The setting is Williamsburg, Brooklyn, in the war years. Reuven (Miller) is the young son of Professor Malter (Schell), an intellectual with a fervent belief in Zionism and the formation of a Jewish state. Danny (Benson) is the Hasidic son of a beloved rabbi (Steiger) who rejects the idea of a Jewish state. Inevitably, there is a clash over values and beliefs, and almost as inevitably, each boy moves to the other side, with introspective Reuven thinking of becoming a rabbi and intellectually curious Danny breaking away from his father's powerful influence. Despite the intensity of the opposing viewpoints, the movie never catches fire. The best feature is Rod Steiger's fine performance as the rabbi; in the film's most eloquent scene, he explains why he has chosen to give his son "the wisdom and the pain of silence." His expression of pride in a son who has become "a righteous man" is a profoundly moving moment in a disappointing film.

Off-Screen: When the movie had its benefit premiere at Radio City Music Hall in New York, author Potok was dismayed that the organizers of the benefit supper failed to arrange for kosher supervision of the food. The menu included many things that were delicious but not quite kosher. Scenes for the film were shot all over New York City but not in actual Hasidic neighborhoods. Steiger acquired a Yiddish accent by listening to a butcher in a Manhattan supermarket. Potok appears briefly as a Talmud teacher. A musical version of the story ran briefly off-Broadway in January 1988.

Christmas in July

Paramount, 1940. (67m.) Dir: Preston Sturges. Sp: Preston Sturges. Cast: Dick Powell, Ellen Drew, Raymond Walburn, William Demarest, Ernest Truex, Franklin Pangborn.

On-Screen: *An early Preston Sturges comedy*. An office worker with a mania for entering contests, young Jimmy (Powell) is deluded into believing that he has won $25,000 in a contest to find a slogan for Maxford House Coffee. Somehow he convinces the dim-witted Maxford people that he is indeed the winner, and he goes on a frenzied shopping spree with the check. When the truth comes out, Jimmy suffers the consequences, until . . . Made immediately after *The Great McGinty*, *Christmas in July* is a minor but amiable comedy, with some Sturgesian touches of satire and knockabout slapstick. The funniest scenes involve members of the up-and-coming Sturges stock company of players, including Raymond Walburn as the befuddled head of Maxford House Coffee and Franklin Pangborn as the overwrought Maxford radio announcer. Jimmy's slogan, incidentally, is "If you can't sleep at night, it isn't the coffee, it's the bunk."

Off-Screen: In 1931, Preston Sturges had written a play called *A Cup of Coffee*, which he turned into a screenplay in 1935. Paramount bought the rights from Universal, and it began filming as *The New Yorkers*. By the time of editing, it was called *Something to Shout About* and finally *Christmas in July*. Sturges was astonished when the censors asked him to delete the word *schlemiel* as being "too Jewish." Somehow the substituted word *schnook* appeased them.

Citizen Kane

RKO, 1941. (119m.) Dir: Orson Welles. Sp: Herman J. Mankiewicz and Orson Welles. Cast: Orson Welles, Joseph Cotten, Ruth Warrick, Dorothy Comingore, Everett Sloane, George Coulouris, Agnes Moorehead, William Alland, Ray Collins, Paul Stewart, Erskine Sanford.

On-Screen: *Orson Welles's enduring classic.* A deeply influential film, still remarkable in its use of cinematic techniques, *Citizen Kane* brought both acclaim and condemnation to wunderkind Orson Welles (then only twenty-five years old). The film begins with the death of Charles Foster Kane (Welles), newspaper tycoon and would-be national force, then flashes back to trace his rise and fall over the years: his audacious takeover of the *National Enquirer*; his failed marriages; his aborted run for governor; and his descent to a life of lonely, empty splendor. Step by step, he loses sight of his goals and ideals, destroyed by his ambitions, his appetites, and his overpowering need to be loved. Books, of course, have been written on the film's technical virtuosity, which absorbed, then redefined the basic elements of film: Robert Wise and uncredited Mark Robson's brilliant editing, with its astonishing use of telescoped time; Gregg Toland's deep-focus cinematography, in which light and shadow are employed for dramatic effect; and Bernard Herrmann's evocative music score. In acknowledging over a half-century of esteem, it is sometimes forgotten

that much of the film is satirical, and some of it is banal. (The final explanation of "Rosebud," for example, is too pat.) But *Citizen Kane* remains a masterpiece, an audacious work whose influence can be seen, overt or implied, in many films that followed it.

Off-Screen: The brouhaha sparked by *Citizen Kane,* especially the vehement objections of its ostensible subject, powerful publishing tycoon William Randolph Hearst, has been recorded in a number of books, most notably Pauline Kael's *The Citizen Kane Book* (Little, Brown, 1971) and Barbara Leaming's biography of Welles (Viking Penguin, 1985). *The Making of "Citizen Kane"* by Robert L. Carringer (University of California Press, 1985) offers a detailed, fascinating study of the making of the movie. Early on, the screenplay was titled *American* and also *John Citizen, U.S.A.* It was awarded the film's only Oscar. See if you can spot young Alan Ladd as a reporter.

City for Conquest

Warners, 1940. (101m.) Dir: Anatole Litvak. Sp: John Wexley, b/o novel by Aben Kandel. Cast: James Cagney, Ann Sheridan, Donald Crisp, Arthur Kennedy, Anthony Quinn, Frank McHugh, Frank Craven, George Tobias, Elia Kazan.

On-Screen: *A promising boxer faces blindness.* The sort of pulpish, hard-breathing melodrama that was ripe for parody in later years on such television programs as "Your Show of Shows," *City for Conquest* holds the attention, nonetheless, with its driving pace and forceful performances. James Cagney stars as a New York slum youth who takes up boxing to support his composer brother (Kennedy). Abandoned by his ambitious girlfriend (Sheridan), he turns bitter and agrees to a nasty boxing match (a vivid sequence) that leaves him almost totally blind. The screenplay rings every ounce of bathos from the story, but the Warners stock company, as usual, punches it all home. Cagney, in particular, gives an exceptionally moving performance. Try not to laugh at brother Kennedy's perfervid *New York* symphony, and look for director Elia Kazan in an early acting role as a dapper hoodlum. He has a memorable death scene in which, riddled with bullets, he gasps, "Ah, gee, I never figured on that at all."

Off-Screen: For reissues and television showings, the entire prologue of the film, showing the three principal characters as children, was deleted. Frank Craven's scenes as the codger who narrates the story were also cut to ribbons. Cagney, who argued constantly with director Litvak, claimed that the movie failed to do justice to the original novel. He says that he was heartsick when he realized that the studio had cut out the best scenes, leaving only the skeleton of the novel and "a trite melodrama."

City Slickers

Castle Rock, 1991. (110m.) Dir: Ron Underwood. Sp: Lowell Ganz and Babaloo Mandel. Cast: Billy Crystal, Bruno Kirby, Daniel Stern, Jack Palance, Patricia Wettig, Helen Slater, Noble Willingham, Tracey Walter, Josh Mostel.

On-Screen: *Three urban types become cowpokes.* A thoroughly genial movie about three friends (Crystal, Kirby, and Stern) who

are transplanted from the Big Apple to the Wild West. Each of the three has his own problems, and together they decide to get away from it all on a two-week vacation as real, working cowboys. Under a trail boss named Curly (Palance), these city slickers must drive a herd of cattle to a new home in spite of such challenges as an attractive young woman (Slater) and their own klutziness. Half of what's good about *City Slickers* are the clichés it avoids, such as people getting on a horse backward. The other half is that much of the film is original and funny, and the three principals do it full justice. There's also a bonus half, and that's Palance, whose face by now ought to be declared a national monument. Playing a real cowboy with total authority and sly good humor, Palance walks or rides off with every scene he's in. He was given the Best Supporting Actor Oscar for that year.

Off-Screen: Billy Crystal conceived the idea for the movie, and if you can believe the publicity, he had Jack Palance in mind from the very first for the role of Curly. Outlining the story, he wrote, "My character gets involved with the tough trail boss." And in parentheses, he added, "Jack Palance." Months later, he was discussing the role with Palance. (BL)

Cleopatra

Fox, 1963. (C-243m.) Dir: Joseph L. Mankiewicz. Sp: Ranald MacDougall, Sidney Buchman, and Joseph L. Mankiewicz, b/o histories by Plutarch, Suetonius, and Appian, and book by C. M. Franzero. Cast: Elizabeth Taylor, Richard Burton, Rex Harrison, Roddy McDowall, Hume Cronyn, Martin Landau, Pamela Brown, Michael Hordern, Carroll O'Connor, Kenneth Haigh.

On-Screen: *Liz and Dick upstage history.* The hoopla that attended the two-and-a-half-year filming of this movie has long since faded. What remains is a flashy, splashy talkathon brought to occasional life by Taylor's luminous presence as a kittenish, and later regal, Queen of the Nile and Harrison's Julius Caesar, a wise and witty counselor who gives Cleopatra political-science lessons, as well as a child. Burton, as Mark Antony, whose passion for Cleopatra both sustains and dooms him, gives a strong performance. The clumsily staged Battle of Actium is a letdown, but watch Taylor as she and her son, both clad in gold, spectacularly enter Rome on a colossal sphinx. Her sly wink, aimed at an admiring Harrison, proves she's learned her lessons well, and is worth all the rest.

Off-Screen: Early on, Joan Collins was cast as the title temptress. With Taylor finally set, opposite Stephen Boyd and Peter Finch, filming began in England. Production was shut down when she became critically ill, and director Rouben Mamoulian withdrew. Mankiewicz assumed direction, rewrote the script, and began the movie again in Rome. Taylor and Burton's off-camera dalliance (both were married to others at the time), whetted the public's appetite, but the movie opened to disparaging reviews. (The current home-video version is shaved down to 185 minutes.) The movie received nine Oscar nominations, but only four statuettes, for color cinematography, art direction, costume design, and special visual effects. (CFB)

The Clock

MGM, 1945. (90m.) Dir: Vincente Minnelli. Sp: Robert Nathan and Joseph Schrank, b/o story by Paul Gallico and Pauline Gallico. Cast: Judy Garland, Robert Walker, James Gleason, Keenan Wynn, Marshall Thompson, Lucille Gleason, Ruth Brady.

On-Screen: *Two young people meet and fall in love in wartime New York City.* Surprisingly, in the midst of its glittering entertainments of the forties, MGM produced—and, as his first nonmusical film, Vincente Minnelli directed—this small but beguiling tale of a whirlwind wartime romance. A winsome secretary (Garland) meets a gauche, small-town soldier (Walker) on forty-eight-hour leave in Manhattan; they discover an almost immediate rapport as they move through the nighttime city, meeting a few amiable eccentrics along the way. Their idyll ends when they lose each other in the crowd, but they are reunited and decide to marry. They part where they met, in Grand Central Station. With few flourishes, *The Clock* tells a sweetly affecting story. The best scenes take place after their hasty wedding; a highlight is their first breakfast together, acted in pantomime. Garland is enchanting as the girl bewildered by the sudden turn of events, and Walker exudes boyish charm.

Off-Screen: The film was started by Fred Zinnemann after first-choice director Jack Conway fell ill, but Judy Garland was unable to get along with him and asked that he be replaced with Vincente Minnelli. There were cast replacements as well: Ruth Brady substituted for Audrey Totter as Garland's roommate, and James Gleason took over for Hume Cronyn as a friendly milkman. The man from whom Robert Walker cadges a light at the film's beginning is none other than producer-composer Arthur Freed. Largely using rear projection, the movie was shot in Culver City rather than New York. One set was a full-scale replica of the interior of Pennsylvania Station.

Close Encounters of the Third Kind

Columbia, 1977. (C-135m.) Dir: Steven Spielberg. Sp: Steven Spielberg. Cast: Richard Dreyfuss, François Truffaut, Teri Garr, Melinda Dillon, Cary Guffey, Bob Balaban.

On-Screen: *Spectacularly produced culmination of all UFO movies.* The story centers on a group of people in Muncie, Indiana, who experience an eerie manifestation. One, Roy Neary (Dreyfuss), becomes obsessed with the vision of a mountain; others, Jillian Guiler (Dillon) and her small son (Guffey), find their electrical appliances running wild and toys coming to life. Meanwhile, scientific and military experts, led by an eminent researcher (Truffaut), are trying to decipher musical signals emanating from UFOs. Roy's attempts to interpret the vision make for some dull patches, but the climactic sequence, at Wyoming's Devil Tower, is worth the wait. The landing of an immense circular object with hundreds of illuminated windows, the debarking of ethereal aliens, the awe and wonder of the onlookers, including Roy and Jillian, the soaring music— all converge to make this sequence one of the most beautiful and most moving ever conceived for the movies.

Off-Screen: The movie was shot in such far-flung locations as the Mojave Desert, Bombay, Wyoming's twelve-hundred-foot-high Devil's Tower National Monument, and inside a gigantic dirigible hanger in Mobile, Alabama, where the lower portion of the huge mothership was constructed. Spielberg had planned to star Jack Nicholson in *Watch the Skies* (the film's original title), but the actor was unavailable at the time and Richard Dreyfuss replaced him. Famed French director Truffaut (*The 400 Blows, Jules and Jim,* among others), appears as Lacombe. Nominated for eight Oscars, the movie was honored for Vilmos Zsigmond's outstanding cinematography. In 1980 Spielberg released *The Special Edition,* a somewhat shortened version of the film that includes a view of the mothership's interior. Cast member Balaban's *Close Encounters of the Third Kind Diary* (1978) is a fascinating journal of the filming. (CFB)

Coal Miner's Daughter

Universal, 1980. (C-125m.) Dir: Michael Apted. Sp: Tom Rickman, b/o autobiography by Loretta Lynn, with George Vecsey. Cast: Sissy Spacek, Tommy Lee Jones, Beverly D'Angelo, Levon Helm, Phyllis Boyens.

On-Screen: *The story of the queen of country music.* This rags-to-riches account of Loretta Lynn covers basically familiar ground, but Sissy Spacek's Oscar-winning performance is so well-wrought that the movie is worth your attention. Her Loretta begins as a gawky fourteen-year-old in a large coal miner's family in Appalachia, who becomes the child bride of rowdy, ambitious Mooney Doolittle (Jones). (These early scenes are the best.) Four years later, already burdened with four children, she begins singing her country music and rises to stardom. The usual stresses of fame result in complications, including her onstage collapse, but eventually she returns to singing. Spacek, who performs Loretta Lynn's popular songs in her own voice, is entirely persuasive, and Jones is equally good as Mooney. Beverly D'Angelo plays Patsy Cline, the country singer whose story was told five years later in Karel Reisz's *Sweet Dreams* (1985).

Off-Screen: In addition to Spacek's Oscar, *Coal Miner's Daughter* won four other Academy nominations, including Best Picture. Spacek was Loretta Lynn's personal choice for the role, and Tom Rickman wrote his screenplay with the actress in mind. Most of the songs in the film were recorded live as Spacek performed them, rather than in a soundproof studio, which would have required her to lip-synch them on-screen. The film's original director, Joseph Sargent, was replaced by Michael Apted.

Cocoon

Fox, 1985. (C-116m.) Dir: Ron Howard. Sp: Tom Benedek, b/o novel by David Saperstein. Cast: Don Ameche, Wilford Brimley, Hume Cronyn, Brian Dennehy, Jack Gilford, Steve Guttenberg, Maureen Stapleton, Jessica Tandy, Gwen Verdon, Herta Ware, Tahnee Welch, Tyrone Power, Jr.

On-Screen: *Comedy-fantasy concerning aliens and oldsters.* An alien spaceship lands on earth with the goal of retrieving some of the aliens that were left behind aeons ago and who are now encased in cocoons concealed in a deserted Florida pool. Only the pool is not deserted—elderly male residents of a nearby retirement home are using it and becoming physically (and sexually) revitalized by the force generated by the cocoons. Soon the aliens and the oldsters become intertwined in unexpected ways. This disarming comedy-fantasy boasts some cleverly wrought sequences and a first-rate cast headed by veteran actors. (Wonderful Jack Gilford is best as a crotchety resident.) Unfortunately, the script also takes a rather patronizing view toward old age, and the ending is insupportable. It not only panders to its target audience's dream of eternal life but also suggests that this dream is much stronger than any earthly ties. Still, much of *Cocoon* is genial entertainment.

Off-Screen: The movie started under the direction of Bob Zemeckis, who left the project after several preliminary meetings. The company spent three months filming on location in St. Petersburg, Florida. Don Ameche won a Best Supporting Actor Oscar for his performance. Two of the visiting aliens were played by Tahnee Welch, Raquel's daughter, and by Tyrone Power, Jr., son of the popular star of the forties. A 1988 sequel, *Cocoon: The Return,* failed to duplicate the success of the original.

The Collector

Columbia, 1965. (C-119m.) Dir: William Wyler. Sp: Stanley Mann and John Kohn, b/o novel by John Fowles. Cast: Terence Stamp, Samantha Eggar, Maurice Dallimore, Mona Washbourne.

On-Screen: *A dangerously disturbed man kidnaps a beautiful young woman.* A curious and morbid melodrama based on John Fowles's best-selling novel, *The Collector* is essentially a two-character exercise in psychological terror. Freddie Clegg (Stamp), an evident sociopath who has won a huge sum in a football pool, kidnaps Miranda Grey (Eggar), the young woman with whom he is sexually obsessed, and keeps her a prisoner in the cellar of his secluded farmhouse. A frightening cat-and-mouse game ensues in which Miranda tries desperately to escape while enduring the constantly changing moods and whims of her captor. For Freddie, Miranda is the jewel in his collection—he collects butterflies. The terror mounts until it reaches an unsettling denouement. In a surprising change of pace from his earlier films (*The Little Foxes, The Best Years of Our Lives,* etc.), William Wyler directs adroitly, and both Stamp and Eggar give exemplary performances. The screenplay, however, has a few gaps in logic (for example, why doesn't Stamp's neighbor return after one baffling visit?). Still, *The Collector* is a chilling nail-biter.

Off-Screen: Some of *The Collector* was filmed at an isolated Victorian villa in Kent, England. When Samantha Eggar proved disappointing in the first reading, the producers thought of replacing her, perhaps with Natalie Wood. But Wyler, known for his relentless way with actors, took her in hand and tyrannized her into a sterling performance. In interviews at the time the actress said, "He's the hardest man I ever worked with. I guess I was supposed to feel trapped, and I did. I lost ten pounds."

The Color of Money

Touchstone, 1986. (C–119m.) Dir: Martin Scorsese. Sp: Richard Price, b/o novel by Walter Tevis. Cast: Paul Newman, Tom Cruise, Mary Elizabeth Mastrantonio, Helen Shaver, John Turturro, Forest Whitaker, Bill Cobbs, Robert Agins.

On-Screen: *The return of pool shark Fast Eddie Felson.* Twenty-five years after Robert Rossen's *The Hustler* (1961), Eddie Felson (Newman) is back, older and wearier, and now selling liquor rather than hustling pool. Yet he still retains most of his wizardry at the game, and still has his pride, his know-how, and his tough wisdom. Along comes Vincent (Cruise), a cocky young hustler with a gift for pool, whom Eddie takes on as his protégé. ("Pool excellence is not about excellent pool. It's about becoming something . . . a student of human moves.") The relationship between the two men, old and young, forms the center to this pungent, entertaining follow-up to *The Hustler.* Scorsese doesn't aim for the cosmic soul-searching of Rossen's movie, and that may not be a bad thing. The best features are Michael Ballhaus's dazzling cinematography and Paul Newman's perfectly tuned, Oscar-winning performance as Eddie. Tom Cruise is good as the strutting young Vincent.

Off-Screen: Paul Newman's nomination for the Oscar, which he won, was his seventh. Newman had originally sent Martin Scorsese a screenplay that was literally a sequel to *The Hustler,* using scenes from that film. Scorsese came up with a different idea and assigned Richard Price to rework the script. The project was turned down by several studios before a deal was made with Touchstone.

Come Back, Little Sheba

Paramount, 1952. (99m.) Dir: Daniel Mann. Sp: Ketti Frings, b/o play by William Inge. Cast: Burt Lancaster, Shirley Booth, Terry Moore, Richard Jaeckel, Philip Ober, Edwin Max, Lisa Golm.

On-Screen: *Shirley Booth's Oscar as an alcoholic's wife.* On stage since 1925, Shirley Booth was a busy and versatile actress who projected warmth and honesty in every role. In 1950 she scored a singular triumph as Lola, the slovenly housewife who must cope with the pain and terror of an alcoholic husband. Repeating the role in her film debut, she won equal acclaim and an Academy Award. William Inge's slice-of-life play is not distinguished—for one thing, it leans too heavily on the obvious symbolism of the title—but it serves as a tour de force for Booth, who makes every wrenching moment believable and even heartbreaking. Burt Lancaster was hardly the obvious choice to play her hard-drinking husband, but he gives a fairly commendable performance of a weak, desperate man. Terry Moore is also good as the young boarder whose uninhibited sexiness stirs up trouble for Lancaster and Booth. At the end, the movie offers a stronger ray of hope than the play, but on the whole it is faithful, and a worthy effort.

Off-Screen: At first producer Hal Wallis rejected Lancaster for the role, but Lancaster persisted until he won it. The studio worked hard to make the actor look like a broken-down, middle-aged alcoholic. They dressed him in a shapeless sweater, padded his figure to make his trim waistline seem flabby, and gave him baggy trousers that made him look heavy in the hips. He also wore pale makeup over a stubble of beard.

Coming Home

United Artists, 1978. (C-127m.) Dir: Hal Ashby. Sp: Waldo Salt and Robert C. Jones, b/o story by Nancy Dowd. Cast: Jane Fonda, Jon Voight, Bruce Dern, Penelope Milford, Robert Carradine, Robert Ginty, David Clennon.

On-Screen: *An officer's wife falls for a paraplegic veteran.* A searing drama on the physical and emotional devastation inflicted by the Vietnam War, *Coming Home* is strong stuff, served up with force and conviction. Jane Fonda is the dutiful wife of Marine Captain Bruce Dern, who leaves to fight in Vietnam. Volunteer work at a veterans' hospital not only awakens her consciousness but propels her into a romance with bitter and cynical paraplegic Jon Voight. When her husband returns with deep psychic wounds that refuse to heal, the consequences are tragic. Fonda and Voight both won Academy Awards for their sensitive performances, and Dern is also fine as the troubled officer. The ultimate confrontation scene of these three principals is stunningly effective. Robert Carradine contributes a few wrenching scenes as a shattered veteran whose despair cannot be assuaged.

Off-Screen: Not kindly disposed toward Jane Fonda, the Pentagon and the Veterans Administration refused any cooperation in the filming and would not allow use of any government hospital facility. The film was shot at a civilian hospital for spinal-cord injuries in Downey, California. The male lead was turned down by Al Pacino, Jack Nicholson, and Sylvester Stallone before it went to Jon Voight. Nancy Dowd, Waldo Salt, and Robert C. Jones won Academy Awards for their story and screenplay. The film, director Hal Ashby, editor Don Zimmerman, and cast members Bruce Dern and Penelope Milford also received Oscar nominations.

Command Decision

MGM, 1948. (112m.) Dir: Sam Wood. Sp: William R. Laidlaw and George Froeschel, b/o play by William Wister Haines. Cast: Clark Gable, Walter Pidgeon, Van Johnson, Brian Donlevy, Charles Bickford, John Hodiak, Edward Arnold, Cameron Mitchell, Marshall Thompson.

On-Screen: *An Air Force general faces life-and-death decisions.* At an Air Force base in London, 1943, Brigadier-General K. C. ("Casey") Dennis knows that the bombing missions he orders over Germany are essential to winning the war. Yet the missions exact a staggering toll in lives. Tenaciously, he faces a barrage of doubt and protest from everyone, until finally his own personal anguish seeps through his steel-hard veneer. William Wister Haines's Broadway play about the torment of command in wartime was a hit, and the film is a worthy, if rather verbose, adaptation. Wisely, the movie confines itself to the tangled problems at hand without resorting to battle action in the skies. Clark Gable handles the role of Dennis competently enough—he misses much of the depth— but acting honors are won by Walter Pidgeon, whose Major-General Kane is a master of expediency and political maneuvering.

Off-Screen: On the Broadway stage during the 1947–48 season, that estimable actor, Paul Kelly, appeared as General Dennis. His sergeant was played by James Whitmore, who not long afterward went to Hollywood to launch his career in films.

Compulsion

Fox, 1959. (103m.) Dir: Richard Fleischer. Sp: Richard Murphy, b/o novel by Meyer Levin. Cast: Orson Welles, Diane Varsi, Dean Stockwell, Bradford Dillman, E. G. Marshall, Martin Milner.

On-Screen: *A brutal murder rocks Chicago in the twenties.* Adapted from Meyer Levin's best-selling novel, *Compulsion* fictionalizes one of the most shocking events of the twenties, when Nathan Leopold and Richard Loeb, young scions of wealthy Chicago families, were brought to trial for murdering a neighbor's son in cold blood. The movie traces the origins of their crime in their feelings of Nietzschean superiority, coupled with shadowed hints of homosexuality, then proceeds to the crime itself, the police investigation, and the trial. Efficiently directed by Fleischer, the screenplay sorts out all the elements to keep viewers absorbed. The actors are commendable, with Stockwell and Dillman, in particular, conveying both the frightening and pathetic sides of the partners in crime, who believe that "murder is the true test of the superior intellect." At the trial, Orson Welles turns up as their lawyer, Jonathan Wilk (actually a surrogate for famed lawyer Clarence Darrow), and he gets to orate an impassioned speech against capital punishment in that remarkable voice.

Off-Screen: After the film opened, paroled killer Nathan Leopold, contending invasion of privacy, sued Darryl F. Zanuck Productions, author Meyer Levin, and over fifty other defendants for roughly $1.5 million. Leopold asserted that he had agreed to assist Levin in writing a book only on his prison experiences. The suit was finally settled in Leopold's favor in 1964. Levin accused Leopold of showing the "barest gratitude," asserting that his book did more than anything else to get Leopold released on parole.

Coney Island

Fox, 1943. (C-96m.) Dir: Walter Lang. MS: Ralph Rainger and Leo Robin. Cast: Betty Grable, George Montgomery, Cesar Romero, Charles Winninger, Phil Silvers, Paul Hurst, Matt Briggs.

On-Screen: *Betty Grable in a turn-of-the-century musical.* One of the most popular of Fox's Betty Grable musicals of the forties, *Coney Island* has all the ingredients for a breezy, mindless wartime excursion into nostalgia: a gaudily Technicolored turn-of-the-century setting; a batch of old and new songs (the old ones—"Cuddle Up a Little Closer," "Pretty Baby"—are the best); and most of all Grable herself, shapely, immensely likable, and modestly talented. The silly but harmless plot involves two warring saloon owners (Montgomery and Romero) who both love brassy singer Grable. Several musical numbers are staged in the ghastly early-forties style, especially the elaborate finale, "There's Danger in a Dance," which pushes campiness beyond the limits of endurance. But then there's Grable, cheerfully and unpretentiously giving it her all.

Off-Screen: In his autobiography, *I Remember It Well* (Doubleday, 1974), Vincente Minnelli recalls that while *An American in Paris* was in the planning stages, Louis B. Mayer told him that he should "copy the color in *Coney Island*. In fact," he added, "all our color pictures should have that look." Producer Pandro Berman, seated nearby, whispered to Minnelli, "That picture has the most garish and vivid and ugly color in the history of the movie business." Minnelli laughed in agreement. *Coney Island* was remade in 1950 as *Wabash Avenue,* again with Betty Grable in the leading role.

Confessions of a Nazi Spy

Warners, 1939. (102m.) Dir: Anatole Litvak. Sp: Milton Krims and John Wexley, b/o story by Krims and Wexley and materials gathered by former FBI agent Leon G. Turrou. Cast: Edward G. Robinson, George Sanders, Francis Lederer, Paul Lukas, Lya Lys, Henry O'Neill, James Stephenson, Sig Rumann.

On-Screen: *FBI agent Edward G. Robinson exposes the Nazi underground.* In keeping with its reputation for combining socially conscious themes with vigorous action, Warners produced this early exposé of Nazi activities in Europe at the start of World War II. Edward G. Robinson stars as a dogged FBI man who uncovers a Nazi spy ring, including bigwigs George Sanders and Paul Lukas. Lukas, who recruits young people for the Nazi Bund, is kidnapped and beaten senseless when he tries to inform on Sanders. Francis Lederer has the most dramatic role, as a pathetically confused man who is drawn reluctantly into the spy ring. The film includes some documentary footage, including newsreel clips from a 1937 trial in which four Nazis were accused and convicted of espionage.

Off-Screen: Not surprisingly, the film incurred cries of outrage from Nazi Bundists, and from Germany, which banned it immediately. Distributors were warned about the possibility of riots started by Nazi agitators, but there seems to have been little clamor in the theaters.

The Conversation

Paramount, 1974. (C-113m.) Dir: Francis Ford Coppola. Sp: Francis Ford Coppola.

Cast: Gene Hackman, John Cazale, Teri Garr, Allen Garfield, Frederick Forrest, Cindy Williams, Michael Higgins, Harrison Ford, Elizabeth MacRae, Robert Duvall (unbilled).

On-Screen: *Coppola's thriller with a point.* In San Francisco, surveillance expert Harry Caul (Hackman), "the best bugger on the West Coast," is trailing and recording a young couple (Forrest and Williams). The tape leads him to suspect that they are potential murder victims. But are they? Harry allows his professionalism and his anonymity to disappear, and he is soon drawn into a complex and sinister labyrinth of murder and deception. The ending is devastating. *The Conversation* may well be Francis Coppola's best movie to date. Aside from being a riveting melodrama, it has much to say about personal responsibility in an age of sophisticated, modern-day surveillance, where privacy no longer has any meaning. The immediate reference may be Watergate, but the idea reverberates into our own time. Gene Hackman is brilliant as Harry Caul, a man who deliberately strips himself of any personal identity, then finds his life falling apart when he violates his own rules. Allen Garfield stands out in a supporting role as a rival wiretapper. A stunning, haunting movie.

Off-Screen: Coppola first wanted Marlon Brando for the leading role, but the actor wasn't interested. Look for future superstar Harrison Ford as a devious aide to the director, played by an unbilled Robert Duvall. Two years after this film, Cindy Williams started her long run as Shirley on the television series "Laverne and Shirley." *The Conversation* received Academy Award nominations for Best Picture and Best Original Screenplay.

Cool Hand Luke

Warners, 1967. (C-126m.) Dir: Stuart Rosenberg. Sp: Donn Pearce and Frank R. Pierson, b/o novel by Donn Pearce. Cast: Paul Newman, George Kennedy, J. D. Cannon, Lou Antonio, Robert Drivas, Strother Martin, Jo Van Fleet, Dennis Hopper, Wayne Rogers.

On-Screen: *"What we've got here is a failure to communicate."* There's a bittersweet moment at the end of the movie when Luke (Newman), a convict-hero without a cause, echoes defiantly that byline of a brutal prison guard (Martin). Up to then, Luke has been content to be a loner, visited only by his ailing mother (Van Fleet) or accompanying himself on the guitar as he sings, "I don't care if it rains or freezes, long as I got my plastic Jesus." When a fellow prisoner (Kennedy, in an Oscar-winning supporting role) severely beats him in a fight, Luke's "You're gonna have to kill me" earns him the respect of his opponent and the other inmates. When he proves he can eat fifty hard-boiled eggs in an hour, he gains their admiration. This oddly exhilarating movie doesn't explain why Luke is such a very private rebel. What's important is that in Newman's loose, casual performance, you come to believe that even a lonely man can become a hero to others.

Off-Screen: To prepare for his role, Newman got in shape by walking for long periods in leg irons and spent time in the Appalachian region of the Deep South, where the movie takes place. During the guitar-playing scene, the actor muffs a line and expresses anger at himself with tears. The error, and Newman's reaction to it, was so appropriate to the mood of the scene that director Rosenberg kept it in the movie. Novelist and screenplay coauthor Pearce acts the part of Sailor, one of the prisoners. (CFB)

The Corn Is Green

Warners, 1945. (114m.) Dir: Irving Rapper. Sp: Casey Robinson and Frank Cavett, b/o play by Emlyn Williams. Cast: Bette Davis, John Dall, Joan Lorring, Nigel Bruce, Rhys Williams, Rosalind Ivan, Mildred Dunnock, Arthur Shields.

On-Screen: *A Welsh schoolmistress nurtures the genius of a young miner.* In the role originated on stage in England by Dame Sybil Thorndike and in America by Ethel Barrymore, Bette Davis plays Miss Moffat, a discerning Welsh teacher who discovers the innate gifts of a sensitive young miner (Dall). Despite setbacks caused by his indiscretion with a local girl (Lorring), he succeeds, with Miss Moffat's help, in gaining admittance to Oxford. Although somewhat too young for the role at age thirty-six, Davis acts with becoming restraint and warmth, her love and pride shining through her dignified manner. The scenes with her young protégé are handled effectively, if a shade theatrically. ("I shall always remember," he tells Miss Moffat as they part, to which she replies, "I'm glad you think you will.") Mildred Dunnock, Rhys Williams, and Rosalind Ivan repeat the roles they played in the Broadway stage version.

Off-Screen: The studio had wanted Richard Waring to re-create his stage role as the young miner, but his date to be drafted into the service could not be postponed, and the role went to John Dall. Foolishly, Warners decided to create an asinine ad campaign for the film. Showing a glamorous-looking Davis, the ad proclaims, IN HER HEART OF HEARTS, SHE KNEW SHE COULD NEVER HOLD HIM. The title of the film was followed by the legend, A LOVE THAT RIPENED TOO FAST! Many years later, Bette Davis reprised her role in a stage-musical adaptation, *Miss Moffat,* which closed before reaching New York. Katharine Hepburn starred in a 1979 television version, directed by George Cukor as his final film.

The Cotton Club

Orion, 1984. (C-127m.) Dir: Francis Coppola. Sp: William Kennedy and Francis Coppola, b/o story by William Kennedy, Francis Coppola, and Mario Puzo. Cast: Richard Gere, Gregory Hines, Diane Lane, Bob Hoskins, Lonette McKee, Nicolas Cage, James Remar, Fred Gwynne, Maurice Hines, Gwen Verdon, Allen Garfield, Joe Dallesandro, Julian Beck, Lisa Jane Persky.

On-Screen: *Francis Coppola on Harlem's legendary nightclub.* From the early twenties to the late thirties, the Cotton Club flourished as the launching pad for some of the greatest black entertainers. Wealthy whites came "slumming" to Harlem to watch them perform, but no black person was allowed to enter—the owners were white gangsters. Francis Coppola fashions his movie against the background of this club, catching the flashy chorines, the exuberant singers and dancers, and the violent hoods in bursts of color and excitement. If production values were the only consideration, *The Cotton Club* would be wonderful—Richard Sylbert's decor and Stephen Goldblatt's cinematography are masterly. There's also some great dancing, mainly by talented Gregory Hines. Unfortunately, there's also a cliché-ridden plot involving two sets of brothers

(Gere and Cage, Hines and his true brother Maurice) whose lives and romances are tied in with the Cotton Club and its clientele. The film is not the disaster it promised to be during its stormy production history. But for all its heat and energy, it's a dispiriting effort that seldom comes alive.

Off-Screen: The turbulent story behind the making of *The Cotton Club* would fill a book by itself. The principal figures in this imbroglio were producer Robert Evans, director Francis Coppola, and star Richard Gere, supported by a bevy of money people, some with dubious credentials, a cast and crew that went from bewildered to hostile, and many hangers-on who were hoping to ride the coattails of a huge success. That perennial Hollywood conflict over "creative control" seems to have been at the heart of the dispute, but there were also many other power plays between the principals that ended in a barrage of lawsuits.

Country

Touchstone, 1984. (C-109m.) Dir: Richard Pearce. Sp: William D. Wittliff. Cast: Jessica Lange, Sam Shepard, Wilford Brimley, Levi L. Knebel, Matt Clark, Therese Graham.

On-Screen: *A modern farm family battles the Feds.* It sound like the oldest of plots: Wicked bank tries to take over family farm, but the bank is the Federal Housing Administration and the family has gone into debt because the FHA has urged them to do so. Gil and Jewell Ivy (Shepard, Lange) work their farm with their children and Jewell's father (Brimley), get along just fine, and happen to owe the FHA over $90,000. And the FHA squeezes them, harder and harder, until they face the almost certain loss not just of their

farm but also of their roots, their past. It's too much to bear, and in one painful scene, the family shatters. More than that: The entire community begins to fragment under the strain. Shepard seems to be a born farmer; Oscar-nominated Lange, womanly and strong, matches him every step of the way. All in all, the people who made this movie had something to say, and they say it with scope and power. Based on fact, *Country* is an absorbing film.

Off-Screen: Lange had long been interested in a film about the plight of the small American farmer. She carried out some research and discovered that there were many farmers who were living through a depression as bad if not worse than the Great Depression of the thirties. She became determined to make a film that would call attention to the problem. *Country* was filmed largely on location in Waterloo, Iowa, where the company worked under extremely difficult conditions, sometimes in subzero temperatures. Writer and coproducer Wittliff began as director of the movie but was replaced by Pearce. (BL)

The Country Girl

Paramount, 1954. (104m.) Dir: George Seaton. Sp: George Seaton, b/o play by Clifford Odets. Cast: Bing Crosby, Grace Kelly, William Holden, Anthony Ross, Gene Reynolds.

On-Screen: *Broadway playwright Odets's searing backstage drama.* A happy-go-lucky crooner, a patrician beauty, a romantic leading man—each starring player is cast strikingly against type in this story of the harsh world of the Broadway stage. Director Bernie Dodd (Holden) persuades Frank Elgin

(Crosby), a washed-up musical-comedy star, to make a comeback in a play Dodd will direct. He disregards the warning of Elgin's careworn wife, Georgie (Kelly), that her husband is an unreliable drunk. When the pre-Broadway tryout results in disaster, Dodd learns the shocking truth behind Elgin's alcoholism and downfall. Crosby offers a subtle, moving portrait of a dissipated, self-pitying loser. As a woman who made a bad marriage, Kelly's loyal housewife is deeply touching. "The theater and the people in it have always been a complete mystery to me," she admits. "They still are."

Off-Screen: Nominated for Oscars in six categories, including Best Picture and Best Direction, the film won two: for Seaton's adaptation of Odets's play, and for Kelly's finely tuned performance as Georgie. (Lucky for her—Jennifer Jones had been set for the part but relinquished it when she became pregnant.) At first, Crosby was vehemently opposed to playing Elgin ("I'm a crooner!"), but he was finally convinced. He was also nominated for an Oscar but lost to Marlon Brando's dockworker in *On the Waterfront.* Harold Arlen and Ira Gershwin contributed songs for Crosby's role. (CFB)

Cover Girl

Columbia, 1944. (C-107m.) Dir: Charles Vidor. Sp: Virginia Van Upp; adaptation: Marion Parsonnet and Paul Gangelin, b/o play by Erwin Gelsey. MS: Jerome Kern and Ira Gershwin. Cast: Rita Hayworth, Gene Kelly, Phil Silvers, Lee Bowman, Eve Arden, Otto Kruger, Jinx Falkenburg, Anita Colby, Leslie Brooks.

On-Screen: *A screen goddess is born, to the music of Jerome Kern.* An established star by 1944— she had danced with Fred Astaire in two

musicals—Rita Hayworth became a screen icon with this film. It is by no means a great musical, but it does mark an important transition between past and future. The backstage plot is old hat and improbable, and some of the musical numbers are deliriously silly. But the movie also looks ahead to the late forties and beyond with the emergence of Gene Kelly as an important film dancer, and in the lighthearted exuberance of some of the numbers, such as "Make Way for Tomorrow," which foreshadow the later Kelly-Sinatra teamings. Kelly's "alter ego" dance is sensational, and the Kern-Gershwin score includes the hauntingly beautiful "Long Ago and Far Away."

Off-Screen: Columbia studio head Harry Cohn originally balked at casting Gene Kelly. He was said to have shouted, "That tough Irishman with his tough Irish mug! You couldn't put him in the same *frame* with Rita! Besides, he's too short." Happily, he later relented. Cohn also insisted that famed composer Arthur Schwartz produce the movie, which Schwartz did, reluctantly. Later, Schwartz acknowledged Cohn's vulgarity but claimed he had "an instinct for quality." Actually, Schwartz's first choice for composer was Richard Rodgers, but he was unavailable. Popular British singer Gracie Fields coached Hayworth in her cockney accent for the "Poor John" number. Hayworth's songs throughout the film were dubbed by Martha Mears.

Crimes and Misdemeanors

Orion, 1989. (C-104m.) Dir: Woody Allen. Sp: Woody Allen. Cast: Martin Landau, Alan Alda, Mia Farrow, Woody Allen, Anjelica Huston, Claire Bloom, Sam Waterston, Joanna Gleason, Jerry Orbach, Caroline Aaron.

On-Screen: *Woody Allen reflects on morals and ethics in today's society.* Woody Allen's darkest and most complex film to date, *Crimes and Misdemeanors* combines drama and comedy (with decided emphasis on the former) in its view of the perversity and shaky moral structure of our times. Martin Landau is a successful ophthalmologist whose overwrought mistress (Huston) becomes a dangerous nuisance. Desperate, he agrees to have her murdered, then suffers agonies of conscience. He learns to forgive himself, however, and returns to his "protected world of wealth and privilege." Not so lucky are the film's basically decent characters, including an unhappy documentary filmmaker (Allen) who loses the girl (Farrow) he loves to his famous but fatuous brother-in-law (Alda), a TV producer. Another brother-in-law is a saintly rabbi (Waterston) who is going blind. Under God's all-observant but neutral eye, Allen tells us, the wicked prosper and the good suffer. Even the film's final words of hope and affirmation are spoken by a philosophy professor who commits suicide. Much of *Crimes and Misdemeanors* is somber, but Allen still manages to work in some satirical laughter, mostly at the expense of Alda's puffed-up character. And there are some marvelous Allenesque lines: "Show business is dog-eat-dog. It's worse than that. It's dog-doesn't-return-other-dog's-phone-calls."

Off-Screen: Oscar nominations went to Martin Landau for his superb performance as Dr. Judah Rosenthal, and to Woody Allen for his direction and screenplay. A role played by actress Sean Young was edited out of the film.

Crossfire

RKO, 1947. (86m.) Dir: Edward Dmytryk. Sp: John Paxton, b/o novel by Richard Brooks. Cast: Robert Young, Robert Ryan, Robert Mitchum, Gloria Grahame, Paul Kelly, Sam Levene, Steve Brodie, George Cooper, Jacqueline White.

On-Screen: *A murder rooted in bigotry sparks a manhunt.* A compelling *film noir* with a social conscience, *Crossfire* begins with the brutal murder of an unassuming Jew (Levene), beaten to death in his hotel room. A troubled young soldier (Cooper) is suspected, but while his buddies rally to help him, another figure—a viciously anti-Semitic ex-soldier (Ryan)—looms large in the investigation. Heading the manhunt is a police captain (Young) who knows the price of bigotry ("Hate . . . is like a gun. If you carry it around with you, it can go off and kill somebody"). Ultimately, all trails lead to Ryan and a violent showdown. Apart from the rhetoric about prejudice, *Crossfire* has all the familiar trappings of the genre: looming shadows, tough, cryptic dialogue, and offbeat characters who move through big-city streets, seedy barrooms, and run-down hotels. Most striking among the sideline players are a surly bargirl (Grahame) and the peculiar man (Kelly) who may or may not be her husband.

Off-Screen: In adapting portions of Richard Brooks's novel *The Brick Foxhole,* producer Adrian Scott had the idea of changing the victim in the story from a homosexual to a Jew. Director Dmytryk tells of an assistant sound cutter who asked him why he brought in "that stuff about anti-Semitism" when it was such a "fine suspense story." "There is no anti-Semitism in the United

States," the cutter added. "If there were, why is all the money in America controlled by Jewish bankers?" All that Dmytryk could think of saying was, "That's why we made the film." *Crossfire* earned five Oscar nominations.

A Cry in the Dark

Warners, 1988. (C-121m.) Dir: Fred Schepisi. Sp: Robert Caswell and Fred Schepisi, b/o book by John Bryson. Cast: Meryl Streep, Sam Neill, Bruce Myles, Charles Tingwell, Nick Tate, Neil Fitzpatrick.

On-Screen: *Trial by rumor devastates an Australian couple.* The sometimes insidious power of public opinion, coupled with media hysteria, to shatter and destroy lives has seldom been demonstrated as forcefully as in this true-life drama. In Australia a horrified young mother named Lindy Chamberlain (Streep) sees a wild dog carry off her infant. Instead of pity and revulsion, she and her husband Michael (Neill) find themselves the victims of rumor and, fired by nationwide hysteria fanned by the media, they are brought to trial for murder. (Their religion also worked against them.) Despite the lack of a body, or a motive, or a weapon, the trial proceeded in an atmosphere that reviled Lindy as a monster. Fred Schepisi directs this disturbing story in a near-documentary style, and Meryl Streep gives a persuasive performance as a woman who refused to play the grieving, hysterical mother for her suspicious fellow countrymen and paid a terrible price. Sam Neill is also excellent as her bewildered, supportive husband.

Off-Screen: Meryl Streep won her eleventh Oscar nomination for her performance. Reportedly, Streep had to revise her characterization after meeting Lindy Chamberlain. "It was much harder than I imagined," she remarked. Lindy made no effort to appear sympathetic or to invite pity. Her conviction was finally reversed in 1988. Even then, while observers reacted emotionally, she remained stonily silent. The next day, however, she spoke with muted rage about the suffering she had undergone at the hands of the judicial system.

Dames

Warners, 1934. (90m.) Dir: Ray Enright and Busby Berkeley. Sp: Robert Lord and Delmer Daves. MS: Harry Warren, Al Dubin, and others. Cast: Dick Powell, Ruby Keeler, Joan Blondell, ZaSu Pitts, Hugh Herbert, Guy Kibbee.

On-Screen: *Busby Berkeley strikes again.* Another entry in the series of Warners musicals featuring the lavish production numbers of Busby Berkeley, *Dames* contains some of his best work. The staging of that grand old song "I Only Have Eyes for You" is both preposterous and enchanting—how can one forget the finale of chorus girls, each with a board strapped to her back, forming a jigsaw puzzle of Ruby Keeler's face? Also mind-boggling are the title number, which wickedly turns the audience into voyeurs, and "The Girl at the Ironing Board," in which Joan Blondell leads a group of unlikely laundresses in a song-and-dance using underwear and pajamas as movable props ("When I'm off on Sundays, I miss all these undies"). *Dames* also has a plot of sorts—something about putting on a show—but it's the gaudy, crackpot musical numbers that are worth watching.

Off-Screen: Busby Berkeley often disregarded the studio's strict edicts regarding budget. For the "I Only Have Eyes for You" number, the budget called for thirty-six performers and a set cost of $15,000. By the time he was ready to go into production, Berkeley wanted 250 chorus girls and a $50,000 set. Yet the studio acknowledged Berkeley's important contribution to the film by having his name in equal-size credits to director Ray Enright.

A Damsel in Distress

RKO, 1937. (101m.) Dir: George Stevens. Sp: P. G. Wodehouse, S. K. Lauren, and Ernest Pagano, b/o book by P. G. Wodehouse. MS: George and Ira Gershwin. Cast: Fred Astaire, Joan Fontaine, George Burns, Gracie Allen, Constance Collier, Ray Noble, Reginald Gardiner, Montagu Love.

On-Screen: *Fred Astaire and company sing and dance to Gershwin music.* Temporarily deserting Ginger Rogers for RKO starlet

Joan Fontaine, Fred Astaire starred in this moderately diverting musical. The story—concerning an American dancer's involvement with a sequestered English girl—is a tribulation that must be endured to enjoy Astaire's musical numbers and the endearing dimwit comedy of Gracie Allen. Astaire sings the exquisite "A Foggy Day" in an appropriately fog-shrouded setting and tries gallantly to dance with the heavy-footed Fontaine to the strains of "Things Are Looking Up," another charming (and neglected) Gershwin tune. Best of all is the Oscar-winning fun-house number, "Stiff Upper Lip," in which Astaire, Burns, and Allen cavort through a carnival fun house. For those who can't get enough of Gershwin, there's also "Nice Work If You Can Get It" and "I Can't Be Bothered Now."

Off-Screen: Apparently many other actresses were considered for Joan Fontaine's role, among them English musical star Jessie Matthews, Ruby Keeler, Carole Lombard, and Ida Lupino. Fontaine remembers: "Before the film began, I took tap-dancing lessons from Ruby Keeler's brother, who came to the house each day with a portable wooden dance floor. Why these tap lessons, I never knew. I didn't have to do any tap steps in the film."

Dances with Wolves

Orion, 1990. (C-181m.) Dir: Kevin Costner, Sp: Michael Blake, b/o his novel. Cast: Kevin Costner, Mary McDonnell, Graham Greene, Rodney A. Grant, Floyd Red Crow Westerman.

On-Screen: *Kevin Costner's epic, award-winning Western.* "I've always wanted to see the frontier," Lieutenant John Dunbar (Costner) remarks as he sets off to the furthest reaches of the wilderness in 1865. Years later he can say, "I knew for the first time who I really was." This impressive, large-scale Western relates what happens to Dunbar in between: his discovery and embracing of the Sioux civilization and its way of life. He marries the young white woman (McDonnell) who has been raised by the Sioux, participates in their war against the Pawnees, and even destroys the American soldiers bent on wiping out the Indians. In the end, he has found his true identity at the cost of his alienation. The pace is leisurely, and the point of view lacks balance (noble savages versus scurrilous whites), but *Dances with Wolves* has sequences of imposing grandeur, especially a buffalo hunt. The actors are dwarfed by the magnificent scenery, but Mary McDonnell does well as Stands with a Fist, the "white" Indian girl who comes to love Dunbar, and Graham Greene is sympathetic as Kicking Bear, the Sioux holy man who befriends Dunbar. (The Indians speak in their native tongue, with English subtitles.) *Dances with Wolves* is long but satisfying—the equivalent of a good read.

Off-Screen: Many powers in Hollywood were deeply skeptical of a Western made by an actor with no previous directing experience, especially one that ran over three hours and featured subtitles for characters speaking in the Sioux language. Kevin Costner persisted through all the criticism. The movie received a dozen Oscar nominations, winning in seven categories, including Best Picture, Best Director, and Best Screenplay Adapted from Another Medium.

Dangerous Liaisons

Warners, 1988. (C-120m.) Dir: Stephen Frears. Sp: Christopher Hampton, b/o his play and novel by Choderlos De Laclos. Cast: Glenn Close, John Malkovich, Michelle Pfeiffer, Swoosie Kurtz, Uma Thurman, Keanu Reeves, Mildred Natwick, Peter Capaldi.

On-Screen: *Passion, betrayel, and cruelty in eighteenth-century France.* The movie begins stunningly, with the wicked and sensual Marquise de Merteuil (Close) being prepared for the day by the servants. The opulent and elegant images continue, as the story moves into areas of treachery and deceit. The Marquise and the Vicomte de Valmont (Malkovich) are deadly creatures, bored into playing dangerous games with other people's lives. The Marquise wants him to seduce the virginal fiancée (Thurman) of her ex-husband, while he intends to seduce the demure young married woman, Madame de Tourvel (Pfeiffer). If Valmont produces written proof of his seduction, the Marquise promises to give herself to him. Eventually the games of these two diabolical "virtuosos of deceit" go fatally awry, ending in death and ruination. The film is sumptuous indeed, with sets and costumes that dazzle the eye, but it is also chilly and remote, even with its last gratifying view of a distraught Marquise, shunned and disgraced by her deeds. The leading actresses are fine, and a miscast Malkovich does what he can with his reptilian role.

Off-Screen: Christopher Hampton's play, adapted from the famous period novel, appeared on Broadway in 1987. The story was also made into the 1959 French film *Les Liaisons Dangereuses* by Roger Vadim

and filmed again in 1989 as *Valmont*, with Milos Forman as director. Frears's version won Oscars for its screenplay, music score, art direction, and costume design. The movie, Close, and Pfeiffer were all nominated.

Daniel

Paramount, 1983. (C-130m.) Dir. Sidney Lumet. Sp: E. L. Doctorow, b/o his novel. Cast: Timothy Hutton, Mandy Patinkin, Lindsay Crouse, Edward Asner, Amanda Plummer, John Rubinstein, Ellen Barkin, Tovah Feldshuh, Carmen Matthews, Julie Bovasso, Norman Parker.

On-Screen: *A young man confronts his grim heritage.* Derived by E. L. Doctorow from his novel *The Book of Daniel*, this movie is patterned on the famous (and, to many, notorious) case of Julius and Ethel Rosenberg, who were executed for espionage in 1953. Timothy Hutton stars as Daniel, a young man embittered and haunted by the execution of his Communist parents, Paul and Rochelle Isaacson (Patinkin and Crouse). The film moves back and forth in time, from the days of revolutionary idealism, to the searing period of the trial, to the sixties and the anti-Vietnam protest. The intention is to relate one period to the other, and to form a sort of mosaic from the events. The effect, however, is diffuse and disconcerting—the viewer is given little time to digest a scene or to place it in its proper context. Still, there are some powerful moments: Daniel's visit with his mentally ill sister (Plummer), the children's visit to their parents in prison, and the execution of the Isaacsons. Flawed, but worthwhile.

Off-Screen: The "Free the Isaacsons" rally was filmed on 20th Street between Broadway and Fifth Avenue in New York City. Since there were no aluminum lampposts in 1953, the production used some full-size period lampposts left over from an NBC mini-series. Others were covered with a fiberglass "period" skin. As expected, the movie proved highly controversial. Conservatives thought it was too easy on the Rosenbergs, while the Old Left felt that Lumet had not gone far enough in proving their innocence. The Rosenberg sons were displeased with the poetic license the filmmakers took with events. Five songs are performed at appropriate moments by Paul Robeson.

The Dark at the Top of the Stairs

Warners, 1960. (C-123m.) Dir: Delbert Mann. Sp: Harriet Frank, Jr., and Irving Ravetch, b/o play by William Inge. Cast: Robert Preston, Dorothy McGuire, Eve Arden, Shirley Knight, Angela Lansbury, Frank Overton, Lee Kinsolving.

On-Screen: *Family travails from the William Inge play.* Set in 1920s Oklahoma, this adaptation of William Inge's Broadway success concerns what would today be called a seriously dysfunctional family. Mother Cora Flood (McGuire) is judgmental, frigid, and inclined to smother her two withdrawn, lonely children. Her robust husband Rubin (Preston) is sexually frustrated and also anxiously seeking work after losing his salesman's job. Even their relatives are troubled: Cora's sister Lottie (Arden) and her husband Morris (Overton) have been trapped for years in a loveless marriage. All this familial misery may have been affecting onstage, but on-screen it comes across as

heavily theatrical, with an emotional crisis erupting every ten minutes. Even a subplot involving an unhappy young Jewish cadet (Kinsolving) who takes a shine to the Flood daughter (Knight) smacks more of greasepaint than reality. The acting, however, is very good, with an especially appealing performance by Angela Lansbury as a warm-hearted beauty-shop owner who loves Rubin Flood. At least she injects a note of honesty into an essentially fraudulent movie.

Off-Screen: For the film, the studio built an entire Oklahoma community, circa 1920, on a large ranch off the Santa Ana freeway. It included a harness shop, a drugstore, a military school, and a business center. The movie marked Robert Preston's first screen role in over six years. Only Frank Overton was retained from the 1958 Broadway cast.

Dark Victory

Warners, 1939. (106m.) Dir: Edmund Goulding. Sp: Casey Robinson, b/o play by George Emerson Brewer, Jr., and Bertram Bloch. Cast: Bette Davis, George Brent, Geraldine Fitzgerald, Humphrey Bogart, Ronald Reagan, Cora Witherspoon, Henry Travers.

On-Screen: *Bette Davis's tour de force as a dying heiress.* Among the performances given by Bette Davis during the height of her Warners career, few are more electrifying or more poignant than her doomed Judy Traherne in *Dark Victory*. The material is pure soapsuds—a headstrong heiress learns that she has a fatal brain tumor, falls in love with and marries her doctor (Brent), then expires gallantly. Davis, however, invests the story with an honesty and emotional directness that transcends all of her usual mannerisms. From vibrant, heedless young woman to a sensitive young wife, she creates an unforgettable character. Her final scene has had generations of moviegoers sobbing into their handkerchiefs. George Brent is competent as her doctor-husband, while Geraldine Fitzgerald, in her American film debut, turns Judy's sympathetic friend into a warm and believable person. Only Humphrey Bogart, using an unconvincing Irish brogue, is rather absurd as her horse trainer who would also like to become her lover. *Dark Victory* is Bette Davis's film, and she carries it to the forefront of her most memorable work.

Off-Screen: The original play had a brief run on Broadway, with Tallulah Bankhead in the leading role. For a while, it was owned by David O. Selznick, but the film never reached production. Bette Davis had Warners buy it from Selznick as her next vehicle. Jack Warner was not enthusiastic— "Who wants to see a dame go blind?"—but he agreed to acquire it. Davis and writer Casey Robinson wanted Spencer Tracy to play the doctor, but he was unavailable. (He played the role later on radio, in an entry of "Lux Radio Theater.") *Dark Victory* won Oscar nominations for Best Picture, Best Actress (Davis), and Best Score (Max Steiner). It was remade in 1963 as *Stolen Hours* and as a television drama in 1976.

Darling Lili

Paramount, 1970. (C-136m.) Dir: Blake Edwards. Sp: Blake Edwards and William Peter Blatty. MS: Johnny Mercer and Henry Mancini. Cast: Julie Andrews, Rock Hudson, Jeremy Kemp, Lance Percival, Michael Witney, Andre Maranne, Jacques Marin.

On-Screen: *German spy disguises herself as London entertainer in World War I*. A bewildering combination of World War I flying action, romantic comedy, and musical, *Darling Lili* succeeds only intermittently with the first two aspects, while pleasing the ear with the third. Casting quintessentially British Julie Andrews as a spy working for the Germans in World War I was the first mistake. Her abundant charm cannot conceal the fact that she is playing the sort of wicked enemy spy usually assayed by someone like Gale Sondergaard. The story, which involves Andrews with flying ace Rock Hudson as both love interest and spy, is played largely with tongue in cheek, but the plot becomes increasingly incoherent, climaxing in a wild sequence aboard a train. The production is clearly expensive but the fun, on the whole, is spotty. The best feature of *Darling Lili* is the Mancini-Mercer score, especially the truly beautiful theme song, "Whistling Away the Dark."

Off-Screen: The production had many problems. Filming in Paris was interrupted by riots, while filming in Ireland was held up for weeks because of bad weather. In the end, Paramount production head Robert Evans called the movie "the most flagrant misappropriation and waste of funds I've seen in my entire career." Indeed, Edwards spared no expense in making *Darling Lili*—a press release noted that he had rented a chateau at Chantilly and hired a thousand extras just for a single scene showing Lili being awarded the Legion of Honor.

David and Bathsheba

Fox, 1951. (C-116m.) Dir: Henry King. Sp: Philip Dunne. Cast: Gregory Peck,

Susan Hayward, Raymond Massey, Kieron Moore, James Robertson Justice, Jayne Meadows, John Sutton, Dennis Hoey.

On-Screen: *King David covets another man's wife. Uh-oh.* Among the biblical epics that proliferated in the early fifties, *David and Bathsheba* remains a curiosity. Yes, it derives from the Bible, but no, it isn't really an epic with large-scale battle scenes. Instead it's a lavishly costumed soap opera concentrating on David (Peck), king of the Israelites, and his passionate affair with Bathsheba (Hayward), wife to his loyal aide, Uriah the Hittite (Moore). A noble sort who writes psalms, David suffers when he deliberately sends Uriah off to die in battle. Many others, especially the sonorous Nathan the Prophet (Massey) and David's bitter first wife Michal (Meadows), give him a hard time. The screenplay is rather dull and long-winded, and Peck gives a competent performance that only catches fire in his last scenes of atonement ("My sins are many—and terrible!"). Susan Hayward is merely beauteous as Bathsheba, and Raymond Massey does what he can with the one-note role of Nathan.

Off-Screen: Back in 1947, Darryl F. Zanuck had bought the film rights to Jacques Deval's play, *Bathsheba*, in which James Mason and his wife Pamela made their American stage debuts. The play failed, but Zanuck thought a picture could be made of it. It took four years to bring it to the screen, but by that time Philip Dunne's original screenplay was no longer derived from Deval's work. Gwen Verdon (then called Gwyneth) appears briefly as one of the palace dancers. The movie received five Oscar nominations.

David Copperfield

MGM, 1935. (130m.) Dir: George Cukor. Sp: Howard Estabrook and Hugh Walpole, b/o novel by Charles Dickens. Cast: Freddie Bartholomew, Frank Lawton, W. C. Fields, Lionel Barrymore, Basil Rathbone, Maureen O'Sullivan, Roland Young, Edna May Oliver, Elizabeth Allan, Madge Evans, Jessie Ralph, Lewis Stone.

On-Screen: *Bull's-eye version of the Dickens classic.* Gratifyingly faithful to Dickens's intertwined plots of love and cruelty, self-sacrifice and greed, this adaptation serves up most of the plum-pudding narrative. As the hero grows from boy (Bartholomew) to man (Lawton), he encounters a gallery of unforgettable characters. From such eccentrics as his great-aunt Betsey Trotwood (Oliver) and the forever impecunious Wilkins Micawber (Fields), Copperfield learns what kindness is. From Mr. Murdstone (Rathbone), his cold, rapacious stepfather, and Uriah Heep (Young), a handwringing, hypocritical clerk, Copperfield learns about evil. He moves from infatuation with Dora Spenlow (O'Sullivan) to lasting love for Agnes Wickfield (Evans). Cukor's tight direction, which extracts the essence of the sprawling Victorian work, and the seemingly heaven-ordained casting represent Hollywood at its Golden Age peak.

Off-Screen: Producer David O. Selznick at first intended releasing the lengthy film as two separate movies. He and Cukor finally persuaded studio boss Louis B. Mayer not to cast child star Jackie Cooper as young Copperfield, but Bartholomew, a ten-year-old Briton, instead. Charles Laughton reluctantly accepted the role of Micawber, but after a few days of filming, the actor realized he was wrong for the role and bowed out. Selznick was then inspired to cast Fields, whose screen image of a shrewd bumbler was ideal for the part. Except for a few scenes, the entire movie was made at the studio. It was nominated as Best Picture of the year but lost to *Mutiny on the Bounty*. A musical adaptation of the novel failed on Broadway in 1981. (CFB)

A Day at the Races

MGM, 1937. (111m.) Dir: Sam Wood. Sp: Robert Pirosh, George Seaton, and George Oppenheimer, b/o story by Robert Pirosh and George Seaton. MS: Bronislau Kaper, Walter Jurmann, and Gus Kahn. Cast: Groucho, Chico, and Harpo Marx, Allan Jones, Maureen O'Sullivan, Margaret Dumont, Douglass Dumbrille, Sig Rumann, Leonard Ceeley, Esther Muir.

On-Screen: *The Marxes at a sanitarium and a race-track (yes, both).* Following directly after the successful *A Night at the Opera* (1935), *A Day at the Races* may not be up to the high level of its predecessor, but Marx fans will not quibble. Blissful hilarity is still rampant, as the lunatic brothers help to keep Maureen O'Sullivan's sanitarium out of the villain's clutches while simultaneously dealing with High Hat, the horse owned by O'Sullivan's fiancé, Allan Jones. Groucho is Dr. Hackenbush, the newly appointed sanitarium head (actually, he's a veterinarian), Chico is a racetrack tout, and Harpo is a jockey. Memorable quips abound, along with classic Marxian sequences: Chico selling a library of racing tip books to a gullible Groucho ("Get your tutsi-frutsi ice cream!"), or Groucho's examination of Harpo ("Either he's dead or my watch has stopped!").

Off-Screen: The screenplay went through some eighteen versions before production head Irving Thalberg was satisfied. There was a bitter dispute about writing credits, with final credit gong to Pirosh, Seaton, and Oppenheimer. George S. Kaufman was involved in doctoring the script. "Dr. Hackenbush," a song written for Groucho by Bert Kalmar and Harry Ruby, was deleted from the film, but Groucho later made it part of his musical repertoire.

The Day of the Locust

Paramount, 1975. (C-144m.) Dir: John Schlesinger. Sp: Waldo Salt, b/o novel by Nathanael West. Cast: Karen Black, Donald Sutherland, William Atherton, Burgess Meredith, Geraldine Page, Billy Barty, Richard A. Dysart, Bo Hopkins.

On-Screen: *A grim vision of thirties Hollywood, by way of Nathanael West's novel.* Evangelism. Cockfights. Stag movies. Wild and dangerous excess—and shattered dreams. These are all part of the world of Hollywood in the thirties, encountered by artist (and would-be art director) Tod Hackett (Atherton) in John Schlesinger's adaptation of Nathanael West's book. Through Tod's eyes we observe the monstrous vulgarity and desperate manufacturing of dreams that West intended to symbolize the decline and fall not only of the movie colony but of America itself. Major sequences support that symbol: the horrifying collapse of a set during the filming of the battle of Waterloo; a hideous, bloody cockfight; and a premiere that turns into an apocalyptic riot. Top performances include Karen Black as a self-absorbed blonde extra; Donald Sutherland as an eccentric, repressed accountant; and Burgess Meredith as Black's tippling ex-vaudevillian father. Geraldine Page plays an evangelist who fancies herself as running "God's gas station." *The Day of the Locust* is a repellent but fascinating film.

Off-Screen: Oscar nominations went to Burgess Meredith (Best Supporting Actor) and to cinematographer Conrad Hall. Billy Barty, who plays a nasty-tempered dwarf in the movie, had a long career in films—fans of the Busby Berkeley musicals may remember him as a leering toddler in several numbers. To play Big Sister, Geraldine Page spent three weeks listening to recordings by evangelist Aimee Semple McPherson. In the scene of the giant movie premiere, Dick Powell, Jr., appears as his father, and Ginger Rogers was played by a hostess at Universal Studios.

The Day the Earth Stood Still

Fox, 1951. (92m.) Dir: Robert Wise: Sp: Edmund H. North, b/o story by Harry Bates. Cast: Michael Rennie, Patricia Neal, Hugh Marlowe, Sam Jaffe, Billy Gray, Frances Bavier, Lock Martin.

On-Screen: *Klaatu barada nikto!* At a time when many American films were equating the menace of Communism with the threat of alien invasion, one science-fiction movie took a drastically different approach and became a cult favorite. Robert Wise's *The Day the Earth Stood Still* had an intriguing premise: Klaatu (Rennie), a reasonable, dignified alien from a distant planet, comes to Earth in a spaceship and declares that its citizens must learn to live in peace or be obliterated. With the help of a young Washington widow (Neal) and her son (Gray), the ultimate disaster is averted. The movie has a few patches of absurdity, and some sequences, especially those involving crowds, are staged awkwardly, but there are diverting moments, such as when Klaatu cuts off the world's supply of electricity for thirty minutes to demonstrate his power. And how does Patricia Neal save the Earth from destruction? Look above.

Off-Screen: The spaceship, twenty-five feet high, was built on a studio backlot. It had to show no visible openings or hatches, yet had to open at certain times. The art directors incorporated an invisible split in its sides that was sealed over with soft plastic and coated with silver paint. Every time the dome of the ship was opened or closed, workmen had to reseal the split. The first choice for the role of Klaatu was Claude Rains, but he was committed to a play in New York City.

Days of Heaven

Paramount, 1978. (C-95m.) Dir: Terrence Malick. Sp: Terrence Malick. Cast: Richard Gere, Brooke Adams, Sam Shepard, Linda Manz, Robert Wilke, Jackie Shultis, Stuart Margolin.

On-Screen: *A fatal love triangle in the Texas panhandle.* The images are stunningly beautiful: an isolated farmhouse in a vast expanse of land; wheat dancing in the wind; simple folk holding church services in the fields; a nighttime square dance. Cinematographer Nestor Almendros (with additional photography by Haskell Wexler) fully deserved his

Oscar for *Days of Heaven*. The story is simple: In 1916, traveling south from Chicago, Gere, his girlfriend Adams, and his teenage sister Manz find work in the wheat fields of Shepard, a wealthy young farmer. Shepard falls for Adams, with consequences that are ultimately deadly. The bleak tragedy of the story is offset in part by Manz's quirky, ingenuous narration. After a while, the scenes begin to seem too artfully arranged, like a series of slide entries in a photography contest, but they are beautiful nonetheless. Gere seems too contemporary for his role, but Shepard is the very embodiment of the raw-boned farmer whose ordered life is suddenly changed.

Off-Screen: Alberta, Canada, stood in for Texas in the film. It took two years for Malick to complete the film, since he waited for the actual change of seasons in the area. John Travolta was the original choice for the role that went to Richard Gere.

Days of Wine and Roses

Warners, 1962. (117m.) Dir: Blake Edwards. Sp: J. P. Miller, b/o his television play. Cast: Jack Lemmon, Lee Remick, Jack Klugman, Charles Bickford, Alan Hewitt, Jack Albertson, Debbie Megowan.

On-Screen: *Powerful drama of a couple's descent into alcoholism.* "We get drunk, and we stay drunk most of the time," Joe (Lemmon) states flatly to his wife, Kirsten (Remick). When the two first meet, their problem hasn't surfaced; but as Joe's work pressures mount (he's an advertising executive), he finds both relief and release in the bottle. Soon, Kirsten joins her husband in drunken bouts, and as Joe loses job after job, they also lose touch with their daughter, Debbie

(Megowan). How this pair fight their addiction is shown graphically and without sentimentality. Though Remick is effective as the tormented Kirsten, it's Lemmon's portrayal of a ravaged alcoholic that gives the movie its starkly realistic quality. Coming after his series of richly comic performances, most notably in *Some Like It Hot*, the film reveals the actor's first-rate dramatic talents.

Off-Screen: Although Lemmon and Remick were nominated for Best Actor and Actress Oscars, the film's sole award went to Henry Mancini and Johnny Mercer for their haunting title song. Initially Fox was set to produce Miller's adaptation of his 1958 "Playhouse 90" television drama, in which Cliff Robertson and Piper Laurie gave outstanding performances (Bickford is the only holdover from that cast). However, the heavy costs of the studio's *Cleopatra*, as yet unreleased, resulted in the sale of the property to Warners, who were willing not only to film their downbeat story, but to cast funnyman Lemmon as well. (CFB)

Dead Again

Paramount, 1991. (C-108m.) Dir: Kenneth Branagh. Sp: Scott Frank. Cast: Kenneth Branagh, Emma Thompson, Andy Garcia, Derek Jacobi, Hanna Schygulla, Robin Williams (unbilled).

On-Screen: *Gripping thriller-romance merges past with present.* Gumshoe Mike Church (Branagh) meets up with Grace (Thompson), an amnesiac haunted by nightmares of a concert pianist murdered by her jealous husband, a famous conductor-composer. Trouble is, Grace herself is the victim in her dreams and Mike's a ringer for her killer.

Are Grace and Mike reincarnations from the scandal that rocked Los Angeles forty years before? Reversals and surprises abound, supplied by an eccentric hypnotist with an odd interest in antiques (Jacobi), a romantic reporter (Garcia) involved in the long-ago murder who's now barely alive, and a gurulike butcher (Williams). The cast shines, though a few startling plot twists are a bit murky. Film buffs will revel in echoes of classic creepers such as *Rebecca*, *Laura*, and *Vertigo*.

Off-Screen: Originally, Frank's screenplay was written for four actors to play the past and present-day couples. Though Branagh is Belfast-born and Thompson is English, their American accents are flawless (Branagh also manages a soft German inflection for one of his roles). The youth who tries to abscond with Thompson-as-Grace is played by Campbell Scott, son of George C. Scott and Colleen Dewhurst. (CFB)

Dead End

United Artists, 1937. (93m.) Dir: William Wyler. Sp: Lillian Hellman, b/o play by Sidney Kingsley. Cast: Sylvia Sidney, Joel McCrea, Humphrey Bogart, Claire Trevor, Marjorie Main, Wendy Barrie, Allen Jenkins, Ward Bond, The Dead End Kids.

On-Screen: *The lives of New York slum residents undergo many changes.* This once-hailed film version of the 1935 Broadway hit seems tame in contrast with today's dramas of inner-city violence. Still, the gritty realism of Hellman's adaptation and Wyler's first-rate cast continue to stir our emotions. Sidney, in her customary long-suffering, slum-girl role, and McCrea, a struggling ar-

chitect, are the film's nominal leads, but it is a charismatic Bogart who steals the limelight as "Baby Face" Martin, a swaggering killer and hero to young gangs roaming his former turf. There are also outstanding performances from Main, Martin's bitter mother who despises her born-loser son, and Trevor, an old girlfriend, now a prostitute. Richard Day's production design— seedy tenements abutting posh apartment houses along New York's East River—and Gregg Toland's photography were nominated for Oscars. The film itself and Trevor (Best Supporting Actress) also won Oscar nominations.

Off-Screen: George Raft left the door ajar for Bogart when he turned down the movie's pivotal role, as he would again when he rejected leading parts in *High Sierra* and *The Maltese Falcon*. Wyler had counted on using actual New York locations for the movie, but producer Samuel Goldwyn assigned Day, his "house" designer, to create the gigantic set. Main reprised her intensely dramatic Broadway performance, as did the six Dead End Kids, who thrived variously in later movies as The East Side Kids, The Little Tough Guys, and The Bowery Boys. (CFB)

Dead Poets Society

Touchstone, 1989. (C-128m.) Dir: Peter Weir. Sp: Tom Schulman. Cast: Robin Williams, Robert Sean Leonard, Ethan Hawke, Josh Charles, Gale Hansen, Dylan Kussman, Allelon Ruggiero, Norman Lloyd.

On-Screen: *A new teacher causes an upheaval at a prep school.* The year is 1959. At Welton School, an exclusive prep school for boys where individualism and initiative are discouraged, English teacher John Keating (Williams) is a startling new arrival. Charismatic and audacious, he urges his students to "seize the day" and find "their own voice." He tells them about the Dead Poets Society, a secret group dedicated to poetry and to evoking its romantic spirit. Keating's approach challenges his students but, inevitably, it leads to trouble and, eventually, tragedy. Tom Schulman's Oscar-winning screenplay is provocative (and also rather predictable) but its ambivalence raises the question of whether encouraging impressionable youngsters to think and to act on their feelings can be hazardous as well as stimulating. Keating himself learns that there are risks as well as rewards. In his Oscar-nominated performance, Robin Williams keeps reasonable control of his usual manic personality, and the young actors are just right in their roles. The other adult characters, however, are incredibly obtuse and stuffy.

Off-Screen: At first Robin Williams rejected the role of John Keating until director Peter Weir was signed to direct and the screenplay was revised. The original version had Keating dying of leukemia. Tom Schulman set his screenplay in 1959 because, he said, "I believed there was a certain innocence there; it was a time when many things were about to happen."

The Deer Hunter

Universal, 1978. (C-183m.) Dir: Michael Cimino. Sp: Deric Washburn, b/o story by Michael Cimino, Deric Washburn, Louis Garfinkle, and Quinn K. Redeker. Cast: Robert De Niro, Christopher Walken, Meryl Streep, John Savage, George Dzunda, John Cazale, Chuck Aspegren.

On-Screen: *Three steelworker friends feel the impact of the Vietnam War.* An often stirring if somewhat self-indulgent drama, *The Deer Hunter* traces the lives of three men (De Niro, Walken, Savage) in a Pennsylvania steel town before, during, and after their tribulations in the Vietnam War. Mike (De Niro) is the fulcrum of the trio, and the film's central character—as "macho" as the others, but with his own code of responsible behavior. After a long (actually overlong) section establishing what is good and traditional in their lives (Savage's wedding, a deer hunt that becomes a ritual of manhood), the film veers shockingly into the men's harrowing experiences in Vietnam. Their lives will never be the same, and although Mike is the only one who escapes without physical or emotional scars, even he is drastically changed. Although he allows some scenes to run too long, Michael Cimino does a masterful job of tying together the film's many complex elements. The acting is splendid—De Niro creates a fully rounded character in Mike and Walken won a Supporting Oscar for his stunning performance as the doomed, despairing Nick.

Off-Screen: On the whole, *The Deer Hunter* was widely praised, although its themes and attitudes were deemed highly controversial by some critics. Many objected (and Cimino himself admitted) that the terrifying Russian roulette sequence was purely fictional. In addition to Walken's Oscar, *The Deer Hunter* was honored as the year's Best Picture, and other Oscars were awarded for direction, sound, and editing. Chuck Aspegren, who plays Axel, was an actual steelworker in the U.S. Steel plant in Gary, Indiana.

The Defiant Ones

United Artists, 1958. (97m.) Dir: Stanley Kramer. Sp: Nathan E. Douglas and Harold Jacob Smith. Cast: Tony Curtis, Sidney Poitier, Cara Williams, Lon Chaney, Jr., Theodore Bikel, Charles McGraw, Claude Akins, Carl Switzer.

On-Screen: *Southern fugitives are caught in a racial conflict.* Johnny (Curtis), white and bigoted, and Cullen (Poitier), black and belligerent, must do two things: outrun the sheriff (Bikel) and smash the wrist-binding shackles that join them in mutual hatred. A sympathetic ex-con (Chaney) saves them from a lynching, and a lonely young mother (Williams), with an agenda of her own, separates them. Or so she thinks. Curtis and Poitier's intense performances (both were nominated for the Best Actor Oscar) make this "message" film worth seeing, despite its glaring improbabilities. The fugitives never lack cigarettes nor need a shave, the woman displays an unlikely calm in the presence of the gun-waving cons, and a swamp conveniently fails to live up to its reputation. But Chaney's empathy with the fleeing duo and Poitier's singing of the poignant blues classic "Long Gone" are moments to cherish.

Off-Screen: Some thought that Smith and Douglas's dialogue had more than its share of Tennessee Williams's sultry Southern style; others regarded the story's plea for racial tolerance as dangerously leftist. (Douglas, whose face is seen in the opening credits, was actually the blacklisted writer Nedrick Young.) However, the writers received an Oscar for Best Original Screenplay. Gossip-monger Hedda Hopper sniffed that if it won, outraged former Oscar winners would relinquish their statuettes. None did.

Sam Leavitt also won an Oscar for his black-and-white photography, and the movie received a number of other nominations, including one for Best Picture. The story was remade as a television movie in 1986. (CFB)

Deliverance

Warners, 1972. (C-109m.) Dir: John Boorman. Sp: James Dickey, b/o his novel. Cast: Jon Voight, Burt Reynolds, Ned Beatty, Ronny Cox, Billy McKinney, Herbert "Cowboy" Coward.

On-Screen: *Atlanta businessmen confront primitive evil on a canoe trip.* As a break from office routine, four friends set out for a weekend of white-water canoeing in Georgia's magnificently scenic Appalachian region. Tragedy overtakes them when one of the trekkers plunges into the swift-flowing river. More to be reckoned with than nature, however, is mankind itself, as one of a pair of psychopathic mountain men (McKinney, Coward) sexually attacks the hapless member (Beatty) of the group. The entire cast couldn't be more convincing. Reynolds plays the macho, nature-loving weekender; Voight, his buddy forced by ever-mounting dangers to become a leader. Both become killers. It falls to Cox, the gentle member of the party, to provide one of the film's few moments of repose and tenderness when, early on, he plays guitar in a duet with a retarded, but gifted, youngster and his banjo. This disturbing, grimly brilliant movie will remain with you for a long, long time.

Off-Screen: British director Boorman and cinematographer Vilmos Zsigmond shot the movie on the Chattooga River and at Tallulah Falls, in northern Georgia's Rabun County. Poet-novelist Dickey not only got to adapt his work for the screen (a rare privilege for a writer), but also plays Sheriff Bullard. Boorman's son Charley (spelled "Charlie" in the credits) appears briefly as Voight's son. "Duelling Banjos," based on "Feudin' Banjos," was arranged and played by Eric Weissberg and Steve Mandel. The movie was Oscar-nominated for Best Picture, Director, and Film Editing. (CFB)

The Desperate Hours

Paramount, 1955. (112m.) Dir: William Wyler. Sp: Joseph Hayes, b/o his novel and play. Cast: Humphrey Bogart, Fredric March, Martha Scott, Arthur Kennedy, Dewey Martin, Mary Murphy, Gig Young, Richard Eyer, Robert Middleton.

On-Screen: *Vicious escaped convict Humphrey Bogart versus home-and-hearth Fredric March.* You've seen it before: A nice American family, held captive in their home by hoodlums on the run, triumph over their adversaries through their pluck and resourcefulness. *The Desperate Hours*, derived by Joseph Hayes from his own novel and Broadway play, has escaped hood Humphrey Bogart hiding out in the home of family man Fredric March. Guess who wins the day. Surprisingly, since the movie was directed by the usually unfailing William Wyler, it seems all wrong. Many of the actors, including leads Bogart and March, are years too old for their roles, some of the plot details are handled clumsily, the police are exceptionally inept and overbearing, and, most importantly, the decision of paterfamilias March not to contact the police once he's allowed to leave his house seems

rather dubious. In his next-to-last role, Humphrey Bogart returns to the sort of nasty gangster he often played early in his career, most notably in *The Petrified Forest* (1936).

Off-Screen: The behavior of Fredric March in failing to contact the police once he's allowed out of his besieged home was questioned by critic Bosley Crowther in a follow-up review of the movie in *The New York Times*. Crowther wondered whether author Joseph Hayes really believed that March did the right thing, or was it "a temporary assumption" he had made "for the purposes of plot?" Hayes responded with a letter to the *Times* in which he defended his premise. Judge for yourself. Paul Newman played Bogart's role in the 1955 stage version. *The Desperate Hours* was poorly remade in 1991, with Mickey Rourke and Anthony Hopkins.

Destination Moon

Eagle-Lion, 1950. (C-91m.) Dir: Irving Pichel. Sp: Rip Van Ronkel, Robert A. Heinlein, and James O'Hanlon, b/o novel by Robert A. Heinlein. Cast: John Archer, Warner Anderson, Tom Powers, Dick Wesson, Erin O'Brien Moore.

On-Screen: *A group of men travel to the moon—and back.* Producer George Pal's company won a 1950 Oscar for the imaginative special effects created for this modestly made but amusing pioneer film on space exploration. Unavoidably naive and simplistic (but fun), *Destination Moon* takes a group of men on the first voyage to the moon, then drums up a fair amount of suspense as to whether they can return to Earth. The early portions of preparation for the trip are the best (there's even a Woody Woodpecker cartoon to explain the principle of rocket propulsion), but the latter part bogs down in unconvincing theatrics. Inevitably, someone is on hand to offer the expected hortatory remarks about space exploration ("The race is on, and we'd better win it!"), but the Technicolor is vivid, and the rocket-ship hardware should entertain space buffs.

Off-Screen: The film's moonscape was the combined effort of astronomical painter Chesley Bonestell and art director Ernst Fegte. It took one hundred men over two months to build. George Pal fought with the backers, who, fearing that the movie would fail, wanted drastic changes. Pal won, and the movie represents his vision.

Destry Rides Again

Universal, 1939. (94m.) Dir: George Marshall. Sp: Felix Jackson, Gertrude Purcell, and Henry Myers, b/o novel by Max Brand. Cast: James Stewart, Marlene Dietrich, Brian Donlevy, Charles Winninger, Mischa Auer, Una Merkel, Billy Gilbert, Samuel S. Hinds, Irene Hervey, Jack Carson.

On-Screen: *A rowdy new Dietrich invades the Wild West.* After years as an exotic if rather remote movie queen, Marlene Dietrich revitalized her fading career by starring as the coarse, lusty saloon singer Frenchy in this lively, enormously popular Western comedy. Whether singing "The Boys in the Back Room" in that inimitable voice, or grappling with Una Merkel in an unladylike free-for-all, she surprised moviegoers with her new, more accessible personality. Her Frenchy also has a heart of gold, as she

changes sides to help Destry (Stewart), Bottleneck's gawky, mild-mannered new sheriff, defeat the wicked town boss (Donlevy). *Destry Rides Again* is great entertainment as it pokes fun at the familiar Western conventions, ending with a noisy brawl in which club-wielding women do battle with the town's corrupt element. Jimmy Stewart is amiable in the role that cowboy star Tom Mix had played earlier (1932) and that Audie Murphy would play again (1954). But it's Dietrich's hot-tempered Frenchy that everyone recalls.

Off-Screen: The famous cat fight left both Dietrich and Una Merkel badly bruised. Dietrich refused to have a stand-in; she pulled Merkel's hair and wrestled, punched, and kicked her incessantly. The scene required five days of shooting. Originally, Dietrich had laughed at the very idea of being cast in a Western, but after much cajoling by producer Joe Pasternak, she accepted the role. The durable story even became a short-lived Broadway musical in 1959.

Detective Story

Paramount, 1951. (103m.) Dir: William Wyler. Sp: Philip Yordan and Robert Wyler, b/o play by Sidney Kingsley. Cast: Kirk Douglas, Eleanor Parker, William Bendix, Horace McMahon, Lee Grant, Joseph Wiseman, Michael Strong, Cathy O'Donnell, Bert Freed, George Macready.

On-Screen: *Matters of life and death at a New York police station.* Although its stage origins show—it was a hit Broadway play—*Detective Story* still impresses with its vigorous, if melodramatic, story of a cop (Douglas) at the end of his tether. The son of a criminal who drove his wife to insanity, Douglas is a relentless, unforgiving "one-man army against crime." When his own wife (Parker) reveals a sordid incident in her past, his moral world collapses. As the tormented protagonist, Douglas gives his usual intense, coiled-spring performance, but he undoubtedly commands the attention. Repeating her stage role, Lee Grant is marvelous (and was Oscar-nominated) as a pathetic shoplifter, and you aren't likely to forget Joseph Wiseman (also repeating from the stage) as a psychopathic hoodlum.

Off-Screen: Dashiell Hammett first worked on the screenplay, but he dropped out. In spite of director Wyler's authoritarian ways, Kirk Douglas found working with him a rewarding and instructive experience. After the filming, he wrote Wyler: "For the first few days, you . . . seemed to be wrapped in an impenetrable shell, and I'm a guy who needs a very personal contact. But once, when you didn't know it, you had your guard down, and I saw under it a very warm, human person. . . . This won me over completely, and for this I forgive all the whiplashes across the back that you gave me during the course of the picture."

Dial M for Murder

Warners, 1954. (C-105m.) Dir: Alfred Hitchcock. Sp: Frederick Knott, b/o his play. Cast: Grace Kelly, Ray Milland, Robert Cummings, John Williams, Anthony Dawson.

On-Screen: *Ray Milland's scheme to murder Grace Kelly takes an unexpected turn in Alfred Hitchcock's thriller*. Originally a stage hit in London and on Broadway, *Dial M for Murder* is a taut and tidy melodrama that Hitchcockians would place among the middle range of the director's movies. Working from Knott's stock characters, Hitchcock achieves much of the film's tension by confining virtually all the action to a comfortable London flat (similar to the single-set restrictions of *Rope* and *Rear Window*). The film's chief suspense follows Kelly's disposal of her would-be murderer (Dawson), hired by scheming husband Milland. Though Milland's plan has backfired, he can still eliminate Kelly through the courts of law. John Williams's shrewd police inspector ("People don't commit murder on credit"), Robert Cummings's American writer, and an all-important latchkey bring this neatly plotted nail-biter to its conclusion.

Off-Screen: Although the movie is a gripping, almost-perfect crime thriller, Hitchcock dismissed it as a time-marker while he waited to move on to *Rear Window*. It was shot in a then-faddish 3-D process (special glasses merged two images), and Hitchcock took shrewd advantage of the gimmick when Grace Kelly reaches out from the screen, groping for a weapon with which to fend off Anthony Dawson. When the film was released, the 3-D novelty had already passed, and most audiences saw it in the conventional format. You can glimpse Hitchcock's "signature" appearance in the reunion photograph; he is seated to the left of the right-hand table. A television remake of *Dial M for Murder* turned up in 1981. (CFB)

The Diary of Anne Frank

Fox, 1959. (170m.) Dir: George Stevens. Sp: Frances Goodrich and Albert Hackett, b/o their play and book by Anne Frank. Cast: Joseph Schildkraut, Millie Perkins, Shelley Winters, Richard Beymer, Lou Jacobi, Ed Wynn, Gusti Huber, Diane Baker.

On-Screen: *Two Jewish families hide out from the Nazis.* First it was a book, derived from the actual diary of Anne Frank, a Jewish girl living in Amsterdam during World War II and forced to hide in an attic with her family. Then it was a long-running Broadway play. Beautifully handled by George Stevens, the film version conveys the claustrophobic terror, the petty squabbling, and the fleeting moments of happiness experienced by the Franks and their neighbors, the Van Damms. Scenes of simple joys (dancing to the music from a new radio, celebrating Chanukah with little handmade presents) alternate with scenes of almost unbearable suspense when they fear they have been discovered. Perkins works hard to capture Anne's sweetness, naïveté, and idealism, but neither she nor Beymer, as young Peter Van Damm, are up to their roles. The adults fare much better: Schildkraut repeating his stage role as Mr. Frank, Wynn as a vexing dentist who joins the group, and Winters in her Oscar-winning performance as the shrill Mrs. Van Damm.

Off-Screen: George Stevens brought Anne's father Otto from Europe to assist in the film's production. After visiting the Frank hideaway in Amsterdam, he built a cutaway, four-story replica of the apartment house. To simulate the effects of an air raid, he had the attic reconstructed on wooden pillars and steel locomotive springs, so that when the crew pulled out the supports, the entire room dropped six inches and bounced. William C. Mellor's cinematography won an Oscar, as did the art direction. There were a number of nominations, including Best Picture. A television remake appeared in 1980.

Dick Tracy

Touchstone, 1990. (C-105m.) Dir: Warren Beatty. Sp: Jim Cash and Jack Epps, Jr., b/o characters created by Chester Gould. Cast: Warren Beatty, Madonna, Al Pacino, Dustin Hoffman, Glenne Headly, Charlie Korsmo, James Caan, Charles Durning, Mandy Patinkin, Dick Van Dyke, William Forsythe.

On-Screen: *Beloved comic strip brought to life, more or less.* For all the makeup piled on Pacino, Caan, Forsythe (Big Boy Caprice, Spaldoni, Flattop, respectively), and other guest stars masquerading as Gould's endearing grotesques, this movie is less a cartoon infused with new life (as *Batman* was) than a dead weight. Lacking the snappy spirit of the original strip, Beatty's direction is as lifeless as his yellow-trenchcoated police detective. Headly's Tess Trueheart fades into the sets; Madonna, who performs Stephen Sondheim songs, breathes little life into Breathless Mahoney. Only Korsmo, as the homeless Kid adopted by Tracy and Trueheart, creates a person whom you really care about. Richard Sylbert's production design, stylishly evoking urban 1938, is the best (maybe the only) reason to see the movie.

Off-Screen: It took over ten years to transfer Cash and Epps's script to the screen. In 1977 rights had been acquired to film the Gould comic strip, which began life in the Detroit *Mirror* in 1931. John Landis was set to direct, but he moved on to other projects when Clint Eastwood declined to play

Tracy. The production finally got under way when Beatty agreed both to direct and star. The movie won Oscars for makeup, art direction, and for Sondheim's "Sooner or Later (I Always Get My Man)". Jut-jawed Ralph Byrd played the crime-stopper in thirties and forties serials and cofeatures, and on television in the 1950–51 season. (CFB)

Die Hard

Fox, 1988. (C-131m.) Dir: John McTiernan. Sp: Jeb Stuart and Steven E. de Souza, b/o novel by Roderick Thorp. Cast: Bruce Willis, Alan Rickman, Bonnie Bedelia, Alexander Godunov, Reginald VelJohnson, De'voreaux White, William Atherton, Hart Bochner.

On-Screen: *A cop tangles with terrorist thieves in a catch-your-breath thriller.* Christmas Eve at a party given by a large corporation in an ultramodern building in Los Angeles. Suddenly a band of mostly German terrorists, led by Hans Gruber (Rickman) breaks in with the goal of stealing $600 million worth of negotiable bonds locked in the vault. Unknown to the terrorists, John McClane (Willis), a New York cop visiting his ex-wife (Bedelia) who works for the company, has eluded them and is desperately trying to let the outside world know what's taking place. Soon McClane and the terrorists are engaged in an explosive, deadly, cat-and-mouse game that spreads throughout the building. *Die Hard* churns up so much suspense and anxiety that you may not have time to notice its many absurdities. Bruce Willis gives the story some welcome humor by applying the smart-aleck persona of his television "Moonlighting" character to the straight-action role of cop McClane. *Die*

Hard is formula material, but also a genuine nail-biter.

Off-Screen: Most of the movie was filmed in and around the thirty-four-story Plaza Building, which towers over Century City, California, and also on a spectacular indoor set on Stage 15 at Fox. Three models of the Plaza Building were constructed, including one about twenty-five feet high. These substituted for the actual building in several major sequences. *Die Hard 2*, a sequel duplicating the same situations at a different locale (Washington's Dulles Airport) was released in 1990, with Willis, Bedelia, VelJohnson, and Atherton repeating their roles. *Die Hard 3* turned up in 1993.

Diner

MGM/UA, 1982. (C-110m.) Dir: Barry Levinson. Sp: Barry Levinson. Cast: Steve Guttenberg, Daniel Stern, Mickey Rourke, Ellen Barkin, Kevin Bacon, Timothy Daly, Paul Reiser, Michael Tucker.

On-Screen: *A group of Baltimore friends share their lives.* Baltimore. Christmas 1959. Perched at the close of one decade and about to enter another, a group of close friends gather daily at the Fells Point Diner to chat, argue, and contemplate an uncertain future. Among them are Eddie (Guttenberg), about to be married but only if his wife-to-be can pass a football quiz; Boogie (Rourke), a soft-spoken womanizer who has shady dealings with gamblers; Fenwick (Bacon), intelligent, wealthy, and burdened with private despair; and the uneasily married Shrevie (Stern). During the course of the film, relationships shift and change as the young men move toward the serious concerns of adulthood. Secretly terrified by new challenges, these characters seek ways to avoid facing them, from Eddie's football quiz for his fiancée to Shrevie's beloved record collection, the center of his emotional life. Marking Barry Levinson's debut as a director, *Diner* is an exuberant, affectionate, and touching view of the shaky bridge between adolescence and maturity. Anyone for french fries with gravy?

Off-Screen: Barry Levinson admitted to basing many of his characters on friends from his early years in Baltimore. The movie fared poorly in previews until critics began shouting its praises. Ellen Barkin and Paul Reiser both made their film debuts in this movie. In 1983, a pilot film based on the movie was shown on CBS, but it never developed into a series.

Dinner at Eight

MGM, 1933. (133m.) Dir: George Cukor. Sp: Frances Marion, Herman J. Mankiewicz, and Donald Ogden Stewart, b/o play by George S. Kaufman and Edna Ferber. Cast: Marie Dressler, John Barrymore, Wallace Beery, Jean Harlow, Lionel Barrymore, Billie Burke, Lee Tracy, Edmund Lowe, Madge Evans.

On-Screen: *A glittering cast serves up a tasty comedy-drama.* Host Lionel Barrymore and hostess Burke are unaware of the tangled lives of the guests they've invited to a dinner party at their posh Manhattan apartment. John Barrymore is cast perfectly as a has-been movie idol who's been philandering with his hosts' engaged daughter (Evans). And Beery is just right as a boorish wheeler-dealer about to sink their shipping business. The movie, though, really belongs to comediennes Harlow and Dressler. Har-

low is hilarious as Beery's brash wife, a socially ambitious ex–hatcheck girl, and Dressler is magnificent as an aging, celebrated actress. When Harlow makes a game try at light conversation—"I was reading a book the other day"—Dressler's lurch-and-stagger double take is a classic moment in movies. Her scene with Lionel Barrymore, in which she talks about the vanished golden days, is also indelible. The lines sparkle, the cast gleams, the movie enthralls. *Bon appetit!*

Off-Screen: Producer David O. Selznick, having seen the 1932 Kaufman-Ferber play, asked writer Stewart to provide a more upbeat ending for the movie version, which resulted in the memorable closing exchange between Dressler and Harlow. Beery and Harlow despised each other even more than their on-screen characters; he thought she was a tramp, and she loathed his crude ways. Clark Gable was slated to play the adulterous Dr. Talbot, but studio chief Louis B. Mayer feared that movie fans would be disappointed to see their rugged hero in an unsympathetic role. The name of Marie Dressler's dog was changed from Mussolini to Tarzan when the Italian government objected. *Dinner at Eight* was remade for television in 1989. (CFB)

Dirty Dancing

Vestron, 1987. (C-97m.) Dir: Emile Andolino. Sp: Eleanor Bergstein. Cast: Patrick Swayze, Jennifer Grey, Jerry Orbach, Cynthia Rhodes, Jack Weston, Jane Brucker, Kelly Bishop, Lonny Price, Charles "Honi" Coles.

On-Screen: *A young girl learns about life and dancing.* Coming to a summer resort with her family, young Francis Kellerman (Grey), known as "Baby," discovers the mysteries of sex, a few of the hard truths about life, and the techniques of dancing as entertainment. That's a lot of ground to cover, and much of the material is familiar, but *Dirty Dancing* has a nice sense of detail about time and place (summer of 1963, Kellerman's Mountain Lodge), and it offers up the story with some honesty and conviction. The dancing (dirty or otherwise) is more linked to the eighties than the sixties, but it hardly matters, since it's very good indeed (courtesy of Kenny Ortega). Patrick Swayze, in a charismatic performance, plays Johnny Castle, the streetwise but actually sensitive young man with whom Baby falls in love. They perform several sensual dances together.

Off-Screen: *Dirty Dancing* was filmed mostly at a hotel in Mountain Lakes, Virginia, in September of 1986. One of the film's songs, "(I've Had) The Time of My Life," won an Academy Award. In 1988, the movie became the basis for a short-lived television show with the same title.

The Dirty Dozen

MGM, 1967. (C-150m.) Dir: Robert Aldrich. Sp: Nunnally Johnson and Lukas Heller, b/o novel by E. M. Nathanson. Cast: Lee Marvin, Ernest Borgnine, John Cassavetes, Robert Ryan, Telly Savalas, George Kennedy, Donald Sutherland, Jim Brown, Ralph Meeker, Richard Jaeckel, Clint Walker, Trini Lopez.

On-Screen: *An army major leads twelve criminals on a wartime mission.* An enormously successful war film in its time, *The Dirty Dozen* even had some clout several decades later when a series of television specials used it as a jumping-off point. The question is why, since the movie is dreadful. For one thing, the premise is ridiculous: During World War II, a maverick army major trains a dozen criminals—murderers, rapists, etc.—for a mission to destroy a German-occupied chateau in France. Whoever survives *may* be given amnesty. For another thing, a surprising amount of footage over a very long movie is given over to raucous, unfunny comedy involving the one-upmanship of the disreputable, dangerous dozen. Even the ramshackle World War II comedies did it better. And as the topping on a rancid cake, the climax involves the actual mission, as sadistic and repellent a sequence as you will ever see. (Highlight: Scores of German officers and their women are immolated in an underground bunker.) Lee Marvin heads the cast in his usual hard-bitten style, but poor Robert Ryan is burdened with the butt-of-the-humor role that usually went to someone like Paul Ford or Ernie Kovacs.

Off-Screen: Nunnally Johnson was dismayed when Robert Aldrich brought in his own writer, Lukas Heller, during filming to revise the screenplay. The question of screen credit had to be arbitrated by the Writers Guild. It was decided that both names should appear on the credits. John Wayne was offered the leading role but declined in favor of *The Green Berets*. Jack Palance turned down the role that went to Telly Savalas.

Dirty Harry

Warner, 1971. (C-102m.) Dir: Don Siegel. Sp: Harry Julian Fink, R. M. Fink, and Dean Riesner, b/o story by Harry Julian Fink and

R. M. Fink. Cast: Clint Eastwood, Harry Guardino, Reni Santoni, Andy Robinson, John Larch, John Vernon, John Mitchum.

On-Screen: *Gun smoking, "Dirty" Harry Callahan enters the movie scene.* If film technique were all, *Dirty Harry* would rank high among tough police melodramas. Don Siegel's direction takes us into the less glamorous heart of San Francisco, and his editor (Carl Pingitore) and cinematographer (Bruce Surtees) make it vivid and compelling. But then there's the story to consider, and all that expertise appears to be in the service of a very dubious premise. Clint Eastwood introduces his character of Inspector Harry Callahan, an uncompromising cop who has his own code of justice and retribution. At the moment he's obsessed with tracking down a deranged serial killer (Robinson) who is threatening the entire city. Harry's belief that the police should not be restricted in any way when pursuing evil—a kind of vigilante justice—leads him into trouble with the authorities. Limited space cannot permit a discussion of the dangers inherent in Harry's philosophy. If we ignore its point of view, *Dirty Harry* is exciting entertainment. But even two decades later, we may ignore it at our peril.

Off-Screen: Audiences clearly loved *Dirty Harry* (both film and man), and a number of sequels followed, including *Magnum Force* (1973), *The Enforcer* (1976), *Sudden Impact* (1983), and *The Dead Pool* (1988). Eastwood himself has defended his character: "I think the appeal of the Dirty Harry–type character is that he's basically for good, and he's got a morality that's higher than society's morality. He hates bureaucracy and he thinks that the law is often wrong. If that's

being called fascistic, as several critics have called it, they're full of it."

Divorce American Style

Columbia, 1967. (C-109m.) Dir: Bud Yorkin. Sp: Norman Lear, b/o story by Robert Kaufman. Cast: Debbie Reynolds, Dick Van Dyke, Jason Robards, Jean Simmons, Van Johnson, Joe Flynn, Shelly Berman, Martin Gabel, Lee Grant, Tom Bosley.

On-Screen: *A couple faces the consequences of their broken marriage.* The movie begins brilliantly: Standing alone on a hillside, a man dons his judicial robe and conducts the chorus of marital bickering below. The rest of *Divorce American Style* is almost, but not quite, as clever. After fifteen years of marriage, Debbie Reynolds and Dick Van Dyke agree to split up—she is courted by a television huckster (Johnson), and he meets Robards, a divorced man anxious to marry off his ex-wife (Simmons) so that he can stop paying alimony and marry his new girlfriend. Along the way to a frenetic climax, there are some wryly observant sequences: an early pantomime scene in which the antagonistic duo vent their spleen; an encounter with a pompous psychologist (Gabel); and, best of all, a hilarious scene in which the extended families of divorce come together and try to sort out the various children.

Off-Screen: Norman Lear's screenplay won an Oscar nomination. Old-time radio counsellor John J. Anthony, who would advise people about their marital or family problems, plays a judge in the film. Dick Van Dyke's comment on the movie: "It's a comedy with some hard-hitting truths and a running current of pathos about American couples who get bored with each other, or tired of each other, and head for the divorce courts."

Do the Right Thing

Universal, 1989. (C-120m.) Dir: Spike Lee. Sp: Spike Lee. Cast: Danny Aiello, Ossie Davis, Ruby Dee, John Turturro, Richard Edson, Giancarlo Esposito, Spike Lee, Bill Nunn, Paul Benjamin, John Savage.

On-Screen: *Spike Lee's controversial film on racial tensions.* Everybody does "the right thing" in Spike Lee's movie set in the Bedford-Stuyvesant black ghetto of Brooklyn—and the result is a police murder and a riot. Spike Lee does the right thing as well: turning out a high-energy, controversial film that asks the viewer to look at both sides of the racial issue. This double vision not only pervades the movie—it practically *is* the movie. Sal (Aiello), the Italian owner of the neighborhood pizzeria, has two sons, one (Edson) who likes blacks, the other (Turturro) who hates them. Mookie (Lee), Sal's delivery boy, is the only one in Bed-Stuy who seems to have a job, but he hardly works at it. Da Mayor (Davis), the block's self-styled mayor, is a drunkard and braggart who turns out to be a hero. Early on the cops avert what might have turned into a riot— and near the end of the film they kill a black youth. *Do the Right Thing* sharply emphasizes these contrasts, and as tensions rise in the summer heat, an inevitable riot leads to the destruction of Sal's pizzeria. Spike Lee's point of view can (and has been) hotly debated, but there is no denying the inventiveness of his writing or the power of the performances, particularly by Danny Aiello, whose Sal holds the film together with his innate presence, strength, and decency. *Do the Right Thing* is funny, sad— and troubling.

Off-Screen: The film created a stir at the forty-second Cannes Film Festival in 1989, and the furor continued after its release in New York City soon afterward. Shortly before the film's opening, Spike Lee commented, "Essentially what I hoped was that it would provoke everybody, white and black." And it did. Aiello was nominated for a Best Supporting Actor Oscar, and Lee was also cited for his original screenplay. (BL)

The Doctor

Touchstone, 1991. (C-125m.) Dir: Randa Haines. Sp: Robert Caswell, b/o book by Ed Rosenbaum, M.D. Cast: William Hurt, Christine Lahti, Elizabeth Perkins, Mandy Patinkin, Wendy Crewson, Adam Arkin, Charlie Korsmo, Bill Macy.

On-Screen: *A hotshot doctor becomes a patient.* Yet another addition to the early-nineties films about the Perils of Selfishness and the Need to Find One's True Self, *The Doctor* is a credible, reasonably intelligent entry in the series. William Hurt is Dr. Jack McKee, a smug, unfeeling, affluent heart surgeon who develops cancer of the larynx and suddenly finds himself on the opposite side of the scalpel as a patient. He learns all about the evasions, humiliations, and sheer indifference to their feelings that many patients must endure. He shuts out his wife (Lahti) and strikes up a friendship with a young, dying cancer patient (Perkins). It's not much of a surprise when he develops an entirely new attitude toward his patients and his fellow doctors, one that shows compassion and regard for seriously ill people. Hurt is persuasive as the doctor-turned-patient, and Lahti, one of the best actresses in films today, is equally good as his agonized wife. Perkins, also a fine actress, is obliged to play the cliché role of the young woman who is made noble and wise by her illness.

Off-Screen: The movie is based on the true experiences of Dr. Ed Rosenbaum, an Oregon internist who developed throat cancer at age seventy and wrote about the ordeal in *A Taste of My Own Medicine*. Dr. Rosenbaum makes a brief appearance in the film as a hospital physician. Many doctors objected to the opening sequence in which McKee and other doctors engage in horseplay in the operating room, singing and indulging in black humor while performing surgery.

Doctor Zhivago

MGM, 1965. (C-180m., originally 197m.) Dir: David Lean. Sp: Robert Bolt, b/o novel by Boris Pasternak. Cast: Omar Sharif, Julie Christie, Rod Steiger, Alec Guinness, Ralph Richardson, Geraldine Chaplin, Tom Courtenay, Rita Tushingham, Siobhan McKenna.

On-Screen: *Sweeping world events shape a young Russian doctor's life.* Based on Boris Pasternak's best-selling book, *Doctor Zhivago* is essentially a tragic romance set against the background of the Russian Revolution. Moist-eyed Omar Sharif stars as Yuri Zhivago, idealistic doctor and poet, whose over-the-years passion for the beautiful Lara (Christie) is buffeted not only by the tumultuous Revolution, but also by World War I. Among the other characters who affect his life are his patient wife Tonya (Chaplin),

the ardent, later ruthless revolutionary Pasha (Courtenay), and the sinister bureaucrat Komarovsky (Steiger) who lusts for Lara. Although the Zhivago-Lara romance takes up a good part of the footage, it has a curiously remote air for all of the soulful glances and warm embraces. David Lean fares much better with the massive, splendidly filmed set pieces—czarist troops attacking the revolutionary marchers, or swarms of desperate exiles being deported on a train to the distant regions of the Urals. These sequences spark the emotional involvement lacking in the personal drama. Maurice Jarre's "Lara" theme is lovely but ubiquitous.

Off-Screen: For the film, a replica of a Russian town as it looked around 1905 was built on the outskirts of Madrid. It had two- and three-story buildings of the period, a tram line, and an equestrian statue of Czar Alexander II. Since Soviet government officials would not allow Pasternak to accept the Nobel Prize for Literature for his novel in 1958, they were less than happy with the movie version and refused to permit any filming inside Russia. Finland was used instead for many of the snow-laden scenes. Oscars were awarded for the film's screenplay, cinematography, music score, costume design, and art direction.

Dodsworth

Goldwyn–United Artists, 1936. (101m.) Dir: William Wyler. Sp: Sidney Howard, b/o his play and on novel by Sinclair Lewis. Cast: Walter Huston, Ruth Chatterton, Mary Astor, Paul Lukas, David Niven, Maria Ouspenskaya, Gregory Gaye, Spring Byington, John Payne.

On-Screen: *Dissension in a midwestern marriage, via Sinclair Lewis's novel.* First adapted to the stage by Sidney Howard in 1934, with Walter Huston and Fay Bainter in the leading roles, Sinclair Lewis's book finally reached the screen in this intelligent, beautifully made film, one of the really adult dramas of the thirties. Huston recreated his role as the retired auto tycoon whose vain and shallow wife (Chatterton) instigates a series of affairs and flirtations when they travel to Europe. Eventually, after much soul-searching, he leaves her for a sympathetic woman (Astor) ("Love has to stop someplace short of suicide!"). Huston is superb as Dodsworth and Chatterton etches a convincing portrait of the frivolous Fran, but Astor's performance stays in the mind; she demonstrates a rare ability to make a "good" woman interesting rather than vapid. Repeating her stage role as a German baroness, venerable Maria Ouspenskaya has one brilliant scene with Chatterton.

Off-Screen: The film rights cost Samuel Goldwyn $160,000 (in some accounts, $165,000), at that time one of the highest amounts ever paid. The movie was a *succès d'estime*, but Goldwyn was not a happy man: "Don't talk to me about *Dodsworth*. I lost my goddamn shirt. I'm not saying it wasn't a fine picture. It was a *great* picture, but nobody wanted to see it. In *droves*." David Niven recalls that William Wyler "was a Jekyll-and-Hyde character. Kind, fun, and cozy at all other times, he became a fiend the moment his bottom touched down in the director's chair." Look for young John Payne in his first screen role as Dodsworth's son-in-law. Richard Day won an Oscar for his art direction, and there were four other nominations, including Best Picture.

Dog Day Afternoon

Warners, 1975. (C-130m.) Dir: Sidney Lumet. Sp: Frank Pierson, b/o article by P. F. Kluge and Thomas Moore. Cast: Al Pacino, Charles Durning, James Broderick, John Cazale, Chris Sarandon, Sully Boyar, Penny Allen, Carol Kane, Lance Henriksen.

On-Screen: *Al Pacino robs a bank—and triggers a citywide uproar.* Director Sidney Lumet's affinity for the gritty side of New York life is vividly displayed in this pungent melodrama. Based on an actual incident, *Dog Day Afternoon* relates what happens when a born loser (Pacino) holds up a Brooklyn bank to obtain money for his lover's sex-change operation. The holdup spirals into a media event involving the bank employees, the police, and a mob of cheering bystanders. Around this single event, Lumet and Oscar-winning writer Pierson construct a memorable mosaic of city life. Pacino won an Oscar nomination as the hapless Sonny—absurd, pathetic, and funny as he briefly enjoys his celebrity status. He is joined by a ripe collection of eccentric characters, notably his dull-witted but dangerous confederate (Cazale) and his bewildered lover Leon (Sarandon, also Oscar-nominated), who shares a telephone scene with Sonny that is a highlight of the movie. Mostly one remembers Pacino, shouting "Attica! Attica!" as he struts before the cheering crowd, or dictates his last will and testament to a bank employee.

Off-Screen: The actual robbery took place on a sweltering day in August 1972 at a small branch of the Chase Manhattan Bank in Brooklyn. The full story appeared in an article in *Life* magazine entitled "The Boys in the Bank," which came to the attention of the film's producer. Sidney Lumet later asserted that the phone call in the barbershop between Pacino and Sarandon was completely improvised by the actors. The true person played by Al Pacino was released from prison after serving six years for armed robbery.

The Dolly Sisters

Fox, 1945. (C-114m.) Dir: Irving Cummings. Sp: John Larkin and Marian Spitzer. MS: James Monaco and Mack Gordon. Cast: Betty Grable, John Payne, June Haver, S. Z. Sakall, Reginald Gardiner, Frank Latimore, Gene Sheldon.

On-Screen: *Betty Grable and June Haver as the legendary vaudeville stars*. Back in the golden age of vaudeville, Rose and Jenny Dolly were top-ranking stars, a popular sister act that drew in the crowds. With scant relation to the truth, Fox turned them into the studio's curvaceous, singing-and-dancing blondes, Betty Grable and June Haver. The lamebrain plot traces their rise to fame (with romantic problems along the way), but moviegoers came to see the glitzy musical numbers. One of them reaches some sort of nadir in forties musical style: in "Don't Be Too Old-Fashioned," the Dolly Sisters sing the praises of the "new-style" woman, then chorus girls emerge one by one, dressed as various forms of makeup (Lady Lipstick, Patricia Powder, etc.). Better wait, if you can, for the simple renditions of such standards as "I'm Always Chasing Rainbows."

Off-Screen: Reputedly, Betty Grable wanted Dick Haymes for the male lead but Zanuck substituted Perry Como. Grable thought he was "too short" and agreed to the casting of John Payne. Producer George Jessel submitted June Haver for the role of the other sister. During the filming, there was ill feeling between the two actresses, a sort of quietly smoldering battle of the blondes.

Double Indemnity

Paramount, 1944. (107m.) Dir: Billy Wilder. Sp: Billy Wilder and Raymond Chandler, b/o novel by James M. Cain. Cast: Barbara Stanwyck, Fred MacMurray, Edward G. Robinson, Tom Powers, Porter Hall, Jean Heather.

On-Screen: *Stanwyck lures MacMurray into murdering her husband*. If a *film noir* can be defined briefly as a movie lacking any trace of love or pity, then *Double Indemnity* is the preeminent example of the genre. Basing their screenplay on Cain's story, Wilder and Chandler turned a sizzler into a masterpiece that burns with the cold fire of a fine diamond. The plot is disarmingly simple: Stanwyck, a Los Angeles housewife as hardboiled as a ten-minute egg, lures insurance salesman MacMurray, whose mind is clouded by lust, into a pact to kill her husband (Powers). Their murder plot seems to have worked perfectly, until Robinson, claims investigator for MacMurray's company, starts to question the facts in the case. His dogged investigation—and the couple's mutual suspicion and resentment—lead to an uncompromising ending. The dialogue, much of it laden with sexual innuendo, crackles, and there are many gripping moments. Wilder's direction is taut and lean, and the three stars are brilliant.

Off-Screen: Although Wilder and Chandler's script is silken-smooth, their relationship during the collaboration was scratchy.

Wilder thought Chandler prissy; Chandler resented Wilder's brashness. After George Raft rejected the male lead, Dick Powell (later to play Chandler's private eye Philip Marlowe in *Murder, My Sweet*) wanted to step in. But the role went to MacMurray after his initial misgivings about playing a heel. Originally, he was to die in the gas chamber (the scene was shot), but Wilder decided that it was out of keeping with the film's generally understated tone, so he and Chandler wrote a new, and far more effective ending. The film was nominated for five Academy Awards. A television remake surfaced in 1973. (CFB)

A Double Life

Universal, 1947. (104m.) Dir: George Cukor. Sp: Ruth Gordon and Garson Kanin. Cast: Ronald Colman, Signe Hasso, Edmond O'Brien, Shelley Winters, Ray Collins, Philip Loeb, Millard Mitchell, Joe Sawyer.

On-Screen: *Ronald Colman's Oscar-winning performance*. Usually cast in debonair or romantic roles that took advantage of his dulcet voice, Ronald Colman switched gears to play a renowned actor with a schizoid personality. He earned a Best Actor Academy Award for his efforts. In George Cukor's smoothly made melodrama, he is Anthony John, who steeps himself all too intensely in his stage roles. Unfortunately, he is now acting the role of Othello, churning up a violent, even homicidal streak in his nature. Believing that he *is* Shakespeare's Moor, he strangles a waitress (Winters), then blanks out the act in his mind. Bill Friend (O'Brien), the publicity agent for the play, becomes suspicious and ultimately exposes John's crime, leading to the actor's demise by his own hand. Under George Cukor's expert direction, Colman performs with an intensity and power seldom revealed in his other roles. Signe Hasso is the wife who loves John but fears his irrational and potentially dangerous side. In all, a crackerjack psychological melodrama.

Off-Screen: Colman's role was intended for Laurence Olivier, but he was unavailable. Colman's comment: "It was the most satisfying role I ever had. . . . It tested my total range, and all my resources." Miklos Rozsa also won an Oscar for his music score, and the screenplay was nominated. Although Shelley Winters had appeared in films for several years, *A Double Life* gave her the breakthrough role that attracted studio attention. When the actress tried to add some glamour to her frumpy role, Cukor urged her to take off her false eyelashes and heavy makeup. She was grateful for the advice. Actor John Derek can briefly be seen as a photographer.

Down and Out in Beverly Hills

Touchstone, 1986. (C-103m.) Dir: Paul Mazursky. Sp: Paul Mazursky and Leon Capetanos, b/o play by Rene Fauchois. Cast: Nick Nolte, Bette Midler, Richard Dreyfuss, Little Richard, Tracy Nelson, Elizabeth Pena, Evan Richards, Mike the dog.

On-Screen: *Bum Nick Nolte changes the lives of a Beverly Hills family*. Simply put, Jerry Baskin (Nolte) is a bum, scruffy, irreverent, and with a self-proclaimed mysterious background. When he tries to drown himself in the pool of the affluent Whiteman family, Dave Whiteman (Dreyfuss) rescues him and makes him a house guest. Soon Jerry is affecting everyone's life, showing Dave a freer, more relaxed way of life and awakening the sleeping sexuality of Dave's wife, Barbara (Midler), and releasing the budding sexuality of his daughter (Nelson). Others, too, come under Jerry's spell. Suggested by Jean Renoir's 1932 French film, *Boudu Saved From Drowning, Down and Out in Beverly Hills* is a broad, hectic, and occasionally funny farce with some clever if obvious patches of satire. The overdecorated Whiteman house is in itself a satirical statement. The two best performances come from Bette Midler, hilarious as the repressed Barbara, and by Mike the Dog as Matisse, a canine in the great tradition of "Blondie" 's Daisy. Moviegoers of a certain vintage need no further explanation.

Off-Screen: Paul Mazursky's original title was *Jerry Saved From Drowning,* but a month before shooting began, he changed it to *Down and Out in Beverly Hills.* He also thought of Jack Nicholson for the role of Jerry, but Nicholson was unavailable. Mike the Dog drew the most press attention. A veteran of television commercials, he appeared to have enjoyed what *The New York Times* called his "Oscar-caliber work." A television series, suggested by the film, had a short run in 1987.

Down Argentine Way

Fox, 1940. (C-90m.) Dir: Irving Cummings. Sp: Karl Tunberg and Darrell Ware, b/o story by Rian James and Ralph Spence. MS: Harry Warren and Mack Gordon. Cast: Betty Grable, Don Ameche, Carmen Miranda, Charlotte Greenwood, J. Carrol Naish, Henry Stephenson, Leonid Kinskey.

On-Screen: *Betty Grable sings and dances south of the border.* A minor blonde performer in the thirties, Betty Grable came into her own as a movie star when she replaced Alice Faye in this cheerfully mindless, gaudily Technicolored musical. Playing a rich American girl who finds romance with an Argentinean horsebreeder (Ameche), she revealed a modest singing and dancing talent but an appealing presence that American audiences found attractive. The movie also introduced that improbable "Brazilian bombshell," Carmen Miranda, whose songs and outlandish costumes became a fixture of Fox musicals in the forties. Best number: "Sing to Your Señorita," performed exuberantly by long-legged Charlotte Greenwood. Prettiest song: "Two Dreams Met."

Off-Screen: Desi Arnaz was originally scheduled to costar with Grable, but he was forced to turn down the role for "personal" reasons. Also, Cesar Romero was going to play Tito, the fawning escort who squires Grable and Greenwood around Buenos Aires. When he became ill, the role went to Leonid Kinskey.

Dr. Jekyll and Mr. Hyde

Paramount, 1932. (97m.) Dir: Rouben Mamoulian. Sp: Samuel Hoffenstein and Percy Heath, b/o novel by Robert Louis Stevenson. Cast: Fredric March, Miriam Hopkins, Rose Hobart, Halliwell Hobbes, Edgar Norton, Tempe Pigott.

On-Screen: *Stylish version of the Victorian horror classic.* Unlike the lumbering, overly Freudianized remake a decade later, this is a swiftly paced, though as richly mounted, account of Stevenson's psychological thriller. While Mamoulian stresses the story's potential for innovative—and frighteningly real—camera wizardry, he gives due emphasis to the overtly sexual nature of the tale. Suggestively simmering lab equipment as well as erotic art objects do well enough to symbolize Jekyll's thwarted libido. March's dapper doctor-about-London, impatient to wed his virginal fiancée (Hobart), convinces. Jekyll's evil counterpart, the apish, snaggletoothed Hyde, horrifies. Georgia-born Hopkins adds a zesty dash of Dixie to her pitiable Cockney tart. Predictably, March won an Oscar for his performance as the man who lived a double life.

Off-Screen: Of the many camera tricks that Mamoulian conceived for the film, the early Jekyll-into-Hyde transformations are among the most ingenious. The changes were achieved by colored lights and lens filters that, when manipulated, gradually revealed more and more of Wally Westmore's makeup applied to March's face. As Hyde's appearance became increasingly simian, requiring heavy makeup, body hair, and alterations in stature, stop-motion photography and adroit methods of cutting were used. One of the many exotic sounds accompanying Jekyll's agonized changes into Hyde is that of Mamoulian's own heartbeat. (CFB)

Dr. Jekyll and Mr. Hyde

MGM, 1941. (114m.) Dir: Victor Fleming. Sp: John Lee Mahin, b/o novel by Robert Louis Stevenson. Cast: Spencer Tracy, Ingrid Bergman, Lana Turner, Donald Crisp, Ian Hunter, C. Aubrey Smith.

On-Screen: *A Freudian treatment of the scary classic.* Credit Tracy with a game try at a role he wasn't born to play. He's believable as the compassionate though headstrong physician; but his eye-popping and teeth-gnashing make the sadistic Hyde, Jekyll's alter ego, more raving madman than evil incarnate. In the forties, Hollywood "discovered" the murkier aspects of Freud's probing into the human psyche. As a result, this elaborately mounted film, set in London of the 1880s, contains painfully obvious inserts meant to depict Jekyll's dual nature: white flowers symbolize Turner, the good doctor's unsullied betrothed; Bergman, object of Hyde's unbridled lust, wallows in a mud pit. Turner is nobody's idea of Victorian maidenhood, but Bergman, also cast against type, is electrifying. As the barmaid who is trapped in a waking nightmare at the hands of the increasingly bestial Hyde, she walks off with the movie.

Off-Screen: Originally, Turner and Bergman's roles were reversed. But the imported Swedish star persuaded Fleming and Tracy that she would enjoy the challenge of playing the terrified prostitute. A decade earlier, Fredric March won an Academy Award for his far subtler performance as Jekyll and Hyde, although his Hyde was more heavily made up than Tracy's. This 1941 version earned nominations for Joseph Ruttenberg's photography, Franz Waxman's score, and Harold F. Kress's editing. (CFB)

Dr. Strangelove or: How I Learned to Stop Worrying and Love the Bomb

United Artists, 1964. (93m.) Dir: Stanley Kubrick. Sp: Stanley Kubrick, Terry Southern, and Peter George, b/o novel by Peter George. Cast: Peter Sellers, George C. Scott, Sterling Hayden, Keenan Wynn, Slim Pickens, Peter Bull, James Earl Jones.

On-Screen: *Stanley Kubrick's jet black comedy about nuclear annihilation.* Madness reigns at Burpelson Air Force Base when Gen. Jack D. Ripper (Hayden), the deranged base commander, becomes convinced that the Russians have launched a full-scale invasion of America. He orders a squadron of planes to hit Russian targets with atom bombs, not knowing that the bombing of Russia will set off a "doomsday" device that will destroy all life on earth for over a century. Involved in his mad act are a sensible British captain (Sellers), a belligerent general (Scott), and America's ineffectual president (Sellers again). On the sidelines is the decidedly peculiar German scientist Dr. Strangelove (Sellers in a third role), whose mechanical arm insists on giving the Nazi salute. Wickedly funny and chilling, *Dr. Strangelove* brilliantly satirizes the sort of primeval thinking that would lead to nationwide protest and alienation in later years. Sellers is remarkable in all three of his roles, and Scott plays General Turgidson with manic exuberance. Watch for Keenan Wynn, hilarious as Corp. "Bat" Guano.

Off-Screen: The original climax of the film had everyone engaged in a custard-pie fight, ending with the president and the Russian ambassador sitting on the floor in the imposing war room, waist deep in custard pies and singing "For He's a Jolly Good Fellow" about Dr. Strangelove. Kubrick decided that the sequence was at odds with the rest of the movie and deleted it.

Dracula

Universal, 1931. (75m.) Dir: Tod Browning. Sp: Garrett Fort, b/o novel by Bram Stoker and play by Hamilton Deane and John L. Balderston. Cast: Bela Lugosi, Helen Chandler, David Manners, Dwight Frye, Edward Van Sloan.

On-Screen: *The legendary vampire stalks the night.* With *Frankenstein* and *The Mummy* to follow, this is the first of the studio's memorable trio of ground-breaking (in more ways than one) "walking dead" films of the early thirties. Just as Karloff's lumbering monster gained him screen immortality, so Lugosi's suave Count Dracula assured him lasting fame as moviegoers' vampire of choice. Karl Freund uses his camera creatively when he floats us eerily about the dank, cobwebby vaults of Dracula's castle or shows Dracula and his mistress-victims rising from their coffins to greet a new night. But it's Lugosi's fixed stare and the florid lilt of his Hungarian accent that not only make the film, but also made him an icon of horror. "Listen to them," he says affectionately of the howling wolves. "Children of the night. What music they make." Or: "I never drink . . . wine," leaving us to guess what his preferred beverage is. As Lugosi utters the lines—once heard, never forgotten.

Off-Screen: Lon Chaney was set to play the title role, but his untimely death opened the door for Lugosi, who first appeared in the part on Broadway, in 1927. Bram Stoker's 1897 novel was filmed several other times, most notably as *Nosferatu,* F. W. Murnau's silent expressionistic German version of 1922. In 1979, Universal released a refurbished version of the play, with Frank Langella reprising his Broadway role as the dapper vampire. And in 1992, Francis Coppola directed *Bram Stoker's Dracula,* his erotic and blood-soaked adaptation of the story. Still, this slightly creaky but still creepy 1931 version has remained the most popular, prompting two sequels, *Dracula's*

Daughter (1936) and *Son of Dracula* (1943), neither with Lugosi. (CFB)

Dressed to Kill

Filmways, 1980. (C-105m.) Dir: Brian De Palma. Sp: Brian De Palma. Cast: Michael Caine, Angie Dickinson, Nancy Allen, Keith Gordon, Dennis Franz, David Margulies, Brandon Maggart.

On-Screen: *A psychopathic killer stalks two women.* Still deep in his Hitchcock phase —he would later move beyond it in films such as *The Untouchables* (1987)—writer-director De Palma emulates the master in this high-tension but none too credible thriller. No doubt *Psycho* will leap to mind when the apparent heroine is dispatched early on, and other sequences—one in a museum, another in the subway—mimic Hitchcock's techniques. Still, the movie has enough harrowing moments of its own as a clearly deranged killer stalks and murders one woman, then goes after another woman who is helping the victim's son to find her killer. Tossing one red herring after another, De Palma strives for lurid effects rather than logic, and sometimes he succeeds in raising goose bumps. But then, after an explanation lifted straight out of *Psycho,* he adds a bogus and unforgivable shock ending. Michael Caine gives a flamboyant performance as a psychiatrist with a secret.

Off-Screen: The role played by Angie Dickinson was turned down first by Liv Ullmann, who thought that the screenplay was too violent. Sean Connery was up for Michael Caine's part, and Keith Gordon was chosen over Matt Dillon and Cameron De Palma, the director's nephew. De Palma wanted director and sometime actor Paul Mazursky to play the obnoxious detective Marino, but Mazursky was about to start one of his own films. Dennis Franz got the part. A body double replaced Dickinson during the intimate close-ups in the opening shower scene.

Driving Miss Daisy

Warners, 1989. (C-99m.) Dir: Bruce Beresford. Sp: Albert Uhry, b/o his play. Cast: Morgan Freeman, Jessica Tandy, Dan Aykroyd, Patti LuPone, Esther Rolle.

On-Screen: *The over-the-years relationship of an elderly Southern widow and her black chauffeur.* *Driving Miss Daisy* won the Academy Award as the Best Picture of its year, and how could it miss? As heartwarming as it is predictable, it tells a simple but affecting story, it is acted with consummate skill, and it even offers the reassuring illusion that racial disharmony can be overcome with patience and time. Albert Uhry adapted his Pulitzer Prize–winning play about a wealthy Jewish Southern widow (Tandy), stubborn and testy, and the innately wise black chauffeur (Freeman) she is forced to hire. Over a quarter of a century, their relationship changes and deepens, mirrored by historic changes in the South, which sometimes affect them directly. In the end, the aged, nearly senile woman can say, "Hoke, you're my best friend." As the proud widow, Jessica Tandy gives a richly detailed performance that deserved the Best Actress Oscar, and Morgan Freeman is every bit as fine as the chauffeur. Smoothly directed by Bruce Beresford, *Driving Miss Daisy* offers few surprises, but it lingers in the mind.

Off-Screen: Much of the film was shot on location in a house in a section of Atlanta called Druid Hills. Producers Lilli and Richard Zanuck found it extremely difficult to sell the play to the studios, which considered it uncommercial. They finally persuaded Warners to back the film by agreeing to slash its production budget by almost half. An unexpected hit, the film grossed many millions. It also won Oscars for Best Screenplay and Best Makeup.

Drugstore Cowboy

Avenue, 1989. (C-100m.) Dir: Gus Van Sant, Jr. Sp: Gus Van Sant, Jr., and Daniel Yost, b/o novel by James Fogle. Cast: Matt Dillon, Kelly Lynch, James Remar, James Le Gros, Heather Graham, Beah Richards, Grace Zabriskie, Max Perlich, William S. Burroughs.

On-Screen: *A drug addict and his family.* "I was once a shameless full-time dope fiend" are the first words we hear from Bob (Dillon). And the last words we hear from him are "I'm still alive. I hope they can keep me alive," as he's taken away in an ambulance. In between is Gus Van Sant, Jr.'s unsparing, uncommonly vivid picture of the drug culture in 1971. In Portland, Oregon, Bob and his friends—a "family" of addicts—rob drugstores to pay for their habit. Diane (Lynch) is his loving wife and partner in crime and drugs, Rick (Le Gros) is his dimwitted pal, and Nadine (Graham) is the girl whose death from an overdose frightens Bob so much that he tries to give up drugs. His pathetic monologue in a methadone clinic is one of the movie's most powerful moments. His efforts pay off, but he cannot fully leave the drug scene, and he ends up

critically wounded by a junkie's bullet. Dillon gives one of his best performances in a film that is sometimes awkward but always riveting. Most painful scene: Bob visits his mother (Zabriskie).

Off-Screen: Author William S. Burroughs has a role in the movie as an addicted priest. He rewrote his dialogue in his own style. The screenplay is based on an unpublished autobiographical novel by James Fogle, a Portland penitentiary inmate who was serving time for drug-related crimes. Not surprisingly, Van Sant had a great deal of trouble selling the script to studio executives, who were afraid of the subject matter.

Drums Along the Mohawk

Fox, 1939. (C-103m.) Dir: John Ford. Sp: Lamar Trotti and Sonya Levien, b/o novel by Walter D. Edmonds. Cast: Claudette Colbert, Henry Fonda, Edna May Oliver, Ward Bond, John Carradine, Arthur Shields, Eddie Collins, Jessie Ralph, Robert Lowery.

On-Screen: *Pioneers fight for survival in colonial America.* John Ford's first color film, *Drums Along the Mohawk* deals impressively with pioneer life in the early years of the American Revolution. Henry Fonda plays a young farmer who settles with wife Claudette Colbert in the Mohawk Valley in upstate New York; together they must endure the rigors of the wilderness, marauding Indians, and treacherous Tories. Ford never allows his familiar themes—the enduring strength of America's founders, the bonds of community life, the rituals of life and death—to interfere with a rousing adventure story. The movie abounds in authentic period detail, and the photography bathes every scene in vivid Technicolor. Although Colbert seems rather artificial in her role as a refined Eastern girl who becomes a staunch frontier wife, Henry Fonda excels as the determined farmer. As a feisty widow, marvelous Edna May Oliver steals every scene in which she appears. (She received an Oscar nomination.) *Drums Along the Mohawk* displays John Ford's matchless skill with American themes.

Off-Screen: Much of the film was shot in northern Utah. Ford brought his cast and crew into high country, about eleven thousand feet above sea level. Miles of woods had to be cut through to make roads in the wilderness. At the end, Ford was required to tear down every building he had erected for the film. Since it was difficult to destroy the sturdy fort, Ford added a few climactic scenes in which the besieged colonials are attacked by Indians and British irregulars, who blow up most of the fort with gunpowder.

Duck Soup

Paramount, 1933. (70m.) Dir: Leo McCarey. Sp: Bert Kalmar and Harry Ruby. Cast: Groucho, Chico, Harpo, and Zeppo Marx, Margaret Dumont, Louis Calhern, Raquel Torres, Leonid Kinskey, Verna Hillie.

On-Screen: *"Hail, Freedonia!"* Regarded by Marx fans as the summit of their screen work, *Duck Soup* was a flop when it was first released. Audiences were put off by its satirical barbs at government leaders who would plunge their countries into war over trifling matters. Now Groucho's wicked quips, Harpo's brilliant pantomime, and Chico's garbled English are viewed with total delight. Groucho plays Rufus T. Firefly, named Freedonia's newest president by Mrs. Teasdale (Dumont), the country's richest citizen. Zeppo is his secretary, for those who care, and Harpo and Chico are unlikely spies. The memorable moments are too numerous to mention—only wait for the inspired mirror scene, in which Harpo must pretend to be Groucho's mirror image, or the delirious war sequences. When Mrs. Teasdale offers moral support, Groucho's comment is, "Remember, you're fighting for this woman's honor, which is probably more than *she* ever did!" But why go on? You are bound to enjoy every drop of *Duck Soup*.

Off-Screen: When citizens of the *real* Freedonia, New York, objected to the name being used, Groucho advised the mayor to change the town's name: "It is hurting our picture." At the time of its release, the film's indifferent critical reaction and poor audience response threatened to end the Marxes' career. When Zeppo left the act to become a theatrical agent, the outlook seemed bleak. Irving Thalberg, MGM's head of production, came to their rescue by signing them to a long-term contract. Their first MGM film was *A Night at the Opera* (1935).

Duel in the Sun

Selznick International, 1947. (C-130m.) Dir: King Vidor. Sp: David O. Selznick, b/o novel by Niven Busch. Cast: Gregory Peck, Jennifer Jones, Joseph Cotten, Lionel Barrymore, Lillian Gish, Charles Bickford, Herbert Marshall, Walter Huston, Butterfly McQueen, Tilly Losch, Harry Carey.

On-Screen: *David O. Selznick's epic western.* "Lust in the dust" is what the wags of the day called this grandiose western, and lust is what the audience witnesses when no-account Lewt McCanles (Peck) grapples with tempestuous half-breed Pearl (Jones). An audacious gamble for producer-writer Selznick, *Duel in the Sun* swirls around the McCanles clan: domineering cattle baron Barrymore, his cowed wife (Gish), and their two sons, lecherous Lewt and honorable Jesse (Cotten). There's plenty of trouble when Pearl comes into the family, and even more trouble when the elder McCanles opposes the encroaching railroads. Virtually every scene in the movie is charged with high-powered emotion that teeters dangerously on the edge of parody, from the portentous opening to the notorious final sequence in which Lewt and Pearl engage in a bloody love-hate shoot-out in the mountains. Best scene: the gathering of the men of Barrymore's ranch to offer armed resistance to the railroads.

Off-Screen: *Duel in the Sun* has a stormy production history. Determined to duplicate his success with *Gone With the Wind,* Selznick took charge of every aspect of the film. He bombarded director Vidor and others with constant memorandums, brought in director Josef von Sternberg to act as "special visual consultant," and kept demanding that Jennifer Jones, his protégé and wife-to-be, be given maximum attention. Following an altercation with Selznick, Vidor walked off the film, and director William Dieterle was hired to complete it. (After arbitration, Vidor received sole credit.) On its release, the movie caused a furor among Catholic and Protestant leaders across the country.

Dumbo

Disney-RKO, 1941. (C-64m.) Supervising Dir: Ben Sharpsteen. Sp: Joe Grant and Dick Huemer, b/o book by Helen Aberson and Harold Pearl. MS: Frank Churchill, Oliver Wallace, and Ned Washington.

On-Screen: *Disney's floppy-eared baby elephant.* A charming, if minor, feature film from the Disney studios, *Dumbo* recounts the tale of an adorable baby elephant who is teased by the other circus animals because of his huge ears. When little Dumbo's mother is enraged by the teasing, she has to be restrained and placed behind bars. A desolate Dumbo is befriended by Timothy Mouse, while a group of black crows teach him how to use his ears for flying. In time, flying Dumbo becomes a circus star, reunited with his mother. The simple story is nicely told and well animated, but there are a few problems. As in the superior *Bambi,* the little hero's separation from his mother has to be traumatic for tiny viewers. Also, the crows, who sing "When I See an Elephant Fly," are depicted as caricatures of blacks, which may sit less well with today's audiences than those of half a century ago. Still, there are wonderful moments, the best being the famous "Pink Elephants on Parade," which has little to do with the story and everything to do with showing off Disney's animation techniques. Dumbo and Timothy become tipsy on champagne and have an animated nightmare highlighted by pink dancing elephants. It's a surrealistic delight.

Off-Screen: Among the distinctive voices used in *Dumbo*, including those of Herman Bing, Sterling Holloway, and Verna Felton, one is especially inimitable: the New York tones of Edward Brophy as Timothy Mouse. *Dumbo*, originally planned as a thirty-minute featurette, was expanded to feature length. Walt Disney refused to add another ten minutes of footage, insisting that the movie was just the right length. He turned out to be right. Frank Churchill and Oliver Wallace won an Oscar for Best Scoring of a Musical Picture.

Each Dawn I Die

Warners, 1939. (92m.) Dir: William Keighley. Sp: Norman Reilly Raine and Warren Duff, b/o novel by Jerome Odlum. Cast: James Cagney, George Raft, Jane Bryan, George Bancroft, Maxie Rosenbloom, Stanley Ridges, Alan Baxter, Thurston Hall.

On-Screen: *Framed reporter James Cagney faces a hellish life in prison.* Another entry in the series of hard-hitting prison dramas produced by Warners and other studios in the thirties, *Each Dawn I Die* is suitably grim if not altogether convincing. Cagney stars as a crusading reporter who is framed into prison and must cope with the hard, violent life within its walls. Reluctantly, he becomes involved in a breakout masterminded by big-shot gangster George Raft. Cagney's role calls for some unrestrained scenery chewing, from bitter defiance in the warden's office to a tearful breakdown before the parole board, but as usual, he gives a vital, driving performance. Best scene: a stoolie is stabbed in the prison theater.

Off-Screen: Warners originally intended to have John Garfield play the reporter and Cagney the tough con. But then they gave the tough con to George Raft—he had just become a studio contract player—and switched Cagney to the reporter role.

East of Eden

Warners, 1955. (C-115m.) Dir: Elia Kazan. Sp: Paul Osborn, b/o novel by John Steinbeck. Cast: James Dean, Julie Harris, Raymond Massey, Jo Van Fleet, Burl Ives, Richard Davalos, Albert Dekker.

On-Screen: *A Hollywood legend's first major role, as a "generation gap" rebel.* Set in California's Salinas Valley around World War I, this is a powerfully acted, if at times stagily so, updating of the biblical Cain and Abel tale. The story focuses on the tormented relationship of rival brothers, insecure Cal Trask (Dean) and favored son Aron (Davalos), with their stern, puritanical father, Adam (Massey). Harris plays Aron's sweetheart, Abra, though it's the unloved Cal who worships her. At the heart of the movie is Cal's intensely dramatic confrontation with his gauntly evil mother, Kate (Fleet), who abandons her family to establish a brothel. Though Kazan's direction tends to call attention to itself—tilted camera angles and moody lighting underline familial turmoil that's made clear in the dialogue and acting—Dean's highly individualistic (some say mannered) performance as the tortured Cal will linger in your memory.

Off-Screen: During the shooting of the movie, Dean repeatedly forgot his lines, missed cues, and arrived late on the set, thus failing to endear himself to other cast members. (Kazan had originally considered Marlon Brando as Cal.) Massey, however, was impressed by Dean's ability to improvise action. At the end of the scene in which Adam spurns his son's birthday gift of money, the camera registers the seasoned actor's look of genuine surprise at Dean's unexpected reaction. Dean, Kazan, and Osborn, for his adaptation of Steinbeck's 1952 novel, were Oscar nominated, but it was Van Fleet who captured the statuette as Best Supporting Actress. In 1968, the story was turned into a short-lived Broadway musical, *Here's Where I Belong;* in 1981, it was presented as a television miniseries. (CFB)

Easter Parade

MGM, 1948. (C-103m.) Dir: Charles Walters. Sp: Sidney Sheldon, Frances Goodrich, and Albert Hackett, b/o story by Frances Goodrich and Albert Hackett. MS: Irving Berlin. Cast: Judy Garland, Fred Astaire, Ann Miller, Peter Lawford, Jules Munshin, Clinton Sundberg.

On-Screen: *A matchless musical trio: Judy, Fred, and Irving Berlin.* Brimming over with lilting Berlin melodies, *Easter Parade* is, on the whole, a musical delight, and a movie to be cherished as the only teaming of Fred Astaire and Judy Garland. The time is 1912, and the stars play entertainers who form a shaky team until love finally blossoms. (For Astaire, it takes the entire movie.) It's all foolish and predictable, but the musical numbers are frequent and sometimes wonderful: Astaire's dance to "Steppin' Out With My Baby"; the Astaire-Garland duet of "A Couple of Swells"; and Garland's heartfelt "Better Luck Next Time." Ann Miller is on hand to offer a sizzling song and dance to "Shakin' the Blues Away," and early in the film, she teams up with Astaire for a lovely song, "It Only Happens When I Dance With You." Although it cannot be counted among MGM's best musicals, *Easter Parade* is top-notch entertainment.

Off-Screen: Judy Garland's then-husband Vincente Minnelli was originally scheduled to direct, but with Garland recently released from a sanatorium, where she had been treated for emotional disturbances and drug dependency, her doctor felt that it would be risky for her to be directed by him. (He believed that Minnelli symbolized all her problems with the studio.) Charles Walters was substituted. Then Gene Kelly, who was scheduled to costar with her, broke his ankle and Astaire replaced him. In 1992, a laser disc of the film was released in which Garland's deleted musical number, "Mr. Monotony," was restored.

Easy Living

Paramount, 1937. (86m.) Dir: Mitchell Leisen. Sp: Preston Sturges, b/o story by Vera Caspary. Cast: Jean Arthur, Ray Milland, Edward Arnold, Franklin Pangborn, William Demarest, Mary Nash, Luis Alberni.

On-Screen: *A sable coat turns Jean Arthur into Cinderella.* Many romantic comedies in the thirties revolved about a working girl who dreams of romance and riches—and may or may not find them. *Easy Living* is one of the brightest of these comedies, graced with two main virtues: a charming screenplay by Preston Sturges and the delectable presence of Jean Arthur. She plays a working girl who literally has a sable coat dropped into her lap when an irate financier (Arnold) flings it out a window. (His wife bought it for a mere $58,000.) Before long, the bewildered girl is sitting in the lap of luxury, treated as Cinderella by those who believe she's Arnold's mistress. She also finds love with a young man (Milland) who turns out to be Arnold's son. *Easy Living* shows evidence of the style Preston Sturges would bring to his later, better-known screenplays, especially in the famous sequence in a New York City Automat. When all the food slots open suddenly, the patrons erupt into a comic frenzy that is a model of sustained slapstick.

Off-Screen: Hired as a writer by Paramount, Preston Sturges was first assigned to turn Vera Caspary's story into a screenplay. When he presented his finished script to a Paramount executive, he was told that the time was not right for comedies; the project would be abandoned. Sturges disagreed ("Anytime is a good time for comedies") and took it to Mitchell Leisen, who decided to direct it. For the Automat scene, Leisen had "every stuntman in Hollywood taking pratfalls."

Easy Rider

Columbia, 1969. (C-94m.) Dir: Dennis Hopper. Sp: Peter Fonda, Dennis Hopper, and Terry Southern. Cast: Peter Fonda, Dennis Hopper, Jack Nicholson, Karen Black, Luke Askew, Luana Anders, Robert Walker, Jr., Phil Spector.

On-Screen: *The counterculture landmark film of the sixties.* Alienated from society of the late sixties, Wyatt (Fonda), who calls himself Captain America, and Billy (Hopper) are two young, long-haired motorcyclists—and occasional drug dealers—riding across the country in search of "the American dream." Instead, they find a nightmare, rife with open hostility and ending in obliteration. Along the way, they are joined by George (Nicholson), a strange alcoholic lawyer who, in talking to Wyatt and Billy, sounds the movie's theme, all too explicitly: "This used to be a great country. They are scared of what you represent. What you represent is freedom." *Easy Rider* dates badly, but at the time it sounded a clarion call to the country's disaffected young people and was a great success. It also inspired a slew of inferior imitations. Jack Nicholson, who had only appeared in low-budget movies since 1960, scored a triumph as the oddball who believes that aliens called Venutians are now on Earth. He may have been right.

Off-Screen: Oscar-nominated Jack Nicholson won the role that was first slated for Rip Torn and was also offered to Bruce Dern. The hippie commune leader is played by Robert Walker, Jr., son of the forties actor (*Bataan,* etc.). The New Orleans cemetery scene, in which a drugged Fonda talks angrily to a statue of the Madonna, was difficult for the actor to shoot since it reminded him of his mother's suicide when he was a child. The movie's screenplay was also nominated for an Oscar.

The Elephant Man

Paramount, 1980. (125m.) Dir: David Lynch. Sp: Christopher De Vore, Eric Bergren, and David Lynch, b/o writings by Sir Frederick Treves and Ashley Montagu. Cast: Anthony Hopkins, John Hurt, Anne Bancroft, John Gielgud, Wendy Hiller, Freddie Jones.

On-Screen: *A doctor befriends a hideously deformed man in turn-of-the-century London.* This film is not adapted from the Bernard Pomerance play that had a long Broadway run, although it tells the same factual story of John Merrick (Hurt), the grotesquely deformed man who was rescued by a doctor, Frederick Treves (Hopkins), from his life as an abused carnival freak, and who proved to be both sensitive and intelligent. The movie shows both the bright and dark sides of Merrick's sad, brief life: his lionization by turn-of-the-century London society and the humiliation and pain he suffers from those who still regard him as a monster. The screenplay attempts to add some depth by having Dr. Treves briefly agonize over his motives for helping Merrick, but coscenarist and director David Lynch seems more involved in evoking the bleaker side of the Victorian era, which he does in vivid detail, than in probing the characters. Freddie Francis's black-and-white photography is brilliant, and the acting is mostly superb and in the case of Oscar-nominated Hurt, extraordinary. With only his voice and gestures, he suggests the rare quality of the man behind the deformed body.

Off-Screen: There was a heated legal battle over the film's title between the producers of the Pomerance play and Mel Brooks, whose company produced this film. The matter was settled privately out of court. It took nine hours to fit John Hurt with his elaborate makeup for the first time. Later, makeup artist Christopher Tucker was able to reduce the time to five or six hours. Hurt was unable to eat and could only drink through a straw. *The Elephant Man* received a number of other Oscar nominations, including Best Picture, Best Direction, Best Adapted Screenplay, and Best Art Direction–Set Decoration.

Elmer Gantry

United Artists, 1960. (C-146m.) Dir: Richard Brooks. Sp: Richard Brooks, b/o novel by Sinclair Lewis. Cast: Burt Lancaster, Jean Simmons, Arthur Kennedy, Shirley Jones, Dean Jagger, Patti Page, Edward Andrews, Hugh Marlowe, John McIntire, Rex Ingram.

On-Screen: *Charismatic evangelist proves to be corrupt.* "Torn From Today's Headlines!"as exposé-movie ads used to shout. Viewing this adaptation of Lewis's 1927 novel in the light of recent scandals involving rapscallion preachers gives this film a contemporary spin. Ideally cast, Lancaster is galvanizing as a flamboyant Midwestern salesman turned fire-and-brimstone religion merchant. Simmons is winsome as the pure, dedicated evangelist (reversing the character in the novel) who is Gantry's true love. Cast effectively against type, Jones earned an Oscar as Gantry's wronged sweetheart who turns vengeful prostitute. Otherwise, this overproduced and overlong movie disappoints. Most important, Lewis's searing satire of rip-off revivalists, and their flocks who create them unwittingly, is softened.

Off-Screen: Director-adapter Brooks discarded much of Lewis's novel in preparing his screenplay, even altering some of the characters—Simmons's role in particular. Lancaster, who was universally praised for his performance, said that he modeled Gantry's high-energy mannerisms on those of Billy Sunday, the renowned and respected revivalist minister. For the religious assembly scenes, Brooks rounded up senior citizens from Long Beach, California, who regularly went to Baptist meetings and who responded avidly to Lancaster's fervent sermonizing. The movie won three Oscars: Lancaster for Best Actor, Jones for Best Supporting Actress, and Brooks for Best Adapted Screenplay. Robert Shaw starred in a short-lived stage musical version in 1970. (CFB)

Empire of the Sun

Warners, 1987. (C-152m.) Dir: Steven Spielberg. Sp: Tom Stoppard, b/o book by J. G. Ballard. Cast: John Malkovich, Christian Bale, Miranda Richardson, Nigel Havers, Joe Pantoliano, Leslie Phillips, Masato Ibu, Emily Richard, Rupert Frazer, Ben Stiller.

On-Screen: *A boy lives through the ordeal of World War II.* Shanghai, late 1941, shortly before the bombing of Pearl Harbor. Jamie, later Jim (Bale), a young British boy living with his parents in ease and affluence, suddenly finds himself alone when the Japanese invade the city. These early scenes of chaos and mass evacuation are stunning in their scope and power, and nothing that follows quite matches their impact. Jim spends four years at a Japanese prison camp, where his mentor is the wily, self-serving American named Basie (Malkovich). The boy learns the art of survival, but always in his mind is his reverent, almost mystical attitude toward airplanes and flight, which makes it difficult for him to distinguish between friend and enemy. Steven Spielberg's film received mixed, sometimes hostile reviews, but it's an impressive, absorbing work, with some moving sequences and a fine performance by young Bale. Now if someone had only suggested cutting down on those irksome heavenly voices! An underrated movie.

Off-Screen: *Empire of the Sun* became the first major Hollywood movie to be made in the People's Republic of China. This required long, face-to-face negotiations that took a year to complete. Thousands of Chinese nationals wanted to act in the film; one day five thousand extras appeared, only to be replaced the next day by five thousand others. Other filming took place in Spain and England. Tom Stoppard's screenplay is based on J. G. Ballard's autobiographical novel. Ballard himself appears briefly in beefeater costume in an early party scene.

The Empire Strikes Back

Paramount, 1980. (C-124m.) Dir: Irvin Kershner. Sp: Leigh Brackett and Lawrence Kasdan, b/o story by George Lucas. Cast: Mark Hamill, Carrie Fisher, Harrison Ford, Billy Dee Williams, Anthony Daniels, Peter Mayhew, David Prowse, Kenny Baker, Frank Oz, Alec Guinness.

On-Screen: *Installment two of the Star Wars epic trilogy.* The first sequel to the phenomenally successful *Star Wars* (1977), *The Empire Strikes Back* assumes that you've seen the original entry. But even if you haven't, you should enjoy this extravagant, high-spirited fantasy-adventure. This time the evil Galactic Empire, headed by the evil Lord Darth Vader (Prowse), is still determined to capture and destroy the Rebel Alliance, especially the stalwart Luke Skywalker (Hamill), feisty Princess Leia (Fisher), and the flip, cynical mercenary Han Solo (Ford). Still along for the ride (and for comic relief) are the 'droids, R2D2 (Baker) and C3PO (Daniels), the hairy Wookie, Chewbacca (Mayhew), and—for a touch of mysticism—the ghostly vision of Ben Kenobi (Guinness). The story moves swiftly from one crisis or narrow escape to another, pausing for some words of wisdom from a beguiling new character called Yoda (Oz), the wizened old Jedi master. Billy Dee Williams also makes an appearance as Solo's raffish pal, Lando Calrissian. As in *Star Wars,* the acting and dialogue are rudimentary, and the "philosophical" content is, to say the least, simplistic. But fans of the trilogy won't care.

Off-Screen: Brian Johnson and Richard Edlund received a special Oscar for their impressive special effects. The movie also won an award for sound. Frank Oz, who played Yoda under tons of makeup (*New York* magazine said that he looked like "a squashed Theodore H. White"), was a prominent member of the Muppets team and has since gone on to direct a number of feature films. Once again James Earl Jones provided the sepulchral voice of Darth Vader.

The Enchanted Cottage

RKO, 1945. (92m.) Dir: John Cromwell. Sp: DeWitt Bodeen and Herman J. Mankiewicz, b/o play by Sir Arthur Wing Pinero. Cast: Dorothy McGuire, Robert Young, Herbert Marshall, Mildred Natwick, Spring Byington, Hillary Brooke, Richard Gaines.

On-Screen: *Two lonely souls find love in a mystical setting.* Many people have retained a special fondness for this romantic fantasy, but it is difficult to understand why. Straining for sensitivity and poignancy, it only ends up seeming lugubrious and maudlin: perfumed sentiment passing as profoundly emotional drama. Robert Young and Dorothy McGuire play lonely misfits—he is a maimed war veteran, she is a homely spinster—who come to see each other through the eyes of love, but only when they are together in an enchanted cottage. Although the leads work well together, they seemed more compatible as the husband and child-wife of *Claudia* (1943). Herbert Marshall is simply unctuous as the blind pianist who understands the lovers' special vision. Apparently, the movie requires a suspension of disbelief that many viewers can make. Others beware.

Off-Screen: Pinero's play opened on Broadway in March of 1922. A silent film version appeared in 1924, with Richard Barthelmess and May McAvoy in the leading roles. The *New York Times* reviewer found it "much more satisfying" than the stage version, "due to the modern magic of the camera, resourceful direction, and thoroughly competent acting."

Enemies: A Love Story

Morgan Creek, 1989. (C-119m.) Dir: Paul Mazursky. Sp: Roger L. Simon and Paul Mazursky, b/o novel by Isaac Bashevis

Singer. Cast: Anjelica Huston, Ron Silver, Lena Olin, Margaret Sophie Stein, Alan King, Judith Malina, Rita Karin, Phil Leeds, Paul Mazursky, Elya Baskin.

On-Screen: *A man copes with three wives.* It's 1949, and Coney Island resident Herman Broder (Silver) is in deep trouble. A Holocaust survivor who lost his wife and children, Herman is married to plodding Yadwiga (Stein), the Polish woman who saved his life during the war, while also enjoying a fiercely passionate relationship with Masha (Olin), another Holocaust survivor. Then suddenly he learns that his first wife, Tamara (Huston), is alive in New York City. Bewildered, indecisive Herman is soon saddled with three wives, trying to juggle his lies and deceptions. If this sounds like the stuff of farce, guess again. *Enemies: A Love Story,* derived from Isaac Bashevis Singer's novel, has humor and a vividly recreated background, but it's essentially a sad tale of lives permanently destroyed by the Holocaust. Herman is tormented by terrible memories of the past, cynical Tamara says, "I'm not alive, and I'm not dead," and Masha asks, "Why wasn't I cremated like all the other Jews?" The movie ends, however, on a life-affirming note. A haunting movie, and one of director Paul Mazursky's best.

Off-Screen: Both Anjelica Huston and Lena Olin were nominated for Oscars, for Best Supporting Actress, as were Roger L. Simon and Mazursky for their screenplay adaptation. Production designer Pato Guzman found many of the artifacts for 1949 New York—stoves, refrigerators, dinnerware—in Canada. Replicas of the forty-year-old streetlights on the Coney Island boardwalk were installed, then removed when the shooting was done. The Stillwell Avenue subway station in Brooklyn had to be repainted an authentically ugly green to cover up the new decorator hues. Director Mazursky plays Masha's first husband.

E.T.: The Extra-Terrestrial

Universal, 1982. (C–115m.) Dir: Steven Spielberg. Sp: Melissa Mathison. Cast: Dee Wallace, Henry Thomas, Peter Coyote, Robert Macnaughton, Drew Barrymore, Sean Frye, K. C. Martel.

On-Screen: *An endearing outer-space creature is lost on planet Earth.* Analyze it if you insist. (Is it a religious parable? An updated *Wizard of Oz?*) Criticize it if you must. (The sentiment gets rather thick and its attitude toward parents is questionable.) Never mind—*E.T.* remains a magical movie that is destined to enchant generations of moviegoers. Everyone knows the story: endearing little E.T., lost on an alien planet, is befriended by ten-year-old Elliott (Thomas) and his family. When his presence is discovered, a race is on to get him "home" before he dies. The many unforgettable sequences include E.T.'s encounters with Elliott and his siblings; the Halloween adventure of E.T. in which Elliott's bicycle soars into the air with joyful ease; and the final, frantic race to bring E.T. to his spaceship. E.T.'s near-death scene, with a tearful Elliott watching nearby ("I'll believe in you all my life, every day") is infinitely touching. One of the highest-grossing movies in film history, *E.T.: The Extra-Terrestrial* could hardly fail to delight young viewers, but it also touched a wellspring of emotion for adults who still retained even a small portion of their sense of childhood wonder.

Off-Screen: Oscars went to Melissa Mathison for her screenplay, to John Williams for his exhilarating score, and to the film's sound and visual effects teams. E.T. was created by special effects wizard Carlo Rambaldi. He built three E.T.'s: a mechanical model operated by cables, an electronic model for the finer facial movements, and the so-called "walking" E.T. for the freestanding scenes, this one operated by two dwarfs and a legless boy. All the models were aluminum-and-steel skeletons covered by layered fiberglass, polyurethane, and rubber. Rambaldi stated that E.T.'s eyes were inspired by his Himalayan cat. E.T.'s vocal sounds were produced by various means. For example, when E.T. sees Elliott for the first time and screams, it's an otter's shriek, electronically processed.

Executive Suite

MGM, 1954. (104m.) Dir: Robert Wise. Sp: Ernest Lehman, b/o novel by Cameron Hawley. Cast: William Holden, June Allyson, Barbara Stanwyck, Fredric March, Walter Pidgeon, Paul Douglas, Shelley Winters, Louis Calhern, Nina Foch, Dean Jagger.

On-Screen: *A star-studded excursion into the corporate life.* Films often enjoy depicting the world of business and high finance as a place where throat-cutting and backbiting are every day activities. MGM's adaptation of this best-selling novel is no exception: When the head man of a top corporation dies suddenly, the race is on among the candidates to replace him, and ruthless maneuvering is the order of the day. William Holden heads an impressive cast as the idealistic company man—married to June Allyson—who gets caught up reluctantly in the battle. The movie marked Holden's first appearance since *Golden Boy* with his mentor, Barbara Stanwyck, who plays the daughter of the corporation's founder and the mistress of the just-deceased tycoon. As the manipulations and deceptions continue, each cast member plays an emotional or revealing scene. Smooth but shallow, *Executive Suite* is an entertaining stroll through the corporate corridors.

Off-Screen: Producer John Houseman's first choice for the leading role was Henry Fonda, but he dropped out to train for a Broadway musical that was never produced. Production head Dore Schary suggested that the movie use the sounds of the city—church bells, sirens, the roar of traffic, etc.—instead of the conventional musical score. Houseman approved of the idea and worked closely with the sometimes reluctant sound-department chief, Douglas Shearer.

Exodus

United Artists, 1960. (C-213m.) Dir: Otto Preminger. Sp: Dalton Trumbo, b/o novel by Leon Uris. Cast: Paul Newman, Eva Marie Saint, Lee J. Cobb, Ralph Richardson, Sal Mineo, Peter Lawford, Jill Haworth, John Derek, Felix Aylmer, Hugh Griffith, David Opatoshu.

On-Screen: *The violent birth throes of Israel, adapted from Leon Uris's best-selling novel.* Long, *very* long, and determined to be fair (virtually every conflicting point of view is carefully advanced), *Exodus* depicts the desperate efforts of Europe's Jewish refugees to reach Palestine, the clashes within Palestine's warring factions, and the violence that followed the creation of Israel in 1948. Director Preminger handles the large-scale sequences well (especially a prison breakout), but Dalton Trumbo's dialogue is either flat or hortatory, and the characters are one-dimensional. They seem to wear signs: Fierce Freedom Fighter (Newman); Sympathetic British Officer (Richardson); Unsympathetic British Officer (Lawford); Saintly Martyr (Haworth), and so on. There's also a perfunctory romance between Newman and Eva Marie Saint as an American, non-Jewish nurse and widow. As a tormented young refugee, Oscar-nominated Sal Mineo has the strongest scene, in which he is forced to recall the horrors of the concentration camps. Ernest Gold's Oscar-winning score is stirring.

Off-Screen: Otto Preminger tried to write the screenplay with author Leon Uris but then discharged him, claiming that Uris had no idea of how to write a screenplay. After the film was released, Uris declared that Preminger had ruined his book. *Exodus* marked the first time that Dalton Trumbo, one of the Hollywood Ten, was able to use his real name after being blacklisted for years. Paul Newman had difficulty with Preminger—the director's dictatorial style clashed with Newman's painstaking attention to detail. At a first screening of the movie, after it had run for three hours, comedian Mort Sahl stood up and pleaded, "Let my people go!" A stage musical version, entitled *Ari,* failed to make the grade in 1971.

The Exorcist

Warners, 1973. (C-121m.) Dir: William Friedkin. Sp: William Peter Blatty, b/o his novel. Cast: Ellen Burstyn, Linda Blair, Max Von Sydow, Lee J. Cobb, Kitty Winn, Jason Miller, Jack MacGowran.

On-Screen: *State-of-the-art shocker, and then some.* Moviemaking at its scariest, this film is obscene at times, and often revolting, but undeniably fascinating as well. Ellen Burstyn is Mrs. MacNeil, mother to seemingly normal, twelve-year-old Regan (Blair). When Regan begins behaving oddly, then lapses into increasingly violent behavior and gruesome appearance, doctors can't explain the reason. In desperation, Mrs. MacNeil takes the advice of Father Karras (Miller) and calls upon the exorcising skills of Father Merrin (Von Sydow). The venerable priest, adept at expelling evil spirits from their tormented victims, gets results, but at a terrible cost. The production creates a suitably ominous mood, with shadowed lighting and eerie music, and the cast performs with the solemnity befitting a true horror tale. The climax will leave you shaken.

Off-Screen: As audiences crowded the theaters to see *The Exorcist,* accounts of viewers fainting and vomiting in reaction to the film added to its cachet. Ticket sales reached $90 million, setting a record for Warners up to that time. Pea soup lost its appeal for a while when audiences learned that it substituted for the real thing when Blair regurgitates green slime. The unearthly sound of the demon who speaks through her is the throaty voice of actress Mercedes McCambridge; the screams of the exorcised demon are actually cries of pigs being led to slaughter. The movie received Oscars for its screenplay and sound. *Exorcist II: The Heretic* (1977) and *The Exorcist III* (1990) were dismal sequels. (CFB)

The Fabulous Baker Boys

Fox, 1989. (C-113m.) Dir: Steve Kloves. Sp: Steve Kloves. Cast: Jeff Bridges, Michelle Pfeiffer, Beau Bridges, Elie Raab, Jennifer Tilly.

On-Screen: *Two piano-playing brothers and a singer.* This long, smoky, absorbing romantic comedy relates what happens when Frank and Jack Baker (Beau Bridges, Jeff Bridges), two small-time nightclub pianists, have singer Susie Diamond (Pfeiffer) join their act. Frank has a family to support; Jack has broken dreams to forget; Susie has a past to climb out of; and what happens is predictable in outcome but touching and unexpected along the way. Music winds through the film, mostly meditative jazz, superbly chosen and played. Pfeiffer sings for herself, well enough, but no threat to Streisand; call her a more vulnerable Dietrich. Her version of "Makin' Whoopee" lets you know what *whoopee* means, but there's a love scene that shows how to be really sexy with both partners clothed, silent, and hardly moving. The Bridges brothers capture Frank's uptightness and Jack's cynicism with perfect pitch, and the direction is at once unsparing and romantic. Seeing *The Fabulous Baker Boys* is like being in a small club at two A.M. with your best friend or lover, watching a trio play their hearts out. You may stay longer than you want to, but you won't regret a minute of it.

Off-Screen: Writer-director Steve Kloves held out for five years to get the film made the way he intended. It was suggested that Chevy Chase and Dan Aykroyd should play the leads, or someone thought that Michelle Pfeiffer's character should become a singing star. There was other "input" along the way, but Kloves said no to it all. As we can see from the evidence, tenacity sometimes pays. The piano playing is by Dave Grusin. Michelle Pfeiffer won a Best Actress Oscar nomination for her performance. (BL)

A Face in the Crowd

Warners, 1957. (125m.) Dir: Elia Kazan. Sp: Budd Schulberg, b/o his story. Cast: Andy Griffith, Patricia Neal, Walter Matthau, Anthony Franciosa, Lee Remick, Kay Medford, Howard Smith, Percy Waram, Marshall Neilan.

On-Screen: *A corrupt drifter becomes a national power through television.* Back in 1957, Budd Schulberg's cautionary tale created something of a stir with its cynical view of the gullibility of the American public, as well as of the insidious power of television to make and break idols. Elia Kazan was generally praised for his direction, as was Andy Griffith (in his film debut) for his performance as Larry "Lonesome" Rhodes, the guitar-playing hobo who stars as a folksy voice on a small Arkansas station and becomes a power-hungry celebrity on national television. Today, *A Face in the Crowd* seems heavy-handed, and its once-blistering satire of television comes across as painfully obvious. Patricia Neal gives a sharp edge to her role as the woman who creates and finally destroys Lonesome, and Lee Remick makes her movie debut as an air-headed drum majorette. Walter Matthau is rather ludicrous as an intellectual TV writer (complete with pipe and horn-rimmed glasses) who has Lonesome's number.

Off-Screen: Elia Kazan worked closely on the screenplay with Budd Schulberg, and unlike their collaboration on *On the Waterfront,* where Schulberg was seldom near the camera, Kazan insisted that the writer remain at his side on every day of the shooting. Marshall Neilan, a once-prominent director fallen on hard times because of alcoholism, plays the role of scheming Senator Fuller in the film. Rip Torn can also be spotted in the cast.

Fail Safe

Columbia, 1964. (111m.) Dir: Sidney Lumet. Sp: Walter Bernstein, b/o novel by Eugene Burdick and Harvey Wheeler. Cast: Henry Fonda, Dan O'Herlihy, Walter Matthau, Frank Overton, Fritz Weaver, Edward Binns, Larry Hagman, Dom DeLuise, Sorrell Booke.

On-Screen: *A nuclear failure triggers disaster.* What would happen if America's nuclear deterrent system suddenly failed and bombers with atomic weapons were accidentally aimed toward Moscow—and nothing could be done to retrieve them? The thoroughly chilling answer is provided in this taut, sober adaptation of the best-selling novel. Henry Fonda has the central role as the U.S. president, isolated in a cell-like room as he desperately attempts to avoid further catastrophe by convincing the Soviet premier that it was an accident. In his intense hot-line conversations, Fonda provides the core of the film's meaning ("We're paying for our mutual suspicions"), but others give expert performances within their limited roles, including Frank Overton as a top SAC general, Fritz Weaver as a colonel who cracks under the strain, and Larry Hagman as an interpreter. The concept, happily, remains in the realm of science fiction, but *Fail Safe* is written, directed, and performed so persuasively that it can still provide more than a few frightening moments.

Off-Screen: Quite a different view of a nuclear holocaust was provided earlier in the year with the release of Stanley Kubrick's *Dr. Strangelove.* Afterward, Henry Fonda admitted that he "flipped" over the black humor of *Dr. Strangelove* and would have been unable to do *Fail Safe* if he had first seen Kubrick's movie.

Fame

MGM, 1980. (C-134m.) Dir: Alan Parker. Sp: Christopher Gore. MS: Michael Gore,

Leslie Gore, and others. Cast: Irene Cara, Lee Curreri, Barry Miller, Maureen Teefy, Gene Anthony Ray, Eddie Barth, Laura Dean, Paul McCrane, Antonio Franceschi, Anne Meara, Albert Hague.

On-Screen: *Aspiring young performers share their fears and dreams.* Scratch *Fame* and you'll find a Mickey Rooney–Judy Garland musical with angst. The setting is Manhattan's High School for Performing Arts where hopeful young performers learn their craft and dream of "making it big" in show business. The movie follows the lives of eight youngsters over four years, including Irene Cara as a talented black singer bent on stardom, Barry Miller as a Puerto Rican with a wretched family background, Paul McCrane as a troubled gay, Maureen Teefy as a Jewish girl with a possessive mother, and Gene Anthony Ray as an angry, gifted black dancer. Periodically, the film curtails all the adolescent suffering for musical numbers that, while staged expertly and performed exuberantly, seem at odds with the rest of the material. The Oscar-winning title tune was the standout. Ironically, none of the young performers in *Fame* achieved fame, though some went on to successful careers.

Off-Screen: *Fame* also won an Academy Award for its score and was nominated for its screenplay, film editing, and sound. The movie became a popular television series that ran from 1982 to 1986. Lee Curreri, Gene Anthony Ray, and Albert Hague (as a music teacher) were picked up from the original cast. When the New York City Board of Education refused permission to film at the High School for Performing Arts, the producers settled for two other New York schools, Haaren High on Tenth Avenue and P.S. 122 on East Ninth Street.

Inside these schools they recreated the hallways, classrooms, and studios of Performing Arts.

Fantasia

Walt Disney, 1940. (C-120m., animated) Production Supervisor: Ben Sharpsteen. With Deems Taylor and Leopold Stokowski and the Philadelphia Orchestra.

On-Screen: *Walt Disney and company animate the musical classics.* One of Disney's most ambitious—and also most controversial—projects, *Fantasia* continues to enthrall many viewers, while irritating many others. A number of musical compositions, ranging from Tchaikovsky's *Nutcracker Suite* to Moussorgsky's *Night on Bald Mountain,* are visually interpreted by Disney artists. The result is uneven but always imaginative and often enchanting. Highlights include Tchaikovsky's *Nutcracker Suite,* with its sinuous "Arabian Dance" and clever "Chinese Dance"; Paul Dukas's *The Sorcerer's Apprentice,* in which a delightful Mickey Mouse makes the mistake of assuming the powers of his master; and Igor Stravinsky's *The Rite of Spring,* where the animation depicts no less than the creation of the earth and the dawn of history. The latter segment is extraordinarily compelling, especially when the prehistoric creatures, expiring in the blazing heat, raise their heads to the pitiless sun. Favorite portion: Ponchielli's "Dance of the Hours," interpreted as a zany, hilarious ballet performed by a corps of ostriches, hippos, elephants, and crocodiles. Other segments, such as Beethoven's *Pastoral Symphony,* are less successful. Composer and musicologist Deems Taylor provides on-screen commentary.

Off-Screen: *Fantasia* began with *The Sorcerer's Apprentice,* which Disney animated to Stokowski's conducting. Stokowski suggested to Disney that they expand the idea to include a wide range of musical compositions that would be interpreted in animation by Disney's artists. The final production cost $2,280,000, and it did not return its heavy investment for many years. A segment using Debussy's "Clair de Lune" did not appear in the final film; the animation turned up years later, with new music, in *Make Mine Music* (1946). For the complete story of the production, see *Walt Disney's Fantasia,* by John Culhane (Abrams, 1988).

A Farewell to Arms

Paramount, 1932. (78m.) Dir: Frank Borzage. Sp: Oliver H. P. Garrett and Benjamin Glazer, b/o novel by Ernest Hemingway. Cast: Gary Cooper, Helen Hayes, Adolphe Menjou, Mary Philips, Jack LaRue, Blanche Frederici.

On-Screen: *Ernest Hemingway's tragic love story set during World War I.* This first try at transferring Hemingway to the screen downplays much of the antiwar novel's biting realism, emphasizing instead the love affair between an American lieutenant (Cooper), serving with an Italian ambulance unit, and a British nurse (Hayes). As a soldier whose desperate search for happiness and revulsion at war's brutalities drive him to desert the army, Cooper is more petulant than introspective. Hayes is radiant, if somewhat affected, as the doomed nurse; Menjou is fine as the Italian major who befriends and then betrays Cooper. Hemingway's characters are more interesting and less sentimental

than the screenplay and Borzage's direction make them. Yet audiences at the time responded to this moist tale of wartime romance.

Off-Screen: No actors—not even Fredric March and Claudette Colbert, for whom the screenplay was written—could have mitigated Hemingway's displeasure with this adaptation. One of the author's annoyances involved the fate of his heroine: in the novel, she dies at the end; the movie's ambiguous conclusion plays it safe. Bells joyously ringing out news of the armistice suggest her eventual recovery, or flight to heavenly rest. The movie received four Oscar nominations (including Best Picture), but won only two, for photography and sound recording. A ponderous, epic-scaled remake, with Jennifer Jones and Rock Hudson, was released in 1957. (CFB)

The Farmer's Daughter

RKO, 1947. (97m.) Dir. H. C. Potter. Sp: Allen Rivkin and Laura Kerr, b/o play by Juhni Tervataa. Cast: Loretta Young, Joseph Cotten, Ethel Barrymore, Charles Bickford, Rose Hobart, Rhys Williams, Harry Davenport, Tom Powers, Lex Barker, William Harrigan.

On-Screen: *A Minnesota farm girl runs for Congress.* Since making her film debut in the late twenties, beautiful Loretta Young could be counted on to give pleasing if unexceptional performances in a great many movies. In 1947, she came into her own, winning the Best Actress Oscar over such strong contenders as Joan Crawford, Susan Hayward, Dorothy McGuire, and Rosalind Russell. In *The Farmer's Daughter,* she plays a Minnesota farm girl of Swedish stock who gets a job as a maid in the home of a congressman (Cotten) and ends up not only running for Congress herself but winning the heart of her charmed employer (Cotten). It's purely a fairy tale, of course, but so agreeably played and written that you shouldn't mind the fanciful ideas about government and politics. Ethel Barrymore appears as Cotten's politically wise mother, and Charles Bickford is the rather informal butler in the house.

Off-Screen: Ingrid Bergman had been scheduled to play the leading role when the story was known as *Katie for Congress,* but she turned it down. David O. Selznick, who had originally purchased the play and was part owner of the property, had Sonja Henie in mind for the role, but luckily, it went to Loretta Young. Producer Dore Schary convinced Young that she could handle the Swedish accent. *The Farmer's Daughter* became a television series that ran from 1963 to 1966.

Fatal Attraction

Paramount, 1987. (C-119m.) Dir: Adrian Lyne. Sp: James Dearden, b/o his short subject "Diversion." Cast: Michael Douglas, Glenn Close, Anne Archer, Fred Gwynne, Ellen Hamilton Latzen, Mike Nussbaum, Stuart Pankin, Ellen Foley, Meg Mundy.

On-Screen: *A married man's one-night stand turns into a nightmare.* Fair warning to married men: never cheat on your wives, not even for a night, or you're liable to end up with a psychotic harridan, bent on your destruction. Or is the movie saying that a sexually active woman can be a devouring, terrifying

creature? Take your pick. In this harrowing melodrama, lawyer Michael Douglas's existence becomes a living hell after a casual fling with a dangerously disturbed woman (Close). As she intrudes further into the lives of Douglas's wife (Archer) and daughter (Latzen), Close's revenge for his neglect turns horrifying. The climax is gory if not entirely credible. The plot has more holes than Swiss cheese, but you may not notice as the movie gallops from one scary situation to another. Key sequences are edited for maximum impact, especially one in which Archer searches frantically for her kidnapped daughter while the girl rides a roller coaster with the serenely oblivious Close.

Off-Screen: Glenn Close was not the first choice to play Alex Forrest, but she asked for an audition and won the role when she proved in minutes that she could play a seriously disturbed woman. To understand her character, she consulted with several psychiatrists about the nature of her obsession. The original ending had Alex committing suicide, but the reaction of a preview audience convinced the filmmakers to change it.

Father of the Bride

MGM, 1950. (93m.) Dir: Vincente Minnelli. Sp: Albert Hackett and Frances Goodrich, b/o novel by Edward Streeter. Cast: Spencer Tracy, Joan Bennett, Elizabeth Taylor, Don Taylor, Billie Burke, Leo G. Carroll, Moroni Olsen, Russ Tamblyn, Melville Cooper.

On-Screen: *Spencer Tracy experiences the joys and tribulations of his daughter's wedding.* A perfect fantasy of American suburban life circa 1950, *Father of the Bride* depicts a world in which father only *thinks* he knows best while mother and daughter exert their tyrannical hold over him. Still, it's a vastly likable movie, with Oscar-nominated Tracy as hapless Stanley Banks, who must cope with the various traumas of daughter Taylor's wedding. Lightly satirical touches concerning the event ("An experienced caterer can make you ashamed of your house in fifteen minutes") are nicely blended with Banks's ambiguity about losing a daughter. ("Something inside me was beginning to hurt.") The best sequence involves his nightmare vision of a disastrous wedding ceremony. Elizabeth Taylor is radiantly beautiful as the bride-to-be, and her kitchen scene with Tracy over a bottle of milk ("Kitten" with her "Pops") is a well-remembered gem.

Off-Screen: Before signing Spencer Tracy to play Stanley Banks, Vincente Minnelli was obliged to test Jack Benny at production head Dore Schary's request. (Schary had promised Benny a chance at the part.) This prompted Tracy to refuse the role when it was finally offered, but he was persuaded to accept by Minnelli. The director said of Tracy: "Spencer was an inspiration. His instincts were infallible. He knew how to throw the unimportant things away, and he knew how to create the illusion of throwing the important things away, too, so that they were inscribed in your mind. His way of speaking made you feel you'd stumbled on a great truth." A television version surfaced in 1961. The film was remade in 1991 with Steve Martin and Diane Keaton.

Father's Little Dividend

MGM, 1951. (82m.) Dir: Vincente Minnelli. Sp: Albert Hackett and Frances Good-rich, b/o characters created by Edward Streeter. Cast: Spencer Tracy, Joan Bennett, Elizabeth Taylor, Don Taylor, Billie Burke, Moroni Olsen, Russ Tamblyn.

On-Screen: *Stanley Banks learns the joys and perils of becoming a grandfather.* A rose-colored view of suburban life in 1950, *Father of the Bride* enjoyed a huge success and won a fourth Oscar nomination for Spencer Tracy. A sequel was inevitable, and here again is Tracy as Stanley Banks, gruff, harassed, and lovable, as he learns that daughter Kay (Taylor) is about to become a mother. His reactions are predictable but also amusing, and in some ways *Father's Little Dividend* is an improvement on the original. This time around, Stanley Banks is somewhat less of a buffoon and a fall guy for the humor, and the situations are a mite closer to reality. He must contend with the uproar over a name for the baby, his pregnant daughter's tearful return to his household after a quarrel with her husband, and, inevitably, the brouhaha caused by the birth itself. Once again, Joan Bennett plays Stanley's distracted but loving wife, and Elizabeth Taylor makes a beautiful expectant mother. Good fun.

Off-Screen: Spencer Tracy frequently balked at the roles he was offered, and *Father's Little Dividend* was no exception. He didn't want to repeat the role and felt that sequels were never as good as the original. As she did many other times, Katharine Hepburn stepped in to change his mind. With the sets still up, and the players under contract, the film was completed in twenty-two days.

A Few Good Men

Columbia-Castle Rock, 1992. (C-140m.) Dir: Rob Reiner. Sp: Aaron Sorkin, b/o his play. Cast: Tom Cruise, Jack Nicholson, Demi Moore, Kevin Bacon, Kevin Pollak, Keifer Sutherland, James Marshall, J. T. Walsh, Wolfgang Bodison, Christopher Guest.

On-Screen: *A military trial, via the Broadway stage.* On an American naval base on the coast of Cuba at Guantanamo Bay, two young marines (Marshall and Bodison) are accused of murdering a fellow marine when what starts as a hazing incident turns deadly. Lieut. (j.g.) Kaffee (Cruise), a young hotshot naval lawyer, is assigned to defend the marines, assisted by Lieut. Comdr. Galloway (Moore). Were the defendants acting on orders from higher up, as high, perhaps, as the base's commander, Col. Jessup (Nicholson)? In its concern with military ethics and questions of guilt and responsibility, *A Few Good Men* recalls *The Caine Mutiny* and other films, but a finely tuned screenplay, skillful direction, and top-notch performances turn it into a smashing movie. Playing his usual character, Tom Cruise moves convincingly from flip indifference to nostril-flaring dedication, and Jack Nicholson, who seems to be turning more granitelike with every new role, is properly scary in his few scenes as the tough, arrogant officer. In an explosive climax, when the two men inevitably confront each other in the courtroom, the screen fairly bristles with high-voltage tension. *A Few Good Men* is first-rate entertainment.

Off-Screen: Articles published at the time of the movie's release told how director Reiner worked intensely and sometimes heatedly with writer Sorkin and others to reshape the hit Broadway play for the screen. Sorkin later acknowledged that he was so pleased with the result that he went back and re- vised his original play. Michelle Pfeiffer was first considered for the part of Jo Galloway, and other actresses who read for the role included Julie Warner, Penelope Ann Miller, Linda Hamilton, and Elizabeth Perkins. The movie won three Oscar nominations, including Best Picture and Best Supporting Actor (Nicholson).

Fiddler on the Roof

United Artists, 1971. (C-181m.) Dir: Norman Jewison. Sp: Joseph Stein, b/o his musical play and stories of Sholem Aleichem. MS: Jerry Bock and Sheldon Harnick. Cast: Topol, Norma Crane, Leonard Frey, Molly Picon, Paul Mann, Rosalind Harris, Neva Small, Michael Glaser.

On-Screen: *Tevye and his family on the screen. "L'chayim!"* Beginning its extraordinarily long run on Broadway in 1964, the stage musical *Fiddler on the Roof* was widely acclaimed for the beauty and poignancy of its book and score. This film version appeared seven years later, and despite some negative appraisals, it reaffirmed the show's stature as a towering achievement. A musical fable, both harsh and tender, concerning the milkman Tevye (Topol), his family, and neighbors, in the beleaguered town of Anatevka in Russia, *Fiddler on the Roof* deals with family traditions shattered by religious persecution. Yet many of the film's most unforgettable moments are musically joyous: the exquisite "Sabbath Prayer," Tevye's exultant dream of wealth and glory ("If I Were a Rich Man"), and the wedding of Tevye's daughter ("Sunrise, Sunset"). Other sequences, such as Tevye's parting from another daughter ("Far From the Home I Love"), are deeply touching. The Oscar-nominated Israeli actor Topol, who had appeared in the London production of the musical, gives expressive shadings to Tevye, and the rest of the cast remains solidly immersed in the tradition of *Fiddler on the Roof.*

Off-Screen: Anatevka's fiddler on the roof was played by a British actor and choreographer named Tutte Lemkow. His fiddle playing was dubbed by Isaac Stern. The movie was shot at Pinewood Studios, just outside London, and exteriors were filmed in Yugoslavia. It was nominated for eight Oscars (including Best Picture) and won for Cinematography, Sound, and Scoring (Adaptation). Topol reprised his role on Broadway many years later. *Tevye* (a.k.a. *Tevya*), a Yiddish-language version starring famed actor Maurice Schwartz, was released in 1939.

Field of Dreams

Universal, 1989. (C-106m.) Dir: Phil Alden Robinson. Sp: Phil Alden Robinson, b/o novel by W. P. Kinsella. Cast: Kevin Costner, Amy Madigan, James Earl Jones, Ray Liotta, Burt Lancaster, Timothy Busfield, Gaby Hoffman.

On-Screen: *Baseball, faith, and Kevin Costner.* If you hear voices, make a movie. When Iowa farmer Roy Kinsella (Costner) hears the voice of God (or whomever) saying, "If you build it, he will come," he somehow knows that "it" is a baseball diamond in the middle of his cornfields. He's right. The "he" turns out to be Shoeless Joe Jackson (Liotta), the legendary star of the infamous Chicago Black Sox, the team accused of throwing a World Series. Soon, long-departed baseball stars are joining Shoeless Joe in playing real

ball games on Roy's field. There are other complications, including a few more cryptic messages and several very real and serious family crises, before a happy resolution. With all the voices, all the miracles, all the sweetness and understanding on most everyone's part, you may find *Field of Dreams* indigestible and manipulative. Or you may put aside your cynical impulses and surrender to its mood. Many viewers did, and the film was a great success.

Off-Screen: After reading W. P. Kinsella's novel *Shoeless Joe* in 1981, writer-director Phil Alden Robinson spent the next eight years trying to get the movie made. The baseball field built on Don Lansing's farm in Dyersville, Iowa, has become a kind of shrine and tourist attraction. Many people drive to this remote place twenty-five miles west of Dubuque, drawn to the diamond with its edges of red brick and an outfield outlined by an eight-foot-high wall of corn. (BL)

The Fighting 69th

Warners, 1940. (90m.) Dir: William Keighley. Sp: Norman Reilly Raine, Fred Niblo, Jr., and Dean Franklin. Cast: James Cagney, Pat O'Brien, George Brent, Jeffrey Lynn, Dennis Morgan, Alan Hale, Dick Foran, Frank McHugh.

On-Screen: *The exploits of the famous World War I fighting unit.* Just about as corny as a war film can get, *The Fighting 69th* purports to tell the story of the brave men, mostly Irishmen from New York, who performed heroic deeds in World War I. The movie concentrates on Cagney as the arrogant but cowardly private who inevitably (and unconvincingly) proves his heroism by the film's end. Cagney's frequent costar Pat O'Brien plays the unit's chaplain, saintly Father Duffy, and Jeffrey Lynn appears as Joyce Kilmer, the ill-fated poet who wrote the perennial "Trees." The thick leavening of Irish humor and sentiment is almost as heavy as in a John Ford western. With America on the verge of involvement in another war, the film emphasizes the patriotic virtues of honor and duty, but there's enough battle action to keep viewers awake.

Off-Screen: When Fox said that it was planning a film on the same regiment after Warners had announced its intention of making *The Fighting 69th,* Jack Warner sent Darryl Zanuck a warning letter telling him that he did not have "the moral right" to make the picture. Fox dropped the project. Warners spent heavily to re-create Camp Mills, French villages, and the battlefields of World War I. Armies of extras took over the studio's entire Calabasas Ranch for the production.

Finian's Rainbow

Warners, 1968. (C-145m.) Dir: Francis Ford Coppola. Sp: E. Y. Harburg and Fred Saidy, b/o their musical play. MS: Burton Lane and E. Y. Harburg. Cast: Fred Astaire, Petula Clark, Tommy Steele, Don Francks, Keenan Wynn, Al Freeman, Jr., Barbara Hancock.

On-Screen: *Leprechauns, gold, and racism—from a Broadway musical.* Back in 1947, Broadway audiences were enchanted by this musical concerning an old Irishman (Astaire) who comes to the mythical state of Missitucky and becomes involved with an imp-

ish leprechaun (Steele), a bigoted senator (Wynn), and a number of Missituckians. The mixture of whimsy and political significance may have worked in 1947, but twenty years later, in this maladroit production, it makes for heavy going. The familiar songs—"How Are Things in Glocca Morra?" "Something Sort of Grandish," "Look to the Rainbow," etc.—are still delightful, but those offbeat lyrics, with words like *animules* and *Eisenhowerish,* begin to pall after a while. Fred Astaire looks haggard, but his very presence gives the movie a badly needed lift. Tommy Steele grins and grins as the leprechaun, but his charm, at least on-screen, is elusive. *Finian's Rainbow* might have best remained in Broadway memory.

Off-Screen: At the time, Francis Ford Coppola recognized the pitfalls inherent in the book, but he believed that he could overcome them. Wrong. Although Hermes Pan, Fred Astaire's longtime associate, is credited as choreographer, he was fired by Coppola not long after production began, and his absence shows. (Coppola: "The choreography was abysmal, let's be honest.") Also the studio blew the 35mm original up to 70mm, going from a normal-screen ratio to a wide-screen ratio. The effect was to crop the top and bottom of the screen so that Fred Astaire's feet couldn't be seen when he danced.

A Fish Called Wanda

MGM, 1988. (108m.) Dir: Charles Crichton. Sp: John Cleese, b/o story by John Cleese and Charles Crichton. Cast: Jamie Lee Curtis, John Cleese, Kevin Kline, Michael Palin, Maria Aitken, Tom Georgeson, Patricia Hayes.

On-Screen: *A British barrister becomes involved with criminal activity*. A delightfully ditsy Monty Pythonesque comedy, *A Fish Called Wanda* is an extremely broad farce, a caper film in which sexy con artist Jamie Lee Curtis seduces barrister John Cleese into unwittingly helping her with a bank robbery. Kevin Kline, who won a Best Supporting Oscar, plays Curtis's hilariously stupid, clumsily crafty boyfriend. Curtis provides the main charm of this slapstick folly, whether turned on with mounting fervor at the sound of phrases spoken in foreign tongues, or crawling behind furniture when caught in a tryst with Cleese. A stuttering Michael Palin (like Cleese, a Monty Python alumnus) is underemployed in an able cast, but he has a few hilarious moments of physical awkwardness. Cleese is delightful as the conservative lawyer who is more than ready to chuck everything for sin, sex, and profit with his inamorata. Warning: animal-cruelty jokes include squashed dogs and eating pet fish.

Off-Screen: Charles Crichton, aged seventy-eight, received two Oscar nominations (Best Direction, Best Original Story) for his first film in many years. Best known for the films he directed at England's Ealing studios (*The Lavender Hill Mob, The Titfield Thunderbolt*), Crichton worked for British television after the demise of these comedies. *A Fish Called Wanda* received many complaints about its depiction of stuttering and even produced pickets at MGM's studios. (JMK)

The Fisher King

TriStar, 1991. (C-135m.) Dir: Terry Gilliam. Sp: Richard LaGravenese. Cast: Jeff Bridges, Robin Williams, Mercedes Ruehl, Amanda Plummer, Michael Jeter, Harry Shearer.

On-Screen: *Terry Gilliam's oddball mixture of mythology, hard-edged realism, and romance*. Cluttered, sometimes incoherent, but also fascinating, *The Fisher King* is a film that will reap rewards for those who are willing to stay with its quirkiness. Jeff Bridges plays Jack Lucas, a radio talk-show host whose heartless insults provoke a deranged man to commit mass murder in a bar. Years later, a wrecked, alcoholic Lucas meets Parry (Williams), the husband of one of the victims, now a mad derelict who believes he is a knight searching for the Holy Grail in today's world. After many fanciful, bizarre, and starkly realistic events, Parry becomes the source of Jack's redemption. The film veers off its sin-and-redemption course to take up Parry's courtship of the eccentric Lydia (Plummer). Yet this section boasts the film's two most wonderful sequences: in the throes of love, Parry envisions hundreds of couples waltzing in Grand Central Station; in the second, hoping to woo Lydia, Parry sends a homeless gay man (Jeter) to her office, where he does a wickedly funny, yet oddly touching impression of Ethel Merman in *Gypsy*.

Off-Screen: Much of *The Fisher King* was shot in New York City under very difficult conditions. The most difficult, logistically, was shooting one thousand waltzing extras in Grand Central Station. According to the director, they had visited dancing schools in search of people who supposedly know how to waltz, only to discover that most of them *didn't*. Gilliam recalls sitting in the station with the extras and the choreographer trying to teach them how to waltz. Williams won an Oscar nomination as Best Actor, and Mercedes Ruehl, as his earthy girlfriend, took home the statuette as Best Supporting Actress.

Five Easy Pieces

Columbia, 1970. (C-96m.) Dir: Bob Rafelson. Sp: Adrien Joyce, b/o story by Bob Rafelson and Adrien Joyce. Cast: Jack Nicholson, Karen Black, Susan Anspach, Billy Green Bush, Fannie Flagg, Sally (Ann) Struthers, Lois Smith, Helena Kallianiotes.

On-Screen: *A disaffected man returns to his family.* Rude, cynical, intolerant, and above all, self-hating, Robert (Bobby) Dupea leaves his job as an oil worker to visit his family at their island home in Puget Sound. Traveling with dim-witted Rayette Dipesto (Black), Bobby is determined to divest himself of all responsibilities. (At one time he was a promising concert pianist, and his family is musical.) During his visit home, he moves further away "from things that get bad if I stay." Bob Rafelson's well-made portrait of alienation was probably overrated at the time of its release, but several sequences linger in the mind. One, of course, is the diner scene in which Bobby has a funny encounter with a hostile waitress. Another is Bobby's agonized soliloquy with his mute, dying father. Jack Nicholson's many-faceted performance won an Oscar nomination. Helena Kallianiotes is hilarious as a lesbian hitchhiker who has a diatribe against the "filth" destroying the country.

Off-Screen: Voted the year's best film by New York film critics, *Five Easy Pieces* was Bob Rafelson's first film after his debut with the rock film *Head* (1968). (Rafelson also won as Best Director, and Karen Black was cited as Best Supporting Actress.) "Adrien Joyce" was a pseudonym for writer Carol Eastman. Sally Struthers, billed here as Sally Ann Struthers, achieved fame the following year in television's "All in the Family."

The Fly

Fox, 1958. (C-94m.) Dir: Kurt Neumann. Sp: James Clavell, b/o story by George Langelaan. Cast: Al Hedison, Patricia Owens, Vincent Price, Herbert Marshall, Kathleen Freeman.

On-Screen: *Sci-fi horror concerning man-into-fly.* Preposterous as the premise may be, and it numbers among the silliest in the genre, *The Fly* proved to be popular with viewers who liked a good fright for their money. Al Hedison plays one of those overambitious scientists who dares to probe the secrets of the universe and pays a bitter price. He invents a "disintegrator-integrator" apparatus that can transmit solid matter from one place to another with no apparent damage. Trouble is, when he experiments on himself, a fly gets into the machine, and he ends up a horrible creature, with the head and one arm of a fly! His distraught wife (Owens) finally puts an end to his misery. The cast acts out the story with a straight face, and a few moments have some shock value, none more than the climax in which Hedison's brother (Price) and the police inspector (Marshall) come upon the ghastly result of Hedison's experiment. Even viewers who had laughed their way through the movie recalled that final cry for help with a few goose bumps.

Off-Screen: The screenplay was written by James Clavell, who later wrote the epic novel *Shogun*. Reportedly, Price and Marshall could not contain their laughter during the filming of that climactic scene with the trapped fly, and many takes were necessary. Al Hedison later changed his name to David Hedison. The popularity of *The Fly* prompted two sequels, *Return of the Fly* (1959) and *Curse of the Fly* (1965). The original movie was remade in 1986, with Jeff Goldblum as the hapless hero. It was much more elaborate, and infinitely more gory. This remake was followed in 1989 by its own sequel, *The Fly II*. Somebody get the flyswatter.

Flying Down to Rio

RKO, 1933. (89m.) Dir: Thornton Freeland. Sp: Lou Brock. MS: Vincent Youmans, Gus Kahn, and Edward Eliscu. Cast: Gene Raymond, Dolores Del Rio, Fred Astaire, Ginger Rogers, Raul Roulien, Franklin Pangborn, Eric Blore.

On-Screen: *Introducing Fred and Ginger*. An inane and cluttered musical, *Flying Down to Rio* enjoys two claims to fame. One is "The Carioca," in which Fred Astaire and Ginger Rogers danced together on-screen for the first time, and the other is the astonishing sequence in which chorus girls perform on the wings of airplanes in midair to the music of the title song. (Although we know that the girls are only a few feet from the ground, the effect is a bit frightening.) The rest is rather tiresome nonsense about the romance between sultry Dolores Del Rio and bandleader Gene Raymond. But what joy when Astaire and Rogers dance together with the rapport and the wit that would soon make them famous. In other musical numbers, Rogers sings (and later Astaire dances to) "Music Makes Me," and Del Rio and Astaire perform a brief, insinuating tango to

"Orchids in the Moonlight." But you'll remember Fred and Ginger cavorting to "The Carioca," and those absurd and amazing wing-dancers.

Off-Screen: Actress Dorothy Jordan had originally been cast in the role of band singer Honey Hale. When she chose to marry producer Merian Cooper instead and go off on her honeymoon, the role went to Ginger Rogers, who had already made a few films for RKO. She had known Astaire in New York. The wing-dancing number was filmed in an airplane hangar, using wind machines and a few planes suspended from the ceiling. Authentic background footage of Rio was mixed with aerial views of the more accessible Malibu Beach.

Follow the Fleet

RKO, 1936. (110m.) Dir: Mark Sandrich. Sp: Dwight Taylor and Allan Scott, b/o play by Hubert Osborne. MS: Irving Berlin. Cast: Ginger Rogers, Fred Astaire, Randolph Scott, Harriet Hilliard, Astrid Allwyn, Harry Beresford, Russell Hicks, Lucille Ball, Betty Grable.

On-Screen: *Sailor Astaire woos dancer Rogers to the music of Irving Berlin*. The third dance musical costarring Rogers and Astaire, *Follow the Fleet* takes the team out of the posh pavilions and into the two-bit dance halls—but with the irresistible lilt of the Berlin music to guide them, the change does them little harm. Fred's a self-confident, gum-chewing sailor who is reunited with former partner Ginger, now a dance hall hostess. Their quarrels and misunderstandings also involve his shipmate Scott and her mousy sister, Hilliard. What really matters, of course, are the songs and the dances, and they are splendid, among them the team's deft comedy-in-dance routine for "I'm Putting All My Eggs in One Basket"; Astaire's dazzling nautical tap dance to "I'd Rather Lead a Band"; and their incomparable final number, "Let's Face the Music and Dance," which is staged as a self-contained miniature drama at a benefit performance. *Follow the Fleet* is top-notch entertainment.

Off-Screen: Hubert Osborne's play *Shore Leave,* which is the source of the screenplay, was first filmed in 1925, with Richard Barthelmess. It then became the basis for Vincent Youmans's 1928 stage musical *Hit the Deck.* RKO filmed *Hit the Deck* in 1930 and MGM remade it in 1955. (Are you following this?) For the "Let Yourself Go" number at the Paradise Ballroom, choreographer Hermes Pan recruited a number of nonprofessionals who performed exhibition dances in the dance halls of the period. Two Berlin songs, "Moonlight Maneuvers" and "There's a Smile on My Face," were dropped from the film.

Footlight Parade

Warners, 1933. (104m.) Dir: Lloyd Bacon. Musical numbers directed by Busby Berkeley. Sp: Manuel Seff and James Seymour. MS: Sammy Fain, Irving Kahal, Harry Warren, and Al Dubin. Cast: James Cagney, Joan Blondell, Dick Powell, Ruby Keeler, Guy Kibbee, Ruth Donnelly, Frank McHugh.

On-Screen: *Busby Berkeley in full bloom.* One of the best of the Warners musicals of the thirties, *Footlight Parade* combines the familiar "let's put on a show" story line with some eye-popping and marvelously absurd pro-

duction numbers. Heading the cast is James Cagney, pugnacious and fast on his feet as a producer of "prologues," short stage presentations between film showings. Those who can tolerate the narrative will be rewarded with three back-to-back "prologues" coming at the end: "Honeymoon Hotel," a cheerfully vulgar piece about an emporium where "Cupid is the night clerk"; the mind-boggling "By a Waterfall," involving Dick Powell, Ruby Keeler, and one hundred chorus girls gamboling at a giant waterfall; and best of all, "Shanghai Lil," in which Cagney excels as a sailor looking for his "Lil" in a sleazy bar choked with sailors and prostitutes. A heady mixture of the exotic, the erotic, and the bizarre, this number is not to be missed.

Off-Screen: James Cagney had to argue with Jack Warner to get his role in *Footlight Parade.* Claire Dodd, who plays Cagney's nasty ex-wife, was taller than him, so a box had to be slipped under him in their scenes together to make him appear taller. When Dick Powell had throat trouble, he was replaced by Stanley Smith (*Honey, Good News,* both 1930). But Powell recovered, and Warners decided to scrap all the footage with Smith and use their original star. Star-to-be John Garfield is clearly visible as a sailor in the "Shanghai Lil" number.

For Me and My Gal

MGM, 1942. (104m.) Dir: Busby Berkeley. Sp: Richard Sherman, Sid Silvers, and Fred Finklehoffe, b/o story by Howard Emmett Rogers. MS: various writers. Cast: Judy Garland, Gene Kelly, George Murphy, Marta Eggerth, Ben Blue, Keenan Wynn, Richard Quine.

On-Screen: *Judy and Gene, together for the first time*. Moviegoers of a certain vintage will recall the scene in which Judy Garland and Gene Kelly (in his film debut) pool their talents to perform the title song in a restaurant. Their rapport was apparent to everyone, and their recording of the song was one of the year's surprise hits. Audiences responded favorably to Kelly's charm and dancing, despite the unsympathetic character he was playing. The rest of the movie is modest but tolerable corn about a vaudeville singer (Garland) and an ambitious dancer (Kelly) who shirks his duty in World War I. (Of course he later proves his heroism and redeems Garland's love.) Murphy is Garland's song-and-dance partner who gives her up for Kelly. A goodly number of old tunes ("After You've Gone," "When You Wore a Tulip," "Ballin' the Jack," etc.) helps to dilute the sticky wartime sentiment.

Off-Screen: Kelly's role in the film was originally intended for costar George Murphy, but both Judy Garland and Arthur Freed, who had seen Kelly in *Pal Joey* on Broadway, convinced studio executives to switch the roles. (At the time, Kelly was under contract to David O. Selznick.) Garland taught Kelly to tone down some of his stage-actor gestures. At the same time, Kelly was able to help Garland with their dance routines. They became good friends.

For the Boys

Fox, 1991. (C-148m.) Dir: Mark Rydell. Sp: Marshall Brickman, b/o story by Neal Jimenez and Lindy Laub. Cast: Bette Midler, James Caan, George Segal, Norman Fell, Patrick O'Neal, Christopher Rydell, Melissa Manchester.

On-Screen: *Two showbiz entertainers over fifty years*. Bette Midler's presence—that bawdy manner, toddling walk, and beaming smile —has galvanized many a recent movie, and here she is virtually the entire movie. Both funny and touching, she plays Dixie Leonard, a brassy singer who teams up with Eddie Sparks (Caan) to entertain troops in World War II and stays with him through fifty embattled years of the Korean War, blacklisting, Vietnam, and the combat deaths of her husband and son. Even in hideous old-age makeup, Midler gives a powerhouse performance, but she has little to play against in Caan, who is ineffectual as Eddie. (He looks embalmed, even when "young," and you never understand what made him a beloved star.) The movie is good at depicting America's changing attitude toward war (it starts as bravura patriotism and ends as numbed horror). But it's best as a showcase for Bette Midler's varied talents. George Segal is fine as a gagwriter who is purged during the McCarthy period.

Off-Screen: *For the Boys* began as merely an idea in Bette Midler's mind after her film debut in *The Rose* (1979). Nothing materialized until Fox picked it up around 1986. A screenplay was written by Neal Jimenez and Lindy Laub, but when Mark Rydell finally agreed to direct, he insisted that the script be entirely rewritten by Marshall Brickman, coauthor of *Annie Hall* and *Manhattan*. Brickman devised the central premise of long flashbacks from Dixie's point of view. The movie was an unexpected disappointment at the box office.

For Whom the Bell Tolls

Paramount, 1943. (C-130m.) Dir: Sam Wood. Sp: Dudley Nichols, b/o novel by Ernest Hemingway. Cast: Gary Cooper, Ingrid Bergman, Katina Paxinou, Akim Tamiroff, Joseph Calleia, Vladimir Sokoloff, Mikhail Rasumny, Arturo de Cordova, Fortunio Bonanova.

On-Screen: *Passions flare in a film version of Hemingway's novel.* Balancing the merits and demerits of this elaborate adaptation of the Hemingway book, one still comes out slightly on the plus side of the ledger. The setting is Spain in 1937, during the devastating civil war, and Gary Cooper is the stalwart American who is assigned to blow up a strategic bridge for the Loyalists, here called Republicans. He joins a group of guerrillas in the mountains, where he meets and falls in love with Maria (Bergman), a pathetic victim of the conflict. Their passionate but ill-fated encounter ends with the bridge's destruction. Hemingway's political content is largely absent in Dudley Nichols's screenplay, and the novelist's oddly mannered dialogue comes across as merely strange on the screen, especially when delivered by so many diverse accents. Also, Cooper is not entirely persuasive as the hero. Still, there are scenes of vigorous action and several fine performances. Bergman glows as Maria, while Oscar-winning Paxinou is powerfully compelling as Pilar, the woman with the "head of a bull and the heart of a hawk." Credit also a rousing score by Victor Young.

Off-Screen: Sam Wood replaced Cecil B. De-Mille as director. Also, after two weeks of shooting, dancer Vera Zorina was replaced by Ingrid Bergman in the role of Maria. An earlier adaptation had been written by novelist Louis Bromfield, but it was not used. The film was photographed in the isolated highlands of the Sierra Nevadas. In addition to Paxinou's Oscar, it was nominated for six others, including Best Picture, Best Actor (Cooper), and Best Actress (Bergman).

Forbidden Planet

MGM, 1956. (C-98m.) Dir: Fred McLeod Wilcox. Sp: Cyril Hume, b/o story by Irving Block and Allen Adler. Electric tonalities by Louis and Bebe Barron. Cast: Walter Pidgeon, Leslie Nielsen, Anne Francis, Warren Stevens, Earl Holliman, Jack Kelly.

On-Screen: *Shakespeare's* The Tempest *becomes a science-fiction adventure.* Fondly remembered by fans of science-fiction movies, *Forbidden Planet* is a most unusual entry to have emerged from MGM. The concept is clever: transposing *The Tempest* to a futuristic world, the story has Walter Pidgeon as Dr. Morbius, a scientist who is the lord and master of Altair-4, a distant planet inhabited two thousand centuries ago by a master race. The only other resident of Altair-4 is his daughter Altaira (Francis). In the year 2200, a disabled spaceship, headed by Leslie Nielsen, lands on Altair-4, searching for survivors of a previous space mission. After mysterious deaths occur, Dr. Morbius reveals the origin of the monstrous force that threatens them all. The acting is stiff, and some of the details are patently absurd, but the sets (especially Dr. Morbius's laboratory) are imaginative, the electronic score is intriguing, and the *Tempest* analogies are fun to follow. And three cheers for Robby the Robot.

Off-Screen: The eerie atmosphere on Altair-4 was achieved largely by means of a ten-thousand-foot cyclorama painting. Arnold "Buddy" Gillespie, MGM's special-effects supervisor, and art director Arthur Lonergan also created a six-foot-eleven-inch Robby the Robot, with a clear plastic head that allows the viewer to see the crackling electronic waves of the brain. The Disney Studio's special-effects animation department, headed by Joshua Meador, created the Id monster for the film.

A Foreign Affair

Paramount, 1948. (116m.) Dir: Billy Wilder. Sp: Charles Brackett, Billy Wilder, and Richard Breen. Cast: Jean Arthur, Marlene Dietrich, John Lund, Millard Mitchell, Peter Von Zerneck, Stanley Prager.

On-Screen: *A prim lady from Congress finds romance in postwar Berlin.* A member of a delegation sent to West Berlin to investigate military morale, Congresswoman Phoebe Frost (Arthur) becomes romantically involved with Capt. John Pringle (Lund), an officer who has made bombed-out Berlin his own profitable domain. Pringle's true intention is to keep Phoebe from investigating his mistress (Dietrich), a sultry nightclub singer and a former consort of Nazi bigwigs. By the time Phoebe learns that she has been Pringle's patsy, she has fallen in love with him. Billy Wilder's harshly cynical (and to some critics, callous) comedy somehow manages to squeeze many laughs out of a potentially depressing situation, thanks in no small part to Jean Arthur, expert as always despite her disfiguring makeup and hairdo, and Marlene Dietrich, who delivers several songs in her inimitable voice.

Off-Screen: If Jean Arthur's descent on Berlin in *A Foreign Affair* reminds you of Greta Garbo's mission to Paris in *Ninotchka* (both somber women find liberation and romance), it could be because Billy Wilder co-authored both films. Many years later, Dietrich wrote that Wilder was "a master builder who knew his toolbox and used it in the best way possible to set up the framework on which he hung the garlands of his wit and wisdom."

Foreign Correspondent

United Artists, 1940. (120m.) Dir: Alfred Hitchcock. Sp: Charles Bennett and Joan Harrison. Cast: Joel McCrea, Laraine Day, Herbert Marshall, George Sanders, Albert Basserman, Edmund Gwenn, Eduardo Ciannelli.

On-Screen: *World War II theme, dated now, but the Hitchcock touches still dazzle.* The real stars of this anti-Nazi thriller are the many excitingly staged scenes: the phony political assassination in a rain-splattered, umbrella-filled public square in Amsterdam, or the view from the cockpit of a transatlantic clipper as it nose-dives into the sea. Yet these stunning images never overpower the cloak-and-dagger story, thanks largely to McCrea's impassioned American journalist, caught up in a Nazi plot to kidnap a Dutch diplomat (Basserman), and Marshall's silk-smooth double agent. Watch for Gwenn's ill-timed lunge at McCrea atop London's Westminster Cathedral, and keep your eyes on that windmill's revolving sails.

Off-Screen: This was Hitchcock's second Hollywood movie, following the same year's *Rebecca.* The original intent had been to film

Personal History, political observer Vincent Sheean's acclaimed book on events prior to the war. Instead, Bennett and Harrison came up with a story dramatizing the urgent need for the United States to abandon its pre-1941 noninterventionist stand. According to Ben Hecht's biographer, Hecht, John Howard Lawson, Budd Schulberg, and Harold Clurman all contributed to the screenplay, uncredited. First-choice Gary Cooper's reluctance to play the male lead gave McCrea one of his best-remembered roles. The movie won six Oscar nominations, including one for Best Picture. That's Hitchcock, with a newspaper, passing McCrea on a street. (CFB)

Fort Apache

RKO, 1948. (127m.) Dir: John Ford. Sp: Frank S. Nugent, b/o story by James Warner Bellah. Cast: Henry Fonda, John Wayne, Shirley Temple, John Agar, Ward Bond, George O'Brien, Victor McLaglen, Pedro Armendariz, Anna Lee.

On-Screen: *John Ford's first major cavalry western.* John Ford's lifelong affection for the professional soldier and for the rituals of military life permeates this popular western drama. Cast against his usual type, Henry Fonda plays Colonel Thursday, a stern, implacable martinet whose rabid hatred of Indians and stubborn refusal to compromise ultimately plunge him and his troops into a fatal encounter with the Apaches. His most vigorous opposition comes from Capt. Kirby York (Wayne), a levelheaded army veteran. Ford builds the film slowly, taking time to savor life at the fort. (Highlight: a stirring grand march at the regimental dance). The pace quickens as the threat of Indian attack increases and Thursday and his troops sweep into action. After Colonel Thursday's unyielding ways have triggered a fearsome ambush of his men, Captain York still eulogizes him out of respect for the army and its traditions. Ford directs with his usual authority, but the film's ultimate point of view is questionable, suggesting that the disastrous behavior of military blunderers should be discounted in our need to believe in heroes.

Off-Screen: Conditions were rough in Monument Valley during the filming of *Fort Apache.* Most of the company were required to live in tents pitched outside the one ranch-style inn. The temperature soared to 115 degrees at midday, cooling only to 90 degrees at night. The shooting was continually delayed by high winds and desert storms. Tempers flared, and the sharp-tongued Ford found a principal target in Shirley Temple's young and inexperienced husband, John Agar.

Fort Apache, the Bronx

Fox, 1981. (C-125m.) Dir: Daniel Petrie. Sp: Heywood Gould. Cast: Paul Newman, Edward Asner, Ken Wahl, Rachel Ticotin, Danny Aiello, Kathleen Beller, Pam Grier.

On-Screen: *A veteran cop endures the horrors of a ravaged neighborhood.* It begins with the cold-blooded murder of two policemen by a deranged prostitute, and it ends with a siege in which hospital workers are held hostage by drug dealers. In between, veteran cop John Murphy (Newman) must cope with the day-to-day violence, corruption, and traumatic events surrounding his South Bronx precinct, which is called Fort Apache—"a fort in hostile territory." Murphy's main problems are twofold: dealing with his new by-the-book captain (Asner), and with a sadistic fellow cop (Aiello), whom he witnessed throwing a boy off a roof. He also has a brief, doomed romance with an addicted nurse (Ticotin). Daniel Petrie's film presents an unsparing portrait of urban life, which, sadly, hasn't changed drastically in the decade since the movie was released. Newman gives a strong performance as a hardened battle veteran who undergoes a crisis of conscience. Most compelling scene: a truly brutal fight between Newman and Aiello.

Off-Screen: Steve McQueen had turned down the leading role seven years earlier, and Nick Nolte had also rejected it. To prepare for his part, Newman rode around the South Bronx in a squad car with the former officers upon whose exploits the story was based. Newman had wanted John Travolta to play his younger partner, but when it didn't work out, Ken Wahl got the role. The hostility of South Bronx residents while the film was being shot resulted in media coverage, but an angry Newman insisted that the situation had been blown far out of proportion to the actual events.

The Fortune Cookie

United Artists, 1966. (125m.) Dir: Billy Wilder. Sp: Billy Wilder and I. A. L. Diamond. Cast: Jack Lemmon, Walter Matthau, Ron Rich, Judi West, Cliff Osmond, Lurene Tuttle.

On-Screen: *Meet Whiplash Willie.* The very definition of a shyster lawyer, Willie Gingrich is described by one character as "a man who could find a loophole in the Ten Commandments." Devious and proudly corrupt, Willie believes he has the case of a lifetime

when Harry Hinkle (Lemmon), his brother-in-law and a TV cameraman, is injured by a football player (Rich). The ensuing commotion involves worried lawyers for the insurance company, doctors with conflicting opinions, the dismayed football player, and Harry's greedy, ambitious ex-wife (West). Sparked by a funny, cynical Wilder-Diamond screenplay, Walter Matthau gives a performance that won him an Oscar as Best Supporting Actor. Judi West, in her first and last movie role, does a fair impersonation of Marilyn Monroe.

Off-Screen: Jack Lemmon fully understood that Walter Matthau would walk away with the movie, but it didn't matter. ("I'll play straight man to him anytime.") Realizing that Matthau had the showier role, Billy Wilder added several scenes for Lemmon during the shooting and even put the film back into production to give him more. But Whiplash Willie prevailed. Watch for a brief appearance as a doctor by William Christopher, who played Father Mulcahy on "*M★A★S★H.*"

48HRS.

Paramount, 1982. (C-97m.) Dir: Walter Hill. Sp: Roger Spottiswoode, Walter Hill, Steven E. de Souza and Larry Gross. Cast: Nick Nolte, Eddie Murphy, Annette O'Toole, James Remar, Frank McRae, David Patrick Kelly, Sonny Landham.

On-Screen: *Eddie Murphy's film debut in a fast-paced cop melodrama.* Sassy, street-smart crook Reggie Hammond (Murphy) is released from prison for forty-eight hours to help policeman Jack Cates (Nolte) trap two escaped convicts with a really mean streak. Naturally, Hammond and Cates despise each other, until a series of shoot-outs and chases forces them to form a loose alliance. Director Walter Hill knows how to stage violent action, and he keeps the highly predictable story moving at a fast, exciting pace. He gets an ingratiating performance from Eddie Murphy—his Reggie Hammond seems brighter and more resourceful than anyone else in the film, and in one very funny sequence he pretends to be a policeman taking over a redneck bar ("I'm your worst nightmare. I'm a nigger with a badge!"). Nick Nolte is also good as the rough-hewn cop who keeps making mistakes and getting into trouble, leaving Murphy, of course, to set things right.

Off-Screen: The screenplay for *48HRS.* went through a legion of writers over a number of years before reaching its final form. Inevitably, there was some dispute about the final writing credits. Nolte and Murphy made their own improvised contributions to the script, which many people felt should have been acknowledged. At one distant point, Clint Eastwood and Richard Pryor were being considered as the protagonists. A sequel, *Another 48HRS.,* was released in 1990.

42nd Street

Warners, 1933. (89m.) Dir: Lloyd Bacon. Musical numbers directed by Busby Berkeley. Sp: Rian James and James Seymour, b/o story by Bradford Ropes. MS: Harry Warren and Al Dubin. Cast: Warner Baxter, Dick Powell, Ruby Keeler, Bebe Daniels, Ginger Rogers, George Brent, Una Merkel, George E. Stone.

On-Screen: *The landmark in backstage movie musicals.* After several years of disrepute, the movie musical bounced back in the Depression era with this refreshing romp. The backstage milieu was realized with some crisp, slangy dialogue, the cast was ready and eager (Warner Baxter even contributed a poignant note as an ill and weary producer putting together his last show), and the songs ("You're Getting to Be a Habit With Me," "Shuffle Off to Buffalo," and others) were lively. But what created the sensation was Busby Berkeley's gigantic musical numbers in which the camera was used in new and innovative ways. Audiences gasped as chorus girls formed kaleidoscopic patterns in "Young and Healthy," or a stageful of performers enacted a minidrama of New York's nightlife in the title song. The enthusiastic response to *42nd Street* prompted more of the same from Warners, and not a few imitations from their competitors. But this was the granddaddy of them all.

Off-Screen: Sensing that musical films could be revived, Darryl Zanuck bought the rights to *42nd Street,* a yet-unpublished novel about an obsessive stage director, and had it turned into a musical. Although he had prepared the production, an exhausted Mervyn LeRoy had to be replaced by Lloyd Bacon. Busby Berkeley staged his gigantic musical numbers in a separate studio with his own unit of dancers. A former army drill instructor, he reverted to army ways for the movie. Chorus girls were put on an extensive training program, with a strict diet (no between-meal snacks or desserts) and fast rules concerning sleeping hours. When an influenza epidemic broke out in Hollywood, Berkeley's girls didn't even get the sniffles. A lavish stage version of the movie was a big hit on Broadway in 1980, running for years.

Foul Play

Paramount, 1978. (C–116m.) Dir: Colin Higgins. Sp: Colin Higgins. Cast: Goldie Hawn, Chevy Chase, Dudley Moore, Rachel Roberts, Burgess Meredith, Eugene Roche, Marilyn Sokol, Billy Barty.

On-Screen: *A detective and a librarian try to thwart an assassination.* A helter-skelter comedy-thriller, *Foul Play* doesn't make much sense, yet somehow it generates more laughter than many more straightforward movies. Deep in her dizzy-blonde mode, Goldie Hawn plays a scatterbrained San Francisco librarian who inadvertently becomes involved in a plot to assassinate visiting Pope Pius XIII. Chevy Chase, in his first leading-man role, is the bumbling detective who finally comes to believe her stories about attempts on her life. Inevitably, there's a wild car chase (what else are those hills for?) and a theater climax lifted unabashedly from Alfred Hitchcock. Among the funniest characters who have the misfortune to cross Hawn's path are Dudley Moore (his first major American film) as a world-class swinger who turns out to be an orchestra conductor, and Billy Barty (everyone's favorite short person) as a hapless encyclopedia salesman. Goldie Hawn is pertly adorable, and Chevy Chase is actually likable, but this was before his smirky, put-on attitude became a permanent feature of his acting style.

Off-Screen: The pope in jeopardy was played by a San Francisco socialite named Cyril Magnin. A short-lived television series based on the movie appeared in 1981.

Four Daughters

Warners, 1938. (90m.) Dir: Michael Curtiz. Sp: Julius J. Epstein and Lenore Coffee, b/o story by Fannie Hurst. Cast: Claude Rains, Priscilla Lane, John Garfield, Rosemary Lane, Lola Lane, May Robson, Gale Page, Frank McHugh, Dick Foran.

On-Screen: *Four sisters in a close-knit family encounter romance and tragedy.* An enormously popular film and the first in a series of three, *Four Daughters* gives a smooth treatment to the tale of the Lemp sisters (the Lane sisters, plus Page), daughters to an eccentric musician (Rains), who each find love amid the warmth of their family. The central story involves the youngest (Priscilla), whose marriage to a dark-natured, fatalistic pianist (Garfield) ends tragically. The film's surprise was Garfield, a New York actor from the Group Theater. Seated at the piano, a cigarette dangling from his lips as he talked about the "fates" who are out to "get" him, he displayed an arresting presence and a dynamic personality that made audiences sit up and take notice. He became a major star until his untimely death in 1952 at age forty.

Off-Screen: Originally written by Lenore Coffee, the screenplay, based on a Fannie Hurst story called "Sister Act," was reworked by Julius Epstein. Errol Flynn was scheduled to play the Jeffrey Lynn role of Priscilla Lane's patient boyfriend, but when the role was not expanded to his satisfaction, he bowed out. Epstein built up the role of the brooding pianist for Van Heflin, but when Heflin was tied up onstage with *The Philadelphia Story,* Eddie Albert was considered. Finally, Garfield won the part, modeling his performance on the cynical, bitingly witty pianist Oscar Levant. *Four Daughters* was later musicalized as *Young at Heart* (1954).

The Four Seasons

Universal, 1981. (C-107m.) Dir: Alan Alda. Sp: Alan Alda. Cast: Carol Burnett, Alan Alda, Rita Moreno, Jack Weston, Len Cariou, Sandy Dennis, Bess Armstrong.

On-Screen: *Three couples share their vacations and their lives.* A perceptive and extremely likable comedy, *The Four Seasons* deals with three married couples who have been devoted friends for years, sharing each other's joys and sorrows and taking vacations together with every change of season. Alan Alda's screenplay shows what happens when one of their number (Cariou) divorces his wife (Dennis) and marries a much younger woman (Armstrong). As director, star, and writer, Alda keeps the tone humorous, touching on the competitiveness among the men and the wives' clear-eyed acceptance of their husbands' foibles, but his movie also has a serious side, especially when it concerns the men's fear of growing old and dying that lurks at the edges of their boisterous behavior. Jack Weston embodies this theme as a hypochondriacal dentist who is a chubby mass of perpetual apprehension. He gives the movie's best performance, but most of the others are just fine, with a special nod to Rita Moreno's cheerful, patient Italian wife to Weston.

Off-Screen: *The Four Seasons* was briefly turned into a television situation comedy in 1984, with Jack Weston repeating his movie role and Marcia Rodd as his wife,

Claudia. The cast included Allan Arbus, Barbara Babcock, Tony Roberts, and Joanna Kerns.

Frankenstein

Universal, 1931. (71m.) Dir: James Whale. Sp: John L. Balderston, Garrett Fort, and Francis Edwards Faragoh, b/o novel by Mary Shelley and play by Peggy Webling. Cast: Colin Clive, Mae Clarke, John Boles, Boris Karloff, Edward Van Sloan, Dwight Frye, Marilyn Harris.

On-Screen: *A man-made monster mistakenly receives an abnormal brain.* Arguably *the* classic horror movie, *Frankenstein* continues to startle us with the grotesque appearance of its central character—the lumbering gait, the boxy head with shuttered eyes and a snarling gash of a mouth. The monster's first stirrings of life, its unintentional drowning of a child, the raging windmill fire in which it and its creator are trapped— these are among the scenes that unfailingly shock as well as fascinate. Colin Clive is properly impassioned in the title role as the overreaching scientist, Mae Clarke is convincingly distraught by her husband's obsession, and dwarfish Dwight Frye is almost endearing as Clive's bumbling grave-robber assistant. But the movie belongs to Karloff, whose sensitive portrayal of the monster is unforgettable.

Off-Screen: Bela Lugosi, who objected to the cumbersome makeup, and John Carradine turned down the part of the monster. Bette Davis was rejected for the Clarke role because director James Whale considered her, understandably, "too aggressive" for the character. Sets from the studio's recent *All Quiet on the Western Front* provided *Frankenstein* with its picturesque village. Robert Florey, originally engaged to write the screenplay and direct, got the idea for the film's climactic scene from the windmill logo of an L.A. bakery. Jack Pierce's elaborate facial makeup and costuming— platform boots and quilted suit—for Karloff weighed nearly fifty pounds and took four hours to apply. Clive's exultant cry, "Now I know what it feels like to be God!" and the scene of little Marilyn Harris's drowning, both long deleted from circulated prints, are restored in the video release. (CFB)

The French Connection

Fox, 1971. (C-104m.) Dir: William Friedkin. Sp: Ernest Tidyman, b/o novel by Robin Moore. Cast: Gene Hackman, Roy Scheider, Fernando Rey, Tony LoBianco, Marcel Bozzuffi.

On-Screen: *Oscar-winning melodrama on the thwarting of an international drug deal.* Exciting, expertly staged, and fast, fast, fast, *The French Connection* brought a measure of distinction to the usually routine police melodrama. It also had a most unorthodox central character: Popeye Doyle (Hackman) is a profane, seedy, and brutish cop who works in any way he can to apprehend a kingpin drug dealer (Rey) based in Marseilles and to confiscate his large shipment of heroin to New York City. The basic situation is hardly original, but the film's pace is relentless, the New York locations are well used, and Hackman creates a memorable character in the sneering, hard-nosed Popeye. The most celebrated sequence involves Popeye's heart-stopping pursuit of a

hijacked elevated train. Brilliantly edited (Jerry Greenberg) and photographed (Owen Roizman), it is a symphony of screeching brakes, shrieking passengers, and colliding cars. The movie won the year's Academy Award as Best Picture, and other Oscars went to Hackman, Friedkin, Tidyman, and Greenberg.

Off-Screen: Popeye Doyle was based on an actual New York City policeman named Eddie Egan, who, with his partner Sonny Grasso, destroyed a drug ring and confiscated 120 pounds of heroin worth over $30 million. Both cops had small roles in the film. Friedkin's first choice for Popeye was columnist Jimmy Breslin, and Friedkin even rehearsed with him. But it turned out that Breslin "couldn't sustain from one day to the next" and also couldn't drive a car. Others considered for the role included Jackie Gleason and Peter Boyle. For the chase sequence, every shot and every stunt was planned carefully to keep the risk at a minimum, while maximizing the filmmaking possibilities. It took five weeks to film. A sequel, *The French Connection II,* was released in 1975, and *Popeye Doyle,* a failed pilot film, turned up on television in 1986.

Freud

Universal, 1962. (139m.) Dir: John Huston. Sp: Charles Kaufman and Wolfgang Reinhardt. Cast: Montgomery Clift, Susannah York, Larry Parks, Susan Kohner, Eileen Herlie, David McCallum, Rosalie Crutchley, Eric Portman.

On-Screen: *A brave attempt at a difficult subject.* Viewing the movie, you may feel as if you're taking an accelerated course in the early history of psychoanalysis. Restricted to a five-year period (1890–95) in the life of Sigmund Freud (Clift), the film is imaginatively conceived and produced, if overcrowded with incident in trying to cover as much ground as possible. As the discoverer of the sexual origin of hysterical neuroses, Clift is properly intense, and Parks is passable as a doubting colleague. York's fictional, tormented patient, a walking casebook of psychic disorders, is riveting, and the scenes in which Freud probes deeply into the source of her illness are the best in the film. While treating her, Freud also discovers crucial truths about himself. Huston's approach is somewhat too reverential, but it gives the story the importance it deserves.

Off-Screen: Huston had long wanted to direct a biography of the father of psychoanalysis, but was forced by censorship problems to defer the project. His World War II documentary, *Let There Be Light,* cowritten with Charles Kaufman and dealing with psychic disorders of battle-scarred soldiers, gave him added impetus. A 1959 screenplay by French writer Jean-Paul Sartre proved unmanageably lengthy. Instead, Kaufman, his wartime colleague, and Reinhardt furnished a new (and Oscar-nominated) script. During filming, Clift himself suffered emotional and physical difficulties stemming from his near-fatal automobile accident a few years earlier. When the movie was not a popular success, Huston trimmed it and retitled it *Freud: The Secret Passion,* to no avail. (CFB)

Fried Green Tomatoes

Universal, 1991. (C-130m.) Dir: Jon Avnet. Sp: Fannie Flagg and Carol Sobieski, b/o novel by Fannie Flagg. Cast: Kathy Bates, Mary Stuart Masterson, Mary-Louise Parker, Jessica Tandy, Cicely Tyson, Chris O'Donnell, Stan Shaw, Gailard Sartain.

On-Screen: *A two-tiered story of the South.* The setting is Alabama in the twenties. Tough-girl Idgie (Masterson) and pretty Ruth (Parker) open the Whistle Stop Cafe, where life is beautiful until the Klan and Ruth's abusive husband arrive. Their story is told in the present by Ninnie (Tandy), living in a nursing home, to Evelyn (Bates), a visitor. Evelyn wants desperately to get through to her husband, Ed (Sartain), whose consciousness needs raising by about a mile, and through Ninnie she finds the courage she has been looking for. Parker and Masterson are capable, but the film belongs to Bates and Tandy. Bates manages to be totally appealing without an ounce of cuteness, and Tandy is by now transparent, every emotion coming through with no barrier. We are given a prettified, sanitized South here, but if some of the details are unconvincing, the feelings are genuine and welcome.

Off-Screen: Jessica Tandy, a Best Actress Oscar winner in 1989 for *Driving Miss Daisy,* received a Best Supporting Actress nomination for her performance in this film. Fannie Flagg and the late Carol Sobieski were also nominated for their screenplay. (BL)

Friendly Persuasion

Allied Artists, 1956. (C-138m.) Dir: William Wyler. Sp: Michael Wilson (uncredited), b/o book by Jessamyn West. Cast: Gary Cooper, Dorothy McGuire, Anthony Perkins, Phyllis Love, Richard Eyer, Mark Richman, Marjorie Main.

On-Screen: *Drama of Quaker family's involvement in the Civil War.* The title of this unusual film refers to the peace-loving practices of the Society of Friends, the religious sect whose members are often called Quakers. Set in southern Indiana, the movie chiefly concerns the moral dilemma facing a Quaker family when Confederate troops invade their farmland. To prove his mettle, young Josh Birdwell (Perkins) joins the fight against the intruders. Violent circumstances eventually force his parents (Cooper, McGuire) to choose between the dictates of their pacifist faith and the demands of survival. On occasion, this loving look at a fascinating, if little-known, sidelight of American history rambles a bit (a jarring, played-for-laughs episode, for example, involves Main's Widow Hudspeth and her man-hungry daughters). Overall, though, it's a compelling, beautifully made movie that makes you care very much about what happens to the Birdwells.

Off-Screen: West, whose collection of sketches, *The Friendly Persuasion,* was published in 1945, was herself a Quaker. As technical adviser on the movie, she kept a journal later published as *To See the Dream.* The film was released with no screenwriter credit because of Wilson's having pleaded the Fifth Amendment before the House Un-American Activities Committee in 1952. Oscar nominations included Best Picture, Best Director, Best Supporting Actor (Perkins) and for Best Song, Paul Francis Webster and Dimitri Tiomkin's title tune, sung by Pat Boone on the sound track. In 1975, Richard Kiley and Shirley Knight appeared as the elder Birdwells in a made-for-television movie based on other material in West's book. (CFB)

From Here to Eternity

Columbia, 1953. (118m.) Dir: Fred Zinnemann. Sp: Daniel Taradash, b/o novel by James Jones. Cast: Burt Lancaster, Montgomery Clift, Deborah Kerr, Frank Sinatra, Donna Reed, Philip Ober, Ernest Borgnine, Mickey Shaughnessy, Jack Warden.

On-Screen: *Scorching drama of the regular army, just before Pearl Harbor.* Like the novel, the movie focuses on a group of people living in or near Honolulu's Schofield Barracks. Flawlessly cast and directed, it takes an unvarnished view of the dehumanizing of soldiers by the military machine. The central character is Private Prewitt (Clift), a sensitive loner with three loves: the army, his bugle, and Lorene (Reed), who's "two steps up from the pavement." Sergeant Warden (Lancaster), tough and cynical, is romantically involved with Karen (Kerr), wife of the base's gung ho captain (Ober). No less vital to the movie's theme of a regimented world of casual cruelty are easy-going Maggio (Sinatra) and "Fatso" (Borgnine), his brutal nemesis. The film climaxes with the bombing of Pearl Harbor, leaving one of the characters dead. Deservedly, this powerful movie was voted Best Picture.

Off-Screen: The movie reaped seven additional Academy Awards, Best Supporting Oscars going to Sinatra (Maggio was an important dramatic breakthrough for him) and to Reed. Zinnemann and Taradash were also honored with statuettes. Deborah Kerr replaced Joan Crawford, who fell out with studio boss Harry Cohn over her wardrobe demands. Burt Lancaster was chosen over Robert Mitchum, and Montgomery Clift over Aldo Ray. Eli Wallach was signed to play Maggio but withdrew, and Frank Sinatra won the role he coveted. Authenticity was gained by filming much of the action at the real Schofield Army Barracks. In 1979, a well-received television miniseries followed the wartime fortunes of some of Jones's characters; the following year, a regular weekly series lasted a month. (CFB)

Full Metal Jacket

Warners, 1987. (C-116m.) Dir: Stanley Kubrick. Sp: Stanley Kubrick, Michael Herr, and Gustav Hasford, b/o novel by Gustav Hasford. Cast: Matthew Modine, Lee Ermey, Adam Baldwin, Vincent D'Onofrio, Dorian Harewood, Arliss Howard, Kevyn Major Howard, Ed O'Ross.

On-Screen: *Stanley Kubrick's corrosive drama on war's dehumanization*. Although it lacks the cohesiveness and impact of Oliver Stone's *Platoon* (1986), this powerful film on the Vietnam experience deserves to be seen. The screenplay tries to crowd too many themes and ideas into its two-hour running time, creating an oddly splintered effect. Yet many scenes are unforgettable. The pivotal character is a young Marine called Joker (Modine), who trains at Parris Island under a DI (Ermey) grimly determined to turn his men into fighting and killing machines. Tragically, this dehumanizing process works too well with a pathetically inept recruit (D'Onofrio), turning this butt of all the jokes into a terrifying killer. The film's second part takes Joker into the thick of combat, where the hardened shell he has acquired in training helps him to survive. Much of the movie is a scathing indictment of the insanity and corruption of war, but like Joker, who writes "Born to Kill" on his helmet and also wears a peace button, it tries to strike a realistic balance. Oddly enough,

although the battle scenes are well-handled, the film's first section is somehow more engrossing, thanks in good part to the performances by Ermey and D'Onofrio.

Off-Screen: Although set in Parris Island and Vietnam, much of the movie was shot in England. Lee Ermey was actually a drill instructor in the Marines, making his performance that much more frightening.

Funny Face

Paramount, 1957. (C-103m.) Dir: Stanley Donen. Sp: Leonard Gershe. MS: George and Ira Gershwin, also Roger Edens and Leonard Gershe. Cast: Fred Astaire, Audrey Hepburn, Kay Thompson, Michel Auclair, Robert Flemyng, Suzy Parker, Ruta Lee.

On-Screen: *Astaire, Hepburn, Gershwin, and high fashion*. One of the most stylish musical films of the fifties, *Funny Face* offers an irresistible combination: a mature but still agile Fred Astaire; Audrey Hepburn at her most ravishing; a Hollywood-eye view of Paris; and a number of marvelous Gershwin tunes. The fashions are dated, and the story line (fashion photographer Astaire turns duckling Hepburn into a swan, then falls for her) is only adequate, even with a measure of wit. But greatly aided by Richard Avedon's spectacular work as color consultant, the musical numbers are pure enchantment: Hepburn's song and dance to "How Long Has This Been Going On?" her dark-room duet with Astaire to "Funny Face," and most unforgettably, their rhapsodic countryside dance to "He Loves and She Loves." As a brash magazine editor, Kay Thompson contributes to the fun, singing, and dancing with enormous verve. Her duet with Astaire to "Clap Yo' Hands" is another of the movie's highlights. *Funny Face* is high-class moviemaking, and a musical treat.

Off-Screen: Many years later, at the occasion of Astaire's Lifetime Achievement Award, Audrey Hepburn recalled her first meeting with the dancer: "One look at this most debonair, elegant, and distinguished of legends, and I could feel myself turn to solid lead, while my heart sank into my two left feet. Then suddenly I felt a hand around my waist, and with his inimitable grace and lightness, Fred literally swept me off my feet." Astaire's character was modeled on Richard Avedon, and Kay Thompson's character resembled Diana Vreeland of *Vogue* magazine. The film's original title was *Wedding Day,* which was the title of an unproduced stage musical on which the screenplay was based.

Funny Girl

Columbia, 1968. (C-155m.) Dir: William Wyler. Sp: Isobel Lennart, b/o musical play by Bob Merrill. MS: Jule Styne and Bob Merrill. Cast: Barbra Streisand, Omar Sharif, Kay Medford, Anne Francis, Walter Pidgeon, Lee Allen, Mae Questel, Gerald Mohr.

On-Screen: *Barbra as funny Fanny in her film debut.* From the moment Barbra Streisand stepped in front of a mirror as gifted comedienne-singer Fanny Brice and announced "Hello, gorgeous!" it was clear that a unique film star had arrived. Throughout this film version of her 1964 stage triumph, Streisand's vibrant, expressive voice soars across the sound track and washes away the soapiness of the story. The tiresome plot involves Brice's rise to stardom and her love affair, then marriage, with gambler Nick Arnstein (Sharif) and the end

of their troubled relationship. But it's Streisand's rendition of the music that matters: her first song that affirms "I'm the Greatest Star," her lovely version of "People," her trumpeting of "Don't Rain on My Parade" in the movie's most remarkable sequence, and her final, eloquent "My Man." Omar Sharif is acceptable if rather oleaginous as Arnstein, and Walter Pidgeon appears as impresario Florenz Ziegfeld. Still, Streisand is the show, and she earned the Best Actress Oscar she shared with Katharine Hepburn, who won for *The Lion in Winter. Funny Girl* received seven other nominations, including Best Picture.

Off-Screen: Barbra Streisand won her star-making role of Fanny Brice in the Broadway production over such actresses as Anne Bancroft, Carol Burnett, and Mitzi Gaynor. When Egyptian actor Omar Sharif was signed to play Arnstein, he was vilified by the Egyptian press, and there was talk of revoking his citizenship. The movie became the highest-grossing musical since *The Sound of Music.*

Funny Lady

Columbia, 1975. (C-137m.) Dir: Herbert Ross. Sp: Jay Presson Allen and Arnold Schulman, b/o story by Arnold Schulman. MS: John Kander and Fred Ebb. Cast: Barbra Streisand, James Caan, Omar Sharif, Roddy McDowall, Ben Vereen, Carole Wells.

On-Screen: *Barbra Streisand returns as Fanny Brice.* A disappointing sequel to William Wyler's *Funny Girl* (1968), *Funny Lady* continues the offstage problems and onstage triumphs of entertainer Fanny Brice. It begins after Brice's divorce from gambler Nick

Arnstein (Sharif) and ends with her final separation from showman Billy Rose (Caan). The trouble lies mainly with the cliché-ridden screenplay, in which the relationship of Fanny and Billy never seems to get beyond a certain spikiness and grudging respect. Caan, who in no way resembles Rose, cannot do much with his underwritten role. A luckier Streisand can resort to singing, which she does in her best belting style. The old songs—"Am I Blue?" "More Than You Know," etc.—make for marvelous listening, and some of the new Kander-Ebb tunes are also fine, especially "How Lucky Can You Get?" Nevertheless, in between the music, the viewer must tolerate Brice's continual mooning over Nick Arnstein and her dull sparring with Rose.

Off-Screen: Despite less than enthusiastic reviews, *Funny Lady* won five Oscar nominations, including Best Cinematography (James Wong Howe), Best Scoring, and Best Costume Design (Ray Aghayan and Bob Mackie).

Fury

MGM, 1936. (94m.) Dir: Fritz Lang. Sp: Bartlett Cormack and Fritz Lang, b/o story by Norman Krasna. Cast: Spencer Tracy, Sylvia Sidney, Walter Abel, Bruce Cabot, Edward Ellis, Walter Brennan, Frank Albertson.

On-Screen: *An innocent man confronts mob violence*. One of the most memorable social dramas of the thirties, *Fury* is a corrosive, blistering account of a small Midwestern town overwhelmed by the bloodlust of its citizens. Spencer Tracy plays the hapless man who is falsely arrested on a charge of kidnapping, then must face the hysteria generated by a local rabble-rouser. He nearly loses his life and ends up a ravaged man, with no faith in his country or its system of justice. Sylvia Sidney is his distraught girlfriend. Director Fritz Lang's first American film, *Fury* occasionally veers into melodramatic excess, but the scenes involving the revenge-minded mob, screaming for a lynching, are truly terrifying. Tracy gives one of his best thirties performances, reaching an apex in the climactic courtroom scene in which he vents his bitterness and rage.

Off-Screen: The film was first titled *The Mob* and then *Mob Rule,* but the Hays Office rejected them both. The origin of the film is a tangled web that probably nobody will ever unravel. The questions remain as to how much Norman Krasna actually contributed to the story (although he won an Oscar for it), or how much of the screenplay was written by Fritz Lang. There is no question, however, that the cast and crew of *Fury* loathed the Austrian-born director for his autocratic demands. At one point the electricians plotted to drop a lamp on his head. After the film was completed, Lang was barred from the studio for the next twenty years.

The Gang's All Here

Fox, 1943. (C-103m.) Dir: Busby Berkeley. Sp: Walter Bullock, b/o story by Nancy Winter, George Root, Jr., and Tom Bridges. MS: Harry Warren and Leo Robin. Cast: Alice Faye, Carmen Miranda, James Ellison, Charlotte Greenwood, Edward Everett Horton, Eugene Pallette, Benny Goodman and His Orchestra.

On-Screen: *Busby Berkeley rampant on a field of Technicolor.* After directing several films at MGM, Busby Berkeley, who had revolutionized the musical at Warners in the thirties, took a side trip to Fox to direct this movie, his first in color. The result was delirious, which is not to say good. Given full control, Berkeley staged musical numbers that almost defy reason with their special effects. The most spectacular, "The Lady in the Tutti Frutti Hat," features the Brazilian bombshell, Carmen Miranda, in a musical orgy that prominently involves bananas. (Don't ask.) There are a few quieter moments, notably Alice Faye's throaty rendition of "No Love, No Nothing." The story line—something about a chorus girl and a soldier—is a nuisance, but wait for Berkeley's hallucinatory creations.

Off-Screen: During the filming of "The Lady in the Tutti Frutti Hat," there was a near disaster when Berkeley swooped down on the scene with his camera boom, overshot his mark, and dislodged Miranda's towering headpiece. The remnants of her hat lay strewn at her feet. Reluctantly, a furious Miranda agreed to try it again, but was quoted as telling Berkeley, "Knock one banana off my head and I will make of you the flat pancake!" This was Alice Faye's last musical for many years. Pregnant at the time, she decided to make one more film, the melodrama *Fallen Angel,* and then retire.

Gaslight

MGM, 1944. (114m.) Dir: George Cukor. Sp: John Van Druten, Walter Reisch, and John S. Balderston, b/o play by Patrick Hamilton. Cast: Ingrid Bergman, Charles Boyer, Joseph Cotten, Angela Lansbury, Dame May Whitty.

On-Screen: *Bergman's first Oscar, as a trusting wife driven to the edge of madness.* Two superstars give bravura performances in this elegant suspense thriller set in Victorian London. Bergman is riveting as the victimized child-woman infatuated with worldly husband Boyer, whose true passion is reserved for the jewels hidden in their richly appointed town house. His insistent denials that the gaslights dim in the evening and that there are unsettling sounds coming from the attic are only part of his scheme to destroy his wife's sanity. The movie's dramatic highlight comes when Scotland Yard detective Cotten lets Bergman gloriously turn the tables on her tormentor. As the cunning villain, Boyer manages the shift from seductiveness to menace very persuasively. Lansbury's saucy housemaid provides a comic touch singing "Up in a Balloon, Boys." Joseph Ruttenberg's photography conveys a sense of ever-lurking menace, and George Cukor's direction makes it all crackle.

Off-Screen: The movie began its tortuous life as *Gaslight,* a 1938 London stage hit (it was filmed in England under that title in 1939), then enjoyed a long run on Broadway in 1941 as *Angel Street.* Columbia bought the property for Irene Dunne, then sold it to MGM, which decided to borrow David O. Selznick's Swedish-born "discovery." When the studio released its version in England, it became *The Murder in Thornton Square.* Now-surviving prints of the original British film version are called *Angel Street.* In addition to its Best Actress award, the movie also won Oscars for black-and-white art direction and set decoration. Boyer, Lansbury (in her first acting role), the screenplay, the cinematography, and the film itself were all Oscar-nominated. (CFB)

The Gay Divorcee

RKO, 1934. (107m.) Dir: Mark Sandrich. Sp: George Marion, Jr., Edward Kaufman, and Dorothy Yost, b/o musical play by Dwight Taylor. MS: Cole Porter, Mark Gordon, Harry Revel, Con Conrad, and Herb Magidson. Cast: Fred Astaire, Ginger Rogers, Edward Everett Horton, Alice Brady, Erik Rhodes, Eric Blore.

On-Screen: *Astaire and Rogers in their second dance musical.* A year after their success in *Flying Down to Rio,* RKO costarred the dance team in the film that established them in the public eye. Adapted from Astaire's stage musical, the movie retained the lightheaded book, which had Astaire as an amorous dancer who is mistaken by Rogers for the professional gigolo (Rhodes) she has hired in order to win a divorce from her long-absent husband. It's all extremely silly, but thankfully, some of the musical numbers are wonderful. The most outstanding—and one of the great musical numbers of the screen—is their romantic duet to Cole Porter's "Night and Day," danced rapturously in the deserted ballroom of a Brighton resort hotel. The movie's musical climax is "The Continental," a lavish production number that features not only Astaire and Rogers but nearly one hundred dancers and several solo singers in seemingly interminable reprises of the song. This number claimed two firsts: at seventeen and a half minutes, it was the longest musical number in films to that date, and it was the first song to win an Oscar.

Off-Screen: The Broadway version had been called *The Gay Divorce,* but the studio felt it was too risqué for the screen and renamed it *The Gay Divorcee.* Edward Everett Horton's role was originally considered for Charles Ruggles, but Astaire felt he was not British enough. Helen Broderick was the first choice for Alice Brady's role, but she was committed to *As Thousands Cheer* on Broadway. Eric Blore and Erik Rhodes had both appeared with Astaire in the stage version.

Gentleman's Agreement

Fox, 1947. (118m.) Dir: Elia Kazan. Sp: Moss Hart, b/o novel by Laura Z. Hobson. Cast: Gregory Peck, Dorothy McGuire, John Garfield, Celeste Holm, Anne Revere, Sam Jaffe, June Havoc, Albert Dekker, Dean Stockwell.

On-Screen: *Hollywood tackles a "forbidden" subject.* When Phil Green (Peck) agrees to write a series of magazine articles on anti-Semitism in America, he gets more than he bargained for. A gentile himself, Phil gets "inside" his subject by posing as a Jew. In researching his exposé, he becomes increasingly angry as he encounters, for example, carefully phrased rebuffs by clerks at "restricted" hotels. Even his supposedly sophisticated fiancée, Kathy (McGuire), finds that her social set is guilty of the "gentleman's agreement" to exclude Jews from their circle. The movie is well acted and directed, but its central flaw is that for all the humiliation Phil experiences, as a non-Jew he remains, after all, safely outside the condition he's investigating. Only when his Jewish friend Dave (Garfield) is degraded by a bigoted restaurant patron do the true horror and sadness of anti-Semitism seem as real and repellent as they are.

Off-Screen: Today, when it seems that every social aberration has been explored in films, it should be borne in mind that it took con-siderable daring for Fox's Darryl Zanuck to bring the then-taboo subject of Hobson's novel to the screen. A number of screen moguls, including Louis B. Mayer and the brothers Warner, urged Zanuck to stay away from the topic, but he persisted. It became clear that the studio's courage was not misplaced when the movie became a box-office and critical hit and won Oscars for Best Picture, Kazan's direction, and for the Best Supporting Actress performance by Holm. The movie seems tame and naive now, but it was a brave beginning in Hollywood's coming of age. (CFB)

Gentlemen Prefer Blondes

Fox, 1953. (C-91m.) Dir: Howard Hawks. Sp: Charles Lederer, b/o musical play and novel by Anita Loos. MS: Jule Styne and Leo Robin (also Hoagy Carmichael and Harold Adamson). Cast: Marilyn Monroe, Jane Russell, Charles Coburn, Elliott Reid, Tommy Noonan, George Winslow.

On-Screen: *Monroe and Russell on the prowl for millionaires.* A splashy, moderately entertaining musical film, *Gentlemen Prefer Blondes* is clearly designed as a vehicle to display the obvious charms of its leading ladies. Anita Loos's popular twenties novel had been filmed once before in 1927, then turned into a stage musical in 1949, with Carol Channing as the gold-digging Lorelei. This recycled version eliminates the flapper-era background, setting a contemporary Lorelei and her friend on a luxury liner bound for Europe and in a strictly backlot Paris. A few of the stage songs are retained, particularly "Diamonds Are a Girl's Best Friend," which gives Monroe a golden opportunity for an extravagant display of hip-waving, purring, and incidental singing. Jane Russell gets some good sharp dialogue and a musical number with musclemen. In any case, two cheers for those little girls from Little Rock.

Off-Screen: An insecure Marilyn Monroe insisted on many takes for the "Bye, Bye, Baby" musical sequence, even after director Hawks had approved the first take. This happened many times, which did not endear her to Hawks. Publicity stills for the movie showed a musical number in which the leading ladies wore tights (with a huge flower on each seat) and exaggerated Napoleonic headgear. Although the number could be seen in the advertising clips, it did not appear in the movie.

Ghost

Paramount, 1990. (C-122m.) Dir: Jerry Zucker. Sp: Bruce Joel Rubin. Cast: Patrick Swayze, Demi Moore, Whoopi Goldberg, Tony Goldwyn, Vincent Schiavelli, Rick Aviles, Gail Boggs, Armelia McQueen, Phil Leeds.

On-Screen: *A ghost tries to warn his endangered lover.* Jerry Zucker's film was the most popular of 1990—and small wonder. Shrewdly, it blends tender romance, violent melodrama, brash comedy, and more than a touch of the supernatural. To top it all, it offers the same reassuring vision of death that moviegoers have found palatable for decades. Patrick Swayze plays a rising young stockbroker who is brutally murdered and then, as a ghost, must warn his beloved, Demi Moore, of the threat to her life. Enter Whoopi Goldberg as a fake spiritualist who discovers, to her amazement,

that she *does* have psychic powers. The movie is too long and contrived but is entertaining, thanks mainly to Goldberg's feisty, Oscar-winning performance. (Bruce Joel Rubin's screenplay also won an Oscar.) Vincent Schiavelli gives a funny, over-the-top performance as a ferocious ghost who teaches Swayze some of the tricks of the trade.

Off-Screen: It's not generally known, but at first the producers wanted to replace Demi Moore with Swoozie Kurtz. The thought was to generate some catchy advertising: "Swoozie and Swayze are swell together." But Whoopi Goldberg vetoed the idea because the names sounded funny. Exteriors were filmed for five weeks in New York City: in Bedford-Stuyvesant, SoHo, and Wall Street. The movie featured close to one hundred special-effects sequences supplied by three units.

Ghostbusters

Columbia, 1984. (C-107m.) Dir: Ivan Reitman. Sp: Dan Aykroyd and Harold Ramis. Cast: Bill Murray, Dan Aykroyd, Sigourney Weaver, Rick Moranis, Harold Ramis, William Atherton, Ernie Hudson, Annie Potts.

On-Screen: *Three "paranormal investigators" battle ghosts and demons in New York City.* If you're in a relaxed frame of mind, or if you're a bright prepubescent with a fondness for scary and slimy things, you should enjoy this large-scale fright comedy. Aykroyd, Murray, and Ramis (later joined by Hudson) are off-the-wall, self-described "ghostbusters" who—to their amazement—find themselves battling all sorts of ghostly—and ghastly—creatures suddenly at large in New York City. The creatures are bent on not only destroying the city but also the world in an apocalyptic judgment day. "Spook Central" is an apartment house inhabited by the beautiful Weaver and her nerdy neighbor Moranis, who both become agents of the demonic forces. Forget the dumb plot and concentrate on the special effects, which are sometimes astonishing, especially in the climactic sequences. (The giant Sta-Puf marshmallow man is fun.) Aykroyd and Ramis are adequate, but Bill Murray's usual smirky response to every situation grows tiresome long before the movie ends.

Off-Screen: *Ghostbusters* was originally intended as a Dan Aykroyd–John Belushi–Bill Murray vehicle called *Ghostsmashers* before Belushi's death in 1982. John Candy was first scheduled to play Rick Moranis's role. The movie required an enormous number of special visual effects, including the design and execution of matte paintings, miniatures, creature costumes, stop-motion animation, cable-operated monsters, and optically created ghosts. The visual effects and the title song won Oscar nominations. The success of the film eventually led to a sequel, *Ghostbusters II* (1989), and to an animated cartoon series.

Giant

Warners, 1956. (C-201m.) Dir: George Stevens. Sp: Fred Guiol and Ivan Moffat, b/o novel by Edna Ferber. Cast: Elizabeth Taylor, Rock Hudson, James Dean, Carroll Baker, Chill Wills, Jane Withers, Dennis Hopper, Mercedes McCambridge, Sal Mineo.

On-Screen: *The sweeping saga of a Texas family*. As expansive and, in some ways, as impressive as the state it celebrates, *Giant* is perhaps best remembered today as the final film of James Dean, that surly icon of fifties rebelliousness. Based on Edna Ferber's novel, the film relates the across-the-decades story of Bick and Leslie Benedict; he (Hudson) is a wealthy, conservative rancher steeped in tradition, and she (Taylor) is the feisty, liberal Easterner he brings to Texas. Over the years, they confront the problems of their independent-minded children, racial bigotry, and especially the burgeoning power of Jett Rink (Dean), their former ranch hand, who becomes a greedy oil tycoon. The film is long, lavish, and undeniably absorbing, but the screenplay has a pulpish quality that might be suitable for a miniseries on today's television. The emoting of Taylor and Hudson is more than competent, even though they fail to age convincingly. As for James Dean, he gives his customary mannered performance, on the verge of exploding from all that coiled intensity.

Off-Screen: Grace Kelly was the first choice for the Taylor role, but she was unavailable. William Holden believed that he had the inside track for the lead and was bitterly disappointed when the role went to Hudson. During the filming, James Dean created a brouhaha by battling incessantly with director Stevens or riding his motorcycle around the soundstages, performing stunts on the handlebars. *Giant* won ten Oscar nominations, including Best Picture and Best Actor (Hudson), but only George Stevens won for his direction.

Gigi

MGM, 1958. (C-116m.) Dir: Vincente Minnelli. Sp: Alan Jay Lerner, b/o novel by Colette. MS: Alan Jay Lerner and Frederick Loewe. Cast: Maurice Chevalier, Leslie Caron, Louis Jourdan, Hermione Gingold, Isabel Jeans, Eva Gabor, Jacques Bergerac.

On-Screen: *Turn-of-the-century Paris comes alive in Lerner and Loewe's musical.* Sumptuous, witty, and tuneful, *Gigi* represents a peak among MGM's memorable series of fifties musicals. For once, everything is right: Cecil Beaton's exquisite sets and costumes of fin de siècle Paris; Lerner and Loewe's blithe and lilting score, and an impeccable cast. The charming screenplay, derived from Colette's novel, concerns a family of courtesans and especially the youngest, Gigi (Caron), an elfin girl on the verge of womanhood, who decides that being a wife is better than being a mistress. Louis Jourdan brilliantly portrays the dashing boulevardier who is stunned to discover that Gigi is no longer a child; Maurice Chevalier is his debonair uncle. *Gigi* overflows with memorable moments: Jourdan's splendid rendition of the Oscar-winning title song; Chevalier's duet of "I Remember It Well" with Hermione Gingold as Gigi's grandmother; Chevalier's entrancing paen to old age, "I'm Glad I'm Not Young Anymore"—these are only a few. In all, thank heaven for *Gigi*.

Off-Screen: *Gigi* swept the Academy Awards during its year, winning a total of nine Oscars, including Best Picture. Yet the production had many problems before reaching the screen. The censors objected to the "immoral" elements in Colette's story before finally approving of producer Arthur Freed's treatment. At first, Paris refused to allow filming in and about the city, and even after consent was finally given, there were so many setbacks in the location filming that the movie went far over budget. After a disastrous preview, roughly one-quarter of the movie was reshot. Yet somehow it all came together, triumphantly. Side note: Famed actress Ina Claire was originally offered the role of Gigi's aunt, played by Isabel Jeans, but decided to stay in retirement. Previous, nonmusical versions of Colette's novel appeared on screen (French, 1950) and on Broadway in 1951, with Audrey Hepburn.

Gilda

Columbia, 1946. (110m.) Dir: Charles Vidor. Sp: Marion Parsonnet; adaptation: Jo Eisington, b/o a story by E. A. Ellington. Cast: Rita Hayworth, Glenn Ford, George Macready, Joseph Calleia, Steven Geray, Joe Sawyer, Gerald Mohr, Robert Scott.

On-Screen: *Rita Hayworth at her most alluring in a steamy love triangle.* "It's the most curious love-hate pattern I've ever had the privilege of witnessing," police chief Joseph Calleia remarks—and he's right on target. In this absurd but fascinating melodrama, Hayworth (in her most famous role) plays the new wife of a sinister Argentinean casino owner (Macready), who meets an old flame (Ford) and rekindles their old spark of mutual hatred and attraction. The three-way relationship (husband, wife, former lover) takes on some unmistakably perverse implications, but the movie concentrates on Hayworth and Ford, and their alternating feelings of loathing and desire. (Ford: "I hated her so much I couldn't get her out of my mind for a minute!") With her voluptuous figure and cascading red hair, Hayworth became America's love goddess, and her modified striptease to "Put the Blame on Mame" was a memorable highlight of moviegoing in the forties.

Off-Screen: Author Ben Hecht is alleged to have made some uncredited contributions to the screenplay. Choreographer Jack Cole modeled Hayworth's provocative dances after a professional stripper he had once seen. Suspecting that Hayworth and Ford were having an affair, studio mogul Harry Cohn had microphones hidden in her dressing room. When the stars discovered them, they teased eavesdropping Cohn with risqué conversation. Anita Ellis dubbed Hayworth's songs; however it is the star who is heard in a reprise of "Put the Blame on Mame," as she accompanies herself on the guitar.

Girl Crazy

MGM, 1943. (99m.) Dir: Norman Taurog. Musical numbers directed by Busby Berkeley. Sp: Fred Finklehoffe, b/o the 1930 musical play. MS: George and Ira Gershwin. Cast: Mickey Rooney, Judy Garland, Gil Stratton, Nancy Walker, Rags Ragland, June Allyson, Guy Kibbee, Tommy Dorsey and His Orchestra.

On-Screen: *Mickey and Judy in the musical West.* Marking their ninth appearance together, *Girl Crazy* transposed Mickey Rooney and Judy Garland to the wide-open spaces for their next round of music and romance. Derived from the Gershwin stage show first filmed in 1932, the movie has Mickey as a girl-chasing playboy banished by his father to a ramshackle Western college, and Judy is

the school's postmistress and the dean's granddaughter. Musical highlights include Garland's lazy, drawling "Bidin' My Time"; her wistful rendition of "But Not for Me"; her sprightly duet with Rooney, "Could You Use Me?" (with top-notch lyrics by Ira Gershwin); and a large-scale production number to "Embraceable You." Busby Berkeley staged the eye-popping finale, "I Got Rhythm," which, among other things, involves whips, guns, and the energetic stars.

Off-Screen: Busby Berkeley was the original director, but after working for three weeks on a single number (which became the finale), he was replaced by Norman Taurog. Some of the film was shot near Palm Springs, using cutouts of saguaro cacti to make the landscape look more like Arizona. Good friends off-screen, Rooney and Garland joked incessantly on the set, even during the filming. *When the Boys Meet the Girls* was an inferior 1965 remake. *Girl Crazy* also inspired the 1992 Broadway musical *Crazy for You.*

Glengarry Glen Ross

New Line, 1992. (C-100m.) Dir: James Foley. Sp: David Mamet, b/o his play. Cast: Al Pacino, Jack Lemmon, Alec Baldwin, Ed Harris, Alan Arkin, Kevin Spacey, Jonathan Pryce.

On-Screen: *The bleak lives of real estate salesman, by way of the Broadway stage.* Eking out a meager and sometimes respectable income hustling home sites in Florida and Arizona, the salesmen of *Glengarry Glen Ross* live in fear and not-so-quiet desperation. Forever searching for all-important "leads," badgered and humiliated by their superiors, they are a sorry lot. David Mamet's screen adaptation of his Pulitzer Prize–winning play conveys the hopelessness of their situation, yet somehow it lacks the raw, stinging power of the stage version. Mamet keeps his machine-gun dialogue intact, but the director opts for either close-up arias by each man or quick back-and-forth cuts, like a Ping-Pong match. The effect is to dissipate the potential impact of a brilliant ensemble cast. *Glengarry Glen Ross* becomes largely an exercise in bravura acting, with Jack Lemmon leading the way in an all-stops-out performance as the oldest and most desperate of the salesmen. (It's the ultimate Jack Lemmon role.) Oscar-nominated Al Pacino and the other players have their moments to shine, and they are all highly adept at Mamet's patented style, in which profanity becomes a kind of musical accompaniment to the action. But ultimately, the movie is never quite as involving as intended.

Off-Screen: For years, David Mamet's play was considered unfilmable. The high-caliber cast agreed to take minimal salary for the opportunity to appear in the film. The actors rehearsed for weeks before shooting began. Repeated takes were often necessary to capture the rhythm of Mamet's dialogue. Alec Baldwin plays the only character not in the play—a hotshot bully from the main office.

The Glenn Miller Story

Universal International, 1954. (C-116m.) Dir: Anthony Mann. Sp: Valentine Davies and Oscar Brodney. MS: Various writers. Cast: James Stewart, June Allyson, Charles Drake, George Tobias, Henry Morgan, Frances Langford, Louis Armstrong, Gene Krupa.

On-Screen: *The life and music of bandleader Glenn Miller.* The sweet, warm sound of Glenn Miller and his orchestra permeated American life in the early forties, and this film attempts to re-create that vanished time. As biodrama, *The Glenn Miller Story* is conventional, largely tracing Miller's search for that special sound and ending with his wartime disappearance on a military plane. June Allyson plays his steadfast wife. Stewart and Allyson make an appealing duo—they were teamed two other times—but their charm gives way to the wonderful Miller music. Many of the well-loved standards are here, including "Tuxedo Junction," "String of Pearls," "Moonlight Serenade," and others. Miller's colleagues Louis Armstrong and Gene Krupa surface occasionally to join in the music.

Off-Screen: Jimmy Stewart did not play the trombone, but he later recalled that he was determined to at least *look* like a trombone player. He was assigned a coach, a fine trombone player named Joe Yukl. After five days, his coach wanted to quit, claiming that the noises Stewart was making with the trombone were affecting him mentally and making him use "terrible language" to his wife. Stewart convinced him to stay and eventually licked the problem.

Glory

TriStar, 1989. (C-122m.) Dir: Edward Zwick. Sp: Kevin Jarre. Cast: Matthew Broderick, Morgan Freeman, Denzel Washington, Cary Elwes, Jihmi Kennedy, Andre

Braugher, John Finn, Donovan Leitch, Bob Gunton, Cliff De Young, John David Cullum.

On-Screen: *An all-black regiment proves its heroism in the Civil War.* Here is a war film with a crucial difference: based on fact, it concerns the exploits and unheralded heroism of the first black unit in the Civil War. Sweeping, stirring, and marvelously detailed, the film tells how the 54th Regiment, made up of former slaves, discovers "courage, spirit, and honor" under the leadership of a young, inexperienced white Northerner (Broderick). In a sense, the characters duplicate those we remember from many previous war films; they include the rebel and troublemaker (Washington, in an Oscar-winning performance), the intellectual (Braugher), the wise older man (Freeman), and the naive youngster (Kennedy). But under Zwick's assured direction, *Glory* attains scope and stature. Best are the battle scenes, especially the final one, in which the regiment launches a bloody assault on a virtually impregnable fort in Charleston harbor.

Off-Screen: In addition to Denzel Washington's Supporting Oscar, *Glory* received Academy Awards for Cinematography (Freddie Francis) and Sound. Jane Alexander makes a brief uncredited appearance as Matthew Broderick's mother, and Raymond St. Jacques can also be seen, uncredited, as Frederick Douglass.

The Godfather

Paramount, 1972. (C-175m.) Dir: Francis Ford Coppola. Sp: Francis Ford Coppola and Mario Puzo, b/o novel by Mario Puzo.

Cast: Marlon Brando, Al Pacino, James Caan, Richard Castellano, Diane Keaton, John Cazale, Talia Shire, Robert Duvall, Sterling Hayden, John Marley, Richard Conte, Abe Vigoda, Morgana King, Alex Rocco.

On-Screen: *Francis Ford Coppola's blockbuster on the life and times of a Mafia family.* One of the most extraordinary films of the seventies, *The Godfather* carried the gangster movie to a new level of bravura and theatrical intensity. Dramatizing the idea that organized crime thrived on, and indeed depended on, "'the family," this gripping melodrama centers on Vito Corleone (Brando), the godfather and revered head of the family, who, despite his professed love for his adopted country, draws his sons (Caan, Pacino, Cazale) into a network of murder and vengeance. The violent scenes in *The Godfather* are not bloodless as in thirties gangster films, nor do they have the "aesthetic" overtones of *Bonnie and Clyde*—they are depicted graphically as ugly, grotesque, and horrifying. Marlon Brando's performance as the godfather is somewhat self-conscious—he appears to be acting in a different film from anyone else—but Al Pacino is outstanding as Michael Corleone, who is transformed from a dutiful son into the all-powerful don. *The Godfather* abounds in vivid, brutal scenes, skillfully staged by Coppola. A winner all the way, and one of the great crime films.

Off-Screen: In casting the role of Vito Corleone, the studio apparently went far afield, even considering such wildly unlikely choices as Danny Thomas, Melvin Belli, and Carlo Ponti. Other possibilities included Anthony Quinn, George C. Scott, and Laurence Olivier. Studio executives were strongly opposed to Brando, but they were finally convinced after he did a test in full makeup. The producer wanted Robert Redford to play Michael, but he turned it down. Jill Clayburgh tested for the role of Kay, as did Susan Blakely and Michelle Phillips. Vic Damone was first cast as singer Johnny Fontane but withdrew. Academy Awards went to the film, to Brando, and to Coppola and Puzo for their screenplay. (The words *Mafia* and *Cosa Nostra* were deleted after a protest by the Italian-American Civil Rights League.) *The Godfather II* turned up in 1974, and *The Godfather III* in 1990.

The Godfather, Part II

Paramount, 1974. (C-200m.) Dir: Francis Ford Coppola. Sp: Francis Ford Coppola and Mario Puzo. Cast: Al Pacino, Robert De Niro, Robert Duvall, Diane Keaton, John Cazale, Talia Shire, Lee Strasberg, Michael V. Gazzo, G. D. Spradlin, Morgana King, Abe Vigoda, Troy Donahue, Danny Aiello, Fay Spain, Harry Dean Stanton.

On-Screen: *The Godfather saga continues.* That rare film: a sequel superior to the original. This second installment of the epic Corleone story is a movie of staggering dimensions and near-operatic power. Sweeping both backward and forward in time, the story begins in Sicily in 1901, with little Vito Corleone as the only survivor of a bloody vendetta, and ends in 1958 in Lake Tahoe, with Michael Corleone (Pacino) as the undisputed don, feared and alone. In between the film depicts crime, not as a family affair as in *The Godfather,* but as big business and a corruption of the American dream.

The early scenes, depicting slum life in 1917 New York, have an astonishing verisimilitude, and Robert De Niro gives a brilliant performance as young Vito Corleone. The impact of the later portions rests squarely with Al Pacino's riveting performance as Michael; his character develops into the godfather who can deal as ruthlessly with senators and dictators as he can with petty thugs, and who can place family ties above personal feelings. A masterpiece of filmmaking.

Off-Screen: Paramount wanted Marlon Brando back in the film, but this never happened. He asked for a huge amount of money and was also feuding with the head of the studio. Richard Castellano (Clemenza) was also cut because of his exorbitant demands. At first Al Pacino hated the screenplay, until revisions further humanized his character. To play young Vito Corleone, Robert De Niro watched tapes of Brando's performance, trying to pick up his mannerisms. Director Elia Kazan, who had been an actor, was the first choice to play Hyman Roth, but he declined. *The Godfather, Part II* won that year's Oscars for Best Picture, Director, Screenplay, Supporting Actor (De Niro), Music Score, and Art Direction/Set Decoration.

The Godfather, Part III

Paramount, 1990. (C-161m.) Dir: Francis Ford Coppola. Sp: Mario Puzo and Francis Ford Coppola. Cast: Al Pacino, Diane Keaton, Talia Shire, Andy Garcia, Eli Wallach, Joe Mantegna, George Hamilton, Bridget Fonda, Sofia Coppola, Raf Vallone, Franc D'Ambrosio, Donal Donnelly, Don Novello.

On-Screen: *The bitter end of the Corleone saga.* After innumerable delays and countless stories about the Sturm und Drang on the set, the third and final part of Coppola's *Godfather* trilogy finally appeared and turned out to be the least effective of the three. Despite the epic-scale production and several extraordinarily powerful sequences, the movie could not surmount a muddled and cluttered story line that was often difficult to follow. The year is 1979, and Michael Corleone (Pacino) is an aging Mafia don who has sold off all his enterprises, both criminal and legitimate. His only love is his daughter, Mary (Coppola). Against his will, he is drawn back into the world of violent crime and even more dangerously, into the treacherous world that links the Catholic Church with international business. In the end, a shattered man, he loses everything. The film often has the scope and even the grandeur of the first two movies, most especially in the stunning climactic sequence staged at Milan's famous La Scala opera house. The overall effect, however, is unsatisfying. And, yes, Sofia Coppola is painfully inadequate as Mary, but she doesn't wreck the movie.

Off-Screen: When Francis Coppola was reluctant to undertake another sequel, many other directors were considered, including Costa-Gavras, James Bridges, and Robert Benton. After Al Pacino demanded $7 million to do the role, Coppola announced that he would start the movie with Michael's funeral. Pacino's price went down, and he joined the film. Originally cast as Mary, Winona Ryder was replaced by Sofia after pleading mental and physical exhaustion. Robert Duvall declined to return to his role as Tom Hagen, the Corleone legal eagle, after the studio refused to give him equal billing and equal money with Al Pacino. The movie won some Oscar nominations, including Best Picture, but received no awards.

Going My Way

Paramount, 1944. (126m.) Dir: Leo McCarey. Sp: Frank Butler and Frank Cavett, b/o story by Leo McCarey. Cast: Bing Crosby, Barry Fitzgerald, Rise Stevens, Frank McHugh, Jean Heather, Gene Lockhart, William Frawley, Stanley Clements.

On-Screen: *Crosby's Oscar-winning role as a progressive parish priest.* Sure, and it's Irish blarney you want? Then this winner of seven Oscars is the way to go. Father O'Malley (Crosby) must save a decaying inner-city parish from financial ruin, and in doing so he runs against the conservative ways of aging, crotchety Father Fitzgibbon (Fitzgerald). Eventually, of course, the two men form a touching bond, as each works in his own way to save the parish. The actors blend marvelously, Crosby easygoing yet forceful, Fitzgerald cantankerous yet lovable. Woven into the story are Met Opera diva Stevens, the Robert Mitchell Boys Choir, and the perennial favorite "Swinging on a Star." There's a surefire climax in which Father Fitzgibbon is reunited with his elderly Irish mother while Father O'Malley croons "Too-ra-loo-ra-loo-ral." The good-humored cast of supporting players adds to the fun. Sure, and it's grand entertainment for all.

Off Screen: When James Cagney and Spencer Tracy proved unavailable to play Father O'Malley, McCarey was inspired to cast Crosby in his first dramatic role. The actor modeled his portrayal on a priest he knew while attending Gonzaga University. McCarey called his story *The Padre,* its main characters being priests he knew in Santa Monica. But the studio, wary of the Catholic Church's reaction to the film, released it under a more secular title. Academy Award rules let Fitzgerald be doubly nominated: as Best Actor (thus competing with Crosby), and the category in which he won, Best Supporting Actor. A movie-history footnote: Gibson Gowland, who starred as the doomed hero of *Greed,* Erich von Stroheim's silent masterpiece, appears as a churchgoing extra. (CFB)

Gold Diggers of 1933

Warners, 1933. (96m.) Dir: Mervyn Le Roy. Sp: Erwin Gelsey and James Seymour, b/o play by Avery Hopwood. MS: Harry Warren and Al Dubin. Cast: Dick Powell, Joan Blondell, Warren William, Ruby Keeler, Ned Sparks, Aline MacMahon, Ginger Rogers, Guy Kibbee.

On-Screen: *Wisecracks, chorus girls, and Busby Berkeley.* Warners' quick follow-up to the sensational *42nd Street* turned out to be a top-notch musical in its own right. The story of three down-on-their-luck actresses had been filmed twice before, but this variation had some sharp dialogue and astonishing musical numbers, staged again by Busby Berkeley. It all begins with Ginger Rogers and the chorus, wearing skimpy coin-covered costumes as they proclaim "We're in the Money." Other highlights include "Pettin' in the Park" and "The Shadow Waltz," in which Ruby Keeler and the girls "play" violins in a lavish white setting. Best of all is "Remember My Forgotten Man," a bold plea on behalf of America's desperate war veterans on the country's breadlines, rendered imploringly by a dubbed Joan Blondell in a stylized Depression setting. It received mixed notices at the time, but remains a stunning reminder of those bleak years.

Off-Screen: Originally, the film was meant to have a semidocumentary montage opening, showing the impact of the Depression on show business, with closed theaters and empty ticket agencies. This was eventually scrapped and the opening evolved into the famous "We're in the Money" number. It was Ginger Rogers, "getting a little slaphappy" on the set, who thought of singing a chorus of that song in Pig Latin, with Darryl Zanuck's approval.

Golden Boy

Columbia, 1939. (99m.) Dir: Rouben Mamoulian. Sp: Lewis Meltzer, Daniel Taradash, Sara Y. Mason, and Victor Heerman, b/o play by Clifford Odets. Cast: Barbara Stanwyck, Adolphe Menjou, William Holden, Lee J. Cobb, Joseph Calleia, Sam Levene, Edward Brophy.

On-Screen: *A young man is torn between boxing and music.* Often imitated and parodied onscreen and on television (and even musicalized for the stage), *Golden Boy* is the one about the gifted young musician (Holden) who chooses to box instead of pursuing a career as a violinist, to the anguish of his Italian-immigrant father (Cobb). On hand is his manager's tough-minded girlfriend (Stanwyck), who falls hard for the boxer. A tragic event in the ring devastates the boxer, but with the girl's help, he finds himself again and returns to the violin. Transposed to the screen, Clifford Odets's Broadway play gets a happy ending while losing some of the social content, but much of Odets's pseudopoetic dialogue, so ripe for parody, is retained. Stanwyck gives the best performance, etching a rounded portrait of an experienced dame who finds salvation in love. In his first screen role, Holden is awkward but likable; Cobb, however, gives an atrocious performance, affecting an Italian accent that would make Henry Armetta seem like Laurence Olivier. The fight sequences are exceptionally well staged.

Off-Screen: Harry Cohn's first choices for the role of Joe Bonaparte, John Garfield and Tyrone Power, were unavailable. Many other actors were tested before William Holden was selected. Nervous and inexperienced, Holden found a true mentor in Barbara Stanwyck. She coached him tirelessly in his lines and helped him develop his characterization. They remained friends for many years. At the 1978 Academy Award ceremonies, he acknowledged his debt to her, and four years later, after he was dead, Stanwyck, in accepting her special Oscar, spoke warmly of Holden, saying, "He always wished I would get an Oscar. And so tonight, my Golden Boy, you got your wish!" A stage musical version of *Golden Boy,* with Sammy Davis, Jr., ran on Broadway in 1964.

Gone With the Wind

David O. Selznick–MGM, 1939. (C-222m.) Dir: Victor Fleming. Sp: Sidney Howard, b/o novel by Margaret Mitchell. Cast: Clark Gable, Vivien Leigh, Leslie Howard, Olivia de Havilland, Hattie McDaniel, Thomas Mitchell, Butterfly McQueen, Ona Munson, Victor Jory, Barbara O'Neil, Harry Davenport, Ann Rutherford, Evelyn Keyes, Carroll Nye, Laura Hope Crews, Isabel Jewell.

On-Screen: *Still champion after more than five decades.* What can be said about *GWTW* at this late date? For over fifty years, *Gone With the Wind* has retained its hold on the public imagination, not necessarily as Hollywood's *greatest* movie but rather as *Hollywood's* greatest movie, a masterly distillation of that magical combination of glamour, technical expertise, and hoopla unique to America's film colony. What is the source of its mythic fame? Certainly there have been more spectacular movies since *GWTW* was made, although its story of Southern belle Scarlett O'Hara (Leigh) and dashing Rhett Butler (Gable) in the antebellum and Civil War South has its share of large-scale sequences. Probably the key to its perennial fascination lies in the Scarlett-Rhett relationship, a sexually charged, contentious fusion of two well-matched people. Credit for the film's durable fame is also due to its obsessed producer, David O. Selznick, and to the performances by Leigh, brilliant in her transition from pouting belle to resourceful woman; Gable, who radiates charisma from his first moment on film; and McDaniel, who makes a memorable figure of her tenacious Mammy. De Havilland also does wonders with the too-good-to-be-true Melanie. *GWTW* has its undeniable shortcomings (a shameless distortion of history; a soap-operatic second half; Howard's wan performance as Ashley), yet somehow it remains one of the handful of films that has taken a permanent place in our collective memory.

Off-Screen: Possibly no film has been written about more than *Gone With the Wind*. (Only *The Wizard of Oz* might come close.) Detailed information on this staggering project can be found in many books, among them *GWTW: The Making of "Gone With the Wind"* by Gavin Lambert (Little, Brown, 1973); *The Art of "Gone With the Wind"* by Judy Cameron and Paul J. Christman (Prentice Hall Press, 1989); *GWTW: The Screenplay* by Sidney Howard (Collier Books, 1980); *Scarlett Fever: The Ultimate Pictorial Treasury* by William Pratt (Collier Books, 1977); and many others. *GWTW* took home eight Oscars, including statuettes for Best Picture, Best Director, Best Actress (Leigh), and Best Supporting Actress (McDaniel). Over the years, several unsuccessful attempts have been made to musicalize the story for the stage. Alexandra Ripley's 1991 novel, *Scarlett,* later a television miniseries, purported to continue the heroine's adventures.

The Good Earth

MGM, 1937. (138m.) Dir: Sidney Franklin. Sp: Talbot Jennings, Tess Slesinger, and Claudine West, b/o novel by Pearl S. Buck. Cast: Paul Muni, Luise Rainer, Walter Connolly, Keye Luke, Tilly Losch, Jessie Ralph, Charley Grapewin.

On-Screen: *Eye-filling drama of Chinese farmer's struggle to attain wealth*. This adaptation of the Pulitzer Prize–wining novel still holds up as spectacular, and often moving, entertainment. It traces the calamitous events that befall Wang Lung (Muni) as he moves from desolate poverty to uneasy prosperity: fierce storms, a devastating drought and famine, and a revolution that rocks the country. Ul-timately, he comes to understand his deep need and love for the land, represented by O-Lan (Rainer), the shy but resilient slave he takes as his wife. Muni is fine, if rather too American as the ambitious peasant; the Austrian actress, though, gives the best performance of her brief career, lending her role both poignancy and dignity. In its day, the terrifying attack of buzzing locusts on Wang's land was considered an awesome technical achievement. It still is.

Off-Screen: Pearl Buck's novel was dramatized for the stage in 1933, with Claude Rains and Nazimova. It was seen by MGM's legendary producer Irving Thalberg, who wanted to turn it into an epic for the screen. In 1934, Chiang Kai-shek's Nationalist government gave the studio reluctant permission to film inside China and to export authentic gear, equipment, and artifacts. When the production finally got under way, the studio purchased five hundred acres in the San Fernando Valley. Rolling fields terraced after the Chinese fashion were created, along with farmers' huts and an artificial river. A walled city was also built complete with streets and shops. Nominated for Best Picture, the movie won Oscars for Rainer's sensitive portrayal and for Karl Freund's cinematography. Fittingly, *The Good Earth* is dedicated to the memory of Thalberg, who died just before production was completed. (CFB)

Good Morning, Vietnam

Touchstone, 1987. (120m.) Dir: Barry Levinson. Sp: Mitch Markowitz. Cast: Robin Williams, Forest Whitaker, Bruno Kirby, Chintara Sukapatana, Robert Wuhl, Tung Thanh Tran.

On-Screen: *Robin Williams on the loose in Vietnam.* Your reaction to this movie will largely depend on your feeling about Robin Williams. As the real-life Adrian Cronauer, an irreverent, rapid-fire disc jockey for Armed Forces Radio during the Vietnam War, Williams relies largely on the sort of manic, freewheeling humor he employs in his stand-up comedy routines. Depending on your inclination, the result will be irritation or admiration for his bursts of brilliance. In the tradition of service comedies, the antiestablishment Cronauer tangles with the uptight, humorless military types. He also becomes involved with a young Vietnamese boy (Tung Thanh Tran) and his sister (Sukapatana), which ultimately costs him his job. Much of the material is uneven or heavy-handed, but Williams's flights of free association are often dazzling and hilarious.

Off-Screen: The real Adrian Cronauer is not at all like the character played by Robin Williams. A very subdued man, he is said to have remarked after seeing the film, "You made me look so funny. That wasn't me at all." Williams, who had been an antiwar activist during the Vietnam War, balked at having to say the line, "We're here to help these people." Barry Levinson believed it was necessary and convinced Williams to speak it.

Good News

MGM, 1947. (C-95m.) Dir: Charles Walters. Sp: Betty Comden and Adolph Green, b/o musical play by Lawrence Schwab and B. G. DeSylva. MS: B. G. DeSylva, Lew Brown, Ray Henderson, and others. Cast: June Allyson, Peter Lawford, Joan McCracken, Patricia Marshall, Ray McDonald, Mel Torme, Donald MacBride, Clinton Sundberg.

On-Screen: *College life in the twenties, MGM musical style.* A Broadway stage hit in 1927, then a 1930 film musical, *Good News* became a lesser but entertaining MGM musical in 1947. A never-never-land view of higher education in the Jazz Age, complete with flappers, raccoon coats, and gin flasks, this *Good News* might have been better news with a little more imagination and style. It's a pleasant vehicle for June Allyson and Peter Lawford, two of MGM's popular players of the time, and the songs ("Just Imagine," "The Best Things in Life Are Free," "The Varsity Drag," etc.) are fun. Highlights include Allyson and Lawford's "French Lesson," written for the film by Comden and Green (music by Roger Edens), and an energetic song and dance to "Pass That Peace Pipe," led by a talented vixen from Broadway named Joan McCracken. Look for singer Mel Torme as one of Tait College's students.

Off-Screen: Claiming that he was not only British but couldn't sing a note, a terrified Peter Lawford tried to beg off from appearing in the movie, but the studio persisted. (Earlier, they had considered Van Johnson and Mickey Rooney.) When Gloria De Haven declined to appear as the college siren, newcomer Patricia Marshall was substituted. "Pass That Peace Pipe" was originally written for *Ziegfeld Follies* but never made it into the score. A stage revival of the musical, starring movie veterans Alice Faye and John Payne, had a brief Broadway run late in 1974.

Goodbye, Columbus

Paramount, 1969. (C-105m.) Dir: Larry Peerce. Sp: Arnold Schulman, b/o novella by Philip Roth. Cast: Richard Benjamin, Ali MacGraw, Jack Klugman, Nan Martin, Michael Meyers, Lori Shelle.

On-Screen: *Young man falls for Jewish princess.* What's a man in love to do? When Bronx librarian Neil (Benjamin) falls madly in love with Brenda Patimkin (MacGraw), a rich, spoiled, and beautiful Jewish girl from Westchester, he must find a way to cope with her family's wildly materialistic lifestyle. Soon he is deeply immersed in their world of over-decorated furniture, overstuffed freezers, and overelaborate wedding receptions. (The latter is a depressing orgy of consumption.) Neil, like many film heroes of the late sixties, is aimless and unfocused, ready to sail with the prevailing wind. A biting, often funny look at upwardly mobile Jewish suburban life, *Goodbye, Columbus* follows Roth's novella fairly closely, but it also tends to allow some of the characters to lapse into caricature; however, there are some wickedly accurate sequences. Benjamin and MacGraw (in their film debuts) are adequate, and Jack Klugman is better than adequate as Brenda's exasperated father, but the movie is stolen by Michael Meyers as Brenda's dim-bulb brother.

Off-Screen: The movie changed Neil's hometown from Newark to the Bronx and settled the Patimkins in Purchase, New York, in Westchester County rather than Short Hills, New Jersey. The grand ballroom of Delmonico's Hotel on Park Avenue was used for the wedding and reception scenes. The rabbi at the wedding was actually a cantor who also served as the coach and recital accompanist for the director's father, singer Jan Peerce, and for other opera singers. Michael Meyers never made another film; instead he went on to become a doctor.

The Goodbye Girl

MGM-UA, 1977. (C-110m.) Dir: Herbert Ross. Sp: Neil Simon, b/o his play.

Cast: Richard Dreyfuss, Marsha Mason, Quinn Cummings, Paul Benedict, Barbara Rhoades.

On-Screen: *An aspiring actor and a dumped-on divorcée share a New York apartment.* Neil Simon's best original screenplay to date, *The Goodbye Girl* is funnier and warmer than most of the mechanical, juiceless adaptations of his Broadway plays. Dreyfuss gives a charismatic, Oscar-winning performance as a young actor who is obliged to share an apartment with Mason, a divorcée and ex-dancer with a young daughter (Cummings). Their mutual hostility eventually gives way to love. Both Dreyfuss and Mason create fully rounded characters, he as the voluble actor for whom all life is a kind of stage (he even flings a scarf around his neck theatrically), and she as the wary "goodbye girl" who is constantly being deceived or deserted by the men in her life. Their best scene, romantic and funny, is a rooftop party organized by Dreyfuss to celebrate his finding a new job.

Off-Screen: A sequel with Richard Dreyfuss, Marsha Mason, and Quinn Cummings was planned but never materialized. There was also an attempt to turn the property into a television series, and a pilot film called "Goodbye Doesn't Mean Forever," with Karen Valentine and Michael Lembeck, was shown in June 1982. The series, however, never made it on the schedule. A stage musical adaptation opened on Broadway in 1993.

Goodbye, Mr. Chips

MGM, 1939. (114m.) Dir: Sam Wood. Sp: R. C. Sherriff, Claudine West, and Eric Maschwitz, b/o novel by James Hilton.

Cast: Robert Donat, Greer Garson, Paul von Hernreid (Henreid), Terry Kilburn, John Mills.

On-Screen: *A teacher's life across the years.* Published in 1934, James Hilton's sentimental novel concerning a much-loved schoolmaster won enthusiastic acclaim around the world. Brought to the screen five years later, it proved to be every bit as popular: a touching story centering on Mr. Chipping (Donat), who, at age eighty-three in 1928, recalls his fifty-eight years as a teacher at Brookfield School. We see him as an eager young man arriving at the school, ardent husband to Katherine (Garson), who dies tragically in childbirth, and then as a fussy but revered codger. Many sequences are calculated to draw tears from viewers, but Robert Donat plays the beloved "Chips" with such warmth and finesse that the heavy sentiment can easily be forgiven. Perhaps most affecting is Chips's retirement ceremony. ("Remember me sometimes. I shall always remember you.") Donat won a well-deserved Academy Award, and the film received five other nominations. Paul Henreid, here called Paul von Hernreid, appears as an Austrian teacher at Brookfield.

Off-Screen: To serve as the setting for the film, MGM chose the 382-year-old Repton School, which also provided several hundred boys to appear as extras for a week. To create costumes for the 153 speaking roles, the studio's designers pored over files of illustrated magazines, fashion books, and family albums. Charles Laughton was first considered to play Chips, but mercifully Donat was cast instead. Louis B. Mayer saw British actress Garson in a London play and, stunned by her beauty and auburn hair, signed her to a contract. An unsuccessful musical version of the story was filmed in 1969, with Peter O'Toole as Chips.

GoodFellas

Warners, 1990. (C-146m.) Dir: Martin Scorsese. Sp: Nicholas Pileggi and Martin Scorsese, b/o book by Nicholas Pileggi. Cast: Robert De Niro, Ray Liotta, Lorraine Bracco, Joe Pesci, Paul Sorvino, Frank Sivero, Tony Darrow, Mike Starr, Chuck Low.

On-Screen: *Inside the Mafia, Scorsese-style.* While many gangster movies of the past have given crime a sort of left-handed attractiveness or treated crime as merely a large-scale business enterprise, Martin Scorsese's *GoodFellas* takes us deep into the ugly heart of the Mafia and its "wiseguys" or "goodfellas." Based on the true story of half-Irish, half-Italian Henry Hill, the movie traces Hill's rise from gofer to trusted mob member, his relations with his wife (Bracco), and with the mob's kingpins (De Niro, Sorvino). Brilliantly handled for the most part, it exposes the machismo, the flamboyant lifestyle, and mostly the stomach-churning violence that makes up the lives of these brutal, heedless men. They represent the corruption of the American dream: for Hill, being a gangster was "better than being president of the United States," and graduation came with your first arrest. Some sequences are extraordinary, notably Hill's visit to the Copacabana nightclub where all the giddy "glamour" of being a known mobster is revealed by the tracking camera. Other scenes, such as a conversation between the Mafia wives, are funny indeed. The acting is vivid throughout, and Joe Pesci is truly terrifying as a short-fused, psychotic hood.

Off-Screen: *GoodFellas* is based on Nicholas Pileggi's 1985 best-seller, *Wiseguy*. Pileggi, who coauthored the screenplay, called it "a mob home movie." Martin Scorsese spoke of the wiseguys as "sociopaths—violence is the key to their lifestyle and power." Joe Pesci won an Oscar as Best Supporting Actor, and Lorraine Bracco was nominated for Best Supporting Actress. Other nominations went to the picture, the director, the screenplay, and the editing.

Gorillas in the Mist

Universal, 1988. (C-129m.) Dir: Michael Apted. Sp: Anna Hamilton Phelan, b/o story by Anna Hamilton Phelan and Tab Murphy, and on the work by Dian Fossey and an article by Harold T. P. Hayes. Cast: Sigourney Weaver, Bryan Brown, Julie Harris, John Omirah Miluwi, Iain Cuthbertson, Constantin Alexandrov.

On-Screen: *The true account of Dian Fossey's obsessive mission to protect Africa's mountain gorillas.* Sigourney Weaver gives a remarkable, Oscar-nominated performance as Dian Fossey, a young woman who went to central Africa to observe the mountain gorillas in danger of extinction and remained to become their fierce defender. This beautifully shot, often powerfully moving film relates how Fossey came to love and admire the gentle creatures who were being exterminated by poachers, and how her need to protect them drove her to near-madness and drove others to regard her as a threat. Except for Fossey's romantic idyll with a *National Geographic* photographer (Brown), the movie concentrates on her relationship with the gorillas. Among the memorable moments, none is more touching than the one in which Fossey and a gorilla finally make hand-to-hand contact. You are not likely to forget the shot of Sigourney Weaver weeping in the rain, surrounded by her gorilla friends, nor the scene in which she must part from the baby gorilla she has nurtured back to health.

Off-Screen: All but one of the scenes were filmed with genuine, untamed gorillas. Jessica Lange was considered for the role but became pregnant. Cast and crew spent many arduous weeks in the mountainous jungles of central Africa, where Dian Fossey lived and died. Sigourney Weaver learned how to communicate with the gorillas using sounds and gestures. The film also received Oscar nominations for Best Adapted Screenplay, Best Film Editing, Best Original Score, and Best Sound.

The Graduate

Joseph E. Levine/Embassy, 1967. (C-105m.) Dir: Mike Nichols. Sp: Buck Henry and Calder Willingham, b/o novel by Charles Webb. Cast: Anne Bancroft, Dustin Hoffman, Katharine Ross, Murray Hamilton, William Daniels, Elizabeth Wilson, Brian Avery, Norman Fell, Marion Lorne, Alice Ghostley.

On-Screen: *"Award-winning scholar" Benjamin Braddock faces life.* One of the key films of the late sixties, *The Graduate* seemed to crystallize, in hilarious and pungent terms, the alienated mood of many young people of the time. In his first major role, Dustin Hoffman plays twenty-one-year-old Benjamin Braddock, a recent college graduate who is the pride of his upper-middle-class parents (Daniels and Wilson). In reality,

Ben is in limbo, uncertain of where his life is heading. It heads for trouble in the person of his parents' neurotic, alcoholic friend Mrs. Robinson (Bancroft), who seduces him. When Ben falls for her daughter, Elaine (Ross), there's hell to pay. Written with wit and perception, and directed adroitly by Mike Nichols (his second film), *The Graduate* abounds in memorable moments: Ben, wearing a diving suit and drifting alone in his parents' pool, the very image of alienation; or Ben's first bedroom encounter with Mrs. Robinson. Hoffman's star-making performance never falters, and Anne Bancroft etches a blistering portrait of a hard-as-nails virago.

Off-Screen: Dustin Hoffman, Anne Bancroft, and Katharine Ross were all nominated for Oscars (and there were other nominations), but the only award was given to Mike Nichols for his direction. Robert Redford turned down the part that went to Hoffman. Charles Grodin auditioned for the role and for a while he was the leading contender. He lost to Hoffman when it was erroneously perceived that it would be difficult to work with him. Patricia Neal was the first choice for Mrs. Robinson, but felt that she hadn't recovered sufficiently from her stroke. Another turndown was Doris Day. Coauthor Buck Henry appears as a hotel clerk, and there are walk-on appearances by Mike Farrell and Richard Dreyfuss. The film's evocative songs were written by Paul Simon and sung by Simon and Art Garfunkel.

Grand Canyon

Fox, 1991. (C-134m.) Dir: Lawrence Kasdan. Sp: Lawrence Kasdan and Meg Kasdan. Cast: Kevin Kline, Danny Glover, Steve Martin, Mary McDonnell, Mary-Louise Parker, Alfre Woodard.

On-Screen: *On life and Los Angeles in the nineties.* Living in today's perilous urban world generates terror and alienation. Everything is fraught with danger—from a driving lesson in congested traffic to a violent street attack, from an earthquake to emotional upheavals. Yet the winds of chance blow both ways—and a fleeting moment can also bring friendship, romance, and most of all, hope. These are only a few of the themes in Lawrence Kasdan's ambitious, brilliant film that ties together a group of Los Angeles residents in various ways. An ensemble cast does full justice to the Kasdans' provocative, many-faceted screenplay, including Kevin Kline as an immigration lawyer; Danny Glover as the auto mechanic who becomes his friend; Steve Martin as a filmmaker; and Mary McDonnell as Kline's wife, who finds and adopts an abandoned baby. The film tries to cover too much territory, but since most movies cover little or nothing at all, this should not be construed as a defect. And an affirmative ending will leave you with the exuberant feeling that there are some things, such as the Grand Canyon, that remain eternal after all.

Off-Screen: Coauthor and director Kasdan was disturbed and angered by some critics who claimed that the characters suffer from nothing more than yuppie angst. In a *New York Times* article, he stated, "If you make a movie about some subject that's distant from our lives, a movie about a spaceship or a gangster or a serial killer, something that people don't experience on an everyday basis, then nobody challenges that reality. But there are certain subjects, like everyday life in urban America, where everybody is an expert. Suddenly your view is put up against everyone else's view. So you're open to criticism."

Grand Hotel

MGM, 1932. (112m.) Dir: Edmund Goulding. Sp: William A. Drake, b/o novel and play by Vicki Baum. Cast: Greta Garbo, John Barrymore, Joan Crawford, Wallace Beery, Lionel Barrymore, Jean Hersholt, Lewis Stone.

On-Screen: *Star-filled, Oscar-winning Best Picture.* Some of the histrionics have dated; still, there's much to enjoy in this glittering drama of guests whose stories, both tragic and life-affirming, intertwine at a ritzy Berlin hotel. Garbo, luminous as always, is less persuasive as a suicidal Russian ballerina than as the sexually released woman she becomes after a one-night fling with jewel thief John Barrymore. Their scene together is magical and a trifle absurd, with the camera moving in for a close-up of the screen's two greatest profiles. Beery makes his boorish "industrial magnate" surprisingly sympathetic, but Lionel Barrymore, as his terminally ill accountant, shreds the scenery. The most impressive performance is Crawford's stunning, on-the-make stenographer who discovers that, after all, she has a heart. Yes, this is the movie in which Garbo, that fabled force of nature, wants "to be alone."

Off-Screen: Before the final cast was assembled, John Gilbert was considered for John Barrymore's role, and after he was rejected, Robert Montgomery tested for the part. Buster Keaton was Edmund Goulding's first choice to play the doomed accountant, but his heavy drinking made him unreliable. Clark Gable was first thought of for Beery's role, but was finally considered too young. To her chagrin, Crawford had no scenes with Garbo, who filmed all her major scenes on a separate soundstage. In 1945, MGM produced a glossy remake with Ginger Rogers in the Garbo role, switching the locale to New York and calling it *Weekend at the Waldorf.* In 1958, a stage musical adaptation entitled *At the Grand* failed to make an impression, but in 1989, Baum's story finally became a long-running Broadway show. (CFB)

The Grapes of Wrath

Fox, 1940. (129m.) Dir: John Ford. Sp: Nunnally Johnson, b/o novel by John Steinbeck. Cast: Henry Fonda, Jane Darwell, John Carradine, Charley Grapewin, Dorris Bowden, Russell Simpson, John Qualen.

On-Screen: *Stirring drama of dust bowl Okies.* No movie has expressed the plight of the rural poor in the depressed thirties with greater power than this adaptation of Steinbeck's novel. The Joads, together with other drought-plagued Oklahoma farmers, head for jobs and a new life in the "promised land" of California. Tom Joad (Fonda), just released from prison, rejoins his family as they move from one transient camp to another, only to find himself once more in trouble with the police. Fonda's loping gait and steady gaze bring Tom to vivid life, but it's Darwell's indomitable Ma Joad who gives the movie its greatest strength. Though a simple eulogy by an itinerant preacher (Carradine) is among the film's most poetic moments, for many the most poignant scene shows Darwell burning all her possessions, then putting on a pair of earrings as she smiles at memories of happier days. A classic, unforgettable movie.

The film was nominated for seven Academy Awards (including Best Picture and Best Screenplay), with both Ford and Best Supporting Actress Darwell winning. Surprisingly, the Academy overlooked Gregg Toland's stunning, documentarylike photography. Ford wanted Beulah Bondi to play Ma Joad, but Fox head Darryl Zanuck insisted on contract player Darwell instead. Zanuck himself wrote the affirmative lines that end the movie. Because banks and farm interests regarded Steinbeck's novel as dangerously subversive, the studio shot the movie under the title *Highway 66*. Touted in the Soviet Union as an exposé of capitalist oppression, it was suppressed when Russian viewers observed enviously that at least the Joads owned an automobile. A stage adaptation of the novel ran on Broadway in 1990. (CFB)

Grease

Paramount, 1978. (C-110m.) Dir: Randal Kleiser. Sp: Bronte Woodard; adaptation: Allan Carr, b/o musical play by Jim Jacobs and Warren Casey. MS: Jim Jacobs and Warren Casey, and other writers. Cast: John Travolta, Olivia Newton-John, Stockard Channing, Jeff Conaway, Didi Conn, Eve Arden, Sid Caesar, Joan Blondell, Dody Goodman, Edd Byrnes, Alice Ghostley, Michael Tucci, Frankie Avalon.

On-Screen: *High-school extracurricular activities in the fifties, by way of the musical stage.* Fresh from his sensational success in *Saturday Night Fever,* John Travolta starred in this lively adaptation of the long-running Broadway musical. He plays Danny, kingpin of the Rydell High School crowd in the fifties, whose summer romance with Sandy (Newton-John) turns alternately sweet and sour when it resumes during the school year. That's merely the jumping-off point for a series of elaborate, nostalgic musical numbers, many of them staged with distracting photographic gimmickry. The titles tell all: "Beauty School Dropout," "Look at Me, I'm Sandra Dee," "Alone at a Drive-in Movie," etc. In effect, *Grease* is not much different from a Mickey-Judy musical of the forties, only with much racier dialogue and a driving fifties beat. Older viewers not so inclined to sit through the noisy activities of the energetic young cast will welcome the presence of such veteran actors as Eve Arden, Sid Caesar, Joan Blondell, and Dody Goodman.

Off-Screen: John Travolta had appeared on Broadway in *Grease* before he began his featured role in television's "Welcome Back, Kotter." One song from the movie, "Hopelessly Devoted to You," won an Oscar nomination. Venice High School in California was used for the exteriors of Rydell High. A sequel, *Grease 2* (1982), starring Michelle Pfeiffer and Maxwell Caulfield, failed to cause even a ripple at the box office. It was directed by Patricia Birch, who contributed the vigorous choreography to the original movie.

The Great Caruso

MGM, 1951. (C-109m.) Dir: Richard Thorpe. Sp: Sonya Levien and William Ludwig, b/o book by Dorothy Caruso. MS:

Various writers. Cast: Mario Lanza, Ann Blyth, Dorothy Kirsten, Jarmila Novotna, Carl Benton Reid, Eduard Franz, Ludwig Donath, Alan Napier.

On-Screen: *The life and music of famed singer Enrico Caruso*. Having created a sensation in two previous MGM musicals with his robust operatic voice, it was inevitable that the studio would cast Mario Lanza as the renowned Italian tenor Enrico Caruso. In its usual fashion, MGM uses more fiction than fact in telling Caruso's story, trotting out the usual obscurity-to-fame plot—Caruso goes from café singer to opera star in record time—but ending, as it must, in Caruso's death. Luckily, much of the film is given over to Lanza's singing, and his powerful voice soars through twenty-seven arias and traditional songs. One song, "The Loveliest Night of the Year," adapted from "Over the Waves," became a popular hit, and the movie was one of the top-grossing films of the year. It also marked the peak of Lanza's brief career.

Off-Screen: Mario Lanza's first meeting with his costar Ann Blyth was a touchy affair. Lanza was known to swear profusely, and Blyth was demure and highly religious. The ice was broken when Lanza reminded her that Caruso, too, was known to yell and swear. The two got along well during the filming, although Lanza disrupted the proceedings many times with his boorish, volatile behavior. He often declared, "I am Caruso!"

The Great Dictator

United Artists, 1940. (128m.) Dir: Charles Chaplin. Sp: Charles Chaplin. Cast: Charlie Chaplin, Paulette Goddard, Jack Oakie, Henry Daniell, Reginald Gardiner, Billy Gilbert, Maurice Moscovich.

On-Screen: *Charlie Chaplin's often biting satire on the lunacy of totalitarianism*. Chaplin takes on two roles in this rather conventionally staged but daring (for its day) send-up of Hitler and his Third Reich cronies. As the humble Jewish barber and his egomaniacal look-alike, Adenoid Hynkel, ruler of Tomania, Chaplin is both funny and poignant as the one, pompous and fanatical as the other. The barber's tonsorial skills performed to a Brahms "Hungarian Dance" and Hynkel's self-intoxicated ballet with a buoyant terrestrial globe are among the movie's classic moments. Goddard is affecting as the Jewish girl the "little man" protects from storm troopers; Daniell and Gilbert as Garbitsch and Herring, Hynkel's stooges, and Oakie, as jut-jawed Napaloni, dictator of Bacteria, make the most of their caricature roles. Viewers tend to regard the courageous barber's final speech espousing peace and universal love as either high-flown or still relevant.

Off-Screen: *The Great Dictator* is Chaplin's first true talkie, his previous sound-era films, *City Lights* (1931) and *Modern Times* (1936), being silent, except for sound effects, nonsense speech, and music scores. Produced before the true horrors of the Third Reich were widely known, the film's acknowledgment of the very existence of dictators—and treatment of them in a humorous, unflattering way in the bargain—caused many to fear the film was too controversial. Nevertheless, the movie won a number of Oscar nominations, including one for Best Picture. Getting the musical shave is former Keystone Kop Chester Conklin. Goddard was Mrs. Chaplin at the time. (CFB)

The Great Escape

The Mirisch Company/United Artists, 1963. (C-168m.) Dir: John Sturges. Sp: James Clavell and W. R. Burnett, b/o book by Paul Brickhill. Cast: Steve McQueen, James Garner, Richard Attenborough, James Coburn, Charles Bronson, James Donald, Donald Pleasence, Angus Lennie, Hannes Messemer, David McCallum.

On-Screen: *Allied servicemen plot escape from a German prison*. The movie begins by announcing, "This is a true story." Well . . . it may be true that over seventy Allied military men of various nationalities managed to escape during World War II from a high-security German prison. *The Great Escape*, at least for its first half, seems more like Hollywood derring-do, a mite closer to *Stalag 17* or even "Hogan's Heroes" than the documented truth. Led by British officer Attenborough, the prisoners plot many clever ploys and distractions to keep their captors from knowing that they are digging a tunnel to freedom. Their first effort fails, but not their second, and the film picks up momentum after the escape, with many suspenseful scenes. Among the prisoners are Steve McQueen, as a cocky pilot whose failed attempts to escape keep sending him to the solitary cell called the Cooler, and James Garner, as a light-fingered man who steals valuable tools.

Off-Screen: Although the plot seems far-fetched, a letter to the *New York Times* in August 1963 from one of the participants in the actual escape from Stalag Luft III confirmed that "the American and British flying officers were as arrogant and defiant as depicted in this film. Not romantic or Rover Boyish but determined to harass the Germans in every possible way. . . ." Another man who had been in charge of the tunneling at the Stalag insisted that "Mr. Sturges and his company of actors and writers truly captured the spirit of the prisoners, of their humor and dedication." A television sequel turned up twenty-five years later.

The Great Gatsby

Paramount, 1974. (C-144m.) Dir: Jack Clayton. Sp: Francis Ford Coppola, b/o novel by F. Scott Fitzgerald. Cast: Robert Redford, Mia Farrow, Bruce Dern, Sam Waterston, Karen Black, Scott Wilson, Lois Chiles, Howard da Silva, Edward Herrmann.

On-Screen: *Third adaptation of F. Scott Fitzgerald's Jazz Age novel*. The Great Gatsby has no shortage of style. All aglitter with John Box's opulent production design, the film takes the viewer to the swank Long Island mansions of the twenties, where filthy-rich couples dance the night away. But style, as we know, is not all, and this becalmed version of Fitzgerald's book has few other virtues. Robert Redford is Gatsby, the rich young man of mysterious background and romantic nature. Obsessed with Daisy (Farrow), the golden girl he once loved and lost, Gatsby pursues his dream of winning her. Daisy, in love with the *idea* of Gatsby's adoration, is married to Tom Buchanan (Dern), a boorish lout whose cheating ultimately has fatal consequences. The Buchanans, to Fitzgerald, are emblematic of the twenties: heedless, hedonistic, and destructive. The movie's opulence cannot conceal the screenplay's inability to breathe life into the characters. Nor can Redford do much with his cryptic Gatsby, while Farrow, though lovely in her twenties garb, soon irritates with her fluting voice and petulant manner.

Off-Screen: Previous adaptations of *The Great Gatsby* were released in 1926 and 1949. This 1974 version went through some tangled casting procedures. Marlon Brando was considered for Gatsby, but his price was too high. Steve McQueen wanted the role, but Redford was already signed. Ali McGraw had been slated to play Daisy, and when she withdrew, many other actresses, including Faye Dunaway, Katharine Ross, and Candice Bergen, were tested. After Truman Capote's adaptation of the novel was rejected, he sued the studio. The movie failed to draw customers, but it won Oscars for Theoni V. Aldredge's costumes and Nelson Riddle's score.

The Great Lie

Warners, 1941. (107m.) Dir: Edmund Goulding. Sp: Lenore Coffee, b/o novel by Polan Banks. Cast: Bette Davis, George Brent, Mary Astor, Lucile Watson, Hattie McDaniel, Grant Mitchell, Jerome Cowan, Thurston Hall, Russell Hicks.

On-Screen: *Two women share a secret that changes their lives.* It is difficult to believe that any actor could outdistance Bette Davis, but Mary Astor did just that in *The Great Lie,* winning a Supporting Actress Oscar as well. She plays a temperamental pianist who has a baby out of wedlock with Brent. When he is presumed dead in a plane crash, she gives her baby to friend Davis to raise. But Brent returns (oddly, with gray hair and lined face after less than a year) and marries Davis, whom he has always loved, and now the two women battle for possession of Brent and the baby. It's all arrant nonsense, noisily scored, but Astor gives such a vivid performance that she makes the movie at least watchable.

Off-Screen: Desperately unhappy with the screenplay, Bette Davis worked on her own to improve it. Mainly, she strengthened Mary Astor's part so that the character became the stronger and more vivid of the two women. She had wanted Astor for the role from the beginning, knowing that she could not only play the piano well but could also invest the character with all the hauteur and bitchiness it required. All through the filming, Davis was entirely supportive of her costar.

The Great McGinty

Paramount, 1940. (8lm.) Dir: Preston Sturges. Sp: Preston Sturges. Cast: Brian Donlevy, Akim Tamiroff, Muriel Angelus, William Demarest, Allyn Joslyn, Louis Jean Heydt, Arthur Hoyt.

On-Screen: *A bum rises in the political ranks in Preston Sturges's debut comedy as director.* Although it lacks the polish and sustained fun of Sturges's later movies, *The Great McGinty* shows clear evidence of his originality and wit. In this satirical view of political chicanery, Brian Donlevy plays a bum who is elected mayor, then governor, with the backing of the state's all-powerful boss (Tamiroff). His political career crumbles when he turns honest under the influence of his wife (Angelus). Sturges's amusing screenplay has all the ingredients he would use in his later movies: bursts of slapstick, quotable lines of dialogue ("This is the land of opportunity. Everybody lives by chiseling everybody else"), and above all, a deeply rooted affection for the world's blowhards, frauds, and nincompoops. William Demarest, delightful as the boss's right-hand man, sums up the prevailing point of view: "If you didn't have graft, you'd have a lower class of people in politics."

Off-Screen: Originally called *Biography of a Bum,* the screenplay was turned down by every major studio. Sturges decided that he would not sell it unless he could direct it. "It only took six years," he said later. After finally getting his big chance from Paramount, Sturges promptly contracted pneumonia. To his enormous relief, the studio decided to wait until he recovered. *The Great McGinty* won an Oscar as Best Original Screenplay.

The Great Ziegfeld

MGM, 1936. (176m.) Dir: Robert Z. Leonard. Sp: William Anthony McGuire. MS: Walter Donaldson and Harold Adamson. Cast: William Powell, Myrna Loy, Luise Rainer, Frank Morgan, Virginia Bruce, Ray Bolger, Fanny Brice, Reginald Owen.

On-Screen: *The story of theatrical impresario Florenz Ziegfeld.* Long, lavish, and as heavy as a Christmas fruitcake, *The Great Ziegfeld* was one of MGM's most prestigious productions of the thirties. It purports to tell the life story of the master showman famous for his extravagant yearly "Follies," which "glorified" the American girl and which introduced such luminaries as Eddie Cantor, Will Rogers, and Fanny Brice. As biography, the movie is largely balderdash, but it also represents the zenith of MGM's opulent phase in the thirties. One outsize production number, "A Pretty Girl Is Like a Melody," a gaudy, delirious mixture of ballet, opera, and spectacle, must be seen to be believed. William Powell and Myrna Loy

(as Billie Burke) do a charming reprise of their Nick-and-Nora act, but Luise Rainer, in her Oscar-winning performance as Anna Held, is insufferably coy and petulant. Her famous telephone monologue (she is learning that her beloved "Flo" is no longer available) will move you to either tears or the nearest exit.

Off-Screen: The singer in the "Pretty Girl" number is Dennis Morgan, then billed as Stanley Morner. Although his light singing voice would later be used in other musicals, it was dubbed for this number by Allan Jones. Ziegfeld stars Will Rogers and Eddie Cantor are impersonated, but Fanny Brice plays herself. *The Great Ziegfeld* also won the Best Picture award for that year, and Seymour Felix's dance direction for the "Pretty Girl" number received an Oscar.

The Greatest Show on Earth

Paramount, 1952. (C-153m.) Dir: Cecil B. DeMille. Sp: Fredric M. Frank, Barre Lyndon, and Theodore St. John, b/o story by Frank Cavett, Fredric M. Frank, and Theodore St. John. Cast: Charlton Heston, Betty Hutton, James Stewart, Cornel Wilde, Dorothy Lamour, Gloria Grahame, Lyle Bettger, Lawrence Tierney.

On-Screen: *Cecil B. DeMille glorifies the Big Top.* Was this the best picture of 1952? The Motion Picture Academy thought so and voted it the Oscar. Today, we might hope that wiser heads would prevail. It's certainly lavish: Cecil B. DeMille's all-out tribute to the gaudy and giddy pleasures of the circus, particularly Ringling Bros. and Barnum & Bailey, which provided the acts. The trapeze artists, the clowns, the acrobats, etc., are all fun to watch, and with DeMille himself providing the narration in sonorous tones, the movie provides some colorful glimpses of the circus's modus operandi. But then someone had to provide a narrative about the backstage lives of the principals, and it's quite dreadful, replete with bad acting and preposterous dialogue. Heston (in his second film) is the gruff circus manager, and Hutton is the aerialist who adores him. Enter egotistic trapeze king Wilde (sporting an unconvincing French accent), and there's romance and rivalry. A spectacular circus-train wreck (actually staged in miniature) makes for a suitable climax.

Off-Screen: In addition to its Best Picture Oscar, *The Greatest Show on Earth* won an award for its story. DeMille spent weeks traveling in John Ringling North's private car to learn about the circus. Burt Lancaster, Marlene Dietrich, Hedy Lamarr, and Kirk Douglas were among the many stars who were considered for roles in the film, and Gloria Grahame was selected over Paulette Goddard for the part of the elephant girl. Hutton was able to handle the trapeze, but Wilde learned that he had a fear of heights. Bing Crosby, Bob Hope, and Mona Freeman can be spotted among the spectators in the Big Top audience.

The Green Pastures

Warners, 1936. (92m.) Dir: William Keighley and Marc Connelly. Sp: Sheridan Gibney and Marc Connelly, b/o play by Marc Connelly and stories by Roark Bradford. Cast: Rex Ingram, Oscar Polk, Eddie Anderson, Frank Wilson, George Reed, Abraham Gleaves, Myrtle Anderson, the Hall Johnson Choir.

On-Screen: *"Gangway for de Lawd God Jehovah!"* Hailed by the *New York Times* in 1930 as "a play of surpassing beauty," and winner of a Pulitzer Prize, *The Green Pastures* was finally transposed to film in 1936. Faithful to the concept of the Bible as interpreted by poor Southern blacks, *The Green Pastures* first takes the viewer to a fish fry in heaven, presided over by "de Lawd" (Ingram), then moves to the familiar stories of Noah and the flood, Moses' liberation of his people from slavery in Egypt, the fall of Babylon, and the appearance of Jesus on earth. Today, our sensibilities are quite different from what they were over a half century ago, and much of *The Green Pastures* now seems crude and patronizing. Still, there are some indelibly moving moments: Noah (Anderson) confronting the Lord ("I should have known you, Lord. I should have seen the glory"), or the Lord discovering compassion for sinners through his own suffering. ("Even bein' God ain't no bed of roses.") The Hall Johnson Choir offers a number of stirring hymns and spirituals.

Off-Screen: Since most of the cast members came from Los Angeles, a coach had to be hired to teach them the Louisiana bayou accent. Author and codirector Marc Connelly wanted to shoot the film on location in the South, but he was overruled, and it was made on indoor studio sets. Despite its mild and reverent tone, the movie was boycotted by many exhibitors, especially in the South.

Greystoke: The Legend of Tarzan, Lord of the Apes

Warners, 1984. (C-129m.) Dir: Hugh Hudson. Sp: P. H. Vazak and Michael Austin, b/o story by Edgar Rice Burroughs. Cast: Ralph Richardson, Christopher Lambert, Ian Holm, Andie MacDowell, James Fox, Cheryl Campbell, Ian Charleson, Nigel Davenport.

On-Screen: *Hugh Hudson's new version of the long-standing Tarzan legend.* Imagine shedding tears at the death of a large ape. Then imagine that the ape *isn't* King Kong but the "father" of the hero, Greystoke, or Tarzan, Lord of the Apes. This poignant scene occurs at the climax of this sober, handsomely produced, if somewhat disjointed version of the Tarzan legend. Here John Clayton, heir to the Greystoke fortune, is raised by apes in the jungle after surviving a shipwreck. When fully grown, he (Lambert) is found and returned to the ancestral estate, where his primitive and civilized instincts clash painfully. Eventually, despite loving his grandfather's ward, Jane (MacDowell), he returns to his home in the jungle. The film's first part is much the best, a fascinating account of his life with the apes (Rick Baker's special makeup effects are marvelous). When the story moves to the Greystoke estate in England, there are charming and funny sequences as the Ape Man reacts to the strange new world, but the action becomes sluggish. Top acting honors go to Ralph Richardson, who was Oscar-nominated for his last role as John's loving grandfather.

Off-Screen: The movie's African scenes were filmed in Cameroon. Writers Austin and Vazak won an Oscar nomination for Best Adapted Screenplay, although Vazak was actually Robert Towne, who removed his name from the screenplay. The part of John's ape "father" was played by Peter Elliot, who choreographed the movie's ape sequences. (He was billed as Elliot W. Cane.) Only the babies among the chimps were real; the others were actors made up ingeniously. The actors playing chimps had to wear body stockings with rubber chimp musculature molded onto them to force the actors into an apelike posture. Andie MacDowell's voice was dubbed by Glenn Close.

The Grifters

Cineplex Odeon, 1990. (113m.) Dir: Stephen Frears. Sp: Donald E. Westlake, b/o novel by Jim Thompson. Cast: Anjelica Huston, John Cusack, Annette Bening, Pat Hingle, Henry Jones, J. T. Walsh.

On-Screen: *Three con artists clash with deadly results.* A film noir for the nineties—ice-cold, relentlessly tough, and explicitly violent—*The Grifters* does a brilliant new turn on the old nest-of-vipers theme. The story revolves about three grifters on a fatal collision course: a seasoned and hardened woman (Huston) working her scam at the racetrack; her young son (Cusack), whose cons to date have only been petty; and a girl (Bening) whose ambitions coincide with her utter ruthlessness. As their fast-buck schemes succeed or backfire, the three move in and out of trouble, until the rivalry between mother and girl turns deadly. The twists and turns of the plot come so swiftly, and the atmosphere is so thick with covert menace, that the film is likely to leave you unsettled but fascinated. Anjelica Huston gives a stunning, Oscar-nominated performance as a woman who knows everything and trusts nobody, and John Cusack and Annette Bening (also nominated) match her every step of the way. *The Grifters* may be filmed in bright color, but it's as *noir* as they come.

Off-Screen: To find the look and the feel of her elusive character of Lily, Anjelica Huston frequented the windowless, smoke-filled card parlors in forgotten pockets of Los Angeles County. Those who had neither the money nor the inclination to travel to Las Vegas would gamble there every day. She would watch the lady dealers to find out what had drawn these women to these places. She discovered "a lot of Lily" in them. Other Oscar nominations went to Frears and Westlake.

The Group

Columbia, 1966. (C-150m.) Dir: Sidney Lumet. Sp: Sidney Buchman, b/o novel by Mary McCarthy. Cast: Candice Bergen, Joan Hackett, Shirley Knight, Elizabeth Hartman, Jessica Walter, Joanna Pettet, Kathleen Widdoes, Mary-Robin Redd, Larry Hagman, Hal Holbrook, James Gregory, Richard Mulligan.

On-Screen: *Mary McCarthy's over-the-years chronicle of Vassar graduates.* Meet the class of Vassar College, 1933, and follow their rising and falling fortunes over the years as they experience romance, marriage, career changes, and the world around them. Sidney Buchman's long, soap-operatic screenplay takes the young women from hope to disillusionment and despair. Kay (Pettet) is tied to her alcoholic, cheating playwright-husband; radical Priss (Hartman) suffers marriage to a Republican with advanced "ideas" on bearing and raising children; Lakey (Bergen) dabbles in lesbianism; Polly (Knight) has an unhappy romance with a married editor (Holbrook); and so on. Most of the men in the film, in fact, are fools and/or scoundrels, and the women's in-

volvement with them is neither credible nor interesting. The period costumes for the women, incidentally, are supremely hideous.

Off-Screen: Writer Sidney Buchman, who also produced, enjoyed a long and distinguished career at Columbia as the author of such notable films as *Mr. Smith Goes to Washington* and *The Talk of the Town*. Unfortunately, he was blacklisted in 1951 when he acknowledged former membership in the Communist Party to the House Un-American Activities Committee and refused to name others. He later resumed his career. Making their debuts in the film are Candice Bergen, Joan Hackett, Joanna Pettet, Kathleen Widdoes, and Hal Holbrook.

Guess Who's Coming to Dinner

Columbia, 1967. (C-108m.) Dir: Stanley Kramer. Sp: William Rose, b/o his story. Cast: Spencer Tracy, Katharine Hepburn, Sidney Poitier, Katharine Houghton, Cecil Kellaway, Beah Richards, Roy E. Glenn, Sr., Isobel Sanford, Virginia Christine.

On-Screen: *Hepburn and Tracy, together for the last time.* Back in 1967, *Guess Who's Coming to Dinner* seemed fairly audacious in its theme of an interracial romance and the impact of the romance, and impending marriage, on the couple's parents. Yet even at the time, it was criticized for stacking the cards by making the black groom-to-be virtually perfect in every respect. Today, despite the best of intentions and an intelligent, Oscar-winning screenplay, the movie seems more decorous than ever: a drawing-room comedy with social pretensions. Its principal value is that it marks the last teaming of

Spencer Tracy and Katharine Hepburn, the screen's most memorable acting couple. As the San Francisco newspaper publisher whose liberal beliefs are tested, Tracy looks worn and tired, but his artistry is intact, and Hepburn's Oscar-winning performance as his caring wife matches him all the way. Tracy's long final speech, as he comes to realize that he cannot oppose his daughter's marriage to a black man, is highly affecting, especially with a tearful Hepburn in the background. (A viewer can be forgiven for reading personal implications into the speech.)

Off-Screen: In addition to its Oscars for Katharine Hepburn and William Rose, the movie won nominations for Spencer Tracy, Cecil Kellaway (as a sympathetic priest), and Beah Richards (as Poitier's understanding mother). There were several other nominations as well. Katharine Houghton, who played Hepburn's daughter, is actually her niece. On the last day of filming, Tracy made a rare speech to the crew in which he thanked them for their help and support. Two weeks later, he was dead.

Guilty by Suspicion

Warners, 1991. (C-105m.) Dir: Irwin Winkler. Sp: Irwin Winkler. Cast: Robert De Niro, Annette Bening, George Wendt, Patricia Wettig, Sam Wanamaker, Luke Edwards, Chris Cooper, Martin Scorsese, Ben Piazza.

On-Screen: *A Hollywood director becomes a victim of the blacklist.* A trenchant if uneven drama on an appalling period in American history, *Guilty by Suspicion* is set in the early fifties, when the House Un-American Activities Committee sought to root out Communists in the entertainment industry. Robert De Niro plays a rising Hollywood director—the new golden boy of the movies, who is suddenly plunged into a nightmare. Accused of Communist sympathies in the past, he finds that his reluctance to name others costs him his career. The insidious blacklist also destroys the lives and careers of good friends. Writer-director Irwin Winkler conveys the fear, unease, and anguish of the period, managing to touch on all the possible attitudes and responses. A problem lies in the central character played by De Niro, who, despite several angry outbursts, never seems to react as drastically to the experience as others around him and therefore never invites as much sympathy. De Niro doesn't help with a performance that is adequate but not among his best. Still, the movie zeroes in on a tragic time that has not had much coverage in films.

Off-Screen: *Guilty by Suspicion* has a tortured history that began in 1986 when producer-director-writer Irwin Winkler got together with blacklisted writer Abraham Polonsky and director Bernard Tavernier to do a film about the blacklisting of the fifties. Polonsky insisted that the leading character should be a former Communist. Several years later, Winkler wrote his own script in which the character under siege became a political naif, and Polonsky had his name removed from the credits. Winkler, ordinarily a producer, decided to direct the movie himself.

Gunfight at the O.K. Corral

Paramount, 1957. (C-122m.) Dir: John Sturges. Sp: Leon Uris. Cast: Burt Lancaster, Kirk Douglas, Rhonda Fleming, Jo

Van Fleet, John Ireland, Lyle Bettger, Earl Holliman, Frank Faylen.

On-Screen: *The legend lives on: Wyatt Earp and Doc Holliday vs. the Clantons.* Over the years, there have been many variations on the western legend of stalwart marshal Wyatt Earp's loose partnership with alcoholic, tubercular Doc Holliday, ending with their joining together for that showdown in Tombstone at the O.K. Corral. (The date was October 26, 1881.) John Ford's *My Darling Clementine* leads the rest, but this version has several strong action sequences and the star power of Lancaster (Earp) and Douglas (Holliday). The screenplay concentrates on the scratchy relationship between the two men, starting with wary hostility and ending with their mutual trust and admiration. ("If I'm goin' to die, let me die with the best friend I ever had.") The movie has no shortage of western clichés, but the well-staged climactic episode at the O.K. Corral compensates in part for the rest.

Off-Screen: Shot near Tucson, Arizona, the film had its share of problems. According to producer Hal Wallis, both strong-willed stars attempted to override director Sturges, who was apparently a match for them. Wallis wanted the film to have the burned-out, brown look of a Remington painting, which cinematographer Charles Lang, Jr., provided. The climactic gunfight was choreographed like a ballet, with every move carefully plotted. (The actual fight was much shorter and duller.)

The Gunfighter

Fox, 1950. (84m.) Dir: Henry King. Sp: William Bowers and William Sellers, b/o story by William Bowers and Andre de Toth. Cast: Gregory Peck, Helen Westcott, Millard Mitchell, Jean Parker, Karl Malden, Skip Homeier, Verna Felton, Richard Jaeckel, Ellen Corby.

On-Screen: *A famous gunslinger tries to live down his reputation.* A brooding, somber western, appropriately filmed in black and white, *The Gunfighter* stars Gregory Peck in one of his best roles as Jimmy Ringo, a famous but weary gunfighter whose reputation follows him wherever he goes. He comes into town to see his estranged wife (Westcott) and son, where he has a fatal confrontation with the town's swaggering young bully (Homeier). Western-film purists tend to dismiss melancholy, end-of-an-era stories such as *The Gunfighter,* and indeed the movie substitutes character interplay for the usual shoot-outs and horseback pursuits. But the film has many strong moments, and Gregory Peck's laconic, understated style of acting makes his stoical Jimmy Ringo that much more believable. Many other out-of-their-time Westerners would follow him in the years ahead.

Off-Screen: Gregory Peck agreed to do *The Gunfighter* if Henry King, who had directed him so well in *Twelve O'Clock High,* would also direct this film. Peck grew a mustache for the role, which displeased producer Nunnally Johnson, who worried that it would diminish Peck's box-office appeal. "That mustache," as it came to be known at the studio, also angered Fox president Spyros Skouras, but when he learned the cost of reshooting without it, the mustache remained.

Gunga Din

RKO, 1939. (117m.) Dir: George Stevens. Sp: Joel Sayre and Fred Guiol, b/o story by

Ben Hecht and Charles MacArthur, from poem by Rudyard Kipling. Cast: Cary Grant, Douglas Fairbanks, Jr., Victor McLaglen, Sam Jaffe, Joan Fontaine, Eduardo Ciannelli, Montagu Love, Robert Coote.

On-Screen: *Rousing adventure classic.* Set in the late nineteenth century amid India's mountained splendor, this lavishly staged epic follows the exploits of three comrades-in-arms in the British army. Cutter (Grant), the cockney cutup, hopes to find treasure and live "like a bloomin' duke," while the romantic Ballantine (Fairbanks) yearns to wed lovely Emmy Stebbins (Fontaine). Brawny MacChesney (McLaglen) wants to keep the trio together, boozing and brawling. You'll love the spindly-legged Gunga Din (Jaffe), the regiment's lowly Indian water carrier who longs to become a soldier, too. You'll be moved by his courageous act when the fanatical guru (Ciannelli) and his murderous cult of Thuggees threaten to destroy the British troops. Stevens's fast-paced direction expertly blends high spirits and deep-dyed villainy.

Off-Screen: A version of Kipling's poem was filmed in 1911 as a silent short. In 1936, RKO planned a production, but Howard Hawks withdrew as director. Eventually, Stevens took over, with Grant cast as Ballantine and comedian Jack Oakie as Cutter. After Oakie was dropped and Fairbanks joined the cast, Grant wisely opted to play the irrepressible prankster, Cutter. Sabu, the popular teenage Indian actor, was an obvious choice to play the brave water boy, but he was already involved with *The Thief of Bagdad.* After the considerably older Jaffe replaced him, filming went forward in the Sierras, where fierce dust storms often delayed production. The movie was loosely remade as *Soldiers Three* (1951) and *Sergeants 3* (1962). Blake Edwards's *The Party* (1968) begins with Peter Sellers doing a hilarious spoof of Jaffe's Gunga Din. (CFB)

Guys and Dolls

Goldwyn-MGM, 1955. (C-150m.) Dir: Joseph L. Mankiewicz. Sp: Joseph L. Mankiewicz, b/o musical play by Abe Burrows and Jo Swerling, and on characters created by Damon Runyon. MS: Frank Loesser. Cast: Marlon Brando, Frank Sinatra, Jean Simmons, Vivian Blaine, Stubby Kaye, Robert Keith, Sheldon Leonard, B. S. Pully, Regis Toomey.

On-Screen: *Film version of the long-running stage musical.* A Broadway sensation in 1950, *Guys and Dolls* combined a superb Frank Loesser score with Abe Burrows and Jo Swerling's tangy version of Damon Runyon's raffish New York sharpsters and show girls. Finally brought to the screen five years later by Sam Goldwyn, it turned out to be largely a misfire. The wonderful score is intact, but the ebullience is missing. The garish, stylized sets are no help, and the central male roles are miscast. Brando seems ill at ease as gambler Sky Masterson, and Sinatra captures little of the warm, likable quality that Sam Levene brought to Nathan Detroit, master of the floating crap game. Vivian Blaine repeats her stage role as Adelaide and gives the film's best performance; her musical "Lament" about the psychosomatic effects of long engagements is a highlight. Jean Simmons is appealing as Salvation Army "doll" Sarah Brown, and Stubby Kaye pleases with his reprised role as "Nicely Nicely" Johnson. But this *Guys and Dolls* doesn't make it.

Reportedly, Gene Kelly was bitterly disappointed when the role of Sky Masterson went to Marlon Brando. During the filming, there was some animosity between Brando and Sinatra, with Sinatra still smarting about losing the *On the Waterfront* lead to Brando. Sinatra, who was best on the first take, objected to Brando's agonized Method style of acting. Sam Goldwyn decided to have Brando and Simmons do their own singing. He told Simmons, "Maybe you don't sound so good. But it's *you*." A Broadway revival of the musical play was an enormous hit in 1992.

Gypsy

Warners, 1962. (C-149m.) Dir: Mervyn Le-Roy. Sp: Leonard Spigelgass, b/o musical play by Arthur Laurents. MS: Jule Styne and Stephen Sondheim. Cast: Rosalind Russell, Natalie Wood, Karl Malden, Paul Wallace, Betty Bruce, Roxanne Arlen, Faith Dane, Ann Jillian.

On-Screen: *Mama Rose claws her way to the top in this backstage musical.* On the Broadway stage in 1959, *Gypsy* was a deserved hit—it had color, pace, superb Styne-Sondheim songs, and the incomparable Ethel Merman. Then what went wrong with the film version? The movie retains the book's sharp edges—Mama Rose fighting ruthlessly to move daughter Gypsy Rose Lee into the big time—and the songs—"Everything's Coming Up Roses," "Small World," "You'll Never Get Away From Me," etc.—are still marvelous. And yet it all seems disconcertingly flat and juiceless. Part of the fault rests with Rosalind Russell, who is simply not up to the role. Working gamely, she gives her all to the bitter, defiant "Rose's Turn" near the film's end, but the impact is missing. Natalie Wood fares better as Gypsy, making the transition from lonely waif to assured burlesque queen. Best number: three strippers demonstrate that "You Gotta Have a Gimmick."

Off-Screen: Gypsy's sister June Havoc raised a fuss about the actress who played her as a child, insisting that she must be exactly five years old. The issue was settled out of court. The musical number "Together," a highlight of the stage show, was filmed with Russell, Malden, and Wood, but it was dropped when the movie went into general release. Look sharp for a bit appearance as a press agent by future television comedian Harvey Korman.

Hail the Conquering Hero

Paramount, 1944. (101m.) Dir: Preston Sturges. Sp: Preston Sturges. Cast: Eddie Bracken, Ella Raines, William Demarest, Raymond Walburn, Freddie Steele, Elizabeth Patterson, Franklin Pangborn, Jimmy Conlin, Al Bridge.

On-Screen: *A small-town army reject returns home as a "hero."* Preston Sturges's most fully sustained satire, *Hail the Conquering Hero* aims at a number of targets, including mindless hero worship, wartime hysteria, and even the gentle tyranny of motherhood. Eddie Bracken plays Woodrow Lafayette Pershing Truesmith, a hapless 4–F whose father was a famous marine hero. Taken under the wing of a group of sympathetic marines, Woodrow is dragged kicking and screaming into a deception—he is returned home as a war hero. Things spin out of control until he is nominated to replace the town's corrupt mayor (Walburn). Once again Sturges mocks the world's blowhards and opportunists, while at the same time reveling in slapstick. The funniest sequence is the town's reception for Woodrow, a model of disorganization in which four bands battle to gain the upper hand while the organizer (Pangborn) gives way to hysteria. Sturges's irreverence spares nobody; even the marines get short shrift—one (Demarest) is a fanciful liar, and another (Steele), cruelly nicknamed Bugsy, is a shell-shocked fellow with a mother complex. *Hail the Conquering Hero* is Sturges at his sardonic best.

Off-Screen: Paramount producer B. G. De Sylva wanted to fire Ella Raines, who was playing Woodrow's girlfriend, but Sturges remained adamant about retaining her. De Sylva also questioned Sturges's use of the same players in his films—his "stock company." Sturges argued that since they had contributed so much to his first successes, they had a moral right to work in his subsequent films. The battle continued as De Sylva insisted on personally editing the film. Sturges persevered, but his relations with Paramount finally ended. An attempt to turn the story into a Broadway musical *(The Conquering Hero)* failed early in 1961.

Hair

United Artists, 1979. (C-121m.) Dir: Milos Forman. Sp: Michael Weller, b/o musical play by Gerome Ragni and James Rado. MS: Gerome Ragni, James Rado, and Galt MacDermot. Cast: John Savage, Treat Williams, Beverly D'Angelo, Annie Golden, Cheryl Barnes, Dorsey Wright, Nicholas Ray, Charlotte Rae.

On-Screen: *Welcome to the Age of Aquarius.* In 1968, the rock musical *Hair* created a sensation on and off Broadway with a startling view of the hippie generation and its call for flower power to end war and violence. A decade later, Czech director Milos Forman turned it into a musical film that drew general acclaim. The slight story is basically the same—at the height of the Vietnam War, a naive farm boy (Savage) comes to New York to enter the army and is taken over by a band of unrestrained hippies who change his life forever. The musical numbers are the real attraction: driving rock songs that celebrate untrameled freedom or mock conventional ideas about war, sex, etc. For all its undeniable pleasures, *Hair* now seems like a quaint anachronism, and the park hippies appear to be ghosts out of their own time, playing a game that has ended. Still, there are some effective musical sequences, such as the opening number, "Aquarius," and the affirmative closing song, "Let the Sunshine In." Favorite moment: the white horses of the park policemen, prancing in time with the music.

Off-Screen: The times they are a-changing: The original stage show was thought to be subversive. For the film version, Milos Forman was given permission to film on a National Guard base in the California desert. And in Washington, the National Park Service allowed the filmmaker to use the area around the Washington Monument and Reflecting Pool where, only six or seven years earlier, thousands of angry demonstrators were arrested. The cast of this movie version includes Nell Carter, Melba Moore, and Michael Jeter (now of television's "Evening Shade").

Halloween

Compass International, 1978. (C-93m.) Dir: John Carpenter. Sp: John Carpenter and Debra Hill. Cast: Jamie Lee Curtis, Donald Pleasence, Nancy Loomis, P. J. Soles, Charles Cyphers, Kyle Richards.

On-Screen: *"Lock your windows! Bolt your doors! Turn off the lights!"* Sensible advice when you're watching this modestly made but artful, genuinely scary thriller. "Death has come to your little town," says Dr. Loomis (Pleasence) to the police chief of Haddonfield, Illinois. And he should know. For fourteen years, he has been treating Michael Myers (Cyphers), a purely evil, conscienceless killer. And now Myers has escaped and returned to his hometown, where he will stalk new victims. Teenaged Laurie (Curtis) is one of them, and she experiences the nightmare on Halloween. Carpenter's chilling movie unsettles the viewer by using a subjective camera to follow the victims from the killer's point of view, or by never showing the killer in his entirety (we are given a quick glimpse of his arm or his masked face, or he appears as a shadowy figure in the background). The climax, with Myers stalking a terrified Curtis through and around the house at which she is babysitting, is a bona fide nail-biter. The four subsequent sequels (none directed by Carpenter) were poor—and increasingly gory—imitations.

Off-Screen: Carpenter and Hill wrote the screenplay in approximately ten days. According to Carpenter, it was based on an idea by producer Irwin Yablans about a killer who stalks baby-sitters. Then Yablans suggested that the story take place on October 31, and that *Halloween* might be a good title for an exploitation horror movie. Carpenter composed the film's score, which was admittedly influenced by Bernard Herrmann and Ennio Morricone.

Handle With Care (Citizens Band)

Paramount, 1977. (C-98m.) Dir: Jonathan Demme. Sp: Paul Brickman. Cast: Paul LeMat, Candy Clark, Ann Wedgeworth, Marcia Rodd, Roberts Blossom, Charles Napier, Bruce McGillis, Alix Elias.

On-Screen: *All about the lives of a group of dedicated CB operators.* The continual buzz of voices of ham radio operators as they talk over their CBs serves as a background for this rambling but funny and engaging comedy from Jonathan Demme. Paul Brickman's screenplay pinpoints a group of these cheerfully obsessed people, especially Paul LeMat, a truck driver who must cope with a cantankerous father (Blossom), a resentful brother (McGillis), and an ex-girlfriend (Clark) with a surprising CB secret. A secondary plot involving a bigamous trucker (Napier) and his two wives (Rodd and Wedgeworth) is by far the best part of the film, quirky and hilarious as the three (with the aid of his newest girlfriend, Elias) try to resolve the situation. Under any name, *Citizens Band* (or *Handle With Care*) deserved a better fate.

Off-Screen: The movie first opened in May 1977 and was a disastrous failure. It was then called *Citizens Band.* When *Film Comment* mentioned it favorably, the Lincoln Center Film Society, which sponsors the magazine, decided to show the movie at its annual film festival. Thrilled, the studio changed the title to *Handle With Care* and rereleased it with a truncated ending, without the director's blessing. (The original ending was a CB wedding in which all the participants sat in separate cars.) Despite some enthusiastic reviews, the movie still didn't draw business.

Hannah and Her Sisters

Orion, 1986. (C-106m.) Dir: Woody Allen. Sp: Woody Allen. Cast: Mia Farrow, Woody Allen, Michael Caine, Dianne Wiest, Barbara Hershey, Lloyd Nolan, Maureen O'Sullivan, Carrie Fisher, Max von Sydow, Julie Kavner, Daniel Stern, Sam Waterston, Tony Roberts.

On-Screen: *Woody Allen looks at the intertwined lives of three New York sisters.* One of Woody Allen's finest films, *Hannah and Her Sisters* injects a warm and generous note into his usual mix of urban angst. A richly perceptive, Chekovian mixture of comedy and drama, the film centers on a family that has known both grief and happiness; at the center are three sisters: nurturing Hannah (Farrow), Lee (Hershey), a reformed alcoholic, and Holly (Wiest), once a drug addict, now continually distracted and unsure of herself. Around them swirl the many people in their lives, including their parents (Nolan and O'Sullivan) and their husbands, ex and otherwise (Allen, Caine). Events expose the subtle, bristling, occasionally poignant relationships between these people and their friends. Allen brings a virtuosic style and rhythm to many of the movie's sequences, especially two Thanksgiving dinners, two years apart, and a scene in which the sisters lunch together. Add Gordon Willis's glowing photography and a score of wonderful old songs, and you have a treasurable film from Woody Allen.

Off-Screen: Supporting Oscars went to Michael Caine for his witty performance as Mia Farrow's husband, and to Dianne Wiest for her glorious performance—funny and touching—as Holly. Woody Allen's original screenplay also received an Academy Award. Allen, however, was not happy with the ending, which found the principal characters reasonably content with their lot. Life, he felt, was never as neatly or nicely resolved as that. Still, the ending left viewers glowing with pleasure.

Hans Christian Andersen

Goldwyn–RKO, 1952. (C-120m.) Dir: Charles Vidor. Sp: Moss Hart, b/o story by Myles Connolly. MS: Frank Loesser. Cast: Danny Kaye, Farley Granger, Renee Jeanmaire, Roland Petit, Joey Walsh, John Qualen, Philip Tonge.

On-Screen: *Danny Kaye plays the Danish storyteller, to Frank Loesser's music.* Although bandbox pretty and graced with a richly melodic score by Frank Loesser ("Thumbelina," "Wonderful Copenhagen," "Anywhere I Wander," etc.), Sam Goldwyn's lavish musical still manages to miss the mark. Blame must be divided between the rather dull book, which has shoemaker Hans, a fictional version of the great writer of children's stories, finding adventure and unrequited love in Copenhagen, and an oddly dispirited Danny Kaye in the leading role. Renee Jeanmaire plays a temperamental ballerina (and the object of Hans's affections) and dances beautifully in sequences choreographed by her husband, Roland Petit. (Best is the seventeen-minute "Little Mermaid.") There are pleasures to be had from *Hans Christian Andersen,* but it seldom soars.

Off-Screen: Over a fifteen-year period, producer Sam Goldwyn was obsessed with making a musical built around Hans Christian Andersen. Sixteen different screenplays were commissioned, including one by ubiquitous author Ben Hecht, and at one point Gary Cooper was scheduled to star. When the film finally got under way, dancer Moira Shearer was expected to play the ballerina, but she became pregnant and was replaced by Jeanmaire. The movie won six Oscar nominations.

Harold and Maude

Paramount, 1971. (C-90m.) Dir: Hal Ashby. Sp: Colin Higgins. Cast: Ruth Gordon, Bud Cort, Vivian Pickles, Cyril Cusack, Charles Tyner, Ellen Geer.

On-Screen: *An early April–late December romance.* Harold (Cort) is a distinctly odd twenty-year-old who is obsessed with death ("I go to funerals") and apparently enjoys faking his suicide, over and over again. Maude (Gordon) is nearing eighty, still feisty, exuberant, and given to large, hollow pronouncements ("It's best not to be too moral. You cheat yourself out of too much life"). They meet at a funeral, fall in love, and carry out a number of pranks together. Eventually, they marry, but their romance ends on a sadly ironic note.

Harold, however, has been restored to the real world of life-affirming possibilities. *Harold and Maude* is now regarded as a cult classic, and you may find yourself laughing at its dark humor, especially at Harold's bogus suicide attempts. Others will be bewildered or irritated but not bored. By this time Ruth Gordon had honed her one-note performances of eccentric biddies to a fare-thee-well, and she tries to make us like her aged flower child. It isn't easy. Vivian Pickles gives the funniest performance as Harold's unflappable mother, and Charles Tyner is broadly amusing as Harold's uncle, a loose-hinged military man who is determined to straighten Harold out.

Off-Screen: *Harold and Maude* was originally a twenty-minute script written as a graduate thesis by UCLA student Colin Higgins. As expected, the movie failed in its first release despite a few rave reviews. After a while, however, it became phenomenally popular in many college towns, and the studio re-released it with a new campaign designed for the youth market.

Harper

Warners, 1966. (C-102m.) Dir: Jack Smight. Sp: William Goldman, b/o novel by Ross MacDonald. Cast: Paul Newman, Lauren Bacall, Shelley Winters, Julie Harris, Robert Wagner, Janet Leigh, Arthur Hill, Pamela Tiffin, Robert Webber, Strother Martin.

On-Screen: *A cool private eye is hot on the trail of a kidnapped millionaire.* Most of the familiar Hammett-Chandler ingredients are here: wealthy clients, vulnerable to blackmail, whose money hasn't brought them happiness; acquiescent women from every strata of society, and of course, the sardonic, world-weary detective ready with a fist or a wisecrack. It's all been seen before, but a good-looking production and a slick cast give this heavily plotted movie about L.A.'s upper crust and underbelly the kick it needs to hold one's interest. Winters and Harris are especially good as, respectively, a washed-up movie actress and a junkie piano bar "chantoozy." Bacall stands out as the woman who hires Newman. ("You say you're good at finding things. My husband is missing.") Newman, who pays more attention to his job than to his wife (Leigh) is fast with the quips, slow to figure out the guilty party.

Off-Screen: In *The Moving Target,* the novel that the film is based on, author MacDonald's private eye is named Lew Archer. But Newman preferred a last name beginning with *H,* as a good-luck charm in view of his success with *The Hustler* and *Hud.* Bacall's role is a sort of homage to the younger part she had played years before in *The Big Sleep* (opposite Bogart's shamus), that of a spoiled, acid-tongued woman who is at the same time enormously likable. Screenwriter Goldman has related that in the scene in which Newman insults Wagner's girlfriend to his face, Wagner produced real tears. Newman was so taken aback that he blew some of his lines. But the result was so effective that the shots were used in the movie. (CFB)

Harry and Tonto

Fox, 1974. (C-115m.) Dir: Paul Mazursky. Sp: Paul Mazursky and Josh Greenfeld. Cast: Art Carney, Ellen Burstyn, Geraldine Fitzgerald, Larry Hagman, Phil Bruns, Joshua Mostel, Melanie Mayron, Chief Dan George, Arthur Hunnicutt.

On-Screen: *An elderly man begins a cross-country odyssey.* Art Carney, Jackie Gleason's long-time second banana, won an Academy Award for his performance in this loosely structured, amiable, and occasionally affecting comedy-drama. He plays Harry Coombs, a crusty old widower who goes to live with his son (Bruns) when his apartment building is torn down. When life with his son's family becomes intolerable, he travels cross-country to visit his other children. On his journey, with his cat, Tonto, as his companion, he comes across the usual Mazursky mix of eccentrics, including a runaway teenager (Mayron), a displaced Indian (George), and an old flame (Fitzgerald), now a nursing home resident. He also sees his children (Burstyn and Hagman), neither of whom have led happy or rewarding lives. Although one tires of the cranky or lovable oddballs who turn up regularly, Carney's Harry keeps the film on an even keel with his mixture of irascibility and spirit, tinged with melancholy.

Off-Screen: For the scenes in the house of Harry's son, the movie used the home of a New York police sergeant in the Riverdale section of the Bronx. Other scenes were shot at Newark's then-new International Airport, and at the edge of the Grand Canyon in Arizona. For a short time, there was talk of turning *Harry and Tonto* into a half-hour television series for the 1976–77 season, but it never materialized.

Harvey

Universal-International, 1950. (104m.) Dir: Henry Koster. Sp: Mary Chase and Oscar Brodney, b/o play by Mary Chase. Cast: James Stewart, Josephine Hull, Peggy Dow, Charles Drake, Victoria Horne, Cecil Kellaway, Jesse White, Wallace Ford, Nana Bryant.

On-Screen: *Concerning Elwood P. Dowd and his odd friend Harvey.* The happiest of drunkards, tippling Elwood P. Dowd (Stewart) enjoys a simple life with his sister, Veta (Hull), often sitting in a bar with his best friend, a six-foot-three-and-one-half-inch invisible rabbit named Harvey. Trouble ensues, however, when Veta, frantically embarrassed by her brother's daft but winning ways, tries to have him committed to an asylum. Elwood, of course, is the character originated by Frank Fay in Mary Chase's long-running, prize-winning Broadway comedy. Here, Jimmy Stewart gives the role a disarming sweetness that almost (but not quite) makes alcoholism an endearing character flaw rather than a devastating illness. *Harvey* is stolen, waddle and all, by the wonderful Josephine Hull, who repeats her stage role as the bewildered, scatterbrained Veta. The movie is rather drably made, and the whimsy sometimes gets too thick for comfort, but thanks to the two leading players, *Harvey* is enjoyable.

Off-Screen: Josephine Hull was rightfully awarded an Oscar as the year's Best Supporting Actress. James Stewart was nominated for Best Actor. Stewart replaced Frank Fay on Broadway for a limited time in the summer of 1947. In 1970, he returned to the stage to play Elwood once more, with Helen Hayes as sister Veta. He and Hayes repeated their roles in a 1972 television production. Victoria Horne and Jesse White also appeared in the original stage version. (This was White's first movie.)

The Harvey Girls

MGM, 1946. (C-101m.) Dir: George Sidney. Sp: Edmund Beloin, Nathaniel Curtis, Harry Crane, James O'Hanlon, and Samson Raphaelson, b/o book by Samuel Hopkins Adams. MS: Harry Warren and Johnny Mercer. Cast: Judy Garland, John Hodiak, Angela Lansbury, Marjorie Main, Virginia O'Brien, Ray Bolger, Kenny Baker, Preston Foster, Cyd Charisse, Chill Wills.

On-Screen: *Judy Garland helps to civilize the musical West.* An entertaining MGM musical, *The Harvey Girls* pays tribute to the intrepid young women who came to the untamed West to work as waitresses for the Harvey House restaurants—and thereby brought a touch of civilization. Judy Garland plays the girl who comes West as a mail-order bride and stays to become a Harvey girl. She and the other girls tangle with the bawdy, lawless element in town, but it all works out, and she finds romance. The musical numbers provide the real treat, the most famous being the rousing production number to the Oscar-winning "On the Atchison, Topeka, and the Santa Fe." Another fine musical moment is "It's a Great Big World," sung by Garland, Virginia O'Brien, and Cyd Charisse as they shiver together in their nightgowns. Amusingly, Angela Lansbury, known to today's television viewers as Jessica Fletcher on "Murder, She Wrote," plays a hard-boiled saloon queen.

Off-Screen: Angela Lansbury's songs were dubbed by Virginia Rees, and when the score was later recorded by most of the original cast, she was conspicuously absent. Ms. Lansbury's comment: "In Hollywood, they thought I had a reedy little voice."

A Hatful of Rain

Fox, 1957. (109m.) Dir: Fred Zinnemann. Sp: Michael V. Gazzo, b/o his play. Cast: Don Murray, Eva Marie Saint, Anthony Franciosa, Lloyd Nolan, Henry Silva, Gerald S. O'Loughlin, William Hickey.

On-Screen: *A drug addict undergoes living hell.* Until the midfifties, films about drug addiction were virtually nonexistent. Then, in 1955, Frank Sinatra starred in Otto Preminger's adaptation of Nelson Algren's *The Man With the Golden Arm* as a desperate junkie experiencing the terrors of withdrawal. Following revisions in the production code, it was now possible to show the nightmare of addiction in its most harrowing form. Adapted from the Broadway play, *A Hatful of Rain* was strong stuff in its day, and although its attitude seems almost simplistic in light of today's drug epidemic, it still retains considerable impact. Don Murray plays the tortured young husband fighting desperately—and failing—to contain his addiction while his naive, bewildered wife (Saint) and anxious brother (Franciosa) suffer on his behalf. Nolan is expert as Murray's rough-hewn father, who learns the terrible truth about his son. As an early spotlight on a national tragedy, *A Hatful of Rain* still warrants attention.

Off-Screen: Anthony Franciosa and William Hickey were repeating their stage roles in the film. During impromptu rehearsals at the Actors Studio, before the play reached Broadway, Eva Marie Saint read the wife's role. (Shelley Winters played it on Broadway.) The movie was partly filmed at sixteen New York sites from the Brooklyn Bridge to uptown Manhattan.

The Heartbreak Kid

Fox, 1972. (C-104m.) Dir: Elaine May. Sp: Neil Simon, b/o story by Bruce Jay Friedman. Cast: Charles Grodin, Cybill Shepherd, Jeannie Berlin, Eddie Albert, Audra Lindley, William Prince, Augusta Dabney.

On-Screen: *A newly married man meets the girl of his dreams.* Shallow, self-absorbed, and manipulative, Lenny (Grodin) has just married Lila (Berlin), a plain, awkward Jewish girl. Then, only three days after the wedding, he meets wealthy and beautiful Kelly (Shepherd), abandoning Lila and launching a relentless courtship of the golden WASP of his dreams. Nothing stops him, neither her initial indifference or the frank loathing of her bigoted father (Albert). Incredibly, he wins the prize, but in the end he is no less of a hollow man. Neil Simon's adaptation of a Bruce Jay Friedman story is maliciously funny, but the laughter often sticks in the throat due to harsh undercurrents. This is especially true of the scenes involving Lila, whose desertion by her brand-new husband is much too cruel to draw even a smile. Charles Grodin is very good as Lenny, catching all of his earnest insincerity. Shepherd is every inch the radiant and vacuous rich girl, and Berlin, who seems to be related to the character played by her mother in *A New Leaf* (1971), gives the hapless Lila a touch of poignancy. Mother, of course, is Elaine May, who directed this movie with style.

Off-Screen: *The Heartbreak Kid* marked the first time that a woman director had ever directed her daughter in a leading role. Berlin won an Oscar nomination as Best Supporting Actress.

Heaven Can Wait

Fox, 1943. (C-112m.) Dir: Ernst Lubitsch. Sp: Samson Raphaelson, b/o play by Lazlo Bus-Fekete. Cast: Don Ameche, Gene Tierney, Charles Coburn, Laird Cregar, Allyn Joslyn, Eugene Pallette, Marjorie Main, Spring Byington, Louis Calhern, Signe Hasso, Dickie Moore.

On-Screen: *An elderly roué reviews his life.* In the thirties and early forties, the collaboration of director Lubitsch and screenwriter Raphaelson resulted in several imcomparably wry and witty romantic comedies and musicals. *Heaven Can Wait* is no less wry or witty, but bathed in vivid Technicolor, it has a warmer, more nostalgic glow than the others. A diverting comedy-fantasy, it involves elderly Henry Van Cleve (Ameche), recently deceased and resigned to being sent to the nether regions. Appearing before the devil (Cregar), here called His Excellency, he remembers a life devoted mainly to philandering. Yet there are those who would place him on the side of the angels, especially his adored wife (Tierney) and crusty grandfather (Coburn). Against a well-realized background of late nineteenth-century New York, the movie recounts, by way of Henry's birthdays, the pivotal events in his life. The film sags at times, but most often is deliciously sly and funny, especially when Tierney's squabbling Midwestern parents (Pallette and Main) are briefly on the scene. Their battle over the comics at breakfast is a classic sequence in an enjoyable film.

Off-Screen: *Heaven Can Wait* was Ernst Lubitsch's first film in color. D. W. Griffith was said to have remarked, "I like the way Ernst Lubitsch used color in *Heaven Can*

Wait.'' The director called it "a three-haircut movie,'' that being the length of time it took to make it. This film is not to be confused with Warren Beatty's 1978 film of the same name.

Heaven's Gate

United Artists, 1980. (C-149m.) Dir: Michael Cimino. Sp: Michael Cimino. Cast: Kris Kristofferson, Christopher Walken, Jeff Bridges, Isabelle Huppert, John Hurt, Sam Waterston, Brad Dourif, Joseph Cotten, Geoffrey Lewis, Mickey Rourke.

On-Screen: *Michael Cimino's epic western—and a disaster of epic proportions.* First, the virtues: no other western drama has been more successful in capturing the sweep and the turbulence of the Western frontier. The sets and costumes are magnificent, and Vilmos Zsigmond's stunning photography bathes them all with a burnished splendor. End of virtues. Cimino's muddled screenplay centers on a Bostonian named Jim Averill (Kristofferson), who, twenty years after graduating from Harvard, inexplicably turns up as a marshal in the untamed West. He becomes embroiled in the violent Johnson County War between the Stock Growers Association and European immigrant homesteaders. He also becomes involved in a triangular relationship with a madam (Huppert) and a former friend (Walken). In the ensuing warfare, only Averill survives. Despite several impressively staged sequences, *Heaven's Gate* suffers from a trite story and indecipherable characters. A viewer leaves this lumbering film with a melancholy sense of what might have been.

Off-Screen: The original title was *The Johnson County War.* After the film's initial hostile reception in 1980, a shorter, trimmer version was released in April of the following year. The result was not appreciably better. A full account of the making of this film can be found in Steven Bach's book *Final Cut* (Morrow, 1985).

Heidi

Fox, 1937. (88m.) Dir: Allan Dwan. Sp: Walter Ferris and Julien Josephson, b/o novel by Johanna Spyri. Cast: Shirley Temple, Jean Hersholt, Arthur Treacher, Helen Westley, Pauline Moore, Thomas Beck, Mary Nash, Mady Christians, Marcia Mae Jones, Delmar Watson.

On-Screen: *Shirley Temple as Johanna Spyri's well-loved heroine.* Across the years, young viewers have enjoyed this tale of Heidi (Temple), the sweet, self-reliant little girl who lives with her beloved grandfather (Hersholt) in the Swiss Alps of the eighteenth century. The two are separated as Heidi becomes a companion to Clara (Jones), a crippled girl, and is also subjected to the nasty whims of Clara's housekeeper (Nash). Is Heidi reunited with her grandpa? Need you ask? One of Shirley's more pleasing vehicles, *Heidi* tells the story quite nicely and gives its adorable star every opportunity to shine.

Off-Screen: Lake Arrowhead substituted for the Swiss Alps in the movie. Shirley's mother asked Darryl Zanuck to enliven the film by adding a musical number, "In Our Little Wooden Shoes,'' but many credit Shirley herself with some of the number's best features. Actor Delmar Watson (Peter) recalled years later that Shirley's mother insisted that absolutely everything pass by her before reaching her daughter. "But," he hastened to add, "she was never unpleasant." *Heidi* was also filmed in 1952, 1965, and 1968, and *Heidi's Song,* an animated version, was released in 1982. Busy girl, that Heidi.

The Heiress

Paramount, 1949. (115m.) Dir: William Wyler. Sp: Ruth and Augustus Goetz, b/o their play and novel by Henry James. Cast: Olivia de Havilland, Montgomery Clift, Ralph Richardson, Miriam Hopkins, Mona Freeman, Vanessa Brown, Ray Collins, Selena Royle, Betty Linley.

On-Screen: *A shy spinster takes revenge on those who wronged or betrayed her.* Exquisitely filmed, and acted with rare artistry, *The Heiress* adapts the Broadway play (taken from Henry James's novel *Washington Square*) into a splendid movie. Olivia de Havilland won a Best Actress Oscar for her beautifully modulated performance as a painfully shy spinster in mid-nineteenth-century New York, whose father (Richardson) treats her with icy contempt. She falls ardently in love with a dashing suitor (Clift), only to be betrayed by him and crushed by her father's cruelty. In the end, she has her revenge on those who hurt her. ("I can be very cruel. I have been taught by masters.") Except that she is much too beautiful to be convincing as a plain Jane, de Havilland offers a persuasive portrait of a woman whose pathetic vulnerability turns to steel, and Richardson is marvelously adept at revealing the human side of his iron-willed father. Only Montgomery Clift seems out of synchronization with the rest of the cast.

Off-Screen: Apparently, the actors in *The Heiress* were not overly enchanted with each other. De Havilland has described Richardson as "a wicked, selfish man" who used every dirty trick in the book to steal their scenes together. (Hopkins was adept at this as well.) She also complained that Clift "was thinking almost entirely of himself and leaving me out of the scene." Nevertheless, in addition to de Havilland's Academy Award, Oscars went to Aaron Copland for his score, to Edith Head and Gile Steele for their costumes, and to Harry Horner, John Meehan, and Emile Kuri for their art direction.

Hello, Dolly!

Fox, 1969. (C-146m.) Dir: Gene Kelly. Sp: Ernest Lehman, b/o on musical play by Michael Stewart, which was adapted from Thornton Wilder's play *The Matchmaker.* MS: Jerry Herman. Cast: Barbra Streisand, Walter Matthau, Michael Crawford, Tommy Tune, Marianne McAndrew, E. J. Peaker, Louis Armstrong.

On-Screen: *Streisand plays Dolly in the long-running stage musical.* Surely one of the most maligned musical films of recent memory, *Hello, Dolly!* has its undeniable faults. It's too long and wildly overproduced, and Barbra Streisand is seriously miscast as Dolly Levi, matchmaker extraordinaire. In addition, Gene Kelly's direction is cumbersome. Still, there are pleasures to be enjoyed. The production is truly sumptuous, the score includes some lilting and charming tunes, and if Streisand overdoes her Mae West inflections, she gives the role a game try, and her singing, of course, is superb. Walter Matthau appears disinterested as Streisand's costar, but there are some nice song-and-dance turns by Michael Crawford and especially the tall and talented Tommy Tune. Worth waiting for: Louis Armstrong wanders in from nowhere to join Streisand in an infectious rendition of the title song. *Hello, Dolly!* is far from a great musical, but "hello" all the same.

Off-Screen: Before Barbra Streisand was cast as Dolly, Fox considered Julie Andrews, surely a disconcerting contender. Ernest Lehman thought of Elizabeth Taylor, but his first choice was Carol Channing, who, of course, had originated the role on the musical stage. He was persuaded that she could not carry an over-two-hour film musical. There was much bitter wrangling between Streisand and Walter Matthau during the filming. She called him Old Sewermouth; he labeled her Miss Ptomaine. (With about $24 million at stake, *everyone* was nervous.) Matthau's later comment: "I'd like to work with Barbra Streisand again, in something appropriate. Perhaps *Macbeth*."

Hell's Angels

United Artists, 1930. (129m.) Dir: Howard Hughes. Story by Marshall Neilan and Joseph Moncure March; adaptation and continuity by Howard Estabrook and Harry Behn. Cast: Ben Lyon, James Hall, Jean Harlow, John Darrow, Lucien Prival, Douglas Gilmore, F. Schumann-Heink.

On-Screen: *Spectacular World War I epic, and Harlow's first major role.* "Would you be shocked if I put on something more comfortable?" It's doubtful if Hughes, the industrial-tool tycoon and film producer,

intended that artfully casual question—delivered by Harlow, in a slinky evening dress, to Lyon—to be the most startling moment in a movie that had cost him $4 million to make. Despite thrillingly staged aerial skirmishes and German zeppelin raids over London, the torrid scenes involving the Platinum Blonde riveted audiences most. The plodding plot focuses on two brothers who leave their Oxford studies to join the Royal Flying corps. Lyon plays a fast lad with the ladies who dallies with the sluttish fiancée (Harlow) of his unsuspecting brother (Hall). Crashing behind enemy lines, one of the men proves a coward, the other a hero. Time has tamed the wanton ways of the thirties' sex queen, but the realistically staged dogfights still impress.

Off-Screen: The movie was begun in 1927, with Greta Nissen as the female lead; talkies were fast become a rage, however, and the Norwegian actress's heavy accent led Hughes to replace her with Harlow. Although he received full director's credit, Hughes handled only the aerial sequences; the ground story was directed by James Whale. Red-tinted battle scenes, a ball sequence in two-color Technicolor, and in some theaters, a screen that enlarged at times for even more stunning effects helped ensure the movie's success. (Tinted and Technicolor scenes were restored in 1989.) The actor who plays the zeppelin's first officer is a son of the great German diva Ernestine Schumann-Heink. (CFB)

Here Comes Mr. Jordan

Columbia, 1941. (93m.) Dir: Alexander Hall. Sp: Sidney Buchman and Seton I.

Miller, b/o play by Henry Segall. Cast: Robert Montgomery, Evelyn Keyes, Claude Rains, James Gleason, Edward Everett Horton, Rita Johnson, John Emery.

On-Screen: *Comedy-fantasy returns dead man to earth.* Thanks to a scatterbrained heavenly messenger (Horton), boxer Joe Pendleton (Montgomery) dies in a plane crash fifty years before his time. Since it's Joe's destiny to become the next world heavyweight champion, celestial bookkeeper Mr. Jordan (Rains) sends him back to earth to take up residence in another man's body. Complications arise when Joe discovers that the body he now inhabits belonged to a wealthy crook, murdered by his wife (Johnson) and her lover (Emery). Somehow it all works out for Joe and the girl (Keyes) he has come to love. The film's combination of whimsy, sentiment, and romance works well for the most part, losing ground only toward the end. Montgomery's Oscar-nominated performance is both amusing and touching; Gleason (also nominated) makes Max Corkle, Joe's bewildered manager, hilarious.

Off-Screen: Fantasies often die a quick death at the box office, but this tale was carried out with such finesse that it turned out to be both a hit and a Best Picture Oscar nominee. Segall and the Buchman-Miller team won Oscars for their Original Story and Screenplay. In *Down to Earth* (1947), a kitschy musical spin-off created for Rita Hayworth, the studio reintroduced Gleason and Horton in their Corkle and messenger roles, with British actor Ronald Culver as Mr. Jordan. A 1978 remake, called *Heaven Can Wait* (the title of Segall's original play), starred Warren Beatty (as a

football player), Jack Warden, and James Mason. (CFB)

Hero

Columbia, 1992. (C-112m.) Dir: Stephen Frears. Sp: David Webb Peoples, b/o story by Laura Ziskin, Alvin Sargent, and David Webb Peoples. Cast: Dustin Hoffman, Geena Davis, Andy Garcia, Joan Cusack, Chevy Chase, Warren Berlinger, Susie Cusack.

On-Screen: *A comedy about heroism in the modern world.* Speaking bluntly, Bernie Laplante (Hoffman) is a "no-goodnik." A petty thief and a con man, not to mention a world-class misanthrope, Bernie is also in serious trouble with the law. Then one rainy night, he becomes a reluctant hero by rescuing people trapped in a plane crash. Only someone else—a down-and-out Vietnam vet named John Bubber (Garcia)—seizes the spotlight instead and claims to be "the Angel of Flight 104." With the help of Gale Gayley (Davis), a beautiful television newswoman, Bubber becomes a media sensation, while Bernie sulks helplessly in the background. Fate, plus some convoluted plotting by the writers, intervene to set things reasonably right. *Hero* tries to blend Frank Capra's feel-good comedy with Preston Sturges's wicked satire, but the mixture turns rancid. Despite a prolonged climax that aims at telling us that we can all be heroes at the right moment, the movie seems sour and cynical. The actors try, but only Geena Davis and Joan Cusack (as Bernie's angry ex-wife) come across with true conviction. *Hero* aims to be seriocomic reflection on the elusive, ambiguous nature of heroism, as well as an attack on the crassness of media coverage, but it falls flat.

Off-Screen: The idea for *Hero* started with producer Laura Ziskin, who recalled an actual plane crash in the Potomac River in which a man rescued some people, then drowned with his identity unknown. David Webb Peoples wrote the role of Bernie with Dustin Hoffman in mind, but Stephen Frears saw other actors, including Billy Crystal. Reportedly, Hoffman had great difficulty finding his character. Kevin Costner was considered for Bubber, but Andy Garcia won the role.

The High and the Mighty

Warners, 1954. (C-147m.) Dir: William Wellman. Sp: Ernest K. Gann, b/o his novel. Cast: John Wayne, Claire Trevor, Laraine Day, Robert Stack, Jan Sterling, Phil Harris, Robert Newton, David Brian, Paul Kelly, John Howard.

On-Screen: *John Wayne saves an imperiled airliner.* Long before there was *Airport* or *Airplane!* or any of the high-flying disaster movies, there was *The High and the Mighty*, William Wellman's airborne melodrama about a plane in flight from Honolulu to San Francisco. John Wayne stars as the pilot, second-in-command, whose cool professionalism keeps the plane from crashing when an on-board gunfight causes a bullet to explode one engine. Much of the movie concerns the passengers, their individual stories and their various reactions in the face of danger. Among them are a couple (Day and Howard) on the verge of divorce; a shady lady (Trevor) with a good amount of grit; a cowardly playboy (Brian); and a demoralized atomic scientist (Kelly). Robert Stack plays the plane's unhinged captain. None of them is really believable, and the suspense is churned up mechanically at regular intervals. Nevertheless, the movie was popular, and everyone in 1954 was humming Dimitri Tiomkin's theme. Tiomkin's score received an Academy Award.

Off-Screen: John Wayne coproduced the movie and wanted Spencer Tracy to play the leading role. When Tracy turned it down, Wayne took it over himself. Wayne whistles the theme, which was played at his funeral. Novelist Ernest Gann worked on the screenplay and was dismayed and angered when he saw that the final script was cited as "William Wellman's *The High and the Mighty.*" He remarked, "I knew then the chilling ways of Hollywood and left town immediately."

High Anxiety

Fox, 1977. (C-94m.) Dir: Mel Brooks. Sp: Mel Brooks, Ron Clark, Rudy DeLuca, and Barry Levinson. Cast: Mel Brooks, Madeline Kahn, Harvey Korman, Cloris Leachman, Dick Van Patten, Ron Carey, Howard Morris, Jack Riley, Charlie Callas.

On-Screen: *Mel Brooks takes on Alfred Hitchcock.* An affectionate, intermittently funny parody of Alfred Hitchcock's films, *High Anxiety* aims at the sort of psychological melodrama at which the master director excelled. As usual, Brooks aims with a blunderbuss, which is guaranteed to hit its target once in a while. Brooks stars as Dr. Richard Thorndyke, a psychiatrist who takes over the top position at the Institute for the Very, Very Nervous and finds a hornet's nest of kinkiness and murder. Harvey Korman is the scheming villain, and Cloris Leachman plays the grim head nurse whose breasts could penetrate steel. Hitchcock fans will recognize Brooks's parodies of scenes from *Psycho, The Birds,* and especially *Vertigo* (Thorndyke has a morbid fear of heights), but recognition alone does not necessarily earn laughs.

Off-Screen: The bellboy in the parodied shower scene is played by coauthor Barry Levinson, who would launch his career as a director in a few years.

High Noon

United Artists, 1952. (84m.) Dir: Fred Zinnemann. Sp: Carl Foreman, b/o story by John W. Cunningham. Cast: Gary Cooper, Grace Kelly, Katy Jurado, Thomas Mitchell, Lloyd Bridges, Otto Kruger, Lon Chaney, Jr., Lee Van Cleef, Ian MacDonald.

On-Screen: *Sheriff Gary Cooper stands alone against revenge-minded killers.* A landmark western, lean, taut, and compelling, *High Noon* takes place in "real time." On a fateful day in Hadleyville, retiring sheriff Will Kane (Cooper) learns that Frank Miller (MacDonald), newly released from prison, is returning to town with the sworn goal of killing Kane. Standing tall against Miller and his thugs, despite the fact that he is about to marry a lovely Quaker girl (Kelly), Kane finds only cowardice and betrayal from the townspeople. He survives the shoot-out but leaves town with contempt. With firm direction by Fred Zinnemann, austere black-and-white photography by Floyd Crosby, and expert, Oscar-winning editing by Elmo Williams and Harry Gerstad, *High Noon* is an exemplary western. Gary Cooper also won an Oscar by making apt use of his stoic demeanor and unadorned acting style.

Off-Screen: At the time Carl Foreman was writing his screenplay, Hollywood was being investigated by the House Un-American Activities Committee, and Foreman expected to be called up as an uncooperative witness. Shunned by many friends, Foreman wrote *High Noon* to express his outrage at the cowardice and vacillation of many Hollywood figures in response to the HUAC investigation. During the filming, Gary Cooper was ill with a bleeding ulcer and an injured hip, and the pain was reflected in his craggy face. He was far from the first choice for the role of Will Kane—Marlon Brando and Charlton Heston were earlier candidates. The film's popular theme song and music score also won Oscars. A television sequel turned up in 1980.

High Sierra

Warners, 1941. (100m.) Dir: Raoul Walsh. Sp: John Huston and W. R. Burnett, b/o novel by W. R. Burnett. Cast: Humphrey Bogart, Ida Lupino, Alan Curtis, Arthur Kennedy, Joan Leslie, Henry Hull, Henry Travers, Jerome Cowan, Barton MacLane, Cornel Wilde.

On-Screen: *Humphrey Bogart's first major break.* As "Mad Dog" Roy Earle, a tough, bitter ex-con with a streak of compassion and sensitivity, Bogart gives one of his best early performances. Although Bogey as a world-class loser may seem unlikely casting, he turns Earle, recently sprung from prison and on his way to rob a California resort hotel, into a complex, strangely sympathetic character who can confess, "Sometimes I feel like I don't know what it's about anymore." Earle is smitten with a crippled girl (Leslie), but his love is unreturned;

when he does find a loyal companion (Lupino), time is already running out. Walsh stages the violent climax atop a mountain with breath-catching suspense. You'll long remember Lupino's final, triumphant cry: "He's free! He's free!"

Off-Screen: Bogart's portrayal of doom-ridden Roy Earle proved he was well on his way to full-fledged stardom, a promise fulfilled by *The Maltese Falcon,* released after *High Sierra.* The studio's other "house gangsters," Edward G. Robinson, James Cagney, John Garfield, and George Raft, as well as Paul Muni, all turned down the role. The concluding sequence was filmed on Mount Whitney, highest peak of California's Sierra Nevada. Watch for Cornel Wilde in the small but crucial role of the hotel clerk. The studio recycled the movie as *Colorado Territory* (1949), Walsh again directing, and as *I Died a Thousand Times* (1955). (CFB)

High Society

MGM, 1956. (C-107m.) Dir: Charles Walters. Sp: John Patrick, b/o play by Philip Barry. MS: Cole Porter. Cast: Bing Crosby, Frank Sinatra, Grace Kelly, Celeste Holm, Louis Calhern, Louis Armstrong, Sidney Blackmer, Margalo Gilmore.

On-Screen: The Philadelphia Story—*musicalized by Cole Porter*. The idea of turning Philip Barry's airy comedy into a Cole Porter movie musical must have seemed a good idea at the time. In execution, the result is only intermittently successful, due mainly to inappropriate casting. In the Katharine Hepburn role of the rich, lofty girl who learns humility, Grace Kelly looks stunningly beautiful—this was her last film

role—but she appears a bit wan and bloodless. As her bemused ex-husband, Bing Crosby is badly miscast, and Frank Sinatra is not much better as a magazine writer who, to his surprise, falls for Kelly. The score included a big hit, "True Love," and many of the other songs, though not top-drawer Porter, have his expected wit and insouciance. Personal favorite: the seductive ballad "You're Sensational," sung by Sinatra to Grace Kelly. In general, *High Society* lacks the spark and the spice of the original.

Off-Screen: Bing Crosby on his "True Love" duet with Grace Kelly: "I had a great deal of trouble with the studio. They didn't want her to sing on the record; they thought it should have a better voice. Of course, I was determined to have Grace on a record that I thought had a chance to be a gold one, and we had quite a squabble about it. She didn't care whether she sang on it or not." The record sold a million copies and was Crosby's twentieth gold disc.

His Girl Friday

Columbia, 1940. (92m.) Dir: Howard Hawks. Sp: Charles Lederer and Ben Hecht (uncredited), b/o play by Hecht and Charles MacArthur. Cast: Rosalind Russell, Cary Grant, Ralph Bellamy, Gene Lockhart, Helen Mack, Ernest Truex, Clarence Kolb, John Qualen, Porter Hall, Billy Gilbert.

On-Screen: The Front Page—*with switched sexes*. Hecht and MacArthur's rowdy newspaper stage play had been filmed before in 1931 with Adolphe Menjou as the conniving editor Walter Burns and Pat O'Brien as his star reporter, Hildy Johnson. In an inspired move, this remake turned Hildy into a woman (Russell) who is not only Walter's best reporter but also his ex-wife. The plot remains the same: Walter tries to prevent Hildy from quitting the newspaper and remarrying, while the embattled duo become involved with an escaped convict on the eve of his execution for murder. One of the funniest comedies of the period, *His Girl Friday* is also one of fastest ever: The entire film moves at a dizzying, headlong pace, and the dialogue, especially the exchanges between Grant and Russell, often sputters like a machine gun out of control. In her pin-striped suit and absurd hat, Russell confirms her forte in this sort of aggressively comedic role, and Grant matches her every step of the way with his usual aplomb.

Off-Screen: The role of Hildy Johnson was turned down by many actresses, including Katharine Hepburn, Jean Arthur, Margaret Sullavan, Irene Dunne, and Claudette Colbert. Wisely, Rosalind Russell leaped at the chance. It was clear that she was not Howard Hawks's choice, and after a while, she finally leveled with him, saying, "You don't want me, do you? Well, you're stuck with me, so you might as well make the most of it." He did, Russell persevered, and the result was a hilarious performance that enhanced her star quality.

Hoffa

Fox, 1992. (C-140m.) Dir: Danny DeVito. Sp: David Mamet. Cast: Jack Nicholson, Danny DeVito, Armand Assante, J. T. Walsh, John C. Reilly, Frank Whaley, Kevin Anderson, Robert Prosky, Natalija Nogulich.

On-Screen: *The life of the controversial labor leader.* Danny DeVito's most ambitious film to date, *Hoffa* relates the story of James R. Hoffa (Nicholson), the tough, relentless labor leader who bullied his way to the head of the powerful Teamsters Union, then vanished under mysterious circumstances. Despite the film's attempt at objectivity, Nicholson's Hoffa comes across as a blustering bully, unworthy of an audience's sympathy or attention for over two hours. Screenwriter David Mamet tries to soften the central character by having him viewed in flashback through the eyes of his worshipful aide (actor DeVito in a ludicrously overextended role), but the device fails to work. And director DeVito attempts to give the story an epic feel by staging several large-scale sequences (a violent labor-management encounter, a Teamsters rally), but this also fails to give the movie the necessary momentum. Jack Nicholson gives a galvanic performance as Hoffa, but after a while his single note of rage and aggression begins to pall. What works best in the film are well-etched performances in minor roles, such as Robert Prosky as an early Hoffa ally who meets a tragic end, and J. T. Walsh as Hoffa's self-serving successor. In the end, *Hoffa* is an uninvolving biodrama.

Off-Screen: After reading David Mamet's screenplay, Danny DeVito campaigned for the directing assignment and won it only after Barry Levinson declined. Nicholson and DeVito began their association when they appeared together in *One Flew Over the Cuckoo's Nest* in 1975. DeVito worked on the film for three years. Stephen H. Burum's cinematography won an Oscar nomination.

Hold Back the Dawn

Paramount, 1941. (115m.) Dir: Mitchell Leisen. Sp: Billy Wilder and Charles Brackett, b/o story by Ketti Frings. Cast: Olivia de Havilland, Charles Boyer, Paulette Goddard, Walter Abel, Rosemary DeCamp, Victor Francen, Mikhail Rasumny.

On-Screen: *Deceitful gigolo Charles Boyer marries naive Olivia de Havilland—with unexpected results.* Although he was a fine actor, Charles Boyer was best known for the seductive Gallic charm that devastated his leading ladies. In this effective romantic drama, playing a Romanian gigolo, he uses that charm as a weapon to snare spinsterish teacher Olivia de Havilland, who is touring Mexico with a busload of students. His only intention is to get across the border with his new American wife. However, her decency and genuine love for him overwhelm his selfishness, and ultimately he risks everything to be at her side when she needs him. On the fringes of their story are the hapless refugees waiting to be admitted to the United States. Mitchell Leisen directs ably (he also plays a role as the film director who listens to Boyer's story), and de Havilland shows that she is more than a decorative heroine for Errol Flynn swashbucklers.

Off-Screen: The story was loosely based on a true-life romance between free-lance writer Katharine Hartley and a German refugee named Kurt Frings. They fell in love and married, but Frings was unable to enter the United States since he had once falsified a date when applying for a visa. Along with many other desperate refugees, they languished in Tijuana, waiting for the official documents. Katharine (now Ketti) Frings wrote her story for a Paramount producer, who bought it. Brackett and Wilder changed her noble hero into a deceitful gigolo. Although Frings was furious, the filming proceeded. De Havilland won an Oscar nomination for her performance but lost to

her sister Joan Fontaine in *Suspicion*. The film was also nominated but lost to *How Green Was My Valley*.

Holiday

Columbia, 1938. (93m.) Dir: George Cukor. Sp: Sidney Buchman and Donald Ogden Stewart, b/o play by Philip Barry. Cast: Katharine Hepburn, Cary Grant, Lew Ayres, Doris Nolan, Edward Everett Horton, Henry Kolker, Binnie Barnes, Jean Dixon, Henry Daniell.

On-Screen: *Society girl Katharine Hepburn falls for Cary Grant, her sister's fiancé.* Filmed once before in 1930, Philip Barry's brittle comedy of manners receives superior treatment in this adaptation. The premise is dated but still workable: Hepburn, a discontented rich girl, finds herself enchanted by Grant, her haughty sister's fiancé, who scorns the family millions. Grant's attitude—earn a lot of money quickly, then take an extended "holiday"—dismays the stuffed shirts but enchants Hepburn, who wins him in the end. Hepburn is appealing in the role she understudied onstage a decade earlier, and Grant makes an ideal romantic partner. With its thirties attitude that wealthy people are obsessed only with money and position, *Holiday* now seems like a musty artifact. Yet much of the dialogue still sparkles. Lew Ayres contributes an incisive portrait as Hepburn's bitter, alcoholic brother.

Off-Screen: Columbia studio mogul Harry Cohn wanted Irene Dunne to play the lead, but director Cukor insisted on Hepburn. After Hepburn was named "box-office poison" by theater exhibitors, Columbia used this as part of their advertising campaign for the movie, with the headline "Is it true what they say about Hepburn?" Grant admired Hepburn greatly, saying that she was "a joy to work with" and "the most completely honest woman I've ever met." A 1980 musical version of *Holiday,* entitled *Happy New Year,* had a brief Broadway run.

Holiday Inn

Paramount, 1942. (101m.) Dir: Mark Sandrich. Sp: Claude Binyon, b/o idea by Irving Berlin. MS: Irving Berlin. Cast: Bing Crosby, Fred Astaire, Marjorie Reynolds, Virginia Dale, Walter Abel, Louise Beavers.

On-Screen: *A cornucopia of Irving Berlin music.* It's the constant flow of soothing-to-the-ear tunes by the masterly Irving Berlin that makes this musical a recurring holiday treat. Don't look for any sense in the story about a laid-back crooner (Crosby) who opens a country inn only on holidays, and who becomes involved in an over-the-years romantic triangle with his hoofer friend (Astaire) and a girl singer (Reynolds). Instead, relax and enjoy such songs as "Be Careful, It's My Heart," "You're Easy to Dance With," and of course, the timelessly beautiful "White Christmas." Fred Astaire has a thankless role, but he has one wonderful number, "Say It With Firecrackers," in which he summons up all his old verve and dash to execute a dance in which his steps are punctuated by exploding firecrackers. Crosby is his usual genial self, but it's the Berlin music that makes *Holiday Inn* enjoyable.

Off-Screen: Marjorie Reynolds's singing voice was dubbed by Martha Mears. The story goes that when Berlin first presented "White Christmas" to producer-director Mark Sandrich, he said, "I have an amusing

little number here." The "amusing little number" turned out to be the most successful popular song ever written. *White Christmas* (1954), Paramount's partial remake of *Holiday Inn,* also starred Bing Crosby, this time with Danny Kaye, but it was inferior to the original, despite the Berlin score.

Hollywood Canteen

Warners, 1944. (124m.) Dir: Delmer Daves. Sp: Delmer Daves, b/o his original story. Cast: Joan Leslie, Robert Hutton, Janis Paige, Dane Clark, and many guest stars including Bette Davis, Joan Crawford, John Garfield, Barbara Stanwyck, Sydney Greenstreet, Peter Lorre, Jimmy Dorsey and his band.

On-Screen: *Warner stars pay tribute to—and give a home away from home to—America's fighting men.* Another self-congratulatory exercise from the movie industry, *Hollywood Canteen* was designed, like the other all-star tributes from the major studios, to boost the morale of America's servicemen. There's a wisp of a plot about a soldier (Hutton) with a crush on Joan Leslie, who wins a date with her, but the attraction is the glittering star lineup assembled at the popular Hollywood Canteen. Apart from the expected patriotic numbers, there are a few nondescript tunes rendered by such people as Dennis Morgan and Jane Wyman, and even a smattering of classical music for the highbrows. Best is Roy Rogers's introduction of that most unlikely Cole Porter song "Don't Fence Me In."

Off-Screen: Bette Davis, one of the Canteen's founders, had a scene with Warners' resident ingenue Joan Leslie in which she was merely required to play herself. According to Leslie, "She blew her lines a few times.

Finally, she exclaimed, 'Oh, I just don't think I could do this. I can't play myself! If you give me a gun, a cigarette, a wig, I can play any old bag, but I can't play myself!' "

Hombre

Fox, 1967. (C-111m.) Dir: Martin Ritt. Sp: Irving Ravetch and Harriet Frank, Jr., b/o novel by Elmore Leonard. Cast: Paul Newman, Fredric March, Richard Boone, Diane Cilento, Barbara Rush, Cameron Mitchell, Martin Balsam, Peter Lazer, Margaret Blye.

On-Screen: *An Indian-raised white man confronts a bigoted western world.* In this darkly pessimistic western, Paul Newman stars as John Russell, a white man raised by Apaches who has come to terms with the hatred his Indian heritage provokes in bigoted whites. Circumstances cause him to join a group of largely contemptible people on a stagecoach ride that results in robbery, gunfights, and death for both the villains and himself. The irony stems from his giving up his life to save an Indian-hating woman (Rush) who has been left by the robbers to die in the blazing sun. Newman does another variation on his sixties outcasts, and the rest of the cast performs well as mostly unadmirable types. *Hombre* is helped by James Wong Howe's spare, unfussy photography.

Off-Screen: Paul Newman traveled to the location site weeks ahead of the shooting schedule to immerse himself in the local culture. He stayed on an Indian reservation for five days: "I drove past a general store, and there was this guy standing there in front with one foot up and his arms crossed. He was in exactly the same position when I drove back four hours later. That whole character came out of that."

Home Alone

Fox, 1990. (C-103m.) Dir: Chris Columbus. Sp: John Hughes. Cast: Macaulay Culkin, Joe Pesci, Daniel Stern, John Heard, Roberts Blossom, Catherine O'Hara, John Candy, Angela Goethals, Devin Ratray.

On-Screen: *A boy's all-by-himself adventure.* Small wonder that this preteen comedy became one of the year's most widely attended movies, as well as the largest-grossing comedy to date. How could it miss? Every child who has ever felt shunned or neglected (and that means every child) had to respond with glee to this amusing tale of an eight-year-old boy (Culkin) who is inadvertently left home alone by his family when they travel to Paris. Of course he proves to be brave, resourceful, and capable, especially in routing two inept thieves (Pesci and Stern). The heart of the movie is little Kevin's ingenious ploys for disconcerting, humiliating, or hurting his would-be foes, all carried out in the style of an animated cartoon. (This may explain, without excusing, the audience's acceptance of its pain-inflicting humor.) Is it curmudgeonly to note that the movie is padded out with some easy sentiment about Kevin's strange old neighbor (Blossom)? Never mind. *Home Alone* is really about a small boy's self-reliance in the face of danger, and that was enough to keep the box office humming until the inevitable sequel came along.

Off-Screen: Macaulay Culkin has been acting since the age of four. His father is an actor, and his aunt is actress Bonnie Bedelia. According to the director, young Macaulay was rewarded with a game of Nintendo after each day of rehearsal in the Chicago studio where the film was shot. *Home Alone 2: Lost in New York* turned up for the Christmas season in 1992.

Homicide

Triumph, 1991. (C-100m.) Dir: David Mamet. Sp: David Mamet. Cast: Joe Mantegna, William H. Macy, Natalija Nogulich, Ving Rhames, Vincent Guastaferro, Rebecca Pidgeon.

On-Screen: *The personal turmoil of a Jewish cop.* Bobby Gold (Mantegna) is a tough, seasoned cop in an unspecified city. But he's also Jewish, and he's always felt like an outsider, needing to prove his value and his courage by being "the first one through the door." Bobby doesn't "belong." Then he becomes assigned to the case of a murdered old Jewish shopkeeper, and he becomes drawn into a tangled web of treachery and deceit. His suddenly obsessive need to establish his identity as a Jew leads him to acts that betray his sworn duty as a cop and have tragic consequences. David Mamet directs his own bleak, compelling screenplay, but there's a central flaw that ultimately defeats him: Bobby Gold's transformation from self-hating but hardened cop to vengeful Jew is never believable, despite Joe Mantegna's strong performance. Also, Mamet's attempt to graft his familiar style of clipped, cryptic dialogue onto a police drama is only intermittently successful—some key scenes, such as Bobby's final encounter with a cornered drug dealer, seem heavily contrived.

Off-Screen: *Homicide* is set in an unnamed city, but it was shot in Baltimore. The city's old waterworks offices were transformed into a police station. The movie is David Mamet's third as a writer/director, after *House of Games* and *Things Change*. A bit role as "Rookie Cop at the Variety Store" is played by Mamet's brother Tony.

Honey, I Shrunk the Kids

Buena Vista, 1989. (C-93m.) Dir: Joe Johnston. Sp: Ed Naha and Tom Schulman, b/o story by Stuart Gordon, Brian Yuzna, and Ed Naha. Cast: Rick Moranis, Matt Frewer, Marcia Strassman, Kristine Sutherland, Thomas Brown, Jared Rushton, Amy O'Neill, Robert Oliveri.

On-Screen: *Four youngsters are miniaturized.* They're your typical American suburbanite family, except that Dad Szalinski (Moranis) is a dangerously compulsive tinkerer. His latest folly is a gadget that—oops!—accidentally zaps his and the neighbors' kids down to a quarter-inch size. This movie gets its sci-fi fantasy bounce from down-to-earth dangers lurking in the towering grass of the family backyard. That's where the plucky Szalinski youngsters (O'Neill, Oliveri) and their unlucky neighbors (Brown, Rushton) wind up after being tossed out with trash. (Dad's botched it again.) In their struggle to survive the long trek back to the house (about sixty feet), they meet a friendly ant and a "monstrous" bumblebee. A critical moment: Oliveri, aswim in a bowl of cereal, is threatened with being gobbled up. Persuasive visual effects, a likable cast, and a tad of teenage romance make this outstanding family fare. Keep your eyes on that pooch.

Off-Screen: Thanks to a team of movie-magic wizards, employing both special effects and outsize mock-ups, even the smallest creatures and objects in the seemingly vast expanse of the backyard take on menacing attributes. Hoping to repeat the movie's success, in 1992 the studio released *Honey, I Blew Up the Kid* (its original title, *Honey, I Blew Up the Baby,* didn't send the right message). Of course Dad blunders anew, turning his two-year-old son into a lumbering Brobdingnagian with a height of 112 feet. This huge tyke, however, lacks the appealing vulnerability of the tiny, earlier kids. (CFB)

Hook

TriStar, 1991. (C-144m.) Dir: Steven Spielberg. Sp: Jim V. Hart and Malia Scotch Marmo, b/o story by Jim V. Hart and Nick Castle. Cast: Dustin Hoffman, Robin Williams, Julia Roberts, Bob Hoskins, Charlie Korsmo, Maggie Smith, Caroline Goodall, Dante Basco.

On-Screen: *Steven Spielberg's ten-ton fantasy.* What went wrong? The idea for an elaborate fantasy film would seem to be feasible: Peter Pan (Williams), now a middle-aged, work-obsessed lawyer named Banning, is required to return to Never-Never Land to rescue his children from the clutches of the revenge-minded Captain Hook (Hoffman). In doing so, he must recall the wonder and magic of his childhood days as a soaring sprite. Sadly, there is very little wonder or magic in the movie. The production is cluttered and elephantine (Never-Never Land looks like a giant, ugly amusement park), and embedded in this bloated movie are some banal ideas about parenting and childhood. Some of the material seems secondhand—the ending is borrowed from *The Wizard of Oz.* Robin Williams is adequate as the earthbound Peter, although much of his dialogue sounds as if it were written for one of his comedy routines. Dustin Hoffman is

neither funny nor menacing as Hook, when he should have been both, and Julia Roberts as Tinker Bell simply relies on the enchanting Roberts grin. *Hook,* alas, is a Spielberg mistake.

Off-Screen: Nick Castle, coauthor of the story, was originally signed to direct but was replaced by Steven Spielberg. The pirate ship, the *Jolly Roger,* was 170 feet long, 35 feet wide, and 70 feet high. The cannons were replicas of those on the real H.M.S. *Bounty.* The ship was constructed at an estimated cost of $1 million, and after the film's completion, the producers intended to move it to a projected theme park. It turned out, however, that the *Jolly Roger* wasn't built to hold thousands of theme park visitors and was too big to be removed from the soundstage. Eventually, it was scrapped. *Hook* won Oscar nominations for Costume Design and Art Direction.

Horse Feathers

Paramount, 1932. (68m.) Dir: Norman Z. McLeod. Sp: Bert Kalmar, Harry Ruby, S. J. Perelman, and Will B. Johnstone. MS: Bert Kalmar and Harry Ruby. Cast: Groucho, Chico, Harpo, and Zeppo Marx, Thelma Todd, David Landau, Florine McKinney, Nat Pendleton, James Pierce, Reginald Barlow, Robert Greig.

On-Screen: *The Marx Brothers go to college.* The halls of ivy will never be the same after these academia nuts take over the campus. *Horse Feathers,* the Marxes' collegiate romp, has a wider range of satirical humor than their previous movies. As Prof. Quincy Adams Wagstaff, the newly appointed head of Huxley College, Groucho gets to poke fun at the pomposity and long-windedness often associated with higher education. Zeppo is his secretary, and Chico and Harpo are over-age students who enjoy disrupting every class. The movie has many well-remembered highlights: a tumultuous classroom sequence in which the brothers take over a session in biology ("My students will bear me out," the teacher says. And they do); the "password" scene at a speakeasy, in which Groucho and Chico reach heights of delirium; and the climactic football game that has Harpo bringing down the opposing team with banana peels. Thelma Todd is fun as the seductive "college widow." *Horse Feathers* stirs some satire into the Marxian insanity and comes up with a tasty brew.

Off-Screen: A few comments by the writers of *Horse Feathers* on working for the Marxes: S. J. Perelman: "As far as temperaments and their personalities were concerned, they were capricious, tricky beyond endurance, and altogether unreliable. They were also megalomaniac to a degree which is impossible to describe." Harry Ruby: "In a Marx Brothers movie, there was no law and order. Everything went."

The Hospital

United Artists, 1971. (C-103m.) Dir: Arthur Hiller. Sp: Paddy Chayefsky. Cast: George C. Scott, Diana Rigg, Barnard Hughes, Stephen Elliott, Richard Dysart, Nancy Marchand, Robert Walden, Roberts Blossom, Frances Sternhagen, Lenny Baker.

On-Screen: *Paddy Chayefsky's jet-black comedy.* "It's a Roman farce! . . . The incompetence here is absolutely radiant!" These are some of the kinder words leveled by Dr. Herbert Bock (Scott) at the hospital he serves as chief of medicine. Beset with malpractice, misdiagnosis, and pilfering, the hospital must also cope with a strike, a riot, and (as a topper) a homicidal maniac on the loose. And bitter, burned-out Dr. Bock is in no condition to help. Along comes Barbara Drummond (Rigg), the beautiful daughter of a patient, and a sexual encounter restores Dr. Bock to life. Chayefsky's screenplay is verbose but also scathing and mordantly funny, with one lunatic situation following another. Few groups are spared the author's poisoned arrows—he aims at money-mad doctors, inept administrators, and noisy activists. George C. Scott is in his element here, whether bellowing "We cure nothing! We heal nothing!" out a hospital window or relating the grim facts about his dysfunctional family to a fascinated Rigg. Clearly, the movie intends the beleaguered hospital to represent what Chayefsky calls "the whole wounded madhouse of our times."

Off-Screen: Paddy Chayefsky's original screenplay won a well-deserved Academy Award. Look quickly for Stockard Channing as a nurse. Many years after playing the dubious and corrupt Dr. Welbeck, Richard Dysart became respectable as the head of the law firm in the long-running television series "L.A. Law."

House of Games

Orion, 1987. (C-102m.) Dir: David Mamet. Sp: David Mamet, b/o story by David Mamet and Jonathan Katz. Cast: Lindsay Crouse, Joe Mantegna, Mike Nussbaum, Lilia Skala, J. T. Walsh, Steve Goldstein, Willo Hausman.

On-Screen: *A psychiatrist in deep water.* If you accept the central premise, you will probably enjoy this stylish and intriguing melodrama. Writer-director David Mamet (in his directorial debut) casts his wife, Lindsay Crouse, as a tightly wound psychiatrist and best-selling author of a book on obsessive behavior. On the pretext of helping a patient, she ventures into the sleazy, dangerous world of con men and gamblers and finds it not only sexually arousing but also compulsively exciting. Mike (Mantegna) is the suave con man who leads her into forbidden territory, with devastating results. You have to believe that this highly intelligent woman would freely venture into a place as obviously sinister as the House of Games, and that she would be so utterly dense about the con games being played on her. Having swallowed this, you should appreciate the offbeat dialogue, the twists and turns of a convoluted plot, and a startling climax in a deserted area of an airport. Lindsay Crouse's repressed shrink could use a shade or two more subtlety, but Joe Mantegna excels as the devious hustler.

Off-Screen: *House of Games* was filmed in Seattle, although the location is never identified. Joe Mantegna's association with David Mamet, notably in the Broadway stage version of Mamet's *Glengarry Glen Ross,* continued in the 1991 film *Homicide.*

How Green Was My Valley

Fox, 1941. (118m.) Dir: John Ford. Sp: Philip Dunne, b/o novel by Richard Llewellyn. Cast: Walter Pidgeon, Maureen O'Hara, Donald Crisp, Roddy McDowall, Sara Allgood, Barry Fitzgerald, Anna Lee, Patric Knowles, Rhys Williams.

On-Screen: *John Ford's towering drama of a Welsh mining family.* "How green was my valley then—and the valley of those who have gone." These final poignant words echo in the minds of everyone who has seen this wonderful film. Many Ford aficionados prefer his western movies, but in terms of simple human drama, the director never surpassed this story of a close-knit Welsh mining family, and its painful disintegration over the years. Many of the incidents are viewed through the eyes of Huw (McDowall), the youngest Morgan son, as he witnesses bitter strikes, death in the mines, and bruising family squabbles—all the while groping toward manhood. Donald Crisp won a richly deserved Oscar for his sterling performance as the strong family patriarch, but it is difficult to forget Sara Allgood as his tenacious, loving wife. Once again Ford is concerned with a favorite theme: the role of the family and its place in a turbulently changing community. Alfred Newman's haunting score and Arthur Miller's beautiful black-and-white photography (please, no colorizing) add to the film's durable quality. It won five Academy Awards, including Best Picture and Best Director.

Off-Screen: According to Roddy McDowall, William Wyler was originally set to direct the film, which then concentrated on the grown-up Huw, to be played by Tyrone Power. When Wyler left the project, Philip Dunne rewrote the screenplay to focus entirely on Huw's childhood. Darryl Zanuck wanted to make the film in Rhondda Valley in Wales but was prevented by World War II. Instead he had an entire Welsh village, a coal mine, and adjacent buildings constructed on eighty acres in California's San Fernando Valley. More than 150 men worked for six months on the set. A stage musical version, called *A Time for Singing*, had a brief run on Broadway in 1966.

How to Marry a Millionaire

Fox, 1953. (C-95m.) Dir: Jean Negulesco. Sp: Nunnally Johnson, b/o plays by Zoë Akins, Dale Eunson, and Katherine Albert. Cast: Betty Grable, Marilyn Monroe, Lauren Bacall, William Powell, David Wayne, Rory Calhoun, Cameron Mitchell.

On-Screen: *Three girls search for rich husbands in a CinemaScopic New York.* Designed to show off CinemaScope, Fox's new wide-screen process, *How to Marry a Millionaire* attempts to conceal its old-hat story under a glittering production. (Its origins, in fact, can be traced back to a 1932 movie entitled *The Greeks Had a Word for Them* (a.k.a. *Three Broadway Girls*), which amusingly began life as Zoë Akins's play *The Greeks Had a Word for It*.) It's the old gold-digger tale, all gussied up, with Grable, Monroe, and Bacall as three girls who set themselves up in a swank apartment to snare wealthy husbands. By the film's end, they have learned that romance and money do not necessarily mix. Grable is appealing in her unabashed hearty-girl manner, Bacall gets all the caustic lines, and Monroe, Grable's successor in the Fox Blonde Sweepstakes, coos and pouts fetchingly as a nearsighted dimwit. William Powell brings a note of class to the film as Bacall's wryly realistic suitor. At its first release, the movie was preceded by a prologue in which Alfred Newman conducted his "Street Scene" theme to show off stereophonic sound.

Off-Screen: In a 1953 letter, producer-author Nunnally Johnson wrote: "The two Bettys [Grable and Bacall] have gone out of their way to make friends with Marilyn, but Miss Monroe is generally something of a zombie. Talking to her is like talking to somebody underwater. She's very honest and ambitious and is either studying her lines or her face during all of her working hours, but she's not material for warm friendship."

How to Succeed in Business Without Really Trying

United Artists, 1967. (C-121m.) Dir: David Swift. Sp: David Swift, b/o musical play by Abe Burrows, Jack Weinstock, and Willie Gilbert and book by Shepherd Mead. MS: Frank Loesser. Cast: Robert Morse, Rudy Vallee, Michele Lee, Anthony Teague, Maureen Arthur, Sammy Smith, Ruth Kobart, Murray Matheson, Paul Hartman.

On-Screen: *The musical rise of J. Pierpont Finch.* A virtual duplication of the long-running 1961 stage musical, *How to Succeed in Business* takes a satirical look at the business world (a novel setting for a musical) and finds it chock full of sycophants, opportunists, and fools. Robert Morse repeats his Broadway role as J. Pierpont Finch, a striving young man whose boyish grin conceals a wicked mind. Manipulating his way to the top ranks of the Worldwide Wicket Company, he romances a secretary (Lee) and ingratiates himself with the company's addled president (Vallee), all the while exuding charm to spare. The farcical interludes are quite funny, and Frank Loesser's clever score includes "I Believe in You," Finch's hymn of self-esteem; a sly, company-wide tribute to "The Brotherhood of Man"; and Worldwide employee Sammy Smith's enthusiastic expression of obeisance to "The

Company Way." On the whole *How to Succeed in Business* captures the verve and satirical bite of the Broadway original.

Off-Screen: In addition to Robert Morse, Rudy Vallee, Sammy Smith, and Ruth Kobart also repeated their stage roles. Two versions of the movie were filmed, one with the performers singing their songs, the other with "dialogue bridges" that would allow the musical numbers to be eliminated if overseas audiences didn't like them.

Hud

Paramount, 1963. (112m.) Dir: Martin Ritt. Sp: Irving Ravetch and Harriet Frank, Jr., b/o novel by Larry McMurtry. Cast: Paul Newman, Patricia Neal, Melvyn Douglas, Brandon de Wilde, John Ashley, Whit Bissell.

On-Screen: *Harsh, stinging drama of the new West.* A man of ethical scruples, Homer Bannon (Douglas) knows he must destroy the diseased cattle on his Texas ranch. His son, Hud (Newman), a "Cadillac cowboy," wants to sell the animals quickly, take over the ranch, and drill for oil. That Hud is brutally selfish is made shatteringly clear to his hero-worshiping nephew (de Wilde) when Hud tries to rape Alma (Neal), the Bannon housekeeper. The movie wants to elegize the passing of old-West values, embodied in the elder Bannon, and to condemn Hud's me-generation selfishness. Newman, however, makes his lean and mean nonhero so fascinating that Douglas's passionately moral patriarch comes across as a platitudinizing old-timer. A topsy-turvy movie, but splendidly acted and stunningly photographed. Most memorable scene: the killing of the cat-

tle (old Homer remarks, "It don't take long to kill things, not like it takes to grow").

Off-Screen: In the years since this adaptation of McMurty's novel *Horseman, Pass By,* Neal remains grateful to director Ritt for his sympathetic understanding during a troubled time. Neal and writer-husband Roald Dahl had recently lost their young daughter when production began. Ritt arranged for Neal to appear in her exterior scenes, shot near Claude in the Texas Panhandle, before returning to London to be with her family. She won the Academy Award as Best Actress, and other Oscars went to Douglas as Best Supporting Actor, and to James Wong Howe, for his black-and-white cinematography. Newman received a Best Actor nomination. (CFB)

The Human Comedy

MGM, 1943. (118m.) Dir: Clarence Brown. Sp: Howard Estabrook, b/o novel by William Saroyan. Cast: Mickey Rooney, Frank Morgan, Fay Bainter, James Craig, Marsha Hunt, Van Johnson, Ray Collins, Donna Reed, Jackie "Butch" Jenkins.

On-Screen: *The war changes the lives of small-town inhabitants.* In this almost plotless evocation of small-town America during World War II, Mickey Rooney plays a hardworking telegraph boy whose job touches many of the town's residents. His is an ideal American family: saintly mom (Bainter), sweet sister (Reed), inquisitive little brother (Jenkins), and an older brother (Johnson), fighting in the army. These characters—plus Frank Morgan as a boozing telegrapher who dies on the job—are calculated to wring tears and an occasional smile from the audience. Made during World War II, *The Human Comedy* can be forgiven some of its sticky sentimentality by virtue of the boosterism of the period and the nation's genuine desire to support its troops. Rooney's manic energy is put to good use, and there are a few magical moments involving freckled little "Butch" Jenkins. Robert Mitchum, Barry Nelson, and Don DeFore can be spotted briefly as three soldiers on the loose in town.

Off-Screen: Taken with William Saroyan, the eccentric Armenian writer whose plays and stories were all the rage in the late thirties and early forties, MGM head Louis B. Mayer hired him to write a story for the movies. The result was *The Human Comedy*, which Mayer adored. ("Sentiment is the heart of America," he told Saroyan.) Their relationship soured when Saroyan's screenplay had to be rewritten, and Mayer refused to let him direct the film. After three months of screening all the MGM movies he had missed as a youth, Saroyan left the studio. A Broadway musical version of the novel had a ten-day run in 1984.(JMK)

Humoresque

Warners, 1946. (125m.) Dir: Jean Negulesco. Sp: Clifford Odets and Zachary Gold, b/o story by Fannie Hurst. Cast: Joan Crawford, John Garfield, Oscar Levant, J. Carrol Naish, Ruth Nelson, Tom D'Andrea, Joan Chandler, Craig Stevens, Paul Cavanagh, Peggy Knudsen.

On-Screen: *Ill-fated romance of violinist and socialite.* Take your pick. You will find this film either overripe high camp or a mesmerizing emotional melodrama. In either case, chances are you will not be bored. John Garfield plays an intense, gifted violinist whose career is sponsored by Joan Crawford, an unhappy and alcoholic married socialite. His obsession with music clashes inevitably with her obsession with him, leading to a tragic outcome. In roles that are the very essence of their familiar movie personas, both actors give worthy performances in a beautifully photographed production. It is hard, however, to take it all very seriously, especially with a delirious climax that has Crawford marching into the ocean while Garfield plays Wagner's "Liebestod" at his concert. Oscar Levant is on hand to lighten the heavy tone with his usual brand of sarcastic humor. ("Tell me, Mrs. Wright, does your husband interfere with your marriage?")

Off-Screen: The screenplay combined Fannie Hurst's original "Humoresque" story and the 1920 film version with large portions of Clifford Odets's unused original screenplay for *Rhapsody in Blue*. Isaac Stern dubbed the violin-playing for John Garfield. At the first meeting of the two stars, Garfield said, "So you're Joan Crawford, the big movie star!" Crawford smiled and held out her hand, whereupon Garfield gave her a playful pinch on the breast. "Why, you insolent son of a . . . ," she exclaimed, then stopped herself. She smiled again and said, "I think we're going to get along just fine."

The Hunchback of Notre Dame

RKO, 1939 (115m.) Dir: William Dieterle. Sp: Sonya Levien and Bruno Frank, b/o novel by Victor Hugo. Cast: Charles Laughton, Maureen O'Hara, Thomas Mitchell, Edmond O'Brien, Sir Cedric Hardwicke,

Alan Marshal, Walter Hampden, Harry Davenport.

On-Screen: *Spectacular drama of medieval Paris.* The versatile British actor audiences had come to both love and hate, as, respectively, the affable gentleman's gentleman in *Ruggles of Red Gap* and the sadistic Captain Bligh in *Mutiny on the Bounty* (both 1935), transformed himself yet again to become one of the screen's most unusual heroes. As the grotesquely deformed Quasimodo, deaf from years of ringing Notre Dame's enormous bells, Laughton gives a moving, if rather florid, performance, perfectly mirroring the all-stops-out production. The strong supporting cast includes Hardwicke, as Frollo, the villainous brother of the archbishop of Paris (Hampden); O'Hara as Esmerelda, the beautiful, imperiled gypsy girl whom Quasimodo thrillingly rescues from Frollo's lustful attentions ("Sanctuary! Sanctuary!"); and O'Brien as a dashing, François Villon–like poet. Alfred Newman's magnificent score adds enormously to the movie's pathos and excitement.

Off-Screen: Charles Laughton fought bitterly with Perc Westmore, the famous Hollywood makeup artist, who was personally assigned to him. Westmore came up with version after version for Quasimodo's makeup, but the actor rejected them all. Finally, he was satisfied. In that extraordinary movie year of 1939 (*Gone With the Wind, The Wizard of Oz,* and others), *The Hunchback of Notre Dame* won only two Oscar nominations, for Newman's score and for sound recording. Earlier adaptations of Hugo's novel appeared in 1917 and 1923 (the latter with the legendary Lon Chaney), and it was remade with Anthony Quinn in a 1957 French version and again in 1982 for British television, with Anthony Hopkins as the Hunchback. The must-sees remain the Chaney and Laughton versions. (CFB)

The Hurricane

Goldwyn-United Artists, 1937. (102m.) Dir: John Ford. Sp: Dudley Nichols; adaptation: Oliver H. P. Garrett, b/o novel by Charles Nordhoff and James Norman Hall. Cast: Dorothy Lamour, Jon Hall, Raymond Massey, Mary Astor, C. Aubrey Smith, Thomas Mitchell, John Carradine, Jerome Cowan.

On-Screen: *A miscarriage of justice and a holocaust of nature devastate a South Seas island.* One of the best-remembered, most impressive "disaster" films of the thirties, *The Hurricane* adapts the Nordhoff-Hall novel into a compelling tale that ends with a wallop. Don't look for a realistic view of life in the islands of the South Seas; Manikoora is an idyllic paradise of swaying palms and happy people until Terangi (Hall), its best-loved citizen, is imprisoned unjustly, leaving behind his distraught bride, Marama (Lamour in her famous sarong). Harshly opposing Terangi's release, and insisting on his recapture when he escapes in desperation, is DeLange (Massey), the implacable governor of the islands. Yet all the personal drama pales beside the climactic hurricane that destroys the island. Staged by James Basevi, who also masterminded the earthquake in *San Francisco* and the locust attack in *The Good Earth,* this hurricane is an eye-popping marvel of special effects.

Off-Screen: Filming the hurricane sequence was an ordeal for the cast. The actors were drenched by fire hoses and nearly blown apart by the studio wind machines. In the studio-created storm, Ford directed the Hawaiian extras to climb the coconut trees to save themselves from the artificial waves; later, when a real hurricane and tidal wave destroyed their island, they were able to survive by remembering this technique. The film marked the debut of Jon Hall, who was part-Tahitian and a neighbor of John Ford's. A 1979 remake was disastrous.

Husbands and Wives

TriStar, 1992. (C-107m.) Dir: Woody Allen. Sp: Woody Allen. Cast: Woody Allen, Mia Farrow, Judy Davis, Sydney Pollack, Juliette Lewis, Liam Neeson, Lysette Anthony, Blythe Danner, Benno C. Schmidt, Jr.

On-Screen: When Jack (Pollack) and Sally (Davis) suddenly announce to their best friends, teacher Gabe Roth (Allen) and his wife, Judy (Farrow), that they are splitting up, the apparently seamless marriage of Gabe and Judy begins to unravel as well. Each becomes involved with other people, Gabe with one of his young students (Lewis), Judy with an editor (Neeson). On this premise, Woody Allen fabricates his bleakest film to date, a blistering comedy-drama (actually there are only scattered laughs) that views marriage and romance with a jaundiced eye. Shorn of the usual Allen wit and devoid of the warmth and generosity of the characters in a movie such as *Hannah and Her Sisters,* these New Yorkers come across as a joyless lot. The ensemble cast is excellent, with the best performance coming from Oscar-nominated Judy Davis as a woman whose emotions are constantly at war with her intellect. Film director Syd-

ney Pollack is also surprisingly good as Jack. One scene with his young girlfriend (Anthony) is the most wrenchingly violent in any Allen film. *Husbands and Wives* is often brilliant and perceptive, but it would have been more effective without Carlo Di Palma's jittery, endlessly swooping hand-held camera.

Off-Screen: Inevitably, in the summer of 1992, it was difficult for many viewers to separate *Husbands and Wives* from the sordid true-life Woody-and-Mia story. Scores of magazine and newspaper articles (even editorials) buzzed about Allen's romance with Farrow's twenty-one-year-old adopted Korean daughter, and the scandalous allegations that followed. Everyone, it seemed, had an opinion on the couple and what had transpired. Many who had confused the endearing intellectual nebbish on the screen with the real-life writer, director, and actor felt betrayed. In the long run, despite dire predictions that the scandal would damage his career, the gifted Allen continues to make his special sort of movie. His screenplay won an Oscar nomination.

Hush ... Hush, Sweet Charlotte

Fox, 1965. (133m.) Dir: Robert Aldrich. Sp: Henry Farrell and Lukas Heller. Cast: Bette Davis, Olivia de Havilland, Joseph Cotten, Agnes Moorehead, Victor Buono, Mary Astor, Cecil Kellaway, Bruce Dern.

On-Screen: *A former Southern belle reaches old age believing she murdered her boyfriend.* Director Robert Aldrich capitalized on the success of *What Ever Happened to Baby Jane?* by casting Bette Davis in a second role as a Grand Guignol madwoman. This time she's an aging

Southern belle who, haunted by the early grisly death of her fiancé (Bruce Dern in one of his early roles), has fantasies involving severed body parts and hatchets that have a horrifying basis in reality. De Havilland is the comforting cousin who may not be what she seems. The atmosphere drips with Southern gothic moss, shattered mirrors, and ghostly music. The film takes a long time getting to the point, with many asides about the presumed good intentions of the characters, which, of course, turn out to be false. The stars, who have fun playing their wicked, dotty, or just plain cruel roles, are better than the direction. Still, *Charlotte* is good, creepy fun.

Off-Screen: Robert Aldrich had expected to reunite the stars of *Baby Jane,* but Joan Crawford claimed illness after the filming began and was replaced by Olivia de Havilland. Before Crawford left, there was the usual antagonism between her and Davis, with each jockeying for top position or vying for ways to annoy or humiliate the other. When the company finished rehearsals and left for location shooting in Louisiana, Aldrich remarked, "I hope we live through it." Mary Astor appears in a small but key role that was originally offered to Barbara Stanwyck. It turned out to be her last. (JMK)

The Hustler

Fox, 1961. (135m.) Dir: Robert Rossen. Sp: Robert Rossen and Sidney Carroll, b/o novel by Walter Tevis. Cast: Paul Newman, Jackie Gleason, Piper Laurie, George C. Scott, Myron McCormick, Murray Hamilton, Michael Constantine, Jake LaMotta, Vincent Gardenia.

On-Screen: *Pungent drama set in the world of pool sharks.* Rossen and Carroll's screenplay, together with Eugene Shuftan's Oscar-winning camerawork, brilliantly expresses the tense, sleazy, and boozy atmosphere in which small-time pool hustlers rub shoulders with would-be and true champions, gamblers, and hangers-on. Dominating the movie is Newman's Fast Eddie Felson, a cynical young shark obsessed with winning a billiards match against the deceptively calm Minnesota Fats (Gleason), the country's top player. Also contributing superb performances to this taut drama are Scott, as a manipulative, malevolent gambler, and Laurie, as Fast Eddie's crippled, alcoholic girlfriend. Except for touching romantic interludes between the lovers, the movie offers little to warm the heart; instead, it serves up an authentic, unflinching look at practitioners of the pool-hall hustle. One of Newman's best movies.

Off-Screen: The principal action was filmed in New York's Ames Billiard Academy, where legendary pro Willie Mosconi (he plays a bit part as "Willie") provided his own expert hands as Newman's for pool-table close-ups. The movie won Oscars for black-and-white cinematography and art direction and received nominations for picture, director, actor, actress, and supporting actor (Gleason and Scott). Six nominations and twenty-five years later, Newman won an Oscar when he repeated his role of Fast Eddie Felson in the movie's sequel, *The Color of Money* (1986). (CFB)

I Am a Fugitive from a Chain Gang

Warners, 1932. (93m.) Dir: Mervyn LeRoy. Sp: Sheridan Gibney and Brown Holmes, b/o autobiographical story by Robert E. Burns. Cast: Paul Muni, Glenda Farrell, Helen Vinson, Preston Foster, Edward Ellis, Allen Jenkins.

On-Screen: *An innocent man is brutalized by the justice system*. Crude but still powerful, *I Am a Fugitive from a Chain Gang* created quite a stir in its day with its unsparing view of America's insensitive method of dealing with criminals. Paul Muni plays a World War I veteran who innocently becomes involved with a robbery and finds himself trapped in a pitiless justice system until he is little more than a hunted animal. The scenes in the primitive, corrupt prison, where men are chained together, are harrowing, a vision of hell. Paul Muni gives an intense, moving performance, almost devoid of the hamminess that often marred his acting. The women in his life (Farrell and Vinson) are only sketchily characterized, and some points are made with a sledgehammer. But *I Am a Fugitive* has some memorable moments, none more so than the famous ending in which Muni, in a last furtive meeting with his fiancée (Vinson), is asked how he lives. "I steal!" Muni hisses, and disappears into the darkness.

Off-Screen: Bought for the screen, Robert E. Burns's true story of life in a chain gang was originally called "I Am a Fugitive from a Georgia Chain Gang." For obvious reasons, "Georgia" was deleted in the film version. While still a fugitive, Burns came to California under an alias to help with the screenplay. Guaranteed safety, he was housed at the studio and only a few people knew of his whereabouts. The film created a public uproar and a clamor for immediate legislation. When Burns was finally arrested in New Jersey, a flood of appeals called for leniency, and three governors refused to extradite him to Georgia. His story was told in the television movie *The Man Who Broke 1,000 Chains* (1987).

I Remember Mama

RKO, 1948. (134m.) Dir: George Stevens. Sp: DeWitt Bodeen, b/o play by John Van Druten and book by Kathryn Forbes. Cast:

Irene Dunne, Barbara Bel Geddes, Oscar Homolka, Philip Dorn, Cedric Hardwicke, Edgar Bergen, Rudy Vallee, Barbara O'Neil, Ellen Corby, Florence Bates.

On-Screen: *A young woman recalls her immigrant family and her indomitable mother*. Irene Dunne began her long career depicting noble, sacrificial wives/mothers/lovers, then graduated to playing delectable, independent-minded ladies in screwball comedies. By the late forties she had returned to playing mothers, in *Life with Father* (1947) and in this long, rambling but charming nosegay. Dunne is endlessly resourceful Mama, holding her Norwegian immigrant family together and coping with periodic crises in turn-of-the-century San Francisco. Derived from Kathryn Forbes's reminiscences and John Van Druten's Broadway play, the movie is sluggish at times, but the characters surrounding Mama are delightfully eccentric, especially Oscar Homolka as a boisterous uncle and Sir Cedric Hardwicke as a flamboyant and insolvent actor. Dunne's Oscar-nominated Mama outshines them all.

Off-Screen: The film was scheduled to play Radio City Music Hall in New York when an argument erupted about its length. The Music Hall wanted the film cut to exactly two hours to accommodate its stage show, but George Stevens would cut only ten minutes, no more. Production head Dore Schary also refused to cut more, although he had the authority to override Stevens. *Mama,* a television series based on the story, turned up in 1956, with Peggy Wood as Mama. It ran for eight years. Richard Rodgers's musical adaptation had a modest run on Broadway in 1979.

I Walked with a Zombie

RKO, 1943. (69m.) Dir: Jacques Tourneur. Sp: Curt Siodmak and Ardel Wray, b/o story by Inez Wallace. Cast: Tom Conway, Frances Dee, James Ellison, Edith Barrett, James Bell, Christine Gordon, Sir Lancelot, Theresa Harris.

On-Screen: *Voodoo shadows the lives of a group of people in the West Indies*. Hired to look after Tom Conway's catatonic wife (Gordon) on the island of St. Sebastian, nurse Frances Dee finds herself caught up not only in family intrigue but in mysterious and frightening voodoo rites. The natives believe that Gordon is a zombie—a member of the living dead—and so does Ellison, Conway's troubled, alcoholic half-brother. After a series of bizarre incidents, the truth is finally revealed. One of Val Lewton's best-known horror films, *I Walked with a Zombie* uses the power of suggestion rather than explicit gore—one recalls, in particular, Dee's late-night walk through the cane fields to witness a voodoo ceremony. What matters here is not the rather muddled story which, surprisingly, was suggested by Charlotte Brontë's *Jane Eyre,* but the unsettling atmosphere that permeates this modest but often intriguing little movie.

Off-Screen: At the time of their release, Val Lewton's now well-regarded horror films for RKO were treated scornfully, and *I Walked with a Zombie* was no exception. The *New York Times* dismissed it as "a dull, disgusting exaggeration of an unhealthy, abnormal concept of life." (Earlier, the *Times* had called Lewton's best film, *Cat People,* "a labored and obvious attempt to induce shock.")

I Want to Live!

United Artists, 1958. (120m.) Dir: Robert Wise. Sp: Nelson Gidding and Don M. Mankiewicz, b/o articles by Ed Montgomery and the letters of Barbara Graham. Cast: Susan Hayward, Simon Oakland, Theodore Bikel, Virginia Vincent, Philip Coolidge.

On-Screen: *Susan Hayward's Oscar as a good-time, bad-luck woman*. A grim true story, as well as a blistering attack on the death penalty, *I Want to Live!* traces the sordid life and last harrowing days of Barbara Graham, a prostitute-crook who was executed for a crime she never committed. In and out of trouble with the police, deserted by her junkie husband and left with a baby, hard-luck Barbara (Hayward) is convicted of participating in a murder and sentenced to death in the gas chamber. The last (and best) portion of the film spares nobody in its unflinching, detailed look at the execution. Other, earlier sections are less successful, particularly in their overwrought, unconvincing depiction of a vicious press ("How does it feel to see your baby knowing that you're going to the gas chamber?"). Susan Hayward pulls out all stops in an electrifying performance that justifiably earned her an Academy Award.

Off-Screen: Ed Montgomery, the reporter who championed Barbara Graham in her fight to have her sentence overturned or commuted, is played in the film by Simon Oakland. Montgomery served as adviser and was often consulted by Susan Hayward. The film was first banned in England, then shown in a watered-down version. Writer Albert Camus asserted that the movie should be seen by future generations as a document of prehistoric cruelty. There were five other Oscar nominations. A television remake turned up in 1983.

I'll Cry Tomorrow

MGM, 1955. (117m.) Dir: Daniel Mann. Sp: Helen Deutsch and Jay Richard Kennedy, b/o book by Lillian Roth. Cast: Susan Hayward, Richard Conte, Eddie Albert, Jo Van Fleet, Don Taylor, Ray Danton, Margo, Virginia Gregg.

On-Screen: *Susan Hayward portrays the alcoholic ordeal of Lillian Roth*. In her totally candid autobiography *I'll Cry Tomorrow,* actress-singer Lillian Roth bared her nightmarish life as an alcoholic for sixteen years. Brought to the screen, her story holds a grim fascination, tracing the impact of a relentless stage mother (Van Fleet), the devastating death of an adored young lawyer (Danton), and husbands (Taylor, Conte) who either lead her to alcoholism or abuse her viciously. Lillian finally finds solace and redemption with Alcoholics Anonymous and a kindly member (Albert). It's certainly a harrowing tale, but much of the dialogue is preposterous and overblown. As Lillian Roth, Susan Hayward gives a bravura, Oscar-nominated performance, working hard to convey the torment and helplessness of a woman living in alcoholic hell. Her scenes of all-out drunkenness and her "drying-out" scenes with AA ("I can't live—and I can't die!") are played with stinging force and conviction.

Off-Screen: Susan Hayward was always Lillian Roth's first choice to portray her, but she had to campaign vigorously for the role. Rather than have Roth dub her singing, Hayward used her own voice in the musical numbers. Roth was bitterly disappointed at not being used, but the studio was so pleased with the result that it devoted an entire credit panel to announcing MISS HAYWARD SINGS!, then listed her songs. Hayward credits director Mann with her success in the role: "Danny checked every detail. He wouldn't let me cheat with lipstick or even a curl. . . ." The movie won an Oscar for costume design (black-and-white).

I'm No Angel

Paramount, 1933. (87m.) Dir: Wesley Ruggles. Sp: Mae West; adaptation: Harlan Thompson. MS: Harvey Brooks, Gladys du Bois, and Ben Ellison. Cast: Mae West, Cary Grant, Edward Arnold, Ralf Harolde, Russell Hopton, Gertrude Michael, Kent Taylor, Gregory Ratoff, Gertrude Howard.

On-Screen: *Lion tamer Mae West tames Cary Grant and other men*. Generally regarded as West's best movie, *I'm No Angel* has a flavorsome carnival background in the early scenes, a goodly batch of quotable lines from the lady herself, and her best leading man, Cary Grant. Mae plays Tira, the carnival queen who's seen it all and wants her share of it. Bumping and grinding on the midway, she murmurs to the palpitating spectators, "A penny for your thoughts." In no time at all, she rises to the big time, where she entrances a socialite (Taylor) but ends up with his cousin (Grant). "Do you mind if I get personal?" he asks her. "I don't mind if you get familiar," she answers. Mae's best scene is in the courtroom, where she's suing Grant for breach of promise. Wearing a black gown, a fur stole, and a feathered hat, she brazenly reduces every male witness to total bewilderment. Her

credo: "When I'm good, I'm very good. But when I'm bad, I'm better." In *I'm No Angel,* she's at her best.

Off-Screen: Cary Grant acknowledged that he learned much about film acting from West: "She instinctively knew everything about camera angles and lighting, and she taught me all I know about timing." Of her personality, however, he was less than complimentary: "I thought she was brilliant with that one character she portrayed, but she was an absolute fake as a person. . . . She wore so much makeup and all that figure and those tall high heels. You couldn't find Mae West in there. I'm not attracted to artificiality. I'm not attracted to makeup. And certainly Mae wore more of it than anyone I've ever seen in my life."

In a Lonely Place

Columbia, 1950. (91m.) Dir: Nicholas Ray. Sp: Andrew Solt, b/o story by Dorothy B. Hughes and adaptation by Edmund H. North. Cast: Humphrey Bogart, Gloria Grahame, Frank Lovejoy, Carl Benton Reid, Art Smith, Jeff Donnell, Martha Stewart, Ruth Gillette.

On-Screen: *Bogart as a volatile murder suspect*. A taut and well-written *film noir, In a Lonely Place* casts Humphrey Bogart as a screenwriter whose violent temper and erratic behavior get him into trouble, notably as a prime suspect in the murder of a hatcheck girl (Stewart). Despite the *noir* aspects— dark streets, clipped, cryptic dialogue, whiff of decadence—the film is not really a mystery but a study of the writer's passionate and possibly dangerous affair with Gloria Grahame, his sultry neighbor, who realizes that he is a ticking bomb about to explode. Bogart and Grahame make an interesting team, his barely restrained fury playing against her coolly insinuating manner. Many *noir* fans recall Bogart's epitaph for their relationship: "I was born when she kissed me. I died when she left me. I lived a few weeks while she loved me." Note Ruth Gillette's performance as a slightly sinister masseuse.

Off-Screen: Although it seems unlikely, director Ray claimed that he first sought Ginger Rogers for the female lead. Ray was married to Gloria Grahame at the time, and, reportedly, he rewrote the screenplay extensively to reflect their disintegrating relationship.

In Cold Blood

Columbia, 1967. (134m.) Dir: Richard Brooks. Sp: Richard Brooks, b/o book by Truman Capote. Cast: Robert Blake, Scott Wilson, John Forsythe, Paul Stewart, Gerald S. O'Loughlin, Jeff Corey, Will Geer.

On-Screen: *Truman Capote's harrowing account of a true crime and its aftermath.* The banality of evil has seldom been presented more chillingly than in Richard Brooks's grim, relentless drama. Truman Capote's self-styled "nonfiction novel" told the true story of a dreadful 1959 murder in Kansas in which Perry Smith and Dick Hickok (Blake and Wilson), two deeply troubled ex-convicts, wiped out the Clutters, a Kansas farm family. The film version cuts steadily between the family and their killers, moves swiftly through the murders (later returning to the act in horrifying detail), then deals with the pursuit, the capture, and the execution of

the killers. Along the way, the film touches on the terrible past lives of the killers, offering them not as excuses but as cold, inexorable facts. The numbing amorality of the killers is summed up when one of them says, "It had nothing to do with the Clutters. They just happened to be there. Mr. Clutter was a very nice gentleman—up until the time I cut his throat."

Off-Screen: Much of *In Cold Blood* was filmed in Kansas at the scene of the crime and its environs. A neighbor of the Clutter family remarked, "It's true. The thing happened. You ain't gonna erase it. It's part of history. The only thing you can do is tell it straight." Although many local citizens resented the intrusion and the hoopla, others worked as extras. Brooks was relentless in his pursuit of authenticity, insisting on accurate detail for every scene.

In Old Chicago

Fox, 1938. (95m.) Dir: Henry King. Sp: Lamar Trotti and Sonya Levien, b/o story by Niven Busch. Cast: Tyrone Power, Alice Faye, Don Ameche, Alice Brady, Brian Donlevy, Andy Devine, Phyllis Brooks, Tom Brown, Sidney Blackmer, Berton Churchill, Gene Reynolds.

On-Screen: *Events (Fox says) leading to the Great Chicago Fire.* Having had the San Francisco earthquake rudely usurped by MGM, Fox elected to produce an elaborate fiction concerning the origins of the Chicago fire of 1871. And elaborate is indeed the word for this lusty, entertaining period drama that takes the legend literally: The fire starts when Mrs. O'Leary's cow kicks over a lantern in the barn. Alice Brady plays the widow O'Leary, but her sons are the central characters, one (Power) an unscrupulous, power-hungry rascal, the other (Ameche) the honest, forthright type who wants to reform a rowdy, corrupt Chicago. Faye plays the saloon singer who loves and ultimately marries Power but hates his disreputable ways. It all ends with the twenty-minute climactic conflagration, impressively staged.

Off-Screen: Faye's role of Belle Fawcett was intended for Jean Harlow, on a loan-out deal with MGM, but Harlow died in mid-1937. Although the movie was actually released in 1938, it competed in the 1937 balloting for Academy Awards, receiving six nominations, including Best Picture. It won two awards: Alice Brady as Best Supporting Actress and Robert Webb as Best Assistant Director (a category eliminated after 1937). During the filming of the fire sequence, no women were allowed on the set, and men wearing bonnets and long skirts doubled for the women called for in the screenplay.

In Name Only

RKO, 1939. (92m.) Dir: John Cromwell. Sp: Richard Sherman, b/o novel by Bessie Breuer. Cast: Carole Lombard, Cary Grant, Kay Francis, Charles Coburn, Helen Vinson, Katharine Alexander, Nella Walker, Peggy Ann Garner.

On-Screen: *Carole Lombard and Cary Grant, caught up in a romantic triangle.* A glossy soap opera, somewhat more intelligent than most, *In Name Only* pits a gallant young widow against a scheming wife for the love of her husband. In a rare dramatic role, Carole Lombard plays the widow who falls for Cary Grant, trapped in a loveless marriage to Kay Francis. Husband and wife squabble and the lovers face an anguished separation, but a near-fatal illness resolves everything happily. Lombard and Grant do well in their roles, but surprisingly Francis wins the acting honors, etching a skillful portrait of an icy, grasping woman. Most interesting character: Lombard's neurotic sister, played by Katharine Alexander. And look for a marvelously bitchy turn by Helen Vinson as Francis's gossiping friend.

Off-Screen: RKO had bought the novel for Katharine Hepburn but Hepburn had left Hollywood by this time to take a chance on the Broadway stage. Lombard had read the book and liked it very much. The film was her first under her new contract with RKO.

In the Good Old Summertime

MGM, 1949. (C-102m.) Dir: Robert Z. Leonard. Sp: Albert Hackett, Frances Goodrich, and Ivan Tors, b/o screenplay by Samson Raphaelson and play by Nikolaus Laszlo. MS: Various writers. Cast: Judy Garland, Van Johnson, S. Z. Sakall, Spring Byington, Buster Keaton, Clinton Sundberg.

On-Screen: *Judy Garland and Van Johnson have a romance-by-mail in a period musical.* A cozy little bandbox of a musical, *In the Good Old Summertime* is a remake with songs of the memorable 1940 comedy *The Shop Around the Corner.* Don't look for the charm or the elegance of the original film by Ernst Lubitsch, and neither Garland nor Johnson, despite their geniality, can approach Margaret Sullavan and James Stewart as the store co-workers who dislike each other but are unaware that they are pen pals exchanging friendly letters. Still, there are diverting compensations: an attractive setting (turn-of-the-century Chicago instead of Budapest), some nice old tunes, and Garland to belt them out in her full-throated style. It is sad to see the great Buster Keaton in a supporting role, but he manages one hilarious pratfall.

Off-Screen: In the film's postscript, Garland and Johnson, now happily married, appear with their little daughter, played by Garland's real-life daughter, two-year-old Liza Minnelli. In 1963, the story was turned into a delightful Broadway musical called *She Loves Me*.

In the Heat of the Night

United Artists, 1967. (C-109m.) Dir: Norman Jewison. Sp: Stirling Silliphant, b/o novel by John Ball. Cast: Sidney Poitier, Rod Steiger, Warren Oates, Lee Grant, James Patterson, Quentin Dean, Larry Gates, William Schallert.

On-Screen: *They call him Mr. Tibbs.* The leading citizen in Sparta, Mississippi, has been murdered, and Sheriff Bill Gillespie (Steiger) must find the killer. Enter Virgil Tibbs (Poitier), a cool, intelligent black policeman from Philadelphia. Tibbs goes from suspect to investigator as the town seethes and finally explodes with racial tension. A taut, exciting, and moody thriller, *In the Heat of the Night* mixes its melodrama with a muted message on racism. Poitier is commanding as Tibbs, and Steiger, although he sometimes seems to be defining his role by chewing gum energetically, is also fine, winning a Best Actor Oscar for his perfor-

mance. Other awards went to the film itself and to the screenplay and the editing.

Off-Screen: Rod Steiger, who was always battling with his excessive weight, was actually required to *gain* weight for his role: "Even my normal girth wasn't enough for Norman Jewison. . . . Norman kept saying, 'I'd like to see your stomach over your belt.' That's all I had to hear. I gladly sacrificed myself to art. If I had only two pieces of pecan pie, they went mad. So I gorged myself." Steiger also credits Sidney Poitier for much of his success in the film: "We had a great relationship. He underplayed and made me look good." Poitier reprised his role in *They Call Me MISTER Tibbs!* (1970) and *The Organization* (1971), and a television series based on the movie premiered in 1988.

The Incredible Shrinking Man

Universal, 1957. (81m.) Dir: Jack Arnold. Sp: Richard Matheson, b/o his novel. Cast: Grant Williams, Randy Stewart, April Kent, Paul Langton, William Schallert, Billy Curtis.

On-Screen: *An atomic accident wreaks havoc on an unsuspecting man.* One of the recurring themes of the fifties was the possibly devastating effects of the atom bomb. In the glaring light of the bomb, strange, mutant creatures were formed, and innocent men suffered terrible consequences. *The Incredible Shrinking Man,* one of the best-remembered movies to draw on this theme, has a reasonably coherent script, some very good special effects, and even a cosmic ending. Caught up in an atomic mist that interacts with the insecticide in his system,

Scott Carey (Williams) begins to shrink until he is only a few inches tall. While his wife (Stuart) looks on in helpless horror, Scott finds himself in a terrifying new world where cats, mousetraps, and spiders become deadly enemies. The movie starts awkwardly, and the acting throughout is barely passable, but as the tiny hero fights to survive, there is some genuine suspense (best moment: Scott versus the spider). The message is clear: While man has only an infinitesimal place in "the vast mystery of creation," even the smallest of beings has a value and a purpose. "To God, there is no zero."

Off-Screen: For the early shrinking scenes, Williams was surrounded by oversized furniture, scaled to make him look slightly shorter than his normal, six-foot height. As the character decreased in size, the furniture on the sets grew bigger. During the final scenes, Williams was surrounded by amazing oversized sets containing giant blocks of cheese, mammoth coffee cans, huge spools of thread, and much more.

Indiana Jones and the Last Crusade

Paramount, 1989. (C-127m.) Dir: Steven Spielberg. Sp: Jeffrey Boam, b/o story by George Lucas and Menno Meyjes. Cast: Harrison Ford, Sean Connery, Denholm Elliott, Alison Doody, John Rhys-Davies, Julian Glover, River Phoenix, Alex Hyde-White.

On-Screen: *Indy and dad in a final adventure.* This third and last entry in the popular Indiana Jones series has all the familiar ingredients: nonstop action in exotic locations; flip, comic-strip dialogue; and "Indy" himself (Ford), complete with rumpled hat and whip. This entry has fewer gross-outs than *Indiana Jones and the Temple of Doom,* but also far too many climaxes that come tumbling upon each other at a breathless pace. The best new feature is Sean Connery, engaging as Indy's father. Set in 1938, the story has Indy leaving his post as a teacher of archaeology to find his father, who has disappeared while searching for the Holy Grail. It turns out, not unexpectedly, that the Nazis, in league with a rich, nasty collector (Glover), are also after the Grail. Following a hair-raising adventure in Venice (involving, among other things, swarms of repulsive rats), Indy locates Dad in a Nazi-occupied castle on the German-Austrian border, and they are off on escapades that take them to Berlin and the Republic of Hatay, where Indy has a final, nerve-racking encounter with the Grail. It's all scenic, exhausting, and—if you liked the other films—entertaining. River Phoenix plays teenage Indy in a prologue set in 1915.

Off-Screen: Making the movie called for even more perilous stunts than usual. For the scene in which Indy, on horseback, pursues a Nazi tank in which his father is being held captive, stunt coordinator Vic Armstrong had to jump from a horse onto a moving tank. He also had to hold onto the tank for dear life while the Nazis inside tried to crush him against an embankment. The dangerous stunt had never been attempted before, but Armstrong carried it off without a hitch.

Indiana Jones and the Temple of Doom

Paramount, 1984. (C-118m.) Dir: Steven Spielberg. Sp: Willard Huyck and Gloria Katz, b/o story by George Lucas. Cast: Harrison Ford, Kate Capshaw, Ke Huy Quan, Amrish Puri, Roshan Seth, Philip Stone.

On-Screen: *Steven Spielberg's follow-up adventures of Indiana Jones.* Any movie that begins over the credits with Kate Capshaw and a Busby Berkeley chorus singing "Anything Goes" in a Shanghai nightclub, then follows with a preposterous melee and chase, is not intended to be taken seriously. This sequel (more accurately, prequel) to Spielberg's successful *Raiders of the Lost Ark* follows intrepid archeologist Indiana Jones (Ford) on new adventures in 1935. Accompanied by the screaming Willie (Capshaw) and a spunky boy (Quan), Indy rescues enslaved children from a monstrously evil cult and returns a sacred stone to their village. As in *Raiders,* Spielberg is out to make a giant-size version of the old cliff-hanger serials, and he piles one breathtaking sequence on another. The movie lacks the variety and surprise of its predecessor, and a few of the scenes are needlessly gross. The dialogue is also more comic-book than ever, with quips traded by the characters while their lives are in danger. After a while, you'll find yourself either exhausted and glum, or laughing at the sheer outrageousness of it all.

Off-Screen: Some of the movie was shot on location in Macao, Sri Lanka, London, and San Francisco. The jungles and elephants were in Sri Lanka, but all the exteriors of the palace were paintings and miniatures. Most of the movie was shot on soundstages in London. Working with cinematographer Douglas Slocombe, production designer Elliott Scott, and costume designer Anthony Powell, Spielberg chose a color scheme that deliberately resembled the bright, gaudy Technicolor of classic old movies.

The Informer

RKO, 1935. (91m.) Dir: John Ford. Sp: Dudley Nichols, b/o novel by Liam O'Flaherty. Cast: Victor McLaglen, Heather Angel, Preston Foster, Margot Grahame, Wallace Ford, Una O'Connor, Donald Meek, Joseph Sawyer.

On-Screen: *Grim, Dublin-set drama of betrayal and vengeance.* Although this sometimes "arty" movie is far from John Ford's best, it deserves more praise than some critics have recently granted it. It depicts the last hours in the life of Gypo Nolan (McLaglen), a brutish, childlike giant who, during the Irish "troubles" in 1922, betrays his best friend, Frankie (Ford), to the Black and Tans for money to emigrate to America. Some of the symbolism is obvious—Gypo seemingly pursued by a blind, cane-tapping "Destiny" figure, Gypo as a Judas-like betrayer accepting twenty pounds' payment for his betrayal. Other, more dramatic moments work splendidly, as when a sweating Gypo tries to convince the tribunal of rebels that a timid tailor (Meek) is the real informer. It may be labored to have Gypo assuming a crucified Christ posture in the final scene, but his final outcry in the presence of Frankie's bereaved mother (O'Connor) is unforgettable. McLaglen's performance is powerful.

Off-Screen: Realizing that its production of O'Flaherty's offbeat, if prestigious, morality tale would not be a moneymaker, the studio gave Ford a small budget to suggest Dublin's fog-shrouded streets and mean dwellings. Nevertheless, the movie, shot in about three weeks, won Oscars for Ford, McLaglen, and Nichols, and for Max Steiner's score. A British version had appeared in

1929, and in 1968 a remake called *Up Tight* set the story in an American black ghetto. (CFB)

Inherit the Wind

United Artists, 1960. (127m.) Dir: Stanley Kramer. Sp: Nathan E. Douglas and Harold Jacob Smith b/o play by Jerome Lawrence and Robert E. Lee. Cast: Spencer Tracy, Fredric March, Gene Kelly, Florence Eldridge, Dick York, Donna Anderson, Harry Morgan, Claude Akins.

On-Screen: *Rousing courtroom drama inspired by the 1925 Scopes "monkey trial."* Tracy and March are in top form playing characters based on Clarence Darrow and William Jennings Bryan, defender and prosecutor, respectively, of a public-school biology teacher (York) accused of teaching Darwin's theory of evolution. Adapted from the Broadway stage hit, the movie focuses on the famous Dayton, Tennessee case that rocked America. It's clear from the start that the townspeople favor March's emotional, Bible-thwacking attack on the teacher. When crafty Tracy puts fundamentalist March on the stand, allowing him to trap himself by declaring his personal view of the Bible to be the only true one, we see two opposing legal titans locked in battle. Kelly, in a small but key role as a thinly disguised H. L. Mencken, is a cynical reporter covering the trial. But it's Tracy and March who bring history to vivid life.

Off-Screen: When Spencer Tracy was nominated for an Oscar (along with three other Oscar nominations for the film), he remarked, "I need another award like I need ten pounds." To heighten the tension of the movie's climax, Tracy's eleven-minute summation to the jury was filmed in a single take. During the filming, Tracy and March had a grand time vying with each other for the camera's attention; each time Tracy would begin an oration, March would fan himself vigorously, and, during March's summation to the jury, Tracy kept pulling at his nose. Eldridge, March's wife, played his spouse in the movie. A 1988 television remake starred Kirk Douglas and Jason Robards. (CFB)

Interiors

United Artists, 1978. (C-93m.) Dir: Woody Allen. Sp: Woody Allen. Cast: Diane Keaton, Geraldine Page, Mary Beth Hurt, E. G. Marshall, Maureen Stapleton, Kristin Griffith, Sam Waterston, Richard Jordan.

On-Screen: *Woody Allen's first drama as writer-director.* Talk about dysfunctional families. Lawyer Marshall has left and is about to divorce Page, a neurotic interior decorator prone to nervous breakdowns and suicide attempts. Their three daughters are unhappy in various degrees: Keaton is a blocked poet married to Jordan, an angry writer-teacher. Hurt, unsettled and caustic, lives with Waterston, a political scientist. And Griffith is a film actress with little belief in her talent. Their father's remarriage to a life-affirming woman (Stapleton) sends Mother over the edge. Woody Allen's first drama is mainly patterned after Swedish filmmaker Ingmar Bergman, although the influence of other directors is clear. The writing is literate if somewhat overfancy, and the production is elegant. But in the end the film is so austere and so bloodless that it is difficult to become emotionally involved with the characters. Geraldine Page won a Best Actress nomination but Mary Beth Hurt's performance is the one that stays in the mind. Refusing to soften a thoroughly unlikable character, she has a long soliloquy, addressed to her silent mother, that is a highlight of the film. *Interiors* seems more like an exercise in style than anything else.

Off-Screen: Much of the filming was done at a turn-of-the-century thirty-room beachfront house in Southampton, said to have been designed by architect Stanford White. The house was transformed by the crew into the setting for the film. The changes were meticulous: Eighty-one windowpanes were replaced because they were cracked and they obscured the view of the ocean. And for the desired pale look in one room of the house, a rented $10,000 Aubusson rug was turned upside down. Allen's direction and screenplay were nominated for Oscars.

Intermezzo: A Love Story

Selznick, 1939. (70m.) Dir: Gregory Ratoff. Sp: George O'Neil, b/o story by Gosta Stevens and Gustav Molander. Cast: Leslie Howard, Ingrid Bergman, Edna Best, John Halliday, Cecil Kellaway, Ann Todd, Douglas Scott.

On-Screen: *Ingrid Bergman makes her American film debut in a tale of clandestine romance.* When Ingrid Bergman's rapturously beautiful face appeared on American screens for the first time in this film, it was clear that a major star had been born. As talented as she was beautiful, Bergman had been seen by producer David O. Selznick in a Swedish-language version of the same story and he signed her immediately. She plays a young music student who has a brief but passion-

ate love affair with a celebrated violinist (Howard). Howard, however, is married with two small children, and their love cannot thrive on guilt. Ultimately they part, and a family crisis reunites Howard with his wife. Rather touching in spite of Ratoff's placid direction and the underdeveloped characters, *Intermezzo: A Love Story* still glows when Bergman is on-screen.

Off-Screen: David Selznick instructed director Ratoff (who took over from a slower-paced William Wyler) to copy the original virtually shot for shot. Even composer Heinz Provost's haunting title theme was retained, and with the addition of Robert Henning's English words, it became a national favorite. Howard's apparent instrumental virtuosity was provided on the soundtrack by Toscha Seidel, while his bowing and fingering dexterity was achieved by two unseen violinists standing on either side of him, his own arms held closely to his sides. The film received a couple Oscar nominations: Lou Forbes for his musical direction and Gregg Toland for his black-and-white photography.

Intruder in the Dust

MGM, 1949. (87m.) Dir: Clarence Brown. Sp: Ben Maddow, b/o novel by William Faulkner. Cast: Claude Jarman, Jr., David Brian, Juano Hernandez, Elizabeth Patterson, Porter Hall, Will Geer.

On-Screen: *Tidy film version of a Faulkner novel.* In a small Mississippi town, a man has been found murdered, and Lucas Beecham (Hernandez), a proud, dignified black man who owns his own land, is accused of the crime. An oddly matched group of skeptical citizens, including a young boy (Jarman), a reluctant lawyer (Brian), and a feisty old woman (Patterson), joins together to prove Lucas's innocence before he is lynched by a hostile crowd. A modestly made but effective adaptation of William Faulkner's novel, *Intruder in the Dust* is a rather surprising entry from the glossy MGM studios. The most compelling scene takes place at the grave site of the murder victim, where the determined group exhumes his body in the hope of extracting the fatal bullet. There's a chilling climax in which Lucas is threatened with lynching in a circus atmosphere while his intrepid old defender guards the jail ("I'm goin' for eighty, and I ain't tired yet"). Apart from some awkward dialogue, *Intruder in the Dust* is a small but estimable version of the Faulkner story.

Off-Screen: Director Clarence Brown was eager to make the film, but Louis B. Mayer was opposed: "He was ready to throw me off the lot just for suggesting it, but I had been through the Atlanta race riots when I was sixteen, and this was a picture I had to make. So I kept after him. I wasn't going to back off just because Mayer dumped on the idea."

Invasion of the Body Snatchers

Allied Artists, 1956. (80m.) Dir: Don Siegel. Sp: Daniel Mainwaring, b/o novel by Jack Finney. Cast: Kevin McCarthy, Dana Wynter, Carolyn Jones, King Donovan, Virginia Christine, Larry Gates.

On-Screen: *Space pods turn people into emotional drones.* One of the classic science-fiction films of the fifties is both a warning against becoming loveless conformists and a horror story cautioning us to watch out for every generation's Senator Joseph McCarthy.

Pods drift into Santa Mira from outer space and soon turn into exact replicas of townsfolk, but without any emotions whatever. The story details the efforts of a doctor (Kevin McCarthy) to halt the growing threat, his betrayal by his girl, his friends, and his terrifying isolation as the last real human being in town. The film ends with McCarthy (Kevin, that is) screaming "You're next!" into the camera. Good performances, especially by the leads, help to retain the paranoid atmosphere. Most frightening moment: The good doctor looks into the blank, staring eyes of his fiancée and realizes that she is now one of "them."

Off-Screen: Kevin McCarthy's stark warning at the film's end was originally softened by a studio-added prologue and epilogue, which both director Siegel and writer Mainwaring opposed. These were dropped in Philip Kaufman's 1978 version. Both McCarthy and Seigel appeared in this version in cameo roles that echoed the earlier film. Look for future director Sam Peckinpah as a meter reader in the basement. Another remake, this time entitled *Body Snatchers,* turned up in 1993. (JMK)

The Invisible Man

Universal, 1933. (71m.) Dir: James Whale. Sp: R. C. Sherriff, b/o novel by H. G. Wells. Cast: Claude Rains, Gloria Stuart, William Harrigan, Henry Travers, Una O'Connor.

On-Screen: *Humor and terror combine in a classic fantasy.* Jack Griffin has a problem. A deluded, overweening scientist, he has injected himself with "monocaine," an Indian drug producing invisibility. To find an antidote in secret, he lodges at an English inn where his peculiar appearance (head swathed in bandages, eyes concealed by dark glasses—all to render him visible) drives the village busybodies to distraction. Unfortunately, a side effect of the drug is galloping megalomania, and soon Griffin has turned into a homicidal maniac with a plan for world domination. After a rampage that includes robbery and murder, a providential snowfall releases him from madness. Although Wells's cautionary point regarding misuse of mankind's godlike potential is retained, an occasionally witty screenplay as well as ingenious camera tricks give the film a curious mixture of playfulness and horror. In his movie debut, Rains is virtually unseen, yet he uses his distinctive voice to both comic and moving effect.

Off-Screen: When Boris Karloff demurred at playing Griffin because of the limited time he would be actually seen, Whale, who had also directed *Frankenstein,* engaged Rains. (Actually Whale was not very keen on Karloff, since he believed that the movie was not in the horror vein.) An odd lapse occurs when we see Rains's shod footprints in the snow; logically, we should see prints of his bare feet. The success of the movie's special effects, achieved by double exposure, masked negatives, and other wizardry, inspired the studio to follow up with other *Invisible* movies, but they lacked the power and poignancy of the original. (CFB)

Ironweed

TriStar, 1987. (C-144m.) Dir: Hector Babenco. Sp: William Kennedy, b/o his novel. Cast: Jack Nicholson, Meryl Streep, Carroll Baker, Michael O'Keefe, Diane Venora, Fred Gwynne, Margaret Whitton, Tom Waits.

On-Screen: *Two derelicts share their grim fates.* An unrelievedly bleak, though not uninteresting, adaptation of William Kennedy's novel (Kennedy himself wrote the screenplay), *Ironweed* casts two pitiable souls into the lower depths of late-Depression America. The time: 1938. The place: Albany. Francis (Nicholson) is a once-prominent baseball player who abandoned his family over twenty years ago after the accidental death of his infant son. Now he is continually haunted by visions of the past. Helen (Streep) is a once-gifted pianist with a troubled past. Both are now destitute and living in an alcoholic haze, clinging to each other for bare survival. In the film's weakest section, Francis returns to his family for one last painful visit, but Helen comes to a tragic end. Nicholson and Streep are both splendid in Oscar-nominated performances, best in their solo scenes (he at his son's grave site, she in a church monologue). In the most memorable sequence, Helen delivers a rendition of "He's Me Pal" at a bar, or at least the rendition she imagines herself delivering. Brazilian Hector Babenco (*Kiss of the Spider Woman*) directs this provocative but utterly depressing film with a keen sense of revealing detail.

Off-Screen: Gene Hackman, Jason Robards, and Sam Shepard were considered early possibilities for the role of Francis. But, according to William Kennedy, "Nicholson had that toughness, that Irishness." Much of the film was shot in Albany over a three-month period. Thousands of residents auditioned for extra roles, and one city councilman even won a small part. Streep's song, a popular 1905 ballad, required eighteen takes. William Kennedy and his wife appear in this scene.

Ishtar

Columbia, 1987. (C-107m.) Dir: Elaine May. Sp: Elaine May. Cast: Dustin Hoffman, Warren Beatty, Isabelle Adjani, Charles Grodin, Jack Weston, Tess Harper, Carol Kane, Aharon Ipale.

On-Screen: *Two would-be songwriters embark on an adventure in North Africa.* Well, there's always the blind camel. One of the legendary disasters in film history (and we don't mean fire, flood, or earthquake, although those might have helped), *Ishtar* tries to recover the antic mood of the old Crosby-Hope "road" movies. No way. Hoffman and Beatty play two wildly untalented songwriters who accept a job in North Africa and find themselves caught up in the civil war raging in Ishtar. Soon, they are the targets of bumbling CIA agents, fiery left-wing terrorists, and others who would like to see them dead. Don't try to follow the incoherent story; concentrate, if you must, on the funny bits: the duo's idiotic songs ("Telling the Truth," etc.), a scene in a marketplace where everyone is an agent, a desert sequence in which Beatty tries to convince a flock of vultures that Hoffman is still alive ("Not dead. Just resting"), and some slapstick moments with that blind camel. The movie's "MacGuffin," as Hitchcock would call it, is a map that "can lose us Ishtar and inflame the Middle East." Favorite line: When a distraught Hoffman tries to leap off a ledge, Beatty reassures him, "It takes a lot of nerve to have nothing at your age." *Ishtar,* however, is a mess.

Off-Screen: The tortuous road that led to *Ishtar* has been described in many an article, especially at the time of the movie's release. Among the off-screen tidbits: The studio thought of over forty titles, including *Blind Camel,* before coming up with *Ishtar.* The production crew found the perfect camel but when they finally returned to buy it, it had been eaten. Throughout the production, no journalists were allowed on the set, not even friends of the stars. Apparently director Elaine May's deliberate pace and frequent takes (more than fifty on some scenes) created serious problems during the filming. And more, much more took place, leading eventually to what is known as "the *Heaven's Gate* of movie comedies."

It Happened One Night

Columbia, 1934. (105m.) Dir: Frank Capra. Sp: Robert Riskin, b/o story by Samuel Hopkins Adams. Cast: Clark Gable, Claudette Colbert, Walter Connolly, Roscoe Karns, Alan Hale, Ward Bond.

On-Screen: *Classic comedy of runaway heiress and earthy reporter.* For her own very good reasons, rich, spoiled, and newsworthy Ellie Andrews (Colbert) leaps from the yacht belonging to her father (Connolly), and swims for the Florida shore. Boarding a New York–bound bus, she stumbles right into the lap of Peter Warne (Gable). A headline-hungry journalist, he stays hot on her trail to get an exclusive story. Their eventful trip is filled with scenes that are now part of movie lore: Gable teaching Colbert the art of doughnut-dunking; a suspended blanket serving as "the Walls of Jericho" when they're forced to share a motel cabin; the pair hitchhiking, as she proves that "the limb is mightier than the thumb." This captivating romp has dated surprisingly little; the characters remain real and the screwball situations are deftly handled in Riskin's screenplay and in Capra's direction. An unalloyed delight, right up to that final trumpet blast.

Off-Screen: Neither star wanted to make the movie. To make its favorite, but balky, son more appreciative of his posh home studio, MGM temporarily exiled Gable to less prestigious Columbia. Though Myrna Loy and Margaret Sullavan, among others, rejected offers to play Ellie, Colbert grabbed the chance to double her per-picture Paramount salary. With this film, Capra, hardly a household name at the time, entered the permanent annals of movie history. The film, based on Adams's short story "Night Bus," won five Oscars, for picture, actor, actress, director, and writer. Though it set back the men's underwear industry for awhile—Gable, stripping off his shirt, exposed a bare chest—it helped boost the budding motel business. *Eve Knew Her Apples* (1945) and *You Can't Run Away from It* (1956) were lackluster remakes. (CFB)

It Should Happen to You

Columbia, 1954. (87m.) Dir: George Cukor. Sp: Garson Kanin, b/o his story. Cast: Judy Holliday, Jack Lemmon, Peter Lawford, Michael O'Shea, Vaughn Taylor, Connie Gilchrist.

On-Screen: *Judy Holliday makes a name for herself.* Judy Holliday's special brand of dumb-as-a-fox charm is well-served in this amiable satirical comedy. She's an aspiring actress who decides to "be somebody" by placing her name on a billboard in New York's Columbus Circle. With the help of a conniving publicity agent (O'Shea), she becomes a media celebrity, much to the annoyance of the photographer (Lemmon) who has come to love her. By now the film's satire is rather lame

and dated, and at times Holliday comes close to being irritatingly dumb rather than innocently beguiling, as intended. But her appeal manages to shine through, and she gets exceptionally strong support from Lemmon in his film debut. His fresh good looks and expert comedy timing mark him as a star-in-the-making. The film's most memorable moment occurs when he joins Holliday in a rendition of "Let's Fall in Love."

Off-Screen: Jack Lemmon thought he was acting well, but every time he began his lines, George Cukor came over to him with emphatic instructions about not going over the top. "Don't you want me to act at all?" Lemmon asked the veteran director. "Ah, dear boy," said Cukor. "You're finally getting it." Many years later, Cukor called Lemmon "a brilliant comedy performer."

It's a Gift

Paramount, 1934. (73m.) Dir: Norman Z. McLeod. Sp: Jack Cunningham, b/o story by Charles Bogle (W. C. Fields) and J. P. McEvoy. Cast: W. C. Fields, Jean Rouverol, Julian Madison, Kathleen Howard, Tommy Bupp, Tammany Young, Baby LeRoy, Charles Sellon.

On-Screen: *W. C. Fields at a comic peak.* One of Fields's best films, *It's a Gift* has the master comedian as Harold Bissonette, a small-town grocer who is constantly abused by his wife, his relatives, and his customers. Out of desperation, he buys an orange ranch in California, which proves to be something of a goldmine. That's the plot—and now you can concentrate on either its hilarious set-pieces or on trying to figure out exactly *why* they should be so funny. One involves a blind man (Sellon), who systematically demolishes Harold's store with his cane (yes, a blind man, and it's still funny rather than tasteless). The other concerns Harold's futile attempts to fall asleep on his porch, highlighted by his mounting frustration with an insistent insurance salesman looking for one "Karl La Fong." Of course there's also Harold's running battle with little Baby LeRoy. For Fields fans, *It's a Gift* is a gift indeed.

Off-Screen: Several of the movie's set-pieces, including the grocery store sketch, the back-porch routine, and a picnic skit, came from Fields's 1925 stage comedy *The Comic Supplement*. Fields also used these set-pieces the following year in the silent film *It's the Old Army Game*. According to Fields's son Ronald, the story that his father spiked Baby LeRoy's milk with gin is true. Fields exclaimed, "The kid's no trouper!" when the groggy tot was removed from the set.

It's a Mad Mad Mad Mad World

United Artists, 1963. (C-154m.) Dir: Stanley Kramer. Sp: William and Tania Rose. Cast: Spencer Tracy, Milton Berle, Sid Caesar, Jimmy Durante, Buddy Hackett, Ethel Merman, Mickey Rooney, Dick Shawn, Phil Silvers, Terry-Thomas, Jonathan Winters, Dorothy Provine, Edie Adams.

On-Screen: *A parade of comedy stars in a madly extravagant movie.* A long, essentially mean-spirited, but occasionally funny movie, Stanley Kramer's gargantuan farce pays tribute to movie slapstick by duplicating every physical gag, every collision, explosion or chase that ever turned up on the screen. Spencer Tracy, of all people, plays a cop who's trailing a greedy horde bent on finding a stash of loot stolen by Smiler Grogan

(Durante). With his last breath, Smiler divulged a clue to its whereabouts, and nearly everyone in the enormous cast of comedians is making a run for his money. By the time the climax is reached, with most of the principals swinging on an extension ladder high above the city, the premise—and your patience—may have been exhausted. Watch for fleeting appearances by Buster Keaton, ZaSu Pitts, the Three Stooges, Jack Benny, and Jerry Lewis, in addition to all the other funsters.

Off-Screen: According to Ernest Gold, who composed the film's score, Kramer's original version of the movie was over five-and-a-half hours long. It was then cut to three hours and forty minutes, but United Artists kept after Kramer to cut it some more, and he did. The first released version, shot in the Cinerama process, ran 192 minutes. According to Gold, "Most of Spencer Tracy's motivation for turning crooked cop disappeared." The movie received six Academy Award nominations, but only one Oscar, for Best Sound Effects. (CFB)

It's a Wonderful Life

RKO, 1946. (129m.) Dir: Frank Capra. Sp: Frances Goodrich, Albert Hackett, and Frank Capra, with additional scenes by Jo Swerling, b/o story by Philip Van Doren Stern. Cast: James Stewart, Donna Reed, Lionel Barrymore, Thomas Mitchell, Henry Travers, Beulah Bondi, Gloria Grahame, H. B. Warner.

On-Screen: *Ordinary Joe learns what might have happened had he never been born.* An ace director and a beloved actor with a boyish crack in his voice bring passionate commitment to this tale of a decent family man in deep trouble. George Bailey (Stewart), a small-town bank manager whose books don't balance, is driven to the brink of suicide by a mean old banker (Barrymore). Just in time, his guardian angel (Travers) shows him how wretched the community would be had he never lived. His kindly mother (Bondi), for starters, would have been a heartless harridan, his loving wife (Reed) a withered spinster, and the town flirt (Grahame) a brazen prostitute. Depending on the extent to which you view Bailey's importance as role model for Bedford Falls, this sugary slice of Americana will either turn your tear ducts on, or turn you off.

Off-Screen: James Stewart almost didn't get to play Bailey. The studio had bought the story, "The Greatest Gift," for Cary Grant, with Jean Arthur as a possible costar, but, happily, Stewart won the role. Years later he said: "[The movie] didn't do well at all. I don't think it was the type of story people wanted right after the war. . . . Our movie just got lost. It was television, years later, that made it a classic." The film, Capra, and Stewart won Oscar nominations, but could not compete with *The Best Years of Our Lives*. Everything you ever wanted to know about this movie can be found in *The "It's a Wonderful Life" Book* by Jeanine Basinger (Knopf, 1986). Don't bother with a television remake called *It Happened One Christmas* (1977). (CFB)

It's Always Fair Weather

MGM, 1955. (C-102m.) Dir: Gene Kelly and Stanley Donen. Sp: Betty Comden and Adolph Green. MS: Andre Previn, Betty Comden, and Adolph Green. Cast: Gene Kelly, Cyd Charisse, Dan Dailey, Dolores Gray, Michael Kidd, David Burns, J. C. Flippen.

On-Screen: *Three wartime buddies reunite in an MGM musical.* A sort of follow-up to Comden and Green's *On the Town* (1949), *It's Always Fair Weather* concerns three soldier friends who meet again a decade after their discharge and discover that they are not so compatible after all. One (Kelly) finds romance with an advertising girl (Charisse). Surprisingly, the Comden-Green book has a rather sourish, dispirited tone, and the incidental satire, mainly of television, dates badly. Good musical numbers compensate, however—the three buddies (Kelly, with Dailey and Kidd) dance exuberantly around the streets of New York; Cyd Charisse has her own sizzling dance number in Stillman's Gym ("Baby, You Knock Me Out"); and Dan Dailey mocks the advertising game in "Situation-Wise." As a gushing television hostess, Dolores Gray gives the movie a needed lift when she sings and dances to "Thanks a Lot But No Thanks." Gene Kelly's roller-skate dance is another highlight. *It's Always Fair Weather* offers ample, if not top-drawer, entertainment.

Off-Screen: Made toward the end of MGM's "golden" musical era, *It's Always Fair Weather* shows signs of the studio's severe budget cuts at the time. Still, it manages to make good use of the wide-screen Cinema-Scope process in sequences that employ split screens and masking within the frame. There were problems with the split screen, since the three cameras had to move at exactly the same speeds to keep the figures from appearing to be jumping about haphazardly.

Jailhouse Rock

MGM, 1957. (96m.) Dir: Richard Thorpe. Sp: Guy Trosper, b/o story by Ned Young. MS: Mike Stoller and Jerry Leiber, and others. Cast: Elvis Presley, Judy Tyler, Mickey Shaughnessy, Dean Jones, Vaughn Taylor.

On-Screen: *Ex-con Elvis hits the musical big time.* Elvis Presley's third movie, *Jailhouse Rock* is generally regarded as one of his best (if not his best), but (pardon the pun) it's no great shakes. At least Presley makes a stab at playing an identifiable human being, but since the character is so bullheaded and obnoxious, there's not much of a gain. He's Vince Everett, a construction worker sent to prison for accidentally killing someone in a bar brawl. He comes out embittered and fights his way to musical stardom, alienating everyone along the way until he's shown the error of his ways. The dialogue is awesomely dumb, Richard Thorpe's direction is clumsy, and Presley's ability to play an ex-con with a chip on his shoulder is less than nil. But then there's the music—a batch of Leiber-Stoller songs ("Treat Me Nice," "Don't Leave Me Now," etc.) rendered by Presley in his most intense, hip-swiveling style, and for many viewers, that should be enough. Best is the production number built around the title song, which at least shows some imagination in the staging.

Off-Screen: Judy Tyler, who played the movie's heroine, had appeared on Broadway in 1955 in the Rodgers and Hammerstein musical *Pipe Dream*. Tragically, she was killed in a car accident in July 1957, not long after finishing the film. *Jailhouse Rock* was rereleased on the day Elvis was discharged from the army.

Jaws

Universal, 1975. (C-124m.) Dir: Steven Spielberg. Sp: Peter Benchley and Carl Gottlieb, b/o novel by Peter Benchley. Cast: Roy Scheider, Richard Dreyfuss, Robert Shaw, Lorraine Gary, Murray Hamilton, Jeffrey Kramer, Susan Backlinie, Carl Gottlieb.

On-Screen: *Don't go into the water!* At night, at the tranquil beach resort of Amity Island, a solitary swimmer is viciously attacked and killed by a shark. With this sequence, skillfully edited for maximum suspense and horror, Steven Spielberg begins the sensational movie that put his name on the movie map. From this point *Jaws* moves into high gear, as Police Chief Brody (Scheider) suspects the presence of a deadly great white shark, but runs into opposition from the cautious, worried mayor (Hamilton). A few more shark attacks convince Brody to bring in a determined shark-hunter (Shaw) and an oceanographer (Dreyfuss) who knows the ways of sharks. Together, in a riveting, nerve-shattering climax, the three engage in a monumental battle with the shark. At heart, *Jaws* is little more than your basic horror movie, with the jolting shocks artfully spaced, but Steven Spielberg's confident direction and Verna Fields's brilliant, Oscar-winning editing make it all seem better than it really is. There's also John Williams's relentless, Oscar-winning score.

Off-Screen: Steven Spielberg insisted that the film be shot on location, and Martha's Vineyard was selected. Three hydraulically operated sharks were created at a cost of $150,000 each. It took thirteen scuba-geared technicians to handle them. Author Benchley appears briefly as a reporter on the beach. The huge success of *Jaws* led to three sequels, none as good as the original. (JMK)

The Jazz Singer

Warners, 1927. (89m.) Dir: Alan Crosland. Sp: Jack Jarmuth (titles), adapted by Alfred A. Cohn from play by Samson Raphaelson. Cast: Al Jolson, May McAvoy, Warner Oland, Eugenie Besserer, Otto Lederer.

On-Screen: *"You ain't heard nothin' yet!"* Yes, but after this movie milestone, the screen could never stop talking again. The first feature film to contain sound sequences, *The Jazz Singer* was a lachrymose tale concerning Jakie Rabinowitz (Jolson), whose deep love for jazz music conflicts with the burning desire of his cantor father (Oland) that he follow in his footsteps. The characters are given to much hand-wringing and eye-rolling, and the titles (the movie is largely silent) are sometimes excruciating ("God made her a woman and love made her a mother!"). Still, audiences in October, 1927, were wildly enthusiastic when Jolson broke into song ("Dirty Hands, Dirty Face," "Toot, Toot, Tootsie") or addressed an emotional monologue to his adoring mother (Besserer). The climax, with Jakie rushing from the theatre to his dying father's bedside, had viewers sobbing. From this time on, silent movies were headed for obsolescence.

Off-Screen: The brothers Warner were unable to get George Jessel to repeat his stage role in *The Jazz Singer* and signed Al Jolson in his place. In later years, Swedish-born Warner Oland played detective Charlie Chan in a series of low-budget features. Look for young Myrna Loy in a brief appearance as a chorus girl. *The Jazz Singer* was remade in 1953, with Danny Thomas and Peggy Lee, and in 1980, with Neil Diamond and Lucie Arnaz. In the latter version, Laurence Olivier played the father.

Jesse James

Fox, 1939. (C-105m.) Dir: Henry King. Sp: Nunnally Johnson. Cast: Tyrone Power, Henry Fonda, Randolph Scott, Nancy Kelly, Brian Donlevy, Slim Summerville, J. Edward Bromberg, John Carradine, Donald Meek, Jane Darwell, Henry Hull.

On-Screen: *The notorious outlaw gets the Hollywood treatment.* Nowhere in this Technicolor Western will you find the true ruthless gunman who left a trail of human suffering as he robbed banks and trains. Instead, Hollywood opted for a purely fictionalized version in which poor Jesse (Power) turns to crime to wreak vengeance on those who were responsible for his mother's murder. Veracity aside, *Jesse James* is a churning, vigorous movie, directed at a fast clip by Henry King. A sequence in which the James boys and their gang ride into an ambush while attempting a bank robbery could stand as a model of its kind. Tyrone Power acts competently, but he is edged out by Henry Fonda as Jesse's laconic, quiet-spoken brother, Frank. *Jesse James* fits handily into the recurring late-thirties theme that a corrupt society breeds criminal behavior. Nevertheless, it survives as one of the better Western films of its day.

Off-Screen: Much of the film was shot in and around the town of Pineville in the Missouri Ozarks. A plain old farmhouse was converted to the James house for the movie. For a while, controversy raged over the film's treatment of the local livestock. The American Humane Society protested against the killing of horses and several hundred prize guineas. On a more positive note for the community, by the time the company left Pineville, nearly a quarter of a million dollars had been spent locally.

Jezebel

Warners, 1938. (103m.) Dir: William Wyler. Sp: Clement Ripley, Abem Finkel, and John Huston, b/o play by Owen Davis. Cast: Bette Davis, Henry Fonda, George Brent, Donald Crisp, Fay Bainter, Margaret Lindsay, Henry O'Neill, John Litel, Spring Byington, Richard Cromwell.

On-Screen: *Bette Davis's second Oscar.* After losing her bid to play Scarlett O'Hara in *Gone with the Wind*, Bette Davis was awarded, as compensation, a very similar role—that of willful Southern belle Julie Marsden in this floridly romantic drama of the pre–Civil War South. Giving it her customary flair and vitality, she won her second Academy Award. The story is really magnolias-and-cotton nonsense: Having alienated her beau (Fonda) by insisting on wearing red instead of virginal white to the Olympus Ball, the tempestuous Julie ultimately finds redemption in sacrifice. But with Davis at the mercurial center of a lavish production, ably directed by William Wyler and beautifully photographed by Ernest Haller, *Jezebel* makes compelling viewing. Fay Bainter won an Oscar as Best Supporting Actress for her performance as Julie's aunt.

Off-Screen: Davis's archrival Miriam Hopkins had played Julie in the 1933 Broadway play and was furious when Davis won the role. During the filming, when the shooting schedule had fallen far behind because of Wyler's insistence on repeated takes—he made Davis repeat the opening shot forty-five times—Jack Warner decided to replace him with another director. Despite her frequent battles with Wyler, Davis insisted that she would leave the film if he was fired. He stayed on. Fonda's role was first offered to Franchot Tone, but he was unavailable. Fonda accepted the role only on the provision that his scenes would be finished in time for his return to New York for the birth of his baby (Jane).

J.F.K.

Warners, 1991. (C-188m.) Dir: Oliver Stone. Sp: Oliver Stone and Zachary Sklar, b/o book by Jim Garrison and other sources. Cast: Kevin Costner, Sissy Spacek, Joe Pesci, Tommy Lee Jones, Jay O. Sanders, Michael Rooker, Jack Lemmon, Walter Matthau, Donald Sutherland, Kevin Bacon, John Candy, Edward Asner.

On-Screen: *On the events and people swirling about the assassination of President Kennedy.* Who killed President Kennedy? Oliver Stone's film, based on unsubstantiated evidence, would have us believe that it was a massive conspiracy involving the C.I.A., the military, the F.B.I., the mob, and even the White House. The chief proponent of this theory, a discredited New Orleans district attorney named Jim Garrison (Costner), is depicted as a valiant seeker of truth, battling against a monstrous cover-up. There are two ways of looking at this film: as a brilliantly orchestrated exercise in special pleading, performed in Stone's hyperbolic style by an impressive cast; or as an irresponsible exercise that offers material that is speculative at best as the gospel truth. (Will future generations at revival theaters regard it as a documentary?) Taken either way, *J.F.K.* proved to be one of the year's most widely argued-over films, either praised or condemned, and one that opened up new discussions of the assassination. In the long run, that may be its most significant achievement.

Off-Screen: Few films in recent years have created such a firestorm of controversy. Many people condemned it vigorously, including Dan Rather, Arthur Schlesinger, Jr. ("a reckless, paranoid, really despicable fantasy"), and Tom Wicker ("heavily weighted storytelling"). Oliver Stone responded just as vigorously to the "thousand and one vultures out there, crouched on their rocks. History," Stone wrote at one point, "may be too important to be left to newsmen." Hollywood usually shies away from honoring films as controversial as *J.F.K.,* but the movie received a number of Oscar nominations, including one for Best Picture. It won two Oscars, for editing and for cinematography. The documented screenplay, plus reactions and commentaries, appear in *J.F.K.: The Book of the Film,* by Oliver Stone and Zachary Sklar (Applause Books, 1992). In January, 1993, *J.F.K.: The Director's Cut* was released on two cassettes. It added seventeen minutes of previously cut material.

Johnny Belinda

Warners, 1948. (102m.) Dir: Jean Negulesco. Sp: Irmgard von Cube and Allen Vincent, b/o play by Elmer Harris. Cast: Jane Wyman, Lew Ayres, Charles Bickford, Agnes Moorehead, Stephen McNally, Jan Sterling.

On-Screen: *Jane Wyman won an Oscar for her incandescent performance as a deaf-mute.* Fans of television's "Falcon Crest" know her as the powerful matriarch, Angela Channing. But Wyman's role in *Johnny Belinda* allows her to display the true depth and range of her acting ability. She plays Belinda, the deaf-mute daughter of a surly farmer (Bickford) on Nova Scotia's bleak Breton Island. Called "the Dummy" by villagers, Belinda is befriended by a kindly doctor (Ayres) who recognizes her mind and heart by instructing her in sign language and lipreading. Raped by the town bully (McNally), Belinda bears a child. When he tries to wrest the child from her protection, the film explodes in a violent climax leading to a heart-wrenching trial. Wyman's most luminous moment: reciting the Lord's Prayer in sign language at her dead father's bedside. Throughout the film, her restrained playing, awarded with an Oscar, helps to keep the heavy sentiment from becoming oppressive.

Off-Screen: Director Jean Negulesco made a personal pitch for the movie after reading the screenplay and finding it "one of the most exciting, human, and colorful scripts I have ever read." Jane Wyman has related that although she closely observed the hearing-impaired for six months to prepare for her role as Belinda, it was wearing earplugs during much of the film's shooting that dramatically brought home to her the feeling of isolation that deaf-mutes experience. Mendocino, in northern California, stood in for Nova Scotia's windswept coast. An updated version of the story appeared on television in 1982. (CFB).

The Jolson Story

Columbia, 1946. (C-128m.) Dir: Alfred E. Green. Sp: Stephen Longstreet; adaptation: Harry Chandlee and Andrew Solt. MS: Various writers. Cast: Larry Parks, Evelyn Keyes, William Demarest, Bill Goodwin, Ludwig Donath, Tamara Shayne.

On-Screen: *Great entertainer Al Jolson sings his heart out in a musical biography.* One of the most popular entertainers in show-business history, Jolson riveted every audience's attention with his flamboyant personality and emotional singing style. He was also known for his arrogance and outsize ego, but the movie takes pains to soften these unpleasant traits. Instead, it trots out a series of hoary clichés about the rise of an entertainer so obsessed with his career that he is deserted by his wife (Keyes, playing a surrogate for Ruby Keeler). The songs, of course, provide the cream, with Jolson himself providing the voice for Parks's credible impersonation. Most of the performer's classic renditions are here, ranging from "My Mammy" to "California, Here I Come," and one, "The Anniversary Song," became a nationwide hit and a staple at anniversary parties for decades.

Off-Screen: When columnist Sidney Skolsky tried to sell a biography of Jolson to the studios, only Columbia was interested. (Studio head Harry Cohn adored the singer.) However, Jolson proved to be something of a problem. Although he was receiving fifty percent of the profits, he insisted on an additional $25,000 for recording the songs. He wanted desperately to play himself, but Cohn offered the role to James Cagney and Danny Thomas, who turned it down. (Thomas refused to change his nose.) Cohn finally opted for contract player Larry Parks, who studied all of Jolson's movies and listened to all of his recordings. Jolson can be seen as himself in a long shot during the "Swanee" number.

Journey for Margaret

MGM, 1942. (81m.) Dir: W. S. Van Dyke II. Sp: David Hertz and William Ludwig, b/o book by William L. White. Cast: Robert Young, Laraine Day, Margaret O'Brien, Fay Bainter, Nigel Bruce, William Severn.

On-Screen: *A displaced war child finds a home.* One of the most gifted child actresses of her generation, Margaret O'Brien created quite a stir when she appeared in this modest but affecting drama as a war orphan finally adopted by an American newspaperman and his wife (Young and Day). Although the story really hinges on Young's conversion from detachment about children en masse to his emotional involvement in the plight of little Margaret and her friend (Severn), it is O'Brien who steals the show with her persuasive acting. The key scene in which she finally releases her long-suppressed tears will surely drench many a handkerchief. Young and Day are competent, but Fay Bainter, as the refugee superintendent of an orphan's nursery, gives a painfully condescending, nobler-than-thou performance.

Off-Screen: Little Ms. O'Brien had made her film debut a year earlier in a small role in *Babes on Broadway* (1941). She had been modeling since the age of three, but MGM recognized her potential as a child star and assigned her to the meaty role in this film. *Journey for Margaret* was based on William White's true experience with a young British orphan named Margaret, whom he adopted in 1940.

Juarez

Warners, 1939. (132m.) Dir: William Dieterle. Sp: John Huston, Wolfgang Reinhardt, and Aeneas MacKenzie, b/o play by Franz Werfel and novel by Bertita Harding. Cast: Paul Muni, Bette Davis, Brian Aherne, Claude Rains, John Garfield, Donald Crisp, Gale Sondergaard, Joseph Calleia, Gilbert Roland.

On-Screen: *A Mexican leader fights for "truth, liberty, and justice."* In keeping with its concern with the spreading totalitarianism in the world, Warners used this elaborate historical drama to express the belief that democracy must be defended. The story of Mexico's Benito Juarez (Muni) and his clash with the forces of Louis Napoleon (Rains) was balanced against the pathetic plight of Archduke Maximilian of Austria (Aherne), who is duped by Napoleon into heading a puppet regime in Mexico. His tragic fate is shared by his wife Carlotta (Davis). Although handsomely produced and well-intentioned, *Juarez* lacks cohesion and dramatic impact, mainly due to its splintered screenplay, which divides the audience's sympathy between Juarez and Maximilian. Muni never breathes fire into his role, but Davis, in what is actually a large supporting role, gets to perform several vivid scenes. Aherne gives the film's best performance as gentle, ineffectual Maximilian. As Juarez's chief aide Porfirio Diaz, John Garfield is patently absurd.

Off-Screen: This lavish production required fifty-four sets, the largest a recreation of a miniature, eleven-acre Mexico on a ranch at Calabasas. Muni could often be difficult, and he insisted on fattening his role even after filming had been completed. This required the cutting of some of Davis's scenes with Aherne. According to John Huston, it also ruined the screenplay. Garfield's Bronx intonations caused concern, and the studio considered replacing him but decided to keep him for box-office clout.

Judgment at Nuremberg

United Artists, 1961. (178m.) Dir: Stanley Kramer. Sp: Abby Mann, b/o his television play. Cast: Spencer Tracy, Burt Lancaster, Marlene Dietrich, Richard Widmark, Maximilian Schell, Judy Garland, Montgomery Clift, William Shatner, Edward Binns.

On-Screen: *German judges are tried as war criminals.* Strong, searing, and, most importantly, a film that has not lost its potency, *Judgment at Nuremberg* recounts the 1948 trial of a group of German judges who were charged with "crimes committed in the name of the law." Abby Mann's Oscar-winning screenplay touches on virtually every aspect of a complex and painful situation (perhaps straining to encompass too much), and an eminent cast plays it out with enormous conviction. Spencer Tracy excels as the presiding judge from Maine, but equally good are Marlene Dietrich as the widow of an executed Nazi general, Richard Widmark as the prosecuting attorney, and Maximilian Schell (Best Actor Oscar–winner) as the defense attorney. Burt Lancaster is not entirely convincing as a distinguished defendant, although he rises to the occasion in his climactic speech to the tribunal. Judy Garland, as a hausfrau at the center of a notorious case, and Montgomery Clift, as a man sterilized by the Nazis, do well in smaller roles. (Both were Oscar-nominated.) *Judgment at Nuremberg* is a flawed but still powerful film.

Off-Screen: Laurence Olivier was originally sought for Burt Lancaster's role, but he proved to be unavailable. (He was in the process of marrying Joan Plowright.) Some of the film was shot on location in Germany, but the Nuremberg courtroom was constructed in exact detail in Hollywood. During the filming, Montgomery Clift's deteriorating physical and mental state made him unable to shoot his scene, until a compassionate Spencer Tracy seized him by the shoulders and assured him that he was the greatest young actor of his generation. Tracy urged Clift to look into his eyes and play to him, to forget the precise lines and express their meaning. Other Oscar nominations included Best Picture and Best Actor (Tracy).

Julia

Fox, 1977. (C-118m.) Dir: Fred Zinnemann. Sp: Alvin Sargent, b/o story by Lillian Hellman. Cast: Jane Fonda, Vanessa Redgrave, Jason Robards, Maximilian Schell, Hal Holbrook, Rosemary Murphy, Meryl Streep, Cathleen Nesbitt, John Glover, Lisa Pelikan.

On-Screen: *Lillian Hellman's story concerning her unusual friend Julia.* In her memoir *Pentimento,* playwright Lillian Hellman wrote about her abiding friendship with a remarkable woman named Julia. Adapted for the screen, *Julia* turned out to be a memorable combination of nostalgic reminiscence, wartime suspense drama, and mystery detection. Jane Fonda plays Hellman, who recalls her happy childhood days with Julia, her relationship with writer Dashiell Hammett (Robards), and, most especially, her harrowing and perilous involvement with Julia (Redgrave) when her friend was dangerously committed to the fight against Fascism in the early days of Hitler. Fonda gives Hellman strength and conviction, but Redgrave, in a much smaller role, dominates the film with an eloquent, beautifully modulated performance. She won an Academy Award as Best Supporting Actress, and other Oscars went to Robards (Best Supporting Actor) and to screenwriter Sargent. Most indelible scene: Lillian and Julia's brief, final meeting in a Berlin café, in which they must both suppress their feelings.

Off-Screen: To prepare for her role as Lillian Hellman, Jane Fonda visited the writer on Martha's Vineyard, sat out a hurricane with her, and learned all the Hellman mannerisms. However, in a later interview, Fonda made the mistake of saying that Hellman was a homely woman who nonetheless carried herself like Marilyn Monroe. Although Fonda meant it as a compliment, Hellman took umbrage and a chill existed between the two women for the rest of the project. *Julia* marked Meryl Streep's film debut.

Jungle Fever

Universal, 1991. (C-132m.) Dir: Spike Lee. Sp: Spike Lee. Cast: Wesley Snipes, Annabella Sciorra, Ossie Davis, Ruby Dee, Samuel T. Jackson, John Turturro, Spike Lee, Lonette McKee, Anthony Quinn, Tim Robbins, Brad Dourif.

On-Screen: *An interracial romance disrupts many lives.* Spike Lee's *Jungle Fever* is one of his best films to date: a pungent if rather over-busy comedy-drama involving an interracial romance between a black married architect (Snipes) and his Brooklyn Italian assistant (Sciorra). Their passionate affair creates havoc among family and friends, including Snipes's indignant wife (McKee) and Sciorra's volatile father and brothers. Lee's screenplay adds too many subplots to the central story, but actually these are the most effective. As Snipes's crack-addicted brother, Samuel T. Jackson gives the movie's best performance, and one sequence, in which Snipes searches for his brother in a crack house, is a waking nightmare. John Turturro is especially good as Sciorra's frustrated, gentle would-be boyfriend, adding a welcome note of reason and common sense to the rampant racial bigotry. The film's pervading tone, however, is harsh and bitter—there appears to be an irreparable division between the races. Snipes's final cry of anguish sums up a striking, troubling movie.

Off-Screen: Spike Lee asserted that the idea for *Jungle Fever* came to him when Yusef Hawkins, a black Brooklyn youth, was shot and killed by white youths who mistakenly thought he was visiting a girlfriend in Brooklyn's Italian neighborhood of Bensonhurst. Lee's first cut had a scene in which Snipes makes a foray into Bensonhurst in the manner of Hawkins, but he decided that the sequence was implausible and deleted it. The movie is dedicated to Hawkins.

Keeper of the Flame

MGM, 1943. (100m.) Dir: George Cukor. Sp: Donald Ogden Stewart, b/o story by I. A. R. Wylie. Cast: Katharine Hepburn, Spencer Tracy, Richard Whorf, Margaret Wycherly, Forrest Tucker, Frank Craven, Audrey Christie, Percy Kilbride, Howard da Silva, Darryl Hickman.

On-Screen: *Journalist Spencer Tracy unravels the dark secret of widow Katharine Hepburn*. Not long after their first teaming in *Woman of the Year,* Hepburn and Tracy reunited for a change of pace: a psychological melodrama laced with a timely warning about the dangers of homegrown Fascism. Hepburn plays the widow of a revered national figure who dies in an accident, and Tracy is the noted journalist who, in spite of her resistance, delves into the man's background and comes up with a shocking surprise about his true intentions. He also finds the widow more than fascinating. A rather pretentious and talky film, with resemblances to *Citizen Kane* and *Rebecca, Keeper of the Flame* manages to work up a fair amount of suspense about the mystery surrounding the great man. As the troubled widow desperately trying to conceal the truth, Hepburn strikes attitudes instead of creating a character, but Tracy is solid as the curious journalist.

Off-Screen: Years later, in Gavin Lambert's book *On Cukor* (G. P. Putnam's Sons, 1972), director Cukor remarked, "The story was basically fraudulent. . . . Hepburn had to float in wearing a long white gown and carrying a bunch of lilies. That's awfully tricky, isn't it? . . . Well, I think she finally carried a slightly phony part because her humanity asserted itself, and her humor. They always did." Cukor also praised Spencer Tracy's believability in "a difficult part." Still, he admitted that the movie had "a waxwork quality."

Key Largo

Warners, 1948. (101m.) Dir: John Huston. Sp: John Huston and Richard Brooks, b/o play by Maxwell Anderson. Cast: Humphrey Bogart, Edward G. Robinson, Lauren Bacall, Claire Trevor, Lionel Barrymore, Thomas Gomez, Jay Silverheels.

On-Screen: *Bogart versus Robinson at a Florida hotel*. This adaptation of Maxwell Anderson's Broadway play retains some of the symbolic intention of the original but concentrates more on the vigorous, Warners-style action. Bogart stars as a disillusioned World War II hero who comes to a decrepit Florida hotel, where he finds he must deal with a brutal kingpin gangster (Robinson). He not only learns that the war was fought to rid the world of hoods like Robinson, but also discovers romance with the hotel owner's widowed daughter (Bacall). Some of the bones of Anderson's morality play shine through (freedom versus corruption or Hitlerism), but most of the movie has the requisite melodrama, with people held at bay, bursts of gunfire, and desperate attempts to escape. As Robinson's boozy mistress, Claire Trevor comes across with a bravura performance that won her a Best Supporting Actress Oscar. (She clinched the award with her singing of "Moanin' Low," rendered in desperation to win her a drink from Robinson.) The movie contains one of the memorable images from the forties: Robinson sitting in a bathtub with a cigar clenched in his teeth.

Off-Screen: John Huston was unenthusiastic about filming the play until Richard Brooks suggested deleting the Spanish Civil War background and changing the villainous gambler in the play into a big mobster. Huston kept putting off rehearsing Trevor's song until one day he simply shot it. An embarrassed Trevor gamely sang "Moanin' Low" and won the Oscar. Her character was modeled on Lucky Luciano's mistress, Gay Orlova. The yacht in the film is called the *Santana,* which was Bogart's name for his own boat.

The Killers

Universal, 1946. (105m.) Dir: Robert Siodmak. Sp: Anthony Veiller and John Huston (uncredited), b/o story by Ernest Hemingway. Cast: Burt Lancaster, Ava Gardner, Edmond O'Brien, Albert Dekker, Sam Levene, Virginia Christine, William Conrad, Charles McGraw.

On-Screen: *Hemingway-inspired tale of violence and vengeance*. This thriller ranks among the best of the *film noir* genre that flourished during the forties—dark, downbeat stories often set in grubby hotels, dingy rooming houses, and sleazy nightclubs (here, Atlantic City's "The Green Cat"). Directed by Siodmak in his customary shadowy, Germanic style, the story explains in a series of flashbacks why a boxer called Swede (Lancaster, in a stunning film debut) holds fast to his sense of personal honor in a corrupt world. As his past is gradually revealed, it becomes clear that his nemesis is Kitty Collins (Gardner), a sexy femme fatale ("I'm poison—to myself and everybody around me!"). O'Brien is an insurance man determined to solve the ugly puzzle involving Swede, Kitty, and Big Jim Colfax (Dekker), a kingpin crook. The beginning of the movie is a superb replica of the original story, complete with Hemingway's menacing, staccato dialogue.

Off-Screen: It's fortunate for Lancaster's career, as well as the movie's effectiveness, that lighter-weight actors Wayne Morris and Sonny Tufts were unavailable to play the tormented ex-fighter. Oscar nominations went to Siodmak, composer Miklos Rozsa, and solely to Veiller for the script he and Huston collaborated on (the latter was under contract to Warners at the time). Fans of the old radio and television series "Dragnet" will recognize Rozsa's often parodied dum-da-da-dum theme later used in those shows. Popular television actor Conrad also made his debut in this movie. The 1964 remake is worth noting only for the last movie appearance of Ronald Reagan, as a crooked big shot. (CFB)

The Killing

United Artists, 1956. (83m.) Dir: Stanley Kubrick. Sp: Stanley Kubrick and Jim Thompson, b/o novel by Lionel White. Cast: Sterling Hayden, Coleen Gray, Vince Edwards, J. C. Flippen, Marie Windsor, Ted de Corsia, Elisha Cook, Joe Sawyer, Tim Carey.

On-Screen: *The anatomy of a robbery, from Stanley Kubrick.* Small but compact, taut, and quite exciting, this early film from director Kubrick (his third) has become a cult classic. It centers on the robbery of a racetrack, carried out by a sleazy group not unlike the men in John Huston's *The Asphalt Jungle*: ex-con Hayden; meek cashier Cook, saddled with a trampish wife (Windsor); crooked cop de Corsia; nasty killer Carey; and an old friend of Hayden's (Flippen). The $2-million robbery takes place, but a combination of bad timing, bad luck, and treachery by Windsor's secret lover (Edwards) does all the gang members in, one way or another. The movie's budget was obviously small, but Kubrick, cinematographer Lucien Ballard, and editor Betty Steinberg create a documentary-like feeling that holds the viewer's attention in a vise. Hayden repeats his *Asphalt Jungle* role, and acting honors go to Cook as a drab, pathetic little

man and Windsor, whose performance recalls the wicked ladies of forties *film noir*.

Off-Screen: After directing *Fear and Desire* (1953) and *Killer's Kiss* (1956), Stanley Kubrick finally won serious critical attention with *The Killing*. Kubrick later admitted that he was influenced by the work of French director Max Ophuls, whose smooth camerawork he emulates. Five years after *The Killing*, Vince Edwards became well-known as television doctor "Ben Casey."

The King and I

Fox, 1956. (C-133m.) Dir: Walter Lang. Sp: Ernest Lehman, b/o musical play by Oscar Hammerstein II, which was adapted from book by Margaret Landon and film *Anna and the King of Siam*. MS: Richard Rodgers and Oscar Hammerstein II. Cast: Deborah Kerr, Yul Brynner, Rita Moreno, Martin Benson, Terry Saunders, Rex Thompson, Alan Mowbray.

On-Screen: *Opulent adaptation of Rodgers and Hammerstein's Broadway musical.* Stunningly produced and richly melodic, *The King and I* does full justice to the long-running stage musical. Deborah Kerr plays the widowed teacher who, in 1862, comes to Siam with her son (Thompson) to teach the many children of the king (Brynner). Liberal-minded and compassionate, she comes into contention with the stubborn king, who is making a groping attempt to learn the new "scientific" ways. Oscar-nominated Kerr (dubbed by Marni Nixon) is radiant as a woman who comes to admire and even love the king, but it is Brynner's legendary, Oscar-winning performance that gives the musical its texture and strength. Torn between two worlds, his fierce but baffled ruler is literally destroyed by the conflicting points of view raging in his mind. Memorable, too, is the score, with such wonderful songs as "Hello, Young Lovers," "Getting to Know You," and "Shall We Dance?" The film won other Oscars for its art direction, costume design, and scoring of a musical picture.

Off-Screen: Director Walter Lang had problems with Yul Brynner, who felt that everything Lang was doing was wrong: "[Brynner] would claim that he was really the picture's director, that I wasn't needed. That without him calling the shots the movie would wind up being second rate." Costar Deborah Kerr had nothing but praise for Brynner: "His imaginative suggestions and instructions were responsible for turning *The King and I* into a great movie. If not for him, it would have wound up being just another pleasant Hollywood musical." One song from the stage version, "Shall I Tell You What I Think of You?" was talk-sung by Kerr but later deleted. (It remained in the LP record of the film.)

King Kong

RKO, 1933. (103m.) Dir: Merian C. Cooper and Ernest B. Schoedsack. Sp: James Creelman and Ruth Rose, b/o idea conceived by Edgar Wallace and Merian C. Cooper. Cast: Fay Wray, Robert Armstrong, Bruce Cabot, Frank Reicher, Sam Hardy, Noble Johnson, James Flavin.

On-Screen: *The original movie Beauty and the Beast*. Generations of moviegoers have been awed by the climax of this classic film: The giant ape Kong strides atop New York's Empire State Building, swiping at planes bent on killing him, while his beloved Ann cowers on the precipice. After six decades, the special effects of *King Kong*, and its primitive but powerful story of a creature destroyed by love, have remained a source of wonder and amazement. Following a desultory opening, the film moves into high gear as an expedition headed by producer Carl Denham (Armstrong) comes to Skull Island. Once the towering Kong comes crashing out of the jungle to claim the beautiful Ann Darrow (Wray), the excitement mounts as he is captured and turned into a pitiable "freak" attraction. Few can forget his awesome rampage against the forces out to topple him from his urban mountain. Carl Denham's summary line, "It was beauty killed the beast!" like Kong himself, has entered permanent movie lore. For many years, pundits have speculated on the film's allegorical meanings, but *King Kong* defies all interpretations to remain a thrilling adventure story.

Off-Screen: Much of the phenomenal success of *King Kong* can be attributed to a special-effects wizard named Willis H. O'Brien, whose "stop-motion" process could bring inanimate objects to life on the screen. Full details on the making of the film, plus critical assessments and speculation on its meaning, can be found in *The Making of "King Kong"* by Orville Goldner and George E. Turner (A. S. Barnes, 1975), and in *The Girl in the Hairy Paw*, edited by Ronald Gottesman and Harry Geduld (Avon Books, 1976). A sequel, *Son of Kong*, made no impact whatsoever later in 1933, and an abysmal remake was released in 1976.

The King of Comedy

Fox, 1983. (C-109m.) Dir: Martin Scorsese. Cast: Robert De Niro, Jerry Lewis, Diahnne Abbott, Sandra Bernhard, Shelley Hack, Tony Randall, Ed Herlihy, Fred de Cordova.

On-Screen: *Would-be stand-up comic kidnaps talk-show host.* Meet Rupert Pupkin—even if you may not want to. Obnoxious and self-deluding, Rupert fancies himself as a master of stand-up comedy, and he's determined to win a spot on the popular late-night television program hosted by Jerry Langford (Lewis). Often moving into his fantasy world of fame and fortune, Rupert finally balks at rejection by kidnapping Langford with the help of a crazed fan (Bernhard). A sardonic reflection on America's obsession with celebrity and the sometimes dangerous consequences of this obsession, Scorsese's film asks the viewer to spend every minute with a man we would ordinarily avoid like the plague, and this may be too much to ask, especially since the material surrounding him, though sometimes pungent, is not especially compelling. De Niro is convincingly repellent as Rupert, and Jerry Lewis surprises with a noncomedic portrayal of a man whose cheerfully manic public image is belied by his lavish but coldly antiseptic home. The ending is intended as massive irony, but it merely leaves you with a feeling of glum disbelief.

Off-Screen: Martin Scorsese's mother plays Rupert Pupkin's off-screen mother, while his brother shows up as a bar patron. Initially, Scorsese wanted Johnny Carson to play Jerry Langford but he declined. Robert De Niro haunted the New York comedy clubs to watch young, undiscovered talent while preparing for his role.

King Solomon's Mines

MGM, 1950. (C-102m.) Dir: Compton Bennett and Andrew Marton. Sp: Helen Deutsch, b/o novel by H. Rider Haggard. Cast: Deborah Kerr, Stewart Granger, Richard Carlson, Hugo Haas.

On-Screen: *The old jungle adventure, smoothly turned.* Richly bolstered by eye-filling on-location photography in Africa, this second version of the Haggard novel is great fun from start to finish—an exciting adventure story with a keen appreciation of its high hokum content. The story is purely conventional: A safari headed by hunter-guide Allan Quatermain (Granger) ventures into the jungle in search of a lost explorer who has been seeking a legendary diamond mine. On the safari is the man's wife (Kerr), whose hostility toward Quatermain ripens into love. All well and good, but with such sights as roaring falls, roaming jungle creatures, breathtaking landscapes, and such events as a battle between two giant Watusi warriors and a wild-animal stampede, who needs a plot? The cast members go through their paces efficiently, but it's the scenery and the action that really count.

Off-Screen: *King Solomon's Mines* was previously filmed in a 1937 British production with Paul Robeson, and it was remade in 1985 with Richard Chamberlain. This 1950 version won Oscars for editing and for cinematography (Robert Surtees). Deborah Kerr had wanted to play Rose in *The African Queen*, but MGM production head Dore Schary cast her instead in this other African tale. The company spent five months in the Belgian Congo in temperatures that ranged from freezing to sweltering. Kerr complained about her perfectly coiffed hair, to no avail.

Kings Row

Warners, 1942. (127m.) Dir: Sam Wood. Sp: Casey Robinson, b/o novel by Henry Bellamann. Cast: Ann Sheridan, Robert Cummings, Ronald Reagan, Betty Field, Claude Rains, Charles Coburn, Judith Anderson, Nancy Coleman, Maria Ouspenskaya.

On-Screen: *A turn-of-the-century town hides its unsavory secrets*. The film begins ironically, with a shot of a roadside billboard proclaiming, KINGS ROW . . . A GOOD TOWN TO LIVE IN. In fact, Kings Row is the setting for some sordid goings-on. Adapted from Henry Bellamann's best-selling novel, the film focuses on Parris Mitchell (Cummings), the young doctor who discovers the ugliness, fear, and repression lurking within the town's neat, orderly houses. Among the people who affect his life are Dr. Tower (Rains), whose promising career was cut short by his wife's insanity; his daughter Cassie (Field), who has inherited her mother's madness; Dr. Gordon (Coburn), a physician with a penchant for performing needless surgery; and the town rake Drake McHugh (Reagan), whose romance with Gordon's daughter (Coleman) is thwarted in a terrible way. Luckily, there's Randy Monoghan (Sheridan), who loves Drake though she's from the wrong side of the tracks. All this melodrama would be heavy going were it not for superior production values, including Erich Wolfgang Korn-gold's melodic score. The cast is exemplary, although Cummings is rather callow as the town's pillar of strength.

Off-Screen: Joseph Breen, head of Hollywood's Production Code office, was horrified even by Robinson's toned-down version of the novel, calling it "a very questionable undertaking." Many changes had to be made before it could be deemed acceptable. Darryl F. Zanuck, Fox studio head, refused to loan Tyrone Power for the Parris Mitchell role; Cummings was borrowed from Universal instead. Bette Davis wanted the role of Cassie, as did Olivia de Havilland, but it was considered too brief for the former and too youthful for the latter. Ida Lupino was asked, but she refused, pleading overexposure in neurotic parts. Even such unlikely Cassies as Priscilla Lane and Joan Leslie were considered before Betty Field was signed. The movie won three Oscar nominations. (CFB)

Kiss Me Kate

MGM, 1953. (C-109m.) Dir: George Sidney. Sp: Dorothy Kingsley, b/o musical play by Sam and Bella Spewack. MS: Cole Porter. Cast: Howard Keel, Kathryn Grayson, Ann Miller, Tommy Rall, James Whitmore, Keenan Wynn, Bobby Van, Bob Fosse, Kurt Kasznar, Carol Haney, Ron Randell.

On-Screen: *Cole Porter's musical* Shrew *from Broadway*. Graced with one of Cole Porter's wittiest scores, *Kiss Me Kate* opened on Broadway at the end of 1948 to wide acclaim and a long run. Transferred to the screen, the show's purely theatrical conceit—a battling divorced couple is appearing in a musical version of Shakespeare's *The Taming of the Shrew*—doesn't work as well. The backstage bickering is rather tedious, and Kathryn Grayson is inadequate as a temperamental diva. (Howard Keel, in fine voice, fares much better as her vis-à-vis.) Still, there are compensations, especially in the shapely form of Ann Miller, who brightens the scene with her dancing. And best of all, there's the splendid score containing such durable gems as "So in Love," "Where Is the Life That Late I Led?" and "Always True to You in My Fashion." (Personal favorite: The bewitching "Were Thine That Special Face.") The most exciting dance number has three couples (including Bob Fosse and Carol Haney) cavorting to "From This Moment On." If not top-drawer, *Kiss Me Kate* is still most entertaining.

Off-Screen: *Kiss Me Kate* was the first Cole Porter musical to retain most of the songs from the original stage version. It was filmed in the 3-D process, but this was dropped after the initial release. (Objects are still thrown at the camera.) "From This Moment On" was first written by Porter for his 1950 stage musical, *Out of This World*. A year after appearing in *Kiss Me Kate,* Carol Haney created a sensation on Broadway in *The Pajama Game*.

Kiss of Death

Fox, 1947. (98m.) Dir: Henry Hathaway. Sp: Ben Hecht and Charles Lederer, b/o story by Eleazar Lipsky. Cast: Victor Mature, Richard Widmark, Coleen Gray, Brian Donlevy, Taylor Holmes, Robert Keith, Karl Malden, Anthony Ross, Mildred Dunnock, Millard Mitchell.

On-Screen: *A "stoolie" confronts the consequences of his actions.* Tommy Udo is a sadistic killer with a maniacal giggle. Cross him, and he'll push your old wheelchair-bound mother down a flight of stairs. As played by Richard Widmark in his movie debut, he's the demonic character who caused a sensation in this vivid crime thriller. The movie is really about Nick Bianco (Mature), a hoodlum who, to keep himself out of prison and near his young daughters, spills the goods on the psychotic Udo. Now he must deal with the revenge-minded killer, which he does in an explosive climax. *Kiss of Death* now seems tame in light of recent gangster films, but it remains a solid movie, filmed in actual locations in Fox's semidocumentary style of the time. By making Bianco a loving family man, the movie avoids dealing with the moral quagmire of the "squealer"—he, in effect, is indirectly responsible for that old lady's plunge down the stairs.

Off-Screen: The original version of the movie had Patricia Morison playing Victor Mature's suicidal first wife. Her role was cut, although she appeared in magazine photo spreads at the time. The film marked the debut of Anthony Ross; it was also Mildred Dunnock's first film after her debut two years earlier in *The Corn Is Green* (1945). Richard Widmark won an Oscar nomination as Best Supporting Actor.

Kiss of the Spider Woman

Island Alive, 1985. (C-117m.) Dir: Hector Babenco. Sp: Leonard Schrader, b/o novel by Manuel Puig. Cast: William Hurt, Raul Julia, Sonia Braga, Jose Lewgoy, Nuno Leal Maia, Herson Capri.

On-Screen: *Political activist and homosexual share prison cell.* Although this movie is of Brazilian origin and is directed by an Argentinian, it was filmed in English and stars two leading American actors. Hurt's brilliant performance, in fact, earned him an Academy Award as Best Actor. The story, which takes place in an unspecified Latin American country, mainly concerns the contrasting personalities of Valentin (well-acted by Julia), imprisoned for antifascist writings, and Molina (Hurt), doing time on a morals charge. The pair are diametric opposites: The macho revolutionary yearns for his girlfriend (Braga); the other, an effeminate movie fan, diverts his cellmate with accounts of imaginary films in which Braga stars. (Acted out on the screen, these fanciful, intentionally kitschy movies provide some welcome comic relief.) The conclusion, a consequence of Molina's political awakening, is both shattering and strangely exhilarating.

Off-Screen: This remarkably faithful adaptation of the widely read novel by Puig, an Argentinian writer, was shot in its entirety in São Paolo, Brazil. Originally, Burt Lancaster was to play Molina, but heart surgery forced his withdrawal from the project. Although Julia expressed interest in that part, Hurt took over the role. In addition to winning a Best Actor Oscar for Hurt, the movie received nominations in the Best Picture, Best Director, and Best Screenplay (Based on Material from Another Medium) categories. (CFB)

Kitty Foyle

RKO, 1940. (107m.) Dir: Sam Wood. Sp: Dalton Trumbo and Donald Ogden Stewart, b/o novel by Christopher Morley. Cast: Ginger Rogers, Dennis Morgan, James Craig, Gladys Cooper, Eduardo Ciannelli, Ernest Cossart, Odette Myrtil, Mary Treen, Nella Walker.

On-Screen: *Ginger Rogers's Oscar as a working-class heroine.* After years as Fred Astaire's partner in a string of memorable musicals, Ginger Rogers turned to playing pert, sensible but inwardly romantic-minded heroines in such comedies as *Vivacious Lady* and *Bachelor Mother.* With *Kitty Foyle,* she tried her hand at emotional drama, and her heartfelt performance earned her an Oscar. She portrays a working-class girl who reviews her life in flashback when she must choose between the Philadelphia scion (Morgan) who loves and marries her, but who clings to his privileged Main Line life, and a dedicated but insolvent young doctor (Craig). Her final choice is not exactly a surprise. The movie has stretches of tedium, but Rogers props it up by giving the sort of sturdy, straightforward performance that characterized her acting in the late thirties and early forties, before she adopted her *grande dame* manner. Best scene: Kitty meets Morgan's snobbish family.

Off-Screen: At first Ginger Rogers rejected the role of Kitty Foyle, claiming that the novel was "highly suggestive and too lurid." An extensive rewriting made it much more palatable to her, and she agreed to play the part. A story about the making of the film appeared in *Life* magazine on December 9, 1940.

Klute

Warners, 1971. (C-114m.) Dir: Alan J. Pakula. Sp: Andy K. and Dave Lewis. Cast: Jane Fonda, Donald Sutherland, Charles Cioffi, Roy Scheider, Dorothy Tristan, Rita Gam, Jean Stapleton.

On-Screen: *A detective, a call girl, and a killer in New York City.* A high-voltage melodrama, *Klute* enhances its standard stalking-killer plot with some in-depth characterization of the principal characters. Jane Fonda stars in a vivid, Oscar-winning performance as Bree Daniel, a call girl who appears to be the next victim of a homicidal sadist. Enter strangely silent detective Klute (Sutherland), whose investigation of a missing friend leads him to Bree. Their growing relationship actually surpasses in interest the pure thriller aspects of the story. For thriller fans, however, there is a suspenseful if rather contrived climax in a deserted garment factory. Fonda creates a rounded character in a girl whose sordid life makes her long for a kind of oblivion ("I'd like to be faceless and bodyless and be left alone.")

Off-Screen: During the filming, some of the crew members viewed Jane Fonda with hostility, hanging an American flag to demonstrate their animosity. As research for the role, she spent a month with $1,000-a-night call girls, and with madams and pimps. "They didn't know who I was," she noted, "because I had cut my hair." Accepting the Oscar to a chorus of applause and boos, Fonda simply thanked those who applauded and said, "There's a lot I could say tonight. But this isn't the time or the place."

Kramer vs. Kramer

Columbia, 1979. (C-104m.) Dir: Robert Benton. Sp: Robert Benton, b/o novel by Avery Corman. Cast: Dustin Hoffman, Meryl Streep, Jane Alexander, Justin Henry, Howard Duff, George Coe, JoBeth Williams.

On-Screen: *Award-winning drama of divorce and its consequences.* An emotionally stirring film, *Kramer vs. Kramer* relates what occurs when advertising man Ted Kramer (Hoffman) is suddenly left by his wife (Streep) and obliged to raise his young son (Henry) by himself. In his Oscar-winning performance, Hoffman displays a perfect blend of exasperation and tenderness as he copes with the needs and demands of a child. An inevitable high point of the film is the custody trial, in which both parents expose their crumbling relationship while trying to assert their rights. Meryl Streep also won an Oscar (Best Supporting Actress) as the wife and mother who leaves to "find" herself, then returns to claim the child she wants so desperately. Scene after scene wrenches the heart, none more so than one in which Hoffman tries to explain to his troubled son why his mother left him. Their embrace in a moment of sorrow and mutual need is deeply affecting. *Kramer vs. Kramer* earns honest tears with its sensitive treatment of a difficult problem.

Off-Screen: The film's producer wanted François Truffaut to direct, but Robert Benton, who wrote the screenplay, insisted that he himself be allowed to make his debut as a director. Reportedly, Hoffman assisted with the rewrites and the editing, while Streep wrote much of her own dialogue. Justin Henry was chosen to play Kramer's son from a field of over two hundred candidates, including forty finalists who screen-tested with Dustin Hoffman. Henry became the youngest person ever nominated for an Oscar. Academy Awards were also bestowed for Best Picture, Best Director, and Best Screenplay (Based on Material from Another Medium).

L.A. Story

TriStar, 1991. (C-95m.) Dir: Mick Jackson. SP: Steve Martin. Cast: Steve Martin, Victoria Tennant, Richard E. Grant, Marilu Henner, Sarah Jessica Parker, Susan Forristal, Kevin Pollak, Sam McMurray.

On-Screen: *Steve Martin's loving, satirical look at the City of Angels.* A romantic comedy that works in spite of itself, *L.A. Story* is also a virtual encyclopedia of Things That Worked in other films of the late eighties: a touch of the supernatural, a large serving of "kookiness" (we used to call it being dumb), a lot of moonlight, a nod to eggheads, and a nice dose of satire. Martin, the "Kookie Weatherman" of an L.A. television station, meets a British reporter (Tennant) at a tony Hollywood lunch (spoofed hilariously). After a few complications, and some cryptic advice from a freeway traffic signal (yes, a traffic signal), boy gets girl. *L.A. Story* is ramshackle, but it has a number of funny situations and witty lines, no malice at all, and a few sly moments that will have you looking twice. (Check the names of a Sausalito motel and that expensive Hollywood restaurant.) Most of all, it has Steve Martin at his most engaging, and an enchanting leading lady in Tennant.

Off-Screen: British director Mick Jackson's only previous movie was a barely seen drama entitled *Chattahoochee* (1990), concerning a man's mental breakdown due to post-Korea combat stress. Steve Martin began thinking of an homage to Los Angeles some years earlier, when he first met co-star and wife Tennant. The name of Martin's character, Harris Telemacher, would suggest a reference to Telemachus, the mythical son of Odysseus and Penelope. Martin insists, however, that the name was completely made up. (BL)

The Lady Eve

Paramount, 1941. (94m.) Dir: Preston Sturges. Sp: Preston Sturges, b/o story by Monckton Hoffe. Cast: Barbara Stanwyck, Henry Fonda, Charles Coburn, William Demarest, Eugene Pallette, Eric Blore, Melville Cooper, Janet Beecher, Martha O'Driscoll.

On-Screen: *Lady cardsharp sets her sights on a millionaire.* One of Preston Sturges's deftest comedies, *The Lady Eve* brims with sparkling dialogue and one-of-a-kind Sturgesian characters. Henry Fonda is the young, cotton-headed millionaire whose only interest is snakes until his shipboard meeting with Barbara Stanwyck, a seductive card-sharp bent on taking his money with the help of her father (Coburn). Love blossoms instead, until Fonda learns the truth and tells her off angrily. Out for revenge, Stanwyck concocts an elaborate impersonation as a bewitching Englishwoman named Lady Eve Sidwich. Her intention: to seduce, marry, and dump Fonda. Of course romance wins out in the end. The fun is not so much in the farfetched premise as in the bursts of inventive slapstick and the twists and the turns of surprising dialogue (Sturges had his very own way of saying things). Most fondly remembered sequence: the wedding night on the train, when Stanwyck confesses about her many lovers to an increasingly horrified Fonda.

Off-Screen: Paramount wanted either Paulette Goddard or Madeleine Carroll to play the leading role, but Sturges insisted on Stanwyck. He had promised her that he would write a great comedy for her someday. Years later, Stanwyck affirmed, "I think there was a great, compatible feeling between Sturges and myself. . . . I loved the script . . . and I had an enormous plus by the name of Henry Fonda." The movie was poorly remade in 1956 as *The Birds and the Bees,* with George Gobel, Mitzi Gaynor, and David Niven.

Lady for a Day

Columbia, 1933. (96m.) Dir: Frank Capra. Sp: Robert Riskin, b/o story by Damon Runyon. Cast: May Robson, Warren William, Glenda Farrell, Jean Parker, Walter Connolly, Ned Sparks, Nat Pendleton, Barry Norton.

On-Screen: *Damon Runyon's fable about "Apple Annie," by way of Frank Capra.* Damon Runyon's raffish, softhearted New York characters have surfaced periodically in movies, notably in *Guys and Dolls.* This adaptation of a Runyon story marked director Capra's first major success. Unabashedly sentimental, it revolves about old Apple Annie, a derelict with a secret: She has a young daughter (Parker) who thinks her mother is a society dowager, and who is now coming to America with her wealthy fiancé (Norton) and his father (Connolly), a Spanish nobleman. Led by top gambler Dave the Dude (William), Annie's friends rally to her side and transform her into a *grande dame* for the occasion. After a few setbacks, the ruse is carried off with the help of city officials. May Robson is wonderful as the salty apple-vendor, and she gets top-notch support from William, Farrell as a brassy nightclub singer, and Ned Sparks as a character whose dour continence and snarling monotone immediately qualify him for the nickname of "Happy."

Off-Screen: Frank Capra's first choice for the role of Annie was Marie Dressler, but MGM's Louis B. Mayer was not about to relinquish his biggest star. Seventy-year-old stage star May Robson was selected. *Lady for a Day* was nominated for Oscars in four categories: Best Film, Best Actress (Robson), Best Directing, and Best Writing. The story was remade by Capra himself in 1961 as *A Pocketful of Miracles,* with Bette Davis as Apple Annie.

The Lady from Shanghai

Columbia, 1948. (89m.) Dir: Orson Welles. Sp: Orson Welles, b/o novel by Sherwood King. Cast: Rita Hayworth, Orson Welles, Everett Sloane, Glenn Anders, Ted de Corsia, Erskine Sanford, Gus Schilling.

On-Screen: *Guillible Irish adventurer is framed for murder.* If you become too absorbed in the Wellesian flourishes—extreme close-ups, overlapping dialogue, abrupt cutting—you'll get lost in this labyrinthine whodunit. Concentrate instead on what is going on between a seductive woman (Hayworth), her crippled husband (Sloane), and his off-the-wall business partner (Anders) who wants to fake his own murder with the help of an easily deceived seaman (Welles). Although the brain-melting puzzles are more or less solved, only Sloane's reptilian lawyer and Anders's effeminate weirdo breathe life into the movie. Welles is improbable as a world-class sap, and Hayworth is stunning as a fire-and-ice enchantress. The brilliantly realized climactic shoot-out in an amusement park's hall of mirrors is worth nearly all the rest of this overheated, but undercooked, *film noir*.

Off-Screen: Welles impulsively had the studio acquire rights to King's 1938 mystery, *If I Die Before I Wake,* only to declare after reading it that it was "horrible." He wrote the adaptation in three days, then learned that studio chief Harry Cohn wanted Hayworth, from whom Welles was legally separated, to costar with the actor-director. (Ida Lupino previously had been promised the role.) To create a new image for Hayworth, Welles had her luxuriant red tresses cut and dyed chromium blonde, which enraged Cohn. Afterward, Cohn stated: "The six people who saw what Orson Welles did to

Rita in *The Lady from Shanghai* wanted to kill him, but they had to get behind me in line." (CFB)

Lady in the Dark

Paramount, 1944. (C-100m.) Dir: Mitchell Leisen. Sp: Frances Goodrich and Albert Hackett, b/o musical play by Moss Hart. MS: Kurt Weill and Ira Gershwin. Cast: Ginger Rogers, Ray Milland, Warner Baxter, Jon Hall, Mischa Auer, Barry Sullivan, Mary Philips.

On-Screen: *A woman fantasizes about her troubled life in this lavish musical.* A 1941 Broadway hit starring Gertrude Lawrence, *Lady in the Dark* intrigued audiences with its mixture of psychoanalysis and musical fantasy. The movie version cast Ginger Rogers as a hard-driving fashion magazine editor haunted by buried memories of the past and confused about the men in her life. The story is basically a variation on the many "boss-lady" comedies of the thirties and forties, but director Leisen submerges it in a series of elaborate production numbers representing the heroine's dreams. The sets and costumes for these numbers—"Girl of the Moment," "Liza's Wedding Day," etc.—assault the eyes with their garishness. Unfortunately, Ginger Rogers is another liability; she looks grim and uncomfortable, even after she discovers that she would rather be a pliant woman than a driven editor. Some of the wit of the Gershwin-Weill score is retained, although the wicked "Saga of Jenny" (who *would* make up her mind) is abridged from the original version.

Off-Screen: A set decorator and art director before becoming a full-fledged director, Mitchell Leisen suggested many of the extravagant costumes designed by Raoul Pene du Bois for *Lady in the Dark*'s dream sequences. Ginger Rogers filmed a version of the crucial, haunting "My Ship," but it was deleted at the insistence of producer Buddy De Sylva. Her rendition of "Suddenly It's Spring" was also cut.

Lassie Come Home

MGM, 1943. (C-88m.) Dir: Fred M. Wilcox. Sp: Hugo Butler, b/o novel by Eric Knight. Cast: Roddy McDowall, Donald Crisp, Edmund Gwenn, Dame May Whitty, Nigel Bruce, Elsa Lanchester, Elizabeth Taylor, J. Patrick O'Malley, Ben Webster.

On-Screen: *Eric Knight's well-loved tale of a boy and his dog.* Shimmering with MGM's most vivid Technicolor hues of the forties, and aglow with the unselfish love of a boy for his dog, *Lassie Come Home* is perfectly unreal—and perfectly delightful. The simple story has Lassie as the devoted dog to an impoverished Yorkshire family (father Crisp, mother Lanchester, son McDowall). Sold to the local Duke (Bruce), Lassie keeps returning home, until she is forced to make her way from Scotland. Her journey is frought with danger and adventure (plus some benign help and a host of heavenly voices), but a badly injured Lassie manages to crawl back to her beloved young owner. Children and adults alike sobbed at his heartfelt "You're my Lassie come home!" Smoothly handled and satisfying, *Lassie Come Home* has the added bonus of featuring little Elizabeth Taylor, radiant in her second movie role, as Bruce's granddaughter.

Off-Screen: By now everyone knows that Lassie was a male dog named Pal, chosen to replace the female dog that was originally cast. Many dogs have played Lassie in subsequent films and on the popular television program. (There was also a radio program.) Elizabeth Taylor had made one minor film for Universal (*There's One Born Every Minute*), after which her contract was dropped by the studio. MGM signed her and launched her long career. Lassie was turned into a horse for a minor 1954 remake called *Gypsy Colt*.

The Last Detail

Columbia, 1973. (C-105m.) Dir: Hal Ashby. Sp: Robert Towne, b/o novel by Darryl Poniscsan. Cast: Jack Nicholson, Otis Young, Randy Quaid, Clifton James, Michael Moriarty, Carol Kane, Nancy Allen.

On-Screen: *Two sailors transport a third to prison.* A ribald comedy, with strongly melancholy overtones, *The Last Detail* contains one of Jack Nicholson's best early performances. He's Billy ("Bad Ass") Buddusky, a career sailor who, along with buddy Mulhall (Young), is assigned to transport young Meadows (Quaid) to naval prison in Portsmouth. Meadows—naive and bewildered—has been sentenced to eight years for stealing forty dollars from a favorite charity of the admiral's wife. Their trip to the prison turns into a movable party, with stop-offs in Richmond, Trenton, New York, and Boston. They drink, brawl, attend oddball religious services, and end up visiting a whorehouse. All the while their pity and affection for Meadows grows, so that turning him over to the authorities becomes a deeply painful matter. Much of *The Last Detail* is raucously funny, with free-flowing profanity, but the feeling persists that these petty officers are leading petty lives, with little or no chance to express their true emotions. As Buddusky, Jack Nicholson gives a sharply etched, Oscar-nominated performance, allowing small glimmers of feeling to surface from that hard-boiled exterior.

Off-Screen: Otis Young replaced Rupert Crosse (*The Reivers*), who was terminally ill. The production languished for a while at Columbia when executives grew suddenly frightened by its extremely raunchy dialogue. Robert Towne, however, refused to change anything, and Jack Nicholson was willing to go along with anything he wanted. Not surprisingly, the Navy would not cooperate with the filming in any way: "We don't feel it's flattering to the Navy." Gilda Radner appears briefly in the church sequence.

The Last Hurrah

Columbia, 1958. (121m.) Dir: John Ford. Sp: Frank Nugent, b/o novel by Edwin O'Connor. Cast: Spencer Tracy, Jeffrey Hunter, Dianne Foster, Pat O'Brien, Basil Rathbone, Donald Crisp, James Gleason, Edward Brophy, John Carradine, Frank McHugh, Ricardo Cortez, Jane Darwell, Anna Lee, Frank Albertson.

On-Screen: *Popular mayor Spencer Tracy runs his last election.* John Ford always adored the Irish—he was the thirteenth child of Irish immigrants—and *The Last Hurrah* is yet another tribute to their lusty, life-embracing ways. Based on the best-selling novel by Edwin O'Connor, the movie records "the last hurrah" of Frank Skeffington (Tracy), the popular four-term mayor of a New England city, whose freewheeling, hands-on style has made him a legion of friends and

some enemies. Skeffington's campaign for a final fifth term ends in defeat, followed by his lingering death, but his mark on his constituency remains indelible. A sprawling, immensely enjoyable movie, *The Last Hurrah* features a choice supporting cast of veteran actors, many of them Ford favorites. As Ditto Boland, Skeffington's loyal, dimwitted aide, Edward Brophy caps a long career with an unforgettable performance. Favorite scene: the wake for disreputable old crony Knocko ("A lovable man. His friends were legion"). Favorite line: Skeffington's last.

Off-Screen: The character of Frank Skeffington was modeled on Boston's longtime mayor, James Curley. Tracy had this comment on the movie: "It was like aspirin to me after a very bad headache. It was just what I needed, the kind of story I'd done before and was comfortable with. And I had a lot of my old buddies in it. . . . It was like an alumni meeting of the Boys' Club from back in the 1930s."

The Last of the Mohicans

Fox, 1992. (C-110m.) Dir: Michael Mann. Sp: Michael Mann and Christopher Crowe, b/o novel by James Fenimore Cooper. Cast: Daniel Day-Lewis, Madeleine Stowe, Russell Means, Wes Studi, Jodhi May, Eric Schweig, Steven Waddington, Maurice Roeves, Patrice Chéreau.

On-Screen: *James Fenimore Cooper's heroic Hawkeye, back on the screen.* A lavish new adaptation of the famous (but now largely unread) novel, *The Last of the Mohicans* is short on subtlety but long on stirring action. The time is 1757, when the French and the English are at war in North America, and American Indian tribes have aligned themselves with the combatants. Daniel Day-Lewis, performing in the old-fashioned tradition of stalwart movie heroes, is Hawkeye, the scout raised by Indians, now bent on defending Cora (Stowe) and Alice (May), the daughters of British officer Munro (Roeves) during their dangerous trek through the wilderness. At first, it is a bit difficult to sort out the various alliances, but soon the story settles into a series of violent, rousingly staged battles between British and Indians, French and British, etc., with a side romance between Hawkeye and Cora as added spice. As the treacherous Magua, Wes Studi, a founder of the American Indian Movement, makes a striking impression, and Russell Means has the proper stoic authority as Hawkeye's adopted father, Chingachgook. On the whole, *The Last of the Mohicans* surprises by making something impressive out of Cooper's old warhorse of a book.

On-Screen: *The Last of the Mohicans* was filmed on location in North Carolina. Daniel Day-Lewis spent a grueling month preparing for his role at the Special Operations Center in Alabama. A number of conflicts developed during the production—the director of photography was fired midway through the project, and the first costume designer quit. To date, there have been four previous versions of the Cooper novel: a silent version made in 1920, directed by Maurice Tourneur; a 1936 adaptation with Randolph Scott as Hawkeye; a loose 1947 version called *The Last of the Redmen*; and a television adaptation in 1977, with Steve Forrest as Hawkeye. This newest version won an Oscar for Best Sound.

The Last Picture Show

Columbia, 1971. (118m.) Dir: Peter Bogdanovich. Sp: Larry McMurtry and Peter Bogdanovich, b/o novel by Larry McMurtry. Cast: Timothy Bottoms, Jeff Bridges, Cloris Leachman, Ben Johnson, Cybill Shepherd, Ellen Burstyn, Eileen Brennan, Randy Quaid, Sam Bottoms.

On-Screen: *Peter Bogdanovich's probing study of intertwining, small-town lives.* In the dusty, eroding backwater town of Anarene, Texas, in the fifties, life appears to be changing forever. Torn between restlessness and lethargy, young and old mirror the town's aimless drift toward oblivion. The school coach's lonely wife (Cloris Leachman) dallies with high-school senior Timothy Bottoms; spoiled, social-climbing tease Cybill Shepherd loses her virginity to Jeff Bridges; Shepherd's mother (Ellen Burstyn) reflects on Sam the Cowboy (Ben Johnson), the past love of her life, who himself represents the death of the pioneer spirit. By the film's end, most of the characters remain caught in the same web of bitterness and regret. Bogdanovich's astute direction, Bruce Surtees's evocative black-and-white photography, and the fine ensemble performances succeed in creating an honest and sensitive portrait of small-town life in the years after World War II and before the tumultuous sixties.

Off-Screen: Cloris Leachman and Ben Johnson both won Supporting Oscars for their performances. The film also earned six other nominations, including Best Picture and Best Direction. Many acting careers were launched or resuscitated with this film. Ellen Burstyn previously acted under the name of Ellen McRae. John Hillerman, who later costarred with Tom Selleck in television's "Magnum, P.I.," appears briefly as a teacher. (CFB)

Last Summer

Warners, 1969. (C-97m.) Dir: Frank Perry. Sp: Eleanor Perry, b/o novel by Evan Hunter. Cast: Barbara Hershey, Bruce Davison, Richard Thomas, Cathy Burns, Ralph Waite.

On-Screen: *A parable of innocence and evil*. At Fire Island one summer, three teenagers—willful Sandy (Hershey) and friends Dan (Davison) and Peter (Thomas)—idly pass the time, swimming, playing games, and tending to a wounded bird. Sexuality hovers in the air, becoming increasingly palpable as time passes. Along comes Rhoda (Burns), shy, lonely, and very vulnerable, who reveals a painful secret from her past. Inexorably, the streak of cruelty in Sandy combines with the overwhelming sexual longings of Dan and Peter, with violent results. Derived from Evan Hunter's novel, Frank Perry's small-scaled and occasionally awkward film is disturbing in its view of the thin line separating innocence and evil, and the four young actors are very good indeed. Cathy Burns is exceptionally moving, especially in a monologue about her mother's death by drowning.

Off-Screen: Three of the young leading players managed to achieve successful careers: Barbara Hershey as the star of *Hannah and Her Sisters* (1986), *Beaches* (1988), and other films; Davison as a stage and film actor, notably in *Longtime Companion* (1990); and Thomas as a star of TV's "The Waltons" and numerous films and television plays.

Oscar-nominated Cathy Burns (Best Supporting Actress) made only one other film appearance, billed as Catherine Burns in *Red Sky at Morning* (1970).

The Last Temptation of Christ

Universal, 1988. (C-163m.) Dir: Martin Scorsese. Sp: Paul Schrader, b/o novel by Nikos Kazantzakis. Cast: Willem Dafoe, Harvey Keitel, Barbara Hershey, Harry Dean Stanton, David Bowie, Verna Bloom, Andre Gregory.

On-Screen: *Powerful, controversial version of the Christ story*. What Scorsese and Schrader achieve in this intensely religious retelling is a sense of immediacy. Avoiding customary biblical-movie piety and pageantry, the film brings to startling life all the grittiness of real people existing at a real time in a real place. To point up the dual nature of Jesus (Dafoe), He is shown as attracted to but unable to love the youthful Mary Magdalene (Hershey). When He rejects her, she becomes the prostitute described in the Scriptures. Dafoe and Keitel, as Judas, are compelling, though most of the cast too often speak in distractingly contemporary Americanese. Christ's agony on the cross, a tempting vision of a happy, mortal life that might have been, is imaginatively, and stirringly, presented.

Off-Screen: Greek author Kazantzakis's book was brought to Scorsese's attention by actress Hershey as early as 1972. Ten years later, the director was ready to make the film for Paramount, with Aidan Quinn as Christ. But the studio yielded to pressure from evangelical groups, and dropped the project. Finally, under the aegis of Universal, Scorsese began once again. Robert De Niro proved unavailable, so the director chose Dafoe, and filming got under way in Morocco. Receiving generally favorable reviews, the movie gained much publicity from picketing groups who protested what they believed to be its irreligiosity. Scorsese received a Best Director Oscar nomination. (CFB)

The Last Tycoon

Paramount, 1976. (C-125m.) Dir: Elia Kazan. Sp: Harold Pinter, b/o novel by F. Scott Fitzgerald. Cast: Robert De Niro, Robert Mitchum, Tony Curtis, Jack Nicholson, Jeanne Moreau, Ray Milland, Ingrid Boulting, Theresa Russell, Dana Andrews, Donald Pleasance, Peter Strauss, Anjelica Huston, John Carridine.

On-Screen: *F. Scott Fitzgerald's tale of power plays and lost love in 1930s Hollywood.* Here's proof positive that a truly impressive cast and a handsome production are not enough to create a superior movie. British playwright Harold Pinter adapted F. Scott Fitzgerald's last novel (unfinished at the time of his death) concerning Monroe Stahr (De Niro), a young, hard-working, and talented film studio head, modelled on MGM's Irving Thalberg, who eventually loses both his all-powerful position and the one true love of his life. Pinter's screenplay conveys much of the frenetic activity of thirties Hollywood, but most of the characters (ambitious second-in-command, temperamental star, frantic writer, etc.) are banal, and the romance between Stahr and his dream girl (Boulting) flattens long before it is ended. The stellar cast works hard to overcome the lulls, with De Niro leading the way in an uncharacteristically subdued performance as Stahr. Jack Nicholson has one strong scene as a Communist labor organizer from the East.

Off-Screen: Mike Nichols was the studio's first choice to direct the movie but he ultimately bowed out. The leading role was offered to Al Pacino, Dustin Hoffman, and Robert De Niro. Pacino said that the script wasn't for him, and Hoffman, though interested, delayed too long in committing himself to the role. De Niro accepted enthusiastically, even agreeing to lose over forty pounds to play the fragile Stahr. Ingrid Boulting is the daughter of Roy Boulting, the British director and producer who formed a team with his brother John to make many notable films over several decades.

The Late Show

Warners, 1977. (C-94m.) Dir: Robert Benton. Sp: Robert Benton. Cast: Art Carney, Lily Tomlin, Bill Macy, Eugene Roche, Joanna Cassidy, John Considine, Howard Duff, Ruth Nelson.

On-Screen: *A private eye and a "kook" are caught up in skulduggery and murder.* What, you may ask, are top-flight comic actors Carney and Tomlin doing in this twisty, clever, and surprisingly violent crime thriller? The answer is very well, thank you. Carney is Ira Wells, an aging detective with many ailments, who teams up with Lily Tomlin's Margo Sperling, an odd woman with a questionable background, to find the culprit, or culprits, in a series of murders. Squarely in the tradition of the old Dashiell Hammett–Raymond Chandler mysteries, the plot gets very complicated as corpses turn up everywhere while Ira and Margo scramble about trying to figure out what's happening without getting killed themselves. The familiar characters are part of the puzzle: the seductive woman (Cassidy) with shady motives, the disreputable clod (Macy) who is a natural-born victim, and all the other figures on the wrong side of the law. It all ends with bursts of gunfire and more dead bodies, but the unlikely hero and heroine manage to survive all the mayhem.

Off-Screen: *The Last Show* was Lily Tomlin's first movie after her debut in *Nashville,* and Art Carney's first since his Oscar-winning triumph in *Harry and Tonto.* Bill Macy played Bea Arthur's husband in the long-running television series "Maude." The Carney-Tomlin combination would seem to lend itself to further Wells-Sperling adventures, but nothing ever materialized.

Laura

Fox, 1944. (85m.) Dir: Otto Preminger. Sp: Jay Dratler, Samuel Hoffenstein, and Betty Reinhardt, b/o novel by Vera Caspary. Cast: Gene Tierney, Dana Andrews, Clifton Webb, Vincent Price, Judith Anderson.

On-Screen: *The elegant veneer of a Manhattan social set masks a world of greed, decadence, and murder.* Still one of the most stylish mysteries to come out of Hollywood, *Laura* is unusual on several counts. The title character (Tierney), a beautiful, successful career woman, is seen mostly in flashbacks or in the large portrait adorning her lavish apartment. Observed or not, her presence is eerily felt throughout the film, as David Raksin's haunting "Laura's Theme" is played repeatedly. Offbeat, too, are the story's three morally seedy members of the upper crust, any one of whom could be the killer. Besides Waldo Lydecker (Webb), the prissy, peevish newspaper columnist and radio commentator who is infatuated with Laura, there's Shelby Carpenter (Price), the effeminate gigolo whose cynical engagement to Laura rouses the jealousy of her aunt (Anderson), Shelby's dominating mistress and former meal ticket. Even the detective (Andrews) assigned to the case is not your typical gumshoe. As he investigates the murder, he comes to be romantically, and rather ghoulishly, obsessed with Laura, whom he's never met. Under Preminger's assured direction, these murky characters and their ambivalent relationships give *Laura* its disturbing *film noir* ambience. But it's Webb, with his patrician bearing and acid-tongued delivery—"I don't use a pen. I write with a goose quill dipped in venom" —who dazzles.

Off-Screen: The movie version of Caspary's 1943 novel was originally conceived as a run-of-the studio release. After Fox chief Darryl F. Zanuck became interested in the property, he quarreled with its director, Rouben Mamoulian, substituting Otto Preminger. Zanuck wanted Jennifer Jones as Laura (Hedy Lamarr was also considered) and Laird Cregar as Lydecker, who was modeled on the well-known theater critic Alexander Woollcott. Preminger, scrapping the scenes Mamoulian had shot, not only cast Tierney in the role for which she is best remembered, but also insisted that Webb, making his sound-film debut, play Lydecker. The actor was nominated for a Supporting Oscar; Joseph LaShelle won the award for his crisply atmospheric black-and-white cinematography. A stage adaptation had a brief Broadway run in 1947. (CFB)

Lawrence of Arabia

Columbia, 1962. (C-222m.) Dir: David Lean. Sp: Robert Bolt, b/o book by T. E. Lawrence. Cast: Peter O'Toole, Alec Guinness, Anthony Quinn, Jack Hawkins, Jose Ferrer, Anthony Quayle, Claude Rains, Arthur Kennedy, Donald Wolfit, Omar Sharif.

On-Screen: *David Lean's epic film on the British soldier who became an Arab leader during World War I.* Magnificent photography, a swashbuckling performance by Peter O'Toole as the enigmatic T. E. Lawrence, and a stellar supporting cast are enough to offset Bolt's turgid screenplay and its sprawling, over-indulgent length. Focusing on the "Arabian" period in his life, the movie traces Lawrence's progress from minor government official to obsessed leader of the Arabs in revolt against the Turks. The film offers some of the finest action sequences ever filmed, especially the storming of a military installation at Aqaba and the Arab army's bloody attack on a Turkish train. White-robed, piercing blue eyes ablaze with fanatical zeal, O'Toole makes the most of a script and direction that hint only vaguely at why Lawrence moved from visionary to collapsed wreck to bloodthirsty monster and finally to a man defeated by duplicitous officials, both British and Arab.

Off-Screen: Over an eighteen-month period, the movie (based largely on Lawrence's autobiographical work, *The Seven Pillars of Wisdom*) was shot in Saudi Arabia, Jordan, Spain, Morocco, and London. Its seven Oscars included Best Picture and Director, and Fred A. Young's spectacular color cinematography and Maurice Jarre's stirring music score. The film was rereleased in 1971, with twenty minutes shorn from its original running time; in 1989, it was released again to theaters, this time in a fully restored version. Damage to the master negative, however, required O'Toole and other cast members to repeat some of their dialogue. (CFB)

Lenny

United Artists, 1974. (111m.) Dir: Bob Fosse. Sp: Julian Barry, b/o his play. Cast: Dustin Hoffman, Valerie Perrine, Jan Miner, Stanley Beck, Gary Morton.

On-Screen: *Ground-breaking film about a controversial comedian.* "You need the deviate!" screamed comedian Lenny Bruce at those who accused him of scatology and pornography. It seems he was right, for almost thirty years after his death, audiences can hear the words he went to jail for saying in the privacy of their own homes, courtesy of cable TV and video rentals. Bruce railed, not just at the police who hounded him, but at the hypocrisy of a system he, paradoxically, never ceased to admire. Bruce's power to shock may be diluted by the passage of time, but this scathingly funny film remains a powerful indictment of pretense. As the tormented, druggy comedian, Dustin Hoffman gives a riveting, manic performance, babbling strings of obscenities one minute and taking on his own defense in court the next. Director Bob Fosse never loses sight of Bruce's humor in portraying the comedian's harrowing quest for vindication. Some still argue that Bruce was a sick man who pandered to America's prurience, but *Lenny* makes a convincing plea for the view that he was unjustly maligned for being well ahead of his time.

Off-Screen: Cliff Gorman, who had played Lenny on Broadway, was considered for the film, along with Ron Liebman and Al Pacino. Other candidates for the role of Lenny's wife Honey were Tuesday Weld, Joey Heatherton, and Ann-Margret. The film received six Oscar nominations: for Best Picture, Best Actor (Hoffman), Best Supporting Actress (Perrine), Best Director, Best Screenplay, and Best Cinematography (Bruce Surtees). It failed to receive an award in any of these categories. (JMK)

Les Girls

MGM, 1957. (C-114m.) Dir: George Cukor. Sp: John Patrick, b/o story by Vera Caspary. MS: Cole Porter. Cast: Gene Kelly, Mitzi Gaynor, Kay Kendall, Taina Elg, Jacques Bergerac, Leslie Phillips, Henry Daniell.

On-Screen: *A Cole Porter musical with a* Rashomon *theme.* Boasting attractive stars, songs by Cole Porter, and an amusing, original premise, *Les Girls* somehow should have been better than it is. Still, while it is lacks the spark of the great screen musicals, it is undoubtedly enjoyable and stylishly presented. The idea is clever: At a slander trial, two former dancers (Kendall and Elg) remember their association (both professional and romantic) with Kelly, the manager of their touring dance troupe, Les Girls. In *Rashomon* fashion, each woman recalls the past differently. In the end, Kelly goes off with Gaynor, the third member of Les Girls. Echoing past endeavors, Cole Porter's

songs are not top-drawer, but several musical numbers permit the cast to shine, and every moment with Kay Kendall is a treat. Kendall, in fact, is the film's greatest asset. A gifted comic actress and a beautiful woman whose untimely death marked a serious loss, she can play a witty sophisticate at one moment and then a low-comedy clown at another. Watch *Les Girls* for her.

Off-Screen: Dancer Jack Cole was in charge of the film's choreography until he became ill during production and was replaced partly by Gene Kelly. The film marked Kelly's last acting job for MGM, and also Porter's last Hollywood score. Orry-Kelly's costumes for the movie won an Academy Award.

Lethal Weapon

Warners, 1987. (C-110m.) Dir: Richard Donner. Sp: Shane Black. Cast: Mel Gibson, Danny Glover, Gary Busey, Mitchell Ryan, Tom Atkins, Darlene Love, Traci Wolfe.

On-Screen: *Two cops team up to break a drug ring.* Fast, furious, and unrelievedly violent, *Lethal Weapon* occasionally succeeds in covering its senseless plot with slam-bang action. After the drug-induced murder of a prostitute, two cops—one (Gibson), a near-psychopathic, suicidal man ("Doin' my job keeps me alive"), the other (Glover) a happily married family man—team up to investigate. Their mutual hostility turns to friendship as their investigation leads to a powerful and deadly drug ring. Except for Gibson's death wish (induced by the demise of his beloved wife), the good cop–bad cop material is familiar, but Richard Donner keeps things moving at a breathless pace. Be warned—the brutality is rampant and excessive, and one sequence in which the cops are tortured is almost unwatchable. Gary Busey, once so impressive in *The Buddy Holly Story* (1978), plays the requisite demented hit man whose showdown fight with Gibson is one of the movie's several climaxes.

Off-Screen: The success of this movie led inevitably to two sequels, *Lethal Wespon 2* (1989) and *Lethal Weapon 3* (1992). Both featured the same mix of violent action and buddy-banter between Gibson and Glover. Joe Pesci scored a hit in *Lethal Weapon 2* as a hustler with a fondness for cops. He turned up again in *Lethal Weapon 3*.

The Letter

Warners, 1940. (95m.) William Wyler. Sp: Howard Koch, b/o play by W. Somerset Maugham. Cast: Bette Davis, Herbert Marshall, James Stephenson, Frieda Inescort, Gale Sondergaard, Willie Fung, Bruce Lester, Cecil Kellaway.

On-Screen: *Bette Davis spins a web of murder and deceit.* From its famous opening scene, with Davis pumping her lover full of lead, to the final moment when she meets her fate, this is moviemaking at its most stylish and compelling. A hard-edged, even savage melodrama, it makes brilliant use of its sultry setting of a Malayan plantation and of the twisted emotions of its charactrers. Often given to placid performances, Marshall is touching as the wronged husband, and Stephenson is fine as the defense lawyer torn between loyalty to friends and self-loathing. Sondergaard makes her blackmailing Eurasian widow both menacing and sympathetic. In the central role of Leslie Crosbie, Davis won a deserved Oscar nomination.

Coolly lying at her trial or cruelly flaunting her infidelity before her forgiving husband ("With all my heart, I still love the man I killed!"), she's magnificent.

Off-Screen: In addition to Davis's, other Academy Award nominations went to the movie, Wyler, and Stephenson, and to Max Steiner and Tony Gaudio for the original music score and black-and-white photography, respectively, as well as to the editing. Gladys Cooper was the mendacious adulteress on the London stage, and Katharine Cornell played her on Broadway. This movie is the second of three film versions of Maugham's drama. In 1929, Jeanne Eagels starred, with Marshall playing her doomed lover. The third came along in 1947 as *The Unfaithful,* with Ann Sheridan. A superfluous television remake appeared in 1982, with Lee Remick. (CFB)

Letter from an Unknown Woman

Universal, 1948. (89m.) Dir: Max Ophuls. Sp: Howard Koch, b/o story by Stefan Zweig. Cast: Joan Fontaine, Louis Jourdan, Mady Christians, Art Smith, Marcel Journet.

On-Screen: *An old-world love story, told with grace and sensitivity.* In such films as *Madame Bovary* and *Gigi,* Louis Jourdan played the jaded lover, not old, but prevented from fully enjoying romance by his own sophistication. Joan Fontaine was often the wide-eyed innocent, blonde and virginal (*Rebecca, Suspicion,* etc.), who comes to realize the horrible truth about her paramour. No such revelation awaits her in Max Ophuls's Hollywood evocation of old Vienna: The love-struck woman she plays dies without revealing her secret, or that of her lover, except through the epistle of the title. Until her death, she adores the man who courted and then deserted her; only then does he understand how cruelly indifferent he was. Under Ophuls's masterful direction, Jourdan gives a rounded performance as the matinee-idol musician. Although too old to portray the heroine convincingly as a gawky, worshipful adolescent, Fontaine matures beautifully into the woman who loves, as the cliché has it, "not wisely, but too well."

Off-Screen: Writer Howard Koch agreed to write the script only if the renowned Max Ophuls would direct. The German-born director had fled his native country after the Reichstag fire and became a naturalized French citizen in 1938. He came to Hollywood in 1941. After this production was ended, studio executives cut twenty minutes from the film, which were restored when all participants registered their indignation. (JMK)

A Letter to Three Wives

Fox, 1949. (103m.) Dir: Joseph L. Mankiewicz. Sp: Joseph L. Mankiewicz; adaptation: Vera Caspary, b/o novel by John Klempner. Cast: Jeanne Crain, Linda Darnell, Ann Sothern, Kirk Douglas, Paul Douglas, Jeffrey Lynn, Thelma Ritter, Connie Gilchrist, Florence Bates.

On-Screen: *Three wives learn that one of their husbands has strayed.* One of the wittiest comedies of the late forties, *A Letter to Three Wives* has an intriguing premise: On a fateful afternoon, three country-club wives (Crain, Darnell, Sothern) learn that one of their husbands has run off with a friend.

During the afternoon, each wife reflects on her marriage, and flashbacks reveal the married status of each couple. Scenarist Mankiewicz offers some pungent observations in the segment involving radio writer Ann Sothern and her teacher husband Kirk Douglas, but the movie's real prize goes to poor girl Linda Darnell and rough-hewn businessman Paul Douglas, two well-matched battlers in the marital arena, whose tough, scratchy relationship provides the movie's best moments. Three cheers as well for Connie Gilchrist as Darnell's earthy mother and Thelma Ritter as her beer-guzzling neighbor.

Off-Screen: Celeste Holm provided the voice of Addie Ross, the woman who runs off with one of the husbands. Originally, a *Cosmopolitan* story had been expanded by its author, John Klempner, into a novel about four wives, but when it was bought for the screen, studio head Darryl Zanuck ordered the deletion of one wife. At first, Zanuck wanted Ernst Lubitsch to direct the film, but Mankiewicz won the assignment that brought him fame and two Oscars for his screenplay and direction. A 1985 television remake sank without a trace.

Libeled Lady

MGM, 1936. (98m.) Dir: Jack Conway. Sp: Maurine Watkins, Howard Emmett Rogers, George Oppenheimer, b/o story by Wallace Sullivan. Cast: William Powell, Myrna Loy, Jean Harlow, Spencer Tracy, Walter Connolly, Charley Grapewin, Cora Witherspoon.

On-Screen: *Bright, bouncy thirties comedy and, with this cast, pure star dust.* Tracy, a New York newspaper editor, mistakenly brands

Loy a notorious home-wrecker. When she slaps the paper with a megabucks lawsuit, Tracy has Harlow, his longtime fiancée, wed Powell, an irresistible ladies' man. The plan is for Powell to play up to Loy, who'll naturally fall for him and thus prove she's a husband-chasing predator. Of course, Tracy's harebrained scheme goes haywire. The dialogue, much of it sounding surprisingly contemporary, crackles. When Loy begs Harlow to give up Powell, telling her she "can't build love on hate or marriage on spite," Harlow snaps, "Why on earth not?" Tracy's desperate newspaperman, Loy's other woman, Powell's suave gigolo, and Harlow's hapless pawn make for a rousing comedy classic.

Off-Screen: Although the movie teams Tracy with Harlow, film buffs will take particular pleasure in watching Powell and Harlow in their scenes together. Powell, nearly twenty years older than the legendary Platinum Blonde, appears to find as much delight in Harlow the woman as he does in Harlow the actress. Their off-screen romance was the talk of Hollywood and often mentioned in the press. They had apparently planned to marry, but Harlow died the following year. The movie was nominated for an Academy Award as Best Picture, but lost to *The Great Ziegfeld,* also with Powell and Loy. Ten years later, the studio remade the film as *Easy to Wed* with Esther Williams, Van Johnson, Lucille Ball, and Keenan Wynn. Technicolor didn't make up the difference. (CFB)

The Life and Times of Judge Roy Bean

First Artists, 1972. (C-120m.) Dir: John Huston. Sp: John Milius. Cast: Paul New-man, Jacqueline Bisset, Anthony Perkins, Tab Hunter, John Huston, Stacy Keach, Roddy McDowall, Ned Beatty, Ava Gardner.

On-Screen: *The notorious hanging judge, with a few new twists.* Three decades after Walter Brennan depicted the real-life Judge Roy Bean as a grizzled rascal in *The Westerner* (1940), Paul Newman takes the hanging judge into the seventies with this iconoclastic and essentially tongue-in-cheek approach. Blending boisterous comedy and Western action with touches of surrealism, John Huston's movie involves Judge Bean over the years in a series of adventures with various colorful characters. The judge still dispenses his own brand of summary "justice" and still worships actress Lily Langtry (Gardner), but that's where the similarity to Brennan's Bean ends. In a curious finale, Bean becomes the champion of the old order, an avenging angel who destroys the trappings of an advancing but greedy civilization. You may be irritated by the movie's playful approach to Western lore, but it's still one of the most striking Western films of the seventies.

Off-Screen: John Milius, who wrote the screenplay, would have also liked to direct but the producer wanted John Huston. Milius was convinced that Huston "ruined it because I don't think he was terribly interested in making the movie." Paul Newman asserted that *Judge Roy Bean* was "one of the best experiences I ever had as an actor." He did believe, however, that the ending was "a problem we never did lick. Maybe it has no ending. But if we had found one, then the picture might have been a serious classic."

The Life of Emile Zola

Warners, 1937. (116m.) Dir: William Diet-
erle. Sp: Norman Reilly Raine, Heinz Her-
ald, and Geza Herczeg, b/o story by Heinz
Herald and Geza Herczeg. Cast: Paul Muni,
Gale Sondergaard, Joseph Schildkraut, Glo-
ria Holden, Donald Crisp, Erin O'Brien
Moore, John Litel, Henry O'Neill, Morris
Carnovsky.

On-Screen: *Famed novelist Emile Zola defends
Captain Dreyfus.* Widely acclaimed in its day
(the *New York Times* called it "the finest
historical film ever made"), *The Life of
Emile Zola* still has considerable merit. Meticulously detailed and elaborately staged,
the film portrays Emile Zola's rise to fame
as a novelist, followed by his passionate defense of the unjustly accused Captain Alfred
Dreyfus and his own embattled day in
court. Zola's trial is the film's best sequence,
vividly conveying the vituperation that as-
sails him from every quarter and his unwa-
vering courage as he braves the mob to
address the court. Dreyfus's plight is also
well-handled, and Joseph Schildkraut, in an
Oscar-winning performance, gives him pathos and dignity. (Evasively, the screenplay
never mentions that Dreyfus was Jewish,
which was, in good part, the reason for his
persecution.) The movie won the Oscar as
the year's Best Picture, and an award also
went to Raine, Herald, and Herczeg for
their screenplay. Muni was nominated but
lost to Spencer Tracy (*Captains Courageous*).

Off-Screen: Paul Muni read everything available about Emile Zola and every word of
the Dreyfus trial transcripts. Through research, he even adopted some of Zola's
gestures and idiosyncrasies. Every day before shooting, he spent over three hours in

the makeup department. (In 1924, when he
was twenty-nine, he had played Dreyfus in
a production by Maurice Schwartz's Yiddish Art Theatre.) Bette Davis asked to
play the role of Nana but was refused.
Dreyfus's son at first was disturbed by the
film, but it turned out that he was more
concerned about the portrayal of the
French military than of his father. He and
Mme. Dreyfus, who was still alive, were
both reassured.

Life with Father

Warners, 1947. (C-118m.) Dir: Michael
Curtiz. Sp: Donald Ogden Stewart, b/o
play by Howard Lindsay and Russel Crouse
and the writings of Clarence Day. Cast:
William Powell, Irene Dunne, Edmund
Gwenn, ZaSu Pitts, Elizabeth Taylor,
Jimmy Lydon, Martin Milner.

On-Screen: *Film version of the long-running
Broadway play.* On the stage for many years,
Life with Father pleased audiences with its
account of Clarence Day's life with his
family (particularly father) in turn-of-
the-century New York. Transposed to the
screen, the Lindsay-Crouse play retained all
of its charm and warmth in an exceptionally
handsome production. William Powell stars
as the crusty, overbearing paterfamilias of
the redheaded Day family, whose household is well-managed by his levelheaded
wife, Vinnie (Irene Dunne). There was
never much plot—Father reveals that he was
never baptized, Mother falls briefly ill—but
the many small, amusing details of the Day
family life made up for the lack of substance.
Dunne is winning, if perhaps a bit arch, as
Mother, and Powell bellows and blusters
with great authority. On loan from MGM,

Elizabeth Taylor appears as a flirtatious young cousin who drives the eldest Day son (Lydon) to distraction.

Off-Screen: William Powell was the unanimous choice to play Father, but many actresses, including Mary Pickford and Bette Davis, wanted to play Mother. Davis even made a test for Michael Curtiz, but the role went to free-lancer Irene Dunne. For the film's initial release, the two stars shared alternate first billing on main titles, publicity, advertising, and theater displays.

Lifeboat

Fox, 1944. (96m.) Dir: Alfred Hitchcock. Sp: Jo Swerling, b/o story by John Steinbeck. Cast: Tallulah Bankhead, William Bendix, Walter Slezak, Mary Anderson, John Hodiak, Henry Hull, Heather Angel, Hume Cronyn, Canada Lee.

On-Screen: *"Hitch," that sly fox, does it again.* A lifeboat adrift in the mid-Atlantic—not much, it would seem, to keep you glued to the screen for an hour and a half. What's more, the movie's "big" moment, the sinking of an Allied passenger-freighter by a Nazi submarine, comes at the very outset. This taut, splendidly acted drama really begins when glamorous journalist Connie Butler (Bankhead) manages to heave herself, her jewels, and her typewriter, aboard the small craft. Joining her are eight more survivors, including, of all people, the captain (Slezak) of the U-boat, which also went down in the attack. The disparate personalities clash and conspire, but the suspense—surprisingly, there's lots of it—arises from the irony that the survivors' fate is in the experienced hands of the Nazi seaman.

Hitchcock-watchers won't have to look hard for the portly director's "bit" appearance: He's in a newspaper ad for a reducing aid.

Off-Screen: When the movie was released (World War II was well under way), Hitchcock and writers Steinbeck and Swerling were surprised by some viewers' objections not only to giving the Nazi the upper hand among the lifeboat occupants, but also to making Hodiak's character, a crew member of the doomed freighter, appear to be a left-leaning liberal. What they overlooked, of course, was that Slezak hardly emerges as the hero of the film, and Hodiak's role represented only one view among the survivors' spectrum of political attitudes. Everyone, though, agreed that the single-set movie (filmed in the studio tank against footage shot in Florida) was a triumph of artistic realism and that Lee's moving recitation of the Twenty-third Psalm was one of the movie's highlights. Hitchcock, Steinbeck, and Glen MacWilliams's black-and-white photography were nominated for Oscars. (CFB)

Lili

MGM, 1953. (C-81m.) Dir: Charles Walters. Sp: Helen Deutsch, b/o story by Paul Gallico. MS: Bronislau Kaper and Helen Deutsch. Cast: Leslie Caron, Mel Ferrer, Jean Pierre Aumont, Zsa Zsa Gabor, Kurt Kasznar, Amanda Blake, Alex Gerry, Ralph Dumke.

On-Screen: *A French orphan joins a carnival.* A beguiling and becomingly small-scaled musical, *Lili* stars Leslie Caron as a wistful, sixteen-year-old French waif who joins a carnival. She becomes friends with the puppets created by Ferrer, who, bitter and crippled, can only express his true feelings, including his love for Lili, through the objects he manipulates. Young Lili has a yen for magician Aumont, but she realizes the truth about Ferrer in due time. Caron is enchanting in her first good role since *An American in Paris,* giving Lili a touching quality that never cloys, and others offer firm support. Although not really very musical—Caron dances in a dream ballet and the puppets sing the hit tune "Hi-Lili, Hi-Lo"—the movie is an agreeable diversion with charm to spare.

Off-Screen: Bronislau Kaper received an Oscar for his music score, and Caron won an Oscar nomination as Best Actress. Other nominations were for direction, writing, cinematography, and art direction (color). In 1961, *Lili* was adapted into the stage-musical hit *Carnival,* starring Anna Maria Alberghetti.

Lilies of the Field

United Artists, 1963. (93m.) Dir: Ralph Nelson. Sp: James Poe, b/o novel by William E. Barrett. Cast: Sidney Poitier, Lilia Skala, Stanley Adams, Dan Frazer, Isa Crino, Francesca Jarvis.

On-Screen: *Black handyman builds a chapel for some nuns.* Sidney Poitier was the first black actor to win a Best Actor Oscar for his ingratiating performance in this small, sweetly sentimental film. He's Homer Smith, a man drifting westward, who comes upon a meager mission at the edge of the Arizona desert run by five nuns who are refugees from behind the Iron Curtain.

Soon, against his will, he is building them a badly needed chapel. There are setbacks and some mild contention between Homer and the mission's tough but warmhearted mother superior (Skala). But (surprise!) the chapel gets built. The nuns in the film are of the standard Hollywood variety—they giggle, chirp, and gape a lot—but the movie has a decency and optimism that will please many viewers. And it's fun to watch Poitier teaching the nuns a "down-home meetin' " song called "Amen."

Off-Screen: Actress Lilia Skala was a stage star in pre-Hitler Vienna. In 1970, *Lilies of the Field* was turned into an unsuccessful stage musical called *Look to the Lilies,* with Shirley Booth as the mother superior. *Christmas Lilies of the Field,* a television sequel with a new cast, appeared in 1979.

Limelight

United Artists, 1952. (145m.) Dir: Charles Chaplin. Sp: Charles Chaplin. Cast: Charlie Chaplin, Claire Bloom, Sydney Chaplin, Nigel Bruce, Buster Keaton.

On-Screen: *Chaplin's "story of a ballerina and a clown."* Chaplin's last creditable film (the inferior *A King in New York* and *A Countess from Hong Kong* followed in 1957 and 1967, respectively), *Limelight* fairly drips with the Victorian sentimentality that permeated his career. The time is 1914, the place London, and Chaplin is Calvero, a once-famous, now alcoholic and forgotten comedian who rescues Terry (Bloom), a despairing young ballerina, from suicide. Inspired by his windy bromides about life, she is cured of her hysterical paralysis and eventually triumphs as a ballet star. Although buoyed by

Terry's love for him, Calvero fails wretchedly at a comeback until his very last performance, when he is received rapturously at a benefit in his honor. Chaplin spreads the pathos with a trowel, asking us at every turn to pity Calvero's plight, but the character becomes wearisome long before the tragic finale. Not surprisingly, the very best moments are Calvero's comic routines, one an act with invisible performing fleas that Chaplin had performed in his music-hall days, and the other his hilarious closing musical sketch in which he is joined by the masterly Buster Keaton. Claire Bloom glows in her film debut.

Off-Screen: Known as *Footlights* in its early stages, *Limelight* was a family affair for Chaplin. His son Sydney appears in a large role as a young composer who loves Terry; another son, Charles, Jr., plays a clown in the ballet; and children Geraldine, Michael, and Josephine can be seen fleetingly as street urchins who watch a drunken Calvero stagger home. A scene in which Calvero shares his dressing room with a famous real-life juggler named Cinquevalli was later eliminated by Chaplin. Dancer Melissa Hayden doubled for Claire Bloom in the ballet scenes. Chaplin's theme for the movie became the popular hit song "Eternally."

The Lion in Winter

Avco Embassy, 1968. (C–132m.) Dir: Anthony Harvey. Sp: James Goldman, b/o his play. Cast: Peter O'Toole, Katharine Hepburn, Anthony Hopkins, Timothy Dalton, John Castle, Jane Merrow, Nigel Terry.

On-Screen: *A squabbling royal family, from the Broadway stage.* "What family doesn't have its ups and downs?" asks Queen Eleanor of Aquitaine (Hepburn) at a climactic point in *The Lion in Winter*. True enough, but how many families could claim patricide, treason, incest, and sodomy as part of their lives? An offbeat but fascinating combination of historical pageant, family drama, and drawing-room comedy, *The Lion in Winter* brings together the family of King Henry II (O'Toole)—his imprisoned wife Eleanor and their three sons (Hopkins, Terry, Castle)—on Christmas Eve in 1183. Detesting or plotting against each other, they bicker over succession to the throne, ending with no resolution but the promise of more battles to come. A witty, stinging screenplay by Goldman, adapted from his play, gives the two leading players, in particular, the opportunity to shine. Hepburn has a fine soliloquy before her mirror, and O'Toole makes a strong Henry II, especially in one anguished review of his life. The stars play off each other in high style ("I could listen to you lie for hours"), and their final confrontation is handled brilliantly. *The Lion in Winter* is not everyone's beaker of ale, but it's intriguing entertainment.

Off-Screen: Katharine Hepburn and Peter O'Toole got along quite well, but on the last day of shooting O'Toole remarked, half-jokingly, "Kate was sent by heaven to make my life a hell." Hepburn read every available book on Eleanor of Aquitaine, even adding many touches to the screenplay. The film was shot in Ireland, Wales, and France. There were frequent setbacks: Anthony Hopkins broke several bones when he fell off his horse, director Harvey became ill with hepatitis, and the changeable weather often played havoc with filming. Hepburn won her third Oscar for her performance, sharing it with Barbra Streisand for *Funny Girl*. Oscars also went to

James Goldman and to John Barry for his score.

Little Boy Lost

Paramount, 1953. (95m.) Dir: George Seaton. Sp: George Seaton, b/o novel by Marghanita Laski. Cast: Bing Crosby, Claude Dauphin, Nicole Maurey, Christian Fourcade, Gabrielle Dorziat.

On-Screen: *A father searches France for his missing son.* Late in his career, Bing Crosby undertook a few roles that contrasted sharply with the happy-go-lucky crooner he had played throughout his career. The first was *Little Boy Lost,* in which he is an American reporter, still in love with his dead wife, who returns to France after World War II to search for his son (Fourcade). Shot on location, the movie convincingly depicts the grimness of postwar France and especially the meager hopes and longings of the war's displaced children. Dismissed as a tearjerker when it opened, the film is, in fact, rather tough-minded in its exploration of the conflicting emotions assailing Crosby. The amiable, laid-back personality the actor usually displayed is at odds with the father's tension, but the conflict works for the role. With his thin, tired face, old beyond its years, Christian Fourcade is intensely affecting as the boy.

Off-Screen: George Seaton was so taken with Marghanita Laski's story that he decided to adapt it himself for the screen. He also believed that Crosby was right for the leading role, although both Laski and Paramount executives insisted that audiences would not find him convincing. Dixie Lee, Crosby's wife of twenty-two years, died during the making of the film. (JMK)

Little Caesar

Warners, 1930. (80m.) Dir: Mervyn LeRoy. Sp: Francis Edwards Faragoh and others, b/o novel by W. R. Burnett. Cast: Edward G. Robinson, Douglas Fairbanks, Jr., Glenda Farrell, Stanley Fields, Sidney Blackmer, George E. Stone, Ralph Ince, William Collier Jr..

On-Screen: *The rise and fall of a kingpin gangster.* One of the two most famous gangster films of the Depression years (*The Public Enemy* is the other), *Little Caesar* still packs a considerable wallop. Although there had been other movies about America's crime lords, none riveted the attention as much as this sordid tale of Caesar Enrico Bandello (Robinson), a mobster whose ruthlessness takes him to the top of the Chicago underworld, and whose arrogance and pride send him plummeting to defeat and death. Edward G. Robinson's performance as the snarling Little Caesar made him a star. (This was actually his eighth film.) Much of the action has the crude, overemphatic style of many pioneer sound movies, but no viewer is likely to forget the final scene depicting Little Caesar's ignominious end, nor his last gasping words. Douglas Fairbanks, Jr. appears as Joe Massara, Rico's closest friend, whose desire to leave the mob triggers Rico's murderous rage.

Off-Screen: Memory clouds over when it comes to claiming credit for discovering and buying the book. Jack Warner, Hal Wallis, and Mervyn LeRoy each insisted that it was *he* who was responsible. LeRoy would have preferred Clark Gable to play the role of Joe Massara, but production head Darryl Zanuck objected to Gable's ears. Many years later, LeRoy wrote that his only objection to Robinson was that he blinked when he fired his gun. He finally had to affix transparent tape to his eyelids.

The Little Foxes

Goldwyn-United Artists, 1941. (116m.) Dir: William Wyler. Sp: Lillian Hellman, Arthur Kober, Dorothy Parker, and Alan Campbell, b/o play by Lillian Hellman. Cast: Bette Davis, Herbert Marshall, Teresa Wright, Patricia Collinge, Charles Dingle, Carl Benton Reid, Dan Duryea, Richard Carlson.

On-Screen: *Bette Davis stars in a film version of Lillian Hellman's play.* A hit on Broadway early in 1939, Lillian Hellman's corrosive study of avarice and corruption in the deep South of 1900 was turned into an equally powerful film. The story revolves about the Hubbards, a vicious family dominated by Regina (Davis), who is married to the ill, submissive Horace Giddens (Marshall). Regina's down-and-dirty battle with her greedy brothers (Dingle and Reid) for control of Horace's money constitutes the heart of the movie. Davis's strong, occasionally mannered performance scorches the screen, culminating in a final fatal clash between Regina and her husband (a sequence that remains a model of filmmaking craftsmanship). Other performances are splendid, especially Patricia Collinge's pitiful, alcoholic wife to Reid. She was recreating her Broadway role, as were Dingle, Reid, and Duryea. Gregg Toland's superb deep-focus photography conveys a sense of the menace lurking in the plush surroundings.

Off-Screen: Bette Davis clashed frequently and bitterly with director Wyler over the interpretation of her role. She wanted to model her performance after Tallulah Bankhead's hard, implacable Regina on the stage, but Wyler encouraged her to add touches that would make her character softer, more human. Davis refused to play it Wyler's way. As Regina's daughter, Teresa Wright made her film debut. *The Little Foxes* received eight Oscar nominations, including Best Picture and Best Actress (Davis), but no awards. The play has been revived several times, once with Elizabeth Taylor; composer Marc Blitzstein turned it into an opera called *Regina* in 1949.

The Little Mermaid

Disney, 1989. (C–82m., animated) Dir: John Musker and Ron Clemente. Sp: John Musker and Ron Clemente, b/o story by Hans Christian Andersen. MS: Alan Menken and Howard Ashman.

On-Screen: *Disney feature concerning a mermaid and her adventures under the sea and on land.* Walt Disney's craftsmen return close to their old form with this delightful animated feature. Loosely based on Hans Christian Andersen's story, it concerns Ariel, a blithe young mermaid, who longs to be human (especially after seeing Prince Erik) and gets her wish for three days. The catch: The wish is granted by Ursula the Sea Witch, who is scheming to take over the undersea kingdom of Ariel's father, King Triton. In exchange for being human, Ariel must also surrender her voice to Ursula. Not to worry—it all turns out happily for everyone except Ursula. As usual, Disney's animal characters—Sebastian the Jamaican crab, Scuttle the sea gull, and others—are much more entertaining than the human figures. The Menken-Ashman songs are lively and tuneful, and two—"Under the Sea" and "Kiss the Girl"—are featured in beautifully animated, imaginative sequences. The funniest section has the crab Sebastian frantically trying to elude Louis, the palace chef, who is determined to catch and cook him.

Off-Screen: *The Little Mermaid* won Oscars for Best Original Score (Alan Menken) and Best Song ("Under the Sea" by Menken and Howard Ashman). Hans Christian Andersen's story was also used as the basis for the ballet with Jeanmaire in Sam Goldwyn's 1952 film *Hans Christian Andersen*. Among the voices used are Jodi Benson as Ariel, Samuel E. Wright as Sebastian, Pat Carroll as Ursula, and Buddy Hackett as Scuttle.

The Little Princess

Fox, 1939. (C-91m.) Dir: Walter Lang. Sp: Ethel Hill and Walter Ferris, b/o novel by Frances Hodgson Burnett. Cast: Shirley Temple, Richard Greene, Anita Louise, Ian Hunter, Cesar Romero, Arthur Treacher, Mary Nash, Sybil Jason, Beryl Mercer.

On-Screen: *A screen "first"—Shirley Temple sings, dances, and emotes in color.* Although her extraordinary gifts were still intact at the ripe old age of twelve, Shirley Temple's box-office draw was starting to dwindle. To boost her popularity, Fox starred her in this lavish Technicolor film, a remake of the novel previously filmed in 1917 with another movie sweetheart, Mary Pickford. It turned out to be one of her best films: a charming Victorian fable about a spunky, resourceful little girl who refuses to believe that her father (Hunter) has died in the Crimean War. She makes some friends, and a few enemies as well, but ultimately, with

the intervention of Queen Victoria (Mercer), no less, she is reunited with her beloved, shell-shocked daddy. Shirley is in top form; she fights back the tears (when she can), sings and dances engagingly to "The Old Kent Road" with Arthur Treacher, and performs in tutu and ballet slippers in a lavish fantasy sequence. She made three more films for Fox, none as good as *The Little Princess*.

Off-Screen: Studio head Darryl Zanuck was so convinced that *The Little Princess* would be a success that he budgeted $1.5 million for the film, twice the cost of her previous film, and scheduled it to be her first in Technicolor. Fox hired little Sybil Jason to play Shirley's Cockney friend, assuming that she was British. It turned out that she was actually born in Capetown, South Africa, and had to be taught how to speak with a Cockney accent. The studio ran *Pygmalion* for her, and soon she was prepared to play the role.

Little Women

RKO, 1933. (115m.) Dir: George Cukor. Sp: Victor Heerman and Sarah Y. Mason, b/o novel by Louisa May Alcott. Cast: Katharine Hepburn, Joan Bennett, Paul Lukas, Frances Dee, Edna May Oliver, Jean Parker, Spring Byington, Douglass Montgomery.

On-Screen: *Louisa May Alcott's classic story lives on the screen.* Those who have only seen MGM's lacquered 1949 version of the novel would do well to watch this enchanting, definitive adaptation. Katharine Hepburn, all quicksilver and girlish enthusiasm, seems born to play the irrepressible Jo March, surrounded by her beloved "Marmee"

(Byington) and her sisters, and finding independence and love with a shy professor (Lukas). Exquisitely photographed by Henry Gerrard and impeccably directed by George Cukor, *Little Women* even manages to make its heavily maudlin and sentimental passages, such as the demise of little Beth (Parker), not only tolerable but moving. Every member of the cast, with the exception of the insufferable Douglass Montgomery, is just fine. Writers Heerman and Mason received a well-deserved Academy Award, and the film and Cukor were also nominated.

Off-Screen: Thrilled to be playing one of her favorite fictional heroines, Katharine Hepburn did thorough research on Louisa May Alcott, family life in Massachusetts of the 1860s, Christmas customs, and the modes and manners of the Civil War. She modeled the character on the maternal grandmother she knew only from her mother's stories. During the filming, Hepburn insisted on having picnics or afternoon teas for both cast and crew. Joan Bennett was pregnant during the filming, and when a strike of sound technicians took three weeks, her dresses had to be remade to accommodate her burgeoning figure. A 1978 television version benefited from the presence of Dorothy McGuire as Marmee and Greer Garson as Aunt March.

The Lives of a Bengal Lancer

Paramount, 1935. (109m.) Dir: Henry Hathaway. Sp: John L. Balderston, Waldemar Young, and Achmed Abdullah; adaptation: Grover Jones and William Slavens McNutt, b/o novel by Major Francis Yeats-Brown. Cast: Gary Cooper, Franchot Tone, Richard Cromwell, Sir Guy Standing, Douglass Dumbrille, C. Aubrey Smith, Kathleen Burke, Akim Tamiroff.

On-Screen: *High adventure with the British in India.* During the thirties, Hollywood's Anglophilic bent resulted in a series of adventure films involving soldiers of the British Empire in heroic deeds against the "heathens." *Gunga Din* (1939) was the best of these films, but *The Lives of a Bengal Lancer* made an impression with its rousing action sequences. Ignore the emphasis on the "white man's burden," and you'll enjoy the story of Lancers McGregor (Cooper) and Forsythe (Tone), stationed in colonial India, and their involvement with a new arrival, the colonel's callow son (Cromwell). Their mission to foil the villainous Mohammed Khan (Dumbrille) leads to a spectacular climax. Aging moviegoers will remember the scene in which the captured lancers are tortured by Mohammed Khan's men. The film won six Oscar nominations, including Best Picture and Best Director, but only assistant directors Clem Beauchamp and Paul Wing received the award.

Off-Screen: After buying the rights to Major Yeats-Brown's book in 1930, Paramount realized that once they extracted the references to polo and mysticism, there was little left. Various writers spent the next five years grappling with the screenplay while background footage shot in India gathered dust. Director Hathaway shot some of this footage himself which he wove seamlessly into the film.

Lolita

MGM, 1962. (152m.) Dir: Stanley Kubrick. Sp: Vladimir Nabokov, b/o his novel. Cast: James Mason, Shelley Winters, Peter Sellers, Sue Lyon, Marianne Stone.

On-Screen: *Comedy-drama of middle-aged man's obsession with teenage girl.* Mason makes Humbert Humbert, a lecture-circuit celebrity who falls madly in love with an adolescent (Lyon), both funny and pitiable. Unfortunately, to make the film version of his novel less shocking for mass audiences, Nabokov was forced to advance the age of the teasing "nymphet" (Lyon) from twelve to full-blooming adolescence, thus blunting the edge of his strangely compelling story. Still, Kubrick's direction is full of surprises (the staging of the violent beginning, for example). Lyon's Lolita is lackluster, but Winters, as her intellectually pretentious, and sex-starved, mother, is so likable that her fate turns out to be the most upsetting event in the movie. The brightest element of all is Sellers' Clare Quilty, the predatory cad-of-many-disguises, who wants Lolita for himself. For many, the movie may prove a more lively experience than the book.

Off-Screen: Paradoxically, the studio decided that the movie, set, like the novel, in America, would be less expensive to film in England, but the locations are not always convincing. Despite the apparent raising of Lolita's age, both Noël Coward and Cary Grant still rejected the role of the child-lusting Humbert. Although Kubrick made radical changes in Nabokov's script during shooting, the author's screenplay was nevertheless nominated for an Oscar. *Lolita, My Love,* a stage musical adaptation, closed during its road tour in 1971. (CFB)

Lonely Are the Brave

Universal-International, 1962. (107m.) Dir: David Miller. Sp: Dalton Trumbo, b/o novel by Edward Abbey. Cast: Kirk Douglas, Gena Rowlands, Walter Matthau, Michael Kane, Carroll O'Connor, William Schallert, George Kennedy, Bill Bixby.

On-Screen: *A misfit modern cowboy meets his fate.* A well-regarded contemporary Western with a point of view, *Lonely Are the Brave* centers on Jack Burns (Douglas), an amiable cowpoke who still rides his horse in a world of automobiles. When circumstances land him in jail, he finds life behind bars unendurable and escapes. Ironically, and all too symbolically, Jack and his horse are struck down by a highway truck. Despite working too hard at its effects and symbols, Dalton Trumbo's screenplay offers a convincing portrait of a man completely at odds with modern society. Kirk Douglas gives a strong, not overly hypertense performance as Burns, and Walter Matthau is sympathetic as the sheriff assigned to capture him. Lest we miss the import of the story, the script has Matthau remarking, "I think we're chasing a ghost." Still, *Lonely Are the Brave* (a meaningless title) is a better-than-average latter-day Western with some affecting moments.

Off-Screen: Kirk Douglas had brought Edward Abbey's novel *Brave Cowboy* to the studio and put up some of his own money to get it made. When the film was allowed to expire after a few engagements, despite favorable reviews, Douglas was angry. He told *The New York Times,* "I don't say they should spend a lot of money on it. Try it in the smaller theaters, in the art houses, so people can see it."

Long Day's Journey into Night

Embassy, 1962. (174m.) Dir: Sidney Lumet. Sp: Eugene O'Neill, b/o his play. Cast:

Katharine Hepburn, Ralph Richardson, Jason Robards, Jr., Dean Stockwell, Jeanne Barr.

On-Screen: *America's great playwright lays bare his turbulent background.* This long but absorbing movie is a faithful transcription of the play that triumphed on Broadway in the fifties. A searing autobiographical drama (the O'Neills become the Tyrones), it takes a troubled new England family through a harrowing day and evening in 1912. Playing against the type of strong-woman roles that characterize her career, Hepburn is heartbreaking as Mary Tyrone, who finds surcease from pain in memories and morphine addiction. As James, her bombastic, miserly husband, a once-famous actor now lost to alcohol, Richardson is even more convincing. No less tortured are young Jamie (Robards), a hard-drinking wastrel, and Edmund (Stockwell), a budding writer haunted by the specter of tuberculosis. Robards, repeating his stage role, is splendid; Stockwell is a bit callow as the young Eugene. Not a happy film, but a powerful and memorable one.

Off-Screen: Because of its sensitive, personal nature, O'Neill specified that his drama, "a play of old sorrow, written in tears and blood," not be produced until twenty-five years after his death, which occurred in 1953. His widow, Carlotta, however, relented and the work was triumphantly produced on Broadway in 1956, with Fredric March, Florence Eldridge, Robards, and Bradford Dillman. The film's interiors were shot in a Manhattan studio, and a large, old house on City Island in the Bronx provided the exterior of the Tyrone/O'Neill residence in New London, Connecticut. Hepburn was Oscar-nominated. (CFB)

The Long Goodbye

United Artists, 1973. (C-113m.) Dir: Robert Altman. Sp: Leigh Brackett. Cast: Elliott Gould, Nina Van Pallandt, Sterling Hayden, Mark Rydell, Henry Gibson, Jim Bouton.

On-Screen: *Famed sleuth of the forties and fifties, adrift in contemporary L.A.* Wisecracking his way through a police interrogation on suspicion of being an accessory to murder, roughed up by hoods employed by a sadistic gangster (Rydell), and pursuing rich but morally bankrupt suspects (Hayden, Van Pallandt), it's business as usual for private eye Philip Marlowe (Gould), right? No way. In this updated—and brilliantly upended—version of the 1953 novel, Chandler's uncorruptible loner is now a frazzled, shambling anachronism. Only when his client and pal (Bouton) betrays him does this Marlowe snap to life, and, in one shocking moment, set matters right. Chandler, who always knew his latter-day Galahad was "out of his time and place," might have well approved.

Off-Screen: When first released, the movie's reception proved disappointing, and it was withdrawn from theaters. Rereleased a few months later, it met with somewhat more success, thanks to rave reviews, word-of-mouth, and some clever advertising. Van Pallandt, a Danish baroness, had figured in the trial of Clifford Irving, whose bogus Howard Hughes "memoirs" caused a stir in the early seventies. Rydell is a film director as well as an actor, and Bouton is the baseball-player-turned-sportscaster. Watch for unbilled appearances by David Carradine as Gould's chatty cellmate, and, as Rydell's muscular hood, a youthful Arnold Schwarzenegger. (CFB)

The Long Hot Summer

Fox, 1958. (C-117m.) Dir: Martin Ritt. Sp: Irving Ravetch and Harriet Frank, Jr., based on stories and novel by William Faulkner. Cast: Paul Newman, Joanne Woodward, Orson Welles, Lee Remick, Anthony Franciosa, Angela Lansbury, Richard Anderson, Sarah Marshall.

On-Screen: *Steamy doings in Faulkner country*. Based on two of William Faulkner's short stories, "Barn Burning" and "The Spotted Horses," and on part of his novel *The Hamlet, The Long Hot Summer* is a florid, over-baked movie. However, in their first film together, Paul Newman and Joanne Woodward do strike some sparks, he as an insolent, smoldering drifter, rumored to be a "barn-burner," who ambles into a Mississippi town, she as the outspoken daughter of the overbearing man (Welles) who runs the town. The lusty Welles covets a grandchild, and when he tries to force a match between Newman and Woodward and dismisses his weak son (Franciosa), there's plenty of heated trouble. Everything happens at a fever pitch, with many noisy or melodramatic confrontations, and none of it has a semblance of life except in some crackling Newman-Woodward exchanges. Welles gives an outrageously hammy performance; his face twisted into a permanent scowl, he appears to be in a black fury that never abates, and after a while you long for him to be off the screen. The climax, involving a barn on fire and all-around reconciliations, is preposterous.

Off-Screen: Although the setting is Mississippi, *The Long Hot Summer* was largely filmed on location in Clinton, Missouri. Paul Newman spent much of his time there absorbing local color and listening for local speech patterns. His performance earned him the Best Actor award as the 1958 Cannes Film Festival. Newman and Joanne Woodward were married in January 1958. The film was remade for television in 1985.

The Long Voyage Home

United Artists, 1940. (105m.) Dir: John Ford. Sp: Dudley Nichols, b/o one-act plays by Eugene O'Neill. Cast: John Wayne, Thomas Mitchell, Ian Hunter, Ward Bond, Barry Fitzgerald, Wilfred Lawson, Mildred Natwick, John Qualen, Arthur Shields.

On-Screen: *John Ford's drama of men at sea—by way of Eugene O'Neill*. Eugene O'Neill's plays have seldom fared well on-screen, but this adaptation drawn from four of his short plays has enough merit to warrant a viewing. *The Long Voyage Home* is a brooding drama concerning the men who are sailing aboard the S.S. *Glencairn*, bound for London with a cargo of explosives. The ship is attacked by a German warplane but makes it to its destination. However, a boisterous pub crawl later brings trouble for some of the men. John Wayne has one of his better early roles as good-natured Swedish seaman Ole Olsen, who dreams of returning home, and other members of John Ford's stock company, including Ward Bond, Barry Fitzgerald, and John Qualen, acquit themselves well. Gregg Toland's superb black-and-white photography obscures the studio sets and accentuates the solemn mood of the film.

Off-Screen: Eugene O'Neill was said to have approved of this film more than any other made from his work. Before the production began, he had met both Ford and author Nichols and had given them his full trust.

Ford gave him a print of the film, which he ran over and over again until it wore out.

The Long Walk Home

New Visions, 1990. (C-97m.) Dir: Richard Pearce. Sp: John Cork. Cast: Sissy Spacek, Whoopi Goldberg, Dwight Schultz, Ving Rhames, Dylan Baker, Erika Alexander, Lexi Randall.

On-Screen: *Civil-rights unrest affects an Alabama housewife.* The time is 1955; the place, Montgomery, Alabama. Fired by the need for change, blacks have inaugurated a boycott of the city's buses, launching "a war of wills in the cradle of the Confederacy." Miriam Thompson (Spacek) is a complacent, well-to-do Montgomery wife and mother whose life is altered forever by the events that transpire. When her devoted maid Odessa (Goldberg) becomes part of the boycott, Miriam's consciousness is finally raised, and defying the racism of her husband and the town, she finally takes her stand with Odessa. *The Long Walk Home* effectively dramatizes some of the frightening and brutal incidents that took place (one involving Odessa's daughter is especially nerve-racking), and director Pearce gets solid performances from Spacek and Goldberg. The movie may have some of the cut-and-dried tendencies of a television movie-of-the-week, but it's a worthy recreation of a difficult time.

Off-Screen: Veteran cinematographer John Bailey began directing this film but was replaced by Richard Pearce due to "creative differences." Sissy Spacek's comment on the movie: "This is not an issue-oriented film. It's a movie about relationships and individuals. The only way we're going to change things, or have any hope of making a dent in the world, is if individuals believe they can make a difference."

The Longest Day

Fox, 1962. (180m.) Dir: Ken Annakin, Andrew Marton, and Bernhard Wicki. Sp: Cornelius Ryan, b/o his book. Cast: John Wayne, Robert Mitchum, Henry Fonda, Richard Burton, Peter Lawford, Red Buttons, Robert Ryan, Eddie Albert, Edmond O'Brien, Jeffrey Hunter, Rod Steiger, Sean Connery, Curt Jurgens.

On-Screen: *An epic-scale recreation of the invasion of Normandy in World War II.* The great battle to break the Nazi hold on France in the Second World War began on June 6, 1944, with the Allied invasion of Normandy. On this monumental day, forces on land, sea, and air converged on the beaches to engage in fierce combat with Germany's entrenched troops. Producer Darryl F. Zanuck recreated this "longest day" with a film of staggering scope and enormous impact. The first part concerns the vast preparation for the invasion of Normandy, and the days of tense, anxious waiting. The pace quickens with the actual invasion, scene after scene offering stunning images of battle: the sky turning white as advance paratroopers descend on the towns below; a German plane, dispensing sudden death as it roars across the men swarming on the beach; the spectacular arrival of the boats on the shore; the fierce battles as precious ground is won and lost, and many others. The enormous cast, which includes many well-known actors in cameo roles, is dwarfed by the panoramic action. *The Longest Day* is long indeed, but well worth the viewing.

Off-Screen: Although Darryl Zanuck gave Cornelius Ryan a lucrative contract to adapt his book, the two men disliked each other intensely and argued frequently. Zanuck secretly enlisted the aid of other authors, including James Jones and Romain Gary. Ryan, however, was instrumental in getting valuable footage of the U.S. Sixth Fleet landing exercises in the Mediterranean, which he used in the film to simulate the D–Day invasion. *The Longest Day* was nominated for the Best Picture Oscar and won Academy Awards for its outstanding special effects and black-and-white cinematography.

Longtime Companion

American Playhouse Films, 1990. (C-96m.) Dir: Norman René. Sp: Craig Lucas. Cast: Bruce Davison, Stephen Caffrey, Patrick Cassidy, Brian Cousins, John Dossett, Mary-Louise Parker, Campbell Scott, Mark Lamos, Dermot Mulroney, Michael Schoeffling.

On-Screen: *The AIDS epidemic devastates a group of gay men.* Insightful, heartbreaking, and frequently witty, *Longtime Companion* traces the impact of AIDS on a close group of gay men in New York City. It begins with casual references to a mysterious illness in 1981 and concludes in 1989 with the shattered men, clinging to each other in their misery, yet affirming their need for each other. While the story is undeniably affecting, the direction is rather awkward, and for a while it's difficult to sort out the characters. But there are a number of touching sequences, none more so than Bruce Davison's tenacious attendance at the deathbed of his lover. The note of fantasy at the end, as all the AIDS victims gather for a joyful reunion, will move you to tears. A noteworthy film on a painful subject.

Off-Screen: After commissioning Craig Lucas to write the screenplay, American Playhouse was unable to find financial backing to make the film. For the first time in its history, it became the sole financial backer of one of its movies. Even after the film was completed, no company could be found to distribute it, until the Samuel Goldwyn Company came along. The film's producer acknowledged that "Hollywood is afraid of AIDS, and they don't know how to handle it or deal with it."

Lost Horizon

Columbia, 1937. (132m.) Dir: Frank Capra. Sp: Robert Riskin, b/o novel by James Hilton. Cast: Ronald Colman, Jane Wyatt, Edward Everett Horton, John Howard, Thomas Mitchell, Margo, Isabel Jewell, H. B. Warner, Sam Jaffe.

On-Screen: *Travelers in Tibet discover a serene, faraway world.* Yes, the theme—in everyone's heart is a longing for Shangri-La, a world without struggle—is simplistic and rather dubious, and yes, Shangri-La resembles a high-price resort hotel with a vaguely Oriental motif. Yet *Lost Horizon* remains a striking and impressive film, beautifully directed by Frank Capra. Mellifluous-voiced Ronald Colman stars as idealistic dreamer Robert Conway, who, escaping from war-torn China with four other travelers, is brought to Shangri-La, a place of perfect peace and harmony in the remote, snowy wastes of Tibet. All but one of the travelers find contentment, and Conway finds love and his life's purpose. *Lost Horizon* has no more profundity than proverbs stitched on a sampler ("Be kind," the High Lama tells Conway, "the one simple rule of Shangri-La"), but viewers will no doubt continue to fall under its spell, as they did in the Depression years.

Off-Screen: Ronald Colman was always Capra's first choice to play Conway, but when Colman hesitated too long in accepting, Capra almost signed Brian Aherne. In recent years, the film has been restored to its original length, although several scenes are still missing and are represented only by stills. Broadway actor Sam Jaffe, aged thirty-eight, was cast as the two-hundred-year-old High Lama only after several other candidates had died. After a disastrous preview in Santa Barbara, at which the audience howled with laughter, Capra decided to discard the first two reels. From then on, the film was a huge success and a nominee for the Best Picture Oscar. It won Oscars for art direction and film editing. *Shangri-La,* a stage-musical version, failed in 1956, and there was a wretched movie-musical adaptation in 1973.

The Lost Weekend

Paramount, 1945. (101m.) Dir: Billy Wilder. Sp: Charles Brackett and Billy Wilder, b/o novel by Charles Jackson. Cast: Ray Milland, Jane Wyman, Philip Terry, Howard da Silva, Doris Dowling, Frank Faylen, Mary Young.

On-Screen: *Oscar-winning drama of an alcoholic writer.* Known for years as a lightweight actor of debonair and romantic roles, Ray Milland switched gears for this harrowing film on the perils of excessive drinking and won a well-deserved Oscar. He's Don Birnam ("Boinam" to sympathetic bartender da Silva), a writer who turns to liquor when his creative juices cease to flow. He tumbles into a nightmare world of desperation and degradation, a ravaged man who cannot be helped by the love of his fiancée (Wyman) or the ministrations of his brother (Terry). Today much of the movie seems contrived but it does present an unsparing view of the hell-bent drunkard, a character seldom covered in films except as a source of humor. The most memorable scene: Birnam has a hallucination in which a bat attacks and kills a squealing mouse, and the mouse's blood stains the wall of his room. Second best performance: Frank Faylen as a vicious male nurse in the alcoholic ward. Despite its flaws, a one-of-a-kind landmark.

Off-Screen: Billy Wilder had great difficulty getting Paramount to agree to do this film. To make the story more palatable, Brackett and Wilder wrote in a love interest and changed Don Birnam's hang-up from latent homosexuality to writer's block. The liquor industry was not eager to have the movie released, and reportedly offered to pay the studio millions of dollars for the negative. For the film, the New York saloon P. J. Clarke's was reconstructed to the last detail on a studio lot. In addition to Milland's award, Oscars also went to the film, Wilder (direction), and Brackett and Wilder (screenplay).

Love Affair

RKO, 1939. (87m.) Dir: Leo McCarey. Sp: Delmer Daves and Donald Ogden Stewart, b/o story by Mildred Cram and Leo McCarey. Cast: Irene Dunne, Charles Boyer, Maria Ouspenskaya, Lee Bowman, Astrid Allwyn, Maurice Moscovich.

On-Screen: *Two people share a tender shipboard romance.* A nightclub singer (Dunne) and a debonair playboy (Boyer), meeting on an ocean voyage and engaged to other people, fall deeply in love and promise to meet again six months later. Tragedy intervenes, but the two are finally reunited. On this frail premise, *Love Affair* builds a delightful, well-remembered love story. The first part is played as airy comedy, as Dunne and Boyer banter or exchange confidences with artful ease. Midway, the film leaves comedy behind and moves into sentimental drama that works only if a viewer is inclined to suspend disbelief. Still, Dunne and Boyer make a fine team, and their scenes together, especially a long, languid sequence with Boyer's grandmother (Ouspenskaya) in Madeira, are performed with skill and conviction.

Off-Screen: Donald Ogden Stewart received coauthor credit, but he actually worked mainly on the early shipboard sequences. In keeping with his improvisational style, director McCarey made daily changes in the script, embellishing some parts and abandoning others. The movie won a number of Oscar nominations, including one for Best Picture, but received no awards. The story was recycled in 1957 as *An Affair to Remember,* with Cary Grant and Deborah Kerr in the leading roles and Leo McCarey again in the director's chair. A second remake stars Warren Beatty and Annette Bening.

Love and Death

United Artists, 1975. (C–82m.) Dir: Woody Allen. Sp: Woody Allen. Cast: Woody Allen, Diane Keaton, Harold Gould, Alfred Lutter, Olga Georges-Picot, Zvee Scooler, C. A. R. Smith.

On-Screen: *Woody Allen takes on Russian literature.* One of Allen's least-known, yet most inventive, comedies, *Love and Death* is not only a spoof of classic Russian novels but also a tribute to great foreign filmmakers from Eisenstein to Bergman. Allen plays a cowardly, bookish young Russian named Boris who lives through the Napoleonic Wars, only to be executed for killing Napoleon. (Well, not really, but the charge remains.) Narrating the story from his prison cell, Boris relates his experiences on the battlefield, his unrequited love for his cousin Sonia (Keaton), and his collusion with Sonia in the plan to assassinate Napoleon. Outrageous—and often hilarious—anachronisms abound: blinis are hawked during battle, a black drill sergeant badgers poor Boris, etc. Allen also pokes fun at the agonized soul-searchings and dense philosophical discussions prevalent in Russian literature. Other characters include Boris's dim-bulb father (Scooler), who owns a plot of land a few inches wide and hopes to build on it someday, and a priest (Smith) who dresses entirely in black (Boris: "For years I thought he was an Italian widow").

Off-Screen: Locations in and around Budapest and Paris were used to evoke nineteenth-century Russia. In Budapest, the company filmed at the famed Opera House and on Castle Hill around the old castle of Franz Joseph, Emperor of Austria and King of Hungary. In Paris, locations included the Old Russian Church on the Rue des Russes and a thatched Russian cottage (Chaumière Russe) at Les Mesnuls.

Love Finds Andy Hardy

MGM, 1938. (90m.) Dir: George B. Seitz. Sp; William Ludwig, b/o stories by Vivien

R. Bretherton and characters created by Aurania Rouverol. Cast: Mickey Rooney, Judy Garland, Lewis Stone, Cecilia Parker, Ann Rutherford, Lana Turner, Fay Holden, Don Castle, Gene Reynolds, Marie Blake.

On-Screen: *America's perennial teenager has romantic problems*. In the late thirties and through much of the forties, filmgoers embraced MGM's movie family the Hardys, especially the assertive, energetic Hardy son, Andy (Rooney). In that more innocent era, viewers liked to think of him and his stern but loving father, Judge Hardy (Stone), as typical Americans. The series not only prospered but also became the springboard for the careers of Lana Turner (seen here as a redheaded tease), Kathryn Grayson, Esther Williams, and other MGM starlets. *Love Finds Andy Hardy* is one of the more tolerable entries in the series, mainly because it features Judy Garland as a visitor to Andy's hometown of Carvel. Her memorable first lines are "Hello! I'm Betsy Booth. I *sing*, you know!" And she does, three times. She appeared in two more Hardy films, usually hovering wistfully in the background as Andy fumed about his none-too-earthshaking dilemmas.

Off-Screen: The fourth entry in the series (there were sixteen in all), *Love Finds Andy Hardy* brought Rooney and Garland together after they had appeared in a minor horse-racing movie called *Thoroughbreds Don't Cry* (1938). They were both in between assignments at the studio. For a while MGM considered changing the title, but Rooney's soaring popularity convinced them to keep the emphasis on Andy.

Love in the Afternoon

Allied Artists, 1957. (130m.) Dir: Billy Wilder. Sp: Billy Wilder and I. A. L. Diamond, b/o novel by Claude Anet. Cast: Audrey Hepburn, Gary Cooper, Maurice Chevalier, John McGiver.

On-Screen: *An aging roué falls in love with a detective's daughter*. The setting: Paris. Gary Cooper is a bored American plutocrat who routinely seduces women to the strains of "Fascination." Audrey Hepburn is a cello-playing gamine. When she bursts into Cooper's hotel room to warn him of an approaching jealous husband bent on mayhem, he is entranced and mystified by the girl's elusiveness and her stories about legions of admirers. Unknowingly, he hires Hepburn's detective father (Chevalier) to find out who she really is. His attempts at seduction inevitably give way to true romantic feeling. Cooper was fifty-three at the time, and Hepburn twenty-eight, and although the age difference is noted in the script, it still strains credulity to see them together. This caveat aside, the film has all the hallmarks of a Billy Wilder comedy: cynicism, sophistication, and biting wit, with more than a touch of Lubitsch-style sexual innuendo thrown in for spice.

Off-Screen: Billy Wilder's first choices for the male lead were Cary Grant and Yul Brynner; he settled on Cooper when both were unavailable. To soften Cooper's aging visage, gauzy filters were used, and his face was often photographed in shadow, or scenes were shot with the camera behind his shoulder. The film was designed by Alexandre Trauner, who took over almost the whole of the studios at Boulogne to recreate the entire second floor of the Ritz Hotel in

Paris, with working elevators and a fully furnished suite. (JMK)

Love Me or Leave Me

MGM, 1955. (C-122m.) Dir: Charles Vidor. Sp: Daniel Fuchs and Isobel Lennart, b/o story by Daniel Fuchs. MS: Various writers. Cast: James Cagney, Doris Day, Cameron Mitchell, Robert Keith, Tom Tully, Harry Bellaver, Richard Gaines.

On-Screen: *A new Day as torch singer Ruth Etting*. Having established herself as a demure heroine of Warners musicals in the early fifties, Doris Day took a chance by moving to MGM for a turn at playing Ruth Etting, the singer and Ziegfeld Follies star who flourished in the twenties and thirties. As an ambitious, tough-fibered woman in thrall to Chicago gangster Moe Snyder (Cagney), Day offered a new and grittier, sexier image that impressed critics and surprised her fans. In fact, she gives a commendable performance, moving through the dramatic portions with professional ease. Although she sounds not at all like Etting, she also renders a number of songs associated with Etting, including "You Made Me Love You," "Mean to Me," and "It All Depends on You." Her version of "Ten Cents a Dance," performed in a tight black dress with sequins, would no doubt shock all the "Goody Two-Shoes" she played previously. As the crippled hood who is obsessed with her, Cagney does his usual high-voltage acting.

Off-Screen: In her autobiography, Ava Gardner claims that she was placed on suspension for refusing to play Ruth Etting. James Cagney asked many of Snyder's friends and associates to demonstrate the extent of his limp. "What I did was simple," he said afterward. "I slapped the foot down as I walked and turned it out . . . that's all. And I knew that those so afflicted tend to exaggerate their limp when they're tired. So I varied it as I saw fit. That kept it from being monotonous." The movie received six Oscar nominations but only Daniel Fuchs won for Best Original Story.

Love Me Tonight

Paramount, 1932. (96m.) Dir: Rouben Mamoulian. Sp: Samuel Hoffenstein, Waldemar Young, and George Marion, Jr., b/o play by Leopold Marchand and Paul Armont. MS: Richard Rodgers and Lorenz Hart. Cast: Jeanette MacDonald, Maurice Chevalier, Myrna Loy, Charlie Ruggles, C. Aubrey Smith, Charles Butterworth, Robert Greig.

On-Screen: *Champagne set to music, via Mamoulian, MacDonald, and Chevalier*. One of the glories of the American musical film, *Love Me Tonight* enchants with every viewing. Witty, tuneful, and innovative, the film weaves magic even in its frivolous plot: A bored princess (MacDonald) falls for a Parisian tailor (Chevalier), whom she mistakes for a baron. Love conquers all, of course. In a style rarely attempted at the time, the musical numbers advance and comment on the plot. The rendition of "Isn't It Romantic?" is most memorable—the song travels from Maurice to various others until it arrives at Princess Jeanette's castle, linking hero to heroine. "Mimi" becomes a song of joyful spirits as it moves from one cast member to another. Mamoulian uses the medium in imaginative ways, especially in the celebrated opening in which the sounds of the city take on a musical beat. Add Victor Milner's shimmering camerawork and splendid supporting performances, especially by Myrna Loy as a love-hungry countess and Charles Butterworth as Jeanette's woebegone suitor, and you have a durable musical treasure.

Off-Screen: Reportedly, Rouben Mamoulian was not eager to direct the film and suggested Ernst Lubitsch, who was unavailable. Mamoulian later recalled that "all the songs were carefully planned with the lyrics to advance the story line, and their place in the story itself designed before the writers of the screenplay were engaged." Many years later, Myrna Loy remembered Chevalier as "an enigma . . . a very, very strange man, keeping completely to himself." But then she added, "He would walk onto the set, the lights would go on, and this thing would happen—this marvelous thing that everyone adored."

Love Story

Paramount, 1970. (C-100m.) Dir: Arthur Hiller. Sp: Erich Segal. Cast: Ali McGraw, Ryan O'Neal, John Marley, Ray Milland, Russell Nype, Tom (Tommy) Lee Jones.

On-Screen: *"Love means never having to say you're sorry."* Not exactly oven-fresh now, this is the line that had audiences fumbling for fresh tissues as the movie drew to its misty close. As lachrymose as the film seems now, many moviegoers, burned out from watching such contemporary student-protest or druggie sagas as *The Strawberry Statement* and *Easy Rider,* welcomed its squeaky-clean story. Oliver Barrett IV

(O'Neal), a Harvard law student, is no longer bankrolled by his rich and snobbish father (Milland) when the young scion weds lower-class Jenny Cavilleri (McGraw). That she's a Radcliffe music major cuts no ice with Oliver's dad. They work hard and make sacrifices to get Oliver his degree, only to learn that fate can be merciless. McGraw and O'Neal work hard, too, to make us care, and for most viewers, their efforts pay off. Now get out those hankies.

Off-Screen: Reversing the usual sequence, Segal, a Yale classics professor at the time, wrote the screenplay before turning it into a best-selling novel. In 1977, he published *Oliver's Story,* a less enthralling follow-up, and O'Neal also appeared in the 1978 movie version of that one. Movie buffs will relish seeing former matinee idol Milland, albeit without his hairpiece. The picture, McGraw, O'Neal, and Hiller were among the Oscar nominees, but only Francis Lai, who composed the original score, walked off with a statuette. (CFB)

The Loved One

MGM, 1965. (116m.) Dir: Tony Richardson. Sp: Terry Southern and Christopher Isherwood, b/o novel by Evelyn Waugh. Cast: Robert Morse, Jonathan Winters, Rod Steiger, Anjanette Comer, Dana Andrews, Milton Berle, Margaret Leighton, John Gielgud, Liberace, Roddy McDowall, James Coburn, Robert Morley, Lionel Stander, Ayliene Gibbons.

On-Screen: *Outrageous satire on the American way of death.* Advertised as "the movie to offend everyone," *The Loved One* works hard to live up to its promise. Derived from Evelyn

Waugh's novel, the film aims its satirical fire at America's (and specifically Los Angeles's) foibles and rituals, particularly in matters of death and burial. Dennis Barlow (Morse) is the young British poet who comes to America and finds himself caught up in the activities at Whispering Glades, an extravagant and bizarre cemetery very much like Forest Lawn. Demented characters at this place include the Blessed Reverend (Winters), the unctuous, greedy founder of Whispering Glades; the effete chief embalmer (Steiger); and an oily casket salesman (Liberace) ("Rayon chafes, you know"). As Steiger's grotesquely fat mother, who wallows orgasmically in food, Ayliene Gibbons is especially memorable, in a horrifying way. Who knows, *The Loved One* may be your cup of formaldehyde.

Off-Screen: A famous estate called Greystone, just off Sunset Boulevard in Los Angeles, vacant for many years, was converted into Whispering Glades for the movie. The broad lawns and numerous fountains were augmented by classical Greek statuary. The bottom floor of the estate was fitted out as a funeral home, and the once-celebrated kitchen was temporarily converted into an embalming room. Coauthor Terry Southern recorded his thoughts while making the film in *The Journal of "The Loved One"*, with photographs by William Claxton (Random House, 1965).

Lover Come Back

Universal-International, 1962. (C-107m.) Dir: Delbert Mann. Sp: Stanley Shapiro and Paul Henning. Cast: Doris Day, Rock Hudson, Tony Randall, Edie Adams, Jack Kruschen, Ann B. Davis, Joe Flynn, Jack Albertson, Howard St. John.

On-Screen: *Business rivals Doris Day and Rock Hudson fall in love*. An underrated comic actress, Doris Day could project a pert, unforced charm in her early-sixties romantic and marital comedies. In *Lover Come Back*, she is reunited with *Pillow Talk* costar Rock Hudson for a highly amusing movie. She's an advertising executive who clashes with unethical, womanizing Hudson, who works for a rival agency. Further plot complications involve a deception about an imaginary product ("Vip") and, inevitably, some coy sexual maneuverings. Featuring a few satirical flourishes at the idiocies of the advertising game, *Lover Come Back* manages a breezy style that makes it one of the best of the Day-Hudson teamings. As the bumbling vice-president of Hudson's agency, Tony Randall contributes his usual comic flair. In a sense, *Lover Come Back* merely repeats the *Pillow Talk* formula (oversexed Hudson versus undersexed Day), but it's still good fun.

Off-Screen: If we are to believe the comments of the participants, making *Lover Come Back* was a source of unbridled hilarity. Delbert Mann's comment: "Rock and Doris would keep breaking up. There was a scene on the beach—shot in a sandbox on the set—in which they had to kiss, and they could not carry it off because they were laughing so loud." Doris Day added, "Our teeth bumped one time, and after that, we got hysterical every time we tried to kiss."

Lust for Life

MGM, 1956. (C-122m.) Dir: Vincente Minnelli. Sp: Norman Corwin, b/o novel by Irving Stone. Cast: Kirk Douglas, Anthony Quinn, James Donald, Pamela Brown, Everett Sloane, Niall MacGiniss, Noel Purcell, Henry Daniell, Lionel Jeffries.

On-Screen: *The torment and exultation of artist Vincent van Gogh.* Few films have been made about the world's great artists—*Rembrandt* (1935) and *Moulin Rouge* (1952) come to mind—but *Lust for Life* can be counted among the best. Adapted from Irving Stone's best-selling 1934 novel, the film deals with the anguished life of Dutch artist Vincent van Gogh. Kirk Douglas portrays him as a man who moved from bottomless despair and self-loathing to creative exultation when he could express his passionate feelings in his paintings. Norman Corwin's rambling screenplay takes van Gogh through the highs and lows, including the notorious episode in which he severed his ear in rage and frustration. Anthony Quinn won an Oscar as Best Supporting Actor for his performance as van Gogh's lusty friend and sparring partner, artist Paul Gauguin. The movie's best feature is the beautiful color photography by F. A. (Freddie) Young and Russell Harlan, which reproduces many of van Gogh's paintings in exquisite detail.

Off-Screen: Kirk Douglas was Oscar-nominated for his intense performance as van Gogh. MGM owned the novel for years and at one time intended to film it with Spencer Tracy. Many of the scenes were shot at the places where van Gogh had lived and worked. Kirk Douglas found that playing the artist was, on the whole, a painful and exhausting experience. The film was made in the wide-screen CinemaScope process, against Vincente Minnelli's wishes. He did insist, however, on using the subtler Ansco color process rather than the Eastman color film usually employed by MGM.

Madame Bovary

MGM, 1949. (115m.) Dir: Vincente Minnelli. Sp: Robert Ardrey, b/o novel by Gustave Flaubert. Cast: Jennifer Jones, Van Heflin, Louis Jourdan, James Mason, Christopher Kent, Gene Lockhart, Gladys Cooper, George Zucco, Henry (Harry) Morgan.

On-Screen: *Flaubert's tragic heroine on the screen.* French novelist Gustave Flaubert's Emma Bovary, destroyed by her dreams of romance, springs vividly to life in this well wrought, absorbing adaptation. Jennifer Jones portrays the nineteenth-century farm girl who marries a dull provincial doctor (Heflin) while longing for a world of love and luxury. Fired by "images of beauty that never existed," Emma enters into a clandestine romance with a dashing suitor (Jourdan) that, coupled with her extravagances, leads inexorably to her terrible fate. Her story is framed by the trial of Flaubert (Mason), who was accused of writing a "corrupt, loathsome" book. Minnelli's production is exceptionally attractive (color is neither needed nor missed), and one sequence in which Emma attends a ball and is overwhelmed and nearly suffocated by its splendor, is one of the finest in any film. (Miklos Rozsa wrote a haunting waltz for this scene.) Subduing some of her usual mannerisms, Jennifer Jones gives a persuasive performance as Emma, and Van Heflin is reliable as always as her drab but well-intentioned husband.

Off-Screen: Vincente Minnelli and producer Pandro Berman considered Lana Turner for the role of Emma Bovary, until a representative of the Breen office objected, stating that it would be "a difficult story to tell at best, and it'll be much harder for you if you use a sex symbol like Miss Turner." MGM borrowed Jennifer Jones from her husband, David Selznick who, as usual, had a lot to say, by way of lengthy memos, about his wife's performance and the production. Previous versions of *Madame Bovary* appeared in 1932 (as *Unholy Love*), 1934 (French, directed by Jean Renoir), and 1937 (German, with Pola Negri). A French remake was released in 1991.

Made for Each Other

Selznick–United Artists, 1939. (93m.) Dir: John Cromwell. Sp: Jo Swerling. Cast: Carole Lombard, James Stewart, Charles Coburn, Lucile Watson, Eddie Quillan, Harry Davenport, Louise Beavers, Ward Bond.

On-Screen: *A young married couple weathers many tribulations*. Smoothly turned out and often touching, *Made for Each Other* traces the travails of Jane and John Mason (Lombard and Stewart) in the first years of their marriage. The clichés abound and, after a while, the movie threatens to drown in soapsuds, but the stars bring such conviction to their roles that the story stays afloat. The screenplay has them worrying about money, coping with John's bossy mother (Watson), and finally anguishing over their baby's critical illness. The climax, which has a plane winging through a blizzard to deliver a lifesaving serum to the baby, is the ripest of corn. Not surprisingly, it all ends with happy smiles. Stewart uses his unforced charm to make his essentially irritating character sympathetic, and Lombard is radiant in a rare dramatic role.

Off-Screen: The movie's cliff-hanger climax was added by producer David O. Selznick after disappointing previews. He remembered using a similar plot device in *Night Flight* (1933) which, in turn, had been based on a true incident. His brother Myron (Lombard's agent) had fallen ill in California and required a serum found only in New York City. The chartered plane completed the flight in record time, and Myron's life was saved. With the crisis ended, David declared, "This is too good to waste on Myron. Let's put it in the picture." The device was revived for *Made for Each Other*.

The Magnificent Ambersons

RKO, 1942.(88m.) Dir: Orson Welles. Sp: Orson Welles, b/o novel by Booth Tarkington. Cast: Joseph Cotten, Dolores Cos-

tello, Agnes Moorehead, Tim Holt, Anne Baxter, Richard Bennett, Ray Collins, Erskine Sanford.

On-Screen: *The decline and fall of an affluent small-town family*. Although it is not much more than a fragment of the original film, Orson Welles's adaptation of Booth Tarkington's novel is still a splendid movie, in many ways as fascinating as Welles's landmark *Citizen Kane* (1941). As in *Kane*, Welles makes fresh and innovative use of cinematic techniques that were in no way brand-new at the time. Light and shadow, frequent close-ups, and overlapping dialogue bring impact to the story of the Ambersons, a midwestern town's most prominent family, its decline due to industrialization, and the final "comeuppance" of its arrogant, bullheaded son (Holt). Holt gives a rather stiff performance as George Amberson Minifer, who keeps his weak, gentle mother Isabel (Costello) from consummating her lifelong romance with Eugene Morgan (Cotten). Agnes Moorehead is exceptionally vivid, if a bit over the top, as George's hysterical, repressed Aunt Fanny, who loves Eugene. Beautifully photographed by Stanley Cortez, *The Magnificent Ambersons* contains memorable sequences, especially the last great ball at the Amberson mansion.

Off-Screen: What actually happened to Orson Welles's film? The truth will probably never be absolutely clear. Apparently, while Welles was working in South America on a documentary called *It's All True,* there was a change of management at RKO, and the new production head, who regarded Welles as an antiestablishment provocateur, had *Ambersons* severely cut and thrown on a double bill. Welles claimed that the film now looked "as though somebody had run a lawnmower through the celluloid." The film's editor, Robert Wise (later the director of *West Side Story* and *The Sound of Music*), who was deeply involved in making changes, insists that the movie was not "mutilated": "I feel that all of us tried sincerely to keep the best of Welles's concept and still lick the problems." A silent version of the story, called *Pampered Youth,* had appeared in 1925, and Welles himself had done a radio adaptation in 1939.

The Major and the Minor

Paramount, 1941. (100m.) Dir: Billy Wilder. Sp: Charles Brackett and Billy Wilder, b/o story by Fannie Kilbourne. Cast: Ginger Rogers, Ray Milland, Rita Johnson, Robert Benchley, Diana Lynn, Norma Varden, Lela Rogers.

On-Screen: *A young woman impersonates a twelve-year-old, with comic results.* After years as a top screenwriter, Billy Wilder took the plunge as a director with this saucy and still amusing comedy. Finding herself without sufficient fare on her trip home from New York City, Ginger Rogers dresses up as a big-for-her-age preteen and becomes involved with an army major (Milland) who thinks she really *is* twelve. Life becomes even more complicated when she stays at his military school. As Major Milland takes on inexplicable yearnings for the "little kid," the movie veers into pre-*Lolita* territory, but the Brackett-Wilder screenplay manages to avoid the danger by a narrow margin. Early in the film, Robert Benchley does a comic turn as a lecherous New Yorker ("Why don't you get out of that wet coat and into a dry martini?"), and Diana Lynn gets many of the movie's best lines as Milland's knowing sister, who is *really* twelve.

Off-Screen: Years later, asked if she took the role as a favor to Billy Wilder, Ginger Rogers replied, "Hell, no. I didn't do it to help anybody. I did it because it was one hell of a good script and I knew Charlie Brackett and Billy Wilder were the best writers in the business, and they had written one hell of a part for me." She also admired Wilder's "wonderful sense of the ridiculous." In the movie's last scene, Rogers's true-life mother Lela plays her mother. (Spring Byington was unavailable.) In a sex reversal, Jerry Lewis played the Ginger Rogers role in a 1955 remake called *You're Never Too Young.*

Make Way for Tomorrow

Paramount, 1937. (92m.) Dir: Leo McCarey. Sp: Viña Delmar, b/o novel by Josephine Lawrence and play by Helen and Nolan Leary. Cast: Victor Moore, Beulah Bondi, Thomas Mitchell, Fay Bainter, Porter Hall, Barbara Read, Louise Beavers.

On-Screen: *An elderly couple faces a sad parting.* Is the title ironic or, under the circumstances, merely pointless? Never mind. *Make Way for Tomorrow* is a small but poignant drama about the tragedy of old age, a subject seldom covered in films. The story concerns an elderly couple (Moore and Bondi) who must sell their house and separate after many devoted years together. She moves in with her son (Mitchell) and becomes a well-meaning nuisance; finally she agrees to go into an old-folks' home. They have one last meeting before they are parted, probably forever. It's as simple as that, but the screenplay, and McCarey's sensitive direction, turn the situation into a heartbreaking experience, with nobody really to blame. Bondi and Moore are both splendid, and their long final sequence is deeply moving.

Off-Screen: Astonishingly, Beulah Bondi was only in her mid-forties when she played this, her only starring role. One of the screen's best, most reliable character actresses, she enjoyed a career that spanned more than three decades. Victor Moore's forte, in films and on stage, was bumbling comedy; this was his only dramatic role.

Malcolm X

Warners, 1992. (C-199m.) Dir: Spike Lee. Sp: Arnold Perl and Spike Lee, b/o Malcolm X's autobiography. Cast: Denzel Washington, Angela Bassett, Al Freeman, Jr., Delroy Lindo, Albert Hall, Spike Lee, Theresa Randle, Kate Vernon, Lonette McKee.

On-Screen: *From sinner to saint: the odyssey of the black activist leader.* Spike Lee's most ambitious effort to date, *Malcolm X* is an impressive film that sweeps the viewer through nearly three decades of turbulent black history as seen through the experiences of one of its most charismatic, most controversial leaders. The movie traces the life of Malcolm X (Washington): his early years as a thief and convict; his role as a rising star in the Nation of Islam, in service to its leader, Elijah Mohammad (Freeman); the profound pilgrimage to Mecca that altered his separatist views; and his assassination in February, 1965. Inevitably, the question arises as to how much of the story is fiction and how much is dramatic license. To his credit, Lee avoids preaching at the audience until the movie's end,

when he indulges in some ill-advised proselytizing. Denzel Washington dominates the film with an impassioned performance; most of the other characters are merely ciphers. There are some non-fatal flaws: the movie is excessively long—the early scenes, in particular, repeat their points too often, and the Harlem dance sequence seems to have been lifted out of a musical movie. On the whole, however, *Malcolm X* succeeds in offering a full-bodied portrait of its subject.

Off-Screen: The release of *Malcolm X* prompted a flood of articles and books (some reissued) on Malcolm and the long, tortuous process of getting the film made. The two most essential publications are probably *The Autobiography of Malcolm X,* written with Alex Haley (Ballantine, 1965), and *By Any Means Necessary: The Trials and Tribulations of the Making of Malcolm X,* by Spike Lee and Ralph Wiley (Hyperion, 1992). At one time or another, David Mamet, Calder Willingham, David Bradley, and Charles Fuller worked on the screenplay. Credited co-author Arnold Perl died in 1971. In the movie's earliest stages, Norman Jewison was scheduled to direct. Many articles have recorded Lee's difficulties in getting the film made exactly as he envisioned it, including his insistence on directing it himself, his battles over budget, and his turning to wealthy black celebrities for additional funds to complete the film.

The Maltese Falcon

Warners, 1941. (100m.) Dir: John Huston. Sp: John Huston, b/o novel by Dashiell Hammett. Cast: Humphrey Bogart, Mary Astor, Sydney Greenstreet, Peter Lorre,

Elisha Cook, Jr., Lee Patrick, Gladys George, Jerome Cowan, Barton MacLane.

On-Screen: *Huston's on-target directorial debut.* As Sam Spade, Hammett's laconic, hard-boiled private eye, Bogart found the role that shaped his superstar screen image. Perfectly matching his character's mocking cynicism ("The cheaper the crook, the gaudier the patter") is Astor's beautiful but duplicitous Brigid O'Shaughnessy. Through her, Spade gets involved with portly Kasper Gutman (Greenstreet), hysterical Joel Cairo (Lorre), and bug-eyed Wilmer (Cook), as fascinatingly repellent a group of "pocket-edition desperadoes" as ever crawled across a movie screen. More concerned with characterization than mystery, Huston's screenplay and direction, as well as his heaven-sent cast, made the film a classic. Memorable scenes abound, among them Spade's encounters with Brigid, with their mixture of danger and sexual tension. The final close-up is unforgettable, as Brigid's tear-streaked face is darkened by the shadow of the closing elevator gate.

On-Screen: The studio had filmed Hammett's story twice before, in 1931 under its original title, and again in 1936 as *Satan Met a Lady*. George Raft had been slated to play Sam Spade, but felt strongly that *The Maltese Falcon* was "not an important picture." He was replaced by Bogart, and originally cast Geraldine Fitzgerald was replaced by Mary Astor. By meticulously preparing every camera setup in advance, Huston was able to complete the film in thirty-four days at a cost of only $324,000. As an inside "joke," Huston cast his father, Walter, in the unbilled role of Captain Jacobi, who staggers into Spade's office with the statue of the black bird, then falls dead of

bullet wounds. The movie won three Oscar nominations, including Best Picture. (CFB)

Man Hunt

Fox, 1941. (105m.) Dir: Fritz Lang. Sp: Dudley Nichols, b/o novel by Geoffrey Household. Cast: Walter Pidgeon, Joan Bennett, George Sanders, Roddy McDowall, John Carradine, Ludwig Stossel, Heather Thatcher.

On-Screen: *A big-game hunter stalks his most unusual prey.* Shortly before the outbreak of World War II, big-game hunter Alan Thorndike (Pidgeon) has decided to stalk Adolf Hitler purely for sport. His gun aimed at the Führer, he is deciding whether to shoot when he is captured by Nazi guards. So begins Fritz Lang's exciting, if hardly credible, melodrama. Thorndike is interrogated by a treacherous Nazi agent (Sanders) and manages to escape to England, where he himself becomes the prey, stalked by the sinister Mr. Jones (Carradine) and abetted by a Cockney streetwalker (Bennett). The often illogical turns of plot demand complete suspension of disbelief, but Lang covers up the holes with swift action and suspense. The story was remade in 1976 as a British television movie, *Rogue Male*, which was the title of Geoffrey Household's novel.

Off-Screen: *Man Hunt* was first offered to John Ford, who declined because he disliked the subject matter. Because Joan Bennett's prostitute character was depicted as both honest and compassionate, the Hays office feared that her profession would be placed in a "glamorous" light. The censors insisted on placing a sewing machine in her room, to give the impression that she was really a "seamstress." *Man Hunt* was Roddy McDowall's first American film.

The Man in the Gray Flannel Suit

Fox, 1956. (C-153m.) Dir: Nunnally Johnson. Sp: Nunnally Johnson, b/o novel by Sloan Wilson. Cast: Gregory Peck, Jennifer Jones, Fredric March, Arthur O'Connell, Marisa Pavan, Lee J. Cobb, Keenan Wynn, Ann Harding, Connie Gilchrist, Gene Lockhart, Gigi Perreau.

On-Screen: *A writer comes to a turning point in his life.* In this adaptation of Sloan Wilson's best-seller, Gregory Peck plays the "man," a symbol in opposition to everything that is supposedly wrong with American corporate life, especially its overweening ambition and ruthlessness. Jennifer Jones is his wife, a woman who, in the unliberated fifties, expresses her own ambitions through her husband. Fredric March is the network tycoon and Peck's boss, who confesses that his own success has been won at the cost of his family's happiness. That confession, plus the devastating revelation that he sired a child by Marisa Pavan during a romantic idyll in World War II, leads Peck to a crisis of decision and conscience. Peck plays the writer in his usual sincere style, as a questioning corporate everyman. Jones is frantic but loving, and March is touching as an older man who sees all too clearly the results of his own mistakes.

Off-Screen: During the filming, David O. Selznick, Jennifer Jones's husband, kept sending long telegrams to Nunnally Johnson demanding that the cameraman be fired, the script be altered, and his wife be given more close-ups. At one point, Johnson sent Selznick a note reading, "In case your wife is too modest to tell you this, I think the scene she did today was absolutely superb, and she couldn't have been better. Please do not answer this." (JMK)

The Man in the Moon

MGM, 1991. (C-99m.) Dir: Robert Mulligan. Sp: Jenny Wingfield. Cast: Sam Waterston, Tess Harper, Reese Witherspoon, Gail Strickland, Emily Warfield, Jason London, Bentley Mitchum.

On-Screen: *Two teenage sisters love the same boy.* At first glance, *The Man in the Moon* would appear to be merely a reworking of an old formula that might have costarred Jeanne Crain and June Haver in a Fox color movie of the forties. But this small film makes something lovely and moving out of that formula. In a rural Louisiana town in 1957, fourteen-year-old Dani (Witherspoon) is excruciatingly aware of her budding sexuality and distressed by her "inferiority" to her pretty older sister, Maureen (Warfield). Trouble ensues when both girls fall in love with a handsome young neighbor (London). An unexpected tragedy shatters their lives and ultimately brings them closer together. The story is as simple as that, but Jenny Wingfield's perceptive screenplay and Robert Mulligan's sensitive direction make it seem almost newly minted. Sam Waterston and Tess Harper are fine as the girls' parents, and both young actresses are luminous. *The Man in the Moon* may cover familiar territory, but it's worth your time and attention.

Off-Screen: Director Mulligan spent several months searching for a location and finally settled on Natchitoches, Louisiana, several hundred miles from New Orleans and adjacent to author Wingfield's hometown of Robilene. One scene was shot at the Robilene church where her father had served as minister. Jeremy London, the twin brother of Jason London, played Sam Waterston's older son in the television series "I'll Fly Away."

Man on the Flying Trapeze

Universal, 1935. (65m.) Dir: Clyde Bruckman. Sp: Ray Harris, Sam Hardy, Jack Cunningham, and Bobby Vernon, b/o story by Charles Bogle (W. C. Fields). Cast: W. C. Fields, Mary Brian, Kathleen Howard, Grady Sutton, Vera Lewis, Lucien Littlefield, Oscar Apfel, Walter Brennan.

On-Screen: *W. C. Fields versus the American family.* Meet office worker Ambrose Wolfinger, a.k.a. W. C. Fields. Burdened with a shrewish wife (Howard), a nasty mother-in-law (Lewis), and a shiftless brother-in-law (Sutton), with only a daughter (Brian) to love him, Ambrose needs a break, and never gets one. When he becomes drunk on applejack with burglars who break into his cellar, he is charged with not having a license to make applejack. When he is given one day off from his job in twenty-five years to attend a wrestling match, he gets into trouble again. That's all there is, but as usual Fields manages to generate hilarity out of very little. Fields had no use for domesticity, and it shows in the venom with which he depicts Ambrose's hideous clan. Best line: When Ambrose lies that he wants to take the day off to attend his mother-in-law's funeral, his sympathetic boss remarks, "It must be hard to lose a mother-in-law." "Yes, it is," Ambrose replies. "Almost impossible."

Off-Screen: In the small role of his admiring secretary, Fields cast Carlotta Monti, his real-life mistress, with whom he lived for over twelve years. Ambrose's brother-in-law is called "Claude," which was Fields's middle name as well as the name of his son, who was also known as W. C. Fields, Jr. The movie is based on Fields' 1927 silent feature, *Running Wild.*

The Man Who Came to Dinner

Warners, 1941. (112m.) Dir: William Keighley. Sp: Julius J. and Philip G. Epstein, b/o play by George S. Kaufman and Moss Hart. Cast: Bette Davis, Ann Sheridan, Monty Woolley, Jimmy Durante, Reginald Gardiner, Billie Burke, Richard Travis, Grant Mitchell, Mary Wickes, Elizabeth Fraser.

On-Screen: *An overbearing celebrity invades an Ohio household.* A Broadway hit in October 1939, Kaufman and Hart's comedy *The Man Who Came to Dinner* delighted critics and playgoers with its wickedly funny tale of the eccentric author and raconteur Alexander Woollcott (here named Sheridan Whiteside). Forced to stay with an Ohio family when he breaks his hip on their doorstep, the vitriolic, truculent Whiteside disrupts everyone's lives while his celebrated friends come to visit. Transferred to the screen, the comedy retains much of its crackling wit, although Warners, in its usual fashion, insists on hitting every comic point with an anvil. Happily, the studio had the good sense to cast the original star, Monty Woolley, as Whiteside, and he is wonderful. Bette Davis is uncharacteristically self-effacing as his secretary whose romance with the local newspaper editor (Travis) sparks the action. Others have their own field day: Ann Sheridan as a flamboyant actress (read Gertrude Lawrence), Jimmy Durante as the cheerful lunatic based on Harpo Marx, and Reginald Gardiner as a Noël Coward–like Englishman.

Off-Screen: There were many candidates for the role of Sheridan Whiteside. Charles Laughton tested for it but was ruled as too effeminate by Jack Warner. Also tested were Laird Cregar, Robert Benchley, and John Barrymore. Barrymore was strongly considered, but he would have had to read his dialogue from "idiot cards"—his memory had been ruined by all the heavy drinking he had done over the years. Orson Welles was nearly signed, but RKO finally refused to lend him to Warners. Olivia de Havilland was originally announced to play Bette Davis's role. *Sherry!*, a stage-musical version, failed to make the grade on Broadway in 1967.

The Man Who Knew Too Much

Paramount, 1956. (C-120m.) Dir: Alfred Hitchcock. Sp: John Michael Hayes, b/o story by Charles Bennett and D. B. Wyndham-Lewis. Cast: James Stewart, Doris Day, Brenda De Banzie, Bernard Miles, Ralph Truman, Christopher Olsen, Daniel Gelin, Alan Mowbray, Hillary Brooke.

On-Screen: *Alfred Hitchcock remakes his tale of a man caught in a web of conspiracy and murder.* Although it is generally regarded as less than top-drawer Hitchcock, this thriller offers a fair amount of suspense and a few brilliantly executed sequences. A remake of Hitchcock's 1934 British film, it stars James Stewart and Doris Day as an American couple on vacation in French Morocco. When Stewart learns about the planned assassination of a top political figure in London, his young son (Olsen) is kidnapped as insurance against his speaking out. He sets about rescuing his son while thwarting the assassination. Curiously, there are two climactic sequences: one at London's Albert Hall, where an agonized Day is torn between jeopardizing her son's life and stopping the assassination, the other at an embassy ball, where the couple finally free their son. Both are staged with the expected Hitchcock bravura.

Off-Screen: The film's song "Que Sera, Sera (Whatever Will Be, Will Be)", which figures in the plot, won that year's Academy Award. The man playing the nearly assassinated prime minister was a prominent actor in Copenhagen. Having never before left the United States, Doris Day was understandably rattled by the strange food and lack of hygiene in Marrakesh, where some filming was done. She also worried about Hitchcock's never speaking to her, until he explained gently that he didn't say anything because she had done everything perfectly.

The Man Who Shot Liberty Valance

Paramount, 1962. (119m.) Dir: John Ford. Sp: Willis Goldbeck and James Warner Bellah, b/o story by Dorothy Johnson. Cast: John Wayne, James Stewart, Vera Miles, Lee Marvin, Edmond O'Brien, Andy Devine, Woody Strode, Jeanette Nolan, Ken Murray, John Qualen.

On-Screen: *How the West was civilized—and at what cost.* Saddened by the encroachments of old age, and by the more realistic, less mythic view of the Western traditions in recent movies, director John Ford made this melancholy and haunting Western. It contrasts the Old West, represented by gunfighter Wayne, with the New West personified by lawyer Stewart, who has a more reasoned, more "civilized" point of view. When Stewart seems to kill the evil Liberty Valance (Marvin), who is in league with the cattle barons, he becomes a national hero and, ultimately, a senator. But it was Wayne who actually did the shooting, and his secrecy costs him everything he values in life. Less expansive than Ford's usual Westerns, *The Man Who Shot Liberty Valance* relies more on character than on action—there are hardly any outdoor scenes—but it contains deeper insights than many of his more polished efforts. As usual, Ford draws sterling performances from his seasoned stock company of players.

Off-Screen: From all reports, a weary, aging John Ford directed *Liberty Valance* with much less than his usual vigor and enthusiasm. Although he relished filming outdoors, he shot most of the movie on a soundstage. Usually a stickler for fastidious detail, he appeared to have complete disregard for background effects. Yet many critics regard the film as one of the most fascinating efforts of Ford's late, dark-hued career.

The Man with the Golden Arm

United Artists, 1955. (119m.) Dir: Otto Preminger. Sp: Walter Newman and Lewis Meltzer, b/o novel by Nelson Algren. Cast: Frank Sinatra, Kim Novak, Eleanor Parker, Darren McGavin, Arnold Stang, Robert Strauss, Doro Merande, John Conte, Emile Meyer, George E. Stone, George Mathews.

On-Screen: *Drug addict Frank Sinatra goes through the wringer.* Considered bold and innovative in its day, Otto Preminger's adaptation of Nelson Algren's novel about drug addiction now seems crude and heavy-handed, with one notable exception: Frank Sinatra. As card dealer Frankie Machine, the "man with the golden arm," he slides back into the nightmare of drug addiction with a power and conviction that can still grip the viewer. The rest is overcooked, with a shrill Eleanor Parker as Frankie's neurotic, possessive wife and Darren McGavin as a drug dealer so obvious you expect him to twirl his little black mustache. Kim Novak seems uneasy as the girl who loves and helps Frankie. The movie belongs to Sinatra, whose bravura "cold turkey" scene is harrowing. There's one other memorable performance: Arnold Stang as Frankie's loyal little friend, Sparrow.

Off-Screen: Inevitably, the movie was denied the Production Code seal because of its controversial content. Frank Sinatra won a Best Actor Oscar nomination but lost to Ernest Borgnine's *Marty*. According to Otto Preminger, an uncompleted script was sent to both Sinatra and Marlon Brando. Sinatra agreed to do the film, without seeing the rest, and Preminger signed him. Brando's agent, says Preminger, was angry that he hadn't waited. Sinatra was patient with an extremely nervous Novak—some of her scenes had to be shot as many as thirty-five times.

The Manchurian Candidate

United Artists, 1962. (126m.) Dir: John Frankenheimer. Sp: George Axelrod, b/o novel by Richard Condon. Cast: Frank Sinatra, Laurence Harvey, Janet Leigh, Angela Lansbury, Henry Silva, James Gregory, John McGiver, Leslie Parrish, James Edwards.

On-Screen: *Brainwashed G.I. is programmed for assassination.* Bennett Marco (Sinatra) and Raymond Shaw (Harvey) are among a group of Korean War veterans who were captured by Chinese Communists and survived. Or did they? During their captivity, both men were subjected to highly sophisticated psychological programming techniques, Shaw ending up a walking time bomb. Back in the States, he's assigned to kill one of the presidential nominees. The cast is first-rate, with Harvey as the zombielike pawn who's "set to go off" at the sight of a queen of diamonds playing card, and Lansbury as his domineering, diabolical mother, taking top acting honors. Most of all, it's Frankenheimer's dazzling direction—you'll be reminded of Hitchcock and Welles at the top of their form—that will glue your eyes to the screen. The climax, a rally in Madison Square Garden, and its aftermath are devastating. A suspenseful and disturbing what-if drama.

Off-Screen: At first, the studio was unwilling to film Axelrod's adaptation of Condon's controversial political thriller. At the suggestion of Sinatra, who was already set to play Marco, his friend President Kennedy let it be known that he had liked the novel and encouraged the studio to produce it. The movie was released little more than a year before Kennedy's assassination and was eventually removed from circulation. In 1988, the film was revived to even greater acclaim than on its initial release. Lansbury received a Best Supporting Actress Oscar nomination. (CFB)

Manhattan

United Artists, 1979. (96m.) Dir: Woody Allen. Sp: Woody Allen and Marshall Brickman. Cast: Woody Allen, Diane Keaton, Michael Murphy, Mariel Hemingway, Meryl Streep, Anne Byrne.

On-Screen: *New York neurotics, Woody Allen style.* A brilliant, bittersweet comedy, *Manhattan* takes a perceptive look at the tangled lives of a group of neurotic New Yorkers. Author-director-star Woody Allen plays a comedy writer who is plagued by his ex-wife (Streep) at the same time that he is having a difficult affair with a seventeen-year-old girl (Hemingway). Along comes a third woman (Keaton), the intensely neurotic mistress of his married friend (Murphy). Nothing is resolved satisfactorily; unable to develop durable relationships, Allen ends up baffled, regretful, and dissatisfied with his life. Beautifully photographed in black and white by Gordon Willis, and richly scored with Gershwin music, *Manhattan* has more than the requisite number of laughs for a Woody Allen movie; still, a melancholy air pervades the film, as characters experience hurt and bewilderment while they grapple with their lives. The last shot of Allen, his face expressing sorrow, confusion, and a glimmer of hope as his young girlfriend leaves him, is clearly modeled after the ending of Chaplin's *City Lights*. As usual, Allen's ensemble cast carries out every quip or nuance with enormous skill.

Off-Screen: The stunning opening shots of Manhattan end with a view of fireworks over Central Park, which was added after the filming was nearly completed. Woody Allen enjoyed photographing Manhattan in a glamorous way: "I had a real urge to show

New York as a wonderland and I completely exorcised that feeling in *Manhattan*." His screenplay was nominated for an Oscar.

Marathon Man

Paramount, 1976. (C-120m.) Dir: John Schlesinger. Sp: William Goldman, b/o his novel. Cast: Dustin Hoffman, Laurence Olivier, Marthe Keller, Roy Scheider, William Devane, Fritz Weaver.

On-Screen: *Dustin Hoffman, trapped in a waking nightmare. Marathon Man* should keep you absorbed, even when you're aware of its contrivances and its lack of plausibility. Dustin Hoffman stars as Babe Levy, a Columbia graduate student who discovers, to his horror, that his brother (Scheider) is fatally involved with international skulduggery, mostly with a notoriously evil ex-Nazi named Szell (Olivier). When Szell comes to America in search of a secret cache of jewels, violence becomes the order of the day. Hapless Babe becomes ensnared in Szell's insidious web, leading to some suspenseful—and also repellent—sequences. Even those who have forgotten this movie will wince at the memory of the harrowing scene in which Szell, a dentist by profession, tortures Babe with dental instruments ("Is it safe?"). Marthe Keller is the inevitable mysterious woman who figures importantly in the story. The best scene has Szell frantically trying to elude Babe and the police in New York's garment district.

Off-Screen: John Schlesinger's first choice to play Babe Levy was Keith Carradine, but William Goldman wrote a draft with Dustin Hoffman in mind, and Schlesinger accepted Hoffman reluctantly. After the film attracted controversy with its graphic violence, the actor offered this comment on the notorious dental scene: " . . . I wish that the ones who are screaming the loudest would be more honest with themselves. The truth is they *do* want to see that dental scene. They want to be titillated by it; but they don't want to be screwed into the wall in such a way that they have to say, 'Jesus, what's the matter with me, am I a coward or a sadist?' "

Marked Woman

Warners, 1937. (99m.) Dir: Lloyd Bacon. Sp: Robert Rossen and Abem Finkel. Cast: Bette Davis, Humphrey Bogart, Eduardo Ciannelli, Jane Bryan, Lola Lane, Isabel Jewell, Henry O'Neill, Rosalind Marquis, Mayo Methot, Allen Jenkins.

On-Screen: *A dance-hall "hostess" exposes a sordid crime ring.* Younger film buffs who would like to watch one of Warners' definitive hard-boiled melodramas of the thirties might do well to choose *Marked Woman*. Blistering and fast-paced, and suggested by the real-life case of gangster "Lucky" Luciano, the story focuses on a group of girls euphemistically called "hostesses," who are in thrall to vicious kingpin gangster Ciannelli. When the innocent kid sister (Bryan) of hostess Davis is killed, Davis risks her life to expose Ciannelli, with dire consequences for herself. Davis's portrait of a jittery, high-strung woman vivifies the film (deep in her thirties style, she sometimes overemotes), and Ciannelli is truly chilling as the crime lord. Only Bogart, in a straight role as a sympathetic district attorney, fails to convince.

Off-Screen: After being mutilated in the film by Eduardo Ciannelli, Bette Davis did not like the way she had been bandaged. She went to her own doctor, who applied realistic bandages. When she drove through the front gate at Warners, the frantic gate guard called the front office to report that Davis had been in a terrible accident. Hal Wallis ran down to see her and was relieved to find that she was all right. Davis remarked, "We film this makeup, or we don't film *me* today!" Everyone associated with the film knew that it was really about "Lucky" Luciano and his prostitutes, but this had to be shown only by innuendo. Davis later commented, "We made the audience know that we were whores!"

Married to the Mob

Orion, 1988. (C-103m.) Dir: Jonathan Demme. Sp: Barry Strugatz and Mark Burns. Cast: Michelle Pfeiffer, Matthew Modine, Dean Stockwell, Mercedes Ruehl, Alec Baldwin, Joan Cusack, Trey Wilson.

On-Screen: *A gangster's widow remains linked to the mob.* Few films can claim that they draw their biggest laughs from their sets, but *Married to the Mob* is a conspicuous exception. A raucous, disheveled, and frequently amusing farce, it is set in the garishly overdecorated, hilariously vulgar homes and hotel rooms inhabited by well-to-do Mafia "families." Michelle Pfeiffer plays a murdered hood's widow who cannot escape her connections with the mob. The mob boss (Stockwell) who killed her husband lusts for her, and a genial but inept young F.B.I. man (Modine) is following her, hoping to nail the boss. Misunderstandings lead to a number of complications, many of them funny, until a protracted and clumsy climax. Jonathan Demme directs breezily and gets good performances from all, especially Mercedes Ruehl, who plays Stockwell's fe-

rociously jealous wife with comic zest and a shriek that could penetrate steel.

Off-Screen: In an interview about the film, Jonathan Demme remarked, "I've always wondered why people are so fascinated by the mob—and the bottom line may be that gangsters wear such great outfits. Their style is so fantastic that you almost forget what the people are like inside their clothes."

The Marrying Kind

Columbia, 1952. (93m.) Dir: George Cukor. Sp: Ruth Gordon and Garson Kanin. Cast: Judy Holliday, Aldo Ray, Madge Kennedy, Sheila Bond, John Alexander, Rex Williams, Phyllis Povah, Peggy Cass, Mickey Shaughnessy.

On-Screen: *A divorcing couple review their married life.* Judy Holliday's unique combination of comic brashness and poignant vulnerability was never better realized than in this perceptive comedy-drama. She plays Florence Keefer, wife of post-office worker Chet (Aldo Ray in his second film), who joins with him in recalling their married life as they prepare to divorce. The expert Gordon-Kanin screenplay focuses on the small everyday activities in their scratchy relationship, as well as the tragic event that split them asunder. Events are seen from contrasting viewpoints, and at the end there is a promise of reconciliation. A deft mixture of comedy and drama, *The Marrying Kind* benefits from Holliday's special qualities and also from the earthy personality of her gravel-voiced costar, Aldo Ray.

Off-Screen: The Kanins had written the screenplay with Sid Caesar in mind, but his television commitments made that impossible, and Aldo Ray was signed for the role. George Cukor wanted veteran actress Ina Claire to play the judge, but Garson Kanin objected, and Madge Kennedy was cast instead. The company spent two weeks filming in actual locations, including Times Square and Central Park.

Marty

United Artists, 1955. (91m.) Dir: Delbert Mann. Sp: Paddy Chayefsky, b/o his television play. Cast: Ernest Borgnine, Betsy Blair, Esther Minciotti, Jerry Paris, Joe Mantell, Karen Steele.

On-Screen: *"Comes New Year's Eve, everybody starts arranging parties, I'm the guy they got to dig up a date for."* Ordinary people leading ordinary lives—unpromising dramatic material, perhaps. But that's what *Marty* is all about. The title character is a Bronx butcher and likable lug who lives with his mother (Minciotti) and spends long, lonely evenings with his card-playing pals. Marty knows something is missing from his life when he meets an unmarried schoolteacher (Blair). Although they are both plain and painfully shy, their relationship matures into tenderness, then flowers into love. Chayefsky's dialogue catches precisely the rhythms and nuances of everyday speech: "What do you feel like doing tonight?" "I don't know, Ange. What do *you* feel like doing?" Delbert Mann sensitively directs a superb cast in a funny and moving portrait of ordinary people with very special needs and feelings.

Off-Screen: When Paddy Chayefsky's play first appeared on television, Rod Steiger played the title role. The refreshing, unpretentious slice-of-life realism of the movie version brought it instant acclaim. Among its many awards: Grand Prix at the Cannes Film Festival and four Oscars, for Best Picture, Best Actor (Borgnine), Chayefsky's screenplay, and Mann's direction. *Marty* was also the first major American-made film to be shown in Moscow since the end of World War II. (CFB)

Mary Poppins

Disney, 1964. (C-140 m.) Dir: Robert Stevenson. Sp: Bill Walsh and Don Da Gradi, b/o books by P. L. Travers. MS: Richard M. and Robert B. Sherman. Cast: Julie Andrews, Dick Van Dyke, Glynis Johns, David Tomlinson, Matthew Garber, Karen Dotrice, Ed Wynn, Arthur Treacher, Reginald Owen, Hermione Baddeley.

On-Screen: *A magical nanny comes to London in this musical fantasy.* The operative word for *Mary Poppins* is enchanting. From first frame to last, this Disney production spills out an abundance of musical and visual riches. The story, based on P. L. Travers's popular children's stories, concerns Mary Poppins (Andrews), a "practically perfect," magic-dispensing nanny who arrives in 1910 London and enters the lives of the father-dominated Banks family. With the help of a friendly street musician (Van Dyke) of many talents, she introduces the Banks children (Dotrice and Garber) to her world of fantasy and trickery, unbends their starchy father (Tomlinson), then goes on her way. The Oscar-winning score, including "Chim Chim Cheree," is a total delight, and the production numbers are splendid. Highlights include a long but imaginative "Jolly Holiday," which combines animation and reality, and "Step in Time," a dancing romp across London's rooftops. Julie Andrews won the Best Actress Academy Award, and other Oscars were received for visual effects and film editing. In all, a musical to be cherished.

Off-Screen: Among the supporting cast of notable character actors, the wonderful Jane Darwell appears in her last role, as the Bird Woman in "Feed the Birds." Composer Richard Sherman said that the song "Supercalifragilisticexpialidocious" originated when he and his brother recalled their time at a summer camp in 1937, when the nonsense word was regarded as a test of one's verbal agility. *Mary Poppins* was the last feature film completed by Walt Disney.

M*A*S*H

Fox, 1970. (C-116m.) Dir: Robert Altman. Sp: Ring Lardner, Jr., b/o novel by Richard Hooker. Cast: Elliott Gould, Donald Sutherland, Sally Kellerman, Robert Duvall, Tom Skerritt, Rene Auberjonois, Gary Burghoff, Jo Ann Pflug, John Schuck, Roger Bowen.

On-Screen: *The antics of a medical unit during the Korean War. M★A★S★H* was an innovative film in its use of overlapping dialogue, long traveling shots, and deliberate ugliness. All of these factors, plus the witty, irreverent screenplay and the superb ensemble playing turned *M★A★S★H* into director Altman's first big hit. Ironically, Ring Lardner, Jr., won an Oscar for a script Altman and the cast virtually improvised as they went along. There is no plot, merely a series of events, with the surgery that takes place all the time as a unifying thread. Surgeons "Hawkeye" Pierce (Sutherland) and "Trapper" John McIntyre (Gould) set the tone— they are carnal, bitter, skeptical, funny, and

even cruel. Like all the men and women of the M*A*S*H unit, they have no time for mock heroics and they despise hypocrisy. Their big mission in life is to hang on to their sanity amid the chaos of the Korean War swirling around them. Made while the war in Vietnam was causing a huge schism in the U.S., *M★A★S★H* uses a late-sixties sensibility to comment on that conflict.

Off-Screen: Robert Altman's directorial style was to have the cast rehearse and improvise a scene until a consensus emerged and it was committed to film. Actors were encouraged to alter, replace, or drop their lines as new main characters were introduced. The movie was turned into a hugely successful television series that ran for eleven years. (JMK)

Mask

Universal, 1985. (C-120m.) Dir: Peter Bogdanovich. Sp: Anna Hamilton Phelan. Cast: Cher, Sam Elliott, Eric Stoltz, Laura Dern, Estelle Getty, Richard Dysart, Lawrence Monoson, Marsha Warfield, Ben Piazza.

On-Screen: *A teenager and his mother cope with his disfiguring disease.* Based on a true story, *Mask* focuses largely on Rocky Dennis (Stoltz), a gentle, intelligent teenage boy inflicted with craniodiaphyseal dysplasia, a rare disease that gives him a grotesque appearance and casts the shadow of a short life over him. Cher plays his mother, Rusty, tough, feisty, and into drugs, but mostly generous in her devotion to Rocky. Anna Hamilton Phelan's discursive but often touching screenplay traces Rocky's relationship with his mother, his time in school, and his tender romantic summer idyll with a young blind girl (Dern). Cher gives an honest, unsentimental performance, and Eric Stoltz, under what must been pounds of makeup, matches her every step of the way. Most affecting scene: Rocky stares in a distorted fun-house mirror and sees a normal reflection.

Off-Screen: During the filming, Cher argued frequently with director Bogdanovich, each seeking control. Halfway through the production, they finally reached some accord. After the movie was completed, however, there was more contention, this time about some of the music. Universal wanted to remove the Bruce Springsteen songs from the soundtrack and replace them with songs by Bob Seger. Bogdanovich was angered by this, especially since Cher sided with the studio. To Bogdanovich's dismay, the Seger songs were substituted.

Maytime

MGM, 1937. (132m.) Dir: Robert Z. Leonard. Sp: Noel Langley, b/o musical play by Rida Johnson Young. MS: Sigmund Romberg, with special lyrics by Bob Wright and Chet Forrest. Cast: Jeanette MacDonald, Nelson Eddy, John Barrymore, Herman Bing, Tom Brown, Lynne Carver, Rafaela Ottiano, Paul Porcasi, Sig Ruman.

On-Screen: *The most fragrant of the MacDonald-Eddy nosegays*. Younger viewers who are curious about the popularity of the Jeannette MacDonald–Nelson Eddy operettas of the thirties might do well to screen *Maytime*. True, the sentiment is thick, the production heavily ornate in the MGM style, and the leads are not exemplary actors. But the movie's story, concerning the tragic romance of an opera star (MacDonald) and an improverished singer (Eddy), can still move die-hard romantics to tears, the Sigmund Romberg songs, especially "Will You Remember (Sweetheart)," are beautiful, and the photography bathes the entire production in a silvery glow. As the heroine's insanely jealous husband and mentor, John Barrymore dominates every scene in which he appears. Few viewers will be able to resist the ending, in which the heroine, now aged, joins her lover in death amid a shower of falling blossoms.

Off-Screen: *Maytime* had started shooting with a different director (Edmund Goulding) and cast (Paul Lukas, Frank Morgan), but after MGM production head Irving Thalberg died, Louis B. Mayer halted the production and resumed shooting with *his* director and cast. By this time, John Barrymore was well on the road to self-destruction, wasted by drink and indulgence, and he could barely stand up for some scenes. Although he had to read his lines from giant cue cards, he somehow managed to gave a strong, if hammy, performance.

McCabe and Mrs. Miller

Warners, 1971. (C-121m.) Dir: Robert Altman. Sp: Robert Altman and Brian McKay, b/o novel by Edmund Naughton. Cast: Warren Beatty, Julie Christie, Rene Auberjonois, Corey Fischer, Bert Remsen, Shelley Duvall, William Devane, Keith Carradine.

On-Screen: *Unvarnished view of the winning of the West*. Around 1900, in the wryly named mining town of Presbyterian Church, John McCabe (Beatty), a seedy cowboy-turned-gambler, joins forces with Constance Miller, a Cockney, opium-smoking whore (Christie), to set up a combination casino and brothel. When crooks move in, the pair's idyllic enterprise is thrown into jeopardy. Depending on how you take it, Altman's movie is either a grittily realistic Western that refreshens Hollywood's customary view of homespun frontier values, or a wrenchingly updated, hip horse opera in which greed and corruption inevitably trample pure-hearted naïveté. Either way, you'll enjoy the old-time look of Vilmos Szigmond's color photography, Leon Eriksen's picturesquely ramshackle sets, and the electricity generated between the stars. The British actress was nominated for an Academy Award.

Off-Screen: Add this movie to Altman's list of revisionist films—especially *M★A★S★H, The Long Goodbye, Nashville*—in which conventional views are questioned and inverted. For this film, the director, cast, and crew went to West Vancouver, British Columbia, for three months of shooting, much of it improvised on the set, departing not only from Naughton's novel *McCabe,* but also from Altman and McKay's prepared script. Altman chose Beatty over the studio's choice, George C. Scott, to play the bearded, derby-hatted male lead. The songs heard during the course of the movie were written and performed by Canadian folksinger Leonard Cohen. (CFB)

Mean Streets

Warners, 1973. (C-110m.) Dir: Martin Scorsese. Sp: Martin Scorsese and Mardik Martin. Cast: Robert De Niro, Harvey Keitel, David Proval, Amy Robinson, Richard Romanus, Cesare Danova, George Memmoli, Robert Carradine, David Carradine.

On-Screen: *Martin Scorsese's vivid early film on hoods in Little Italy.* Scorsese's third feature film, and the first to attract strong critical attention, *Mean Streets* is a scalding, ugly, but undeniably compelling melodrama set in the "mean streets" of New York's Little Italy. Charlie (Keitel) is a small-time hood who works for his Mafia uncle but spends much of his time looking after his wild, dangerously incautious friend, Johnny Boy (De Niro). While trying to keep Johnny Boy from being destroyed for his unpaid debts, Charlie finds time to court Johnny Boy's epileptic cousin, Teresa (Robinson). He is also continually haunted and occasionally tormented by his strict Catholic upbringing. (His sinner's guilt forms a crucial subtext in the film.) The showdown with Johnny Boy's nemesis ends inevitably in violence. In *Mean Streets,* Martin Scorsese begins the ongoing relationship with Robert De Niro that continued with *Taxi Driver* in 1976, peaked with *Raging Bull* in 1980, and continued most recently with *Goodfellas* (1990) and *Cape Fear* (1991). As a film, *Mean Streets* shows early evidence of Scorsese's ability to vivify the screen with his nervous, energetic style.

Off-Screen: *Mean Streets* marked Martin Scorsese's third feature film after *Who's That Knocking at My Door?* (1968), also set in Little Italy, and *Boxcar Bertha* (1972). The film was shot largely on New York locations—Scorsese spent three days photographing the San Gennaro Festival on the east side of the city. The director himself appears briefly as the mysterious assassin hired by Johnny Boy's old gang to kill him. Scorsese's reverence for other filmmakers keeps turning up in the film. Visible are posters for John Boorman's *Point Blank* and for John Cassavetes's *Husbands.*

Meet John Doe

Warners, 1941. (132m.) Dir: Frank Capra. Sp: Robert Riskin, b/o story by Robert Presnell and Richard Connell. Cast: Gary Cooper, Barbara Stanwyck, Edward Arnold, Walter Brennan, James Gleason, Spring Byington, Gene Lockhart, Regis Toomey, Ann Doran, Sterling Holloway.

On-Screen: *Frank Capra's comedy-drama on the dangers of native-grown Fascism.* Following not long after Capra's successful *Mr. Smith Goes to Washington* (1939), *Meet John Doe* is another attempt by the director to extol the virtues of America's "little people" and their ability to triumph over homegrown tyranny. Gary Cooper plays a hobo and ex–baseball player who is used by reporter Barbara Stanwyck as a tool to raise her paper's circulation. His fake "John Doe" letter, berating the state of the world and announcing his "suicide" on Christmas Eve, creates a sensation and starts a nationwide chain of "John Doe" clubs. There's trouble when Fascist-minded publisher Edward Arnold, with an eye on the White House, uses Cooper and his followers as a step toward his goal. When Cooper tries to denounce Arnold and his cronies, he is publicly humiliated and, a broken man, moves toward a genuine suicide. The ending is illogical and unconvincing. *Meet John Doe* has some dull and sticky patches, and a muddled point of view, but there are good performances, notably by James Gleason as a newspaper editor who sees through Arnold's scam.

Off-Screen: Earlier titles for the movie were *The Life and Death of John Doe* and *The Life of John Doe*. Robert Riskin tried—and Frank Capra filmed—a number of different endings for the movie. All were discarded. In desperation, Capra consulted writer and noted "script doctor" Jules Furthman, who told him bluntly that he had no ending because he had no story in the *first* place. Finally, Capra settled on the upbeat conclusion now in the film. *Meet John Doe* won only one Oscar nomination—for Best Original Story. Capra dropped plans for a sequel after the movie's disappointing reception.

Meet Me in St. Louis

MGM, 1944. (C-113m.) Dir: Vincente Minnelli. Sp: Fred Finklehoffe and Irving Brecher, b/o stories by Sally Benson. MS: Hugh Martin and Ralph Blane. Cast: Judy Garland, Margaret O'Brien, Mary Astor, Tom Drake, Lucille Bremer, Leon Ames, Marjorie Main, Harry Davenport, Joan Carroll.

On-Screen: *Judy Garland loves "the boy next door" in this nostalgic turn-of-the-century musical.* Forget the elaborate but lifeless 1989 stage version and bask in the warm glow of the classic original: a lovely, tuneful valentine to an America that probably never existed. The story is paper-thin, skimming lightly over the tribulations, romantic and otherwise, of the Smith family in 1903 St. Louis. But the film is aglow with bandbox settings, a lilting score ("The Trolley Song," "The Boy Next Door," etc.), and expert performances. Judy Garland is enchanting as Esther Smith, but tiny Margaret O'Brien steals the show as the youngest Smith, a precocious, oddly morbid-minded tot named Tootie. Her justly famous Halloween sequence evokes the very real terrors of childhood. Favorite moment: Gazing out wistfully at a winter scene, Esther sings, "Have Yourself a Merry Little Christmas" to a mournful Tootie.

Stars are often not the best judge of suitable roles. Case in point: At first Judy Garland refused to make the movie, claiming that she was too old to play Esther and that Tootie was the main character. Vincente Minnelli not only persuaded her but also married her, over a year after the film was completed. Garland was frequently ill or energized by pills, but Margaret O'Brien was the real problem. Occasionally, Minnelli had to resort to drastic measures to elicit an emotional response from little Margaret. To make her cry in a crucial scene, he told her that her dog was going to be killed. Margaret turned on the tears, and Minnelli felt like a monster. Her reward for all this anguish came in the form of a miniature Oscar, given to her that year in recognition of her acting achievements at the ripe old age of seven.

Melvin and Howard

Universal, 1980. (C-95m.) Dir: Jonathan Demme. Sp: Bo Goldman. Cast: Paul LeMat, Jason Robards, Mary Steenburgen, Pamela Reed, Jack Kehoe, Michael J. Pollard, Dabney Coleman, Gloria Grahame.

On-Screen: *Jonathan Demme's off-beat treat.* Genial, none-too-bright, and frequently insolvent, Melvin Dummar (LeMat) is driving across the Arizona desert when he finds and helps an apparent derelict (Robards) who claims to be billionaire Howard Hughes. After Hughes's death, Melvin comes into possession of a will that names him as one of Hughes's beneficiaries. Is it authentic or a sham? The incident actually occurred, and Jonathan Demme uses it as a focal point for his quirky, delightful comedy. Actually, the movie is more about Melvin's haphazard life, and especially his relationships with wife Lynda (Steenburgen) and friends. These simple, foolish, endearing people are seen as having real hopes and dreams, and Bo Goldman's screenplay portrays them without a trace of mockery or condescension. Mary Steenburgen is best as the resolute Lynda; her hilarious performance at a television talent show is a highlight of the movie. At the end, Dummar gets his day in court, but nobody, including the judge (Coleman), believes him. A true original, *Melvin and Howard* may not be as satirical or malicious as a Preston Sturges movie, but it certainly belongs in that vein of American humor.

Off-Screen: Writer Bo Goldman and Mary Steenburgen both received Academy Awards, she as Best Supporting Actress. Jason Robards was nominated as Best Supporting Actor. Veteran actress Gloria Grahame has a small, wordless role as Melvin's mother-in-law. She had a courtroom scene with Paul LeMat, but it was deleted, allegedly because of problems with LeMat. According to Dummar, the movie was accurate in almost all the details. He insisted, however, that he was not as naive as the movie made him appear. You can spot the real Dummar behind a bus-station lunch counter.

The Men

United Artists, 1950. (85m.) Dir: Fred Zinnemann. Sp: Carl Foreman, b/o his story. Cast: Marlon Brando, Teresa Wright, Everett Sloane, Jack Webb, Richard Erdman, Arthur Jurado, Virginia Farmer, Howard St. John.

On-Screen: *Marlon Brando's film debut as a paraplegic.* Following his Broadway triumph in *A Streetcar Named Desire,* Marlon Brando made his first film appearance in this strong drama. He plays Ken, a paraplegic veteran of World War II who struggles to readjust to life after his injury. The film concentrates not only on Ken's personal anguish but on the many other men who have to battle fear, loneliness, and feelings of inadequacy in order to achieve even a small triumph. Carl Foreman's screenplay captures the frustration and pain of men whose paralysis below the waist confines them to beds or wheelchairs. Moving from bitter silence to passionate rage, Marlon Brando rivets the attention. Teresa Wright is fine playing yet another of her supportive wives, and Everett Sloane is sympathetic as the doctor who understands and deals with the plight of the paraplegic men. No doubt the treatments and attitudes will seem antiquated today, but *The Men* is still a forceful drama.

Off-Screen: Much of the film was made at the Birmingham Veterans Hospital near Los Angeles, where Marlon Brando lived for weeks, learning what it felt like to be unable to move without aid. At first Marlon Brando's eccentric acting style caused tension on the set between him and some of the other actors. Director Zinnemann recruited some of the minor players from the hospital's residents.

Mermaids

Orion, 1990. (C-111m.) Dir: Richard Benjamin. Sp: June Roberts, b/o novel by Patty Dann. Cast: Cher, Bob Hoskins, Winona Ryder, Christina Ricci, Michael Schoeffling, Caroline McWilliams, Jan Miner.

On-Screen: *Cher and her daughters struggle to remain a family.* A small, cheerful comedy, set mostly in a small, cheerful Massachusetts town in 1963, *Mermaids* centers on Mrs. Flax (Cher) and her two fatherless daughters. The Flaxes are Jewish, but with Cher as mother, they are as kosher as a ham-and-butter sandwich. Fifteen-year-old Charlotte (Ryder) is in love with Catholicism and dreams of being a nun; younger Katie (Ricci) is a swimmer with Olympic potential. By sheer coincidence, the Flaxes' nearest neighbor is a nunnery; by another coincidence, the nunnery handyman (Schoeffling) is excessively handsome, Charlotte is torn between G–d and s–x. Mrs. Flax finds Lou (Hoskins), a Jewish shoe-store owner, who is very nice and also very sexy. (Score one for short, bald, fat men!) The Flax family finally resolves its conflicts in the expected, comforting ways, but *Mermaids* is an enjoyable film. Cher as the flamboyant Mrs. Flax and Ryder as the incredibly naive Charlotte are fine, separately and together, and there are enough modest insights and funny lines to keep you smiling.

Off-Screen: The film was first set for production in 1988, with young British actress Emily Lloyd as the older daughter and Swedish director Lasse Halström at the helm. The production was postponed when Cher became ill. It was resumed in February 1989, with Winona Ryder as the daughter and Frank Oz as director. Oz clashed with his leading ladies, however—reportedly, he wanted to make the material "darker"—and he was replaced by Richard Benjamin after two weeks of shooting. (BL)

The Merry Widow

MGM, 1934. (99m.) Dir: Ernst Lubitsch. Sp: Samson Raphaelson and Ernst Vajda, b/o operetta by Victor Leon and Leo Stein. MS: Franz Lehar, with new lyrics by Lorenz Hart and Gus Kahn. Cast: Jeanette MacDonald, Maurice Chevalier, Edward Everett Horton, Una Merkel, George Barbier.

On-Screen: *MacDonald and Chevalier waltz to Lehar music.* At one moment in this glorious musical, the "Merry Widow Waltz" plays as dozens of couples whirl to the music down a mirrored hall. If you fail to respond to this rapturous image, you are watching the wrong movie. A champagne cocktail that bubbles from first frame to last, *The Merry Widow* is the best film version to date of Lehar's everpopular operetta. Jeanette MacDonald and Maurice Chevalier sparkle as the couple—she plays Marshovia's richest widow, he a dashing captain—whose stratagems and deceptions end inevitably in romance. One delightful musical number follows another: Chevalier's jaunty "I'm Going to Maxim's," or his joyful tribute to "Girls! Girls! Girls!", and MacDonald's beguiling rendition of "Villa." As director, Ernst Lubitsch contributes many of the sly and witty touches that made his films so diverting. *The Merry Widow* is memorable—and merry indeed.

Off-Screen: Singer Grace Moore wanted the title role badly. She pleaded with Irving Thalberg, but he rejected her. (She fared well, however, going to Columbia to score a success in *One Night of Love.*) MacDonald and Chevalier did not like each other; she thought he was too frisky with his hands, and he thought she was too prissy and lofty. The censor objected to a scene in which Chevalier picks up MacDonald, deposits her on a couch, and sits beside her. After creating a fuss, he decided to let the scene play if MacDonald kept her feet on the floor. The

1952 remake, with Lana Turner, was lavish but lifeless.

Midnight

Paramount, 1939. (94m.) Dir: Mitchell Leisen. Sp: Charles Brackett and Billy Wilder, b/o story by Edwin Justus Mayer and Franz Schulz. Cast: Claudette Colbert, Don Ameche, John Barrymore, Mary Astor, Francis Lederer, Rex O'Malley, Hedda Hopper, Elaine Barrie.

On-Screen: *A Cinderella in Paris finds wealth and romance in unexpected ways.* One of the brightest comedies of the thirties, *Midnight* combines a cynically witty screenplay with a set of stylish performances from an expert cast. Claudette Colbert stars as a sort of Cinderella in reverse—a penniless girl in Paris who is given her own prince and castle, then settles for a man from the lower classes. Along the way she becomes involved with a cuckolded aristocrat (Barrymore), his cheating wife (Astor), and an amorous playboy (Lederer). She also attracts a taxi driver (Ameche) who follows her to a chateau in Versailles for further complications. There are many twists and turns to the lightheaded plot; what really matters, however, is the sparkling, frequently sardonic dialogue that Brackett and Wilder keep spinning throughout the film. John Barrymore contributes the best performance. As Georges Flammarion, who loves his straying wife, he not only draws the biggest laughs but also invests the character with touches of irony and rue.

Off-Screen: Claudette Colbert replaced Barbara Stanwyck in the leading role. Mary Astor, playing Helene Flammarion, was pregnant during the filming and had to be swathed in furs or photographed behind furniture. John Barrymore, weakened by long bouts with alcohol and illness, was uncharacteristically quiet and reserved on the set. The production's most severe problem came from the clear enmity between director Mitchell Leisen and coscripter Billy Wilder. The two argued bitterly and continually about the screenplay and other matters. *Midnight* was remade in 1945 as *Masquerade in Mexico,* with Leisen repeating as director.

Midnight Cowboy

United Artists, 1969. (C-113m.) Dir: John Schlesinger. Sp: Waldo Salt, b/o novel by James Leo Herlihy. Cast: Dustin Hoffman, Jon Voight, Sylvia Miles, John McGiver, Brenda Vaccaro, Barnard Hughes, Ruth White, Jennifer Salt, Bob Balaban.

On-Screen: *Two homeless drifters move through New York's tawdry night world.* At its first release, John Schlesinger's *Midnight Cowboy* startled and disturbed audiences (and received an X rating) with its powerful, candid view of life's underside. Now it can be seen as a hardly shocking but ultimately poignant drama of two friends. Joe Buck (Voight) is a naive Texas "cowboy" who dreams of being a "stud" to New York City's rich women; "Ratso" Rizzo (Hoffman) is a chronically ill, street-smart part-time pimp who shows him the ropes. Together they share grubby adventures as they move through the sleazy night world, vividly illuminated by Salt's screenplay and Schlesinger's direction. Eventually, the two come to have a grudging regard for each other that only ends with Ratso's death. Jon Voight fleshes out his bland character admirably, but it is Dustin Hoffman who aston-

ishes with his remarkable portrayal of a pathetic loser. His wheedling pleas for pity and his fleeting attempts at pride are like the last gasps of a drowning man. A first-rate movie.

Off-Screen: The film, John Schlesinger, and Waldo Salt all won Academy Awards, and Jon Voight, Dustin Hoffman, and Sylvia Miles (as an aging hooker) were nominated. Most television stations will not show an unedited version of this film; usually any language deemed foul has been excised, along with any material judged obscene. Hoffman told *The New York Times:* "Ratso Rizzo was not character acting. That was just an autobiography of subjective feelings about oneself."

Midnight Express

Columbia, 1978. (C-121m.) Dir: Alan Parker. Sp: Oliver Stone, b/o book by Billy Hayes and William Hoffer. Cast: Brad Davis, John Hurt, Randy Quaid, Mike Kellin, Irene Miracle, Bo Hopkins, Paolo Bonacelli, Paul Smith.

On-Screen: *A nerve-jangling melodrama set in a Turkish prison.* This movie is "based on a true story," the opening legend tells us, and while we might quibble with its veracity, we cannot ignore its impact as a grim and nightmarish viewing experience. In 1970, young Billy Hayes (Davis), from Babylon, Long Island, was arrested for attempting to smuggle drugs out of Turkey and spent five shattering years in one of the nastiest of human hells, a Turkish prison. Eventually he escaped to Greece by way of what the inmates called the "midnight express." Under Alan Parker's relentless direction, the film spares no sordid detail in telling a story of depravity and sadism at the hands of the Turkish prison guards and officials. The most searing moments involve Billy's bitter, eloquent speech before the court, after which he is sentenced to thirty *additional* years, and the various encounters with the prison's evil informer, Rifka (Bonacelli), the last one especially brutal. That estimable actor, John Hurt, has an important role as Max, a drugged-out convict who has only a few remaining sparks of life after seven years of imprisonment.

Off-Screen: *Midnight Express* received Academy Awards for its screenplay (by future director Oliver Stone) and for its music score by Giorgio Moroder. Filmed mostly in a nineteenth-century British barracks on the island of Malta, it inevitably raised a roar of enraged protest from the Turkish government. Apparently, many of the incidents were not based on the exact truth, and Billy Hayes's book was not as anti-Turkish.

A Midsummer Night's Dream

Warners, 1935. (117m.) Dir: Max Reinhardt and William Dieterle. Sp (or "arranged for the screen"): Charles Kenyon and Mary C. McCall, Jr., b/o play by William Shakespeare. Cast: James Cagney, Olivia de Havilland, Dick Powell, Joe E. Brown, Mickey Rooney, Anita Louise, Ross Alexander, Jean Muir, Ian Hunter, Victor Jory, Hugh Herbert, Verree Teasdale, Frank McHugh, Arthur Treacher.

On-Screen: *Warner Bros. does Shakespeare.* On rare occasions in the thirties, Hollywood decided to turn "cultural" by producing a film version of a Shakespeare play. (MGM's *Romeo and Juliet* comes to mind.) Warners took the quantum leap with this elaborate, star-filled adaptation of the Bard's *A Midsummer Night's Dream.* Directed by the renowned Max Reinhardt (with help from his former student William Dieterle), the movie is a mixed bag, ludicrous in some portions and lovely in others. The sets are opulent but strangely gloomy, and the ballet sequences are self-consciously "arty." Still, there are haunting moments, as when the fairies and elves retreat into the night as dawn breaks. The cast members range from trying (Dick Powell as Lysander) to hilarious (Joe E. Brown as Flute the Bellows-Mender). James Cagney is clearly out of his element as Bottom, and Mickey Rooney makes a giddy but increasingly irritating Puck. The ladies are all vapid but beautiful.

Off-Screen: Warners imported Max Reinhardt from Germany to turn the play into a film spectacle. A year earlier, he had directed a stage production of the play at the Hollywood Bowl, in which Olivia de Havilland appeared. When Reinhardt proved to be ignorant about film techniques, Dieterle was made codirector. During production, Mickey Rooney broke his leg while tobogganing and came back to the set with his leg in a cast. All of his subsequent scenes had to be shot from the waist up, with a double used for long shots. Hal Mohr won an Academy Award for his shimmering photography.

Mildred Pierce

Warners, 1945. (109m.) Dir: Michael Curtiz. Sp: Ranald MacDougall, b/o novel by James M. Cain. Cast: Joan Crawford, Ann Blyth, Jack Carson, Zachary Scott, Eve Arden, Bruce Bennett, Lee Patrick, Butterfly McQueen.

On-Screen: *Joan Crawford's Oscar-winning role as a sacrificial mother.* From its famous opening (in a beach house at night, an unseen hand fires a bullet at scoundrel Zachary Scott, who mutters "Mildred!" before he dies), *Mildred Pierce* grips the attention. An intriguing combination of *film noir* and soap opera, it affords Joan Crawford her finest hour as a woman who will go to any lengths to pamper and protect her vicious and ungrateful daughter Veda (Blyth). (The lengths begin with a loveless marriage and end with murder.) While much of the cynical dialogue and murky atmosphere belong to *film noir,* Mildred's devotion to her wretched daughter has the texture of soapsuds. It's all compulsively watchable, even if Crawford is not really convincing as a household drudge or waitress. Shedding the ingenue image of her earlier career, Ann Blyth also does her best in a preposterous role. The movie's sharpest lines go to Eve Arden as Mildred's friend ("Veda's convinced me that alligators have the right idea. They eat their young").

Off-Screen: The record is unclear, but apparently a number of other actresses either wanted or were considered for the title role before it went to Joan Crawford. (Among them: Bette Davis, Barbara Stanwyck, and Rosalind Russell.) Seven writers worked on the screenplay, but no version could pass the censors. Ranald MacDougall thought of the idea of telling the story in flashback. At first Curtiz was extremely reluctant to direct Crawford, and their first days on the set were stormy. ("You and your damned Adrian shoulder pads!" he reportedly shouted at her.) But he learned to work with her, and they ended on a friendly basis.

One source claims that Shirley Temple was considered for the role of Veda. (The mind boggles.)

Miller's Crossing

Fox, 1991. (114m.) Dir: Joel Coen. Sp: Joel and Ethan Coen. Cast: Gabriel Byrne, Marcia Gay Harden, Albert Finney, John Turturro, Jon Polito, J. E. Freeman.

On-Screen: *Gangsters battle for supremacy in Prohibition days.* Either a scorecard or a nimble brain is required to follow the twists and turns of this offbeat gangster film. After creating the fascinating *film noir Blood Simple* in 1984, followed by the raucously amusing *Raising Arizona* in 1987, the brothers Coen turned to the gangster genre with *Miller's Crossing.* The film summons up the familiar characters from the old gangster melodramas—the burly crime boss, the seductive moll, the ambitious henchman, etc.—but seems to view them under the influence of some hallucinogenic drug. Their double crosses and acts of treachery and violence are so convoluted that they become difficult to follow. The central figure is tough, laconic Gabriel Byrne, hired gun for kingpin Albert Finney, who plays both sides in a gang war and manages to survive the mayhem. The photography is striking, and there are several viscerally powerful scenes; still the movie makes one long for Warners' unadorned approach to the underworld of gangsters and hoodlums.

Off-Screen: The Coen brothers followed their usual pattern for this movie, with Joel directing, Ethan producing, and both brothers writing the screenplay. Gabriel Byrne's comment: "The film itself, though an homage to the gangster movies of previous years, deals with relationships in a very complex way. It's not simply a pastiche of previous films."

Million Dollar Legs

Paramount, 1932. (64m.) Dir: Edward Cline. Sp: Henry Myers and Nick Barrows, b/o story by Joseph L. Mankiewicz. Cast: W. C. Fields, Jack Oakie, Andy Clyde, Lyda Roberti, Susan Fleming, Ben Turpin, Hugh Herbert, George Barbier, Billy Gilbert.

On-Screen: *W. C. Fields and other lunatics at large in Klopstokia.* A madcap farce, one of the weirdest ever to come from Hollywood, *Million Dollar Legs* should keep you laughing with its array of sight gags and non sequiturs. W. C. Fields is the crackpot president of Klopstokia, a mythical country overrun with nuts and goats, mostly the former. To raise badly needed funds, President Fields enters the country in the Olympics, with himself as a champion weight lifter and his majordomo (Clyde) as the world's fastest runner (the "legs" of the title). Also involved are brush salesman Jack Oakie, and Lyda Roberti as a slinky spy named Mata Machree ("The Woman No Man Can Resist"). In a fast sixty-four minutes, the movie pokes fun at crazy bureaucratic governments, seductive Mata Hari–like spies, and Olympic contests where anything goes. Fields is by no means the star, but he gets his laughs, and Roberti is hilarious as the lady who "is only resisted from two to four in the afternoon."

Off-Screen: The controversy remains as to how much Joseph Mankiewicz's brother Herman, who is the film's uncredited producer, actually contributed to the screenplay of *Million Dollar Legs.* Herman *did* contribute to two previous Marx Brothers films at Paramount, *Monkey Business* and *Horse Feathers,* and *Million Dollar Legs* is undoubtedly reminiscent of the Marxes' movies. However, Henry Myers, one of the credited writers, strongly denied Herman's involvement in the script. Joseph Mankiewicz recently acknowledged that he named the kingdom of Klopstokia after the eighteenth century German poet Friedrich Klopstock, whom his father always quoted.

The Miracle of Morgan's Creek

Paramount, 1944. (99m.) Dir: Preston Sturges. Sp: Preston Sturges. Cast: Betty Hutton, Eddie Bracken, William Demarest, Diana Lynn, Porter Hall, Almira Sessions, Jimmy Conlin, Alan Bridge.

On-Screen: *Preston Sturges assaults some sacred cows in wartime.* Sturges's boldest film—it was made in 1942 but held up for release— *The Miracle of Morgan's Creek* dared to take aim at some of America's most cherished illusions at a time when such illusions were essential to wartime morale. Betty Hutton plays Trudy Kockenlocker, a small-town party girl who becomes pregnant one evening by a soldier she cannot even identify. To keep her reputation, Trudy wheedles hapless 4-F Norval Jones (Bracken) into marrying her. Many frantic situations later, she gives birth to sextuplets! Much of the movie is downright hilarious in Sturges's antic, satirical style, and Betty Hutton and Eddie Bracken work strenuously to keep the fun moving. The movie is stolen, however, by William Demarest as Trudy's deeply suspicious and cantankerous father, the town's constable. Despite its flaws, *The Miracle of*

Morgan's Creek stays in the mind as Preston Sturges's Bronx cheer to small-town America.

Off-Screen: As expected, the movie stirred up some controversy. Some viewers denounced the studio as immoral, believing that the heroine's sextuplets were the result of her being promiscuous with six different men. (Sturges's comment: "Education, though compulsory, seems to be spreading slowly.") Sturges wrote that he was required to delete one scene in which the rector of the town's church warns the young women in his congregation to "beware . . . of confusing patriotism with promiscuity." The studio was apparently nervous about showing a clergyman in a humorous light.

Miracle on 34th Street

Fox, 1947. (96m.) Dir: George Seaton. Sp: George Seaton, b/o story by Valentine Davies. Cast: Maureen O'Hara, John Payne, Edmund Gwenn, Natalie Wood, Gene Lockhart, Porter Hall, William Frawley, Thelma Ritter, Jerome Cowan.

On-Screen: *An old gent claims that he is really Santa Claus.* As cheerful, brightly wrapped, and welcome as a Christmas gift, *Miracle on 34th Street* centers on Edmund Gwenn, a white-bearded oldster who insists that he really *is* Kris Kringle. Hired as the holiday Santa for Macy's department store, he soon has everyone in an uproar over his claim. Most involved with old Kris are a divorcée (O'Hara) who works for Macy's, her too-sensible young daughter (Wood), and a neighborly lawyer (Payne). This hugely popular movie draws much of its fun from Kris's interaction with those who question

his sanity, notably Macy's resident psychiatrist (Hall). (Hollywood in the forties insisted on oversimplifying or ridiculing psychiatry.) Everything converges at a sanity hearing for Kris, which resounds with all of the reassuring sentiment of a Frank Capra film. By this time even the judge believes that Kris is truly Santa.

Off-Screen: Gwenn, Davies, and Seaton (screenplay) all won Oscars. Look for Thelma Ritter in her film debut as a customer, and for Jack Albertson as a young postal employee. In 1963, the story was adapted by Meredith Willson for the musical stage as *Here's Love*. A 1973 television remake was scarcely noticed.

The Miracle Worker

United Artists, 1962. (107m.) Dir: Arthur Penn: Sp: William Gibson, b/o his play. Cast: Anne Bancroft, Patty Duke, Victor Jory, Inga Swenson, Andrew Prine, Beah Richards.

On-Screen: *The story of young Helen Keller and her teacher Annie Sullivan.* As on Broadway in 1959, the centerpiece of this powerful drama is the acting, notably the two extraordinary performances by Anne Bancroft as Annie Sullivan, a feisty teacher of the handicapped with her own sorrowful history, and young Patty Duke as Helen Keller, her blind and deaf pupil. As Annie fights to gain authority over the wildly uncontrollable Helen, and to make her link words with objects, their relationship reaches a riveting crescendo in the famous battle sequence. Their exhausting fight to the finish is easily the film's highlight, but the triumphant ending will move you to tears. Both Bancroft and Duke richly deserved their Oscars (Duke for Best Supporting Actress), and except for Victor Jory's strident performance as Helen's father, the rest of the cast does as well as can be expected in the shadow of the two leading players. "One word—and I can put the world in your hands!" Annie tells Helen. She did just that, with results that enhanced the world.

Off-Screen: The story was first seen as a television play on the program "Playhouse 90" in 1957, with Teresa Wright and Patty McCormack in the leading roles. Seventeen years after the 1962 film of *The Miracle Worker,* the story came full circle with another television version of the play, with Patty Duke (then Patty Duke Astin) as Annie Sullivan and Melissa Gilbert as Helen. William Gibson wrote a sequel, *The Monday After the Miracle,* which ran briefly on Broadway in 1982.

Misery

Castle Rock, 1990. (107m.) Dir: Rob Reiner. Sp: William Goldman, b/o novel by Stephen King. Cast: James Caan, Kathy Bates, Frances Sternhagen, Richard Farnsworth, Lauren Bacall.

On-Screen: *A writer is held captive by a deranged woman.* Paul Sheldon (Caan), author of a series of hugely popular novels about a character named Misery Chastaine, has a serious auto accident deep in the snowbound wilderness of Colorado. He is rescued by Annie Wilkes (Bates), a onetime nurse who lives alone and is his "number-one fan." She also turns out to be a dangerous psychotic who makes him her prisoner when she

learns that her beloved Misery is about to die. The two begin a deadly cat-and-mouse game that ends violently. *Misery* is undoubtedly gripping, and Bates's Oscar-winning performance is excellent, but except for a gory conclusion, the film is really not much different—or better—than a television "Movie of the Week." Also, the situation contains all sorts of gaps in logic that you should try to ignore if you want to suspend disbelief. Lauren Bacall appears briefly as Caan's worried agent.

Off-Screen: Annie Wilkes's house, where most of the story takes place, was built in Nevada, where exteriors were shot for four weeks, then reconstructed in Los Angeles. At one point Rob Reiner considered Bette Midler for the role of Annie Wilkes, but she was afraid that it would spoil her image. Reiner also worked on the script for several months with Warren Beatty before finally signing James Caan.

The Misfits

United Artists, 1961. (124m.) Dir: John Huston. Sp: Arthur Miller, b/o his story. Cast: Clark Gable, Marilyn Monroe, Montgomery Clift, Eli Wallach, Thelma Ritter, Kevin McCarthy, Estelle Winwood.

On-Screen: *Sentimental, but compelling, tale of rootless Nevadans.* They've all seen better days: Gay (Gable), an aging cowboy who's through with "roping a dream"; Perce (Clift), a burned-out rodeo star; and Guido (Wallach), the embittered member of the trio who ropes his pals into rounding up wild horses to sell as food. Into their lives comes Roslyn (Monroe), an ex-stripper-with-a-soul, whose life-affirming innocence gives Gay and herself hope for happiness together. Until this happens, however, there are emotional obstacles to overcome, not the least Roslyn's hysterical reaction to the cowboys' roundup of the wild horses. Ultimately, you'll find Gay's reassurance to Roslyn about their uncertain future—"Just head for that big star straight on. . . . It'll take us right home"—a poignant reminder that not long after completing the film, the two screen legends were themselves to "head for that big star." *The Misfits* is a curious, uneven, yet haunting movie.

Off-Screen: John Huston first thought of Robert Mitchum for the lead but Mitchum told him that the screenplay made no sense. Gable was also baffled until Huston explained, "It's sort of an eastern Western. It's about our lives' meaninglessness and maybe how we got to where we are." Gable didn't live to see what was to be his final performance, having succumbed to heart failure two weeks after shooting was finished. Filming in Nevada was fraught with difficulties: Playwright Miller and Monroe's marriage was breaking up, and her unprofessionalism in repeatedly keeping Huston and fellow cast members waiting on the set made the fifty-nine-year-old veteran actor's physically active role all the more exhausting. See *The Story of "The Misfits"* by James Goode (Bobbs Merrill, 1963). (CFB)

Missing

Universal, 1982. (C-122m.) Dir: Constantin Costa-Gavras. Sp: Constantin Costa-Gavras and Donald Stewart, b/o book by Thomas Hauser. Cast: Jack Lemmon, Sissy Spacek, John Shea, Melanie Mayron, Charles Cioffi, David Clennon, Joe Regalbuto, Janice Rule, Richard Venture.

On-Screen: *A man searches for his missing son in a volatile South American country*. Based on a true story, director Costa-Gavras's first American movie is a taut, riveting political thriller. After Charlie Horman (Shea), an impetuous young American, vanishes during a military coup in a Latin-American country (presumably Chile in 1973), his father, Ed (Lemmon), begins a search to find him. Stiff-backed and conservative, and resentful of Charlie's blunt-speaking counterculture wife, Beth (Spacek), Horman changes as he comes up against not only the violence and brutality of the country but also the political expediency and possible duplicity of American officials, both in the coup and in his son's murder. Costa-Gavras clearly has no liking for American policy, but he does create a few sympathetic American characters, including Mayron as a friend of Shea's (who is seen only in flashback) and Spacek. His most electrifying scenes recreate the terrifying, disorienting atmosphere of a country in upheaval. In a dramatic role, Jack Lemmon uses the coil-spring edginess he usually brings to his comedy playing and gives a deeply felt performance.

Off-Screen: Jack Lemmon refused to meet Ed Horman until after the movie was completed, stating, "If I can treat him as if he was fictional, as most characters are, then I'm not inhibited." Mexico served as a stand-in for Chile. Costa-Gavras and Stewart (with an uncredited contribution by John Nichols) won an Oscar for their screenplay. The film, Lemmon, and Spacek were all nominated.

Mississippi Burning

Orion, 1988. (C-125m.) Dir: Alan Parker. Sp: Chris Gerolmo. Cast: Gene Hackman,

Willem Dafoe, Frances McDormand, Brad Dourif, R. Lee Ermey, Gailard Sartain, Stephen Tobolowsky, Michael Rooker.

On-Screen: *An FBI investigation sparks a firestorm of racism and violence.* In 1964, three civil-rights workers were murdered in Philadelpia, Mississippi. After an investigation, seven of the nineteen men arrested, including the town's deputy sheriff, were convicted of conspiracy to murder. Drawing on that incident, without recreating it or its consequences, Alan Parker fashioned this compelling drama. When the workers disappear in a virulently racist Mississippi town, two FBI agents are sent to investigate. One (Hackman) is a Southerner, a former Mississippi sheriff who knows how to bend the rules to get results; the other (Dafoe) is a by-the-book man, determined to stay within the law. As their investigation provokes resentment, anger, and finally more violence, the two battle each other bitterly until Hackman's methods prevail and they uncover the ugly truth. The central concept—two radically different men unite in a common cause—is banal, and reasonable questions do arise about the film's distortion of historical fact. But Parker's feverish style does create a vivid atmosphere and some exciting scenes. Oscar-nominated Gene Hackman is brilliant as a man whose "good ol' Southern boy" exterior conceals a caring, committed man.

Off-Screen: *Mississippi Burning* was nominated for seven Academy Awards, including Best Picture, but only Peter Biziou won for his cinematography. Milos Forman and John Schlesinger were proposed to direct, but Orion settled on Alan Parker. Many of the scenes were filmed in areas of Mississippi over a ten-week period; derelict churches and other structures were set ablaze, and the final funeral anthem was sung by the choir of a small church in Jackson. A former Mississippi sheriff sued the producers, claiming that he was the model for the film's sheriff and was done "terrible harm."

Mister Roberts

Warners, 1955. (C-123m.) Dir: John Ford and Mervyn LeRoy. Sp: Frank Nugent and Joshua Logan, b/o play by Joshua Logan and Thomas Heggen. Cast: Henry Fonda, James Cagney, William Powell, Jack Lemmon, Betsy Palmer, Ward Bond, Nick Adams, Harry Carey, Jr.

On-Screen: *Comedy-drama aboard a Navy cargo ship.* Its setting—the Pacific during World War II—has dated this movie not at all. The main reason it still entertains are the terrific performances turned in by the four principals of the virtually all-male cast. Stuck "between the islands of Tedium and Ennui" are the officers and crew of the U.S.S. *Reluctant,* whose chief contribution to the war effort is delivering toothpaste and toilet paper to other ships. Fonda plays the pensive, well-loved Lieutenant (jg) Roberts, who openly defies the sputtering, tyrannical captain (Cagney) while aching to see combat. Lemmon is hilarious as the irrepressible Ensign Pulver, and Powell makes a suave ship's doctor, adept at improvising "cocktails." Highlights include the crew's rapturous discovery of nurses on a nearby island and Pulver's rebellious destruction of the ship's laundry. Fonda's moving portrayal is one of his most memorable.

Off-Screen: Fonda, star of the 1948 play, performed the title role on Broadway and on tour for three-and-a-half years. Ford insisted on Fonda for the movie, although others preferred Marlon Brando or William Holden. Ironically, a combination of illness and bitter disagreements with Fonda over the actor's interpretation of the role led to Ford's withdrawal, and LeRoy took over. After the film was completed, Jack Warner called in Joshua Logan to refilm two key scenes, including the one in which the laundry blows up. Lemmon won a Best Supporting Oscar. A television series based on Heggen's work appeared in 1965, and a needless movie sequel, *Ensign Pulver,* was produced in 1964. (CFB)

Moby Dick

Warners, 1956. (C-116m.) Dir: John Huston. Sp: Ray Bradbury and John Huston, b/o novel by Herman Melville. Cast: Gregory Peck, Richard Basehart, Leo Genn, Orson Welles, James Robertson Justice, Harry Andrews, Bernard Miles, Mervyn Johns, Friedrich Ledebur.

On-Screen: *A New England sea captain's search-and-destroy obsession.* Maybe Gregory Peck is right about the futility of trying to dramatize Melville's nineteenth-century symbolic allegory: "I still think it all belongs between the covers of a book." And some moviegoers may have a point in noting that Peck's gaunt, bewhiskered Captain Ahab distractingly resembles "Honest Abe" Lincoln. No matter. Huston's eye-filling, extraordinarily powerful movie comes as close to capturing Melville's vision of a God-defying monomaniac as we're likely to get. The cast is generally fine, with a standout cameo by Orson Welles as Father Mapple, whose faith in God's goodness contrasts with Ahab's view. The climax, as the *Pequod* overtakes and is attacked by the great white whale that mutilated Ahab long ago, is one of the most thrilling sequences ever filmed. Seeing the movie, you may find yourself in disagreement with critic Peck.

Off-Screen: The studio had filmed the novel in 1926 (as a silent, *The Sea Beast*) and in 1930, both times with John Barrymore as Ahab. Huston had hoped to star his father, Walter Huston, but by the time production got under way, the actor had died. Youghal, Ireland, stood in for the New Bedford, Massachusetts, waterfront, with the Irish Sea and the waters off the coasts of Madeira and the Canary Islands substituting for the Pacific. The Great White Whale is a ninety-two-foot-long, electronically controlled rubber model. In 1992, coscenarist (and science-fiction writer) Ray Bradbury published a novel, *Green Shadows, White Whale,* based on his time in Ireland working on the screenplay. (CFB)

Modern Times

United Artists, 1936. (85m.) Dir: Charles Chaplin. Sp: Charles Chaplin. Cast: Charlie Chaplin, Paulette Goddard, Henry Bergman, Chester Conklin, Stanley Sanford, Hank Mann.

On-Screen: *The Tramp tangles with industrialized society.* Chaplin introduces his "little fellow" to hazards of up-to-date factory methods—a tic-inducing, mass-production conveyor belt and a wildly out-of-order feeding machine. In another hilarious scene, he's mistaken for a flag-waving Communist agitator. Of course, Charlie remains the seedy but gallant gent; this time, though, he has the adoring companionship of an equally resilient, homeless waif (Goddard). You'll laugh at his involvement with the trappings of modern mechanization—he daintily serves lunch to a factory worker (Conklin) enmeshed in the cogs of a giant machine; a television monitor in the men's room reprimands him for snatching a smoke—and you'll both chuckle and gasp as he blithely roller-skates, blindfolded, in a department store, nearly breaking his neck. The movie's satiric edge may have dulled over the years, but the feisty Tramp's antics are as rib-tickling as ever.

Off-Screen. Continuing his preference for images over words, Chaplin used sound-film techniques sparely in making the movie: his original music score, occasional sound effects, voices coming from the radio, phonograph, and the television set, and, for the first time, his own voice singing a nonsense version of the song "Titina." Goddard, who was to become Mrs. Chaplin soon after the movie was completed, had already appeared, inconspicuously, in three films (most noticeably an Eddie Cantor comedy, *The Kid from Spain,* in 1932). She was Chaplin's only leading lady to go on to a starring career of her own. It seems incredible now, but the movie stirred up a fuss among some sectors as being anticapitalist. The truth of the matter is simpler: It's a spoof of mechanization, not an indictment. (CFB)

Mogambo

MGM, 1953. (C-115m.) Dir: John Ford. Sp: John Lee Mahin, b/o his 1932 screenplay and play by Wilson Collison. Cast: Clark Gable,

Ava Gardner, Grace Kelly, Donald Sinden, Philip Stainton, Eric Pohlmann, Laurence Naismith.

On-Screen: *Clark Gable returns to Africa—via John Ford.* Over two decades after appearing opposite Jean Harlow in *Red Dust* (1932), Clark Gable starred in the same role in this lusty, colorful remake. Looking amazingly fit, he plays a rugged hunter—in *Red Dust,* he headed a rubber plantation—who tangles with ferocious animals, ferocious natives, and two women. One (Kelly) is a married and very proper British lady, ripe for a jungle fling; the other (Gardner) is a ribald, wisecracking playgirl named "Honey Bear" Kelly. As Honey Bear, Gardner gets the best lines, and she gives a funny, expert performance (considerably less vulgar than Harlow's) that earned her an Oscar nomination. One of the movie's prime attractions is Robert Surtees and Freddie Young's magnificent photography of African scenery and wildlife.

Off-Screen: The location filming in Africa generated many problems and several serious incidents. An enraged rhinoceros rammed a jeep carrying the three stars, almost turning it over before the animal was shot. Three crew members were killed when their jeep overturned in the jungle; at various times, dozens of others were injured. Natives who performed their ceremonies for the cameras would suddenly turn threatening. And both cast and crew suffered from intense heat, maddening mosquitoes, tropical infections—and the blunt, autocratic style of director John Ford.

Mommie Dearest

Paramount, 1981. (C-129m.) Dir: Frank Perry. Sp: Frank Yablans, Frank Perry,

Tracy Hotchner, and Robert Getchell, b/o book by Christina Crawford. Cast: Faye Dunaway, Diana Scarwid, Steve Forrest, Mara Hobel, Howard da Silva, Rutanya Alda, Harry Goz.

On-Screen: *"No wire hangers!"; or, Joan Crawford, monster mother*. For many years, actress Joan Crawford, whether playing shopgirls or society swells, epitomized Hollywood glamour. Behind the greasepaint, however, there was apparently a driven virago who abused her adoptive daughter, Christina. Christina related the whole sordid story in her book, and Frank Perry turned it into this film. *Mommie Dearest* has become a cult classic, mainly because of the harrowing sequence in which a nearly demented Crawford, her face a Kabuki-like mask of cold cream, beats her terrified daughter (Hobel) for using wire hangers for her clothes. Actually, the movie deserves a better fate, mainly because of Dunaway's stunning performance. Although the screenplay never delves very deeply into the reasons for Crawford's behavior, Dunaway manages to convey a blend of the pathetic and the horrific. Diana Scarwid is merely adequate as the older Christina, which weakens the latter portions of the movie, but there's a climactic confrontation between mother and daughter that scorches the screen.

Off-Screen: Anne Bancroft was first signed to play Crawford, but after many problems developed she was replaced by Faye Dunaway. Apparently, Dunaway created her own share of problems, wanting to portray Crawford in a more sympathetic light. Not to worry about little Mara Hobel's hanger scene—the girl was fortified with a layer of cotton, a layer of leather, a second layer of cotton, with pajamas over all that.

Monkey Business

Paramount, 1931. (77m.) Dir: Norman Z. McLeod. Sp: S. J. Perelman and Will B. Johnstone, with additional dialogue by Arthur Sheekman. Cast: Groucho, Harpo, Chico, and Zeppo Marx, Thelma Todd, Douglass Dumbrille, Rockcliffe Fellowes, Tom Kennedy, Ruth Hall, Harry Woods, Ben Taggart.

On-Screen: *The maniac Marxes, on ship and shore*. For this, their third movie, the Marx Brothers moved to Hollywood and Paramount Studios, where they could take advantage of the larger resources. They also took on the writing services of the brilliant humorist, S. J. Perelman. The result was a much less stage-bound effort, and uproariously funny as well. Here the brothers are stowaways on an ocean liner who tangle with bootleggers. Groucho's principal foil is not Margaret Dumont but voluptuous blonde Thelma Todd, and their tango in her stateroom is a treasured moment in the Marx movies. Another memorable sequence has the brothers attempting to leave the ship, with each of them pretending to be Maurice Chevalier. (Resourceful Harpo straps a phonograph to his back.) There's also a riotous scene in a barbershop in which the Marxes give the works to a hapless customer. *Monkey Business* is funny business indeed.

Off-Screen: Producer Joseph L. Mankiewicz warned S. J. Perelman in advance about the perils of working with the Marxes: "This is an ordeal by fire. Make sure you wear asbestos pants." Perelman later wrote, "It took five months of drudgery and Homeric quarrels, ambuscades, and intrigues that would have shamed the Borgias, but it finally reached the cameras, and the result was *Monkey Business,* a muscular hit."

Monkey Business

Fox, 1952. (97m.) Dir: Howard Hawks. Sp: Ben Hecht, Charles Lederer, and I. A. L. Diamond. Cast: Cary Grant, Ginger Rogers, Charles Coburn, Marilyn Monroe, Hugh Marlowe, Henri Letondal, Larry Keating.

On-Screen: *Scientist Cary Grant discovers a rejuvenation serum.* In many of his comedy films, director Howard Hawks enjoyed humiliating or embarrassing men of science or academia. *Bringing Up Baby* (1937) and *Ball of Fire* (1942) are well-known examples. Keeping with that tradition, *Monkey Business* (not to be confused with the 1931 Marx Brothers comedy of the same name) has Cary Grant as an absentminded chemist (shades of *Baby!*) who accidentally discovers the formula for a serum that causes a reversion to childhood. One sip turns him into an energetic teenager, and soon his wife (Rogers) joins him in a bad case of galloping adolescence. The movie strains to be a carefree farce, but the sight of the stars behaving like children is merely embarrassing. As Grant's boss at the chemical works, Charles Coburn gets the movie's only memorable lines. Handing a letter to secretary Marilyn Monroe, he says "Find someone to type this." Then, ogling her well-rounded contours, he adds, "Anybody can type!"

Off-Screen: The movie started shooting under the title, *Darling, I Am Growing Younger.* Cary Grant later offered this comment on Marilyn Monroe: "I found her a very interesting child. I was able to have several chats with her on the set and I thought her most attractive, very shy and very eager to learn her job. We discussed books and I mentioned a few she might want to read."

Monsieur Verdoux

United Artists, 1947. (123m.) Dir: Charles Chaplin. Sp: Charles Chaplin. Cast: Charlie Chaplin, Martha Raye, Isobel Elsom, Marilyn Nash, Mady Correll, Fritz Leiber.

On-Screen: *Chaplin's unexpectedly macabre comedy-drama.* A jobless bank clerk living in Paris during the thirties, Verdoux (Chaplin) is charming and devoted to his family. He also woos and weds rich and foolish women, then murders them for their money. If wars can be countenanced, he argues, why should a loving, desperate man be executed for supporting his family? Despite its grim goings-on, the movie is very funny at times, as when Verdoux bungles his attempt to drown the bumptious Annabella Bonheur (Raye). Such clownish antics are offset by dreary philosophical exchanges between Verdoux and (a Chaplin hallmark) the pretty street girl (Nash) whom he befriends. For all its faults—some primitive sets and photography—it's a courageous attempt to make a black comedy before that genre became fashionable. Credit Chaplin with tackling an ambitious, Shavian theme, even though the result lacks Shaw's corrosive wit.

Off-Screen: The elements of this "comedy of murders," as Chaplin terms it, were suggested by Orson Welles, who wanted to cast

Chaplin in a movie based on the infamous career of Henri Landru, the French "Blue-beard" who killed at least ten widows during World War I. Reluctant to work under Welles's direction, Chaplin bought the rights instead. At first, Chaplin called his seriocomic screenplay *Lady Killer*. Because the movie came along so soon after World War II (a justifiable armed conflict), special-interest groups denounced the film as unpatriotic. Many critics and moviegoers, however, applauded its daring theme. Chaplin's original screenplay was nominated for an Oscar. (CFB)

The Moon Is Blue

United Artists, 1953. (95m.) Dir: Otto Preminger. Sp: F. Hugh Herbert, b/o his play. Cast: William Holden, David Niven, Maggie McNamara, Tom Tully, Dawn Addams, Fortunio Bonanova.

On-Screen: *A virginal young thing attracts two men.* Once upon a time, in the dear dead days certainly beyond recall, the movie censors, in their infinite wisdom, objected vociferously to this movie's flippant use of such words as "virgin" and "pregnant." Indeed, their disapproval caused a brief uproar in the media. Viewed all these years later, this film version of the Broadway comedy now seems laughably tame, a lightweight trifle concerning a militantly virginal actress (McNamara), a bachelor (Holden), and a lecherous neighbor (Niven). In the end, of course, the bachelor, worn down by the girl's relentless purity, proposes marriage. On the strength of all the publicity, *The Moon Is Blue* scored a hit, but it was hardly worth all the fuss. Still, it remains a footnote in film history.

Off-Screen: United Artists wanted someone other than Niven in the third leading role, claiming that the actor was "all washed up." But Preminger insisted on keeping him. Five years later, Niven won an Academy Award for *Separate Tables* (1958). After the Catholic Legion of Decency condemned *The Moon Is Blue* and the Breen office denied it the Production Code Seal, director Preminger defied one and all by sending it quickly into release.

Moonstruck

MGM, 1987. (C-102m.) Dir: Norman Jewison. Sp: John Patrick Shanley. Cast: Cher, Nicolas Cage, Olympia Dukakis, Vincent Gardenia, Danny Aiello, Julie Bovasso, John Mahoney, Louis Guss, Feodor Chaliapin, Anita Gillette.

On-Screen: *Norman Jewison's warmhearted toast* a la famiglia. A thoroughly delightful comedy—observant, pungent, and very funny—*Moonstruck* stars Cher in her Oscar-winning role as a young widow who becomes engaged to the dim but decent Aiello, then finds herself inexplicably drawn to his estranged, eccentric younger brother (Cage). Their love affair develops against the background of Cher's effusive, close-knit Italian-American family. John Patrick Shanley's screenplay (also an Oscar-winner) sparkles with comically offbeat touches and richly rounded characters, including Olympia Dukakis (yet another Oscar winner, for Best Supporting Actress) as Cher's plain-speaking mother; Vincent Gardenia as her straying yet loving father; and Feodor Chaliapin as her befuddled grandfather. Cher dominates the film as a woman transformed by love into a confident beauty. In the end, as the camera pans across the shelf of family photographs, you may find yourself as "moonstruck" as the characters.

Off-Screen: John Patrick Shanley originally wrote the screenplay for Sally Field—it was then called *The Bride and the Wolf*—but by the time it reached MGM for production, Cher took over the leading role. She was coached in her Brooklyn accent by Julie Bovasso, who plays her aunt in the film. Despite strenuous objections, Cher insisted on Nicolas Cage for her leading man.

The More the Merrier

Columbia, 1943. (104m.) Dir: George Stevens. Sp: Richard Flournoy, Lewis R. Foster, Robert Russell, and Frank Ross, b/o story by Robert Russell and Frank Ross. Cast: Jean Arthur, Joel McCrea, Charles Coburn, Richard Gaines, Bruce Bennett, Ann Savage, Ann Doran, Grady Sutton.

On-Screen: *Romance and housing in wartime Washington.* In the World War II years, a number of comedies (*Standing Room Only, The Doughgirls,* etc.) touched on the dire shortage of housing in the nation's capital. One of the brightest entries, *The More the Merrier* concerns three people (a working girl, an army sergeant, and an elderly millionaire) who share a single Washington apartment. Inevitably, there are complications, with the old gentleman playing Cupid to the girl and the sergeant. Arthur and McCrea play the lovers with charm and ease to spare, but Coburn steals the show in an Oscar-winning performance as the genial Mr. Dingle. The best scenes: Arthur and Coburn turn their attempt at a morning schedule into a comic shambles, and Arthur

and McCrea behave amorously on the stoop of their apartment house. A popular wartime film, *The More the Merrier* won a Best Picture nomination, and Arthur was also nominated as Best Actress.

Off-Screen: For a deftly handled rooftop scene, the studio built a "rooftop" that covered the entire floor of a soundstage, complete with water tanks, chimney tops, ventilator outlets, and other items. The movie was remade in 1966 as *Walk, Don't Run,* with Cary Grant in Coburn's role. (It was the actor's last film.) The story was moved from Washington to Tokyo during the 1964 Olympics.

Morning Glory

RKO, 1933. (74m.) Dir: Lowell Sherman. Sp: Howard J. Green, b/o play by Zoë Akins. Cast: Katharine Hepburn, Adolphe Menjou, Douglas Fairbanks, Jr., C. Aubrey Smith, Mary Duncan.

On-Screen: *Katharine Hepburn in her Oscar-winning role as an aspiring actress.* You may choose to admire Katharine Hepburn or have the urge to throttle her, but you can hardly ignore her tremulous performance as Eva Lovelace in this, her third film. Playing a hopeful, inexperienced young woman who is seeking her chance in the Broadway theater, she twangs her way through the role with assurance, ultimately impressing everyone who comes into her life. Adolphe Menjou is the producer who is understandably baffled by her at first, and Douglas Fairbanks, Jr., is the playwright who finds her fascinating. C. Audrey Smith plays the veteran actor who befriends her and ultimately warns her about becoming a "morning glory" that "fades before the sun is very high." Hepburn's big moment comes at a party where she stuns the guests with the balcony scene from *Romeo and Juliet*. Later, the actress would modify the prattling, quicksilver style she uses in *Morning Glory,* but it impressed everyone enough to award her the year's Best Actress Oscar.

Off-Screen: Working swiftly and never deviating from the continuity of the screenplay, Lowell Sherman rehearsed and shot the film in three weeks. Hepburn found this helpful—she had difficulty adjusting to the out-of-sequence shooting of her previous films. After seeing the film forty years later, Hepburn remarked, "I should have stopped then. I haven't grown since." The film was remade unsuccessfully as *Stage Struck* in 1958, with Susan Strasberg in Hepburn's role.

The Mortal Storm

MGM, 1940. (100m.) Dir: Frank Borzage. Sp: Claudine West, Andersen Ellis, and George Froeschel, b/o novel by Phyllis Bottome. Cast: Margaret Sullavan, James Stewart, Robert Young, Frank Morgan, Maria Ouspenskaya, Bonita Granville, Irene Rich, Gene Reynolds, Dan Dailey.

On-Screen: *A German family confronts the terrors of Nazism.* Before America entered World War II, some studios (notably Warner Bros.) offered cautionary films concerning the rising Nazi threat. *The Mortal Storm,* adapted from Phyllis Bottome's best-selling novel, is one of the most potent: a moving, if slightly overbaked, story of the destruction of a German-Jewish family during the early years of Hitler. Frank Morgan gives one of his best performances as the family

head, a renowned professor who is sent to a concentration camp as his family disintegrates. His two stepsons become Nazis, while his brave daughter (Sullavan) joins with the young man (Stewart) she loves in fighting the oppressors. Their efforts end tragically. Superficial and evasive (the word "non-Aryan" is used instead of "Jew"), *The Mortal Storm* still contains affecting scenes. One, in which Stewart's mother (Ouspenskaya) "marries" the fleeing couple in her mountain home, is especially touching. As usual, Sullavan gives a sensitive performance, adding an extra measure of poignancy with her inimitable voice.

Off-Screen: After remaining silent for years, MGM decided that it was "safe" to have an anti-Nazi film. (They also noted the success of Warners' *Confessions of a Nazi Spy.*) Alarmed by the number of anti-Nazi films that appeared after *The Mortal Storm,* the isolationist America First Association, spearheaded by Charles Lindbergh, protested that these films were propaganda to force America into the war. Dan Dailey, billed as Dan Dailey, Jr., made his film debut.

Mother Wore Tights

Fox, 1947. (C-107m.) Dir. Walter Lang. Sp: Lamar Trotti, b/o book by Miriam Young. MS: Josef Myrow and Mack Gordon. Cast: Betty Grable, Dan Dailey, Mona Freeman, Connie Marshall, Vanessa Brown, Veda Ann Borg, Señor Wences.

On-Screen: *A retired vaudeville couple has child problems in this nostalgic musical.* One of Betty Grable's most popular musicals, and the first of several that teamed her with amiable Dan Dailey, *Mother Wore Tights* is a thin but sweetly sentimental family tale about a married vaudeville team who retire to raise their two daughters (Freeman and Marshall), and then must cope with their older girl's resentment of their "show-biz" background. That's about all, but the score has several hit numbers ("You Do" and "Kokomo, Indiana") and some pleasant turns by Grable and Dailey, individually or in tandem. Gift-wrapped in Fox's ultrabright Technicolor, the movie was a nice diversion. The indefatigible Alfred Newman won an Oscar for Best Scoring of a Musical Picture.

Off-Screen: The production was delayed while Fox negotiated with Warner Bros. for the services of James Cagney. The negotiations failed, as did a bid for Fred Astaire. Fox finally bought up Dan Dailey's contract with MGM. The voice of the film's narrator belongs to Anne Baxter.

Moulin Rouge

United Artists, 1952. (C-123m.) Dir: John Huston. Sp: Anthony Veiller and John Huston, b/o novel by Pierre La Mure. Cast: Jose Ferrer, Colette Marchand, Suzanne Flon, Zsa Zsa Gabor, Katherine Kath, Muriel Smith, Eric Pohlmann.

On-Screen: *The life and art of tortured genius Henri de Toulouse-Lautrec.* If color were the only or even the principal factor in evaluating a film, *Moulin Rouge* might be judged a masterwork. Exquisitely photographed by Osward Morris, in collaboration with special color consultant Eliot Elisfon and fashion artist Marcel Vertes, this movie stuns the eye with its vision of Paris in the 1890s. The reproductions of Toulouse-Lautrec's paintings are meticulous, and the scenes at the Moulin Rouge alone are breathtaking in their vividness. Dramatically, however, *Moulin Rouge* is less successful. Toulouse-Lautrec (Ferrer) is portrayed as a bitter, cynical alcoholic whose growth was stunted by a childhood accident. Desperately unhappy, he becomes obsessed with a perverse prostitute (Marchand) who torments and humiliates him. Later, he is involved with a sympathetic woman (Flon) whom he alienates with his harsh behavior. Jose Ferrer is perfectly competent as Toulouse-Lautrec, but hindered by a static screenplay, he fails to capture the full anguish of the artist, and his destruction by the willful Marchand is never quite as moving as intended. Zsa Zsa Gabor plays Jane Avril, the beautiful, giddy chanteuse at the Moulin Rouge, whom Toulouse-Lautrec immortalized in his paintings.

Off-Screen: To play Toulouse-Lautrec, Jose Ferrer had to wear a special rig that strapped his calves backward painfully so that he could wear his shoes on his knees. Ferrer reached the point where he could walk naturally in the rig, but when he took it off, his legs had to be massaged for long periods to return enough circulation so that he could walk normally. The movie won deserved Oscars for art direction—set decoration and for costume design. It was also nominated in the categories of Best Picture, Best Actor, and Best Director. Georges Auric's lilting theme song was given new lyrics ("Theme from *Moulin Rouge*—Where Is Your Heart?") and became a popular hit.

Mr. & Mrs. Bridge

Miramax, 1990. (C-127m.) Dir. James Ivory. Sp: Ruth Prawer Jhabvala, b/o novels by Evan S. Connell. Cast: Paul Newman, Joanne Woodward, Blythe Danner, Simon Callow, Kyra Sedgwick, Robert Sean Leonard, Margaret Walsh, Austin Pendleton, Saundra McClain.

On-Screen: *A midwestern couple and their children, over the years.* Walter Bridge (Newman) is a well-to-do lawyer, stodgy, conservative, and more than a little dense, but with deeply hidden pockets of lasciviousness. India Bridge (Woodward) is timid, gentle, and a little vague, but with submerged wells of emotion. The Bridges of Kansas City, Missouri, would seem an unlikely couple to form the center of a film, but this adaptation of two Evan Connell novels manages to make them fascinating and even complex. Ruth Prawer Jhabvala's screenplay moves from 1937 to the war years, touching on crucial and not-so-crucial moments in the lives of the Bridges and their three children. Their story is necessarily episodic, but subtleties abound: Mrs. Bridge, suddenly trying to make her feeling of invisibility known to her oblivious husband; Mr. Bridge, smiling slightly as he watches can-can dancers in a Paris nightclub; Mrs. Bridge, her face aglow as she pores over the contents of a safety deposit box. Paul Newman is singularly fine as Mr. Bridge, but it's Joanne Woodward's repressed, eternally hopeful India Bridge you're likely to remember. And cheers to Blythe Danner as Mrs. Bridge's unhappy friend.

Off-Screen: Joanne Woodward's performance won her a Best Actress Oscar nomination. Many of the scenes were shot on location in Kansas City. To rehearse the scene in which he enacts a scene from *Romeo and Juliet* with his aspiring actress daughter, Paul Newman had Kansas Senator Robert Dole recite part of the balcony scene into a tape recorder to get the accent right.

Mr. and Mrs. Smith

RKO, 1941. (95m.) Dir: Alfred Hitchcock. Sp: Norman Krasna. Cast: Carole Lombard, Robert Montgomery, Gene Raymond, Lucile Watson, Philip Merivale, Jack Carson.

On-Screen: *A marital comedy directed by whom?* The one and only surprise of this film is its director. After establishing his reputation as a master of suspense, Alfred Hitchcock took a vacation from mayhem with this moderately amusing comedy. The fun begins when Anne and David Smith (Lombard and Montgomery) learn that they were never legally wed and David wonders aloud whether he would do it again. Big mistake. Inevitably, he is forced to pursue and win Anne all over again. Somewhere at midpoint, the movie turns strained, but there are a few bright spots under Hitchcock's routine direction. It all roars to a showdown in a Lake Placid cabin—comedies of that era often wound up in either a country home or a courtroom. Those who fancy world's fairs will be interested in a sequence in which Anne and her new suitor (Raymond), who is also David's business partner, are trapped on the Parachute Ride at the 1940 World's Fair in New York City. Otherwise, *Mr. and Mrs. Smith* is merely an offbeat entry in the Hitchcock filmography.

Off-Screen: It was Carole Lombard who got the extraordinary notion to ask Alfred Hitchcock to direct this film. Both Lombard and Hitchcock wanted Cary Grant for the lead, but he was unavailable, so they chose Robert Montgomery instead. When Lombard overheard someone remark that Hitchcock "herded his actors like cattle," she rigged up a tiny corral near the set and brought in three young heifers whom she labeled "Lombard," "Montgomery," and "Raymond."

Mr. Blandings Builds His Dream House

RKO, 1948. (94 m.) Dir: H. C. Potter. Sp: Norman Panama and Melvin Frank, b/o novel by Eric Hodgins. Cast: Cary Grant, Myrna Loy, Melvyn Douglas, Sharyn Moffett, Connie Marshall, Louise Beavers, Reginald Denny, Lurene Tuttle.

On-Screen: *Cary Grant confronts a real-estate nightmare.* After more than four decades, the ordeal of advertising man Jim Blandings (Grant) as he builds a house may seem positively quaint, but it's also quite amusing. The premise is as simple as can be: Blandings has the dream of residing in a spacious, spanking-new Connecticut home with wife Loy and daughters Moffett and Marshall. Instead, his dream turns into a nonstop nightmare of well-digging, price-gouging, hostile weather conditions, and unreliable workmen. One disaster after another—he walks through the freshly painted living room or gets locked in a tiny supply closet with his wife—causes him to lose his temper and his patience. Loy makes a deft Mrs. Blandings, innocently choosing the exact shades of paint she wants. (The workmen believe in basic colors.) Melvyn Douglas brings a welcome wryness to his role of the family lawyer and friend who arouses Blandings's feelings of jealousy.

Off-Screen: Many years later, Myrna Loy remembered that making this film was "a joy, sheer heaven from beginning to end. . . . The picture was as smooth as glass." She marveled at her costar: "Cary's impeccable timing and delivery, his seemingly effortless performances, resulted from hard work, concentration, and a driving demand for perfection." Grant returned the compliment: "Myrna kept that spontaneity in her acting, a supreme naturalness that had the effect of distilled dynamite."

Mr. Deeds Goes to Town

Columbia, 1936. (115m.) Dir: Frank Capra. Sp: Robert Riskin, b/o story by Clarence Budington Kelland. Cast: Gary Cooper, Jean Arthur, George Bancroft, Lionel Stander, Douglass Dumbrille, Raymond Walburn, H. B. Warner, Mayo Methot.

On-Screen: *Capra's small-town eccentric overcomes the powers of cynicism and corruption.* The first of Frank Capra's true populist heroes, Longfellow Deeds (Cooper) is a guileless young greeting-card poet who inherits millions from his uncle. Assailed by a venal lawyer (Dumbrille), greedy people, and a reporter (Arthur) out to make him a laughingstock, bewildered Deeds tries to give his money to the desperate poor and is called insane. This being another of Capra's tributes to the common man, Deeds triumphs in the end and wins the reporter's love. Capra's 'Oscar-winning movie now seems naive and unsubtle, but the director's characteristic warmth and humor, plus Cooper's Oscar-nominated performance, makes it very palatable indeed. Most audiences remember the rousing climax, in which a depressed Deeds, termed "pixilated" by the old biddies of his town, finally rallies to his own defense. Add another charming performance by the delectable Jean Arthur, and you have a slightly faded movie that still has its rewards.

Off-Screen: *Mr. Deeds Goes to Town* was the first movie for which Frank Capra had his name above the title and also earned him his second Oscar as Best Director. Gary Cooper was always his first choice for the role of Longfellow Deeds. Capra later remarked: "Cooper *was* Longfellow Deeds. I can't imagine anyone playing the part any better. Who in Hollywood could play honest, humble, 'corn-tossed poet' Mr. Deeds? Only one actor: Gary Cooper." A short-lived television series based on the film surfaced in 1969.

Mr. Saturday Night

Columbia, 1992. (C-110m.) Dir: Billy Crystal. Sp: Billy Crystal, Lowell Ganz, and Babaloo Mandel. Cast: Billy Crystal, David Paymer, Julie Warner, Helen Hunt, Mary Mara, Jerry Orbach, Ron Silver, Sage Allen.

On-Screen: *The life and career of a self-destructive comedian.* You remember Buddy Young, Jr. (Crystal). In the fifties, he was a regular performer on television—the brash, hectic, sharp-tongued comedian who would do just about anything for a laugh. Somehow he never made the big time. *Mr. Saturday Night* tells Buddy's story, a sometimes funny, more often painful, account of a man who lived only to perform but who was his own worst enemy, destroying every chance with obnoxious behavior. The screenplay moves back and forth in time, revealing Buddy's relationship with his cowed, decent brother

Stan (Paymer), his patient wife, Elaine (Warner), and troubled daughter, Susan (Mara). Crystal directs competently and unobtrusively, perhaps milking too much sentiment in a vain attempt to make Buddy more sympathetic and understandable. A tour de force in some respects, Crystal's performance ultimately seems to be a patchwork of the characters he has created in his television appearances. Oscar-nominated Paymer is outstanding, never overplaying the pathos of Stan's situation and giving the movie its strongest emotional pull. *Mr. Saturday Night* draws laughs and tears, and occasionally a little blood, and that should be enough for most viewers.

Off-Screen: At the time of the movie's release, interviews with everyone associated with the production bent over backward to avoid pinpointing the true-life model for Buddy Young, Jr. Nevertheless, there were many candidates, including Milton Berle, Alan King, and Jerry Lewis (who makes a cameo appearance). Actually it was more of a composite of all those hopeful comics—doubtlessly all veterans of "The Ed Sullivan Show"—who never made it to the top rung of the ladder.

Mr. Skeffington

Warners, 1944. (127m.) Dir: Vincent Sherman. Sp: Philip G. and Julius J. Epstein, b/o novel by "Elizabeth." Cast: Bette Davis, Claude Rains, Walter Abel, Richard Waring, George Coulouris, Marjorie Riordan, Robert Shayne, John Alexander, Jerome Cowan.

On-Screen: *The changing life and times of a New York society belle.* "A woman is beautiful only if she is loved!" This dubious pronouncement forms the theme (and the cautionary sentiment) of *Mr. Skeffington,* a long and well-produced soap opera featuring one of Bette Davis's better performances. Davis portrays Fanny Trellis, a vain, frivolous belle of 1914 New York society, who marries wealthy Jewish banker Job Skeffington (Rains), then comes to loathe him for reasons involving her disreputable brother (Waring). Many years after her divorce and her estrangement from her daughter (Riordan), Fanny learns that Job has been a victim of the Nazis and is now blind. Now disfigured by age and illness, she embraces her husband, who sees her as still beautiful. Some of the film's sequences teeter at the edge of parody, but Davis, as always, invests the material with her unflagging energy and drive. Helped considerably by Claude Rains (one of her best costars), she keeps viewers awake and interested in the life of Fanny Trellis Skeffington.

Off-Screen: Bette Davis created many difficulties on the set. (One coworker remarked that filming was "five months of hell, sheer hell, with no casualties taken.") The actress demanded approval on every facet of the production. Makeup for the aged Fanny centered on a rubber mask which had to be applied each day in a two-hour process. Cinematographer Ernest Haller noted that the mask "made her look like something out of a horror movie, but she insisted on wearing it."

Mr. Smith Goes to Washington

Columbia, 1939. (129m.) Dir: Frank Capra. Sp: Sidney Buchman, b/o story by Lewis R. Foster. Cast: James Stewart, Jean Arthur, Claude Rains, Edward Arnold, Thomas Mitchell, Eugene Pallette, Harry Carey, Beulah Bondi, Guy Kibbee, H. B. Warner.

On-Screen: *Capra's naive senator finds the Devil in the nation's capital.* Not Frank Capra's best-loved film—that honor must go to *It's a Wonderful Life*—but quite possibly his best, *Mr. Smith Goes to Washington* offers a hearty dose of Americana. Jefferson Smith (Stewart) is the wide-eyed young man who is appointed senator from his state and is nearly crushed by the political machine that exercises control with an iron fist. The movie relates how Jeff, with the help of his loving assistant (Arthur), topples the dangerously powerful empire of an ambitious publisher (Arnold). Capra drains every drop of heart-stirring emotionalism from the story, especially in the climactic filibuster sequence. Sensibly, he laces it all with humor while extracting splendid performances from his cast. In his star-making role, James Stewart is the very model of gawky earnestness that can turn into righteous fervor, and Jean Arthur cuts through the heavy sentiment and flag-waving with her wry delivery.

Off-Screen: Now regarded as a classic comedy-drama, the film ran into serious trouble at its Washington, D.C., premiere. Much of the audience was outraged that Capra could show the U.S. Senate in such a bad light, and later he was vilified by Washington's press correspondents for making such a scurrilous film. Leading senators were urging Columbia to withdraw the movie from circulation. Capra defended his movie vehemently, assembling hundreds of favorable opinions. Columbia's top man, Harry Cohn, also stood his ground, and the film was released. It received a number of Oscar nominations, but only Lewis R. Foster won for his original story. The story was remade in 1977 as *Billy Jack Goes to Washington* and was also the basis for a brief television series in 1962.

Mrs. Miniver

MGM, 1942. (134m.) Dir: William Wyler. Sp: Arthur Wimperis, George Froeschel, James Hilton, and Claudine West, b/o novel by Jan Struther. Cast: Greer Garson, Walter Pidgeon, Teresa Wright, Dame May Whitty, Henry Travers, Richard Ney, Reginald Owen, Henry Wilcoxon, Helmut Dantine.

On-Screen: *A stalwart British family confronts the ordeal of World War II.* During World War II, especially in the early years, Hollywood studios liked to pay tribute to the courage and tenacity of the invaded nations. Once America joined the fray, the studio floodgates opened to films that were, in essence, propaganda efforts designed to strengthen the Allied resolve. MGM's *Mrs. Miniver* was one of the most popular, celebrating the bravery of the British populace in the face of repeated bombings and personal sacrifices. As the strong wife and mother whose well-ordered life is disrupted by the war, Kay Miniver (Garson) embodied all the virtues that were traditionally associated with her countrymen. The film takes Mrs. Miniver and her devoted husband, Clem (Pidgeon), from the tranquility of afternoon teas and flower shows to the harrowing reality of wartime. Although the British were either amused or irritated by the movie's rose-colored view of life before the war, the result was undeniably uplifting and often moving under William Wyler's polished direction.

Off-Screen: After Louis B. Mayer decided to turn the popular novel into a prestige production, Norma Shearer was offered the role of Mrs. Miniver but wouldn't consider playing a mother. Greer Garson, only thirty-three, accepted the part reluctantly. Richard Ney, who appeared as her son, married the actress in 1943. An unsuccessful sequel to the film, *The Miniver Story* (1950), had Mrs. Miniver expiring of cancer.

The Mummy

Universal, 1932. (72m.) Dir: Karl Freund. Sp: John L. Balderston, b/o story by Nina Wilcox Putnam and Richard Schayer. Cast: Boris Karloff, Zita Johann, David Manners, Arthur Byron, Edward Van Sloan, Bramwell Fletcher, Noble Johnson.

On-Screen: *An ancient Egyptian battles scientists for possession of a long-dead princess.* This chiller is notable both for its stunning visual quality and for its grisly, but oddly touching, story of the revivified mummy (Karloff) who pursues a young Englishwoman (Johann), the reincarnation of his beloved from the distant past. Freund, famed for his camera work, first in Germany and then in Hollywood (*Dracula* and *The Good Earth*, e.g.), here makes his directorial debut, and although the photography is not credited to him, his influence is clearly seen in the macabre style of this distinctly offbeat horror classic. The mummy's awakening, among the most terrifying sequences ever filmed, is unforgettable: An incantation is read over the bandaged corpse, the encrusted eyelids slowly lift, and rotted fingers move with restored life. Karloff is superb as the resuscitated mummy and, reincarnated in human form, as the sinister, modern-day Egyptian.

Off-Screen: Freund triumphed over a limited budget with unusual camera angles, bizarre lighting effects, and ingeniously designed sets, some of them in flashbacks to ancient Egypt. The gruesome makeup for the mummy and his parchment-faced incarnation as an archeologist was created by Jack Pierce, who also "designed" Dr. Frankenstein's monster. The star is billed as "Karloff" in the credits, thus allowing him to share last-name-only prestige with Garbo. Before he retired, Freund was director of photography for the "I Love Lucy" television series. Like the studio's *Dracula, Frankenstein,* and *The Invisible Man,* the movie set off a barrage of sequels, spin-offs, and remakes. Unsurprisingly, the original *Mummy* remains the most memorable. (CFB)

Murder, My Sweet

RKO, 1944. (95m.) Dir: Edward Dmytryk. Sp: John Paxton, b/o novel by Raymond Chandler. Cast: Dick Powell, Claire Trevor, Anne Shirley, Otto Kruger, Mike Mazurki, Esther Howard, Miles Mander.

On-Screen: *Private eye Philip Marlowe's auspicious screen debut.* This gratifyingly faithful adaptation of *Farewell, My Lovely* is distinguished by its crisp dialogue, imaginative direction, and starkly contrasted black-and-white photography. As the tough, incorruptible Los Angeles detective Philip Marlowe, Powell lacks the grittiness Bogart brought to the role in *The Big Sleep* (1946), but he perfectly catches Marlowe's chipper-whatever-the-odds, surface insouciance. Caught up in a typically complex Chandler plot, Marlowe helps an ex-con (Mazurki) search for his former girlfriend,

now the rich and decadent Mrs. Grayle (Trevor), who is lethally intent on keeping her wealth intact and her past hidden. Only a concession to Hollywood convention that romantically links Powell and Shirley, as Trevor's stepdaughter, mars a genuinely Chandlerian movie, and a mystery classic.

Off-Screen: Previously cast in musicals and frothy comedies, Dick Powell was eager to play Chandler's hard-boiled detective, and RKO, initially skeptical, finally signed him for the role. The movie opened as *Farewell, My Lovely,* but when the public avoided it as one more Dick Powell musical, it was quickly given its more atmospheric title. The studio had filmed the novel in 1942 as *The Falcon Takes Over,* an awkward merging of Michael Arlen's suave hero (George Sanders) with Chandler's down-at-the-heels outsider. In 1975, still another version was released, this time bearing the novel's title. Robert Mitchum was the somewhat sluggish Marlowe. (CFB)

The Music Man

Warners, 1962. (C-151m.). Dir: Morton Da Costa. Sp: Marion Hargrove, b/o musical play by Meredith Willson. MS: Meredith Willson. Cast: Robert Preston, Shirley Jones, Paul Ford, Buddy Hackett, Hermione Gingold, Timmy Everett, Ronny Howard, Pert Kelton, Susan Luckey.

On-Screen: *Musical Americana via the Broadway stage.* Exuding confidence to spare, Robert Preston recreates his stage role in this bountifully entertaining adaptation of the long-running Broadway musical. He's "Professor" Harold Hill, a cunning traveling salesman who, in 1912, convinces the citizens of River City, Iowa, to buy his band instruments and uniforms for a boys' band he will train and lead. In fact, he cannot read a note of music. Ultimately, he is exposed, but not before charming everyone, especially the demure town librarian (Jones). Many colorful musical numbers submerge this undernourished plot, from Preston's irresistible "Trouble" to the splendidly staged "Marian the Librarian." The folksiness is rather calculated, and the characters are cartoonish and sometimes excruciatingly "cute," but the production is bandbox pretty, the music is lively, and Robert Preston ties it all up with his seemingly inexhaustible energy.

Off-Screen: Shirley Jones's lisping little brother is played by Ronny Howard, who became popular on television in "The Andy Griffith Show" and "Happy Days," then became even better known as the director of such films as *Splash, Parenthood,* and *Far and Away.* Jones's mother is Pert Kelton, an unheralded but funny comic actress of the thirties.

Mutiny on the Bounty

MGM, 1935. (132m.) Dir: Frank Lloyd. Sp: Talbot Jennings, Jules Furthman, and Carey Wilson, b/o novels by Charles Nordhoff and James Norman Hall. Cast: Clark Gable, Charles Laughton, Franchot Tone, Herbert Mundin, Eddie Quillan, Dudley Digges, Donald Crisp, Movita, Mamo, Ian Wolfe.

On-Screen: *Best-remembered version of the rousing sea adventure.* This long but flavorsome movie, set in the late eighteenth century, has more than enough to keep you enthralled from start to finish. In one of his strongest roles, Gable plays Fletcher Christian, first officer of the H.M.S. *Bounty,* who leads the mutiny against the ship's strutting, sadistic captain (Laughton). Tone is cast as Byam, a foppish officer, who finally speaks out against the brutal conditions of life in the British navy. Gable delivers a virile performance in this lavishly mounted production; it's Laughton's movie, though, not only because of his formidable presence, but also because Bligh is the most complex figure in the story. A cruel martinet, he is at the same time a courageous, if demonically obsessed, born leader. The British actor lays on the histrionics with a trowel at times, but he makes the role his own and creates an unforgettable character in a terrific movie.

Off-Screen: The story of the famous mutiny was filmed earlier as *In the Wake of the Bounty* (1933). An Australian semidocumentary, it starred a young Errol Flynn as Christian. Director Lloyd's classic version is based on the first two novels of Nordhoff and Hall's trilogy—*Mutiny on the Bounty* (1932) and *Men Against the Sea* (1934). (The disastrous 1962 remake, with Marlon Brando playing a dandified Christian, includes material from the 1934 third volume, *Pitcairn's Island*.) California's Santa Catalina Island, as well as Tahiti, provided tropical background for the Oscar-winning movie. By an odd coincidence, Mexican actress Maria Castenada, billed as "Movita" in the role of a Polynesian native, many years later became Brando's second wife. In 1984, *The Bounty* (unrelated to the Nordhoff-Hall books) retold the story yet again. (CFB)

My Darling Clementine

Fox, 1946. (97m.) Dir: John Ford. Sp: Samuel G. Engel and Winston Miller, b/o story by Sam Hellman and book by Stuart N. Lake. Cast: Henry Fonda, Victor Mature, Linda Darnell, Walter Brennan, Cathy Downs, Tim Holt, Ward Bond, Alan Mowbray, Jane Darwell.

On-Screen: *The definitive Wyatt Earp–Doc Holliday Western, from John Ford.* One of the greatest Western films, and one of director Ford's finest achievements, *My Darling Clementine* will satisfy every moviegoer's desire for lusty action, while exploring deeper feelings about America and the land. Stoic and sturdy Wyatt Earp (Fonda) comes to lawless Tombstone, where he becomes marshal after his brother is murdered by the vicious Clanton gang. Aided by the darkly brooding, tubercular Doc Holliday (Mature), Earp succeeds in restoring law and order to Tombstone. The climactic shoot-out at the O.K. Corral remains the most durable version of that much-replayed incident. Some of the film's most memorable sequences, such as Earp's funeral for his brother and the town's celebration of its new church, reveal Ford's deep regard for family and community. As Wyatt Earp, Henry Fonda offers one of his most indelible performances. Joseph MacDonald's superb black-and-white photography and Dorothy Spencer's editing contribute to the film's excellence.

Off-Screen: The source material for *My Darling Clementine* was Stuart N. Lake's biography, *Wyatt Earp, Frontier Marshal,* which was also used for two earlier movies, released in 1934 and 1939. Ford, however, veered greatly from the truth about Earp, giving him a mythic quality he never really had. The director later claimed that the film's ending, in which Wyatt rides away from Tombstone, was not done by him: "I wanted Wyatt to stay there and become permanent marshal—which he did."

My Fair Lady

Warners, 1964. (C-170m.) Dir: George Cukor. Sp: Alan Jay Lerner, b/o his musical play and play by George Bernard Shaw. MS: Alan Jay Lerner and Frederick Loewe. Cast: Rex Harrison, Audrey Hepburn, Stanley Holloway, Wilfrid Hyde-White, Gladys Cooper, Jeremy Brett, Theodore Bikel.

On-Screen: *Lerner and Loewe's musical version of* Pygmalion, *brought sumptuously to the screen.* A memorable triumph on Broadway in 1956, *My Fair Lady*, the musical version of Shaw's *Pygmalion,* enjoyed a record run of 2,717 performances. Finally turned into a film, the musical fully retained its principal virtues: a score of infinite beauty and variety; an elaborate, elegant production; and Rex Harrison's stunning performance as Henry Higgins, the linguistics professor who turns a guttersnipe into a lady, then finds himself inexplicably falling in love with her. In the film, Harrison recaptures the crackling wit and impeccable style of his stage performance and talk-sings his way through Lerner's lyrics with ease and charm. Audrey Hepburn's Eliza Doolittle is more successful as the post-Higgins lady than the pre-Higgins Cockney flower-vendor, but she looks ravishingly beautiful in Cecil Beaton's gowns. Stanley Holloway repeats his inimitable stage portrait of Eliza's rascally father, Alfred Doolittle. *My Fair Lady* may lack the heartbeat of a great movie musical, but it's a stunning achievement nonetheless.

Off-Screen: In addition to Harrison's Oscar, *My Fair Lady* received Academy Awards in the categories of picture, director, cinematography (Harry Stradling), costumes (Cecil Beaton), score adaptation (Andre Previn), and art direction (Beaton and Gene Allen). Producer Jack Warner wanted Cary Grant to play Higgins but finally agreed to Rex Harrison. (He also fancied James Cagney as Alfred Doolittle.) Audrey Hepburn's voice was dubbed by Marni Nixon. During the filming, many conflicts raged between George Cukor and Cecil Beaton. At first cold and remote with Audrey Hepburn, Rex Harrison finally warmed to her and became friendly. Years later, he conceded that she had given "an enchanting performance."

My Favorite Wife

RKO, 1940. (92m.) Dir: Garson Kanin. Sp: Sam and Bella Spewack, b/o their story. Cast: Irene Dunne, Cary Grant, Gail Patrick, Randolph Scott, Donald McBride, Ann Shoemaker, Scotty Beckett, Granville Bates.

On-Screen: *Cary Grant finds himself with one wife too many.* Three years after teaming for the classic screwball comedy *The Awful Truth,* Irene Dunne and Cary Grant were reunited for this lesser, but still amusing, romp. *My Favorite Wife* has Dunne as Grant's wife, long considered dead in a shipwreck, who turns up very much alive. The problem is that Grant has just remarried. Most viewers will be able to predict the situations and the outcome, but the screenplay has a degree of wit, and the leads are charming, as always. Grant is especially funny as he reacts to the first view of his "dead" wife, tries desperately to avoid bedding down his new bride (Patrick),

or fantasizes about the man (Scott) with whom Dunne shared a deserted island for seven years. It all ends in the courtroom, where the judge (Bates) presides over the brouhaha with a hilariously grumpy and suspicious demeanor. Donald McBride also wins laughs as a confused hotel manager.

Off-Screen: Garson Kanin replaced Leo McCarey as director after McCarey was injured in a car accident. McCarey supervised much of the production from his hospital bed. The film was remade in 1963 as *Move Over, Darling,* with Doris Day and James Garner. It had originally been started as *Something's Got to Give,* with Marilyn Monroe and Dean Martin in the leading roles. Monroe was dismissed from the production and died shortly afterward.

My Favorite Year

MGM/UA, 1982. (C-92m.) Dir: Richard Benjamin. Sp: Norman Steinberg and Dennis Palumbo, b/o story by Dennis Palumbo. Cast: Peter O'Toole, Mark Linn-Baker, Jessica Harper, Joseph Bologna, Bill Macy, Lainie Kazan, Adolph Green, Anne DeSalvo, Lou Jacobi, Selma Diamond, George Wyner, Cameron Mitchell.

On-Screen: *A drunken British film star disrupts a TV variety show.* Back in the 1950s, the television program "Your Show of Shoes," starring Sid Caesar and Imogene Coca, was widely applauded for its innovative wit and style. *My Favorite Year* looks back at that time, and that program, with more affection than malice, but it's an extremely genial and often funny movie. Mark Linn-Baker is a fledgling writer with a variety program very much like "Your Show of

Shows" who is asked to watch over the week's guest star, a flamboyant, hard-drinking British film actor named Alan Swann. Peter O'Toole is hilarious in his Oscar-nominated role, reeling from one rowdy incident to the next as he thoroughly confounds or embarrasses his watchdog, Linn-Baker. Some of the characters are clearly meant to suggest "Your Show of Shows": Joseph Bologna as the show's burly, Sid Caesar–like top banana, or Adolph Green as a sort of surrogate for producer Max Liebman. O'Toole's Alan Swann resembles Errol Flynn, or any devil-may-care, frequently soused superstar. Lainie Kazan contributes a broad bit as Linn-Baker's exuberant mother.

Off-Screen: *My Favorite Year* marked the directorial debut of actor Richard Benjamin. For a number of seasons, Mark Linn-Baker starred with Bronson Pinchot in the television series "Perfect Strangers." The woman who dances with Peter O'Toole in a nightclub is the lovely thirties actress Gloria Stuart. A musical adaptation of the movie turned up on Broadway in the fall of 1992.

My Little Chickadee

Universal, 1940. (83m.) Dir: Edward Cline. Sp: Mae West and W. C. Fields. Cast: Mae West, W. C. Fields, Joseph Calleia, Dick Foran, Margaret Hamilton, Donald Meek, Ruth Donnelly.

On-Screen: *Fields meets West out West.* It's a memorable encounter: On a train to Greasewood City, W. C. Fields, the audacious King of Con Men, comes upon Mae West, the bawdy Queen of Sex. "Ah, what sym-metrical digits," he cries, fondling her fingers. The fun begins, but what should have been a historic occasion turns out to be only intermittently funny. Fields is Cuthbert J. Twillie, confidence man with a penchant for cards, liquor, and women like West, who plays shady lady Flower Belle. Together, the two ignore a silly plot line and a ramshackle production to toss around lines that sometimes draw hearty laughter. Their solo sequences work best: Fields at a card game or regaling bar patrons with his tall stories, West as an unlikely schoolteacher. When they marry—West only wants his money—he becomes an eager bridegroom to her reluctant bride. Locked from their room, he peers through the keyhole and bellows, "My dear, I have some definite pear-shaped ideas to discuss with you." Most of the time, however, their comedy styles fail to mesh. Still, it's always fun to see these icons perform.

Off-Screen: Throughout the filming, there was unmistakable tension and hostility between the two stars. Fields insisted on adding many of his own touches to the screenplay, some of which, West claimed, had nothing to do with the movie. He also circumvented West's "no liquor" clause by bringing his whiskey onto the set in a Coke bottle. Each feared and was continually wary of the other's screen-stealing tricks.

My Man Godfrey

Universal, 1936. (95m.) Dir: Gregory La Cava. Sp: Morrie Ryskind and Eric Hatch, b/o novel by Eric Hatch. Cast: William Powell, Carole Lombard, Alice Brady, Gail Patrick, Eugene Pallette, Alan Mowbray, Mischa Auer, Franklin Pangborn.

On-Screen: *Rich girl Lombard chases butler Powell.* An enormously diverting Depression comedy, *My Man Godfrey* makes the popular assumption of the time that rich folk are addled, irresponsible infants who don't deserve their wealth. Carole Lombard is the light-headed Park Avenue girl who finds a suave hobo (Powell) during a scavenger hunt and makes him the butler to her madcap family. Of course he is not what he seems, and by film's end, he has turned every family member into a recognizable human being. He also wins the heart of Lombard. The movie closes on a note of pure Depression fantasy, but the dialogue sparkles and the players are impeccable. Mischa Auer is hilarious as a permanent guest who loves to imitate a gorilla, and Alice Brady, as the mother of this brood, is the funniest of dim bulbs. A truly dismal 1956 remake starred June Allyson and David Niven.

Off-Screen: The movie's working title was *1011 Fifth Avenue,* the name of the *Liberty* magazine serial on which it was based. Both Bennett sisters, Joan and Constance, were also considered for the leading role, but Powell insisted on ex-wife Lombard. Powell had enormous praise for director Gregory La Cava: "Probably no one ever lived who was like Godfrey. But La Cava . . . made the man seem quite plausible. Actually, that was La Cava's picture. Every morning he'd give us some dialogue that he'd written during the night, and it was good dialogue. . . ."

My Sister Eileen

Columbia, 1942. (96m.) Dir: Alexander Hall. Sp: Joseph Fields and Jerome Cho-

dorov, b/o their play and stories by Ruth McKinney. Cast: Rosalind Russell, Brian Aherne, Janet Blair, George Tobias, Allyn Joslyn, Elizabeth Patterson, June Havoc.

On-Screen: *Two Ohio sisters invade New York's Greenwich Village.* Having established herself as a top-notch comic actress in *The Women* (1939), Rosalind Russell went on to play energetically funny roles in such movies as *His Girl Friday* (1940) and this rollicking farce. She carries the film as Ruth, an aspiring writer who comes to New York City with her naive sister Eileen (Blair) and becomes quickly entangled with a host of eccentrics and crackpots. Ultimately, she also finds romance with a magazine editor (Aherne). Whether coping with a noisy basement apartment or the Portuguese merchant marine, Russell plays it all with good cheer, a refreshingly acid tongue, and perfect comic timing. Commenting on eating lots of roughage on her limited diet, she comments, "I'd like to mix it with a little smoothage." Janet Blair is appropriately dewy-eyed as sister Eileen, and the rest of the cast is just fine.

Off-Screen: Over two decades, *My Sister Eileen* proved to be an extremely durable property. It was turned into a Broadway musical play called *Wonderful Town* in 1953, with Russell repeating her role, then made into a musical film with Betty Garrett in 1955 (with a different score from the stage version). It was even a television comedy series in 1960, featuring Elaine Stritch as Ruth.

The Naked City

Universal-International, 1948. (96m.) Dir: Jules Dassin. Sp: Albert Maltz and Malvin Wald, b/o story by Malvin Wald. Cast: Barry Fitzgerald, Howard Duff, Don Taylor, Dorothy Hart, Ted de Corsia, House Jameson, Adelaide Klein.

On-Screen: *The police stalk a killer in the heart of New York City.* The last film produced by columnist-journalist Mark Hellinger before his untimely death in 1947, *The Naked City* holds the distinction of being the first to be filmed largely on location in New York City. Despite William Daniels's Oscar-winning photography, which captures the grittiness and clutter of the city, the story itself is merely routine: A shady blonde is brutally murdered, and the New York police, led by Lieutenant Dan Muldoon (Fitzgerald), launches a massive manhunt to track down the killer. The investigation leads to a nest of vipers, and in an exciting climax, the killer (de Corsia) is finally trapped on the Williamsburg Bridge. Mark Hellinger himself speaks the rather corny narration: "There is a pulse to the city . . . and it never stops beating." The cast is merely competent, with Fitzgerald not entirely convincing as the dogged police lieutenant.

Off-Screen: Cameraman Daniels shot most of his scenes from inside a parked van, using a one-way mirror and tinted windows so that passersby would not be aware of the camera. Although the movie was reviewed favorably, director Dassin was not happy with the result: "I said I would do it if they let me film in the streets of New York, in real interiors, with unknown actors. They agreed, but when it came to the editing the very heart of the film was cut out. . . . I could have wept." Ironically, Paul Weatherwax won an Oscar for his editing. *The Naked City* was the springboard for a television series that ran from 1958 to 1963.

Nashville

Paramount, 1975. (C-159m.) Dir: Robert Altman. Sp: Joan Tewkesbury. Cast: Keith Carradine, Lily Tomlin, Henry Gibson, Karen Black, Ronee Blakley, Geraldine Chaplin, Michael Murphy, Barbara Harris,

371

Shelley Duvall, Ned Beatty, Barbara Baxley, Gwen Welles, Scott Glenn, Jeff Goldblum, Allen Garfield, Keenan Wynn.

On-Screen: *Robert Altman's stunning mosaic of American life, by way of country music.* This brilliant film combines scathing satire, implied political commentary, and a basically unattractive view of the nation's mores. Set at a music festival in "the country musical capital of the world," it brings together twenty-four people whose lives intertwine in a mad mélange that begins with a patriotic song ("We Must Be Doin' Somethin' Right to Last Two Hundred Years") and ends with the onstage assassination of a popular country singer (Blakley). In between the music and the violence, we witness the antics of country-music stars and their sycophants, frustrated dreamers and drifters, and even an unseen candidate for the presidency. The huge and talented cast includes Keith Carradine as a guitar-strumming womanizer, Lily Tomlin as a gospel singer who is the only white member of her group, Henry Gibson as a self-satisfied singing star, and Geraldine Chaplin as an inane reporter for the BBC. The film's many songs are either sprightly or hilarious and sometimes both; one of them, "I'm Easy," won that year's Academy Award. A triumphant film.

Off-Screen: The movie, Altman, Tomlin, and Blakley were nominated for Oscars, Tomlin and Blakley for Best Supporting Actress. Reportedly, much of the dialogue for the film was contributed by the players themselves. The actors also wrote many of the songs they perform. The men at the stag party at which Gwen Welles does her striptease were actually members of the Nashville Chamber of Commerce.

National Lampoon's Animal House

Universal, 1978. (C-109m.) Dir: John Landis. Sp: Harold Ramis, Douglas Kenney, and Chris Miller. Cast: Tim Matheson, John Belushi, Thomas Hulce, John Vernon, Verna Bloom, Peter Riegert, Karen Allen, Stephen Furst, Cesare Danova, Donald Sutherland.

On-Screen: *Fun and games at Delta House.* Bawdy, outrageous, and sporadically funny, *National Lampoon's Animal House* found its audience and became an enormous hit. At Faber College in 1962, the fraternity members at Delta House are the disgrace of the school, loathed by the nasty Dean (Vernon) who wants to expel them and by snobbish Omega House, which would like to destroy them. Leading the Delta pack in their non-stop parties, stunts, and practical jokes are makeout artist Otter (Matheson) and lunatic slob Bluto (Belushi). When the fraternity is finally expelled, the Delta men plot an elaborate revenge. The gags are scattershot, and there's not an ounce of subtlety, but some scenes may have you laughing helplessly. (Favorite moment: At a raucous toga party, Bluto listens as a guest strums his guitar and sings "I Gave My Love a Cherry," that perennial of folksingers everywhere. Bluto raises one quizzical eyebrow, then promptly demolishes the guitar. His simple apology: "Sorry.") In the closing sequence the Delta men wreck the school's big homecoming parade, and there are scattered laughs that rise above the din of crashing floats and shrieking bystanders.

Off-Screen: Most of the movie was filmed in Eugene, Oregon, where the citizens were wary of the cast and crew, not without good reason. The film's huge popularity led to nationwide toga parties, and a number of rowdy, dim-witted imitations. *National Lampoon,* the humor magazine that sponsored *Animal House,* also gave its name to a series of later films that starred Chevy Chase as a fool forever getting himself and his family in trouble. "Delta House," a television spin-off from *Animal House,* had a brief run in 1979.

National Velvet

MGM, 1944. (C-125m.) Dir: Clarence Brown. Sp: Theodore Reeves and Helen Deutsch, b/o novel by Enid Bagnold. Cast: Mickey Rooney, Elizabeth Taylor, Donald Crisp, Anne Revere, Angela Lansbury, Reginald Owen, Jackie "Butch" Jenkins, Norma Varden.

On-Screen: *A young girl rides her horse to victory.* In a picture-postcard British village, young Velvet Brown (Taylor) has a dream of riding her beloved horse Pi in the famed Grand National Steeplechase. In films such as this, dreams have a way of coming true, and with the help of Mi Taylor (Rooney), a footloose horse trainer with a checkered past, Velvet manages to triumph. *National Velvet* made Elizabeth Taylor a star, and one can see why: She radiates a youthful glow and beauty that commands our attention. The film is ideal family entertainment—unreal, to be sure, but comforting, prettily Technicolored, and uniformly well-acted. Donald Crisp and Anne Revere are stalwart as Velvet's parents (Revere won a Supporting Oscar for her wise, plain-speaking mother, her specialty in these years), and you'll be amused to see the future Jessica Fletcher of "Murder, She Wrote" as Velvet's older, flirtatious sister.

Off-Screen: Years before, MGM had thought of making *National Velvet* with Spencer Tracy and Maureen O'Sullivan as father and daughter, but the project was shelved. Producer Pandro Berman considered Elizabeth Taylor too short for the role of Velvet, but Taylor was determined to play it. She began a determined regimen to grow three inches, which she did. She also spent many hours developing her horsemanship. In the film, only difficult jumps were performed by a professional jockey; Taylor did the rest of her own riding. A television series built around young Velvet Brown had a two-year run starting in 1960. A sequel entitled *International Velvet,* with Tatum O'Neal as a grown Velvet's niece, appeared in 1978.

The Natural

TriStar, 1984. (C-134m.) Dir: Barry Levinson. Sp: Robert Towne and Phil Dusenberry, b/o novel by Bernard Malamud. Cast: Robert Redford, Glenn Close, Robert Duvall, Kim Basinger, Barbara Hershey, Wilford Brimley, Richard Farnsworth, Darren McGavin, Robert Prosky.

On-Screen: *Myth, baseball, and Robert Redford.* An extraordinary baseball player, capable of demolishing baseballs with the force of his swing, rises to national fame. On one side is his demure childhood sweetheart, urging him on to victory. On the other is a sexy blonde in conspiracy with corrupt forces to destroy him. Will he win the Big Game, or will he "throw" it, as the villains demanded? This may sound like the tired plot of a forties film from Warners, but it's actually the main story line of *The Natural.* This adaptation of Bernard Malamud's novel has a curious prologue, set sixteen years earlier in which Roy Hobbs (Redford), then a promising player, is shot by a mysterious woman (Hershey). But for all the fancy, mythical trimmings, including glowing photography, portentous music, and a star-heavy cast, *The Natural* is a surprisingly banal film. The actors strive to bring some conviction to the material, but they are defeated by one-dimensional characters.

Off-Screen: The movie's baseball sequences were shot in the War Memorial Stadium in Buffalo, New York. The uniforms and baseball gloves were recreated from period photographs. Oddly, Darren McGavin, who plays a scheming big-league bookie in the film, receives no billing and was never mentioned in the press material.

Naughty Marietta

MGM, 1935. (106m.) Dir: W. S. Van Dyke II. Sp: Albert Hackett, Frances Goodrich, and John Lee Mahin, b/o operetta by Victor Herbert and Rida Johnson Young. MS: Victor Herbert. Cast: Jeanette MacDonald, Nelson Eddy, Frank Morgan, Elsa Lanchester, Douglass Dumbrille, Cecilia Parker.

On-Screen: *The first of the MacDonald-Eddy musical teamings.* At the time it seemed unlikely that pairing MGM's resident soprano, Jeanette MacDonald, with a stocky, wooden baritone named Nelson Eddy would draw much of a response from movie audiences. Yet *Naughty Marietta* proved to be a sensation—and the first of many musicals teaming the pair. Based on the popular 1910 operetta by Victor Herbert, the movie touched a romantic chord in viewers, who responded enthusiastically to their singing of such lovely melodies as "Ah, Sweet Mystery of Life," "I'm Falling in Love with Someone," and "Neath the Southern Moon." The story is

airy nonsense about a disguised French princess and a leader of mercenary scouts in pre-Revolutionary America, which the stars play with what would become their approach—she over-emoting and he under-emoting. Still, audiences paid to bask in the Herbert music and the romantic glow, and they were not disappointed.

Off-Screen: Studio head Louis B. Mayer had urged MacDonald to do this film, telling her that he would costar her with singer Allan Jones. When Jones was unavailable, the project was shelved, then later revived with Eddy. During the filming, MacDonald and director Van Dyke worked hard to instill confidence in a nervous Eddy. Later, Van Dyke was reputed to have remarked, "I've handled Indians, African natives, South Sea Islanders, rhinos, pygmies, and Eskimos and made them act—but not Nelson Eddy." The scene in which Eddy bumps into a tree was actually accidental, but Van Dyke decided to keep it in the film.

Network

United Artists, 1976. (C-120m.) Dir: Sidney Lumet. Sp: Paddy Chayefsky. Cast: Faye Dunaway, William Holden, Peter Finch, Robert Duvall, Ned Beatty, Beatrice Straight, Wesley Addy, William Prince.

On-Screen: *A blistering view of the television industry.* In *Network,* writer Paddy Chayefsky uses a razor's edge to lacerate the soulless wasteland of television journalism. At the UBS network, when deranged anchorman Howard Beale (Finch) proclaims, "I think I'd like to be an angry prophet denouncing the hypocrisies of our times," ratings soar for the faltering news division. Diana Christensen (Dunaway), an ambitious executive with the division, turns Beale's messianic denunciations of practically everything into a nationwide phenomenon that energizes countless numbers of America's angry, disenchanted citizens. However, when network chiefs (Duvall, Beatty) become less than pleased with Beale's popular tirades, Diana and the media moguls devise a violently dramatic solution for silencing the "spokesman for the people." Lumet's direction, an ice-cold Dunaway, and a white-hot Finch perform brilliantly, and William Holden also excels as a seasoned newsman at UBS whose affair with Diana strains his marriage to Beatrice Straight. *Network* is a savage, satirical comedy-drama that somehow seems more plausible with the passage of time.

Off-Screen: A huge box-office success, the movie brought Oscars to Dunaway, Finch, Straight, and Chayefsky. A melancholy note was sounded, however, when Finch's widow, Eletha, came to the stage to accept her husband's Oscar. The British actor had died of a massive heart attack in January 1977, just two months before the award ceremonies. It was the first time an actor had been presented with an Oscar posthumously. His role had first been offered to Henry Fonda, who rejected it. Exterior locations and office scenes were photographed in New York, although the broadcasting scenes were shot in a Toronto television studio. (CFB)

Never Give a Sucker an Even Break

Universal, 1941. (71m.) Dir: Edward Cline. Sp: John T. Neville and Prescott Chaplin, b/o story by Otis Criblecoblis (W. C. Fields). Cast: W. C. Fields, Gloria Jean, Leon Errol, Margaret Dumont, Susan Miller, Franklin Pangborn, Jody Gilbert, Mona Barrie.

On-Screen: *W. C. Fields on the loose in Hollywood.* The master comedian's last starring film, a piece of rampant lunacy that will have you either laughing uncontrollably or shaking your head with bewilderment. The story makes no sense whatever: something about Fields trying to sell his script to producer Pangborn, then enacting his bizarre tale about landing in a mountain retreat owned by the imperious Dumont. Somehow it also involves Fields's singing niece, Gloria Jean, that marvelous low comedian Leon Errol, and other bewildered souls. It all ends with a beautifully executed car chase. Watch for Fields's hilarious enounter with an obnoxious waitress (Gilbert). There are also some great Fieldsian remarks: Told that someday he will drown in a vat of whiskey, he quips, "Drown in a vat of whiskey? Death, where is thy sting?" *Never Give a Sucker an Even Break* is Fields's final effort to thumb his nose at the Hollywood establishment.

Off-Screen: The title remark is usually credited to writer–con man Wilson Mizner, although it is said to have been uttered by Fields in the 1923 stage version of *Poppy*. "Otis Criblecoblis" is, of course, another of Fields's many pseudonyms. The censor excised many of his references to drinking, which Fields acknowledges in the movie when at one point he turns to the camera and says, "This scene was supposed to be in a saloon but the censor cut it out. It'll play just as well."

New York, New York

United Artists, 1977. (C-164m.) Dir: Martin Scorsese. Sp: Earl MacRauch and Mardik Martin, b/o story by Earl MacRauch. MS: John Kander and Fred Ebb.

Cast: Liza Minnelli, Robert De Niro, Lionel Stander, Mary Kay Place, Georgie Auld, Barry Primus, George Memmoli, Diahnne Abbott, Dick Miller, Larry Kert.

On-Screen: *Two performers battle their way through the big-band era. New York, New York* is undeniably different. A musical of sorts, a romance of sorts, and a marital drama of sorts, it somehow never succeeds in cohering all three into the movie its makers obviously intended. Instead we get a joyless musical drama concerning a singer (Minnelli) who meets a saxophonist (De Niro) on V-E Day in 1945 (one of the most tedious "meeting cute" encounters ever), marries him, and then fights with him over the years. The main problem is that De Niro is so terminally obnoxious and Minnelli so annoyingly self-effacing that you keep hoping in vain that they will tear at each other out of camera range. For much of the movie, Liza Minnelli's songs are interrupted to advance the story, but toward the end she is given full-scale musical numbers. Although her mother's influence is all too apparent, she delivers vibrant renditions of such fine Kander-Ebb songs as "And the World Goes Round" and the now-ubiquitous title tune. The production number "Happy Endings" (see below) is elaborate but uninspired. And so is this movie.

Off-Screen: At one point Barbra Streisand was considered for the role of Francine, with Ryan O'Neal as Jimmy. The "Happy Endings" number, featuring Larry Kert, was cut from the release print so that the film would run under two hours. It was later restored for the 1981 rerelease. Robert De Niro spent many hours learning to play the saxophone from jazz musician Georgie Auld, who has

a role in the movie. In the scene in which De Niro proposes to Minnelli, a spontaneous moment of improvisation occurred when the actor, to show his desperate sincerity, threw himself in front of a moving taxi. Scorsese kept it in the film.

New York Stories

Touchstone, 1989. (C-123m.) "Life Lessons"—Dir: Martin Scorsese. Sp: Richard Price. Cast: Nick Nolte, Rosanna Arquette. "Life Without Zoe"—Dir: Francis Coppola. Sp: Francis Coppola and Sofia Coppola. Cast: Heather McComb, Talia Shire, Giancarlo Giannini. "Oedipus Wrecks"—Dir: Woody Allen. Sp: Woody Allen. Cast: Woody Allen, Mia Farrow, Mae Questel, Julie Kavner.

On-Screen: *An omnibus movie from three famous directors.* These tales of New York City, each guided by a well-known filmmaker, are uneven in content, but they have their moments, and one, "Oedipus Wrecks," has more than its share of laughs. Martin Scorsese's "Life Lessons" stars Nick Nolte in a fine performance as a famous painter, a rumpled, shaggy bear of a man, and his obsession with his young assistant-lover (Arquette). Francis Coppola's "Life Without Zoe" is an airy trifle about a rich girl (McComb) living in the Sherry Netherland Hotel. Woody Allen's "Oedipus Wrecks" is a minor work, but funny. Allen plays a fifty-year-old corporate lawyer whose Mother from Hell (Questel) suddenly disappears during a magic act, then reappears as a figure looming over the entire city and continuing her litany of humiliation. More could be said about Allen's usual love-hate attitude toward his Jewishness, but the smile that comes involuntarily to his face when he realizes that his mother has vanished gives us a cherishable movie moment.

Off-Screen: Francis Coppola wrote "Life Without Zoe" with his then seventeen-year-old daughter, Sofia, who later starred in Part Three of Coppola's *Godfather* trilogy. In "Oedipus Wrecks," for the hilarious scene in which Allen's mother and aunt make an unannounced visit to his office, it was Allen's inspired idea to add Gene Krupa's drum solo on the classic recording of "Sing, Sing, Sing" to the soundtrack.

Night and Day

Warners, 1946. (C-128m.) Dir: Michael Curtiz. Sp: Charles Hoffman, Leo Townsend, and William Bowers. MS: Cole Porter. Cast: Cary Grant, Alexis Smith, Monty Woolley, Ginny Simms, Jane Wyman, Eve Arden, Mary Martin, Alan Hale, Victor Francen.

On-Screen: *Cole Porter through the meat grinder.* Among the rash of composer "biographies" turned out by the Hollywood studios in the forties, *Night and Day* easily ranks as one of the most dreadful. Only the imperishably beautiful Porter music survives, although it's mangled or misinterpreted at almost every opportunity. Except for his crippling accident and his marriage to Linda (and yes, he did attend Yale), the story line bears little resemblance to the real Porter, and Cary Grant gives a stiff, uneasy performance in the role. The sequence in which Porter composes the title song is one of the most quintessentially absurd in all movie musicals. Monty Woolley, a true friend of Porter's, comes off best playing himself and talk-

singing "Miss Otis Regrets." One highlight: Mary Martin reprises her delicious rendition of "My Heart Belongs to Daddy."

Off-Screen: Apparently, no less than seventeen writers labored for two years to come up with an acceptable screenplay. All failed. Cary Grant knew that he had given an inept performance as Porter and remarked much later that he had "shown little understanding of such extraordinary talent or the graciousness of its possessor." Grant loathed Michael Curtiz, and after the film was completed, he told him, "If I'm ever stupid enough to be caught working with you again, you'll know that I'm either broke or I've lost my mind."

A Night at the Opera

MGM, 1935. (92m.) Dir: Sam Wood. Sp: George S. Kaufman and Morrie Ryskind; additional material: Al Boasberg, b/o story by James Kevin McGuinness. MS: Nacio Herb Brown and Arthur Freed. Cast: Groucho, Harpo, and Chico Marx, Allan Jones, Kitty Carlisle, Margaret Dumont, Walter Woolf King, Sig Ruman.

On-Screen: *Culture gets the boot from the Marx Brothers.* One of the funniest Marx Brothers romps, *A Night at the Opera* sets those inspired maniacs loose in the world of opera, which they soon reduce to tatters. Groucho appears as Otis P. Driftwood, business manager to wealthy Mrs. Claypool (Dumont), who enlists the dubious help of Fiorello (Chico) and Tomasso (Harpo) in keeping the lady's fortune from straying elsewhere. The boys also help a young tenor (Jones) find his niche in the opera world. So what if the plot is a big unwieldy—as usual, the Marxes go their own way, puncturing the balloon of pomposity in one hilarious sequence after another. Everyone's favorite, of course, is the celebrated stateroom scene, a peak of inspired Marxian slapstick, but other memorable scenes include the Groucho-Chico encounter over a contract and the climactic tumult in the opera house, where the brothers gleefully demolish a performance of "Il Trovatore" with their antics.

Off-Screen: To sharpen the Marxes' material, MGM production head Irving Thalberg, who brought them to the studio, had the brothers tour the vaudeville circuit in western cities in advance of filming. Writers Kaufman and Ryskind, who had worked on the Marxes' first movies, were hired at Groucho's suggestion, after other writers had failed to come up with a workable screenplay.

Night Must Fall

MGM, 1937. (117m.) Dir: Richard Thorpe. Sp: John Van Druten, b/o play by Emlyn Williams. Cast: Robert Montgomery, Rosalind Russell, Dame May Whitty, Alan Marshal, Kathleen Harrison, E. E. Clive, Beryl Mercer.

On-Screen: *A killer stalks an English estate.* Usually cast in debonair comedy roles, Robert Montgomery switched gears to play the charming murderer Danny in this chilling adaptation of Emlyn Williams's psychological stage thriller. Montgomery is eerily convincing as the young man who ingratiates himself with crotchety old recluse May Whitty and intrigues her repressed companion, Rosalind Russell, against her better judgment. Ultimately, Danny claims an-

other victim. Also playing against her usual type—until *The Women,* she was cast as lofty, composed, upper-class women—Russell creates an interesting character in the mousy spinster who is sexually aroused by the danger and excitement Danny represents. Although modest in scope and rather stagy, this *Night Must Fall* is far superior to the 1964 remake with Albert Finney.

Off-Screen: Louis B. Mayer was strongly opposed to this film and allowed it to be made very reluctantly. (He felt that it projected the wrong MGM image.) He kept the film on a very stringent budget, and even after it was completed, he virtually disowned it. He personally supervised a trailer in which he admitted making the movie, but added that it was a purely experimental project, removed from the usual glossy MGM fare. Robert Montgomery won a Best Actor Oscar nomination for his offbeat role.

The Night of the Hunter

United Artists, 1955. (93m.) Dir: Charles Laughton. Sp: James Agee, b/o novel by Davis Grubb. Cast: Robert Mitchum, Shelley Winters, Lillian Gish, Evelyn Varden, Peter Graves, James Gleason, Billy Chapin, Sally Jane Bruce.

On-Screen: *Crazed backwoods "preacher" marries—and murders—for money.* Renowned actor Laughton turns director for this period thriller set in the rural South. Mitchum, adept at playing deceptively languid characters, makes an ideal smooth-talking Preacher Powell, psychotic right down to his fingers tattooed with the words *love* and *hate*. After wedding and then killing a gullible widow (Winters) for the money her thief of a husband (Graves) left her, he sets out in pursuit of her terrified children (Chapin and Bruce). The film pays tribute to D. W. Griffith not only in style—clear distinctions between good and evil, starkly contrasted black-and-white photography, archaic camera devices such as iris-outs—but also by the casting of Gish, the luminous star of that great director's masterpieces. As the gentle, hymn-singing spinster who shelters the children from the murderous minister, the actress is sublime.

Off-Screen: Although James Agee is credited as the author of the screenplay, producer Paul Gregory related that Agee was often too drunk to write and turned in a script four times thicker than the book. With help from Davis Grubb, Charles Laughton edited and rewrote the screenplay until it fully reflected the novel. In her autobiography, Lillian Gish recalls that during a visit to New York, Laughton "ran and reran D. W. [Griffith's] films at the Museum of Modern Art" in order to "capture some of the excitement . . . in his own film." Walter Schumann's folk-oriented musical score and Stanley Cortez's stunning cinematography contributed greatly to the film's impact. The story was remade for television in 1991. (CFB)

The Night of the Iguana

MGM, 1964. (118m.) Dir: John Huston. Sp: Anthony Veiller and John Huston, b/o play by Tennessee Williams. Cast: Richard Burton, Deborah Kerr, Ava Gardner, Sue Lyon, Grayson Hall, Cyril Delevanti, Skip Ward.

On-Screen: *Three people reach a crossroads in their lives at a run-down hotel.* More interesting for its casting than for its plot, this adaptation of Tennessee Williams's play records the events at Ava Gardner's ramshackle Mexican beach resort, where lonely souls gather with a busload of lady tourists. Richard Burton plays their guide, a defrocked minister and frightened alcoholic who needs the comfort of his lusty old friend Gardner. Deborah Kerr is the sensitive, down-on-her-luck sketch artist who accompanies her grandfather (Delevanti) to his last resting place. Tennessee Williams concocted this uneasy mixture of sex and heavy-handed symbolism—the sea is the cradle of life, the iguana tethered on the porch is, like Burton, "one of God's creatures at the end of his rope." The acting, for the most part, is superb. Burton plays the priest as a desperate wayfarer; Kerr, ever the lady, observes tactfully; and Gardner, as a blowsy earth mother, has a field day with the last good role of her career.

Off-Screen: Marlon Brando, Richard Harris, and William Holden were briefly considered before Richard Burton took the role. Most of the film was shot in the yet undiscovered Mexican coastal town of Puerto Vallarta and also on a remote peninsula called Mismaloya some eight to ten miles further away. Puerto Vallarta soon became the site of a media frenzy, with everyone expecting something to happen because of all the volatile personalities assembled. When there weren't any fireworks, reporters began to write about the town. Dorothy Jeakins's costumes won an Oscar. (JMK)

Night of the Living Dead

Image Ten, 1968. (96m.) Dir: George A. Romero. Sp: John A. Russo, b/o story by George A. Romero. Cast: Duane Jones, Judith O'Dea, Russell Streiner, Karl Hardman, Marilyn Eastman, Keith Wayne, Judith Ridley.

On-Screen: *Flesh-eating zombies wreak havoc.* A cult horror film for many years, *Night of the Living Dead* is everything its admirers and detractors claim: tacky, repellent, and thoroughly unsettling. Filmed in and around Pittsburgh on a shoestring, it concerns an aberration (caused, it is hinted, by radiation following a satellite explosion) in which the unburied dead become hideous, flesh-eating ghouls. Seven people are trapped in an abandoned house, fighting against these abominable creatures. Since its release, many films have surpassed it in explicit gore, but the sight of the ghoulish beings devouring human remains as they roam the countryside is still unnerving. And remember, "they're coming to get you, Barbara!" Years later, Romero followed this film with *Dawn of the Dead* (1979) and *Day of the Dead* (1985).

Off-Screen: Produced for less than $150,000 and filmed in grainy black and white (which somehow enhances the horror), *Night of the Living Dead* turned out to be one of the most successful independent films ever made. Not surprisingly, it had great trouble finding a distributor, and when it was released, it received mostly scathing reviews. Its cult status grew over the years. A 1990 remake (in color) made little impression.

Nightmare Alley

Fox, 1947. (111m.) Dir: Edmund Goulding. Sp: Jules Furthman, b/o novel by William Lindsay Gresham. Cast: Tyrone Power, Joan Blondell, Coleen Gray, Helen Walker, Taylor Holmes, Mike Mazurki, Ian Keith.

On-Screen: *The rise and fall of a carnival hustler.* After more than a decade of playing mainly dashing romantic heroes, Tyrone Power switched gears with a strikingly good performance as Stan Carlisle, a disreputable, ambitious carnival hustler, in this moody drama. A no-good drifter who joins a traveling carnival, Stan becomes partners in a mind-reading act with Zena (Blondell) after plying her boozy husband with a fatal dose of alcohol. With the help of a smitten psychologist (Walker), he rises in the ranks to become a fake but popular spiritualist. He also marries a trusting carnival girl (Gray). His downfall, when it comes, is truly harrowing—he ends up at a sleazy carnival, working as a "geek," the lowest form of carnival life. *Nightmare Alley* sloughs off toward the end, but its early portions are handled vividly, with fine shadowy photography by Lee Garmes that helps to create a sense of foreboding.

Off-Screen: Darryl Zanuck was appalled when Tyrone Power said he wanted to play Stan Carlisle. But Power was anxious to prove that he was a good actor. Zanuck urged director Henry King to talk him out of the idea, but Power was adamant. Years later, he remarked, "Stan Carlisle fascinated me. He was such an unmitigated heel. I've played other disreputable fellows, but never one like Carlisle. Here was a chance to create a character different from any I had ever played before. . . ."

Ninotchka

MGM, 1939. (110m.) Dir: Ernst Lubitsch. Sp: Billy Wilder, Charles Brackett, and Walter Reisch. Cast: Greta Garbo, Melvyn Douglas, Ina Claire, Bela Lugosi, Sig Ruman, Felix Bressart, Alexander Granach.

Garbo's Russian wren turns into a swan. After years of playing tragic heroines, Greta Garbo turned to comedy for the first time with this delectable romantic comedy. She plays Nina Ivanovna Yakushova, a somber Russian emissary who is sent to Paris on a government mission and succumbs to the beauty and magic of the City of Lights. Romance also arrives in the person of Count Leon d'Algout (Douglas), who begins as her adversary and ends up as her ardent lover. By now the satire of Soviet rigidity and lack of humor is somewhat frayed, but with a witty screenplay, Lubitsich's adroit direction, and—above all—Garbo's bewitching transformation from wren to swan, *Ninotchka* remains a joy forever. Douglas is suave and charming, and stage star Ina Claire gives a wonderfully dry and stylish performance as the exiled Grand Duchess Swana, whose confiscated jewels are the story's point of contention. The ads for *Ninotchka* proclaimed "Garbo Laughs!" and, happily, the world laughed with her. So will you.

Off-Screen: It must have been interesting filming Garbo's scenes with Ina Claire. For years Garbo had been actor John Gilbert's romantic interest both on and off the screen, while Claire was his widow. There was much opposition to making *Ninotchka* at MGM. Studio head Louis B. Mayer felt that Garbo was inexperienced at playing comedy and also found the entire subject of Communism objectionable. He finally relented, but afterward, when *Ninotchka* fared only moderately well at the box office, he continued to point out that he was right all along ("*Ninotchka* got everything but money"). The story was turned into a 1955 stage musical entitled *Silk Stockings,* which was filmed

two years later with Fred Astaire and Cyd Charisse.

No Way Out

Fox, 1950. (106m.) Dir: Joseph L. Mankiewicz. Sp: Joseph L. Mankiewicz and Lesser Samuels. Cast: Richard Widmark, Linda Darnell, Sidney Poitier, Stephen McNally, Mildred Joanne Smith, Harry Bellaver, Stanley Ridges, Dots Johnson, Bill Walker, Ruby Dee, Ossie Davis.

On-Screen: *Racial hatred sparks a riot*. Once considered a bold, searing attack on racial bigotry, Joseph L. Mankiewicz's *No Way Out* now has considerably less voltage but is still an effective, if somewhat contrived, melodrama. Sidney Poitier makes his film debut as a young doctor, the only nonwhite at a metropolitan hospital, who treats an injured man he believes is suffering from a brain tumor. When the man dies, his violently bigoted brother (Widmark) accuses the doctor of deliberately murdering the patient. With another brother, he sets about generating a riot to wipe out "Nigger Town." Ultimately, the doctor, in order to force an autopsy of his patient, gives himself up to the police on the charge of murder. As directed by Joseph Mankiewicz, the scenes of the preparation for the riot have a frightening intensity. Sidney Poitier demonstrates the dignity and strength that would make him a leading star in the years ahead, and Linda Darnell excels as the ex-wife of Widmark's dead brother.

Off-Screen: In a scrapped version of the film's climax, Widmark forced Poitier to dig his own grave in a coal bin while calling him "Sambo." Mankiewicz later noted that *No*

Way Out was "the first time racial violence was shown on screen—except for *Birth of a Nation*—in modern times." The film met opposition from censors in Chicago, and also from censorship boards in Pennsylvania, Virginia, and Ohio.

No Way Out

Orion, 1987. (C-116m.) Dir: Roger Donaldson. Sp: Robert Garland, b/o novel by Kenneth Fearing. Cast: Kevin Costner, Gene Hackman, Sean Young, Will Patton, George Dzunda, Jason Bernard, Iman, Fred Dalton Thompson.

On-Screen: *A high-tension thriller set in the world of Washington politics.* Loosely adapted from Kenneth Fearing's book *The Big Clock,* which became a taut 1948 melodrama, *No Way Out* entangles Navy Commander Tom Farrell (Costner) in a web of political intrigue and murder. It seems that the sexy woman (Young) he is seeing is also the secret mistress of David Brice (Hackman), the new secretary of defense. When Brice kills Young in a rage of jealousy, the elaborate cover-up entraps Farrell, who is assigned to Brice, in an increasingly dangerous situation. Not only is his life threatened but also the lives of everyone who is involved in the investigation. The Pentagon and its surrounding Washington area are used as backdrops for exciting chase scenes and tense confrontations that, if you can accept the premise, will have you at the edge of your seat. Will Patton is especially chilling as Scott Pritchard, the defense secretary's aide whose deadly machinations are the result of an overzealous devotion to his employer. The film's ending is a shocker but also an outrageous cheat that threatens to trash everything that came before it.

Off-Screen: The film was originally called *Deceit.* The director, Roger Donaldson, is a New Zealander who was unable to keep *The Bounty* (1984), a remake of *Mutiny on the Bounty,* from crashing on the rocks. The film's cinematography was by John Alcott, who died only weeks after the shooting was completed. He was responsible for the stunning photography of *2001: A Space Odyssey* (1968).

None But the Lonely Heart

(113m.) RKO, 1944. Dir: Clifford Odets. Sp: Clifford Odets, b/o novel by Richard Llewellyn. Cast: Cary Grant, Ethel Barrymore, Barry Fitzgerald, June Duprez, Jane Wyatt, George Coulouris, Dan Duryea.

On-Screen: *Cockney drifter Cary Grant seeks peace but finds only trouble in London's slums.* Featuring one of Grant's rare dramatic performances, *None But the Lonely Heart* adapted Richard Llewelyn's novel into a moody and sometimes striking film. Playwright Clifford Odets wrote and directed the story of Ernie Mott (Grant), a genial but shiftless rover in London's prewar East End who yearns for "a decent human life" but finds he must cope with a dying mother (Barrymore) and a girl (Duprez) in thrall to a nasty gangster (Coulouris). Murky and a mite pretentious, the movie suffers from too much windy dialogue, especially with some misplaced wartime sentiment at the end, but occasionally a moment seems poetically right. Grant is commendable in an Oscar-nominated performance as Ernie, and Barrymore, who won the Best Supporting Actress Oscar, is affecting if a bit too regal as Ma Mott. Their climactic scene in a prison hospital should move you to tears.

Barry Fitzgerald is around to do his familiar turn as Eddie's sympathetic friend.

Off-Screen: Cary Grant on this film: "I got an Oscar nomination for playing a poor Cockney in *None But the Lonely Heart,* but it wasn't the big acting—what do they say today—'stretch' that critics seemed to think. I felt closer to that guy than to most of the well-turned-out characters I was known for. . . ." Grant wanted Laurette Taylor for the role of his mother, but the veteran actress, though tested, was bloated from excessive beer guzzling. To obtain the services of Ethel Barrymore, RKO had to pay all expenses incurred by temporarily closing down the touring company of *The Corn Is Green.*

Norma Rae

Fox, 1979. (C-113m.) Dir: Martin Ritt. Sp: Irving Ravetch and Harriet Frank, Jr. Cast: Sally Field, Ron Leibman, Beau Bridges, Pat Hingle, Barbara Baxley, Gail Strickland, Lonny Chapman, Grace Zabriskie.

On-Screen: *Sally Field's Oscar-winning performance.* In a Southern town where the textile mill provides the only employment, Norma Rae (Field) is a problem: a tough, outspoken woman with two children and no husband. Enter Reuben (Leibman), a labor organizer who changes her life forever. The movie traces Norma Rae's marriage to Sonny (Bridges) and especially her feisty, unpopular role in organizing a union. A workmanlike film, *Norma Rae* gains momentum toward the end, when Norma Rae resists the mill bosses ("I started this and I'm going to finish it!"). Inevitably, in this sort of movie, Norma Rae and Reuben succeed in establishing the union. Sally Field is excellent as Norma Rae, especially in the scene in which she must level with her children about her less-than-perfect life and prepare them for the ignominy they will now face on her behalf. The movie's theme song, "It Goes Like It Goes," also won an Oscar.

Off-Screen: Fox's first choice to play Norma Rae was Jane Fonda, but she declined, as did Jill Clayburgh, Marsha Mason, and Diane Keaton, either because of prior commitments or because they felt the role just wasn't right for them. In addition to her Oscar, Sally Field also won, among others, the Cannes Film Festival award, the New York Film Critics' Circle award, and the Golden Globe for Best Dramatic Actress.

North by Northwest

MGM, 1959. (C-136m.) Dir: Alfred Hitchcock. Sp: Ernest Lehman. Cast: Cary Grant, Eva Marie Saint, James Mason, Jessie Royce Landis, Leo G. Carroll, Martin Landau, Adam Williams, Philip Ober.

On-Screen: *Alfred Hitchcock's crackerjack comedy-suspense thriller.* Dapper Roger Thornhill (Grant) is a victim of mistaken identity (a favorite Hitchcock theme), pursued by enemy agents and the FBI who are out to kill or arrest him. His flight takes him from New York (the UN, Grand Central Station) to Chicago, via the elegant Twentieth Century Limited, and to South Dakota for a hair-raising finale. The entire movie, in fact, takes you on a perilous, and thoroughly entertaining, roller coaster: Thornhill driving down a mountain road after being forced to drink a bottle of liquor; the famous cropdusting sequence (without crops but with a deadly airplane pursuing him); his desperate flight with the mysterious Eve Kendall (Saint) across the chiseled faces of Mount Rushmore. The plot has some holes, but you won't mind them as you follow the hero eluding villains Mason and Landau, or savor the suggestive banter between him and Eve on their cross-country train ride. And three cheers for "George Kaplan."

Off-Screen: The United States Department of the Interior turned down Hitchcock's request to film the climactic sequence on the presidential faces that form Mount Rushmore's National Monument. Full-size replicas were used instead. (The director resisted the temptation to film Grant having a sneezing fit in one of Lincoln's nostrils.) The studio wanted contract star Cyd Charisse to play the enigmatic heroine, but Hitchcock, who preferred blonde leading ladies, cast Saint. Watch for his traditional brief appearance as a man hurrying to a bus, which shuts its door in his face.

Northwest Passage

MGM, 1940. (C-125m.) Dir: King Vidor. Sp: Laurence Stallings and Talbot Jennings, b/o novel by Kenneth Roberts. Cast: Spencer Tracy, Robert Young, Ruth Hussey, Walter Brennan, Nat Pendleton, Louis Hector, Isabel Jewell, Lumsden Hare, Regis Toomey, Donald McBride.

On-Screen: *Spencer Tracy leads his men through the rigors of the colonial frontier.* Based on part of Kenneth Roberts's best-selling novel, *Northwest Passage* is a lusty adventure tale concerning Major Robert Rogers (Tracy), who takes his men on a perilous expedition to defeat a murderous Indian tribe in 1759,

during the French and Indian Wars. Rogers's Rangers undergo numerous hardships and frustrations as they venture deep into uncharted country, and their return journey is even more hazardous. The vivid Technicolor photography captures the beauty of the Oregon countryside where much of the movie was filmed. Robert Young plays the effete Easterner who becomes a hardened veteran under Rogers's tutelage. Many older viewers will surely recall the horrifying scene in which a crazed ranger insists on playing with the severed head of an Indian.

Off-Screen: After the company spent twelve grueling weeks in the wilderness, Spencer Tracy refused to work any longer with director Vidor, and the production was shut down with only half of the screenplay filmed. The movie ends with Rogers preparing for a new journey in search of the Northwest Passage, which was originally intended to be the more important section of the film. This was the first color film for both Tracy and Vidor.

Nothing Sacred

United Artists, 1937. (C-75m.) Dir: William Wellman. Sp: Ben Hecht, b/o story by James H. Street. Cast: Carole Lombard, Fredric March, Charles Winninger, Walter Connolly, Sig Ruman, Frank Fay, Monty Woolley, Margaret Hamilton.

On-Screen: *A biting, classic thirties comedy.* America's mania for celebrities, no matter how bizarre their claim to fame, is only one of the targets of this slyly satirical movie. Hazel Flagg (Lombard) is mistakenly diagnosed as dying of radium poisoning. Although she knows she's perfectly well, she accepts the offer made by newspaper reporter Wally Cook (March) of an all-expenses-paid visit to New York City. Lionized by the media and the public, she lives out her "last days" gloriously. A budding romance between Hazel and Wally is severely tested, though, when Wally learns the truth, and in one of the movie's funniest scenes, they literally come to blows. Hecht's screenplay aims its barbs at incompetent medical rogues (Winninger), exploitative newspaper owners (Connolly), and human gullibility. In one of her best "screwball" roles, Lombard is at her feisty and feminine best; March, often cast in wooden historical parts, displays a rarely tapped gift for boisterous comedy.

Off-Screen: Hecht based his script on Street's *Cosmopolitan* magazine story "Letter to the Editor." He claims to have written it in five days on trains between New York and Los Angeles. When Hecht quit after his ending was rejected, producer David O. Selznick brought in uncredited Ring Lardner, Jr., and Budd Schulberg, who devised an acceptable climax. In 1953, the movie became a Broadway musical, *Hazel Flagg;* a year later, it was turned into a Jerry Lewis–Dean Martin vehicle, *Living It Up,* with Lewis playing the Lombard part, Janet Leigh cast as the reporter, and Martin as the erring doctor. Sig Ruman repeated his role as Dr. Eggelhoffer. (CFB)

Notorious

RKO, 1946. (101m.) Dir: Alfred Hitchcock. Sp: Ben Hecht. Cast: Ingrid Bergman, Cary Grant, Claude Rains, Louis Calhern, Madame Konstantin, Reinhold Schunzel, Moroni Olsen.

On-Screen: *Sex, suspense, and superstars in a top-notch spy thriller.* Hecht's swiftly paced, Oscar-nominated story ideally showcases Hitchcock's genius for intrigue and sudden plot turns. Bergman, daughter of a convicted Nazi spy, wants to right her father's wrongs. Grant is an American agent who enlists her aid in uncovering a secret plan being hatched by a band of Nazi refugees in Rio de Janeiro. Although their relationship develops into a love affair, Bergman must marry rich and powerful Rains in order to help destroy the plotters' scheme for another world war. Among the film's memorable scenes are the stars' marathon kiss, and cameraman Ted Tetzlaff's virtuoso continuous descending shot at the party, from high over the milling guests down to Bergman's hand clutching the key to that all-important wine cellar. Another great moment: A humiliated Rains tells his mother (Konstantin) the truth about his wife ("Mother, I am married to an American agent").

Off-Screen: Claude Rains was Oscar-nominated for his performance as the despicable yet oddly sympathetic Nazi schemer. His casting proved ideal, though Hitchcock's original choice had been Clifton Webb. When Ethel Barrymore rejected the role of Rains's merciless mother, she was replaced by European actress Leopoldine Konstantin (billed as Madame Konstantin). For the movie's most talked-about scene, Hitchcock got around the Hollywood code limiting a kiss to three seconds by having Grant and Bergman rapidly alternate passionate kisses with more mundane activities, resulting in "the longest kiss in history," as ads proclaimed. Hitchcock can be seen standing by a punch bowl in the lavish party sequence. Disregard the 1992 television remake. (CFB)

Now, Voyager

Warners, 1942. (117m.) Dir: Irving Rapper. Sp: Casey Robinson, b/o novel by Olive Higgins Prouty. Cast: Bette Davis, Paul Henreid, Claude Rains, Gladys Cooper, Bonita Granville, John Loder, Ilka Chase, Mary Wickes, Franklin Pangborn.

On-Screen: *Ugly duckling Bette Davis becomes a swan*. Well-cooked and deliciously seasoned corn, *Now, Voyager* remains one of Bette Davis's best-loved, best-remembered films. In this moth-to-butterfly tale, she plays a repressed, desperately unhappy Boston spinster under the thumb of a tyrannical mother (Cooper). With the guidance of a wise psychiatrist (Rains), she blossoms into an assured beauty who finds love with an unhappily married man (Henreid). The premise is Hollywood nonsense, of course, but Davis, at the peak of her form, makes it work with an assured, deeply felt performance, and she is ably abetted by everyone, particularly Cooper, who freezes the blood with her incisive portrait of a cruel and cunning woman. The pivotal scene in which she confronts her transformed daughter is a marvel of acting finesse. The two-cigarettes scene with Davis and Henreid is now a permanent part of movie lore.

Off-Screen: Irene Dunne and Norma Shearer had both been considered for the leading role but declined. (Shearer had decided to retire.) Bette Davis went to production head Hal Wallis and asked for the part. Paul Henreid's first test for the role of Jerry Durrence was a disaster; his hair was brilliantined, and he wore layers of pancake makeup. Davis insisted on having him retested in a more natural state, and he was signed. Henreid is usually credited with thinking of the famous two-cigarettes scene, but others have been given (or taken) the credit as well. Davis maintained that she made crucial changes in the screenplay; scenarist Robinson bitterly denied this, insisting that not a line of his dialogue was ever altered.

The Nun's Story

Warners, 1959. (C-149m.) Dir: Fred Zinnemann. Sp: Robert Anderson, b/o book by Kathryn Hulme. Cast: Audrey Hepburn, Peter Finch, Edith Evans, Peggy Ashcroft, Dean Jagger, Mildred Dunnock, Beatrice Straight, Patricia Collinge, Barbara O'Neil, Colleen Dewhurst.

On-Screen: *A young woman's trials in becoming a nun*. A beautifully made film, *The Nun's Story* concentrates on Audrey Hepburn as a young Belgian woman who goes through the rigors of becoming a nun, then leaves the order when she finds that she cannot endure its discipline. The first part is almost documentary-like in its amazingly detailed depiction of how a young woman becomes a nun, taking Hepburn from her entrance into a nunnery to her final vows. In the Congo as a nursing nun, violent incidents shake her faith and an agnostic doctor (Finch) criticizes her religious practices. When she is not allowed to avenge her slain father by serving as a nurse with the Belgian underground in World War II, she asks to be released from her vows. As Sister Luke, Audrey Hepburn gives a radiant performance that can surely be numbered among her best. Edith Evans has strength and authority as the mother superior, and other distinguished actresses—among them, Mildred Dunnock, Peggy Ashcroft, and Patricia Collinge—play nuns. Exquisite photography by Franz Planer.

Off-Screen: Nominated for six Academy Awards, including Best Picture and Best Actress (Hepburn), *The Nun's Story* did not receive any. To prepare for her difficult role, Hepburn spent a great deal of time with author Kathryn Hulme and with Marie-Louise Habets, the nun who inspired the story. Gerard Philipe and Yves Montand were considered for the role of the doctor, but Australian actor Peter Finch was finally cast. There were negotiations for Katharine Cornell to play the mother superior, but the role went to Edith Evans.

Nuts

Columbia, 1988. (C-116m.) Dir: Martin Ritt. Sp: Tom Topor, Darryl Ponicsan, and Alvin Sargent, b/o play by Tom Topor. Cast: Barbra Streisand, Richard Dreyfuss, Maureen Stapleton, Karl Malden, Eli Wallach, James Whitmore, Robert Webber, Leslie Nielsen, William Prince.

On-Screen: *A prostitute's mental competence is investigated.* How you respond to this movie depends entirely on your feelings about Barbra Streisand. Standing firmly at center stage, she plays Claudia Draper, a high-priced hooker, foulmouthed, aggressive, and defiant, who demands the right to stand trial on a charge of manslaughter. The trouble is, everyone, including her parents (Stapleton and Malden), believes that she is not in her right mind and needs medical treatment instead of jail. A Legal Aid lawyer named Aaron Levinsky (Dreyfuss) defends her at a competency hearing. It soon becomes clear that Claudia is tormented by a terrible and buried family secret that led her to a degraded life. Streisand pulls out all stops, delivering an over-the-top perfor-

mance that will leave you either stunned by its power or ready for aspirin and a hearing aid. Her climactic testimony on the stand is an emotional tour de force. She gets able support from an exceptionally fine cast, especially Stapleton as her anguished mother. But it's Streisand's show most of the way. (She also produced the film and composed the score.)

Off-Screen: Tom Topor's play had its premiere off-off-Broadway in February 1980, then moved to Broadway's Biltmore Theatre in April 1980 for a three-month run. Mark Rydell was first scheduled to direct, and he considered many actresses, including Bette Midler, for the leading role. He worked on the property for several years before relinquishing the direction to Martin Ritt. Rydell also wanted to change the title, feeling that audiences would think that the film was a comedy.

The Nutty Professor

Paramount, 1963. (C-107m.) Dir: Jerry Lewis. Sp: Jerry Lewis and Bill Richmond. Cast: Jerry Lewis, Stella Stevens, Del Moore, Kathleen Freeman, Henry Gibson.

On-Screen: *Jerry Lewis meets Jekyll and Hyde.* Regarded by many as Jerry Lewis's best movie, *The Nutty Professor* is certainly a departure from his usual idiot-at-large solo efforts. This is not to say that it is good. Lewis plays Julian Kelp, a bumbling, gargoyle-like professor who is forever wreaking havoc. Experimenting with a secret formula, he turns himself into Buddy Love, an egotistical, obnoxious singer who may have been modeled on Lewis's former partner, Dean Martin. (See below.) Eventually, the two personalities begin to interact, causing all sorts of confusion. Lewis works hard to little effect; neither Julian Kelp nor Buddy Love is a funny or even identifiable human being, and the few passing attempts to add a poignant note simply do not work. When Love suddenly starts talking in Kelp's voice, it isn't amusing or touching, merely spooky. In the leading feminine role, Stella Stevens has the unenviable task of pretending to be in love with Kelp, a creature even a mother might reject.

Off-Screen: In his book *Jerry Lewis in Person* (Atheneum, 1982), Jerry Lewis denied vehemently that Buddy Love was a vengeful attack on Dean Martin: "Buddy Love was a composite of all those rude, distasteful, odious, crass, gross, imbecilic clowns we can spot instantly at any large gathering. We know him only too well. . . . He isn't Dean. He's Buddy Love, infinitely for himself, and disliking all other humans."

Obsession

Columbia, 1976. (C-98m.) Dir: Brian De Palma. Sp: Paul Schrader. Cast: Cliff Robertson, Genevieve Bujold, John Lithgow, Sylvia Kuumba Williams, Wanda Blackman.

On-Screen: *A New Orleans developer confronts mystery and deception years after losing his family.* Brian De Palma has spent part of his career ripping off Alfred Hitchcock. This film has the ominous bedrooms from *Psycho* and *Rebecca,* and the master's interest in stairs (those two and *Suspicion*), but here De Palma uses them as red herrings—symbols that lead nowhere. De Palma steals the older director's swirling, vertiginous camera work, but fails to employ the wit that animated Hitchcock. The story: Kidnappers abduct Cliff Robertson's wife and daughter; years later he finds his wife miraculously alive as an Italian artist (Bujold) in Florence. What is the sinister plot behind it all? The movie is good, silly fun if you don't ask too many questions, such as why doesn't Robertson get wise to the plot before it smacks him in the eyes? Bernard Herrmann's score is great heard out of context; in the film it calls attention to itself, blaring at the most inappropriate moments.

Off-Screen: Not the happiest of productions. From all reports Cliff Robertson and Genevieve Bujold disliked each other intensely during the filming. Paul Schrader was bitter about De Palma's changes in his screenplay, claiming that they sacrificed character to plot. He felt particularly betrayed by De Palma's ending, which was vastly different from the one he had written in his screenplay. Schrader's ending had Robertson arrested and confined to an asylum for fifteen years. On his release, he goes to Florence to kill his daughter but ends up being reconciled with her. All this was dropped from the film. (JMK)

The Odd Couple

Paramount, 1968. (C-105m.) Dir: Gene Saks. Sp: Neil Simon, b/o his play. Cast: Jack Lemmon, Walter Matthau, Herb Edelman, John Fiedler, David Sheiner, Larry Haines, Monica Evans, Carol Shelley.

On-Screen: *Neil Simon's stage hit on the screen.* What happens when two divorced men of radically different temperaments decide to share an apartment? The answer proved to be a gold mine for playwright Neil Simon, who parlayed his successful Broadway play into this movie and then a long-running television series. (See below.) The premise, of course, has countless comic possibilities, and the hilarious play touched on many of them. The movie reconstructs the play as sloppy sportswriter Oscar Madison (Matthau) must cope with fussy, hypochondriacal photographer Felix Unger (Lemmon), and vice versa. They find that the same hang-ups, biases, and eccentricities that drove them away from their respective mates are still present in full force. Bleary-eyed and contemptuous, Matthau is delightful as Oscar, but Lemmon plays Felix glumly and too realistically, so that the character becomes somewhat more intolerable than comic. Yet there's still a great deal of fun to be had, and yes, there are always those English secretaries, the Pidgeon sisters (Evans and Shelley).

Off-Screen: With Tony Randall and Jack Klugman in the leading roles, *The Odd Couple* was turned into one of the more durable television comedies (1970–75). In 1982, the series was revived as "The New Odd Couple," with two black actors in the roles, but it was short-lived. In the late eighties, Simon rewrote the play for two women, played by Sally Struthers and Rita Moreno.

Of Human Bondage

RKO, 1934. (83m.) Dir: John Cromwell. Sp: Lester Cohen, b/o novel by W. Somerset Maugham. Cast: Leslie Howard, Bette Davis, Frances Dee, Kay Johnson, Reginald Denny, Reginald Owen, Alan Hale.

On-Screen: *Bette Davis's star-making performance in an adaptation of Maugham's novel.* After years of acting in poor or indifferent films for Warners, Bette Davis was loaned reluctantly by Jack Warner to RKO to appear opposite Leslie Howard in the film version of Maugham's book. Grateful for the opportunity, Davis pulled out all stops to play Mildred, the slatternly, grasping waitress who becomes the obsession of a sensitive, clubfooted artist (Howard). His life, and his other relationships with women, are nearly wrecked by his bondage to Mildred. Ranging from the flirtatious tearoom waitress at the beginning to the shattered shell of a woman dying in a hospital charity ward, Davis gives a bravura performance that threatens to become excessive at every turn, and Howard, though overpowered by her star turn, is quietly effective.

Off-Screen: At first, Leslie Howard was coolly disdainful with Davis, believing that she was just another assembly-line blonde. Her intense performance startled him into respect and admiration. Surprisingly, she did not receive an Oscar nomination, but in the following year, possibly as a gesture for having overlooked her, the Acadamy gave her the award for her much less successful performance in *Dangerous*. When preview audiences laughed, RKO decided it was the score and had Max Steiner write a completely new score for the film. *Of Human Bondage* was remade badly in 1946 and 1964.

Of Mice and Men

United Artists, 1939. (107m.) Dir: Lewis Milestone. Sp: Eugene Solow, b/o play by

John Steinbeck. Cast: Burgess Meredith, Betty Field, Lon Chaney, Jr., Charles Bickford, Roman Bohnen, Bob Steele, Noah Beery, Jr., Granville Bates.

On-Screen: *John Steinbeck's tragic tale of two drifters.* Adapted from the prize-winning play that had a successful run on Broadway in the 1937–38 season, *Of Mice and Men* concerns two migrant workers who come to work on a ranch. George (Meredith) looks after the feebleminded Lennie (Chaney), who was "kicked in the head by a horse." Lennie's fondness for "soft things" leads him to the accidental killing of the foreman's sluttish wife (Field), and to a poignant and inevitable ending. Lewis Milestone directs a commendable, straightforward transcription of the play, and the atmosphere of the ranch and its inhabitants is enhanced by Aaron Copland's score. Burgess Meredith gives a sturdy, unmannered performance as George, and Lon Chaney, Jr., is surprisingly good as the pathetic Lennie. A sad reflection on man's inhumanity to his own kind, and to other creatures as well, the movie is well worth a look.

Off-Screen: The original stage version starred Wallace Ford as George and Broderick Crawford as Lennie, with Claire Luce, who had danced on Broadway with Fred Astaire in *The Gay Divorce,* as the ill-fated Mae. A television version of the play was shown in 1981, with Robert Blake as George and Randy Quaid as Lennie. John Malkovich played Lennie and Gary Sinise was George in a 1992 remake.

An Officer and a Gentleman

Paramount, 1982. (C-125m.) Dir: Taylor Hackford. Sp: Douglas Day Stewart. Cast: Richard Gere, Debra Winger, Louis Gossett, Jr., David Keith, Lisa Blount, Robert Loggia, Lisa Eilbacher.

On-Screen: *An aspiring naval officer finds romance and rough times.* Moviegoers with long memories will recall the one about the pugnacious guy—say, Jimmy Cagney—who joins the service and learns about life, honor, etc., from a tough superior—say, Pat O'Brien—and all about love from an adoring girl—say, Ann Sheridan. Extract the explicit sex scenes and "bad" language from *An Officer and a Gentleman,* and you'll discover that the old war-horse is alive and well. Still, the movie is expertly made and entertaining. Richard Gere is the scrappy young man who is determined to make it through Naval Officer Candidate School, and Louis Gossett, Jr., is the seemingly hard-as-nails instructor who puts him through the grueling training and turns him into a true navy man. Husky-voiced Debra Winger is highly appealing as the local girl who loves him. There's a tragic subplot involving another officer candidate (Keith) who fails to make the grade, and whose romance with another local girl (Blount) ends badly. *An Officer and a Gentleman* works reasonably well as a new spin on an old formula.

Off-Screen: Louis Gossett, Jr., won the year's Best Supporting Actor Oscar for his performance as the relentless drill instructor, and the movie's theme song, "Up Where We Belong," also received an award. Gossett's role was originally written for a white actor. Paramount was turned down by the navy when it asked for a base at which they could film. The navy objected to the movie's sexual explicitness and to the opening sequence showing a sailor gone to seed. The producer finally found a deserted base on which to film.

Oklahoma!

Magna, 1955. (C-145m.) Dir: Fred Zinnemann. Sp: Sonya Levien and William Ludwig, b/o musical play by Oscar Hammerstein II. MS: Richard Rodgers and Oscar Hammerstein II. Cast: Gordon MacRae, Shirley Jones, Rod Steiger, Charlotte Greenwood, Gloria Grahame, Eddie Albert, Gene Nelson, James Whitmore, J. C. Flippen, Bambi Linn.

On-Screen: *The classic Rodgers and Hammerstein musical, brought to the screen.* A surprise hit on Broadway in 1943, Rodgers and Hammerstein's melodious musical ran for many years and became a landmark that forever changed and influenced American musical theater. It took twelve years for *Oklahoma!* to reach the screen in this lavish production, filmed in the Todd-AO process. There's only a sliver of a plot—who will take pretty Laurey (Jones) to the social: cowboy Curley (MacRae), who loves her, or nasty farmhand Jud (Steiger), who merely covets her? But those lilting Rodgers and Hammerstein songs and those innovative Agnes DeMille dances are still intact for everyone to enjoy. There are flaws. Some of the sequences are staged in cumbersome fashion, rather than in the airy style required, and the grandiose on-location settings somehow work against the small, stylized nature of the musical. Ah, but there's the music and that may be enough.

Off-Screen: Years later, director Zinnemann admitted that he hadn't done a good job with *Oklahoma!:* "It was my first musical and I was in awe of Dick and Oscar. But I shouldn't have been." Although Richard Rodgers wanted Gloria Grahame for Ado Annie, the actress hated doing the role and fought everyone involved with the production. At the wrap party, nobody would even speak to her. Robert Russell Bennett, Jay Blackton, and Adolph Deutsch won an Oscar for their music scoring.

The Old Maid

Warners, 1939. (95m.) Dir: Edmund Goulding. Sp: Casey Robinson, b/o play by Zoë Akins and novella by Edith Wharton. Cast: Bette Davis, Miriam Hopkins, George Brent, Jane Bryan, Donald Crisp, Louise Fazenda, Jerome Cowan, William Lundigan.

On-Screen: *Two cousins clash across the years.* One of Bette Davis's most impressive films of the thirties, this glossy soap opera adapted Zoë Akins's Pulitzer Prize–winning drama into a moist tale of mother love and sacrifice. Davis is the ardent young woman whose indiscretion with her cousin's rejected fiancé (Brent) results in the birth of a baby. Her cousin (Hopkins) charitably agrees to raise the child as her own, with Davis as the disapproving maiden aunt. Years later, a conflict erupts when the now-grown daughter (Bryan) is about to be wed. Set in the magnolia-and-mint-julep South of the 1860s, *The Old Maid* is hardly cinematic art, but it is effective drama, handsomely mounted and well acted, especially by Davis. Her aging spinster, concealing feelings that occasionally break through her drab exterior, is one of her most artful creations. Hopkins manages to keep up with her in their emotional encounters, and Bryan is lovely as the daughter who innocently precipitates the trouble.

Off-Screen: Davis and Hopkins were acquaintances but scarcely friends when they agreed to costar in *The Old Maid*. During filming, Hopkins was her usual demanding, disruptive self, making life on the set almost unendurable by insisting on having dialogue rewritten, by moving arbitrarily and spoiling many shots, or by changing her makeup to make herself look younger. Humphrey Bogart was originally signed to play George Brent's role, but he was dismissed after a few weeks of filming. Alan Marshal was considered to replace him, but the part went to Brent.

The Omen

Fox, 1976. (C-111m.) Dir: Richard Donner. Sp: David Seltzer. Cast: Gregory Peck, Lee Remick, David Warner, Billie Whitelaw, Harvey Stephens, Leo McKern, Patrick Troughton.

On-Screen: *A shock-filled thriller concerning a demonic child.* What's a father to do? Pity Robert Thorn (Peck), America's ambassador to England, when he learns that his adopted son, Damien (Stephens), is the spawn of the devil, the Antichrist come to earth to destroy it. The full horror strikes him after a series of hideous deaths perpetrated by Damien, and his investigation leads him to forbidding places. Ultimately he is unable to save either his wife (Remick) or himself. The story goes its grim, inexorable way, punctuated by shocking moments that are not for the queasy, but it all seems like a pointless, if well-managed, exercise in horror. Actually, the most frightening sequences involve animals out of control rather than the explicitly gory deaths: an assault on Remick's car by shrieking baboons in Windsor Safari Park, or an attack on Peck and inquisitive photographer Warner by a pack of wild dogs in a cemetery. The film's resolution is *not* comforting or reassuring, but it guaranteed sequels.

Off-Screen: Jerry Goldsmith's music score received an Oscar. The popularity of *The Omen* resulted in three much less successful sequels, *Damien-Omen Two* (1978), *The Final Conflict* (1981), and *Omen IV: The Awakening* (television, 1991) which proved irrevocably that Damien did not mellow with age.

On a Clear Day You Can See Forever

Paramount, 1970. (C-129m.) Dir: Vincente Minnelli. Sp: Alan Jay Lerner, b/o his musical play. MS: Burton Lane and Alan Jay Lerner. Cast: Barbra Streisand, Yves Montand, Larry Blyden, Bob Newhart, Jack Nicholson, Simon Oakland, John Richardson.

On-Screen: *Barbra Streisand in the stage musical about reincarnation.* On Broadway in 1965, *On a Clear Day You Can See Forever* promised more than it delivered. It had a melodic Lane-Lerner score, but its story about Daisy Gamble, a girl with extrasensory perception whose psychiatrist discovers that she had a previous life in the eighteenth century, was not exactly involving. The film version is designed as a vehicle for Barbra Streisand as Daisy, but while Streisand is in fine voice, the story is no less wearisome, and costar Montand as the psychiatrist is an unfortunate choice. The film becomes opulent when Daisy reverts to her eighteenth-century double, Melinda Tentrees, but by then interest has waned. Many of the songs (including several new entries) are lovely or witty, and Vincente Minnelli's unfailing sense of color and design is evident in sequences set in the past. Yet despite a talented star and director, *On a Clear Day* is not a superior musical.

Off-Screen: Richard Harris was scheduled to play the lead opposite Barbra Streisand, but after reading the script, he declined, feeling that the role would be secondary to hers. The regression sequences were photographed at the Royal Pavilion in Brighton, England. Jack Nicholson's role as Tad Pringle, Streisand's sitar-playing step-brother (a character not in the original play), was severely cut before the film's release.

On Golden Pond

Universal/AFD, 1981. (C-109m.) Dir: Mark Rydell. Sp: Ernest Thompson, b/o his play. Cast: Henry Fonda, Katharine Hepburn, Jane Fonda, Doug McKeon, Dabney Coleman, William Lanteau.

On-Screen: *The twilight summer of an elderly couple.* Unabashedly sentimental and occasionally touching, Ernest Thompson's adaptation of his play *On Golden Pond* is more of a tribute to two screen icons than a thoughtful reflection on old age. But since Henry Fonda and Katharine Hepburn richly deserve the tribute, why quibble? In his last role, Fonda is splendid as cantankerous, eighty-year-old Norman Thayer, who shares summers with his wise, devoted wife, Ethel (Hepburn), at their lakefront Maine home. Terrified that he is losing his faculties, Norman must also cope with his contentious relationship with his daughter, Chelsea (Jane Fonda). The summer on Golden Pond brings renewed fears of mortality but also a tentative reconciliation with

Chelsea. Fonda gives a fine performance as Norman, seldom stooping to soften the character but giving him a kind of scratchy lovability nonetheless. Saddled with the role of a woman who embraces all the virtues, Hepburn is somewhat less successful, allowing some artifice to show through. However, she has several indelible moments, especially one in which she dances alone in the woods.

Off-Screen: Hepburn's comment on meeting Fonda was "Well, it's about time," although she was certain that they must have met before: "I'm sure I must have said, 'How do you do?' to Henry Fonda at one time or another. I felt as though I knew him." Fonda was deeply touched when Hepburn gave him Spencer Tracy's favorite old hat, which he wore in the movie. Fonda's climactic scene with his daughter contained much of their private and public feelings about each other, and it was difficult for them to shoot. Although the setting is Maine, the movie was filmed on Big Squam Lake in New Hampshire. Hepburn, Henry Fonda, and Ernest Thompson all won Oscars. Fonda died five months later.

On the Beach

United Artists, 1959. (133m.) Dir: Stanley Kramer. Sp: John Paxton, b/o novel by Nevil Shute. Cast: Gregory Peck, Ava Gardner, Fred Astaire, Anthony Perkins, Donna Anderson, John Tate, Guy Doleman.

On-Screen: *A group of people confront the end of the world.* The year is 1964, and the world is approaching doomsday. A nuclear war has enveloped the earth, spreading a lethal cloud of atomic dust that will annihilate all traces of mankind. In Australia, one group of people await the inevitable end in five months. Those who face their doom with courage and tenacity include an American submarine captain (Peck), a worldly, dissipated woman (Gardner) who loves him, a cynical atomic scientist (Astaire in his first dramatic role), and others. John Paxton's cautionary tale, based on Nevil Shute's novel, stresses the value of life in the face of doom, but you are likely to remember the scenes of man's last days on earth: Peck's submarine passing by a destroyed San Francisco, or Astaire in his beloved racing car, pushing it to the limit in one final race. Other images are memorably stark, but the film's overall power is somewhat diminished by Stanley Kramer's slow pacing. Ernest Gold's musical score uses the Australian tune "Waltzing Matilda" as its theme.

Off-Screen: Much of the film was shot on location in Australia, where the temperature often soared. Reportedly, novelist Nevil Shute was unhappy with the film and stayed away from the set and from any public showing of the movie. Peck felt that it was a mistake to have his character go to bed with Ava Gardner, but Kramer insisted. Peck: "My character goes out the window when I do the expected thing and go to bed with Ava. The eccentricity of the character, the peculiar twist that makes him interesting and different, goes down the drain."

On the Town

MGM, 1949. (C-98m.) Dir: Gene Kelly and Stanley Donen. Sp: Betty Comden and Adolph Green, b/o their musical play. MS: Leonard Bernstein, Roger Edens, Betty Comden, and Adolph Green. Cast: Gene Kelly, Frank Sinatra, Vera-Ellen, Ann Miller, Jules Munshin, Betty Garrett, Alice Pearce.

On-Screen: *From the Broadway musical: three sailors on leave in New York.* Opening at the end of 1944, the Bernstein, Comden, and Green stage musical *On the Town,* derived from Jerome Robbins's ballet *Fancy Free,* took Broadway by storm. Five years passed before it reached the screen, but when it did, the wait seemed worth it. Exuberant, entertaining, and in some ways, innovative, it has the simplest of premises: three sailors (Kelly, Sinatra Munshin), on a weekend leave in New York, find romance. One (Kelly) discovers, loses, and then, with the help of his friends, rediscovers the girl (Vera-Ellen) of his dreams. A few of the sequences were filmed on location in New York City, giving them an air of immediacy and excitement. Musical highlights include the wonderful "New York, New York" opening and the engaging Kelly–Vera-Ellen duet to "Main Street." There are a few flaws: the added songs by Roger Edens are inferior to the original songs, and the final chase sequence is more frantic than funny. Still, *On the Town* remains a landmark musical that brought new vitality to the genre.

Off-Screen: Considering that Louis B. Mayer disliked the stage show and that Arthur Freed didn't care for Leonard Bernstein's original score, it's something of a miracle that this musical is as good as it is. Credit should probably go to directors Kelly and Donen, and to Comden and Green for preserving the spirit. Kelly, who wanted to make the entire film in New York City, was allowed only one frantic week to shoot against actual sites with the cast. The movie won a single Oscar for Best Scoring of a Musical Motion Picture.

On the Waterfront

Columbia, 1954. (108m.) Dir: Elia Kazan. Sp: Budd Schulberg, b/o articles by Malcolm Johnson. Cast: Marlon Brando, Eva Marie Saint, Karl Malden, Lee J. Cobb, Rod Steiger, Martin Balsam, Pat Henning.

On-Screen: *Brando's Oscar-winning role as a rebellious dock worker.* Kazan's masterly "orchestration" of the movie's components—Schulberg's screenplay, Boris Kaufman's photography, Leonard Bernstein's music—gives the film its now-classic status. The story deals with labor racketeering on New York City's docks; the real drama, though, concerns Terry Malloy (Brando). An ex-boxer and now a lackey to dock boss Johnny Friendly (Cobb), Terry turns stoolie when he learns of Friendly's murderous power. He's helped by a feisty priest (Malden) and a girl (affectingly played by Saint) whom he comes to love. The taxicab scene, in which Terry faces the bitter truth about life with brother Charley (Steiger), a mob lawyer, is part of movie legend. "I coulda been a contender," Terry tells him. "I coulda been somebody." Finally acknowledging his own value ("They tell me I'm a bum. Well, I ain't a bum"), Brando makes his barely articulate character both believable and moving.

Off-Screen: Filmed along the banks in Hoboken, New Jersey, the movie won eight Oscars, including those for Best Picture, Direction, and Story and Screenplay (Schulberg's script was inspired by Johnson's Pulitzer Prize–winning articles written for the *New York Sun*). Acting honors went to Brando and Saint (Best Supporting Actress, in her film debut). Frank Sinatra was originally scheduled to play Terry under Kazan's direction, but the role went to Brando (a bigger name at the time), to Sinatra's great disappointment. Shot in a local studio, the taxicab scene was hated by Brando, who thought it was phony. Years later, he recognized its universal theme of regret and disappointment. Even so, it required many takes before it was completed satisfactorily. (CFB)

One False Move

I.R.S. Media, 1992. (C-105m.) Dir: Carl Franklin. Sp: Billy Bob Thornton and Tom Epperson. Cast: Bill Paxton, Cynda Williams, Billy Bob Thornton, Michael Beach, Jim Meltzer, Earl Billings.

On-Screen: *Three people leave a trail of murder and mayhem.* It begins with a bloodbath, with the gangland-style execution of some partygoers, and ends with a violent shootout between killers and a sheriff. In between is a modest but oddly effective crime melodrama that attracted much critical attention on its release. At first the plot seems conventional: Murderous drug dealers Ray (Thornton) and Pluto (Beach), accompanied by Ray's girlfriend, Fantasia (Williams), travel to a small town in Arkansas, where Ray and Fantasia (actually Lila) have family. Waiting for them are the town's sheriff (Paxton) and two Los Angeles cops. But then the story takes some unexpected turns that give new facets to the characters and make their involvement with each other more intriguing than one might imagine. The direction is not polished, but the acting is competent, especially by Bill Paxton as the sheriff who may not be the down-home "good ol' boy" he appears to be, and Cynda Williams as a girl who is actually more than just another drugged-out gun moll. *One False Move* is something of a sleeper, but you won't be caught napping.

Off-Screen: Financed independently, *One False Move* was directed by Carl Franklin, a former actor who was a semiregular on television's "The A-Team." The movie's wide release was due in part to the enthusiastic support of critics Gene Siskel and Roger Ebert.

One Flew Over the Cuckoo's Nest

United Artists, 1975. (C-133m.) Dir: Milos Forman. Sp: Lawrence Haubman and Bo Goldman. Cast: Jack Nicholson, Louise Fletcher, Brad Dourif, William Redfield, Michael Berryman, Peter Brocco, Will Sampson, Scatman Crothers, Dean R. Brooks, Danny DeVito, Christopher Lloyd.

On-Screen: *A freewheeling asylum patient fights conformism.* "I'm senseless, out of it, gone-down-the-road wacko," Randle McMurphy (Nicholson) tells a doctor (Brooks) at the mental hospital. "Mac" exaggerates. Disreputable, defiant, and off-center he surely is; he's also a life-affirming, formidable threat to the deadening rigors of the social establishment. The movie concerns Mac's pitched battle with the chillingly sinister, unflappable Nurse Ratched (Fletcher), who represents the evil of repression. Nicholson and Fletcher are brilliant as the strongly opposing forces. Forman gets fine performances, too, from the supporting cast, especially from Dourif, as the mother-dominated patient, and Sampson, as the supposedly mute inmate who's able at last,

under disastrous circumstances, to honor Mac's celebration of human dignity and freedom.

Off-Screen: In 1963, Kirk Douglas appeared on Broadway in an adaptation of Kesey's acclaimed novel. Douglas had secured film rights, but the actor's prior commitments delayed production. By the time he was ready to make the movie, Douglas felt he was too old to play McMurphy again, and so he turned the rights over to son Michael, who became the film's coproducer. Marlon Brando, Gene Hackman, and Burt Reynolds turned down the principal role, and Anne Bancroft and Angela Lansbury were among those who declined to play Nurse Ratched. Sampson is a well-known Creek Indian artist; Dr. Dean R. Brooks (Dr. Spivey) was superintendent of the Oregon State Hospital where the movie was filmed. The film won all five Oscars in the major categories (*It Happened One Night* was the only previous movie to do so), for picture, director, actor, actress, and screenplay adaptation. (CFB)

100 Men and a Girl

Universal, 1937. (84m.) Dir: Henry Koster. Sp: Bruce Manning, Charles Kenyon, Hans Kraly, and James Mulhauser, b/o story by Hans Kraly. MS: Various writers. Cast: Deanna Durbin, Leopold Stokowski, Adolphe Menjou, Alice Brady, Eugene Pallette, Mischa Auer, Billy Gilbert, Frank Jenks.

On-Screen: *Deanna Durbin sings and schemes in her second musical.* After her success in her first feature film *Three Smart Girls* (1936), perky young Deanna Durbin starred in this charming, melodic musical. The sort of movie that Jane Powell would make at

MGM about a decade later (with more lavish sets and with Jose Iturbi replacing Leopold Stokowski), *100 Men and a Girl* has Deanna as yet another warbling Miss Fix-It. This time she schemes to have her indigent musician father (Menjou) and his fellow musicians audition for none other than Stokowski. There are several good orchestral renditions by Stokowski, and Deanna warbles a few pleasing songs and arias in her girlish soprano. The climactic scene works best: The out-of-work musicians gather on the staircase of Stokowski's home to play for him, and the maestro, carried away by the music, begins to lead them. Charles Previn and his Universal Studio Music Department earned an Oscar for the film's score.

Off-Screen: In order to add visual interest to the classical music numbers, director Koster used the swooping and gliding camera crane devised for the musical *Broadway* (1929), the studio's first all-talkie. The movie was such a box-office success that Durbin's salary was increased to $3,000 a week, with a $10,000 bonus for each following film. It received five Oscar nominations, including Best Picture.

One, Two, Three

United Artists, 1961. (108m.) Dir: Billy Wilder. Sp: Billy Wilder and I. A. L. Diamond, b/o play by Ferenc Molnar. Cast: James Cagney, Arlene Francis, Horst Buchholz, Pamela Tiffin, Lilo Pulver, Howard St. John, Hans Lothar, Leon Askin, Red Buttons.

On-Screen: *James Cagney takes on Berlin. Guess who wins.* Cagney's last film for twenty years, *One, Two, Three* fairly crackles with the actor's seemingly boundless vitality. And since it was directed and cowritten by Billy Wilder, it also has more than its share of caustic wit. Cagney plays the high-powered head of Coca-Cola's operations in West Berlin, who is forced to deal with the perils of life in a divided, occupied city. (Remember?) When his boss's daughter (Tiffin) marries an East German Communist (Buchholz), there are countless complications, especially when the boss himself (St. John) arrives for a visit. Soon Cagney finds himself frantically sprinting from one side of the Berlin wall to the other. Played in rapid-fire style, with Cagney leading the way, *One, Two, Three* takes the viewer on a giddy ride into Wilder's world of liars, cheats, and fools. Cagney still has his pugnacious Irish charm, even if he's playing an amoral rascal. The Cold War may be over, but this movie merrily skewers its obvious absurdities.

Off-Screen: Filming in Berlin proved to have many problems, largely due to wary, suspicious authorities in the Eastern sector. When they asked to read the script, Wilder replied, "I wouldn't even let President Kennedy read my script." And when a sequence at the Brandenburg Gate turned out to be untenable, Wilder shot it on a studio backlot in Munich where art director Alexander Trauner built an exact duplicate. During the filming, Cagney complained to Billy Wilder about Horst Buchholz's "scene-stealing didoes," which were soon curtailed.

One-Eyed Jacks

Paramount, 1961. (C-141m.) Dir: Marlon Brando. Sp: Guy Trosper and Calder Willingham, b/o novel by Charles Neider. Cast:

Marlon Brando, Karl Malden, Katy Jurado, Ben Johnson, Pina Pellicer, Slim Pickens.

On-Screen: *Marlon Brando as star and director in a revenge western.* Having chosen to both direct and star in this outsize western, Marlon Brando gave himself a formidable task, but he succeeds only intermittently. Brando plays Rio, a loner bent on avenging himself against Dad Longworth (Malden), the former friend who betrayed his love and trust. His dream of revenge is complicated when he discovers that Longworth is now a trusted sheriff; Rio also falls in love with Longworth's stepdaughter (Pellicer). The showdown ends inevitably in violent death. A number of intense scenes will keep you interested, but the movie lacks the sustained and unified force of a great western film. Mostly, it suffers from the director's indulgence of his star—Brando stays front and center for most of the film, and after a while, his brooding, sensitive face becomes oppressive. *One-Eyed Jacks* has merit, but it also needed a restraining hand.

Off-Screen: Brando, who replaced Stanley Kubrick as director, dominated all aspects of the production. Reportedly, he shot a million feet of film for an original version that ran nearly five hours, even after extensive cutting. The story is told that for a scene in which Rio sits on a rock and gazes out at the surf, Brando spent hours waiting for "the right wave." Apparently, he also worked on the screenplay with Guy Trosper and Calder Willingham.

Only Angels Have Wings

Columbia, 1939. (121m.) Dir: Howard Hawks. Sp: Jules Furthman, b/o story by Howard Hawks. Cast: Cary Grant, Jean Arthur, Richard Barthelmess, Thomas Mitchell, Rita Hayworth, Allyn Joslyn, Sig Ruman, Noah Beery, Jr., John Carroll.

On-Screen: *Pilots share the stress and adventure of flying.* Renowned for his vigorous adventure films and westerns that often emphasized male camaraderie and bonding, Howard Hawks made one of his best in this high-flying tale. Dressed more like a gaucho than an airman, Cary Grant plays Geoff Carter, the head of a group of pilots who risk their lives daily by flying mail and freight high over the Andes in South America. Stoic in the face of death, these men have a private code of behavior. Along comes Bonnie Lee (Arthur), a stranded show girl who falls for Geoff and has to learn the hard way about the pilots' code. A subplot involves Barthelmess, a pilot with a troubled past, and his seductive wife, an old flame of Geoff's (Hayworth, in an important early role). As Kid Dabb, Geoff's closest friend, Thomas Mitchell comes close to stealing the film, and his death scene is the most affecting in the movie. There are a few excellent flying sequences, but *Only Angels Have Wings* is more concerned with relationships among the characters.

Off-Screen: For the film, a complete walled village, representing the port town of Barranca in Ecuador, was built on the Columbia lot in the San Fernando Valley. The movie represented a comeback effort for Richard Barthelmess, who had been a major star in the silent years. He failed to make the transition to sound, however. A contract player at Columbia in minor films, Rita Hayworth campaigned actively for the role of Judy McPherson, reportedly donning a form-fitting dress and going to the restaurant where Hawks and Columbia head Harry Cohn were dining.

Operation Mad Ball

Columbia, 1957. (105m.) Dir: Richard Quine. Sp: Arthur Carter, Jed Harris, and Blake Edwards, b/o play by Arthur Carter. Cast: Jack Lemmon, Ernie Kovacs, Kathryn Grant, Mickey Rooney, Dick York, Arthur O'Connell, Roger Smith, James Darren.

On-Screen: *Soldiers plan a monster party.* Service comedies are often cut from the same cloth, but *Operation Mad Ball* is funnier than most. The material is basically familiar—the rowdy, take-charge private vs. the nasty, uptight officer—but the screenplay gives the old situations a few fresh spins. The setting is Normandy right after the end of World War II. Under the nose of by-the-book Captain Lock (Kovacs), Private Hogan (Lemmon) and his cohorts in revelry plot to stage "the maddest mad ball in the history of the United States army" at a local inn. The consequences, of course, are wildly unexpected. Many of the sequences have the pace and vitality of good farce; the funniest (if not the most tasteful) involves the substitute for a misplaced corpse in the post mortuary. In his first movie role, Ernie Kovacs plays the sort of blustery comic villain he would repeat in later films.

Off-Screen: One scene between Jack Lemmon and Mickey Rooney (as the post's wild transportation sergeant) required thirty takes because Lemmon kept breaking up. Director Quine remembered: "Mickey never did the scene twice the same way, and every time he'd add a new touch, Jack would just fall over backwards. It was the only time I saw Lemmon unable to handle an acting chore."

Ordinary People

Paramount, 1980. (C-123m.) Dir: Robert Redford. Sp: Alvin Sargent, b/o novel by Judith Guest. Cast: Mary Tyler Moore, Donald Sutherland, Timothy Hutton, Judd Hirsch, Elizabeth McGovern, Dinah Manoff, M. Emmet Walsh, James B. Sikking.

On-Screen: *A family is torn asunder by a son's death.* In an affluent Chicago suburb, the members of the Jarrett family, shattered by the drowning death of an older son, are being torn apart by deeply rooted antagonism and resentment. Frosty mother Beth (Moore) smothers her feelings in propriety; father Calvin (Sutherland) is well-meaning but weak; and younger son Conrad (Hutton) blames himself for his brother's death. Wracked with guilt and tormented by the belief that his mother hates him, Conrad manages to grope toward a new beginning with the help of a compassionate psychiatrist (Hirsch). His parents, however, have irreparable wounds. Actor Redford's first effort as a director, *Ordinary People* is an uncommonly fine film, powerful in expressing the private demons that lurk in the shadows of well-ordered lives. The acting is exemplary, but Timothy Hutton rates top honors in the pivotal role. His Conrad's anguish is palpable in every scene, and his explosion in the psychiatrist's office wrenches the heart.

Off-Screen: The company spent two months on location in Lake Forest, an affluent suburb in Chicago. For the scene in which Moore and Sutherland fly to relatives in

Texas, Redford opted to rent out one section of the commercial jetliner that was taking the cast back to California. Judd Hirsch's scenes were shot out of sequence and back-to-back so that he would not be out of the cast of "Taxi" for more than a few weeks. *Ordinary People* won Oscars for Hutton, Redford, and writer Alvin Sargent; it was also cited as the year's Best Picture.

Our Town

United Artists, 1940. (90m.) Dir: Sam Wood. Sp: Thornton Wilder, Frank Craven, and Harry Chandlee, b/o play by Thornton Wilder. Cast: Frank Craven, William Holden, Martha Scott, Thomas Mitchell, Fay Bainter, Guy Kibbee, Beulah Bondi, Stuart Erwin, Doro Merande.

On-Screen: *The rituals of life and death in a small New Hampshire town.* In 1938, Thornton Wilder's Pulitzer Prize–winning play had dispensed with scenery in order to emphasize the eternal verities in the everyday events occurring over the years in Grovers Corners, New Hampshire. Transformed to the screen, the story was much less stylized but just as warm and moving. Frank Craven repeated his Broadway role as the Narrator who leads the viewers through the crucial episodes in the lives of the characters. Although patently too old for their roles, Martha Scott (also from the stage cast) and William Holden are charming as the Grovers Corners youngsters who fall in love and marry. Their moonlight conversation and their drugstore courtship are among the film's highlights, and later, Scott figures in the most memorable scene, when, having presumably died in childbirth, she is allowed to return to earth for one day of her life and chooses her sixteenth birthday. Aaron Copland's evocative score contributes greatly to the movie's effectiveness.

Off-Screen: In transposing the play to the screen, the most pressing problem was determining whether Emily, the heroine, should live or die. (She died in the play.) After considerable thought, it was decided, with Thornton Wilder's approval, to let her live. A musical adaptation of the play appeared on television in 1955, with Frank Sinatra as the Narrator and Paul Newman and Eva Marie Saint as the young couple. *Grovers Corners*, a stage musical version by Tom Jones and Harvey Schmidt, was produced at the Lincolnshire Theater in Illinois in 1987, and in 1989, a Broadway production was announced, with Mary Martin starring as the Narrator, but she became ill, and the show never opened.

Out of Africa

Universal, 1985. (C-161m.) Dir: Sydney Pollack. Sp: Kurt Luedtke, b/o books by Isak Dinesen and book by Judith Thurman. Cast: Meryl Streep, Robert Redford, Klaus Maria Brandauer, Michael Kitchen, Malick Bowens, Michael Gough, Rachel Kempson, Suzanna Hamilton.

On-Screen: *Multi-Oscar winner about a woman's African experiences.* Long, sprawling, and leisurely paced, *Out of Africa* is derived from the writings of Isak Dinesen, who, under her true name of Karen Blixen, lived for a number of years in Kenya, East Africa, where she ran a coffee plantation. In the film, Karen (Streep) engages in a marriage of convenience with her lover's brother,

Baron Bror Blixen (Brandauer), undergoes various trying experiences, and later has a passionate romance with British hunter Denys Finch-Hatton (Redford). Despite its length and slow pace, *Out of Africa* is seldom dull and is also ravishing to look at; David Watkin's African photography is breathtaking. In addition, Meryl Streep gives a lovely, finely tuned performance as Karen. (We are mesmerized the moment we hear her intone, "I had a farm in Africa, at the foot of the Ngong Hills," in her lightly accented voice.) The movie's most serious liability is Redford, who gives a flat performance as a scarcely credible Englishman. Still, romanticists should cherish his love scenes with Karen under the African stars, or their flight across the landscape, all set to John Barry's beautiful score.

Off-Screen: Years before *Out of Africa* was produced, others had been interested in adapting Isak Dinesen's memoirs to films. Orson Welles and David Lean had considered the project, and Nicolas Roeg had thought of making a film with Julie Christie as Karen. Much of the film was shot on location in Africa. Local workers recreated the city of Nairobi as it appeared in the early 1900s, and a group of women built the circular cottages of the Kikuyu village. The movie won an Academy Award as Best Picture, and other Oscars went to Pollack, Luedtke, Watkin, and Barry. There were Oscars as well for Art Direction and Sound. Nominations went to Streep and Brandauer.

Out of the Past

RKO, 1947. (97m.) Dir: Jacques Tourneur. Sp: Geoffrey Homes (Daniel Mainwaring), b/o his novel. Cast: Robert Mitchum, Jane Greer, Kirk Douglas, Rhonda Fleming, Steve Brodie, Dickie Moore.

On-Screen: *A woman of sexual mystery lures a former private eye into a disastrous encounter.* Rivaling *The Big Sleep* in its dizzying plot convolutions, this top-notch, if gloomy, thriller plays fairer with the viewer, avoiding the earlier *film noir's* narrative ellipses. In a role seemingly tailor-made for him, languid, sleepy-eyed Mitchum is perfect as the morally ambiguous detective whose fate is sealed the moment he sees Greer's psychotic siren walking into a streetside cantina in Acapulco. Like Barbara Stanwyck in *Double Indemnity,* Greer is chillingly convincing as a woman with no qualms about betraying, framing, or killing her lovers. Douglas is fine as the reptilian gangster who sparks the events by sending Mitchum to Mexico to find errant girlfriend Greer. Tourneur's direction makes the dialogue snap and sting: "Don't you believe me?" Greer purrs. "Baby, I don't care," Mitchum replies, kissing her.

Off-Screen: Because he had appeared as a private eye in *The Maltese Falcon* and *The Big Sleep,* Humphrey Bogart was first choice for the male lead, followed by John Garfield, then Dick Powell, who had also scored as a gumshoe in *Murder, My Sweet.* None of them expressed interest, thus giving Mitchum one of his best roles. Scenes were shot on location sites as disparate as New York City, Lake Tahoe, San Francisco, Mexico City, and Acapulco. Thirties child star Moore plays the deaf-mute youth at Mitchum's rural gas station. An off-target remake, *Against All Odds,* with Jeff Bridges and Rachel Ward, was released in 1984. Its main point of interest is that Jane Greer appears as the mother of her character in the original. (CFB)

The Ox-Bow Incident

Fox, 1943. (75m.) Dir: William A. Wellman. Sp: Lamar Trotti, b/o novel by Walter Van Tilburg Clark. Cast: Henry Fonda, Dana Andrews, Anthony Quinn, Mary Beth Hughes, William Eythe, Henry Morgan, Jane Darwell, Harry Davenport, Frank Conroy, Francis Ford.

On-Screen: *Western townsmen organize a lynching*. More of a reflection on mob violence than a traditional western, *The Ox-Bow Incident* is unusually stark material to emerge from a major studio. When a popular rancher is presumably murdered by horse thieves, three hapless, innocent men (Andrews, Quinn, and Ford) are apprehended, then summarily executed by an angry mob of townspeople spurred on by a bogus Confederate colonel (Conroy). Only a few, including an itinerant cowpoke (Fonda), question the terrible deed. Grim and harrowing, the movie stays relentlessly with the lynchers and their victims, conveying the brutality and the terror with compelling force. There are flaws. The scenery (especially an artfully gnarled hanging tree) is obviously phony, and a victim's letter to his wife, read aloud after his lynching, introduces a false note. (In the novel, the contents are never revealed.) But *The Ox-Bow Incident* is a cautionary tale worth watching.

Off-Screen: Several studios refused this project, but director Wellman was determined to see Clark's novel filmed. He found that Fox's Darryl Zanuck "was the only one with the guts to do [the film] for the prestige rather than the dough." Wellman's deal with Fox required him to provide Zanuck with two "commercial" movies, *Thunder Birds* and *Buffalo Bill*.

The Pajama Game

Warners, 1957. (C-101m.) Dir: George Abbott and Stanley Donen. Sp: George Abbott and Richard Bissell, b/o their musical play and novel by Bissell. MS: Richard Adler and Jerry Ross. Cast: Doris Day, John Raitt, Carol Haney, Eddie Foy, Jr., Reta Shaw, Barbara Nichols, Thelma Pelish, Ralph Dunn.

On-Screen: *Romance and labor relations in a pajama factory.* A Broadway hit in 1954, the musical *The Pajama Game* finally reached the screen three years later, with all of its ebullience and most of its great score intact. The plot, which may seem antediluvian today, centers on labor agitation at a pajama factory and on the romance between the factory foreman (Raitt, repeating his Broadway role) and the head of the union's grievance committee (Day). Day fairly glows in the musical portions, offering first-rate renditions of such tunes as "Hey, There" and "I'm Not At All in Love." She also joins Raitt in several numbers, especially the exuberant "There Once Was a Man." As good as these two are, the musical is stolen by pixieish Carol Haney, reprising her Broadway numbers—"Steam Heat" and "Hernando's Hideaway"—and turning them into showstoppers. A highlight of the movie is the picnic sequence, in which the workers joyfully celebrate their "Once-a-Year Day" to Bob Fosse's dazzling choreography.

Off-Screen: Sadly, the happy spirit of the movie did not carry over to some of the creators and cast. Jerry Ross, co-composer and lyricist of the musical, died in 1955 at twenty-nine. And Carol Haney died in 1964 at age thirty. Eddie Foy, Jr., Reta Shaw, Ralph Dunn, and Thelma Pelish also repeated their Broadway roles.

Pal Joey

Columbia, 1957. (C-111m.) Dir: George Sidney. Sp: Dorothy Kingsley, b/o musical play and stories by John O'Hara. MS: Richard Rodgers and Lorenz Hart. Cast: Frank Sinatra, Rita Hayworth, Kim Novak, Hank Henry, Barbara Nichols, Bobby Sherwood, Elizabeth Patterson.

On-Screen: *Rodgers and Hart's musical about an enormous heel.* Back in 1940, Gene Kelly had scored his first major success playing the heel-hero of Rodgers and Hart's musical, derived from John O'Hara's stories. Seventeen years later, the musical reached the screen in somewhat altered form. Some of the bite and bawdiness of the original was extracted, with Sinatra playing a much nicer, although still self-centered, fellow. As the restless society woman who dallies with him, Rita Hayworth still looks alluring—a mature love goddess—but Kim Novak is hopeless as the sweet young thing who loves the wayward hero. The Rodgers and Hart songs—some not from *Pal Joey*—include "Bewitched," "My Funny Valentine," and "The Lady Is a Tramp." Some are treated well; others are trashed by misinterpretation. *Pal Joey* is no model musical, but it's easy on the ears.

Off-Screen: For years, writers had attempted to bring this acerbic story to the screen without success. When director Sidney moved his independent company to Columbia in 1956, he commissioned a new screen treatment from Dorothy Kingsley. The setting was moved from Chicago to San Francisco, and the central characters were made somewhat more sympathetic. The change of locale caused the elimination of the song "Our Little Den of Iniquity," since Joey was no longer set up in an apartment by his rich, predatory benefactor but in a yacht on San Francisco Bay.

The Palm Beach Story

Paramount, 1942. (90m.) Dir: Preston Sturges. Sp: Preston Sturges. Cast: Claudette Colbert, Joel McCrea, Rudy Vallee, Mary Astor, Sig Arno, Robert Dudley, Franklin Pangborn, William Demarest, Jack Norton, Robert Greig, Roscoe Ates, Dewey Robinson.

On-Screen: *Three cheers for the Ale and Quail Club!* Can the reputation of a movie be secured largely by one sequence? Probably. Case in point: Preston Sturges's madcap marital comedy, *The Palm Beach Story*. Many viewers recall with special fondness the scene in which a group of rowdy hunters who call themselves the Ale and Quail Club romp with their dogs through the train bearing Claudette Colbert to Florida. It's a comedy gem in an only fitfully amusing movie. Colbert plays the wife who flees from husband McCrea and finds herself in Palm Beach, involved with crackpot billionaire Vallee and his oversexed sister Astor. *The Palm Beach Story* has some diverting moments, and Astor is delightful as a much-married princess ("I grow on people—like moss"), but the principal characters lack appeal, and some of the fun is rather strained. Still, the movie has its partisans.

Off-Screen: Preston Sturges derived the Ale and Quail Club train sequence from his happy boyhood memories of traveling with his mother on the Twentieth Century from Chicago to New York. ("How I loved the porters and the dining-car waiters. How kind they were to little boys.") Palm Beach was also familiar to him from the time he spent there with rich folk in earlier years. ("Millionaires are funny.")

Paper Moon

Paramount, 1973. (102m.) Dir: Peter Bogdanovich. Sp: Alvin Sargent, b/o novel by Joe David Brown. Cast: Ryan O'Neal, Tatum O'Neal, Madeline Kahn, P. J. Johnson, John Hillerman, Burton Gilliam, Randy Quaid.

On-Screen: *A con man and a young girl travel across Depression America.* A hugely entertaining comedy, *Paper Moon* stars Ryan O'Neal as Moze, a resourceful, fly-by-night con man and Bible salesman who finds himself burdened with Addie (his real-life daughter Tatum), an orphaned tyke who is even more resourceful—and larceny-minded—than he is. Along the way, they encounter a variety of eccentrics, especially a shrill, flamboyant, "entertainer" named Trixie Delight (Kahn, hilarious in the role) and her black maid (Johnson). Perhaps the movie is a bit self-conscious about evoking the period (sobering signs of Kansas during the Depression, period music on the sound track, stark black-and-white photography), but it all works, especially with the help of young Tatum's Oscar-winning performance as Addie. With her fierce glints, pursed lips, and steely voice, she makes a formidable adversary and then partner for Moze's schemes. *Paper Moon* is pure pleasure, and with some scrubbing, it might have made a good Shirley Temple–James Dunn vehicle back in 1934.

Off-Screen: The screenplay changed the novel's locale from Georgia to Kansas. It was the suggestion of Polly Platt, Peter Bogdanovich's wife and the film's production designer, that eight-year-old Tatum O'Neal play Addie Pray. Bogdanovich agreed to direct only if Tatum's father, Ryan, would play Moze. At first Bogdanovich fought the story, feeling that the characters weren't believable, then he "became interested in doing that kind of travel movie with a story that is really rather picaresque." A short-lived television series based on the movie turned up in 1974.

Parenthood

Universal, 1989. (C-124m.) Dir: Ron Howard. Sp: Lowell Ganz and Babaloo Mandel, b/o story by Lowell Ganz, Babaloo Mandel, and Ron Howard. Cast: Steve Martin, Mary Steenburgen, Dianne Wiest, Rick Moranis, Jason Robards, Tom Hulce, Martha Plimpton, Keanu Reeves, Harley Kozak, Dennis Dugan, Jasen Fisher, Leaf Phoenix.

On-Screen: *Steve Martin and siblings cope with the trauma of being parents.* The complex, exasperating, and often infinitely rewarding business of being a parent (and a child) comes under close comic scrutiny in this cluttered but highly enjoyable movie. Steve Martin stars as Gil Buckman, husband of Steenburgen and father of three, whose troubled young son (Fisher) is giving him headaches and heartaches. Swirling around him is his family (father Robards; sisters Wiest and Kozak; brother Hulce), all of whom have to cope in one way or another with parenthood. The screenplay tries to absorb too much and occasionally loses its grip, but there are many perceptive insights and some pricelessly funny moments. Steve Martin shines as the well-meaning dad (his fantasies about his son are on target), and others in the large and talented cast contribute solid performances. Dianne Wiest is exceptionally good as a much put-upon mother who seems to be able to smile and cry simultaneously. The all-smiles ending is too pat, but *Parenthood* is almost as much fun as the real thing.

Off-Screen: Dianne Wiest won a Best Supporting Actress nomination for her performance. Another Oscar nomination went to Randy Newman for his song "I Love to See

You Smile." Some in-family casting: Ron Howard's brother Clint plays an obnoxious parent at the Little League game, and his father has the small role of the college president in Gil's fantasy about his son. A television series based on the film, starring Ed Begley, Jr., as Gil Buckman, had a brief run in 1990.

Pat and Mike

MGM, 1952. (95m.) Dir: George Cukor. Sp: Garson Kanin and Ruth Gordon. Cast: Katharine Hepburn, Spencer Tracy, Aldo Ray, William Ching, Jim Backus, Sammy White, George Mathews, Loring Smith.

On-Screen: *Hepburn and Tracy dabble in sports and romance.* "Nicely packed, that kid. Not much meat on her, but what's there is *cherce!*" That's sports promoter Spencer Tracy's assessment of his newest client, world-class athlete Katharine Hepburn. He's attracted, all right, but there are problems: Hepburn appears to be under the thumb of her smugly superior fiancé (Ching), and she's also much too assertive for Tracy's macho ways. ("I like a he to be a he, and a she to be a she!") Not to worry—it all works out satisfactorily. Breezily entertaining, *Pat and Mike* marks the team's seventh pairing, and if it's not in the top rank of their films together, it seems to get better every year. The stars play together comfortably, and George Cukor's direction is smoothly professional. Aldo Ray draws laughs as another of Tracy's clients, a punch-drunk boxer.

Off-Screen: The film's producer, Lawrence Weingarten, later recalled: "Gar [Garson Kanin] had written a line in which Spencer said of Kate, 'She's pretty well stacked.' I said, 'Do you know the meaning of the word? Kate is not well stacked. She has a small bust.' I pressured him, George [Cukor] pressured him, and he came up with another line: 'Not much meat on her, but what's there is *cherce!*' It got the biggest laugh in the movie."

Paths of Glory

United Artists, 1957. (86m.) Dir: Stanley Kubrick. Sp: Stanley Kubrick, Calder Willingham, and Jim Thompson, b/o novel by Humphrey Cobb. Cast: Kirk Douglas, Ralph Meeker, Adolphe Menjou, George Macready, Wayne Morris, Joseph Turkel, Timothy Carey, Richard Anderson.

On-Screen: *Searing drama of military politics in World War I.* One of the finest antiwar movies, this lean, tautly characterized film packs a wallop. Some of the action takes place on the battlefield, but the real combat is waged in the headquarters of the French High Command. Scheming General Broulard (Menjou) flatters the vain General Mireau (Macready) into ordering a doomed attack on an impregnable German stronghold. When some of the troops falter, their commander, Colonel Dax (Douglas), is ordered to try three soldiers—a corporal (Meeker) and two privates (Turkel and Carey)—for treason as an example to the others. As their defense counsel, Douglas acts with his customary intensity; but it's Menjou's falsely hearty Broulard, Macready's maniacally patriotic Mireau, and the trio of hapless enlisted men whom you'll long remember.

Off-Screen: After Kirk Douglas was shown the screenplay by Stanley Kubrick, he insisted that the film *had* to be made, even if it didn't make a dime. (It had been turned down everywhere.) When he arrived in Munich to begin shooting, he found that the script had been cheapened to make it more commercial. Furious, he insisted that the original screenplay be restored. It was, and the movie became a cult classic. Based on an actual occurrence, *Paths of Glory* was banned in France for fifteen years, and for a brief period on United States military bases. (CFB)

Patton

Fox, 1970. (C-170m.) Dir: Franklin J. Schaffner. Sp: Francis Ford Coppola and Edmund H. North, b/o books by Ladislas Farago and Omar N. Bradley. Cast: George C. Scott, Karl Malden, Karl Michael Vogler, Stephen Young, Michael Strong, Frank Latimore, Tim Considine.

On-Screen: *Epic war drama and full-length portrait of the controversial general.* Scott brings fire and eloquence to his role of Gen. George S. Patton, the charismatic, war-loving tyrant whose contempt for cowards and incompetents extended to physical violence. In also depicting the World War II warrior as a forceful military leader with the audacity and imagination to win great battles, the movie balances fairly both facets of this complex man, providing ample material for drawing your own conclusion. Schaffner opens his film with "Blood and Guts" Patton standing before an enormous American flag as he harangues the troops and closes with him walking away from the army, while the sails of a giant windmill (suggesting the erratic idealism of Don Quixote) turn slowly behind him. The movie conveys the awesome quality of military battles, but rarely strays from the formidable,

gritty presence of Scott's Patton. A brilliant film.

Off-Screen: Based on material from Farago's *Patton: Ordeal and Triumph* and General Bradley's autobiography, *A Soldier's Story,* the Coppola-North screenplay received one of the movie's seven Oscars, as did the movie itself, director Schaffner, and Scott. The actor, however, declined his Best Actor award (the first actor to do so), expressing a perfectionist's dissatisfaction with his performance. Shooting took place in many locations, including Spain, Greece, Sicily, Morocco, and England. In 1986, Scott appeared in *The Last Days of Patton,* a television sequel. (CFB)

The Pawnbroker

Landau/Allied Artists, 1965. (116m.) Dir: Sidney Lumet. Sp: David Friedkin and Morton Fine, b/o novel by Edward Lewis Wallant. Cast: Rod Steiger, Geraldine Fitzgerald, Brock Peters, Jaime Sanchez, Thelma Oliver, Marketa Kimbrell, Juano Hernandez, Raymond St. Jacques.

On-Screen: *A war victim's tormented life and the shattering events that redeem it.* This emotion-wrenching drama concerns Sol Nazerman (Steiger), a pawnshop owner in New York's Harlem. The loss of his family in the Holocaust has so traumatized him that he has no compassion for the customers, whom he regards as "rejects, scum." A prostitute (Oliver) who offers herself to him only evokes memories of his wife's rape by concentration camp guards. Nor can he respond to a compassionate social worker (Fitzgerald) who would like to help him. Only when his young Puerto Rican assistant (Sanchez) is killed during a robbery attempt is Nazerman painfully recalled to life. His voiceless cry of rage and anguish is a searing moment in the film. Lumet makes the going a little self-consciously arty at times, but the cast brings the story to vivid life, with Steiger giving an uncommonly powerful performance as the deeply scarred survivor.

Off-Screen: The film's sole Academy Award nomination was for Best Actor. The recognition was well deserved, Steiger having subordinated his often mannered, in-your-face acting style to the role's complex demands. An outstanding feature of the movie is Boris Kaufman's cinematography, which used New York City sites such as Harlem, Lincoln Center for the Performing Arts, and Jericho, Long Island.(CFB)

Peggy Sue Got Married

TriStar, 1986. (C-104m.) Dir: Francis Coppola. Sp: Jerry Leichtling and Arlene Sarner. Cast: Kathleen Turner, Nicolas Cage, Barry Miller, Barbara Harris, Don Murray, Catherine Hicks, Joan Allen, Kevin J. O'Connor, Leon Ames, Maureen O'Sullivan, John Carradine.

On-Screen: *A middle-aged woman travels back magically to her past*. Forty-three and on the verge of divorce, Peggy Sue (Turner) attends her high school reunion (class of 1960), where she collapses and finds herself transported back to that year. Her eighties attitudes and reactions mystify everyone, but mostly she attempts to change the future by changing her relationships, especially with her husband-to-be (Cage). In the end, she returns to the present with new perceptions about herself and her life. Francis Coppola's film has some amusing and

poignant moments, although the time-travel device begins to creak toward the end. Kathleen Turner makes a fine Peggy Sue, but Nicolas Cage is a serious liability, turning her boyfriend-husband into an even less appealing character than he is intended to be. *Peggy Sue Got Married* marked another failed attempt by director Francis Coppola to return to the glory of his *Godfather* days.

Off-Screen: *Peggy Sue Got Married* has a complicated preproduction history. At first Jonathan Demme was signed to direct the film, with Debra Winger as the star. Winger, however, wanted Penny Marshall to direct, and Marshall came in as the replacement for Demme. Then Marshall quit, and Winger withdrew after a back injury. Kathleen Turner was signed to replace her. Contenders for the Nicolas Cage role included Judge Reinhold and Martin Short.

Pennies From Heaven

MGM, 1981. (C-107m.) Dir: Herbert Ross. Sp: Dennis Porter, b/o his television play. MS: Various writers. Cast: Steve Martin, Bernadette Peters, Jessica Harper, Vernel Bagneris, Christopher Walken, John McMartin, John Karlen, Tommy Rall, Jay Garner.

On-Screen: *A musical drama set in the Depression years*. Most viewers were baffled or troubled by this one-of-a-kind film, but in many ways it's a remarkable achievement, artfully produced and played to perfection. Dennis Potter adapted his acclaimed British television miniseries about Arthur (Martin), a sheet-music salesman in Chicago, 1934, whose sexual frustration with his wife (Harper) leads him to an assignation with Eileen (Peters), a gentle schoolteacher.

Arthur and Eileen's fate is bleak, and so is this Depression tale, but then, astonishingly, the movie is also a lavish musical. The characters express their dreams and illusions by lipsynching to popular tunes of the era, rendered by such stars as Bing Crosby, Connie Boswell, and Arthur Tracy. The musical numbers are staged brilliantly and opulently; highlights include Vernel Bagneris's song and dance to the title tune and the Martin-Peters reconstruction of an Astaire-Rogers number from *Follow the Fleet*. It's true that the grim story clashes with the exuberant musical numbers, but *Pennies From Heaven* remains a true original that warranted a much friendlier reception.

Off-Screen: The British miniseries starred Bob Hoskins at a time when he was not yet familiar to American audiences. Many viewers will recognize the visual images reproducing the thirties photographs of Walker Evans and others, and the paintings of Edward Hopper and Reginald Marsh. Vernel Bagneris, who plays the Accordian Man, was recruited from the Los Angeles company of the musical *One Mo' Time*, which he wrote and directed. *Pennies From Heaven* won Oscar nominations for its screenplay, sound, and costume design.

Penny Serenade

Columbia, 1941. (125m.) Dir: George Stevens. Sp: Morrie Ryskind, b/o story by Martha Cheavens. Cast: Irene Dunne, Cary Grant, Edgar Buchanan, Beulah Bondi, Eva Lee Kuney.

On-Screen: *A young married couple experiences joy and tragedy over the years.* After appearing together in several successful comedies (*The Awful Truth,* 1937; *My Favorite Wife,* 1940), Irene Dunne and Cary Grant turned to emotional drama with this tale of a married couple who survive one tragedy after another. It would be easy for this sort of soap opera to tumble into bathos (and sometimes it gets perilously close), but somehow George Stevens, aided by Morrie Ryskind's moist but tasteful screenplay and the expert performances by the leads, succeeds in making this film quite affecting. If you cannot guess what will happen to the couple's adopted daughter when she gets to play an angel in her school play, you have never been to the movies. Nevertheless, *Penny Serenade* will touch your heart, and Dunne and Grant are always a pleasure to watch together. (Grant received an Academy Award nomination as Best Actor.)

Off-Screen: Years later, Irene Dunne described what it was like to work with Cary Grant: "He was very apprehensive about nearly everything. So apprehensive, in fact, that he would get almost physically sick. If the script, the director, an actor, or a particular scene displeased him, he would be greatly upset. I remember one scene in *Penny Serenade* where he had to plead with a judge to keep an adopted baby. He was so disturbed. I had to talk to him and talk to him." The scene clinched his Oscar nomination.

People Will Talk

Fox, 1951. (110m.) Dir: Joseph L. Mankiewicz. Sp: Joseph L. Mankiewicz, b/o play by Kurt Goetz. Cast: Cary Grant, Jeanne Crain, Walter Slezak, Hume Cronyn, Finlay Currie, Sidney Blackmer, Margaret Hamilton.

On-Screen: *An unorthodox doctor in love and trouble*. How many films can you recall that discuss such topics as medical ethics, the role of teachers in today's world, and the processing and packaging of food? Few indeed, and Joseph L. Mankiewicz touches on them all, and others as well, in his comedy-drama. Cary Grant is a highly unorthodox teacher of gynecology whose rival and nemesis (Cronyn) considers him a dangerous charlatan. Cronyn, it seems, is most perturbed by Grant's very odd right-hand man (Currie), who has a mysterious past. While all this is happening, Grant also courts and marries Crain, a pregnant, unmarried student. *People Will Talk* has a verbose but intriguing screenplay, and while it cannot be counted among Mankiewicz's best films, it is seldom dull. Grant makes the most of his offbeat role, and Walter Slezak is amusing as his friend, an atomic scientist and occasional bull-fiddle player.

Off-Screen: The film is a remake of a popular 1933 German play and movie *Dr. Praetorius*. Joseph Mankiewicz first called his screenplay *Doctor's Diary*, but Darryl Zanuck renamed it *People Will Talk*. Jeanne Crain's role was intended for Anne Baxter, but ironically, Baxter became pregnant.

The Petrified Forest

Warners, 1936. (83m.) Dir: Archie Mayo. Sp: Charles Kenyon and Delmer Daves, b/o play by Robert E. Sherwood. Cast: Leslie Howard, Bette Davis, Humphrey Bogart, Genevieve Tobin, Dick Foran, Charley Grapewin, Porter Hall.

On-Screen: *An escaped killer holds people at bay in a desert café*. The stage origins of this taut melodrama are evident as Duke Mantee (Bogart), a gangster on the loose, comes charging into an Arizona café with his henchmen and places a group of people under his gun. Among his prisoners are a burned-out writer (Howard) and the proprietor's yearning daughter (Davis), who come to share a brief but tender relationship. Although the situation is tense and threatening, the film, like the play, has more on its mind than creating suspense. Howard's world-weary, enervated intellectual and Bogart's vicious killer are poles apart; yet they are both as obsolete in the contemporary world as the trees of the nearby petrified forest. The movie is stage-bound and too heavily symbolic, but still worth a look for its star chemistry.

Off-Screen: Howard and Bogart re-create their stage roles in the film. Howard insisted that Bogart play the part, which marked his first major chance after years of floundering in minor films. Bogart modeled his character on gangster John Dillinger, studying newsreels to learn how he walked and dressed. The story was remade in 1945 as *Escape in the Desert*, and there was a television version in 1955, with Bogart, Henry Fonda, and Lauren Bacall.

Petulia

Warners–Seven Arts, 1968. (105m.) Dir: Richard Lester. Sp: Lawrence B. Marcus; adaptation: Barbara Turner, b/o novel by John Haase. Cast: Julie Christie, George C. Scott, Richard Chamberlain, Shirley Knight, Arthur Hill, Pippa Scott, Kathleen Widdoes, Joseph Cotten.

On-Screen: *A doctor's involvement with a "kook."* Recently separated from his wife, a world-weary surgeon named Archie (Scott) meets the rich, "kooky," and unhappily married Petulia (Christie) at a charity ball and finds himself deeply involved in her life. Petulia's husband (Chamberlain) is a weak, despicable sadist who abuses her, and Archie tries in vain to rescue her. For director Lester, this frail plot is clearly not the essence of *Petulia*. What's really intended in the screenplay and in Lester's direction is a mosaic of urban upper-class life in the late sixties, where people behave coolly or eccentrically to avoid recognizing that their relationships, like Petulia's, are unrewarding, disoriented, and painful. The movie indicates this point of view by having many of the characters indulge in visualized flashes of thought or memory as they move through their empty days and frenetic nights. After a while, the device becomes more distracting than illuminating, however. Much of the film is dated, but there's no faulting the performances, especially by Christie and Knight (as Scott's wife).

Off-Screen: While many reviewers praised the film, *Petulia* drew some unusually harsh reviews when it was first released. Critic Pauline Kael called it "obscene, disagreeable, dislikable," and *Newsweek* dismissed it as a "rather dishonest comedy" and said that Lester was "an opportunistic deracinated entertainer." Since then, its reputation has improved to the extent that it is now regarded by many as one of the outstanding films of its time. *Petulia* was photographed by Nicolas Roeg, later a notable director (*Don't Look Now,* etc.).

Peyton Place

Fox, 1957. (C-157m.) Dir: Mark Robson. Sp: John Michael Hayes, b/o novel by Grace Metalious. Cast: Lana Turner, Lee Philips, Diane Varsi, Hope Lange, Lloyd Nolan, Arthur Kennedy, Russ Tamblyn, Terry Moore, Mildred Dunnock, Leon Ames, Lorne Greene, Betty Field, Barry Coe.

On-Screen: *Scandalous doings in a New England town.* Back in the fifties, Grace Metalious's best-selling novel perpetuated the long-standing notion that small American towns were hotbeds of lurid secrets. Today, the book, and this film version, are not half as steamy as the average television soap opera. Still, the movie is decent pulp fiction, written and played in broad, obvious strokes but fairly riveting and handsomely produced. Set just before and after the start of World War II (although there is no sense of period), the story exposes the long-buried secrets, the peccadilloes, and the violent clashes of a group of Peyton Place citizens. Lana Turner (in an Oscar-nominated performance) heads the cast as a repressed woman whose daughter (Varsi), an aspiring writer, narrates the story. Along the way to a climactic murder trial, the movie manages to touch on such topics as suicide, rape, and sexual hang-ups. There are some pluses: William C. Mellor's camerawork captures the beauty of the New England countryside, and Franz Waxman's score, including the familiar theme, enhances the shifting moods. Several sequences, especially a Labor Day picnic, evoke the pleasures of small-town communal life. *Peyton Place* is a glossy soap opera, but you won't be bored.

Off-Screen: *Peyton Place* won nine Oscar nominations in all, including Best Picture and Best Director. Russ Tamblyn, Arthur Kennedy, Hope Lange, and Diane Varsi were nominated in the Supporting Actor/Actress categories. Amazingly, the film received an A (Acceptable for All) rating from the Catholic Legion of Decency, and the National Board of Review cited it as "an example of how a fine motion picture can be made out of a cheap and dirty book."

The Philadelphia Story

MGM, 1940. (112m.) Dir: George Cukor. Sp: Donald Ogden Stewart, b/o play by Philip Barry. Cast: Katharine Hepburn, Cary Grant, James Stewart, Ruth Hussey, Roland Young, John Howard, John Halliday, Virginia Weidler, Mary Nash, Henry Daniell.

On-Screen: *Romance and revelry among the Philadelphia rich.* A literate, sparkling comedy, *The Philadelphia Story* adapts Philip Barry's Broadway play into one of the screen's durable treasures. Reprising her stage role, Katharine Hepburn enchants as Tracy Lord, a haughty Philadelphia rich girl, on the verge of marrying again, who not only learns to have humility and heart but also rediscovers the virtues of her first husband (Grant). Cary Grant is at his most debonair as wry C. K. Dexter Haven, and James Stewart, in his Oscar-winning role, is enormously likable as Mike Connor, a reporter for *Spy* magazine who begins by disdaining "the rich and the mighty," then comes to adore Tracy. The movie is heavy on talk, but it's such witty talk that you won't mind, and the supporting players are perfectly cast, especially Roland Young as a lecherous uncle and Ruth Hussey as a knowing photographer. Favorite scene: Hepburn and Stewart at poolside in the moonlight ("You're the golden girl, full of warmth and delight!") *The Philadelphia Story* is a story worth telling, many times.

Off-Screen: Hepburn wanted Spencer Tracy to play C. K. Dexter Haven, but MGM refused to cast him, and when George Cukor suggested Cary Grant, she accepted him readily. She also agreed to Grant's insistence on top billing. In addition to Stewart's Oscar, the movie received four other Academy Award nominations: for Best Picture, Best Actress, Best Director, and Best Screenplay. The movie was remade as a musical called *High Society* in 1956. A glittering cast (Bing Crosby, Grace Kelly, Frank Sinatra) and Cole Porter music were unable to dim the glow of the original film.

Picnic

Columbia, 1955. (C-113m.) Dir: Joshua Logan. Sp: Daniel Taradash, b/o play by William Inge. Cast: William Holden, Rosalind Russell, Kim Novak, Betty Field, Susan Strasberg, Cliff Robertson, Arthur O'Connell.

On-Screen: *Sexual stirrings in a small Kansas town.* It's Labor Day, and everyone's set for the annual picnic. If Hal Carter (Holden) hadn't hopped a freight train and breezed into town, it might have been just another holiday. He only wants his ex-college pal (Robertson) to help him get a job; instead, Hal, who exudes virility from every sinew, ends up turning around the life of just about everyone he meets. Russell is both sublimely funny and touching as an unmarried schoolteacher whose sexual repression is released just by the sight of the handsome hunk. Thanks to Hal's satyrlike power, she lands a husband (O'Connell). Novak plays Robertson's girlfriend, and when she and Hal team up for a steamy dance at the picnic, their lives are changed, too. Holden, though possessing an athletic build, is a bit old for Hal; Novak, while beautiful, is rather vapid as a woman ready to kick over the traces. Logan makes all these whistle-stop lives matter.

Off-Screen: This was Logan's first job as film director in eighteen years—in 1937, he had codirected *I Met My Love Again* with Arthur Ripley. (Logan had directed Kansas-born Inge's play on Broadway in 1953.) Russell was so eager to play the lonely spinster that she accepted a lesser "costarring" billing. Many of her scenes landed on the cutting-room floor. The seduction dance scene had to be filmed on a Hollywood soundstage after a hailstorm ruined the shooting in Hutchinson, Kansas. "Moonglow," a popular song from 1934, took a new lease on life when it was revived for the movie. *Picnic* won a Best Picture nomination and received Oscars for Art Direction (Color) and Film Editing. A stage musical version, called *Hot September,* failed in 1965. (CFB)

The Picture of Dorian Gray

MGM, 1945. (110m.) Dir: Albert Lewin. Sp: Albert Lewin, b/o novel by Oscar Wilde. Cast: Hurd Hatfield, George Sanders, Angela Lansbury, Donna Reed, Peter Lawford, Lowell Gilmore.

On-Screen: *A youth's desire to remain young wreaks havoc in Victorian London.* Scandalous from the day of its publication in 1891, Wilde's novel was still deemed sufficiently steamy to require some ironing out of its kinky wrinkles when it reached the screen more than half a century later. An updated version of the Faust legend, the story relates how handsome Dorian Gray (Hatfield),

fallen under the spell of corrupt Lord Henry Wotton (Sanders), strikes an unholy bargain that not only allows him to pursue a dissolute life without aging, but also results in his life-size portrait (shown in Technicolor) depicting, finally and horribly, his true nature. Hatfield and Sanders are perfect, but Lansbury, as the winsome music-hall singer ruined by the dissolute Dorian's cruelty, steals this stylish movie.

Off-Screen: Worried about how the film would be received, MGM decided to sell it as a thriller, with ad copy that screamed, "Behind his fascinating face lived the soul of a killer!" Malvin and Ivan Albright, the famous artist twins, painted the portraits showing Dorian Gray's gradually deteriorating "soul." Harry Stradling won an Academy Award for his black-and-white cinematography, while Angela Lansbury received a second Oscar nomination for her performance as the hapless Sibyl Vane. (The year before, at age nineteen, she was nominated for her first movie role as the saucy maid in *Gaslight*.) Many years later, in an episode of the television series "Murder, She Wrote," the actress, doubling as a relative of her starring character, Jessica Fletcher, reprised her *Dorian Gray* rendition of "Little Yellow Bird." The story was remade in 1970 as a multinational film. (CFB)

Pillow Talk

Universal-International, 1959. (C-105m.) Dir: Michael Gordon. Sp: Stanley Shapiro and Maurice Richlin, b/o story by Russell Rouse and Clarence Greene. Cast: Doris Day, Rock Hudson, Tony Randall, Thelma Ritter, Nick Adams, Julia Meade, Allen Jenkins, Lee Patrick, Marcel Dalio.

On-Screen: *The first Doris Day–Rock Hudson teaming.* An airily amusing romantic comedy, once considered quite bold in its approach to sexual matters, *Pillow Talk* brought perky Doris Day and stolid Rock Hudson together for the first time. Audiences liked the combination, and they went on to costar in two more movies. Day plays a chic interior decorator who shares a party line with Hudson, a womanizing Broadway composer. When she lodges a complaint against his hogging of their party line, he exacts his own kind of revenge: He impersonates a shy Texan who releases Day's long-dormant libido. Of course the two actually love each other. The situations are only mildly risqué, but the screenplay takes such a leering attitude toward them that sixties audiences were persuaded they were seeing a titillating sex farce instead of a conventional comedy. The stars are attractive, however, and Tony Randall as Hudson's befuddled friend and Day's suitor manages to earn some laughs. The best lines fall to Thelma Ritter as a plain-speaking, perpetually tipsy maid.

Off-Screen: Surprisingly, the story and screenplay for *Pillow Talk* received Academy Awards. Rock Hudson had serious misgivings about appearing in a comedy—this was his first—but director Gordon convinced him that he only need play the role with the utmost seriousness to earn laughs. Day, Hudson, and Randall were teamed again for *Lover Come Back* (1961), the best of their films, and for *Send Me No Flowers* (1964).

The Pink Panther

United Artists, 1964. (C-113m.) Dir: Blake Edwards. Sp: Maurice Richlin and Blake Edwards. Cast: David Niven, Peter Sellers, Capucine, Robert Wagner, Claudia Cardinale, Brenda De Banzie, Fran Jeffries.

On-Screen: *Introducing the world's worst detective, Jacques Clouseau.* Stumbling from one disaster to another, the monumentally stupid, hugely funny Inspector Clouseau made his film debut in this scenic caper comedy. Played by the gifted Peter Sellers, Clouseau immediately found favor with audiences, and although he doesn't dominate the proceedings as he would in his later movies, he draws the largest laughs. Here, Clouseau comes with his wife (Capucine) to the Riviera where a group has gathered for both frivolous and larcenous reasons. Among them are Niven, a debonair Englishman with a secret identity as a notorious jewel thief, and a beautiful princess (Cardinale), whose fabulous diamond the Pink Panther is sought by Niven. The cream of the jest is that Clouseau's wife is Niven's confederate! Everyone finally converges on a lavish masquerade party that involves two men dressed as gorillas, a policeman disguised as a zebra, and Clouseau in full armor. (Don't ask.) It's the highlight of a moderately entertaining movie that gave Clouseau to the world.

Off-Screen: The role of Inspector Clouseau was originally intended for Peter Ustinov, with Ava Gardner as his wife. Robert Wagner commented on David Niven: "That first *Panther* was supposed to be his picture, and when they suddenly brought in Sellers instead of Ustinov, he could see it being taken away from him scene by scene. He just sat back and watched Sellers take it from him because he knew there was nothing he could do." Friction between Blake Edwards and Peter Sellers developed on the set because of their opposite approaches to their work, with Sellers as the perfectionist who wanted many retakes and Edwards as someone more inclined to improvise.

Pinocchio

Disney-RKO, 1940. (C-88m.-animated) Supervising Dir: Ben Sharpsteen and Hamilton Luske. b/o story by Carlo Collodi. MS: Leigh Harline, Ned Washington, and Paul J. Smith.

On-Screen: *Walt Disney's timeless tale of a puppet's adventures*. One of Disney's most fondly remembered feature films, *Pinocchio* boasts technically brilliant animation, a story with some exciting (and potentially frightening) sequences, and even a lilting score. Loosely derived from the Collodi story, it relates the adventures of the puppet Pinocchio, who, in answer to the prayer of his creator, the wood-carver Geppetto, is given life by the Blue Fairy. But he can't become "a real boy" until he proves himself "brave, truthful, and unselfish." Before he can achieve his goal, innocent Pinocchio undergoes many perilous experiences. Most terrifying are his sojourn on Pleasure Island, where bad boys are turned into enslaved donkeys, and his fearsome encounter with Monstro the Whale. *Pinocchio* abounds in memorable characters, including Pinocchio's engaging little friend and official conscience, Jiminy Cricket, the flamboyantly wicked fox, J. Worthington Foulfellow, and Geppetto's mischievous cat, Figaro. One song from the lively score, "When You Wish Upon a Star," won that year's Academy Award.

Off-Screen: Dickie Jones provided the voice of Pinocchio, and character actor Christian Rub was the voice of Geppetto. J. Worthington Foulfellow was played, unmistakably, by the inimitable Walter Catlett, the befuddled con man and crook of many a movie. Cliff Edwards voiced (and sang) the role of Jiminy Cricket. The movie was reissued in 1992 after a yearlong restoration project that included cleaning the original negative frame by frame, removing accumulated scratches, reviving the colors, and eliminating distortions on the sound track.

The Pirate

MGM, 1948. (C-102m.) Dir: Vincente Minnelli. Sp: Frances Goodrich and Albert Hackett, b/o play by S. N. Behrman. MS: Cole Porter. Cast: Judy Garland, Gene Kelly, Walter Slezak, Gladys Cooper, Reginald Owen, George Zucco, the Nicholas Brothers.

On-Screen: *Garland and Kelly in a splashy Cole Porter musical*. Among the blooms in Vincente Minnelli's musical garden, *The Pirate* could be considered a hothouse flower: colorful and exotic, but perishable when exposed to the light. Derived from a 1942 play that starred Alfred Lunt and Lynn Fontanne, the movie casts Judy Garland as a romantic-minded West Indian lass in thrall to the legend of the dangerous pirate known as Mack the Black. Her arranged marriage to the portly town mayor (Slezak) is interrupted when Gene Kelly, a traveling actor, appears and pretends to be Mack the Black. Garland gives a strained performance, but when she sings Porter's "Mack the Black" or "Love of My Life," she is peerless, as always. Kelly comes off much better with his imitation of Douglas Fairbanks, Jr., and his dancing is top-notch. Porter's score is far from his best, but even second-string Porter has more wit and panache than the songs of most other composers.

Off-Screen: MGM had originally purchased the property back in 1942, expecting to film it as a songless farce starring William Powell, Hedy Lamarr, and Charles Laughton. (Later, Myrna Loy substituted for Lamarr.) There were a number of screen treatments, but after some years of false starts, it was decided to turn the play into a musical vehicle for Judy Garland. The name of the leading male character was changed from Estramundo to Macoco because Cole Porter had a friend by that name, nicknamed Mack the Black, and always wanted to write a song about him. Judy Garland was in poor shape throughout the filming of *The Pirate*. She was often absent because of illness, and when she appeared, she was either extremely tense or incoherent due to pills. Several of her numbers, including one called "Voodoo," were cut from the release print.

A Place in the Sun

Paramount, 1951. (122m.) Dir: George Stevens. Sp: Michael Wilson and Harry Brown, b/o novel by Theodore Dreiser and play by Patrick Kearney. Cast: Montgomery Clift, Elizabeth Taylor, Shelley Winters, Anne Revere, Raymond Burr, Keefe Brasselle.

On-Screen: *A youth tries desperately to climb the social ladder.* Updating Dreiser's powerful novel *An American Tragedy,* this compelling film traces the steps by which one man meets his inexorable fate. Montgomery Clift plays George Eastman, who turns his back on a life of poverty and the fierce puritanism of his mother (Revere). He goes to work in a factory, where he meets and has an affair with frumpy Alice Tripp (Winters). But then he meets the beautiful Angela Vickers (Taylor), and as they fall in love, he enters her glamorous world of social privilege. When Alice reveals her pregnancy, George finds himself torn between duty to her and desire for Angela and all she represents. How George resolves his dilemma provides the dramatic action that decides his destiny. Stevens's direction stresses the sensual interplay between Clift and Taylor, while submerging the social commentary in Dreiser's novel beneath lush cinematography (by William C. Mellor) and rapt fascination with the wealthy. Still, Clift's and Taylor's performances are electrifying, and Winters's pitiable, nagging Alice is superb.

Off-Screen: A previous version of Dreiser's novel, under the title *An American Tragedy,* was released in 1931, under Josef von Sternberg's direction. To placate the studio, George Stevens discarded the negative title of the book for the more upbeat *A Place in the Sun.* Anne Revere maintained that her two best scenes as Clift's mother were cut over Stevens's objections. Both Clift and Winters, as well as the film itself, were nominated for Academy Awards. They lost, but Oscars were presented for direction, screenplay, editing, score, cinematography (black-and-white) and costumes (black-and-white). (CFB)

Places in the Heart

TriStar, 1984. (C-102m.) Dir: Robert Benton. Sp: Robert Benton. Cast: Sally Field, Danny Glover, John Malkovich, Lindsay Crouse, Ed Harris, Amy Madigan, Lane Smith, Terry O'Quinn.

On-Screen: *Sally Field's Oscar as a Texas farmwoman battling the Depression.* Of the trio of films released in 1984 that concerned the

417

plight of American farmers at different points in their history (*Country* and *The River* were the others), *Places in the Heart* is the most sentimental and predictable. Yet it is a memory play, after all—Robert Benton's fictionalized recollection of his great-grandmother's life in Waxahachie, Texas. At the height of the Depression, Edna Spaulding (Field) is a suddenly widowed woman with two small children. On the verge of having to sell her farm, she opts to grow cotton, and with the help of a knowledgeable itinerant black man (Glover) and a blind, testy, but sympathetic boarder (Malkovich), she overcomes the terrible odds. There's also a subplot involving Edna's brother-in-law (Harris) in an extramarital affair with a local married teacher (Madigan). No real surprises, but the film has some nicely observed period details, a few well-staged sequences (especially a tornado that shatters the community), and an odd but moving ending in which all the characters, living and dead, join hands in the church. Sally Field's Oscar-winning performance is on target.

Off-Screen: Robert Benton's family lived in Waxahachie for over a century. John Malkovich's character was based on Benton's great-uncle, from whom he borrowed mannerisms, habits, and even the profession of caning chairs and making brooms. The filmmaker updated the story to the Depression years so that he could call upon his childhood memories. In addition to Field's Oscar, Benton's original screenplay won a statuette. The movie was also nominated for Best Picture, Benton for Best Director, and both John Malkovich and Lindsay Crouse (as Field's sister) were cited for their supporting roles.

The Plainsman

Paramount, 1936. (113m.) Dir: Cecil B. DeMille. Sp: Waldemar Young, Harold Lamb, and Lynn Riggs, b/o stories by Frank J. Wilstach and book by Courtney Riley Cooper and Grover Jones. Cast: Gary Cooper, Jean Arthur, James Ellison, Helen Burgess, Porter Hall, Anthony Quinn.

On-Screen: *Cecil B. DeMille's fanciful epic western about Wild Bill Hickok. The Plainsman* has nothing to do with American Western history and everything to do with perpetuating the legend of that pioneer and Indian fighter James Butler "Wild Bill" Hickok. The truth is much different, but Cecil B. DeMille makes Hickok (Cooper) the centerpiece of a churning, elaborate movie. Cooper plays Hickok as a stoic, quietly forceful man whose brave deeds include rescuing the lovelorn Calamity Jane (Arthur) from hostile Indians. Unfortunately, he never forgives her when she is unable to bear seeing him tortured and reveals the position of the cavalry. Hickok's famous death scene, in which "Calam" kisses him farewell after he expires on the barroom floor, moved thirties audiences to tears. Most viewers attended, however, for DeMille's obligatory action scenes, well staged as usual.

Off-Screen: Listing the many inaccuracies in *The Plainsman* would fill many pages. For one, Calamity Jane was actually a vulgar, ugly virago, much different from the winsome charmer played by Jean Arthur. To his credit, DeMille did refuse to spare Hickok at the film's end, or to have him killed by a character other than cowardly Jack McCall (Hall). Anthony Quinn made his film debut in *The Plainsman*. The film was poorly remade in 1966, with Don Murray as Hickok.

Planet of the Apes

Fox, 1968. (C-112m.) Dir: Franklin J. Schaffner. Sp: Michael Wilson and Rod Serling, b/o novel by Pierre Boulle. Cast: Charlton Heston, Roddy McDowall, Kim Hunter, Maurice Evans, James Whitmore, James Daly, Linda Harrison.

On-Screen: *Adventure-fantasy, with a sharp satiric edge.* The tables are turned for astronaut George Taylor (Heston) when he's taken prisoner on a planet run by highly intelligent apes. Although most of his simian captors regard human beings as savages fit only for slavery, Taylor is befriended by sympathetic apes Cornelius (McDowall) and Dr. Zira (Hunter). Heston is tough and strong-jawed as the arrogant time-traveler who must assert his supposed superiority over the socially developed apes. Even more convincing are the surprisingly "human" performances of the planet's rulers. Some dialogue strains for easy laughs—"Humans see, humans do," "I never met an ape I didn't like," for example. Otherwise, this serious, intensely dramatic science-fiction movie recalls *Gulliver's Travels* in its slyly Swiftian inversions of our accepted values and attitudes. The conclusion is as startling as it is unforgettable.

Off-Screen: Though the film has an appropriately otherworldly look to it (deceptively so, as it turns out), exteriors were shot at Lake Powell, Utah; in Page, Arizona; and, for the surprising ending, at Point Dume, California. Maurice Evans replaced Edward G. Robinson in the role of Dr. Zaius, when Robinson could not tolerate the elaborate makeup. Jerry Goldsmith's score was nominated for an Oscar, but because there was no Best Makeup category that year, an honorary statuette was presented to John Chambers for his "outstanding achievement" in creating the simians. Four film sequels and two television series follow-ups were nowhere as successful as their progenitor. (CFB)

Platoon

Orion, 1986. (C-120m.) Dir: Oliver Stone. Sp: Oliver Stone. Cast: Tom Berenger, Willem Dafoe, Charlie Sheen, Forest Whitaker, Francesco Quinn, John C. McGinley, Richard Edson, Kevin Dillon, Reggie Johnson, Keith David, Johnny Depp.

On-Screen: *Oliver Stone's powerful, haunting war film.* Narrating the harrowing events in letters to his grandmother, Pvt. Chris Taylor (Sheen) begins by saying, "Someone once wrote: 'Hell is the impossibility of reason.' That's what this place is like." The place is Vietnam, the time 1967, and Taylor is a newly arrived member of Bravo Company, Twenty-fifth Infantry. Through the course of this searing film, we follow his platoon through a nightmarish vision, caught up in the terror, disorientation, and sudden violent death of close combat. Taylor is the central figure as he moves from knowing too little to knowing too much, but the film's theme is embodied in two contrasting sergeants: the tough, cold-blooded, and vicious Barnes (Berenger) and the equally tough but compassionate Elias (Dafoe). Their opposing attitudes toward behavior in combat make up the heart of *Platoon*. The battle scenes are as vivid as any you will ever see, and one sequence in a village is almost unendurable in its cruelty and ugliness. There are flaws: Taylor's letters to his grandmother are a rather overfancy literary device, and the central Barnes-Elias conflict is a bit too schematic (good vs. evil), but *Platoon* is one of the durable war films.

Off-Screen: Oliver Stone shot two endings, one in which Sergeant Elias lives and one in which he is martyred. Stone finally chose the ending that "felt more realistic." In preparation for the filming, the entire company participated in intense and grueling field training in the Philippines. The Philippine government supplied the military hardware and equipment for the film. Since the Vietnam War was a forbidden subject for many years, it took ten years to get the movie made. The rewards included eight Oscar nominations. The movie received top honors (Best Picture, Best Director) and also won in the categories of Sound and Film Editing. Berenger and Dafoe were both nominated for Supporting Oscars. Samuel Barber's "Adagio for Strings" was used hauntingly throughout the movie.

The Player

Fine Line Features, 1992. (C-123m.) Dir: Robert Altman. Sp: Michael Tolkin, b/o novel by Michael Tolkin. Cast: Tim Robbins, Greta Scacchi, Fred Ward, Whoopi Goldberg, Peter Gallagher, Brion James, Cynthia Stevenson, Vincent D'Onofrio, Dean Stockwell, Sydney Pollack, Dina Merrill, Lyle Lovett.

On-Screen: *Robert Altman takes on Hollywood's wheeler-dealers.* Who's sending young, ambitious movie producer Griffin Mill (Robbins) all that threatening mail? Mill figures it's a disgruntled screenwriter (D'Onofrio); in a violent encounter, he eliminates the source of those pesky postcards. (Or so he thinks.) Mill's troubles, though, have only begun. His career jeopardized by a hotshot rival producer (Gallagher), Mill devises an ingenious way to get rid of him, too. (Or so he thinks.) With boyish charm, Mill seduces his victim's lover (Scacchi), betrays his girlfriend (Stevenson), and undermines colleagues and scripts alike. Finally, two persistent detectives (Goldberg and Lovett) and the real nemesis close in. His fate? You may find the movie less a thriller than a challenge to pick up on its multitude of inside-Tinseltown jokes and jabs. The huge cast—"players" both on screen and off—clearly relishes its chance to shout, along with Altman and Tolkin, "Two cheers for Hollywood!"

Off-Screen: Film fans will have a field day spotting the sixty-five actors (Nick Nolte, Julia Roberts, Susan Sarandon, Bruce Willis, among others), writers, and directors playing themselves in cameo walk-ons and bit parts. Famed director Pollack plays a famed showbiz lawyer. Altman used the tenth of thirteen takes (note the clapboard) for the virtuoso eight-minute, uncut opening tracking shot of a busy studio street. (One of the superabundant inside jokes: A security guard laments that directors no longer stage lengthy single takes, as Orson Welles did in *Touch of Evil*.) Viewers who want to know who may be sending those postcards should pay close attention to the eulogist at the funeral. The movie won three Oscar nominations, including one for Best Director. (CFB)

Point Blank

MGM, 1967. (C-92m.) Dir: John Boorman. Sp: Alexander Jacobs, David Newhouse, and Rafe Newhouse, b/o novel by Richard Stark (Donald E. Westlake). Cast: Lee Marvin, Angie Dickinson, Carroll O'Connor, Keenan Wynn, Lloyd Bochner, John Vernon, Michael Strong, Sharon Acker.

On-Screen: *Mobster Lee Marvin seeks revenge and retribution.* A taut, violent, hard-edged crime melodrama, now regarded as one of the best of the sixties, *Point Blank* stars Lee Marvin, at his meanest and surliest, as Walker, a gangster who is betrayed, shot, and left for dead by his wife (Acker) and her lover (Vernon). Two years later, he returns, hell-bent on revenge and on getting the $93,000 he is owed. His mission takes him deep into the crime organization and involves him with his wife's seductive sister (Dickinson). A top cop (Wynn) waits in the wings to see who will survive the bloodbath. With its relentless pace and spectacular camerawork, *Point Blank* brings a stylized (perhaps overstylized) note to the subgenre. An exciting climax at a deserted Alcatraz is marred only by an oddly indecisive ending. Carroll O'Connor appears in one of his pre–"All in the Family" roles as a kingpin gangster.

Off-Screen: The original screenplay by the Newhouses was refashioned by Alexander Jacobs. Jacobs was not entirely satisfied with the finished movie; he wanted to introduce more variations of tone into the film and to soften Marvin's harsh character. For the film, Alcatraz, which had been closed in 1963, was rented by the producers for $2,000 a day.

Poltergeist

MGM/UA, 1982. (C-114m.) Dir: Tobe Hooper. Sp: Steven Spielberg, Michael Grais, and Mark Victor, b/o story by Steven Spielberg. Cast: Craig T. Nelson, JoBeth Williams, Beatrice Straight, Dominique Dunne, Heather O'Rourke, Zelda Rubinstein, Oliver Robins, James Karen.

On-Screen: *Unfriendly spirits invade a family.* Strange things are happening in the Freeling household. Pieces of furniture are moving of their own free will. Cutlery is suddenly bent out of shape. The house begins to shake as if in an earthquake. And strangest of all, Carol Anne, the youngest Freeling (O'Rourke), stares at the television set and announces, "They're here!" But who are they and what do they want? When Carol Anne mysteriously disappears and seems to have been kidnapped by poltergeists—unfriendly spirits in the house—the true horror begins for the Freelings. Yes, it's all nonsense, but what truly scary nonsense it is—with many artfully handled special effects that should have you cowering with terror. (Watch out for a tree outside a bedroom window and a normal-seeming kitchen sink.) Thankfully, too, the movie has a sense of humor as well as a sense of what frightens viewers. Zelda Rubinstein is amusing as Tangina, a tiny lady with the power to exorcise poltergeists (or so she believes). The climax is horrific, but in the style of films of this sort, a second climax follows soon after the first.

Off-Screen: How much of the movie's direction was actually handled by coproducer Steven Spielberg? During the shooting, rumors were rife that he had played a large role, to the extent that Spielberg felt it necessary to send an open letter to Tobe Hooper, which was printed in *Variety* in June 1982. Spielberg said, in part, "I enjoyed your openness in allowing me, as a producer and writer, a wide berth for creative involvement, just as I know you were happy with the freedom you had to direct *Poltergeist* so wonderfully." According to on-the-set visitors, Hooper let Spielberg do most of the preparatory work for each shot, stepping forward only at the last minute to assume control. Spielberg's on-the-set presence ended before the shooting was completed, and Hooper received sole directorial credit. Two mediocre sequels followed in 1986 and 1988, neither directed by Hooper.

Porgy and Bess

Goldwyn-Columbia, 1959. (C-138m.) Dir: Otto Preminger. Sp: N. Richard Nash, b/o folk opera by DuBose Heyward and play by DuBose and Dorothy Heyward. MS: George and Ira Gershwin and Du Bose Heyward. Cast: Sidney Poitier, Dorothy Dandridge, Sammy Davis, Jr., Brock Peters, Pearl Bailey, Diahann Carroll.

On-Screen: *Expansive film version of the Gershwin folk opera.* A sensational, but also controversial, stage success in 1935, the Gershwin-Heyward folk opera finally reached the screen in 1959, as Samuel Goldwyn's last production. The result was only fitfully successful. Filmed in the wide-screen Todd-AO process, the movie caught the teeming intensity of life in the black Charleston slum called Catfish Row and extracted every ounce of melodrama from the story of the crippled Porgy (Poitier) and his doomed love for Bess (Dandridge). Although most of the beautiful Gershwin music ("Summertime," "Bess, You Is My Woman," "It Ain't Necessarily So," etc.) soars on the sound track, there is too much evidence of director Preminger's heavy hand—opera is always difficult to transpose to the screen. Poitier and Dandridge are attractive but somewhat too sophisticated for their roles. Brock Peters, Diahann Carroll, and Pearl Bailey are helpful, but Sammy Davis, Jr. stands out as that insinuating snake in the grass called Sportin' Life.

Off-Screen: At first Sidney Poitier was extremely reluctant to appear in *Porgy and Bess* because of its "inherent racial attitudes," but he finally agreed, asserting that his "reservations" had been "washed away" by Goldwyn and original director Rouben Mamoulian, who first staged the opera. (Mamoulian was later replaced by Otto Preminger.) Controversy over the production continued to rage, however, and then disaster struck when the set and costumes were destroyed in a fire in July 1958. Dorothy Dandridge's singing was dubbed by Adele Addison, Poitier's by Robert McFerrin. Diahann Carroll's singing voice belonged to Loulie Jean Norman. Andre Previn and Ken Darby won an Oscar for their music scoring.

Portrait of Jennie

Selznick, 1948. (86m.) Dir: William Dieterle. Sp: Paul Osborn and Peter Berneis; adaptation: Leonardo Bercovici, b/o novel by Robert Nathan. Cast: Jennifer Jones, Joseph Cotten, Ethel Barrymore, David Wayne, Lillian Gish, Cecil Kellaway, Felix Bressart, Henry Hull.

On-Screen: *An artist is haunted and inspired by a ghostly vision.* Many people regard *Portrait of Jennie* as one of their favorite films, and it's difficult to understand why. A fine cast tries earnestly to bring conviction to Robert Nathan's romantic fantasy about Eben Adams (Cotten), a penniless artist who continues to meet Jennie (Jones), a mysterious, elfin young girl who appears to live in the past. Despite all evidence that Jennie is the ghost of a long-dead girl, he falls in love with her, and she inspires his painting. Their otherworldly romance ends in a furious hurricane off the New England coast. Some excellent actors (Barrymore as an art dealer; Wayne as a philosophical cabbie; Gish as a nun) are obliged to smile beatifically while mouthing fatuous platitudes, and it's all rather foolish. Producer David Selznick gives the film high-toned production values, including a Dimitri Tiomkin score based on themes by Debussy, and he stages a convincing hurricane for the climax, but *Portrait of Jennie* is little more than romantic pap.

Off-Screen: Selznick went all out for his climactic hurricane, striving for "a real D. W. Griffith effect." (For the movie's original release, the sequence was tinted green.) His reward was an Oscar for Special Effects. Striving to make Jennie ethereal, famed cinematographer Joseph August obtained some of the primitive equipment he had developed for the movies of William S. Hart and used it in place of sophisticated modern lenses. Author Ben Hecht wrote the foreword that was added to the film at the last minute.

The Poseidon Adventure

Fox, 1972. (C-117m.) Dir: Ronald Neame. Sp: Stirling Silliphant and Wendell Mayes, b/o novel by Paul Gallico. Cast: Gene Hackman, Ernest Borgnine, Red Buttons, Carol Lynley, Roddy McDowall, Stella Stevens, Shelley Winters, Jack Albertson, Leslie Nielsen, Arthur O'Connell.

On-Screen: *Spectacular disaster at sea.* After a slow start in which you're introduced to passengers and crew members of the SS *Poseidon,* it's anything but smooth sailing for the luxury liner as a humongous tidal wave flips it over, literally turning upside down the lives of those aboard. The fun in watching disaster films—aside from gasping at the special effects—is seeing how the doomed perish and how the survivors get to survive. Hackman is a take-command minister who rallies the panicky victims when it's found that escape from the inverted ship is possible through a certain area in the hull. Explosions, fire, sealed iron doors, flooded compartments—all contribute to the mounting suspense. The cast, representing various walks of life and personality traits, does its job convincingly. You'll remember longest Winters's Oscar-nominated performance as the courageous, unstylishly stout Belle Rosen ("In the water, I'm a very skinny lady").

Off-Screen: If the ship at times looks familiar, it's the *Queen Mary,* berthed in Long Beach, California. For some storm scenes, hoses and a swaying camera give the illusion that the famous liner is actually in peril; for others, miniatures were used in a studio tank. Interiors, many constructed upside down, were modeled on those of the *Queen Mary.* The movie, which inspired a series of big-budget disaster epics in the seventies, won an Oscar for Al Kasha and Joel Hirschhorn's theme song, "The Morning After," as well as a "Special Achievement Award" for visual effects. In 1979, a dismal sequel, *Beyond the Poseidon Adventure,* sank. (CFB)

Postcards from the Edge

Columbia, 1990. (C-101m.) Dir: Mike Nichols. Sp: Carrie Fisher, b/o her novel.

Cast: Meryl Streep, Shirley MacLaine, Dennis Quaid, Gene Hackman, Richard Dreyfuss, Rob Reiner, Mary Wickes, Annette Bening, Conrad Bain, Simon Callow, Gary Morton.

On-Screen: *Mother and daughter at odds in Tinseltown.* Poor Suzanne Vale (Streep) is having a terrible time. A minor movie actress with a bad reputation as a cocaine addict, she is finding it difficult to function on her new film. She is also having an affair with Jack Falkner (Quaid), a producer who cheats on her with impunity. Most of all, she must contend with her pushy, alcoholic mother, Doris (MacLaine), a fading but still famous movie star. As she moves back into sobriety, Suzanne becomes acutely aware of the treachery and opportunism of everyone around her. Her battles with her mother are especially lacerating, and they constitute the heart of this enjoyable, witty black comedy. Streep gives a persuasive performance, even getting to sing creditably, and MacLaine pulls out all stops as Momma, allowing herself to appear without wig or makeup in one scene. ("I don't mind *getting* old. What I mind is *looking* old.") If the actresses seem to be an unlikely mother and daughter, their professionalism carries them through. An expert supporting cast does well by Carrie Fisher's screenplay, based on her novel. Favorite performance: veteran actress Mary Wickes as Doris's salty, no-nonsense mother.

Off-Screen: Readers and viewers of Carrie Fisher's novel and screenplay might be forgiven for believing that the story resembled Fisher's life with her mother, Debbie Reynolds. Streep won a Best Actress Oscar nomination, and her song, "I'm Checking Out," was also nominated. Conrad Bain, who plays Streep's senile father, is best known for his television work in "Maude" and "Diff'rent Strokes."

The Postman Always Rings Twice

MGM, 1946. (112m.) Dir: Tay Garnett. Sp: Harry Ruskin and Niven Busch, b/o novel by James M. Cain. Cast: Lana Turner, John Garfield, Cecil Kellaway, Hume Cronyn, Leon Ames, Audrey Totter.

On-Screen: *Passion and murder, fired by Turner-Garfield chemistry.* Despite some sanitizing, this earlier Hollywood adaptation of Cain's steamy melodrama remains gripping entertainment, owing in large measure to the casting of its costars. In what is probably her best role, Turner is sultry and seductive as Cora, the restless wife of Nick (Kellaway), amiable, elderly owner of a California roadside diner. Garfield makes Frank, the tough but pliable drifter whom Cora lures into helping her kill Nick, surprisingly sympathetic. From the start, you know big trouble lies ahead the moment Garfield spots the fateful MAN WANTED sign. After he meets Turner, sexily clad in white shorts, halter, and turban (the camera travels up her body, following Garfield's appreciative gaze), there's no turning back for either of them. A final, ironic twist explains the title. Kellaway and Cronyn, as a manipulative lawyer, stand out among the supporting cast.

Off-Screen: The novel was filmed twice before, as *Le Dernier Tournant* (France, 1939) and *Ossessione* (Italy, 1942). The latter version, directed by neorealist Luchino Visconti and relocated to Fascist Italy (where it ran into trouble with the authorities), is generally regarded as being the most faithful to Cain's tale. To make their 1946 version more contemporary in its appeal, the writers updated the novel, moving it ahead from the Depression era to just after World War II. Curiously, the second Hollywood version (1981), costarring Jack Nicholson and Jessica Lange, was more sexually explicit, yet generated less heat. (CFB)

Presumed Innocent

Warners, 1990. (C-127m.) Dir: Alan J. Pakula. Sp: Frank J. Pierson and Alan J. Pakula, b/o novel by Scott Turow. Cast: Harrison Ford, Brian Dennehy, Raul Julia, Bonnie Bedelia, Greta Scacchi, John Spencer, Joe Grifasi, Tom Mardirosian, Anna Maria Horsford.

On-Screen: *A prosecuting attorney is accused of murder.* Fans of Scott Turow's best-selling novel should probably be pleased with this gripping adaptation. A very dour and intense Harrison Ford stars as Rusty Sabich, a rising prosecuting attorney who becomes the prime suspect in a murder case. The victim (Scacchi) was a ravishing, ambitious attorney with whom Rusty was having a clandestine affair, and eventually all clues point to him as the killer. His worried wife (Bedelia) stands by his side, but colleagues and others desert him out of political expediency or sheer dislike, or the conviction that he is guilty. The incriminating evidence mounts, even as it becomes clear that Rusty is being framed for the crime. The denouement will startle you if you haven't read the book, but it's hardly believable. *Presumed Innocent* is a workmanlike if unexceptional thriller, ably directed by Alan J. Pakula.

Off-Screen: Although the director considered other well-known actors for the leading role, he offered it first to Harrison Ford: "Indiana Jones may be his primary image, but Harrison comes across as an Everyman. To play Rusty convincingly, you can't be exotic, and you have to be bright as well." The all-important courtroom in the film was modeled after an actual courtroom in Cleveland that was spotted by the director and his production designer during location scouting.

Pretty Woman

Touchstone, 1990. (C-117m.) Dir: Garry Marshall. Sp: J. F. Lawton. Cast: Richard Gere, Julia Roberts, Ralph Bellamy, Jason Alexander, Laura San Giacomo, Hector Elizondo, Alex Hyde-White, Elinor Donahue.

On-Screen: *A hooker is transformed by a business tycoon.* Julia Roberts may not yet be a seasoned actress, but her infectious grin and unforced charm light up the screen in this predictable but entertaining comedy. In a variation of the Pygmalion story, she plays Vivian, a Hollywood hooker with a sad past and a romantic streak who entrances a wealthy young businessman (Gere). During the course of the movie, he transforms her, Galatea-style, into a stylish, ravishing young woman, while she teaches him humanity and generosity. The premise is improbable, and the choice of a heroine is curious, to say the least, but *Pretty Woman* manages some amusing moments, particularly when Vivian moves into the posh, snobbish world of Beverly Hills. The movie is essentially another version of the Cinderella tale, but with Julia Roberts as the prostitute-turned-princess, it's diverting entertainment.

Off-Screen: The movie's original screenplay was much darker. It made Roberts a drug user and even had a downbeat ending in which Prince Charming dumps his Cinderella back on the street. Roberts was nominated for an Academy Award but lost to Kathy Bates's performance in *Misery*.

Pride and Prejudice

MGM, 1940. (118m.) Dir: Robert Z. Leonard. Sp: Aldous Huxley and Jane Murfin, b/o novel by Jane Austen and play by Helen Jerome. Cast: Greer Garson, Laurence Olivier, Mary Boland, Edmund Gwenn, Edna May Oliver, Maureen O'Sullivan, Ann Rutherford, Melville Cooper, Frieda Inescort, Heather Angel, Karen Morley, Marsha Hunt.

On-Screen: *Jane Austen's comedy of manners, well served by MGM.* The studio's versions of great novels could sometimes be heavy-handed, but this adaptation of Jane Austen's novel is pure delight: a witty, elegant comedy revolving about the Bennets and their five marriageable daughters. As in the novel, the focus is on the verbal sparring and eventual romance of the eldest Bennet girl, Elizabeth (Garson), and the insufferably snobbish Mr. Darcy (Olivier). Capturing the spirit if not the letter of Jane Austen, the movie offers many moments of delicious absurdity as well as some glancing comments on manners and morals. Mary Boland and Edmund Gwenn are wonderful as the Bennet parents, and the other players are aptly cast as well. Garson's haughty and refined manner finally finds the right role, and Olivier's Darcy could not be bettered. (Darcy: "I'm in no humor tonight to give consequence to the middle classes at play.")

Off-Screen: Norma Shearer and Clark Gable were first thought of as possibilities to play Elizabeth and Darcy; thankfully, the thought passed. Robert Donat was also briefly considered, but he returned to stage acting in England. When Laurence Olivier was signed, he wanted Vivien Leigh to play Elizabeth, but Louis B. Mayer preferred Garson. Cedric Gibbons and Paul Groesse won an Oscar for their splendid art direction. Some years later, MGM considered doing a musical version, but it never materialized. An unsuccessful stage musical adaptation was produced as *First Impressions* in 1959.

Pride of the Marines

Warners, 1945. (119m.) Dir: Delmer Daves. Sp: Albert Maltz, b/o story by Roger Butterfield. Cast: John Garfield, Eleanor Parker, Dane Clark, John Ridgely, Rosemary DeCamp, Ann Doran, Tom D'Andrea, Anthony Caruso.

On-Screen: *True story of a blinded soldier's ordeal.* In the years directly after World War II, films began addressing the problems—physical and psychological—of returning war veterans. *Pride of the Marines* is one of the strongest: a true account of how blinded marine Al Schmid (Garfield), a hero of Guadalcanal, learned to live with his affliction after months of bitterness and self-pity. The movie is, in essence, a two-hour pep talk aimed at the country's returning veterans—in scene after scene, Schmid is exhorted to go on, to cope with his blindness. Garfield is fine in one of his best tough-sensitive roles ("Why don't God strike me dead?"), and Eleanor Parker is touching as his girl, Ruth, who pleads desperately for his understanding. The movie has too much proselytizing, and too many cheery family scenes, but it worked well in its time and is still reasonably effective today. Best sequence: the hellish battle at Guadalcanal early in the film.

Off-Screen: Before filming began, John Garfield lived with the Schmid family for several weeks, closely observing the movements and gestures of a blind man, so that he could bring as much conviction to his performance as possible. Scenarist Albert Maltz was one of the Hollywood Ten, who, in 1947, was convicted on charges of contempt of Congress for refusing to testify about his affiliation with the Communist Party.

Pride of the Yankees

Goldwyn-RKO, 1942. (127m.) Dir: Sam Wood. Sp: Jo Swerling and Herman J. Mankiewicz, b/o story by Paul Gallico. Cast: Gary Cooper, Teresa Wright, Walter Brennan, Dan Duryea, Elsa Janssen, Ludwig Stossel, Babe Ruth, Addison Richards.

On-Screen: *Triumph and tragedy in the life of baseball star Lou Gehrig.* Films about baseball seldom fare well at the box office, but this movie, with its built-in drama surrounding Gehrig, was a notable exception. Although undoubtedly well-intentioned, the film is plodding and cliché-ridden. It traces Gehrig's story from his early years as apparently the world's oldest college student, saddled with a benignly tyrannical mother (Janssen), through his courtship of and marriage to Eleanor (Wright) and his years as a top-flight baseball star, to his tragic early death. Until the last poignant scenes, very little occurs, and the screenplay tries in vain to in-

ject some drama by playing up Mama Gehrig's interference in the lives of Lou and Eleanor. Inevitably, the re-creation of Gehrig's famous farewell to his fans and teammates is the film's highlight, and a genuinely touching sequence. Teresa Wright gives the best performance, creating a supportive and ultimately anguished woman in Eleanor Gehrig.

Off-Screen: There was justified concern that Cooper was too old (forty-one) to play Gehrig in the early scenes. Cameraman Rudolph Maté decided to light Cooper from below during the early part of the film to remove the wrinkles in the actor's face. As time passed in the film, Maté reduced and finally removed the special lighting. Cooper threw right-handed, and Gehrig was a southpaw, so a photographic trick was devised to make it seem as if the actor were throwing the ball with his left hand. The movie received ten Oscar nominations but won only for Daniel Mandell's editing.

Prince of the City

Warners, 1981. (C-167m.) Dir: Sidney Lumet. Sp: Jay Presson Allen and Sidney Lumet. Cast: Treat Williams, Jerry Orbach, Richard Foronjy, Don Billett, Kenny Marino, Carmine Caridi, Bob Balaban, James Tolkan, Lindsay Crouse.

On-Screen: *The life of a whistle-blowing cop becomes a nightmare.* Based on a true story, this long (actually too long), emotionally charged drama concerns the harrowing ordeal of a cop named Danny Ciello (Williams). Asked to cooperate with a committee investigating corruption in the police force, Ciello agrees, but only if he doesn't involve his fellow policemen. His anguish increases, however, as his testimony tightens the net around his friends and colleagues, resulting in suicide and disgrace. Inevitably, he comes under fire himself, and though he is ultimately exonerated, his reputation is soiled forever. Without ever condoning cops on the take, *Prince of the City* takes a fascinating look at their motives and their lives in constant jeopardy. It also points up the moral ambiguity in which the investigating government officials are largely seen as cold, harsh, and manipulative, while the cops on the beat, while corruptible, are caring men, sensitive to each other's needs. Treat Williams gives a forceful performance as Ciello, and Bob Balaban is particularly repellent as one of the investigators.

Off-Screen: The film is based on the true experiences of a New York detective named Bob Leuci, who, in 1971, volunteered his services to lawyers working for the Knapp Commission on Police Corruption. Originally, it was to have been a Brian DePalma film with a screenplay by David Rabe (based on Robert Daley's book of the same name). John Travolta and Robert De Niro were considered for the lead. Eventually, Lumet and Jay Presson Allen created a new script with Treat Williams as the star. The production used over 130 different sites in New York and on Long Island.

The Prince of Tides

Columbia, 1991. (C-132m.) Dir: Barbra Streisand. Sp: Pat Conroy and Becky Johnston, b/o novel by Pat Conroy. Cast: Nick Nolte, Barbra Streisand, Blythe Danner, Kate Nelligan, Jeroen Krabbe, Melinda Dillon, George Carlin, Jason Gould, Brad Sullivan.

On-Screen: *A troubled man comes to terms with his life and his past.* His marriage shaky, football coach Tom Wingo (Nolte) is called suddenly from his home in South Carolina to New York City because his sister (Dillon) has attempted suicide, and her analyst, Susan Lowenstein (Streisand), needs help in understanding her. With Susan, Tom relives the trauma of his childhood and simultaneously becomes emotionally involved with her and her teenaged son (Gould). Ably directed by Streisand, *The Prince of Tides* makes generous room for some memorable moments: Tom and his brother and sister, underwater, holding hands in a magic circle; a farfetched but marvelously bitchy party to which Tom is invited by Susan; and many others. Holding the film together is Nolte's strong, sensitive performance, his finest to date. Kate Nelligan is perfect as his steel-willed mother, and the rest of the cast is not far behind. The only exception is Streisand herself, whose performance seems more assembled than organic. As a director, however, she gives us a film of visual beauty and honest emotions.

Off-Screen: *The Prince of Tides* won seven Oscar nominations, including Best Picture, Best Actor (Nolte), and Best Supporting Actress (Nelligan). No awards were forthcoming, however. Inexplicably, Barbra Streisand's direction was not cited. Jason Gould, playing Streisand's son, is her real-life son; his father is actor Elliott Gould. (BL)

The Princess Bride

Fox, 1987. (C-98m.) Dir: Rob Reiner. Sp: William Goldman, b/o his novel. Cast: Cary Elwes, Mandy Patinkin, Chris Sarandon, Christopher Guest, Robin Wright, Wallace Shawn, Andre the Giant, Fred Savage, Peter Falk, Peter Cook, Billy Crystal, Carol Kane.

On-Screen: *An off-center fairy tale and adventure.* It's difficult to determine the audience for which this odd film was intended. Part fable, part swashbuckling adventure, and part spoof, it leaps from one to the other, generating more exasperation than pleasure. As related by a grandfather (Falk) to his ailing grandson (Savage), the movie basically concerns a farm boy turned pirate (Elwes) and his true love, the reluctant Princess Bride (Wright). Their adventures also involve, among many others, a nasty prince (Sarandon), his insidious aide (Guest), a master criminal (Shawn), and a revenge-minded Spaniard (Patinkin). There are a few moments of magic and fantasy that should please young viewers, but then perversely, the screenplay folds in a few dollops of horror (monstrous swamp reptiles), sadism (the prince's torture machine), and Borscht Belt humor (Billy Crystal's turn as old Miracle Max). At least most of the film avoids the coarse shtick that Mel Brooks would have brought to the proceedings. But it doesn't work.

Off-Screen: The screenplay for *The Princess Bride* had made the Hollywood rounds for years, and several times it almost found its way to the screen. Much of the filming was done at Haddon Hall, an English castle originally built by William the Conqueror, and at other locations in England and Ireland.

The Prisoner of Zenda

Selznick International–United Artists, 1937. (101m.) Dir: John Cromwell. Sp: John L. Balderston, b/o novel by Anthony Hope. Cast: Ronald Colman, Madeleine Carroll, Douglas Fairbanks, Jr., Mary Astor, David Niven, Raymond Massey, C. Aubrey Smith, Montagu Love.

On-Screen: *Ronald Colman in the definitive version of the old swashbuckler.* Films such as this—elaborate costume adventures set in mythical lands—are seldom made anymore, and what a pity when they can be done this well. The third, and best, version of Anthony Hope's novel (filmed again in 1952 and 1979), *The Prisoner of Zenda* relates a stirring tale of treachery, heroism, and romance, all served up in lavish settings. Ronald Colman stars in a dual role as Rudolf Rassendyll and his cousin, King Rudolf V, whom he must impersonate in order to rout the conspirators who plot the king's overthrow. The complications mount, but Rassendyll discovers one definite bonus in his ordeal in the lovely person of Princess Flavia (Carroll). With his celebrated mellifluous voice, Colman makes a most dashing hero, and both Massey and Fairbanks are worthy opponents. (Fairbanks is especially amusing as the swaggering Rupert of Hentzau.) James Wong Howe's photography clearly illustrates the virtues of black and white—the 1952 version added Technicolor and was not nearly as good as this one.

Off-Screen: The excellence of the film belies the fact that the production did not go smoothly. Donald Ogden Stewart's screenplay was so heavily reworked that he lost his screen credit. Director Cromwell complained to producer David Selznick that Fairbanks and Niven appeared on the set "overindulged and lazy," and he also asserted that Colman never knew his lines. And after the production was presumably completed, Selznick insisted on refilming several sequences, bringing in directors

Woodrow (Woody) Van Dyke and George Cukor for retakes. *Zenda,* a 1963 musical version with Alfred Drake, closed during its pre-Broadway tryout.

Prizzi's Honor

Fox, 1985. (C-129m.) Dir: John Huston. Sp: Richard Condon and Janet Roach, b/o novel by Richard Condon. Cast: Jack Nicholson, Kathleen Turner, Anjelica Huston, Robert Loggia, William Hickey, John Randolph, Lee Richardson.

On-Screen: *Comedy-melodrama about Mafia "family" matters.* "Do I ice her? Do I marry her?" Charley Partanna (Nicholson) decides to ignore his suspicions about Irene Walker (Turner) and opts for wedding bells. Charley's a likable, if somewhat dim, Brooklyn-based hitman, and silky Irene's a bright woman in the same line of work. The trouble is, they're competitors. This is a tremendously black—and funny—movie that works on several levels: as a sly satire on the traditional mobster film, as an offbeat romance with several nasty shocks along the way, and as a demonstration of director Huston's astonishing skill with actors. Nicholson and Turner are in prime form as the ill-matched professional pair. Supporting-cast top honors go to Hickey, as the wizened, wily old don of the Prizzi family, and—most of all—to Anjelica Huston's Maerose, his equally crafty granddaughter who decides, after once jilting Charley, to reclaim him for herself.

Off-Screen: In pursuit of authenticity, Huston filmed much of the movie on the home ground of the Prizzi family. The opening wedding sequence was shot in Brooklyn Heights, at the Episcopal Church of Saint Ann and the Holy Trinity; a nearby mansion, overlooking New York Harbor, served as the don's oppressively ornate home. The wedding reception was filmed at the YWCA in the Boerum Hill section of the borough. Nicholson and Hickey, the movie, and its director and screenplay were among the Oscar nominees. Huston, making the third of four appearances in her father's films, was named Best Supporting Actress. Alex North's music score makes wry use of the overture to Rossini's opera *The Thieving Magpie.* (CFB)

The Producers

Embassy, 1968. (C-88m.) Dir: Mel Brooks. Sp: Mel Brooks. Cast: Zero Mostel, Gene Wilder, Dick Shawn, Kenneth Mars, Lee Meredith, Estelle Winwood, Renee Taylor, Christopher Hewett, Andreas Voustinas.

On-Screen: *Mel Brooks's first feature film.* Blimpish Broadway producer Max Bialystock (Mostel) finances his shows by romancing rich elderly women. He and his overwrought accountant, Leo Bloom (Wilder), conspire to make a fortune by getting Max's doting backers to oversubscribe a sure flop, then skimming off the surplus money after production costs. Murphy's Law takes over when *Springtime for Hitler,* the most abysmally tasteless musical in showbiz history, is a smash hit. Love the movie for its brash, over-the-top antics or hate it for the same reason (movie fans are about equally divided), you'll probably find Mostel's roaring, outsize screen presence off-putting, Wilder's frantic schemer endearing, and *Springtime for Hitler,* the brainchild of Mars's die-hard Nazi, a truly awesome example of superkitsch. Even funnier (or, depending on your point of view, inevitably better) films lay ahead for Brooks.

Off-Screen: Brooks had proved himself an ace comedy writer for Sid Caesar's "Your Show of Shows," a memorable variety program of the fifties, when *The Critic,* an animated short that he scripted, won an Academy Award in 1963. The screenplay for *The Producers,* his first full-length movie, brought him his own Oscar, as well as a nomination for supporting player Wilder. Dustin Hoffman had expressed interest in playing the die-hard Nazi, but opted to appear in *The Graduate.* You can spot Brooks among the chorus members of the musical, which was filmed in New York's Playhouse Theatre. (CFB)

Psycho

Paramount, 1960. (109m.) Dir: Alfred Hitchcock. Sp: Joseph Stefano, b/o novel by Robert Bloch. Cast: Anthony Perkins, Janet Leigh, Vera Miles, John Gavin, Martin Balsam, John McIntire, Frank Albertson.

On-Screen: *Prime Hitchcock.* Expect to be frightened—even deeply disturbed—by this classic suspense thriller. It takes place somewhere west of Phoenix, where lanky, likable Norman Bates (Perkins) runs a motel adjoining his musty Victorian house. His attractive, and only, guest is Marion Crane (Leigh). She's having an affair with a married man (Gavin), and she's stolen a payroll to finance his divorce and their marriage. Norman exudes patience and simple goodness whether putting up with his cranky mother or talking Marion into returning the

money. But wait—there's horror ahead, and one jolt after another. The movie, brilliantly shot and edited (the motel shower scene and the episode on the staircase of the grim house are waking nightmares), calls your bluff at every turn.

Off-Screen: Hitchcock regarded the movie as "a serious story told with tongue in cheek," referring, perhaps, to his outrageous way of playing with viewers' expectations. Filmed by a television crew on a modest budget, the movie nevertheless earned four Oscar nominations—including ones for Hitchcock, Leigh, and the photography—but oddly, none for Bernard Herrmann's eerie and often imitated score. The notorious forty-five-second shower sequence, which took a week to film, is composed of seventy camera setups. The equally breathtaking staircase scene was, surprisingly, shot before a process screen. Unsurprisingly, none of the movie's sequels have had the impact of the original. Yes, that's Hitchcock himself early on, wearing a cowboy hat. (CFB)

The Public Enemy

Warners, 1931. (84m., originally 96m.) Dir: William Wellman. Sp: Kubec Glasmon and John Bright, b/o story by John Bright. Cast: James Cagney, Jean Harlow, Edward Woods, Joan Blondell, Mae Clarke, Donald Cook, Beryl Mercer.

On-Screen: *The meteoric rise and grisly demise of a gangster.* Yes, this is the movie in which tough-as-nails Jimmy Cagney, annoyed at breakfast, pushes a grapefruit into the face of girlfriend Mae Clarke. It's a raw, startling moment in a primitive but seminal gangster film. In his fifth movie for

Warners, Cagney rose to major stardom as Tom Powers, a slum kid who goes from petty thief to public enemy, then meets an ignominious end. Cagney's performance is so powerful and riveting that his vicious character towers above everyone else in the cast, including his brooding brother (Cook) and his simpleminded mother (Mercer). The women in his life haven't a chance, although Jean Harlow, in an amateurish performance as a brassy upper-class blonde, gets to tell him a thing or two. Apart from that celebrated grapefruit, *The Public Enemy* has some powerful moments, not the least being the final one, in which Cagney's mummified corpse, bound in rope, falls through the door before the eyes of his horrified brother.

Off-Screen: The screenplay was based on a story called "Beer and Blood," and there was plenty of both in the movie. Cagney was originally scheduled to play Tom Powers's best friend, now played by Edward Woods, but after the first day's rushes, writers Glasmon and Bright suggested that he switch roles with Woods, and director Wellman and reluctant production head Darryl Zanuck finally agreed. Wellman and Zanuck both claimed credit for thinking of the grapefruit scene, but Cagney insisted that it originated with a real Chicago hood who plastered his moll with an omelet.

The Purple Rose of Cairo

Orion, 1985. (C-82m.) Dir: Woody Allen. Sp: Woody Allen. Cast: Mia Farrow, Jeff Daniels, Danny Aiello, Dianne Wiest, Van Johnson, Zoe Caldwell, John Wood, Milo O'Shea, Edward Herrmann, Karen Akers.

On-Screen: *A movie-mad Depression wife has an odd experience*. In the eighties, Woody Allen occasionally softened his usually astringent tone to offer a gentler view of man's foolish ways. *The Purple Rose of Cairo* is a slender but sometimes affecting fable that pays tribute to moviegoers whose longing for dreams, romance, and laughter finds fulfillment at the movies. Cecilia (Farrow) is an unhappy Depression housewife whose only refuge from her boorish husband (Aiello) is the local bijou. One night, while she is watching *The Purple Rose of Cairo,* the character played by movie idol Gil Shepard (Daniels) descends from the screen to proclaim his love for Cecilia. The resulting brouhaha brings the real and very vain Gil Shepard from Hollywood, and soon a bewildered Cecilia must cope with two identical suitors, one fictional. The movie's tone is bittersweet, never more so than in the final shot that finds Cecilia gazing raptly at the screen while Astaire and Rogers dance. Lost in her dream, she has discovered solace and a measure of joy in those flickering images.

Off-Screen: In the film-within-a-film that Cecilia watches, the characters who address her from the screen are played by a group of notable actors, including Zoe Caldwell, Milo O'Shea, and onetime movie idol Van Johnson. Woody Allen's screenplay received an Oscar nomination.

Queen Christina

MGM, 1933. (97m.) Dir: Rouben Mamoulian. Sp: Salka Viertel, H. M. Harwood, and S. N. Behrman, b/o story by Salka Viertel and Margaret P. Levino. Cast: Greta Garbo, John Gilbert, Ian Keith, Lewis Stone, Elizabeth Young, C. Aubrey Smith.

On-Screen: *Garbo as the seventeenth-century Swedish queen.* One of Greta Garbo's best-remembered movies, *Queen Christina* is less notable for its excellence as a film than for its scenes that define the Garbo mystique. Lavish, or more accurately, over-stuffed in the MGM style, it purports to deal with the imperious seventeenth-century Swedish monarch Christina (Garbo), and her ill-fated romance with Don Antonio (Gilbert), a Spanish envoy. Renouncing her throne for a love that ends in tragedy, Christina ends up a lonely exile. *Queen Christina* is famous for two moments: one in which the queen, besotted with love for Antonio, "memorizes" all the artifacts in the bedroom in which she has experienced the only passion of her life, the other the movie's final shot, in which the camera lingers on Christina's face as a ship carries her away from Sweden forever. The rest of the movie is rather starchy and leaden, but the legion of Garbo admirers will not object.

Off-Screen: Garbo insisted on John Gilbert as her leading man, when the studio actually favored Laurence Olivier. For that final shot of Garbo, director Mamoulian has said that he asked the actress to make her face "a blank sheet of paper," adding, "I want the writing to be done by every member of the audience." Viewers have been "writing" ever since. Ben Hecht and Gene Fowler contributed to the screenplay without credit. The Swedish historical adviser complained bitterly about the inaccuracies in every sequence, to no avail.

The Quiet Man

Republic, 1952. (C-129m.) Dir: John Ford. Sp: Frank S. Nugent, b/o story by Maurice Walsh. Cast: John Wayne, Maureen O'Hara, Barry Fitzgerald, Ward Bond, Victor McLaglen, Mildred Natwick, Francis Ford, Eileen Crowe, Arthur Shields.

On-Screen: *John Ford's rowdy and gorgeous Irish comedy.* Sean Thornton (Wayne) is an American boxer who, having accidentally killed an opponent, has hung up his gloves and returned to his native Ireland for a quiet life. He woos and wins fiery Mary Kate Danaher (O'Hara), but in a quarrel over land ownership, he incurs the wrath of her brother Will (McLaglen), who refuses to part with his sister's dowry. "Until y'have my dowry," she tells her "quiet" groom, "y'haven't got any bit of me." To prove he's no coward, Sean takes on Will in a hilarous marathon donnybrook that involves practically the whole village. The story is all blather and blarney—Fitzgerald, as always, takes top honors in that regard—but Wayne, O'Hara, and company, and the breathtaking photography, make this fairy tale believable and endearing. Sure, and it's grand entertainment for all.

Off-Screen: Director Ford made the movie something of an interfamily affair; cast members include his brother, long-time actor Francis; son-in-law Ken Curtis; four of Wayne's seven children, including son Patrick; O'Hara's brother Charles FitzSimons; and brothers Fitzgerald and Shields. The film was shot principally in County Mayo, Ireland, as well as in Hollywood. Oscars went to Ford, and for their color cinematography, to Winton C. Hoch and Archie Stout. *Donnybrook!*—a musical version of the film—failed on Broadway in 1961. (CFB)

Quo Vadis

MGM, 1951. (C-171m.) Dir: Mervyn LeRoy. Sp: John Lee Mahin, S. N. Behrman, and Sonya Levien, b/o novel by Henryk Sienkiewicz. Cast: Robert Taylor, Deborah Kerr, Leo Genn, Peter Ustinov, Finlay Currie, Patricia Laffan, Abraham Sofaer, Buddy Baer.

On-Screen: *Be it ever so colossal, there's no place like first-century-A.D. Rome.* The real stars of this extravagant epic are the sprawling sets swarming with extras, the spectacular fire, and the climactic sequence in which Christians are served up to hungry lions. Close second to the scenery and special effects is Ustinov, whose blubbery, blubbering Emperor Nero, childlike and cruel, is outrageously off-the-wall. The story is comic-book simple: Gruff Roman officer Marcus Vinicius (Taylor) falls for prim and pretty Lygia (Kerr), but his acceptance of her Christian faith jeopardizes both their lives. Among the waxworks, martyrs, and meanies, Genn, as Petronius, Nero's cynical sycophant, and Currie, as Apostle Peter, are gratifyingly human. Miklos Rozsa's martial music is heart-racing.

Off-Screen: The expensive movie received eight Oscar nominations—Best Picture and Supporting Actor (both Genn and Usinov) among them—but failed to win a single award. Although the novel had been filmed abroad in two silent versions (and would be again in 1985), MGM began planning a production in 1939, but postponed it during World War II. Afterward, John Huston was to direct Gregory Peck and Elizabeth Taylor, but studio chief Louis B. Mayer rejected Huston's script. At director LeRoy's invitation, Taylor, honeymooning in Italy with husband Nicky Hilton, appeared as an extra, as did also future star Sophia Loren. Walter Pidgeon narrates off-screen. (CFB)

Rachel, Rachel

Warners, 1968. (C-101m.) Dir: Paul Newman. Sp: Stewart Stern, b/o novel by Margaret Laurence. Cast: Joanne Woodward, Estelle Parsons, James Olson, Kate Harrington, Donald Moffat, Terry Kiser, Geraldine Fitzgerald, Nell Potts.

On-Screen: *One crucial summer in a woman's life.* Pity Rachel Cameron (Woodward). Lonely, repressed, and burdened by the unchanging rituals of her small-town life, this thirty-five-year-old spinster schoolteacher faces what she calls her "last ascending summer." ("I'm exactly in the middle of my life.") But during that summer, things change; mostly she finds sexual fulfillment at last with an old high-school friend (Olson) who has returned to town. The consequences change her life forever and give her the strength to face an uncertain future. ("I may be afraid always. I may be lonely always. What will happen? What will happen?") Woodward's expressive, beautifully modulated performance is the centerpiece of this film, skillfully directed by her husband, Paul Newman. There are fine performances as well by Estelle Parsons as Rachel's best friend and fellow teacher, and by Kate Harrington as Rachel's foolish, frightened, and demanding mother. Stewart Stern's screenplay has a sharp ear for the daily conversational exchanges of small-town life.

Off-Screen: The making of the film in a studio built inside a gymnasium in Danbury, Connecticut, was virtually a family affair. The eldest Newman daughter, Elinor, using the name Nell Potts, played Rachel as a child. Newman's brother Arthur worked as associate producer. Friends of the Newmans filled out the cast and crew. Newman was eager to face the challenge of his first job as director.

Radio Days

Orion, 1987. (C-85m.) Dir: Woody Allen. Sp: Woody Allen. Cast: Mia Farrow, Michael Tucker, Julie Kavner, Dianne Wiest, Seth Green, Josh Mostel, Wallace Shawn, Danny Aiello, Jeff Daniels, Diane Keaton, Tito Puente, Kitty Carlisle Hart, Kenneth Mars.

On-Screen: *Radio's golden age, recalled by Woody Allen*. More of a freewheeling series of anecdotes and sketches than a sustained narrative, *Radio Days* is Woody Allen's fond, funny tribute to radio at its golden peak in the late thirties and early forties. Written and played with on-target accuracy, the movie returns most often to the members of one family, including mother (Kavner), father (Tucker), and their young son (Green), whose life revolves around the radio. Around them swirl the popular radio stars of the day, remembered with affectionate parody, plus a squeaky-voiced hatcheck girl (Farrow) who rises to radio stardom at the beginning of World War II. The many vignettes may be unfocused, but filtered through Allen's wit, they are also never less than amusing and are sometimes hilarious. Favorite sequence: young Green's first awed visit to New York's Radio City Music Hall. The performances are all splendid, but special kudos to Dianne Wiest as Kavner's unmarried sister; she makes something touching out of ever-hopeful spinsterhood. Pleasing period music is a bonus.

Off-Screen: It is clear that Seth Green's character is intended as a surrogate for young Woody Allen. Many of the film's details are autogbiographical. Allen's deft screenplay for *Radio Days* was nominated for an Academy Award. Santo Loquasto was given a British Academy of Film and Television Arts Award for his sets.

Raging Bull

United Artists, 1980. (128m.) Dir: Martin Scorsese. Sp: Paul Schrader and Mardik Martin, b/o book by Jake La Motta with Joseph Carter and Peter Savage. Cast: Robert De Niro, Joe Pesci, Cathy Moriarty, Frank Vincent, Nicholas Colasanto, Theresa Saldana.

On-Screen: *The rise and fall of a true-life boxer*. A dormant volcano forever on the verge of erupting, Jake La Motta fought his way to the middleweight boxing championship. Yet his volatile nature alienated everyone who ever cared for him, and he ended as a grotesque and pitiable clown, performing in sleazy nightclubs. The screenplay strives to find remnants of dignity and even heroism in La Motta, and it succeeds to a surprising degree. (Beaten to a pulp, he cries, "I never went down! You never got me down!") Directing in a near-documentary style that vivifies the grubby settings, Martin Scorsese extracts an electrifying performance from Robert De Niro. Watching his Jake La Motta banging his head against a prison wall in 1957 as he cries, "Why? Why? I'm not an animal!" we can actually feel pity for this repellent man. Joe Pesci is also fine as his loyal brother, Joey, and Cathy Moriarty, with her carefully coiffed blond hair and dark red lips, is emblematic of the film's period as Vickie, La Motta's second wife. Michael Chapman's boxing photography is brilliantly graphic.

Off-Screen: *Raging Bull* won Oscars for Robert De Niro and editor Thelma Schoonmaker. The film, Scorsese, Pesci, and Moriarty were also nominated, as were the cinematography and sound. To box convincingly in the ring, De Niro worked out for a year with La Motta at a gym on East Fourteenth Street in New York City. To play La Motta at the end of his career, De Niro ate heavily, pigging out on ice cream and gorging himself in France's best restaurants until he gained fifty-five pounds.

Ragtime

Paramount, 1981. (C-156m.) Dir: Milos Forman. Sp: Michael Weller, b/o novel by E. L. Doctorow. Cast: Howard E. Rollins, Jr., James Cagney, Brad Dourif, Mary Steenburgen, James Olson, Kenneth Mc-Millan, Elizabeth McGovern, Mandy Patinkin.

On-Screen: *Zesty but overbaked slice of Americana*. Doctorow's best-seller, set just prior to World War I, is a dazzling, crazy-quilt novel in which real and fictional characters, both everyday and famous, cross paths. Despite its length, the movie captures only portions of the book's charm and variety. It focuses primarily on the intensely dramatic story of a black musician, Coalhouse Walker (Rollins), driven to rage and mayhem by a bigot (McMillan). Rollins (Oscar-nominated) is splendid as the wronged man; Cagney's New York City police commissioner, ordered to quell the violence, is riveting. You'll meet fictional characters, such as the immigrant silhouette cutter (Patinkin) who becomes an early movie director, as well as historical figures such as the fatally beautiful show girl Evelyn Nesbit (McGovern), Houdini, and Teddy Roosevelt.

Off-Screen: Robert Altman was originally set to direct, but a falling-out with producer Dino De Laurentiis resulted in Forman's taking over for Altman and Weller's replacing Doctorow as scriptwriter. Eighty-one-year-old Cagney emerged from retirement to play the top cop—his sixty-third role in a movie career that began in 1930. Another revered old-timer, Pat O'Brien, appears as the corrupt lawyer for playboy Harry K. Thaw (Robert Joy), who murdered famed architect Stanford White (novelist Norman Mailer). Other cameo performers include Donald O'Connor and silent-screen star Bessie Love. (CFB)

Raiders of the Lost Ark

Paramount, 1981. (C-115m.) Dir: Steven Spielberg. Sp: Lawrence Kasdan. Cast: Harrison Ford, Karen Allen, John Rhys-Davies, Wolf Kahler, Paul Freeman, Ronald Lacey, Denholm Elliot.

On-Screen: *Introducing Indiana Jones*. Crackerjack entertainment, and the first of Steven Spielberg's popular Indiana Jones series, *Raiders of the Lost Ark* deliberately harked back to the old matinee adventure serials of the thirties and forties. Harrison Ford became a superstar playing Jones, a resourceful (and not a little crabby) professor of archaeology who teams up with the daughter (Allen) of a celebrated archaeologist to locate the lost Ark of the Covenant before Nazi scientists can seize it. Before they win the day, the intrepid adventurers are subjected to numerous attempts on their lives by means of asps and cobras, poisoned darts, violent explosions, and torture with a red-hot poker. One jolting surprise follows another, but they emerge unscathed, of course. There are a few gory moments, but little of the grossness that marred the sequels. The religiously oriented climax is too solemn for the rest of the film, which is designed only to reconstruct the old cliff-hangers on a lavish scale. It succeeds admirably, and audiences everywhere responded to the formula with enthusiasm.

Off-Screen: Steven Spielberg shot the film in Hawaii, France, Tunisia, and at Elstree Studios in England in a mere seventy-three days at a cost of $22.8 million. The movie won Oscars for Editing and Special Effects. Sequels to *Raiders of the Lost Ark* were guaranteed, and *Indiana Jones and the Temple of Doom* (1984) was followed by *Indiana Jones and the Last Crusade* (1989). "The Young Indiana Jones Chronicles," a television series featuring a teenage Indy in wild adventures, began a run in 1991.

Rain Man

MGM/UA, 1988. (C-140m.) Dir: Barry Levinson. Sp: Ronald Bass and Barry Morrow, b/o story by Barry Morrow. Cast: Dustin Hoffman, Tom Cruise, Valeria Golino, Jerry Molden, Jack Murdock, Michael D. Roberts.

On-Screen: *A wheeler-dealer must cope with his autistic brother.* Dustin Hoffman's expert, Oscar-winning performance as an autistic man constitutes the bone and the sinew of this enjoyable if highly predictable movie. He's Raymond Babbitt, an idiot savant who can function at only a minimal level but who has a genius for dealing with numbers. When his selfish wheeler-dealer brother, Charlie (Cruise), learns of his existence and finds that Raymond has inherited their father's fortune, he takes him out of the asylum. Their cross-country adventures, including a sojourn in Las Vegas, lead inevitably to a change of heart for Charlie. There are few surprises along the way, but some of the incidents are funny or touching. (Best is Charlie's effort to teach Raymond how to dance.) Cruise is convincing as the hustling Charlie, baffled and exasperated by his brother, but Hoffman rivets our attention with his shuffling gait, fixed stare, and verbal tics. *Rain Man* is essentially a "road" movie with a twist, but with Hoffman front and center most of the time ("Uh-oh. Five minutes to Wapner"), it's worth your attention.

Off-Screen: *Rain Man* went through many changes and convolutions before finally reaching the screen. One of the first directors to decline was Barry Levinson, who eventually took the assignment and also made significant changes in the screenplay. Other interested directors along the way included Martin Brest, Steven Spielberg, and Sydney Pollack. Although both writers are credited, Ronald Bass came on as a replacement for Barry Morrow and wrote several drafts. The screenplay also earned an Oscar, as did the film and the director. Levinson also appears near the film's end in a climactic scene as an examining psychiatrist. In that scene, Hoffman's referring to Cruise as "main man" was ad-libbed by the actor.

The Rainmaker

Paramount, 1956. (C-121m.) Dir: Joseph Anthony. Sp: N. Richard Nash, b/o his play. Cast: Katharine Hepburn, Burt Lancaster, Wendell Corey, Lloyd Bridges, Earl Holliman, Cameron Prud'homme, Wallace Ford.

On-Screen: *Spinster Hepburn meets con man Lancaster.* If you can accept Katharine Hepburn as a plain old maid and homespun farm girl, you should enjoy N. Richard Nash's adaptation of his stage play. Actually, Hepburn is far from plain as Lizzie Curry, who serves as housekeeper on the Kansas farm she shares with her father (Prud'homme) and two brothers (Bridges, Holliman) in the twenties. Content to have Lizzie make a home for them, they look upon her as an unmarriageable spinster. Along comes Starbuck (Lancaster), a fast-talking con man and rainmaker in a dry land, who in one magical evening transforms her into a woman eager for love. The newly awakened spinster is a rather tired creation, and Hepburn is somewhat too tremulous as Lizzie, but the production is attractive, and the long, crucial barn scene between Lizzie and Starbuck, despite its often high-flown dialogue, is well-handled by the stars. ("There are all kinds of dreams, Mr. Starbuck. Mine are small ones—like my name. Lizzie. But they're *real* like my name—*real!*").

Off-Screen: *The Rainmaker* began life as a television play in 1952. Joseph Anthony also directed the 1954 stage version with Geraldine Page and Darren McGavin. With their different approaches to acting, hers derived from stage experience, his from Hollywood films, Katharine Hepburn and Burt Lancaster did not get along well during the filming. Hepburn received an Oscar nomination, as did Alex North for his music score. A musical adaptation called *110 in the Shade* had a brief run on Broadway in 1963 and was later revived, more successfully, in 1992.

The Rains Came

Fox, 1939. (104m.) Dir: Clarence Brown. Sp: Julien Josephson and Philip Dunne, b/o novel by Louis Bromfield. Cast: Myrna Loy, Tyrone Power, George Brent, Brenda Joyce, Maria Ouspenskaya, Nigel Bruce, Jane Darwell, Henry Travers, Joseph Schildkraut, Marjorie Rambeau, H. B. Warner, Laura Hope Crews.

On-Screen: *Passion and disaster in India.* A spectacularly staged earthquake and flood constitute the only real reasons to see this exotic

romantic drama. A watered-down version of Louis Bromfield's best-selling novel, *The Rains Came* is set in the Indian province of Ranchipur in 1938. Mainly, it concentrates on the "forbidden" but passionate romance between Loy, the bored, restless wife of stuffy Englishman Bruce, and an Indian doctor (Power) who is destined to lead his people. ("Who's the pale copper Apollo?" Loy asks as she spies him for the first time.) The cholera plague that follows the earthquake brings out Loy's nobler instincts, and you can guess the rest. George Brent is the world-weary observer who was once Loy's lover, and Maria Ouspenskaya plays the only Indian maharani with a heavy Russian accent. A viewer must plow through some heavy dialogue to reach the special effects, but they are almost worth the effort.

Off-Screen: The special effects by Fred Sersen and E. H. Hansen were *so* notable, in fact, that they received an Academy Award. According to Myrna Loy, such actresses as Marlene Dietrich, Rosalind Russell, and Tallulah Bankhead campaigned to play Lady Esketh. The movie was remade in 1955 as *The Rains of Ranchipur,* with Lana Turner and Richard Burton as the romantic couple.

A Raisin in the Sun

Columbia, 1961. (128m.) Dir: Daniel Petrie. Sp: Lorraine Hansberry, b/o her play. Cast: Sidney Poitier, Claudia McNeil, Ruby Dee, Diana Sands, Ivan Dixon, John Fiedler, Louis Gossett, Stephen Perry.

On-Screen: *Tribulations of a black family, from the Broadway stage.* A faithful transcription of Lorraine Hansberry's successful play, *A Raisin in the Sun* concerns the Younger family, living in a Chicago slum and longing to improve their lot. Walter Lee (Poitier) is the angry son, crushed by his environment and his thwarted aspirations, and Lena (McNeil) is his patient, pious, and tenacious mother. Walter Lee's desperation leads him to an act that betrays his mother's dream of a respectable home. Although the production is stagebound and uncinematic (Claudia McNeil's performance, in particular, is obviously aimed at the rafters), many of the scenes have a simple eloquence that makes the viewer care about the family's plight. Diana Sands is especially good as the Younger daughter, who is seeking her identity in studying medicine. John Fiedler sounds the film's one false note as a segregation-minded white who nervously tries to encourage the Youngers to stay out of his neighborhood.

Off-Screen: Most of the cast members of *A Raisin in the Sun* were repeating their roles from the 1959 stage version. A musical adaptation of the play, entitled *Raisin,* appeared in 1974. Tragically, both Lorraine Hansberry and Diana Sands died at an early age.

Raising Arizona

Fox, 1987. (C-92m.) Dir: Joel Coen. Sp: Ethan and Joel Coen. Cast: Nicolas Cage, Holly Hunter, John Goodman, Trey Wilson, William Forsythe, Sam McMurray, Frances McDormand, Randall "Tex" Cobb.

On-Screen: *Two born losers kidnap a baby, with comic consequences.* Having made their movie mark with the artful *film noir Blood Simple* (1984), the brothers Coen turned to flat-out farce with *Raising Arizona.* Chronic thief Cage and ex-policewoman Hunter, neither of them overly bright, learn that their marriage is going to be childless. To please his distraught wife, Cage kidnaps one of the brand-new quintuplets of furniture mogul Nathan Arizona. Unforeseen consequences involve Cage's scruffy convict pals (Goodman and Forsythe), just escaped from prison, a weirdly demonic motorcyclist (Cobb) bent on recovering the baby at any cost, and Arizona himself. The comedy is off-the-wall, but it often works, especially in one hilarious slapstick sequence of a foiled robbery in which the police, hapless drivers, and a pack of barking dogs all get into the act. Cage, who can be an irritating actor, is perfectly cast as the dim-witted, chronically criminal Hi, and Hunter makes a delightful Ed, teary-eyed at the prospect of having a baby of her own (or anyone else's).

Off-Screen: Nathan Arizona, Jr., the tot in contention, was played by twenty-month-old T. (Thomas) J. (Joseph) Kuhn, Jr., the son of a Phoenix, Arizona, couple. John Goodman, who plays the burly convict Gale, is, of course, Roseanne Arnold's husband on the television series "Roseanne" and also appeared in the Coen brothers' 1991 film, *Barton Fink.*

Random Harvest

MGM, 1942. (126m.) Dir: Mervyn LeRoy. Sp: Claudine West, George Froeschel, and Arthur Wimperis, b/o novel by James Hilton. Cast: Ronald Colman, Greer Garson, Susan Peters, Philip Dorn, Henry Travers, Reginald Owen, Bramwell Fletcher, Margaret Wycherly.

On-Screen: *An amnesiac recovers his lost life, but loses another.* There's not a genuine or lifelike moment in this extremely popular adaptation of James Hilton's equally popular novel. The film is meticulously produced in the MGM tradition, and the cast is first-rate, but the story remains pulpish nonsense. Colman plays a World War I amnesiac who loves and marries a music hall entertainer (Garson), then recovers his true identity as the scion of an aristocratic British family. Years later, after he has been declared legally dead, the still-devoted Garson becomes his secretary, then his wife (again) as he rises to a seat in Parliament. By film's end, he has remembered their idyllic life in the past. Colman's mellifluous voice gives the dialogue more credibility than it deserves, and Garson is all dignity and forbearance as the woman in his life. But together they generate little emotional heat.

Off-Screen: Director LeRoy had nothing but praise for Ronald Colman: "There was nothing of the ham in him. He'd make a lot of suggestions about script and dialogue, always good ideas. . . . He was very businesslike on the set, a real pro." James Hilton loved the film adaptation of his book and offered to speak the narration that opens the film.

The Razor's Edge

Fox, 1946. (146m.) Dir: Edmund Goulding. Sp: Lamar Trotti, b/o novel by W. Somerset Maugham. Cast: Tyrone Power, Gene Tierney, Anne Baxter, Clifton Webb, John Payne, Herbert Marshall, Lucile Watson, Elsa Lanchester, Frank Latimore.

On-Screen: *The spiritual odyssey of "a very remarkable creature."* "The road to salvation is difficult to pass over . . . as difficult as the sharp edge of a razor." These words are ut-

tered by a saintly Indian guru to Larry Darrell (Power), and indeed they prove to be indisputably true as Larry searches for the meaning of life in the post–World War I years. His journey to spiritual wisdom is the heart of this windy, turgid adaptation of Maugham's popular novel, but there are juicier portions that will no doubt interest you more, notably the personal tragedy of Larry's friend Sophie (Baxter), who sinks to the lower depths after the accidental deaths of her husband and child. Gene Tierney is Larry's upper-class fiancée, whom he leaves to find himself, and whose lifelong unrequited passion for him turns her later into a kind of Dragon Lady. As novelist Maugham, Herbert Marshall narrates and observes the events with an air of weary worldliness. They are certainly competent, but Clifton Webb steals the film as Tierney's snobbish uncle whose death scene turns him finally into a pitiable figure.

Off-Screen: Webb's character of Elliott Templeton was based on Sir Henry "Chips" Cannon, an American who lived most of his life in England and took British citizenship. The film's two main themes—"Isabel's Waltz" and "Sophie's Theme," which became the hit song "Mam'selle"—were composed by director Goulding. One sequence taken from the book, involving Larry and a young farm girl (Colleen Townsend), was cut from the film. Anne Baxter won an Oscar as Best Supporting Actress for her performance as Sophie. The film itself was nominated, as was Clifton Webb. A dreary 1984 remake starred Bill Murray, of all people.

Rear Window

Paramount, 1954. (C-112m.) Dir: Alfred Hitchcock. Sp: John Michael Hayes, b/o story by Cornell Woolrich. Cast: James Stewart, Grace Kelly, Wendell Corey, Thelma Ritter, Raymond Burr, Judith Evelyn.

On-Screen: *A room with a view, Hitchcock style.* To pass the time while a broken leg confines him to a wheelchair, photographer J. B. (Jeff) Jeffries (Stewart) has taken to peering through binoculars into apartments across the courtyard. Soon, his conviction that a neighbor (Burr) has butchered his wife forces him to become personally involved. Hitchcock slyly plays with our loyalties. We root for Jeff—he wants justice, after all; still, we are put off by his morbid preoccupation with complete strangers' lives. The director tricks us again by casting Stewart against type. The actor's usual laid-back persona is replaced by a reckless compulsiveness that overtakes his romantic commitment to his delectable fiancée (Kelly). A crackling suspense thriller, a bold cinematic experiment, and a reflection on the dangers of prying too deeply into the private lives of others, *Rear Window* is one of the director's most intriguing works.

Off-Screen: As he had in *Lifeboat* (1944) and *Rope* (1948), Hitchcock reduces locale to a seeming minimum. The cast inhabits an ingeniously designed set consisting of Stewart's apartment, the building opposite showing windows of the thirty-odd apartments within, and that all-important garden in between. But Hal Pereira's striking art direction was overlooked at Oscar-nomination time. The movie was cited, however, for its direction, screenplay, color cinematography, and sound recording, but won no statuettes. Blooper spotters will notice that Stewart's cast appears briefly on the wrong leg during a tense scene with Kelly. (CFB)

Rebecca

Selznick International, 1940. (130m.) Dir: Alfred Hitchcock. Sp: Robert E. Sherwood, Joan Harrison, b/o novel by Daphne du Maurier. Cast: Joan Fontaine, Laurence Olivier, Judith Anderson, George Sanders, Nigel Bruce, Reginald Denny, Gladys Cooper, Florence Bates.

On-Screen: *A dead woman's memory torments Joan Fontaine and Laurence Olivier in Hitchcock's auspicious American movie debut.* The new mistress of Manderley (Fontaine), married to dashing Max de Winter (Olivier), lord of the ancestral manor, learns that the mysterious death of Rebecca, the first Mrs. de Winter, remains a painful memory to her husband. What's more, Mrs. Danvers (Judith Anderson), Manderley's imperious housekeeper, is openly hostile toward her. In the film's most chilling scene, Mrs. Danvers urges her to jump to her death because she can never replace Rebecca as the true mistress of Manderley. ("He doesn't love you—he wants to be alone again with *her*. . . . Look down there. It's easy, isn't it? . . . Go on. Don't be afraid!") Fontaine shines in her first great damsel-in-distress role; Olivier, Anderson, and the rest of the virtually all-British cast are splendid. After the famous opening line ("Last night I dreamt I went to Manderley again"), there's no turning back.

Off-Screen: After Hitchcock completed *Jamaica Inn,* based on another du Maurier novel, he took up Selznick's offer to work in Hollywood, and *Rebecca* became his first American movie. Loretta Young, Margaret Sullavan, Vivien Leigh, and Anne Baxter were considered for the female lead, but Fontaine's lower fee (at that time) and ready-made English accent tipped the scales in her favor. William Powell and Ronald Colman were interested in playing de Winter, but Selznick wanted Olivier. Anderson won the Danvers role over Flora Robson and Nazimova. You can spot Hitchcock, in his customary cameo appearance, standing by a phone booth as George Sanders makes a call. *Rebecca* won two Oscars, for Best Picture and for George Barnes's atmospheric black-and-white cinematography. (CFB)

Rebel Without a Cause

Warners, 1955. (C-111m.) Dir: Nicholas Ray. Sp: Stewart Stern; adaptation: Irving Shulman, b/o story by Nicholas Ray. Cast: James Dean, Natalie Wood, Sal Mineo, Jim Backus, Ann Doran, Rochelle Hudson, William Hopper, Corey Allen, Dennis Hopper.

On-Screen: *Drama of misunderstood, alienated teenagers*. You could drive a truck through the generation gap that separates Jim Stark (Dean) from his conformist parents (Backus, Doran), residents of a comfortable Los Angeles suburb. The youth feels responsible for the death of Buzz (Allen) in a "chicken run" car race, but his quarreling, self-absorbed parents give higher priority to social status than their son's grief and guilt. Jim's girl (Wood) has her own problems with an unloving father (William Hopper); his unhappy pal (Mineo), son of divorced parents, finds solace in a crush on Jim. What saves the film from being a near-parody of soap opera (the adult characters come off as cartoonish boobs) are the young players'—especially Dean's—moving portrayals of barely articulate rebels against their elders'

hypocrisy and indifference. Highlight: the three youngsters explore a deserted house, with tragic results.

Off-Screen: So potent was Dean's screen image as a misunderstood loner (despite criticism that his acting style strongly resembled Marlon Brando's) that he became an icon for the restless youth of the midfifties and beyond. Both Wood, a former child actress in her first adult role, and Mineo earned Oscar nominations as best supporting players. Movie buffs will recognize Hudson, who plays Wood's mother, from her many ingenue roles in the thirties, as well as the deserted house and swimming pool (the Getty estate in Los Angeles) from *Sunset Boulevard*. Inside joke: Dean's imitation of the fuddy-duddy Mr. Magoo voice that Backus used in the well-known UPA cartoon shorts of the period. (CFB)

The Red Badge of Courage

MGM, 1951. (69m.) Dir: John Huston. Sp: John Huston, b/o novel by Stephen Crane. Cast: Audie Murphy, Bill Mauldin, John Dierkes, Royal Dano, Arthur Hunnicutt, Andy Devine, Douglas Dick.

On-Screen: *John Huston films Stephen Crane's classic Civil War story*. At the climax of his trouble-plagued film, writer-director Huston stages a Civil War battle that conveys its disorientation, terror, and sudden death in stunning images. The rest is a reasonable and sometimes moving adaptation of the Crane novel about a frightened youth (Murphy) who overcomes his "visions of a thousand-tongued fear" to find his courage in battle. Considering the many tribulations in making the film, Huston manages some effective scenes, especially the one in which the Tall Soldier Jim Conklin (Dierkes), mortally wounded, refuses to fall down, and—like a Messiah undaunted by death—stumbles along until he collapses. With a narrator periodically breaking into the action to read passages from Crane's novel, the film sometimes takes on an academic air that tends to dissipate the emotional impact of the young soldier's experiences. Still, Murphy, the much-decorated hero of World War II and an actor of very limited range, has been directed by Huston to reveal some of the terror and anguish of war with only his facial expression.

Off-Screen: The complete story of the making of *The Red Badge of Courage* and the mutilation it suffered on the way to the screen will be found in Lillian Ross's 1952 classic study, *Picture,* available from Limelight Editions. Some scenes were altered drastically, some material was rearranged to "fix" the story, and a narration by James Whitmore was added. Most of the battle scenes were filmed on John Huston's own ranch. An excellent 1974 television version starred Richard Thomas.

Red Dust

MGM, 1932. (83m.) Dir: Victor Fleming. Sp: John Lee Mahin, b/o play by Wilson Collison. Cast: Clark Gable, Jean Harlow, Mary Astor, Gene Raymond, Donald Crisp.

On-Screen: *The King and the Platinum Blonde scorch the jungle foliage.* The first of the sizzling duo's five costarring movies and, thanks to Fleming's fast-paced direction, at the top of the list. Gable oversees a rubber plantation and has welcoming arms for Harlow, a tough-talking floozy he's harboring from the Saigon authorities. Sexual rivalry rears its head when he dumps her for the more sophisticated charms of Astor, the refined woman who has come to the plantation with husband Raymond. The movie's memorable moments include Harlow bathing in a rain barrel, to Gable's ogling delight ("Scrub my back," she orders him); her furious scraping of the bottom of a parrot's cage, yelling, "Whaddya been eatin', cement?"; and her recounting to Gable in excruciating baby talk the exploits of Peter Rabbit, as his hand advances up her leg. The scene is like most of the movie, funny and erotic.

Off-Screen: The original play had been bought for John Gilbert, who was to costar with Harlow. Then writer John Lee Mahin saw Gable on the screen and knew he was the right actor for the role. During the making of the movie, Harlow experienced personal tragedy when her second husband, producer Paul Bern, fatally shot himself for reasons never explained satisfactorily. A year later, she wed cameraman Harold Rosson, who had photographed *Red Dust*. The movie was remade in 1940 as *Congo Maisie* with Ann Sothern and again in 1953 as *Mogambo,* with Gable repeating his role opposite Ava Gardner and Grace Kelly. (CFB)

Red River

United Artists/Monterey, 1948. (133m.) Dir: Howard Hawks. Sp: Borden Chase and Charles Schnee, b/o story by Borden Chase. Cast: John Wayne, Montgomery Clift, Joanne Dru, Walter Brennan, John Ireland, Noah Beery, Jr., Paul Fix, Coleen Gray, Harry Carey, Jr., Hank Worden.

On-Screen: *Howard Hawks's sweeping western drama*. Widely regarded as one of the great western films, *Red River* combines a strong personal story with epic views of a cattle drive. In a basically unsympathetic role, John Wayne stars as Tom Dunson, a rugged man obsessed with building a cattle empire on his own terms. Opposed by his adopted son, Matt (Clift), he becomes a darkly vengeful figure, bent on killing Matt for rendering him powerless. In the end, they are reconciled by the girl (Dru) who loves Matt. Dunson's complex character becomes the catalyst for vividly dramatic scenes, and Wayne's sterling performance invests him with shading and dimension. On the other hand, Montgomery Clift, in his first film role, is not exactly at home on the range. (He seems to have landed out West in a time machine.) What we remember most are the large-scale sequences, especially the start of the cattle drive and the resulting stampede. Russell Harlan's photography is breathtaking, and Dimitri Tiomkin contributes a rousing score.

Off-Screen: *Red River* was shot in Rain Valley, sixty miles east of Tucson, Arizona. Gary Cooper was first offered the role of Tom Dunson but turned it down because he thought that the character was too ruthless. *The Search*, Montgomery Clift's second film, was released before *Red River*. Wayne and Clift did not like each other very much, although they maintained a cautious politeness on the set. The screenplay and editing were nominated for Oscars. A television remake turned up in 1988.

Reds

Paramount, 1981. (C-200m.) Dir: Warren Beatty. Sp: Warren Beatty and Trevor Grif-

fiths. Cast: Warren Beatty, Diane Keaton, Jack Nicholson, Edward Herrmann, Jerzy Kosinski, Maureen Stapleton, Paul Sorvino, Gene Hackman, Nicolas Coster, William Daniels, Max Wright, George Plimpton, Ian Wolfe.

On-Screen: *Romance and revolution, from Warren Beatty*. Essentially a love story set against the massive canvas of world history, Warren Beatty's *Reds* offers a true account of American radical leader John (Jack) Reed (Beatty)—whose book, *Ten Days That Shook the World*, is regarded as the best account of Russia's 1917 revolution—and his relationship with writer and feminist Louise Bryant (Keaton). This long, spectacular film covers five years of their lives (1915–20), especially their prewar involvement with such writers as Eugene O'Neill (Nicholson) and Max Eastman (Herrmann) and their experiences during and after the tumultuous October Revolution. The sweeping large-scale scenes are beautifully staged, but too much time is spent on tedious ideological clashes. Nor are Reed and Bryant fully rounded characters who can sustain our interest for over three hours. An effective feature is the periodic introduction of testimony or reminiscences by "witnesses" (Rebecca West, Henry Miller, Will Durant, and others) who knew Reed and Bryant.

Off-Screen: Warren Beatty worked on the screenplay with British playwright Trevor Griffiths, but it was found unacceptable by the studio. Robert Towne and Elaine May were brought in as script doctors (without screen credit), and they refashioned the script until it was approved. Although not a box-office success, *Reds* earned Oscars for Beatty's direction, Vittorio Storaro's cinematography, and Maureen Stapleton's supporting performance as Emma Goldman. The film itself was nominated, as were Beatty, Keaton, and Nicholson. The witnesses were not identified as they spoke in the film (Beatty didn't want to suggest a documentary), but placards with photos of the witnesses were placed in lobbies of theaters around the country. A Soviet version of John Reed's story was filmed by Russian director Sergei Bondarchuk in 1982.

Reflections in a Golden Eye

Warners, 1967. (C–108m.) Dir: John Huston. Sp: Gladys Hill and Chapman Mortimer, b/o novel by Carson McCullers. Cast: Elizabeth Taylor, Marlon Brando, Brian Keith, Julie Harris, Robert Forster, Zorro David.

On-Screen: *Taylor and Brando in a tale of strange obsessions*. The film begins and ends with the legend: "There is a fort in the South where a few years ago a murder was committed." The blunt statement gives little indication of the bizarre events that occur in this adaptation of the Carson McCullers novel. Sporting a thick Southern accent, Marlon Brando plays Maj. Weldon Penderton, an army officer married to contemptuous Leonora (Taylor). While Leonora dallies with another officer (Keith, excellent as always), the major has a secret obsession for a surly private (Forster). The private himself is no stranger to obsession, being fascinated by Leonora, stealing into her room at night to crouch at the foot of her bed while she sleeps. Add to this unsavory mix Keith's disturbed, self-destructive wife (Harris) and you have the makings of a highly unconventional, but not very satisfactory, film. Brando works strenuously to convey the

anguish of his closeted character, and Taylor mixes her Southern belles of the fifties with more than a touch of the promiscuous bitch-wife she played a year earlier in *Who's Afraid of Virginia Woolf?* (1966).

Off-Screen: The film was shot in southern Italy, using an Italian crew and Italian extras. At Elizabeth Taylor's insistence, Montgomery Clift was scheduled to play Major Penderton, but he died in 1966 and was replaced by Brando. Huston experimented with the film's color, aiming for a muted, desaturated effect that was only used in the original release prints.

Regarding Henry

Paramount, 1991. (C–107m.) Dir: Mike Nichols. Sp: Jeffrey Abrams. Cast: Harrison Ford, Annette Bening, Bill Nunn, Mikki Allen, Donald Moffat, Nancy Marchand, Bruce Altman, Rebecca Miller, Elizabeth Wilson.

On-Screen: *A lawyer rebuilds his shattered life*. Another entry in the early-nineties Feel-Good-About-Yourself Movie Sweepstakes, *Regarding Henry* offers a familiar message: forget the greed and selfishness of the eighties and get in touch with your true feelings about the Things That Matter: love, family, helping others. Henry Turner (Ford) is a wealthy, mean-spirited lawyer who is shot in the head during a random robbery. Now he must not only learn to talk and walk again but he must also rediscover his wife (Bening) and daughter (Allen). In the process, he becomes a whole new person; he buys a puppy, makes cookies, and most importantly, he is overcome with a burst of integrity that alienates him from his firm. The movie is an utter sham: Henry's transformation is so all-encompassing that it is hardly believable. And his therapist (Nunn) is so warmly supportive that you keep expecting him to sprout wings. Toward the end, reality intrudes when Henry learns about his wife's infidelity, as well as his own, during the time before his injury, but by then it's too late to save the movie.

Off-Screen: Much of the movie was filmed on location in New York City: at the Metropolitan Museum of Art, the Edwardian and Oak Rooms at the Plaza Hotel, the law offices of Rogers and Wells in the Pam Am Building, and the Ritz Carlton Hotel. The boarding school scenes were shot at the Millbrook School, ninety minutes north of New York City in Millbrook, New York. The school was previously used in *The World According to Garp* (1982).

Return of the Jedi

Fox, 1983. (C-133m.) Dir: Richard Marquand. Sp: Lawrence Kasdan, b/o story by George Lucas. Cast: Mark Hamill, Harrison Ford, Carrie Fisher, Peter Mayhew, Anthony Daniels, Sebastian Shaw, David Prowse, Kenny Baker, Alec Guinness, Frank Oz, Denis Lawson.

On-Screen: *The third and final Star Wars adventure.* More of the same, and if you enjoyed *Star Wars* and *The Empire Strikes Back* (and followed the plot), you are sure to like the last escapades of Luke Skywalker, now a Jedi knight, and his friends. While Darth Vader constructs a more powerful Deathstar, Luke (Hamill), Princess Leia (Fisher), and their friends are desperately trying to free Solo (Ford) from the clutches of the repulsive, toadlike Jabba the Hutt on the planet of Tatooine. The

intrepid group succeeds, and after a startling revelation about Leia's identity, they set about to finally destroy the Deathstar. A final confrontation between Luke and Darth Vader has an unexpected twist, but all ends well. Leia and Solo come to a romantic understanding, after all that banter and bickering. Most prominent of the new creatures are the cuddly koala/teddy bears called Ewoks. The special effects are still state-of-the-art, but it's clear that all those duels, battles, and intergalactic flights are beginning to pall. So much for the Force.

Off-Screen: Once again the special effects received an Academy Award. The Ewoks found their way to television, where, under George Lucas's auspices, they appeared in two television films, *The Ewok Adventure* (1984) and *Ewoks: The Battle for Endor* (1985).

Reversal of Fortune

Warners, 1990. (C-120m.) Dir: Barbet Schroeder. Sp: Nicholas Kazan, b/o book by Alan Dershowitz. Cast: Jeremy Irons, Glenn Close, Ron Silver, Annabella Sciorra, Uta Hagen, Fisher Stevens, Christine Baranski.

On-Screen: *All about the notorious von Bulow case.* Here are the facts, as they appear, in the case of Claus von Bülow (Irons), convicted of attempting to murder his wife (Close) and later granted an appeal for a retrial, which he went on to win. Based on a book by von Bülow's lawyer, Alan Dershowitz, played by Ron Silver, the film tracks Dershowitz's team of colleagues and students as they wrestle with the truth, the legalities, and the morality of the case. Silver is first-rate as the brilliant, ebullient Dershowitz, and Irons shows why he received the Best Actor Oscar for his performance. Cold and impassive, he projects an inner intensity that moves and baffles us at the same time. In what is essentially a cameo role, Glenn Close is superb as the troubled, self-indulgent Sunny von Bülow. There are no emotional heights in *Reversal of Fortune,* but watching a team of very bright people chipping away at a seemingly impervious case, you are likely to be fascinated.

Off-Screen: Although Jeremy Irons never met Claus von Bülow, he did speak with many people who knew him, watched him on television, and read all the police statements and courtroom transcripts. "This sort of research," Irons said, "is like being a detective. You get a hunch and follow it. I think I found him, but I'm probably very arrogant to say that. I found *a* Claus, anyway . . . and I thought about him a lot. I came to conclusions about him. He had a sort of slow, rather pompous, somewhat snobbish, center-of-the-stage European quality." (BL).

Rhapsody in Blue

Warners, 1945. (139m.) Dir: Irving Rapper. Sp: Sonya Levien, Howard Koch, and Elliot Paul. MS: George Gershwin, Ira Gershwin, and others. Cast: Robert Alda, Joan Leslie, Alexis Smith, Charles Coburn, Oscar Levant, Rosemary DeCamp, Morris Carnovsky, Al Jolson, Paul Whiteman, Julie Bishop, Albert Basserman.

On-Screen: *The life and music of George Gershwin, more or less.* It would be damning with faint praise to say that *Rhapsody in Blue* is marginally better than Warners' other composer "biography," *Night and Day,* which trashed Cole Porter. Once again, the depiction of the composer's life is more fiction than fact, and clichéd fiction at that, and Robert Alda is wan and inexpressive as Gershwin. Too many of the great Gershwin songs are rendered ineffectually, although Al Jolson shakes the rafters with "Swanee" ("That ain't a bad ditty," he tells Gershwin), and Anne Brown, the original Bess in *Porgy and Bess,* does a splendid version of "Summertime." Gershwin's symphonic music fares best, especially with a full-scale performance of "Rhapsody in Blue," led (as in its first performance) by Paul Whiteman. Playing himself—he was one of Gershwin's closest friends—Oscar Levant is amusing in his dyspeptic fashion.

Off-Screen: Playwright Clifford Odets was hired to write a screenplay loosely based on the life of Gershwin. In the end, very little of his script was used, but producer Jerry Wald took it, changed the names of the characters, and retitled it *Humoresque,* combining it with elements of Fannie Hurst's original story. To learn how to finger the piano properly, Robert Alda studied four hours a day, seven days a week, for one month. Oddball business: Oscar Levant prerecorded "Rhapsody in Blue," then sat in the audience while Alda "played" it at the inaugural performance.

Ride the High Country

MGM, 1962. (C-94m.) Dir: Sam Peckinpah. Sp: N. B. Stone, Jr. Cast: Joel McCrea, Randolph Scott, Mariette Hartley, Ronald Starr, Edgar Buchanan, R. G. Armstrong, Warren Oates, John Anderson.

On-Screen: *Two aging cowboys take on one last assignment.* A fitting coda to the long screen careers of Randolph Scott (his last movie) and Joel McCrea, *Ride the High Country* is an affecting, beautifully played and produced western that says more about the waning of the West than many more elaborate films. Tired-in-the-saddle cowhands who have seen better days, Scott and McCrea are old friends who come together to deliver a shipment of gold to a bank. Their journey takes them in an unexpected direction, involving them with a girl in jeopardy (Hartley, in her film debut) and some vicious miners. The last scene between the two men is one of the most memorable in the genre. Although there is some lively western action, the film's mood is basically autumnal. Lucien Ballard's superb photography captures this mood, giving appropriate attention to the proudly lived-in faces of the stars.

Off-Screen: Originally, Joel McCrea and Randolph Scott were scheduled to play each other's role, but when they confessed to being uneasy about the casting, the roles were switched. This was Sam Peckinpah's second film, and he agreed to direct if he was allowed to rewrite the screenplay and bring in some of his own experiences. (McCrea's line "All I want is to enter my house justified" was often spoken by Peckinpah's father.) Largely due to poor marketing, the movie failed to do business in America, but it was received enthusiastically in Europe, winning major prizes.

The Right Stuff

The Ladd Company/Warners, 1983. (C-193m.) Dir: Philip Kaufman. Sp: Philip Kaufman, b/o book by Tom Wolfe. Cast: Sam Shepard, Ed Harris, Scott Glenn, Dennis Quaid, Fred Ward, Barbara Hershey, Kim Stanley, Pamela Reed, Donald Moffat, Levon Helm, Scott Wilson, David Clennon, Jeff Goldblum, Mary Jo Deschanel.

On-Screen: *On America's journey into the age of space flight.* Offhand, would you consider the story of America's space pioneers to be the stuff of satire? Probably not, unless you happen to be Philip Kaufman, who adapted Tom Wolfe's best-seller into this frequently stirring but basically schizophrenic film. It begins in 1947 with Chuck Yeager (Shepard), a crackerjack pilot whose mystical view of flying leads to his breaking the sound barrier. Much of the film is then devoted to the first group of astronauts (Shepard, Grissom, Cooper, et al.): their rigorous training, their reluctant transformation into space-age heroes, and finally their first manned flights. When John Glenn (Harris) soars into space for the first time in *Friendship 7,* or Chuck Yeager reenters the picture, *The Right Stuff* conveys the wonder of space flight in extraordinarily beautiful photography (courtesy of Oscar-nominated Caleb Deschanel). Too often, however, the movie shows two faces, mixing low-level humor with high-minded space technology. This may be true to the book, but it makes for a distracting film.

Off-Screen: An earlier screenplay by William Goldman never mentioned Chuck Yeager. When Philip Kaufman was named the director, he jettisoned this screenplay and wrote his own, which restored Yeager. The legendary pilot acted as a consultant during the filming and also appears briefly as a bartender. A Mercury spacecraft was built for the film from the original NASA mold. One error of fact: John Glenn did not sing "Battle Hymn of the Republic" during reentry. *The Right Stuff* received eight Oscar nominations, including Best Picture and Best Supporting Actor (Shepard); Bill Conti won a statuette for his original score.

Rio Bravo

Warners, 1959. (C-141m.) Dir: Howard Hawks. Sp: Leigh Brackett and Jules Furthman. Cast: John Wayne, Dean Martin, Walter Brennan, Angie Dickinson, Ricky Nelson, Ward Bond, John Russell, Claude Akins, Bob Steele.

On-Screen: *Sheriff John Wayne and his "deputies" rout the villains.* Once casually dismissed by the critics, *Rio Bravo* is now regarded as one of Howard Hawks's best westerns, a distillation of his ideas about men in groups and the bond that links them together. When beleaguered sheriff John T. Chance (Wayne) must protect his jail against assault by thugs who want to break out their friend, he forges a trustworthy alliance out of an alcoholic has-been (Martin), a lame, toothless codger (Brennan), and a callow boy (Nelson). Under pressure, the men either recover (Martin) or discover (Nelson) their manhood and integrity. Also on hand is a feisty dance-hall girl (Dickinson). The movie has some action sequences, but the screenplay doesn't stint on character relationships. *Rio Bravo* may not be a classic example of the genre—it meanders too often and also lacks the visual splendor of the great westerns—but Sheriff Chance has the stature of a classic western lawman.

Off-Screen: *Rio Bravo* was made partly as Howard Hawks's response to *High Noon* (1952), which he found reprehensible. Hawks's idea of a good sheriff was not one who ran around the town asking for help from its citizens. He made *Rio Bravo* the "exact opposite" of *High Noon*. Hawks liked the central idea of the film so much that he used it twice more in *El Dorado* (1967) and *Rio Lobo* (1970). Neither film, however, can be considered an actual remake of *Rio Bravo*. Featured in the cast is Bob Steele, who starred in many low-budget westerns in the thirties and early forties.

River's Edge

Hemdale, 1987. (C-99m.) Dir: Tim Hunter. Sp: Neal Jimenez. Cast: Crispin Glover, Keanu Reeves, Ione Skye Leitch, Daniel Roebuck, Dennis Hopper, Joshua Miller, Roxana Zal.

On-Screen: *Small-town teenagers react to a friend's murder.* Every American town will admit to its share of disaffected teenagers, but one hopes that few contain as many as this disturbing and ultimately oppressive film. Based on a true incident, the story involves the brutal murder of a teenage girl and especially the oddly disengaged, even indifferent way in which her friends respond to her killing before the body is discovered. In thrall to their drugged, out-of-control leader (Glover), who urges them to remain silent, they continue to go about their empty and pointless lives. They apparently inhabit a frightening moral vacuum in which there are no authorities or role models. Only one boy (Reeves) is troubled, and when he tells the police, he is treated hostilely by them and denounced by his demonic younger brother (Miller). Also involved is a drug-crazed hermit (Hopper) who claims to have also killed a girl twenty years earlier. The film is undeniably fascinating, but after a while the deliberately creepy approach begins to pall, and one begins to wonder whether any happy or productive people inhabit this bizarre town.

Off-Screen: The film was based on the real murder of a fourteen-year-old junior high school student in Milpitas, California, in 1981. When her body was discovered, some of her friends buried it in leaves, and for two days, nobody called the police. The screenplay was turned down by many studios until it was taken by Hemdale. Even when completed, the movie was extremely difficult to market.

Road to Singapore

Paramount, 1940. (84m.) Dir: Victor Schertzinger. Sp: Don Hartman and Frank Butler, b/o story by Harry Hervey. Cast: Bing Crosby, Bob Hope, Dorothy Lamour, Charles Coburn, Anthony Quinn, Jerry Colonna, Judith Barrett.

On-Screen: *Crosby and Hope travel down their first "road."* Claiming easygoing, mellow-voiced Bing Crosby and quipping Bob Hope as two of their biggest stars, Paramount decided to team them in this lighthearted (also light-headed) caper, adding Dorothy Lamour for decoration. Viewers responded enthusiastically, launching a series of *Road* movies that extended into the early sixties. The format is usually the same: Hope and Crosby play friends and partners who find themselves in an exotic location, caught up in some perilous dilemma involving the sultry Lamour. Gags, quips, and wisecracks abound, some forced, others funny. Oddly, the *Road* movies always

showed Hope and Crosby with a disregard or even contempt for each other's well-being or safety, but laughing audiences never seemed to notice. Crosby, in particular, seemed to go out of his way to con, humiliate, or betray his "pal." Yet *Road to Singapore* is a pleasant introduction to the series.

Off-Screen: Paramount originally intended the film as a minor effort to star Fred MacMurray and Jack Oakie, but decided instead to give it to Hope and Crosby. The movie introduced the "pat-a-cake" routine that Hope and Crosby used in every *Road* film to extricate themselves from a dilemma. *Road to Singapore* was followed by travels to *Zanzibar* (1941), *Morocco* (1942), *Utopia* (1945, actually Alaska), *Bali* (1952), and much later, *Hong Kong* (1962).

The Roaring Twenties

Warners, 1939. (103m.) Dir: Raoul Walsh. Sp: Jerry Wald, Richard Macaulay, and Robert Rossen, b/o story by Mark Hellinger. Cast: James Cagney, Priscilla Lane, Humphrey Bogart, Jeffrey Lynn, Gladys George, Frank McHugh, Paul Kelly.

On-Screen: *Gangster James Cagney finds violence—and sacrificial love—in the days of Prohibition.* In one of his most sympathethic gangster roles, Cagney plays an ex–World War I doughboy who becomes a criminal when society turns its back on him. Rising in the ranks to kingpin hood, he clashes with rival Bogart and falls for demure singer Lane, who only has eyes for a rising young attorney (Lynn). In the end Cagney meets his doom, while the blowsy chanteuse (George) who loved him intones, "He used to be a big shot." The movie is unquestionably hackneyed, but in the hard-hitting Warners style, it holds the attention. And Cagney rewards his fans with a vigorous performance, all coiled tension and energy. Best scene: The gang robs a shipment of liquor confiscated by the government. *The Roaring Twenties* is so generic that it has been emulated and parodied many times.

Off-Screen: Anatole Litvak was originally slated to direct, but Raoul Walsh won the assignment at the last minute. This was Walsh's first film with Cagney, and Cagney's last gangster film for a decade. Cagney's role was based on the rise and fall of a New York gangster named Larry Fay, who promoted the career of Texas Guinan. Gladys George's character in the film strongly resembles Guinan. Ann Sheridan, Lee Patrick, and Glenda Farrell were also considered for this part.

The Robe

Fox, 1953. (C-135m.) Dir: Henry Koster. Sp: Philip Dunne, b/o novel by Lloyd C. Douglas. Cast: Richard Burton, Jean Simmons, Michael Rennie, Victor Mature, Jay Robinson, Torin Thatcher, Dean Jagger, Richard Boone, Betta St. John, Ernest Thesiger.

On-Screen: *A biblical epic concerning Christ's robe.* As a weapon against the inroads of television, Darryl F. Zanuck decided to use the new wide-screen process of CinemaScope, which didn't require special glasses or a gigantic screen. *The Robe,* his first CinemaScope film, is nothing less than the story of Christ's crucifixion, and its impact on the Roman centurion (Burton) who presides

over it, and who wins Christ's scarlet garment in a dice game. Although nominated for a Best Picture Oscar, the movie is a huge, vulgar mess, the sort of spectacle that Cecil B. DeMille would enjoy creating. The sets are enormous, dazzling the eye and dwarfing the actors. Nobody is really required to act, only to pose against the mighty halls of Roman power or vast landscapes. His hair in curls, Richard Burton looks stiff and pained (although he won an Oscar nomination), Jean Simmons is lovely and worried, and Michael Rennie is tall and imposing. Surprisingly, the actor who comes off best is Victor Mature, who was usually thought of as a ham with muscles. His performance earned him the leading role in a sequel, *Demetrius and the Gladiators* (1954). *The Robe* did earn one Oscar, for Costume Design (Color).

Off-Screen: Tyrone Power had first been scheduled to play Marcellus, and Laurence Olivier, next in line for the part, rejected it. Richard Burton campaigned actively for the role, claiming that he was "the poor man's Olivier." Long after the film was released, Darryl F. Zanuck admitted that CinemaScope was a mistake, acknowledging that "it was all wrong, mechanically." Still, *The Robe* was an enormous hit and established Burton as an international star.

Roberta

RKO, 1935. (85m.) Dir: William A. Seiter. Sp: Jane Murfin, Sam Mintz, and Allan Scott, b/o musical play by Otto Harbach and novel by Alice Duer Miller. MS: Jerome Kern, Otto Harbach, Dorothy Fields, and Jimmy McHugh. Cast: Irene Dunne, Randolph Scott, Fred Astaire, Ginger Rogers, Helen Westley, Claire Dodd.

On-Screen: *The dancing duo—plus Kern music and high fashion.* Although Astaire and Rogers play supporting roles in this adaptation of the stage musical, the movie ends with their dancing, showing that the studio knew when they had a sure thing. The plot is a bore—Scott inherits a Paris dress shop from his aunt, then falls in love with the shop's beautiful manager (Dunne), a displaced Russian princess. Astaire is a member of Scott's band; Rogers is a slangy American girl passing herself off as a Polish countess. Happily, the songs and dance numbers, especially the team's performance to "I Won't Dance," compensate for the story portions. Irene Dunne, a charming actress in comedy, is much less accomplished in musicals, but she gamely renders three of Jerome Kern's most beautiful melodies, "Smoke Gets in Your Eyes," "Yesterdays," and "Lovely to Look At." The movie ends with a fashion show, originally filmed in color, that is now the very essence of camp.

Off-Screen: Four of the songs from the original stage musical ("Let's Begin," "Smoke Gets in Your Eyes," "Yesterdays," and "I'd Be Hard to Handle") were retained for the movie version. When producer Pandro Berman thought that more songs were necessary, he brought Jerome Kern to Hollywood to collaborate with Dorothy Fields and Jimmy McHugh on the Oscar-nominated "Lovely to Look At." Rogers called Kern "the shyest, most unpretentious composer" she had ever met. *Roberta* was remade in 1952 as *Lovely to Look At.*

Robin Hood, Prince of Thieves

Warners, 1991. (C-138m.) Dir: Kevin Reynolds. Sp: Pen Densham and John Watson, b/o story by Pen Densham. Cast: Kevin Costner, Morgan Freeman, Christian Slater, Alan Rickman, Mary Elizabeth Mastrantonio, Nick Brimble, Micheal McShane.

On-Screen: *The legendary hero returns to fight against tyranny.* For whom was this elaborate recycling of the Robin Hood legend intended? Those old enough to remember the classic Errol Flynn version of 1938 will find little of that film's storybook exhilaration in this heavily oppressive, if realistic, view of medieval England. Parents of young children should be warned about the movie's graphic bloodletting. And teenagers in search of a new swashbuckling hero had best look elsewhere, since Kevin Costner gives an embarrassingly inept performance as Robin Hood. The familiar characters have been given new wrinkles for the nineties: Maid Marian (Mastrantonio) is feisty rather than demure, Will Scarlett (Slater) is no amiable aide to Robin but a surly sort with a secret agenda, and the Sheriff of Nottingham (Rickman) is no bumbling oaf but the chief villain, ambitious to wrest the throne from absent King Richard. Rickman gives the film's best performance, being hilariously over-the-top as a snarling, sadistic creature who enjoys being mean to everyone. ("Call off Christmas!" he yells at one point.) He provides the only real diversion in a somber movie.

Off-Screen: Viewers will be pleased to know that at the film's end, Sean Connery makes a brief, uncredited appearance as King Richard, returning from the Crusades. In that short time, he conveys all of the style and panache missing from the previous two hours.

Rocky

United Artists, 1976. (C-119m.) Dir: John G. Avildsen. Sp: Sylvester Stallone. Cast: Sylvester Stallone, Talia Shire, Burgess Meredith, Burt Young, Carl Weathers, Thayer David.

On-Screen: *First of the five, and still champ*. You don't have to be a slugfest fan to respond to this rousing charmer of a movie. Set in Philadelphia, the story follows the road to self-discovery of Rocky Balboa (Stallone), from strong-arm man for a local numbers racket to hard-won fame as contender for the world heavyweight title. Rocky, fortunately, is a lucky guy. When a chance at the crown comes along—his name is picked from the boxing registry by reigning champ Apollo Creed (Carl Weathers)—he not only has a loving and supportive girlfriend Adrian (Shire) rooting for him, he also has Mickey (Meredith), a seasoned trainer with tanbark in his blood. Because Stallone's well-endowed physique and understanding of his character make you believe Rocky's "not just another bum from the neighborhood," it's easy to enjoy this fast-paced, stirring movie. Meredith's portrayal won him a Best Supporting Actor Oscar nomination. Yo! Rocky!

Off-Screen: After appearing in eight films—*Bananas* (1971) and *The Lords of Flatbush* (1974) among them—Stallone, already thirty, with a pregnant wife and little money in the bank, figured it was time to star in his own movie. In less than a week, he wrote *Rocky,* his thirty-third attempt at scriptwriting. Though the producers wanted box-office names for the lead (Burt Reynolds and James Caan were among those considered), Stallone held out and won. *Rocky* itself won, also, as Best Picture, with Avildsen receiving an Oscar as Best Director. The movie is something of a family affair, with Stallone's father, Frank, and brother, Frank, Jr., appearing as a timekeeper and street singer, respectively. Four Roman-numeraled sequels followed, from 1979 through 1990. (CFB)

Roman Holiday

Paramount, 1953. (119m.) Dir: William Wyler. Sp: Dalton Trumbo, originally credited to Ian McLellan Hunter and John Dighton, b/o story by Trumbo, also credited to Hunter. Cast: Gregory Peck, Audrey Hepburn, Eddie Albert, Hartley Power, Laura Solari, Harcourt Williams, Tullio Carminati.

On-Screen: *Audrey Hepburn as a Cinderella in reverse*. Young Audrey Hepburn had appeared in several British films and on Broadway in *Gigi* when she was signed to play a princess in *Roman Holiday*. Audiences and critics responded enthusiastically to the lithe and enchanting actress, and she won an Academy Award for her performance. The movie is a charming bauble in which Hepburn, as a princess on a state visit to Italy, escapes her gilded prison to find adventure and romance with newspaperman Gregory Peck. As the incognito princess sheds her bonds, she gets an eye-catching tour of Rome, and luckily, so does the audience. Soberly laid-back as usual, Gregory Peck plays well against Hepburn's naive radiance, and Eddie Albert is ingratiating as a bearded photographer. Director William Wyler wraps it all up as a pleasurable gift for moviegoers.

Off-Screen: After four decades, it was finally acknowledged that blacklisted author Dalton Trumbo wrote the screenplay, using his close friend Ian McLellan Hunter as a front.

The Oscar that went to Hunter for Best Motion Picture Story should have gone to Trumbo. Filming in Rome was difficult: In addition to the intense noise and heat, and the day-to-day logistics of clearing the streets, the cast and crew found themselves in the midst of a citywide battle between Fascists and Communists. A 1987 television remake seemed pointless.

Rope

Paramount, 1948. (C-80m.) Dir: Alfred Hitchcock. Sp: Arthur Laurents; adaptation: Hume Cronyn, b/o play by Patrick Hamilton. Cast: James Stewart, John Dall, Farley Granger, Joan Chandler, Cedric Hardwicke, Constance Collier, Douglas Dick.

On-Screen: *Two friends murder for danger and thrills*. One of Alfred Hitchcock's least-viewed films, *Rope* begins with a strangulation: Brandon (Dall) and Philip (Granger), believing themselves to be superior intellects above the law, murder a friend "for the sake of danger and for the sake of killing." Perversely, they invite the victim's father, aunt, and girlfriend to have supper in their apartment, with the body in the room, hidden in a chest. During the film's course, their former headmaster (Stewart), who is responsible for inculcating their ideas about "superior beings," is horrified to uncover their crime. *Rope* is less of a fully rounded film than a Hitchcockian exercise in film technique. There are some suspenseful and clever moments, but despite Hitchcock's best cinematic efforts, the movie's stage origin is obvious. Playing against his usual ingratiating persona, Stewart is the most provocative character: a rather lofty and sardonic man whose words to the killers ("Murder is, or should be, an art") come back to haunt him.

Off-Screen: This film was Hitchcock's first in color. In order to create eighty seamless minutes of real time, he shot in continuous ten-minute takes, using actors to pass in front of the camera and black out the scene between takes. This was an unprecedented technique, but much later, Hitchcock admitted to director François Truffaut that the movie was "a stunt . . . I really don't know how I came to indulge in it."

The Rose

Fox, 1979. (C-134m.) Dir: Mark Rydell. MS: Bo Goldman and William Kerby, b/o story by William Kerby. MS: Various writers. Cast: Bette Midler, Alan Bates, Frederic Forrest, Harry Dean Stanton, Barry Primus, David Keith, Sandra McCabe, Will Hare, Don Calfa, Doris Roberts, James Keane.

On-Screen: *Bette Midler's debut as a self-destructive singer*. Any disclaimer to the contrary, *The Rose* was clearly suggested by the short, tragic life of raspy-voiced rock singer Janis Joplin, who died in October 1970 at age twenty-seven from an overdose of heroin. In an all-stops-out performance, Bette Midler makes an impressive screen debut as The Rose, a driven, vulnerable rock star whose dissipation from drugs and alcohol eventually spells her doom. Alan Bates is her coldhearted, ambitious manager whose refusal to let her take time off sends her reeling into the lower depths, and Frederic Forrest plays an AWOL soldier turned chauffeur who, for a while, becomes the one stable influence in her life. Midler has the bawdy, over-the-top style that makes Rose a suitable role for her, and later in her film career, she would use the bawdy side to move her roles in the direction of raucous comedy. Here, her performance is no laughing matter but an Oscar-nominated tour de force. The movie, however, is not half as good as her performance.

Off-Screen: Bette Midler insisted that the character was not based on Janis Joplin but rather on a composite of hard-rock singers who died tragically. Her comment: "There is a certain superficial resemblance between The Rose and Janis, but nothing is intended. She was so spectacular, I really don't think I could imitate her." Frederic Forrest won an Oscar nomination for Best Supporting Actor.

Rose Marie

MGM, 1936. (110m.) Dir: W. S. Van Dyke II. Sp: Frances Goodrich, Albert Hackett, and Alice Duer Miller, b/o musical by Rudolf Friml, Otto Harbach, and Oscar Hammerstein II. MS: Rudolf Friml and Herbert Stothart. Cast: Jeanette MacDonald, Nelson Eddy, James Stewart, Reginald Owen, Allan Jones, Una O'Connor, Alan Mowbray, Gilda Gray.

On-Screen: *America's Singing Sweethearts in the Canadian Rockies.* The second film version of the popular stage operetta, *Rose Marie* followed hard on the heels of *Naughty Marietta,* which catapulted MacDonald and Eddy to fame. More expansively produced than *Naughty Marietta,* yet without the ornate bric-a-brac that often weighed down MGM musicals, the film is overlong but actually quite pleasing. MacDonald is still given to coy overstatement, and since Eddy reacts to everything with blank understatement, a balance is struck that makes the pairing more than tolerable. MacDonald plays opera star Marie de Flor, who flees into the Canadian wilderness in search of her fugitive brother (young Stewart in his second film role) and finds romance and trouble with Eddy, the Mountie assigned to track him down. Everyone waits, of course, for their glorious and much-parodied duet on "Indian Love Call."

Off-Screen: David Niven (billed as David Nivens) can be spotted in a small role as one of MacDonald's rejected suitors. At Nelson Eddy's insistence, some of the footage with singer Allan Jones in the opera-within-the-story sequences was trimmed. Much of the movie was filmed in the Lake Tahoe area of northern California. Totem poles forty feet high were built on a state-owned area at Emerald Bay for the Indian totem-pole dance number. An inferior remake, starring Howard Keel and Ann Blyth, was released in 1954. The plot was completely different.

The Rose Tattoo

Paramount, 1955. (117m.) Dir: Daniel Mann. Sp: Tennessee Williams; adaptation: Hal Kanter, b/o play by Tennessee Williams. Cast: Anna Magnani, Burt Lancaster, Marisa Pavan, Ben Cooper, Jo Van Fleet, Virginia Grey.

On-Screen: *A volcanic force of nature named Magnani.* Written by Tennessee Williams expressly for Italian actress Anna Magnani, *The Rose Tattoo* came to Broadway in February 1951, but with Maureen Stapleton in the leading role instead of Magnani. The film version gave the role to Magnani, who came through with a powerful performance. With virtually nonstop ferocity, she plays Serafina Della Rose, a long-grieving Sicilian widow whose memory of her glorious husband is shattered by her learning of his infidelity. A clownish trucker named Mangiacavallo (Lancaster), who resembles her late husband in some ways (he even tattooes the same rose on his chest), finally manages to reawaken Serafina to life. Magnani's performance is so riveting that you may not notice that her character is something of a monster obsessed beyond reason with her dead husband's sexual prowess. The film has serious flaws—some scenes are clumsily staged—and Burt Lancaster, either grinning or stammering, is never convincing as the ardent trucker. But there's always Magnani, and she is something to behold.

Off-Screen: Anna Magnani received the Best Actress Oscar in that year, winning over such strong contenders as Susan Hayward (*I'll Cry Tomorrow*) and Katharine Hepburn (*Summertime*). James Wong Howe's cinematography and the film's art direction were also honored. The movie was nominated, but the big winner that year was *Marty*. When Magnani signed for the role, she spoke virtually no English, but working with Tennessee Williams over several weeks, her English improved remarkably. Much of the film was shot near Williams's home in Key West, Florida.

Rosemary's Baby

Paramount, 1968. (C-137m.) Dir: Roman Polanski. Sp: Roman Polanksi, b/o novel by Ira Levin. Cast: Mia Farrow, John Cassavetes, Ruth Gordon, Sidney Blackmer, Maurice Evans, Ralph Bellamy, Patsy Kelly, Elisha Cook, Jr., Charles Grodin.

On-Screen: *An innocent young woman is chosen to bear Satan's child.* Were she a less devoted mother, Rosemary Woodhouse (Farrow) might have thrown her Antichrist baby out

with the bathwater. But being the compliant wife she is, she's agreed to fulfill the terms of an unholy pact that her husband (Cassavetes) has made with a coven of witches in exchange for success as a Broadway actor. What gives the movie its special fascination and also increases the sense of dread is that the witches and warlocks, also residing in the couple's old Manhattan apartment house, are ordinary-seeming people. They don't have ugly warts and they're not snaggletoothed. They are such friendly neighbors as gabby Gordon, genial Blackmer, and dumpy Kelly. And just plain folks, such as Bellamy, a kindly old obstetrician. The movie terrifies by juxtaposing the dark, sinister images of ancient diabolism with the bright, colorful images of a bustling metropolis.

Off-Screen: A huge box-office success, this was Polish director Polanski's first Hollywood film, although locations were shot in and around New York's famed Dakota apartments on Central Park West. Polanski's adaptation of Levin's novel received an Oscar nomination, and Gordon won the Best Supporting Actress award for her performance. Some casting notes: Polanski's wife, Sharon Tate, and Jane Fonda were first considered for Farrow's role, and Robert Redford and Warren Beatty were candidates for Cassavetes's part. The voice of "Donald Baumgart" belongs to Tony Curtis. And look for actor Charles Grodin in his movie debut. (CFB)

Roxanne

Columbia, 1987. (C-106m.) Dir: Fred Schepisi. Sp: Steve Martin, b/o play by Edmond Rostand. Cast: Steve Martin, Daryl Hannah, Rick Rossovich, Shelley Duvall,

John Kapelos, Fred Willard, Michael J. Pollard, Damon Wayans.

On-Screen: *Steve Martin as an updated Cyrano.* Who would have thought that Steve Martin, the "wild and crazy" comedian of many television appearances, had the talent to become one of the deftest, most engaging actors in films? In *Roxanne,* as writer and star, he adapts Rostand's old war-horse, *Cyrano de Bergerac,* into a winning movie that demonstrates his gift for physical comedy. He plays C. D. Bales, the grotesquely long-nosed fire chief in a Washington State ski town, who adores the enchanting Roxanne (Hannah) from afar. He uses one of his firemen, a dim-witted hulk (Rossovich), as a surrogate to court his ladylove. The truth eventually comes out, this time leading to a happier ending than in the play. Martin plays his modern-day Cyrano with a grace and dexterity that recalls the great silent comedians—only watch him demolish several town fools with his tennis racket, or confound an oaf who mocks his nose with a display of verbal pyrotechnics. Hannah makes a ravishing Roxanne, and other cast members respond to the movie's warmth and sweetness.

Off-Screen: A town in British Columbia substituted for the Washington State town in the film. Notable stage Cyranos over the years have included Richard Mansfield, Walter Hampden, Jose Ferrer, and Derek Jacobi. Ferrer won an Oscar when he repeated the role in a 1950 film. A silent version of the story was released in 1925, and in the thirties, there was even an abortive attempt to musicalize it for the stage.

Royal Wedding

MGM, 1951. (C-93m.) Dir: Stanley Donen. Sp: Alan Jay Lerner. MS: Burton Lane and Alan Jay Lerner. Cast: Fred Astaire, Jane Powell, Peter Lawford, Sarah Churchill, Keenan Wynn, Albert Sharpe.

On-Screen: *Fred Astaire finds love in London during the royal nuptials.* Built around the 1947 marriage of England's Princess Elizabeth to Prince Philip, *Royal Wedding* is a medium-range MGM musical with a weak book and a superior Lane-Lerner score. Fred Astaire and Jane Powell play an unlikely brother and sister, a popular musical comedy team, who travel to London to entertain at the time of the gala event. Of course they both find romance, she with a young aristocrat (Lawford) and he with a dancer (Sarah Churchill, Winston's daughter, in her only film role). The musical numbers compensate for a lame plot. Highlights include Astaire's ingenious dance on the walls and ceiling of his hotel room and the raucous Astaire-Powell duet to "How Could You Believe Me When I Said I Loved You When You Know I've Been a Liar All My Life," one of the longest song titles on record. Loveliest song: "Too Late Now."

Off-Screen: For Fred Astaire's dance on the ceiling, the room was built so that it could be rotated at the same speed as the camera. The camera operator was strapped to his chair, and when Astaire seems to be dancing on the ceiling, it's actually the floor, while the cameraman and his camera are upside down. For "You're All The World to Me," the song to which Astaire performed this number, composer Burton Lane recycled the song he had used in *Kid Millions* (1934), where it was called "I Want to Be a Minstrel Man." June Allyson was first scheduled to play Astaire's sister, but when she became pregnant, the studio turned to Judy Garland. Garland had to be let go because of behavioral problems, and the role finally went to Jane Powell. MGM wanted to sign ballerina Moira Shearer for the part played by Sarah Churchill, but she was otherwise engaged.

Ruggles of Red Gap

Paramount, 1935. (92m.) Dir: Leo McCarey. Sp: Walter De Leon and Harlan Thompson; adaptation: by Humphrey Pearson, b/o novel and play by Harry Leon Wilson. Cast: Charles Laughton, Mary Boland, Charles Ruggles, ZaSu Pitts, Roland Young, Leila Hyams, Maude Eburne.

On-Screen: *A very British butler out West.* Won in a poker game by the Flouds (Ruggles and Boland), a vulgar, newly rich American couple, the very proper British butler Marmaduke Ruggles (Laughton) finds himself unhappily transplanted to the wild West. But he discovers America's spirit of free enterprise and equality—and likes it. He also courts a widow (Pitts) and, after a few setbacks, opens a successful restaurant. Leo McCarey's leisurely comedy has charm to spare and a noteworthy, even rather restrained, performance by Laughton. His best-remembered highlight comes when he offers a heartfelt recitation of the Gettysburg Address as the camera pans across the faces of awestricken barflies and cowhands. As the nouveaux riches Flouds, Charles Ruggles and Mary Boland are delightful, his amiable befuddlement meshing nicely with her light-headed dithering.

Off-Screen: Harry Leon Wilson's story was also filmed in 1918 and 1923; in the latter version, directed by James Cruze (*The Covered Wagon*), the inimitable Edward Everett Horton played Ruggles. It was remade in 1950 as *Fancy Pants,* with Bob Hope. Charles Laughton arranged to have Paramount invite his old friend, the writer Arthur Macrae, to come to Hollywood to keep an eye on the screenplay, checking occasional lapses into Americanisms in his character's dialogue, and also to make suggestions about the other characters to Leo McCarey. A musical version of the story turned up on television in 1956.

Running on Empty

Warners, 1988. (116m.) Dir: Sidney Lumet. Sp: Naomi Foner. Cast: Christine Lahti, River Phoenix, Judd Hirsch, Martha Plimpton, L. M. Kit Carson, Augusta Dabney, Steven Hill, Jonas Arby, Ed Crowley.

On-Screen: *Sixties radicals flee from the law with their sons.* Because a janitor was blinded when they planted a bomb in a napalm lab, the family headed by Christine Lahti and Judd Hirsch is condemned to live on the lam, supported by their "network" and changing towns and identities whenever the FBI gets too close. They forge a tight-knit bond that nothing can penetrate until older son River Phoenix becomes interested in Martha Plimpton and in pursuing a career in music. The acting is the thing here; it is never less than superb, always convincing and deeply moving. Lahti is profoundly affecting as the mother, her sad eyes telling more than her words about a life where no house is home, where her only friends are her family. Even at her toughest, she's pliant and feminine; her wide smile softens the harshest remarks. The other miracle of casting is River Phoenix, who changes moods with lightning speed, at one moment hard, bitter, the next, as he plays the piano, tense, concentrated.

The producers began to think about the movie after reading a newspaper story on the arrest of two underground radicals in upstate New York. What impressed them was the comments of neighbors about how normal and polite their children appeared to be. Writer Naomi Foner interviewed people who had lived underground, and she incorporated details from their lives into her screenplay. In the script, the 1971 bombing of a napalm factory that triggered the flight of the Pope family referred to a real and similar incident at the University of Wisconsin, in which a man was killed. (JMK)

The Russians Are Coming! The Russians Are Coming!

United Artists, 1966. (C-126m.) Dir: Norman Jewison. Sp: William Rose, b/o novel by Nathaniel Benchley. Cast: Carl Reiner, Eva Marie Saint, Alan Arkin, Brian Keith, Jonathan Winters, Paul Ford, Theodore Bikel, John Philip Law, Tessie O'Shea, Ben Blue, Doro Merande, Parker Fennelly.

On-Screen: *Comic pandemonium in a New England coastal town.* Can a cast of talented comic actors carry off a one-joke movie? Judging by such films as *It's a Mad Mad Mad Mad World* (1963) and *1941* (1979), the answer is usually no. And *The Russians Are Coming!* is not the exception that proves the rule. On Gloucester Island off the New England coast, a Russian submarine is grounded by its captain (Bikel). As the Russian sailors scramble ashore, the islanders become convinced that a Soviet invasion is in progress. Soon comic chaos reigns, involving, among many others, a visiting writer (Reiner) and his family. In the nature of unbridled farce, the characters behave like idiots, and the fun begins to wear thin around midpoint. The players work hard (Alan Arkin is best in his feature debut as a Russian sailor), but the only true pleasure comes from a few of the old-timers in the cast, such as dear old Doro Merande as the postmistress who is bound, gagged, and strapped to a wall by the Russians.

Off-Screen: The movie was shot almost entirely in northern California, where the coastline bears a similarity to the intended site of Nantucket. Norman Jewison tried to get actors from Russia and Czechoslovakia to play the Russians, but their governments turned him down. To fill the roles, he had to turn to the Broadway theater and television. When the film was shown at the Berlin Film Festival, nervous West Berliners asked to have the title changed. But Jewison stood his ground.

Ruthless People

Touchstone, 1986. (C-93m.) Dir: Jim Abrahams, David Zucker, and Jerry Zucker. Sp: Dale Launer. Cast: Danny DeVito, Bette Midler, Judge Reinhold, Helen Slater, Anita Morris, Bill Pullman, William G. Schilling.

On-Screen: *A man's murder scheme goes comically awry.* In a certain kind of role, Bette Midler is a comic pleasure. Here, as wealthy, obnoxious Barbara Stone in a slapdash farce, she wins hearty laughs cutting loose with vulgar abandon. It seems that Sam Stone (DeVito), Barbara's tightly wound husband, despises her and has hatched a scheme to kill her. Instead, Barbara is kidnapped by an inept couple (Reinhold and Slater) who have a business grievance against Sam. A series of mistakes, mishaps, and misinterpretations leads to comic chaos involving not only the kidnappers and the Stones but also Sam's mistress (Morris), her dimwit boyfriend (Pullman), and the chief of police (Schilling). The plot gets hectic and out of hand, but there are some priceless moments: Midler shrieking, "I've been kidnapped by K Mart!" when her kidnappers keep lowering their ransom price; and DeVito (as always, a frenzied bantam) trying to conceal his disappointment when the body he's identifying at the morgue proves to be someone other than his despised wife.

Off-Screen: The screenplay went through extensive revisions and a rethinking on casting the female lead. At first Madonna was considered to play Barbara Stone, until it was agreed that it would be difficult to persuade an audience that DeVito would want to kill his sexy wife. Madonna agreed that maybe the movie wasn't right for her. Bill Pullman auditioned originally for the role of the serial killer, but when the directors saw his hair, they cast him as dim-bulb Earl. Half of his hair was dark where it had grown back after being dyed blond for a role in a play. Abrahams and the Zuckers also directed the hilarious *Airplane!* in 1980.

Sabrina

Paramount, 1954. (113m.) Dir: Billy Wilder. Sp: Ernest Lehman, Billy Wilder, and Samuel Taylor, b/o play by Samuel Taylor. Cast: Humphrey Bogart, Audrey Hepburn, William Holden, Martha Hyer, Walter Hampden, John Williams, Francis X. Bushman, Nancy Kulp.

On-Screen: *A chauffeur's daughter finds unexpected romance*. Audrey Hepburn's first film after her triumph in *Roman Holiday, Sabrina* spins the Cinderella tale of a chauffeur's daughter (Hepburn) who pines for wealthy playboy William Holden. Holden's conservative older brother (Bogart), alarmed by his sibling's inconvenient attraction to Sabrina, decides to divert their romance by wooing the girl himself. Naturally, he falls in love with her, while she ultimately switches her affections to Bogart. Adapted from the Broadway play *Sabrina Fair,* the film sparkles, on the whole, although Billy Wilder adds characteristic traces of cynicism and melancholy to the comic mix. The film's most serious problem is the casting: Hepburn makes a lovely heroine, but Bogart is clearly miscast as the stodgy Linus Larrabee, and William Holden is some years too old to play the often-married David Larrabee. Much better are John Williams as Sabrina's father and Walter Hampden as the senior Larrabee.

Off-Screen: Cary Grant was originally offered Humphrey Bogart's role but declined. The filming was troubled by Bogart's unhappiness with the role, and by his feeling that all of the Paramount regulars regarded him as an intruder. Irritable and edgy, he stalked off the set at one point and refused to report for work, forcing Wilder to shut down production. Holden was cast when it was decided that an actor closer to Bogart's age was needed to play his brother.

Sahara

Columbia, 1943. (97m.) Dir: Zoltan Korda. Sp: John Howard Lawson and Zoltan Korda, b/o story by Philip MacDonald and incident in Soviet film *The Thirteen*. Cast: Humphrey Bogart, Bruce Bennett, J. Carrol Naish, Rex Ingram, Dan Duryea, Lloyd Bridges, Richard Nugent.

On-Screen: *Bogart leads a group of Allied soldiers through the Sahara Desert*. In June 1942, an American tank crew fighting in Africa with the British army finds itself cut off from its unit. Led by a tough sergeant (Bogart) and joined by soldiers from other countries (plus an Italian prisoner and a downed Nazi pilot), the group struggles for survival in the desert. Eventually, they must stand alone against a German battalion that desperately needs the water they have found. An exceptionally gritty, unrelenting war drama, *Sahara,* like John Ford's *The Lost Patrol,* which it resembles, derives its impact from concentrating on a small group of men rather than on epic battle scenes. Made at the height of World War II, the movie contains the requisite number of patriotic speeches. The all-male cast acquits itself admirably, with Bogart giving one of his best performances as battle-hardened Sgt. Joe Gunn.

Off-Screen: An American battalion training at Camp Young was enlisted to play German soldiers in the climactic battle sequence. Rex Ingram, who plays a Sudanese soldier, was best known for his portrayal of "De Lawd" in the film version of *The Green Pastures* (1936). *Sahara* was remade as a western, *The Last of the Comanches,* in 1952.

San Francisco

MGM, 1936. (115m.) Dir: W. S. Van Dyke. Sp: Anita Loos, b/o story by Robert Hopkins. Cast: Clark Gable, Jeanette MacDonald, Spencer Tracy, Jack Holt, Jessie Ralph, Ted Healy, Shirley Ross, Al Shean.

On-Screen: *Gable, the Barbary Coast, and an earthquake.* This movie has so much going for it, you won't care that, as a team, Gable and MacDonald don't exactly set the screen afire. The scenes, though, between Gable's Blackie Norton, a shady charmer on San Francisco's turn-of-the-century Barbary

Coast, and Tracy's two-fisted priest, have plenty of snap and sizzle. When Father Tim Mullin persists in trying to make Blackie tread the straight and narrow in order to be worthy of Mary Blake (MacDonald), a minister's daughter and aspiring opera diva, he's rewarded with a bloody nose. Apart from enjoying the rugged male leads' sparring, you'll also relish MacDonald's game attempts to belt out music-hall ditties (including the familiar title tune) for Blackie's rowdy patrons. Of course, the real star of the movie is the all-out staging of the earthquake and fire that leveled "the wicked, ribald, licentious" city that fateful April day in 1906. It's still one of the screen's great spectacles.

Off-Screen: Because Gable was convinced that his part wouldn't stand a chance against MacDonald's vocal prowess, Tracy's role was added to the script to give Gable a man's man part to play against. Although Gable got along with Tracy, he was rather cool toward MacDonald, even though she had specifically requested him as her costar. All of the studio's ingenuity was mustered for the twenty-minute earthquake sequence. Portions of sidewalks, for example, were actually hydraulic platforms, wrenched apart by powerful cables, with geyserlike hoses providing the illusion of burst water lines. The film, Van Dyke, Tracy, and Hopkins's story were Oscar-nominated, with an award going for sound recording, probably for the simulated seismic rumblings of the earthquake. (CFB)

The Sand Pebbles

Fox, 1966. (C-179m.) Dir: Robert Wise. Sp: Robert Anderson, b/o novel by Richard McKenna. Cast: Steve McQueen, Richard

Attenborough, Richard Crenna, Candice Bergen, Mako, Marayat Andriane, Simon Oakland, Larry Gates, Gavin MacLeod.

On-Screen: *A sailor becomes embroiled in a Chinese revolution.* The unusual historical setting, and Steve McQueen's fine performance, are the principal virtues of this overlong but well-produced film. In China of 1926, the Nationalist Revolution led by Chiang Kai-shek is causing an upheaval throughout the country. Cruising down the Yangtze River, the U.S. gunboat *San Pablo* (nicknamed the *Sand Pebbles*) tries to follow the American policy of neutrality but finds itself drawn inexorably into the violence. Steve McQueen plays Jake Holman, a cynical, disaffected sailor aboard the ship. A capable actor who was able to project considerable feeling behind his laid-back style, McQueen frequently keeps the movie from sagging. A subplot involving sailor Attenborough's tragic romance with a Chinese girl (Andriane) is overly reminiscent of *Sayonara* and *South Pacific*. Although the time and setting are distant, *The Sand Pebbles* is clearly intended to relate to the Vietnam War by making the point that only devastating results can be expected when America, in an effort to protect its interests and its citizens, becomes involved in a foreign country's political turmoil.

Off-Screen: After months of negotiation, the producers were given permission—the first ever—to film in Taiwan. Taiwan's port of Keelung had to be extensively rebuilt to resemble Shanghai in the twenties. Most of the junks on the Yangtze River had to be built to order. There was some trouble with the Chinese extras. One spoiled a scene by flashing a silver wristwatch, and the permanent waves of many female extras had to be

straightened out. *The Sand Pebbles* received seven Oscar nominations, including Best Picture, but won no awards.

Sands of Iwo Jima

Republic, 1949. (110m.) Dir: Allan Dwan. Sp: Harry Brown and James Edward Grant, b/o story by Harry Brown. Cast: John Wayne, John Agar, Adele Mara, Forrest Tucker, Wally Cassell, James Brown, Richard Webb, Arthur Franz, Julie Bishop.

On-Screen: *A squad of marines in World War II.* Made four years after the end of World War II, this movie continued to reflect the jingoistic attitude that prevailed during the war. John Wayne, in his first Oscar-nominated performance, stars as John Stryker, a tough but ultimately sympathetic sergeant who leads his squad of marines through major Pacific battles, especially the pivotal battle on Iwo Jima. The other characters are worn clichés out of every World War II movie, and their dialogue induces more than a few winces. The enemy soldiers—or "Nips"—are called "lemon-colored characters," and a mortally wounded marine finds the time to say, "I'll get a good night's sleep tonight!" The wisecracks turn up even in the heat of battle ("Sure ain't like Brooklyn!"). Some good documentary footage is folded into the movie-made sequences, but as a view of what war is really like, *Sands of Iwo Jima* is not four decades removed from *Platoon* but eons.

Off-Screen: Thousands of California-based marines took part in the battle sequences. In the concluding scene, duplicating that celebrated moment when marines raised the American flag on Mt. Suribachi, three of the marines shown were actually involved: Rene A. Gagnon, Ira H. Hayes, and John J. Bradley. Hayes's story as an American Indian was told in *The Outsider* (1961), with Tony Curtis. Mt. Suribachi was actually an artillery observation post at Camp Pendleton.

Saturday Night Fever

Paramount, 1977. (C-119m.) Dir: John Badham. Sp: Norman Wexler, b/o story by Nik Cohn. Cast: John Travolta, Karen Lynn Gorney, Barry Miller, Donna Pescow, Joseph Cali, Julie Bovasso.

On-Screen: *John Travolta's electrifying big-screen film debut.* You'll succumb willingly to disco fever, at least while you're watching handsome Tony Manero (Travolta), paint-store clerk by day, strutting dance king at night as he burns up the floor at the 2001 Odyssey dance palace. There are enough subplots for a couple of movies in this one—a gang war and a suicide, for starters. Mainly, though, it's about how Tony comes of age after meeting Stephanie (Gorney), his more worldly dance partner. Through her, he comes to learn there's more to life than dancing Saturday nights away as a temporary escape from his drab Brooklyn existence. Chances are that the movie's melodramatic and sentimental flourishes will fade from memory, but you'll never forget Travolta's white-suited, black-shirted teenage terpsichorean tornado.

Off-Screen: The screenplay was inspired by "Tribal Rites of the New Saturday Night," Cohn's article that appeared in *New York* magazine in 1976. To producer Stigwood, Travolta seemed a natural to play Tony in

Wexler's fictionalized version of the article, having recently played the rambunctious Vinnie Barbarino in the television sitcom "Welcome Back, Kotter." In his first starring screen role, Travolta gave such a stunning performance that he earned an Oscar nomination as Best Actor. A sound-track album containing songs by the Bee Gees sold a staggering 35 million copies. In 1983, actor Sylvester Stallone directed Travolta in *Staying Alive,* a disappointing sequel. (CFB)

Save the Tiger

Paramount, 1973. (C-101m.) Dir: John G. Avildsen. Sp: Steve Shagan. Cast: Jack Lemmon, Jack Gilford, Patricia Smith, Laurie Heineman, Normann Burton, William Hansen, Thayer David, Harvey Jason, Lara Parker.

On-Screen: *Jack Lemmon's Oscar as an anguished businessman.* Jack Lemmon's comic persona (*The Odd Couple, The Prisoner of Second Avenue,* etc.) has often been that of the dithering urbanite at the end of a very short rope. In *Save the Tiger,* he tilted the same persona in the direction of drama and won a Best Actor Academy Award. He plays Harry Stoner, a weary, despairing clothing manufacturer whose business is collapsing. Against the wishes of his ethical partner (Gilford), he hires a professional arsonist to burn down his plant. All the while he is obsessed by recollections of a past when life was simpler and happier. Lemmon gets several bravura scenes, designed for emotional impact; instead they are distressingly awkward, and one, in which he falls apart while addressing his customers at his annual show, is embarrassing but not in the way intended. That wonderful actor Jack Gilford does a memorable turn as the one oasis of morality amid all the corruption.

Off-Screen: After the script was rejected by many studios as too downbeat, Paramount finally agreed to underwrite the movie, but at a low $1 million budget. Lemmon waived his fee, working instead for minimum scale. The actor's comment: "The best part I've ever had, and the best film I've ever done." Jack Gilford received a Best Supporting Actor nomination for his performance. Steve Shagan's screenplay was also nominated.

Sayonara

Warners, 1957. (C-147m.) Dir: Joshua Logan. Sp: Paul Osborn, b/o novel by James Michener. Cast: Marlon Brando, Miiko Taka, James Garner, Red Buttons, Miyoshi Umeki, Ricardo Montalban, Patricia Owens, Kent Smith, Martha Scott.

On-Screen: *Air force major falls for Japanese entertainer.* Undeniably scenic (it won an Oscar for Art Direction/Set Decoration), *Sayonara* adapts James Michener's novel into a romantic and sometimes touching story of an air force major (Brando), ordinarily a by-the-book career officer, who comes to Japan and finds himself falling in love with a beautiful and renowned Japanese actress/dancer (Taka). The off-limits romance spells deep trouble. A subplot involves an enlisted man (Buttons) and his Japanese bride (Umeki), and its tragic resolution sparks the major's ultimate decision. Sporting a corn-pone accent, Brando gives a persuasive performance, and the desperate plight of Buttons and Umeki (both actors winning Supporting Oscars) is genuinely affecting. Yet Joshua Logan directs rather indifferently, so that the film is never as in-volving as intended. There are some fringe benefits in the views of the colorful Japanese theater, but *Sayonara* is not much more than *Madame Butterfly* with a happy ending.

Off-Screen: Audrey Hepburn turned down the role played by Miiko Taka. Taka, a Seattle-born nisei, was discovered working for a travel agency in Los Angeles. The production was beset with problems from the start, not only from objections by U.S. military personnel and the Japanese government, but also from mechanical failures on location. Also, Marlon Brando rewrote the screenplay extensively, but most of his suggestions were discarded. The film won ten Oscar nominations (including Best Picture and Best Actor). The title song was written by Irving Berlin.

Scarface

United Artists, 1932. (90m.) Dir: Howard Hawks. Sp: Seton I. Miller, John Lee Mahin, and W. R. Burnett, b/o story by Ben Hecht and novel by Armitage Trail. Cast: Paul Muni, Ann Dvorak, George Raft, Boris Karloff, Karen Morley, Vince Barnett, Osgood Perkins, C. Henry Gordon.

On-Screen: *The rise and fall of mobster Tony Camonte.* One of the classic gangster movies of the early thirties, *Scarface* still retains its raw power after more than six decades. Paul Muni pulls out all stops as Tony Camonte, a swaggering, simianlike gangster who murders his way to the top and dies on the gallows, a pathetic figure who loved only one person in his life, his sister Cesca (Dvorak). The brutal killings, many executed in boldly expressionistic style, and the strong hint of incest in Tony's feelings for Cesca, created a storm of protest when the film was released. With his facial scar, coarse Italian-immigrant's manner, and love of Italian opera, Tony bears an obvious resemblance to "Scarface" Al Capone, but Muni makes the character his own. Most memorable sequence: the execution of gangster Boris Karloff in a bowling alley. For all of its primitive style, *Scarface* is still a riveting crime film.

Off-Screen: Produced by an eccentric young millionaire named Howard Hughes, *Scarface* was filmed in 1930, but its release was held up by censorship. The Hays Office insisted on a great many cuts and changes, including the ending now seen. (Originally, Camonte, a blubbering coward after the death of his sister, was shot down in the street.) The censors also demanded the addition of a subtitle—*The Shame of the Nation.* George Raft, playing Tony's top henchman, won stardom with his coin-flipping routine, which was suggested by Howard Hawks. Brian De Palma remade the movie atrociously in 1983.

Scarlet Street

Universal, 1946. (103m.) Dir: Fritz Lang. Sp: Dudley Nichols, b/o novel and play by Georges de la Fourcharliere. Cast: Edward G. Robinson, Joan Bennett, Dan Duryea, Margaret Lindsay, Rosalind Ivan.

On-Screen: *Edward G. Robinson is propelled into a world of deception and murder.* After the success of *The Woman in the Window* (1945), the stars and director of that movie were reunited (at another studio) for this steamy *film noir.* Robinson is a meek, unhappily married clerk (and Sunday painter) who falls into the clutches of seductive Joan Bennett and her sadistic boyfriend, Dan Dur-

yea. Taunted beyond endurance, he finally kills Bennett, but Duryea is charged with the murder and executed. Robinson becomes a guilt-ridden derelict, unable to identify himself as the artist of now highly valued paintings. *Scarlet Street* is not as persuasive as *The Woman in the Window,* but its doom-laden Langian atmosphere is still compelling. Coming full circle from his early gangster roles, Edward G. Robinson is superb as the hapless clerk drawn into the spider's web.

Off-Screen: Because the main character is not prosecuted, the censors were unhappy, until it was pointed out that he does suffer for his sins. The paintings in the film were done by John Decker, an artist who was one of the rowdy friends of Errol Flynn, W. C. Fields, and John Barrymore (Gene Fowler wrote about his life in *Minutes of the Last Meeting*). The story of *Scarlet Street* was filmed before by French director Jean Renoir as *La Chienne* (1931).

Scent of a Woman

Universal, 1992. (C-149m.) Dir: Martin Brest. Sp: Bo Goldman. Cast: Al Pacino, Chris O'Donnell, James Rebhorn, Gabrielle Anwar, Philip S. Hoffman, Richard Venture, Bradley Whitford, Rochelle Oliver.

On-Screen: *Peak Pacino.* Corrosively bitter and blinded in an accident caused by his own stupidity, Lieut. Col. Frank Slade (Pacino) has his private agenda: to spend a totally pleasurable weekend in New York City, then take his own life. Accompanying him is young Charlie Simms (O'Donnell), a student at a snobbish New England prep school, who has his own serious problem with honor and betrayal at the school. The outcome, for both Slade and Charlie, is entirely predictable, and the movie takes too long to reach its inevitable yet bogus feel-good ending. But there's a huge bonus, and it makes *Scent of a Woman* (a dreadful title) well worth viewing. Al Pacino's performance as Slade is his best to date: an electrifying combination of vitriol, arrogance, and pain. Watching him as he mocks a niece and her family, with whom he lives, or dances the tango with a beautiful young woman (Anwar) he meets in a chance encounter, we see this intense actor at the peak of his powers. Chris O'Donnell's role is essentially as straight man to Pacino's withering broadsides, but he turns Charlie Simms into a likable and sympathetic figure. *Scent of a Woman* occasionally strains credulity (a blind man driving a Ferrari through the streets of New York?), but Pacino succeeds in making it all worthwhile.

Off-Screen: Al Pacino's performance earned him a long-overdue Oscar as Best Actor. The movie received three other nominations: for Best Picture, Best Director, and Best Adapted Screenplay.

The Sea Hawk

Warners, 1940. (127m.) Dir: Michael Curtiz. Sp: Howard Koch and Seton I. Miller, b/o novel by Rafael Sabatini. Cast: Errol Flynn, Brenda Marshall, Claude Rains, Donald Crisp, Flora Robson, Alan Hale, Henry Daniell, Gilbert Roland.

On-Screen: *Errol Flynn at a swashbuckling peak.* Once again, dashing, daring, devil-may-care Flynn leaps into the fray to save England and its royalty. Here he plays Geoffrey Thorpe, a marauding privateer in the service of Elizabeth I (Robson) who rescues England from invasion by the Spanish Armada. As in Flynn's first major film, *Captain Blood* (1935), Curtiz crowds the screen with action—sea battles, duels, romance, all to Erich Wolfgang Korngold's stirring music. Watch especially for the first lusty sea battle in which Thorpe takes over a Spanish ship, and the sequence in which Thorpe and his men are ambushed by the Spaniards in a Panama swamp. As Queen Elizabeth, Robson contributes a fiery performance. One of Flynn's most popular films, *The Sea Hawk* was also a timely reminder (in 1940) of the dangers of appeasing a potential enemy.

Off-Screen: Much more elaborately produced than *Captain Blood,* this film required construction of two full-scale square-rigged ships, as well as use of the studio's enormous, newly built indoor tank to float them in. Barely detectable are brief inserts of sea-battle footage from the two versions of *Captain Blood* (the first in 1924) and an earlier *The Sea Hawk* (1924). Also utilized were costly sets, props, and costumes created for *The Private Lives of Elizabeth and Essex* (1939). Relying very little on the Sabatini novel, writer Koch based his story instead on an unproduced screenplay by Miller, concerning the exploits of a character inspired by the real-life Sir Francis Drake. (CFB)

The Sea Wolf

Warners, 1941. (90m.) Dir: Michael Curtiz. Sp: Robert Rossen, b/o novel by Jack London. Cast: Edward G. Robinson, Ida Lupino, John Garfield, Alexander Knox, Barry Fitzgerald, Gene Lockhart, Stanley Ridges.

On-Screen: *A brutish captain tyrannizes his ship.* Jack London's novel has been filmed many times, but this version is the best: a grim and often powerful tale of Wolf Larsen, the captain who controls his ship with an iron hand, and whose belief in his own godlike superiority ultimately spells his doom. Alexander Knox is the writer and accidental passenger who matches wits with Larsen, and John Garfield and Ida Lupino are the lovers—he a seaman, she a fugitive from the law—who try to free themselves from Larsen's grip. This time around, the malevolent Larsen is clearly meant to suggest the sort of totalitarian personality who was ravaging Europe in the early forties, but the message is not pressed unduly, and director Curtiz concentrates on the seaborne action and on Robinson's forceful portrayal of Larsen. The actor succeeds in turning a potential monster into a believable if not sympathetic human being.

Off-Screen: A production of *The Sea Wolf* was planned back in 1937, with Paul Muni as Wolf Larsen, but it was canceled. George Raft rejected the role that John Garfield played. Jack Warner wanted to change the film's title to *The Law of the Sea,* but after many back-and-forth memorandums, the original title was retained. Remakes of the durable story include *Barricade* (1950) and *Wolf Larsen* (1958), and a 1993 television version.

The Search

MGM, 1948. (105m.) Dir: Fred Zinnemann. Sp: Richard Schweizer, in collaboration with David Wechsler. Cast: Montgomery Clift, Ivan Jandl, Jarmila Novotna, Aline MacMahon, Wendell Corey.

On-Screen: *A mother searches for her son in post-war Europe.* The tragic plight of displaced children in a war-ravaged Europe was seldom dramatized with greater poignancy than in Fred Zinnemann's film. Montgomery Clift stars as the young soldier who finds and "adopts" a Czech boy (Jandl) who has been separated from his mother. Meanwhile, his mother (Novotna) searches tirelessly for her son. Filmed against a background of the actual ruins, the film conveys the heartbreak and the desperation of parents and children caught up in the backwash of a terrible war. Clift, Novotna, and Aline MacMahon (as a compassionate woman helping the children) are all fine, but it is little Ivan Jandl, with his frightened eyes and timid manner, who carries most of the emotional weight on his frail shoulders. He was awarded a special Oscar for his performance, and an Academy Award also went to Schweizer and Wechsler for Best Motion Picture Story. Clift and Zinnemann were nominated.

Off-Screen: To prepare for his role, Montgomery Clift lived in an army engineer's unit outside Zurich, dressing in army fatigues and developing a soldier's gait. With Zinnemann he also toured the U.N. Relief and Rehabilitation camps in Germany, meeting some of the homeless Jewish children. He also fought often and bitterly with producer Lazar Wechsler, father of the cowriter, about his proposed changes in the screenplay. Paul Jarrico contributed additional dialogue.

The Searchers

Warners, 1956. (C-119m.) Dir: John Ford. Sp: Frank S. Nugent, b/o novel by Alan

LeMay. Cast: John Wayne, Jeffrey Hunter, Vera Miles, Ward Bond, Natalie Wood, Harry Carey, Jr., Olive Carey, Antonio Moreno, Hank Worden, Henry Brandon, Lana Wood.

On-Screen: *John Ford's towering western of one man's obsessive search*. A classic western drama, arguably John Ford's finest in the genre, *The Searchers* is a richly textured film that warrants repeated scrutiny. John Wayne excels as Ethan Edwards, a lone Texan who discovers his brother's family murdered by Indians, then sets out to find his kidnapped nieces. With a mission that combines revenge, shattered family ties, and a hatred born of bigotry, Ethan finds himself undergoing a voyage of self-discovery, a search for inner peace. When he discovers that his surviving niece (Wood) has become an Indian squaw, he must make the most wrenching decision of his life. Beautifully photographed by Winton C. Hoch, *The Searchers* has its full share of western action, but the characters are unusually complex, and some sequences have a haunting power rare in westerns. John Wayne gives one of his finest performances as Ethan—he projects a man who can never be part of civilization, a loner whose anguish and shifting attitudes are reflected in his craggy face. Those who downgrade westerns should watch *The Searchers,* more than once.

Off-Screen: John Wayne believed that *The Searchers* was John Ford's best film, "a story of the harsh reality of the West, where you're faced with a real enemy." Ford had two units on the film—one photographed seasonal footage; the other worked in Monument Valley, where the cast and crew were plagued by 115-degree temperatures, summer sandstorms, and driving winds. Yet Ford loved it all—he was at his favorite location, surrounded by actors and technicians he admired. The movie has been remade or imitated many times, but never matched.

Separate Tables

United Artists, 1958. (99m.) Dir: Delbert Mann. Sp: Terence Rattigan and John Gay, b/o play by Terence Rattigan. Cast: Burt Lancaster, Rita Hayworth, David Niven, Deborah Kerr, Wendy Hiller, Gladys Cooper, Felix Aylmer, Cathleen Nesbitt, Rod Taylor, Audrey Dalton, May Hallatt.

On-Screen: *Life at a British resort hotel*. Onstage in 1954, Terence Rattigan's *Separate Tables* provided an acting exercise for two British actors, Margaret Leighton and Eric Portman, in which they undertook different roles in two separate plays set at the same resort hotel. The film version eliminated the gimmick and cast four leading film stars in the roles. The result was a much smoother work in a familiar *Grand Hotel* vein. The private lives of a group of people are revealed during their stay at the genteel Beauregard Hotel on the south coast of England. Lancaster is an alcoholic journalist, Hayworth is his glamorous but secretly lonely ex-wife, and their love-hate relationship is not exactly absorbing. Best are David Niven as a blustering, bogus British major whose dirty little secret scandalizes the guests, and Deborah Kerr as an overwrought spinster dominated by her snobbish mother (Cooper). Their hesitant but deep compassion for each other's plight is handled with sensitivity. Wendy Hiller is the proprietor of the hotel and Lancaster's mistress. The ending, in which all the guests except Cooper rally around the major, is heartwarming but as bogus as his character.

Off-Screen: The film began shooting with Laurence Olivier, as director and star, playing both male roles and then-wife Vivien Leigh costarring in both female roles. The studio wanted more bankable stars in the film and signed David Niven and Deborah Kerr for two of the roles. Olivier and Leigh quit in anger, and their roles went to Burt Lancaster and Rita Hayworth. It's fair to say that there are other versions of what happened. The climactic scene referred to above took four days to shoot, and when it was completed, the cast applauded Niven. The movie won a Best Picture Oscar nomination, and Academy Awards went to Niven (Best Actor) and to Hiller (Best Supporting Actress). Kerr was nominated as Best Actress.

Sergeant York

Warners, 1941. (134m.) Dir: Howard Hawks. Sp: John Huston, Harry Chandlee, Howard Koch, and Abem Finkel, b/o diary of Sergeant York, edited by Tom Skeyhill. Cast: Gary Cooper, Joan Leslie, Walter Brennan, Margaret Wycherly, George Tobias, Ward Bond, Howard da Silva.

On-Screen: *Gary Cooper portrays the World War I hero.* At a time when America's entry into World War II was imminent, Warner Bros. lost not a minute in turning out a rousing, patriotic tribute to Alvin York, one of the heroes of the First World War. In an Oscar-winning performance, Gary Cooper plays York as a deeply religious young Tennessee farm boy who discards his pacifist beliefs in the heat of battle. Under fire, he destroys or captures an entire German battalion single-handed. ("There weren't nothin' to do but stop those guns.") Despite the corn-pone dialogue, the first and better part offers a finely detailed if highly idealized view of rural life; the film becomes less persuasive when it dramatizes York's conversion to a hard-fighting soldier who shoots men with impunity. Best moment: As York returns from the war, his mother (Wycherly) greets him taciturnly, only her eyes expressing joy and relief.

Off-Screen: Since Sergeant York's early life was undramatic, the writers took liberties with his backwoods rearing and his courtship of a neighbor girl. When Gary Cooper was reluctant to play a conscientious objector (albeit later hero), producer Jesse Lasky faked a telegram from York himself, urging him to take the role. ("I have great admiration for you as an actor and as a man.") The movie received ten Oscar nominations, but Cooper and editor William Holmes were the only winners.

Serpico

Paramount, 1973. (C-129m.) Dir: Sidney Lumet. Sp: Waldo Salt and Norman Wexler, b/o book by Peter Maas. Cast: Al Pacino, John Randolph, Jack Kehoe, Biff McGuire, Barbara Eda-Young, Tony Roberts, Lewis J. Stadlen, F. Murray Abraham, M. Emmet Walsh.

On-Screen: *The painful true odyssey of an honest cop.* It all actually happened: Frank "Paco" Serpico, a dedicated and conscientious New York cop, not only refused to conform in his dress or behavior but also blew the whistle on the rampant corruption in the police force. His reward: isolation, hostility from his fellow policemen, and a nearly fatal gunshot wound in his head. (He did testify before the Knapp Commission investigating police corruption.) Relating this sorry true tale, director Lumet displays his usual skill at depicting the violence and disorientation of urban life. He also finds his ideal actor in Al Pacino, whose intense, feverish Serpico is the only fully developed character in the movie. Serpico's dedication to being a good and honest cop seems to be the sole propelling force of his life. When he learns that the sleazy character he has arrested is a "friend" of his precinct, his rage almost shatters the screen. (Two years later, Lumet and Pacino would reunite for the excellent *Dog Day Afternoon*.)

Off-Screen: John G. Avildsen was first hired to direct, but he quit after quarreling with the producers. Sidney Lumet replaced him. Playwright Sidney Kingsley's New York loft was used for a party scene in the film. Frank Serpico found his way to the small screen, first in a made-for-television movie, *Serpico: The Deadly Game* (1976), with David Birney as Serpico, and then as a short-lived television series (1976–77), with Birney again in the role.

The Set-Up

RKO, 1949. (72m.) Dir: Robert Wise. Sp: Art Cohn, b/o poem by Joseph Moncure March. Cast: Robert Ryan, Audrey Totter, George Tobias, Alan Baxter, Wallace Ford, Percy Helton, Darryl Hickman.

On-Screen: *A washed-up boxer faces his greatest challenge.* One of the best boxing films ever made, Robert Wise's compact little drama has several unusual aspects. For one, it is based on a narrative poem by Joseph Moncure March; for another, it takes place in real time, as indicated by the opening and closing shots. That splendid actor Robert

Ryan plays Stoker Thompson, a has-been boxer who defies a kingpin gangster (Baxter) by refusing to take a fall. Still believing that he is "one punch away" from the big time, he endures a brutal beating in the ring to win the fight. His dignity and pride intact, he faces the consequences of his act. Obviously made on a tiny budget, *The Set-Up* relies heavily on Milton Krasner's moody photography to suggest the sleazy corruption of the fight game at its lowest ebb. Audrey Totter is touching in the cliché role of Stoker's worried, resilient wife.

Off-Screen: Robert Ryan actually boxed, undefeated, during his four years at Dartmouth College. At a seminar for student filmmakers in 1980, director Wise noted, "I don't know how many people know that the base material for *The Set-Up* is a poem. I find that to be most interesting and unusual. It was a long narrative poem by Joseph Moncure March. He wrote two outstanding things in the late twenties; one was *The Set-Up*, which was a poem that tells very much our story, except that it was a black fighter in the poem. The other was *The Wild Party*, which is an extraordinary work about a party in Greenwich Village during Prohibition." *The Wild Party* was filmed in 1975.

Seven Brides for Seven Brothers

MGM, 1954. (C-103m.) Dir: Stanley Donen. Sp: Albert Hackett, Frances Goodrich, and Dorothy Kingsley, b/o story by Stephen Vincent Benet. MS: Johnny Mercer and Gene dePaul. Cast: Jane Powell, Howard Keel, Jeff Richards, Russ Tamblyn, Tommy Rall, Virginia Gibson, Julie Newmeyer, Marc Platt, Matt Mattox.

On-Screen: *Seven backwoods brothers go a-courtin' in this MGM musical.* Dancing—skillful, energetic dancing staged by Michael Kidd—is the keynote to the success of this delightful musical. Based on Stephen Vincent Benet's story "The Sobbin' Women," the film stars Howard Keel as a rugged Oregon farmer who takes Jane Powell as his wife and then persuades his six lonesome brothers to marry also, only by force. The brothers abduct six town girls they just happen to love and hold them prisoner for the winter. By spring thaw, a group wedding is in the offing. This rather dubious plot is only needed to support the spirited and engaging musical numbers, built around such songs as "Wonderful, Wonderful Day" and "Goin' Courtin'." Since the roles of the rambunctious brothers were filled mostly by professional dancers, the dance routines could hardly be bettered. Wait especially for the celebrated barn-raising sequence, a breathtaking display of acrobatics and ballet.

Off-Screen: Actress Julie Newmeyer later changed her name to Newmar and appeared in Broadway shows, several other movies, and on television, notably as Catwoman on the "Batman" series. Dancer Marc Platt had made an impressive debut a decade earlier in *Tonight and Every Night* (1944), but then had few opportunities to shine until this film. The movie, the screenplay, the cinematography, and the editing won Oscar nominations, and Adolph Deutsch and Saul Chaplin were awarded statuettes for Best Scoring of a Musical Picture. A stage adaptation had a brief Broadway run in 1982.

Seven Days in May

Paramount, 1964. (118m.) Dir: John Frankenheimer. Sp: Rod Serling, b/o novel by Fletcher Knebel and Charles W. Bailey II. Cast: Burt Lancaster, Kirk Douglas, Ava Gardner, Fredric March, Edmond O'Brien, Martin Balsam, George Macready, Hugh Marlowe, Whit Bissell, John Houseman.

On-Screen: *High-tension melodrama about a Washington conspiracy.* Query: What are the insidious plans of popular air force general James M. Scott (Lancaster) and his cohorts? The shocking answer: to forcibly seize control of the government on a certain day in May. (They fear the consequences of a nuclear disarmament treaty with Russia.) Based on the best-selling novel, *Seven Days in May* relates the development of the conspiracy, its detection by an air force colonel (Douglas), and its ultimate collapse. Rod Serling's crisp, intelligent screenplay not only fulfills all the suspenseful possibilities of the concept but also adds a few sobering comments on the nuclear age. Happily, the preconceptions of the plot no longer apply, but the movie works as nail-biting apocalyptic fiction of a high order. It is also acted impressively by a cast that includes Fredric March as the troubled president, Ava Gardner as a Washington hostess, and Edmond O'Brien as a senator. Producer–director John Houseman makes his acting debut in a small role.

Off-Screen: President Kennedy cooperated with the producers of the film by leaving the White House for his Hyannisport retreat while the company was shooting a scene in front of the presidential residence. The Pentagon would not cooperate since Frankenheimer refused to show them an advance screenplay. The movie upset many conservatives, and it was attacked on the floor of the House of Representatives by several congressmen.

The Seven Year Itch

Fox, 1955. (C-105m.) Dir: Billy Wilder. Sp: George Axelrod, b/o his play. Cast: Marilyn Monroe, Tom Ewell, Evelyn Keyes, Sonny Tufts, Victor Moore, Oscar Homolka, Doro Merande, Carolyn Jones.

On-Screen: *A summer bachelor indulges his fantasies.* A Broadway success in 1952, *The Seven Year Itch* came to the screen three years later as a vehicle for Marilyn Monroe. It was never more than an amusing conceit, but coarsened and vulgarized en route to film, it now seems like a magnified locker-room joke. Tom Ewell repeats his stage role as a New York publisher whose family leaves for the summer. His incessant sexual fantasies suddenly lurch toward reality when a wildly sexy but light-headed blonde (Monroe) turns up as his upstairs neighbor. She now figures in his guilt-ridden fantasies, but (surprise!) nothing really happens between them. And when he acts on his delusions about his wife (Keyes), he simply makes a fool of himself. *The Seven Year Itch* may pass muster as the study of an infantile middle-aged man with an overactive imagination. As comedy, however, the film is worthless—astonishingly so when you consider that the director is that master of acerbic wit, Billy Wilder.

Off-Screen: Billy Wilder's first choice for the leading role was Walter Matthau, but he was overruled by Darryl F. Zanuck, who insisted on Tom Ewell. Ewell, he claimed, already had some film experience (*Adam's Rib,* 1949; *Up Front,* 1951; etc.), while Matthau was just beginning his film career. The famous "skirt scene" was filmed in New York City at Fifty-second Street and Lexington Avenue, in front of the Trans-Lux Theatre sometime after two A.M.

The Seven-Per-Cent Solution

Universal, 1976. (C-113m.) Dir: Herbert Ross. Sp: Nicholas Meyer, b/o his novel. Cast: Nicol Williamson, Alan Arkin, Robert Duvall, Vanessa Redgrave, Joel Gray, Charles Gray, Georgia Brown, Samantha Eggar, Jeremy Kemp.

On-Screen: *Sherlock Holmes and Sigmund Freud team up for a case.* "In 1891, Sherlock Holmes was missing and presumed dead for three years. This is the true story of that disappearance. Only the facts have been made up." Thus begins Herbert Ross's stylish and fanciful movie, derived by Nicholas Meyer from his novel. Imagine illustrious detective Sherlock Holmes (Williamson) being lured to Vienna so that the eminent Sigmund Freud (Arkin) can cure him of his cocaine addiction. Then imagine the two men joining together to rescue a lady in distress (Redgrave) from a fate worse than death. It's all patently absurd, and in fact the movie shifts distractingly from serious drama (Holmes's drug-withdrawal nightmare) to tongue-in-cheek melodrama (How about Holmes dueling a villainous baron atop a speeding train?). Williamson and Arkin are good as the Daring Duo, but Robert Duvall's accent as Dr. Watson seems peculiarly off-center. Laurence Olivier makes a brief but notable appearance as a prissy old Professor Moriarty. Don't look for many of the usual Holmesian deductions, but the movie is diverting entertainment.

Off-Screen: *The Seven-Per-Cent-Solution* was shot in Vienna and in England's Pinewood Studios. Director Herbert Ross's comment in a *New York News* interview is worth quoting: "[The movie] will show all the characters before they became clichés. There isn't one single thing in it that will remind anyone of Basil Rathbone." "The Madame Song" ("I Never Do Anything Twice"), performed in a brothel, was written by Stephen Sondheim.

sex, lies, and videotape

Outlaw, 1989. (C-100m.) Dir: Steven Soderbergh. Sp: Steven Soderbergh. Cast: Peter Gallagher, Andie MacDowell, James Spader, Laura San Giacomo.

On-Screen: *The lives of four people are sexually intertwined.* A fascinating, elegantly made, but also rather remote and uninvolving film, *sex, lies, and videotape* created a stir on its release. The first feature by young writer-director Steven Soderbergh, it concerns two men and two women whose inability to express their true thoughts and feelings results in destructive lies and deceptions. John (Gallagher) is a selfish, affluent lawyer who is cheating on his repressed wife, Annie (MacDowell), with her brazen sister, Cynthia (San Giacomo). Enter Graham (Spader), an old college friend of John's, who claims to be impotent and who can only relate to women by taping them as they talk about their sexual experiences. He becomes the catalyst that changes their lives drastically. Much of the film's dialogue is witty and perceptive, and the performances by the four players cannot be faulted. Still, for all the sexual activity, there is little heat generated, and you may not care a whit about these characters and their obsessions.

Off-Screen: *sex, lies, and videotape* surprised the film world by winning the Best Film award at the 1989 Cannes Film Festival. James Spader was also named Best Actor. The movie's screenplay was nominated for an Oscar. Soderbergh, a native of Louisiana, wrote the screenplay while traveling to Los Angeles to seek a place in film. The movie was shot in Baton Rouge.

Shadow of a Doubt

Universal, 1943. (108m.) Dir: Alfred Hitchcock. Sp: Thornton Wilder, Sally Benson, and Alma Reville, b/o story by Gordon McDonell. Cast: Teresa Wright, Joseph Cotten, Macdonald Carey, Patricia Collinge, Henry Travers, Hume Cronyn, Wallace Ford, Edna May Wonacott.

On-Screen: *A young girl suspects her beloved uncle of being a killer.* One of Alfred Hitchcock's personal favorites among his films, *Shadow of a Doubt* delineates (perhaps more than any of his other movies) his central theme of the dual nature of man, and the close linkage between good and evil. A brilliant nailbiter, the movie concerns a naive small-town girl (Wright) who must cope with the devastating knowledge that her dearly loved uncle (Cotten)—they are both named Charlie—is the sinister Merry Widow murderer sought by the police. Hitchcock disturbs us with his vision of the dark underside in the placid California town of Santa Rosa, and he rivets our attention with superbly handled sequences, such as a family dinner that turns chilling when Uncle Charlie reflects on his victims. At the film's end, young Charlie has come full circle from sunny innocence to threatened violence, and so has the viewer. A parable of paradise lost and innocence destroyed, *Shadow of a Doubt* is a stunning entry from the master of suspense.

Off-Screen: The story was based on a real-life Merry Widow murderer named Earle Leonard Nelson, a mass strangler of the twenties. Thornton Wilder's screenplay was reworked by Sally Benson and Alma Reville (Ms. Hitchcock), and then some uncredited finishing touches were made during the filming by Patricia Collinge, who plays young Charlie's mother. Young Charlie's kid sister was played by a nonprofessional Santa Rosa girl named Edna May Wonacott. Teresa Wright received a Best Actress Oscar nomination. The story was remade in 1958 as *Step Down to Terror,* and on television in 1991, under its original title.

Shadows and Fog

Orion, 1992. (86m.) Dir: Woody Allen. Sp: Woody Allen. Cast: Woody Allen, Mia Farrow, Jodie Foster, John Cusack, Kathy Bates, Madonna, John Malkovich, Julie Kavner, Lily Tomlin, Kenneth Mars, Kate Nelligan, Donald Pleasence, Fred Gwynne, David Ogden Stiers.

On-Screen: *Woody Allen takes on Kafka—but why?* Part pastiche of German expressionist movies, part mystery thriller with comic patches, and all vanity film, *Shadows and Fog* is a Woody Allen misfire. In a town in (presumably) Eastern Europe, Kleinman (Allen) is taken from his home during a fog-ridden night to join in the hunt for a serial killer. A stammering, Kafkaesque ninny ("Why me? Where *is* everybody?"), Kleinman is badgered, humiliated, and threatened by everyone he meets except a group of raucous prostitutes. During the night he befriends Irmy (Farrow), a sword-swallower with a traveling circus who is fleeing her cheating lover (Malkovich). The cast is studded with well-known names who have little more than walk-on roles, and the black-and-white photography is highly evocative. The total effect is baffling, irri-

tating, and ultimately tiresome, a nightmare comedy that lacks the terror of a nightmare and the laughs of a comedy. All that remains is Allen's self-indulgence.

Off-Screen: The film was shot entirely in New York City, despite the Old World atmosphere of narrow cobblestone streets, gaslights, and arched bridges. Kurt Weill's score adds some badly needed flavor to the movie. *Shadows and Fog* had its world premiere in Paris.

Shall We Dance

RKO, 1937. (116m.) Dir: Mark Sandrich. Sp: Allan Scott and Ernest Pagano, b/o story by Lee Loeb and Harold Buchman. MS: George and Ira Gershwin. Cast: Fred Astaire, Ginger Rogers, Edward Everett Horton, Eric Blore, Jerome Cowan, Harriet Hoctor.

On-Screen: *Ginger, Fred, and the Gershwins.* Even a lesser Astaire-Rogers musical is superior to most others. Witness *Shall We Dance,* an often delightful and always tuneful confection featuring a lovely score by George and Ira Gershwin. This time the plot is even sillier than usual—ballet star Astaire and musical comedy queen Rogers must pretend to be married—and the comedy elements are a little tiresome. However, most of the musical numbers are splendid, especially the team's dance to "They All Laughed," in which they demonstrate their matchless rapport and execute steps in an astonishing variety of styles. They also sing and dance on roller skates to the witty tune "Let's Call the Whole Thing Off," and in the engine room of a transatlantic ocean liner, Astaire diverts the stokers by executing an intricate tap routine to "Slap That Bass." Inexplicably, Astaire dances to the exquisite "They Can't Take That Away From Me" with a dancer named Harriet Hoctor rather than Rogers. Despite its shortcomings, *Shall We Dance* remains top-grade entertainment.

Off-Screen: Until late in production, the movie had the unfortunate title *Stepping Toes*. It's hard to imagine an Astaire-Rogers musical having trouble with the censors, but the Breen Office objected to the attempt to make comedy out of the suggestion—even the patently untrue suggestion—that the unmarried Rogers was pregnant. Breen considered this "highly offensive," but it remained in the plot.

Shampoo

Columbia, 1975. (C-109m.) Dir: Hal Ashby. Sp: Robert Towne and Warren Beatty. Cast: Warren Beatty, Julie Christie, Goldie Hawn, Lee Grant, Jack Warden, Carrie Fisher, Tony Bill.

On-Screen: *Warren Beatty leads a sexual roundelay in Beverly Hills* The time is 1968 on the eve of Richard Nixon's election. In the giddy whirl of activity in Beverly Hills, hairdresser George Roundy (Beatty) is used by his clients as a sounding board, confessor, and always available sexual partner. At the moment, the women in his life are pert Goldie Hawn, married Lee Grant, and his ex-lover Julie Christie. To complicate matters, Grant is married to Jack Warden, whose current mistress is Christie. Despite all the sexual games, *Shampoo* aims at being more than a bawdy farce. It is also a satirical comment on the rotting society of the late

sixties in which many people resided in a moral and emotional vacuum. George is at the vortex of this society: unfulfilled for all his sexual prowess, he ends up alone, deserted by everyone. *Shampoo* does not always succeed—it often presses too hard to make its points—but it rates a look as telling social commentary.

Off-Screen: Lee Grant won an Oscar as Best Supporting Actress for her performance as a sexually voracious Beverly Hills matron. Her blunt-speaking teenaged daughter is played by seventeen-year-old Carrie Fisher in her movie debut. Future television star Howard Hesseman has a walk-on in the film.

Shane

Paramount, 1953. (C-118m.) Dir: George Stevens. Sp: A. B. Guthrie, Jr., b/o novel by Jack Schaefer. Cast: Alan Ladd, Jean Arthur, Van Heflin, Brandon de Wilde, Jack Palance, Ben Johnson, Elisha Cook, Jr., Edgar Buchanan.

On-Screen: *A stalwart gunslinger defends homesteaders in a classic western.* Western purists of the grittier Ford-Hawks school may scoff at this idealized frontier drama (Alan Ladd as a knight in shining buckskin), but most viewers will be enthralled by its lavish view of the legendary West. Shane is the taciturn gunman who drifts into the home of the Starretts (Arthur, Heflin, and son de Wilde), then stays to help them defeat a powerful rancher and his murderous hoodlums. Seen through the eyes of young Joey Starrett, Shane becomes a Western prince, riding out of a mysterious past to defend and protect the homeless. Like Ford, director George

Stevens takes pleasure in depicting the rituals of Western life: a funeral, a Fourth of July party, quiet dinners in a simple home. A. B. Guthrie, Jr. enshrines these rituals in his screenplay, and Loyal Griggs's beautiful cinematography gives them all a lustrous sheen. Ladd's usual inexpressive acting works for him in the role of Shane, and Jack Palance is memorable as a cold-blooded killer in black.

Off-Screen: *Shane* was largely filmed in Jackson Hole, Wyoming, amid the beauty of Grand Teton National Park. The film garnered five Oscar nominations, including one for Best Picture, but only Loyal Griggs won for his cinematography. Oscar-nominated Jack Palance, who seemed to have been born to ride (see *City Slickers,* nearly four decades later), was actually nervous around horses and had to go through a great many takes before being able to mount or dismount them convincingly. *Shane* briefly became a television series in 1966.

Shanghai Express

Paramount, 1932. (80m.) Dir: Josef von Sternberg. Sp: Josef von Sternberg and Jules Furthman, b/o story by Harry Hervey. Cast: Marlene Dietrich, Clive Brook, Warner Oland, Anna May Wong, Eugene Pallette, Louise Closser Hale.

On-Screen: *Dietrich's Shanghai Lily rides the rails in strife-torn China.* One of the best-remembered of Marlene Dietrich's films, under the direction of her mentor, Josef von Sternberg, *Shanghai Express* may seem rather stale and musty today, but it still fascinates. Artfully photographed by Oscar-winner Lee Garmes, Dietrich plays a traveling trollop ("It took more than one man to change my name to Shanghai Lily") who is reunited with an old flame, British officer Clive Brook, on the train journey from Peiping to Shanghai. Also aboard are a Eurasian merchant (Oland) who turns out to be a revolutionary warlord, and a Chinese courtesan (Wong) with her own ideas about summary justice. The screenplay by Sternberg and Furthman is simultaneously absurd and intriguing, but mostly we remember the soulful close-ups of Dietrich trying to hide her pain and vulnerability as she sacrifices herself for a lost love. *Shanghai Express* may creak, but it's still worth the ride.

Off-Screen: Sternberg has asserted that the original treatment for *Shanghai Express* consisted of a single page written by Harry Hervey. In fact, Hervey wrote a twenty-two-page treatment containing some of the elements that appeared in the completed film. In his autobiography, Sternberg never mentions either Furthman's or Garmes's contributions to the movie. The film was remade in 1951 as *Peking Express,* with Corinne Calvet in the Dietrich role.

She Done Him Wrong

Paramount, 1933. (66m.) Dir: Lowell Sherman. Sp: Harvey Thew and John Bright, b/o play by Mae West. Cast: Mae West, Cary Grant, Gilbert Roland, Noah Beery, Rafaela Ottiano, Rochelle Hudson, David Landau.

On-Screen: *The inimitable Mae in her most famous role.* After creating a stir with her movie debut in *Night After Night* (1932), Mae West won her first starring role in this film. With her undulating hips and insinuating manner on full display, she repeated her stage role of Diamond Lil (here known as Lou), Queen of the Bowery, and by her own admission, "one of the finest women who ever walked the streets." Caught up in a melodramatic mix of passion, skulduggery, and murder, she tangles with her dangerous admirers and spars with an upright Salvation Army officer (Grant) who is not what he seems. Lou is West's first bold woman, an unabashed sexual aggressor who can look Grant up and down and ask him, "Why don't you come up sometime and see me? I'm home every evening." She also brays a few songs, including "I Wonder Where My Easy Rider's Gone." In all, she's audacious, very funny, and at the peak of her voluptuous form.

Off-Screen: Other titles that were considered for the film include *Diamond Lady, Honky Tonk,* and *Ruby Red.* Cary Grant's comments on Mae West were not always kind, but he did admit, "I learned everything from her. Well, no, not quite *everything,* but almost everything. She knows so much. Her instinct is so true, her timing so perfect, her grasp of the situation so right." West demanded approval of every scene or line that veered from her play, and there was constant battling over the screenplay, mostly with writer John Bright.

She Wore a Yellow Ribbon

RKO, 1949. (C-103m.) Dir: John Ford. Sp: Frank Nugent and Laurence Stallings. Cast: John Wayne, Joanne Dru, John Agar, Ben Johnson, Harry Carey, Jr., Victor McLaglen, Mildred Natwick, George O'Brien, Arthur Shields, Francis Ford.

On-Screen: *John Ford's heartfelt tribute to the U.S. cavalry.* One of John Ford's finest films, *She Wore a Yellow Ribbon* richly embodies his principal themes and attitudes. Drenched in reverence for the cavalrymen of the Old West, the movie stars John Wayne as Capt. Nathan Brittles, a tough, seasoned officer on the verge of enforced retirement. His final mission with the men who revere him ends in disaster, but in a war with hostile Indians, he leads them unofficially to a sweeping victory. This battle is the last in a series of climaxes that tumble one after the other in the movie's second half. Wayne plays Brittles as Ford's ultimate man of valor and honor, and a cast of Ford favorites supports him all the way. Winton C. Hoch's Oscar-winning photography captures the full scope and beauty of the director's beloved Monument Valley. Sentimental, yes, but also stirring, *She Wore a Yellow Ribbon* is a treat for western aficionados.

Off-Screen: Ford clashed often with his cinematographer Winton Hoch, who would fiddle endlessly with his camera while the cast waited under the blazing sun. Ford later told Peter Bogdanovich that he had modeled the physical look of the film on the Western paintings of Frederic Remington: "I tried to get his color and movement, and I think I succeeded partly."

The Shining

Warners, 1980. (C-142m.) Dir: Stanley Kubrick. Sp: Stanley Kubrick and Diane Johnston b/o novel by Stephen King. Cast: Jack Nicholson, Shelley Duvall, Danny Lloyd, Scatman Crothers, Barry Nelson, Philip Stone, Joe Turkel, Anne Jackson, Tony Burton.

On-Screen: *Stanley Kubrick's horrific haunted hotel.* Warning: Don't take a job as a winter caretaker at an isolated Colorado resort hotel. You may end up murderously stalking your terrified wife and son. Writer Jack Torrance (Nicholson) ignores this advice and pays the terrible price. Soon after arriving at the Overlook Hotel, he starts losing his mind, affected by a prior caretaker's slaughter of his family. In addition, Torrance's troubled young son, (Lloyd), is a clairvoyant frightened by visions involving the old murder. Adapted from Stephen King's novel, *The Shining* is intended as a stylish exercise in horror, and there are some nerve-racking scenes in the marvelous set of the hotel. But it goes on much too long, and by the time Torrance, grinning diabolically and loping through the hotel like some crazy Quasimodo, is chasing his hapless family, you may find yourself resisting the temptation to chuckle rather than scream. Both Nicholson and Duvall (as his horrified wife) try to make their absurd roles convincing, to no avail. Score one, however, for John Alcott's superb photography.

Off-Screen: The interiors were shot at Elstree Studios in North London. According to Jack Nicholson, it was his idea to say "Hereeeee's Johnny!" "Stanley [Kubrick] lives in England," he remarked, "so he really didn't know what it meant." Nicholson also claimed to have written the scene in which he becomes enraged when Duvall interrupts his work at the typewriter. It reflected an actual incident in his own life during his marriage to actress Sandra Knight.

Ship of Fools

Columbia, 1965. (149m.) Dir: Stanley Kramer. Sp: Abby Mann, b/o novel by Katherine Anne Porter. Cast: Vivien Leigh, Oskar Werner, Simone Signoret, Jose Ferrer, Lee Marvin, Jose Greco, George Segal, Elizabeth Ashley, Michael Dunn, Heinz Ruhmann, Lilia Skala.

On-Screen: *Floating "Grand Hotel."* This two-and-a-half-hour movie is long—much too long—on message. Still, you'll enjoy watching the stellar cast go through its paces as it travels from Vera Cruz to Bremerhaven. The time is the early thirties (just as Nazism is getting up to speed), the ship is German, and the passenger list is as varied an assemblage of "fools" as you're likely to meet. Leigh is a lonely divorcée (you may wince as the fragile actress gamely attempts the Charleston); Signoret, a shopworn countess and drug addict; Werner, the ship's doomed physician; Ferrer, a raucous anti-Semite; Segal and Ashley, a pair of lovers, Ruhmann, an unwisely optimistic Jew. Marvin plays the most interesting passenger of all, a bitterly disappointed professional ballplayer who's not good enough for the major leagues. A dwarf (Dunn) announces at the outset (and again at the end, should you miss the point) that not just the "tub" is loaded with fools.

Off-Screen: Published in 1962, Porter's novel is similar in its satirical intent to German moralist Sebastian Brant's famous allegory, *Das Narrenschiff* (1494), which attacked the vices and villainies of his time. When Katharine Hepburn turned down the role of the divorcée (Spencer Tracy was ill at the time), Leigh was engaged for the part, which marked that actress's final screen appearance. Though the movie, as well as Signoret, Werner, Dunn, and Mann were nominated for Oscars, the film's two awards were given for black-and-white art direction and for black-and-white cinematography (Ernest Laszlo). (CFB)

Shoot the Moon

MGM, 1982. (C-123m.) Dir: Alan Parker. Sp: Bo Goldman. Cast: Diane Keaton, Albert Finney, Karen Allen, Peter Weller, Dana Hill, Viveka Davis, Tracey Gold, Tina Yothers, Leora Dana.

On-Screen: *The wrenching dissolution of a marriage*. On the surface, George and Faith Dunlap (Finney and Keaton) have a picture-perfect marriage. He is a prize-winning author, and they live with their four daughters in a well-appointed California home. Their lives, however, are unraveling. In love with another woman (Allen), George is about to leave his family, bringing anguish to Faith and especially their oldest daughter, Sherry (Hill). His guilt and misery provokes him to acts of destruction and near-violence that leave everyone shattered. Bo Goldman's screenplay is bleak and sometimes piercingly honest, but toward the end, the movie bogs down in too many climaxes that follow one another, leaving the viewer bewildered and exhausted. (The worst involves a shrill restaurant quarrel that defies all logic and reason.) Although Diane Keaton persists in using her familiar mannerisms, she is highly effective as Faith, reaching an emotional peak when she sits alone in the bathtub and begins to cry. Albert Finney is fine in a basically unsympathetic role, and Dana Hill is heartrending as the troubled daughter. An uneven but striking movie that might have benefited from some restraint.

Off-Screen: The Dunlap home was actually a once-prosperous, 114-year-old house called Roy Ranch. Its decaying shell, which sat on the eighth fairway of the San Geronimo National Golf Course, was cut into pieces, loaded onto trucks, and dispatched to a new location a dozen miles away. In six weeks, the house was reassembled, restored, renovated, and decorated, and much of the film was shot there. Some scenes were filmed at the Napa County Courthouse, the second-oldest court building in California.

The Shootist

Paramount, 1976. (C-99m.) Dir: Don Siegel. Sp: Miles Hood Swarthout and Scott Hale, b/o novel by Glendon Swarthout. Cast: John Wayne, Lauren Bacall, Ron Howard, James Stewart, Richard Boone, Sheree North, Hugh O'Brian, Harry Morgan, John Carradine, Scatman Crothers.

On-Screen: *Aging, stricken gunslinger John Wayne tries to end his life with dignity*. This was John Wayne's last performance—three years after the movie was released, he died of cancer, the disease he has in the story. Wayne plays J. B. Books, a legendary gunman who has outlived his time. Mortality is all around him, from the fatal diagnosis he receives from the doctor (Stewart) to the autumnal glow with which director Don Siegel bathes the film. The sense of a vanishing era even extends to Books's passing along his heritage to his landlady's son (Howard), instructing him in a gunman's skills. Here the movie deviates from the Swarthout novel in which the Howard character becomes a hardened "shootist" and guns Wayne down; in the film he defends Wayne in the final shoot-out that kills the man who was his hero. An elegiac western, *The Shootist* is both a tribute to—and a swan song for—its durable star. (It even begins with tinted clips from old Wayne westerns.)

Off-Screen: The film was offered to George C. Scott, who had read the book but refused to sign for the part unless the screenplay was made more faithful to the original novel, which was realistic and earthy. During the filming, there was much contention between Wayne and Siegel, who complained bitterly that the actor interfered continually with his direction. Wayne insisted that his character should be diagnosed with cancer of the prostate, not of the bladder. "Bladder," he said, "sounds so ugly and unmanly."

The Shop Around the Corner

MGM, 1940. (97m.) Dir: Ernst Lubitsch. Sp: Samson Raphaelson, b/o play by Nikolaus Laszlo. Cast: Margaret Sullavan, James Stewart, Frank Morgan, Joseph Schildkraut, Sara Haden, Felix Bressart, William Tracy.

On-Screen: *Two coworkers in a Budapest shop become "pen pals."* Noted for the sly sophistication he brought to such films as *Trouble in Paradise,* director Ernst Lubitsch was in a gentler, more reflective mood when he made this utterly enchanting comedy. Samson Raphaelson's screenplay beautifully captures the small joys and sorrows of life in its story of Sullavan and Stewart, coworkers in Morgan's Budapest shop who heartily detest each other without knowing that they are ardent correspondents. Both stars are captivating, but as fine as they are, it is Morgan who steals the film as the cuckolded shop owner. Forgoing his usual dithering ways, he cuts a poignant figure as he talks on the telephone with his cheating wife or learns the identity of her clandestine lover. A lovely performance in a lovely film.

Off-Screen: According to Ben Hecht's biographer, Hecht made an uncredited contribution to the screenplay. The story has had several reincarnations over the years. MGM remade it in 1949 as the musical *In the Good Old Summertime,* with Judy Garland and Van Johnson, and it was adapted for the Broadway stage in 1963 as the musical *She Loves Me,* with Barbara Cook in the Sullavan role.

A Shot in the Dark

United Artists, 1964. (C-101m.) Dir: Blake Edwards. Sp: Blake Edwards and William Peter Blatty, b/o plays by Harry Kurnitz and Marcel Archard. Cast: Peter Sellers, Elke Sommer, George Sanders, Herbert Lom, Tracy Reed, Graham Stark.

On-Screen: *Bumbling Inspector Clouseau investigates a murder at a château.* The second film to feature that clumsiest of detectives, Inspector Jacques Clouseau, is also one of the funniest in the series. On his new case, he is sent to investigate the killing of a chauffeur at the château of wealthy M. Ballon (Sanders). The obvious suspect is the saucy maid Maria (Sommer), but Clouseau, immediately smitten, insists she is innocent. A few more murders point to Maria, but Clouseau refuses to change his mind, while his bumbling ineptness drives his superior, Chief Inspector Dreyfus (Lom) to near-madness. This time, Clouseau's antics make up the heart of the film, and luckily, most of them are cues for laughter. Clouseau becomes both victim and victimizer as he stumbles through a series of sight gags and slapstick sequences. Sellers succeeds in making Clouseau's stupidity endearing, and Lom matches him as a man deep in the throes of a nervous breakdown.

Off-Screen: Actor Graham Stark, who plays Hercule Lajoy in the film, recalled that the atmosphere on the set was always "'relaxed." At one point a scripted line had Sellers telling Stark, "Let us synchronize our watches," at which point director Blake Edwards interrupted to ask, "Who decides what time you synchronize to?" Sellers and Stark laughed, and when Edwards said, "Make it up without rehearsal," the actors improvised the entire scene, which became a highlight of the movie.

Show Boat

Universal, 1936. (113m.) Dir: James Whale. Sp: Oscar Hammerstein II, b/o his musical play and novel by Edna Ferber. MS: Jerome Kern and Oscar Hammerstein II. Cast: Irene Dunne, Allan Jones, Helen Morgan, Paul Robeson, Charles Winninger, Hattie Mc-Daniel, Helen Westley.

On-Screen: *The river—and the Kern-Hammerstein musical—keep rollin' along.* The second—and by far the best and most faithful —of the film versions of the classic 1927 musical play, this *Show Boat* is memorable in almost every respect. The score, probably the greatest ever written for a home-grown American musical, is presented magnificently; highlights include Robeson's powerful "Old Man River," Morgan's plaintive rendition of "Bill," and the Dunne-Jones duet of "Make Believe." The story of the showboat and its people may get a bit florid, especially toward the end, but it touches honestly on such matters as miscegenation, and occasionally it has an emotional resonance, notably in the performance of Helen Morgan as the tragic mulatto Julie. (She had originated the role in

1927.) All in all, a marvelous movie transcription of a great musical play, superior to the more elaborate 1951 Technicolor version.

Off-Screen: The first film version of *Show Boat* appeared in 1929 as a part-talkie. A new version was discussed again in 1933, with Irene Dunne, Charles Winninger, and crooner Russ Columbo, but was eventually dropped. For this version, W. C. Fields was considered briefly for the role of Cap'n Andy, but it went to Winninger, who was splendid in his original Broadway role. Edna May Oliver rejected the part of Parthy Ann, which she had played on the stage. John Boles and Walter Pidgeon were candidates to play Gaylord Ravenal, and Irene Dunne favored Nelson Eddy. Thankfully, the role went to Allan Jones.

Show Boat

MGM, 1951. (C-107m.) Dir: George Sidney. Sp: John Lee Mahin, b/o musical play by Oscar Hammerstein II and novel by Edna Ferber. MS: Jerome Kern and Oscar Hammerstein II. Cast: Kathryn Grayson, Howard Keel, Ava Gardner, Joe E. Brown, Marge Champion, Gower Champion, Agnes Moorehead, William Warfield.

On-Screen: *The third trip down "old man river."* Lushly produced in the grand MGM style, and cast with players who could do reasonable justice to the glorious Kern-Hammerstein score, this third version of *Show Boat* is still a good distance from the second (and to date, definitive) film. The story of the Mississippi showboat people, and their troubles that range from marriage to miscegenation, remains unusually strong for a musical, and the songs are everlastingly beautiful. Yet there is something hollow at the center of this lacquered production. Howard Keel makes a robust Gaylord Ravenal, and Ava Gardner is surprisingly touching as the ill-fated Julie, but Kathryn Grayson's Magnolia is rather insipid. William Warfield gives a stirring rendition of "Old Man River." Joe E. Brown's Cap'n Andy is amiable, although not in a league with Charles Winninger's memorable performance in the 1936 version. Despite its shortcomings, this *Show Boat* offers an enjoyable ride with a cherished friend.

Off-Screen: For this production, a showboat was constructed at a cost of more than $125,000. It was over 170 feet long and nearly 60 feet high. Ava Gardner was anxious to do her own vocals in the movie. She studied with a coach and sang her songs well enough. But it was decided to dub her singing with Annette Warren's voice, although Gardner's voice can be heard on the soundtrack album.

The Silence of the Lambs

Orion, 1991. (120m.) Dir: Jonathan Demme. Sp: Ted Tally, b/o novel by Thomas Harris. Cast: Jodie Foster, Anthony Hopkins, Scott Glenn, Ted Levine, Anthony Heald, Brooke Smith, Diane Baker.

On-Screen: *A gripping, grisly tale of murder and evil.* FBI trainee Clarice Starling (Foster) is sent to establish a relationship with a convicted serial murderer, Dr. Hannibal Lecter (Hopkins), a former psychiatrist with cannibalistic impulses. The idea is to learn something from Lecter about "Buffalo Bill" (Levine), a current serial killer with his own

ugly eccentricities. The tension starts early, with a memorable walk by Starling along a row of underground prison cells, and it never really lets up. Somewhere at midpoint, the film's emphasis lurches from Lecter to Buffalo Bill. But the heart of the movie is the Starling-Lecter relationship, and the acting of Foster and Hopkins is remarkable. Barely changing the expression on his face or the tone of his voice, Hopkins tells us everything about a man holding all emotions in check, except the need to murder. Jodie Foster is also fine, although the film's second half forces her into some rather absurd "perils-of-Pauline" predicaments. Less skillfully done, *The Silence of the Lambs* would have been another spool of forgettable gore; as it is, it hints at a human darkness that leaves us both disturbed and fascinated.

Off-Screen: The role of Clarice Starling was first offered to Michelle Pfeiffer, who turned it down. The character of Hannibal Lecter had already appeared on the screen, played by Brian Cox in *Manhunter* (1986), based on another Harris novel, *Red Dragon*. Lecter's holding cell, located in the middle of a wood-paneled room, was built in the Allegheny County Soldier's and Sailor's Memorial Hall in Pittsburgh. The death's-head moths that are an important element in the story were actually the more common tomato hornworms, made up to resemble their more exotic relations. (BL)

Silk Stockings

MGM, 1957. (C-117m.) Dir: Rouben Mamoulian. Sp: Leonard Gershe and Leonard Spigelgass, b/o musical play by George S. Kaufman, Leueen MacGrath, and Abe

Burrows, and film *Ninotchka*. MS: Cole Porter. Cast: Fred Astaire, Cyd Charisse, Janis Paige, Peter Lorre, Jules Munshin, Joseph Buloff, George Tobias, Barrie Chase.

On-Screen: *Fred Astaire stars in a musicalized* Ninotchka. Marking Astaire's last appearance in a musical until *Finian's Rainbow* in 1968, *Silk Stockings* adapted Ernst Lubitsch's classic comedy *Ninotchka* into an often pleasing but ultimately middle-drawer movie. The plot was altered, but the basic premise was the same: A dour Communist representative (Charisse) comes to Paris on official business and finds romance instead. Fred Astaire plays the movie director who provides the romance. Although too old for the role, he is ageless when he dances: with Charisse to "Fated to Be Mated," and with Janis Paige (peppery as a movie star) to "Stereophonic Sound." Other songs from the original stage score ("All of You," the title song) have vestiges of the Cole Porter magic. Yet *Silk Stockings* has the elegiac air of a genre that was fast fading from the movie scene.

Off-Screen: Although Astaire's solo to "The Ritz Roll 'n' Rock" may show all of his old agility, he was extremely unhappy with the result: "I overdid, overplayed it. I could have simplified it more. But you get keyed up on a certain day and maybe do something that doesn't please you. I hope nobody noticed it as much as I did, because it made me so angry." The song was one of two ("Fated to Be Mated" is the other) written by Porter especially for the film.

Silkwood

Fox, 1983. (C-128m.) Dir: Mike Nichols. Sp: Nora Ephron and Alice Arlen. Cast: Meryl Streep, Kurt Russell, Cher, Craig T. Nelson, Diana Scarwid, Fred Ward, Ron Silver, Charles Hallahan, Josef Sommer, Sudie Bond.

On-Screen: *A woman fights to expose serious negligence at a plant.* Based on a true story, *Silkwood* focuses on Karen Silkwood, a slangy, irreverent divorced mother of three who works at a plutonium plant in Oklahoma. After she is contaminated with radioactive materials, she begins to suspect the plant's willful negligence is exposing workers to potentially dangerous levels of radiation. Her investigation generates hostility from both workers and management, and as she falls ill from internal contamination, she is ostracized by everyone and possibly even betrayed by her friend (Cher). Eventually, she is killed in a car crash under mysterious circumstances. Absorbing in spite of the audience's likely knowledge of the sad ending, *Silkwood* features a stunning performance by Meryl Streep. Playing against her usual type, she makes a convincing transition from a feisty, tough-talking woman to a pathetic, helpless victim of intangible forces. The film is cautious to avoid the hearsay and innuendo that surrounded the Silkwood case, neither laying the blame on the plutonium company nor on Karen herself. This ambiguity is necessary, but it weakens the film.

Off-Screen: To convey the ill Karen Silkwood, Meryl Streep went on a strict diet, drinking from a concoction in her trailer; makeup artist Roy Helland contributed the finishing touches to suggest her deterioration. Karen's parents were not happy with the movie, claiming that their daughter was more intelligent than the character depicted in the film. Kerr-McGee, the company involved in the case, issued a statement that the film was "a highly fictionalized Hollywood dramatization scarcely connected to the facts." *Silkwood* won Oscar nominations for Streep, Cher, and Nichols, as well as for the writers and editor.

Silverado

Columbia, 1985. (C-132m.) Dir: Lawrence Kasdan. Sp: Lawrence Kasdan and Mark Kasdan. Cast: Kevin Kline, Scott Glenn, Danny Glover, Kevin Costner, John Cleese, Rosanna Arquette, Brian Dennehy, Jeff Goldblum, Linda Hunt.

On-Screen: *A group of ill-assorted men battle a band of outlaws.* This large-scale western—the first in years—attempts to blend the familiar conventions of the western genre with a modern-day spoof of these very same conventions. The result is an entertaining hybrid. Men who have nothing in common except their past history in western movies come together to take on a nasty family of outlaws. Among them are a loner (Kline) with a secret past, a quick-drawing gunslinger (Glenn), and his trigger-happy younger brother (Costner, in prestardom days). Only a black man (Glover) battling frontier racism is relatively new. Nostalgia is speckled with satire as a jailbreak turns into slapstick farce, or a shoot-out and stampede hover between homage and spoof. Even some of the casting is deliberately perverse: British comedian Cleese as a sheriff, or Linda Hunt as a barmaid. *Silverado* is an enjoyable ride down the old dusty trails—with a few bumps along the way.

Off-Screen: Director Lawrence Kasdan wrote the screenplay with his brother Mark. His comment on the film: "We wanted this to be almost like a primer of westerns—to teach kids and remind adults. It consciously embraces all the archetypical western situations. It says, 'These are the pleasures we've been missing—taste them!' This is an attempt to get back to what excited me when I was twelve years old."

Since You Went Away

Selznick, 1944. (172m.) Dir: John Cromwell. Sp: David O. Selznick, b/o book by Margaret Buell Wilder. Cast: Claudette Colbert, Jennifer Jones, Joseph Cotten, Shirley Temple, Robert Walker, Monty Woolley, Agnes Moorehead, Lionel Barrymore, Keenan Wynn, Nazimova, Guy Madison, Craig Stevens.

On-Screen: *An American family endures the tribulations and tragedies of World War II.* At the height of World War II, women who might have been seeking a primer on how they were expected to act during the conflict could have turned to David O. Selznick's film. A long, sentimental, but meticulously produced, often affecting drama, it focuses on one family headed by matriarch Claudette Colbert, whose husband is fighting overseas. The story involves her two daughters (Jones and Temple) and the people in their lives, including a shy sailor (Walker) who courts the older daughter, his crusty grandfather (Woolley), and a family friend (Cotten) who has always loved Colbert. The movie trots out every conceivable home-front crisis and dilemma, from inconvenient to deeply tragic, and if it now seems synthetic, maudlin, and unreal, the performances, for the most part, are expert, the photography by Lee Garmes and Stanley Cortez gives the film a creamy glow, and

Max Steiner's Oscar-winning score dips it all in schmaltz. Best scene: the railroad parting of Jones and Walker.

Off-Screen: Stage star Katharine Cornell expressed interest in playing the mother, but a long, discreet telegram from David O. Selznick expressed doubts about her suitability for the role. Selznick was anxious that the film not be regarded solely as a comeback vehicle for Shirley Temple, who had not made a film in two years. He was more concerned with Jennifer Jones, whom he would later marry and whom he was hoping to build into a major star. Making their film debuts are Guy Madison (as a sailor) and John Derek (as an extra).

Singin' in the Rain

MGM, 1952. (C-102m.) Dir: Gene Kelly and Stanley Donen. Sp: Betty Comden and Adolph Green. MS: Arthur Freed and Nacio Herb Brown. Cast: Gene Kelly, Debbie Reynolds, Donald O'Connor, Jean Hagen, Cyd Charisse, Millard Mitchell, Douglas Fowley, Rita Moreno.

On-Screen: *Musical high jinks at the dawn of Hollywood's sound era.* Widely regarded as the greatest of all film musicals, *Singin' in the Rain* richly deserves the accolade. The Comden and Green screenplay about the birth of talking movies is fresh and funny, if not necessarily accurate, and the cast, headed by Kelly as a film star making the transition to sound, bursts with exuberance and sheer performing joy. Highest marks, perhaps, go to Jean Hagen as a shrill-voiced and dim-witted silent screen idol, but Debbie Reynolds makes an adorable heroine. The musical portions range from good to

wonderful. Kelly's dance in the rain is a heart-lifting classic, of course, but so is Donald O'Connor's slapstick number, "Make 'Em Laugh," one of the funniest ever recorded on film. The "Broadway Ballet," staged in typically opulent (and slightly overblown) MGM style, contains some stunning moments, some of them provided by long-legged Cyd Charisse. In all, who could ask for anything more?

Off-Screen: Under contract to MGM, Betty Comden and Adolph Green were asked to write an original musical about the early days of sound, using the catalog of songs by Arthur Freed and Nacio Herb Brown. The final, glorious result was *Singin' in the Rain.* Some off-screen tidbits: Arthur Freed, head of the prestigious musical unit at the studio, wanted Oscar Levant to play Cosmo, but Donald O'Connor was happily cast instead. Nina Foch tested for the role of Lina Lamont, but Jean Hagen was chosen. Debbie Reynolds's jalopy in the movie was the one used by Mickey Rooney in the Hardy-family series. During the five-o'clock dress rehearsal of the famous title number, the water came out a tired drizzle rather than a downpour. It was discovered that the residents of Culver City turned on their sprinkler systems at this time, depleting the water supply. A stage version of the musical ran on Broadway for nearly a year in 1985.

Sitting Pretty

Fox, 1948. (84m.) Dir: Walter Lang. Sp: F. Hugh Herbert, b/o novel by Gwen Davenport. Cast: Robert Young, Maureen O'Hara, Clifton Webb, Richard Haydn, Louise Allbritton, Randy Stewart, Ed Begley.

On-Screen: *Enter Lynn Belvedere, baby-sitter extraordinaire.* An elegant performer in such Broadway musicals as *The Little Show* and *Three's a Crowd,* Clifton Webb was past fifty when he made his sensational sound debut in *Laura* (1944). Nearly three years later, he made this movie, his first comedy, and audiences responded enthusiastically to his lofty, waspish, and monumentally efficient Lynn Belvedere. (He even won a Best Actor Oscar nomination.) A self-proclaimed genius, Mr. Belvedere arrives at the home of Robert Young and Maureen O'Hara as a most unlikely baby-sitter and proceeds to confound, outrage, and ultimately delight the couple and their neighbors. Sparked by Webb, *Sitting Pretty* is amiable light entertainment. (Funny moment: Tired of being splattered by his tiny charge, Belvedere overturns the bowl of cereal on the infant's head.) Young and O'Hara are a pleasant pair, but watch out for Richard Haydn, who almost gives Webb a run for his money as an obnoxious snoop with a clogged nose.

Off-Screen: The popularity of Webb and *Sitting Pretty* led to two inferior sequels, *Mr. Belvedere Goes to College* (1949), which brought Shirley Temple back to her home studio for the last time, and *Mr. Belvedere Rings the Bell* (1951), adapted from the Broadway play *The Silver Whistle.* "Mr. Belvedere," a TV situation comedy very loosely based on the film character, began in 1985 and lasted several seasons.

Sleeper

United Artists, 1973. (C–88m.) Dir: Woody Allen. Sp: Woody Allen and Marshall Brickman. Cast: Woody Allen, Diane Keaton, John Beck, Mary Gregory, Don Keefer, John McLiam.

On-Screen: *Woody Allen in the year 2173.* One of Allen's best films of the seventies, *Sleeper* mixes science fiction and satire with hilarious results. In 1973, Miles Monroe (Allen) goes into the hospital for a minor operation and, after being frozen when complications develop, wakes up in the year 2173. In a futuristic world where every turn brings another verbal or visual joke, Miles becomes embroiled in a rebellion against the totalitarian government. He also falls for a light-headed girl named Luna (Keaton). The screenplay constructs a mosaic of sight gags and bursts of slapstick around all this inspired silliness. You are likely to remember the outsize vegetables, the peculiar robots, and Allen's comments on the personalities of the midseventies. ("Billy Graham knew God personally. They went on double dates together.") *Sleeper* resembles a Buster Keaton comedy in its badgered hero confronting a hostile world, accompanied by a none-too-bright heroine. But it's also a comedy classic in its own right.

Off-Screen: To keep the movie a manageable length, entire sequences of the story line had to be edited out. The film's excellent score is performed by the renowned Preservation Hall Jazz Band. All but one of the band members were over sixty-five years old.

Smile

United Artists, 1975. (C–113m.) Dir: Michael Ritchie. Sp: Jerry Belson. Cast: Bruce Dern, Barbara Feldon, Michael Kidd, Geoffrey Lewis, Nicholas Pryor, Colleen Camp, Joan Prather, Annette O'Toole, Maria O'Brien, Denise Nickerson, Eric Shea.

On-Screen: *Shenanigans during a beauty pageant.* Widely disregarded at its release despite some enthusiastic reviews, *Smile* deserved a much better fate. A funny and perceptive satire, it centers about a teenage beauty pageant held in Santa Rosa, California, where twenty-five adolescent girls compete in an atmosphere of merchandising, boosterism, and backstage politics. Bruce Dern is the aggressively cheerful mobile-home dealer and the contest's chief judge. Barbara Feldon plays the girls' mother hen who is too busy with the pageant to notice that her marriage is falling apart, and Michael Kidd is the pageant's choreographer, whose career is in decline. *Smile* attacks its targets without demolishing them—there is a residue of sympathy for the beleaguered characters. The highlight of the movie is the pageant itself—we won't spoil the hilarious surprises provided by the eager contestants except to mention that a clear favorite is the girl who demonstrates how to pack a suitcase. *Smile* evokes smiles, and also abundant laughter.

Off-Screen: The movie was actually filmed in Santa Rosa, where Alfred Hitchcock's *Shadow of a Doubt* and Walt Disney's *Pollyanna* were also shot. The pageant was staged before paying viewers who knew they were participating in a film. No one, except the director, the writer, and the executive producers, knew who the actual winner would be. Seventeen-year-old Melanie Griffith appears as one of the contestants—she does an Egyptian dance. A stage musical version of *Smile* had a brief Broadway run late in 1986.

The Snake Pit

Fox, 1948. (108m.) Dir: Anatole Litvak. Sp: Frank Partos and Millen Brand, b/o novel by Mary Jane Ward. Cast: Olivia de Havilland, Leo Genn, Mark Stevens, Celeste Holm, Glenn Langan, Helen Craig, Leif Erickson, Beulah Bondi, Lee Patrick, Ruth Donnelly, Betsy Blair.

On-Screen: *One woman's ordeal in a mental institution.* By now this film's approach to caring for and curing the mentally ill will seem laughably simplistic. Yet as drama it still has some powerful moments. Olivia de Havilland shines as a young psychotic woman who undergoes a harrowing experience as a patient at a public mental hospital. Through flashbacks, we learn the origins of her illness, and with the help of a wise doctor (Genn), she works her painful way back to reason. Some of the scenes in the dingy, prisonlike hospital are still effective, perhaps none more so than the famous moment in which the camera pulls back from de Havilland, surrounded by babbling inmates, until she appears to be at the bottom of a horrifying snake pit. The principal "sane" characters, including the pipe-smoking, all-wise doctor and de Havilland's patient husband (Stevens), seem much too good to be true, but with de Havilland's exemplary performance leading the way, *The Snake Pit* retains some of its emotional force.

Off-Screen: After purchasing the film rights to Mary Jane Ward's novel, director Litvak could not find a studio willing to back the production, until Fox agreed. Litvak insisted that the leading players and the technical staff join him in visiting state mental institutions around the country. Hairdressers were banished from the set, and the women players had strict orders to leave their girdles and brassieres in the dressing rooms. Both the film and de Havilland were nominated for Oscars, but *Hamlet* and Jane Wyman in *Johnny Belinda* won. However, the film did win the New York Film Critics Award as Best Picture.

Sneakers

Universal, 1992. (C-125m.) Dir: Phil Alden Robinson. Sp: Lawrence Lasker, Walter F. Parkes, and Phil Alden Robinson. Cast: Robert Redford, Sidney Poitier, Dan Aykroyd, River Phoenix, Ben Kingsley, Mary McDonnell, David Strathairn, George Hearn, Timothy Busfield.

On-Screen: *A computer hacker and his friends in hot water.* A sort of high-tech "Mission Impossible" for the nineties, *Sneakers* doesn't make much sense, but it's lively, suspenseful, and sometimes quite funny. Robert Redford plays a once-notorious computer hacker who now runs a company that tests security systems. His all-star colleagues have something shady in their pasts, but they are all experts in their fields. Soon Redford and friends (plus his ex-wife, McDonnell) are dangerously enmeshed in high-level intrigue involving a black box that can break *any* existing computer code. The villain is odd-accented Kingsley, a former friend and colleague of Redford's who was imprisoned for computer hacking, while Redford escaped. Now Kingsley is bent on revenge. The box, of course, is merely the "McGuffin" to spark a series of break-ins, narrow escapes, and near-fatal encounters of the sort that were popular in caper movies a few decades ago. Now it's all done with state-of-the-art technology that is sometimes difficult to follow. *Sneakers* is lightweight but fun.

Off-Screen: Phil Alden Robinson's previous movie (his first as writer-director) was the popular baseball fantasy *Field of Dreams* (1989). Coauthors Lasker and Parkes were the authors of the 1983 film *WarGames,* which also revolved about the use of computers to trigger world disorder.

Snow White and the Seven Dwarfs

Disney-RKO, 1937. (C-83m., animated) Supervising Dir: David Hand. MS: Frank Churchill, Leigh Harline, Paul J. Smith, and Larry Morey.

On-Screen: *Walt Disney's historic first feature-length movie. Snow White and the Seven Dwarfs* may seem primitive by the standards of today's state-of-the-art animation (witness Disney's own *Beauty and the Beast*), but its charm endures, as does its ability to amuse and involve children. Disney was taking a huge gamble in making the film, and many were ready to tell him he was foolhardy, but he organized a team of talented people and developed new animation techniques to tell the well-loved tale of Snow White, her prince, the wicked queen who would destroy her, and of course, the lovable dwarfs who befriend her. The gamble paid off not only in returns at the box office but in establishing Disney as a master of popular folklore. For many years afterward, viewers could still recall the antics of the seven dwarfs or sing such infectious tunes as "Whistle While You Work," "Some Day My Prince Will Come," and "Heigh-Ho." There was some criticism at the time of its release of its occasionally frightening images, but most critics and viewers were enchanted. And animation history was made.

Off-Screen: Disney's main technical achievement for the movie was the development of the multiplane camera, which gave greater depth to the animated figures. All but two of the dwarfs were given names that stayed with them from the first. Jumpy was changed to Sneezy, and one nameless dwarf was finally called Dopey. To make Snow White seem more lifelike, a girl was photographed as she walked and danced; the girl was Marjorie Belcher, later known as Marge Champion. Eighteen-year-old Adriana Caselotti became the voice of Snow White. Deanna Durbin was rejected by Disney as sounding "too mature."

The Snows of Kilimanjaro

Fox, 1952. (C-117m.) Dir: Henry King. Sp: Casey Robinson, b/o story by Ernest Hemingway. Cast: Gregory Peck, Susan Hayward, Ava Gardner, Hildegarde Neff, Leo G. Carroll, Torin Thatcher, Ava Norring, Helene Stanley, Marcel Dalio, Vincente Gomez.

On-Screen: *A critically wounded man reviews his life.* One of the more successful adaptations of Ernest Hemingway's work, *The Snows of Kilimanjaro* draws not only on his famous story but on other material evolving out of the author's background. Gregory Peck is Harry, a wealthy, famous author whose leg has been seriously wounded during an African safari. With wife Helen (Hayward) at his side, a near-delirious Harry reflects on the past losses and failures that have made his life meaningless, mostly his ill-fated romance with Cynthia (Gardner), the beautiful woman with whom he restlessly roams Africa and Spain during the bullfights. Their final, fateful encounter occurs during the Spanish Civil War. His marriage to Helen is haunted by the memory of Cynthia. Eventually, Harry comes to terms with his troubled past. Casey Robinson's screenplay makes reasonably intelligent use of Hemingway's themes, and the cast works skillfully. Hildegarde Neff is the possessive countess with whom Harry dallies on the French Riviera.

Off-Screen: Ava Gardner later commented that she was "comfortable" in her role: "She was a good average girl with normal impulses. I didn't have to pretend." The part was originally slated for Anne Francis, but studio head Darryl Zanuck felt that Francis wasn't sexy enough. Casey Robinson called the screenplay "one-third Hemingway, one-third Zanuck, and one-third myself." Hemingway disliked the film, saying that it should have been titled *The Snows of Zanuck.*

The Solid Gold Cadillac

Columbia, 1956. (99m.) Dir: Richard Quine. Sp: Abe Burrows, b/o play by George S. Kaufman and Howard Teichman. Cast: Judy Holliday, Paul Douglas, Fred Clark, John Williams, Hiram Sherman, Neva Patterson, Arthur O'Connell.

On-Screen: *Judy Holliday turns the business world upside down.* Onstage in the Kaufman-Teichman play, Laura Partridge was an endearing old lady, personified by the waddling and wonderful Josephine Hull. The film version changes her into the pleasingly plump and much younger Holliday, but she's still the same gadfly whose innocent inquisition unnerves and disrupts a corrupt corporation. She even charms the company's rough-hewn founder (Douglas), who not only joins her in bringing down the villains but falls for her as well. Frank Capra would be pleased with the climactic courtroom scene. An amusing comedy, *The Solid Gold Cadillac* uses broad cartoon strokes in place of subtlety—the company board members are merely cardboard targets for Holliday's volleys. But the actress is never less than appealing, and Douglas, her costar in Broadway's *Born Yesterday,* is an enormously likable performer.

Off-Screen: After the play was a Broadway hit, several studios made a bid for the property. Fox wanted it for Marilyn Monroe; Paramount thought of it as a vehicle for Shirley Booth. But Columbia won out and Judy Holliday was cast. To add a little zest to the proceedings, George Burns provides some off-camera narration.

Some Like It Hot

United Artists, 1959. (119m.) Dir: Billy Wilder. Sp: Billy Wilder and I. A. L. Diamond, b/o story by Robert Thoeren and M. Logan. Cast: Tony Curtis, Jack Lemmon, Marilyn Monroe, Joe E. Brown, George Raft, Pat O'Brien, Nehemiah Persoff, Joan Shawlee.

On-Screen: *Band musicians Tony Curtis and Jack Lemmon find mayhem and Marilyn Monroe in the roaring twenties.* Question: Can transvestism, impotence, and gangland murder become suitable subjects for laughter? Answer: a resounding "Yes!" if you consider Billy Wilder's uproarious comedy. From the opening in 1927 Chicago to the famous last line, *Some Like It Hot* keeps an outrageous premise spinning merrily. Two down-and-out musicians (Curtis and Lem-

mon) witness the St. Valentine's Day Massacre and flee to Florida, disguised as members of an all-girl band. One becomes involved with the band's voluptuous singer (Monroe), the other with an eccentric millionaire (Brown). Complications ensue when the Chicago gangsters arrive on the scene. Skirting but never surrendering to tastelessness, the screenplay bubbles like vintage champagne, and a top-notch cast plays it to the hilt. Tony Curtis shows a genuine flair for comedy, and Marilyn Monroe, poured into her Orry-Kelly gowns, makes Sugar Kane both amusing and touching. But the movie belongs to Jack Lemmon, whose manic Josephine is one of the screen's funniest comic creations. A special kudo goes to Brown, whose Osgood Fielding III reaches delirious heights of near-imbecility.

Off-Screen: *Some Like It Hot* brims with surprises, one being that the cast and crew managed to stay sane during the filming. The principal problem seemed to be Marilyn Monroe, who drove everyone to distraction with her lateness, her unpreparedness, and her nervous insecurity. Tony Curtis later remarked, ungallantly, that kissing Marilyn Monroe was "like kissing Hitler." The movie received five Oscar nominations, but only Orry-Kelly won for his costume design. A stage musical version, entitled *Sugar,* ran for over a year on Broadway in 1972.

Son of Frankenstein

Universal, 1939. (99m.) Dir: Rowland V. Lee. Sp: Willis Cooper, b/o characters created by Mary Shelley. Cast: Basil Rathbone, Boris Karloff, Bela Lugosi, Lionel Atwill, Josephine Hutchinson, Edgar Norton.

On-Screen: *Frankenstein's offspring follows in his footsteps*. The third in Universal's Frankenstein series, with the last feature-film appearance by Karloff as the Monster, *Son of Frankenstein* does not measure up to the first two films, but it is considerably better than those that followed. Atmospheric sets and eerie photography highlight this tale of the late Baron Frankenstein's son (Rathbone), who restores his father's monster to full power, with disastrous results for everyone, and near-fatal consequences for his own young son. Karloff's Monster lumbers about in his usual fashion, and Lugosi gives a good performance, possibly his best, as the grotesque, broken-necked Ygor. Lionel Atwill plays the police inspector whose arm was ripped out of its roots by the Monster many years earlier; his stiff false arm was parodied in Mel Brooks's *Young Frankenstein* (1974).

Off-Screen: Disappointed by what he considered the weakening of the Monster's character, Boris Karloff decided that he would never play the role again. During the filming, he celebrated his fifty-first birthday, and the crew threw him a surprise birthday party in which the cast participated while still in their makeup and costumes. One of the major cuts made in the film after completion was the elimination of Dwight Frye's role as one of the villagers. Frye had played Dr. Frankenstein's assistant in the first two films.

The Song of Bernadette

Fox, 1943. (156m.) Dir: Henry King. Sp: George Seaton, b/o novel by Franz Werfel. Cast: Jennifer Jones, William Eythe, Charles Bickford, Gladys Cooper, Anne Revere, Vincent Price, Lee J. Cobb.

On-Screen: *A young French girl has a religious vision*. Reverent and sometimes touching, *The Song of Bernadette* draws on Franz Werfel's novel about Bernadette (Jones), a sweetly innocent young peasant who, in the 1800s, has a vision of the Virgin Mary. Some proclaim her vision a miracle, and a shrine is built on the site; others denounce her as a fraud and a heretic. The film runs too long, and too much time is given over to exploring verbally all aspects of the mystical experience. Also, the attempt to affect the simple speech of the French peasantry is often awkward. Jennifer Jones, who had begun her career inauspiciously under another name (see below), makes an earnest Bernadette Soubirous (she won an Oscar for her performance), but the true acting honors go to such seasoned veterans as Charles Bickford as the Catholic dean of Lourdes and Gladys Cooper as a nun fiercely jealous of Bernadette. Religiosity in films is seldom popular, unless it is well seasoned with generous amounts of DeMillian sex and spectacle, but here it gets respectable treatment.

Off-Screen: Early in her career, Jennifer Jones could be seen in several minor films under her real name, Phyllis Isley. In addition to her Oscar, Academy Awards were given for Cinematography, black-and-white (Arthur Miller), Music Score (Alfred Newman), and Art Direction, black-and-white. The film was also nominated for Best Picture. Linda Darnell appears, unbilled, as the Virgin Mary.

A Song to Remember

Columbia, 1945. (C-113m.) Dir: Charles Vidor. Sp: Sidney Buchman, b/o story by Ernest Marischka. Cast: Paul Muni, Merle Oberon, Cornel Wilde, Nina Foch, Stephen

Bekassy, George Coulouris, George Macready.

On-Screen: *Chopin's life and music. Life, no. Music, yes.* Among the screen's biographies of classical composers, *A Song to Remember* must surely rank as the most absurd. The production is lavish, the color is striking, and the music (which accounted for the film's enormous popularity) is glorious. End of virtues. The screenplay bears little or no resemblance to the life of the great Polish composer, and the dialogue is frequently inane. Cornel Wilde makes a vapid Chopin, and Merle Oberon is lovely but not much else as novelist George Sand. Worst of all is Paul Muni as Chopin's fictional teacher, Professor Eisner. Often given to hamminess, the actor uses a dismaying variety of grimaces and vocal flourishes in his over-the-top performance. If you can dismiss the dramatic portions and revel in the outpouring of waltzes, études, polonaises, and other music, you may enjoy *A Song to Remember*.

Off-Screen: First titles for the film were *The Song That Lived Forever* and *A Love of Madame Sand*. The piano-playing in the film was performed by José Iturbi, who could not be credited because he was under contract to MGM. Miklos Rozsa adapted the music. Frank Capra had written a treatment for a proposed life of Chopin, which was dusted off and turned over to Sidney Buchman. Cornel Wilde received a Best Actor Oscar nomination.

Sons of the Desert

MGM, 1933. (69m.) Dir: William A. Seiter. Sp: Byron Morgan, b/o story by Frank Craven. Cast: Stan Laurel, Oliver Hardy, Charlie Chase, Mae Busch, Dorothy Christy, Lucien Littlefield.

On-Screen: *Laurel and Hardy in hot water.* One of the most highly regarded of the team's feature films, *Sons of the Desert* builds a number of hearty laughs around the simplest of premises: In order to attend the convention of the fraternal order of Sons of the Desert without their wives' consent, Stan and Ollie construct a series of lies that spiral comically out of control. At the convention, they are plagued by an overhearty conventioneer (Chase), and at home they must elude their formidable wives (Busch and Christy). That's about it, but notice how meticulously the sight gags are constructed, and how perfectly tuned Stan and Ollie are to every comic nuance, and to each other. As always, Stan's behavior exasperates Ollie, who watches as his dim-bulb friend consumes a wax apple with gusto or uses multisyllabic words in the manner of an idiot savant.

Off-Screen: Mae Busch (Hardy's wife) was at one time a major star in silent films, most notably in Erich von Stroheim's *Foolish Wives* (1922). Then starting his career, Robert Cummings can be spotted fleetingly in one scene. The movie's working title was *Fraternally Yours*. Two trade papers, *Film Daily* and *The Motion Picture Herald,* cited this modest little movie as one of the year's top grossers.

Sophie's Choice

Universal/AFD, 1982. (C-157m.) Dir: Alan J. Pakula. Sp: Alan J. Pakula, b/o novel by William Styron. Cast: Meryl Streep, Kevin Kline, Peter MacNichol, Rita Karin, Stephen D. Newman, Josh Mostel.

On-Screen: *Tormented lovers in postwar Brooklyn, via William Styron's novel.* Stingo (MacNichol), a young Southern writer, comes to Brooklyn in 1947 for his personal "voyage of discovery." He becomes deeply involved in the lives of Sophie (Streep), a Polish refugee with dark and terrible secrets, and Nathan (Kline), her manic and ultimately insane Jewish lover. Shrouded in mystery, Sophie gradually reveals the lies and deceptions about her past and exposes the unbearable guilt that ties her to the often abusive Nathan, who is her penance and the catalyst for her tragic fate. Meryl Streep's Oscar-winning performance is the stunning centerpiece of this long, leisurely paced film—she expresses every facet of her tortured and complex character. Kline is also excellent as the volatile Nathan. The long flashback sequence near the film's end, in which Sophie's true experience is recounted, is superb filmmaking. *Sophie's Choice* has many detractors and much of the film requires patience, but its somber story lingers in the mind.

Off-Screen: Writer-director Pakula at first wanted unknowns for the leading roles, but he was finally persuaded that at least one star was necessary. Liv Ullmann was his first choice, but when the movie was postponed, the actress was no longer available. Polish director Andrzej Wajda suggested Streep, who was eager to play the role. The Auschwitz scenes were filmed in Zagreb, Yugoslavia, at the Jadran Studios. The boardinghouse was a gray Victorian mansion on Rugby Road in Brooklyn. In addition to Streep's Oscar, the movie won nominations for its screenplay, cinematography, and costume design.

Sorry, Wrong Number

Paramount, 1948. (89m.) Dir: Anatole Litvak. Sp: Lucille Fletcher, b/o her radio drama. Cast: Barbara Stanwyck, Burt Lancaster, Ann Richards, Wendell Corey, Ed Begley, Leif Erickson, William Conrad.

On-Screen: *A terrified Stanwyck as a potential murder victim.* Leona Stevenson (Stanwyck) is rich, married, neurotic, and confined to a bed in her luxurious New York apartment. She's also alone. When Leona rings up her husband (Lancaster) to learn why he hasn't returned home from his office, she gets a crossed line and overhears a conversation about a murder that's to be committed that night. From the description of the victim-to-be, it could only be—yes!—Leona herself. Frantic phone calls for help are unavailing, but a conversation with a close friend (Richards) reveals the terrible truth behind the murder plan. Dramatically, this spine-tingler costars Stanwyck with her bedside phone, and the actress rises splendidly to the challenge of what amounts to a one-woman show. Litvak's tautly paced direction and Sol Polito's shadowy photography lend a chilling atmosphere to Leona's claustrophobic surroundings. Wait for that chilling last line.

Off-Screen: Fletcher's original script, the source of the screenplay, was written in 1943 for the popular half-hour radio series "Suspense" and had Agnes Moorehead soloing as the besieged invalid. At Stanwyck's request, Litvak shot all the actress's emotionally charged scenes in sequence over a twelve-day period, thus lending an authenticity to the character's mounting terror. For her harrowing portrayal, Stanwyck was awarded her fourth Academy Award nomination. In 1989, Loni Anderson appeared in an ill-advised television production. (CFB)

The Sound of Music

Fox, 1965. (C-174m.) Dir: Robert Wise. Sp: Ernest Lehman, b/o musical play by Howard Lindsey and Russel Crouse. MS: Richard Rodgers and Oscar Hammerstein II. Cast: Julie Andrews, Christopher Plummer, Eleanor Parker, Peggy Wood, Richard Haydn, Charmian Carr, Daniel Truhitte, Anna Lee, Portia Nelson.

On-Screen: *A singing Austrian family flees the Nazis.* For nearly three decades, Robert Wise's adaptation of the long-running Rodgers and Hammerstein stage musical has been adored, scorned, and frequently revived on television (in a slightly abridged version). The fact is, it does have many virtues: a lilting score (the music is hard to forget, even if one wants to); a lovely, sometimes breathtaking physical production (the opening number in the Austrian Alps is justifiably famous); and a fine, non-saccharine performance by Julie Andrews as the young postulant nun who becomes the governess to the seven Von Trapp children, stays to marry their widowed father (Plummer), and escapes with them from Nazi oppression in 1938. The story, based on the experiences of the renowned Von Trapp Family Singers, has a sugar content high enough to make the teeth rot, but apparently most moviegoers have an insatiable sweet tooth. Christopher Plummer is rather chilly as Captain Von Trapp, and the children are either adorable or off-putting—take your pick. All in all, those hills are certain to be alive with *The Sound of Music* for many years to come.

Off-Screen: The movie was filmed on location for eleven weeks in Salzburg, with interiors at the Fox lot in West Los Angeles. Two new songs—"Something Good" and "I Have Confidence"—were added to the film score, while three stage songs were deleted. Christopher Plummer's songs were dubbed by Bill Lee, while Margery McKay sang for Reverend Mother Peggy Wood. Catch the error: Although the film is set in the thirties, some publicity stills show an orange crate stamped "product of Israel." The movie won five Oscars, including Best Picture and Best Director.

Sounder

Fox, 1972. (C-105m.) Dir: Martin Ritt. Sp: Lonnie Elder III, b/o novel by William Armstrong. Cast: Cicely Tyson, Paul Winfield, Kevin Hooks, Carmen Mathews, Taj Mahal, Janet MacLachlin, James Best.

On-Screen: *The tribulations of black Southern sharecroppers in the Depression years.* A beautifully wrought, if somewhat idealized, film, *Sounder* relates the poignant story of the Morgans, a poor black sharecropping family in 1933 Louisiana. When desperate father Nathan Morgan (Winfield) steals some food for his starving family and is sent to prison, his resilient wife, Rebecca (Tyson), and sensitive son, David Lee (Hooks), must assume the burden. David Lee's journey to find his father's labor camp also leads him to discover his own worth and manhood. Martin Ritt creates lovely sequences out of small events—a father-son hunting trip, or a happy baseball game played by the blacks—and he makes the big emotional moments affecting. Cicely Tyson is the film's strength—her proud, wary, tenacious

Rebecca is most memorable in the scene in which her husband returns home from prison. You are not likely to forget her cry of elation as she rushes to meet him. (Sounder, by the way, is the name of the family dog—a symbol of the family's power to survive.)

Off-Screen: *Sounder* received four Academy Award nominations, for Best Picture, Best Actress (Tyson), Best Actor (Winfield), and Best Screenplay from another source (Elder). The movie was filmed on location in Louisiana's St. Helena Parish and East Feliciana Parish. Taj Mahal, the actor who plays Ike, composed the movie's evocative musical score. A sequel, *Part 2, Sounder,* with different leading players, was released in 1976.

South Pacific

Fox, 1958. (C-151m.) Dir: Joshua Logan. Sp: Paul Osborn, b/o musical play by Oscar Hammerstein II and book by James A. Michener. MS: Richard Rodgers and Oscar Hammerstein II. Cast: Mitzi Gaynor, Rossano Brazzi, John Kerr, Ray Walston, France Nuyen, Juanita Hall, Russ Brown, Jack Mullaney.

On-Screen: *Rodgers and Hammerstein's enchanted evening.* Following its enthusiastic reception on Broadway in 1949, *South Pacific* went on to become one of the most durable and beloved musicals of the American theater. Audiences responded joyfully to its lovely score and its story of the wartime romance between a French planter and young American nurse. When the screen version finally arrived nine years later, did it receive the same approval? In a word, no. The Rodgers-Hammerstein songs are still soaringly beautiful, the production is elaborate, and Gaynor and Brazzi (dubbed by Giorgio Tozzi) are perfectly adequate if unexciting leads. But Joshua Logan directs with little finesse, and worst of all, he resorts to distracting photographic gimmickry to achieve his effects. Working with the film's cinematographer, Leon Shamroy, Logan saturates every musical scene with rainbow hues. "Bali Ha'i," for example, is staged against a background of green and purple colors filtered over the natural beach setting. One blessing: Juanita Hall (dubbed by Muriel Smith), repeating her stage role of pragmatic, lusty Bloody Mary.

Off-Screen: Despite the criticism of his photography, Leon Shamroy won an Oscar nomination. The movie did receive an Academy Award for its sound. John Kerr's voice was dubbed by Bill Lee. Joshua Logan considered Elizabeth Taylor for the role of Nurse Nellie Forbush, but when she auditioned for Richard Rodgers, she was so frightened, her voice was more of a croak.

Spartacus

Universal, 1960. (C-197m.) Dir: Stanley Kubrick. Sp: Dalton Trumbo, b/o novel by Howard Fast. Cast: Kirk Douglas, Laurence Olivier, Jean Simmons, Charles Laughton, Tony Curtis, Peter Ustinov, John Gavin, John Ireland, Woody Strode, Nina Foch, Herbert Lom.

On-Screen: *Spectacular sword-and-toga saga.* Overlong and overburdened with its down-with-oppressors message, this cinemarathon is nevertheless a visual and dramatic treat. As the gladiator who leads a revolt against Rome's decadent leaders, Douglas makes an ideal hero, noble and virile, yet introspective. Olivier and Laughton lend prestigious luster as rival Roman senators, one sadistic, and the other merely corrupt. Ustinov, as the wily head of a gladiator-training school, plays his juicy role for all its worth, and more. Amid the tumult of intrigue and battle, Strode's self-sacrificing gladiator makes a lasting impression. Simmons plays a slave smitten with Spartacus; Curtis, a houseboy who's caught Olivier's eye; and Gavin, a crafty Julius Caesar. Trumbo's literate script is preachy, even ponderous at times; overall, however, Kubrick's direction maintains a spirited narrative drive.

Off-Screen: When first released, the movie's running time was trimmed to a still-lengthy 184 minutes. Now, lost footage and suggestive dialogue between Olivier and Curtis are back in place, thanks to the American Film Institute's painstaking restoration, completed in 1991. Because the sound track of the Olivier-Curtis scene is missing, redubbing was necessary; Anthony Hopkins read the lines delivered by the late actor, and Curtis repeated his dialogue. Douglas, the movie's executive producer, made a point of hiring Trumbo, blacklisted as a result of the 1950s' Red scare, to adapt Fast's novel. The movie won four Oscars: Best Supporting Actor (Ustinov), color Cinematography (Russell Metty), Art Direction–Set Decoration, and Costume Design. (CFB)

Spellbound

Selznick–United Artists, 1945. (111m.) Dir: Alfred Hitchcock. Sp: Ben Hecht, b/o novel by Francis Beeding. Cast: Ingrid Bergman, Gregory Peck, Leo G. Carroll, Michael Chekhov, Rhonda Fleming, John Emery.

On-Screen: *Psychiatrist helps guilt-ridden amnesiac return to sanity.* This "manhunt story wrapped up in pseudopsychoanalysis," as Hitchcock himself termed it, is far from the director's best. Bergman plays the prim, bespectacled psychiatrist who must delve into Peck's deeply troubled past to convince him that he is not a murderer. She also falls in love with him. The actress copes gamely with such excruciating lines as "I have done a great deal of research on emotional problems and love difficulties." Her costar's wooden performance hardly helps. There are virtues in Miklos Rozsa's lush score and especially in George Barnes's striking cinematography. Visually exciting are the subjective flashback in which Peck recalls his brother's gruesome death, and the scene in which Carroll tries to kill Bergman, his gun turning toward the camera, firing a subliminal Technicolor burst of red. The pivotal dream sequence designed by surrealist Salvador Dalí is classic kitsch. At one point, told that a mental patient has gone berserk, Bergman inquires, "Is it bad?" The answer, regrettably, is yes.

Off-Screen: Producer David O. Selznick at first considered Dorothy McGuire, Joseph Cotten, and Paul Lukas for the main roles. Chekhov, as Bergman's wise old former professor, was the nephew of Russian playwright Anton Chekhov. Composer Rozsa made effective use of the theremin, an eerie-sounding electronic instrument, throughout his Oscar-winning score. The movie received five other Oscar nominations. Watch for Hitchcock's minicameo appearance as he exits from an elevator, carrying a violin case. (CFB)

The Spiral Staircase

RKO, 1946. (83m.) Dir: Robert Siodmak. Sp: Mel Dinelli, b/o novel by Ethel Lina White. Cast: Dorothy McGuire, George Brent, Ethel Barrymore, Kent Smith, Rhonda Fleming, Elsa Lanchester, Gordon Oliver, Sara Allgood, Rhys Williams.

On-Screen: *Adroit thriller about a deaf-mute in peril.* The setting: a New England town, circa 1906. Acting as companion and servant to bedridden old Ethel Barrymore, deaf-mute Dorothy McGuire comes to believe that the local killer who preys on handicapped women may be one of Barrymore's two sons. She suspects the wrong son, of course, placing herself in dire peril and leading to a chilling finale that unlocks her power of speech. Always an appealing actress, Dorothy McGuire gives an expert performance as the girl in peril, expressing all emotions with only her face until the climax. Skillfully directed by Robert Siodmak, with appropriately dark-shadowed cinematography by Nicholas Musuraca, *The Spiral Staircase* is a riveting melodrama in a Hitchcockian vein.

Off-Screen: Originally called *Some Must Watch,* the title of the novel on which it was based, this movie was the first in a coproduction venture between RKO and David O. Selznick's Vanguard Films. Profits were shared fifty-fifty, with each partner assuming responsibility for aspects of the production. In 1975, the film was poorly remade in England, with Jacqueline Bisset as the mute heroine.

Splash

Buena Vista, 1984. (C-111m.) Dir: Ron Howard. Sp: Lowell Ganz, Babaloo Mandel, and Bruce Jay Friedman. Cast: Tom Hanks, Daryl Hannah, John Candy, Eugene Levy, Dody Goodman, Richard B. Shull, Shecky Greene, Howard Morris.

On-Screen: *Man loves mermaid.* "All my life I've been waiting for someone, and when I find her, she's a fish!" An understandable lament from Alan (Hanks), a lonely New York bachelor who is rescued from drowning in Cape Cod waters by a comely mermaid (Hannah). When the mermaid follows him to the city, he falls for the bewitching creature, who takes the name of Madison (after the avenue). There are many amusing complications, some predictable, others not, but all in the way of disarming, sweet-natured fun. Both Hanks and Hannah are engaging as the unlikely lovers, but the secondary characters steal the movie: John Candy as Alan's cheerfully oafish, lecherous brother; Eugene Levy as a manic scientist who is determined to prove that Madison is a mermaid; and Dody Goodman as Alan's slow-witted secretary. Funny moments include Madison at Bloomingdale's, where her mermaid language shatters a number of television sets, and Madison eagerly consuming a lobster shell at a restaurant.

Off-Screen: *Splash* was a huge hit, but four years after its release, the Disney organization made the mistake of attempting a television follow-up entitled *Splash, Too.* It had Alan and his mermaid wife trying to make a go of it in New York City. The consensus was that the happy couple should have stayed underwater.

Splendor in the Grass

Warners, 1961. (C-124m.) Dir: Elia Kazan. Sp: William Inge. Cast: Natalie Wood, Warren Beatty, Pat Hingle, Audrey Christie, Sean Garrison, Sandy Dennis, Barbara Loden, Zohra Lampert, Gary Lockwood.

On-Screen: *Teenagers in love are sexually frustrated in twenties Kansas.* In many American movies, young love is treated as the stuff of comedy, cute, cuddly, and sometimes drenched in bubble-gum music. Not so in the films and plays of William Inge (*Picnic, The Stripper, The Dark at the Top of the Stairs*), where teenage sex is intense or repressed or, as in the case of this film, intense *because* it's repressed. Wood and Beatty are youngsters in 1920s Kansas, passionately in love but thwarted at every turn by the puritanical conventions and attitudes of the time. Mostly, they are saddled with incredibly obtuse parents. He goes for sexual relief to a "bad" girl, she has a mental breakdown, and years later, with their lives going separate ways, they have a bittersweet reunion. William Inge's screenplay is more than a little overcooked, and Elia Kazan saturates the material with his hyperbolic style, playing almost every scene at such high voltage that the movie occasionally edges toward parody. There are some strong moments, however, and (except for Pat Hingle's overacting) a good cast. Oscar-nominated Wood is lovely and touching as the desperate Deanie, and Beatty, in his film debut, is also effective as her frustrated beau.

Off-Screen: In addition to Warren Beatty, Sandy Dennis (as one of Wood's friends) and Phyllis Diller (briefly seen as Texas Guinan) make their movie debuts in this film. The author himself, whose screenplay won an Oscar, appears as the minister. In his autobiography, director Kazan relates that Wood and Beatty began an off-screen love affair while making this movie. A 1981 television version made little impression.

Stage Door

RKO, 1937. (92m.) Dir: Gregory La Cava. Sp: Morrie Ryskind and Anthony Veiller, b/o play by Edna Ferber and George S. Kaufman. Cast: Katharine Hepburn, Ginger Rogers, Adolphe Menjou, Gail Patrick, Andrea Leeds, Constance Collier, Lucille Ball, Ann Miller, Eve Arden, Jack Carson.

On-Screen: *Zesty comedy-drama of young women drawn together by love of the theater.* Welcome to the Footlights Club, a Manhattan theatrical boardinghouse where aspiring actresses struggle for the Big Chance that will land them on Broadway. Cynical Jean Maitland (Rogers), desperate for a part, walks into the clutches of a middle-aged rake, producer Anthony Powell (Menjou), already the "protector" of hardened Linda Shaw (Patrick). Also rivals for the female lead in Powell's upcoming drama are fragile Kaye Hamilton (Leeds) and overconfident Terry Randall (Hepburn). Amid the wisecracks and rivalries, and words of wisdom ("It takes more than greasepaint and footlights to make an actress; it takes heartbreak as well") from old trouper Collier, tragedy strikes and humbling lessons are learned. Though roommates Hepburn and Rogers—one snooty, the other earthy—dominate the story, you may well remember best Leeds's slow, determined walk up that staircase.

Off-Screen: The movie departs considerably from its source, the 1936 play being mainly an attack on Hollywood's worse-than-death siren call to actresses eager to advance their careers. For Rogers, the film provided a welcome dramatic break from her previous seven appearances with Fred Astaire; cast as a hoofer, though, she dances a number with Miller. Hepburn spoofs herself when she recites the speech beginning, "The calla lilies are in bloom again." They're lines from her 1933 Broadway flop, *The Lake*. Among the four Oscar nominations (including Best Picture, Director, Screenplay) was a Best Supporting Actress nod to Leeds. (CFB)

Stagecoach

Walter Wanger/United Artists, 1939. (96m.) Dir: John Ford. Sp: Dudley Nichols, b/o story by Ernest Haycox. Cast: John Wayne, Claire Trevor, Thomas Mitchell, George Bancroft, Louise Platt, John Carradine, Berton Churchill, Donald Meek, Andy Devine, Chris-Pin Martin.

On-Screen: *John Ford's classic western adventure*. One of the greatest western films, and a pervasive influence on many other movies, *Stagecoach* marked John Ford's return to the genre after a thirteen-year hiatus. Its story of a group of stagecoach passengers on a perilous journey through Apache country in New Mexico of the 1880s was not especially new, but a screenplay that fleshed out the characters, beautiful black-and-white photography by Bert Glennon, and most of all, Ford's brilliant direction combined to give *Stagecoach* a mythic significance. Such scenes as the Indian attack on the stagecoach and a climactic shoot-out on a dusty street became the standards against which similar scenes were measured. After years in minor westerns, John Wayne achieved stardom as the revenge-bound Ringo Kid, and Thomas Mitchell won a Supporting Oscar as a tippling doctor. The score also received an Oscar.

Off-Screen: Famed stuntman Yakima Canutt contributed importantly to the film, especially in the scene of the Indian attack. Producer Walter Wanger wanted Gary Cooper to play the Ringo Kid, but John Ford persuaded him to hire John Wayne instead. Yet during the filming, Ford was said to have criticized Wayne constantly and vociferously in front of everyone. The cast and crew spent ten grueling weeks on location, mostly in Ford's beloved Monument Valley, a stretch of desert land astride the Utah-Arizona border. A remake in 1966 and a television retread in 1986 failed to come even close to the original.

Stalag 17

Paramount, 1953. (120m.) Dir: Billy Wilder. Sp: Billy Wilder and Edwin Blum, b/o play by Donald Bevan and Edmund Trzcinski. Cast: William Holden, Don Taylor, Otto Preminger, Robert Strauss, Harvey Lembeck, Richard Erdman, Peter Graves, Neville Brand, Sig Ruman.

On-Screen: *Life at a German prison camp during World War II*. William Holden won an Oscar for his performance as Sefton, an abrasive airman under suspicion as a prison-camp informer, in this rousing comedy-drama. Adapted from the successful 1951 Broadway play, *Stalag 17* moves into the bunkhouse of Barrack 4 in the German camp where American airmen are held prisoner. Apart from the usual cavorting of the service comedy, the movie deals with the conflicts that arise between the men, especially the suspicion that one of their number may be a stoolie who thwarts an attempted escape. Sefton, well played by Holden with an edge of bitter contempt for his fellow prisoners, is the principal suspect. Director and coauthor Billy Wilder improves on the play, retaining the rowdy comedy but also strengthening the main character and focusing more on the contrasting attitudes of men in confinement.

Robert Strauss and Harvey Lembeck repeat their stage roles as the camp clowns, and director Otto Preminger makes a rare acting appearance as the camp commandant.

Off-Screen: Working as an independent producer after breaking up with Charles Brackett, Billy Wilder bought the film rights to the play. He first envisioned Charlton Heston in the leading role, but as the character became more cynical, he thought of William Holden. The exteriors were filmed at a ranch in Calabasas, about forty miles northwest of Hollywood. On the first day of filming, Billy Wilder assembled the cast and announced that "not a word, not a syllable" of his screenplay would be changed. *Stalag 17* later inspired the television series "Hogan's Heroes" (1965–71), where the prisoners were housed in Stalag 13.

Stand by Me

Columbia, 1986. (C–87m.) Dir: Rob Reiner. Sp: Raynold Gideon and Bruce A. Evans, b/o novella by Stephen King. Cast: River Phoenix, Wil Wheaton, Corey Feldman, Jerry O'Connell, Kiefer Sutherland, Richard Dreyfuss.

On-Screen: *A writer recalls a boyhood adventure.* Shocked to read about the violent death of an old friend, a writer (Dreyfuss) recalls the time in 1959 when he was twelve, and he and three other boys (including the one now dead) embarked on a trip into the Oregon woods. Their mission: to find the dead body of a boy who had been struck by a speeding train. Their trip also turns out to be a personal communion of their mutual fears and sorrows. Based on Stephen King's novella *The Body, Stand by Me* is an often affecting little film that captures the rules, rituals, and hang-ups of preadolescent boys in the late fifties. This being a memory play, the characters' attitudes are all heightened: Each boy has his confessional crying scene; the adults are all horribly insensitive and cruel; the bullies are nasty beyond belief. It's all a bit calculated, but pleasing nonetheless. A highlight: The boy (Wheaton) who will become a writer tells a wonderfully gross story about a pie-eating contest.

Off-Screen: Rob Reiner auditioned several hundred boys for the four roles. River Phoenix read for the part that went to Wil Wheaton. For a week before filming began, the boys assembled in an Oregon hotel suite to play improvisational dramatic games that would get them into their characters. "Stand by Me," the 1961 soul song by Ben E. King, had a renewed life because of its use in this movie.

Star 80

The Ladd Company–Warners, 1983. (C–102m.) Dir: Bob Fosse. Sp: Bob Fosse, based in part on an article by Teresa Carpenter. Cast: Eric Roberts, Mariel Hemingway, Cliff Robertson, Carroll Baker, Roger Rees, David Clennon, Josh Mostel, Sidney Miller, Jordan Christopher, Stuart Damon.

On-Screen: *The tragic true tale of a centerfold's murder.* Sordid and unpleasant, but also oddly compelling, Bob Fosse's *Star 80* relates the circumstances surrounding the brutal murder of *Playboy* model Dorothy Stratten (Hemingway) by her sleazy mentor and husband, Paul Snider (Roberts), followed by Snider's suicide. Using a deliberately jagged style, Fosse flashes back from the murder scene to their past association and to reminiscences by those who knew them, including Hugh Hefner (Robertson). It's an admittedly ugly story with boundless possibilities for voyeurism, and the movie's theme—America's twin obsessions of sex and celebrity—is not exactly fresh by now. But for all that, *Star 80* is expertly made, and Roberts gives a brilliant performance as a man dangerously obsessed with the "star" he created. In the final analysis, however, the film asks us to watch with mounting dread as events propel a thoroughly repellent man to a horrific crime. And when the characters lack tragic stature, we are left with little else but revulsion.

Off-Screen: Bob Fosse had great difficulty finding a studio to back him on this project. Richard Gere was a prime candidate for the role of Paul Snider, and Melanie Griffith was considered for Dorothy Stratten. The character played by Roger Rees was modeled on director Peter Bogdanovich. Dorothy's mother was played by Carroll Baker of *Baby Doll* fame. *Star 80* was Fosse's last film; before his death, he reedited it for television showings. Dorothy Stratten's sad story was also told on televison in *Death of a Centerfold* (1981).

A Star Is Born

Selznick International–United Artists, 1937. (C-111m.) Dir: William Wellman. Sp: Dorothy Parker, Alan Campbell, and Robert Carson, b/o story by William Wellman and Robert Carson. Cast: Janet Gaynor, Fredric March, Adolphe Menjou, May Robson, Lionel Stander, Andy Devine, Edgar Kennedy, Franklin Pangborn, Owen Moore, Peggy Wood, Clara Blandick.

On-Screen: *One film star rises as another falls.* Of the (to date) four versions of *A Star Is Born,* including the first partial account of the story in *What Price Hollywood?* (1932), this film is perhaps the purest and most affecting of them all. While it lacks the power of the musical performances given by Judy Garland (1954) and Barbra Streisand (1976), it is also free of these actresses' emotional grandstanding in the dramatic portions. You know the story: As farm girl Janet Gaynor's star rises in Hollywood, the career of her actor-husband Fredric March evaporates due to his alcoholism and his complete unreliability. Gaynor's famous final line is certain to wring a few tears. There's a degree of honesty and perceptiveness in the screenplay that cuts through all the blatant sentimentality and makes the plight of March's Norman Maine wholly believable. Also interesting are some of the views of Hollywood in the thirties.

Off-Screen: Reportedly, Ben Hecht and Gene Fowler contributed to the screenplay, uncredited. The film received Academy Award nominations in a number of categories, including Best Picture, Best Director, Best Actor, and Best Actress. It won an Oscar for Best Original Story, and a special award was given to W. Howard Greene for his color cinematography. The story was suggested by the true-life careers and marriage of silent film actor John Bowers and his actress wife, Marguerite de la Motte. Former silent film star Owen Moore turns up briefly as a director, and Lana Turner appears fleetingly as an extra in one scene.

A Star Is Born

Warners, 1954. (C-154m.) Dir: George Cukor. Sp: Moss Hart, b/o screenplay by

Dorothy Parker, Alan Campbell, and Robert Carson: MS: Harold Arlen and Ira Gershwin, other writers. Cast: Judy Garland, James Mason, Jack Carson, Charles Bickford, Tommy Noonan.

On-Screen: *Judy Garland hits a dramatic and musical peak.* The most elaborate of several versions of the rising star–falling star story, *A Star Is Born* is an electrifying musical drama, with most of the sparks attributable to Judy Garland. The story is (and always was) the ripest of corn, but corn so well cooked and so deliciously seasoned that it's hard to resist. Garland is the up-and-coming actress-singer whose marriage to a deteriorating, alcoholic film star begins with joy and ends in tragedy. She runs the gamut of emotions with extraordinary skill, and her musical numbers are also superb, with her throbbing voice, her audacious gestures, and her sense of showmanship all meshing beautifully. Her rendition of the Oscar-nominated Arlen-Gershwin song "The Man That Got Away" is breathtaking. As her doomed husband, Norman Maine, James Mason gives one of his finest performances, acting with heartbreaking intensity. Jack Carson projects pure venom as his nasty agent.

Off-Screen: This version of *A Star Is Born* has a checkered history. After the film's first engagements at 181 minutes—the famous "Born in a Truck" number was added at the insistence of studio executives—it was butchered by the studio to a shorter and less effective 154-minute version. In 1983, much of the original print was carefully restored, bringing the new version to 170 minutes. (For complete coverage of the restoration, see *A Star Is Born: The Making of the 1954 Movie and Its 1983 Restoration* by Ronald Haver, Alfred A. Knopf, New York, 1988.)

During production, Garland's behavior was extremely erratic, ranging from deep depression to manic euphoria. She won an Oscar nomination, but lost to Grace Kelly in *The Country Girl*. James Mason was also nominated. His role appears to have been either sought or turned down by many leading actors, including Cary Grant and Humphrey Bogart.

Star Trek: The Motion Picture

Paramount, 1979. (C-132m.) Dir: Robert Wise. Sp: Harold Livingston and Gene Roddenberry, b/o story by Alan Dean Foster and TV program "Star Trek." Cast: William Shatner, Leonard Nimoy, DeForest Kelley, Stephen Collins, Persis Khambatta, James Doohan, George Takei, Majel Barrett, Walter Koenig, Nichelle Nichols, Grace Lee Whitney.

On-Screen: *The starship* Enterprise, *boldly going "where no man has gone before."* "Trekkies" throughout the world were waiting breathlessly for this first large-screen version of their beloved program, which had left the air nearly a decade earlier. Once again, they could watch the intrepid crew of the U.S.S. *Enterprise,* somewhere in the twenty-third century, as they explored and protected a region of our galaxy run by the United Federation of Planets. The ship's mission: to "explore strange new worlds, seek out new life and new civilizations," and to "boldly go where no man has gone before." For devoted "Trekkies," the movie may be a treat or only a mild letdown. Others will probably find it talky, tedious, and not especially impressive in its special effects. Here the *Enterprise* crew, led by Admiral (formerly Captain) Kirk (Shatner), battle a strange alien ship headed for Earth and destroying everything in its path. To a non-Trekkie, the acting seems indifferent and the dialogue surprisingly dull. Fans won't mind, however.

Off-Screen: To date, there have been five sequels to this first effort: *Star Trek II: The Wrath of Khan* (1982); *Star Trek III: The Search for Spock* (1984); *Star Trek IV: The Voyage Home* (1986); *Star Trek V: The Final Frontier* (1989); and *Star Trek VI: The Undiscovered Country* (1991). *Star Trek II* and *Star Trek IV* were generally judged to be the best of the group. William Shatner directed *Star Trek V,* and Leonard Nimoy, who plays half-earthling, half-Vulcan Spock, directed numbers III and IV in the series. A new TV series, *Star Trek: The Next Generation,* was launched in 1987, and there was a Saturday-morning cartoon series as well.

Star Wars

Lucasfilm Ltd./Fox, 1977. (C-121m.) Dir: George Lucas. Sp: George Lucas. Cast: Mark Hamill, Carrie Fisher, Harrison Ford, Alec Guinness, Peter Cushing, Anthony Daniels, Kenny Baker.

On-Screen: *"May the Force be with you!"* One of the most phenomenally popular movies of all time, *Star Wars* is a hugely entertaining mix of old-time outer-space serials, movie swashbucklers, comic books, and other pop artifacts. Somehow, instead of being an indigestible mess, it all works, piling one exciting sequence on the other as brave, young Luke Skywalker (Hamill) rallies his rebellious forces against the evil Galactic Empire. With the help of wise old Ben Kenobi (Guinness), a space pilot named Han Solo (Ford), the hairy Chewbacca, and the robots R2D2 and C3PO, he rescues Princess Leia (Fisher). The dialogue is grade-school level, and most of the acting is perfunctory, but there are sequences of high adventure, especially a climactic bombing raid across the surface of the Deathstar. Considering that its targeted audience is young people, there's a surprising amount of violence, but throngs of happy moviegoers never seemed to mind. However one would define the mystical Force, it was "with" them all the way.

Off-Screen: *Star Wars* was filmed at various locales in Guatemala, Tunisia, and Death Valley, with interiors shot at Elstree Studios in England. Originally, it was intended as part of a nine-film cycle, but to date only two others have been filmed: *The Empire Strikes Back* (1980) and *Return of the Jedi* (1983). The ingenious special photographic effects were carried out under the direction of John Dykstra. The movie received seven Oscars, including awards for Art Direction-Set Decoration, Editing, Costumes, Score, Visual Effects, and Sound. Benjamin Burt, Jr., was given a special Oscar for creating the robot voices.

Stardust Memories

United Artists, 1980. (91m.) Dir: Woody Allen. Sp: Woody Allen. Cast: Woody Allen, Charlotte Rampling, Jessica Harper, Marie-Christine Barrault, Tony Roberts, Daniel Stern, Amy Wright.

On-Screen: *Woody Allen takes on his fans and admirers.* One of Woody Allen's most personal, most eccentric movies, *Stardust Memories* left many critics and viewers angered, or at least puzzled. Allen plays Sandy Bates, a filmmaker not unlike himself who agrees to attend a festival of his films at a resort hotel at the New Jersey shore. A quivering bundle of neuroses, Sandy is assaulted on all sides by adoring fans, pompous movie freaks, and academics reading deep meaning into his films. As past and present interact in his mind, he must also deal with tax problems, women problems, and troubles with his new movie. Allen takes a poisonous view of his fans and admirers (see his disclaimer below), turning them into inane, even dangerous grotesques. Yet he's also hard on himself as he mocks the unshakable angst that always seeps into his movies. There are some funny Allenesque lines and moments, but hardly enough to put *Stardust Memories* on the popular side of Allen's body of work.

Off-Screen: In a *New York Times* article, Allen denied that he was showing hostility to his fans by casting them with actors made to look grotesque: "It was purely a visual device. I thought if people were going to sit through an hour-and-a-half movie in which a lot of average people were playing roles, the people ought to be interesting to look at. It wouldn't have been as effective if they were just ordinary-looking." Louise Lasser and Laraine Newman make uncredited appearances.

Starman

Columbia, 1984. (C-115m.) Dir: John Carpenter. Sp: Bruce A. Evans and Raynold Gideon. Cast: Jeff Bridges, Karen Allen, Charles Martin Smith, Richard Jaeckel.

On-Screen: *Adventures of an alien visitor*. It would take more than the fingers on both hands to cite the number of movies that have been inspired by, or suggested by, that phenomenal blockbuster *E.T.: The Extra Terrestrial*. John Carpenter's *Starman* is one of the more blatant examples, but it also happens to be charming and even romantic. Jeff Bridges is a visitor from a distant planet who takes over the body of the husband of grieving young widow Karen Allen. Terrified at first, Allen comes to realize that this odd man out must return to his planet or die. Not surprisingly, she also falls in love with him. Of course those in pursuit of the alien are either nasty (Jaeckel) or supportive (Smith). It's all quite derivative, but Bridges, with his stiff-legged walk, his quick head movements, and his way of imitating everything he hears, makes the character endearing and funny. He won, and richly deserved, an Oscar nomination for Best Performance by an Actor. Favorite incident: Starman and the deer.

Off-Screen: No less than five other directors, including John Badham, Tony Scott, and Adrian Lyne, worked on the film before John Carpenter took over the assignment. A major rewrite of the screenplay was done by Dean Riesner, but he was denied screen credit, to Carpenter's indignation. Three famed makeup men, Dick Smith, Rick Baker, and Stan Winston, created the transformation sequence in which Starman clones his human form. A television adaptation turned up in the 1986–87 season.

Starting Over

Paramount, 1979. (C-106m.) Dir: Alan J. Pakula. Sp: James L. Brooks, b/o novel by Dan Wakefield. Cast: Burt Reynolds, Jill Clayburgh, Candice Bergen, Charles Durning, Frances Sternhagen, Austin Pendleton, Mary Kay Place.

On-Screen: *A divorced man finds new love, but can't forget his ex-wife.* A smartly turned-out and pleasing comedy, *Starting Over* offers some perceptive ideas about love, marriage, and divorce. Playing convincingly against his usual macho type, Burt Reynolds stars as a recently divorced man who falls for a wary, vulnerable nursery-school teacher (Clayburgh), but can't get his ex-wife (Bergen) out of his system. His confused state of mind leads to comic and romantic complications. Brooks's screenplay captures the precarious life of the newly divorced, including the therapy workshops and the new dating rituals. The first encounter of Reynolds and Clayburgh is funny, and late in the film, there's a hilarious scene in Bloomingdale's. The cast is expert, but the real surprise is Bergen; she's marvelous as a "liberated" woman who fancies herself a songwriter. Her intense renditions of her "feminist" songs are highlights of the movie.

Off-Screen: Burt Reynolds was determined to end the macho stereotype with his role in this film. He spent hours convincing director Pakula that he should play the part for which Robert Redford and Dustin Hoffman had been considered. Pakula had doubts but signed him. Reynolds had actually been involved in an incident in which he *did* hyperventilate in a restaurant, as he does in the scene in Bloomingdale's: "I remember asking if anyone had a Valium, and about thirty people responded."

State Fair

Fox, 1945. (C-100m.) Dir: Walter Lang. Sp: Sonya Levien, Paul Green, and Oscar Hammerstein II, b/o novel by Philip Stong. MS: Richard Rodgers and Oscar Hammerstein II. Cast: Dana Andrews, Jeanne Crain, Dick Haymes, Vivian Blaine, Charles Winninger, Fay Bainter, Percy Kilbride, Donald Meek, Frank McHugh.

On-Screen: *Rodgers and Hammerstein in the corn belt.* At the crest of their popularity as a Broadway writing team, Richard Rodgers and Oscar Hammerstein created this musical version of a bucolic novel first filmed in 1933. Regrettably, *State Fair* proved to be somewhat less than it might have been. The story is simple: The Frake family visits the Iowa State Fair, where the parents win prizes and their offspring find either temporary or permanent romance. The cast is attractive, and the Rodgers and Hammerstein songs, including the Oscar-winning "It Might As Well Be Spring," are mostly lilting and appealing. Then what's wrong? Mostly, the production misses every chance to convey some of the fun and excitement of a state fair—everything has a flattened, lacquered look that is emphasized by the bright, bright Technicolor. Worst of all, the songs (with a few exceptions) are staged in a perfunctory, unimaginative way that does them no justice.

Off-Screen: Richard Rodgers had originally written "It Might As Well Be Spring" at a bright, medium tempo, but Fox's musical director wanted it performed as a slow ballad. They argued, until the studio promised to reshoot the number if it did not go over well at a preview performance. The audience loved it, and Rodgers later admitted that the studio was right. The movie was poorly remade in 1962, with Pat Boone and Pamela Tiffin as the young Frakes. Alice Faye came out of retirement to play their mother.

State of the Union

MGM, 1948. (124m.) Dir: Frank Capra. Sp: Anthony Veiller and Myles Connolly, b/o play by Howard Lindsay and Russel Crouse. Cast: Spencer Tracy, Katharine Hepburn, Van Johnson, Adolphe Menjou, Angela Lansbury, Lewis Stone, Raymond Walburn.

On-Screen: *Tracy and Hepburn mix in presidential politics*. Adapted to the screen from the Lindsay-Crouse Broadway play, *State of the Union* takes on a strongly Capraesque coloration. Basically, it's still the story of a liberal-minded man (Tracy) who becomes the Republican presidential candidate under the thumb of power-hungry politician Menjou and his cronies. He is very nearly crushed, until his estranged wife (Hepburn) forces him to remember his long-standing commitment to "principle, integrity, honesty." All of the elements of the thirties Capra film—the good man laid low by corruption, the wisdom of the "little people," the ruthlessness and greed of kingpin politicians—are present, but they ring a bit hollow in 1948. An impressive cast, however, plays the familiar material for all its worth. Best are Van Johnson as Tracy's cynical campaign manager and Angela Lansbury, once again in a role older than her years, as a tough and influential newspaper publisher.

Off-Screen: Originally signed to play Tracy's wife, Claudette Colbert walked off the film when the studio wouldn't allow a stipulation in her contract that she could not work past five P.M. Katharine Hepburn replaced her. There was drama on the set: Adolphe Menjou had cooperated with the House Un-American Activities Committee, which was investigating Communist influence in films.

Scornful of this, Hepburn refused to speak to Menjou, except when they had scenes together.

Steel Magnolias

TriStar, 1989. (C-118m.) Dir: Herbert Ross. Sp: Robert Harling, b/o his play. Cast: Sally Field, Shirley MacLaine, Dolly Parton, Daryl Hannah, Julia Roberts, Olympia Dukakis, Tom Skerritt, Sam Shepard.

On-Screen: *The lives of small-town Southern women intermingle over the years*. If you have not yet had your fill of down-home Southern eccentrics, you may well be entertained and even moved by this comedy-drama, adapted from Robert Harling's long-running off-Broadway play. The story revolves about a group of small-town Louisiana women who congregate at Dolly Parton's beauty parlor. Field is the mother of Roberts, who risks her life by becoming pregnant. Hannah is a religious fanatic, and MacLaine is the town's most sour-natured citizen ("I've just been in a very bad mood for forty years"). The sassy exchanges between the women are often amusing, and the climactic tragedy, echoing but never matching *Terms of Endearment,* will leave few dry eyes in the theater. Harling's screenplay opens up his one-set play rather well and brings in lots of local color. *Steel Magnolias* joins such films as *Crimes of the Heart* (1986), *Miss Firecracker* (1989), and *Fried Green Tomatoes* (1991) in the Crackpot Southerner Sweepstakes.

Off-Screen: Julia Roberts, on the verge of becoming a major star, won an Oscar nomination for Best Supporting Actress. The producers wanted to have a trailer for the film in which Sally Field, on her daughter's wedding day, tells her son, "Don't decorate your sister's car with condoms." The ad would have cut to a car festooned with inflated prophylactics. The MPAA rejected the trailer. In the funeral scene, Shirley MacLaine appears with her mother and her daughter, Sachi. Author Harling plays a minister.

Stella Dallas

Samuel Goldwyn/United Artists, 1937. (106m.) Dir: King Vidor. Sp: Harry Wagstaff Gribble and Gertrude Purcell, b/o novel by Olive Higgins Prouty. Cast: Barbara Stanwyck, John Boles, Anne Shirley, Alan Hale, Barbara O'Neil, Ann Shoemaker, Tim Holt.

On-Screen: *Barbara Stanwyck as the ultimate sacrificial mom.* A remake of the 1925 silent (remade again in 1990 with Bette Midler), this version of the Olive Higgins Prouty novel features one of Stanwyck's most assured and heartfelt performances. She's the flashy, lower-class lady who deliberately alienates her young daughter (Shirley) so that the girl can enjoy a life of luxury with her father (Boles) and his new wife. The corn is ripe for the picking, but many moviegoers have wept at the famous climactic scene, in which downtrodden Stella gazes wistfully through a window at her daughter's high-society wedding. As she smiles through her tears, a policeman sends her on her way to a lonely future. Second-best scene: Stella and her daughter wait for the birthday party that never takes place.

Off-Screen: Several other actresses, including Ruth Chatterton, were considered for the role of Stella before Stanwyck was signed.

(Sam Goldwyn felt that Stanwyck was too young to handle the part.) She was obliged to make a test, which convinced the producer that she was the right choice. Stanwyck won an Oscar nomination but lost to Luise Rainer's peasant wife in *The Good Earth*. Anne Shirley was also nominated.

The Sting

Universal, 1973. (C-129m.) Dir: George Roy Hill. Sp: David S. Ward. Cast: Paul Newman, Robert Redford, Robert Shaw, Charles Durning, Ray Walston, Harold Gould, Dana Elcar, Eileen Brennan, Robert Earl Jones.

On-Screen: *Seasoned con artist Newman teaches greenhorn Redford how to pull off the Big One.* Winner of seven Academy Awards, including Oscars for direction, screenplay, and as the year's best picture, *The Sting* tops the list for most comedy-caper movie fans. Set in and around Chicago of the midthirties, the story begins when Redford, seeking revenge for the murder of his friend by mob boss Shaw, turns for help to Newman, an aging boozer down on his luck. With the aid of pals, they devise an ingenious plan to give Shaw a one-way ticket to the cleaner. Among the best scenes is the poker-game sting, played with obvious relish by Newman and Shaw. The chiselers' scheme works—but watch out for the ultimate surprise twister. Hill's direction handles the plot complications deftly, Marvin Hamlisch's adaptations of Scott Joplin ragtime tunes add to the fun, and Henry Bumstead's Oscar-winning set designs have just the right period flavor. A nod, as well, to Robert Surtees's cinematography, which captures the nostalgic glow of old *Saturday Evening Post* covers.

Off-Screen: Originally, Paul Newman's character of Henry Gondorff was, in director Hill's words, "a burly, oafish slob of a man." The screenplay was rewritten to accommodate Newman's sleeker image. Redford's acting in *The Sting* earned him an Oscar nomination. Richard Boone was originally considered for the part of the mob boss, but when he rejected it, it went instead to burly British actor Shaw. In the close-ups, those aren't Newman's hands shuffling the cards; they belong to gambling expert John Scarne. In 1983, *The Sting II,* a sequel with another cast, was released. Bad deal. (CFB)

A Stolen Life

Warners, 1946. (107m.) Dir: Curtis Bernhardt. Sp: Catherine Turney, b/o novel by Karel J. Benes. Cast: Bette Davis, Glenn Ford, Dane Clark, Walter Brennan, Charlie Ruggles, Bruce Bennett.

On-Screen: *Bette Davis as twin sisters who love the same man.* A soap-operatic variation on the good-twin, bad-twin plot gambit, *A Stolen Life* is a remake of a 1939 film made in England with Elisabeth Bergner. In her bravura, nerves-exposed fashion, Bette Davis plays twin sisters who both fall in love with lighthouse keeper Ford. The bolder, sexier twin wins the contest and marries Ford, but when she is killed in a boating accident, the sweeter, gentler twin takes her place. Inevitably, the ruse leads to emotional complications. Bette Davis is convincing if not very subtle in the dual roles, and as usual she manages to make this sort of nonsense entertaining with the sheer force of her personality. She gets competent support from Glenn Ford, and from Dane Clark as the sort of snarling working-class

artist John Garfield might have played in his prestardom days. The movie offers a double dose of Davis for her fans, but it's not among her best efforts.

Off-Screen: Bette Davis had trouble finding a leading man for the film. She was given the choice of Dennis Morgan or Robert Alda, but rejected both actors. Director Curtis Bernhardt suggested Glenn Ford, whom she liked, and he won the role. Other good twin–bad twin movies include *The Dark Mirror* (1946), *Dead Ringer* (1964), again with Davis, *The Other,* (1972), and *Dead Ringers* (1988).

The Story of Louis Pasteur

Warners, 1936. (85m.) Dir: William Dieterle. Sp: Sheridan Gibney and Pierre Collings. Cast: Paul Muni, Josephine Hutchinson, Anita Louise, Donald Woods, Henry O'Neill, Porter Hall, Fritz Leiber, Halliwell Hobbes.

On-Screen: *Paul Muni as the renowned scientist.* One of Warners' prestigious biographical films of the thirties, *The Story of Louis Pasteur* is a reverent, plodding, and occasionally gripping portrait of the scientist who struggled against great odds to find the deadly microbe that causes hydrophobia. As Pasteur, Paul Muni is commendable if a bit overfussy, and he gets good support from a large cast. There are scenes of high drama in the second half, when Pasteur desperately decides to test his unproven theory on a boy stricken with hydrophobia. But the movie is also replete with film-biography clichés. (Wife to Pasteur: "Didn't you promise me to rest? You haven't closed your eyes in forty-eight hours.") Muni won an Oscar as Best Actor, as did Gibney and Collings for their screenplay. The film itself received a Best Picture nomination.

Off-Screen: Initially, Warners' executives were strongly opposed to making the film. Jack Warner claimed that audiences would not want to see a film about a chemist, and Hal Wallis felt that the public wouldn't accept Paul Muni with a beard: "He'll look like a rabbi." Attempts to create a ludicrous fictional plot about Pasteur were stopped by Muni, who had script approval. Even when the movie was approved, the studio assigned it a relatively small budget and insisted that only redressed sets were to be used. (The Academy of Science amphitheater was originally a nightclub in a Busby Berkeley musical.) Earlier titles for the film included *Enemy of Man* and *The Death Fighter*.

The Story of Vernon and Irene Castle

RKO, 1939. (93m.) Dir: H. C. Potter. Sp: Richard Sherman, Oscar Hammerstein II, and Dorothy Yost, b/o story by Irene Castle. MS: Various writers. Cast: Fred Astaire, Ginger Rogers, Edna May Oliver, Walter Brennan, Lew Fields.

On-Screen: *One famous dance couple portrays another.* For the last of their series of RKO musicals, Astaire and Rogers abandoned the sophistication of their other films and turned to the nostalgic past. For the first time in their dual careers, they played real-life personages: Vernon and Irene Castle, the celebrated dance team that was all the rage in the years before World War I. Cozy and sentimental, *The Story of Vernon and Irene Castle* traces their rise to fame and re-creates some of their most sensational dances, notably the Castle Walk. The best

sequence, called the Montage Medley, demonstrates the Castles' soaring popularity. They dance the tango, the polka, and the maxixe, and in an impressive final shot, they whirl across a huge map of the United States as a swarm of dancing couples follows in their wake. The movie's only original song is a lovely, neglected ballad called "Only When You're in My Arms." A viewer may long for the sparkle and wit of their contemporary dances, but this film offers its own quiet pleasures and makes a pleasing coda for their RKO period.

Off-Screen: Reportedly, Irene Castle disapproved of the casting of Ginger Rogers and threw a royal fit when Rogers refused to have her hair cut in the revolutionary "Castle bob." She also insisted that all of her dancing costumes be reproduced in exact detail, including the same materials and colors. The studio and Rogers were pleased when she was diverted by her interest in antivivisectionist activities.

The Strange Love of Martha Ivers

Paramount, 1946. (117m.) Dir: Lewis Milestone. Sp: Robert Rossen, b/o story by Jack Patrick. Cast: Barbara Stanwyck, Van Heflin, Kirk Douglas, Lizabeth Scott, Judith Anderson, Darryl Hickman, Roman Bohnen, Janis Wilson, Mickey Kuhn.

On-Screen: *A guilty secret haunts several lives.* 1928: A young girl (Wilson) murders her odious aunt (Anderson) in the presence of her tutor's son (Kuhn). Sixteen years later, the two, haunted by the crime, are trapped in a bad marriage; she (Stanwyck) is a wealthy, coldly ambitious woman and he (Douglas) is a weak alcoholic. Enter Heflin, a figure from their past who may or may not know about the crime. Soon all three are caught up in a spider's web of blackmail, passion, and threatened violence. Scott also figures in the sordid tale as a parolee who falls for Heflin. All the ingredients of a taut *film noir* are present, including yards of overheated dialogue, clamorous music, and a blatantly wicked woman, and if the movie lacks the flair of the best in the genre, it still holds our attention. No actress could play hard-boiled dames better than Stanwyck, and here she is in top snarling form. Kirk Douglas makes his film debut as her husband.

Off-Screen: Earlier titles for the film were *Love Lies Bleeding* and *Bleeding Heart*. Director Milestone had nothing but praise for his star: "Stanwyck was very knowledgeable about all phases of film production. She would come on a new set and carefully examine the placement of camera, lights, etc. Then she would call the cameraman over and introduce him to the mysteries of her own favorite key light. She astonished everyone with her knowledge of lighting and her technical know-how in general." Reputedly, Milestone contributed to the screenplay without credit.

The Stranger

International-RKO, 1946. (95m.) Dir: Orson Welles. Sp: Anthony Veiller, b/o story by Victor Trivas and Decla Denning. Cast: Edward G. Robinson, Loretta Young, Orson Welles, Philip Merivale, Richard Long, Martha Wentworth, Billy House, Konstantin Shayne.

On-Screen: *A Nazi hides out in a Connecticut town.* Having placed himself firmly on the permanent movie map with the innovative *Citizen Kane,* Orson Welles was determined to show that he "could put out a movie as well as anyone else." To this end, he directed this taut but ultimately disappointing melodrama. Some bravura touches, especially brilliant camerawork by Russell Metty, cannot conceal the story's serious gaps in credibility. Orson Welles plays an unregenerate Nazi who disguises himself as a teacher in a quiet Connecticut town. He even marries the daughter (Young) of a Supreme Court justice (Merivale). Enter Edward G. Robinson, who is tracking him down for the Allied War Crimes Commission. The two play a cat-and-mouse game that ends in the town's old clock tower. Welles makes good use of shadows to create an ominous mood, and he directs several sequences, notably a murder in the woods, with the flourish of a master director. However, the story is hard to believe, and the climax, involving the revolving figure of an avenging angel with a sword, is preposterous.

Off-Screen: Orson Welles wanted Agnes Moorehead to play the Edward G. Robinson role, but producer Sam Spiegel wouldn't hear of it. The 124-foot clock tower constructed for the film was the highest set built in Hollywood since D. W. Griffith's silent classic *Intolerance* (1916). Welles found the clock, which prior to 1922 had been in the Los Angeles County Courthouse, in the cellar of the Los Angeles County Museum. Uncredited John Huston worked on the screenplay with Anthony Veiller.

Strangers On a Train

Warners, 1951. (101m.) Dir: Alfred Hitchcock. Sp: Raymond Chandler and Czenzi Ormonde; adaptation: Whitfield Cook, b/o novel by Patricia Highsmith. Cast: Farley

Granger, Robert Walker, Ruth Roman, Leo G. Carroll, Marion Lorne, Patricia Hitchcock, Laura Elliot, Jonathan Hale.

On-Screen: *A psychotic's crisscross murder plan runs into trouble.* To wealthy, smooth-talking Bruno (Walker), it's a simple and foolproof scheme: He'll rid socially ambitious Guy (Granger) of his wife (Elliot), leaving him free to marry a senator's daughter (Roman), if Guy will do away with Bruno's hated father (Hale). Each will have a pat alibi and the killings will seem motiveless. When Bruno fulfills his part of the bargain but Guy defaults, Bruno sees to it that Guy is the murder suspect. Brilliant set pieces include the murder of Guy's wife in an amusement park, with the killing reflected in the lens of her dropped eyeglasses. The climax of this dizzyingly involuted Hitchcock thriller takes place, aptly enough, on an out-of-control merry-go-round. Walker's maniacal intensity and Granger's conscience-stricken desperation make it all believable; Lorne, as Bruno's dottily doting mother, provides welcome comic relief.

Off-Screen: Hitchcock first wanted William Holden to play Guy, but he extracted a thoroughly convincing performance from Granger. Chandler was hired to adapt Highsmith's novel, but his script was judged less concerned with the story than with character-revealing dialogue, so two other writers adapted it more to Hitchcock's liking. Robert Burks's stunning photography was Oscar-nominated. Pat Hitchcock is the daughter of the director, who is seen lugging a bass fiddle onto a train. *Once You Kiss a Stranger* (1969) is a forgettable remake, and *Throw Momma From the Train* (1987) attempts to get mileage from the story's comic possibilities. (CFB)

A Streetcar Named Desire

Warners, 1951. (122m.) Dir: Elia Kazan. Sp: Tennessee Williams, b/o his play as adapted by Oscar Saul. Cast: Vivien Leigh, Marlon Brando, Kim Hunter, Karl Malden, Rudy Bond, Nick Dennis, Peg Hillias.

On-Screen: *Tennessee Williams's lost Blanche DuBois on the screen.* "All my life I've had to depend on the kindness of strangers." With these memorable words, former Southern belle Blanche DuBois (Leigh) finally succumbs to the hollow peace of madness. This splendid adaptation of Tennessee Williams's play traces Blanche's descent after she arrives at the home of her sister, Stella (Hunter), in New Orleans, a pitiable wreck grasping at the last vestiges of gentility. Her brutish brother-in-law (Brando) ferrets out her desperate life of promiscuity and ultimately rapes her, sending her reeling into comforting darkness. *A Streetcar Named Desire* shows its stage origins, but the scenes have a cumulative power, and the acting is flawless. Vivien Leigh gives a stunning performance that fully justified her Academy Award as Best Actress, and Brando is mesmerizing in the role that made him a certified star. Kim Hunter and Karl Malden won supporting Oscars as, respectively, Blanche's sister, torn between her devotion to Blanche and her animal attraction to Stanley, and Blanche's shy suitor, Mitch. Alex North contributes a haunting jazz score.

Off-Screen: In addition to the Oscars for Leigh, Hunter, and Malden, Academy Awards were given to Richard Day and George James Hopkins for their art direction and set decoration. Marlon Brando was nominated but lost to Humphrey Bogart. Earlier possibilities for the leading roles were Olivia de Havilland as Blanche, John Garfield as Stanley, and Anne Baxter as Stella. At first, Vivien Leigh repeated her London stage performance in the role, which Laurence Olivier had directed, until Elia Kazan accustomed her to his grittier style. The Breen Office, which controlled censorship, raised serious objections to the film's inclusion of homosexuality and rape. There was also trouble from the Legion of Decency, but the film managed to survive the several cuts. A 1984 television production starred Ann-Margret.

Suddenly

United Artists, 1954. (77m.) Dir: Lewis Allen. Sp: Richard Sale. Cast: Frank Sinatra, Sterling Hayden, Nancy Gates, James Gleason, Kim Charney, Christopher Dark, Paul Frees.

On-Screen: *A disturbed killer attempts to assassinate the president.* In a startling change from his usual affable, mild-mannered persona (and only a year after winning an Oscar for *From Here to Eternity*), Frank Sinatra plays a seemingly ice-cold but actually deeply disturbed assassin who keeps a family imprisoned as he plots to kill the president. (The nation's leader is stopping briefly in the town called Suddenly.) Sinatra does a creditable job of acting in this modest but trim and taut melodrama, etching a portrait of a war hero raging at his psychological discharge from the army and willing to turn assassin for the money. The beleaguered family is made up of basic American types: the worried mother, the spunky son, the crusty grandfather—and the movie's message, that we must learn to defend our rights as Americans, even with arms, is simplistic. Still, the tension is very real, and a deadly Frank Sinatra will chill your blood. And

sadly, of course, this little movie foreshadows the assassination of President Kennedy, a decade later.

Off-Screen: At one point in the filming, Sinatra proposed some changes to producer Robert Bassler. Later, Bassler admitted that he was very wary, since "there is nothing more disturbing than the cerebration of the actor. But Frank wasn't making demands to exploit himself at the expense of the picture. The suggestions he offered made sense for the picture."

Suddenly, Last Summer

Columbia, 1959. (114m.) Dir: Joseph L. Mankiewicz. Sp: Tennessee Williams and Gore Vidal, b/o play by Tennessee Williams. Cast: Elizabeth Taylor, Katharine Hepburn, Montgomery Clift, Albert Dekker, Mercedes McCambridge.

On-Screen: *A terrible secret haunts and disrupts a Southern family.* Bizarre, and possibly fascinating, are the operative words for this adaptation of Tennessee Williams's one-act drama, performed off-Broadway in 1958. Why is wealthy dowager Katharine Hepburn urging brain surgeon Montgomery Clift to perform a lobotomy on her seemingly insane niece, Elizabeth Taylor? The answer, it turns out, involves a horrifying incident in the past, in which Hepburn's homosexual son, traveling on the coast of Spain with Taylor, was murdered and, it is hinted, literally devoured by a pack of angry, hungry street urchins. A somber and lurid sort of mystery play, *Suddenly, Last Summer* fairly chokes on Williams's florid dialogue, but it is undeniably riveting. Elizabeth Taylor pulls out all stops as the tormented girl, especially in her climactic monologue, and Katharine Hepburn seems to be acting in her own private film as the imperious woman whose mind snaps in the end. Montgomery Clift is virtually catatonic as the mystified surgeon.

Off-Screen: *Suddenly, Last Summer* was a most unhappy production in which many of those involved were coping with emotional and physical problems. Director Mankiewicz was suffering from a skin ailment that forced him to wear gloves during shooting. Taylor still mourned the death of husband Mike Todd. And Clift, in poor health due to his abuse of drugs and alcohol, was barely able to function. Mankiewicz wanted to replace him, but close friend Taylor interceded. From the first day of shooting, the director also battled frequently with Hepburn. At the end of the filming, convinced that Mankiewicz had treated Clift badly, Hepburn spat in his face. (Years later, on television with Dick Cavett, she asserted that she spat for the way he treated her, not Clift.) Taylor and Hepburn were both nominated for Oscars.

The Sugarland Express

Universal, 1974. (C-109m.) Dir: Steven Spielberg. Sp: Hal Barwood and Matthew Robbins. Cast: Goldie Hawn, William Atherton, Michael Sacks, Ben Johnson, Gregory Walcott, Louise Latham.

On-Screen: *Steven Spielberg's feature film debut.* After making his mark in television, Steven Spielberg turned to film and attracted attention with this rambunctious comedy-drama. Based on a true incident that took place in Texas in 1969, *The Sugarland Express* centers on Lou Jean Poplin (Hawn), a none-too-bright woman and recent parolee who breaks her husband, Clovis (Atherton), out of prison so that they can retrieve their infant son, who has been taken away from them. Kidnapping a highway patrolman (Sacks), they careen across the state, hotly pursued by a great many police cars. Soon the Poplins have become a media event ("The whole state of Texas is here!"), attracting scores of sympathetic supporters. It all ends noisily but, for the Poplins, not happily. In his first feature film, Spielberg shows a skill with chase scenes that feature snaking, speeding, and crashing cars, but he is saddled with characters who are too familiar from other movies. This includes that old standby, the calm, sympathetic police captain, played by the ever-reliable Ben Johnson. On the whole an enjoyable debut film, with the promise of better things to come.

Off-Screen: *The Sugarland Express* was filmed on location all over Texas. Playing the Poplins' son is two-year-old Harrison Zanuck, son of producer Richard D. Zanuck and actress Linda Harrison and grandson of Darryl F. Zanuck. The baby's foster father is played by Mervin Connally, brother of John B. Connally, former governor of Texas. Judge Michael Curry played himself in a scene filmed in his courtroom in San Antonio.

Sullivan's Travels

Paramount, 1942. (91m.) Dir: Preston Sturges. Sp: Preston Sturges. Cast: Joel McCrea, Veronica Lake, William Demarest, Robert Warwick, Eric Blore, Robert Greig, Jimmy Conlin, Franklin Pangborn, Porter Hall.

On-Screen: *Preston Sturges takes a film director on a journey into self-knowledge.* An odd, disconcerting, but also brilliant blend of slapstick comedy and grim drama, *Sullivan's Travels* is one of Preston Sturges's most unusual efforts. Joel McCrea plays the title character, a movie director who, tired of making frivolous comedies, sets out to discover life as a tramp with ten cents in his pocket. He finds more than he bargained for in a nightmarish experience that puts him in prison. His ultimate lesson—make people laugh with comedy films: "It isn't much, but it's better than nothing in this cockeyed caravan!" *Sullivan's Travels* is uneven—the shifts from knockabout humor to stark reality are rather bewildering—but Sturges's wit and originality shine through all the self-justification. As a nameless girl who helps Sullivan on his journey, Veronica Lake gives her usual toneless reading to the lines. In all, *Sullivan's Travels* is worth the trip.

Off-Screen: Preston Sturges wrote that the film was intended to tell his fellow comedy directors that they were "getting a little too deep-dish; to leave the preaching to the preachers." He later acknowledged that the movie's mixture of comedy and tragedy had a kind of oil-and-water effect. While filming the chain-gang sequences in a swamp about fifty miles from Los Angeles, Sturges learned that his son Solomon had been born.

Summer Holiday

MGM, 1948. (C-92m.) Dir: Rouben Mamoulian. Sp: Frances Goodrich and Albert Hackett; adaptation: Irving Brecher and Jean Holloway, b/o play by Eugene O'Neill. MS: Harry Warren and Ralph Blane. Cast: Mickey Rooney, Walter Huston, Gloria De Haven, Frank Morgan, Jackie "Butch" Jenkins, Agnes Moorehead, Marilyn Maxwell, Selena Royle.

On-Screen: Ah, Wilderness! *set to music.* An unjustly maligned musical film, *Summer Holiday* offers rewards to those willing to seek them out. True, it lacks the warmth and charm of O'Neill's play, and true, Mickey Rooney is too old and rambunctious as the teenaged Richard Miller. Yet the film is a lovely, beautifully observed slice of Americana, well-handled by the masterly Mamoulian. Some of the musical numbers are diverting: "Stanley Steamer," obviously modeled after "The Trolley Song" of *Meet Me in St. Louis* but enjoyable in its own right, and "You Mustn't Be Afraid to Fall in Love," with its wonderful image of Rooney and De Haven scampering across the greenest grass. Walter Huston contributes the film's best performance—quietly authoritative and sensitive—as Nat Miller.

Off-Screen: Warren and Blane wrote "Spring Isn't Everything" for Walter Huston, "Never Again" for Frank Morgan, and "Wish I Had a Braver Heart" for Gloria De Haven. None of these songs appear in the released version of the film. Also, an elaborate daydream sequence called "Omar and the Princess," in which Rooney and De Haven find themselves in a Persian kingdom, was finally excised. Little "Butch" Jenkins was a problem until Mamoulian promised to give him twelve minutes away from the set when he wasn't needed, provided he returned on time. He always did.

Summer of '42

Warners, 1971. (C-102m.) Dir: Robert Mulligan. Sp: Herman Raucher. Cast: Gary Grimes, Jennifer O'Neill, Jerry Houser, Oliver Conant, Katherine Allentuck, Christopher Norris, Lou Frizell.

On-Screen: *A teenager's sexual rite of passage.* This slight but sweetly nostalgic movie won popularity in part for its haunting musical theme, but it has other merits as well. Hermie (Grimes), Oscy (Houser), and Benjy (Conant) are horny teenagers spending the summer at an island resort in 1942. Their dream of making out with a girl occupies almost every waking moment as they pore avidly over a sex manual or grope the local girls in a movie house. In one hilarious sequence, Hermie, the most sensitive of the three, tries to buy a condom. Hermie is also deeply infatuated with Dorothy (O'Neill), a beautiful war bride who lives in a nearby cottage, and it is his relationship with her that culminates in his sexual initiation. Their consummation scene is handled tactfully and even touchingly. The movie is funniest when the boys are discussing their ideas of sexual activity. ("I held her breast for eleven full minutes.") That musical theme is ubiquitous, but *Summer of '42* has unmistakable charm.

Off-Screen: Michel Legrand's music score won an Academy Award. Herman Raucher's autobiographical screenplay and Robert Surtees's cinematography were nominated. Maureen Stapleton's daughter, Katherine Allentuck, played Aggie, and Stapleton provided the voice for Hermie's mother. Director Mulligan did the narration. A sequel, *Class of '44,* was released in 1973.

Summer Stock

MGM, 1950. (C-109m.) Dir: Charles Walters. Sp: George Wells and Sy Gomberg, b/o story by Sy Gomberg. MS: Harry Warren, Mack Gordon, and others. Cast: Judy Garland, Gene Kelly, Eddie Bracken, Phil Silvers, Gloria De Haven, Marjorie Main, Ray Collins, Carleton Carpenter, Hans Conried.

On-Screen: *Garland and Kelly "put on a show."* Just when you thought they had retired the hoary "let's-put-on-a-show" plot of the Mickey Rooney–Judy Garland musicals, MGM brought it back for another round in this cheerful, moderately entertaining musical. This time Judy is a Connecticut farm girl, rather plump and mature-looking, whose farm is invaded by a horde of actors who want to use her barn for their show. Head man is Gene Kelly, and after the initial resistance, love blossoms. From the evidence shown, the show in question would barely survive its premiere, but never mind—there's plenty of lively singing and dancing. For the finale, a suddenly slimmer Garland (the number was filmed months after the film's completion) does a memorable musical turn to "Be Happy," her voice the same glorious trumpet as before. At least it ended the movie on a triumphant note.

Off-Screen: Judy Garland was in especially poor shape during the filming of *Summer Stock.* Emotionally at low ebb, she was often late or failed to appear for retakes or refused to attend rehearsals. Director Charles Walters recalls, "She had always been a neurotic and insecure performer, but not as bad as this." Gene Kelly was unenthusiastic about the movie but agreed to costar as a favor to Garland.

Summer Wishes, Winter Dreams

Columbia, 1973. (C-93m.) Dir: Gilbert Cates. Sp: Stewart Stern. Cast: Joanne

Woodward, Martin Balsam, Sylvia Sidney, Dori Brenner, Ron Rickards, Tresa Hughes, Win Forman, Nancy Andrews, Minerva Pious.

On-Screen: *A woman reflects on her life, past and present.* Occasionally, a creditable film will have limited appeal, finding only those viewers who can respond to its subtlety and perception. Such a film is Gilbert Cates's *Summer Wishes, Winter Dreams.* Superlative actress Joanne Woodward plays Rita Walden, an unhappy middle-aged housewife who is struggling to come to grips with the failures in her life, and who ultimately comes to realize her inherent coldness. Balsam is Harry, her decent optometrist husband, who travels with her to Europe where, in a powerful scene, he relives the horror of his World War II days. Sylvia Sidney is her feisty old mother, who succumbs to a heart attack. Over the course of the movie, Woodward reflects on her earlier years and relives critical moments with her children. The pace is deliberate, but Cates's direction shows an eye for revealing detail, and the performances, especially Woodward's, are first-rate. *Summer Wishes, Winter Dreams* is not a film for every taste, but for some, it's worth savoring.

Off-Screen: The movie's original title was *Death of a Snow Queen.* It was shot in many locales, including a London underground station, a village in rural Belgium, a cemetery in Luxembourg, and an old farm in Newtown, Connecticut. Both Joanne Woodward and Sylvia Sidney (her first movie in seventeen years) won Oscar nominations for their performances.

Summertime

Lopert Films/United Artists, 1955. (C-99m.) Dir: David Lean. Sp: David Lean and H. E. Bates, b/o play by Arthur Laurents. Cast: Katharine Hepburn, Rossano Brazzi, Isa Miranda, Darren McGavin, Mari Aldon, Jane Rose.

On-Screen: *Katharine Hepburn finds love in a glorious Venice.* Venice has never looked more enchanting than in this romantic drama. Neither, for that matter, has the film's heroine, Katharine Hepburn, playing a middle-aged spinster—a "fancy secretary"—who falls in love with Venice and a married man (Brazzi). Based on Arthur Laurents's play, *The Time of the Cuckoo, Summertime* actually relates a slender tale—against her better judgment, Hepburn falls rhapsodically in love, then decides to end the affair and return home, newly fulfilled. But the star's tremulous performance, Jack Hildyard's breathtaking photography of a magical city, and Sandro Cicognini's melodic musical theme combine to weave an irresistible spell. Isa Miranda, an Italian actress briefly touted for American stardom in the late thirties, plays the owner of the *pensione* at which Hepburn stays during her Venetian idyll. Hepburn received her sixth Oscar nomination for her performance.

Off-Screen: In filming the scene in which she falls into the canal, Hepburn covered herself with lotions and disinfectants, but she forgot to cover her eyes. They became inflamed and watery, and she developed an incurable infection. The many technical problems with the production included a slow and inefficient Italian crew and the constant presence of a curious crowd, which often ruined key sequences. Hepburn admired Lean greatly, although he often brushed aside her suggestions. In 1965, the story of *The Time of the Cuckoo* and *Summertime* was adapted for the musical stage as *Do I Hear a Waltz?*

Sun Valley Serenade

Fox, 1941. (86m.) Dir: H. Bruce Humberstone. Sp: Robert Ellis and Helen Logan, b/o story by Art Arthur and Robert Harari. MS: Mack Gordon and Harry Warren. Cast: Sonja Henie, John Payne, Glenn Miller and His Orchestra, Milton Berle, Lynn Bari, Joan Davis, the Nicholas Brothers, Dorothy Dandridge.

On-Screen: *Sonja Henie on ice in a tuneful musical.* For a number of years, Olympic skating champion Sonja Henie pleased audiences with her winsome personality and dazzling skating routines. Her thespian ability, however, was minimal, consisting of a bright smile and a piquant Norwegian accent. *Sun Valley Serenade* was her best film, made after a two-year absence from the screen. The plot is skimpy, but the production numbers are lavish, especially a finale on black ice. The popular Glenn Miller Orchestra helps a great deal, especially with their "Chattanooga Choo-Choo" number, which features knockout singing and dancing by Dorothy Dandridge and the Nicholas Brothers. Not a major musical by any means but curiously, it remains a nostalgic favorite of many older moviegoers.

Off-Screen: While filming the black-ice ballet, Henie crashed into one of the male skaters, fell, and covered herself in black dye. Studio head Darryl F. Zanuck refused to allow the number to be reshot, so just before the skater's fall, the film dissolves to a shot of Henie and John Payne skiing down the slopes instead of the ending originally planned. Lynn Bari's vocals were dubbed by Pat Friday.

The Sundowners

Warners, 1960. (C-113.) Dir: Fred Zinnemann. Sp: Isobel Lennart, b/o novel by Jon Cleary. Cast: Deborah Kerr, Robert Mitchum, Peter Ustinov, Glynis Johns, Michael Anderson, Jr., Dina Merrill, Chips Rafferty, Lola Brooks, Mervyn Johns.

On-Screen: *An itinerant family in Australia of the 1920s.* Stronger on atmosphere than on narrative, *The Sundowners* is still a pleasing film. The Carmodys—father Paddy (Mitchum), mother Ida (Kerr), and son Sean (Anderson)—travel about the Australian "back country" in the twenties. Paddy is a drover, someone who moves sheep for pay, as well as a perennially restless man. The thrust of the story is that both Ida and Sean desperately want to settle down in one place, but can never get Paddy's approval. For a while, the Carmodys work on a sheep ranch, he as a shearer, she as the cook. The rambling screenplay involves a raging forest fire, a sheep-shearing contest, and a horse race with a horse that Paddy has won in a bet. Robert Mitchum rouses himself from lethargy to give a zestful performance as Paddy, and Deborah Kerr, although a bit too genteel to be entirely convincing, makes us understand Ida's eagerness for domesticity. Peter Ustinov is engaging as a genial vagabond who joins the family, but Glynis Johns virtually steals the show as a lusty innkeeper who takes a fancy to Ustinov.

Off-Screen: Fred Zinnemann originally hoped to star William Holden or Gary Cooper, but they were not available. The movie received five Oscar nominations, including Best Picture, Best Director, Best Actress (Kerr), and Best Supporting Actress (Johns). Deborah Kerr was named Best Actress by the New York film critics. Many years later, Kerr commented that the movie "was a little before its time. It was a no-story movie—an observation of life, with a marvelous cast."

Sunset Boulevard

Paramount, 1950. (110m.) Dir: Billy Wilder. Sp: Charles Brackett, Billy Wilder, and D. M. Marshman, Jr., b/o story by Charles Brackett and Billy Wilder. Cast: Gloria Swanson, William Holden, Erich von Stroheim, Nancy Olson, Fred Clark, Jack Webb, Cecil B. DeMille, Hedda Hopper, Buster Keaton, Anna Q. Nilsson, H. B. Warner.

On-Screen: "*I am big. It's the pictures that got small.*" Glamorous, egotistical, and demented, Norma Desmond (Swanson) is a silent-screen goddess obsessed with staging a comeback in a script of her own devising. The decaying Beverly Hills mansion in which she lives with only a butler (von Stroheim, who was once her director and husband) has become a private world where she entertains a ghostlike circle of forgotten stars (Keaton, Nilsson, and Warner). This scathing, masterly classic permits little sympathy for the former screen siren or for opportunistic writer Joe Gillis (Holden), who agrees to work on her script (which even her old friend "Mr. DeMille" has rejected) and eventually becomes her kept lover. Swanson, herself a star of the silent era, gives a bravura performance, making Desmond a forgivable monster, pathetically unaware of her obsolescence. Holden's cynical, doomed Gillis is possibly his finest portrayal. One of the all-time greats.

Off-Screen: Swanson is so identified with Norma Desmond, it seems incredible that she had to be coaxed out of retirement after Mae West, Mary Pickford, and Pola Negri had turned down the part. Holden grabbed the Gillis role when Montgomery Clift and Fred MacMurray expressed distaste for the character. At the film's premiere, an enraged Louis B. Mayer told Wilder, "You have disgraced the industry that made you and fed you! You should be tarred and feathered and run out of Hollywood!" The original opening, which had Gillis's corpse narrating his story to other corpses in the morgue, was scrapped. Desmond's mansion, now demolished, belonged to oil magnate J. Paul Getty. The movie won Oscars for screenplay, art direction (black-and-white), and Franz Waxman's score, but Swanson lost out to Judy Holliday for *Born Yesterday*. A projected stage musical adaptation by British composer Andrew Lloyd Webber is in the works, and is to star Patti Lupone as Norma Desmond. (CFB)

Superman

Warners, 1978. (C-143m.) Dir: Richard Donner. Sp: Mario Puzo and David Newman, b/o story by Mario Puzo. Cast: Christopher Reeve, Marlon Brando, Gene Hackman, Margot Kidder, Ned Beatty, Jackie Cooper, Marc McClure, Glenn Ford, Valerie Perrine, Phyllis Thaxter, Jeff East, Trevor Howard, Susannah York.

On-Screen: *The Man of Steel in an outsize production.* Inaugurated in a 1938 comic book, the ongoing story of Superman and his "fight for truth, justice, and the American way" went through many variations, including movie serials, a television series, and even a stage musical adaptation. This is the most elaborate by far, a large-scale mixture of spectacle and spoof, and it's not as much fun as it should have been. Following a rather long-winded prologue, in which baby Superman is sent off to Earth by his father, Jor-El (Brando), from the exploding planet Krypton, the movie takes on a largely cartoonish tone as Superman assumes his alter ego of "mild-mannered reporter" Clark Kent (Reeve). Clark, of course, is shyly taken with fellow reporter Lois Lane (Kidder) on the *Daily Planet* in Metropolis. Gene Hackman appears to be having a high old time as Lex Luthor, self-described as "the greatest criminal mind of the century," but one could do with less of his bumbling aide (Beatty) and his voluptuous secretary (Perrine). There are some impressive special effects, but the movie never seems to know which way it wants to go.

Off-Screen: A number of uncredited writers, including Robert Benton, David Newman's wife, Leslie, and Tom Mankiewicz, contributed to the screenplay. According to some sources, virtually every major male star in Hollywood was offered the title role, but it went to newcomer Reeve. Reportedly, Marlon Brando was paid one of the largest salaries ever for his appearance. Leslie Ann Warren was a close contender for Lois Lane, and Peter Boyle was originally set for the role played by Beatty. The film's visual effects won a Special Achievement Oscar. There were three sequels: the first, *Superman II* (1980) was an improvement on the original, but the other two (*Superman III,* 1983; *Superman IV,* 1987) were inferior.

Suspicion

RKO, 1941. (99m.) Dir: Alfred Hitchcock. Sp: Samson Raphaelson, Joan Harrison, and Alma Reville, b/o novel by Francis Iles. Cast: Cary Grant, Joan Fontaine, Nigel Bruce, Sir Cedric Hardwicke, Dame May Whitty, Leo G. Carroll, Heather Angel.

On-Screen: *A young wife suspects the worst in this Hitchcock thriller.* Marrying a glib charmer (Grant), a mousy heiress-to-be (Fontaine) forces herself to live with his murky dealings. But her placidity eventually turns to panic and she begins to believe her husband is plotting her demise. By the time the two are grappling in a speeding auto, in a crisply edited climax, the audience has ceased to care about the long-suffering heroine. There are some vintage Hitchcockian touches, however: a game of anagrams in which the word *murder* seems to form itself, and a scene with Grant in which he brings Fontaine a tumbler of milk that seems to glow ominously with the poison she suspects him of administering. (The director inserted a lighted bulb.) Yet all in all, this is off-stride Hitchcock.

Off-Screen: The movie, on which Hitchcock's wife, Alma, collaborated, is based on *Before the Fact,* written under Britisher Anthony Berkeley Cox's pen name. Originally titled *Johnnie,* this was the second Hitchcock film in which Fontaine played the imperiled English beauty. And again, as she'd been for *Rebecca,* she was nominated for the Best Actress Oscar. Although her sister, Olivia de Havilland, was also cited for *Hold Back the*

Dawn, this time Fontaine won. The film itself and Franz Waxman's score were also nominated. To soften Grant's role, a studio executive trimmed the movie down to fifty-five minutes, but Hitchcock insisted that the footage be restored. (CFB)

Sweet Bird of Youth

MGM, 1962. (C-120m.) Dir: Richard Brooks. Sp: Richard Brooks, b/o play by Tennessee Williams. Cast: Paul Newman, Geraldine Page, Shirley Knight, Ed Begley, Rip Torn, Mildred Dunnock, Madeleine Sherwood, Philip Abbott, Corey Allen, Dub Taylor.

On-Screen: *Tennessee Williams's "monsters" converge on a Gulf Coast town.* In this churning adaptation of Tennessee Williams's play, Paul Newman repeats his stage role as Chance Wayne, a strutting stud who has returned to his hometown accompanied by Alexandra Del Lago (Page, also from the stage version), an alcoholic, pill-popping ex–movie star he services and watches over, hoping in vain for a screen test. Chance learns that he is in deep trouble for impregnating, then deserting, Heavenly (Knight), the daughter of the area's vicious political boss Finley (Begley). Now Finley and his sadistic son (Torn) are bent on destroying Chance. On the stage, Newman's and Page's star charisma and Williams's reputation as a major dramatist may have convinced audiences that they were viewing important theater. Up close, *Sweet Bird of Youth* comes across as lurid melodrama, with unappetizing characters.

Off-Screen: The play was changed considerably to accommodate the censors, most notably in the ludicrous ending in which Heavenly's brother "punishes" Chance by delivering one smashing, disfiguring blow to his handsome face. In the play, Chance was castrated. Ed Begley won an Oscar as Best Supporting Actor, and Geraldine Page was nominated for Best Actress. Elizabeth Taylor starred in a 1989 television version.

Sweet Charity

Universal, 1969. (C-133m.) Dir: Bob Fosse. Sp: Peter Stone, b/o musical play by Neil Simon and screenplay by Federico Fellini, Tullio Pinelli, and Ennio Flaiano. MS: Cy Coleman and Dorothy Fields. Cast: Shirley MacLaine, Ricardo Montalban, Chita Rivera, John McMartin, Paula Kelly, Stubby Kaye, Sammy Davis, Jr.

On-Screen: *Film version of the Broadway musical about a put-upon waif.* It comes as no surprise that the dancing in Bob Fosse's debut film as a director is superb. In number after number, the masterly choreographer puts his dancers through their paces, allowing them to perform with exuberance and style. More's the pity that the movie is more exhausting than entertaining. Shirley MacLaine has the role of Charity Hope Valentine, the gullible, ever-hopeful girl who began as a prostitute in Fellini's *Nights of Cabiria,* then graduated to dance-hall hostess on Broadway for *Sweet Charity.* MacLaine is front and center most of the time, giving her professional all to such lively tunes as "I'm a Brass Band" and "If They Could See Me Now." The problem is that most of the movie is empty razzle-dazzle. Nothing much changes in Charity's life—she keeps getting dumped and humiliated by men—and Fosse tries to cover up the hollowness at the center with overbusy camerawork. And the strain shows.

Off-Screen: Very little of the film was shot in its setting of New York City. The bridge from which Charity is tossed at the beginning was not in Central Park but over a California pond. Gwen Verdon, who starred as Charity on Broadway under ex-husband Fosse's direction, coached Mac-Laine in the role. John McMartin repeated his stage role as Charity's shy suitor. Rita Moreno was considered for the part of Charity's best friend, which went to Chita Rivera. Universal wanted Fosse to change the downbeat ending, but he prevailed.

Sweet Dreams

HBO Pictures, 1985. (C-115m.) Dir: Karel Reisz. Sp: Robert Getchell. Cast: Jessica Lange, Ed Harris, Ann Wedgeworth, David Clennon, John Goodman, James Staley, Gary Basaraba.

On-Screen: *The life of country singer Patsy Cline.* Following in the tradition of other biographical films concerning top country singers (*Your Cheatin' Heart, Coal Miner's Daughter,* etc.) *Sweet Dreams* revolves about the too-brief life and career of singer Patsy Cline (Lange). Her clear, strong voice pleased legions of fans in the fifties, but her personal life was rocky, largely due to her marriage to Charlie Dick (Harris), a ne'er-do-well she continued to love despite his volatile, unreliable nature. Their relationship falters and then revives as Patsy rises to stardom. The performances are fine—Ann Wedgeworth is especially good as Patsy's mother—but the material is worn and predictable by now. Patsy Cline's voice is heard on the sound track, and her songs are the movie's best feature. There's a marvelous moment in which Patsy and her entourage, wearily sprawled in their motel room, sing "Rollin' in My Sweet Baby's Arms." You get a true sense of their love for music. Otherwise, *Sweet Dreams* is standard fare.

Off-Screen: Jessica Lange does a first-rate job of lipsynching the songs to Patsy Cline's voice. John Goodman, later a star of TV's "Roseanne" and numerous films, has a role in *Sweet Dreams* as one of Ed Harris's drinking buddies.

Sweet Smell of Success

United Artists, 1957. (96m.) Dir: Alexander Mackendrick. Sp: Clifford Odets and Ernest Lehman, b/o novelette by Ernest Lehman. Cast: Burt Lancaster, Tony Curtis, Susan Harrison, Martin Milner, Sam Levene, Barbara Nichols, Jeff Donnell, Joseph Leon, Edith Atwater.

On-Screen: *A vicious columnist controls and wreaks havoc on many lives.* The underbelly of New York's night life has seldom been exposed more vividly, or with such stinging force, as in this film. The intense (sometimes overbaked) Odets-Lehman screenplay, the striking performances, and the moody James Wong Howe photography all combine to create a nightmare vision of a morally decaying world. Lancaster plays a Winchell-like columnist whose devotion to his sister (Harrison) has an unhealthy aura; Curtis (revealing his acting strength for the first time) is the slimy press agent who will do almost anything for a scoop. When sister falls for a jazz musician (Milner), Lancaster turns ugly. The movie's unsparing harshness is relieved only by Elmer Bernstein's fine jazz score.

Off-Screen: Coproducer Harold Hecht openly admitted his dislike of the movie and predicted (correctly) that it would not be a success. He remarked, "People kept waiting for Burt to jump out of a tree." Burt Lancaster also noted, "It was the greatest failure our company ever made. We lost a fortune on it, but it has become a critics' darling over the years. Not enough moviegoers cared for it. I don't think they understood the background, the rather strange Clifford Odets dialogue."

Sweethearts

MGM, 1938. (C-114m.) Dir: W. S. Van Dyke II. Sp: Dorothy Parker and Alan Campbell. MS: Victor Herbert, Bob Wright, and Chet Forrest. Cast: Jeanette MacDonald, Nelson Eddy, Frank Morgan, Florence Rice, Ray Bolger, Allyn Joslyn, Mischa Auer, Reginald Gardiner, Herman Bing, Lucile Watson, Gene Lockhart.

On-Screen: *Jeanette MacDonald and Nelson Eddy—in modern dress and in Technicolor.* As a refreshing change from their usual costumed and perfumed operettas, MGM cast singing stars MacDonald and Eddy in their first modern roles and dressed the production in the vivid new three-color Technicolor process. It turned out to be one of their more pleasing films. They play a married couple who have been starring for years on Broadway in a production of Victor Herbert's operetta *Sweethearts*. Weary of the grind and saddled with obnoxious relatives, they opt to leave for Hollywood, until their worried producer (Morgan) deliberately breaks them up. They are reunited, of course, for the finale. MacDonald is less coy than usual, and Eddy less wooden—and why not? Their material is relatively brisk, the Victor Herbert songs, with new lyrics by Bob Wright and Chet Forrest, are lovely, and the production numbers are opulent in color.

Off-Screen: Victor Herbert's original *Sweethearts* opened in 1913 for a run of 136 performances. It bore no relation whatever to the backstage story of the film. During the filming, director Van Dyke commented, "Color is perfect for the life and warmth and reality of stars like MacDonald and Eddy," but one studio employee was said to remark, "Don't overlook the fact that tints break lots of icicles off Eddy." Oliver Marsh and Allen Davey won a special Oscar for their color cinematography.

The Swimmer

Columbia, 1968. (C-94m.) Dir: Frank Perry. Sp: Eleanor Perry, b/o story by John Cheever. Cast: Burt Lancaster, Janice Rule, Janet Landgard, Tony Bickley, Kim Hunter, Bill Fiore, Marge Champion, Joan Rivers, Cornelia Otis Skinner.

On-Screen: *A suburbanite swims his way to self-awareness.* On a summer afternoon in suburban Connecticut, Ned Merrill (Lancaster) decides to swim home by way of the neighborhood pools. As he moves from pool to pool, and neighbor to neighbor, it becomes clear that he has lost everything, including his wife, his daughters, and his job. He tries to hold on to his illusions and dreams, but by the end of the day, he is left desolate and alone, sobbing in the rain in front of his deserted house. An odd, interesting, but not altogether successful film, based on a John Cheever story, *The Swimmer* has some powerful moments, as well as some that are forced and unbelievable (some of his neighbors seem too ready to abuse him in public). One sequence, in which Ned spends time with a lovely young girl (Landgard) who represents both his daughter and his vanished youth, is somewhat overfancy. Best is Ned's stinging encounter with Janice Rule, an old flame who still bitterly resents his cavalier treatment.

Off-Screen: *The Swimmer* was made in 1966 but released two years later, due to Columbia's dissatisfaction with the film. Producer Sam Spiegel insisted that Perry reshoot the sequence of Ned's meeting with his former mistress, replacing the original actress, Barbara Loden, with Janice Rule, When Perry protested, Spiegel had director Sydney Pollack film the sequence in his place. Although an accomplished athlete, Lancaster had to take swimming lessons for the role.

Swing Time

RKO, 1936. (103m.) Dir: George Stevens. Sp: Howard Lindsay and Allan Scott, b/o story by Erwin Gelsey. MS: Jerome Kern and Dorothy Fields. Cast: Fred Astaire, Ginger Rogers, Victor Moore, Helen Broderick, Eric Blore, Betty Furness.

On-Screen: *Astaire and Rogers in peak form.* One of the very best of the duo's features, *Swing Time* blends a tolerable plot—gambler and dance instructor team up, break up, then make up—with some marvelous Kern-Fields tunes and a batch of topflight musical numbers. In a dance studio, they sprint delightfully, and with spirited humor, to "Pick Yourself Up"; they glide through "Waltz in Swing Time" in a moonlit setting; and in their final duet, "Never Gonna Dance," they express a variety of emotions in dance against an art deco background. Astaire performs in blackface for the first and last time in the astonishing "Bojangles of Harlem," and he also gets to sing the Oscar-winning tune, "The Way You Look Tonight." Rogers renders the "sarcastic" love song "A Fine Romance" in a lovely winter setting. The team receives expert comic support from Victor Moore, Helen Broderick, and Eric Blore, the latter two veterans of past Astaire-Rogers musicals. All told, *Swing Time* is a special treat for their legion of fans.

Off-Screen: For the stunning "Never Gonna Dance" number, Astaire, always the perfectionist, insisted on so many takes that Rogers's feet began to bleed from the effort. For "The Way You Look Tonight," Rogers had to cover her hair with what would appear to be foaming shampoo. Soaps and egg whites were used to simulate the necessary effect, but all failed until Rogers suggested whipped cream.

Take the Money and Run

Cinerama, 1969. (C-85m.) Dir: Woody Allen. Sp: Woody Allen. Cast: Woody Allen, Janet Margolin, Marcel Hillaire, Lonny Chapman, Jacquelyn Hyde. Narrator: Jackson Beck.

On-Screen: *Introducing triple-threat Woody Allen.* Woody Allen's first movie as director, writer, and star (previously he had only written or acted), *Take the Money and Run* may lack the finesse of his later work, but it's often howlingly funny. Basically a spoof of prison and gangster movies, it establishes Allen's persona as an intellectual nebbish and sets the pattern for Allen's style of combining New York sophistication with a sort of logical lunacy. He plays a monumentally inept would-be robber named Virgil Starkwell whose efforts either land him in prison or keep him in flight from the law. Inevitably, he ends up serving an eight-hundred-year sentence. Choose your own favorite scenes: his attempt to rob a bank (bank teller, reading his note: " 'I have a gub?' What's a gub?''); his prison experience (his punishment: being locked in a box with an insurance salesman); his prison break (he fashions a gun from soap but it melts in the rain). Some scenes are awkwardly staged, and many of the jokes seem to have been lifted from one of Allen's stand-up comedy routines. But you'll probably be laughing too hard to really care.

On-Screen: Before taking over the director's chair, Allen approached Jerry Lewis about the job. Lewis thought that the movie should be in color, while Allen favored black and white. Ultimately, the producers decided not to use Lewis and Allen took the assignment. The prison sequences were filmed at San Quentin, where the guards told Allen, "If you're held hostage, we'll do everything we can to get you out short of opening the gates." For more background on this movie and other Allen movies, see *When the Shooting Stops . . . the Cutting Begins* (Viking, 1979) by editors Ralph Rosenblum and Robert Karen.

A Tale of Two Cities

MGM, 1935. (128m.) Dir: Jack Conway. Sp: W. P. Lipscomb and S. N. Behrman, b/o novel by Charles Dickens. Cast: Ronald

Colman, Elizabeth Allan, Edna May Oliver, Reginald Owen, Basil Rathbone, Blanche Yurka, Henry B. Walthall, Donald Woods, Isabel Jewell.

On-Screen: *London, Paris, the French Revolution.* Dickens's melodramatic story may have lost its luster for modern readers, but this classic adaptation still glows. While the storming of the Bastille remains a thrilling spectacle (17,000 extras!), it's the actors, so aptly cast that they seem preordained to play their roles, who bring the novel to vivid life. In his best-remembered part, Colman is Sydney Carton, whose supreme sacrifice ensures the happiness of his beloved Lucie (Allan), her husband, Charles Darnay (Woods), and their daughter. Dickens would also have applauded Oliver's intrepid servant, Miss Pross; Yurka's sinister revolutionary, Mme. Defarge; Rathbone's cruel marquis; and Jewell's pathetic seamstress. Colman delivers Carton's stirring farewell, "It is a far, far better thing. . . ," unforgettably.

Off-Screen: Over the years, Dickens's tale has been dramatized many times for the stage, the movies (first in 1917, and most recently in 1958), and for television (1980). For good measure, there was a 1926 Felix the Cat cartoon, *A Tale of Two Kitties*. Colman wisely insisted that producer David O. Selznick cast him only as Carton; the actor felt his playing both the hero and Darnay, the doomed aristocrat whom Carton nobly replaces, would result in mood-destroying camera trickery. For a brief time, director Robert Z. Leonard took over when Conway became ill. Movie-history buffs will recall Walthall, who plays Dr. Manette, Lucie's persecuted father, as one of the stars of D. W. Griffith's 1915 silent epic, *The Birth of a Nation*. (CFB)

The Talk of the Town

Columbia, 1942. (118m.) Dir: George Stevens. Sp: Irwin Shaw and Sidney Buchman. Cast: Cary Grant, Jean Arthur, Ronald Colman, Edgar Buchanan, Glenda Farrell, Charles Dingle, Rex Ingram, Lloyd Bridges.

On-Screen: *A professor and a fugitive find themselves in contention over love and the law.* Here is a rarity: a comedy with some meat on its bones. The thoughtful Shaw-Buchman screenplay mulls over the role of law in society, while relating an essentially comic tale about the triangular relationship that develops between a small-town anarchist (Grant), a distinguished law professor (Colman), and the professor's landlady and housekeeper (Arthur). Grant, fleeing from a false charge of murder, hides out in Colman's temporary residence, with Arthur's help. Soon the men are not only arguing about the law but about their mutual admiration for the lady. The film is too long, but the dialogue is often quite literate, and the principals work well together under George Stevens's direction. Colman comes off best in an appealing performance as a man who comes to believe that the law should be humanized and who arrives modestly at fame and prestige. (He is nominated to the Supreme Court.)

Off-Screen: Not being entirely sure who should win Jean Arthur at the film's end, director George Stevens shot two different endings and left it to several preview audiences to decide the winner. See the movie and learn who won.

Tarzan, the Ape Man

MGM, 1932. (99m.) Dir: W. S. Van Dyke II. Sp: Ivor Novello; adaptation: Cyril Hume, b/o characters created by Edgar Rice Burroughs. Cast: Johnny Weissmuller, Maureen O'Sullivan, C. Aubrey Smith, Neil Hamilton, Doris Lloyd, Forrester Harvey.

On-Screen: *Weissmuller's debut as king of the jungle.* One of the most durably popular figures in movie lore, the primitive jungle hero called Tarzan turned up in many films, starting in 1918. *Tarzan, the Ape Man* launched Olympic swimming champion Johnny Weissmuller as the most famous of all Tarzans, and after more than six decades, it's still an entertaining movie. Weissmuller's monosyllabic Tarzan turns up at an African safari camp where he whisks away C. Aubrey Smith's pretty daughter, Jane (O'Sullivan). By film's end, Jane's terror turns to love, and she opts to stay with Tarzan in the jungle. (Presumably, she's his common-law wife.) Along with Jane and comic relief chimp Cheetah, Tarzan undergoes many adventures—he grapples with lions and a leopard, and when the safari members are captured by Pygmies, Tarzan saves them by rallying a herd of elephants to wreck the Pygmy village. Weissmuller was no actor, but he had no need to act—at one point he keeps repeating, "Tarzan, Jane" until Jane, speaking for the audience, must plead with him to stop. The corn is as high as an elephant's eye, but *Tarzan, the Ape Man* is vintage fun.

Off-Screen: W. S. Van Dyke, who directed the successful *Trader Horn* the year before, used some of his African footage from that movie, although most of *Tarzan* was shot in the Toluca Lake area of North Hollywood. Among the many actors considered to play Tarzan were Charles Bickford, Johnny Mack Brown, Joel McCrea, and Clark Gable. Olympic champion Herman Brix was a strong contender—eventually he did get to play Tarzan in a serial later released as two features. (In 1940, he changed his name to Bruce Bennett.) A famous circus aerialist named Alfredo Cordona doubled for Weissmuller in the tree-swinging shots. And animal trainer Bert Nelson doubled for Weissmuller in the lion-wrestling scene. *Tarzan, the Ape Man* was remade in 1959 and 1981, both times abysmally.

Taxi Driver

Columbia, 1976. (C-113m.) Dir: Martin Scorsese. Sp: Paul Schrader. Cast: Robert De Niro, Cybill Shepherd, Harvey Keitel, Peter Boyle, Jodie Foster, Albert Brooks, Leonard Harris.

On-Screen: *A taxi driver in a nighttime hell.* Immersed in the sordid, dangerous world of midtown Manhattan at night, taxi driver Travis Bickle (De Niro) is a ticking bomb waiting to explode. He sublimates his feelings of frustration, rage, and disgust in bodybuilding and in secreting an arsenal of guns. When an attractive political worker (Shepherd) rejects him, he plots to assassinate her candidate, but ends up destroying the "animals" he detests in a ghastly bloodbath. Ironically (and also inexplicably), he is acclaimed a hero and returns to his taxi. A jolting movie about one disturbed man's catharsis through violence, *Taxi Driver* is regarded by many as a thoroughly repellent exercise in horror, devoid of any redeeming quality. Others find it a compelling and chilling view of a world gone mad. In his first collaboration with director Scorsese after *Mean Streets* (1973), De Niro gives a stunning performance ("You talkin' to me? You talkin' to *me?*"), and Jodie Foster is memorable as Iris, the fourteen-year-old prostitute De Niro tries to "free" from her pimp (Keitel). Grim stuff indeed, but fascinating.

Off-Screen: Most of the film was shot at various locations in New York City, including an Eighth Avenue porno shop, the Bellmore Cafeteria at Twenty-eighth Street and Park Avenue South, and the garment district at midday, where the movie company tangled with the heavy traffic. De Niro's Mohican-like shaved head was actually a bald cap covered with adhesive that dried to a matte finish. To give the appearance of stubble, coarsely ground yak hair was sprayed onto the cap while it was still wet. Director Scorsese appears as an irate passenger in Travis Bickle's cab. (His wife is cheating on him.)

Tea and Sympathy

MGM, 1956. (C-122m.) Dir: Vincente Minnelli. Sp: Robert Anderson, b/o his play. Cast: Deborah Kerr, John Kerr, Leif Erickson, Edward Andrews, Tom Laughlin, Darryl Hickman, Dean Jones, Norma Crane.

On-Screen: *A "different" young man is plagued at his school.* Robert Anderson's screen adaptation of his hit Broadway play softens and waters down the material but still retains its power to grip an audience. At a boys' boarding school, Tom Robinson Lee (John Kerr) is a sensitive adolescent mocked for his unmanly interest in music, poetry, and the fine arts. Only Laura, the headmaster's compassionate wife (Deborah Kerr) understands his plight, and after he attempts suicide, she ultimately offers herself to Tom as a resolution. The play's suggestion of Tom's homosexuality is much more muted and ambiguous in the film, and added framing material, which shows Tom, years later, as a family man musing over Laura's sad fate (punishment for her "sin"), is an irritating sop to the Breen censorship office. To his credit, Anderson retains the principal concerns of his play, which include the trauma caused by persecution for being different and the definition of what manhood really is. The two Kerrs and Leif Erickson (as Laura's suspiciously macho husband) reprise their stage roles; only John Kerr, by now too old to play a tortured adolescent, fails to come up to expectations.

Off-Screen: Nervous about the play's strong hint of homosexuality, the Breen office insisted on a number of changes, including the addition of the framing material. Minnelli and Anderson both hated these changes, but were obliged to go along. Tom Laughlin, who plays John Kerr's principal nemesis, later acquired short-lived popularity as the righteous yet violence-prone character of Billy Jack in several movies (*Billy Jack,* 1971; *The Trial of Billy Jack,* 1974, etc.).

10

Orion, 1979. (C-122m.) Dir: Blake Edwards. Sp: Blake Edwards. Cast: Dudley Moore, Julie Andrews, Bo Derek, Robert Webber, Dee Wallace, Brian Dennehy, Max Showalter, Sam Jones, Nedra Volz.

On-Screen: *Dudley Moore spots a perfect "10."* George (Moore), a middle-aged composer, has every reason to be happy: a successful career, a loving fiancée (Andrews), and a fabulous beach house. Then he sees luscious Jennie (Derek) and become totally obsessed with her, to the exclusion of everything and everyone else. Trouble is, he sees Jennie on her wedding day. Most of the comedy stems from George's mishaps in trying to get close to his dream girl: He keeps tripping and falling; he undergoes dental work (Jennie's father is a dentist); he walks on hot sand; etc. After he and Jennie finally meet and make love, he discovers that she's willful and shallow. And back he goes to Andrews, who is no longer very interested. Blake Edwards works strenuously as author and director, but *10* is one of his lamer comedies, a frantic and leering farce in which George's succession of physical mishaps and afflictions becomes progressively less funny. On a scale of one to ten, it rates no better than a three.

Off-Screen: George Segal began filming *10,* but quit due to "creative differences." A charming (and major) star of the sixties in *Mary Poppins* (1964) and *The Sound of Music* (1965), Julie Andrews went into a decline in the seventies and eighties, reaching some sort of nadir, perhaps, in her husband Blake Edwards's execrable *S.O.B.* (1981). Nor did Edwards do well by his wife in *10,* in which she is miscast in what is essentially a supporting role.

The Ten Commandments

Paramount, 1956. (C-220m.) Dir: Cecil B. DeMille. Sp: Aeneas MacKenzie, Jessie Lasky, Jr., Jack Gariss, and Fredric M. Frank. Cast: Charlton Heston, Yul Brynner, Anne Baxter, Edward G. Robinson, Yvonne De Carlo, Vincent Price, Judith Anderson, Debra Paget, John Derek, Martha Scott, John Carradine, H. B. Warner.

On-Screen: *Cecil B. DeMille's gargantuan sin-and-salvation epic.* "Oh, Moses! Moses! You stubborn, splendid, adorable fool!" Princess Nefretiri (Baxter) exclaims to her once-princely, now-enslaved passion (Heston). That's about as memorable as the dialogue gets in this long, massive epic film from Cecil B. DeMille. As usual, DeMille churns up a goodly amount of entertaining hokum as he relates the story of the inspired Hebrew leader who led his people out of bondage. A simplistic screenplay covers the expected events in Moses' life, including, of course, his parting of the Red Sea and his receiving the Ten Commandments. Realizing that all that piety can only go so far, DeMille also serves up at least one outsize orgy. In a movie theater, the Oscar-winning special effects may have been impressive, but on the small screen, they come across as surprisingly ineffectual. Charlton Heston carries his demanding role with quiet strength and dignity.

Off-Screen: Much of the film was shot on location in Egypt. The shooting began on the side of Mount Sinai, as close as possible to the sites on which Moses was presumed to have undergone his divine experiences. The heavy equipment was carried part of the way up the mountain by camel and mule train, then unloaded and shouldered or dragged on ropes by the Arab crews. DeMille assembled ten to twelve thousand Arabs (estimates vary) to play the jubilant Hebrews on their way to the Promised Land. The sequence also required about fifteen thousand animals. Oscar nominations included Best Picture. DeMille's 1923 silent version combined the biblical story with a "modern" tale of sin and redemption.

The Terminator

Orion, 1984. (C-108m.) Dir: James Cameron. Sp: James Cameron and Gale Anne Hurd. Cast: Arnold Schwarzenegger, Linda Hamilton, Michael Biehn, Paul Winfield, Lance Henriksen, Rick Rossovich, Earl Boen.

On-Screen: *A cyborg returns from the future and wreaks havoc.* "That terminator is out there. It can't be bargained with. It can't be reasoned with. It doesn't feel pity or remorse or fear. And it absolutely will not stop—until you are dead." These are the ominous words of Kyle (Biehn) to Sarah Connor (Hamilton), warning her about the Terminator (Schwarzenegger). The Terminator, Kyle tells her, has come back from A.D. 2029 Los Angeles, a world destroyed by nuclear warfare, to kill Sarah so that her future son will not be born to become a leader of the rebels against the all-powerful machines that now control the earth. Are you paying attention? It doesn't matter because this hugely popular movie depends on nonstop action as the Terminator pursues Sarah relentlessly. The body count is high amid car chases, explosions, and shoot-outs, and some of the special effects are very good indeed. But despite the sci-fi aspects, this is a much more conventional movie than the 1991 sequel, *Terminator 2,* which features dazzling, elaborate effects. As the unkillable Terminator, Arnold Schwarzenegger is not called upon to act, which is all to the good. As Sarah says, "a person can go crazy thinking about this." Better not to think, and enjoy.

Off-Screen: Most viewers recall the scene in which the Terminator makes emergency repairs on itself after a gunfight with the hero. Working with special effects wizard Stan Winston, cinematographer Adam Greenberg was able to make the viewer believe he was seeing more than was actually taking place. Winston built the prosthetic arm that the Terminator cuts open, and Greenberg moves quickly from a shot of the Terminator's destroyed eye and his knife to a close-up of the eye lens dropping into a sinkful of water that turns red. The audience is sure that it's seen the Terminator stab himself in the eye.

Terminator 2: Judgment Day

TriStar, 1991. (C-136m.) Dir: James Cameron. Sp: James Cameron and William Wisher. Cast: Arnold Schwarzenegger, Linda Hamilton, Edward Furlong, Robert Patrick, Joe Morton, Earl Boen, Danny Cooksey.

On-Screen: *State-of-the-art special effects in a high-voltage sequel.* In James Cameron's *The Terminator* (1984), murderous cyborg Schwarzenegger was sent back in time from the future with the mission of killing Sarah Connor (Hamilton), the innocent woman whose son would become a resistance leader. Now her son (Furlong) is thirteen, the year is 1997, and two "terminators" return from the future—one to kill him, the other to protect him. The story is sheer nonsense, of course, but what matters are the extraordinary special effects. One terminator is Schwarzenegger, now cast in a heroic, even sacrificial mold—the other is the lethal T-1000 (Patrick), a cyborg who can imitate any person or object he desires. The effects with T–1000 are astonishing and quite beautiful, compensating in part for the many screeching chases and violent encounters. Be warned: The movie contains a high quotient of brutality, and despite all the somber talk about "judgment day" and nuclear annihilation, it's essentially mindless entertainment.

Off-Screen: The creators of *Terminator* at first thought of having Schwarzenegger play both terminators in the sequel, but this idea was abandoned. They also considered many ways of finally killing the seemingly invincible T–1000 and settled on dropping him into a vat of molten steel. A demolished steel plant in Fontana, California, was used to simulate the grim, burned-out setting of a future war, and the Lake View Medical Center in the San Fernando Valley became the film's sterile, inhospitable state hospital for the criminally insane. *The Making of Terminator 2: Judgment Day* (Bantam Books, 1991), by Don Shay and Jody Duncan, offers full behind-the-scene information. The movie won four Oscar nominations and received one statuette for Sound.

Terms of Endearment

Paramount, 1983. (C–132m.) Dir: James L. Brooks. Sp: James L. Brooks, b/o novel by Larry McMurtry. Cast: Shirley MacLaine, Debra Winger, Jack Nicholson, Jeff Daniels, John Lithgow, Danny DeVito.

On-Screen: *A mother-daughter relationship over the years.* *Terms of Endearment* swept the Oscars in 1983, and small wonder. It has all the ingredients for a hugely successful movie: an adroit screenplay that begins with humor and ends with heartbreak; capable direction by James L. Brooks, making his feature-film debut; and splendid performances by everyone. Oscar-winner Shirley MacLaine plays the wildly eccentric, difficult Amelia Greenway, whose over-the-years relationship with daughter Emma (Winger) has its dizzying ups and downs. Jack Nicholson, also an Oscar winner (Best Supporting Actor) as a beer-bellied, girl-chasing ex-astronaut named Garrett Breedlove, earns every raunchy laugh. Indeed, most of the film is funny, veering from Amelia's giddy relationship with Breedlove to Emma's troubles with her teacher husband (Daniels). Like life itself, the movie suddenly becomes messy as it turns from laughter to tears, with the tragic, unexpected demise of a major character. MacLaine's ranting, screeching Amelia would be hard to tolerate in real life, but the actress makes her believable and even quirkily likable, like a relative you might enjoy seeing—but not too often.

Off-Screen: Shirley MacLaine and Debra Winger may have battled their way through the movie, but apparently their wrangling continued off the screen as well. Their conflict seems to have been fierce and continuous. (For one thing, Winger insisted on MacLaine's calling her by her character's name off-camera.) Winger received an Oscar nomination; the movie also won as Best Picture, and Brooks was cited for his direction and screenplay.

Test Pilot

MGM, 1938. (118m.) Dir: Victor Fleming. Sp: Vincent Lawrence and Waldemar Young, b/o story by Lt. Comdr. Frank Wead. Cast: Clark Gable, Myrna Loy, Spencer Tracy, Lionel Barrymore, Samuel S. Hinds, Marjorie Main, Gloria Holden, Louis Jean Heydt.

On-Screen: *Exploits of a dashing test pilot, aloft and below.* Never a subtle or particularly good actor (even by his own admission), Clark Gable projected a virility and directness that kept him King of the Movies throughout the thirties and into the forties. Here he plays a test pilot who boldly flies experimental planes, while romancing Myrna Loy on the ground. Tracy is Gable's mechanic and best friend, and everything that Gable is not: practical, sensible, and low-keyed. Both Loy and Tracy worry about Gable's daredevil antics, but it is Tracy who loses his life in a test plane. (Many older viewers will remember his gimmick of placing a wad of gum on Gable's plane for good luck, a gesture Gable repeats movingly after his friend's demise.) Some exciting aerial scenes combined with the triple-star charisma to make *Test Pilot* popular entertainment.

Off-Screen: Clark Gable greatly admired Spencer Tracy's ability to steal a scene without saying a line or making a hammy gesture. "The guy's good," he said, "and there's nobody in the business who can touch him, so you're a fool to try." Gable did admit, however, that Tracy teased everyone by performing "the slowest, most lingering death in history." Every time he seemed to have expired, Tracy would weakly open one eye or manage a wan smile.

Thank Your Lucky Stars

Warners, 1943. (127m.) Dir: David Butler. Sp: Norman Panama, Melvin Frank, and James V. Kern, b/o story by Everett Freeman and Arthur Schwartz. MS: Frank Loesser and Arthur Schwartz. Cast: Eddie Cantor, Dennis Morgan, Joan Leslie, and guest stars Bette Davis, Humphrey Bogart, Errol Flynn, John Garfield, Ann Sheridan, Ida Lupino, Olivia de Havilland, others.

On-Screen: *A bevy of Warners stars in a wartime mélange of music and comedy.* Another of the multistar musical extravaganzas turned out by Hollywood during World War II to bolster morale and entertain the armed forces, *Thank Your Lucky Stars* is a decidedly mixed bag of the good, the mediocre, and the plainly awful. The thin story line involves Eddie Cantor in a dual role (one is usually more than enough), along with Joan Leslie and Dennis Morgan. Most of the star turns are embarrassing attempts to play against the star's familiar persona (Olivia de Havilland and Ida Lupino do a jitterbug routine, etc.), but a few are entertaining. Highlights are Bette Davis's rendition of the witty song "They're Either Too Young or Too Old" and Ann Sheridan's sassy "Love Isn't Born, It's Made." Stargazers will enjoy this; others beware.

Off-Screen: The stars were each paid $50,000 for their respective appearances, but the money was turned over to the Hollywood Canteen for the war effort. Errol Flynn had not been set to appear in the film, but he implored Jack Warner to be included. Bette Davis's number was filmed with multiple cameras so that retakes would be unnecessary.

That's Entertainment!

MGM, 1974. (C-132m.) Dir: Jack Haley, Jr. Sp: Jack Haley, Jr. MS: Various writers. Narrators: Frank Sinatra, Elizabeth Taylor, Peter Lawford, James Stewart, Mickey Rooney, Gene Kelly, Fred Astaire, Liza Minnelli, Bing Crosby.

On-Screen: *A bouquet of musical memories from MGM.* From the advent of sound until the sixties, MGM presented the most elaborate, most entertaining, and—especially in the fifties—the best musical films ever to come from Hollywood. Sometimes they were elephantine or inane, or both, but when they were good, they were wonderful. *That's Entertainment!* brings together the most memorable sequences, along with some antique curiosities that are fun for movie buffs. As you would expect, some of the best numbers come from the studio's gifted luminaries: Fred Astaire, elegantly twirling through dances with Ginger Rogers or Cyd Charisse; Gene Kelly forever singing and dancing in the rain; Judy Garland in either her plaintive or rousing mode. Among the movie's highlights: Donald O'Connor's hilarious "Make 'Em Laugh" from *Singin' in the Rain* and the brilliant challenge dance performed in *Seven Bridges for Seven Brothers.* Choose your own favorites.

Off-Screen: At the time of the film's release, producer Jack Haley, Jr., estimated that if the musical numbers were to be reproduced, the cost, without even paying the principal actors, would be approximately $250 million. As research, Haley viewed about two hundred MGM musicals. From ten hours of entertainment, he finally assembled a rough cut running three hours, then faced the agony of trimming it down to over two. Elizabeth Taylor's narration was shot in Rome.

That's Entertainment, Part 2

MGM, 1976. (C-126m.) Dir: Gene Kelly. Sp: Leonard Gershe. MS: Various writers. Hosts: Fred Astaire and Gene Kelly.

On-Screen: *More goodies from the MGM vault.* This sequel to the highly popular *That's Entertainment* (1974) may lack the sustained pleasure of the first film, but there is still plenty to enjoy. (Comedy and drama segments are added to the musical mix.) You'll rediscover some marvelous evergreens: Gene Kelly, Debbie Reynolds, and Donald O'Connor, in *Singin' in the Rain,* wishing everyone "Good Morning"; Judy Garland's wistful rendition of "Have Yourself a Merry Little Christmas" in *Meet Me in St. Louis;* Maurice Chevalier telling Hermione Gingold "I Remember It Well" in *Gigi.* You should also enjoy some lesser-known highlights, such as Busby Berkeley's giddy "I Got Rhythm" number from *Girl Crazy* and Bobby Van's wonderful hopping dance in *Small Town Girl.* A few moments are ludicrous, none more so than the sight of Frank Sinatra in a white tuxedo singing "Old Man River" against the background of a glittering MGM set. The comedy and drama excerpts move by too quickly to make any lasting impression. Fred Astaire and Gene Kelly provide the breezy narration.

Off-Screen: The movie was originally called *That's Entertainment, Too.* Excerpts from over seventy films were used, including more than sixty musical numbers. After the first engagements, the film was shortened from 133 to 126 minutes. The "Lonesome Polecat" number from *Seven Brides for Seven Brothers* and Oscar Levant's playing of Concerto in F in *An American in Paris* were deleted.

Thelma and Louise

MGM, 1991. (C-128m.) Dir: Ridley Scott. Sp: Callie Khouri. Cast: Susan Sarandon,

Geena Davis, Harvey Keitel, Michael Madsen, Christopher McDonald, Stephen Tobolowsky, Brad Pitt, Timothy Carhart.

On-Screen: *Two women share adventures on the road.* A road movie with a major difference: The protagonists are women seeking to find themselves. A tough and funny story, the film concerns Louise (Sarandon), a waitress, and Thelma (Davis), a housewife married to the ultimate male chauvinist husband (McDonald). The women leave town for a weekend at a friend's cabin, but an attempted rape and its consequences send them heading for Mexico instead. Soon they are fugitives from justice. The film traces their evolution into women who can finally be themselves, even while the police are closing in. *Thelma and Louise* is a film of contrasts: the expansive scenery of America's Southwest and its grungy underside of seedy motels, cheap diners, and dusty service stations; the cramped lives of the women back home and their freedom on the road. Sarandon is fine, as usual, but this is the film in which Davis proves herself, and the two are a pleasure to watch. *Thelma and Louise* is astringent, invigorating—and surprising.

Off-Screen: Callie Khouri's screenplay attracted wide attention in Hollywood circles. Major studios were interested before it finally found its way to MGM. Khouri's ultimate reward was an Oscar for Best Original Screenplay. Among the actresses who were considered for the title roles were Goldie Hawn, Cher, and Michelle Pfeiffer. Both Sarandon and Davis were nominated as Best Actress, but they lost to Jodie Foster. (BL)

There's No Business Like Show Business

Fox, 1954. (C-117m.) Dir: Walter Lang. Sp: Henry and Phoebe Ephron. MS: Irving Berlin. Cast: Ethel Merman, Dan Dailey, Mitzi Gaynor, Marilyn Monroe, Donald O'Connor, Johnnie Ray, Frank McHugh.

On-Screen: *Irving Berlin's musical valentine to showbiz.* Well, there's always the music—a happy profusion of Irving Berlin's lively, irresistible tunes pours forth from the sound track, and they are a pleasure to hear. Much less of a pleasure is this movie's story about a show business family over the years (mother Merman, father Dailey, and children Gaynor, O'Connor, and Ray). The parents fret and worry, while the kids find romance (O'Connor with show girl Monroe), success, or fulfillment. It's all highly excruciating, especially when Ray (a briefly popular singer of the period) turns to the church. Filmed in wide-screen Cinema-Scope, the musical numbers are lavish and often vulgar, but Gaynor and O'Connor do some expert singing and dancing, and there's always Merman's inimitably brassy voice to keep viewers awake. Marilyn Monroe renders, or rather slinks through, a sexy version of "Heat Wave." Not a good musical film by any means, but Berlin's music makes it endurable.

Off-Screen: When screenwriter Lamar Trotti died before he could complete the script, Phoebe and Henry Ephron took on the assignment reluctantly. Unhappy in her marriage to Joe DiMaggio, Marilyn Monroe was frequently hours late for work or failed to show up at all, to the deep irritation of Ethel Merman. Merman resented this voluptuous young blonde who couldn't sing.

These Three

Goldwyn–United Artists, 1936. (93m.) Dir: William Wyler. Sp: Lillian Hellman, b/o her play. Cast: Merle Oberon, Miriam Hopkins, Joel McCrea, Bonita Granville, Catherine Doucet, Alma Kruger, Marcia Mae Jones, Margaret Hamilton, Walter Brennan.

On-Screen: *A malevolent child nearly destroys the lives of three people.* Considering that Lillian Hellman's play *The Children's Hour* involved the then-taboo subject of lesbianism, it seems unlikely that Samuel Goldwyn would attempt to turn it into a film. Yet with Hellman's cooperation—she loosely adapted her play into a conventional triangular romance—Goldwyn produced this intelligent and effective drama. The theme remains intact: the destructive power of a lie. Oberon and Hopkins run a private girls' school, and McCrea is a local young doctor in love with Oberon. Enter Granville as a vicious, bullying child whose lie about Hopkins and McCrea wreaks havoc on their lives, and Oberon's. Fastidiously produced by Goldwyn, *These Three* is far superior to Wyler's remake, *The Children's Hour* (1962), which restored the lesbian theme. The three leads are fine, but young Bonita Granville walks away with the film as the nasty cause of all the trouble.

Off-Screen: The film's working title was *The Lie*. At one point in the production, rather disappointed by McCrea's performance, William Wyler admitted candidly to the actor that he had wanted Leslie Howard in the role. Sam Goldwyn was continually exasperated by Wyler's habit of shooting many takes with the same camera setup, then printing only a few of them. Goldwyn, whose malapropisms were legendary, also had problems with his temperamental actors. "I'm having more trouble with you stars," he exploded, "than Mussolini is with Utopia!"

They Died with Their Boots On

Warners, 1941. (138m.) Dir: Raoul Walsh. Sp: Wally Klein and Aeneas MacKenzie. Cast: Errol Flynn, Olivia de Havilland, Arthur Kennedy, Charley Grapewin, Gene Lockhart, Anthony Quinn, Sydney Greenstreet, Hattie McDaniel, Stanley Ridges, John Litel.

On-Screen: *The story of George Armstrong Custer, Hollywood style.* Worthless as history but enjoyable (if too long) as a rousing, large-scale Warners western, *They Died with Their Boots On* purports to tell about the military career and personal life of George Armstrong Custer (Flynn). The movie depicts Custer as a Civil War hero whose daring deeds in defiance of military rules bring him nothing but trouble. He finally leads his troops in a courageous but futile battle at Little Bighorn. This climactic battle, staged superbly by Raoul Walsh and photographed beautifully by Bert Glennon, is the movie's unquestionable highlight, and one of the screen's great action sequences. Olivia de Havilland is properly loyal and devoted as Custer's wife. Sydney Greenstreet appears as Gen. Winfield Scott, and Anthony Quinn, usually assigned to playing Mexicans or Indians at this early point in his career, plays Chief Crazy Horse.

Off-Screen: In July of 1941, screenwriter Lenore Coffee wrote to production head Hal Wallis, very disturbed about the number of "shocking inaccuracies" in the screenplay.

Many of these remained in the film, but she was hired to strengthen the scenes between Flynn and de Havilland. Joan Fontaine rejected the role of Custer's wife that was finally played by her sister, de Havilland.

They Drive by Night

Warners, 1940. (93m.) Dir: Raoul Walsh. Sp: Jerry Wald and Richard Macaulay, b/o novel by A. I. Bezzerides. Cast: George Raft, Ann Sheridan, Humphrey Bogart, Ida Lupino, Alan Hale, Gale Page, Roscoe Karns, John Litel, George Tobias.

On-Screen: *Two truck-driving brothers face deep trouble*. A partial remake of Warners' *Bordertown* (1935), *They Drive by Night* is the sort of swiftly paced, hard-bitten melodrama at which the studio excelled. Raft and Bogart play truck-driving brothers with problems—bitter Bogart is crippled in an accident and Raft is wrongly suspected of murdering his boss. The true culprit is the boss's aggressive, sex-hungry wife, played by Ida Lupino at fever pitch. Her climactic court scene, in which she goes to pieces in pyrotechnic fashion, packs quite a wallop (as did Bette Davis's earlier version in *Bordertown*.) Lupino gets the best scene, but as a wisecracking waitress in love with Raft, Ann Sheridan gets the best lines. When a customer comments on her chassis, she remarks, "You couldn't afford the headlights."

Off-Screen: George Raft was furious at Humphrey Bogart's constant needling and refused to work with him in their next assigned movie, *Manpower*. Still, Raft became a hero on one occasion when the truck in which he was riding with Bogart and Sheridan lost its brakes at eighty miles an hour. Raft managed to get the careening truck under control and saved their lives.

They Shoot Horses, Don't They?

ABC Pictures/Cinerama, 1969. (C-121m.) Dir: Sydney Pollack. Sp: James Poe and Robert E. Thompson, b/o novel by Horace McCoy. Cast: Jane Fonda, Michael Sarrazin, Susannah York, Gig Young, Red Buttons, Bonnie Bedelia, Bruce Dern, Allyn Ann McLerie, Madge Kennedy.

On-Screen: *Grim drama of thirties dance marathons*. Not exactly Fred and Ginger, Gloria (Fonda) and Robert (Sarrazin) are among the jobless who, during the depths of the Depression, turned to exhibition dancing to make some honest bucks. She's a frazzled, unemployed Hollywood extra; her partner dreams of becoming a famous movie director. Together in a tacky ballroom at the edge of the Pacific Ocean, they endure their dehumanizing, dance-till-you-drop ordeal until tragedy overtakes them. Fonda (in an Oscar-nominated performance) and Sarrazin are superb as the desperate couple. Young won a supporting-actor Oscar for his hearty but heartless emcee. Also compelling are York (Oscar-nominated) as an aspiring Jean Harlow type, Buttons as a savvy marathon veteran, and Bedelia as a pregnant contender. The movie confuses with an abundance of flashbacks and flashforwards, but the cumulative effect is electrifying.

Off-Screen: Most of the action is supposed to take place in the Aragon Ballroom, in Santa Monica's Ocean Park. Actually, it was filmed in a replica of the dance hall, built on nearby Lick Pier. When Young exhorts the exhausted marathon competitors with "Yowsah! Yowsah!" he's alluding to Ben Bernie, a genial bandleader of the thirties. Among the crowd of marathon spectators, watch for famed director Mervyn LeRoy in an unbilled appearance. The movie also garnered six other Oscar nominations, including one for director Pollack. (CFB)

They Won't Forget

Warners, 1937. (95m.) Dir: Mervyn LeRoy. Sp: Robert Rossen and Aben Kandel, b/o book by Ward Greene. Cast: Claude Rains, Gloria Dickson, Otto Kruger, Edward Norris, Allyn Joslyn, Elisha Cook, Jr., Lana Turner, Clinton Rosemond.

On-Screen: *Mob violence explodes in a Southern town.* Crude and overstated by today's standards, *They Won't Forget* still packs a wallop as a social document. The movie is based on the true—and notorious—Leo Frank case of 1913 in which Frank, superintendent of a Georgia pencil factory and a Northern Jew, was accused of murdering a teenage girl and was lynched by a vengeful mob. In the film, after a teenaged girl (Turner, in her famous "sweater" debut) is brutally murdered, suspicion falls on a Northern teacher (Norris). A mob, prodded to violence by an ambitious prosecuting attorney (Rains), drags him from the jail and hangs him. The victim's wife (Dickson) sounds the keynote as she tells the attorney and his lackeys, "You're the ones who killed him! You're the ones who stirred up all the hatred and prejudice down here!" Unusually blunt for its time, *They Won't Forget* pinpoints the ugliness and mindlessness of an unruly mob and the crass opportunism of those who exploit this mob.

Off-Screen: Casting the role of the victim, director LeRoy asked for "a girl who is sexy and innocent at the same time." The casting director found a scared young fifteen-year-old girl named Judy Turner. "Judy" was changed to "Lana." LeRoy's contract with Warners expired with this film, and he moved to MGM. In 1988, the Leo Frank case was superbly dramatized on television in *The Murder of Mary Phagan*.

Thieves Like Us

United Artists, 1974. (123m.) Dir: Robert Altman. Sp: Calder Willingham, Joan Tewkesbury, and Robert Altman, b/o novel by Edward Anderson. Cast: Keith Carradine, Shelley Duvall, John Schuck, Bert Remsen, Louise Fletcher, Ann Latham, Tom Skerritt.

On-Screen: *Doomed lovers outside the law.* Yet another variation of the Bonnie-and-Clyde theme that has turned up in films at various times, *Thieves Like Us* is Robert Altman's gritty version of the Edward Anderson novel that was made as *They Live by Night* in 1949. More realistically detailed and much less romantic than the earlier film, Robert Altman's movie centers on three none-too-bright and hapless prison escapees (Carradine, Schuck, and Remsen) who are being hunted by the police in Mississippi of the Depression thirties. They hide out with a friend where Bowie (Carradine) takes up with Keechie (Duvall), a plain country girl. Their love affair is clearly doomed, and after one of the other escapees is killed and another recaptured, Bowie is shot down in a hail of bullets while Keechie watches in horror. Jean Boffety's camera captures the bleakness of the Depression years, and Altman extracts solid performances from Carradine and Duvall. *Thieves Like Us* has its partisans, who prefer it to *Bonnie and Clyde*.

Off-Screen: The screenplay was actually written by Joan Tewkesbury, with Altman's input; a previous draft of the script was written by Calder Willingham, but Ms. Tewkesbury said that she never read it. Willingham, however, was given first credit. The one significant departure from the book is that Keechie survives.

The Thin Man

MGM, 1934. (93m.) Dir: W. S. Van Dyke II. Sp: Albert Hackett and Frances Goodrich, b/o novel by Dashiell Hammett. Cast: William Powell, Myrna Loy, Maureen O'Sullivan, Nat Pendleton, Minna Gombell, Cesar Romero, Natalie Moorhead, Edward Ellis, Porter Hall.

On-Screen: *Introducing Nick and Nora Charles.* At first it was regarded as nothing special: a modest film version of a Dashiell Hammett mystery novel with two stars not particularly noted for playing comedy. The mystery itself, in fact, was routine and not very interesting. But something clicked with audiences when Nick and Nora Charles, a high-living couple with a fondness for alcohol, began exchanging quips that suggested their pleasure in being married to each other. It was a refreshing new view of wedded bliss, and with Powell and Loy utterly charming in their roles, the movie was an unexpected hit, prompting five sequels and many imitations. Audiences were delighted when Nick looked admiringly at Nora and declared, "I like lanky brunettes with wicked jaws." Later, the *Thin Man* films

would become frayed around the edges, but this first entry in the series displays Nick and Nora at their wisecracking, sophisticated best.

Off-Screen: Louis B. Mayer agreed to the casting of William Powell as Nick Charles, but he was vehemently opposed to Myrna Loy as Nora. He felt that the role called for someone "flashier" than Loy. Director Van Dyke insisted on Loy, and Mayer finally conceded. Van Dyke had the script refashioned around Powell and Loy. Many years later, Loy wrote: "From the very first scene, a curious thing passed between us, a feeling of rhythm, complete understanding, an instinct for how one could bring out the best in the other."

The Thing

RKO, 1951. (87m.) Dir: Christian Nyby. Sp: Charles Lederer, b/o story by John W. Campbell, Jr. Cast: Kenneth Tobey, Margaret Sheridan, Robert Cornthwaite, Douglas Spencer, James Young, Dewey Martin, Eduard Franz, James Arness.

On-Screen: *A monstrous creature devastates an Alaskan outpost.* Many filmgoers retain memories of cringing in terror at this modest but often frightening science-fiction thriller. It relates what occurs when a massive, unidentifiable creature arrives at a remote scientific outpost in Alaska in some sort of spaceship and proceeds to wreak havoc until it is demolished. It turns out to be an outer-space demon that feeds exclusively on human blood. The movie succeeds by suggesting rather than showing the creature (played by James Arness in his pre-"Gunsmoke" days) until the climax.

Scariest scene: As a guard dozes in the night, the ice encasing the creature begins to melt from a heater. Also known as *The Thing from Another World,* the movie was remade in 1982, with closer attention to the original story and with much more gore.

Off-Screen: Although Christian Nyby is the film's director of record, it has been rumored that the producer, Howard Hawks, worked extensively on the production. It is also possible that Ben Hecht made an uncredited contribution to the screenplay.

The Third Man

London Films, 1949. (104m.) Dir: Carol Reed. Sp: Graham Greene. Cast: Joseph Cotten, Valli, Orson Welles, Trevor Howard, Ernst Deutsch, Bernard Lee, Wilfrid Hyde-White.

On-Screen: *Classic suspense thriller.* Time hasn't dimmed the cold brilliance of Greene's story of corruption and betrayal in post–World War II Vienna. When Holly Martins (Cotten) comes to the battered city seeking his old pal Harry Lime (Welles), he's told that Harry has been killed in an accident. Holly finds, however, that Harry is still very much alive, dealing in black-market, defective penicillin. He also falls for Harry's former lover (Valli). The movie is filled with chilling scenes: Major Calloway (Howard) showing Holly dying victims of Harry's greed; Harry, in a Ferris wheel high above a fairground, purring his cynical "Swiss cuckoo clock" philosophy; a desperate pursuit through the city's sewers (where Robert Krasker's Oscar-winning photography is especially striking). The fade-out is a stunner. The cast is top-notch; Welles's scoundrel, unforgettable. Zither player An-

ton Karas's jaunty score is still heard and hummed.

Off-Screen: To raise funds for his embattled film version of *Othello,* Welles agreed to replace first choice Noël Coward as Harry Lime, joining director Reed and other cast members in Vienna. (He also wrote his own lines for the famous Ferris wheel scene.) He became so identified with his role that for many years afterward, restaurant orchestras played "The Third Man Theme" whenever he entered. Both Reed and Howard claimed credit for discovering Karas, performing in a Vienna wine tavern. With his earnings, the musician-composer bought his own tavern. Welles played Lime in a 1950 radio series spin-off of the movie; a 1960 television series had Michael Rennie appearing in a drastically revised version of the character. (CFB)

Thirty Seconds Over Tokyo

MGM, 1944. (138m.) Dir: Mervyn LeRoy. Sp: Dalton Trumbo, b/o book by Capt. Ted W. Lawson and Robert Considine. Cast: Spencer Tracy, Van Johnson, Robert Walker, Phyllis Thaxter, Robert Mitchum, Louis Jean Heydt, Don DeFore, Horace McNally, Leon Ames, Selena Royle.

On-Screen: *A true account of one man's ordeal and triumph in World War II.* Here is one war film that belongs in a time capsule. An often stirring account of the first bombing raid on Japan in April 1942 and one participant's personal ordeal, *Thirty Seconds Over Tokyo* crystallizes virtually every prevailing attitude during the conflict, while also offering up every World War II war-film bromide. Here are scenes of ardent devotion between Capt. Ted Lawson (Johnson) and his pregnant wife (Thaxter); a documentarylike account of the training given to the men who will go on the mission; and finally the mission itself, a well-wrought simulation of the bombing of Japanese targets. The last, and best, section revolves about Captain Lawson's grievous injury that requires the amputation of a leg—and his effort to deal with his handicap. Van Johnson gives what may be his best screen performance as Lawson, and Spencer Tracy, in a guest-starring role, plays Gen. Jimmy Doolittle, who headed the raid.

Off-Screen: Filmed largely at the Naval Air Station in Pensacola, Florida, the movie won an Oscar for its impressive special effects. This was Robert Mitchum's twenty-second movie, although he was not yet a star. (When the movie was reissued in 1955, his name replaced Robert Walker's in the credits.) Bill Williams can be seen briefly in several scenes, as can Stephen McNally, who is billed here as Horace McNally, his true name. Phyllis Thaxter made her film debut as Ellen Lawson.

This Gun for Hire

Paramount, 1942. (80m.) Dir: Frank Tuttle. Sp: Albert Maltz and W. R. Burnett, b/o novel by Graham Greene. Cast: Alan Ladd, Veronica Lake, Robert Preston, Laird Cregar, Tully Marshall, Marc Lawrence.

On-Screen: *Offbeat thriller, with Ladd and Lake on the brink of stardom.* Although it departs in some ways from Greene's *A Gun for Sale* (1936), this Hollywoodized adaptation doesn't seriously violate the original. In fact the qualities that would become Ladd's trademarks—nearly expressionless good looks and a barely inflected voice—are ide-

ally suited for the role of Raven, a pretty-boy professional killer. The movie, relocated to the United States during World War II, focuses on Raven's betrayal not only by a cowardly double agent (Cregar), but also by a nightclub singer (Lake) working for the FBI, who awakens Raven's suppressed human emotions. The tense action slows to a stop when Lake warbles a pair of songs, but Ladd's psychotic loner, ruthlessly seeking revenge, is consistently fascinating to watch.

Off-Screen: Robert Preston, the detective in pursuit of Ladd, was originally cast as Raven; however, he was too tall to play opposite the diminutive Lake, and the star-making role fell instead to Ladd, a convenient five foot four. The actor (his blond hair dyed black here) had already played bits and minor parts in nearly two dozen movies (watch for him as a reporter in *Citizen Kane,* a year earlier). Making one of her earliest screen appearances, as a nightclub hoofer, is Yvonne de Carlo. A poor remake, called *Short Cut to Hell,* was directed by first-and-only-time director James Cagney in 1957. A 1991 television version starred Robert Wagner. (CFB)

This Is Spinal Tap

Embassy, 1984. (C-82m.) Dir: Rob Reiner. Sp: Christopher Guest, Michael McKean, Harry Shearer, and Rob Reiner. Cast: Rob Reiner, Christopher Guest, Michael McKean, Harry Shearer, Tony Hendra, June Chadwick, R. J. Parnell.

On-Screen: *Rob Reiner spoofs the "rockumentary."* Among the few satirical comedies of the eighties, *This Is Spinal Tap* is one of the funniest. A wickedly accurate parody of the documentary form, it concerns a seventeen-year-old British rock band called Spinal Tap and their whirlwind tour of America. The band is, in fact, not only fictional but dreadful, and the movie reveals their precipitous descent to near-oblivion. A documentary filmmaker (Reiner himself) uses his camera to record the group's dwindling audiences, their ceaseless bickering, and their inane lyrics ("The looser the waistband, the deeper the quicksand"). The band's manager (Hendra) tries in vain to justify the frequent cancellations ("Their appeal is becoming more selective"). The movie uses all the familiar documentary techniques—one-on-one interviews, the roving camera, etc.—to reveal Spinal Tap's blank stupidity and lack of talent. After a modest initial release, *This Is Spinal Tap* found its audience and became a justified cult success.

Off-Screen: Rob Reiner and the actors who performed as Spinal Tap had been nurturing the idea for a long time. Christopher Guest, playing the band's lead guitarist, Nigel Tufnel, began creating Nigel a decade before the film after seeing a Tufnel prototype and his band trying to cope in vain with the simplest problems. The movie's cinematographer, Peter Smokler, had worked on the highly regarded Rolling Stones documentary, *Gimme Shelter* (1970).

This Is the Army

Warners, 1943. (C-121m.) Dir: Michael Curtiz. Sp: Casey Robinson and Claude Binyon, b/o stage presentation by Irving Berlin. MS: Irving Berlin. Cast: George Murphy, Joan Leslie, Ronald Reagan, George Tobias, Alan Hale, Charles Butterworth, Dolores Costello, Kate Smith, Frances Langford, Joe Louis, Irving Berlin.

On-Screen: *Irving Berlin's heartfelt wartime tribute to the army.* On Broadway in 1942, Irving Berlin's revue, *This Is the Army,* had been welcomed enthusiastically by wartime audiences. Brought to the screen the following year, it continued to stir viewers and critics with its mixture of topical songs and sketches, all intended to salute the army and its fighting men. A sketchy plot about two generations of soldiers (George Murphy playing Ronald Reagan's father!) was added, but the Berlin music, the army jokes, and the patriotic feeling were the important factors. Today, some of the musical numbers induce winces rather than cheers (the most embarrassing reinforce racial stereotypes), but there are highlights, notably a few pleasing war-oriented ballads and Irving Berlin's plaintive rendition of his song "Oh, How I Hate to Get Up in the Morning," which he had performed in his World War I show, *Yip Yip Yaphank.* Inevitably, Kate Smith turns up to sing "God Bless America." The film's profits were relegated entirely to the Army Emergency Relief Fund.

Off-Screen: Despite Irving Berlin's reputation for wholesomeness, there were censorship problems with the movie. The Breen Office objected to the lyrics in "Ladies of the Chorus" referring to "willing farmers' daughters," plus other "blue" lines. There was also a brouhaha about Berlin's song for the finale, a rather bloodthirsty song called "Dressed Up to Kill." Through pressure from religious groups, the song was changed to "Dressed Up to Win," although the song, as performed, still has the soldiers baring their bayonets aggressively at the enemy. Berlin had a difficult time filming his number, even forgetting the words at one point.

Thoroughly Modern Millie

Universal, 1967. (C-138m.) Dir: George Roy Hill. Sp: Richard Morris. MS: Jimmy Van Heusen and Sammy Cahn, and others. Cast: Julie Andrews, Mary Tyler Moore, Carol Channing, Beatrice Lillie, James Fox, John Gavin, Jack Soo, Pat Morita.

On-Screen: *Flapper Julie Andrews and friends cavort in the roaring twenties.* Entertaining until it wears out its welcome in silly slapstick and melodramatics, *Thoroughly Modern Millie* is yet another musical romp set in Hollywood's idea of the twenties. Julie Andrews plays a stylish flapper who falls for her boss (Gavin), while Mary Tyler Moore is the sweet young thing who may be the next victim of Beatrice Lillie's white slave racket. Carol Channing has a juicy supporting role as a wealthy, eccentric widow. Some of the musical numbers are sprightly and inventive, notably Andrews's opening rendition of the title song (her clothes change from modest to flapperish during the song) and the requisite tune about the latest dance craze, "The Tapioca." For no discernible reason, Andrews also sings at a Jewish wedding, after which the guests participate in a diverting dance. *Thoroughly Modern Millie* should have been trimmed before release, but even in its bloated state, it affords some pleasure.

Off-Screen: The film was conceived as a straight comedy without music until Julie Andrews fell in love with the project. Afterward, she was less enchanted: "I wish they had cut just twenty minutes and not made it a road show. . . . I think it was blown up too far out of proportion from its original conception." She implored the studio to cut the number at the Jewish wedding, but it was retained. The film received seven Oscar nominations, but only Elmer Bernstein won for Best Original Score.

Three Coins in the Fountain

Fox, 1954. (C-102m.) Dir: Jean Negulesco. Sp: John Patrick, b/o novel by John H. Secondari. Cast: Clifton Webb, Dorothy McGuire, Jean Peters, Louis Jourdan, Maggie McNamara, Rossano Brazzi, Howard St. John, Cathleen Nesbitt.

On-Screen: *Three American women find romance in Rome.* Armchair travelers and lovers of romantic pulp should find some pleasure in this movie. Lushly photographed in the wide-screen CinemaScope process, it is set amidst the splendors of Rome, with a brief side trip to Venice. (Milton Krasner's photography won an Oscar.) The frivolous plot involves three young women (McGuire, Peters, McNamara) who make wishes at the Fountain of Trevi and end up happily in love in the Eternal City. The only romance of moderate interest, if only for its refreshing maturity, pairs secretary McGuire with expatriate novelist Webb, her longtime boss. The other romances (Peters with Brazzi, McNamara with Jourdan) are slickly inconsequential. The beauty of Italy's fabled cities requires a wider screen than any television set can provide, but even so, *Three Coins in the Fountain* offers a scenic trip.

Off-Screen: The ubiquitous title song, sung by an uncredited Frank Sinatra, won an Oscar for Sammy Cahn and Jule Styne. The movie received a Best Picture Oscar nomination but lost to *On the Waterfront*. Reset in Spain, it was remade in 1964 as *The Pleasure Seekers,* again with Jean Negulesco as director.

A 1990 television adaptation, called *Coins in the Fountain,* sank without a trace.

Three Comrades

MGM, 1938. (98m.) Dir: Frank Borzage. Sp: F. Scott Fitzgerald and Edward E. Paramore, b/o book by Erich Maria Remarque. Cast: Margaret Sullavan, Robert Taylor, Franchot Tone, Robert Young, Guy Kibbee, Lionel Atwill, Monty Woolley.

On-Screen: *A tragic romance of post–World War I Germany.* Adapted from Erich Maria Remarque's novel, *Three Comrades* removes much of the book's political content to concentrate on an ill-fated romance. Taylor, Tone, and Young play German World War I veterans, inseparable friends whose lives are touched by the fragile, wistful Sullavan. Deeply in love, Sullavan and Taylor marry, but their idyll is tragically brief. In keeping with Hollywood's cautious policy at the time, the film touches only lightly on the early rise of Nazi hooliganism a few years after the war's end, and the Nazi Party is never mentioned by name. Although Frank Borzage was adept at gauzy romance, much of the film is sluggishly paced, and the male leads are only adequate. What makes the film memorable is the performance of Margaret Sullavan, here at her most poignant. Her distinctively throaty voice infuses her lines with a deep melancholy, especially in the final scene that many film buffs remember with tear-dimmed eyes. She received an Oscar nomination and won that year's New York Film Critics Award as Best Actress.

Off-Screen: Producer Joseph L. Mankiewicz hired famed novelist F. Scott Fitzgerald, believing that he could convey the aura of Germany's postwar generation. Although only a portion of Fitzgerald's screenplay was finally used, it represents his only screen credit out of the many pictures he worked on. Margaret Sullavan had a superstition about not starting work until it rained, and indeed she held up this production for six days because of this phobia. Once, Louis B. Mayer had the special effects department create a realistic rain effect outside the stage door.

The Three Faces of Eve

Fox, 1957. (91m.) Dir: Nunnally Johnson. Sp: Nunnally Johnson, b/o book by Drs. Corbett H. Thigpen and Hervey M. Cleckley. Cast: Joanne Woodward, Lee J. Cobb, David Wayne, Edwin Jerome, Nancy Kulp, Ken Scott, Terry Ann Ross, Douglas Spencer.

On-Screen: *Joanne Woodward's Oscar as a three-part personality.* After appearing in several negligible movies, Joanne Woodward joined Fox and promptly proved that she was a superior actress by playing the troubled housewife in *The Three Faces of Eve.* Married to insensitive Wayne, her Eve goes to psychiatrist Cobb to cure or ease her mental woes. He discovers, to his astonishment, that she has three distinct personalities: one mousy and uncertain, another sexually charged and promiscuous, the third a combination of the other two. After much anguish and psychiatric probing, Eve is cured and begins a new life with a new beau. Woodward moves skillfully from one personality to another, and if the film is rather drab, it is never uninteresting. Cobb, who is really her costar, plays the requisite movie psychiatrist, wise and compassionate. Only

Wayne seems somehow off-center, giving an inappropriate comic edge to his role as Eve's cloddish husband.

Off-Screen: According to producer-writer-director Johnson, his first choice for the role was Judy Garland, and at first she seemed excited by the prospect, then turned it down when there were "all kinds of complications." Johnson found that directing Joanne Woodward was "easy and satisfying." She won the Best Actress Oscar over competition that included Anna Magnani, Deborah Kerr, Elizabeth Taylor, and Lana Turner.

Three Little Words

MGM, 1950. (C-102m.) Dir: Richard Thorpe. Sp: George Wells. MS: Bert Kalmar and Harry Ruby. Cast: Fred Astaire, Red Skelton, Vera-Ellen, Arlene Dahl, Debbie Reynolds, Gloria De Haven, Keenan Wynn, Carleton Carpenter.

On-Screen: *Fred Astaire, Red Skelton, and the music of Kalmar and Ruby.* Although not in a class with Rodgers and Hart, Bert Kalmar and Harry Ruby wrote many bright and hummable tunes, and this pleasant MGM musical features their melodic output. Astaire plays Kalmar, whose first love was magic, and Skelton (much more subdued than usual) plays Ruby, an avid baseball fan. They form a successful songwriting team, quarrel bitterly, and then reunite for a happy ending at the instigation of their wives (Vera-Ellen, Dahl). That's about it, but the music and dancing are fine. Highlights include Astaire and Vera-Ellen performing "Mr. and Mrs. Hoofer at Home" and "Thinking of You," and Debbie Reynolds singing "I Wanna Be Loved by You" in an impersonation of "boop-boop-a-doop" singer Helen Kane (with Kane herself dubbing the voice). Astaire also has one nimble solo dance with a cane.

Off-Screen: Producer Irving Cummings had to convince Red Skelton to take on the largely straight role of Harry Ruby. Having played almost exclusively in comedy, Skelton was extremely reluctant, but after much persuasion, he finally agreed. Astaire had nothing but praise for Vera-Ellen: "She was a real accomplished dancer, that girl. Ballet, tap dancing, anything you wanted to do."

Three Strangers

Warners, 1946. (92m.) Dir: Jean Negulesco. Sp: John Huston and Howard Koch, b/o story by John Huston. Cast: Sydney Greenstreet, Geraldine Fitzgerald, Peter Lorre, Joan Lorring, Robert Shayne, Marjorie Riordan, Alan Napier, Rosalind Ivan.

On-Screen: *A sweepstakes ticket changes three lives.* A taut and compelling melodrama, *Three Strangers* involves three people in a tangled web that leads to deception and murder. Strangers to each other, Greenstreet, Fitzgerald, and Lorre share a sweepstakes ticket that, according to the Chinese goddess of fortune and destiny, is destined to win. Each has a turbulent life: Greenstreet is a crooked lawyer who has been misusing his client's funds; bitterly vindictive socialite Fitzgerald is losing her husband; and lowlife Lorre is innocently involved in a crime. Events alter their lives until the fateful day of the sweepstakes race, when they meet again. Moody and offbeat, *Three Strangers* may have its dull patches, but good acting by the leads and atmospheric photography by Arthur Edeson help to raise the movie from the commonplace.

Off-Screen: Back in 1937, John Huston had sold the story of *Three Strangers* to Warners, where it sat on the shelf for a number of years. After the success of *The Maltese Falcon* in 1941, Huston had reworked the screenplay with Howard Koch and intended to reunite Bogart, Astor, and Greenstreet. However, Huston went off to war, and the property came into other hands. Lorre and Fitzgerald replaced Bogart and Astor.

The Thrill of It All

Universal-International, 1963. (C-108m.) Dir: Norman Jewison. Sp: Carl Reiner, b/o story by Carl Reiner and Larry Gelbart. Cast: Doris Day, James Garner, Arlene Francis, Edward Andrews, Reginald Owen, ZaSu Pitts, Elliott Reid.

On-Screen: *Doris Day comes to television land.* One of the liveliest and funniest Doris Day comedies of the sixties, *The Thrill of It All* (a meaningless title) pokes fun at two familiar movie targets: advertising and television. Day plays a vivacious woman—wife of an obstetrician (Garner) and mother of two small children—who unexpectedly becomes the television spokesperson for a soap company. Hubby is not enchanted with his wife's celebrity, and other complications almost wreck her life and her marriage, but it all ends happily. Reiner's screenplay is inventive and sometimes hilarious—the best scenes involve a car sinking into a pool and an explosion of soapsuds. (You'll see.) Look for longtime radio-television personality Arlene Francis as a delirious expectant mother and for ZaSu Pitts as a jittery housekeeper.

Off-Screen: There were difficulties getting a name for the bar of soap that figured importantly in the story. Originally, the name was to be Thrill, but it turned out that there was already a detergent by that name. Of twenty-one names invented for the soap, seventeen were already in use. The legal department settled on Happy. Since companies have copyrights on shapes, colors, and thicknesses, a special soap had to be designed.

Throw Momma from the Train

Orion, 1987. (C-88m.) Dir: Danny DeVito. Sp: Stu Silver. Cast: Danny DeVito, Billy Crystal, Anne Ramsey, Kim Greist, Kate Mulgrew, Branford Marsalis, Rob Reiner.

On-Screen: *A murder scheme goes comically awry.* Well, it must have seemed like a good idea at the time. Owen Liff (DeVito), a middle-aged man only two short steps away from idiocy, is burdened with a monstrous, emasculating mother (Ramsey) he would like to kill. Owen's creative writing teacher, Larry Donner (Crystal), detests and would love to destroy his successful ex-wife (Mulgrew). When Larry seems to suggest, à la Hitchcock's *Strangers on a Train,* that the two should commit each other's murder (thus removing themselves from suspicion by committing apparently motiveless crimes), Owen takes him seriously, and comic chaos results. With Hitchcock, the viewer goes along for a suspenseful ride. In *Throw Momma from the Train,* the material is played for hectic farce, seldom as funny as intended. Danny DeVito, who also directed, is very good as the slow-witted momma's boy, and there are some clever spots in Stu Silver's screenplay. But the movie also trots out such hoary comedy-thriller devices as the runaway automobile and the man teetering precariously on a high ledge. In a relaxed mood, you may enjoy all this. Otherwise, forget it.

Off-Screen: Anne Ramsey's performance won her a Best Supporting Actress Oscar nomination and placed her in a league with other Movie Mothers From Hell, such as Ayliene Gibbons's grotesque mother in *The Loved One* (1965) and Zelda Rubinstein's monstrous mom in *Anguish* (1987). Of course, there's always Anthony Perkins's testy mother in *Psycho* (1960). Or is there?

Till the Clouds Roll By

MGM, 1946. (C-137m.) Dir: Richard Whorf. Sp: Myles Connolly and Jean Holloway, b/o story by Guy Bolton. MS: Jerome Kern and various lyricists. Cast: Robert Walker, Van Heflin, Lucille Bremer, Dorothy Patrick. Guest stars Judy Garland, Frank Sinatra, Kathryn Grayson, Lena Horne, June Allyson, Cyd Charisse, Angela Lansbury, Dinah Shore, Tony Martin, Virginia O'Brien.

On-Screen: *Jerome Kern survives MGM—barely*. Don't look for much truth in this "biography" of composer Jerome Kern. Simply lean back and enjoy his wonderful, imperishable melodies. Since Kern's life was not particularly eventful, the screenwriters could come up with little more than perfunctory material about Kern's rise to fame, his romance and marriage, and his concern for his mentor's rebellious daughter (Bremer). Played blandly by Walker, this Kern is not very interesting. But then there's his music, performed by MGM guest stars with varying degrees of effectiveness. Judy Garland, as Marilyn Miller, sings "Look for the Silver Lining" affectingly; June Allyson is not too oppressively cute performing "Cleopaterrer" and the jaunty title song; and Dinah Shore does a silken version of "The Last Time I Saw Paris." The movie's nadir comes at the end, when Frank Sinatra, in white tuxedo, sings "Old Man River" in a typically glitzy MGM setting.

Off-Screen: Considering its vapidity, it's surprising to learn that the screenplay went through many uncredited writers. Vincente Minnelli directed the musical numbers with Judy Garland, who was pregnant at the time and felt that she showed. Later Garland recalled that when she sang "Who?" it was funny to run up to each man in the scene and ask him that question.

To Be or Not to Be

United Artists, 1942. (99m.) Dir: Ernst Lubitsch. Sp: Edwin Justus Mayer b/o story by Ernst Lubitsch and Melchior Lengyel. Cast: Jack Benny, Carole Lombard, Robert Stack, Felix Bressart, Sig Ruman, Lionel Atwill, Stanley Ridges.

On-Screen: *The original version, and still the funniest anti-Nazi comedy*. Set in Nazi-occupied Poland, Ernest Lubitsch's audacious, and at the time controversial, movie mixes melodrama and farce in almost equal proportions. As a famous Polish husband-and-wife acting team who outwit the German invaders, Jack Benny is in top form and Carole Lombard is, as always, the screen's most alluring funny lady. Robert Stack plays a dashing Polish pilot who's fallen for flirtatious Lombard. When he leaves Warsaw to join the RAF, he learns that the man whom he's trusted to contact the couple is a German spy. Benny, a hammy Hamlet onstage, comes into his own as an actor when he impersonates both a Nazi officer and the informer. Also on hand are inspired clowns Ruman, an absurdly pompous Nazi bigwig ("So they call me Concentration Camp Ehrhardt?"), and Bressart, a mousy troupe bit player who finally gets to give his greatest performance.

Off-Screen: To some critics' assertion that the movie trivialized the plight of German-occupied Poland, director Lubitsch replied, in part, "What I have satirized . . . are the Nazis and their ridiculous ideology." Miriam Hopkins was originally cast in the lead, but temperamental Hopkins had an uneasy relationship with Benny and was fretting to have her role expanded. When she withdrew, Lombard took over willingly. Less than a month after the film was completed, she died in a plane crash while on a tour selling U. S. war bonds. A just-for-laughs remake was released in 1983, with Mel Brooks and Anne Bancroft.

To Catch a Thief

Paramount, 1955. (C-106m.) Dir: Alfred Hitchcock. Sp: John Michael Hayes, b/o novel by David Dodge. Cast: Cary Grant, Grace Kelly, Jessie Royce Landis, John Williams, Charles Vanel, Brigitte Auber.

On-Screen: *Bubbly tingler gets heavy competition from lush Riviera scenery.* "Set a thief," the adage goes, "to catch a thief," and that's what comfortably retired, ex–cat burglar Grant ("I only stole from people who

wouldn't go hungry") must do to remain this side of the law. A rash of jewel thefts, patterned on his old roof-prowling methods, has erupted on the Côte d'Azur, and the police suspect him. Wealthy dowager Landis, who prefers bourbon to her baubles, and daughter Kelly are his means to trap the copycat. But Kelly's amorous fascination with Grant's past turns to distrust when her mother's jewels vanish. Kelly sputters ("Oh, shut up," Landis tells her at one point) and smolders, and you may find yourself wishing that classy Cary and sassy Jessie (exact contemporaries) had costarred in an even wittier movie.

Off-Screen: The film was nominated for Oscars in three color categories—Cinematography, Art Direction, and Costume Design—but only Robert Burks's photography was a winner. It's easy to see why. In fact, chases through a brightly hued flower market in Nice and along the snaking roads of the Grande Corniche, the opulence of the Carlton Hotel at Cannes, and the abstract-painting quality of the nighttime climactic scene on the rippling rooftops (unconvincingly staged, however) almost eclipse the story. It was while the movie was being made that Kelly met her future husband, Prince Ranier of Monaco, and the viewer cannot help recalling that it was along the same sun-drenched mountain roads shown in the film that Princess Grace met her death, in 1982, in an automobile accident. Hitchcock makes his ritual appearance seated in a bus next to Grant. (CFB)

To Each His Own

Paramount, 1946. (122m.) Dir: Mitchell Leisen. Sp: Charles Brackett and Jacques

Thery. Cast: Olivia de Havilland, John Lund, Roland Culver, Mary Anderson, Philip Terry, Bill Goodwin, Virginia Welles, Frank Faylen, Victoria Horne.

On-Screen: *A mother's secret love survives the years.* Since the silent years, tales of sacrificial mother love could always be counted on for a good cry. (Movie fathers tend to vanish, then reappear, incognito.) *To Each His Own* is among the better variations of the theme, well mounted, persuasively acted, and touching without being overly sticky. Olivia de Havilland is a young woman who becomes pregnant by a soldier (Lund) in World War I, and then, through a tragic mishap, is unable to reveal her identity. Years later, pretending to be her son's sour, tight-lipped old-maid aunt, she lavishes love and attention on him. (Lund, in his film debut, played the son as well.) Can you doubt that he will eventually learn her secret? *To Each His Own* will strike you as either an excruciating exercise in maternal masochism or an excellent tearjerker. In either case, Olivia de Havilland gives a sensitive performance that earned her a Best Actress Oscar.

Off-Screen: De Havilland's comment on the role: "When Paramount sent me the script of *To Each His Own,* I knew immediately that it was a part I had to do. It was a very long part and it offered a lot of opportunities for an actress; it was fascinating to see how the character changed. Yet I knew it would be difficult to make a sentimental story such as this believable."

To Have and Have Not

Warners, 1944. (100m.) Dir: Howard Hawks. Sp: Jules Furthman and William Faulkner, b/o novel by Ernest Hemingway. Cast: Humphrey Bogart, Lauren Bacall, Walter Brennan, Hoagy Carmichael, Marcel Dalio, Dan Seymour, Dolores Moran, Sheldon Leonard.

On-Screen: *Sparks fly in Bogie and Bacall's first teaming.* The best reason to see the movie now is for the simmer and sizzle the stars bring to their scenes together. Neither closely based on Hemingway's novel nor as heart-meltingly romantic as *Casablanca,* which it resembles in some ways, it still packs dramatic punch. Bogart is a politically uncommitted skipper of a fishing boat whose need for money forces him to tangle with pro-Vichy thugs in Martinique. Bacall is a sultry, stranded American who needs cash to help her return to the States. At first, their mutual attraction is casual; after their affair turns serious, she propositions him with the lines that made Bacall an overnight sensation: "You know how to whistle, don't you, Steve? You just put your lips together—and blow." Brennan, as Bogart's boozy buddy, and Carmichael, as a seedy pianist, add to the fun.

Off-Screen: Bacall was nineteen when she and Bogart fell in love while making the movie (her film debut) and were married a year later. The novel was updated to take advantage of wartime concerns, and its setting changed to French Martinique to avoid offending the Cuban government. Accounts differ as to whose voice is heard singing "How Little We Know." Vocalist Andy Williams has stated that although he recorded the song, to be dubbed later for husky-voiced Bacall, selections from various takes of her own singing were edited together and used instead. The novel was filmed again as *The Breaking Point* (1950), with John Garfield and Patricia Neal, and less interestingly, as *The Gun Runners* (1958), an Audie Murphy vehicle. (CFB)

To Kill a Mockingbird

Universal, 1962. (130m.) Dir: Robert Mulligan. Sp: Horton Foote, b/o novel by Harper Lee. Cast: Gregory Peck, Mary Badham, Philip Alford, Robert Duvall, Brock Peters, Rosemary Murphy, John Megna, Collin Wilcox, Frank Overton.

On-Screen: *Two children discover racial violence—and their father's nobility—in a small Southern town.* Told from the viewpoint of six-year-old Scout Finch (Badham) and her ten-year-old brother Jem (Alford), this superb film reveals the fear and hatred lurking beneath the quiet exterior of a Southern town in the thirties. Gregory Peck, in his Oscar-winning role, plays their father, Atticus, a lawyer of rare strength and integrity, who is called upon to defend a black man (Peters) accused of raping a white girl (Wilcox). As the children watch, the explosive trial uncovers the ugly truth, but justice is not possible in the South of the time, and it all ends tragically. The children, however, have come to understand and appreciate their father's quiet heroism. Peck delivers an eloquent, understated performance, and Badham and Alford play their roles with complete reality and not a trace of cuteness. In his first film, Robert Duvall is fine as a mysterious neighbor named Boo Radley, who figures in the story.

Off-Screen: The producers had hoped to film in Harper Lee's hometown of Monroeville, Alabama, but radical changes since the Depression made it impossible, and the town was built on the back lot. The film is narrated by a grown-up Scout in the voice of Kim Stanley. The character of Dill, played by little John Megna, was modeled on author Harper Lee's remembrance of her friend Truman Capote. In addition to Peck's well-deserved Oscar, the film received awards for Best Adapted Screenplay and for Art Direction/Set Decoration (black-and-white). It was also nominated as Best Picture but lost to *Lawrence of Arabia*.

Tom, Dick and Harry

RKO, 1941. (86m.) Dir: Garson Kanin. Sp: Paul Jarrico. Cast: Ginger Rogers, Burgess Meredith, George Murphy, Alan Marshal, Phil Silvers, Lenore Lonergan.

On-Screen: *Ginger Rogers must choose among her three suitors.* Putting aside her dancing shoes after *The Story of Vernon and Irene Castle* in 1938, Ginger Rogers concentrated on her acting career. In such films as *Bachelor Mother* (1939) and *Lucky Partners* (1940), she was a pert and charming comedienne, and she won an Oscar for her performance as *Kitty Foyle* (1940). *Tom, Dick and Harry* marked a falling off—playing a character roughly a decade younger than her chronological age and forcing her voice into a childish singsong, she made her heroine seem rather feebleminded. Too bad, because Paul Jarrico's screenplay has an amusing premise: Janie (Rogers) finds herself engaged to three men: practical car salesman Tom (Murphy), wealthy playboy Dick (Marshal), and down-to-earth but oddball Harry (Meredith), and she dreams about what her life would be with each suitor. The dreams are cleverly staged, but the suitors seem rather long in the tooth and Rogers's performance is charmless. Phil Silvers provides a few needed laughs as an obnoxious ice cream salesman.

Off-Screen: *Tom, Dick and Harry* was Ginger Rogers's second film under Garson Kanin's direction; the first was the much more successful *Bachelor Mother* (1939). Rogers liked Garson Kanin: "Gar's sense of humor swung three hundred and sixty degrees, and he always managed to see something humorous in whatever came up." The story was remade in 1957 as *The Girl Most Likely*.

Tootsie

Columbia, 1982. (C-116m.) Dir: Sydney Pollack. Sp: Larry Gelbart and Murray Schisgal, b/o story by Larry Gelbart and Don McGuire. Cast: Dustin Hoffman, Jessica Lange, Teri Garr, Dabney Coleman, Charles Durning, Bill Murray (uncredited), Geena Davis, George Gaynes, Sydney Pollack, Doris Bellack.

On-Screen: *Dustin Hoffman enjoys being a girl.* One of the brightest, most successful comedies of the eighties, *Tootsie* has an amusing if not totally credible premise: Unable to find a job as an actor, Dustin Hoffman disguises himself as a woman and becomes a sensation on a soap opera as Dorothy Michaels. While falling for a beautiful soap-opera actress (Lange), he also becomes a better man by viewing life through a woman's eyes. Wittily scripted, mainly by Gelbart and Schisgal, and ably directed by Sydney Pollack, who also plays Hoffman's agent, *Tootsie* casts a few satirical barbs at the acting community and its frenzied worlds of television and theater, while also scoring some points for understanding between the sexes. Hoffman gives a brilliant performance ("Nobody does vegetables like me"), and Lange is radiant in her Oscar-winning role. Cheers as well for Teri Garr as Hoffman's hapless girlfriend and Dabney Coleman as a smug director. Only an unconvincing climax keeps *Tootsie* from the top echelon of film comedies.

Off-Screen: The history of *Tootsie*'s screenplay is too tangled to be repeated here; suffice to say that Larry Gelbart and Murray Schisgal were the only credited writers among the many who worked on the script. (One was Elaine May.) Hal Ashby was first scheduled to direct. Sydney Pollack considered Dabney Coleman for the role he eventually played himself. Hoffman claimed that the title came from his mother, who would toss him in the air and say, "Who's my little tootsie-wootsie?" For the complete story behind the film, look for *Making Tootsie* by Susan Dworkin (Newmarket Press, 1983).

Top Gun

Paramount, 1986. (C-110m.) Dir: Tony Scott. Sp: Jim Cash and Jack Epps, Jr. Cast: Tom Cruise, Kelly McGillis, Anthony Edwards, Val Kilmer, Tom Skerritt, Meg Ryan, Michael Ironside, John Stockwell, Barry Tubb, Rick Rossovich, Tim Robbins, James Tolkan.

On-Screen: *Rivalry and derring-do in the wild blue yonder.* Top Gun is the name given Fighter Weapons School, where the best navy pilots are sent for advanced training. The competition to be named number one on the base is intense, and high on the list are cocky Maverick (Cruise) and his more stable partner, Goose (Edwards). On the ground,

Maverick's main interest is Charlie (McGillis), a civilian dogfight expert. Sure. Maverick is doing well when tragedy strikes, robbing him of his confidence. The flying scenes are spectacular, the pilots are stalwart, and there's also a real shoot-'em-down dogfight between three navy pilots and six MIGs. It's a tad hard to believe, as it's hard to believe the romance between Maverick and Charlie, who seems too old and smart for such a young squirt. But the scenes with Goose's wife (Ryan) add a nice note of warmth, Cruise manages to make a pain in the neck almost likable, and as long as *Top Gun* is up in the air, it's hard to fault.

Off-Screen: Much of the movie was shot at the actual "Top Gun" at Miramar Naval Air Station in California, where the movie is set. To simulate a pivotal crash, the special effects team rented a parcel of bare land across the bay from Oakland, California, and photographed models of the jet fighters, usually hung by steel wires, flying and firing their weapons and then exploding in a ball of flames against a natural sky and man-made clouds produced with a fogging agent left over from World War II. The movie's theme song, "Take My Breath Away," won an Oscar. (BL)

Top Hat

RKO, 1935. (99m.) Dir: Mark Sandrich. Sp: Dwight Taylor and Allan Scott. MS: Irving Berlin. Cast: Fred Astaire, Ginger Rogers, Edward Everett Horton, Helen Broderick, Erik Rhodes, Eric Blore.

On-Screen: *The incomparable dancing duo at their peerless best.* Toward the end of the "Cheek to Cheek" number, there is an exhilarating moment in which Astaire and Rogers dance across a bridge as the beat of the orchestra accelerates. In a way, it epitomizes the sheer bliss that Astaire and Rogers generated in their best musicals. And this may well be their very best musical: an enchanting blend of frivolous plot, lilting Berlin songs, and those magical dances. Yes, the mistaken-identity story line is foolish, but what does it matter when the music begins? *Top Hat* abounds in musical riches, from the delightful give-and-take of "Isn't This a Lovely Day (To Be Caught in the Rain)" in a deserted park pavilion to Astaire's quintessential dance to "Top Hat, White Tie, and Tails." Most memorable, perhaps, is the team's romantic dancing to "Cheek to Cheek." The climactic production number, "The Piccolino," runs on too long, but by this time, viewers have been transported to musical heaven. As in *The Gay Divorcee,* Horton, Blore, and Rhodes are on hand to lend comic support to the frail story, while Helen Broderick adds a welcome acidulous note.

Off-Screen: At first, Astaire was not happy with the screenplay, but changes were made until he was satisfied. The "Cheek to Cheek" number caused problems. Rogers wore a dress covered with ostrich feathers that made Astaire sneeze as the dress molted. When it happened a second time, he became angry until the designer spent the night sewing each feather in place. Italian officials were offended by Rhodes's parodied Italian dress designer and banned the movie from the country for some time. *Top Hat* received four Oscar nominations, including one for Best Picture.

Topper

MGM, 1937. (97m.) Dir: Norman Z. McLeod. Sp: Jack Jevne, Eric Hatch, and

Eddie Moran, b/o novel by Thorne Smith. Cast: Cary Grant, Constance Bennett, Roland Young, Billie Burke, Alan Mowbray, Eugene Pallette, Arthur Lake, Hedda Hopper.

On-Screen: *Two mischievous ghosts bedevil their friend.* Today, when playful and even amorous ghosts draw huge crowds to the theaters, ectoplasmic spirits are standard movie fodder. Back in 1937, however, they were a relatively novel idea that this still-enjoyable movie helped to popularize. Marvelous Roland Young is Topper, a timid banker with a nagging wife (Burke). When his friends George and Marion Kerby (Grant and Bennett) are killed in an automobile accident, their ghosts take over. Their mission: to teach Topper how to live. Much of the fun comes from their being invisible to everyone but Topper, and so there are many scenes in which the devilish Kerbys cause an uproar by playing pranks on astonished people. Grant and Bennett are perfectly delightful, and Young makes a memorable Topper. (He won an Academy Award nomination for Best Supporting Actor.)

Off-Screen: Producer Hal Roach wanted W. C. Fields to play Topper and Jean Harlow as Marion Kerby, but both were unavailable. (Harlow died a month before the film's release.) Grant was reluctant to appear in a ghost story, but director McLeod convinced him that it would make a great screwball comedy. The actor enjoyed making the film but later confessed that he didn't care for his performance: "I wasn't very good. I didn't enjoy myself in it at all." The popular movie spawned two sequels—*Topper Takes a Trip* (1939) and *Topper Returns* (1941), as well as a television series in the fifties. A 1979 television movie failed to spark interest in a new series.

Torn Curtain

Universal, 1966. (C-128m.) Dir: Alfred Hitchcock. Sp: Brian Moore. Cast: Paul Newman, Julie Andrews, Lila Kedrova, David Opatoshu, Ludwig Donath, Tamara Toumanova, Wolfgang Kieling, Carolyn Conwell.

On-Screen: *Alfred Hitchcock strikes out.* Even the most dazzling of Alfred Hitchcock's films have been known to contain lapses of logic that are cheerfully glossed over by the master director. But when he falters seriously, the defects are all too visible, and the result is a distressingly lame thriller such as *Torn Curtain*. Paul Newman stars as an American physicist who, in 1965, appears to defect to the Communist regime in East Germany. Actually, he is a true-blue patriot bent on extracting essential information from a prominent German physicist (Donath). His baffled British fiancée (Andrews) insists on following him behind the Iron Curtain, and soon the two are engaged in a long, dangerous flight back to safety in West Berlin. Outside of the fact that Newman and Andrews, though lovers, seem to be barely acquainted, the plot is filled with improbabilities, and worst of all, there is little evidence of Hitchcock's usual bravura technique. Only one scene stands out—Newman and a conspiring German farm woman (Conwell) must kill the Communist bodyguard (Kieling) who is onto their secret, but the man, to their exhaustion and horror, dies hard. The rest of the movie, unfortunately, fails to strike any sparks.

Off-Screen: The original screenplay contained a sequence in which Newman, after killing the guard, meets the victim's brother in a factory and is visibly upset when the man holds a kitchen knife that looks very much like the one that killed his brother. Reports from the set indicated that Hitchcock and Newman did not hit it off very well, but Newman later claimed that the only difficulty lay in a faulty screenplay and not in a lack of communication or a lack of respect.

A Touch of Class

Avco Embassy, 1973. (C-105m.) Dir: Melvin Frank. Sp: Melvin Frank and Jack Rose. Cast: Glenda Jackson, George Segal, Paul Sorvino, Hildegard Neil, Cec Linder, K. Callan, Mary Barclay.

On-Screen: *The pleasures and perils of an illicit affair.* Glenda Jackson won a Best Actress Oscar for her brittle (and rare) comedy performance in this airily amusing romantic comedy. She's Vickie Allessio, a divorcée with two children, and George Segal is Steve Blackburn, a married insurance man working in London. They begin what they believe will be a romantic tryst, flying off to Málaga together. In between some ardent lovemaking, their assignation turns out to be largely disastrous—they destroy a hotel room with their furious quarrels—and even back in London, although they maintain their affair, the logistics of keeping a mistress while coping with his wife and children proves too much for Steve. The film's premise is not exactly fresh, but the stars work well together, her cool, acerbic style meshing on the whole with his boyish eagerness to please. One diverting sequence has him attempting to juggle a visit to Vickie and a concert with his wife on the same evening. Thanks mainly to Glenda Jackson, *A Touch of Class* has a touch of class.

Off-Screen: In the softball game that opens the movie, a number of the players were expatriate Americans who lived in London. In addition to Jackson's Oscar, the movie was nominated for Best Picture, Best Song ("All That Love Went to Waste"), Best Original Screenplay, and Best Original Dramatic Score.

Touch of Evil

Universal, 1958. (93m.) Dir: Orson Welles. Sp: Orson Welles, b/o novel by Whit Masterson. Cast: Charlton Heston, Janet Leigh, Orson Welles, Marlene Dietrich, Joseph Calleia, Akim Tamiroff, Ray Collins, Dennis Weaver.

On-Screen: *A couple is thrown into a terrifying world of drugs and violence.* As director, actor, and adapter, Orson Welles dominates this nightmarish *film noir* set in the grubby border town of Los Robles. Heston plays Mike Vargas, a Mexican narcotics agent who, with his American wife, Susan (Leigh), gets caught up in a scheme to frame his new bride on drug-addiction and murder raps. Hank Quinlan (Welles), the town's chief detective, is a bloated, cigar-chomping avenger of his wife's death, years earlier. Quinlan fakes evidence against anyone, especially Mexicans, who threatens his control of the town. When Vargas investigates a murder, both he and his wife run afoul of Quinlan and the local underworld boss (Tamiroff). As powerful as Welles's performance is, Dietrich, looking great in the cameo role of a world-weary madam and Quinlan's only friend, all but steals the movie. Stunning photography by Russell Metty.

Off-Screen: Welles's spectacular opening sequence is considered one of the greatest continuous-action shots ever filmed, from a bomb being placed in a car trunk to the explosion, more than three minutes later. Viewers' attention is distracted from the shot because of studio insistence that the credits be shown at the outset rather than at the end, as was Welles's intention. During much of the filming, Janet Leigh's broken arm had to be concealed from the camera in various ways. Unbilled performers include Joseph Cotten, Mercedes McCambridge, Keenan Wynn, and Zsa Zsa Gabor. Venice, California, stood in for Los Robles. (CFB)

The Towering Inferno

Warners-Fox, 1974. (C-165m.) Dir: John Guillermin and Irwin Allen. Sp: Stirling Silliphant, b/o novels by Richard Morton Stern and by Thomas N. Scortia and Frank M. Robinson. Cast: Paul Newman, Steve McQueen, Faye Dunaway, William Holden, Fred Astaire, Jennifer Jones, Richard Chamberlain, Robert Vaughn, Susan Blakely, Robert Wagner, O. J. Simpson, Gregory Sierra, Dabney Coleman.

On-Screen: *An all-star scorcher.* When the conflagration begins, fire chief Steve McQueen remarks, "This is one building I figured wouldn't burn." Wrong. In San Francisco, the glittering, 138-story building about to be opened with a monster party for celebrities will soon go up in flames, taking some of the celebrities along in grisly fashion. One of the major releases in the cycle of disaster movies popular in the seventies, *The Towering Inferno* asks viewers to worry about the fates of such luminaries as architect Newman, his fiancée Dunaway, builder Holden, and con man Astaire, not to mention scores of others. The story is rather silly, but the special effects are spectacular, and the action sequences directed by producer Irwin Allen are undoubtedly exciting. The movie, however, generates the wrong kind of suspense: We wait with a sort of numbing dread for the next cast member to be incinerated, so that we begin to wonder why we're watching. Ultimately, *The Towering Inferno* is an exhausting—and even depressing—experience.

Off-Screen: When two novels (*The Tower, The Glass Inferno*) with virtually the same theme (fire in the world's tallest building) were offered for sale at the same time, Fox and Warners decided to join forces to produce *The Towering Inferno,* derived from both books. This became a Hollywood "first." Faye Dunaway was notorious for causing delays in the filming while she restyled her hair or adjusted her makeup. Her punctuality improved after William Holden berated her in no uncertain terms. The fifty-seven sets established a record for a single film on the Fox lot. By the time the movie was completed, only eight were still intact. There were eight Oscar nominations, including Best Picture, and three wins (Cinematography, Editing, Song).

Trading Places

Paramount, 1983. (C-116m.) Dir: John Landis. Sp: Timothy Harris and Herschel Weingrod. Cast: Dan Aykroyd, Eddie Murphy, Jamie Lee Curtis, Ralph Bellamy, Don Ameche, Denholm Elliott, Jim Belushi, Alfred Drake.

On-Screen: *A rich snob and a street hustler trade places.* Eddie Murphy, in his second movie, is the sole reason to watch this contrived comedy. He's a delight as streetwise Billy Ray Valentine, who finds himself part of a wager between the elderly, wealthy Duke brothers (Bellamy and Ameche). To resolve the eternal question about heredity versus environment, the brothers manipulate stuffy financial wizard Louis Winthrope III (Aykroyd) into changing places with Billy Ray. Soon Louis has lost his job, his house, and his fiancée, while Billy Ray is enjoying life as a rich, hotshot businessman. When the two realize that they're part of a nasty scheme, they exact an elaborate revenge. The idea is old hat, of course, and the execution not very funny or inventive. The scenes of Louis's humiliation are, in fact, painful, and the climax on a train (involving, among other things, a caged gorilla) is merely stupid. But then there's Murphy, reacting with unbridled glee to his unlikely new situation, and he's great fun to watch.

Off-Screen: Some older theater-lovers should notice that the small role of the president of the Stock Exchange is played by Alfred Drake, one of the great figures of the musical stage, well remembered for *Oklahoma!* and *Kiss Me Kate. Trading Places* marked Don Ameche's first appearance in a theatrical movie since 1970.

Treasure Island

MGM, 1934. (105m.) Dir: Victor Fleming. Sp: John Lee Mahin, b/o novel by Robert Louis Stevenson. Cast: Wallace Beery, Jackie Cooper, Lionel Barrymore, Lewis Stone, Otto Kruger, Nigel Bruce, Douglass Dumbrille.

On-Screen: *A boy's pirate adventure.* The first sound version of Robert Louis Stevenson's classic novel, this *Treasure Island* has the benefit of an expansive MGM production and makes top-notch entertainment for preteenagers. Young Jackie Cooper, a bit too pouty and exclaiming "Bless my soul" a few times too often, is spunky, resourceful Jim Hawkins, who joins in a search for buried treasure and finds himself entangled with a scurvy band of pirates. As Long John Silver, Wallace Beery displays more ham than an Easter dinner, but he's enjoyable in his rough-hewn, blustery way. The final parting of Jim and Long John is even rather touching. There's a good supporting cast, headed by Lewis Stone as the ship's captain and Lionel Barrymore (nearly outdistancing Beery in hamminess) as Capt. Billy Bones.

Off-Screen: Despite their on-screen compatibility (this was their third teaming), Jackie Cooper once said of Wallace Beery, "He always made me feel uncomfortable." There were two silent versions of *Treasure Island,* one in 1917 and again in 1920. In both films, Jim Hawkins was played by a girl. The story was remade in 1950 and 1972, and Charlton Heston played Long John Silver in a 1990 television version. No doubt there will be other versions in the future.

The Treasure of the Sierra Madre

Warners, 1948. (124m.) Dir: John Huston. Sp: John Huston, b/o novel by B. Traven. Cast: Humphrey Bogart, Walter Huston, Tim Holt, Bruce Bennett, Alfonso Bedoya, Bobby Blake.

On-Screen: *Greed ravages a trio of prospectors.* Early into this powerful film, scruffy old prospector Howard (Walter Huston) intones, "I know what gold does to men's souls." By the film's end, with the gold scattered to the winds, he declares, "The gold has gone back to where we found it!" In between, John Huston offers a corrosive, unblinkered study of greed. As Howard and two other ill-matched prospectors scrounge for gold in a remote part of Mexico in 1925, their basest instincts emerge. Suspicion gives way to paranoia in the case of mean-spirited Fred C. Dobbs (Bogart), and the basically decent Curtin (Holt) surrenders to selfishness. Only the sly old codger Howard can appreciate the irony of their fate. The film strongly suggests von Stroheim's *Greed* in its dissection of the destructive power of gold, and in the final scenes of men trapped in an unyielding desert. But John Huston makes it his own film as well, harsh, gritty, and difficult to forget.

Off-Screen: John Huston appears briefly in the beginning as the tourist who objects to having the bite put on him more than once by Dobbs. Ronald Reagan was originally scheduled for Tim Holt's role, and Zachary Scott for Bruce Bennett's part. The film was shot on location in Mexico, mostly in the barren mountains in the state of Michoacán. The author of the novel, B. Traven, was a mysterious, reclusive figure with whom John Huston corresponded. (Huston may have met him—a strange man who turned up during the filming and called himself Cloves was later identified as Traven.) Oscars went to John Huston for his direction and screenplay, and his father was awarded the Best Supporting Actor prize for his richly nuanced performance. The movie received a Best Picture nomination.

A Tree Grows in Brooklyn

Fox, 1945. (128m.) Dir: Elia Kazan. Sp: Tess Slesinger and Frank Davis, b/o novel by Betty Smith. Cast: Dorothy McGuire, James Dunn, Peggy Ann Garner, Joan Blondell, Lloyd Nolan, Ted Donaldson, James Gleason, Ruth Nelson, John Alexander.

On-Screen: *Brooklyn "a few decades ago," lovingly evoked in Elia Kazan's first feature film.* Betty Smith's hugely popular novel received exemplary treatment in this warm and deeply touching movie. True, its rambling, episodic narrative betrays Kazan's inexperience after a notable career in the theater. Yet this story of the Nolan family, struggling to survive in a Brooklyn tenement, brims with memorable moments. As young Francie Nolan, Peggy Ann Garner is the focus of events (and gives one of the great performances by a child actress) as she adores her rakish, alcoholic father (Dunn), contends with her weary, striving mother (McGuire), or discovers the mysteries of life. One moment in which she gazes at her singing father with pride and sorrow is unforgettable, but there are many others as well. Dorothy McGuire is wrong for her role—too pretty and ethereal—but she gains strength as the film goes on. Both Garner and Dunn won well-deserved Academy Awards (Garner as outstanding child actress of 1945).

Off-Screen: Casting James Dunn as Johnny Nolan was a case of art imitating life. Dunn, a once-promising actor, had wrecked his career with his drinking, and this, plus his abundant charm, made him, in Elia Kazan's mind, ideal for the role. According to Kazan, Dunn didn't drink during the filming—

"except on his days off." Betty Smith's story was musicalized for the stage in 1951, with Shirley Booth in Joan Blondell's role of Aunt Sissy. It was also remade for television in 1974.

The Trip to Bountiful

Island Pictures, 1985. (C-106m.) Dir: Peter Masterson. Sp: Horton Foote, b/o his play. Cast: Geraldine Page, John Heard, Carlin Glynn, Richard Bradford, Rebecca De Mornay, Kevin Cooney.

On-Screen: *Geraldine Page's Oscar-winning performance.* Old Carrie Watts (Page) has only one dream left: to return once more to her beloved hometown of Bountiful, Texas. Living with her cowed son (Heard) and overbearing daughter-in-law (Glynn), Carrie finds her "golden" years lonely and sad. And so she takes off alone from Houston on her trip back to Bountiful. How she manages to get there—and what happens to her along the way—is the substance of this slight, leisurely film. It's essentially a tour de force for Oscar-winning Geraldine Page, who is up close most of the time, remembering her loveless marriage, or her life in Bountiful with her father. She creates some indelible moments, especially when she wanders through the empty shell of her old home, although the actress occasionally supersedes the character. As her well-meaning son, John Heard has one effective monologue in which he ruminates on the disappointments and frustrations of his life. But mostly *The Trip to Bountiful* is all Geraldine Page. And that may be either enough or too much.

Off-Screen: *The Trip to Bountiful* was first seen on the "Goodyear Television Playhouse" in 1953, with Lillian Gish as Carrie. The cast included Eva Marie Saint, John Beal, and Eileen Heckart. It was later staged in both on- and-off-Broadway productions, with Gish repeating her role on Broadway. Kim Stanley played her daughter-in-law.

Trouble in Paradise

Paramount, 1932. (83m.) Dir: Ernst Lubitsch. Sp: Samson Raphaelson and Grover Jones, b/o play by Laszlo Aladar. Cast: Miriam Hopkins, Herbert Marshall, Kay Francis, Charles Ruggles, Edward Everett Horton, C. Aubrey Smith, Robert Greig.

On-Screen: *Two amorous jewel thieves form a part of a romantic triangle.* Pure sparkling champagne, *Trouble in Paradise* is one of the treasured romantic comedies of the thirties: a witty and elegant confection. The screenplay revolves about Lily (Hopkins) and Gaston (Marshall), two resourceful high-society thieves who become lovers. They decide to steal the jewels of a rich and amorous widow (Francis), but jealousy affects their relationship for a while. Both romantic and sardonic, the dialogue is richly abetted by director Lubitsch's subtle, playfully sophisticated style, which often uses the camera to score a point as well as a laugh. All three principals are in top form: Marshall sheds his usual stodginess to give Gaston an abundance of charm, and both actresses play opposite him with finesse. We should also cite Hans Dreier's amusing art deco sets as well as Victor Milner's glistening camerawork.

Off-Screen: Other titles considered for the film include *Finders Keepers, Thieves and Lovers,* and *A Very Private Scandal.* Sharp-eyed viewers may notice that the name of Hungarian playwright Laszlo Aladar, who wrote the play (*The Honest Finder*) on which the screenplay is based, is transposed in the credits. Samson Raphaelson, who wrote several scripts for Lubitsch, wrote of the director: "I doubt if a greater craftsman ever lived . . . he is one who profoundly respects and understands the art of writing."

The Trouble with Harry

Paramount, 1955. (C-99m.) Dir: Alfred Hitchcock. Sp: John Michael Hayes, b/o novel by Jack Trevor Story. Cast: Edmund Gwenn, John Forsythe, Shirley MacLaine, Mildred Natwick, Mildred Dunnock, Jerry Mathers, Royal Dano.

On-Screen: *Hitchcock turns whimsical.* Autumn in a Vermont town. The body of someone named Harry lies in the woods, and a number of locals claim to be responsible for his death: an old sea captain (Gwenn), an artist (Forsythe), a young widow (MacLaine), and a genteel spinster (Natwick). Each of them insists that he/she committed the act, some accidentally and some deliberately, and soon they are linked together in trying to bury the body. Before Harry has been laid to rest, he has been buried and dug up several times. An offbeat entry from the master director, *The Trouble with Harry* depends for its dark humor on the cool dispatch with which the principal characters handle the disposition of the late, unlamented Harry. Gwenn and Natwick are a joy, especially in a charming courtship sequence, and Shirley MacLaine, in her film debut, has a perky appeal as the widow. The movie's best feature is Robert Burks's breathtaking autumnal photography.

Off-Screen: Alfred Hitchcock on the movie: *"The Trouble with Harry* needed special handling. It wouldn't have failed if the people in the distribution organization had known what to do with the picture, but it got into the assembly line and that was that. . . . *Harry* is very personal to me because it involves my own sense of humor about the macabre." Jerry Mathers, who plays MacLaine's young son, went on to television fame as "the Beaver" on "Leave It to Beaver" (1957–63).

True Confessions

United Artists, 1981. (C-108m.) Dir: Ulu Grosbard. Sp: Joan Didion and John Gregory Dunne, b/o novel by John Gregory Dunne. Cast: Robert De Niro, Robert Duvall, Charles Durning, Burgess Meredith, Ed Flanders, Rose Gregorio, Cyril Cusack, Kenneth McMillan, Dan Hedaya, Jeanette Nolan.

On-Screen: *De Niro and Duvall as brothers from opposite worlds.* This labyrinth of a movie—dark, complex, and chilling—will intrigue some and baffle others. It begins in the sixties, with cop Tommy Spellacy (Duvall) visiting his dying brother, Desmond (De Niro), a Catholic priest. It then flashes back to the forties, when the two men become caught up in a tangled web of murder, church politics, and morality. Tommy is a formerly corrupt cop with a burning hatred for big-shot philanthropist Jack Amsterdam (Durning), once a vice lord. When a girl is brutally murdered, Tommy sets out to frame Amsterdam for the crime, despite knowing of his close ties to the church and Desmond. The resulting scandal shatters many lives, especially Des's, who realizes too late the depth of his guilt in the matter. The movie's convoluted plot is sometimes difficult to follow, and the overall effect of so much concentrated corruption, without the usual hard-edged excitement of *film noir,* is dankly depressing. Add to this a highly unflattering view of the Catholic Church, and you have a recipe for failure at the box office.

Off-Screen: The murder in the film (and the novel) was suggested by the notorious "Black Dahlia" case of 1947. For the crucial prologue and epilogue of the movie, a small social hall in the desert near Lancaster, California, was turned into a desolate church where Father Spellacy is passing his last days. Other scenes were filmed at the fashionable Morton Estate in Pasadena and at deserted army barracks at Fort McArthur in San Pedro. Many religious items for the church scenes were purchased in Rome's Vatican City.

True Grit

Paramount, 1969. (C-128m.) Dir: Henry Hathaway. Sp: Marguerite Roberts, b/o novel by Charles Portis. Cast: John Wayne, Kim Darby, Glen Campbell, Robert Duvall, Jeremy Slate, Dennis Hopper, Alfred Ryder, Strother Martin.

On-Screen: *John Wayne's Oscar-winning stint as Rooster Cogburn.* After many years as one of the most durable icons in films, John Wayne played a fat, one-eyed, and ornery old Westerner named Rooster Cogburn and, to his delight and almost everyone's approval, won his first Academy Award. In this adaptation of the popular Charles Portis novel, he gives a strong, colorful performance as the marshal who joins young Mattie Ross (Darby) and Texas Ranger La Boeuf (Campbell) in tracking down the killers of Mattie's father. They share a number of comic and melodramatic adventures, highlighted by Rooster's encounter with gang leader Ned Pepper (Duvall). "Fill your hand, you son of a bitch!" he shouts at Pepper, and then putting his horse's reins in his mouth and cocking his two weapons, he rides full tilt at the gang. *True Grit* has little substance, but it has beautiful outdoor photography by Lucien Ballard and a lively score by Elmer Bernstein. Most of all, there's Duke at the peak of his later years.

Off-Screen: The film was made at picturesque locations in Colorado and California. Wayne claimed that the role of Rooster Cogburn was typecasting, saying that he was "a mean old bastard, a one-eyed, whiskey-soaked, sloppy old son of a bitch—just like me!" In fact, Wayne had tried to buy the movie rights to the novel but was outbid by Paramount. The 1975 sequel, *Rooster Cogburn,* costarred Katharine Hepburn, but was not nearly as good as this. A 1978 television version of *True Grit* failed to launch a series.

The Turning Point

Fox, 1977. (C-119m.) Dir: Herbert Ross. Sp: Arthur Laurents. Cast: Shirley MacLaine, Anne Bancroft, Tom Skerritt, Mikhail Baryshnikov, Leslie Browne, Martha Scott, Anthony Zerbe, Marshall Thompson.

On-Screen: *Rivalry and romance in the world of ballet.* Many years after dancing with the prestigious American Ballet Theatre, two women are reunited. Emma (Bancroft) is a star ballerina, now fading, and Didi (MacLaine) is a housewife and dance teacher whose daughter, Emilia (Browne), is launching her own career in ballet. Amid the glamour and hectic activity of the ballet scene, Emma and Didi reminisce, reveal their unresolved resentments, and finally engage in a furious catfight that purges them of the complex past. Emilia has a brief passionate relationship with the company's star dancer, Yuri (Baryshnikov). Despite all the glittery trappings, the story is essentially banal, and there are some stretches of tedium. MacLaine and Bancroft, however, are excellent (though Bancroft is not exactly convincing as a ballerina), and the dance sequences are beautiful. Leslie Browne is a lovely dancer but not a very good actress, and Mikhail Baryshnikov is simply unintelligible. A treat for ballet fans, but not necessarily anyone else.

Off-Screen: The role played by Shirley MacLaine was first offered to Grace Kelly, who was strongly interested, but husband Prince Ranier said that he didn't want her to go back to work. Joanne Woodward and Audrey Hepburn were also considered for the leading roles. The movie won eleven Academy Award nominations, including Best Picture, Best Actress (Bancroft), Best Director, Best Supporting Actor (Baryshnikov), and Best Supporting Actress (Browne). It won no Oscars.

12 Angry Men

United Artists, 1957. (95m.) Dir: Sidney Lumet. Sp: Reginald Rose, b/o his television play. Cast: Henry Fonda, Lee J. Cobb, Ed Begley, Jack Klugman, Martin Balsam, E. G. Marshall, Jack Warden, George Voskovec, Joseph Sweeney, Edward Binns, John Fiedler, Robert Webber.

On-Screen: *A jury argues a boy's fate.* Director Sidney Lumet's feature film debut, *12 Angry Men* demonstrates his compatibility with nerve-exposed urban characters. The simple story and straightforward presentation betray the television origins: A diverse group of men assemble in a jury room to decide the fate of a boy accused of murdering his father. Virtually all of the jurors are quick to agree to a guilty vote, but one tenacious, reasonable juror (Fonda) finally persuades them to change their minds. At the same time, some of the men, notably blowhard Cobb and bigot Begley, expose their deeply rooted prejudices. It's all reasonably effective and even compelling, but also rather cut-and-dried. The quick-to-judgment jurors are all obnoxious and/or bigoted; the others inevitably fall into line behind Fonda and his humane, liberal stance. (Of course he wears a white suit.)

Off-Screen: Coproducer Henry Fonda hired Sidney Lumet, a seasoned theater and television director, to helm his first film "because he had the reputation of being wonderful with actors. We got a bonus that nobody counted on. He also had incredible organization and awareness of the problem of shooting and not wasting time." With cinematographer Boris Kaufman, Lumet plotted every camera move and also rehearsed his cast for two weeks before the actual twenty-day shoot.

Twelve O'Clock High

Fox, 1949. (132m.) Dir: Henry King. Sp: Sy Bartlett and Beirne Lay, Jr., b/o their novel. Cast: Gregory Peck, Hugh Marlowe, Gary Merrill, Dean Jagger, Millard Mitchell, Robert Arthur, Paul Stewart, John Kellogg.

On-Screen: *Air force general suffers the strain of command.* Although it takes place in a military setting, *Twelve O'Clock High* is not really a war film, but a piercing drama on the burdens and responsibilities of leadership in wartime. Taking charge of an air force bomber group in 1942, Gen. Frank Savage (Peck) drives them to a peak of aggressiveness and pride. He arouses anger and resentment, but remains firm in his position until the hidden pressures of command cause him to collapse into a catatonic state. As the driven officer, Peck gives one of his best, most sensitive early performances, and Dean Jagger (Oscar winner, Best Supporting Actor) is singularly fine as the adjutant who is disturbed by sending the young men into combat to die. ("I couldn't remember what their faces looked like. All alike. Very young. It confused me.") *Twelve O'Clock High* has one action sequence and considerable documentary footage, but the film's emphasis is clearly on the men, not the combat.

Off-Screen: The character played by Gregory Peck was modeled on Gen. Frank A. Armstrong, who led the first American daylight assaults against German targets. Peck agreed to do the film when he was persuaded that it would not be another star-heavy war picture, similar to MGM's recent *Command Decision* (1948). Only recently, Peck revealed that director Henry King wrote the entire final draft of the screenplay.

Twentieth Century

Columbia, 1934. (91m.) Dir: Howard Hawks. Sp: Ben Hecht and Charles MacArthur, b/o their play. Cast: John Barrymore, Carole Lombard, Walter Connolly, Roscoe Karns, Etienne Girardot, Charles Levison (Lane), Edgar Kennedy.

On-Screen: *All aboard for a madcap ride with Barrymore and Lombard.* Delectable from first frame to last, *Twentieth Century* is one of the funniest comedies of the thirties. Hecht and MacArthur adapted their Broadway play about Oscar Jaffe (Barrymore), a flamboyant theatrical impresario and his tumultuous on-and-off relationship with his temperamental star-protégé Lily Garland (Lombard). Self-created monsters, the two alternate between adoring and wanting to destroy each other as they ride the 20th Century Limited from New York to California. Also aboard the train for the merry ride are Oscar's manager (the unfailing Walter Connolly), his acerbic agent (Roscoe Karns), and other screwballs. Moving with the speed of its title, the movie gives Barrymore and Lombard the opportunity to pull out all stops, and under Howard Hawks's fast-paced direction, they give wonderfully outsize performances.

Off-Screen: Ben Hecht confirmed that the character of Oscar Jaffe, played onstage by Moffat Johnston, had been conceived in John Barrymore's flamboyant image, although there were also resemblances to Broadway impresario David Belasco. Barrymore was always director Hawks's first choice for the film version. Not yet a major star, Lombard was more problematic casting, but she came through with flying colors. (Barrymore was said to have wanted British actress Diana Wynyard.) In 1978, *Twentieth Century* was turned into a Broadway musical called *On the Twentieth Century*.

Twice in a Lifetime

Yorkin, 1985. (C-111m.) Dir: Bud Yorkin. Sp: Colin Welland. Cast: Gene Hackman, Ann-Margret, Ellen Burstyn, Amy Madigan, Ally Sheedy, Brian Dennehy, Stephen Lang, Darrell Lawson.

On-Screen: *A man's infidelity devastates his family.* Steelworker Harry Mackenzie (Hackman), just turned fifty, appears to have a happy life, shared by his loving wife, Kate (Burstyn), and their children. His marriage, however, has turned routine and cold, and when he falls for Audrey (Ann-Margret), a warm, giving barmaid, there's no turning back. Harry's infidelity shatters his family, especially his unforgiving older daughter (Madigan). Graced with fine performances and an honest, intelligent screenplay, *Twice in a Lifetime* is a superior family drama. Some sequences ring false—one painful encounter between the principals at Audrey's bar is handled awkwardly—but on the whole, the film avoids many of the expected clichés. Gene Hackman uses his Everyman persona to good advantage, and Ellen Burstyn conveys the anguish and bewilderment of her character. Amy Madigan deserves a special nod for refusing to soften the abrasive young woman she is obliged to play. Incidentally, the movie makes no bones about its moral position: Poor Harry is abandoned by virtually everyone at the end, while Kate gets a new outlook and even a new hairdo.

Off-Screen: *Twice in a Lifetime* marked Bud Yorkin's return to film directing after years in television as a prominent producer/director ("All in the Family," "Sanford and Son," etc.). Yorkin was intent on giving the film a look that resembled Edward Hopper's paintings. Working with cinematographer Nick McLean and production designer William Creber, he studied a book of Hopper paintings that provided the basis for selecting colors, architectural style, and lighting.

Two for the Road

Fox, 1967. (C-112m.) Dir: Stanley Donen. Sp: Frederic Raphael. Cast: Audrey Hepburn, Albert Finney, William Daniels, Eleanor Bron, Claude Dauphin, Nadia Gray, Georges Descrieres, Gabrielle Middleton.

On-Screen: *The rocky road of a twelve-year marriage.* An offbeat and diverting comedy-drama, *Two for the Road* traces the joys and tribulations of the marriage of Joanna (Hepburn) and Mark (Finney). The film's gimmick requires your undivided attention: Instead of following the couple year by year, Frederic Raphael's screenplay splinters the time sequence, leaping back and forth to various points in their marriage, from the romantic, hopeful beginning to what appears to be the bitter ending. Their contentious, loving relationship is revealed through a series of motor trips they take over the years. Hepburn is enchanting (and models a procession of stylish clothes) as Joanna, but Finney is unable to make his scratchy, sour-natured character appealing. Eleanor Bron and William Daniels are funny as an obnoxious American couple with an even more obnoxious daughter (Middleton), with whom Joanna and Mark travel for a while. Stanley Donen does an expert job of juggling the changing time frames. Henry Mancini's musical theme is lush and lovely.

Off-Screen: Director Donen insisted that Hepburn not be dressed by her usual designer, Givenchy. He felt that Givenchy would be beyond the budget of an architect's wife. Other designers, including Paco Rabanne and Mary Quant, were brought in to design Hepburn's wardrobe. For the first bedroom scene, the production unit took over an entire hotel on the Riviera coast near St. Tropez, and the set was closed to everyone but cameramen and production assistants.

2001: A Space Odyssey

MGM, 1968. (C-139m.) Dir: Stanley Kubrick. Sp: Stanley Kubrick and Arthur C. Clarke, b/o story by Arthur C. Clarke. Cast: Keir Dullea, Gary Lockwood, William Sylvester, Daniel Richter, Leonard Rossiter, Douglas Rain.

On-Screen: *Stanley Kubrick's awesome cosmic journey*. The real hero of this movie is mankind itself—always exploring, forever evolving. A prologue sets the theme when primitive man, after encountering a mystical, monolithic slab, grasps the idea that bones can be useful tools and triumphantly hurls one skyward. Spanning eons of human progress in an instant, the artifact becomes another implement of man, the spaceship. The main action occurs aboard the Jupiter-bound *Discovery*, where astronaut Dullea must do battle with HAL 9000, the icy-voiced controlling computer with its own agenda. The stunning conclusion, in which the slab (God? our creative impulse?) reappears, will have you damp-eyed but smiling at the splendor of it all. There's not much dialogue, but the cast is fine; the real stars are the technical wizardry, and Kubrick and Clarke's haunting poetic vision. And that sound track!

Off-Screen: Some critics, expecting a Buck Rogers trip, were bewildered by Kubrick and Clarke's dramatized philosophical treatise; however, it was a great success, winning an Oscar for Best Special Visual Effects. The film (shot in England) used mostly actors in the prologue to portray the animals evolving into human beings. Kubrick explains that the acronym HAL is a combination of *heuristic* and *algorithmic,* the main learning principles. The user-unfriendly computer's voice belongs to Canadian actor Douglas Rain. *2010* (1984) is a relatively earthbound sequel. (CFB)

Unfaithfully Yours

Fox, 1948. (105m.) Dir: Preston Sturges. Sp: Preston Sturges. Cast: Rex Harrison, Linda Darnell, Rudy Vallee, Barbara Lawrence, Kurt Kreuger, Lionel Stander, Robert Greig, Edgar Kennedy.

On-Screen: *Preston Sturges comedy about a jealous symphony conductor and his fantasies.* One of Preston Sturges's last films, written and directed toward the end of his most creative period in the forties, *Unfaithfully Yours* boasts an original idea which is executed unevenly. Famed symphony conductor Harrison is given reason to believe that his beautiful wife (Darnell) is cheating on him with his secretary (Kreuger). In a rage, he fantasizes about three different ways of dealing with the matter, all while he is conducting his orchestra. The fantasies—which involve noble sacrifice, Russian Roulette, and murder—are all enacted in Harrison's mind. They are cleverly done, but Sturges gets the biggest laughs with his offbeat subsidiary characters, including Harrison's obnoxious brother-in-law (Vallee) and a music-loving detective (Kennedy). Sturges also indulges his fondness for slapstick in the sequence in which Harrison tries to actually carry out his plan to murder his wife. Hilariously, he makes a consummate mess of everything, virtually demolishing a room to set up his equipment for entrapping the "guilty" lovers.

Off-Screen: Rex Harrison recalled Preston Sturges as "a true original," an eccentric man who directed wearing a red fez and laughing uncontrollably at his own jokes. Sturges also kept his Doberman pinscher on the set at all times, and the dog would bark at all the wrong moments. According to Harrison, Sturges was "an understanding, very sophisticated, very Europeanized man. . . ." *Unfaithfully Yours* was remade in 1984 with Dudley Moore, who was amiable but no match for Harrison, as the fiercely jealous, fantasizing conductor.

The Unforgiven

United Artists, 1960. (C-125m.) Dir: John Huston. Sp: Ben Maddow, b/o novel by Alan LeMay. Cast: Burt Lancaster, Audrey Hepburn, Audie Murphy, John Saxon, Charles Bickford, Lillian Gish, Albert Salmi, Joseph Wiseman, June Walker.

On-Screen: *A Western with social import.* Set in Texas in the 1850s, John Huston's Western drama adds a measure of concern with racial issues to the usual action mix. The story involves the Zachary family of settlers, headed by steel-willed mother Lillian Gish and including sons Burt Lancaster and Audie Murphy, as well as adopted daughter Audrey Hepburn. The stage is set for conflict when Hepburn, who is secretly loved by Lancaster, is claimed by the Kiowa Indians as one of their own, the survivor of a tribal massacre who was given to the Zachary family to be raised. *The Unforgiven* touches on a subject seldom addressed in Westerns—the virulent bigotry on the plains—and it does so with considerable force and conviction. Audrey Hepburn seems much too sophisticated to play the Indian maiden, but Audie Murphy, usually an indifferent actor, gives his best performance as the Indian-hating brother. The best scene centers on Lillian Gish: Seated outside her besieged ranch, waiting for the Kiowas to attack, she plays the piano as a kind of "magic" that will keep them at bay.

Off-Screen: The film was shot on location in Durango, Mexico. Severe windstorms troubled the cast, but director Huston used them to his advantage, shooting sequences that occurred in actual winds. Lillian Gish disliked Audie Murphy, asserting that he was too free with his gun and would shoot any animal that moved. During the filming, Audrey Hepburn fell off her horse and broke several vertebrae. The production had to be shut down for several weeks.

Unforgiven

Warners, 1992. (C-130m.) Dir: Clint Eastwood. Sp: David Webb Peoples. Cast: Clint Eastwood, Gene Hackman, Morgan Freeman, Richard Harris, Jaimz Woolvett, Saul Rubinek, Frances Fisher, Anna Thomson.

On-Screen: *Clint Eastwood's powerful Western drama.* Wyoming in the 1880s. Once a notorious, cold-blooded killer, William Munny (Eastwood) is now a dirt-poor hog farmer, reformed by the love of his now-dead wife. To help his two young children, Munny becomes a bounty hunter, bent on finding and killing two cowboys who mutilated a whore in Big Whiskey. He meets violent opposition from the town's sadistic sheriff (Hackman), and in the end, though overwhelmed by moral revulsion, he reverts to his old murderous ways. Eastwood's best movie to date, *Unforgiven* combines the expansive, elegiac style of the John Ford films with the later, revisionist style of such films as *The Gunfighter* (reluctant gunman must live down his reputation). To this mix, Eastwood adds a remarkable reversal of his past persona: the icy Man with No Name of his "spaghetti" Westerns is now a man sickened by killing, and disgusted at having to revert—however temporarily—to his former self. Clint Eastwood's direction of the sombre screenplay is impeccable, and he gives his best performance as the brooding Munny. A strong cast helps to make *Unforgiven* a stunning achievement. Photographed magnificently by Jack N. Green.

Off-Screen: Alberta, Canada, substituted for Wyoming in the film. The movie was shot in the towns of Brooks, Drumbeller, Stettler, and Longview. Clint Eastwood commented on the characters in a *New York Times* interview: "Everyone's a little complicated, everyone's gray, there are no black and whites, there aren't any bad guys or good guys." *Unforgiven* won four Oscars, including Best Picture, Best Director, Best Supporting Actor (Hackman), and Best Editing.

The Uninvited

Paramount, 1944. (98m.) Dir: Lewis Allen. Sp: Dodie Smith and Jack Partos, b/o novel by Dorothy Macardle. Cast: Ray Milland, Ruth Hussey, Gail Russell, Donald Crisp, Cornelia Otis Skinner, Dorothy Stickney.

On-Screen: *Spooky doings in a British house.* A trim and sometimes frightening little ghost story, *The Uninvited* unleashes no monsters to achieve its scary effects, but depends rather on such business as flickering candles, creaking doors, the smell of mimosa, and supernatural apparitions. The story centers on a brother and sister (Milland and Hussey), who buy a seaside English house that turns out to be haunted by vengeful spirits. The chief victim appears to be a young girl (Russell) whose mother died at the house under mysterious circumstances. Not all of the plot elements are resolved coherently, but there are moments many filmgoers have remembered over the years, especially one in which French windows open suddenly and without warning. The cast is competent, although Russell (in her film debut) seems awkward and ill-at-ease. Cornelia Otis Skinner stands out as a sort of relation to sinister Mrs. Danvers of *Rebecca*.

Off-Screen: Ms. Skinner, daughter of the famous stage actor, Otis Skinner, and also a noted stage actress and author (*Our Hearts Were Young and Gay*), was playing her first dramatic movie role. (A year earlier, she had appeared as herself in *Stage Door Can-*

teen.) This was also Lewis Allen's first credit as a director. His second was the movie version of *Our Hearts Were Young and Gay*.

Union Pacific

Paramount, 1939. (135m.) Dir: Cecil B. DeMille. Sp: Walter DeLeon, C. Gardner Sullivan, and Jesse Lasky, Jr.; adaptation: Jack Cunningham, b/o novel by Ernest Haycox. Cast: Barbara Stanwyck, Joel McCrea, Robert Preston, Brian Donlevy, Akim Tamiroff, Anthony Quinn, Lynne Overman, Evelyn Keyes, Robert Barrat, Fuzzy Knight, Regis Toomey.

On-Screen: *Cecil B. DeMille's sprawling epic on the building of the Union Pacific Railroad.* Perhaps only master showman DeMille could create a single film that contains a spectacular train crash, several Indian attacks, a breathtaking last-minute rescue, and a triangular romance. All this is crowded into a large-scale Western that purports to be the story of the building of the Union Pacific Railroad. Joel McCrea stars as the overseer of the construction, who must fight the opposition backing the Union Pacific's rival, the Central Pacific. He also finds time to woo Union Pacific postmistress Barbara Stanwyck, a hot-tempered vixen with a wavering Irish brogue. Don't look for subtlety, or credible dialogue, but there are plenty of exciting brawls, scrapes, and chases. One serious shortcoming: In the fashion of the time, the movie portrays Indians as shrieking, infantile savages. *Union Pacific* runs too long, but it works up quite a head of steam.

Off-Screen: The role played by Barbara Stanwyck was originally offered to Vivien Leigh, who declined. DeMille enjoyed the full cooperation of William M. Jeffers, president of the Union Pacific Railroad, who opened his company's archives for research and gave the director some period trains and his fastest track-laying crew to use in crucial scenes. In the scene in which a golden spike is driven into the ground to show the completion of the Union Pacific in May, 1869, the actual spike was used.

An Unmarried Woman

Fox, 1978. (C-124m.) Dir: Paul Mazursky. Sp: Paul Mazursky. Cast: Jill Clayburgh, Alan Bates, Michael Murphy, Cliff Gorman, Pat Quinn, Kelly Bishop, Lisa Lucas, Michael Tucker, Jill Eikenberry, Penelope Russianoff.

On-Screen: *A married woman suddenly faces life alone.* A witty, probing screenplay—more honest than most—and an assured performance by Jill Clayburgh are the principal virtues of Paul Mazursky's film. Clayburgh is Erica, a forty-plus woman who is abruptly informed by her husband (Murphy) that he is leaving her for another woman. Now Erica must face life as a single woman, and it isn't easy. She sees a psychiatrist (Russianoff), copes with a sulky teenaged daughter (Lucas), and has a brief fling with aggressive "swinger" Gorman. She also meets and develops a deepening relationship with British artist Saul (Bates), who is sensitive and understanding. Erica's final decision to maintain her newfound independence generated some heated discussion in moviegoing circles. Mazursky's script includes a number of sharply funny, observant scenes, such as one in which Erica and her girlfriends meet at lunch to chat about their sex lives. Jill Clayburgh gives one of her best performances as Erica, moving from rage and bewilderment to confidence as she finds her way.

Off-Screen: Alan Bates plays an abstract impressionist who paints by standing above a tilted canvas and splashing different colors of paint on it, creating a swirling effect. He learned this technique from Paul Jenkins, a SoHo artist whose loft is used in the movie. Penelope Russianoff was a real-life therapist whose scenes were filmed in her consulting room. The movie was Oscar-nominated in the categories of Best Picture, Best Actress, and Best Original Screenplay.

The Untouchables

Paramount, 1987. (C-120m.) Dir: Brian De Palma. Sp: David Mamet. Cast: Kevin Costner, Sean Connery, Robert De Niro, Andy Garcia, Charles Martin Smith, Jack Kehoe, Richard Bradford, Billy Drago, Patricia Clarkson, Brad Sullivan.

On-Screen: *Eliot Ness and his team take on Al Capone.* A stunning piece of filmmaking, brilliantly guided by Brian De Palma, *The Untouchables* is only vaguely derived from the popular television series that ran from 1959 to 1963. The movie takes Eliot Ness (Costner), the pure-of-heart, straight-arrow hero of the bloodless series, then plunges him into the graphically violent world of Chicago in 1930. The result is exciting, as Ness and his team of Untouchables (Connery, Garcia, Smith) go after Al Capone (De Niro) and his mob. The movie is studded with memorable sequences, none more than the breathtaking shootout in Chicago's Union Station, modeled on the famed Odessa Steps sequence in Eisenstein's *Po-*

temkin (1925). Sean Connery won a Supporting Oscar for his fine performance as seasoned cop Jim Malone, and Robert De Niro makes a riveting Capone, flamboyant and evil. Billy Drago is repellent as Capone's hood Frank Nitti, and his plunge from a rooftop marks the moment when the fabled-hero side of Eliot Ness surrenders to the dark and violent side he has suppressed all along. All praise to De Palma, Mamet, and cinematographer Stephen H. Burum.

Off-Screen: The movie was filmed on location in Chicago and in Great Falls, Montana, which stood in for Canada in one crucial sequence. Harrison Ford and Mel Gibson were considered for the role of Ness, but Costner was recommended by Steven Spielberg and Lawrence Kasdan. Bob Hoskins had been signed to play Malone, and when Connery won the part in his place, Hoskins was paid his entire salary. To play Capone, De Niro went to Italy for ten weeks, where he gained twenty-five to thirty pounds by stuffing himself on giant portions of pasta, potatoes, and desserts.

Up in Arms

Goldwyn-RKO, 1944. (C-106m.) Dir: Elliott Nugent. Sp: Don Hartman, Allen Boretz, and Robert Pirosh, b/o play by Owen Davis. MS: Harold Arlen and Ted Koehler. Also Sylvia Fine and Max Liebman. Cast: Danny Kaye, Dana Andrews, Dinah Shore, Constance Dowling, Louis Calhern, George Mathews.

On-Screen: *Danny Kaye's feature film debut.* By the time he came to *Up in Arms,* ebullient, antic Danny Kaye, a master of comedy patter songs, had already established a reputa-

tion in musical theater, nightclubs, and even some comedy shorts. Starring in a third version of Owen Davis's play *The Nervous Wreck* (the second was Eddie Cantor's *Whoopee!*), he plays a jittery hypochondriac drafted reluctantly into the Army. His misadventures aboard a troop ship and on a Japanese-occupied island make up most of the movie's humor. Kaye's bumbling ineptness wears thin early on, but happily, he gets to perform two funny routines; one a number in a theater lobby, in which he describes the movie showing inside and plays all the roles, the other his trademarked "Melody in 4-F." Dinah Shore sings charmingly, and the Goldwyn Girls, including future star Virginia Mayo, are on hand for decorative purposes. There's also a hideous musical dream sequence for which "Fast Forward" was invented.

Off-Screen: Samuel Goldwyn heard of a brilliant young New York comedian named Danny Kaye, and after seeing him perform onstage in *Lady in the Dark,* signed him to a contract. He wanted Kaye to have his rather prominent nose fixed, but Kaye refused. When a screen test was finally made, the comedian seemed unphotogenic and even menacing, and Goldwyn was being urged to buy off Kaye's contract. Then Goldwyn had the idea of dyeing Kaye's hair blond—and the result turned Kaye into a popular star.

Up the Down Staircase

Warners, 1967. (C-124m.) Dir: Robert Mulligan. Sp: Tad Mosel, b/o novel by Bel Kaufman. Cast: Sandy Dennis, Patrick Bedford, Eileen Heckart, Ruth White, Jean Stapleton, Sorrell Booke, Roy Poole, Jeff

Howard, Ellen O'Mara, Florence Stanley, Jose Rodriguez.

On-Screen: *The perils of life in a New York City high school.* Sadly, the problems of America's inner-city schools—overcrowding, lack of discipline, undermanagement, and threats of violence—have not improved all that much in the more than quarter-century since Bel Kaufman's bestselling book and the film derived from it. *Up the Down Staircase* chronicles the amusing, poignant, and disturbing situations faced by one idealistic teacher (Dennis) at a New York City problem-area school. In her quest to reach the hearts and minds of her students, Sylvia Barrett faces a daily uphill battle that ends with very few glimmers of hope. Sandy Dennis gives one of her more credible performances as this tenacious teacher, and she gets expert support from Eileen Heckart and Ruth White as fellow teachers, and especially from young Ellen O'Mara, who gives a standout performance as a painfully introverted student who reacts drastically when the teacher she adores (Bedford) rebuffs her.

Off-Screen: For on-location sites, the filmmakers used two New York City schools, Margaret Knox Junior High School at 100th Street and First Avenue, and Haaren High School at 58th Street and Tenth Avenue. The author of the novel, Bel Kaufman, was the granddaughter of Jewish humorist Sholom Aleichem.

Urban Cowboy

Paramount, 1980. (C-135m.) Dir: James Bridges. Sp: James Bridges and Aaron Latham, b/o story by Aaron Latham. Cast: John Travolta, Debra Winger, Scott Glenn, Madolyn Smith, Barry Corwin, Brooke Alderson, Mickey Gilley, Cooper Huckabee.

On-Screen: *"Macho" Texas hardhat marries a cowgirl.* The rowdy, flavorsome atmosphere of Gilley's famous Texas honky-tonk, and the virtually nonstop, foot-stompin' music are the chief attractions of this slight but entertaining movie. John Travolta is Bud, a farm boy who moves to a town on the outskirts of Houston where the gathering point is Gilley's and its mechanical bucking bull. He meets and, on impulse, marries cowgirl Sissy (Winger), but his "macho" pride that will not permit him to be tested or challenged by a mere woman tears them apart. Sissy takes up with Wes (Glenn), an abusive, criminal-minded cowboy, and Bud with possessive Pam (Smith). The climax is a bull "rodeo" at Gilley's, in which Bud and Wes vie for top honors. Eventually, "hardheaded and proudful" Bud learns to soften his stance and returns to Sissy. Travolta struts, dances, and courts an appealing Winger in the style that made him a star in the late seventies. *Urban Cowboy* is an amusing spin on the "macho" image and a colorful slice of Americana.

Off-Screen: The movie derived from Aaron Latham's story "The Ballad of the Urban Cowboy: America's Search for True Grit," which appeared in *Esquire* magazine. It focused national attention on Gilley's. The scenes in Gilley's were shot during the day when the bar was not in operation. Hundreds of extras were recruited from the masses of regular patrons. The soundtrack features a bevy of great country music performers, such as Boz Scaggs, Bonnie Raitt, Dan Fogelberg, and Kenny Rogers; the movie's hit song was "Lookin' for Love," sung by Jonny Lee.

Used Cars

Universal, 1980. (C-111m.) Dir: Robert Zemeckis. Sp: Robert Zemeckis and Bob Gale. Cast: Kurt Russell, Jack Warden, Gerrit Graham, Deborah Harmon, Frank McRae, Joseph P. Flaherty, David L. Lander, Michael McKean.

On-Screen: *Wild and woolly doings in the used car business.* Used Cars is preposterous, outrageous, and tasteless. It also happens to be uncommonly funny. Brimming over with characters who haven't even the slightest sense of honesty or fair play, the movie has twin brothers Luke and Roy Fuchs (both played by Warden) battling each other over their facing used car lots (Luke's nice, Roy's nasty). When Luke dies of a heart attack induced by his brother, his star salesman Rudy (Russell) takes over to wreak havoc and revenge on Roy. Rudy is cheerfully, proudly crooked, and his wild ploys and schemes are the stuff from which this knockabout movie is made. Don't look for subtlety, but watch out for dim-bulb car buyers, gleefully unscrupulous salesmen, and even a perky heroine (Harmon, as Luke's daughter). As Roy Fuchs, Jack Warden is marvelous—so rotten that he seems like the villain in an animated cartoon. The climax involves 250 used cars, and you won't believe a minute of it. But who cares?

Off-Screen: Robert Zemeckis's first movie as a writer-director, *I Wanna Hold Your Hand* (1978), was not a success but it showed his penchant for frantic humor. After *Used Cars,* Zemeckis had a string of popular hits with *Romancing the Stone* (1984), the *Back to the Future* movies (1985, 1989, 1990), and *Who Framed Roger Rabbit* (1988). In 1992 he misfired with the bizarre black comedy, *Death Becomes Her. Used Cars* was filmed largely in Mesa, Arizona, a suburb of Phoenix. Look for Al Lewis, remembered for his Grandpa Munster on TV's "The Munsters," in a funny turn as a judge.

The Verdict

Fox, 1982. (C-129m.) Dir: Sidney Lumet. Sp: David Mamet, b/o novel by Barry Reed. Cast: Paul Newman, James Mason, Charlotte Rampling, Jack Warden, Milo O'Shea, Edward Binns, Julie Bovasso, Lindsay Crouse, Roxanne Hart.

On-Screen: *Down-and-out lawyer Paul Newman battles a negligence case.* Somewhere in the seventies, when he could no longer play rebellious studs, Paul Newman began to apply his considerable acting ability to character roles. *The Verdict* gave him one of his best, and he delivers an assured performance as Frank Galvin, a seedy, wrecked Boston lawyer who is given one final chance to redeem himself. He takes on the case of a young woman now in an irreversible coma through hospital negligence. Since the hospital is owned by the church, Galvin faces the overwhelming opposition of the church, the widely admired doctors who caused the coma, and a high-powered law team headed by the formidable Mason. David Mamet's multilayered screenplay is compelling, and if the case's resolution is not totally believable, it makes for a satisfying ending. Newman creates a fully rounded character in Galvin, and his summation to the jury is one of the actor's finest moments on film.

Off-Screen: Robert Redford was the initial choice to play Galvin but he bowed out and was replaced by Newman. Sidney Lumet took over as director after Arthur Hiller and James Bridges left the film. Many legal figures questioned the tactics of an attorney who would refuse a settlement without first consulting his client, or who would break into a mailbox to intercept a letter. But then, as Newman remarked, "(Galvin) is frightened. He's living on the edge and he's panicked." The movie, Newman, Mason, Lumet, and Mamet all won Oscar nominations.

Vertigo

Paramount, 1958. (C-128m.) Dir: Alfred Hitchcock: Sp: Alec Coppel and Samuel Taylor, b/o novel by Pierre Boileau and Thomas Narcejac. Cast: James Stewart, Kim Novak, Barbara Bel Geddes, Tom Helmore, Henry Jones.

On-Screen: *An ex-detective is obsessed with a woman he saw fall to her death.* However one views *Vertigo*—as an exploration of the dark side of the human psyche or as a tall tale made taller in the telling—it remains a compelling film if only because of its striking accumulation of surprises. Acrophobia, suicide, murder, a guilt complex leading to nervous exhaustion, and even hints of necrophilia seem like astonishingly everyday affairs when set against picturesque views of San Francisco and the lush California coast. Even the choice of principals runs counter to the murky deviousness of the plot. Stewart, everybody's all-American guy, is cast as an anxiety-ridden anti-hero. Novak, with her clear gaze and classic beauty, is no one's idea of a woman involved in sordid intrigue. In *Vertigo,* Hitchcock plays with our expectations. Because he is portrayed by Stewart, we expect Scotty to solve the puzzle when he realizes there is one. Instead, his preoccupation with the Novak character becomes even more intense, and, given Stewart's psychological infirmities, she ends up a victim. *Vertigo,* a movie full of disorienting surprises, is more aptly titled than we at first suspected.

Off-Screen: Hitchcock had at first intended Vera Miles to play the enigmatic female lead, but her pregnancy forced her to relinquish the part. Scenes in the mission tower, where Stewart pursues Novak, are presented from his viewpoint. In order to visualize the extreme dizziness and panic his character feels while ascending the tower, Hitchcock had the camera lens zoom forward at the same time that the camera pulled back. As for Hitchcock's usual "fingerprint" appearance, the director can be seen crossing a street. (CFB)

Victor / Victoria

MGM, 1982. (C-133m.) Dir: Blake Edwards. Sp: Blake Edwards. MS: Henry Mancini and Leslie Bricusse. Cast: Julie Andrews, James Garner, Robert Preston, Alex Karras, Lesley Ann Warren, John Rhys-Davies, Graham Stark, Peter Arne.

On-Screen: *Blake Edwards's comedy of sexual identity. And bravo Robert Preston!* Paris, 1934. Victoria Grant (Andrews), a down-and-out singer, comes under the tutelage of Toddy (Preston), a gay night club entertainer, who turns her into a sensation as a female impersonator (a woman pretending to be a man pretending to be a woman!) Along comes King Marchand, a mob-connected Chicago night club owner, who finds himself inexplicably attracted to Victoria. The complications, all triggered by Andrews's ambiguous sexual identity, come thick, fast, and sometimes hilariously. *Victor/Victoria* runs too long, and the premise begins to wear thin, but there are compensations. The few songs are appealing (one, "Crazy World," has a haunting melody), and the amusing characters include King's dumb, brassy girlfriend (a surprising Lesley Ann Warren) and a very funny befuddled waiter (Graham Stark). But the movie's greatest blessing is Robert Preston, who is a total joy as the wise, witty Toddy.

Off-Screen: Blake Edwards's screenplay is based on a 1933 German film entitled *Viktor und Viktoria,* which was also the basis for the 1936 British film musical, *First a Girl,* with Jessie Matthews. *Victor/Victoria* garnered six Oscar nominations, including nods to Andrews (Best Actress) and Preston (Best Supporting Actor). Henry Mancini and Leslie Bricusse won the award for their song score.

Viva Zapata!

Fox, 1952. (113m.) Dir: Elia Kazan. Sp: John Steinbeck, b/o novel by Edgcumb Pinchon. Cast: Marlon Brando, Anthony Quinn, Jean Peters, Joseph Wiseman, Lou Gilbert, Mildred Dunnock, Margo.

On-Screen: *Kazan directs Brando as the Mexican revolutionary*. Emiliano Zapata was a legendary rebel who led an army of peasants against the oppressive Mexican government from 1910 until his assassination in 1919. In Elia Kazan's visually striking, often stirring film, Zapata is virtually sanctified in the person of a dark-skinned, mustachioed Marlon Brando. Novelist John Steinbeck's screenplay covers Zapata's stormy life: his rise to leadership; his triumphs in battle and setbacks in the treacherous political arena; his courtship of and marriage to Josefa (Peters), and his ultimate martyrdom. The film is occasionally verbose, self-consciously "poetic," and also ambiguous, treating revolution as both a futile endeavor—winning power only corrupts the winner—and a rousing call to action by the people. Brando is more persuasive as the fiery rebel than as the illiterate but striving peasant, and Quinn gives a rousing, Oscar-winning performance as his hot-headed brother, Eufemio. A flawed but still worthy movie.

Off-Screen: Julie Harris was Kazan's first choice for the role of Josefa, but after she and Brando made a test in New York, Darryl Zanuck complained that he could not understand either of them. Although Zanuck would have preferred Tyrone Power, Kazan insisted on keeping Brando, but Harris was replaced by Fox contract player Jean Peters. Zanuck's comment on the film: "It's just a big western. *The Scarlet Pimpernel* with a dignified motif." Brando was nominated for an Oscar but lost to Gary Cooper for *High Noon*.

A Walk in the Sun

Fox, 1945. (117m.) Dir: Lewis Milestone. Sp: Robert Rossen, b/o novel by Harry Brown. Cast: Dana Andrews, Richard Conte, George Tyne, John Ireland, Norman Lloyd, Lloyd Bridges, Sterling Holloway, Huntz Hall, Herbert Rudley, James Cardwell.

On-Screen: *A platoon faces battle in World War II.* Fifteen years after directing the landmark film *All Quiet on the Western Front,* Lewis Milestone returned to wartime combat for this generally impressive film. (The year before, he had also directed another war film, *The Purple Heart.*) The story is simple: A platoon of American infantrymen confront peril, sudden death, and their own inner resources as they fight to establish a beachhead near Salerno during World War II. A series of vignettes convey the hopes, fears, and confusions of the men as they move toward a farmhouse occupied by the Germans—their fateful "walk in the sun." Occasionally, the soundtrack of bomb bursts and gunfire is interrupted for ballads extolling the heroism of the men—a device that tends to clash with the realism of the story. Dana Andrews heads a sturdy cast as a sergeant who finds himself leading the group as they move deeper into enemy territory. *A Walk in the Sun* is a mite pretentious but also one of the better films about World War II.

Off-Screen: The movie was first scheduled to be a United Artists release but switched to Fox after enduring many financial complications. Director Milestone followed Harry Brown's novel carefully: "The book was my script," he remarked. He also acknowledged that while *All Quiet on the Western Front* ended on a pessimistic note, *A Walk in the Sun* closes on a message of hope. Huntz Hall, one of the original Dead End Kids, has a featured role in the movie.

Wall Street

Fox, 1987. (C-124m.) Dir: Oliver Stone. Sp: Stanley Weiser and Oliver Stone. Cast: Michael Douglas, Charlie Sheen, Daryl Hannah, Martin Sheen, Sean Young, Hal Holbrook, John C. McGinley, Saul Rubinek, Sylvia Miles, James Spader, Millie Perkins, Terence Stamp, Josh Mostel.

On-Screen: *Oliver Stone skewers the Age of Greed.* "Greed is good. Greed is right. Greed works. . . ." These are the insidious words of Gordon Gekko (Douglas), master manipulator in the world of business, whose siren song lures young Bud Fox (Charlie Sheen) to disaster. Bud wants to be a "player" on Wall Street, and soon his job at a stock brokerage is secondary to his devious—and illegal—activities on behalf of Gekko. Inevitably, his dealings lead to exposure and shame, followed by redemption. Daryl Hannah is the girl (a former mistress of Gekko's) who urges Bud to play the game, and Martin Sheen is his honorable working-class father. The movie's crisp, intelligent screenplay takes the viewer deep into New York's financial heart, taking aim at the self-serving, greedy attitude that permeated life at the upper levels in the eighties. Michael Douglas scores with an Oscar winning, front-and-center performance as the reprehensible Gekko, and Charlie Sheen is excellent as the ambitious Fox, scheming to find his way through the financial jungle.

Off-Screen: To coauthor the screenplay, Oliver Stone consulted with a variety of Wall Street people, including corporate raiders, an admitted insider trader, prosecutors, and even a proxy solicitor. Kenneth Lipper, a well-known New York investment banker, and former Deputy Mayor of New York for finance and technical development, was hired as technical adviser. Lipper advised Stone on everything from the kind of computers to feature on the trading floor to the correct proportion of women at a business meeting. Stone, who himself was the son of a noted stockbroker, can be spotted briefly in the movie.

The War of the Worlds

Paramount, 1953. (C–85m.) Dir: Byron Haskin. Sp: Barré Lyndon, b/o novel by H. G. Wells. Cast: Gene Barry, Ann Robinson, Les Tremayne, Lewis Martin, Robert Cornthwaite, Henry Brandon, Jack Kruschen.

On-Screen: *Aliens from Mars invade the earth.* Produced by special effects wizard George Pal, *The War of the Worlds* is one of the most fondly remembered science-fiction movies of the fifties. A huge meteor lands in a field near a California town, and from it emerges a swan-shaped machine with a snakelike neck that emits disintegrating heat rays. Soon it is clear that the earth has been invaded by scores of these hissing, ticking machines, operated by grotesque Martian creatures bent on destroying everything in their path. As thousands of people flee in terror, loot the stores, or pray in churches, the invaders level Los Angeles. Scientist Gene Barry and teacher Ann Robinson are the principal figures at the center of the Martian holocaust. It's a surprisingly effective movie, with scenes that are frightening on both a small scale (Barry and Robinson being stalked by a Martian machine in a farmhouse) or a large one. (The scenes of mass destruction are handled with exceptional skill.) The dialogue and performances are perfunctory, but it hardly matters once those machines are on the loose.

Off-Screen: George Pal discovered that Paramount owned the rights to H. G. Wells's novel since 1925, but had never filmed it after both Cecil B. DeMille and Russian director Sergei Eisenstein lost interest. The eerie Martian scream was done by scraping dry ice across a microphone, then adding a woman's high-pitched scream, recorded backward. Gordon Jennings won a posthumous Oscar for his special effects (he died soon after filming was completed). The narrator's dulcet voice belongs to Sir Cedric Hardwicke. A television series based on the movie turned up in 1988.

Watch on the Rhine

Warners, 1943. (114m.) Dir: Herman Shumlin. Sp: Dashiell Hammett, b/o play by Lillian Hellman. Cast: Bette Davis, Paul Lukas, Geraldine Fitzgerald, Lucile Watson, Beulah Bondi, George Coulouris, Donald Woods, Henry Daniell.

On-Screen: *Underground anti-Nazi leader is threatened with exposure.* Widely admired in its time, Hellman's 1941 play was a stirring wake-up call to America about the dangers of isolationism. Today, the movie version seems less a timely warning against Fascism than a theatrical period piece. Set in pre-Pearl Harbor Washington, the story centers on the desperate cat-and-mouse game between covert freedom fighter Kurt Muller (Lukas), a European refugee, and a blackmailing Rumanian count (Coulouris). The movie is still worth viewing for Lukas's impassioned, Oscar-winning portrayal. As Muller's loyal wife, Davis gives an affecting, if at times stagey, performance. Among the gripping moments: the villainous Rumanian discovering Muller's briefcase, stuffed with money intended for the underground cause; Nazis and Nazi sympathizers at the German Embassy, discussing a captured underground hero (Muller's closest friend); the confrontation in the garden.

Off-Screen: The studio wisely chose Lukas to repeat his Broadway role, and then co-starred movie-marquee heavyweight Davis in what is essentially a secondary role. Also from the original cast were Coulouris; Watson, as Davis's patrician and courageous mother; and Eric Roberts (not the contemporary actor), as Bodo Muller. Shumlin's lack of film experience led to disputes with Davis; as a result, seasoned cameraman Hal Mohr at times took over the directoral reins. Hellman added some scenes to Hammett's Oscar-nominated adaptation. (CFB)

Waterloo Bridge

MGM, 1940. (103m.) Dir: Mervyn LeRoy. Sp: S. N. Behrman, Hans Rameau, and George Froeschel, b/o play by Robert E. Sherwood. Cast: Vivien Leigh, Robert Taylor, Lucile Watson, Maria Ouspenskaya, Virginia Field, C. Aubrey Smith.

On-Screen: *Touching World War I romantic drama, elegantly produced.* This tear-streaked tale stars Vivien Leigh as Myra, a ballet dancer who sabotages her career by deciding to marry upper-class British army officer Roy (Taylor) at the height of World War I. After Myra believes that he has been killed, despair and poverty force her into prostitution ("Lonely, soldier?" she asks with a steely smile, sashaying through Waterloo Station). Leigh is heartbreaking as the tragic Myra, moving from dancer to streetwalker with delicacy and conviction, and Taylor, becomingly mustached, exhibits a less petulant manner than usual. Watson, as his naive mother, makes a compassionate confidante to Myra's confession, and Ouspenskaya provides a touch of class as the imposing head of the ballet corps. The story is a bit wilted now, but Leigh's performance is one of her best.

Off-Screen: This was Leigh's follow-up movie after winning an Oscar as Scarlett O'Hara. She wanted husband-to-be Laurence Olivier to costar, but the studio cast its surefire romantic lead instead. Though a top-budget film, great billows of studio-manufactured fog eliminated the need to construct an exact replica of Waterloo Bridge. Sherwood's 1930 play had been filmed in 1931 by Universal; in 1956, it was remade as *Gaby*, with Leslie Caron. The story was updated to World War II, and there was a happy, Technicolored ending. (CFB)

Way Out West

MGM, 1937. (65m.) Dir: James W. Horne. Sp: Charles Rogers, Felix Adler, and James Parrott, b/o story by Jack Jevne and Charles Rogers. Cast: Stan Laurel, Oliver Hardy, James Finlayson, Sharon Lynn, Rosina Lawrence, Stanley Fields.

On-Screen: *Stan and Ollie in the wide open spaces.* One of the best of Laurel and Hardy's feature films, *Way Out West* wins many laughs in its trim sixty-five minutes. The boys venture out West to deliver the deed to a gold mine to a sweet young thing (Lawrence), only to be thwarted by a larcenous saloon owner (Finlayson) and his wife (Lynn). But does anyone really care? The fun is in Stan and Ollie's inspired routines, none funnier than their attempt to get to the second floor of a house (where a crucial safe can be found) by way of a rope and a mule. Other memorable moments include Stan's consumption of his hat (as the payoff on a boast) and Stan and Ollie's sublime dance to a tune played by a group of cowhands.

Off-Screen: Working titles for the movie were *Tonight's the Night* and *We're in the Money*. The cowboys who sing "At the Ball, That's All" are actually the Avalon Boys Quartet, one of whom is character actor Chill Wills. (Years later he was the voice of Francis the Talking Mule.)

The Way We Were

Columbia, 1973. (C-118m.) Dir: Sydney Pollack. Sp: Arthur Laurents, b/o his novel. Cast: Barbra Streisand, Robert Redford, Bradford Dillman, Viveca Lindfors, Patrick O'Neal, Murray Hamilton, Lois Chiles, Herb Edelman, Allyn Ann McLerie, James Woods.

On-Screen: *Streisand and Redford, in love and marriage.* One of the best-remembered romantic films of the seventies, *The Way We Were* manages to override its flaws with potent star chemistry and a literate screenplay. Ideally cast and highly effective, Barbra Streisand plays an abrasive, politically active Jewish girl with a serious crush on blond WASP Redford, an aspiring writer. To a lush score by Marvin Hamlisch that won an Oscar (as did his title song with Marilyn and Alan Bergman), the movie traces the couple's lives from the late thirties to the early fifties, as they fall in love and marry and he becomes a Hollywood writer. During the years of blacklisting and the "Red scare," her activism and idealism clash with his practicality and expediency, and they ultimately part. Streisand and Redford are at their best, both exuding a charisma that fairly defines "movie star." Their last brief meeting, years after their separation, has a bittersweet poignancy that many viewers recall with pleasure.

Off-Screen: Reputedly, much of the footage relating to the blacklist years in Hollywood was cut in the final print, which would account for the puzzling sketchiness of the important Lindfors and Hamilton roles. Barbra Streisand was nominated for an Academy Award as Best Actress. The movie's campus scenes were filmed at Union College in Schenectady, New York.

West Side Story

United Artists, 1961. (C–151m.) Dir: Robert Wise and Jerome Robbins. Sp: Ernest Lehman, b/o musical play by Stephen Sondheim. MS: Leonard Bernstein and Stephen Sondheim. Cast: Natalie Wood, Richard Beymer, Rita Moreno, George Chakiris, Russ Tamblyn, Tucker Smith, David Winters, Tony Mordente, Ned Glass, Simon Oakland.

On-Screen: *The towering musical drama, brought to the screen.* It begins magnificently: After an aerial view of Manhattan, the camera swoops down to a New York slum street where a gang erupts into dance. From this point we are swept into the violent world of gang warfare and the tragic romance that springs from it. Adapted from the long-running stage success, *West Side Story* transposes the story of Shakespeare's *Romeo and Juliet* to the slums of Manhattan's West Side. The story itself now seems archaic, but happily, the movie retains the electrifying Leonard Bernstein–Stephen Sondheim score and Jerome Robbins's remarkable choreography and staging. Natalie Wood makes a lovely Maria, and Richard Beymer is a barely adequate Tony, but the movie's true energy comes from Oscar winners Rita Moreno as hot-blooded Anita and George Chakiris as volatile Bernardo. The songs range from bitingly funny to soaringly romantic, and the dances are as fine as any ever shown in films. Favorite moments:

the gang mocks the police ("Gee, Officer Krupke") and the lovers exchange their private vows ("One Hand, One Heart"). Arguably the finest musical film of the sixties.

Off-Screen: Although Robert Wise and Jerome Robbins are credited as codirectors, Robbins choreographed all but two of the dance numbers and then left several months after the filming began. Reportedly, the film's producers wanted Elvis Presley to play Tony but Jerome Robbins persuaded them otherwise. Natalie Wood's voice was dubbed by Marni Nixon, Richard Beymer's by Jimmy Bryant. In addition to the Oscars for supporting players, the film won eight other Academy Awards, including Best Picture, Best Director, Best Art Direction (Color), Best Costume Design (Color), and Best Scoring of a Musical Picture. Robbins received a special Oscar for his choreography.

The Westerner

Samuel Goldwyn–United Artists, 1940. (100m.) Dir: William Wyler. Sp: Jo Swerling and Niven Busch. Cast: Gary Cooper, Walter Brennan, Doris Davenport, Forrest Tucker, Chill Wills, Dana Andrews, Tom Tyler.

On-Screen: *The West's notorious Judge Roy Bean meets his match.* Films, as we know, have a way of turning history into legend, and nowhere more than in the Western. Roy Bean was a crude, portly judge who carried out his own form of "frontier justice" by hanging every defendant who refused to pay his price. This leisurely and flavorsome film transforms Bean from a scoundrel and swindler into a cantankerous rogue played by Walter Brennan. The self-appointed lawmaker "West of the Pecos," he meets his match in Cole Harden (Cooper), a drifter who defies him by becoming the champion of "the little people." Their well-remembered final confrontation in a theater is the movie's highlight. Cooper does his usual understated turn as Harden, leaving the juicier role to Brennan, whose skilled performance earned him an Oscar as Best Supporting Actor (his third). Pay special attention to Gregg Toland's superb photography, which bathes many of the scenes in a warm glow.

Off-Screen: Early on, Gary Cooper realized that he would actually be playing a large supporting role to Walter Brennan and was reluctant to do the film, until director Wyler convinced him that his part was still worthwhile. *The Westerner* marked Forrest Tucker's debut and the third film for Dana Andrews.

The Whales of August

Alive Films, 1987. (C-90m.) Dir: Lindsay Anderson. Sp: David Berry, b/o his play. Cast: Bette Davis, Lillian Gish, Vincent Price, Ann Sothern, Harry Carey, Jr., Tisha Sterling, Mary Steenburgen.

On-Screen: *Two elderly sisters share their lives and memories.* On rare occasions it becomes a privilege to watch great actors practice their art, even at the end of their careers. *The Whales of August* is such an occasion: A small but beautifully crafted, moving film that brings together two screen legends. Bette Davis and Lillian Gish are aged and widowed sisters living in Gish's home on the Maine coast. Davis is blind, cantankerous, and heading inexorably toward senility; Gish is gentle and patient. There's no "plot" as such, only growing tension and exasperation that may lead to their separation. They

receive visitors: Price as a courtly Russian émigré and Oscar-nominated Sothern as a cheerful longtime friend. They are all fine, but the film's most indelible moments are silent: Davis clutching her late husband's pocket watch and running a lock of his brown hair across her cheek; Gish looking over her mementos of the past, including telegrams tied with a pink ribbon.

Off-Screen: Apparently, Bette Davis was hostile to Lillian Gish. Gish introduced herself and Davis growled, "If you want to talk about the work or the script, fine. Otherwise, we have *nothing* to talk about." Gish was hurt, but tried to be sympathetic and forebearing. The coolness between them continued throughout the filming. Ann Sothern's daughter Tisha plays her mother in the opening sequence set in the past. *The Whales of August* was British director Lindsay Anderson's first American film.

What Ever Happened to Baby Jane?

Warners, 1962. (132m.) Dir: Robert Aldrich. Sp: Lukas Heller, b/o novel by Henry Farrell. Cast: Bette Davis, Joan Crawford, Victor Buono, Marjorie Bennett, Maidie Norman, Anna Lee.

On-Screen: *Bizarre Hollywood tale of mayhem and murder.* Batty and on the bottle, Jane Hudson (Davis) delights in tormenting her invalid sister Blanche (Crawford). Living in a crumbling house, both are aging movie star has-beens who retired after Blanche was crippled in an auto accident, and Jane was blamed. When Jane isn't browbeating her helpless sister, or serving her roasted rats for "din-din," they watch their old movies on "The Late Show." In a mad scheme to recapture her childhood fame as winsome Baby Jane, the blowsy ex-star dresses garishly as a little girl and hires a creepy pianist (Buono) to coach her. (You'll chuckle, and shudder, as Davis croaks "I've Written a Letter to Daddy.") This isn't all Jane is planning. As spider and fly, two Golden Age superstars deliver bravura performances in an outrageous camp classic that tops itself with a startling ending.

Off-Screen: Although rumors ran rampant that the temperamental stars were at each other's throats between takes, both actresses denied behaving unprofessionally. Movie buffs will recognize the films shown on television as *Parachute Jumper* and *Ex-Lady,* Davis oldies dating from 1933, and Crawford's *Sadie McKee,* released the following year. Davis received a Best Actress nomination, and many viewers felt that Crawford should have been cited as well. Buono's performance, as Best Supporting Actor, and Ernest Haller's photography were also nominated. Barbara Merrill, as the teenage neighbor, is the daughter of Davis and actor Gary Merrill. A 1991 television remake starred sisters Vanessa and Lynn Redgrave. It was produced by Robert Aldrich's son, William. (CFB)

What's Up, Doc?

Warners, 1972. (C-94m.) Dir: Peter Bogdanovich. Sp: Buck Henry, David Newman, and Robert Benton. Cast: Barbra Streisand, Ryan O'Neal, Madeline Kahn, Kenneth Mars, Austin Pendleton, Sorrell Booke, Liam Dunn, John Hillerman, Michael Murphy.

Off-Screen: *A dizzy girl disrupts the life of an absent-minded archaeologist.* Director Bogdanovich's fond tribute to the "screwball"

comedies of the thirties, especially *Bringing Up Baby, What's Up, Doc?* is a hectic farce that packs a lot of fun into a compact ninety-four minutes. In an obvious echo of Katharine Hepburn's role in *Baby,* Streisand plays a one-woman disaster area who sets her cap for professor Ryan O'Neal. O'Neal has come to San Francisco with his bossy fiancée (Kahn) for a musicologists' convention, and with Streisand's "help," he's soon involved with jewel thieves, government spies, and assorted other lunatics. The slapstick is frequently hilarious, and the obligatory climactic chase that ultimately leads to a courtroom is handled cleverly. For a change, Streisand is more appealing than abrasive, but the movie is almost stolen by Kahn's up-tight fiancée, who was born to be humiliated. Liam Dunn is howlingly funny as a nerve-shattered judge.

Off-Screen: Peter Bogdanovich had originally signed to direct Streisand and O'Neal in a film called *A Glimpse of Tiger.* When that project was canceled, he had Newman and Benton create a new screenplay for the stars, which Buck Henry rewrote. John Byner and Randy Quaid can be seen briefly at the hotel banquet.

When Harry Met Sally . . .

Columbia, 1989. (C-95m.) Dir: Rob Reiner. Sp: Nora Ephron. Cast: Billy Crystal, Meg Ryan, Carrie Fisher, Bruno Kirby, Steven Ford, Lisa Jane Persky, Michelle Nicastro, Harley Kozak.

On-Screen: *An over-the-years friendship eventually ripens into love.* An amiable, essentially lightweight romantic comedy, *When Harry Met Sally . . .* asks the question, "Can men and women just be friends without (as

Harry puts it) 'the sex part' getting in the way?" Harry (Crystal) and Sally (Ryan) spend a full decade grappling with the question and come up with the inevitable answer. After their first hostile encounter in 1977, they meet again at five-year intervals during which time they are drawn closer together, even as their personal lives remain separate. When true love intervenes, they become uneasy and disconsolate. The movie is clearly in Woody Allen territory, but the screenplay lacks Allen's bracing wit and the storyline is rather attenuated, more of an extended sketch than a sustained narrative. Billy Crystal's character comes across as somewhat smart-alecky, while Meg Ryan seems to emulate Diane Keaton's slightly dithering line readings in her performance. *When Harry Met Sally . . .* is a pleasant diversion.

On-Screen: The much-talked about restaurant scene provides the film's funniest line, delivered, no less, by the director's mother, Estelle Reiner. The scene was filmed at Katz's Delicatessen on Houston Street in New York City.

Where's Poppa?

United Artists, 1970. (C-82m.) Dir: Carl Reiner. Sp: Robert Klane, b/o his novel. Cast: George Segal, Ruth Gordon, Ron Leibman, Trish Van Devere, Barnard Hughes, Vincent Gardenia, Paul Sorvino, Garrett Morris.

On-Screen: *Carl Reiner's lunatic black comedy.* More than two decades after its release, this absurdist comedy has lost some of its power to shock and offend. However, you may still find yourself laughing sporadically at its outrageous tale of Gordon Hocheiser (Segal), a thirty-five-year-old lawyer who loathes his senile mother (Gordon) and would like to see her dead, especially when she interferes with his romance with a nurse (Van Devere). He turns for help to his younger brother Sidney (Leibman), who has his own peculiar problems. Sidney is repeatedly mugged in Central Park, and when he is forced to take part in a rape, the incident has, shall we say, unexpected consequences. The humor throughout is jet-black and occasionally funny. George Segal is always adept at playing an amiable nerd, but whether falling into her mashed potatoes or admiring her son's "tush," Ruth Gordon's momma is even more of a trial than intended. Don't look for "poppa"—he's long gone, and can you blame him?

Off-Screen: Elsa Lanchester was an earlier choice for the role of Momma. At first screenings, the movie ended with Segal getting into bed with Gordon and saying "Poppa's come home." This ending was judged too strong and changed to the current one, which has Segal bringing an old nursing home resident to Momma, telling her it's Poppa, and riding off with his girlfriend. A 1979 television pilot film, based on the movie, never developed into a series.

White Christmas

Paramount, 1954. (C-120m.) Dir: Michael Curtiz. Sp: Norman Panama, Melvin Frank, and Norman Krasna. MS: Irving Berlin. Cast: Bing Crosby, Danny Kaye, Rosemary Clooney, Vera-Ellen, Dean Jagger, Mary Wickes, Sig Ruman, Grady Sutton.

On-Screen: *A wilted Berlin bouquet.* Any musical that contains a brace of diverting Irving Berlin tunes can't be all bad, but *White Christmas* comes uncomfortably close. The songs range from delightful ("The Best Things Happen While You're Dancing," "Sisters," and, of course, the perennial title tune) to dismal ("What Can You Do With a General?"). The plotline, however, is excruciating—something to do with Crosby and Kaye as entertainers who conspire to help their beloved Old General (Jagger) whose New England inn is failing. (The movie is a partial reworking of the much better *Holiday Inn.*) Crosby also becomes involved in some sluggish romantic complications with Rosemary Clooney. A bright spot in the movie is Vera-Ellen, whose expert dancing and piquant personality offset the overall blandness.

Off-Screen: Despite mostly negative reviews, the movie was the highest-grossing film of 1954. Donald O'Connor had to be replaced by Danny Kaye after he injured his leg, and John Brascia was required to fill in for O'Connor in the dance numbers. The chorus line behind Rosemary Clooney when she sings "Love, You Didn't Do Right By Me" includes George Chakiris, later to make his mark in *West Side Story* (1961).

White Heat

Warners, 1949. (114m.) Dir: Raoul Walsh. Sp: Ivan Goff and Ben Roberts, b/o story by Virginia Kellogg. Cast: James Cagney, Virginia Mayo, Edmond O'Brien, Margaret Wycherly, Steve Cochran.

On-Screen: *"Made it, Ma. Top of the world!" Cagney in top form.* Of all the gangsters Cagney played in the five decades of his career, Cody Jarrett may well be his most memorably flamboyant. Sure, he's his usual compressed package of dynamite, but this time he's a certifiably insane paranoid, with a galloping case of mother-fixation to boot. Probably nobody else but Cagney could get away with the prison scene in which he goes berserk after learning about his mother's death. Wycherly's gaunt Ma goes a long way toward giving motherhood a bad name. Mayo, as Cody's no-better-than-she-should-be wife, and O'Brien, the T-man masquerading as a crook in order to trap Cody in a payroll heist, are also fine. It all ends in a blaze of glory atop a gasoline-storage tank, with Cagney shouting the now-famous line.

Off-Screen: Cagney himself had the idea of modeling Cody Jarrett on a real-life psychotic, Arthur ("Doc") Parker, an outlaw son of the notorious Ma Barker. It occurred to Cagney, too, that Cody's mother-obsession would be pointed up, if, after one of his epileptic seizures, he were to give Ma Jarrett a hug as he sat in her comforting lap. Director Walsh was also no stranger to violence, having played John Wilkes Booth in D. W. Griffith's silent epic *The Birth of a Nation,* as well as directing Cagney's feisty bootlegger in *The Roaring Twenties.* Kellogg's original story was nominated for an Academy Award. (CFB)

Who Framed Roger Rabbit

Touchstone, 1988. (C-103m.) Dir: Robert Zemeckis. Sp: Jeffrey Price and Peter S. Seaman, b/o novel by Gary K. Wolf. Cast: Bob Hoskins, Christopher Lloyd, Joanna Cassidy, Stubby Kaye, Alan Tilvern, Joel Silver. Voice of Roger Rabbit: Charles

Fleischer; Speaking/singing voices of Jessica Rabbit: Kathleen Turner/Amy Irving.

On-Screen: *Comedy, mystery, and romance in a brilliant blending of live action and animation.* So absolutely convincing is the interaction of cartoon characters (Toons, as the movie calls them) and living actors in this hilarious and inventive thriller, kids and grownups alike will have no trouble believing that it's really taking place in Los Angeles, in 1947. Britisher Hoskins (with a flawless American accent) plays Eddie Valiant, a lovably seedy gumshoe who gets into all sorts of jams as he tries to prove hysterical Toon-movie star Roger Rabbit innocent of murdering the human lover of his sexy wife, Jessica. Eddie also gets involved with creepy Judge Doom (Lloyd), master criminal with a dastardly agenda. The non-stop action gets overly raucous at times, but you'll have so much fun following sudden plot twists, spotting visual puns and inside jokes, and meeting zany characters, like lecherous "child" Toon-star Baby Herman, that you won't mind a bit. It's dazzling, delirious, and completely daffy (as in Duck).

Off-Screen: Based loosely on Wolf's 1981 private-eye thriller, *Who Censored Roger Rabbit?*, the movie not only won three Oscars (for film editing, sound effects editing, and visual effects, with a special award going to animation director Richard Williams) but also became a box-office hit. Audiences were surprised by the story's serious turn toward the end, when a ghetto-like area of Los Angeles is revealed. Evoking the injustice of apartheid, Toon Town is a community where "mere" animated actors are forced to live. A pair of Roger Rabbit cartoon shorts, *Tummy Trouble* and *Roller Coaster Rabbit*, were released in 1989 and 1990, respectively. *Trail Mix-Up* was added in 1993. (CFB)

Who's Afraid of Virginia Woolf?

Warners, 1966. (129m.) Dir: Mike Nichols. Sp: Ernest Lehman, b/o play by Edward Albee. Cast: Elizabeth Taylor, Richard Burton, George Segal, Sandy Dennis.

On-Screen: *Lacerating drama of an embattled marriage.* When Edward Albee's 1962 Tony Award–winning, four-character play finally reached the screen, it proved worth the wait. As Martha, the slovenly, salty-tongued wife of a spineless college professor, Taylor stretches her acting talents, giving a flamboyant, all-stops-out performance. Burton, usually cast in strong, commanding roles, is even more surprisingly effective as her caustic, defeated husband. George and Martha share a marriage of barbs and bitter recriminations: "I swear, if you existed," she taunts him, "I'd divorce you." Visiting the unhappy pair is a naive campus couple (Segal and Dennis) who become pawns in their hosts' night of cruel fun and games. Much of the outlandish dialogue and cavortings are genuinely funny, though you'll be moved by the conclusion, when George liberates both himself and Martha from a strange lie that has nearly wrecked their marriage.

Off-Screen: Because of its startling use of earthy language, the movie was the first one to receive an "R" rating, a distinction that didn't hurt at the box office. Taylor's image-smashing role earned her a Best Actress Oscar. Many moviegoers felt that Burton (her real-life husband at the time), also nominated, should have won a statuette as well.

Other Academy Awards included Dennis (Best Supporting Actress), Haskell Wexler's black-and-white photography, and Alex North's music score. First-time movie director Nichols won a nomination as Best Director, as did the movie itself. Smith College, in Northampton, Massachusetts, was used in "opening up" Albee's one-set drama. (CFB)

The Wild Bunch

Warners-Seven Arts, 1969. (C-134m.) Dir: Sam Peckinpah. Sp: Walon Green and Sam Peckinpah, b/o story by Walon Green and Roy N. Sickner. Cast: William Holden, Robert Ryan, Ernest Borgnine, Edmond O'Brien, Warren Oates, Ben Johnson, Jaime Sanchez.

On-Screen: *Sam Peckinpah's violent, powerful Western.* The year is 1913, in a West no longer burgeoning or hopeful. The movie begins with a group of children watching a swarm of red ants devouring a scorpion, and it ends with the bloody destruction of the Wild Bunch. In between is a Western drama once condemned for its excessive brutality but now considered a classic of the genre. William Holden stars as Pike Bishop, head of a group of scroungy, amoral bank robbers who somehow retain a remnant of the Westerner's creed. They flee to Mexico where they become involved in a revolution, and where they are also pursued relentlessly by Thornton (Ryan), a bounty hunter who was once Bishop's friend. *The Wild Bunch* is undeniably violent, but several decades later, the bloodletting in movies has sadly become even more explicit. What is remembered now from the film is its hard-edged realism, and its unsparing view of a corrupt and dying West. Peck-

inpah's direction is confident—this was his best film, although *Ride the High Country* (1962) comes close.

Off-Screen: Lee Marvin was the first choice to play Pike Bishop, but he was unavailable due to extended shooting on *Paint Your Wagon.* Much of the movie was shot on location in the remote Mexican town of Parras, where Sam Peckinpah drove his cast and crew very hard. Originally filmed at 190 minutes, *The Wild Bunch* was cut down to 142 minutes when preview audiences reacted to the violence, but then exhibitors insisted on further cuts. The 142-minute version was reissued in 1981.

The Wild One

Columbia, 1954. (79m.) Dir: Laslo Benedek. Sp: John Paxton, b/o story by Frank Rooney. Cast: Marlon Brando, Mary Murphy, Robert Keith, Lee Marvin, Jay C. Flippen.

On-Screen: *First of the motorcycle gang movies, with Brando as leader of the pack.* "What are you rebelling against?" Johnny (Brando) is asked after his marauding band of cyclists take over a small California town. "What have you got?" he replies. Though you're not sure just what Johnny, Chino (Marvin), and the rest of the leather-jacketed Black Rebels are really against (growing up, perhaps), you're never in doubt that Brando delivers one of his best performances as a posturing young hood in conflict with society and its established norms. Murphy, as the local sheriff's daughter whose tenderness baffles Johnny, and Keith, who plays her weakling father, also stand out. Benedek's taut direction will rivet your interest, but the ending may strike you as contrived.

Off-Screen: Rooney's story, "The Cyclists' Raid," was based on an actual incident that happened in Hollister, California, in 1947. Brando was drawn to the Paxton script for its graphic depiction of an ugly, and growing, social phenomenon. Brando being Brando, however, the warning message all but disappeared beneath the charismatic actor's screen persona, and many of his youthful fans regarded Johnny as a heroic rebel. To prepare for the role, Brando rode with motorcycle gangs, closely observing the rigid, conformist lifestyle of the "nonconformists." So great was the fear that it would disturb the peace, the movie was not shown in Great Britain until fourteen years later. (CFB)

Wilson

Fox, 1944. (C–154m.) Dir: Henry King. Sp: Lamar Trotti. Cast: Alexander Knox, Geraldine Fitzgerald, Charles Coburn, Cedric Hardwicke, Thomas Mitchell, Vincent Price, Sidney Blackmer, Ruth Nelson, Stanley Ridges, Eddie Foy, Jr., Mary Anderson.

On-Screen: *Biographical drama concerning the 28th President*. Elaborate, impressively detailed, but not especially exciting, *Wilson* traces the story of Woodrow Wilson (Knox) from his tenure as President of Princeton University to his sad retirement from office as America's 28th President. Lamar Trotti's screenplay touches on the major events in his life, including the several Democratic conventions at which he was nominated (spectacularly recreated); the scandal surrounding his courtship and second marriage to Edith Galt (Fitzgerald); his role as President dur-

ing World War I; and, most tellingly, his futile battle to bring America into the League of Nations. Clearly, the film was made at the height of World War II: Wilson is given more than one opportunity to articulate the country's righteous cause during wartime. The direction and the acting are commendable (Knox gives an excellent, Oscar-nominated performance) and the film is a worthy effort. What's lacking, however, is the heartbeat of great movie-making.

Off-Screen: *Wilson* received five Academy Awards: Art Direction, Color Cinematography, Writing—Original Screenplay, Film Editing, and Sound Recording. It was also nominated in the Best Picture, Best Director, and Best Actor (Knox) categories. Despite these accolades, and praise from the critics, the film was a disastrous failure for Fox. A bitterly disappointed Darryl F. Zanuck, who had worked zealously on the production, had to be content with receiving the Irving G. Thalberg Memorial Award. Henry Fonda and Gary Cooper were considered to play Wilson but the role went to the relatively obscure Knox.

The Window

RKO, 1949. (73m.) Dir: Ted Tetzlaff. Sp: Mel Dinelli, b/o story by Cornell Woolrich. Cast: Bobby Driscoll, Barbara Hale, Arthur Kennedy, Paul Stewart, Ruth Roman.

On-Screen: *A boy witnesses a murder*. An unheralded "sleeper" in its year of release, *The Window* is a small-scale but taut variation on the theme of "the boy who cried wolf." Little Bobby Driscoll, a city boy prone to fabricating stories, sees a murder being committed by a neighboring couple, and of course nobody will believe him. His life in jeopardy, he must use resourceful measures to elude the pursuing killers. In its modest way, the movie works up a considerable amount of suspense, and the climactic chase across the city rooftops and into an abandoned building is genuinely harrowing. Hale and Kennedy are maddeningly obtuse as the boy's skeptical parents, but twelve-year-old Driscoll gives a credible and expressive performance as the terrified boy.

Off-Screen: The merit of *The Window* did not go unnoticed. In addition to many good reviews, it was named the Best Mystery Film of the Year by the Mystery Writers of America, and editor Frederic Knudtson was nominated for an Academy Award. Bobby Driscoll was cited as Outstanding Juvenile Actor by the Academy and given a miniature statuette. Sadly, twenty years later, Driscoll was found dead, probably of a drug overdose, in a crumbling New York City tenement. *The Window* was remade in 1966 as a British movie called *The Boy Cried Murder*.

The Witches of Eastwick

Warners, 1987. (C-118m.) Dir: George Miller. Sp: Michael Cristofer, b/o novel by John Updike. Cast: Jack Nicholson, Cher, Susan Sarandon, Michelle Pfeiffer, Veronica Cartright, Richard Jenkins, Keith Jochim, Carel Struycken.

On-Screen: *Three women consort with a devilish visitor.* Who were the intended viewers for this indigestible mix of fantasy, black comedy, and horror? Certainly not the readers of John Updike's novel, from which the screenplay was very loosely adapted. And certainly not moviegoers who cringe at scenes of vomiting, physical pain, or merely revolting behavior. Fans of Jack Nicholson may be pleased to see him as "your average horny little devil"—actually the Devil incarnate—who comes into a New England town and seduces three bored, currently single, and sexually frustrated women (Cher, Sarandon, Pfeiffer). What the Devil doesn't know is that the ladies have witchly powers of their own, and when they find out who he is, they wage a fierce battle to divest him of his power. With his arched eyebrows and satanic grin, Nicholson's Daryl Van Horne is amusing at first, but as the movie gives way to increasingly coarse and repellent special effects, the fun evaporates quickly. The three ladies are attractive but they seem to be at a loss about the nature of the movie they're doing. And so, alas, is the audience.

Off-Screen: Days before shooting began, Cher decided she wanted the role Susan Sarandon was signed for. Her request was granted, and Sarandon had to learn Cher's role. The evident confusion in the movie seems to have been triggered by the producers, who insisted on frequent changes even as the cameras rolled, to the dismay of everyone. Eventually, in an effort to appease the producers, frantic director Miller decided to do eight takes of each scene, ranging from naturalistic to extremely broad. The nightmarish experience sent Miller fleeing back to his native Australia, where he had made his reputation with the *Mad Max* films.

With a Song in My Heart

Fox, 1952. (C-117m.) Dir: Walter Lang. Sp: Lamar Trotti. MS: Various writers. Cast: Susan Hayward, Rory Calhoun, David Wayne, Thelma Ritter, Una Merkel, Helen Westcott, Richard Allen, Lyle Talbot, Max Showalter, Robert Wagner.

On-Screen: *The chequered life of singer Jane Froman, more or less.* Based loosely on the story of Jane Froman, the singer who rose to Broadway stardom in the thirties and early forties, *With a Song in My Heart* concentrates on the pivotal event in her life: her serious injury in a Lisbon plane crash in 1943. The movie traces her courageous fight to survive her ordeal, and her involvement with two men: David Wayne, the husband who helped to build her career, and Rory Calhoun, the pilot who rescued her after the crash. The story is shamelessly sentimental, topped by Froman's singing to a shell-shocked soldier (Wagner), but the music is just fine—a bevy of great standard tunes rendered by Susan Hayward in Froman's vibrant dubbed voice. Hayward gives a good, heartfelt performance, and Thelma Ritter provides a welcome note of acerbic humor as a nurse who becomes a life-long friend of Froman's.

On-Screen: In real life, Jane Froman ultimately married the pilot who saved her, but in the movie she remains married to Wayne. Robert Wagner's small but dramatic role brought him audience attention and helped to make him a star. Susan Hayward actually sang the songs before Jane Froman dubbed them so that her neck muscles and mouth would be authentic. She received an Academy Award nomination as Best Actress, and Alfred Newman won an Oscar for his music score.

Without Love

MGM, 1945. (111m.) Dir: Harold S. Bucquet. Sp: Donald Ogden Stewart, b/o play by Philip Barry. Cast: Katharine Hepburn, Spencer Tracy, Lucille Ball, Keenan Wynn, Patricia Morison, Felix Bressart, Gloria Grahame, Carl Esmond.

On-Screen: *Hepburn and Tracy forego romance. Or so they say.* Derived from Philip Barry's not-very-successful Broadway comedy (starring Hepburn), *Without Love* marks the third Hepburn-Tracy teaming. It's one of their lesser efforts, mainly because of a screenplay that lacks wit, texture, or surprise. Tracy plays a research scientist in Washington who enters into a special arrangement with young widow Hepburn. They will marry on a purely platonic basis, without love, so that she can help him with his experiments. (She has known the best of love, he the worst.) Would you be startled to learn that they fall in love anyhow? The stars are always entertaining to watch, although Hepburn trots out her mannerisms full force ("By gum!" she often exclaims) and Tracy tends to mug too often. Lucille Ball as a real estate agent and Keenan Wynn as Hepburn's cousin are amusing in secondary roles.

Off-Screen: Director Bucquet had this to say: "Directing Mr. Tracy amounts to telling him when you're ready to start a scene. He hasn't let me down yet, and he if he does, perhaps we'll get acquainted. Miss Hepburn requires direction, for she tends to act too much. Her acting is much less economical than Mr. Tracy's but his style is rubbing off on her. The important thing is that I don't coach them on their scenes together. . . ."

Witness

Paramount, 1985. (C-112m.) Dir: Peter Weir. Sp: Earl W. Wallace and William Kelley, b/o story by William Kelley, Pamela Wallace, and Earl W. Wallace. Cast: Harrison Ford, Kelly McGillis, Josef Sommer, Lukas Haas, Jan Rubes, Alexander Godunov, Danny Glover, Patti LuPone.

On-Screen: *A cop's suspicions drive him into hiding.* Suspense, romance, and human drama —this first-rate thriller has them all. Investigating the murder of an undercover cop in the men's room of a Philadelphia railroad station, police detective John Book (Ford) questions the sole witness to the crime, an Amish boy, Samuel Lapp (Haas), traveling with his attractive widowed mother, Rachel (McGillis). After Samuel identifies the killer, Book finds his own life endangered, and seeks refuge in the Lapps's peace-loving community. When Book and Rachel fall in love, the cop is torn between the idyllic Amish way of life, and the knowledge that his pursuers will soon track down and destroy both them and the boy. Some amusing moments help relieve the movie's tension, such as the strikingly photographed barn-raising sequence and, earlier, little Samuel's mistaking a Hassidic Jew for an Amish patriarch.

Off-Screen: Nominated in eight Academy Award "Best" categories, including those for actor (Ford), director, picture, and cinematography, the movie won Oscars for its original screenplay and for editing. The film was shot mainly in Pennsylvania's Lancaster County, where the director, cast, and crew ran into problems when the Amish populace refused to allow filming on their farms. As a result, a non-Amish structure served as Rachel's dairy farm. Alexander Godunov, who plays Ford's rival for McGillis's attentions, was a renowned Russian ballet dancer before becoming an American citizen. (CFB)

Witness for the Prosecution

United Artists, 1957. (114m.) Dir: Billy Wilder. Sp: Billy Wilder and Harry Kurnitz, b/o story and play by Agatha Christie. Cast: Tyrone Power, Marlene Dietrich, Charles Laughton, Elsa Lanchester, John Williams, Norma Varden, Henry Daniell, Torin Thatcher, Una O'Connor, Ian Wolfe.

On-Screen: *Christie's tense courtroom drama, done with style and wit.* Leonard Vole (Power), a handsome smoothie, is accused of murdering a wealthy widow (Varden), whose will leaves him a fortune. Sir Wilfrid Robarts (Laughton), a famous London barrister, agrees to defend him upon learning from Vole that his German-refugee wife, Christine (Dietrich), can prove his innocence and will testify on his behalf. But Christine swears in court that their marriage is bigamous and that Vole confessed his guilt to her. Which one is lying? Why does a mysterious Cockney prostitute offer Sir Wilfrid letters proving that Christine is framing Vole? This classic puzzler will have you guessing right up to the surprise finish. All concerned do Dame Agatha proud.

Off-Screen: A faithful version of Christie's London and Broadway hit, *Witness for the Prosecution* earned Oscar nominations for Best Picture, Best Director, and Best Actor (Laughton). As the ailing barrister's comically nagging nurse, Laughton's wife Lanchester also earned a nomination. Additional nominations were for the film's sound and editing. Because certain crucial plot twists were kept so secret, many felt that Dietrich was unfairly deprived of a nomination as Best Actress. This was Power's last completed movie; he died in 1958 while making *Solomon and Sheba*. O'Connor, as

Varden's maid, repeats her Broadway role. A 1982 television adaptation starred Ralph Richardson, Deborah Kerr, Diana Rigg, and Beau Bridges. (CFB)

The Wizard of Oz

MGM, 1939. (C & B/W, 101m.) Dir: Victor Fleming. Sp: Noel Langley, Florence Ryerson, and Edgar Allan Woolf, b/o book by L. Frank Baum. MS: Harold Arlen and E. Y. Harburg. Cast: Judy Garland, Frank Morgan, Ray Bolger, Jack Haley, Margaret Hamilton, Charley Grapewin, Clara Blandick, Terry (as Toto), and the Munchkins.

On-Screen: *Over the rainbow forever, with Dorothy and her friends.* Probably the most cherished American film of all time, and why not? Its special enchantment has endured from one generation to the next, bringing joy to everyone who relishes fantastic adventure and fun. It hardly matters that the production was plagued with more than its share of problems—we are entranced from the moment Judy Garland's Dorothy of Kansas steps into the Technicolored world of Munchkinland and travels with her friends to Oz. Who could not love the Scarecrow (Bolger), the Tin Man (Haley), and, most especially, the Cowardly Lion (Lahr in an immortal performance), as they dance down the Yellow Brick Road? Even Margaret Hamilton's Wicked Witch is a permanent pleasure. There is no longer any point in quibbling about the occasionally heavy-handed touches, or the banal sentiment that could be stitched on a sampler. Just sit back and revel for the umpteenth time in the color, the special effects, the sprightly songs, and Garland's always poignant emoting as home-bound Dorothy.

Away above the chimney-tops is not a bad place to be.

Off-Screen: Few films have commanded as much attention in print as *The Wizard of Oz*. The most complete account of the production can be found in Aljean Harmetz's *The Making of The Wizard of Oz* (Alfred A. Knopf, 1977), but there are many other more recent books as well. Oscars were awarded for Best Original Score (Herbert Stothart) and Best Song ("Over the Rainbow"). Other sound films based on Baum's books have included the animated *Journey Back to Oz* (1974), *The Wiz* (1978), and *The Return to Oz* (1985). In the fall of 1992, a stage version that adhered very closely to the movie turned up at the Paper Mill Playhouse in Millburn, New Jersey.

The Wolf Man

Universal, 1941. (70m.) Dir: George Waggner. Sp: Curt Siodmak. Cast: Claude Rains, Lon Chaney, Jr., Warren William, Ralph Bellamy, Patric Knowles, Bela Lugosi, Maria Ouspenskaya, Evelyn Ankers.

On-Screen: *A hirsute murderous creature stalks the night.* Probably one of the better lycanthropic horror stories that surfaced on screen in the thirties and forties, *The Wolf Man* generates a fair amount of suspense and atmosphere within its seventy minutes. Lon Chaney, Jr., son of the famous twenties actor, plays a man who is attacked by a werewolf (Lugosi) and is thereby doomed to keep turning into a murderous, wolflike creature against his will. He is finally slain by his father (Rains) with a silver-tipped cane. With his cultured voice and manner, Rains seems an unlikely father to coarse

Chaney, but no more absurd than Lugosi as the werewolf son of gypsy fortuneteller Maria Ouspenskaya. Although this low-budget thriller has its moments, it might have been better with a stronger actor than Chaney in the lead.

Off-Screen: Lon Chaney's Wolf Man makeup took many hours to apply. Created by gifted makeup artist Jack Pierce, who had designed the Frankenstein monster, it included a black shirt and trousers for Chaney so that he could avoid the ordeal of body makeup. The thick fog that permeated the movie was actually a chemical mist that at one time took its toll on heroine Evelyn Ankers, who passed out from the fumes and was only found much later when the set was being struck.

The Woman in the Window

RKO, 1945. (99m.) Dir: Fritz Lang. Sp: Nunnally Johnson, b/o novel by J. H. Wallis. Cast: Edward G. Robinson, Joan Bennett, Dan Duryea, Raymond Massey, Edmond Breon, Bobby (Robert) Blake, Dorothy Peterson, Arthur Loft.

On-Screen: *A professor becomes trapped in crime.* Erudite and sophisticated, Robinson's psychology professor finds himself inextricably involved as a criminal conspirator after he meets beautiful Bennett. When he stabs to death the man who attacked her in a jealous rage, he and the woman decide to cover up the crime. As the police investigate the case, he becomes ensnared in a web from which the only escape appears to be suicide. Playing another of Fritz Lang's driven, apparently ill-fated protagonists, Robinson sheds his tough-guy image of the thirties to give a

sterling performance in this grim *film noir*. Joan Bennett is the perfect *noir* woman: alluring, amoral, and dangerous. The familiar trappings of the genre are also here in full measure: the shadowed streets, the repressed sexuality, the sense of impending doom. There's a surprise ending which nearly wrecks an otherwise first-rate thriller.

Off-Screen: The movie's "trick" ending, which Fritz Lang felt was the only one possible given Hollywood's production code, displeased the studio and angered producer-writer Nunnally Johnson. Trusting Lang's cinematic skill, Johnson later changed his mind and allowed the director to have it his way.

Woman of the Year

MGM, 1942. (112m.) Dir: George Stevens. Sp: Ring Lardner, Jr. and Michael Kanin. Cast: Katharine Hepburn, Spencer Tracy, Fay Bainter, Dan Tobin, Reginald Owen, Roscoe Karns, William Bendix.

On-Screen: *The incomparable Hepburn and Tracy in their first teaming.* There is a moment in *Woman of the Year* in which the stars, in a restaurant booth, gaze raptly at each other, their faces in profile, and reveal a mutual affection and admiration that transcend the characters they are playing. It marks the true beginning of one of the great partnerships in film history. They would make better films together, but here, as colleagues at the *New York Chronicle*—she's a brittle, brilliant political columnist, he's a rough-hewn sports writer—they meet, fall in love, marry, separate, and reunite in a charming and witty film. Feminists will not applaud as Hepburn learns to be more of a wife and less of a highfalutin pundit, but movie fans recall specific scenes with pleasure. Best, perhaps, is the one in which he takes her to her first baseball game and tries to explain what is going on. Much less felicitous, however, is the sequence in which Hepburn makes a thoroughgoing disaster out of her attempt to be housewifely in the kitchen.

Off-Screen: Legend has it that when they met, Hepburn remarked, "I fear I may be a little too tall for you, Mr. Tracy," whereupon producer Joseph Mankiewicz countered, "Don't worry, he'll cut you down to size." Hepburn was nominated for a Best Actress Oscar, and an Academy Award went to Lardner and Kanin for their screenplay, which was originally called *The Thing About Women*. *Woman of the Year* later became a Broadway musical with Lauren Bacall, and a 1976 television version starred Renee Taylor and Joseph Bologna.

The Women

MGM, 1939. (132m.) Dir: George Cukor. Sp: Anita Loos and Jane Murfin, b/o play by Clare Boothe. Cast: Norma Shearer, Joan Crawford, Rosalind Russell, Joan Fontaine, Paulette Goddard, Mary Boland, Marjorie Main, Virginia Weidler, Lucile Watson, Phyllis Povah, Mary Nash, Ruth Hussey, Dennie Moore.

On-Screen: *Rampant all-star bitchery, courtesy of MGM.* Opening on Broadway late in 1936, Clare Boothe's play *The Women* startled, amused, and occasionally displeased critics and audiences with its venomous view of the female sex. Three years later, it reached the screen with some of its claws removed in this glittering, star-heavy MGM production. There is still the atmosphere of min-

gled perfume and poison as the ladies demolish each other in a beauty salon, a dress emporium, and a dude ranch for divorcées, among other locales. Norma Shearer stars as the noble wife and mother whose marriage is wrecked by scheming minx Joan Crawford. Rosalind Russell steals the show in an over-the-top performance as a vicious gossip, and other roles are well filled by Mary Boland, hilarious as a much-married countess, and Paulette Goddard as a frank, knowing showgirl. Despite its negative images about the feminine gender, *The Women* manages to entertain with its lavishly appointed production, sharp-edged dialogue, and cluster of star performances.

Off-Screen: Ernst Lubitsch was originally scheduled to direct, but when George Cukor became available after being fired from *Gone With the Wind*, he took over, and Lubitsch was assigned to *Ninotchka*. There was no love lost between costars Shearer and Crawford—Shearer considered Crawford an ambitious upstart, and Crawford resented getting the roles rejected by Shearer. Rosalind Russell battled for star billing, then won a partial victory with her name above the title, but in smaller letters than the others. *The Women* was poorly remade in 1956 as a musical called *The Opposite Sex*. (CFB)

Words and Music

MGM, 1948. (C-119m.) Dir: Norman Taurog. Sp: Fred Finklehoffe, b/o story by Guy Bolton. MS: Richard Rodgers and Lorenz Hart. Cast: Mickey Rooney, Tom Drake, Janet Leigh, Betty Garrett, Perry Como, Ann Sothern, Judy Garland, June Allyson, Gene Kelly, Vera-Ellen, Cyd Charisse, Lena Horne.

On-Screen: *Rodgers and Hart get the MGM treatment.* The witty, romantic, and bewitching songs of Richard Rodgers and Lorenz Hart will undoubtedly survive the years. That said, viewers should note that their music is the only virtue of this thoroughly silly "biography." But what a virtue! A bevy of MGM stars perform the songs, and sometimes very well indeed. Judy Garland belts out "Johnny One-Note," Lena Horne moves elegantly through a few songs, and June Allyson does a charming rendition of "Thou Swell." Best is Gene Kelly and Vera-Ellen's steamy dancing in the jazz ballet, "Slaughter on Tenth Avenue." However, the story portion is embarrassing, with Tom Drake as a wan Rodgers and Mickey Rooney as a scenery-chewing Hart. Earmuffs are suggested for their scenes, to be taken off when the glorious Rodgers and Hart music soars on the soundtrack.

Off-Screen: On stage, "Slaughter on Tenth Avenue" had been a ballet integrated with the plot. Gene Kelly and Robert Alton restaged the sequence, making it a self-contained ballet about a gangster and his moll. Judy Garland's two numbers show a clear fluctuation in her weight. In one ("Johnny One-Note"), she is thin; by the time she performed "I Wish I Were in Love Again" with Mickey Rooney, she had regained her health—and also gained twenty pounds.

Working Girl

Fox, 1988. (C-113m.) Dir: Mike Nichols. Sp: Kevin Wade. Cast: Melanie Griffith, Harrison Ford, Sigourney Weaver, Alec Baldwin, Joan Cusack, Philip Bosco, Nora Dunn, Oliver Platt, Kevin Spacey, Olympia Dukakis.

On-Screen: *Working girl Melanie Griffith triumphs in love and business.* Meet Tess (Griffith), ambitious, smart, and sexy. (She admits that she has "a mind for business and a bod for sin.") Working as a secretary at a stock brokerage, Tess rises in the ranks by taking over the job, wardrobe, and even the lover (Ford) of her power-hungry boss (Weaver). With a combination of nerve and savvy, she impresses the higher-ups and entrances Ford, a winner all the way. More of a fanciful eighties-style fable than a treatise on Getting Ahead in Business, *Working Girl* manages to entertain, due to Nichols's expert direction, Kevin Wade's clever screenplay, and Griffith's star-making performance. Her Tess wants the power and prestige that comes with success, but in contrast with the Cinderellas of earlier decades, she won't surrender them to a man. The movie also has first-rate comic performances by Weaver as Tess's treacherous boss and Cusack as her frenetic friend.

Off-Screen: The movie was nominated for six Academy Awards, including Best Picture, Director, Actress (Griffith), and two for Supporting Actress (Weaver and Cusack). Carly Simon's song, "Let the River Run," won the Oscar. One scene has Tess McGill taking revenge on some two-timing colleagues by typing out an obscene putdown on the overhead ticker. In reality, this can't be done: The electronic information is fed directly from the New York Stock Exchange and cannot be intercepted.

The World According to Garp

Warners, 1982. (C-136m.) Dir: George Roy Hill. Sp: Steve Tesich, b/o novel by John Irving. Cast: Robin Williams, Glenn Close, John Lithgow, Mary Beth Hurt, Swoosie

Kurtz, Jessica Tandy, Hume Cronyn, Amanda Plummer, Warren Berlinger.

On-Screen: *Watch out for the "undertoad".* Alternating between absurdist comedy and bursts of melodrama, George Roy Hill's film may not please devotees of John Irving's bestselling novel, and it may baffle those who haven't read the book, but there are rewards (and a few jolts) for those who stay with it. Robin Williams is T. S. Garp, a writer whose life is shaped to a large extent by his wildly eccentric feminist mother (Close). At heart a deeply feeling family man, Garp's world is constantly being threatened or shattered by sudden, unexpected events. (Garp's small son gives a name to this—the dangerous "undertoad" at the seashore.) Much of what happens to Garp is funny, some is tragic, and occasionally (as in the business involving his wife's lover) it is disconcertingly both. Robin Williams is capable if rather muted as Garp, and Glenn Close, in her feature film debut, gives the movie's best performance as Jenny. Also fine is John Lithgow, playing a transsexual ex-football player named Roberta Muldoon. Jessica Tandy and Hume Cronyn make a brief appearance as Jenny's bewildered parents.

Off-Screen: Glenn Close and John Lithgow were both nominated for Supporting Oscars. Author John Irving makes a cameo appearance as a referee in a wrestling match scene and director George Roy Hill plays the pilot who crashes into Garp's house. Amanda Plummer has a brief, wordless role as Ellen James, the girl whose terrible experience triggers the growth of the Ellen James Society. (In sympathy with her rape and mutilation, the members have their tongues removed.)

The World of Henry Orient

United Artists, 1964. (C-105m.) Dir: George Roy Hill. Sp: Nora and Nunnally Johnson, b/o novel by Nora Johnson. Cast: Peter Sellers, Paula Prentiss, Tippy Walker, Merrie Spaeth, Angela Lansbury, Tom Bosley, Phyllis Thaxter, Bibi Osterwald, Peter Duchin.

On-Screen: *Two New York teenagers plague a vain pianist.* What happens when two fourteen-year-old girls (Walker and Spaeth) get a wild crush on a conceited, womanizing pianist named Henry Orient (Sellers)? Plenty, according to this delightful comedy. The girls, well-to-do students at a private school in New York's Upper East Side, drive poor Henry to distraction with their determination. A few serious issues intervene: Walker, the more flamboyant of the two, is virtually ignored by her parents (Lansbury and Bosley), and Spaeth is the product of a broken home. Most of the movie, however, generates laughs as the girls pursue their target with relentless glee, even interfering with his daytime assignation with another man's wife (Prentiss). The two girls are enchanting, and Peter Sellers is the very model of fatuous self-importance. You may find yourself shedding a few surprising tears when Walker reaches an understanding with her father. More often, though, you'll be laughing at the antics in *The World of Henry Orient.*

Off-Screen: The authors of the screenplay, Nunnally and Nora Johnson, were father and daughter. Society pianist Peter Duchin, son of famed pianist Eddy Duchin, appears in a small role. Actress Hermione Gingold's part (as a madam) was deleted at the request of New York's Radio City Music Hall, where the film premiered. In 1967, *The World of Henry Orient* was turned into an unsuccessful Broadway musical called *Henry, Sweet Henry,* with Don Ameche as Henry.

Written on the Wind

Universal-International, 1956. (99m.) Dir: Douglas Sirk. Sp: George Zuckerman, b/o novel by Robert Wilder. Cast: Rock Hudson, Lauren Bacall, Robert Stack, Dorothy Malone, Robert Keith, Grant Williams, Edward C. Platt.

On-Screen: *Love and lust amid the Texas rich.* With the oil-rich Hadley kids of Texas, there's always trouble. Kyle Hadley (Stack), "Prince Charming of the oil empire," is an unstable alcoholic; his sister Marylee (Malone) is a nymphomaniac. Kyle marries lovely Lucy (Bacall), who is secretly loved by his best friend, Mitch Wayne (Hudson). To make things worse, Marylee has an unrequited passion for Mitch. Are you following this? Is there any reason you should? Based on Robert Wilder's bestseller, *Written on the Wind* is all gussied up in bright Technicolor and it does have its partisans, but it's a hopelessly silly melodrama. For all the thrashing about, Hudson and Bacall are colorless, since the scenery-chewing roles go to Stack and Malone. Stack's character is something of a nuisance, but he's almost tolerable beside Malone's ludicrous, sex-hungry Marylee. Inexplicably, she won an Oscar as Best Supporting Actress. The movie is chock full of such juicy lines as "Your daughter's a tramp!" and "Get out before I kill you!" On that basis alone, it may be worth watching.

Off-Screen: In addition to Malone's Oscar, Robert Stack was nominated as Best Supporting Actor. Another nomination went to the title song by Victor Young and Sammy Cahn.

The Wrong Man

Warners, 1956. (105m.) Dir: Alfred Hitchcock. Sp: Maxwell Anderson and Angus MacPhail, b/o story by Maxwell Anderson. Cast: Henry Fonda, Vera Miles, Anthony Quayle, Harold J. Stone, Nehemiah Persoff.

On-Screen: *An innocent man undergoes a nightmarish ordeal.* A departure for Alfred Hitchcock, *The Wrong Man* substitutes a sober quasi-documentary approach for the director's usual stylish, fanciful suspense. The movie relates a true story: Early in 1953, musician Manny Balestrero (Fonda) is accused of having committed several armed robberies. A decent working man with a wife (Miles) and two sons, Balestrero is nevertheless identified by several witnesses, arrested, and brought to trial. The harrowing ordeal causes his wife to have a nervous breakdown. Eventually, the true culprit is apprehended, and Balestrero is released. Unfortunately, the viewer's sense of anxiety, which ordinarily comes with a suspenseful thriller, gives way to exasperated questions: Why does Balestrero accept his fate so placidly? Why are the policemen so hostile? The film offers the familiar Hitchcock theme of an innocent man trapped in a suddenly unreal world, but the drab, straightforward approach mitigates against any true involvement. *The Wrong Man* is simply the wrong movie for Alfred Hitchcock.

Off-Screen: Hitchcock filmed many of the sequences in their actual settings, including the Stork Club, streets in Jackson Heights, Queens, and the surrounding police stations and jails. He even used the same psychiatric rest home to which Balestrero's wife was committed. Yet in the end Hitchcock admitted that "it wasn't any kind of picture." You may be able to spot two giggling girls played by budding actresses Bonnie Franklin and Tuesday Weld.

Wuthering Heights

Goldwyn-United Artists, 1939. (103m.) Dir: William Wyler. Sp: Ben Hecht and Charles MacArthur, b/o novel by Emily Brontë. Cast: Laurence Olivier, Merle Oberon, David Niven, Geraldine Fitzgerald, Flora Robson, Leo G. Carroll, Miles Mander, Hugh Williams, Cecil Kellaway.

On-Screen: *The classic love story, brought memorably to the screen.* Few films of the "golden" movie year of 1939 are as warmly remembered as *Wuthering Heights*. Impeccably produced and splendidly acted, this version of the haunting love story covered only part of the Brontë novel. But filmgoers over more than five decades have scarcely missed the rest. Laurence Olivier and Merle Oberon play the doomed couple in pre-Victorian England—he the wild, bedeviled Heathcliff, she the willful Cathy—who swear eternal love on the moors, part, and then reunite under tragic circumstances. They are both stirring, but special notice should be taken of David Niven, who, against all odds, manages to make the effete Edgar a genuinely touching figure, and of Geraldine Fitzgerald's bravura turn as the wretched Isabella. Glenn Toland's luminous Oscar-winning photography and Alfred Newman's sweeping music score contribute to the film's effectiveness.

Off-Screen: At first, producer Sam Goldwyn was reluctant to film the story. ("I don't like stories with people dying in the end. It's a tragedy.") But he was finally convinced. Candidates for Heathcliff included Charles Boyer, Ronald Colman, Douglas Fairbanks, Jr., and Robert Newton. Laurence Olivier wanted Vivien Leigh to play Cathy, and when she was offered the role of Isabella instead, he almost rejected Heathcliff. Much of the movie was shot on 450 acres of desert in the San Fernando Valley. After the movie was completed, Goldwyn insisted on adding a coda showing Heathcliff and Cathy reunited in heaven. Surprisingly, the film won the New York Film Critics Award as Best Picture over *Gone with the Wind*. The story was remade in 1954, 1970, and 1992.

Yankee Doodle Dandy

Warners, 1942. (126m.) Dir: Michael Curtiz. Sp: Robert Buckner and Edmund Joseph, b/o story by Robert Buckner. MS: George M. Cohan. Cast: James Cagney, Joan Leslie, Walter Huston, Richard Whorf, Rosemary DeCamp, George Tobias, Irene Manning, Jeanne Cagney, S. Z. Sakall.

On-Screen: *James Cagney in a musical biography of George M. Cohan.* Don't look for truth, just bountiful entertainment, in this tribute to writer-performer George M. Cohan. *Yankee Doodle Dandy* purports to tell about the life and music of the cocky Cohan, tracing his rise from the youngest member of a performing family to a beloved icon in American musical theatre. James Cagney inhabits the role, transforming Cohan from the vain, cantankerous man he truly was into a hot-headed but lovable, exuberant song-and-dance man. Cagney's light-footed, eccentric dancing style and his bouncy renditions of such great Cohan songs as "Over There," "You're a Grand Old Flag," and the title tune make this performance a durable treasure. The movie is clearly aimed at the wartime audience of 1942—and as such, its flag-waving fervor is understandable. Walter Huston is outstanding as Cohan's father Jerry. But it's Cagney's movie, and as he bustles about "with a trunkful of songs and a heartful of confidence," he's a joy to behold.

Off-Screen: James Cagney won a deserved Academy Award as Best Actor, and other Oscars were bestowed for Best Scoring of a Musical Picture and Best Sound Recording. George M. Cohan chose Cagney to play him after selling Warners the rights to his life story. There were probably many moments when the studio regretted its decision since Cohan proved to be very difficult. Co-scenarist Buckner and Cagney's brother William had spent months convincing Cohan that his life story should be fictionalized for dramatic effect. Afterwards, in a memorandum to Hal Wallis, Buckner wrote that the revised script was "a 250% improvement over Cohan's egotistical epic."

The Yearling

MGM, 1946. (C-128m.) Dir: Clarence Brown. Sp: Paul Osborn, b/o novel by

Marjorie Kinnan Rawlings. Cast: Gregory Peck, Jane Wyman, Claude Jarman, Jr., Chill Wills, Clem Bevans, Margaret Wycherly, June Lockhart.

On-Screen: *A rural boy comes of age.* Life is hard for Pa and Ma Baxter (Peck, Wyman) and their eleven-year-old son, Jody (Jarman). Barely able to scratch a living from their farm in the Florida backwoods, they can ill afford to allow Jody's pet fawn, Flag, to eat their meager crops. When Flag becomes a yearling, and his appetite presents an even greater threat to the Baxter's livelihood, Jody comes to realize that childhood pleasures must yield to the rigors of survival. The climactic scene, in which Jody alone must seal the fate of his beloved fawn, is heartbreaking. The Technicolored scenery at times upstages and undercuts the story's harshness, and the Baxter abode is too MGM tidy, but credit a splendid cast, especially young Jarman, with bringing Rawlings's characters to vivid life. The five fawns who play the orphaned Flag in various stages of growth are adorable.

Off-Screen: In 1941, Spencer Tracy, Anne Revere, and a young actor named Gene Eckman were cast as the Baxters. Shooting was slowed, however, by Florida's rainy weather and swarms of insects. When Tracy clashed with directors Victor Fleming and then King Vidor, the project was shelved. It was revived four years later, with locations shot in Florida's Everglade and Ocala National Parks, as well as Lake Arrowhead in California. The movie, Peck, and Wyman won Academy Award nominations; two Oscars were bestowed for color cinematography and art direction, and Tennessee-born Jarman was presented with a special Oscar as outstanding child actor. A musical version of the story ran briefly on Broadway in 1965. (CFB)

Yentl

United Artists, 1983. (C-134m.) Dir: Barbra Streisand. Sp: Jack Rosenthal and Barbra Streisand, b/o story by Isaac Bashevis Singer. MS: Michel Legrand, Alan and Marilyn Bergman. Cast: Barbra Streisand, Mandy Patinkin, Amy Irving, Steven Hill, Nehemiah Persoff.

On-Screen: *Streisand directs Streisand as a yeshiva boy.* In her first quadruple-threat effort as producer, director, coauthor, and star, Barbra Streisand fares well in some respects, and not so well in others. In this adaptation of a story by Isaac Bashevis Singer, Streisand plays a girl in 1904 Eastern Europe whose deep thirst for knowledge leads her to impersonate a boy so that she can study at a yeshiva. The ruse has unexpected complications when she becomes involved with Avigdor (Patinkin) and his beloved fiancée Hadass (Irving). The production is lavish and exceptionally handsome, but there are serious problems. Streisand is never really believable as a yeshiva boy, and Yentl's impersonation becomes the catalyst for too many sequences based on sexual identity and confusion, which may have been amusing in a Blake Edwards farce but not here. Also, the producer-director-coauthor has seen fit to encumber the story with many musical soliloquies by the star. She renders them expressively in her vibrant voice, but they become monotonous after a while. A few of the songs are lovely, particularly "Papa, Can You Hear Me?" and "The Way He Makes Me Feel." *Yentl* is a brave effort, but far from an unqualified success.

Off-Screen: Streisand had owned the rights to Singer's story for many years, but it was difficult to find a studio willing to take on the project. She worked for a number of years on the film's design. Singer was not happy with the film version and complained bitterly about it. The Bergman-Legrand score won an Academy Award. A nonmusical stage adaptation of the story ran on Broadway in the fall of 1975.

Yolanda and the Thief

MGM, 1945. (C-108m.) Dir: Vincente Minnelli. Sp: Irving Brecher, b/o story by Jacques Thery and Ludwig Bemelmans. MS: Harry Warren and Arthur Freed. Cast: Fred Astaire, Lucille Bremer, Frank Morgan, Mildred Natwick, Leon Ames, Mary Nash.

On-Screen: *Conman Fred Astaire woos rich girl Lucille Bremer in a lavish musical.* Vincente Minnelli's first musical film after the triumphant *Meet Me in St. Louis, Yolanda and the Thief* is a severe letdown. The production is truly opulent—both stylish and excessive in the Minnelli style. There are a few pleasing songs, notably "Angel." And Mildred Natwick is amusing as the heroine's addled aunt. Also, there is one dazzling production number, "Coffee Time", in which Astaire and Bremer dance joyfully to a hand-clapping, Latin-accented beat. But then the movie is burdened with a dreadful book in which conman Astaire (oddly miscast in a Gene Kelly role) attempts to bilk Bremer, the wealthiest girl in Patria, by pretending to be her guardian angel, then falling in love with her. (She seems more dull-witted than naive.) The movie's most ambitious number is a surrealistic dream ballet which is

sometimes striking but more often pretentious and stifling.

Off-Screen: Here are some comments by the participants. Vincente Minnelli: "I tried to get the quality of Bemelmans's book and illustrations, a curious mixture of worldliness in high places and a primitive naïvete, using his sometimes crude prism colors right out of a child's paint box and combining them with beautifully subtle monotones." Lucille Bremer: "We worked very hard and hoped for a good reception, but the reviews were mixed and nobody seemed to want to go. I think it was too fanciful, too much of a fairy tale for the day . . . Vincente Minnelli was a genius, a man of immense taste and imagination. . . ."

You Can't Cheat an Honest Man

Universal, 1939. (76m.) Dir: George Marshall. Sp: George Marion, Jr., Richard Mack, and Everett Freeman, b/o story by Charles Bogle (W. C. Fields). Cast: W. C. Fields, Edgar Bergen, Constance Moore, Mary Forbes, Thurston Hall, Eddie "Rochester" Anderson, John Arledge, Edward Brophy.

On-Screen: *W. C. runs a circus, more or less.* The first of W. C. Fields's four comedies for Universal, this ramshackle but often riotously funny farce has Fields as Larson E. Whipsnade, circus owner and con man extraordinaire. (He displays a short fellow as "the world's shortest giant and tallest midget.") In constant trouble with the law, Whipsnade also has a daughter (Moore) who is willing to make a bad society marriage to help her insolvent father. Also on hand are ventriloquist Edgar Bergen and his impudent dummy, Charlie McCarthy. Fields exchanges nasty wisecracks with Charlie ("Quiet, or I'll throw a woodpecker on you") or fires off his own inimitable quips ("Some weasel took the cork out of my lunch.") The movie's highlight is a big society party at which Whipsnade turns up as an unwelcome guest. He keeps sending his hostess into a dead faint by mentioning the snakes she fears, and he plays a hilarious pingpong game with another guest. Pure delight for Fields fans.

Off-Screen: Although George Marshall is the director of record, Eddie Cline actually directed most of Fields's scenes. Cline was called in after many heated disputes between Fields and Marshall. Fields continued trading insults with dummy Charlie McCarthy on radio appearances with Edgar Bergen. Several scenes in which Fields's character was meant to show his tender side were deleted from the final print, to the comedian's disapproval.

You Can't Take It With You

Columbia, 1938. (127m.) Dir: Frank Capra. Sp: Robert Riskin, b/o play by George S. Kaufman and Moss Hart. Cast: Jean Arthur, James Stewart, Lionel Barrymore, Edward Arnold, Ann Miller, Spring Byington, Mischa Auer, Donald Meek, Halliwell Hobbes, Eddie "Rochester" Anderson, Dub Taylor.

On-Screen: *Kaufman and Hart's stage comedy about an eccentric family*. Reworked by Riskin and Capra, the Pulitzer Prize-winning play reached the screen with its central idea intact: the wildly madcap Sycamore family goes about its freewheeling business, with

each member holding fast happily to his/her own eccentricities. Jean Arthur plays the "normal" daughter whose romance with a tycoon's son (Stewart) triggers trouble. The story works nicely as screwball farce, with Lionel Barrymore leading the way as the family patriarch with his own ideas about life and taxes. But then Robert Riskin's screenplay inserts indigestible gobs of Capra-esque sentiment about "little people" who must fight the nasty, life-denying figures of power. It all gets rather heavy, with a scarcely credible plot device that compels Stewart's mean-spirited father (Arnold) to see the error of his ways. The movie won the year's Best Picture Oscar, and Capra's direction also received an Academy Award (his third). There were five other nominations.

Off-Screen: Columbia bought the play for an at-the-time record price of $200,000, then altered it considerably when Frank Capra saw it as "a golden opportunity to dramatize Love Thy Neighbor in living drama." Fay Bainter was Capra's first choice to play Penny Sycamore, but she was unavailable. Frequently revived on stage, the play even became a short-lived television series in 1987.

You Only Live Once

Walter Wanger-United Artists, 1937. (86m.) Dir: Fritz Lang. Sp: Gene Towne and Graham Baker. Cast: Henry Fonda, Sylvia Sidney, Barton MacLane, Jean Dixon, William Gargan, Jerome Cowan, Chic Sale, Margaret Hamilton.

Off-Screen: *Grim Fritz Lang melodrama of an ill-fated couple*. The central theme of many of director Fritz Lang's films—the relentless, inexorable course of a man's fate—has seldom been dramatized more vividly than in this somber melodrama. Henry Fonda stars as the hapless victim of an injustice; a three-time loser, he is accused of a robbery he did not commit and sent to prison again. Bitter and desperate, he escapes to be with his devoted wife (Sidney), killing a kindly priest (Gargan) in the process. The end for the couple is uncompromisingly bleak. Although Fonda and Sidney give sensitive performances that arouse our sympathy, the movie states its familiar Depression theme—society creates criminals—too bluntly, and also stacks the cards against the hero. Few people treat him with anything but contempt: his new boss fires him, the prison guards despise him, and his sister-in-law (Dixon) would rather see him dead. Small wonder that he turns vindictive. Still, *You Only Live Once* is an arresting example of thirties melodrama-with-a message.

Off-Screen: According to Henry Fonda, the film was "a tortured nightmare to make." Fonda claimed that Fritz Lang pinched actors to get reactions and treated them like puppets. Many years later, he affirmed, "I hated Fritz Lang . . . he was too preoccupied with what everything was going to look like." Like a number of other films over the years, *You Only Live Once* is loosely suggested by the careers of the notorious Bonnie Parker and Clyde Barrow.

You Were Never Lovelier

Columbia, 1942. (97m.) Dir: William A. Seiter. Sp: Michael Fessier, Ernest Pagano, and Delmer Daves, b/o story by Carlos Olivari and Sixto Pondal Rios. MS: Jerome Kern and Johnny Mercer. Cast: Fred As-

taire, Rita Hayworth, Adolphe Menjou, Xavier Cugat, Leslie Brooks, Adele Mara, Isobel Elsom, Larry Parks.

On-Screen: *Astaire and Hayworth dance and romance.* After scoring a success as a dance team in *You'll Never Get Rich* (1941), Fred Astaire and Rita Hayworth were reunited for this entertaining, tuneful musical. The movie works better than the first, mainly because of the lilting Jerome Kern-Johnny Mercer score, which is superior to Cole Porter's score for *You'll Never Get Rich*. Such lovely songs as "Dearly Beloved," and "I'm Old-Fashioned," caress the ear, and the sensuous Astaire-Hayworth dance to the latter tune is the best one in the film. The story, however, is hardly an improvement—something about Astaire as an American entertainer who becomes involved with the family of a wealthy Argentinian (Menjou), especially Menjou's disdainful daughter (Hayworth). Hayworth was not an ideal partner for Astaire—she seems too much of a lofty goddess for his lighthearted, debonair style, but together on the dance floor, they still provide a good deal of pleasure.

Off-Screen: Rita Hayworth's voice was dubbed by Nan Wynn. Forced to find rehearsal space away from an overcrowded studio, Astaire and Hayworth finally settled on an empty hall above a funeral parlor. The two were obliged to stop their tap routines when a funeral was being held below. The movie won Oscar nominations for the song "Dearly Beloved" and for Best Scoring of a Musical Picture.

Young Frankenstein

Fox, 1974. (105m.) Dir: Mel Brooks. Sp: Gene Wilder and Mel Brooks, b/o characters created by Mary Shelley. Cast: Gene Wilder, Peter Boyle, Marty Feldman, Madeline Kahn, Cloris Leachman, Teri Garr, Gene Hackman, Kenneth Mars, Richard Haydn.

On-Screen: *Off-the-wall spoof of venerable horror movies.* They're all here: sputtering gadgets in the castle's hidden laboratory, blundering Igor (pronounced "Eye-gore" to suit Feldman's odd features), panic-stricken Transylvanian villagers. And, yes, even "wipes" and iris-in and -out effects to lend period flavor to the black-and-white photography. This time, though, it's the mad baron's even nuttier grandson, Dr. Frederick "Frahnkenshteen" (Wilder) who fashions the Monster (Boyle), a lumbering creature who seduces the doctor's frigid fiancée (Kahn). Added lunacy comes from a sex-starved lab assistant (Garr) and a housekeeper (Leachman) so grim she even terrifies horses. Hardly rivaling Boris Karloff, his great predecessor in the role, Boyle nevertheless brings a measure of menace and pathos to the beleaguered Monster. You'll love his and Wilder's nifty soft-shoe to "Puttin' on the Ritz."

Off-Screen: Not only does the original *Frankenstein* (1931) get sent up by the Wilder-Brooks writing team, but also its sequels. The blind, bumbling hermit (Hackman, in an unbilled appearance) is based on a character from *The Bride of Frankenstein* (1935); the inspector (Mars) with an artificial arm is modeled on the Lionel Atwill role in *The Son of Frankenstein* (1939); and the notion of endowing the Monster with a scientist's brain is borrowed from *The Ghost of Frankenstein* (1942). If the laboratory equipment looks familiar, it should; it's the original hardware, designed by Kenneth Strickfaden, used in *Frankenstein* and lent by Universal for this movie. Watch for the madcap director's face as a Castle Frankenstein gargoyle. (CFB)

The Young Lions

Fox, 1958. (C-167m.) Dir: Edward Dmytryk. Sp: Edward Anhalt, b/o novel by Irwin Shaw. Cast: Marlon Brando, Montgomery Clift, Dean Martin, Hope Lange, Barbara Rush, May Britt, Maximilian Schell, Lee Van Cleef, Liliane Montevecchi.

On-Screen: *Irwin Shaw's tale of three soldiers in World War II.* A sprawling adaptation of Irwin Shaw's bestselling novel, *The Young Lions* follows the various fates of three soldiers at the peak of World War II: a sensitive blond German ski instructor (Brando), an introspective American Jew (Clift), and a devil-may-care American playboy (Martin). The movie traces their wartime experiences with women and more particularly, the impact of the war on their way of thinking: Brando moving painfully toward utter disillusion with Nazism, and Clift confronting racial bigotry in training camp. There are some action scenes, and an ironic ending, altered from the novel, in which the lives of these men converge. Edward Anhalt's screenplay is most notable for its softening of the Brando character, turning him from the unregenerate Nazi monster of the book into a decent man who becomes increasingly disgusted with his militaristic colleagues. Very blond and affecting a German accent, Brando is not especially convincing, nor does Clift project more than earnestness. Martin is merely adequate in a conventional role.

Off-Screen: Tony Randall was the first choice for the role played by Dean Martin. The softening of the Brando character appears to have been a joint decision by the film's director, Edward Dmytryk, and its screenwriter, Edward Anhalt, who felt that the movie should be more of an anti-war piece than an anti-Nazi tract. Irwin Shaw was reportedly infuriated by this revision. Bad weather plagued the production when it was shooting near Chantilly, about thirty miles north of Paris. Brando and Clift didn't help by being frequently at odds during the filming. A scene between Clift and his dying father (Jacob Ben-Ami) was deleted from the release print.

Young Mr. Lincoln

Fox, 1939. (100m.) Dir: John Ford. Sp: Lamar Trotti. Cast: Henry Fonda, Alice Brady, Marjorie Weaver, Arleen Whelan, Richard Cromwell, Ward Bond, Donald Meek, Francis Ford, Eddie Quillan, Pauline Moore.

On-Screen: *Henry Fonda portrays the Great Emancipator as a young man.* While Abraham Lincoln has turned up in a number of films, often as a sort of *deux ex machina,* few films have been devoted entirely to his life. John Ford's film, a lovingly rendered piece of Americana, deals with the sixteenth president's early years, when he rose from a gangly Illinois backwoodsman to a lawyer with potential for greatness. Much of the movie is concerned with Lincoln's defense of two young brothers (Cromwell and Quillan) accused of murder. Henry Fonda gives an exemplary performance as Lincoln, whether slyly revealing the true murderer at the trial or, in an indelible moment, addressing a cheering crowd of citizens. As he fills the frame with his strong presence, we sense his impending role in history. Bert Glennon's beautiful black-and-white photography and

Alfred Newman's haunting theme help to carry out John Ford's admittedly idyllic vision of a portion of American history.

Off-Screen: At first Fonda turned down the role, claiming that he was "not ready for a part like that." But an encounter with John Ford convinced him to change his mind, with Ford insisting that he would be playing "a young, jack-legged lawyer from Springfield" rather than the Great Emancipator. Fox also faced a legal problem when the Playwrights Company and author Robert E. Sherwood sued the studio, claiming that its property infringed on their play *Abe Lincoln in Illinois.* The suit was ultimately dismissed.

Young Tom Edison

MGM, 1940. (82m.) Dir: Norman Taurog. Sp: Bradbury Foote, Dore Schary, and Hugo Butler. Cast: Mickey Rooney, Fay Bainter, George Bancroft, Virginia Weidler, Eugene Pallette, Victor Kilian, Bobby Jordan.

On-Screen: *The early years of the great inventor.* Loosely (very loosely) derived from the boyhood years of Thomas Alva Edison, this rather leisurely, episodic film portrays young Tom (Rooney) as an eternally questioning trouble-maker in the 1860s town of Port Huron, Michigan. ("Wouldn't it be great if we could keep a sound?") Regarded as "addled" by the townspeople, he gets the loving support of his prophetic mother (Bainter) and his young sister (Weidler). As customary for films of this sort, Father (Bancroft) conceals a heart of pure gold beneath his gruff exterior. Of course Tom finally redeems himself and becomes a hero by using the Morse Code to warn an oncoming train that the bridge is down. Rooney is uncharacteristically restrained as Tom, except when he is overwrought about his mother's near-fatal illness (how Louis B. Mayer must have loved this portion of the story), and the film also has a pleasant if artificial period flavor. (It never claims to be factual.)

Off-Screen: One of the authors of the screenplay was Dore Schary, who would serve as MGM's production head from 1948 to 1956, replacing Louis B. Mayer. Mickey Rooney took time off from his regular chores as Andy Hardy, America's favorite movie teenager, to play young Tom Edison.

Zelig

Orion-Warners, 1983. (C & B/W, 79m.) Dir: Woody Allen. Sp: Woody Allen. Cast: Woody Allen, Mia Farrow, Garrett Brown, Stephanie Farrow, Will Holt, Sol Lomita, Mary Louise Wilson, Michael Jeter.

On-Screen: *Woody's Allen's identity crisis, in spades*. Filmed as a pseudo-documentary with "newsreels," interviews with real people, hidden cameras, and the like, *Zelig* is the odyssey of a man without a center. Leonard Zelig (Allen) is so little his own person that he takes on the characteristics of whomever he's with—their appearance, their language, their entire being. For a few months he enjoys fame and fortune as the Chameleon Man, with articles, stories, and even a new dance step, the Chameleon Hop. He also attracts the attention of Dr. Eudora Fletcher (Farrow), who sets out to cure him. He falls in love with her instead. When it's discovered that in his various lives Zelig has collected wives, children, and debts, he is hounded and disappears. He is finally found by Eudora as one of a crowd of Hitler-heilers at a Nazi rally in Berlin. Although it is certain to baffle many Allen fans and ir-ritate many others, *Zelig* is a funny and satirical film and quite a remarkable technical achievement. It also contains one of Woody Allen's few nonneurotic love affairs, free of the hostility and melancholy that pervade Allen's romances in such films as *Annie Hall* and *Manhattan*.

Off-Screen: In an interview before the film's release, Woody Allen commented, "Leonard Zelig's existence as a human chameleon represented a minor malady almost everyone suffers from, carried to an extreme. It's that need to be liked, just to keep people around you satisfied. I thought that desire not to make waves, carried to an extreme, could have traumatic consequences. It could lead ultimately to fascism." (BL)

Ziegfeld Follies

MGM, 1946. (C-110m.) Dir: Vincente Minnelli (also George Sidney, Roy Del Ruth, Norman Taurog, Lemuel Ayers, Robert Lewis, and Merrill Pye). MS: Various writers. Cast: William Powell, Judy Garland, Fred Astaire, Gene Kelly, Red Skelton, Esther Williams, Kathryn Grayson, Lucille Bremer, Cyd Charisse, Lucille Ball, Fanny Brice, Lena Horne, Edward Arnold, Victor Moore, Hume Cronyn.

On-Screen: *A star-studded musical revue.* MGM's lavish attempt to duplicate a Florenz Ziegfeld extravaganza—William Powell returns from *The Great Ziegfeld* to play the impresario—*Ziegfeld Follies* strikes out more often than it scores. There are scattered highlights: Lena Horne sings "Love" in a gaudy setting suggesting a Martinque bordello, and best of all Fred Astaire and Lucille Bremer dance in a stunningly staged mini-drama to "Limehouse Blues." Judy Garland spoofs Greer Garson's lofty manner in "A Great Lady Gives an Interview," Fred Astaire dances with Gene Kelly in "The Babbitt and the Bromide," and Esther Williams performs a water ballet. In some segments (the finale with Kathryn Grayson, for one), the sets and costumes defy description. They are certainly funnier than the comedy sketches, which are best forgotten.

Off-Screen: Many numbers were filmed for *Ziegfeld Follies* but later deleted. Among them: Fred Astaire performing "If Swing Goes, I Go Too," Lena Horne and Avon Long in "Liza," and Jimmy Durante in a Pied Piper sequence, "Start Off Each Day With a Song." Greer Garson was originally set to do the number "The Interview," but finally declined. (The number, in effect, spoofs her persona.) For the "Limehouse Blues" sequence, the set for *The Picture of Dorian Gray* was repainted and redressed.

Ziegfeld Girl

MGM, 1941. (131m.) Dir: Robert Z. Leonard. Sp: Marguerite Roberts and Sonya Levien, b/o story by William Anthony McGuire. MS: Various writers. Cast: Lana Turner, James Stewart, Judy Garland, Hedy Lamarr, Charles Winninger, Jackie Cooper, Ian Hunter, Tony Martin, Philip Dorn, Eve Arden, Dan Dailey.

On-Screen: *Three Ziegfeld girls share various fates.* A top-heavy blend of lavish spectacle and hard-breathing drama, *Ziegfeld Girl* traces the careers of three girls who become part of Florenz Ziegfeld's musical ménage: exuberant Garland, daughter of vaudevillian Winninger, achieves stardom; beautiful but catatonic Lamarr dallies with singer Martin, then returns to violinist husband Dorn; and Turner, eager for riches and fame, topples off the ladder into alcoholism and death. Turner is required to do most of the heavy emoting, and at this point in her career, it was more than she could handle. She does, however, exude unmistakable star quality. Stewart plays her embittered truck driver boyfriend. There are several eye-popping musical numbers in the gaudy Ziegfeld style, and Garland stars in one of the splashiest, "Minnie From Trinidad."

Off-Screen: The film borrowed several sequences from MGM's earlier production, *The Great Ziegfeld* (1936), including the "wedding cake" set in which Virginia Bruce appeared atop the giant cake. The set was partially reconstructed and in an expert piece of editing, Judy Garland was substituted for Bruce. The musical numbers were staged by Busby Berkeley. Cedric Gibbons's sets and Adrian's costumes might have even impressed Ziegfeld himself.

Zorba the Greek

Fox, 1964. (146m.) Dir: Michael Cacoyannis. Sp: Michael Cacoyannis, b/o novel by

Nikos Kazantzakis. Cast: Anthony Quinn, Alan Bates, Lila Kedrova, Irene Papas, George Foundas.

On-Screen: *Anthony Quinn as the life-embracing Zorba*. Over the years, beginning early in his career when he was everyone's favorite Spaniard or Indian, Anthony Quinn has played many ethnic types. Among these varied roles, none brought him greater acclaim than the lusty, zestful Greek peasant Alexis Zorba in *Zorba the Greek*. Set on the island of Crete, the movie involves Zorba's friendship with a young English writer (Bates), whom he teaches the elemental rules of life, love, and death. Also part of the story are Irene Papas, a beautiful widow who meets a tragic fate, and Lila Kedrova, as Hortense, the aging French prostitute and former lover of admirals, who clings pathetically to her last vestiges of coquetry. All the actors are fine, but Quinn towers above the movie with an exuberant performance that offsets the essentially dark nature of the story. His joyful dance with Bates on the beach is a well-remembered moment. Mikis Theodorakis's score is an irresistible feature.

Off-Screen: *Zobra the Greek* won three Oscars: for Best Supporting Actress (Kedrova), Best Cinematography (black-and-white), and Best Art Direction-Set Decoration (black-and-white). Nominations went to the movie, Quinn, director Cacoyannis, and the screenplay. A stage musical version of the story, entitled *Zorba,* appeared on Broadway in the 1968–1969 season, with Herschel Bernardi as the swaggering peasant and Maria Karnilova as Hortense. Many years later, Anthony Quinn returned to the stage to appear in the role he had made famous, in a revival of the musical.

BIBLIOGRAPHY

Agan, Patrick. *De Niro: The Man, the Myth, and the Movies*. London: Robert Hale, 1989.

Alpert, Hollis. *Burton*. New York: G. P. Putnam's Sons, 1986.

Arce, Hector. *Gary Cooper: An Intimate Biography*. New York: William Morrow and Company, Inc., 1979.

Behlmer, Rudy, editor. *Inside Warner Bros. (1935–1961)*. New York: The Viking Press, 1985.

———. *Memo from David O. Selznick*. New York: The Viking Press, 1972.

Behlmer, Rudy. *America's Favorite Movies: Behind the Scenes*. New York: Frederick Ungar Publishing Co., 1982.

Berg, A. Scott. *Goldwyn: A Biography*. New York: Alfred A. Knopf, 1989.

Bergreen, Laurence. *As Thousands Cheer: The Life of Irving Berlin*. New York: The Viking Press, 1990.

Biskind, Peter. *The Godfather Companion*. New York: Harper Collins Publishers, 1990.

Boller, Paul F., Jr. and Davis, Ronald L. *Hollywood Anecdotes*. New York: William Morrow and Company, Inc., 1987.

Bonderoff, Jason. *Sally Field: A Biography*. New York: St. Martin's Press, 1987.

Braun, Eric. *Deborah Kerr*. New York: St. Martin's Press, 1978.

Brode, Douglas. *The Films of Jack Nicholson*. Secaucus, New Jersey: The Citadel Press, 1987.

Brown, Peter Harry. *Kim Novak: Reluctant Goddess*. New York: St. Martin's Press, 1986.

Cagney, James. *Cagney by Cagney*. Garden City, New York: Doubleday & Company, Inc., 1976.

Capra, Frank. *The Name Above the Title: An Autobiography*. New York: The Macmillan Company, 1971.

Carey, Gary, with Joseph L. Mankiewicz. *More About All About Eve: A Colloquy*. New York: Bantam Books, 1974.

Carey, Gary. *Judy Holliday: An Intimate Biography*. New York: Seaview Books, 1982.

———. *Katharine Hepburn: A Hollywood Yankee*. New York: St. Martin's Press, 1983.

Ciment, Michel. *Kazan on Kazan*. New York: The Viking Press, 1974.

Clarens, Carlos. *Cukor*. London: Secker & Warburg, Limited, 1976.

Clinch, Minty. *Burt Lancaster*. New York: Stein and Day, 1984.

Collier, Peter. *The Fondas: A Hollywood Dynasty*. New York: G. P. Putnam's Sons, 1991.

Cotten, Joseph. *Vanity Will Get You Somewhere*. San Francisco: Mercury House, 1987.

Crist, Judith. *Take 22: Moviemakers on Moviemaking*. New York: Viking-Penguin, 1984.

Cronyn, Hume. *A Terrible Liar: A Memoir*. New York: William Morrow and Company, Inc., 1991.

Curcio, Vincent. *Suicide Blonde: The Life of Glo-*

ria Grahame. New York: William Morrow and Company, Inc., 1989.

Curtis, James. James Whale. Metuchen, New Jersey and London: The Scarecrow Press, 1982.

Davidson, Bill. Jane Fonda: An Intimate Biography. New York: E. P. Dutton, 1990.

———. Spencer Tracy: Tragic Idol. New York: E. P. Dutton, 1987.

Dietrich, Marlene. Marlene. New York: Grove Press, 1987.

DiOrio, Al. Barbara Stanwyck: A Biography. New York: Coward-McCann, Inc., 1983.

Dmytryk, Edward. It's a Hell of a Life but Not a Bad Living. New York: Times Books, 1978.

Douglas, Kirk. The Ragman's Son: An Autobiography. New York: Simon & Schuster, 1988.

Dworkin, Susan. Making "Tootsie". New York: Newmarket Press, 1983.

Eastman, John. Retakes: Behind the Scenes of 500 Classic Movies. New York: Ballantine Books, 1989.

Edwards, Anne. Shirley Temple: American Princess. New York: William Morrow and Company, Inc., 1988.

Eells, George and Musgrove, Stanley. Mae West: A Biography. New York: William Morrow and Company, Inc. 1982.

Eells, George. Robert Mitchum: A Biography. New York, Toronto: Franklin Watts, 1984.

Eyles, Allen. James Stewart. New York: Stein and Day, 1984.

Finch, Christopher. Rainbow: The Stormy Life of Judy Garland. New York: Grosset & Dunlap, 1975.

Fonda, Henry. Fonda: My Life. As told to Howard Teichmann. New York: New American Library, 1981.

Fontaine, Joan. No Bed of Roses: An Autobiography. New York: William Morrow and Company, Inc., 1978.

Fordin, Hugh. The World of Entertainment!: Hollywood's Greatest Musicals. Garden City, New York: Doubleday and Company, Inc., 1975.

Francisco, Charles. Gentleman: The William Powell Story. New York: St. Martin's Press, 1985.

Freedland, Michael. Jack Lemmon. New York: St. Martin's Press, 1985.

———. Gregory Peck. New York: William Morrow and Company, Inc., 1980.

Gardner, Ava. Ava: My Story. New York: Bantam Books, 1990.

Garnett, Tay, with Fredda Dudley Balling. Light Your Torches and Pull Up Your Tights. New Rochelle, New York: Arlington House, 1973.

Geist, Kenneth L. Pictures Will Talk: The Life and Films of Joseph L. Mankiewicz. New York: Charles Scribner's Sons, 1978.

Giles, Sarah. Fred Astaire: His Friends Talk. New York: Doubleday & Company, Inc. 1988.

Givens, Bill. Film Flubs: Memorable Movie Mistakes. New York: Citadel Press, 1990.

Golden, Eve. Platinum Girl: The Life and Legends of Jean Harlow. New York: Abbeville Press, 1991.

Goldstein, Toby. William Hurt: The Man, the Actor. New York: St. Martin's Press, 1987.

Goodwin, Michael and Wise, Naomi. On the Edge: The Life and Times of Francis Coppola. New York: William Morrow and Company, Inc., 1988.

Gottfried, Martin. All His Jazz: The Life and Death of Bob Fosse. New York: Bantam Books, 1990.

Grobel, Lawrence. The Hustons. New York: Charles Scribner's Sons, 1989.

Grubb, Kevin Boyd. Razzle Dazzle: The Life and Work of Bob Fosse. New York: St. Martin's Press, 1989.

Guiles, Fred Lawrence. Tyrone Power: The Last Idol. San Francisco: Mercury House, 1979.

Harris, Warren G. Cary Grant: A Touch of Elegance. New York: Doubleday & Company, Inc. 1987.

Harrison, Rex. A Damned Serious Business. New York: Bantam Books, 1991.

———. Rex: An Autobiography. William Morrow and Company, Inc., 1975.

Harvey, Stephen. Directed by Vincente Minnelli. New York: The Museum of Modern Art/Harper & Row, Publishers, 1989.

Hayne, Donald, editor. The Autobiography of Cecil B. DeMille. New York and London, Garland Publishing, Inc., 1985.

Henreid, Paul, with Julian Fast. *Ladies' Man*. New York: St. Martin's Press, 1984.

Hepburn, Katharine. *Me: Stories of My Life*. New York: Random House, 1991.

Higham, Charles and Moseley, Roy. *Princess Merle: The Romantic Life of Merle Oberon*. New York: Coward-McCann, Inc., 1983.

Higham, Charles. *Audrey: The Life of Audrey Hepburn*. New York: Macmillan Publishing Company, Inc., 1984.

———. *Brando: The Unauthorized Biography*. New York: New American Library, 1989.

———. *Cecil B. DeMille*. New York: Da Capo Press, 1973.

———. *Charles Laughton: An Intimate Biography*. Garden City, New York: Doubleday & Co., Inc., 1976.

———. *Kate: The Life of Katharine Hepburn*. New York: W. W. Norton & Company, Inc., 1975.

Hirschhorn, Clive. *Gene Kelly: A Biography*. London: W. H. Allen, 1974.

Holtzman, William. *Seesaw: A Dual Biography of Anne Bancroft and Mel Brooks*. Garden City, New York: Doubleday & Company, Inc., 1979.

Hunter, Allan. *Gene Hackman*. New York: St. Martin's Press, 1987.

———. *Walter Matthau*. New York: St. Martin's Press, 1984.

Kaminsky, Stuart. *Coop: The Life and Legend of Gary Cooper*. New York: St. Martin's Press, 1980.

Kelley, Kitty. *Elizabeth Taylor: The Last Star*. New York: Simon & Schuster, 1981.

Kobal, John. *Rita Hayworth: The Time, the Place, and the Woman*. London: W. H. Allen, 1977.

Koch, Howard. *As Time Goes By: Memoirs of a Writer*. New York and London: Harcourt Brace Jovanovich, 1979.

LaGuardia, Robert and Arceri, Gene. *Red: The Tempestuous Life of Susan Hayward*. New York: Macmillan Publishing Company, Inc., 1985.

Lambert, Gavin. *Norma Shearer: A Life*. New York: Alfred A. Knopf, 1990.

Lawrence, Jerome. *Actor: The Life and Times of Paul Muni*. New York: G. P. Putnam's Sons, 1974.

Leaming, Barbara. *If This Was Happiness: A Biography of Rita Hayworth*. New York: Viking Press, 1989.

LeRoy, Mervyn. *Take One*. As told to Dick Kleiner. New York: Hawthorn Books, Inc., 1974.

Lewis, Jerry, with Herb Gluck. *Jerry Lewis in Person*. New York: Atheneum, 1982.

Leyda, Jay, editor. *Voices of Film Experience: 1894 to the Present*. New York: Macmillan Publishing Company, Inc., 1977.

Linet, Beverly. *Ladd: The Life, the Legend, the Legacy of Alan Ladd*. New York: Arbor House, 1979.

———. *Susan Hayward: Portrait of a Survivor*. New York: Atheneum, 1980.

Loy, Myrna and Kotsilibas-Davis, James. *Myrna Loy: Being and Becoming*. New York: Alfred A. Knopf, 1987.

MacAdams, William. *Ben Hecht: The Man Behind the Legend*. New York: Charles Scribner's Sons, 1990.

Marx, Arthur. *Red Skelton: An Unauthorized Biography*. New York: E. P. Dutton, 1979.

Mason, James. *Before I Forget: An Autobiography*. London: Hamish Hamilton, 1981.

McClelland, Doug. *Hollywood Talks Turkey*. Boston and London: Faber and Faber, 1989.

———. *The Unkindest Cuts: The Scissors and the Cinema*. South Brunswick and New York: A. S. Barnes and Company, 1972.

McGilligan, Patrick. *George Cukor: A Double Life*. New York: St. Martin's Press, 1991.

———. *Robert Altman: Jumping Off the Cliff*. New York: St. Martin's Press, 1989.

Merman, Ethel. *Merm*. New York: Simon & Schuster, 1978.

Morella, Joe and Epstein, Edward Z. *Jane Wyman: An Autobiography*. New York: Delacorte Press, 1985.

———. *Loretta Young: An Extraordinary Life*. New York: Delacorte Press, 1986.

———. *Mia: The Life of Mia Farrow*. New York: Delacorte Press, 1991.

———. *Paul and Joanne: A Biography of Paul Newman and Joanne Woodward*. New York: Delacorte Press, 1988.

Morley, Sheridan. *The Other Side of the Moon: A Biography of David Niven*. New York: Harper & Row, Publishers, 1985.

Mosley, Leonard. *Zanuck: The Rise and Fall of Hollywood's Last Tycoon*. Boston, Toronto: Little, Brown and Company, 1984.

Mott, Donald and Saunders, Cheryl McAllister. *Steven Spielberg*. Boston: Twayne Publishers, 1986.

Nash, Jay Robert and Ross, Stanley Ralph. *The Motion Picture Guide*. Chicago: Cinebooks, 1985.

Nelson, Nancy. *Evenings with Cary Grant: Reflections in His Own Words and By Those Who Knew Him Best*. New York: William Morrow and Company, Inc., 1991.

Newquist, Roy. *Conversations with Joan Crawford*. Secaucus, New Jersey: The Citadel Press, 1980.

Niven, David. *The Moon's a Balloon: An Autobiography*. New York: G. P. Putnam's Sons, 1972.

Oppenheimer, Jerry and Vitek, Jack. *Idol: Rock Hudson—The True Story of an American Film Hero*. New York: Villard Books, 1986.

Oumano, Elana. *Paul Newman*. New York: St. Martin's Press, 1989.

Parish, James Robert. *The Jeanette MacDonald Story*. New York: Mason/Charter, 1976.

Peary, Danny. *Cult Movies*. New York: Delta Books, 1981.

Preminger, Otto. *Preminger: An Autobiography*. New York: Doubleday & Company, Inc., 1977.

Quirk, Lawrence J. *Norma: The Story of Norma Shearer*. New York: St. Martin's Press, 1988.

———. *Totally Uninhibited: The Life and Wild Times of Cher*. New York: William Morrow and Company, 1991.

———. *Fasten Your Seat Belts: The Passionate Life of Bette Davis*. New York: William Morrow and Company, Inc., 1990.

———. *Margaret Sullavan: Child of Fate*. New York: St. Martin's Press, 1986.

Riese, Randall and Hitchens, Neal. *The Unabridged Marilyn: Her Life from A to Z*. New York and Chicago: Congdon & Weed, Inc., 1987.

Robbins, Jhan. *Yul Brynner: The Inscrutable King*. New York: Dodd Mead & Company, 1987.

———. *Everybody's Man: A Biography of James Stewart*. New York: G. P. Putnam's Sons, 1985.

Robertson, Patrick. *Movie Clips*. Middlesex, England: Guinness Books, 1989.

Rodgers, Richard. *Musical Stages*. New York: Random House, 1975.

Rogers, Ginger. *Ginger: My Story*. New York: Harper Collins Publishers, 1991.

Sackett, Susan. *The Hollywood Reporter Book of Box Office Hits*. New York: Billboard Books, 1990.

Schary, Dore. *Heyday: An Autobiography*. Boston, Toronto: Little, Brown and Company, Inc., 1979.

Schickel, Richard. *Brando: A Life in Our Times*. New York: Atheneum, 1991.

Segaloff, William. *Hurricane Billy: The Stormy Life and Films of William Friedkin*. New York: William Morrow and Company, Inc., 1990.

Shepherd, Donald and Slatzer, Robert, with Dave Grayson. *Duke: The Life and Times of John Wayne*. New York: Doubleday and Company, 1985.

Sheppard, Dick. *Elizabeth: The Life and Career of Elizabeth Taylor*. Garden City, New York: Doubleday & Company, Inc., 1974.

Spada, James. *Grace: The Secret Lives of a Princess*. Garden City, New York: Doubleday & Company, Inc., 1987.

———. *Peter Lawford: The Man Who Kept the Secrets*. New York: Bantam Books, 1991.

Stine, Whitney. *"I'd Love to Kiss You": Conversations with Bette Davis*. New York: Pocket Books, 1989.

———. *Mother Goddam: The Story of the Career of Bette Davis*. New York: Hawthorn Books, Inc., Publishers, 1974.

Strait, Raymond and Robinson, Terry. *Lanza: His Tragic Life*. Englewood Cliffs, New Jersey: Prentice-Hall, Inc., 1980.

Strait, Raymond. *Alan Alda: A Biography*. New York: St. Martin's Press, 1983.

———. *James Garner*. New York: St. Martin's Press, 1985.

Sturges, Preston. *Preston Sturges: His Life in His Words*. Adapted and edited by Sandy Sturges. New York: Simon & Schuster, 1990.

Swindell, Larry. *Body and Soul: The Story of John Garfield*. New York: William Morrow and Company, Inc., 1975.

———. *Screwball: The Life of Carole Lombard*. New York: William Morrow and Company, Inc., 1975.

———. *Spencer Tracy: A Biography*. New York and Cleveland: The World Publishing Company, 1969.

Taylor, John Russell. *Hitch: The Life and Times of Alfred Hitchcock*. New York: Berkley Books, 1978.

Thomas, Bob. *Clown Prince of Hollywood: The Antic Life and Times of Jack L. Warner*. New York: McGraw-Hill Publishing Company, 1990.

———. *Fred Astaire: The Man and the Dancer*. New York: St. Martin's Press, 1984.

———. *Golden Boy: The Untold Story of William Holden*. New York: St. Martin's Press, 1983.

———. *Joan Crawford: A Biography*. New York: Simon & Schuster, 1978.

———. *King Cohn: The Life and Times of Harry Cohn*. New York: G. P. Putnam's Sons, 1967.

Thomas, Tony and Terry, Jim, with Busby Berkeley. *The Busby Berkeley Book*. New York: A & W Visual Library, 1973.

Thomas, Tony. *The Films of Gene Kelly: Song and Dance Man*. Secaucus, New Jersey: The Citadel Press, 1974.

Thompson, Charles. *Bing: The Authorized Biography*. New York: David McKay Company, Inc., 1975.

Thompson, Frank T. *William A. Wellman*. Metuchen, New Jersey and London: The Scarecrow Press, 1983.

Tornabene, Lyn. *Long Live the King: A Biography of Clark Gable*. New York: G. P. Putnam's Sons, 1976.

Ustinov, Peter. *Dear Me*. Boston, Toronto: Little, Brown and Company, 1977.

van Gelder, Peter. *That's Hollywood: A Behind-the-Scenes Look at 60 of the Greatest Films of All Time*. New York: Harper Collins Publishers, 1990.

Walker, Alexander. *Garbo: A Portrait*. New York: Macmillan Publishing Company, Inc., 1980.

———. *Joan Crawford: The Ultimate Star*. Harper & Row, Publishers, 1983.

———. *Peter Sellers: The Authorized Biography*. London: Weidenfeld & Nicolson, 1981.

Wallis, Hal and Higham, Charles. *Starmaker: The Autobiography of Hal Wallis*. New York: Macmillan Publishing Company, Inc., 1980.

Warren, Doug. *Betty Grable: The Reluctant Movie Queen*. New York: St. Martin's Press, 1974.

Wayne, Jane Ellen. *Stanwyck*. New York: Arbor House, 1985.

Widener, Don. *Lemmon*. New York: Macmillan Publishing Company, Inc., 1975.

Wiley, Mason and Bona, Damien. *Inside Oscar: The Unauthorized History of the Academy Awards*. New York: Ballantine Books, 1987.

Woodward, Ian. *Audrey Hepburn*. New York: St. Martin's Press, 1984.

Yablonsky, Lewis. *George Raft*. New York: New American Library, 1974.

Yule, Andrew. *Life on the Wire: The Life and Art of Al Pacino*. New York: Donald I. Fine, 1991.

CAST INDEX

Foronjy, Richard, 427
Forrest, Frederic, 36, 455
Forrest, Steve, 354
Forristal, Susan, 290
Forster, Robert, 446
Forsythe, John, 30, 260, 559
Forsythe, William, 141, 440
Forte, Nick Apollo, 84
Fosse, Bob, 286
Fosse, Nicole, 109
Foster, Dianne, 294
Foster, Jodie, 11, 20, 484, 528
Foster, Preston, 233, 256, 264
Foundas, George, 607
Fourcade, Christian, 308
Fowley, Douglas, 53, 487
Fox, James, 221, 543
Fox, Michael J., 44, 101
Foy, Jr., Eddie, 58, 404, 586
Francen, Victor, 243, 377
Franceschi, Antonio, 170
Franciosa, Anthony, 168, 233, 314
Francis, Anne, 45, 67, 182, 193
Francis, Arlene, 398, 546
Francis, Kay, 261, 558
Francis, Robert, 94
Francks, Don, 176
François, Jacques, 51
Franklin, Bonnie, 596
Franz, Arthur, 464
Franz, Dennis, 70, 154
Franz, Eduard, 216, 539
Fraser, Elizabeth, 330
Fraser, Liz, 28
Frawley, William, 205, 348
Frazee, Jane, 86
Frazer, Dan, 306
Frazer, Rupert, 163
Frederici, Blanche, 171
Frederick, Vicki, 109
Freed, Bert, 139
Freeman, J. E., 346
Freeman, Jr., Al, 176, 327
Freeman, Kathleen, 178, 387
Freeman, Mona, 236, 358
Freeman, Morgan, 74, 154, 202,
    453, 566
Freeman, Paul, 437
Frees, Paul, 514
Frewer, Matt, 246
Frey, Leonard, 174
Frizell, Lou, 517
Frye, Dwight, 153, 188
Frye, Sean, 165
Fung, Willie, 301
Furlong, Edward, 531
Furness, Betty, 525
Furst, Stephen, 372
Furth, George, 90

Gabel, Martin, 145
Gable, Clark, 76, 118, 207, 269,
    349, 353, 366, 444, 463, 532

Gabor, Eva, 200
Gabor, Zsa Zsa, 305, 359
Gaines, Richard, 164, 320, 357
Gallagher, Peter, 420, 475
Galloway, Don, 62
Garber, Matthew, 336
Garbo, Greta, 33, 95, 214, 380, 433
Garcia, Andy, 134, 204, 238, 568
Gardenia, Vincent, 255, 356, 582
Gardiner, Reginald, 126, 149, 216,
    330, 524
Gardner, Ava, 49, 282, 303, 353,
    379, 394, 473, 483, 491
Garfield, Allen, 121, 372
Garfield, John, 17, 73, 187, 197,
    244, 252, 278, 424, 426, 468,
    533
Garfunkel, Arthur, 99, 103
Gargan, William, 59, 600
Garland, Judy, 42, 113, 160, 180,
    201, 233, 261, 279, 319, 340,
    416, 504, 517, 534, 547, 590,
    592, 605, 606
Garner, James, 28, 217, 466, 546,
    573
Garner, Jay, 409
Garner, Peggy Ann, 261, 557
Garrett, Betty, 395, 592
Garrison, Sean, 500
Garr, Teri, 16, 114, 551, 602
Garson, Greer, 211, 364, 426, 440
Gary, Lorraine, 273
Gates, Larry, 262, 267, 464
Gates, Nancy, 514
Gavin, John, 431, 497, 543
Gaye, Gregory, 147
Gaynes, George, 551
Gaynor, Janet, 503
Gaynor, Mitzi, 300, 497, 535
Gazzara, Ben, 29
Gazzo, Michael V., 204
Gear, Luella, 98
Geddes, Barbara Bel, 572
Geer, Ellen, 230
Geer, Will, 85, 260, 266
Gelin, Daniel, 331
Genn, Leo, 352, 434, 489
George, Chief Dan, 231
George, Gladys, 60, 328, 451
Georgeson, Tom, 176
Georges-Picot, Olga, 318
Geray, Steven, 200
Gere, Richard, 121, 133, 391, 425
Gerle, Milton, 321
Gerry, Alex, 305
Getty, Estelle, 337
Getz, John, 69
Ghostley, Alice, 212, 215
Giannini, Giancarlo, 376
Gibbons, Ayliene, 321
Gibson, Henry, 313, 371, 387
Gibson, Mel, 300
Gibson, Virginia, 472

Gielgud, John, 37, 56, 162, 321
Gilbert, Billy, 139, 216, 241, 347,
    397
Gilbert, Jody, 375
Gilbert, John, 433
Gilbert, Lou, 574
Gilchrist, Connie, 270, 302, 329
Gilford, Jack, 103, 115, 465
Gillette, Anita, 356
Gillette, Ruth, 259
Gilley, Mickey, 570
Gilliam, Burton, 68, 405
Gilmore, Douglas, 237
Gilmore, Lowell, 414
Gilmore, Margalo, 241
Gingold, Hermione, 200, 365, 534,
    594
Ginty, Robert, 117
Girardot, Etienne, 562
Gish, Lillian, 156, 378, 422, 565, 580
Glaser, Michael, 174
Glass, Ned, 105, 579
Gleason, Jackie, 255
Gleason, James, 42, 113, 238, 294,
    340, 378, 514, 557
Gleason, Joanna, 123
Gleason, Lucille, 113
Gleason, Russell, 23
Gleaves, Abraham, 220
Glenn Miller and His Orchestra, 519
Glenn, Scott, 372, 449, 484, 486,
    570
Glenn, Sr., Roy E., 222
Glick, Stacey, 83
Glover, Crispin, 44, 450
Glover, Danny, 300, 417, 486, 589
Glover, John, 279
Glover, Julian, 263
Glover, Kevin, 213
Glynn, Carlin, 558
Goddard, Paulette, 102, 216, 243,
    352, 592
Godunov, Alexander, 142, 589
Goethals, Angela, 245
Goldberg, Whoopi, 198, 315, 420
Goldblum, Jeff, 62, 372, 449, 486
Golden, Annie, 228
Goldstein, Jenette, 21
Goldstein, Steve, 248
Gold, Tracey, 481
Goldwyn, Tony, 198
Golino, Valeria, 438
Golm, Lisa, 116
Gombell, Minna, 539
Gomez, Thomas, 281
Gomez, Vincente, 491
Gompf, Alison, 107
Goodall, Caroline, 247
Gooding, Jr., Cuba, 80
Goodman, Benny, and His Orches-
    tra, 195
Goodman, Dody, 215
Goodman, John, 26, 51, 440, 523

Goodwin, Bill, 277
Gorcey, Leo, 31
Gordon, C. Henry, 106, 466
Gordon, Christine, 257
Gordon, Don, 89
Gordon, Keith, 154
Gordon, Ruth, 230, 457, 582
Goring, Marius, 49
Gorman, Cliff, 23, 568
Gorney, Karen Lynn, 465
Gorshin, Frank, 58
Gossett, Jr., Louis, 391, 439
Gottlieb, Carl, 273
Gough, Michael, 53, 401
Gould, Elliott, 72, 88, 313, 337
Gould, Harold, 318, 509
Gould, Jason, 428
Goz, Harry, 354
Grable, Betty, 119, 149, 151, 179,
    250, 358
Grahame, Gloria, 45, 63, 124, 219,
    259, 341, 392, 588
Grahame, Margot, 264
Graham, Gerit, 571
Graham, Heather, 155
Graham, Therese, 122
Granach, Alexander, 380
Granger, Farley, 230, 455, 512
Granger, Stewart, 285
Grant, Cary, 40, 83, 105, 225, 241,
    243, 259, 261, 355, 361, 368,
    377, 382, 383, 385, 399, 410,
    413, 478, 521, 527, 548, 553
Grant, Kathryn, 29, 400
Grant, Lee, 139, 145, 262, 477
Grant, Richard E., 290
Grant, Rodney A., 127
Granville, Bonita, 358, 386, 536
Grapewin, Charley, 97, 208, 214,
    302, 411, 536, 590
Graves, Peter, 17, 378, 501
Gray, Billy, 133
Gray, Charles, 474
Gray, Coleen, 283, 287, 380, 444
Gray, Dolores, 272
Gray, Gilda, 456
Gray, Joel, 474
Gray, Nadia, 563
Grayson, Kathryn, 30, 286, 483,
    547, 605
Gray, Spalding, 54
Greco, Jose, 480
Green, Adolph, 368
Greene, Graham, 127
Greene, Lorne, 412
Green, Seth, 435
Greenstreet, Sydney, 12, 100, 244,
    327, 536, 545
Greenwood, Charlotte, 151, 195,
    392
Greer, Jane, 402
Gregg, Virginia, 258
Gregorio, Rose, 559

Gregory, Andre, 296
Gregory, James, 222, 333
Gregory, Mary, 488
Greig, Robert, 32, 247, 320, 405,
    515, 558, 565
Greist, Kim, 546
Grenfell, Joyce, 28
Grey, Jennifer, 143
Grey, Joel, 87, 93
Grey, Virginia, 456
Griem, Helmut, 93
Grier, Pam, 184
Grifasi, Joe, 425
Griffies, Ethel, 66
Griffith, Andy, 168
Griffith, Hugh, 59, 166
Griffith, Kristin, 265
Griffith, Melanie, 74, 593
Grimes, Gary, 516
Grizzard, George, 15
Grodin, Charles, 234, 269, 457
Guardino, Harry, 145
Guastaferro, Vincent, 246
Guest, Christopher, 174, 428, 541
Guetary, Georges, 28
Guffey, Cary, 114
Guinness, Alec, 82, 147, 163, 299,
    447, 505
Gunton, Bob, 203
Gunty, Morty, 84
Guss, Louis, 356
Guthrie, Arlo, 20
Guttenberg, Steve, 79, 115, 142
Gwaltney, Jack, 101
Gwenn, Edmund, 183, 293, 304,
    347, 426, 559
Gwynne, Fred, 121, 172, 268, 476

Haas, Hugo, 285
Haas, Lukas, 589
Hackes, Peter, 84
Hackett, Buddy, 271, 310, 365
Hackett, Joan, 222
Hackman, Gene, 75, 189, 350, 382,
    423, 424, 445, 520, 562, 566,
    602
Hack, Shelley, 285
Haden, Sara, 482
Hagen, Jean, 13, 38, 487
Hagen, Uta, 79, 447
Hagerty, Julie, 17
Hagman, Larry, 169, 222, 231
Hague, Albert, 170
Haigh, Kenneth, 113
Haines, Larry, 389
Hale, Alan, 14, 175, 269, 377, 390,
    468, 509, 537, 542
Hale, Barbara, 18, 586
Hale, Jonathan, 513
Hale, Louis Closser, 478
Haley, Jack, 18, 590
Haley, Jackie Earle, 81
Hallahan, Charles, 485

Hall, Albert, 36, 327
Hallatt, May, 470
Hall, Grayson, 379
Hall, Huntz, 31, 575
Halliday, John, 266, 413
Hall, James, 237
Hall Johnson Choir, 220
Hall, Jon, 253, 292
Hall, Juanita, 497
Hall, Porter, 12, 149, 241, 266, 326,
    347, 348, 411, 418, 510, 515,
    539
Hall, Ruth, 354
Hall, Thurston, 159, 218, 599
Halop, Billy, 31
Halton, Charles, 12
Hamill, Mark, 163, 447, 505
Hamilton, George, 204
Hamilton, Linda, 531
Hamilton, Margaret, 369, 384, 410,
    536, 590, 600
Hamilton, Murray, 29, 212, 255,
    273, 578
Hamilton, Neil, 528
Hamilton, Suzanna, 401
Hampden, Walter, 25, 462
Hamptom, James, 108
Hancock, Barbara, 176
Hancock, John, 74
Handy, James, 65
Handzlik, Jan, 39
Haney, Carol, 286, 404
Hanks, Tom, 61, 74
Hannah, Daryl, 67, 457, 508, 575
Hansen, Gale, 135
Hansen, William, 465
Harareet, Haya, 59
Harden, Marcia Gay, 346
Harding, Ann, 329
Hardman, Karl, 379
Hardwicke, Cedric, 56, 252, 257,
    455, 521, 586
Hardy, Oliver, 578
Hardy, Sam, 284
Hare, Lumsden, 384
Hare, Will, 455
Harewood, Dorian, 192
Harlow, Jean, 74, 143, 237, 302,
    431, 444
Harmon, Deborah, 571
Harolde, Ralf, 259
Harper, Jessica, 368, 409, 505
Harper, Tess, 269, 329
Harrigan, William, 171, 267
Harrington, Kate, 435
Harris, Barbara, 371, 409
Harris, Ed, 201, 417, 449, 523
Harris, Julie, 159, 212, 231, 446
Harris, Leonard, 528
Harris, Marilyn, 188
Harrison, Kathleen, 378
Harrison, Linda, 419
Harrison, Rex, 32, 112, 367, 565

McNamara, Maggie, 356, 543
Macnaughton, Robert, 165
McNeil, Claudia, 439
MacNichol, Peter, 494
McPhail, Douglas, 42
McQueen, Armelia, 198
McQueen, Butterfly, 94, 157, 207, 346
McQueen, Steve, 89, 217, 463, 555
McRae, Frank, 185, 571
MacRae, Gordon, 99, 392
Macready, George, 139, 200, 407, 473, 494
McShane, Michael, 453
McWilliams, Caroline, 342
Macy, Bill, 146, 297, 368
Macy, William H., 246
Madigan, Amy, 175, 417, 562
Madison, Guy, 486
Madison, Julian, 270
Madonna, 141, 476
Madsen, Michael, 535
Maggart, Brandon, 154
Magnani, Anna, 456
Mahal, Taj, 496
Mahoney, John, 51, 356
Maia, Nuno Leal, 287
Main, Marjorie, 135, 190, 233, 234, 340, 517, 532, 592
Mako, 464
Malden, Karl, 43, 66, 76, 107, 226, 287, 387, 396, 399, 408, 513
Malina, Judith, 14, 165
Malkovich, John, 128, 163, 417, 476
Malone, Dorothy, 64, 595
Mamo, 366
Manchester, Melissa, 181
Mander, Miles, 365, 596
Manners, David, 153, 364
Mann, Hank, 352
Manning, Irene, 597
Mann, Paul, 174
Mann, Terrence, 109
Manoff, Dinah, 400
Mantegna, Joe, 19, 88, 204, 246, 248
Mantell, Joe, 108, 336
Manz, Linda, 133
Mara, Adele, 464, 601
Mara, Mary, 362
Maranne, Andre, 130
Marchand, Colette, 359
Marchand, Nancy, 248, 446
March, Fredric, 33, 60, 138, 151, 166, 245, 265, 329, 384, 473, 503
Mardirosian, Tom, 425
Margo, 258, 574
Margolin, Janet, 34, 526
Margolin, Stuart, 133
Margulies, David, 154
Marin, Cheech, 16
Marin, Jacques, 105, 130
Marino, Kenny, 427

Marion, George F., 33
Marley, John, 203, 321
Marlowe, Hugh, 22, 66, 133, 162, 355, 473, 561
Marquis, Rosalind, 334
Marsalis, Branford, 546
Marshal, Alan, 378, 550
Marshall, Brenda, 468
Marshall, Connie, 358, 361
Marshall, E. G., 94, 118, 265, 561
Marshall, Herbert, 156, 164, 178, 183, 301, 309, 441, 558
Marshall, James, 174
Marshall, Patricia, 209
Marshall, Sarah, 314
Marshall, Tully, 46, 541
Mars, Kenneth, 90, 430, 435, 476, 581, 602
Martel, K. C., 165
Martin, Barney, 37, 106
Martin, Chris-Pin, 501
Martin, Dean, 18, 58, 450, 602
Martin, Dewey, 138, 539
Martin, Lewis, 576
Martin, Lock, 133
Martin, Lori, 96
Martin, Mary, 377
Martin, Nan, 209
Martin, Steve, 213, 290, 406, 409, 457
Martin, Strother, 90, 120, 231, 560
Martin, Tony, 547, 606
Marvin, Lee, 45, 63, 94, 144, 331, 421, 480, 585
Marx, Chico, 32, 132, 156, 247, 354, 377
Marx, Groucho, 32, 132, 156, 247, 354, 377
Marx, Harpo, 32, 132, 156, 247, 354, 377
Marx, Zeppo, 32, 156, 247, 354
Mason, James, 79, 311, 324, 383, 504, 572
Mason, Marsha, 210
Massey, Raymond, 131, 159, 253, 429, 591
Masterson, Mary Stuart, 190
Mastrantonio, Mary Elizabeth, 116, 453
Mather, Aubrey, 46
Mathers, Jerry, 559
Matheson, Murray, 250
Matheson, Tim, 372
Mathews, Carmen, 496
Mathews, George, 332, 407, 569
Matlin, Marlee, 107
Matthau, Walter, 105, 168, 169, 185, 236, 276, 312, 389
Matthews, Carmen, 128
Mattox, Matt, 472
Mature, Victor, 287, 367, 452
Mauldin, Bill, 443
Maurey, Nicole, 308

Max, Edwin, 116
Maxwell, Marilyn, 104, 516
Mayhew, Peter, 163, 447
May, Jodhi, 294
Mayo, Virginia, 60, 583
Mayo, Whitman, 80
Mayron, Melanie, 231, 350
Mazurki, Mike, 365, 380
Mazursky, Paul, 165
Meade, Julia, 414
Meadows, Jayne, 131
Means, Russell, 294
Meara, Anne, 40, 79, 170
Medford, Kay, 91, 168, 193
Meek, Donald, 42, 97, 264, 274, 369, 501, 507, 600, 603
Meeker, Ralph, 144, 407
Megna, John, 550
Megowan, Debbie, 134
Mellish, Jr., Fuller, 36
Meltzer, Jim, 396
Memmoli, George, 339, 376
Menjou, Adolphe, 171, 206, 357, 397, 407, 500, 503, 508, 601
Merande, Doro, 332, 401, 460, 474
Mercer, Beryl, 23, 378, 431
Meredith, Burgess, 15, 132, 187, 391, 454, 550, 559
Meredith, Lee, 430
Merivale, Philip, 360, 512
Merkel, Una, 49, 74, 77, 139, 186, 343, 587
Merman, Ethel, 18, 271, 535
Merrill, Dina, 91, 420, 519
Merrill, Gary, 22, 561
Merrow, Jane, 307
Messemer, Hannes, 217
Methot, Mayo, 334, 361
Meyer, Emile, 67, 332
Meyers, Michael, 209
Michael, Gertrude, 259
Middleton, Gabrielle, 563
Middleton, Robert, 138
Midler, Bette, 54, 150, 181, 455, 460
Mike the dog, 150
Miles, Bernard, 331, 352
Miles, Sylvia, 344, 575
Miles, Vera, 331, 431, 470, 595
Milford, Penelope, 117
Miljan, John, 57
Milland, Ray, 55, 140, 160, 292, 297, 317, 321, 326, 567
Miller, Ann, 160, 286, 395, 500, 600
Miller, Barry, 110, 170, 409, 465
Miller, Dick, 16, 376
Miller, Jason, 167
Miller, Joshua, 450
Miller, Penelope Ann, 65, 104
Miller, Rebecca, 446
Miller, Sidney, 502
Miller, Susan, 375
Mills, John, 211
Milner, Martin, 118, 304, 523

Savage, Fred, 428
Savage, John, 136, 146, 228
Savalas, Telly, 66, 144
Sawyer, Joe, 150, 200, 264, 283
Saxon, John, 565
Scacchi, Greta, 419, 425
Scarwid, Diana, 354, 485
Schallert, William, 262, 312
Scheider, Roy, 23, 189, 273, 334
Schell, Maximilian, 110, 279, 602
Schiavelli, Vincent, 198
Schildkraut, Joseph, 141, 304, 439, 482
Schilling, Gus, 292
Schilling, William G., 460
Schmidt, Jr., Benno C., 254
Schoeffling, Michael, 342
Schuck, John, 337, 538
Schultz, Dwight, 315
Schumann-Heink, F., 237
Schunzel, Reinhold, 385
Schwarzenegger, Arnold, 531
Schweig, Eric, 294
Schygulla, Hanna, 134
Sciorra, Annabella, 280, 447
Scooler, Zvee, 318
Scorsese, Martin, 223
Scott, Douglas, 266
Scott, George C., 29, 152, 248, 255, 408, 411
Scott, Ken, 544
Scott, Lizabeth, 511
Scott, Martha, 59, 138, 401, 466, 530, 560
Scott, Pippa, 411
Scott, Randolph, 179, 274, 368, 448, 452
Scott, Robert, 200
Scott, Zachary, 345
Scourby, Alexander, 63
Seberg, Jean, 18
Sedgwick, Kyra, 77, 360
Seeger, Pete, 20
Segal, George, 181, 480, 554, 582, 584
Sellers, Peter, 57, 152, 311, 415, 482, 594
Sellon, Charles, 270
Sessions, Almira, 347
Seth, Roshan, 264
Severn, William, 277
Seymour, Dan, 549
Shalhoub, Tony, 51
Sharif, Omar, 147, 193, 299
Sharpe, Albert, 458
Shatner, William, 279, 504
Shaughnessy, Mickey, 191, 273, 335
Shaver, Helen, 116
Shawlee, Joan, 35, 492
Shawn, Dick, 271, 430
Shawn, Wallace, 428, 435
Shaw, Reta, 404
Shaw, Robert, 273, 509

Shaw, Sebastian, 447
Shaw, Stan, 190
Shayne, Konstantin, 512
Shayne, Robert, 362, 545
Shayne, Tamara, 277
Shea, Eric, 488
Shea, John, 350
Shean, Al, 463
Shearer, Harry, 177, 541
Shearer, Norma, 592
Sheedy, Ally, 563
Sheen, Charlie, 419, 575
Sheen, Martin, 36, 46, 103
Sheiner, David, 389
Sheldon, Gene, 149
Shelle, Lori, 209
Shelley, Carol, 389
Shepard, Sam, 122, 133, 449, 508
Shepherd, Cybill, 19, 234, 295, 528
Sheridan, Ann, 31, 111, 286, 330, 533, 537
Sheridan, Margaret, 539
Sherman, Hiram, 491
Sherwood, Bobby, 404
Sherwood, Madeleine, 102, 522
Shields, Arthur, 121, 155, 314, 433, 479
Shire, Talia, 203, 204, 376, 454
Shirley, Anne, 24, 365, 509
Shoemaker, Ann, 19, 368, 509
Shore, Dinah, 547, 569
Showalter, Max, 529, 587
Shultis, Jackie, 133
Sidney, Sylvia, 135, 194, 518, 600–601
Siemaszko, Casey, 65
Sierra, Gregory, 555
Signoret, Simone, 480
Sikking, James B., 400
Silva, Henry, 233, 333
Silverheels, Jay, 85, 281
Silver, Joel, 583
Silverman, Jonathan, 83
Silver, Ron, 165, 362, 447, 485
Silvers, Phil, 119, 123, 271, 517, 550
Silvers, Sid, 77
Simmons, Jean, 63, 145, 162, 225, 452, 497
Simms, Ginny, 377
Simon, Paul, 34
Simon, Simone, 24, 103
Simpson, O. J., 555
Simpson, Russell, 214
Sinatra, Frank, 30, 191, 225, 241, 332, 333, 395, 404, 514, 533, 534, 547
Sinden, Donald, 353
Sivero, Frank, 211
Skala, Lilia, 106, 248, 306, 480
Skelton, Red, 37, 545, 605
Skerritt, Tom, 21, 337, 508, 538, 551, 560
Skinner, Cornelia Otis, 524, 567

Skipworth, Alison, 56
Slate, Jeremy, 560
Slater, Christian, 453
Slater, Helen, 112, 460
Sleeper, Martha, 59
Slezak, Walter, 410, 416
Sloane, Everett, 111, 292, 323, 341
Small, Neva, 174
Smith, Alexis, 377, 448
Smith, Art, 259, 301
Smith, Brook, 484
Smith, C. A. R., 318
Smith, C. Aubrey, 74, 152, 253, 311, 320, 357, 429, 433, 528, 558, 577
Smith, Charles Martin, 27, 87, 506, 568
Smith, Howard, 168
Smith, Kate, 542
Smith, Kent, 103, 466, 499
Smith, Lane, 417
Smith, Lois, 178
Smith, Loring, 407
Smith, Madolyn, 570
Smith, Maggie, 247
Smith, Mildred Joanne, 381
Smith, Muriel, 359
Smith, Patricia, 465
Smith, Paul, 344
Smith, Roger, 39, 400
Smith, Sammy, 250
Smith, Tucker, 579
Snipes, Wesley, 280
Sofaer, Abraham, 434
Sokol, Marilyn, 187
Sokoloff, Vladimir, 182
Solari, Laura, 454
Soles, P. J., 100, 228
Somers, Suzanne, 27
Sommer, Elke, 482
Sommer, Josef, 485, 589
Sondergaard, Gale, 32, 102, 278, 301, 304
Soo, Jack, 543
Sorin, Louis, 32
Sorvino, Paul, 211, 445, 554, 582
Sothern, Ann, 60, 302, 580, 592
Spacek, Sissy, 46, 100, 114, 276, 315, 350
Spacey, Kevin, 201, 593
Spader, James, 475, 575
Spaeth, Merrie, 594
Spain, Fay, 204
Sparks, Ned, 206, 291
Spector, Phil, 161
Spencer, Douglas, 539, 544
Spencer, John, 425
Spencer, Kenneth, 52, 94
Sperber, Wendie Jo, 44
Spradlin, G. D., 204
Stack, Robert, 17, 239, 547, 595
Stadlen, Lewis J., 471
Stainton, Philip, 353